David Rose

CASES AND MATERIALS ON THE ENGLISH LEGAL SYSTEM

AUSTRALIA
The Law Book Company Ltd.
Sydney : Melbourne : Brisbane

CANADA AND U.S.A.
The Carswell Company Ltd.
Agincourt, Ontario

INDIA
N. M. Tripathi Private Ltd.
Bombay

ISRAEL
Steimatzky's Agency Ltd.
Jerusalem : Tel Aviv : Haifa

MALAYSIA : SINGAPORE : BRUNEI
Malayan Law Journal (Pte) Ltd.
Singapore

NEW ZEALAND
Sweet & Maxwell (N.Z.) Ltd.
Wellington

PAKISTAN
Pakistan Law House
Karachi

CASES AND MATERIALS
ON THE
ENGLISH LEGAL SYSTEM

By

GEOFFREY WILSON, M.A., LL.B.

*Professor of Law at the University of Warwick,
of Gray's Inn, Barrister-at-Law*

LONDON
SWEET & MAXWELL
1973

Published in 1973 by
Sweet & Maxwell Limited of
11 New Fetter Lane, London
and printed in Great Britain
by The Eastern Press Limited
of London and Reading

SBN Hardback 421 14970 1
      Paperback 421 15000 9

PREFACE

THE English legal system consists of institutions such as courts and prisons; professional people such as barristers, solicitors, judges, policemen, prison warders and probation officers; principles and rules which are used and applied in advising, planning, judging, finding facts, compensating and punishing; remedies and penalties; ideas, assumptions and values which range from a sense of the system's past to current views about its functions, methods and goals; methods for adapting the law to changing conditions, values, expectations and needs, and of applying it to particular cases; criteria for assessing good and bad decisions and good and bad behaviour. It consists, too, of buildings, docks, waiting rooms, wigs, gowns, uniforms, trumpets, rituals, even modes of speech and life styles, books and libraries, syllabuses and examinations, patronage powers and discretions. The list is endless. Each of the parts has some kind of relationship with things not particularly legal yet all can be seen as forming part of a cluster of related activities which can arguably be regarded as a recognisably distinct enterprise. The materials which follow are designed as an introduction to that enterprise and to some of the received lore upon it.

One of the questions which faces anyone attempting to freeze within the covers of one book anything so fragmented, complex, changing, detailed, pragmatic and factual as the English legal system is as to the best perspective to adopt in order to give a balanced account of the system, or indeed whether to attempt to give a balanced account of it at all. Should one rather look at it from a particular point of view such as that of the poor, of minorities, policy-makers or pressure groups? Should one approach it as an apologist or critic? How far should one dig down in search of the values and assumptions on which it rests? I have adopted for the most part what could be described as an official or semi-official view and have relied heavily on official and semi-official material, in particular reports of Royal Commissions and Departmental Committees. This is not because members of committees are necessarily more accurate observers of the way in which the system works, though they do usually have access to more readily assimilable information than they would in their private capacities, nor because their discussions of a problem are necessarily better than those of anyone else. More important is the fact that their reports have often formed the basis of subsequent changes and that their identification of the problems and the way in which they discuss them often give useful clues to the values, assumptions and ideologies which make up the atmosphere in which the system works. They therefore form essential elements in any picture of the system as a whole. They need to be supplemented, however, by observation and research and the reports of observation and research if a real understanding of the way the system actually works in practice is to be obtained. I have also tended to assume that the best introduction to the general ideology of the system and its style is still rooted in the attitudes developed by the practitioners and judges of the Common Law courts even though it is arguable that the work of their successor on the civil side, the Queen's Bench Division of the High Court, is no longer as central to the working of the system as a whole as this might suggest. This has affected the choice of extracts, especially in relation to civil procedure, law making and remedies. It is perfectly arguable that a different starting point would more accurately reflect the legal system as it is today. There has, especially in recent years, been a great shift of interest away from the Queen's Bench Division, and indeed from the High Court altogether, to new courts like the Restrictive Practices Court and the Industrial Relations Court, to lower courts like the county courts and the magistrates' courts, and to the numerous tribunals which have grown up outside the traditional legal system but which the Franks Committee on Administrative Tribunals and Inquiries, for example, in 1955, insisted are part of the machinery of adjudication of the country. It has, however, in my view yet to be seen how this will affect traditional views as to what constitutes the real unity of the English legal system. The shift in interest has not really been matched by the development of a new global approach which would bring into one legal philosophy the varied activities, styles and functions of the old and the new. Indeed to a large extent the new developments have relied on past capital both in terms of standards and of personnel. Although, therefore, many of the examples are taken from within the jurisdiction of the Queen's Bench Division they are still included much more as clues to what is currently regarded as the English legal way of going about things than as something which is characteristic of only one part of it. The assumption here is that all systems have to make some provision for preparation for trial, finding facts, finding, developing and applying law, providing remedies, devising measures of treatment for those who infringe society's rules, and giving opportunities for appeal. The materials have also been arranged so far as possible to keep open the questions which are raised by the very phrase "English legal system," namely, what is "English" about the system, how does it compare with the approach of other countries to the solution of the same problems, to what extent do the materials identify something that can be regarded as distinctively "legal," and in what sense do they make up something which can be called a "system"? One other assumption I have made is that there is still some virtue in trying to see the system as a whole and that there is a sense in which it is possible to see a connection between the various activities discussed in the book without imposing a false unity upon them.

There are some notable omissions, for example, the Restrictive Practices Court and the Industrial Relations Court. They have been omitted simply because even a partial account of them would have taken up too much space. Nor have I attempted to emphasise what elements in the system as a whole are related to the fact that it is part of a Western parliamentary system operating in a mixed economy or to illustrate some of the basic substantive values of the system which, though not part of the machinery of justice, seem to be so much part of the common law heritage that it is difficult to imagine the English legal system without them.

I apologise for the errors of detail that this book is bound to contain and the rapidity with which parts of it will become out of date. Contrary to widespread belief the English legal system is subject to constant and often quite radical change. Being a little out of date is an inevitable result of stopping for a moment to try and catch a glimpse of the system as a whole. The most that I can hope is that the errors will not distort and that readers will find it easy enough to update the materials. I also hope that if they feel compelled to dismantle parts of the book, shore up and repair others, and make additions here and there, they will still be better off than they would have been without it. Hopefully what the extracts will provide is at the least an anthology and at best a handbook with which to set out to observe the system as it really works from day to day in London and the provinces.

My thanks are due to the various publishers and writers listed below who have given me permission to quote from their works and in particular to Her Majesty's Stationery Office for permission to quote so extensively from government publications. I owe personal thanks to Philip Britton, David Farrier and Christina Sachs who have at various stages given me a reassuring hand. Had I relied on them more I should have made fewer mistakes. I am particularly grateful to Elizabeth Anker in the Government Publications Room at the University of Warwick Library whose patient willingness to help far exceeds her passion for sending things for binding. There are others, too, who would I know be puzzled to find their names mentioned in a preface to a law book without whom this book would never have been completed. Someone besides the author always suffers in the production of any book. Dr. Monika Lichtenfeld suffered more than any-one else. Were it not that it would be an inadequate recompense I would dedicate this book to her.

There are two disclaimers I would wish to make. It had been my expectation that the materials would be in the larger print and my contributions in the text smaller. The publishers decided that it would be more economical to reverse this. One result is that my growing illiteracy is revealed more glaringly than I would wish. The second is that although this book was written at Warwick it is not a wholeheartedly Warwick book. It is written more in pious memory of those students at Queen's College, Cambridge, who now form part of the legal system to which it is devoted.

GEOFFREY WILSON.

1973.

CONTENTS

Contents

ACKNOWLEDGMENTS

GRATEFUL acknowledgment is made to the following for permission to reproduce materials from their publications: Her Majesty's Stationery Office, The Bar Council, The Law Society, The Solicitors' Journal and Times Newspapers Ltd. We would also like to express our gratitude for permission to reproduce from the undermentioned works:

ABEL-SMITH, B. AND STEVENS, R., *In Search of Justice: Society and the Legal System* (Allen Lane, The Penguin Press, 1968).

ACKNER, D., Q.C., " Reply " (*Sunday Times*, November 3, 1968).

COHEN, F. S., " Transcendental Nonsense and the Functional Approach," *Columbia Law Review* 35 (1935) (Columbia University).

" Comment on ' Justice out of reach,' " *Law Society Gazette* (1970).

CORRY, J. A., " Administrative Law and the Interpretation of Statutes," *Vol.* I 1935–36 *University of Toronto Law Journal* (University of Toronto Press).

DICKINSON, J., " The Law behind the Law," *Columbia Law Review* 29 (1929) (Columbia University).

FRANK, W. F., " Employers' Liability in Great Britain," *Law and Contemporary Problems, Vol.* 18, *No.* 3 (Duke University School of Law).

HALL-WILLIAMS, *English Penal System in Transition* (Butterworth & Co. Ltd.).

JACKSON, R. M., *Enforcing the Law* (Macmillan).

" Justice for All," *Fabian Research Series* 273 (1968) (Fabian Society).

LANDIS, " Statutes and the sources of Law," *Harvard Legal Essays* 1934 (Harvard University Press).

LAURIE, P., *Scotland Yard* (The Bodley Head Ltd.).

LLEWELLYN, K. N., *Bramble Bush* (Oceana Publications Inc.).

PARKER, RT. HON. LORD, " The History and Development of Commercial Arbitration," *Lionel Cohen Lecture* 1959 (Magnes Press, Jerusalem).

PLUCKNETT, *Concise History of the Common Law* (Butterworth & Co. Ltd.).

POLLOCK, S., " The future of Legal Aid in England," *Law Society Gazette* (March 1969).

POTTER AND STANSFELD, *The National Insurance (Industrial Injuries) Act* 1948, 2nd ed., 1950 (Butterworth & Co. Ltd.).

" Rough Justice " (Conservative Political Centre).

STEPHEN, SIR J. F., *History of the Criminal Law of England* (Macmillan).

WRIGHT, RT. HON. LORD, " Precedent " (1942–44) 8 *Cambridge Law Journal* 118 (Cambridge University Press).

ZANDER, M., " The Lawyer's Pound of Flesh " (*Sunday Times*, 1968).

TABLE OF CASES

[Figures in *italics* refer to the pages on which extracts from judgments appear.]

TABLE OF STATUTES

[Figures in italics refer to the pages on which extracts from Acts appear.]

CHAPTER 1

THE COURTS

INTRODUCTION

THE legal system of a modern industrialised country is bound to be complex. That of the United Kingdom is made somewhat more complicated by the fact that the legal systems of Scotland and England are still to a considerable degree separate, having developed under the influence of Roman law and the common law respectively, and having their separate courts, below the level of the final Appeal Court the House of Lords, and separate legal professions. Northern Ireland also has its own courts. This book is therefore confined to only one section of the United Kingdom, that is England and Wales. The other complicating factor about the English legal system is its age. It still bears the marks of having had its origins in the twelfth century and consciousness of its age still affects the rhetoric and, it may be, some of the attitudes of many of its practitioners. Certainly, in so far as universities have any part to play in shaping attitudes, the lip service which has been paid to the study of legal history as the method *par excellence* of broadening the student's understanding of the law may well have confused the attitudes towards the contemporary shape of things even if it has failed to instil any genuinely historical perspective. Much of the formal structure of the system is in fact a product of the nineteenth century, though many of the raw materials which were built into the structure had roots going back much further, and this is particularly true of the structure of the superior courts, the character of the legal profession and the relationship between it and the judiciary.

THE EARLY BEGINNINGS

If anyone has the right to be called the founder of the English legal system it is probably Henry II. When he came to the throne in 1154 justice was administered for the most part in local courts. These were either the feudal courts held by local lords for their tenants, or the local county and hundred courts, presided over by the sheriff or, where the court had fallen into private hands, by a steward appointed by the person who held the franchise. There was a central royal court, the Curia Regis, but it was not a general court open to all. It was the appropriate feudal court for those who were the tenants-in-chief of the King. It had also been the scene of a number of treason trials and the hearing of such disputes as to who should be the primate of all England. In special cases the right to have one's case heard by it might be granted as a special favour. In general, however, the aggrieved citizen made his complaint in a local court and had it decided by local or feudal custom.

It was Henry who introduced the innovations which led to the appearance of royal courts open to all. In the Assizes of Clarendon (1166)

1

and Northampton (1176) he provided that in future there should be twelve men in every county who should be responsible for presenting to the sheriff all those suspected of serious crime.   These men would then be brought before the royal officials who toured the country from time to time looking after the King's affairs.   They were then to be put to the ordeal and those who did not pass the test were to be punished.   Here for almost the first time on a regular basis royal officials known as justices were given the task of trying criminals and, to perform the task, they were sent round the country at regular intervals on assize.   They were not lawyers as we know them as there was, as yet, no legal profession in England.   They still performed other administrative tasks on the King's behalf but their travels on circuit were the beginnings of the assizes, which continued until their abolition by the Courts Act 1971, and of the travelling High Court judge, who still continues.   Nor were the criminal assizes Henry's only innovation. He also offered for the first time a new remedy, "the assize of novel disseisin" to citizens who complained that their land had been wrongfully seized, and an alternative process to defendants in suits claiming land, known as the "grand assize."   The condition in each case was that the suit must be heard before or transferred to a court presided over by the royal justices.

In this way the royal justices came to have what we would now call a criminal and a civil jurisdiction.   The civil cases too were at first heard by justices travelling around the country, but after a time a distinction appeared between those cases heard before the justices who travelled or remained with the King, and those heard before justices who sat apart and came to settle at Westminster.   During the thirteenth century the latter became known as the Court of Common Pleas and the former the court of King's Bench. These two common law courts, once established, remained in existence until the nineteenth century. A third common law court, the Court of Exchequer, followed later.   It was the product of the financial side of the activities of the Curia Regis.   It had always been the place where disputes might arise between those from whom taxes were claimed and the King, and the barons who made up its staff therefore included some who specialised in deciding such cases.   But like all such bodies in the Middle Ages, once it was clear that it had a staff and procedure which could be useful to private litigants as well as the King and his debtors, steps were taken to open it up to people who were not debtors to the Crown, first in special cases, then to those against whom Crown debtors said they had claims, the non-satisfaction of which prevented them paying their own debts to the Crown.   Finally by a fictitious extension of this principle the court became available to litigants generally.

By the end of the fourteenth century, therefore, many of the features which were to be characteristic of the legal system were already established. There were the three common law courts, Common Pleas, King's Bench and Exchequer which had a continuous history until they were absorbed into the High Court established by the Supreme Court of Judicature Acts 1873–75. At first they had distinct and separate jurisdictions, but over the years these distinctions became blurred as each sought to expand its jurisdiction at the expense of the others, commonly by the use of fictions.   The King's Bench, for example, which had a limited jurisdiction so far as litigants in general were concerned, like other courts had a general jurisdiction over those who were in the custody of the court for one reason or another. It therefore allowed litigants who wished to bring cases before it to sue out a Bill of Middlesex before it which called upon the sheriff of Middlesex to arrest the defendant and, if he was not in Middlesex, it authorised a further writ of *latitat et discurrit* for his attachment wherever he might be. Once within the jurisdiction of the court in this way the plaintiff could bring his true cause of action against him. Provided the defendant accepted the jurisdiction of the court there need not be any actual arrest. The Court of Common Pleas failed in an attempt to defeat this ruse and was eventually itself forced to counter-attack, adopting its own fictitious process using the writ *quare clausum fregit*. The jurisdiction of the Court of Exchequer was largely based on the fiction that the plaintiff was a debtor of the Crown, who, by reason of the defendant's failure to pay what he owed the plaintiff, prevented him in turn paying the Crown. Here the fictitious writ used was " quominus." As a result of these developments the courts gradually came to exercise a similar jurisdiction. This was recognised in effect by a statute in 1585, so far as the King's Bench was concerned, which set up a Court of Exchequer Chamber to hear appeals from the Court of King's Bench when it was exercising its newly acquired general jurisdiction.

At the same time the system of the travelling justice was well established and justices armed with commissions to hear and determine cases and to deliver gaols travelled the country on circuit trying the more serious criminal cases. By virtue of the Statute of Westminster II 1285 they heard civil cases under the provisions known as " nisi prius " which required the sheriff to send a jury to London unless before the due time the royal justices came to hear the case locally, which in fact became the practice. This was the origin of the " nisi prius " system by which cases were opened in London, tried by a jury in the locality, and the verdict recorded in London, which lasted until the nineteenth century. Other criminal cases were already being heard by justices of the peace either summarily or sitting in quarter sessions.

There was also a complicated system of procedure and a large number of actions available in the royal courts though there were already signs of a hardening of the arteries. The separation of the courts from the main-springs of government, and in particular from the Council, seems to have taken much of the sense of initiative from them and increasing professional-ism, reinforced by the fact that it was medieval did the rest. Gone already were the days when Hengham C.J. could tell counsel:

> Ne glosez point le statut; nous le savons meuz de vous, quar nous les feimes.[1]

But Plucknett [2] notes that in 1366:

> Thorpe C.J. recalled that there had been a discussion before him on the interpretation of a statute, " and Sir Hugh Green C.J.K.B. and I went together to the council ... and asked those who made the Statute

---

[1] Y.B. 33–35 Edw. I, R.S. 83 (1305).
[2] *Concise History of the Common Law*, p. 329.

what it meant, [T]he Archbishop told them . . . after remarking (with some justification) that the judge's question was rather a silly one." [3]

By the end of the fourteenth century too there was a legal profession with its Inns of Court and a system of apprenticeship. Maitland has a romantic passage about the significance of this event [4]:

> No, the clergy were not the only learned men in England, the only cultivated men, the only men of ideas. Vigorous intellectual effort was to be found outside the monasteries and universities. These lawyers are worldly men, not men of the sterile caste; they marry and found families, some of which become as noble as any in the land; but they are in their way learned, cultivated men, linguists, logicians, tenacious disputants, true lovers of the nice case and the moot-point. They are gregarious, clubable men, grouping themselves in hospices which become schools of law, multiplying manuscripts, arguing, learning and teaching, the great mediators between life and logic, a reasoning, reasonable element in the English nation.

By that time too the system could claim two distinguished legal writers, the author of the book ascribed to Glanville in the twelfth century and Bracton in the thirteenth century. A comparison of the scope of their books and the number of writs they describe as being available in the royal courts is some measure of the rapid growth of the system in its first 100 years. Here too the pace had begun to slow down even after the encouragement apparently given by the Statute of Westminster 1285 to the clerks in Chancery to extend existing writs by analogy. It was not until actions " on the case " and the use of fictions got into full swing that further developments on any scale were possible.

COURTS OTHER THAN THE COMMON LAW COURTS

The origins of the English legal system are to be found in the common law courts and it is around them that much of the system has developed, but they have never had a monopoly of the administration of justice any more than their successor the Queen's Bench Division of the High Court.

The local courts continued to hear cases long after the royal courts were established and even as they declined—the feudal courts with the decline of feudalism, and the other local courts in the face of competition of the royal courts reinforced by central government policy embodied in statute— there still remained important areas of dispute outside the jurisdiction of the common law courts and the common law. One notable area was that involving mercantile and maritime disputes. Disputes between merchants, foreign and local, which arose at the fairs at which most important commercial business was transacted in the fourteenth century, were tried in courts of the fair or borough (known as " courts of piepowder ") in which the case arose, presided over by the mayor or his deputy, or, if the fair was held as part of a private franchise, the steward appointed by the franchise holder. The rules applied were those of the European law merchant

---

[3] Citing Y.B. 40 Edw. III, f. 34 b.
[4] Cited Plucknett, *Concise History of the Common Law*, p. 220.

developed over the years from the customary practices of merchants and the jury was often made up of merchants. These were supplemented for a time by " staple courts " which sat in the staple towns. These were towns designated by the King as the exclusive centres of trade for such commodities as wine, wool, leather and tin.

Maritime disputes were heard by maritime courts, sitting in major ports like Bristol. These too applied a special European customary law developed from the customary practices of seamen. The common law courts were slow to show an interest in dealing with matters of this kind or in developing rules to deal with them adequately. In part this was due to the notion that their jurisdiction was limited geographically to matters which had arisen in England between English citizens, foreign matters—and many of these disputes did involve either a foreign merchant or a contract made or to be performed abroad—being left to some other body, especially if it might raise questions about the relation between the King and foreign sovereigns where the King's Council might be a more appropriate body. In part too it was due to the fact that the common law courts and the common law had come into existence at a time when land was the most important commodity and the procedures and concerns of the common law courts were adapted to problems arising from disputes about the possession and ownership of land. They were formal and slow and ill adapted to the needs of merchants and seafaring men who wanted a speedier justice administered according to rules with which they were familiar.

In the long run the common law courts could not afford to remain indifferent to the changed economic situation in which commerce came to rival land as a source of wealth and disputes. In the Middle Ages courts behaved as much like private business enterprises as the public institutions we know today, eager to increase their business at the expense of one another and of any other body which looked as if it was enjoying a valuable source of income from the suits with which it was dealing. In the mercantile and maritime sphere this led to a clash with the Court of Admiralty, which from small beginnings in the fourteenth century dealing with cases of piracy and the like on the High Seas, had by the reign of Henry VIII come to absorb much of the jurisdiction of the maritime and mercantile courts. These latter courts had themselves declined with the decline in importance of the fairs. The criminal jurisdiction which it had assumed was taken from it in 1536 and transferred to commissioners of *oyer* and *terminer* (which was one of the normal commissions issued to the travelling royal justices authorising them to hear criminal cases at assizes), to be tried by a judge and jury just as if they had occurred on land. Throughout the sixteenth and in the early part of the seventeenth centuries, the common lawyers conducted a campaign against the Court of Admiralty's exercise of a wide civil jurisdiction ending in a victory in 1660 when its jurisdiction was reduced to more strictly maritime affairs like collisions at sea and disputes about wages. It was left to the common law courts, having won jurisdiction, to develop a set of rules to deal with it adequately. This was achieved partly by fiction. For example, to get over the fact that technically it still lacked jurisdiction over matters arising abroad, the court accepted allegations that something that had occurred abroad had occurred in England within its jurisdiction, *e.g.* by using the fiction that Bordeaux was in Cheapside. It also developed new forms of action from those already existing, to provide a body of law that could cope with the conduct and needs of mercantile men. These ranged from a basic notion that mere agreements should be binding as contracts to the recognition of more complicated transactions like negotiable instruments. These developments were not achieved by means of legislation, as they would be today, but by the exertions of the courts themselves. In fact, so far as mercantile law is concerned, one can even name particular judges who can claim the credit for bringing the common law to a point where the common law court could offer a reasonably acceptable service to the merchants who were now compelled to come before them if they were to have their disputes decided by a court of the realm. Lord Holt for example and, even more conspicuously Lord Mansfield, were such judges. Both of them, and especially the latter, made a practice of consulting merchants to discover what their practices were and what they would regard as acceptable solutions in the commoner commercial situations. The fact that the area was, so far as the common law was concerned, relatively undeveloped proved an advantage in this respect. Other areas in which Lord Mansfield tried to introduce innovations proved too firmly established to be changed and withstood even the reforms of the nineteenth century.

The Court of Star Chamber and The Court of Chancery

The battle between the common law courts and the court of Admiralty over commercial matters was one which was won by the former. However, they were not as successful in all their attempts to secure a monopoly of major litigation in the country. This was particularly true of their struggle with the Court of Chancery.

Rapid as the growth of the common law was in the thirteenth century it proved unable to satisfy the complaints of a large number of aggrieved citizens. In fact the position was worse even than this because often it was the common law courts and the common law about which the complaints were being made. Some of the complaints had to do with the general conditions of the day, the disorder that was common and the general inability of those in power at any particular time to maintain order throughout the country in such a way that the legal system could function as it was meant to. Hence the complaints about the bribery, corruption or oppression of juries, the partiality of sheriffs and the inability of a litigant to enforce a judgment or recover property from his more powerful neighbour. The defects could not properly be laid at the door of the system itself, though in many cases its personnel connived at the perversion of the administration of justice that resulted. Order returned with Henry VII and the Tudors, in the late fifteenth and sixteenth centuries, and the courts began to function normally again. They had however to pay a price for the chaos of the previous century.

When Henry VII came to the throne he charged a committee of his Council with the task of trying and punishing those guilty of oppression and disorder, keeping private armies, of the oppression of jurors and the bringing of suits in which they had no personal interest as a means of harassing their neighbours. And this committee, one is tempted to say inevitably, became a court, the Court of Star Chamber, which by the beginning of the seventeenth century had a regular jurisdiction over a large number of criminal and civil cases. Political circumstances, however, came to the aid of the common lawyers in their battle with this court as they had to some extent in their battle with the Court of Admiralty. Both the Court of Star Chamber and the Court of Admiralty came to be identified with the royal prerogative and to be seen as prerogative courts, as opposed to common law courts. They got caught up in the battle between the Stuart Kings, who relied heavily on royal prerogative powers as a means of governing the country without too frequent recourse to parliament, and who claimed that these powers put them above the ordinary law of the land, and the combination of parliamentarians and common lawyers who insisted that parliamentary approval was necessary for most of the major acts of government, and in particular taxation and legislation. They also claimed that, far from being above the law, prerogative and the King's powers and position in general were a part of the common law and, by implication, subject to the ordinary law of the land, as administered in the ordinary courts. The Court of Star Chamber was bound to be destroyed if the King was defeated in this battle because the King used it as a means of enforcing his will in circumstances in which he could not necessarily have relied on the courts of common law, though in fact in a number of important constitutional cases they served him fairly well. It was abolished in 1640. That part of its jurisdiction which was considered useful, its jurisdiction over criminal offences which it had itself developed, for example criminal libel, was taken over by the common law courts. The rest lapsed.

Disorder was not, however, the only reason why the common law system was defective and not the only ground of complaint. After the rapid developments of the thirteenth century, the common law in the fourteenth century ceased to have the momentum of earlier years. As a legal profession came into existence the judges came to be chosen exclusively from it instead of from a wider variety of royal officials as had been the case in the thirteenth century. The common law courts became more self-conscious about what they were doing and attempted in their medieval way to become more systematic. There was much talk about the proper way of doing things, of not being able to do this or that and much clever reasoning. Reports of cases in the Year Books, the nearest we have to law reports of this time, show a considerable concern with procedural points and niceties, a reluctance to depart from what had become established, a close attention to the observance of proper forms and much less concern with what the circumstances of the particular case demanded if it was to be settled in an appropriate way. Even remedies such as the specific enforcement of an agreement, making a man do what he has promised to do, gave way to the practice of making an award of money damages the only remedy for a successful litigant.

As a result of this hardening up of the system complaints were made by large numbers of people about the inadequacy of the service provided by the courts, the cost, delay, technicalities, refusal to give help in cases of accident, fraud or mistake, adherence to the written word, and emphasis on the exact observance of formalities. The complaints were made to anyone who looked as if they might be able to help, the judges who came round on circuit, the Council, the King and the Lord Chancellor. Quite often complaints which were addressed to someone else, such as the Council or the King, ended up with the Lord Chancellor. It was his office that was responsible for sending out the writs which would often be necessary if any remedy was to be authorised in respect to any particular complaint. He was secretary to the Council, often an ecclesiastic, and someone who was expected to be in a position to give advice on what the just and equitable thing to do might be. Ultimately he came to be talked of as the Keeper of the King's Conscience. In later accounts of the development of the Chancellor's jurisdiction it is in particular this concern with what is " just and equitable " that came to be emphasised, since as the jurisdiction developed parallel to, and often corrective of, the jurisdiction exercised by the common law courts, the distinction between the different jurisdictions was identified with the Aristotelian distinction between law and equity. Law, so the argument ran, was made up of general rules, and general rules were bound to cause hardship and injustice in some particular cases. It was necessary therefore to temper the rules of law with equity which could make exceptions in particular cases to avoid hardship. Even if one accepted this kind of approach to the problems of the administration of justice it did not follow of course that there should be one court or group of courts responsible for the administration of strict law and another to temper that law with equity. However, once the jurisdiction of the Chancellor had grown, inevitably, into the Court of Chancery, it was easy to identify the respective roles of the two jurisdictions in this way, whether the supplementary role of the Chancellor took the form of relieving a litigant when the common law worked a particular hardship in his case, preventing a litigant from making what was regarded as an oppressive use of his formal legal rights, or providing a remedy not provided by the common law courts. In addition the Court of Chancery came to be particularly concerned with a number of institutions not recognised at common law but which it was prepared to recognise and develop, the leading example being the " use," which later became the trust. The concept of the trust and its offshoots was so developed that it totally transformed the whole of property law and the marks of its separate origins remain at the present time.

For their part, in the early days at least, the common lawyers seemed to have been quite sympathetic to the development of this kind of supplementary jurisdiction. At this point their narrower professionalism seemed to have prevailed over their normal desire to increase their jurisdiction. On their side most Chancellors were careful to preserve the form of not providing an open challenge to the common law or the common law courts. They operated, they said, on the conscience of the individual litigant and used methods and offered remedies which were still within the power of the King to offer, though no longer available in his ordinary common law courts. Wolsey was a notable exception to the tradition of conciliatory Chancellors, since he exercised the powers of Chancellor in a manner which the common lawyers found overbearing. His successor Sir Thomas More did much to heal the breach and was in fact one of the long line of lawyer Chancellors who gradually came to be the rule. It was under their influence that equity, *i.e.*, the law administered by the Court of Chancery, came to have the character of a legal system existing side by side with the common law system with many similar features so far as the development of rules and principles and their application were concerned, as well as the regular observance of rules and procedure, and adherence to precedent and the like. Indeed to such an extent had this gone by the nineteenth century, under the benevolent influence of Lord Nottingham in the seventeenth century, of Lord Hardwicke in the eighteenth and the less enlightened influence of Lord Eldon in the late eighteenth and early nineteenth century, that by then there was little to choose between the temper and spirit of the two systems. To the extent that differences of style remained it was probably more in the direction of equity having become the more legalistic and oppressive of the two.

Although, however, this was the way the jurisdiction of the Court of Chancery developed, so that at the time of the great nineteenth century reforms of the courts there existed, by the side of the common law courts and a truncated Court of Admiralty, a flourishing Court of Chancery, it did not reach this position without opposition from the common lawyers. Having rejected the offer of Sir Thomas More to abandon the equity jurisdiction if they would put their own house in order and therefore make it unnecessary, they seem later to have come to regret their decision and resented what they again came to regard as an improper interference with the normal workings and jurisdiction of their own courts. The high point of the controversy again coincided with the constitutional struggle between the protagonists of Parliament and the common law on the one hand, and the King and prerogative on the other. However, the Court of Chancery did not suffer the fate of the other prerogative courts. When Lord Coke offered a direct challenge to the Court of Chancery's jurisdiction, the challenge was taken up, and James I, on the advice of Lord Bacon (then his Attorney-General, and later Lord Chancellor) gave a firm decision in favour of the Court of Chancery, which even the later constitutional defeat of the Stuarts was unable to upset. It might well be argued that by the middle of the seventeenth century the Court of Star Chamber's original purpose, that of assisting the central government to maintain the kind of order in which the ordinary law courts could carry on peacefully with their work, had been completed, and that it was now being used simply as a means of royal oppression, and could and should therefore be dispensed with. It was however far more difficult to argue that the task of the Court of Chancery was completed, since it had already developed a jurisdiction and obtained a foothold in the overall task of providing services for settling disputes, as well as supporting useful institutions and giving useful remedies not available elsewhere. Indeed without it the common law would have been a barbarous anachronism. It could claim to be playing a necessary part in the general administration of justice in a manner which was widely regarded as acceptable and which made it difficult to destroy it as a victim of either constitutional warfare or simple business rivalry between two competing legal enterprises. Even the nineteenth century reforms only succeeded in bringing the common law courts and the Court of Chancery within the same structure, and the Chancery Division survives alongside the Queen's Bench Division when names like Common Pleas and Exchequer have disappeared into the past.

ECCLESIASTICAL COURTS

There was one further area in which the common law courts were not active, and that was in matters which were regarded as the concern of the Church. This was in part the result of an arrangement between William I and the Pope in which William agreed that the affairs of the Church would be kept separate and separate courts would deal with church matters. There were times when the jurisdiction of the ecclesiastical courts went way beyond what would now be regarded as the sphere of the church and indeed what would be regarded as appropriate for any court, both as regards the conduct regulated and the punishments imposed. The administration of the estates of deceased persons, so far as property other than land was concerned, was regarded as within the sphere of the ecclesiastical courts, since the church was interested in seeing that the property was distributed in a proper way. Marriage and the breakdown of marriage, the declaration that a marriage was null, or the authorisation of a separation of spouses following a breakdown, were for a long time regarded as the exclusive concern of the ecclesiastical courts. It was not until the nineteenth century that a divorce was possible as the result of a court proceeding, though before this a divorce could be obtained by private Act of Parliament. This could be obtained in a non-ecclesiastical court, the Court of Matrimonial Causes, which was specially set up for the purpose. The probate jurisdiction was also transferred to a new Court of Probate and Matrimonial Causes in 1857. It was the jurisdiction of this court which was combined with that of a slightly restored jurisdiction of the Court of Admiralty to form the Probate, Divorce and Admiralty Division of the High Court in 1873. There are still ecclesiastical courts but their jurisdiction is now more strictly confined to matters involving the discipline of the clergy and matters affecting the decoration and use of churches.

THE NINETEENTH CENTURY

The English legal system entered the nineteenth century overladen with the accretions of seven centuries. There were five major courts of first instance, the three common law courts, the Court of Chancery and the Court of Admiralty. Apart from these however there were also the ecclesiastical courts and the miscellaneous courts such as the Bristol Tolzey Court, the Liverpool Court of Passage, and the Courts of Chancery of the Duchy of Lancaster and the Bishopric of Durham, which had managed to survive the tendency to centralise the administration of justice in England. Nearly all serious criminal cases and some civil cases were heard locally at the assize towns by travelling justices of the superior courts at Westminster. Criminal cases were also heard by justices of the peace at quarter sessions or dealt with by them summarily. Minor civil cases were heard in what remained of the county, hundred, borough and franchise courts and also, here and there, in courts called Courts of Requests. There were in addition a number of appeal courts. The King's Bench had always had the right to hear appeals from the Court of Common Pleas. There were two courts of Exchequer Chamber, one to hear appeals from the Court of Exchequer, the other to hear appeals from the King's Bench when it was exercising original jurisdiction. Appeals from the Court of Chancery were dealt with mostly by way of rehearing by the Lord Chancellor himself. In addition the House of Lords exercised a general appellate jurisdiction over the common law courts and the Court of Chancery. The Privy Council dealt with appeals from the Court of Admiralty and the ecclesiastical courts.

Each of these courts had its own jurisdiction, sometimes overlapping, sometimes conflicting. This was particularly true of the division between the common law courts and the Court of Chancery. What was even more disconcerting for the litigant was that often neither of the two sides of this division could give a complete remedy in a case, which meant that the litigant had to shuffle to and fro, paying as he went. Each court had its own procedure and even before the same court there were different ways of beginning an action, pleading, and enforcing a judgment. The procedure of the common law courts, complicated in any event, was still further complicated by the roundabout ways that had been used to encroach on one another's jurisdiction and to adapt old legal forms to new needs. Much of the substantive law was enmeshed in these procedural rules since much of it had grown up round particular writs and forms of action. The greater part of the common law could in fact only be described in terms of the forms of action which had been developed to give effect to different classes of claim. The position was further aggravated by the insistence that the forms should be precisely observed and that failure to do so would mean loss of the action. It seems hardly necessary to mention the evils of expense and delay, which were particularly chronic in the Court of Chancery.

This was the inheritance that the Victorians set out to clean up, rationalise and hand over to the twentieth century in the form with which we are familiar today, and it is their work which still forms the foundation on which much of the present system is built. This means of course that what they did is of more than merely historical interest. It is a first possible step towards the understanding of at least the form of the present arrangements and, in some cases the need for their reform.

The Period of Reform

The achievements of the period were formidable. The most obvious was the rationalisation of the relationship between the various superior courts, culminating in the establishment of the Supreme Court in 1873–75, together with the rationalisation and simplification of procedure which led to the formulation of the Rules of the Supreme Court in 1883.[5] At the same time new county courts for the hearing of small causes were established[6] and regular courts of summary jurisdiction established for minor criminal offences. Attempts were made to bring the statute law into some order by modernising the drafting, setting up the office of parliamentary draftsman, beginning the long process of weeding out statutes which had been repealed or become obsolete and by attempting the codification of some areas, *e.g.* of the criminal law. Better provision for the prevention and detection of

---

[5] Below, p. 338 *et seq.*
[6] Below, p. 43.

crime was made in 1829 when the Metropolitan Police force was established to be followed later by county and borough forces. A step was made towards the control of prosecutions in the establishment of a Director of Public Prosecutions. The severe penalties attached to a number of offences were relaxed. Reformatories and industrial schools were established for juvenile offenders and those in need of care and protection.[7] The administration of prisons was put into the hands of the central government and towards the very end of the century in 1895 the Gladstone Committee inaugurated a new era in treatment of prisoners. The lack of legal education in the Inns of Court and the universities was exposed and steps taken to remedy it. The rules of evidence were revised to allow parties to give evidence and the accused in a criminal case was allowed to have counsel to cross-examine witnesses on his behalf. The list is endless. There was hardly a part of the system which was not looked at by one set of royal commissioners or other, and a very large number of their recommendations resulted in changes. The Victorian era was the great age of the Royal Commission. So far as the legal system is concerned three groups were particularly important: those appointed in 1828 after Brougham's reform speech of February 7, 1828, those appointed in 1851 and the Judicature Commissioners appointed in 1869. Extracts from their reports appear later in this book.

THE ORGANISATION OF THE COURTS

THE BASIC STRUCTURE

So far as the structure of the courts is concerned the principal result of the reform agitation of the nineteenth century was the establishment by the Supreme Court of Judicature Acts 1873–75 of a Supreme Court, consisting of the High Court and a Court of Appeal, which replaced the variety of superior trial and appellate courts which had come into existence during the past 600 years. The High Court is still the major civil court of first instance and shares the bulk of the civil work with the county courts which were first introduced by the County Courts Act 1846. The other courts which exercise civil jurisdiction are the magistrates' courts which deal with a small amount of minor, mostly matrimonial, business. Outside the traditional court structure there are the numerous tribunals such as the social insurance tribunals and rent tribunals which have been set up in the twentieth century to deal with the many claims and complaints that arise under modern welfare and regulatory legislation. Within the structure but exercising a specialist jurisdiction are the Restrictive Practices Court, established in 1956, and the Industrial Relations Court established in 1972.

The Judicature Acts 1873–75 which established the Supreme Court and much of the agitation which preceded them were mainly concerned with administration of civil justice. The courts which had traditionally dealt with criminal cases, the courts of assize and quarter sessions, and in the case of the minor (summary) offences, the magistrates' courts were left virtually

[7] Below, p. 539.

untouched, though the magistrates' courts had themselves been made the subject of formal regulation for the first time by the Summary Jurisdiction Act 1848. As a result when the Supreme Court was established it consisted of a High Court and a Court of Appeal both of which were primarily civil courts, though the Divisional Court of the Queen's Bench Division of the High Court heard appeals on points of law from the magistrates' courts and judges of the High Court heard all the most serious criminal cases on assize. Even when a Court of Criminal Appeal was established in 1908 to hear appeals from assizes and quarter sessions, and although again it was staffed by the Lord Chief Justice and judges of the High Court, it was not made a part of the Supreme Court. The position however has been changed as a result of the abolition of the Court of Criminal Appeal by the Criminal Appeal Act 1966 (now replaced by the Criminal Appeal Act 1968), and the transfer of its jurisdiction to the Court of Appeal (Criminal Division) which is now therefore a court of mixed civil and criminal jurisdiction. A second change has been the abolition of assizes and quarter sessions by the Courts Act 1971 and their replacement by a single Crown Court, which is now a part of the Supreme Court. The Supreme Court therefore now consists of the High Court for major civil cases, the Crown Court for major criminal cases and the Court of Appeal which hears appeals from them both. Judges of the High Court share with a newly created body of Circuit judges, part time Recorders, and in some cases justices of the peace, the work of the Crown Court.

At the time of the 1873–75 legislation it had originally been intended to abolish the appellate jurisdiction of the House of Lords. This intention was defeated by a change of government. The House, however, remains formally outside the Supreme Court. Like the Court of Appeal it has a mixed civil and criminal jurisdiction, but does not have a separate criminal division. It hears appeals not only from the Supreme Court but also from the Court of Session in Scotland (and for this reason always contains a number of Scottish judges) and from Northern Ireland. The county courts, which deal with minor civil cases, also remain outside the Supreme Court though they are presided over by Circuit judges who can also sit in the Crown Court, and it is the Court of Appeal which hears appeals from them. The magistrates' courts also remain outside the Supreme Court but are subject to the supervision of the Queen's Bench Division of the High Court. Appeals from their decisions go either to the Crown Court, a divisional court of the Queen's Bench Division or the Family Division. The Privy Council exercises a limited domestic appellate jurisdiction mainly in relation to the ecclesiastical courts and from such tribunals as the Disciplinary Committee of the General Medical Council. Its main appellate jurisdiction from the supreme courts of Commonwealth countries has gradually disappeared as these countries have come to prefer final decisions to be taken by their own courts.

Even though the legislation of 1873–75 was mostly concerned with the administration of civil justice it has always been regarded as a watershed in the development of the English legal system and it is easy to see why. It brought together into one system the courts around which the whole of English law had up to that time been developed. Looking back nearly 100 years later, however, it now seems much more of a half-way house than it did even ten or fifteen years ago. One of the reasons for this is the recent re-examination of the structure of the system by the [Beeching] Royal Commission on Assizes and Quarter Sessions,[8] which was followed by the Courts Act 1971. Interestingly enough it approached its consideration of the system from exactly the opposite perspective of the Judicature Commissioners and their predecessors. Where they were primarily concerned with the administration of civil justice, it was concerned primarily with the administration of criminal justice. Where they concentrated on the central administration of justice in London, it was concerned with the local administration of justice throughout the country. In the case of the Beeching Commission however the division between criminal and civil business was not nearly as sharp as in the case of the Judicature Commissioners. Indeed one of the reasons given for its appointment was to see to what extent the administration of criminal justice could be altered in order to make more time available for the local administration of civil justice, a subject which had already been the concern of a number of previous committees in the twentieth century and for the achievement of which a number of changes had already been made. Whatever the actual results in practice of the recommendations of the Beeching Commission and the Courts Act 1971, the report itself does give an opportunity to look at the system from a different point of view from the one that is suggested by taking 1873–75 as a starting point. This is particularly so in relation to the local administration of justice, the relationship between the administration of civil and criminal justice, the distribution of judges and the allocation of tasks between them to get the business of deciding disputes and trying offenders done as efficiently, economically and fairly as possible.

The administration of civil and criminal justice has always been closely linked in the English legal system by the use of travelling High Court judges to hear civil and criminal cases locally. The English system has always set itself against provincial courts, civil or criminal, staffed by judges resident in the locality. The fears underlying this prejudice were however put aside sufficiently to make possible the establishment of local county courts for smaller civil cases and the establishment of two local " Crown Courts " for criminal business in Manchester and Liverpool. The latter were the subject of strong criticism by the Streatfeild Committee on the Business of the Criminal Courts, though rehabilitated somewhat by the Beeching Commission itself which regarded the previous criticism as premature. The heavy reliance however on a relatively small number of men travelling throughout the country at regular intervals has created serious problems as the amount of business has increased.

A number of proposals had been put before the various commissions and committees which had considered the problem. One was to increase the number of judges, and this has been done, but everyone who has considered the problem has stressed the fact that there is a limit to which this can be done without either lowering the quality of those appointed or denuding the Bar of its leaders. Another suggestion has been to increase the jurisdiction of the county courts. This was for example a proposal made by the Judicature Commissioners in their Second Report in which they also incidentally

8 Cmnd. 4153 (1969).

advocated that the county courts should be made a part of the High Court to facilitate the distribution of business between them. The county courts' jurisdiction has been increased over the years, but here the objection has been that there is a danger that in increasing their jurisdiction one might lose sight of the fact that they had been established originally as small claims courts. They have already been under criticism for no longer providing a reasonably cheap and informal service for the settlement of small claims disputes, especially by consumers. To the extent that their procedure and time had to be geared to more serious cases in order to relieve pressure on the High Court there was a danger that they would become even less suitable for small claims, although this argument has been met to some extent by moving towards the creation of a court within a court. This has been done by giving the registrar, originally merely an administrative officer, more power to deal with small claims, leaving to the county court judge the responsibility for dealing with the more serious cases. One area of work that has been increasingly transferred first to county court judges and later to designated county courts themselves has been matrimonial, and especially undefended divorce work. On the criminal side one expedient, before the Beeching Commission reported, was to increase the jurisdiction of quarter sessions especially where they were presided over by a chairman with legal qualifications, which became the normal position. This however was to some extent counterbalanced by provisions designed to reduce the amount of time that an accused person might be kept in custody while awaiting trial, amongst them one which authorised examining justices to commit them to trial by a High Court judge sitting at assizes if this was more convenient. Some relief was given on the criminal side to both assizes and quarter sessions by increasing the number of offences which though indictable could in a particular case be tried summarily by magistrates' courts sitting without a jury. In addition there had been some tinkering with the actual circuits and the towns at which assizes were held, in an effort to concentrate visits on those places at which a substantial amount of work was likely to arise and to avoid those towns which, though important in the past, no longer provided enough work to justify regular visitation. Progress here was however extremely difficult in the face of strong local loyalties.

None of these remedies proved adequate. Hence the appointment of the Beeching Commission itself. Probably its most important recommendation was that the system of travelling High Court judges should continue. The major problem in its view was then to make sure that their time was used to the best advantage. In the Commission's view this involved two major considerations. First, so to arrange the work to be done, especially on the criminal side, that High Court judges were only used for those cases for which their experience, skill or status was indispensable. Secondly, so to organise the local centres for the administration of civil and criminal justice that it took place at places readily accessible to large numbers of people and that the work to be dealt with was relatively concentrated instead of being distributed unevenly throughout the country. At the same time it made some suggestions of administrative changes which gave responsibility to particular judges to see that the business within the circuit for which they were responsible was organised in the most efficient manner possible. These

presiding judges in relation to their own circuits were, in fact, to play a similar role in this regard to that played by the Lord Chief Justice in London for
the country as a whole. So far as the structure of the courts is concerned
the Commission's most important recommendation was the abolition of the
separate systems of assize and quarter sessions and their replacement by a
single Crown Court which was to become a part of the Supreme Court, and
the appointment of a new class of Circuit judges, to whom criminal business
which did not need the attention of a High Court judge could be allocated.
Although some new Circuit judges were especially appointed as a result of
this recommendation, the bulk of them are county court judges who have
simply been redesignated Circuit judges and authorised, as a result, to sit
not only in the civil county courts but also in the criminal Crown Court.
The result has thus been to carry one step further the assimilation, as regards
personnel at least, of the administration of civil and criminal justice on a
local level.

The English legal system has now for the first time a two tier system
of judges all of whom are capable of exercising both civil and criminal
jurisdiction, the judges of the High Court (though it is in fact mostly the
judges of the Queen's Bench Division who take the criminal cases) and the
Circuit judges. They are supported by part time Recorders in the hearing
of criminal cases. In addition there are the magistrates' courts, staffed by
part time lay justices and in some cases, in London for example, by professional full time stipendiary magistrates, which deal with the summary
trial of criminal offences, including cases involving children and young
persons, and some civil matters. The actual court system too has achieved
a greater formal symmetry, with the House of Lords at the top, then the
Court of Appeal. Below the Court of Appeal there is the High Court and
the Crown Court and finally, and outside to some extent, are the county
courts and magistrates' courts.

One useful thing that the Beeching Report does incidentally to its main
purpose is to bring what one might call the geographical dimension of the
English legal system into focus, in contrast to the more common historical
approach. The legal system for all its formal unity and its different categories of courts, jurisdictions, procedures and personnel is in fact distributed
in towns and cities throughout the country and a map of England would
be as useful a starting point for describing it as any sketch of its long past.
The major centres at which the High Court sits could then be identified
as well as the rather larger number of places in which the Crown Court
is held. Then there are the county courts and magistrates' courts and the
numerous tribunals at their different levels of first instance and appeal.
Nor should the process stop there. There are the local police forces, and
police authorities, the probation service, the local law societies, prisons,
borstals and detention and attendance centres. This approach has the
technical advantage of relating the administration of justice to the other
centrally and locally administered services, and locating the institutions and
personnel where they actually are, around the corner and actually visitable.
It would have the further advantage of revealing the relationship between
the separate agencies and institutions " on the ground." It will be seen that
the Children and Young Persons Act 1969 makes it necessary to take this

relationship into account in a quite specific way since it requires co-operation in any area between the police, the courts and the local authority welfare services. But even where it is not made explicit in legislation in this way, it makes sense to attempt to see the legal system as it is seen by the local inhabitants of a community, instead of over-emphasising the role played by London as a legal and judicial centre. For, although there is a national legal system centred on London, this is not the legal system as it is seen or as it works for the inhabitants, say, of Royal Leamington Spa. They and their friends and neighbours in Coventry and Warwickshire see the legal system as consisting of the police, traffic wardens, solicitors, probation officers, magistrates' courts and the Crown Court, the High Court and county court, the social insurance and rent tribunals, legal aid committees, citizens advice bureaux, neighbourhood law centres, juvenile courts and children's officers, which make up the network of legal and social services to which they will have to appeal for their legal rights and by whom they will be dealt with if they break their legal duties. Not only would this help to emphasise the importance of the local administration of justice, but it would also emphasise those aspects which are most available to observation, most in need of scrutiny and most neglected, as any member of the public who has been asked whether he is a defendent or a witness in a magistrates' court will readily acknowledge. And it is probably as important to see the local legal system as a unity as it is the national system.

It would be tempting in an age of radical optimism to go still further and abandon all talk of the High Court and write only of social insurance tribunals and neighbourhood law centres, just as it would be tempting in a period of rapid Europeanisation to begin a study of the English legal system from Brussels, or rather Luxembourg. But however much progress has been made in rationalising the system it still arrives trailing clouds of history behind it. And although it may not be necessary any more to make the long journey from the Norman Conquest to 1873–75 before beginning to look at the present picture, some historical perspective probably still remains necessary simply to explain how and why it is as it is, and to uncover some of the assumptions and aims underlying its different features either at the time they were introduced or subsequently. Hence the brief historical introduction, and hence, perhaps for the last time, we begin with the High Court.

THE HIGH COURT

The High Court was established by the 1873–75 Judicature Acts. It came as a culmination of a long series of inquiries and reforms concerned with civil administration of justice, starting with Brougham's reform speech in 1828, and was the solution finally adopted to bring into harmony the variety of courts that had developed over the previous 600 years, and in particular to bridge the troublesome gap between the common law courts and the Court of Chancery. The first step towards tackling this last problem had been taken when the common law courts were given the power to use some of the procedural devices of the Court of Chancery such as the putting of interrogatories, and the power to order discovery of relevant documents and to give remedies such as injunction and specific performance. Similarly the Court of Chancery had been given the power to deal with points of common law that came up incidentally in proceedings before it and to give damages in lieu of its usual remedies. But this was only a first step and following the report of the Judicature Commissioners the High Court was established into which the major independent courts were absorbed and re-emerged as Divisions.

First Report of the Judicature Commissioners
1869, P.P. xxv

In commencing the inquiry which we were directed by Your Majesty to make, the first subject that naturally presented itself for consideration was the ancient division of the Courts, into the Courts of Common Law, and the Court of Chancery, founded on the well known distinction in our law between Common Law and Equity. . . .

The evils of this double system of Judicature, and the confusion and conflict of jurisdiction to which it has led, have been long known and acknowledged.

. . . The Commissioners appointed in 1851 to inquire into the constitution of the Court of Chancery . . . state that " a practical and effectual remedy for many of the evils in question may be found in such a transfer or blending of jurisdiction, . . . as will render each Court competent to administer complete justice in the cases which fall under its cognizance."

In like manner the Commissioners appointed in 1850 to inquire into the constitution of the Common Law Courts . . . report that " . . . a consolidation of all the elements of a complete remedy in the same Court was obviously desirable, not to say imperatively necessary, to the establishment of a consistent and rational system of procedure."

In consequence of these Reports several Acts of Parliament have been passed for the purpose of carrying out to a limited extent the recommendations of the Commissioners.

. . . These changes, however, fall far short of the recommendations of the Common Law Commissioners, who in their Final Report expressed the opinion, that power should be conferred on the Common Law Courts " to give, in respect of rights there recognized, all the protection and redress which at present can be obtained in any jurisdiction."

The alterations, to which we have referred, have no doubt introduced considerable improvements into the procedure both of the Common Law and Equity Courts; but, after a careful consideration of the subject, and judging now with the advantage of many years experience of the practical working of the systems actually in force, we are of opinion that " the transfer or blending of jurisdiction " attempted to be carried out by recent Acts of Parliament, even if it had been adopted to the full extent recommended by the Commissioners, is not a sufficient or adequate remedy for the evils complained of, and would at best have mitigated but not removed the most prominent of those evils. . . .

It may be further observed, in illustration of the evils of the double procedure, that whenever a new class of business arises, such as the litigation arising out of railway and other joint stock companies, proceedings, frequently of an experimental character, are commenced both at Law and in Equity by different suitors, leading to the inconvenience of protracted litigation, and the danger of conflicting judgments. We may refer to the litigation lately pending between the sellers of railway shares and the jobbers on the Stock Exchange, by which the sellers sought to obtain an indemnity from the jobbers against calls. The litigation began in a Court of Common Law. A suit in Equity soon followed, by a different plaintiff against the same defendants, both suits asking for similar redress. The Court of Common Law decided in favour of the plaintiff. The Court of Equity shortly after delivered judgment to the same effect. The defendants appealed in both suits; in the one case to the Exchequer Chamber, in the other to the Court of Appeal in Chancery. Both appeals were pending at the same time, but there was no official machinery by which the Judges of Appeal in Chancery and the Court of Exchequer Chamber could enter into communication with the view of arriving at a common result. The Court of Exchequer Chamber reversed the judgment of the Court below; the Court of Appeal in Chancery, acting independently of the Court of Exchequer Chamber, arrived at the same conclusion, and about the same time delivered its judgment, reversing the decision of the Vice-Chancellor. The Defendants were thus subjected to litigation (at the instance, no doubt, of different parties), carried on at the same time in different Courts, and exposed to the risk of conflicting decisions, those Courts operating under different forms of procedure, and being controlled by different Courts of Appeal.

The litigation arising out of Joint Stock Companies has constituted a very large proportion of the business which has engaged the attention of Courts of Law and Equity for some years. Directors of Joint Stock Companies fill the double character of agents and trustees for the companies and shareholders; and the effect of their acts and representations has frequently been brought into question in both jurisdictions, and sometimes with opposite results. The expense thus needlessly incurred has been so great, and the perplexity thereby occasioned in the conduct of business so considerable, as to convince most persons, who have followed the development of this branch of the law, of the necessity that exists for a tribunal invested with full power of dealing with all the complicated rights and obligations springing out of such transactions, and of administering complete and appropriate relief, no matter whether the rights and obligations involved are what are called legal or equitable.

We may refer also to the present condition of the High Court of Admiralty. A conflict, bearing some analogy to that which has so long existed between the Court of Chancery and the Courts of Common Law, seems likely to arise, if it has not already arisen, between the latter Courts and the Court of Admiralty. From ancient times the Courts of Common Law exercised a jealous supervision over the jurisdiction of the Court of Admiralty, and by the issuing of frequent writs of prohibition took pains to confine the jurisdiction of that Court within the narrowest limits. The consequence was, that, except in time of war, when it sat as a Prize Court, there was very little business in the Court of Admiralty until its jurisdiction was extended by recent legislation. Now, however, by virtue of several Acts of Parliament, the first of which was passed so lately as 1840, but more especially by the Admiralty Court Act 1861, the jurisdiction of the Court has been extended to a variety of cases, which had been theretofore considered as exclusively cognizable in Courts of Common Law. As the Court of Chancery, chiefly by means of its power of granting injunctions for threatened as well as actual injuries, has extended its jurisdiction over a large class of cases properly cognizable in Courts of Common Law, the Court of Admiralty, assisted by the recent legislation above mentioned, and enjoying the peculiar advantage of a Court enforcing the law of maritime lien by proceedings in rem, might be expected, if this system were continued, to extend its jurisdiction over many kinds of litigation relating to ships or cargoes, in respect of which the Courts of Common Law have a concurrent jurisdiction, but are not able to afford such convenient redress. The cause of this is manifestly the imperfection of the Common Law system, and the consequent necessity of seeking for a more complete remedy elsewhere.

Not only are the procedure of and the remedies administered by the Courts of Common Law and the Court of Admiralty different, but sometimes the redress to be obtained is regulated by different and conflicting principles. Thus in a collision suit the damages are, in some cases, assessed on one principle in a Court of Common Law, and on an entirely different principle in the Court of Admiralty. At Common Law, if both parties are found to be in fault, the Plaintiff fails. In the Court of Admiralty, the Plaintiff, under exactly similar circumstances, is entitled to recover half his damages from the Defendant; and there being generally in such cases a cross suit, the Defendant is also entitled to recover half his damages from the Plaintiff. This anomaly, if our recommendations are adopted, will require to be corrected by legislation.

The Court of Admiralty, even with the extended jurisdiction conferred on it by recent enactments, still labours under the same defect as the other Courts. It cannot, in many cases, give a complete remedy; the suitor may obtain one portion of his redress in the Court of Admiralty, but he must go into a Court of Common Law, or it may be into the Court of Chancery, for the rest. The Court of Admiralty has jurisdiction over a claim for damage to cargo, where the owner is not domiciled in England, but it has no jurisdiction over the claim of the shipowner for the freight due in respect of the same cargo; the shipowner must proceed for that in a Court of Common Law. It seems plain that these are counter claims, which ought to be capable of being set off against each other in the same suit. In the same way, the jurisdiction of the Court of Admiralty over claims for necessaries supplied to a ship is restricted to the case of a foreign ship, and to that of a British ship where there is not any owner domiciled in England; but if it happens that for some other cause the ship is under arrest, or that the proceeds thereof are in Court, then the Court exercises jurisdiction over all claims for building, equipping, or repairing the ship. All these claims may at the same time be litigated by a different procedure in a Court of Common Law; and hence it may happen not unfrequently that litigation may be proceeding simultaneously in the Court of Admiralty and at Common Law for the adjustment of disputes arising out of the same transaction, between the same parties or those who are liable to indemnify them. The conflict of judicial decisions, which may be thus occasioned, is made more perplexing, by the want of a Common Court of Appeal, as the appeal from the Court of Admiralty is to the Privy Council, and from the Common Law Courts to the Exchequer Chamber and the House of Lords. . . .

Constitution of the Supreme Court

We are of opinion that the defects above adverted to cannot be completely remedied by any mere transfer or blending of jurisdiction between the Courts as at present constituted; and that the first step towards meeting and surmounting the evils complained of will be the consolidation of all the Superior Courts of Law and Equity, together with the Courts of Probate, Divorce, and Admiralty, into one Court, to be called " Her Majesty's Supreme Court," in which Court shall be vested all the jurisdiction which is now exercisable by each and all the Courts so consolidated.

This consolidation would at once put an end to all conflicts of jurisdiction. No suitor could be defeated because he commenced his suit in the wrong Court, and sending the suitor from equity to law or from law to equity, to begin his suit over again in order to obtain redress, will be no longer possible.

The Supreme Court thus constituted would of course be divided into as many Chambers or Divisions as the nature and extent or the convenient despatch of business might require.

All suits, however, should be instituted in the Supreme Court, and not in any particular Chamber or Division of it; and each Chamber or Division should possess all the jurisdiction of the Supreme Court with respect to the subject-matter of the suit, and with respect to every defence which may be made thereto, whether on legal or equitable grounds, and should be enabled to grant such relief or to apply such remedy or combination of remedies as may be appropriate or necessary in order to do complete justice between the parties in the case before the Court, or, in other words, such remedies as all the present Courts combined have now jurisdiction to administer.

We consider it expedient, with a view . . . to make the proposed change at first as little inconvenient as possible, that the Courts of Chancery, Queen's Bench, Common Pleas, and Exchequer should for the present retain their distinctive titles, and should constitute so many Chambers or Divisions of the Supreme Court; and as regards the Courts of Admiralty, Divorce and Probate, we think it would be convenient that those Courts should be consolidated, and and form one Chamber or Division of the Supreme Court. . . .

Between the several Chambers or Divisions of the Supreme Court so constituted it would be necessary to make such a classification of business as might seem desirable with reference to the nature of the suits and the relief to be sought or administered therein, and the ordinary distribution of business among the different Chambers or Divisions should be regulated according to such classification. For the same reason which induces us to recommend the retention for the present of the distinctive titles of the different Courts in their new character, as so many divisions of the Supreme Court, we think that such classification should in the first instance be made on the principle of assigning as nearly as practicable to those Chambers or Divisions such suits as would now be commenced in the respective Courts as at present constituted; with power, however, to the Supreme Court to vary or alter this classification in such manner as may from time to time be deemed expedient.

It should further be competent for any Chamber or Division of the Supreme Court to order a suit to be transferred at any stage of its progress to any other Chamber or Division of the Court, if it appears that justice can thereby be more conveniently done in the suit; but except for the purpose of obtaining such transfer, it should not be competent for any party to object to the prosecution of any suit in the particular Chamber or Division in which it is being prosecuted, on the ground that it ought to have been brought or prosecuted in some other Chamber or Division of the Court. . . .

From the consolidation of all the present Superior Courts into one Supreme Court, it follows, that all the Judges of those Courts will become Judges of the Supreme Court; and thus every Judge (with the exception of those who are to sit exclusively in the Appellate Court hereinafter recommended), though belonging to a particular Division, will be competent to sit in any other Division of the Court, whenever it may be found convenient for the administration of justice.

Here arises an important and difficult question, as to the number of Judges who should ordinarily sit in each Chamber or Division of the Supreme Court. Hitherto the constitution of the Court of Chancery and of the Courts of Common Law, in this respect, has been entirely different. Each Division of the Court of Chancery is presided over by a single judge, who adjudicates on all matters as a Court of First Instance, except in the few cases when he sits as a Court of Appeal from the County Courts. In like manner, a single Judge administers justice in the Courts of Probate, Divorce, and Admiralty respectively. On the other hand, in the Sittings of the Courts of Common Law in Banc, the Court is ordinarily constituted of four Judges. The matters adjudicated upon by the single Judge in the Court of Chancery are in many instances as important as the business transacted before the four Judges in the Courts of

Common Law; so that there would seem to be either a want of power in the Court of Chancery, or an excess of power in the Courts of Common Law; but it must be borne in mind that a considerable proportion of the business of the Courts of Common Law is transacted by one of the Judges sitting at Chambers; much of the business of these Courts also consists of the review of trials which have taken place before a Judge and Jury; they also review the decisions of the Judge sitting at Chambers; they are also empowered to decide various important matters, some of which involve questions of general public interest, on which their determination is in some cases final.

With a Court of Appeal such as we propose to recommend, common to all the Divisions of the Supreme Court, constantly sitting, and easy of access, we think that matters of great importance may properly, as now in the Court of Chancery, be intrusted to the jurisdiction in the first instance of a single Judge; but, having regard to the principles which have guided us in our previous recommendations, and to the importance of avoiding any too violent transition from the modes of conducting judicial business to which the public have been accustomed, and in which they may be presumed to place confidence, we think it will be advisable to authorize a single Judge to exercise the jurisdiction of the Supreme Court, in the despatch of all such business appropriated to the Divisions of the Queen's Bench, Common Pleas, and Exchequer respectively as by general orders, or by the special order of the Court, or the consent of the parties, may be remitted to him; and that all matters now disposed of in banco in those Courts shall be heard and determined by not more than three Judges. We also think that the Judges of each Division or Chamber in which there are several Judges should have power to sit in banco in two sub-divisions at the same time, with the assistance, whenever necessary, of a Judge or Judges from any other Division of the Court. . . .

The main recommendation of the Judicature Commissioners was carried into effect by the Judicature Acts 1873–75 and a Supreme Court consisting of the Court of Appeal and the High Court was established. Those Acts and the Acts which amended them were subsequently repealed and replaced by the Supreme Court of Judicature (Consolidation) Act 1925 which sets out the basic jurisdiction and composition of the High Court at present. A large number of subsequent statutes have enlarged its general jurisdiction and brought its original jurisdiction up to date. What the 1873–75 and the 1925 Acts principally do is to preserve for the High Court all the non-statutory jurisdiction which makes up the " common law " in its widest sense (i.e. in the very general sense which includes equity) which had been developed over the centuries by the courts it had replaced, including their powers of developing and moulding the law to meet changing needs, conditions and views. The old courts became divisions or parts of a division of the new court. All the judges became judges of the High Court and each judge and division had all the powers of the High Court. One of the changes in fact was that in future trials in the High Court would be conducted by a single judge, instead of the small group of judges who when they sat in London constituted the full bench of, for example, the common law courts. This gave proportionately more importance to the Court of Appeal as guardian of the law's quality than its predecessor the Court of Exchequer Chamber had had to assume. A new Rules Committee was established to lay down a common procedure as far as possible for the High Court as a whole. It published the first Rules of the Supreme Court in 1883.

Supreme Court of Judicature (Consolidation) Act 1925

15 & 16 Geo. 5, c. 49

Part II

Jurisdiction and Law

Jurisdiction of the High Court

18.—(1) The High Court shall be a superior court of record.

(2) There shall be vested in the High Court: —

(*a*) Subject as otherwise provided in this Act, the jurisdiction which was formerly vested in, or capable of being exercised by, all or any of the courts following: —

(i) The High Court of Chancery, both as a common law court and as a court of equity, including the jurisdiction of the Master of the Rolls as a judge or master of the Court of Chancery and any jurisdiction exercised by him in relation to the Court of Chancery as a common law court;

(ii) The Court of Queen's Bench;

(iii) The Court of Common Pleas at Westminster;

(iv) The Court of Exchequer, both as a court of revenue and as a common law court;

(v) The Court of Common Pleas at Lancaster;

(vi) The Court of Pleas at Durham;

(vii) The courts created by commissions of assize [9]:

(*b*) All original jurisdiction which, under or by virtue of any enactment which came into force after the commencement of the Act of 1873 and is not repealed by this Act, was immediately before the commencement of this Act vested in or capable of being exercised by the High Court constituted by the Act of 1873:

(*c*) Such other jurisdiction, as is hereinafter in this Act conferred on the High Court.

(3) The jurisdiction vested in the High Court shall, subject as otherwise provided in this Act, include the jurisdiction which was formerly vested in, or capable of being exercised by, all or any one or more of the judges of the courts aforesaid respectively sitting in court or chambers or elsewhere, when acting as judges or a judge, in pursuance of any statute, law or custom, and all powers given to any such court or to any such judges or judge by any statute, and also all ministerial powers, duties and authorities incident to any and every part of the jurisdictions so vested.

. . .

20. Subject to the provisions of this Act the High Court shall, in relation to probates and letters of administration, have the following jurisdiction (in this Act referred to as " probate jurisdiction "), that is to say: —

(*a*) all such voluntary and contentious jurisdiction and authority in relation to the granting and revoking of probate and administration of the effects of deceased persons as was at the commencement of the Court of Probate Act 1857 vested in or exercisable by any court or person in England, together with full authority to hear and determine all questions relating to testamentary causes and matters:

(*b*) all such powers throughout England in relation to the personal estate in England of deceased persons as the Prerogative Court of Canterbury had

[9] s. 18 (2) (*a*) (vii) was repealed by the Courts Act 1971, s. 56 (4), Sched. 11, Pt. IV.

immediately before the commencement of the Court of Probate Act 1857
in the Province of Canterbury or in the parts thereof within its jurisdiction in relation to those testamentary causes and matters and those
effects of deceased persons which were at that date within the jurisdiction
of that court:

(c) such like jurisdiction and powers with respect to the real estate of
deceased persons as are hereinbefore conferred with respect to the
personal estate of deceased persons:

(d) all probate jurisdiction which, under or by virtue of any enactment
which came into force after the commencement of the Act of 1873 and is
not repealed by this Act, was immediately before the commencement of
this Act vested in or capable of being exercised by the High Court
constituted by the Act of 1873:

and the court shall, in the exercise of the probate jurisdiction perform all such
like duties with respect to the estates of deceased persons as were immediately
before the commencement of the Court of Probate Act 1857 to be performed by
ordinaries generally or by the Prerogative Court of Canterbury in respect of
probates, administrations and testamentary causes and matters which were at
that date within their respective jurisdictions.

21. The High Court shall have such jurisdiction—

(a) in relation to matrimonial causes and matters, as was immediately
before the commencement of the Matrimonial Causes Act 1857 vested
in or exercisable by any ecclesiastical court or person in England in
respect of divorce a mensâ et thoro, nullity of marriage, jactitation
of marriage, or restitution of conjugal rights, and in respect of any
matrimonial cause or matter except marriage licences; and

(b) with respect to declarations of legitimacy and of validity of marriage,
as is hereinafter in this Act provided;

and all such jurisdiction in relation to matrimonial causes and matters as, under
or by virtue of any enactment which came into force after the commencement of
the Act of 1873 and is not repealed by this Act, was immediately before the
commencement of this Act vested in or capable of being exercised by the High
Court constituted by the Act of 1873.

. . .

23. The High Court shall be a prize court within the meaning of the Naval
Prize Acts 1864 to 1916, as amended by any subsequent enactment, and shall
have all such jurisdiction on the high seas and throughout His Majesty's
Dominions and in every place where His Majesty has jurisdiction as, under any
Act relating to naval prize or otherwise, the High Court of Admiralty possessed
when acting as a prize court.[10]

. . .

44. Subject to the express provisions of any other Act, in questions relating
to the custody and education of infants and generally in all matters not particularly mentioned in this Act, in which there was formerly or is any conflict or
variance between the rules of equity and the rules of the common law with
reference to the same matter, the rules of equity shall prevail in all courts whatsoever in England so far as the matters to which those rules relate are cognizable
by those courts.

. . .

60. Every proceeding in the High Court and all business arising thereout
shall, so far as is practicable and convenient and subject to the provisions of this

[10] The general Admiralty jurisdiction of the High Court is set out in s. 1 of the Administration
of Justice Act 1956.

Act relating to divisional courts, be heard and disposed of before a single judge, and all proceedings in an action subsequent to the hearing or trial, down to and including the final judgment or order, shall, so far as is practicable and convenient, be taken before the judge before whom the trial or hearing took place.
. . .

63.—(1) Divisional courts may be held for the transaction of any business in the High Court which may be ordered by rules of court to be heard by a divisional court, and in all cases where there is a right of appeal to the High Court from any court or person the appeal shall be heard and determined by a divisional court. . . .

(6) A divisional court shall be constituted of two judges and no more: Provided that—

(a) The decisions of a divisional court shall not be invalidated by reason of the court being constituted of a greater number than two judges; and

(b) If the president of the Division to which the divisional court belongs . . . with the concurrence of not less than two other judges of the Division, is of opinion that the divisional court should be constituted of a greater number of judges than two, the court may be constituted of such number of judges as the president, with such concurrence as aforesaid, thinks expedient; and

(c) A divisional court for hearing such an appeal as aforesaid shall be constituted in accordance with rules of court.

The Divisions of the High Court

The High Court was originally divided into five divisions corresponding to the courts it had replaced: Queen's Bench, Common Pleas, Exchequer, Chancery and Probate, Divorce and Admiralty. In 1881 the first three were amalgamated into the Queen's Bench Division. In 1894 after some dissatisfaction had been expressed about the way in which commercial cases were dealt with in the Queen's Bench Division it was decided that in future, although commercial cases should continue to be tried within the Queen's Bench Division, it should be possible to enter them on a special Commercial List and have them tried by a Commercial judge specially assigned by the Lord Chief Justice to hear such cases. The three divisions in fact remained unaltered. Dissatisfaction was however frequently expressed about the way in which the divisions were organised and in particular the way in which "wills, wives and wrecks" were grouped together in the Probate, Divorce and Admiralty Division.

A number of suggestions had been made for a reorganisation of the divisions. At a time when some two-fifths of divorce work was being heard by King's Bench judges on assize the Hanworth Committee [11] recommended that the divorce work should be transferred completely to the King's Bench Division along with the Admiralty work which could subsequently be dealt with alongside the work of the Commercial Court. The probate work could then be transferred to the Chancery Division. This proposal was however rejected by the Peel Commission.[12] By that time the system under which King's Bench judges heard matrimonial cases on assize was no longer regarded as satisfactory because of the way in which the trial

[11] Business of Courts Committee 1935–36, Cmd. 5066.
[12] Royal Commission on the Despatch of Business at Common Law, 1936, Cmd. 5065.

of these cases was subordinated to the trial of criminal and other civil cases and it feared that any addition to the business of the King's Bench Division would in any event overwhelm it. The Evershed Committee on Supreme Court Practice and Procedure [13] took the view that there was a strong case for the creation of a combined Admiralty/Commercial Court but that there was insufficient reason to make a substantial change of this sort unless some change was proposed in the distribution of the divorce work.

The current division of the High Court into three divisions, Queen's Bench, Chancery and Family, was the result of the Administration of Justice Act, 1970. In introducing it into the House of Lords the Lord Chancellor said [14]:

> Nowadays, it may strike people as very odd to find such a strange assortment as probate, divorce and admiralty proceedings taken by the Judges of a single Division. But this grouping would not have appeared so surprising in 1875. It was then a question of grouping with High Court of Admiralty the court of probate and the court for divorce and matrimonial causes, which had both been ecclesiastical courts as recently as 1857. The jurisdiction of the newly constituted Probate, Divorce and Admiralty Division was by nature and origin unfamiliar to the ordinary common law and chancery courts. The lawyers who had practised in the old ecclesiastical courts were specialists, doctors and proctors and even had their own Inn, known as Doctors' Commons, as your Lordships may remember from the pages of *David Copperfield*.

> In 1875, and indeed for long after that, there was so little matrimonial business that no one would have dreamt of constituting a Division of the High Court especially to deal with it. Indeed, the designers of the Law Courts no doubt thought that they were providing for all future time in providing for four divorce courts when the Division consisted solely of the President and one Judge—now there are the President and 17 Judges. . . .

> Nor has it been seriously suggested until comparatively recent years that a Family Division should be created to deal not only with the matrimonial jurisdiction of the Divorce Division, but also with all the jurisdiction of a family kind which is now fortuitously scattered among the other Divisions of the High Court. . . . We are not simply striving for something that would be tidier and look better on an organisational chart. . . . It is most important that all family matters, whether they involve the parties to a matrimonial dispute or the care, adoption, or guardianship of children, should be dealt with in the most sympathetic atmosphere and by Judges and officials who really understand family problems and how to grapple with them. . . .

The Act created a Family Division and transferred to it the wardship, guardianship and adoption jurisdiction previously exercised by the Chancery Division. The contested probate work was transferred to the Chancery Division which already dealt with the interpretation of wills. The

[13] Cmd. 8878.
[14] 306 H.L.Deb., col. 197; December 4, 1969.

Admiralty work was transferred to the Queen's Bench Division and Admiralty and Commercial Courts were formally created in that Division.

In referring to the present divisions of the High Court it is perhaps worth drawing attention to one which does not exist, though it has had its advocates, namely an Administrative Division which would specialise in disputes involving the government, government departments, Ministers and other public authorities. At the moment disputes between citizens and the state are dealt with either in the course of ordinary proceedings in one of the existing divisions, in which case points of law arising in relation to it are not treated any differently from any other points of law, or, if a party is seeking one of the prerogative orders, in the Divisional Court of the Queen's Bench Division. This is where, for example, he is claiming that a public body is not fulfilling its public duties (mandamus), or that when under a duty to act judicially has failed to do so, or has exceeded its powers, or has made an error of law (certiorari). One result has been that the English legal system has not developed a comprehensive system of administrative law or a specialist administrative law jurisdiction as for example is the case in France. There has been no recognition of the fact that problems involving the administration may require a specialist and experienced approach just as much as shipping and commercial cases do. As a result, problems of administrative law are still dealt with, for the most part, as part and parcel of the ordinary run-of-the-mill civil business of the High Court. This is in keeping with the principle propounded by Professor Dicey in his work *The Law and the Constitution* [15] as part of his definition of the Rule of Law that such problems were best dealt with by the ordinary courts in accordance with the ordinary law of the land in the ordinary way. Where governments have felt the ordinary courts to be unsatisfactory bodies to deal with such problems they have simply attempted to exclude them. Where they have felt the need to provide new remedies against administrative action they have either provided for application to be made to the ordinary courts, as is the case where someone wishes to claim that an order for the compulsory acquisition of his land is invalid because it goes beyond the powers granted to the Minister or because the Minister has failed to observe the proper procedure, or they have set up a separate body of tribunals such as the social insurance tribunals to deal with any disputes that may arise. The matter has been considered by the Law Commission in a report. [16]

Supreme Court of Judicature (Consolidation) Act 1925

15 & 16 Geo. 5, c. 49

5.—(1) His Majesty in Council may from time to time, on a . . . recommendation [of the Lord Chancellor, the Lord Chief Justice, the Master of the Rolls, the President of the Family Division and the Vice-Chancellor] [17] order that any reduction or increase in the number of the Divisions . . . of the High Court . . . may pursuant to such . . . recommendation be carried into effect, and may give all such further directions as may be necessary or proper for that purpose. . . .

[15] 1884.
[16] Cmnd. 4059, No. 20 (1969).
[17] Amended by s. 1 (5), Administration of Justice Act 1970.

(2) An Order in Council under this section shall not come into operation until it has been laid before each House of Parliament for thirty days on which that House has sat, or if within that period of thirty days an address is presented to His Majesty by either House of Parliament, praying that the Order may not come into operation.

55. Without prejudice to any other provision of this Act, all causes and matters in the High Court shall, subject to the power of transfer, be distributed among the several Divisions and judges of the High Court, in such manner as may be directed by rules of court, and subject thereto all such causes and matters shall be assigned . . . in the manner hereinafter provided.

56. Without prejudice to any other provision of this Act, there shall be assigned—

(1) To the Chancery Division—

(a) All causes and matters in respect of which exclusive jurisdiction was under any Act given to the Court of Chancery or to any judge thereof:

(b) All causes and matters for any of the following purposes:
The administration of the estates of deceased persons;
The dissolution of partnerships or the taking of partnership or other accounts;
The redemption or foreclosure of mortgages;
The raising of portions or other charges on land;
The sale and distribution of the proceeds of property subject to any lien or charge;
The execution of trusts, charitable or private;
The rectification or setting aside, or cancellation of deeds or other written instruments;
The specific performance of contracts between vendors and purchasers of real estates, including contracts for leases;
The partition or sale of real estates;
[The appointment of a guardian of a minor's estate alone] [18]:

[(bb) All causes and matters involving the exercise of the High Court's probate jurisdiction otherwise than in respect of non-contentious or common form probate business:] [18]

(c) All causes and matters which under, by virtue of or in pursuance of any enactment for the time being in force are assigned to that Division.[19]

(2) To the King's Bench Division—

(a) All causes and matters, civil and criminal, which, if the Act of 1873 had not passed, would have been within the exclusive cognizance of the Court of Queen's Bench in the exercise of its original jurisdiction, or of the Court of Common Pleas at Westminster, or of the Court of Exchequer, either as a court of revenue or as a common law court [20]:

[18] Amended by Administration of Justice Act 1970, s. 1 (6), Sched. 2, para. 8.
[19] The fact that much of the original jurisdiction of the Court of Chancery involves developing machinery for the investigation of accounts led to it acquiring jurisdiction over company matters. Tax matters are also largely heard in the Chancery Division and since 1921 it has had a bankruptcy jurisdiction. Much of the work is non-contentious and involves applying to the court for, e.g. permission to vary a trust or settlement or to get a point of difficulty in administering a trust or settlement settled.
[20] In 1968 the [Winn] Committee on Personal Injuries Litigation noted (Cmnd. 3691, para. 39): " [O]f all the non-matrimonial civil actions tried in London and at Assizes in 1967 almost 85 per cent. were personal injury actions. Industrial accident cases were twice as numerous as road accident cases."

[(*aa*) All causes and matters involving the exercise of the High Court's
Admiralty jurisdiction, or its jurisdiction as a prize court:] [18]

(*b*) All causes and matters which under, by virtue of or in pursuance of
any enactment for the time being in force are assigned to that
Division.

(3) To the [Family Division] [18]

(*a*) All causes and matters [involving the exercise of the High Court's
jurisdiction in proceedings specified in Schedule 1 to the Administration of Justice Act 1970] [18]:

(*b*) [All causes and maters which under, or by virtue or in pursuance of,
any other enactment for the time being in force are assigned to the
Family Division] [18]:

(*c*) All causes and matters which under, by virtue of or in pursuance of
any enactment for the time being in force are assigned to that
Division.

57.—(1) The Lord Chancellor may, if at any time it appears to him desirable
so to do with a view to the more convenient administration of justice, by order
direct that any jurisdiction vested in the High Court in respect of any [Pro-
ceedings] [21] ...

(*a*) Shall be assigned to such other Division or Divisions as may be specified
in the order ... ; and

(*b*) Shall be exercised either by any special judge or judges or by all the
judges of any Divisoin] : [22]

Provided that an order shall not be made ... except with the concurrence
both of the president of [any] [23] Division to which the jurisdiction is ...
assigned and of the president of [any] [23] Division to which the jurisdiction is to
be transferred [or with which it is to be shared.] [24]

Administration of Justice Act 1970

1970 c. 31

1.—(1) The Probate, Divorce and Admiralty Division of the High Court
shall be re-named the Family Division; and the principal probate registry shall
be re-named the principal registry of the Family Division.

(2) There shall be assigned to the Family Division all causes and matters
involving the exercise of the High Court's jurisdiction in proceedings specified in
Schedule 1 to this Act.

(3) Causes and matters involving the exercise of the High Court's Admiralty
jurisdiction, or its jurisdiction as a prize court, shall be assigned to the Queen's
Bench Division.

(4) As respects the exercise of the High Court's probate jurisdiction—

(*a*) non-contentious or common form probate business shall continue to
be assigned to the Family Division; and

(*b*) all other probate business shall be assigned to the Chancery Division.

2.—(1) There shall be constituted, as part of the Queen's Bench Division of
the High Court, an Admiralty Court to take Admiralty business, that is to say
causes and matters assigned to that division and involving the exercise of the
High Court's Admiralty jurisdiction, or its jurisdiction as a prize court.

[21] Amended by Administration of Justice Act 1928, Sched. I, Pt. 1.
[22] Amended by Administration of Justice Act 1969, s. 23 (2).
[23] Amended *ibid*. s. 23 (3) (*a*).
[24] Amended *ibid*. s. 23 (3) (*b*).

(2) The judges of the Admiralty Court shall be such of the puisne judges of the High Court as the Lord Chancellor may from time to time nominate to be Admiralty Judges.

3.—(1) There shall be constituted, as part of the Queen's Bench Division of the High Court, a Commercial Court to take such causes and matters as may in accordance with rules of court be entered in the commercial list.

(2) The judges of the Commercial Court shall be such of the puisne judges of the High Court as the Lord Chancellor may from time to time nominate to be Commercial Judges.

SCHEDULE 1

HIGH COURT BUSINESS ASSIGNED TO FAMILY DIVISION

Business at first instance

Proceedings consisting of a matrimonial cause, or any matter arising out of or connected with such a cause; proceedings for a decree of presumption of death and dissolution of marriage; and any other proceedings with respect to which rules of court may be made by virtue of section 7 (1) of the Matrimonial Causes Act 1967.

Proceedings for a declaration—

(a) under section 39 of the Matrimonial Causes Act 1965, as to a person's legitimacy, or the validity of a marriage, or a person's right to be deemed a British subject; or

(b) with respect to a person's matrimonial status.

Proceedings in relation to the wardship of minors.

Proceedings under the Adoption Acts 1958 and 1968.

Proceedings under the Guardianship of Infants Act 1886 and 1925 and otherwise in relation to the guardianship of minors, except proceedings for the appointment of a guardian of a minor's estate alone.

Proceedings under section 3 of the Marriage Act 1949 for obtaining the court's consent to the marriage of a minor.

Proceedings under section 17 of the Married Women's Property Act 1882 (determination of title to property in dispute between spouses).

Proceedings in which a parent or guardian of a minor applies for a writ of habeas corpus ad subjiciendum relative to the custody, care or control of the minor.

Proceedings under the following enactments:—

(a) the Maintenance Orders (Facilities for Enforcement) Act 1920 (enforcement in England and Wales of orders made overseas for periodical payments to a man's wife or dependant);

(b) Part II of the Maintenance Orders Act 1950 (enforcement in England and Wales of certain maintenance and other orders made in Scotland or Northern Ireland);

(c) the Maintenance Orders Act 1958 (registration and enforcement of certain maintenance and other orders);

(d) Part III of this Act.

Proceedings under section 1 of the Matrimonial Homes Act 1967 (means whereby a spouse can continue in occupation of, or obtain entry to, a dwelling-house which is, or has been, the matrimonial home).

The Commercial Court and its contemporary role

Reference has already been made to the fact that in 1894 as a result of dissatisfaction which had been expressed about the way in which some of the Queen's Bench judges were handling commercial cases a special Commercial List was established and the cases on it entrusted to a judge who could specialise in commercial cases. The Administration of Justice Act 1970 has now formally established a Commercial Court in the Queen's Bench Division. The question of how the English legal system deals with commercial cases, however, is not simply one of the organisation of divisions or the creation of a special court. It goes much deeper than that and raises several fundamental issues.

Inevitably at the beginning of a book on the English legal system we are concerned with a description of its basic structure. But there is some danger in this. Whatever beauty the system may have itself, its ultimate justification is that it serves a useful purpose. It is important that one should have at the back of one's mind from the very beginning of looking at a legal system the question "What is it good for?" One reason for this is that, if no one uses it, it might as well not exist. A criticism that has been levelled at the English legal system is that it has ceased to play a central role in the life of the community. Two of the areas which have been cited in support of that suggestion are the sphere of administrative and governmental action, including the vast amount of work now entrusted to tribunals, and the sphere of commercial disputes. As regards the latter, it is argued that commercial men prefer arbitration to coming to the ordinary courts, and the suggestion is that it is in some way the courts' fault. They have become marginal because they have failed to give the customer what he wants. All they are good for, and the statistics for the Queen's Bench Division and the county courts bear this out to some extent, is dealing with running down actions, divorce, collection of debts, and the administration of criminal law with the risk that even running down litigation may one day be replaced by some comprehensive scheme of insurance. The question of the role played by the courts, whether it is declining in importance and why, is one that cannot be shirked. Commercial cases provide a kind of test case, though they are not the only point at which potential customers have sometimes been heard to complain that the facilities offered by the system are inadequate. Another, as we shall see later, concerns the facilities offered to consumers with small claims for which it is said the existing arrangements are unable to cater. Some of the problems which these kinds of questions raise are fundamental in a sense other than that of simply questioning the role that the courts play in the important events of the community. They raise fundamental questions about the nature of a legal system, in particular the English legal system, and questions about which of its features are essential and which simply a product of the fact that they were largely developed over the years around the activities of the common law courts and the kind of business with which those courts were accustomed to deal. Problems such as these raise particularly important questions at a time when new demands are frequently being made on the legal system and new tasks invented for it quite unlike those it has traditionally tackled. Two recent examples have been the tasks given to it under the Restrictive Trade Practices Act 1956 and the Industrial Relations Act 1971. Neither of these Statutes entrusted the new tasks to one of the existing courts. Instead each created a new court for the purpose. Both the Restrictive Trade Practices Court and the Industrial Relations Court however are part of the legal system and their existence also raises the question which of those features with which one tends to associate the English legal system, its formal procedures, its rules of evidence and principles of law, its use of rules for deciding cases, its reliance on precedent, its separation between barristers and solicitors and its practice of choosing judges from barristers, are essential features of a legal system, and which are merely essential features of the English legal system, and, further, which are not essential at all and could be abandoned if the efficient performance of new tasks required it?

This short digression on commercial disputes is intended to help drive home the point that one cannot take the success of the legal system for granted because its judges earn salaries which are charged upon the Consolidated Fund, or its practitioners have a large take-home pay. Even at the level of the High Court one has to ask how well adapted is the system to meet the demands which are reasonably made upon it? How far can it adapt or be adapted to meet these demands without losing its essential features? The digression may also serve as a reminder to us that although the High Court is an English court it has to cater for a much wider community than those who live within its borders. Although this foreign element in the administration of justice is not much touched on again it raises important questions of jurisdiction and the determination of the appropriate law to apply and the relationship between the English legal system and the legal systems of other countries. It provides the most extreme alternative perspective to that mentioned earlier which looks at the legal system from the point of view of the man walking down the Parade at Leamington Spa.

Disputes between merchants and commercial problems generally have always caused difficulty for the common law courts. Even after they had won the jurisdiction over such matters previously exercised by the courts of piepowder, the staple courts and the Court of Admiralty, they took a long time digesting it and adapting the traditional forms of action to the needs and customs of merchants, though the fact that it was a new and relatively undeveloped area of the common law did at least make it possible for judges such as Lord Mansfield in the eighteenth century to incorporate many of these customs into the law. In spite however of these great feats of absorption and a more than usual willingness to adapt the law to mercantile needs the courts seem never to have won the wholehearted confidence of the commercial community.

In the nineteenth century there was some demand for the establishment of tribunals of commerce on the continental model which in the view of some commercial men would have been more responsive to the needs and expectations of the business community. The Judicature Commissioners rejected this suggestion in their Third Report. Instead the nineteenth century showed the ordinary courts strengthening their control over arbitration which was the favoured alternative to actions in the superior courts of

law.   When a special Commercial List was created in 1894 and a special
judge assigned to deal with it, it was in the hope that he would bring an
expertise in dealing with such cases to the task, and also that he might be
able to deal with such cases with less formality than was usual.   Some of
the judges assigned in this way gave considerable satisfaction to the commercial community, but satisfaction was by no means constant and the drift
to arbitration both in commercial and admiralty affairs continued.   Commercial men preferred not only the informality of arbitration but also its
privacy.   They complained that litigation in the courts was conducted in a
more combative spirit than they would wish when their dispute was with
someone with whom they wished to continue to do business.   It seems
likely that people do hesitate to do business with those who at the drop of a
hat will take them to court and subject them to the rigours of a public
examination and cross-examination.   Hence for all the fine print in their
contracts they often prefer to arbitrate, at least in the first instance, and
trading associations have made extensive provision for this desire.   Neglect
of the courts however is particularly damaging for a case law system, since
it depends upon frequent cases for the development of the law and the less
it is used the less satisfactory it becomes.   Hence some of the concern at the
drift to arbitration which was considered by the [Evershed] Committee on
Supreme Court Practice and Procedure in 1947–53 and a special Commercial
Court Users' Conference in 1960.

Third Report of the Judicature Commissioners
1874 P.P. xxiv

We think that it is of the utmost importance to the commercial community
that the decisions of the Courts of Law should on all questions of principle be,
as far as possible, uniform, thus affording precedents for the conduct of those
engaged in the ordinary transactions of trade.   With this view it is essential that
the Judges by whom commercial cases are determined, should be guided by the
recognised rules of law and by the decisions of the Superior Courts in analogous
cases; and only Judges who have been trained in the principles and practice of
law can be expected to be so guided.   We fear that merchants would be too apt
to decide questions that might come before them (as some of the witnesses we
examined have suggested that they should do) according to their own views of
what was just and proper in the particular case, a course which from the
uncertainty attending their decisions would inevitably multiply litigation, and
with the vast and intricate commercial business of this country would sooner or
later lead to great confusion.   Commercial questions, we think, ought not to be
determined without law, or by men without special legal training.   For these
reasons, we are of opinion that it is not expedient to establish in this country
Tribunals of Commerce, in which commercial men are to be the Judges.
   ... We are fully alive to the inconveniences that do undoubtedly arise from
the want of adequate technical knowledge in the Court which has to adjudicate
upon cases of a commercial character.   We think there is ground for the complaint that cases are sometimes tried at Nisi Prius before a Judge and jury who
have not the practical knowledge of the trade or business which is necessary
for their proper determination.   We are of opinion that many cases involving
for their comprehension a technical or special knowledge cannot be satisfactorily
disposed of by the ordinary tribunal of a Judge and jury, and that the proper
tribunal for such cases would be a Court presided over by a legal Judge,

assisted by two skilled assessors, who could advise the Judge as to any technical or practical matters arising in the course of the inquiry, and who by their mere presence would frequently deter skilled witnesses from giving such professional evidence as is often a scandal to the administration of justice. This is the kind of assistance which we in our First Report contemplated should be given to the superior Judges on the trial of cases of a scientific or technical character; and which has been provided for by the Supreme Court of Judicature Act.

Lord Parker L.C.J., History and Development of Commercial Arbitration

The Lionel Cohen Lecture (1959)

The 1860s saw an immense expansion of trade. The invention of the steamship made London the financial centre of the world. London bankers, merchants and financiers carried on business, and invested and speculated ever more widely in railways, mines, industry and agriculture over the face of the whole globe. The legal institutions of commerce—bankers' credits, time charters (again due to the arrival of the steamship), contracts for the sale of goods—played an ever more important part; but with the enlargement of trade came a proliferation of disputes; and parliament and the courts were forced to consider modes by which these commercial disputes could be more speedily handled.

Commercial arbitrations were made subject to a systematic code of law by the Arbitration Act 1889 amending and consolidating previous practice.... The increased control of the courts over commercial arbitration carried with it new responsibilities for the courts: for if a dispute depended on a point of law, the power of the court to compel a statement of a Special Case prolonged the arbitration, and in any event, if they proceeded direct to the courts, they were subject to the delays of ordinary litigation. Thus, a speedy trial in the courts both on a Case Stated from arbitration and on direct reference of the dispute was necessary and desirable. Unfortunately, however, the courts were in 1890 suffering from growing pains attendant upon the fusion of law and equity and had failed to produce the desired greater simplicity of practice and procedure. In 1883, Rules of the Supreme Court, dealing with practice and procedure, had been issued, but by 1895 there had been no less than 7,000 decisions on points of practice all obtained at the expense of unfortunate litigants. As can be readily surmised, the reaction of men of business to this situation was not dissimilar from that of their forebears in the seventeenth century. The absence of provision for speedy trials, or for fixing dates for trial, added to the discredit in which the courts were held. Moreover, just as in earlier centuries, many judges were totally ignorant of commercial matters. Though there were famous exceptions like Lord Blackburn, the majority had had little opportunity to become acquainted with the problems of trade and commerce. As Scrutton L.J. said in *Butcher, Wetherly & Co. Ltd.* v. *Norman*, 47 Ll.L.R. 324, " One of the objects of justice is to satisfy the litigants that their cases are fairly and properly heard, and unfortunately, some classes of commercial cases are so complex in their nature that a Judge who is not conversant with that class of commercial business has to have a great many explanations made to him in the course of the case as to matters with which he is quite unfamiliar, and so with every Judge. If I were invited to decide a question of conveyancing turning on the provisions of the Law of Property Act, I should display an amount of ignorance which would entirely disgust the lay clients and solicitors appearing before me, simply because they are practised and experienced in such judicial matters—whereas I have not been conversant with that particular branch of the law. It is not merely that things have to be explained to a Judge in open Court, which lay Clients and solicitors sitting there think that Judges ought to have known without having them explained, but that nobody quite appreciates how little a Judge of that class of case does know, and they do not realise that things which are so obvious to them are not so obvious to everybody and that they are not obvious to every Judge."

An apt example of the effect of bringing cases of a peculiar technicality before a judge unversed in that branch of the law has been noted by Lord Justice Mackinnon in the sphere of commercial law with which we are concerned (60 L.Q.R. 324–325). It involved a case before Mr. Justice J. C. Lawrance, known as " Long Lawrance." I Quote: " When Long Lawrance was trying non-jury cases some time early in 1892, *Rose* v. *Bank of Australasia* was called on. Cohen Q.C. (with him Scrutton) for the plaintiff explained that it was a claim by a shipowner for general average contribution from cargo-owners, based on an immensely complicated adjustment by an eminent firm of adjusters. The defendants, represented by Gorell Barnes Q.C. and J. A. Hamilton, disputed liability, and asserted that the adjustment was not made out on correct principles. The Judge knew as much about the principles of general average as a Hindoo about figure skating. He listened with a semblance of interest to Cohen and Gorell Barnes, reserved judgment and forgot all about the case. After a long delay he was somehow reminded that he ought to give judgment. This he did—in favour of the plaintiff. To his horror Gorell Barnes then rose and said he had failed to deal with a very important point. Not having the least idea what the point was, he pulled himself together and said: ' Oh, Yes; I meant to say that having considered that I think the adjusters took the right view, and in that respect also I think the claim as made out by them ought to succeed.' The defendants went off to the Court of Appeal. Gorell Barnes having been made a Judge in June 1892, Joseph Walton took his place as the defendants' leader. The Court of Appeal reversed Lawrance J. As appears in [1894] A.C. 687, the House of Lords restored the judgment of Lawrance J."

It was these circumstances—outside commercial dissatisfaction and the obvious defects of the Courts as they were—that led to the creation of the " Commercial Court." To what extent *Rose* v. *Bank of Australasia* contributed to that end may be problematical, but it is obviously not without some basis that Scrutton L.J. was wont to refer to " Long Laurence " as " the only Begetter of the Commercial Court." The genesis of the Court was in a resolution of the judges of the Queen's Bench Division in 1894: " That it is desirable that a list should be made of causes to be tried by a Judge alone, or by jurors from the City; and that a Commercial Court should be constituted of judges to be named by the judges of the Queen's Bench Division." On January 11, 1895, the rules for commercial causes were published, and it was announced that Mr. Justice Mathew, chosen for his special acquaintance with commercial matters, would sit daily for the trial of commercial cases. . . .

The position since 1900 has been, therefore, that a commercial dispute can be speedily and efficiently determined in the courts as well as by arbitration. The two systems ought indeed to be properly regarded as co-ordinate rather than rival. Many disputes, like questions as to quality, are clearly more suitable for arbitration. No question of law is involved, and an arbitrator in the trade can, by handling the sample, determine the dispute in a moment without the necessity of hearing advocates, and without the procedure and trappings of a court of law. At the other extreme, a dispute depending solely or mainly on the construction of an exemption clause in a commercial contract is more suitable to be determined by the Commercial Court. This is not to say that an experienced arbitrator, be he lay or legal, might not arrive at a correct decision, but such a case as I have indicated can, and will, no doubt, ultimately come to the courts, and that being so it might as well come there at once, thereby avoiding considerable delay. Between these two extremes, there are of course a mass of disputes in which ultimately the choice will be one of individual preference. In favour of arbitration is the consideration that there will be no publicity unless indeed the matter is ultimately brought before the courts. A further consideration, certainly with us, is that at the moment it is easier to enforce an award abroad than it is to enforce a judgment.

Report of the Committee on Supreme Court Practice and Procedure
Cmd. 8878 (1953)

. . . It is not the function of this Committee to devise a procedure with the object merely of trying to attract disputants away from the commercial arbitral tribunals, which have been established, to the Courts of law. But at the same time it has been pointed out to us that there are substantial disadvantages if disputes of a particular and important kind are commonly determined otherwise than by the ordinary Courts; for in such event the natural development of the law is retarded and the Courts themselves may become out of touch with current business practice and methods.

87. . . . [W]e had the advantage . . . of a discussion with representatives of the London Chamber of Commerce. . . . As we understood their evidence, the main reasons which have created the existing preference for arbitrations among the members of the Chamber are (i) the costs of High Court proceedings, including particularly the impossibility of being able to estimate such costs beforehand, (ii) the relative slowness of High Court proceedings and the uncertainty when the cases would come on for hearing, and (iii) the publicity attached to High Court proceedings; to which was also added the " uncomfortable " circumstances of Court proceedings, particularly the fact that witnesses have to stand up in the witness box when giving evidence. It should also be borne in mind that in a great number of small cases the disputants conduct their own cases and thereby avoid the considerable (and inevitable) cost of professional representation.

892. . . . It is quite clear that at the present time the volume of work both in the Admiralty and Commercial Courts has seriously fallen off. . . . [T]he admiralty work has in recent years occupied about one-third of one Judge's judicial time—say 80 to 90 days in a year. The work of the Commercial Court is more variable but the average of the last five years is approximately the same as the figure for admiralty work. A generation and more ago the figures were enormously greater—three times as great in the case of admiralty work and probably much more than that in the case of the Commercial Court.

893. There is more than one reason, clearly, for this change. Thus, as regards admiralty work the concentration of both shipping and cargoes in the war years in the hands of Departments of the State has been referred to and also the improvement in navigational standards, the practical operation, having regard to the present cost of repairs, of the statutory limit of liability, and the fall in the number of small craft in the Thames estuary, the scene of many collisions. And in the commercial cases the improvement and standardisation of the forms of mercantile documents and the like, the intervention, again, of Government Departments in trade and the virtual loss of the Russian timber trade (a particular source of litigation) were mentioned to us.

894. But above and beyond all these matters and in some measure arising out of them has been the immense growth of arbitration as a preferred means of settling disputes. Thus, to take one instance, an arbitration clause appears in all the Lloyd's forms relating to salvage. It is thus undoubtedly true that a substantial proportion of disputes which were formerly tried in the Courts are now disposed of by arbitration. In this connection it is to be noted that members

of the Admiralty and Commercial Bars spend a considerable portion of their professional time appearing before or sitting as arbitrators, from which it follows that strong and competent Bars are not the less required because the number of admiralty and commercial cases tried in the Courts has heavily fallen.

895. We have been much troubled by this trend to arbitration. If the parties to a dispute desire to have their dispute settled by this means, informally and without publicity, there is *prima facie* no reason to raise objections to their so doing. And many cases, *e.g.* disputes as to quality of goods, peculiarly lend themselves to the method of arbitration. But it has also been suggested to us that the growth of arbitration is in part attributable to reasonable dissatisfaction with the method of trial before the Courts—dissatisfaction based on experience or apprehension of delay and expense. Indeed, there seems no doubt that parties often agree to arbitration because of fears of expense and delay, and in heavy and complicated cases may as a result be disappointed to find that the arbitrations prove in the end more protracted and more costly than would have been trials in the Courts. We think that it is contrary to the public interest that arbitrations should too much replace trials in the Queen's Courts; for the Courts and the law tend to become too remote and out of touch with commercial problems. Further, it has seemed to us that the administration of the law, so far as compatible with vital principles, ought to conform to the requirements of those who seek access to the Courts.

896. Can, therefore, this trend away from the Courts be arrested? We have already referred to what we understand to be the main requirements urged by the commercial community and to achieve these requirements it has been stated to us, time and time again, that what is wanted is a Judge experienced in the kind of work involved, always available in London and able and willing by firm and continuous handling of the cases to arrive at the conclusions speedily, with the maximum relaxation of technical rules of evidence and procedure and the elimination of inessential issues. These desiderata were, it is claimed, achieved by the Commercial Court in what has been referred to as its heyday—the days (and his name has been often cited by way of illustration) of Bailhache J. At the present time and under the control of the present Lord Chief Justice, there is a revival of these conditions. There are now Judges in the Queen's Bench Division whose experience before appointment lay peculiarly in the Commercial Court. But there has in the interval been a loss of the prestige and confidence in the Commercial Court, particularly because the right men were not available for, or were not appointed to preside in, the Commercial Court.

897. It is fair to say that these criticisms have not been made or at least (if made) not established to our satisfaction in the case of the Admiralty Court in which properly qualified Judges have been available throughout. But the fear is that—in the case of the Admiralty Court as a result of the continuing pressure of the divorce work—the necessary conditions cannot be assumed in the future. And for these reasons it has so strongly been urged upon us that only by the creation of a separate Admiralty/Commercial Court manned exclusively by men trained in the classes of work involved can the continuance of the necessary conditions for satisfying and giving confidence to the commercial community be relied upon.

899. . . . The views of the London Chamber of Commerce were . . . given some support by the evidence of the British Insurance Association, and the witnesses from the Protection and Indemnity Clubs thought that there was, by means of a combined Court, some chance of reversing the present tendency away from the Courts to arbitrations. . . . But the weight of evidence (including that of the Bar and the Law Society) was against a removal of the admiralty work . . . to the Queen's Bench Division. . . .

Report of the Commercial Court Users' Conference
Cmnd. 1616 (1962)

The conference was held in November 1960. Those attending fell into seven groups: (1) Commodity Organisations, represented by the Incorporated Oil Seed Association, London Cattle Food Trade Association Inc., London Corn Trade Association Ltd., Baltic Mercantile and Shipping Exchange (Commodity Members); (2) Chambers of Commerce, represented by the Association of British Chambers of Commerce, and the London Chamber of Commerce; (3) Industrial Federations and Councils represented by the Federation of British Industries and the Society of Motor Manufacturers and Traders; (4) Banking, represented by the Committee of London Clearing Bankers; (5) Underwriters and Insurers—Marine and Non-Marine and Aviation, represented by the Institute of London Underwriters, Lloyd's, Liverpool Underwriters' Association, the British Insurance Association, the Protection and Indemnity Associations and the Freight, Demurrage and Defence Associations; (6) Shipowners' and Allied Associations, covering chartering interests, represented by the Baltic Mercantile and Shipping Exchange (Chartering Members) and the Institute of Chartered Shipbrokers, shippers' interests represented by the British Shippers Council, and shipowning interests, represented by the Chamber of Shipping of the United Kingdom, Liverpool Steamship Owners' Association and Cardiff and Bristol Channel Incorporated Shipowners' Association; (7) Ports Docks and Harbours represented by the Dock and Harbour Authorities Association.

Continuance of Commercial Court

7. We are able to report the unanimous opinion of the Conference that the commercial community earnestly desires that the Commercial Court shall continue to be available for the adjudication of commercial disputes. Indeed the evidence given on behalf of the Protecting & Indemnity and Freight, Demurrage & Defence Associations (who are probably the most frequent litigants in the Court) was that it would be " a major disaster " if the facilities afforded by the Commercial Court were to disappear.

At the same time we consider that we should not be justified in predicting that the work of the Commercial Court will necessarily increase in the future, but we are of the opinion that the adoption of the reforms which we advocate below are necessary if the decline in the use of the Court is to be arrested and its greater use encouraged.

We have studied the " Summary of Commercial Actions from 1946 to 1959 " with which we have been supplied (attached in Appendix G) and find that during these years the cases actually tried in the Commercial Court varied from 12 (in 1948) to 32 (in 1954): we find also that in the last decade there has been some increase in the volume of the work. Nevertheless it is the fact that the business of the Commercial Court has much diminished below the level reached between the two World Wars, when the Court not infrequently required the services of more than one Judge simultaneously. We appreciate also that the wide fluctuations of the business of the Court in modern times, as shown by the Summary, must greatly enhance the difficulty of those responsible for the administration of justice.

But litigation and more especially commercial litigation does tend to fluctuate in cycles, owing to the rapid and unforeseeable changes in commercial conditions; and we think that this is not wholly a modern trend, as is shown by the heavy incidence of war risk cases immediately after the First World War and of the scuttling cases engendered by the depression of the nineteen-twenties. Both of these threw a heavy but temporary burden not only upon the Commercial Court but upon the Appellate Courts as well.

8. Turning our attention to present conditions of commerce, we think that a number of factors have recently emerged which have tended and will continue to tend to decrease commercial litigation, not only in the Commercial Court itself but also in Arbitration. The trend, therefore, appears to be the opposite of that which has been manifest in the Common Law Courts since the Second World War.

9. The most important of these factors we consider to be the following.

Trading organisations have, owing to the modern predilection for amalgamation, become larger in size but fewer in number . . . and the effect is that not only are there fewer potential litigants but that there is a greater inclination to compromise disputes. Large organisations will only litigate a dispute if the amount at stake is much larger or the principle involved is much more important than the smaller trading concerns of the past would have tolerated without a contest.

The growth of international business has been rapid during the past fifteen years. In the early reports of Commercial Cases it is rare to find a foreign Plaintiff or Defendant. Now it is the reverse; often both parties are foreigners. And, for the reasons discussed below, foreigners are less inclined to submit their disputes to our Courts than to Arbitration in London.

The accumulation of a wealth of case law afforded by the decisions of the Commercial Court has had a similar effect. It may not be generally appreciated how continually businessmen are assisted in the settlement of problems which might have led to contested disputes by reference to those principles of commercial law which have been so clearly enunciated in those decisions. We consider that it is essential that this invaluable assistance should continue to be available; new methods of business involving new forms of contracts will continue to require the evolution of commercial law; but there is no doubt the past decisions have narrowed the scope of uncertainty upon legal principle. Perhaps the most striking example of this trend, as applied to one particular industry, are the decisions of the Commercial Court upon the many problems which arose under the Carriage of Goods by Sea Act 1924, most of which were solved during the first fifteen years of the Act's existence. It has become increasingly difficult to find a new point for decision under this Act.

The commercial community is also undoubtedly deterred from resort to the Commercial Court by its inherent dislike of publicity and especially of the system of oral examination and cross-examination. . . .

Again, and this a very potent factor, the increasing cost and delays of litigation discourage business men from resorting to it.

Finally we find that the difficulty of enforcing judgments of the Court in foreign countries as opposed to Arbitral Awards has had a serious effect upon the use of the Commercial Court by those whom the Court was established to serve.

10. These deterrent factors apply to all trades and industries alike. But we think that we should mention two others which are peculiar to particular industries.

We find that the Commodity Associations are in a special category. Theirs is essentially an international business. For example, 50 per cent. of the membership of the Incorporated Oil Seed Association is domiciled abroad: one-third of the members of the London Corn Trade Association and of the London Cattle Food Trade Association are also domiciled overseas. Their commodity contracts, which are standard documents of long-standing and of world-wide acceptance, cover movements of commodities from countries of origin mostly outside the United Kingdom to destinations throughout the world. These Associations have long-established arbitration tribunals, both first instance and appellate, to which disputes under these commodity contracts are referred. Most of these disputes concern condition or quality and in the majority of cases one or even both of the parties are domiciled overseas. It is rare that an appeal is made from those tribunals to the Court upon a Special Case: but when this does occur the case is transferred to the Commercial List. We find that the number of such cases, although small, has not diminished since the last War.

In the period between the two Wars much of the work of the Commercial Court was concerned with claims for loss of or damage to cargo, in which the dispute was in effect between Cargo Underwriters on the one side and the Shipowners' Protection & Indemnity Association on the other. In recent years the modern tendency to compromise such disputes has been to some extent assisted by the centralization of the settlement of marine claims in Lloyd's Claims Bureau, in place of the former practice whereby each claim was submitted to each Underwriter concerned, and by the Gold Clause Agreement (which has received full acceptance in this country by the ship and cargo interests concerned and a wide measure of acceptance by Cargo Underwriters in other parts of the Commonwealth and on the Continent).

11. Nevertheless, although the business of the Commercial Court has for the above reasons diminished, its importance to the commercial community has not. We fully appreciate the burden cast upon the administration of justice by the retention of one or more experienced Commercial Judges to be available in London for the adjudication of commercial cases as and when they are ready for trial. . . . But we respectfully urge that the continuance of the Commercial Court is of such paramount importance to the commercial community that it should be kept in being even if these difficulties cannot be completely resolved.

Reforms of the constitution, practice and procedure of the Commercial Court

12. Firstly we regard it as essential . . . that the Judges should be chosen from among those who practised in the Court while at the Bar. . . . We recommend that Commissioners, chosen from the practitioners at the Commercial Bar, should be appointed from time to time as occasion may demand so that, if no Commercial Judge should happen to be available when a commercial case became ready for trial, it would be tried by one of the members of that specialized Bar. . . .

21. One of the important reforms of the practice of the Commercial Court, upon which we are all agreed, is that the Commercial Judge should have power, upon the application of both parties, to sit in private as an Arbitrator. We are of opinion that this practice would greatly enhance the attraction of the Court to the commercial community, as it would meet the objection . . . to the publicity and formality of proceedings in open Court. We think that the attraction might well extend to foreign mercantile interests who trade with this country or who do business on the London Markets. . . .

We think that the Judge's award in such cases should not be published without the consent of the parties; but that, if it were stated in the form of a Special Case on a point of law, there should be an appeal direct to the Court of Appeal.

22. Finally we are of the opinion that more use should be made . . . of the power of the Commercial Judge . . . to sit with Assessors—a power which is regularly used in the Admiralty Court in collision cases . . . [—] in cases, and they are many, where technical questions are involved whether nautical or constructional or concerning the technicalities of a particular trade, industry or Market.

Arbitration

23. . . . . [W]e are unanimously of opinion that Arbitration is an essential part of the mechanism of commerce. We think that the true function of Commercial Arbitration is that it should be complementary to and not in competition with the Commercial Court.

24. We have already referred to the arbitral procedure which has long been operated with success by the Commodity Associations. In the less specialized mercantile community, which forms the membership of Chambers of Commerce, the practice of Arbitration is equally favoured; for example, of the hundreds of disputes adjudicated since the last War by the London Court of Arbitration (which is operated jointly by the London Chamber of Commerce and the Corporation of the City of London) only one found its way to the Court by way of a Special Case.

25. In policies of insurance arbitration clauses are perhaps not so common and Marine Policies do not usually contain such clauses. But arbitration clauses are common in Reinsurance Treaties with foreign Underwriters and in Aviation Policies—under the latter there have only been six disputes referred to Arbitration in the last five years. And salvage remuneration for salvage services to ships insured on the London Market is determined in nearly all cases by Arbitration in London.

Lloyd's Standard Non-Marine Policies on United Kingdom business—other than Motor Insurance Policies—do not contain arbitration clauses: but Non-Marine Underwriters have found it necessary to submit to local jurisdiction clauses in many of the foreign countries to which their business extends, notably in the States and Provinces of the United States and Canada. Non-Marine Policies issued by the Insurance Companies do contain arbitration clauses, but in 1956 the members of the British Insurance Association agreed not to insist, in general, upon arbitration if the Insured prefers to have the question of liability, as distinct from amount, determined by a Court in the United Kingdom. To the limited extent to which their Non-Marine business was affected, Lloyd's Underwriters were also parties to this arrangement.

26. Lastly, as an illustration of the prevalence of Arbitration in commerce, we take the Baltic Mercantile & Shipping Exchange. Nearly 80 per cent. of the world's chartering of ships is still done on this Market, but it is subject to fierce and increasing competition from foreign Markets, notably New York, Paris, Hamburg and Japan. The great majority of Charterparties negotiated on the Baltic Exchange contain the stipulation that any dispute arising under the Charterparty shall be referred to Arbitration in London.

We attach great importance to the maintenance of this type of arbitration clause in Charterparties. Foreign Owners or Charterers who operate on this London Market could not, we are advised by the Chartering Brokers, be induced to agree, under their Charterparties, to settle their disputes in London otherwise than by Arbitration. The reason is that a foreign Owner or Charterer who accepts such an arbitration clause knows that, in the event of a dispute, he can nominate as his Arbitrator a member of the Market with whom he is accustomed to do business and whom he knows and trusts: he has not the opportunity of such knowledge of and confidence in our Courts. It is only through the mechanism of London Arbitration that such disputes come before our Courts by way of Special Case. Any attempt to force foreigners to agree to refer their disputes direct to the Court would not only fail in the desired effect but would seriously prejudice the position of the Baltic Exchange as the leading World Chartering Market.

In view of the importance of maintaining the standard of Arbitration in London in Charterparty cases, the London Maritime Arbitrators' Association has recently been formed, most of whose members are experienced Chartering Brokers and now number about forty. Only those approved by the Association are included in the official list of Baltic Exchange Arbitrators from which Arbitrators in Charterparty cases are normally chosen.

28. There are cases referred to Arbitration which so obviously depend upon a point or points of law that a more expeditious and satisfactory solution would be found by direct reference to the Commercial Court. But this is a matter for the parties concerned: we can devise no mechanism, and we would consider it highly undesirable to make the attempt, whereby the parties could be compelled in advance to relinquish Arbitration in favour of the Court. When, however, Arbitration is resorted to, we find that the delay in obtaining a final award is often as great and as avoidable as the delay in bringing an action in the Court to a conclusion.

29. . . . [T]he commercial community is even more interested in speedy than in perfect justice, and a great deal of formality which at present entrammels Commercial Arbitrations in which practitioners are concerned could well be dispensed with. . . .

30. . . . [W]e consider that the process of what is in effect an appeal to the High Court from an arbitral tribunal on a point of law by way of Special Case is too often abused.

We understand that this procedure is unique to English law: it is certainly not understood by foreigners and is not infrequently the subject of complaint by them. Nevertheless we appreciate that it has long been a fundamental principle of our law that, where the Court has jurisdiction, that jurisdiction cannot be ousted, even by agreement of the parties: we do not desire to make any suggestion in abrogation of this principle. We do, however, recommend that the right of either party to an arbitration to require an arbitral tribunal (under the Arbitration Act, 1950, section 21) to state a question of law arising in the course of a reference or an award in the form of a Special Case for the decision of the High Court, should be conditional upon the requirement being accompanied by a statement in a concise form of the point or points of law which it is desired to raise. . . .

31. The complaint was made to us . . . that arbitral tribunals are too often required to state Special Cases upon vague or indeterminate points of law. . . . In effect this practice may amount to a rehearing of the case already decided by the Arbitrators and too often it necessitates the case being remitted to them for further findings of fact. . . .

[W]e, therefore, recommend that the use of this procedure be more severely controlled.

The Conference went on to recommend that arbitrators be given wider powers to compel parties to prepare the case for arbitration without undue delay and also the amalgamation of the Commercial and the Admiralty Court.

APPENDIX G

SUMMARY OF COMMERCIAL ACTIONS FROM 1946–59

	Cases c/f from previous year	Cases set down	Total col. (1) and (2)	Cases tried	Cases withdrawn or struck out	Total cases disposed of col. (4) & (5)	Carry over to next year
	(1)	(2)	(3)	(4)	(5)	(6)	
1946	7	25	32	15	11	26	6
1947	6	37	43	22	7	29	14
1948	14	35	49	12	17	29	20
1949	20	20	40	25	10	35	5
1950	5	33	38	16	8	24	14
1951	14	28	42	13	16	29	13
1952	13	31	44	18	16	34	10
1953	10	50	60	25	20	45	15
1954	15	39	54	32	17	49	5
1955	5	40	45	27	7	34	11
1956	11	36	47	27	10	37	10
1957	10	27	37	15	12	27	10
1958	10	27	37	21	8	29	8
1959	8	43	51	23	11	34	17

Clause 3 of the Administration of Justice Bill 1969 originally increased the powers of the Commercial Court to dispense with the strict rules of evidence and to sit in private, or rather it conferred the power on the Supreme Court Rule Committee to do this, which would have made experiment possible but the clause was eventually defeated on the grounds that courts should sit in public so that justice could be seen to be done.

THE COUNTY COURTS

The High Court is too expensive and its procedure too cumbrous to be suitable for small claims. These are dealt with by the local county courts which derive their authority at present from the County Courts Act 1959. Like the High Court itself, they too are a nineteenth century creation, introduced by the County Courts Act 1846 to meet the demand for a national system of courts for the recovery of small debts. Their importance is twofold. In the first place they are local courts, locally administered by locally resident judges. The country is divided into a number of county court districts to which the county court judges (now Circuit judges) have been assigned, and within the districts they hold courts at the main centres of population. Secondly they are intended to be courts for small claims, the forum where the ordinary citizen can bring his claims and secure the enforcement of his civil rights. The demand for such courts has been constant. In the earliest days of the legal system it was satisfied by the local county and hundred courts which existed alongside the feudal courts before the royal courts came into existence. The rise of the common law courts and the fall in the value of money led to their decline, the fall in the value of money taking more and more cases outside the monetary limits of their jurisdiction. The need for a substitute was, however, strongly felt. Whenever any court became established it was likely to be besieged by petitioners asking for their small claims to be dealt with. Informal claims of this kind were made when the royal justices travelled the country in the earliest days of the system. Poverty and the expense of law suits in the common law courts were frequent grounds set out in the petitions which formed one of the early bases of the Chancellor's jurisdiction. When the Court of Star Chamber came into existence in the sixteenth century for the suppression of disorder it too acquired a small claims jurisdiction, and throughout the whole period there was a variety of courts going under the name of Courts of Requests which gave some kind of remedy in such cases.

The problem of the recovery of small debts was the subject of the Fifth Report of the Commissioners set up to consider practice and procedure in the common law courts in 1829. Legislation setting up the new county courts was passed in 1846. Almost as soon as they were established they were given a wide variety of tasks to perform until, by the beginning of the twentieth century, they had a very mixed jurisdiction going beyond what had originally been envisaged, and covering all kinds of business which was not considered to merit the attention of a High Court judge or the expense of a High Court trial.

The jurisdiction of the county courts has always been subject to a monetary limit, which at the moment is £750 so far as actions in contract and tort are concerned. As was mentioned above (p. 14) there has been a fairly constant pressure to increase their jurisdiction as a means of relieving the High Court. The Judicature Commissioners in their Second Report in fact recommended that the county courts should become branches of the High Court to facilitate the transfer of business between them and to cater for those cases which were not the small claims for which the county courts had originally been introduced, but which also did not justify the expense of a High Court trial. This suggestion was considered again by the Committee on County Court Procedure which reported in 1909 [26] and the Beeching Commission, but neither recommended its adoption. The main reason against the expansion of the jurisdiction of the county courts has been the fear that the more important claims would be dealt with at the expense of small claims. In recent years however doubts have been felt about the satisfactoriness of the county courts for small claims as it is. From the very beginning the notion that the county courts were a small claims courts for the ordinary citizen has been somewhat misleading. In spite of the reference of the importance of small debts to the poor man, to be found, for example, in the Fifth Report of the Common Law Commissioners, the man-in-the-street has been more likely to appear in the county courts, if he bothered to put in an appearance at all, as a defendant, with shopkeepers and creditors like public utilities, finance houses, professional debt-collecting agencies or mail order firms as the plaintiffs. The report of

[26] H.C. 71 of 1908–09.

the Consumer Council " Justice out of Reach " made much of the inadequacy of the county courts as courts for the small consumer-plaintiff, where the cost of bringing the claim might well exceed the amount that the plaintiff could hope to recover, and recommended a more informal procedure for dealing with these claims. It is interesting to note the fears of the Common Law Commissioners as regards the increasing dependence on the integrity of the judge as the informality of the process increases. In fact the scheme that has been set up in Manchester as an experiment to deal with consumer complaints does have more of a conciliation committee about it than a court. A suggestion that special consumer courts should be established was rejected by the Molony Committee on Consumer Protection in 1962.[27] It recommended a greater reliance on citizens advice bureaux.

In some other cases jurisdiction which might previously have been or had in fact been entrusted to county courts has been entrusted to tribunals created for the purpose. This is particularly the case where the number of claims is likely to be very large and the amounts in issue relatively small, where the law is capable of being fairly well settled in regulations or where some special kind of expertise, knowledge or representative character is felt to be needed in the deciding body. Administrative tribunals of this kind were already recognised when the Committee on Ministers Powers reported in 1932.[28] They were accepted as a normal part of the system of adjudication by the Franks Committee on Tribunals and Inquiries in 1957.[29] A particularly striking example of a case where experience had shown the undesirability of entrusting a jurisdiction to the ordinary courts, in this case the county courts, is in connection with industrial injuries claims under the National Insurance (Industrial Injuries) Act 1948. Here the past experience with the courts in connection with claims under the old Workmen's Compensation Acts 1897 and 1925 led to the creation under the Act of 1948 of national insurance (industrial injury) tribunals. Similar considerations have led to the creation of national insurance tribunals, rent tribunals and industrial tribunals which now play such a large part in dispute determination throughout the country.

The basic jurisdiction of the county courts is set out at present in the County Courts Act 1959 though other statutes have added to the jurisdiction of some or all of them. The 1959 Act sets out the jurisdiction under a number of separate heads, for example, actions of contract and tort and actions for the recovery of land. In each case a monetary limit is set on the amount of the claim that can be brought in the county court without the defendant's consent. It has, for example, a general jurisdiction over actions in contract and tort, other than actions of defamation, up to £750. Provision is however also made for actions to be transferred to the High Court where the sum involved is over £100 if the defendant objects to the case being tried in the county court, provided that the judge certifies that in his opinion some important question of law or fact is likely to arise, and the defendant gives security for the amount claimed and the costs of the trial

27 Cmnd. 1781.
28 Cmd. 4060.
29 Cmnd. 218.

in the High Court.[30] Similarly if an action is begun in the High Court for a sum of not more than £750 the defendant may apply to have the case transferred to a county court and it will be transferred if the judge or master who hears the application thinks fit.[31] If in an action brought in the High Court a sum of less than £100 is recovered the plaintiff will not be entitled to costs.[32] If he recovers less than £500 he will only be awarded costs on the county court scale unless it appears to the judge or master that there was reasonable ground for supposing that he would recover more than he could have claimed in the county court, or if they are satisfied that there was sufficient reason for bringing the action in the High Court, or, of course, if the defendant objected to the case being transferred to a county court.[33] There are also monetary limits on the county courts' jurisdiction over actions for the recovery of land and their equity and probate jurisdiction. Some courts also have a limited admiralty jurisdiction. Amongst the other statutes giving the county courts jurisdiction are the Rent Acts 1965 and 1968 and the Race Relations Act 1968, s. 19 of which provides that the Race Relations Board may bring civil proceedings in any county court " for the time being appointed to have jurisdiction to entertain such proceedings by an order made by the Lord Chancellor."

Some county courts have also been made divorce county courts for the purpose of hearing undefended divorce cases. The history of the allocation of divorce work illustrates quite well some of the tensions between the desire to reserve important work for the High Court and at the same time to prevent it being overburdened. Until 1920 all divorce cases were heard by a judge of the Probate, Divorce and Admiralty Division in London. In 1920 it was provided that undefended and poor persons' cases could be heard by judges of the King's Bench Division on circuit. In 1944 it was decided that all classes of matrimonial work could be heard locally, and judges of the Probate, Divorce and Admiralty Division went on Circuit to take some of these cases at the larger assize towns. Following the Second Interim Report of the Denning Committee on Procedure in Matrimonial Causes [34] new arrangements were made which involved not the transfer of some of these cases to the county courts, but the use of county court judges as Divorce Commissioners with the status of High Court judges for the purpose. (The same device was used in criminal cases when leading barristers were commissioned to take criminal cases at assizes to relieve the burden on the High Court judges.) From 1947 therefore judges of the Probate, Divorce and Admiralty Division dealt with the longer defended cases in London and at the larger assize towns, and judges of the King's Bench Division dealt with those at the smaller assize towns, while special commissioners, including all the county court judges and a number of leading barristers, heard the shorter defended cases and the undefended cases. Finally in 1967 the Matrimonial Causes Act accepted the fact that undefended cases could not merely be heard by county court judges but could actually be assigned to a number of selected county courts.

[30] County Courts Act 1959, s. 44.
[31] *Ibid.* s. 45.
[32] Administration of Justice Act 1969, s. 4.
[33] County Courts Act 1959, s. 47.
[34] Cmd. 6945 (1946).

Fifth Report of the Commissioners on the Practice and Procedure of the Common Law Courts

1833 P.P. xxii [247]

The County Court, once an efficient and important Court for the administration of justice, has now fallen into a state of comparative inutility.

As early at least as the reign of King Edward the First, its general jurisdiction was confined to causes of action below 40s.; a limitation which, combined with the changes and deterioration which have taken place in the value of money, has reduced one of the most ancient Courts to a state of desuetude.

The Hundred Courts and Courts Baron . . . labour under the same or even greater defects than the County Court. . . .

The Courts of different boroughs . . . frequently possess jurisdiction to an unlimited amount. . . .

Their general utility is, however, much fettered by their local limits.

. . . [N]umerous Courts under the description of Courts of Requests or Courts of Conscience, have . . . in populous districts, arisen from a necessity for a more cheap and speedy method of enforcing small claims.

The suspicion entertained, however, by Sir William Blackstone, as to the policy of erecting Courts, " with methods of proceeding entirely in derogation of the Common Law, and whose large discretionary powers make a petty tyranny in a set of standing Commissioners," have not been removed by later experience.

It is a matter of sound moral as well as just legal policy, that no Debtor shall be exempted from the legal obligation to pay a just debt, however small; such an exemption would not only be unjust in reference to the poorer classes of society, to whom small sums may be of great importance, but objectionable in its tendency to weaken the sense of moral obligation.

On the other hand, the due administration of justice in the case of very minute claims is subject to inconvenience. The labour and difficulty of investigation do not depend on the magnitude of the cause of action. . . .

If justice in such cases is to be administered according to the ordinary rules of evidence, in a Court regulated by certain rules of practice, the proceeding ceases to be remedial in its effect. If, on the other hand, all such restraints be dispensed with, the tribunal becomes arbitrary, and its decisions too vague and uncertain to be satisfactory.

Where the cause of suit is too minute to bear the expenses, which, however moderate, are necessarily incident to proceedings conducted according to any certain and methodical rules binding on those who administer justice, the confidence reposed must be altogether of a personal nature, depending on the known ability and integrity of the Judge.

These considerations tend to point out the main objection to which a Court of Requests is, in its nature, subject. So much is left to the discretion of those who decide the cause, that they ought to be persons of considerable ability and learning to perform their functions with propriety. But they consist, in general, of commissioners, whose pursuits in life can give no assurance of their possessing these qualities.

Upon the whole, it is our duty to represent to Your Majesty that the inadequacy of the present Courts, in causes of action from 40s. to at least £20, amounts almost to a denial of justice; and that we believe . . . that creditors are obliged to abandon their just demands; that debtors are from the same cause tempted to a dishonest resistance, and that the result is great injury to public morals and to private rights.

It appears to us to be expedient that the whole Kingdom should be divided into districts, for the purpose of establishing Local Courts, upon an uniform system, and that provision should be made for the trial of causes at such places as shall be best accommodated to public convenience. . . .

To insure the efficiency of the new Local Courts, it is . . . most important that their Judges should be persons of learning and experience, that their tenure of office should be permanent, and that they should be excluded from private practice.

. . . [W]e calculate that the whole number required will probably not exceed twenty. . . .

Some doubts have occurred to us as to the propriety of the permanent residence of the local Judge within his district. It may be objected, that he will acquire local prejudices and local intimacies, which may influence his judgment. We think however that the certain advantages to be derived from the permanent residence of the Judge within his district far outweigh the risk of any disadvantage to the suitors. . . . One of the principal advantages of the proposed Courts would be lost, if the Judge were not at hand to regulate and determine the interlocutory business which must be continually occurring.

We think indeed that . . . in respect of probable partiality and prejudice . . . these feelings are much less likely to affect an individual Judge, who makes his circuit through an extensive district, who administers justice by the medium of a Jury, and who is always liable to account to a superior Court for his judgments, than a standing body of irresponsible Commissioners, like the Judges of the Courts of Requests, resident in the immediate neighbourhood of the litigant parties.

There should also be one or more Registrars of each Court . . . to attend at all the Courts held by the local Judges . . . to take minutes and make entries of all the proceedings, and to assist in the general conduct and arrangement of the business.

. . . [W]hilst the practice of an inferior Court must be regulated by a principle of strict economy, . . . it appears to us that professional aid in the conduct of a cause, even where the demand does not exceed £5 in amount, ought not to be excluded; and that to require all to appear and plead their causes in person, without regard to age, sex, condition or mental capacity, would frequently be productive of hardship, if not of positive injustice.

While we think that no party ought to be debarred from availing himself of professional assistance we recommend . . . that such costs shall not be allowed on taxation in any suit to recover a debt not exceeding £5 in amount.

Report of the Committee on County Court Procedure
H.C. Paper 71 1908–9 P.P. lxxii

XVIII. . . . [I]n considering the relations subsisting between the High Court and the County Courts, . . . the Committee have arrived at the conclusion that the real question for determination is what is the best way of dealing with that work which is, or ought to be, disposed of in the provinces, and is beyond the present jurisdiction of the County Courts.

There appear to us to be four suggestions which have to be considered with regard to this question—

(1) That the County Courts should become part of the High Court with unlimited jurisdiction in actions, but subject to a right on the part of a defendant to have any case in which the amount sought to be recovered should exceed a certain limit transferred to the superior branch of the High Court.

(2) That the County Courts should remain with their present constitution but should have unlimited, or at any rate much enlarged, jurisdiction in actions subject to a right of transfer as aforesaid.

(3) That provincial or district courts should be established for cases not left to the County Courts.

(4) That the Circuit system should be re-modelled so as to concentrate the Civil work in centres, and that more time should be allowed, and more convenient arrangements made for the disposal of business.

1. Dealing with the first suggestion, the Committee are of opinion that it is not desirable that it should be in any way adopted. . . .

The County Courts, with the mass of small cases which are brought in them, must continue to dispose of the poor man's cases. This is their primary business. . . . It is essential that that work should not be interfered with by attempts to deal to any serious extent with larger cases taking up much longer time in hearing, when the courts have already had added to their primary duties a quantity of other work and have their time practically fully taken up.

The procedure in these small and simple cases, mostly uncontested, must be to a considerable extent different from that in difficult and contested cases, and must be such as poor litigants can easily understand and follow; and if the procedure be different, the courts will remain in substances separate. . . . The idea of a code of procedure applicable to all courts in a country appeals, no doubt, to many, but we have to deal with an existing practice which has worked well in the County Courts, . . . though not so suitable for larger cases.

The conditions under which a local Judge must work . . . are not likely to make such a court prove a satisfactory tribunal for the trial of cases of legal difficulty or of importance. In most cases he is out of touch with the other Judges and leaders of the legal profession, without opportunities of discussing legal cases with them, will not have any, or hardly any, opportunity of hearing cases argued by eminent counsel, and, as a rule, has not an adequate library with books or works of authority at hand. . . . It is also to be remembered that, even as matters are, a County Court Judge has to cope with a great variety of work which he individually must deal with, and that work is not divided up among County Court Judges as it is between the Judges of High Court, to each Division of which separate work is assigned so that Judges especially experienced therein may deal therewith.

If the object of constituting the County Courts subordinate branches of the High Court be to hand over to them the bulk of the work which should be done on circuit by the High Court Judges, there is further this very strong objection thereto, that suitors in the provinces are entitled to have, and ought to have, facilities for the trial of their causes within their own districts before Judges of the High Court, as it at present is constituted, similar to those enjoyed by suitors in London. . . . If this be not the object, then there is no substance in the suggestion.

There is, moreover, the very important consideration whether it would be desirable to have two grades of High Court Judges. The possible difficulty of keeping up the very high standard and reputation which has been maintained for centuries by His Majesty's High Court Judges, and the continuance of which is of the greatest moment, has not infrequently been remarked on where questions have arisen as to an increase of their numbers, and if the first suggestion were adopted it might not be without its effect upon this, even though it might have an advantageous effect upon the dignity and position of the Judges of the suggested inferior branch.

2. [M]uch of what we have stated with regard to the first suggestion is applicable to the second suggestion. . . . If the effect of adopting the second

suggestion were to add any considerable amount of work to that now done by the County Courts. . . .

We are strongly of opinion that the true remedy to be sought for is not by encouraging litigants to contest their cases in Courts which were not intended to deal with these cases, . . . but to provide that completely adequate facilities should be given by the High Court for disposing of every case which it is reasonable should be both commenced and continued in it.

3. A provincial Judge dealing in his district with every class of work other than that disposed of in the County Courts would labour under the serious disadvantage of becoming out of touch with other Judges. . . . There would be a tendency in him to be more or less affected by his local surroundings, and if every class of business were brought before him . . . he would find that his knowledge and experience would fail to cope with difficulties which are avoided in the High Court by assigning different varieties of work to different divisions of the Court. . . .

4. It is the opinion of the Committee that in this [the fourth] suggestion is to be found the true solution.

Royal Commission on Assizes and Quarter Sessions
Cmnd. 4153 (1966–69)

205. Since we wished to simplify the structure of the courts, to make them more comprehensible and more flexible in use, we were led to consider, as a counterpart to the single criminal court which we recommend, the establishment of a single civil court of wide jurisdiction and uniform procedure in which the only important variable would be the powers of the judge. We also considered a more modest suggestion which was put to us by several witnesses, including The Law Society, that all civil proceedings might be started in common form and that, at an appropriate stage in the proceedings, an officer of the court should, after hearing the parties, decide whether the case should be heard by a High Court or a County Court judge. . . . We concluded in the end, reluctantly for the most part, that it would be impracticable for us to give effect to either of these possibilities. A partial or total assimilation of the Rules of the Supreme Court and the County Court Rules would have been needed, and this would have involved us in a study for which we are ill-qualified as a body and which would have seriously delayed our report.

206. Although we do not recommend that the High Court and the County Courts should be merged, we do propose a more flexible use of judge power.

207. The distribution of civil cases between the two courts is principally a monetary one. . . . While the sum at issue is plainly an important consideration in determining the tribunal by which a case should be tried, the present system can lead to cases being heard by judges for whom they are not suitable. The sum involved may not be very large, but the point at issue may be one of such importance as to warrant being tried by a High Court judge. Conversely, a case where the sum is somewhat over the monetary limit may raise no question of difficulty whatever and be perfectly suitable for trial before a County Court judge. For these reasons we consider that the allocation of civil cases between different tiers of judges should, to some extent, be determined judicially, in a rather similar way to that which we have already outlined for criminal cases.

208. We recommend that a High Court judge, whether he is sitting in London or in the provinces, should have power to release from his list any case which he considers suitable for trial by a Circuit judge who will have been invited to sit by the Presiding Judge. Among the considerations which the

High Court judge would be likely to take into account as making it undesirable to release a case would be the following: —

(*a*) that the damages are likely to be substantial;

(*b*) that a novel or difficult issue of law is likely to be involved;

(*c*) that an allegation of fraud or dishonest conduct is involved;

(*d*) that either party is entitled to claim trial by jury;

(*e*) that the decision may affect public rights generally or the rights of third parties;

(*f*) that the circumstances are of unusual difficulty or importance in some respect other than those indicated above.

209. We suggest that the Lord Chief Justice, with the concurrence of the Lord Chancellor, should make these criteria known by Practice Directions, and should have power to vary them. . . . [A]ny case which is released will continue to be a High Court case and there will, therefore, be no limitation on the amount of damages that may be awarded, and the costs will follow the normal High Court rules. . . .

Second Interim Report of the Committee on Procedure in Matrimonial Causes

Cmd. 6945 (1946)

4. . . . [W]e desire specifically to re-affirm the principle stated by the Royal Commission of 1912 that " the gravity of divorce and other matrimonial cases, affecting as they do the family life, the status of the parties, the interests of their children, and the interests of the State in the moral and social well-being of its citizens, makes it desirable to provide, if possible, that, even for the poorest persons, these cases should be determined by the Superior Courts of the country, assisted by the attendance of the Bar, which we regard as of high importance in divorce and matrimonial cases, both in the interest of the parties and in the public interest." In our opinion the attitude of the community towards the status of marriage is much influenced by the way in which divorce is effected. If there is a careful and dignified proceeding such as obtains in the High Court for the undoing of a marriage, then quite unconsciously the people will have a much more respectful view of the marriage tie and of the marriage status than they would if divorce were effected informally in an inferior court.

5. The difficulty at the present day is to maintain that principle in the face of the large increase in the number of cases. The fact is that there are not enough High Court Judges to deal with the increased number of cases.

7. (i) There is a number of judges who are available to undertake divorce work if they should be asked to do so, namely, the County Court Judges. . . .

(ii) There is no doubt that the County Court Judges would handle matrimonial cases with efficiency and a full sense of responsibility. The assumption that divorce involves a peculiar discretion which only a few know how to exercise is not valid. The increased number of cases has meant a diffusion of knowledge throughout the profession. Only a few of the past or present Judges of the Probate Divorce & Admiralty Division specialised in divorce work before they were appointed to the Bench. The majority had practised at the Admiralty or Common law bar. Many King's Bench and Chancery Judges and Commissioners have tried divorce cases with no previous experience of them. The counsel who conduct the cases are often members of the common law bar, and especially so on circuit. . . .

8. The foregoing considerations lead us to the following conclusions:

1. The High Court jurisdiction should be maintained in London and the provinces but undefended divorce cases should no longer be tried by King's Bench Judges as part of the ordinary work of Assizes.

2. The County Court Judges should be appointed Commissioners for matrimonial causes so as to supplement the number of Judges available for such cases in London and the provinces.

9. We desire to record that these conclusions correspond in principle with those reached by the Royal Commission of 1912. . . . They rejected the suggestion of trial by the County Courts as such, principally for the reason, which still appears to us sufficient, that it does not pay adequate regard to the significance and the public importance attaching to matrimonial causes of every kind. They reached the conclusion that the problem was to be solved by the High Court jurisdiction being exercised by County Court Judges sitting as Commissioners. . . . They did suggest however, that only 8 or 10 selected County Court Judges should be appointed. . . . The increased number of cases makes that suggestion inapplicable today. . . . [W]e are of opinion that all the County Court Judges should be appointed Commissioners. . . .

10. . . . [T]hat does not mean that other suitable persons should not be appointed . . . if the pressure of work demanded it.

11. Our conclusions in point of principle need, however, to be worked out in detail:

(i) The Commissioners should have all the jurisdiction of a High Court Judge in divorce and matrimonial cases. They should have power to try both undefended and defended cases. If they were restricted to undefended cases, it would mean that they would be regarded as Courts of inferior jurisdiction which in our opinion is undesirable. They will be somewhat restricted in . . . practice, however, because they will not be able to sit long at a stretch owing to the fact that they have also to sit in their County Courts. That means that they will usually confine themselves to the undefended cases and the shorter defended cases leaving the heavier defended cases to the Judges who can sit continuously. . . .

(v) The Commissioners should be accorded all the dignity of a High Court Judge. When sitting in Court they should wear the same robes as a Judge of the Divorce Division and be addressed in the same way as a Judge.

(vi) The Commissioners should receive payment at the same rate as a High Court Judge for the days on which they sit as Commissioners. . . .

Royal Commission on Marriage and Divorce
Cmd. 9678 (1956)

742. The main question which we had to consider is whether jurisdiction in divorce should continue to rest exclusively with the High Court; and, if so, whether any changes should be made in the present arrangements for exercising that jurisdiction. We have come to the conclusion that it should so continue, and that it is desirable that all divorce cases should be tried by judges of the High Court. We therefore recommend:

(a) that the High Court should continue to exercise exclusive jurisdiction in divorce, and

(b) that steps should be taken as soon as possible to enable all divorce cases to be tried by judges of the High Court.

We reached these conclusions after careful consideration of the various proposals submitted to us, which are discussed in the paragraphs below.

743. A limited number of our witnesses recommended the abolition of the present matrimonial jurisdiction of the High Court and (in some instances) the magistrates' courts, the jurisdiction to be assumed instead by a new form of tribunal, which for convenience we refer to as the "Family Court." Their proposal as to the powers and composition of the proposed tribunals varied, but generally it was contemplated that the new courts would operate an informal procedure such as exists in the present juvenile courts and would have available to them the services of specially qualified lay persons. The proposals were not developed at length, but underlying the suggestions of some witnesses was the view that matrimonial proceedings are in some sense different from all other types of litigation and that the legal concepts and procedure followed by the present courts are inadequate for dealing with problems of such an intimate and personal nature. Sometimes, the proposals for "Family Courts" were linked with proposals for the adoption of a new principle, either in addition to, or in substitution for, the present principle on which the divorce law is based.

747. We do not recommend the introduction of any system of "Family Courts." If a radical change were to be made in the basis on which divorce is granted, then it might reasonably be argued that the present judicial system would not be best adapted for the consideration of the issues which would then require determination, issues which would often be basically different from those arising today. But we think that a less formal tribunal, such as the witnesses usually contemplated, would be quite unsuited for the trial of divorce cases under the present law, for which high judicial qualities in our opinion are essential. . . .

748. Some witnesses recommended, as an alternative to their proposals for the institution of "Family Courts," that the county courts should have matrimonial jurisdiction, either exclusively, or concurrently with the High Court. . . . In support of giving such jurisdiction to the county courts it was said that a county court constitutes an adequate, inexpensive and readily accessible local tribunal; that the county court judges at present acting as Special Commissioners in Divorce are proving competent and equal to the task; and that it therefore seems reasonable to end the present compromise by taking the final, logical step of giving jurisdiction in divorce to the county courts as such. . . . The principle which has hitherto prevailed is clearly stated in the following extract from the Report of the Gorell Commission:

> ". . . the gravity of divorce and other matrimonial cases, affecting as they do the family life, the status of the parties, the interests of their children, and the interest of the State in the moral and social well-being of its citizens, makes it desirable to provide, if possible, that, even for the poorest persons, these cases should be determined by the superior courts of the country assisted by the attendance of the Bar, which we regard as of high importance in divorce and matrimonial cases, both in the interests of the parties and in the public interest." [35]

750. We accept that principle as sound, and as being just as applicable today as in 1912. We also agree with the view of the Denning Committee that the manner in which divorce is effected does influence the attitude of the community towards the status of marriage.

755. It was suggested in the evidence submitted by the General Council of the Bar of England and Wales that the time had now come to give up the present scheme of special commissioners. . . .

756. . . . [T]he present system of special commissioners was devised in order to deal expeditiously with the very heavy post-war divorce list. It was not

---

[35] Cd. 6478, para. 106.

intended as a permanent administrative change, but as a temporary measure to deal with an immediate problem.

758. It is in our view desirable that there should be a return as soon as possible to the system under which all cases, defended and undefended, are tried by judges of the High Court. . . .

759. On an estimate we have made, some fifteen additional judges would be required to replace all the special commissioners who are at present trying divorce cases. We do not suggest that it would be advisable to appoint at once so large a number of judges. . . .

760. But we wish to make it plain that whatever number of judges may prove to be necessary, it is our view that that number should be appointed, and that accommodation consistent with the dignity of the High Court should be provided for them.

Matrimonial Causes Act 1967

1967 c. 56

1.—(1) The Lord Chancellor may by order designate any county court as a divorce county court, and any court so designated shall have jurisdiction to hear and determine any undefended matrimonial cause, except that it shall have jurisdiction to try such a cause only if it is also designated in the order as a court of trial. . . .

(3) Every matrimonial cause shall be commenced in a divorce county court, but rules of court—

(a) shall provide for the transfer to the High Court of any matrimonial cause which ceases to be undefended; and

(b) may provide for the transfer to that court of matrimonial causes which remain undefended. . . .

2.—(1) Subject to the following provisions of this section, a divorce county court shall have jurisdiction to exercise any power exercisable under Part II or Part III of the Matrimonial Causes Act 1965 . . . and to exercise any power under section 22 or section 24 of that Act.

(2) . . . [R]ules of court shall provide for the transfer to the High Court of any proceedings pending in a county court by virtue of this section in any case where the transfer appears to the county court to be desirable, . . .

(3) A divorce county court shall not by virtue of this section have jurisdiction to exercise any power under sections 25 to 27 of the Matrimonial Causes Act 1965, but without prejudice to the exercise by virtue of section 7 of the Family Provision Act 1966 of any power exercisable by a county court under section 26 or 27 of the said Act of 1965.

(4) Nothing in this section shall affect the jurisdiction of a magistrates' court under section 24 of the Matrimonial Causes Act 1965.

3. Any provision to be made by rules of court for the purpose of section 5 (2) of the Matrimonial Causes Act 1965 with respect to any power exercisable by the court on an application made before the presentation of a petition shall confer jurisdiction to exercise the power on divorce county courts.

4.—(1) Sections 1 to 3 of this Act shall not prevent the commencement of any proceedings in the principal probate registry, except where rules of court under section 2 (2) of this Act otherwise provide. . . .

5. The jurisdiction conferred by this Act on divorce county courts . . . shall be exercised by such county court judges as the Lord Chancellor may direct. . . .

Royal Commission on Assizes and Quarter Sessions
Cmnd. 4153 (1966–69)

219. The present allocation of matrimonial work between the High Court and the County Court, according to whether a case is defended or not, is simple, and we do not propose to disturb its basis very much. We do recommend, however, that flexibility should be introduced, so that uncomplicated defended cases may be heard before a Circuit judge, and so that difficult ancillary business arising from an undefended action may be transferred to the High Court, particularly when it concerns the custody of children. What we propose is that:

(a) all defended divorce shall continue to be heard in the High Court, but that a High Court judge shall have power to release to a Circuit judge any case, or any ancillary business in connection with a case, which does not appear to raise issues of particular difficulty or importance;

(b) all undefended petitions shall continue to be heard in the County Court, but that ancillary work may be transferred to the High Court:
   (i) by consent of both parties;
   (ii) by decision of a Circuit judge, without the consent of both parties, if he considers that the issues are of such complexity or importance as to warrant his so doing; or
   (iii) by decision of a High Court judge, on application by either party;

(c) the President of the Probate, Divorce & Admiralty Division shall be empowered to make Practice Directions, with the concurrence of the Lord Chancellor, about the criteria to be used in determining the difficulty or importance of cases, for the purpose of the powers referred to in (a) and (b). (We make this proposal, rather than recommending the criteria ourselves, because the law governing matrimonial cases is at present in a transitional stage.)

Justice out of Reach

A case for small claims courts
Consumer Council 1970

. . . We found, in brief, that solicitors do not welcome clients with potential consumer claims; that some solicitors will not accept such clients at all; and that, as a result, people with consumer claims may be shuffled from one solicitor to another. Or else, because of expense, they may be advised that their complaint, however sound, is not worth pursuing. This situation is reflected in the county courts: individuals use the county courts very little for any matter at all, not simply consumer matters; they rarely sue and rarely defend if sued. The county courts are mainly used for collecting debts by firms who sell on credit.

Our research was chiefly concerned with claims involving consumer goods and services. But the situation that we found is without doubt as true for other disputed claims involving relatively small sums of money as for consumer claims. Unless he is backed by a trade union or an insurance company, or unless he is entitled to legal aid and it is granted (which it is usually not in small claims), the individual simply does not take his dispute to a court for decision. And rarely would a solicitor advise him to do so. . . .

After a pilot sampling of records in Shoreditch county court, we selected six county courts for this research, representing different types of community ranging from industrial to predominantly rural. They were: Leeds, Bolton, Leicester, Cambridge, Guildford and Worcester.

Every county court keeps record of the progress of all actions begun in the court. Until this year, these records were kept in minute books. . . .

Any consumer claims or counterclaims would be recorded in the minute books for either ordinary summonses or default summonses. We accordingly examined, in the courts selected, the minute book entry for a random 2 per cent. sample of all the summonses recorded in these two categories of minute book during 1967. The total number of ordinaries and defaults in these six courts was 61,866 (roughly 4 per cent. of the national total); thus we examined 1,238 entries. 72 per cent. of our sample were defaults. Since ordinary and default actions in 1967 made up 95 per cent. of county court work, we were in effect sampling nearly the full range of county court actions; the only major category omitted was actions for possession of land or premises, which are usually recorded in separate minute books. But possession summonses amounted to only 2½ per cent. of county court actions begun in 1967.

We found out that nearly 90 per cent. of the summonses in our sample were taken out by a firm or a utility board (nearly always a gas or electricity board). An individual was the plaintiff in nine per cent. of summonses. The remaining 1·6 per cent. were taken out by local authorities or government departments. . . . [C]ounty courts have since gained jurisdiction in undefended divorce which has added a large category to their work not reflected in our figures.

Where individuals did sue, they mainly sued each other for debt (72 summonses as opposed to 1,075 summonses by companies suing for debt); but a good proportion of the plaintiffs in these 72 cases were probably small businesses suing in the proprietor's name. Damage to person or property was the next biggest category (17 summonses); but probably most of these were car accident cases, where insurance companies would often have been standing behind the individuals. Some others may have been union-supported actions for industrial injuries. . . . The chief purpose for which the county courts are used is for debt collection by firms who sell on credit. Nearly three-quarters (71·5 per cent.) of our total sample of summonses were " trader cases," by our definition: that is, summonses by firms against individuals for debt for goods or services. . . . In contrast, we did not find a single case of an individual suing a firm in a consumer matter, excepting a possible one in Bolton, . . .

There was a remarkable preponderance of mail order houses among the trader plaintiffs. . . . The next biggest groups were far behind. . . .

Most traders sue for petty sums. . . . [M]ore than 70 per cent, of our trader cases were for under £20; approaching half (45 per cent.) were for under £10; and one-fifth were for less than £5. As we know, no solicitor would advise a consumer to bring a claim for anything like as small a sum as these, since, even if he won, the costs recoverable from the other party would not cover the expense of the work involved. But the big firms who use the county courts for debt collecting either have special departments of their own or use solicitors' firms with special departments. Here, debt summonses are processed in hundreds and thousands by mass-production methods. Some courts keep separate minute books for certain firms who take out summonses by the hundred. . . .

The defendant filed a defence or counterclaim in 50 of our sample of trader cases—which amounts to seven per cent. of the summonses actually served by traders on consumers. . . . [I]n 32 cases (64 per cent.) the action was withdrawn after the defence was filed. . . .

Defendants are rarely represented in the county courts. . . . It is clear from our research that consumers with sound legal claims are not having them adjudicated.

Much the same must be true of other kinds of dispute where the sums of money or the injuries are too small to be worth a solicitor's time: a dispute over landlords' dilapidations, for example, or a claim for arrears of wages where the claimant has no trade union, or a claim for minor damage to a car where the claimant does not have full insurance or does not want to lose his no-claims bonus by invoking his insurance company. . . .

Every stage of county court procedure can be a major hurdle for a layman. . . . Before the hearing, he will have to decide what evidence is needed to establish his case. The average person has little ability to judge what is relevant to his case, let alone what the court is likely to find persuasive. . . .

Procedure at a court hearing is quite beyond the capabilities of the average person. . . . The layout of the court is not such as to put a lay litigant at his ease. . . .

In the hands of skilled lawyers, formal trial procedure is no doubt a splendid instrument. But as a means of getting at the truth where one or both of the parties is unrepresented a more inefficient system is difficult to imagine. . . .

The custom in this country, when we want a particular area of the law to be administered informally, is to bypass the courts and to hand that area of the law to a system of tribunals. Workmen's compensation was shifted from the county courts to tribunals in 1946; most of the law governing relations between employers and employees is now administered by tribunals; and successive legislation controlling rents has set up tribunal machinery rather than give jurisdiction to the courts.

The result is that the county courts continue to apply their high judicial standards and awesome procedures to a narrower and narrower range of matters. In terms of actions filed, debt collection and undefended divorce actions between them make up a substantial majority of county court work. In terms of judicial time, summonses for possession of houses and flats and cases arising from car and factory accidents no doubt also figure quite large.

Tribunals meanwhile have proliferated: there are now about 2,000 of them adjudicating on citizens' rights in at least 30 fields of law including rent and security of tenure, redundancy payments, the National Health Service, social security benefits, and national insurance. Their decisions have a greater impact on people's lives and livelihoods than do most decisions of the civil courts. . . .

The advantages of tribunals are, as the Franks Committee put it, " cheapness, accessibility, freedom from technicality, expedition, and expert knowledge of their particular subject." (Franks Committee on Administrative Tribunals, 1957, Cmnd. 218). Most tribunals are not bound by rules of procedure or evidence, people are not usually legally represented, and the chairman (generally a lawyer) questions the parties to elicit their cases. Hearings are held in surroundings less imposing than courtrooms. In many tribunals, one or more of the three members is an expert in the subject—a valuer on a rent assessment panel for example, or a trade unionist on an industrial tribunal. . . . [W]here it is necessary, such as in rent tribunals, the members of the tribunal as a matter of course go and inspect the subject-matter of the dispute. . . . [W]e have considered whether consumer cases might be hived off into a new tribunal system. But there is one major—and it seems to us insuperable—difficulty: that is defining the area of law which a consumer tribunal would cover. . . . Arbitration is another attractive-looking solution . . . [A] few trades run praiseworthy schemes for arbitrating in disputes between their members and individual consumers. One example is that run by the Motor Agents' Association, which covers disputes over secondhand cars and car repairs. . . .

Under the National House-Builders' Registration Council scheme, disputes between registered builders and purchasers are referred to an arbitrator. . . . This form of arbitration is widely used in the building trade on very big disputes between contractors, or between developers and contractors.

However, . . . since arbitration is voluntary, the less reputable firms can simply refuse to submit a dispute to arbitration. Such firms do not join a trade association that runs an arbitration scheme.

Arbitration has its drawbacks, too. For one thing arbitrations are held in private, which . . . makes it impossible to find out what usually happens in arbitrations. . . .

One of the advantages claimed for arbitration is its informality. But how informal is it really? Arbitrators are considered to be bound by the same rules of procedure and evidence as are the courts. So how does an unrepresented party fare? . . . The county courts already have the basic requirements for small claims jurisdiction . . . . They have premises excellently distributed round the country . . . they are well administered and competently staffed; and they have an experienced judiciary. They also have the power to use some of the procedures that at present make tribunals and arbitration cheaper and more informal. . . . [W]e suggest a scheme in which county courts would run small claims courts. If county courts could be persuaded to take these on and run them on truly informal lines, we think that the civil courts would have taken an important step towards bringing themselves back into the mainstream of society, which is where they belong.

In brief, we propose that the registrar of each county court should be charged with running an informal court for small claims, as a branch of the county court, designed for individuals to have their claims adjudicated without legal representation. . . . We suggest that the court might have jurisdiction for claims up to £100 in contract and tort. . . . [C]ompanies, partnerships, associations and assignees of debts should not be allowed to sue . . . to prevent . . . the court's becoming widely used by firms for debt collecting. . . .

If there is any provision for appeal it should be very limited. . . . [T]he court must be able to call for certain evidence, or make certain enquiries itself, where it considers that it does not know enough about the facts of a case. . . . [T]he principle of a judicial body's collecting evidence is already well established in some tribunal systems. . . . A good example is the machinery for setting a " fair rent " under the Rent Act 1965. . . . [T]he registrar's . . . first aim should be to achieve an amicable settlement. . . .

If no settlement was reached, then we think that in most cases the registrar would be able to reach a fair decision. . . . [T]he cost to the parties should be limited to a filing fee (perhaps on a scale ranging from 10s. to £2), which would be recoverable by the winning party. [I]f the registrar needed further evidence . . . the cost should fall on the state. We suggest that local solicitors might provide a rota of arbitrators to adjudicate in the small claims courts.

This would relieve the registrar of some of the extra load of small claims work. . . .

A Comment on " Justice out of Reach "

Law Society Gazette (1970) 586

. . . [W]hat is proposed is " palm-tree justice " for a particular type of case, identified by its monetary value, to be fixed at £100.

. . . [A]djudication, in essence, would be under a simple inquisitorial procedure, tinctured by conciliation. Sensible settlements would be encouraged and decisions made, where settlements proved impossible, on the basis of informal inquiry, consideration of any written material available, examination of defective goods and so forth. There is, of course, nothing to suggest that the only method of trial worthy of consideration within the Anglo-Saxon legal system is the adversary system. Our matrimonial law, for example, might have developed on sounder lines within an inquisitorial procedure, and many have thought that something of this sort would be appropriate in debt collection. Then why not in small claim cases? . . .

If money value is to be the criterion, a hundred pounds is far too high and far too arbitrary. The essence of the problem is not, as is often supposed, the *small* claim but all those types of claim in which the cost of resolving them prices justice out of the market. The most serious type of case is the building dispute in which the builder sues for the amount of his bill and the customer counter-claims because he alleges that the work is shoddy. Such a dispute necessitates expert evidence, and the detail to be considered involves an expenditure of time and effort which is extremely costly. The result is frequently a partial success for both sides and the costs they must bear are very likely to make the whole enterprise an expensive failure for both. . . .

There are some disputes in which a sensible settlement is the best solution, and others in which any sensible person (and particularly an experienced lawyer) can resolve a dispute as fairly as any court with a minimum of formality; but there are others where justice cannot be done without careful prior investigation, preparation and an effective and orderly procedure. The distinguishing marks for these types of case have nothing to do with an arbitrary monetary jurisdiction.

It is all very well for the Report to stigmatise discovery notices to produce and admit and other procedural steps as dispensable but these not infrequently are critical if justice is to be done. It is easy to assume that a fair answer can always, or even usually, be found despite a failure to marshal and present the facts in an ordinary way, but experience shows that this is just not so. To claim that all these steps can be taken by a court of its own initiative is merely to say that the cost of doing the work should be transferred from those who do it now to a staff paid by the State. To suggest that Court fees in small claim cases should be minimal means that other litigants would pay greater fees or that the taxpayers would bear the loss.

TRIBUNALS

Report of the Committee on Tribunals and Inquiries
Cmnd. 218 (1957–59)

The development of tribunals

35. At the time of the Donoughmore Committee (1929–32) there were few kinds of tribunal (although some of them, for example the Courts of Referees under the Unemployment Insurance Acts, dealt with important issues affecting large numbers of the population), and the Committee was able to regard tribunals as somewhat exceptional, to be resorted to only in special circumstances and requiring strict safeguards. The position today is different. The continuing extension of governmental activity and responsibility for the general well-being of the community has greatly multiplied the occasions on which an individual may be at issue with the administration, or with another citizen or body, as to his rights, and the post-war years have seen a substantial growth in the importance and activities of tribunals. In some cases new policies or regulatory legislation have meant new tribunals, for example those established under the Agriculture Act 1947, and under the Rent Acts. In other cases an earlier system has been adapted to wider purposes: for example, the local tribunals under the National Insurance Act 1946 are the successors of the Courts of Referees. In other cases tribunals now perform functions previously carried out by the courts: for example, under the National Insurance (Industrial Injuries) Act 1946, many

of the issues previously tried in the courts under the Workmen's Compensation Acts are now determined by tribunals.

36. Tribunals today vary widely in constitution, function and procedure. Appointments of chairmen and members are usually made by the Minister responsible for the legislation under which they operate, but some are made by the Crown and some by the Lord Chancellor, even though he may have no direct responsibility for the subject-matter of their work. Most tribunals deal with cases in which an individual citizen is at issue with a Government Department or other public body concerning his rights or obligations under a statutory scheme. But a few (for example Rent Tribunals) are concerned with disputes between citizens. Still others (for example the Licensing Authorities for Public Service and Goods Vehicles) have regulatory functions and are therefore just as much administrative bodies as they are adjudicating tribunals. Some tribunals, like the courts, have a detailed code of procedure, with testimony on oath and strict rules of evidence. Most have a simple procedure, usually without the oath and sometimes with a ban on legal representation. Finally, there are differences regarding appeals. Sometimes there is no appeal, and further redress can only be had by seeking a court order to set aside the decision. But in most cases there is an appeal—either to an appellate tribunal, a Minister or the courts.

37. Reflection on the general social and economic changes of recent decades convinces us that tribunals as a system for adjudication have come to stay. The tendency for issues arising from legislative schemes to be referred to special tribunals is likely to grow rather than to diminish. It is true that the Restrictive Trade Practices Act 1956 provides for cases to be determined by a new branch of the High Court, the Restrictive Practices Court, and not by a tribunal, and that the Rent Act 1957, has transferred part of the jurisdiction of Rent Tribunals to the courts. These recent preferences for determinations by courts of law do not, however, alter our general conviction.

The Change from Workmen's Compensation to National Insurance

Until the Workmen's Compensation Act 1897 a workman injured at work was left to sue his employer at common law in an action for negligence. This meant he had to prove fault and he had also to overcome a number of defences open to an employer which could defeat his claim, such as the defence that the injury had been caused by a fellow worker (common employment), contributory negligence (which totally defeated the claim at this time) or that the workman had voluntarily incurred the risk (*volenti non fit injuria*). The Workmen's Compensation Act 1897 provided instead that " if in any employment . . . personal injury by accident arising out of and in the course of employment is caused to a workman, his employer shall . . . be liable to pay compensation." The important part of this was that the workman need not any more prove fault. The Act which was consolidated in 1925 was gradually extended to cover most employment. By the time the scheme came to be considered by Sir William Beveridge in his Report on Social Insurance and Allied Services [36] there had been so much complication and dissatisfaction that he proposed that a totally new scheme should be adopted, one aspect of which was to remove the role of the county court as arbitrator. Instead a system of tribunals has been established with a final appeal to a National Insurance (Industrial Injuries) Commissioner. The details are set out in the National Insurance (Industrial

[36] Cmd. 6404 (1942).

Injuries) Act 1946. The following passages contain some of the criticisms of the old set-up.

Potter : The National Insurance (Industrial Injury) Act 1948
2nd ed. (1950)

What are the defects that led to the system being discarded? They may be roughly classified as follows. . . .

5. Most serious of all the defects of the system was the way in which the provisions of the Acts for the determination of disputes had worked in practice.

In introducing the Bill in 1897 Sir Matthew White Ridley, the Home Secretary, said that the Bill is " defined and limited so that both parties may know where they stand; it provides an inexpensive method of settling questions that must arise, and if it be true that legislation of this kind ought to aim at being simple, immediate and effective, this Bill has been conceived with that object."

These high hopes were not to be fulfilled. As is pointed out in Part II of the White Paper on Social Insurance (Cmd. 6551, September 1944) " it was originally contemplated that disputes would generally be settled by informal arbitration by a Committee representative of the employer and his workmen, or by an arbitrator agreed on by the parties, or by the County Court Judge, a form of procedure which was described by the Attorney-General at the time as something in the nature of a domestic forum which should settle matters in a cheap and expeditious manner. Except in the Cumberland and Durham coalfields, where representative committees have been set up, this intention has not been realised. Disputes are generally settled, subject to appeal on questions of law to the Court of Appeal and the House of Lords, by arbitration in the County Court: and this arbitration has developed into a regular legal proceeding " (paragraph 11).

It could hardly have been otherwise. On the one side was the workman, who naturally wished to get everything to which he was entitled. He was left to make a claim in a way which, for all practical purposes, put him in the position of a plaintiff in an ordinary county court action, and, of course, the onus of proof by admissible evidence according to the ordinary law of evidence rested upon him. On the other side there was not, in practice, in the vast majority of cases, even the employer as a virtual defendant, but an insurance company or mutual insurance society, which was not interested in the workman as a human being at all. It was concerned solely with not paying out more than it was legally liable to pay. Most insurance companies acted fairly, but as malingering and exaggeration (conscious or otherwise) were not unknown, . . . a claims manager had to be careful, and was apt to become a little hard headed at times. The obvious result was that a proceeding which it was innately desirable should be a friendly affair, the chief concern being the workman's well-being and restoration to health, degenerated too often into a protracted wrangle with a long court hearing, sometimes conducted with acrimony on both sides. . . .

On the whole it may be fairly said that the system of claims and settling disputes was one of the worst features of the system, and it added enormously to the total cost of administration.

It is not as if there were but few contentious cases. In the House of Commons debate on the Second Reading of the 1945 Bill (414 H. of C. Official Report 268) the Minister of National Insurance said that there were some 3,000 reported leading cases noted in Willis, and certainly that book, which has gone through 37 editions since August 31, 1897, and the text of which now runs to nearly 1,200 pages, bears witness to the highly contentious nature of this branch of law: it has, in fact, become a branch for specialists, and it has its own set of law reports, which now run to forty-seven volumes (Minton-Senhouse's and Butterworth's Workmen's Compensation Cases).

Nor do the reported cases give a true picture. In 1938, a typical year for which full judicial statistics are available, there were 4,572 applications for arbitration in all (though more than half were settled, withdrawn, or not proceeded with, before the hearing). In addition there were 22,454 memoranda registered, of which 3,136 were for lump sum settlements without there being any previous weekly payments, and 16,499 agreements for the redemption of weekly payments by lump sum settlements. In addition there were 75 appeals to the Court of Appeal.

Social Insurance : Proposals for an Industrial Injury Insurance Scheme

Cmd. 6551 (1944)

23. (i) The Government endorse generally the criticisms of the existing system made in the Report.[37] In particular, they consider it to be too complicated and to allow too much scope for contention between the workman (or his trade union) and the employer (or the insurance company or mutual association with which he is insured); it thus tends to retard the workman's recovery and to prejudice good relations between him and his employer. The cases in which actual legal proceedings are taken form only a small fraction of the total number, but even so they number some thousands annually, and in addition there are numerous cases which are settled, by lump sum payments or otherwise, without legal proceedings but only after considerable negotiation. Moreover, in the event of a dispute the workman is apt to feel that he is placed on an unequal footing with the employer or his insurers, and to suspect that the opposition to his claim is not based on merits but is actuated by motives of financial interest.

(ii) The Government consider it essential to provide that in future claims should be made on an independent authority and settled by a procedure less liable to give rise to friction. This, however, involves a complete change of system. So long as the liability to pay compensation is the liability of the employer it is difficult to justify taking the administration out of his hands, or to substitute for litigation less formal, contentious, and costly methods for the settlement of doubtful cases.

(iii) The principle of placing the liability on the individual employer has had other unfortunate consequences. For example, the employer generally protects himself by insurance, and the premiums or levies are fixed according to the risks of the particular industry or class of employment, so that broadly speaking each industry carries its own risks. The result is that the heaviest liability falls on the hazardous employments, which include certain important industries such as mining and shipping, which have to face foreign competition. It is sometimes claimed that the imposition of the liability on the individual employer conduces to safety by giving a direct financial incentive to employers to adopt greater precautions; but . . . it would not appear that it has, in fact, made any material contribution in this direction. . . .

(iv) The general conclusion reached by the government is that the time has come when the present system should be replaced by a new scheme, the general structure of which should be based on the accepted principles of social insurance.

[37] i.e. the Beveridge Report on Social Insurance and Allied Services, Cmd. 6404 (1942).

The Crown Court

As was mentioned above, until 1972 all serious criminal cases were tried on indictment with a jury either by High Court judges or Commissioners at assizes, or by courts of quarter sessions consisting of lay justices of the peace sitting with a legally qualified part-time chairman in the counties, and a part-time Recorder in those boroughs which had separate courts of quarter sessions. Special arrangements existed in London where the Central Criminal Court was in continuous session, and in Manchester and Liverpool where there were permanent " Crown Courts."

Following the report of the Royal Commission on Assizes and Quarter Sessions, the Courts Act 1971 replaced all these separate courts with a single Crown Court in which High Court judges, Circuit judges, or part-time Recorders sit, sometimes with lay justices of the peace. The constitution varies according to the gravity of the offence or the seriousness or difficulty of the particular case. One of the major objects of the reorganisation has been to secure greater flexibility than existed beforehand in the allocation of offences between the different types of judge. It had usually been the practice in the past to allocate not particular cases but particular classes of offence to different courts, the more serious being reserved for trial by a High Court judge at assizes. In many cases this was a perfectly satisfactory way of defining the jurisdiction of the different courts, but not always. Not every particular example of a class of offence was equally serious and, quite apart from this, seriousness and difficulty do not always go together. It is clear that the Beeching Commission took the view that one of the basic defects of the existing system was that this allocation of jurisdiction by classes of offence was one of the factors which led to High Court judges hearing cases that other judges could have dealt with perfectly satisfactorily. The changes they recommended in this respect are part and parcel of their general view that the most pressing need for the future was to organise the administration of criminal justice in such a way that the time of High Court judges would be used in the most economic and efficient way. The Courts Act 1971 has therefore established a system by which offences which prima facie fall into the " serious " category can be released to a Circuit judge if in the particular circumstances this seems appropriate. There is in fact nothing new about attempting to break down the allocation of jurisdiction by looking beyond the category into which a particular offence falls and considering its particular facts as a method of deciding which court should deal with it. As we shall see there has been a parallel development at the border-line between indictable offences, *i.e.* those which prima facie are serious enough to warrant trial with a jury, and summary offences, those which can be tried by magistrates' courts without a jury. Here too it has been felt that designation by category of offence is often unsatisfactory and this has resulted also in the creation of intermediate categories of offences which, though prima facie indictable, may in certain circumstances be tried summarily. This development is more fully discussed in relation to magistrates' courts.

As has also been mentioned earlier the Report of the Beeching Commission, though primarily concerned with the details of the administration of criminal justice, considered the matter in the context of the legal system as a whole and in particular in the context of the local administration of justice, both civil and criminal. Many of its remarks, therefore, are relevant to a general understanding of the problems with which a legal system has to cope, the limitations within which it has to operate, and the demands that it has to attempt to meet. Much of it could as well come at the beginning of the book as now. Its remarks about judges entering courts by the side doors, encouraging High Court judges to have lunch now and again with Circuit judges, and the difficulty of finding butlers for travelling High Court judges bring us almost as near as these materials get to a sociological account of the English legal system.

Report of the Royal Commission on Assizes and Quarter Sessions
Cmnd. 4153 (1966–69)

The merits and defects of the present pattern of courts

64. It stands out clearly from any survey of the pattern of criminal and civil courts that the system was devised for circumstances which no longer exist and that, in spite of very great changes in the life of the country, in the distribution of population, in the mobility of people, and in national and local government, far too much has been retained only because it is traditional. When change has proved unavoidable, the system has been patched rather than reformed. . . . [T]he resulting defects have been further intensified by a sharp rise in the crime rate over the last few decades. The rise in crime has, more recently, been accompanied by an even greater increase in the call upon court time, both for civil and criminal cases.

. . . [T]he recent overloading of the courts is, to a large extent, the result of greatly extended legal aid, one effect of which has been to increase the proportion of fought criminal cases, which our survey has shown take about ten times as long to hear as pleas of guilty. . . .

67. A major cause of difficulty is the limited availability of High Court judge time, intensified by the inflexibility and inefficiency of the Assize system. . . . Added to this is trouble caused by the outdated and inconvenient location of the courts, by accommodation of archaic squalor, and by uncoordinated sittings of courts, which cause overloading of the services on which they are dependent, in particular those of the Bar. . . .

69. We found ourselves readily convinced, both by our own judgment and by unanimous opinion amongst all who gave evidence to us on the subject, that movement of High Court judges between London and the provinces, for the purpose of hearing the more serious civil and criminal cases, has very great merit and has led to a consistency of judicial standards. During their time in London the judges join in the communal life of their Inns and have the opportunity of exchanging views with their fellow judges and with members of the Bar. While on circuit they are able to dispense justice which is seen to be wholly above local prejudices and problems and, at the same time, they gain knowledge of life in different parts of the country which enables them to bring a wider perspective to bear on their work. In perhaps no other profession is it so important for the practitioners to remain detached, while at the same time dealing at closest hand with the aberrations and weaknesses of mankind. High Court judges are expected to personify the dignity, authority, and impartiality of the law, and they have to accept considerable restriction on the kind of lives they can lead. We think that, in return, they must be treated as

being in a special and privileged position. The danger that this may result in their losing touch with common affairs, and becoming narrow and over-authoritarian in outlook, is diminished by the flexibility forced on them by constant changes of environment and by the mixture of criminal and civil work which they do. Movement of judges also has the advantage of ensuring that, if they do occasionally develop idiosyncrasies as a result of the exalted seclusion in which they live, their foibles move with them and do not become a source of irritation or amusement to any one section of the community. . . .

73. The main criticisms made to us about the Assize system are that it does not, in fact, provide justice when and where it is needed, that it is inflexible, that it makes inefficient use of resources, and that, for these and other reasons, it is inconvenient and wasteful of many people's time.

74. Because of the strong historical link with counties, the Assize courts are poorly located in relation to the distribution of population. . . .

75. Partly for traditional reasons, but mainly because the small load of work resulting from the poor locations of a lot of the Assize courts would make it hopelessly uneconomic to do otherwise, Assizes sit in many towns for only short periods two or three times a year. . . .

76. The straitjacket forced on Assizes by the need for the court to move on, in conformity with a pre-arranged timetable, is a cause of great inconvenience.

77. The inflexibility of the Assize system is made markedly more troublesome for the civil litigant by the priority given to crime. . . . [M]any of the witnesses in civil actions are professional men, such as doctors and engineers, who are not easily able to leave their work at short notice. . . .

79. As the Judicature Commission concluded a hundred years ago, it is extremely wasteful of highly skilled judicial talent to oblige High Court judges to travel to every county in England and Wales, at least twice a year, without regard to the volume of civil or criminal business. . . .

83. . . . [T]he provision of suitable lodging accommodation for peripatetic High Court judges . . . is a troublesome problem. It becomes increasingly difficult to find butlers and cooks who will move round the country with the judges. Also, of course, it is expensive to maintain special lodgings, some of which are occupied for only a few weeks in the year, . . . As a consequence there are a number of towns where judges are lodged in residences which most of the time are used by other people, so that Assizes have to be fixed at dates when the lodgings can be made available. . . .

85. . . . [T]he only merit attributed to the Assize system to which we attach importance, namely that it necessitates movement of the judges, is one which is not dependent upon preservation of the Assize system as a whole. . . . [A]lmost all other features of the system are troublesome rather than beneficial.

87. The part-time use of suitably qualified lawyers as Quarter Sessions judges undoubtedly has some advantages. . . . . [I]t provides a flexible source of judicial capacity to meet the fluctuating demands at a very considerable number of court locations. . . . [I]t makes available a good deal of high judicial potential which it might be difficult to match by permanent appointments. . . . [I]t provides a valuable means of giving judicial experience to successful practising members of the Bar, which both develops their talent and facilitates the Lord Chancellor's selection of new High Court judges. . . . On the other hand, there can be no doubt that dependence on the part-time services of lawyers who are very busy with their own practices, who frequently arrange sittings to suit their own convenience, and who can seldom sit for long at any one time, does cause bunching of court sittings, with resulting overloading of the Bar,

and of others, who provide services to a group of courts. It also causes the trial of cases to be postponed and sometimes transferred unnecessarily, either to Assizes or to another court of Quarter Sessions. Moreover, as can be seen from Appendix 9 where we give details about the numbers and occupations of Quarter Sessions judges, there are nearly 400 part-time posts, held by over 300 people, some of whom sit for very short periods, which makes it difficult to establish reasonable consistency in sentencing. . . .

91. The law recognises that it is rarely possible for a busy Chairman or Recorder to commit himself in advance to a long sitting, or to extend a sitting without great difficulty . . . by providing that magistrates may commit to Assizes any case which seems likely to be a long one, . . . While . . . many long cases are difficult, or concern offences of a serious nature, they do not all warrant the judicial talent of a High Court judge, whose time is in short supply. . . .

94. While we recognise that the use of part-time judges . . . has some merit, which is not overwhelmed by accompanying disadvantages in lightly populated areas, we do not consider this to be true for most of the populous areas of the country. We consider . . . that the courts . . . could be better located, and that sittings could be better co-ordinated if the dependence upon part-time judges . . . were to be greatly diminished. We think also that the position would be further improved if the unnecessary distinction between county and borough Sessions were to be abandoned completely.

What is needed and the problem of achieving it

111. It is fairly easy to set out the characteristics which are wanted in a court system, but it is much harder to decide how best to provide them in practice. Some of them, indeed, are incompatible with one another. . . .

112. If judicial integrity is taken for granted, the following are the features which a good court system should provide.

Convenience	(a) Ease of physical access.
	(b) An early hearing.
	(c) The assurance of trial on a date of which reasonable notice has been given.
Quality	(d) Suitable accommodation.
	(e) Judicial expertise.
	(f) Adequate and dependable legal representation.
Economy	(g) Efficient use of all manpower.
	(h) Optimum use of buildings.

. . . [T]he overall requirement of a good system must be to make high quality justice conveniently available at low cost.

113. . . . [I]t is the need to consider cost and to husband limited resources which makes it impossible to satisfy all the other criteria in full.

115. A factor which is even more restrictive than cost, both in the short and medium term, is the capacity of the Bar. . . . Although, provided there were suitable incentives, the Bar could no doubt be considerably enlarged, an expansion of capacity at all levels of competence and experience would take many years to achieve. Moreover, the last to be affected by a larger recruitment to the Bar would be those levels from which the higher ranks of the judiciary are drawn. The present potential of the Bar, therefore, sets a limit to the possibility of increasing judge power without sacrificing judicial quality, and without denuding the Bar of its leading members, and this limitation will only be

eased slowly because, for many years to come, it will depend upon past changes in the strength of the Bar rather than upon any recent or future increase in the rate of expansion.

The matching of judge power to the case load

134. Our court system is based upon the attempted matching of . . . case seriousness, where seriousness is specified by categories of offence in the case of crime, and largely in terms of money in civil cases, and . . . judicial talent. . . .

139. . . . . [I]t can be argued that seriousness is a very subjective thing; that a small financial sum may represent just as serious a burden to some as a much larger sum would to others; or that the danger of conviction of even a minor crime may be much more serious a matter to one person than to another. Ideally, therefore, there should be no more danger of a miscarriage of justice in supposedly less serious cases than in serious ones. But, to a large extent, it is the difficulty of cases rather than their seriousness which makes demands upon judicial ability, and difficulty should be a major determining factor in the matching of judicial quality to the case. While there is a general tendency for seriousness and difficulty to go together, many individual cases are marked exceptions to this rule. It is not satisfactory, therefore, to match judicial quality against a general and necessarily rather arbitrary classification of the seriousness of cases. This is what is attempted at present and, although the system does permit some exercise of discretion as to the trial of individual cases of exceptional difficulty, it is clear that the use of available judge power would be improved by a more flexible system for allocating cases, in which an assessment of the difficulty as well as the seriousness of the case would play a regular part.

147. The aim must surely be to make the best use of High Court judge power to deal with as much as possible of the top of the case load pyramid. But, because of the fluctuating load at this level, this aim cannot be achieved if rigid limits of jurisdiction are laid down. Either High Court judge capacity must be provided to match the peak of the case load above the boundary and be used below the boundary when there are troughs, or it may be matched to some lower level of load and be supplemented by the appointment of lower tier judges, ad hoc, to deal with surges of High Court work. The recurrent use of both expedients in the past has shown that the present system is designed to be abused. Therefore, on these practical grounds, as well as on the basis of the more theoretical considerations set out in paragraphs 134 to 139, it seems to us better to recognise that the desired result can only be achieved by a more flexible use of judge power than a fixed boundary of jurisdiction is intended to achieve, and to design the system accordingly. . . .

148. . . . . There are some other considerations affecting the way in which judges are employed which we feel condition any solution.

149. It has been represented to us, time and again, that it is highly undesirable for judges to remain continuously on criminal work, especially if they are always in one place. The Streatfeild Committee [39] based its criticism of the Crown Court system on this. . . . It is true . . . that a number of cases were mentioned of judges exposed to such conditions who seemed to suffer no ill effects in themselves, or in reputation. There was, for example, no criticism of the present judges at the Old Bailey, where many of them hear criminal cases all the time. . . . We were, however, convinced by the preponderance of evidence, and by reason, that it is undesirable to impose such conditions if they can be avoided.

[39] Interdepartmental Committee on the business of the Criminal Courts, Cmnd. 1289 (1961).

150. There was no spontaneous expression of opinion that it is bad for judges to do substantially the same kind of civil work continuously. Nevertheless . . . some witnesses were not prepared to agree that there was no equivalent of " prosecution-mindedness," or similar failings, among civil judges. Moreover . . . some County Court judges displayed in their evidence a proprietorial attitude towards [their] courts, and placed emphasis on the value of the expertise which results from specialisation and local knowledge, in a way which we found somewhat disturbing.

151. So far as High Court judges are concerned we encountered an extremely strong conviction, on their part and on the part of others, that they should not be immobilised away from London. There was, also, a general view that it is beneficial for them to do varied work, and that their intellectual capacity is such that they have no difficulty in trying both civil and criminal cases.

152. We were convinced that the argument in favour of a circulation of High Court judges throughout the country, to ensure a uniform application of the law by judges whose impartiality and freedom from local associations is unquestioned, is of such weight that any solution we might propose should provide for it. We were aware, too, that difficulties and dangers might arise if individual High Court judges were required to remain for long periods in isolated positions. What we did not readily accept was that other judges, of lesser calibre, could be exposed to the same conditions with safety. We also considered that the capacity of High Court judges to deal with varied work at their own level must be matched by some capacity to do the same thing among judges of lower rank. . . .

The proposed court system in outline

170. . . . The solution we propose is a radical departure from the present system but . . . our recommendations involve the general application of principles and practices which have already been accepted and applied in some parts of the country or in some circumstances. . . .

173. We propose . . . the reconstitution of the Supreme Court, so that it shall consist of the Court of Appeal, the High Court with civil jurisdiction, and a single court, to be called the Crown Court, for criminal work above the level of the magistrates.

CRIMINAL BUSINESS

174.—(a) We recommend the creation, by statute, of a new superior court of criminal jurisdiction, to be called the Crown Court. We suggest that it shall have jurisdiction throughout England and Wales; that it sit when and where needed; and shall absorb the criminal jurisdiction at present exercised by Courts of Assize, the Central Criminal Court, the Lancashire Crown Courts, and the courts of Quarter Sessions, all of which will cease to exist as separate courts.

(b) We propose that the judges of the Crown Court shall consist of High Court judges and a new bench of judges to be called Circuit judges, supported by a limited number of part-time appointments.

(c) We put forward a procedure, based on judicial decision, for allocating the total case load between the two tiers of judges, at centres regularly served by both, in a manner which will give considerable, but not complete, flexibility.

CIVIL BUSINESS

175.—(a) We recommend a revised split of jurisdiction between the High Court and the County Court, by increasing the jurisdiction of the County Court in actions of contract and tort to £1,000.

(b) We recommend that the High Court shall have jurisdiction, by statute, throughout England and Wales; shall sit when and where needed; and shall normally be presided over by High Court judges.

(c) We propose a flexible method, based on judicial decision, by which a limited number of Circuit judges can help to deal with the simpler High Court cases.

The Judiciary

176.—(a) We recommend no change in the title of High Court judges.

(b) We propose that the new permanent bench of Circuit judges shall be made up of the existing County Court bench and of all whole-time judges (other than High Court judges) exercising criminal jurisdiction in the courts to be replaced by the Crown Court.

(c) We recommend that all existing County Court judges shall become Circuit judges.

(d) We suggest that sufficient additional whole-time appointments shall be made to the Circuit bench to reduce the present dependence on part-time judges very considerably.

(e) To supplement the Circuit judges sitting in the Crown Court, we recommend that some part-time judges, to be called Recorders, shall be appointed, and that they shall agree as a condition of appointment to serve for limited periods which will be settled in advance.

(f) We suggest that two High Court judges, each of whom will be called a Presiding Judge, be assigned special responsibility for each of six Circuits. We propose that they shall, alternately, spend substantial periods in their Circuit so that they may, between them, provide the continuous presence of a judge knowledgeable about the affairs of the Circuit and about the Circuit judges serving there. They will be responsible for a general oversight of the administration and, in particular, for the location and well-being of the judges in the Circuit.

(g) We recommend that District and County Court Registrars shall be relieved of responsibilities in connection with the running of their offices, so as to leave them free for work for which a legal qualification is essential, and that they shall be called Circuit and County Court Masters.

(h) We propose an increase in the jurisdiction of County Court Masters to £100. . . .

The criminal courts

190. We approached the problem of how the hearing of criminal cases should be distributed between High Court and Circuit judges on the basis that the present allocation by types of offence imposed an undesirable rigidity. High Court judges are asked to try cases such as killing by dangerous driving, even where there are no aggravating features, and the less serious robberies, all of which could well be tried by other judges. On the other hand, a case requiring the skill of a High Court judge may at present be tried at Quarter Sessions, simply because the offence comes into the category of those which are triable at that court.

191. In framing our proposals we were anxious to introduce a greater degree of flexibility, while at the same time preserving trial of the great bulk of cases at the same judicial level as at present. . . .

192. *Offences which must come before a High Court judge.* ("*Upper band offences.*") Certain offences are generally regarded, for one reason or another, as being of so grave a nature that they ought never to be tried other than at the

highest judicial level. We accept this view, although in some cases it may mean that a High Court judge tries an offence when the circumstances are such that it does not require the application of his level of judicial talent. At the same time, we think that a distinction should be drawn between certain offences whose nature is so inherently grave that they must always be tried by a High Court judge, and ones which should be so tried unless a High Court judge is satisfied that the particular circumstances of a case are such that it is permissible for him to release it for trial by a Circuit judge. This distinction already exists at the Central Criminal Court, . . .

194. *Offences which may be tried by a High Court or by a Circuit judge.* ("*Middle band offences.*") We refer to all other offences now triable only at Assizes as " middle band offences."

195. *Offences which will normally be dealt with by a Circuit judge.* ("*Lower band offences.*") We refer to all cases which are now triable at Quarter Sessions as "lower band offences." These should generally be tried by a Circuit judge at the nearest location of the Crown Court, but there may be an exceptional case where the circumstances are so serious as to warrant its coming before a High Court judge. . . .

250. We recommend that Circuit judges should change occupation between civil and criminal work from time to time. We envisage, nevertheless, that many of them will, by arrangement, serve predominantly in either the criminal or the civil courts and, moreover, that for a considerable transitional period some may serve in one field only. . . .

271. Although we have received a good deal of evidence about the part to be played by lay magistrates at Quarter Sessions, or any court which we may propose in its place, this is not a subject on which we intend to make any firm recommendations. We found a spread of opinion about the value of such magistrates when sitting with the Chairman at county Quarter Sessions.

273. The most important aspect of this problem appears to us to be an issue of sentencing policy and to involve answering the question whether a court composed in part of lay magistrates is inherently more likely, or no less likely, to arrive at the correct sentence than one presided over by a legally qualified judge sitting alone. This is a matter on which we have received no conclusive evidence and it is for this reason that we make no strong recommendations on the subject. We merely record our recognition of the fact that sentencing is one of the most difficult and responsible tasks of a criminal court, and that it is desirable for such a court to be given all the help that can be provided in carrying it out. We accept that lay justices may provide such help, although we are more impressed by the likelihood that they will themselves benefit from the experience. It is for this reason that we recommend that lay justices should be encouraged to sit with a Circuit judge . . . as assessors.

The distribution of court capacity in relation to population

156. . . . About three-quarters of the population of England and Wales are within possible daily travel distance of the centres of six conurbations and, of the remaining quarter, most are either living in, or can fairly easily reach, a town which would provide a convenient court centre.

167. . . . London, with its own high population and its exceptional position as a centre for radial transport routes, is obviously first in the list, having within daily access a population of thirteen millions. Second is the south Lancashire conurbation with Manchester and Liverpool as transport foci and . . . daily access to a population of seven million. Third is Birmingham which gives daily access to six million people. Fourth is the West Riding conurbation

centred in Leeds, which is within daily reach for a population of five and a half million. Fifth . . . is Bristol, within daily access of two million people, and sixth is Cardiff giving access to rather less than that. Other cities, whose gathering grounds do not in most cases seriously overlap the preceding ones are, in decreasing order of population served, Newcastle, Nottingham, Winchester, Exeter and Norwich. In total, these give daily access to about 80 per cent. of the population.

168. The proposals for the location of courts for High Court civil work, . . . are based upon the foregoing considerations. . . . The spaces that remain are then filled by choosing secondary centres, to give virtually total coverage with the minimum of overlap, from amongst those towns which are the largest remaining centres of population and the best remaining communication centres.

169. We have used the same general basis for selecting centres for criminal work but we propose that there should be more of them, particularly at what is at present the Quarter Sessions level. Our reasons for recommending a larger number are that it is less necessary to strive for concentration in criminal than in civil work, and it is important to bear in mind the convenience of jurors.

277. In our proposals we provide for three different types of centre:—

High Court and Crown Court. At these, visiting High Court judges will sit, either continuously or for substantial periods, to take the more important and difficult civil and criminal cases. They will be assisted in this by Circuit judges, who will be invited to help by the Presiding Judge, and who will hear a proportion of the less serious or complex cases which would at present be heard by High Court judges at Assizes. In addition, Circuit judges will be available to take the types of crime at present normally tried at Quarter Sessions.

Crown Court. (Served by High Court and Circuit judges.) These will differ from the first category only in that no High Court civil work will normally be taken there.

Crown Court. (Served by Circuit judges only.) At these, only Circuit judges will normally sit, to deal with Quarter Sessions-type cases. They will be visited only quite exceptionally by a High Court judge.

Other benefits and effects of the proposals

394. Although we certainly do not advocate the establishment of judgeship as a career, we think it very important to avoid the other extreme of making any judicial appointment below the level of the High Court bench a virtually dead end position, with a resulting danger of limiting recruitment to mediocre younger men or resigned older men. Therefore, although we do not think that promotion of Circuit judges should become the main route to the High Court bench, we think it important that it should be seen as an open one. . . . [O]ur proposals for the flexible use of Circuit judges as having an additional beneficial effect, because it will give more of them criminal and civil experience, it will give them opportunity to apply their judicial powers to some of the less complicated High Court cases, and will bring them into more frequent contact with High Court judges and senior members of the Bar. . . .

395. . . . We recommend that the Lord Chancellor should take steps to see that, wherever possible, adequate facilities exist for High Court and Circuit judges to lunch together. This is of particular importance because of our proposals for Circuit judges to be invited to help the High Court bench.

397. We believe that our proposals for the concentration of court work in fewer places . . . will foster strong local Bars.

The Courts Act 1971

1971 c. 23

1.—(1) The Supreme Court shall consist of the Court of Appeal and the High Court, together with the Crown Court established by this Act. . . .

2.—(1) Sittings of the High Court may be held, and any other business of the High Court may be conducted, at any place in England or Wales.

(2) Subject to rules of court—

(*a*) the places at which the High Court sits outside the Royal Courts of Justice, and

(*b*) the days and times when the High Court sits outside the Royal Courts of Justice,

shall be determined in accordance with directions given by or on behalf of the Lord Chancellor.

The Crown Court

4.—(1) There shall be a Crown Court in England and Wales which shall be a superior court of record.

(2) The jurisdiction and powers of the Crown Court shall be exercised by—

(*a*) any judge of the High Court, or

(*b*) any Circuit judge or Recorder, or

(*c*) subject to and in accordance with the provisions of the next following section, a judge of the High Court, Circuit judge or Recorder sitting with justices of the peace,

and any such persons when exercising the jurisdiction and powers of the Crown Court shall be judges of the Crown Court.

(3) Any judge of the Court of Appeal may, on the request of the Lord Chancellor, sit and act as a judge of the Crown Court, and when so sitting and acting shall be regarded . . . as a judge of the High Court.

(4) Subject to the provisions of the next following section as respects a court comprising justices of the peace, all proceedings in the Crown Court shall be heard and disposed of before a single judge, and—

(*a*) any Crown Court business may be conducted at any place in England or Wales;

(*b*) sittings of the Crown Court at any place may be continuous or inter-mittent or occasional,

(*c*) judges may sit simultaneously to take any number of different cases in the same or in different places, and all or any of them may adjourn cases from place to place at any time.

(5) The cases or classes of cases suitable for allocation respectively to a judge of the High Court, and to a Circuit judge or Recorder, and all other matters relating to the distribution of Crown Court business, shall be determined in accordance with directions given by or on behalf of the Lord Chief Justice with the concurrence of the Lord Chancellor given by him or on his behalf.

(6) The places at which the Crown Court sits, and the days and times when the Crown Court sits at any place, shall be determined in accordance with directions given by or on behalf of the Lord Chancellor.

(7) When the Crown Court sits in the City of London it shall be known as the Central Criminal Court, and, notwithstanding the provisions of sub-section (4) above requiring proceedings to be heard and disposed of before a single judge, the Lord Mayor of the City and any Alderman of the City shall

be entitled to sit as judges of the Central Criminal Court with any judge of the High Court or any Circuit judge or Recorder.

5.—(3) . . . Any jurisdiction or power of the Crown Court may be exercised by a judge of the High Court, Circuit judge or Recorder sitting with not more than four justices of the peace.[40]

(4). . . The cases or classes of cases suitable for allocation to a court comprising justices of the peace . . . shall be determined in accordance with directions given by or on behalf of the Lord Chief Justice with the concurrence of the Lord Chancellor. . . .

(8) When a judge of the High Court, Circuit judge or Recorder sits with justices of the peace he shall preside, and—

(a) the decision of the Crown Court may be a majority decision, and

(b) if the members of the court are equally divided, the judge of the High Court, Circuit judge or Recorder shall have a second and casting vote.

6.—(1) All proceedings on indictment shall be brought before the Crown Court.

20.—(1) Every Circuit judge shall, by virtue of his office, be capable of sitting as a judge for any county court district in England and Wales, and the Lord Chancellor shall assign one or more Circuit judges to each district and may from time to time vary the assignment of Circuit judges among the districts.

(3) . . . Every judge of the Court of Appeal, every judge of the High Court, every Recorder, shall be capable of sitting as a judge for any county court district in England and Wales. . . .

23.—(1) If requested to do so by or on behalf of the Lord Chancellor, a Circuit judge or Recorder shall sit as a judge of the High Court for the hearing of such case or cases or at such place and for such time as may be specified. . . .

24.—(1) If it appears to the Lord Chancellor that it is expedient as a temporary measure to make an appointment under this subsection in order to facilitate the disposal of business in the High Court or the Crown Court he may appoint a person qualified for appointment as a puisne judge of the High Court under section 9 of the Judicature Act 1925 or any person who has held office as a judge of the Court of Appeal or of the High Court to be a deputy judge of the High Court. . . .

(2) If it appears to the Lord Chancellor that it is expedient as a temporary measure to make an appointment under this subsection in order to facilitate the disposal of business in the Crown Court or a county court he may appoint to be a deputy Circuit judge . . .

(a) any person qualified for appointment as a Circuit judge under section 16 above;

(b) any person who has held office as a judge of the Court of Appeal or of the High Court or as a Circuit judge; or

(c) any person who, before the day appointed for the purposes of section 20 above, had retired from office as an official referee or judge of a county court.

---

[40] s. 5 (1) provides that on the hearing of any appeal or proceedings on committal to the court for sentence the court shall consist of a High Court or circuit judge or a Recorder sitting with not less than two nor more than four justices.

The classification of offences

Practice Direction (Crime : Crown Court Business)
[1971] 1 W.L.R. 1535

The direction was issued on October 14 by virtue of sections 4 (5) and 5 (4) of the Courts Act 1971.

1. For the purposes of trial in the Crown Court, offences are to be classified as follows:

Class 1. The following offences, which are to be tried by a High Court judge: (1) Any offences for which a person may be sentenced to death. (2) Misprision of treason and treason felony. (3) Murder. (4) Genocide. (5) An offence under section 1 of the Official Secrets Act 1911. (6) Incitement, attempt or conspiracy to commit any of the above offences.

Class 2. The following offences, which are to be tried by a High Court judge unless a particular case is released by or on the authority of a presiding judge, that is to say, a High Court judge assigned to have special responsibility for a particular circuit: (1) Manslaughter. (2) Infanticide. (3) Child Destruction. (4) Abortion (section 58 of the Offences against the Person Act 1861). (5) Rape. (6) Sexual intercourse with girl under 13. (7) Incest with girl under 13. (8) Sedition. (9) An offence under section 1 of the Geneva Conventions Act 1957. (10) Mutiny. (11) Piracy. (12) Incitement, attempt or conspiracy to commit any of the above offences.

Class 3. All indictable offences other than those in classes 1, 2 and 4. They may be listed for trial by a High Court judge or by a circuit judge or recorder.

Class 4. (1) All offences which may, in appropriate circumstances, be tried either on indictment or summarily. They include—(a) indictable offences which may be tried summarily (section 19 of, and Schedule 1 to, the Magistrates' Courts Act 1952); (b) offences which are both indictable and summary (section 18 of the Magistrates' Courts Act 1952); (c) offences punishable on summary conviction with more than three months' imprisonment where the accused may claim to be tried on indictment (section 25 of the Magistrates' Courts Act 1952).

(2) Conspiracy to commit any of the above offences.

(3) The following offences: (a) Causing death by reckless or dangerous driving (section 1 of the Road Traffic Act 1960). (b) Wounding or causing grievous bodily harm with intent (section 18 of the Offences against the Person Act 1861).[41] (c) Burglary (section 9 of the Theft Act 1968) in a dwelling in circumstances set out in paragraph 11 (c) of Schedule 1 to the Magistrates' Courts Act 1952. (d) Robbery, or assault with intent to rob (section 8 of the Theft Act 1968).[41] (e) Offences under the Forgery Act 1913 (being offences under that Act which are not triable summarily, *i.e.*[41] other than offences under section 2 (2) (*a*) or section 7 where the value of the property does not exceed £100). (f) Incitement, attempt or conspiracy to commit any of the above offences. (g) Conspiracy to commit an offence which is in no circumstances triable on indictment or an act which is not an offence.

(4) Any offence in class 3, if included in class 4 in accordance with directions, which may be either general or particular, given by a presiding judge or on his authority.

---

[41] These offences have since been transferred from Class 4 to Class 3 by a *Practice Direction* issued on June 29, 1972: [1972] 1 W.L.R. 954.

When tried on indictment offences in class 4 may be tried by a High Court judge, circuit judge or recorder but will normally be listed for trial by a circuit judge or recorder.

Committals for trial.

2. (i) A magistrates' court on committing a person for trial under section 7 (1) of the Magistrates' Courts Act 1952 [or under the Criminal Justice Act 1967, s. 1] shall, if the offences, or any of the offences is included in classes 1 to 3, specify the most convenient location of the Crown Court where a High Court judge regularly sits, and if the offence is in class 4 shall, subject to paragraph 2 (ii), specify the most convenient location of the Crown Court.

(ii) If in the view of the justices, when committing a person for trial for an offence in class 4, the case should be tried by a High Court judge, they shall indicate that view, giving reasons, in a notice to be included with the papers sent to the Crown Court, and shall commit to the most convenient location of the Crown Court where a High Court judge regularly sits.

The following considerations should influence the justices in favour of trial by a High Court judge, namely, where: (i) the case involves death or serious risk to life (excluding cases of dangerous driving, or causing death by dangerous driving, having no aggravating features); (ii) widespread public concern is involved; (iii) the case involves violence of a serious nature; (iv) the offence involves dishonesty in respect of a substantial sum of money; (v) the accused holds a public position or is a professional or other person owing a duty to the public; (vi) the circumstances are of unusual gravity in some respect other than those indicated above; (vii) a novel or difficult issue of law is likely to be involved, or a prosecution for the offence is rare or novel. . . .

Allocation of proceedings to a court comprising lay justices

13. In addition to the classes of case specified in section 5 (1) of the Courts Act 1971 (appeals and proceedings on committals for sentence) any other proceedings which, in accordance with these directions, are listed for hearing by a circuit judge or recorder are suitable for allocation to a court comprising justices of the peace.

The Location of Courts

To put into effect the provisions of the Courts Act 1971 England and Wales have been divided up into six circuits. Within these circuits a number of towns have been designated first-tier, second-tier and third-tier centres. The first deal with both civil and criminal cases and are served by High Court and Circuit judges. The second deal with criminal cases only but are also served by both High Court and Circuit judges. The third deal with criminal cases and are served by Circuit judges. The allocations are as follows:

MIDLAND AND OXFORD CIRCUIT

First-tier: Birmingham, Lincoln, Nottingham, Stafford, Warwick.

Second-tier: Leicester, Northampton, Oxford, Shrewsbury, Worcester.

Third-tier: Coventry, Derby, Dudley, Grimsby, Hereford, Huntingdon, Stoke-on-Trent, Walsall, Warley, West Bromwich, Wolverhampton.

Peterborough will replace Huntingdon as a third-tier centre as soon as suitable court accommodation can be provided there.

NORTH EASTERN CIRCUIT

First-tier: Leeds, Newcastle upon Tyne, Sheffield, York.

Second-tier: Durham, Teesside.

Third-tier: Beverley, Bradford, Doncaster, Huddersfield, Kingston upon Hull, Wakefield.

Beverley will cease to be a third-tier centre as soon as additional court accommodation can be made available at Kingston upon Hull.

NORTHERN CIRCUIT

First-tier: Carlisle, Liverpool, Manchester, Preston.

Third-tier: Barrow-in-Furness, Birkenhead, Burnley, Kendal, Lancaster.

SOUTH EASTERN CIRCUIT

First-tier: Greater London, Norwich.

Second-tier: Chelmsford, Ipswich, Lewes, Maidstone, Reading, St. Albans.

Third-tier: Aylesbury, Bedford, Brighton, Bury St. Edmunds, Cambridge, Canterbury, Chichester, Guildford, King's Lynn, Southend.

WALES AND CHESTER CIRCUIT

First-tier: Caernarvon, Cardiff, Chester, Mold, Swansea.

Second-tier: Carmarthen, Newport, Welshpool.

Third-tier: Dolgellau, Haverfordwest, Knutsford, Merthyr Tydfil.

WESTERN CIRCUIT

First-tier: Bodmin, Bristol, Exeter, Winchester.

Second-tier: Dorchester, Gloucester, Plymouth.

Third-tier: Barnstaple, Bournemouth, Poole, Devizes, Newport (I.O.W.), Portsmouth, Salisbury, Southampton, Swindon, Taunton.

In addition the following towns have been designated as towns at which defended divorces are to be heard by judges of the High Court: Birmingham, Bodmin, Bristol, Caernarvon, Cardiff, Carlisle, Chester, Exeter, Lancaster, Leeds, Lincoln, Liverpool, Manchester, Mold, Newcastle, Norwich, Nottingham, Sheffield, Stafford, Swansea, Warwick, Winchester and York.

THE MAGISTRATES' COURTS

Although the Crown Court with its High Court judges, Circuit judges and Recorders tries the most serious criminal cases (all those in fact which are tried on indictment) with a jury, the great bulk of the criminal work of the country is performed in magistrates' courts, staffed by part-time lay justices of the peace. These too are the criminal courts with which the ordinary citizen is most likely to come into contact, at least as a defendant, particularly in relation to motoring offences. Although there is a small number of professional stipendiary magistrates in London and a few provincial towns they are in a very small minority. The administration of the criminal law at this level is almost totally dependent on the voluntary labours of magistrates appointed by the Lord Chancellor after consultation with a local advisory committee.

Not only do they hear the great majority of criminal cases which are tried summarily, *i.e.* without a jury, but they also conduct the " preliminary hearings " which take place before an accused person is committed for trial on indictment in the Crown Court.[42] In addition they staff the juvenile courts and exercise a number of quasi-judicial functions such as authorising the issue of warrants of arrest and search, and a number of administrative functions such as the licensing of the sale of alcohol and the showing of films. In addition they make up half of the police authorities which are responsible for the raising and maintenance of local police forces.

The office of justice of the peace dates from the twelfth century. Keepers of the peace were appointed by the King in 1195. In 1361 they were authorised by a statute which is still on the Statute Book:

> to restrain the offenders rioters and all other barators and to pursue arrest, take, and chastise them according their trespass or offence; and to cause them to be imprisoned and duly punished according to the law and customs of the realm, and according to that which to them shall seem best to do by their discretions and good advisement; . . . and to take of all them that be not of good fame . . . sufficient surety . . . of their good behaviour towards the King and his people . . . [And also to hear and determine . . . all manner of felonies and trespasses done in the same county according to the laws and customs aforesaid; . . .].[43]

At the same time they were required to meet at least once in every quarter to perform their duties—hence the " quarter sessions " at which serious criminal cases continued to be tried, until they were replaced in 1972 by the Crown Court. At first justices of the peace were much more than judicial officers. For several centuries they bore the responsibility for the administration of local government and the local administration of central government in the counties until this was transferred to elected authorities in the nineteenth century. At different times in their history this involved them in supervising the administration of the poor law and the maintenance of highways and bridges, fixing wages and prices, checking the quality of goods and the accuracy of weights and measures, and, more important from the point of view of the legal system, taking general responsibility for the maintenance of order in their districts. This involved them from the sixteenth century in the task of conducting the preliminary investigation into offences and offenders before trial and is one reason for the continued responsibility, which they now share with representatives of the elected local authorities, for maintaining the local police forces. It also involved them, especially in the nineteenth century, in acting as the agent of the central government and of the ruling classes. Their responsibilities included suppressing disorders in their communities, calling in troops, and giving the order to fire when this seemed necessary to protect lives or to

---

[42] These are discussed below, p. 327.
[43] The words in square brackets were repealed by the Criminal Law Act 1967, s. 10 (2), Sched. 3, Pt. II.

prevent serious damage to property. Today they are much more strictly judicial officers and great efforts have been made to play down the element of social status and political reliability which still existed at the beginning of the century and which was a hangover from the days when they were an important part of the local government and the social hierarchy in the counties. Although they still have powers in relation to the maintenance of order it is more usual for the immediate responsibility to be that of the police.

The main statute governing their present judicial activities is the Magistrates' Courts Act 1952. This sets out some of their basic duties in relation to the trial and preliminary hearing of criminal offences. Up until the Summary Jurisdiction Act 1848 their trial of summary offences had been largely unregulated but that Act required them to sit as courts of summary jurisdiction for the purpose. The 1952 Act replaces the Summary Jurisdiction Act of 1879 which had in its turn replaced the Act of 1848.

As was mentioned above in dealing with the Crown Court, although the basic jurisdiction of the magistrates' courts is the summary trial of summary offences there has been a tendency over the last hundred years to blur the distinction between "summary" and "indictable" offences. This makes it possible for magistrates' courts to try some indictable offences summarily if the circumstances of the particular case justify it. This is part of the general tendency to downgrade offences in order to relieve the Crown Court and its predecessors of work, e.g. by taking offences out of the indictable category altogether or by making offences both summary and indictable and allowing the prosecution to make an application to have the case tried summarily. It also springs from a desire to achieve greater flexibility in the allocation of cases for trial than is possible when all offences within a particular category are simply labelled "indictable" or "summary." The Summary Jurisdiction Act 1879 already provided that simple larceny, embezzlement and receiving stolen goods could be tried summarily if the circumstances warranted, and the Summary Jurisdiction Act 1899 added obtaining by false pretences. In each case summary trial was only permitted if the value of the property involved did not exceed £2. Indecent assaults on children under sixteen were added in 1908 and further additions were made by the Criminal Justice Administration Act 1914. A committee appointed to consider alterations in criminal procedure in 1921 [44] criticised the use of the value of the property involved as a criterion for deciding whether a case should be triable summarily. It argued that the issues were just the same and the consequences for the accused just as important whether the value was high or low. They also pointed out that there had been very few appeals from convictions in those cases which the magistrates' courts had already had jurisdiction to hear, which suggested a degree of satisfaction with the way in which they had been handled. They therefore recommended further extensions. These were made by the Criminal Justice Act 1925 and included, for example, grievous bodily harm. The matter was considered again in a general way by the Streatfeild Committee on the Business of the Criminal Courts [45] and by the Criminal Law Revision Committee in their proposals for the revision of the law of

---

[44] Cmd. 1813.
[45] Cmnd. 1289 (1961).

theft.[46] Extracts from their reports are included below as illustrations of the factors which they regarded as relevant to an extension of jurisdiction of this kind.

Where an indictable offence is triable summarily safeguards have been introduced both for the accused and the public. The accused must consent, and if it appears as the case progresses that it is more serious than the magistrates thought at first, then they may discontinue the summary trial and continue to hear the case as examining magistrates. Furthermore, if it appears upon conviction that the record of the accused justifies the imposition of a punishment or form of treatment that the magistrates' court cannot impose then it may commit the offender to the Crown Court for sentence.[47]

Criticisms and Attempts to Meet Them

There have been a number of criticisms of the widespread use of justices of the peace and of the way in which the system operates in practice. Some of it has been traditional and dates from Shakespeare's *Shallow and Silence* and the days, which continued well into the nineteenth century, when the justice of the peace was an important local government and social figure, intent on maintaining his position and that of his class and enforcing the law in a manner which emphasised the social distinctions between himself and those whose conduct he had the power to regulate. At the beginning of this century the chief complaint was that after a long period of Conservative Government there were insufficient Liberals on the Benches. The whole question of political influence and the way in which balanced Benches could be obtained was the subject of the report of a Royal Commission in 1913.[48] The relevance of a justice's political views and the question of political influence on appointments was still a concern of the Royal Commission in 1948 [49] though it took the view that this had become much less of a problem than the more basic one of finding men and women of the right quality and motivation from sufficiently varied backgrounds who were prepared to assume the responsibility of being a justice. Some of the mystery surrounding the identification and appointment of such people has now been dispelled and one can often find advertisements in newspapers inviting people who wish to be considered to volunteer.

Following suggestions made by the Royal Commission in 1948, limited training schemes have been introduced for new magistrates. However, the amount they actually need to know about the law which they are called upon to apply is limited. They are not expected to be experts in the law. For this they rely on their professional clerk, as they do if nice points of procedure arise, or questions as to the methods of disposal which are open to them. The Royal Commission itself noted:

> 89. The law that justices have to administer is extensive and complex and any attempt to give lay justices an adequate knowledge of it

---

[46] Report, Cmnd. 2977 (1966).
[47] See below, p. 330.
[48] Cd. 5250.
[49] Cmd. 7463 (1948).

would not usually succeed. What we think is possible and should be done is to train justices to understand the nature of their duties rather than the substantive law that they administer. In the forefront we should put the meaning of "acting judicially." The Lord Chief Justice . . . Lord Goddard, in his evidence points out that justices do not get reproved for being wrong in law, but that a failure to act judicially is a reason for censure. In the course of court proceedings a justice must be sufficiently instructed to perform his duties without constant reference to the clerk. Thus he must know the procedure in ordinary cases; it is for instance not unknown for a bench to mis-understand the nature of a submission that there is no case to answer. He should know something of the law of evidence, at least enough to enable him to avoid mistakes in any questions that he may ask. When justices know and understand their duties they and their clerk can work satisfactorily together; if they are ignorant the clerk must either watch them make mistakes that may be serious to the parties and to the justices, or intervene and take too much part in the proceedings.

Apart from the training programmes, the Home Office, following suggestions made by the Streatfeild Committee on the Business of the Criminal Courts,[50] issues a handbook, *The Sentence of the Court*, which sets out the various methods available for dealing with convicted offenders and their application. The actual decisions of magistrates' courts are subject to appeal on points of law and fact to the Crown Court, with a further appeal on a point of law to the Divisional Court of the Queen's Bench Division. There is also an appeal on points of law, by way of "case stated," direct to the Divisional Court. The Divisional Court may also quash a decision of a magistrates' court by issuing an order of certiorari if it has exceeded its jurisdiction or failed to observe the proper procedure, including the basic principles of natural justice. The Divisional Court also gives general guidance to magistrates' courts on standards of behaviour and sentences. This also helps in meeting one of the other difficulties which is bound to arise when so many justices are dealing with cases throughout the country, namely that of achieving uniformity of treatment of those convicted of similar offences. The Home Office issues unpublished circulars explaining the purpose of new legislation and giving advice generally. Average sentences for motoring offences are also circulated. The Magistrates Association, which was set up in 1921 with the object of raising the general level of performance of duties by magistrates, also plays an informal part in this by circulating information and arranging con-ferences. Particular cases of departure from the standard of behaviour expected of a justice can be dealt with by the exercise of the Lord Chan-cellor's power to suspend him or her.

Criticism of the age and infirmity of some magistrates made to the Royal Commission in 1946 led to the creation of a Supplemental List to which the Lord Chancellor can transfer a justice if he is satisfied: (i) that by reason of his age or infirmity, or other like cause, it is expedient that he should cease to exercise judicial functions, or (ii) that he has declined or neglected to take a proper part in the exercise of these functions. A

---

[50] See below, p. 502.

justice can also ask to be put on the list. Justices are normally transferred to the list automatically when they reach the age of seventy. They then perform only minor administrative functions.[51]

Other problems which arise in relation to the way in which the magistrates' courts perform their functions are problems which everyone must observe for himself, since it is impossible to generalise about them. It is said that some magistrates' courts are dominated by their clerks or their chairman; that some are too ready to accept the word of the police who appear frequently before them; that in some courts procedural irregularities pass unnoticed and that in many courts members of the public are unwelcome and certainly unexpected. Nor is the criticism confined to lay magistrates. Similar criticisms are made of some stipendiary magistrates as well. Many of these criticisms, which of necessity relate to specific courts and people on specific occasions, are difficult to record in any scientific way although they are the standard gossip of practitioners who appear before them. It is a surprising fact that the law schools of England and Wales, which are strategically placed throughout the country and whose students come from every corner of it, have not taken more advantage of their position to take a more systematic and co-ordinated look at magistrates' courts, and indeed other local examples of the legal system at work. Although it might discourage recruitment, there is still something to be said for a National Magistrates' Courts Observation Month, to be followed by a National Tribunals Month and even a National County Courts Month, in an effort to meet this problem of being unable to generalise about the system as a whole without a detailed examination of all its parts over a period of time.

Report of the Royal Commission on Justices of the Peace
Cd. 5250 (1910)

The voluntary system, no doubt, excludes the existence of a high judicial standard; but such standard may find some equivalent if only men of high character and intelligence be appointed to act as Justices.

Political zeal and decided political convictions in no way represent such equivalent standard.

We therefore express the confident view that political opinion or political services should not be regarded as in any way controlling or influencing the appointment of Justices. . . .

We are aware that we are condemning a practice which has existed in different degrees for a long period.

. . . [I]t is desirable that the area of selection should be wide, and the choice comprehensive, so that the Bench may include men of all social classes and of all shades of creed and political opinion.

. . . [W]e concur in the view which has been presented to us very forcibly that it is in the public interest that working men with a first-hand knowledge of the conditions of life among their own class should be appointed to the County as well as to the Borough Benches.

But the more the area is extended, the more difficult becomes the task of selection; and this difficulty must be recognised in deciding upon the method which should be adopted.

[51] See the Justices of the Peace Act 1949, s. 4, and the Justices of the Peace Act 1968, s. 2.

We are strongly of opinion that the appointment of Justices of the Peace should continue to be made by the Crown. We have received very little evidence in favour of the popular election of Justices, and such evidence as has been given in this direction has been rather as a suggestion of a means for redressing the political balance than as an ideal system.

The appointment of judicial officers of any kind by direct popular election is altogether opposed to English constitutional usage. Popular election would probably mean political election. The influence which we have so strongly condemned would thus be rendered all powerful.

Neither can we accept a popular electorate as furnishing good judgment in the selection of men for magisterial office.

So long as appointments are made by the Crown, the Lord Chancellor is obviously the most suitable Minister to be entrusted with the duty of advising upon the selections to be made. He is not only the Keeper of the Great Seal under which the commissions are issued. He is also the head of the Justiciary. . . . He is Your Majesty's responsible adviser in regard to the appointment of Judges, and in giving such advice he does not act as a politician. . . . He is a Minister of the highest dignity and importance, and as little subject to influence or political pressure as any Minister can be. . . .

We are of opinion that the Lords Lieutenant of Counties should, . . . retain the practice of making recommendations to the Lord Chancellor. . . .

But in order to assist both the Lords Lieutenant in recommending and the Lord Chancellor in appointing Justices, we recommend that in every county one or more Justices' Committees . . . should be appointed by the Lord Chancellor. . . .

In constituting these Committees regard should primarily be had to the importance of giving them a representative character, so as to secure the expression on them of different views and currents of public opinion.

We think it should be within the power of the Lord Chancellor to appoint a similar Committee in every Borough having a separate commission on the peace.

Although we have expressed a strong opinion that no appointments should be made on the ground of political opinions or services, it is even more important that no one should be excluded from the Bench on account of his religious or political opinions. . . .

We strongly urge those who may be the Lord Chancellor or Lords Lieutenant or members of an Advisory Committee that they should firmly refuse to receive any applications, or unasked-for advice to appoint Justices, from Members of Parliament or Candidates in their own constituencies, or from political agents or representatives of political associations. . . .

The representatives of several interests appeared before us and asked that greater consideration should be shown to those interests. For instance, it was strongly urged on behalf of those engaged in the liquor trade that but few of them are appointed Justices. . . . The number of these appointments is entirely within the discretion of the Lord Chancellor, and with the exercise of that discretion we cannot recommend any interference. The same observation applies to the claim of pawnbrokers for greater consideration.

Objection was taken to the appointment of total abstainers and particularly of advocates of total abstinence. . . . It was urged that such persons must be regarded as interested, and therefore that they ought not to be placed in a position to deal with cases affecting the liquor trade. We cannot recommend that an advocate of total abstinence should be disqualified from appointment. His interest is only one of opinion, which does not disqualify any judge. By our law the interest which disqualifies must be pecuniary or material. If such a person refuses to sanction all licences, such negation of his duty would be dealt with by the Lord Chancellor.

Report of the Royal Commission on Justices of the Peace 1946–48
Cmd. 7463 (1948)

The Commission was appointed in June 1946 *inter alia* " (i) to review the present arrangements for the selection and removal of Justices of the Peace in Great Britain, and to report what changes, if any, are necessary or desirable to ensure that only the most suitable persons are appointed to the Commission of the Peace; (ii) to consider and report on the qualifications and disqualifications for appointment . . . and on the tenure of the office of Justice of the Peace and, in particular whether appointments should be made for a term of years or subject to a retiring age, and what provision, if any, should be made for removing from the Commission of the Peace the names of Justices who prove unable or unwilling to discharge the functions of their office. . . ."

The appointment of justices

13. The ordinary process by which a person becomes a justice is the insertion of his name in a commission of the peace either for a county or for a borough having a separate commission of the peace. . . . Appointment by placing a name in the commission is an exercise of the Royal Prerogative, though by constitutional usage the names are not submitted to the King, the action being taken on the fiat of the Lord Chancellor. . . .

14. The Lord Chancellor has to deal with about eleven hundred appointments a year. This volume of work makes it necessary for him to rely upon his staff. But no central government department can have sufficient knowledge of the people and conditions of all parts of the country, and to obtain local advice the Lord Chancellor has advisory committees corresponding approximately with the various county and borough commissions of the peace. . . .

The local committees which he establishes are advisory, and whilst they are an essential part of the present system they do not take away from the Minister the ultimate responsibility for any action that is taken.

15. The present practice is based on the recommendations made by the Royal Commission in 1910. . . .

18. As regards the principles of selection it is not surprising to find that successive Lord Chancellors have found some difficulty in following the recommendations of 1910. If an advisory committee is to be so constituted as to secure the expression upon it of different views and currents of public opinion as recommended by the Royal Commission of 1910 it is hardly possible for the Lord Chancellor to avoid taking into account the political opinions of those whom he appoints: representation of " different views and currents of public opinion " has been interpreted to mean representation of the main political parties. In fact the attempt to carry out the 1910 recommendations has resulted in advisory committees being overwhelmingly political. . . .

19. For the selection of persons for appointment as justices the same difficulty arises. . . . If Benches are to include men of " all shades of political opinion " and on each Bench there is to be " adequate representation of different views in politics " the process of selection cannot ignore the political opinions of proposed justices.

20. So far as the selection of justices is concerned the present system, at its best, works well. . . . A principal weakness of the system is that it may, and in some areas certainly does, lead to " political appointments " in the sense that a recommendation is made not because the proposed justice is better fitted for the office than other persons but mainly because he has a good record of

service to a political party or is regarded as a reliable member of the party. Although we have no reason to think that where this process has occurred political partisanship has affected the decision of cases on the bench, " political appointments " are to be condemned because they are not true selections on merit and because they tend to the exclusion of persons whose political views are either unknown or not aligned with those of any party: the man or woman with no record of political service may be virtually barred from appointment. The extent to which selection has been affected by these factors cannot be stated with precision.

74. We think that too much attention in the appointment of justices has been paid to political opinions, but we do not think that a better practice can be secured by " ignoring politics." . . .

The existence and activities of political parties are facts which cannot be ignored. If because a bench has a preponderance of members of party A, it is thought necessary to add to it a number of justices who belong to party B, it must sometimes follow that appointments are not according to merit. . . . Moreover the danger of political bargaining is a real one, and in some cases different parties represented on the advisory committee fill the vacancies in an agreed proportion, each accepting, with little or no enquiry, the nominees of the others. On the other hand, we are satisfied that if the Lord Chancellor and his advisory committees were to close their eyes to the politics of nominees for the bench, there would be no guarantee against the almost complete exclusion in some districts of persons of a particular political colour. Where that resulted, there would be a natural sense of grievance among members of the party affected, and a corresponding loss of confidence (however little justified it might be) in the impartiality of the bench. . . . At present there are undoubtedly a number of justices who regard their office merely as a mark of distinction carrying no obligations of an onerous nature. So long as that state of affairs is possible some people will regard appointment to the commission as being in the nature of a reward. We trust that our recommendations will end that state of affairs. . . . The problem of " politics " may then disappear. . . .

76. . . . The proportion of members of the committee who are appointed because of their affiliation with political parties should be restricted, so that their influence shall not be predominant and that room may be found for other members whose interests and associations lie in other fields than political work. . . . We do not want to encourage a belief that the main political parties have a right to representation on these committees. At the time when advisory committees were originally constituted after the Royal Commission of 1910 the majority of justices belonged to one political party, and for the purpose of preventing any such discrimination in future the practice was adopted of including . . . members of each of the main political parties. Today . . . there is less reason for thinking that to secure this object it is always necessary to appoint on every advisory committee members of each of the main political parties.

79. . . . The committee may well include persons who are not justices. . . .

80. In practice members of advisory committees are likely to be drawn from justices and others who are well known in public life. . . .

84. The evidence we have heard has satisfied us that it would be well that directions to the following effect should be given to all advisory committees—

(a) That no member of the committee should regard himself as " the representative " of any political party. . . .

(b) That in appointing justices the paramount consideration is the person's fitness for the discharge of judicial duties. . . .

(c) Care must be taken to see that there are persons in the commission representative of various sections of the community. . . .

(d) . . . If, after a preliminary selection has been made, it is found that a considerable majority of the proposed new justices are of one political faith, the list should be revised with a view to seeing whether equally good, or better, nominations can be made from among members of other political parties. If the answer is that they cannot, then the original list should stand. . . .

Stipendiary magistrates

213. Our terms of reference seem to us to assume that the system by which justice is administered in courts of summary jurisdiction mainly by lay justices is to be continued, and we should hardly have considered ourselves free to propose that this system should be wholly superseded by the appointment of enough stipendiary justices to cover the whole country even if we had been disposed to do so. We think it right to say, however, that we are in complete agreement with the view expressed by the Lord Chancellor that, both on principle and on grounds of practical convenience the present system ought to be retained. . . . In the circumstances, we will confine ourselves to a short statement of what we conceive to be the principal reasons against any radical change in the present system.

214. First, we think that . . . it would be impossible at present to find a sufficient body of persons, equipped with knowledge of law and, what is certainly not less important, a judicial temperament and knowledge of the world, to provide the large body of stipendiary magistrates which would be required if the suggested change were made. In saying this we assume that salaries would be on a similar scale to those applicable in the case of judges of county courts, but even if it were practicable to pay much higher salaries we think that the difficulty would remain. A legal training is a valuable asset for a magistrate, but if he has not a legal training he may nonetheless perform his duties efficiently if he has good legal advice. Lawyers themselves would be the last to claim that legal training by itself is a sufficient equipment for one called upon to give decisions on questions of fact where reputation and liberty are at stake. Apart from this practical consideration the present system is to be commended because, like that of trial by jury, it gives the citizen a part to play in the administration of the law. It emphasises the fact that the principles of the common law, and even the language of statutes, ought to be (as in the case of the common law at least, they certainly are) comprehensible by any intelligent person without specialised training. Its continuance prevents the growth of a suspicion in the ordinary man's mind that the law is a mystery which must be left to a professional caste and has little in common with justice as the layman understands it. Further, the cases in which decisions on questions of fact in criminal cases are to be left to one man ought to be, as they now are, exceptional. It must be remembered that even a judge in the High Court is never asked to undertake the heavy responsibility of trying a criminal case except with the assistance of a jury of laymen, to whom alone is left the decision on the facts.

215. . . . The General Council of the Bar suggested that a number of stipendiary magistrates should be appointed to attend magistrates' courts on a circuit. The suggestion was that 15 might be appointed to begin with, and that the number might be gradually raised to about 50. The itinerant stipendiary magistrate would visit various benches and sit as chairman with the lay justices. He would also be available to take difficult cases in his area. It would not be possible to pay more than an occasional visit to each bench, and the visits would be at long intervals. . . . There are undoubtedly occasions when a bench of lay

justices would receive help and valuable instruction if the chairman were an experienced professional magistrate, but these occasions cannot generally be known in advance; the visit from the professional magistrate would more often than not be a waste of his time for lack of any case in which the particular bench was in need of guidance. If the number of these stipendiary magistrates could be raised sufficiently to allow them to make frequent attendance at all benches the effect would probably be to discourage the lay justices from themselves attending since their responsibilities would be diminished and their authority reduced.

216. In our opinion the system calls for improvement, not for radical change. . . .

223. Whether a locality has a stipendiary or whether it relies entirely upon lay justices cannot be said to depend upon the nature of the local magisterial work. Bradford and Hull have stipendiaries, whilst Sheffield and Bristol have not [52]; some county divisions of Glamorgan are included in the area served by a stipendiary whilst other comparable divisions rely on lay justices. The determining factor is not a rational assessment of the present need but the course of past history. Some more recent applications have doubtless been based on the desire to have available a professional magistrate to deal with the more difficult cases, but this is not general. . . .

224. We think that there may be a case for the appointment of a stipendiary magistrate . . . when there is a large number of cases of special difficulty, or . . . when the lay justices are unable to deal adequately with the work that comes before them. Where the volume of cases of special difficulty is substantial there should be a bench with legal qualifications. This generally means a stipendiary but it must be remembered that unpaid justices include a number of persons (some with professional legal qualifications) who have made a special study of magisterial work. . . . We do not think that any precise rule, such as population figure or average number of cases a year, can be laid down as a test for the need of a stipendiary. At present no action can be taken by a Minister of the central government unless the local authority takes the initiative. There is no doubt some danger that a local authority may fail to make an application which would be to the public advantage, and we recognise that in these days of rapid travel the administration of justice is not merely a local affair. On the whole, however, we think that it is best to retain the principle of local option. It would, however, be well to give an opportunity for the expression of local opinion, and we recommend that if the Lord Chancellor is satisfied from representations made to him that a prima facie case exists for the appointment of a stipendiary he should be empowered, after directing an inquiry (which may be private or public, at his discretion) to appoint a stipendiary magistrate. . . .

Report of the Interdepartmental Committee on the Business of the Criminal Courts

Cmnd. 1289 (1961)

72. We are of opinion that the principal considerations which should govern the allocation of offences to the different types of court are the gravity of the offence and the competence of the court to try it. . . .

74. The last general extension of the jurisdiction of magistrates' courts to try indictable offences was made by the Criminal Justice Act 1925, which added

---

[52] When the Commission reported there were 26 metropolitan magistrates and 16 stipendiaries (in Birmingham, Bradford, Cardiff, East and West Ham, Huddersfield, Kingston-upon-Hull, Leeds, Liverpool, Manchester, Middlesborough and Swansea), appointed under the Municipal Corporation Act 1882 and 5 appointed under local Acts in Merthyr Tydfil, Pontypridd, Salford, Stafford Potteries and South Staffordshire.

such offences as causing grievous bodily harm and making a false statement to procure a passport. The additions were based on the recommendations of a departmental committee which reported in 1921. Since 1925 certain changes have, it is generally agreed, greatly increased the efficiency of justices in petty sessions. The Justices of the Peace Act, 1949, overhauled the machinery for appointing justices, fixed 75 as their retiring age and created magistrates' courts committees with administrative responsibility for the organisation of county petty sessional divisions and the duty of making and administering schemes approved by the Lord Chancellor providing courses of instruction for justices of their area. In most counties there is a rota system for sitting at quarter sessions, where justices can see how an experienced and legally qualified chairman conducts proceedings and sums up to a jury....

77. . . . We start by considering [the proposal] that some breaking and entering offences should be triable summarily....

88. In assessing the relative seriousness of an offence it is necessary to take a broad view. The legal definitions cover a wide range of circumstances, and for most indictable offences, including breaking offences, it is easy to point to examples of the offence which should never be tried except at assizes and to others which could, by general consent, be tried at a magistrates' court. In our view the right approach is to look at the whole range of breaking offences and the type of offenders who commit them and then consider whether on balance breaking offences fit more appropriately into the category of offences triable only on indictment or into the category of offences triable summarily; that is, whether breaking offences correspond more closely in seriousness with such offences as attempted rape, using a firearm to resist arrest and embezzlement of considerable sums of money (all of which are triable at quarter sessions but not summarily) or with such offences as receiving, larceny and assault causing actual bodily harm (all of which are triable summarily)....

93. Some witnesses based their opposition to the proposal [that the less serious breaking offences (other than those involving a dwelling-house) should be triable summarily] on the effect which they claimed that the change would have on the general public, on potential offenders and on actual offenders, particularly with this type of crime at its present high level. They argued:

(a) that the public expected the law to try serious offences like breaking offences at a court of superior status, where more majesty and ceremony attended the proceedings, rather than at a court at which minor summary offences were tried; and that the " down-grading " of breaking offences, at a time when they were increasing in number, would be generally deprecated;

(b) that " down-grading would impair the reputation of the law and, consequently, its deterrent effect on potential offenders;

(c) that the atmosphere and greater formality of the superior courts, coupled with the period of waiting before trial and the possibility of a substantial sentence, had a salutary effect on individual offenders; that summary proceedings would be less impressive and more quickly concluded—the case might be taken, especially in some country courts, in between parking and other minor offences, and the defendant was merely lined up with a number of other defendants at the back of a court rather than kept waiting in a cell until he appeared in the dock.

94. We have already recognised that the relative seriousness of an offence is an important factor in determining to which category it should be allocated for jurisdiction purposes, and we have borne in mind the need to sustain respect for the law and confidence in its administration. But an assessment of the seriousness of an offence should be based on the nature of the offence itself, the forms

which it actually takes, and statistics which show how those who commit it are
dealt with,[53] and we have already considered this kind of material in detail. We
cannot accept that breaking offences involve different considerations; nor, indeed,
do we consider that the contentions put to us are supported by reliable evidence.
The view put forward in (a) and (b) above was the personal opinion of a number of our witnesses, but we have not been given any other evidence in support
of this opinion and we have no reason to believe it is generally held. Nor have
these witnesses used it to suggest that some indictable offences triable summarily
(e.g. larceny or assaults) should become triable only on indictment. It was not
suggested to us, for instance, that the nature of the legal processes deterred
potential thieves any less than potential shopbreakers, and we have no reason to
think that this is so.

95. The view that appearance at a superior court has a salutary effect on actual
offenders (see (c) above) was said to be supported by observation of their
demeanour in court, but there is no evidence before us that this immediate effect
of an unusual situation makes a continuing contribution towards checking any
tendency to further crime or that the continuing effect of appearance at a
magistrates' court would be significantly different. On the contrary, the considerable increase in this type of crime in recent years points to the opposite
conclusion; and, even if this were not so, there would be objections of principle to exposing the innocent to the delay, anxiety and expense of a trial on
indictment in order to secure a possible effect on the guilty.

96. In our view the issue before us should not be decided on general impressions and speculative arguments of this kind. Indeed, such general impressions
as we have ourselves formed tend in the opposite direction. Those who are professionally concerned with the law doubtless have a clear picture in their minds
of the distinctive types of court, and these distinctions have a daily importance
for them. But the average layman has probably only a vague idea of what the
basic differences are. When he is interested in an individual criminal case, he
is, we suggest, primarily interested in the detection and punishment of the
offender; and the type of court at which the trial takes place is perhaps more
likely to be criticised because the court-house is inconvenient for witnesses than
because it is not of superior status. Again, we suggest that for the actual offender the sentence he receives is far more important than the court which passes
it; and that this might also be the view of the potential offender if, with
uncharacteristic pessimism, he should contemplate the possibility of detection.
Furthermore, although the maximum sentence open to a magistrates' court is
usually six months' imprisonment, magistrates' courts as a group impose more
sentences of imprisonment than all the superior courts taken together. These
observations are not in conflict with the principle that the seriousness of an
offence is an important factor in determining the type of court at which it should
be tried, but they tend to show that in practice the emphasis should be on the
general picture rather than on each individual feature in it.

97. It would not be right to infer that we are proposing to " down-grade "
breaking offences in order to meet the difficulties caused by the recent increase
in their number. . . . The present pressure on the superior courts is not the
justification for the changes discussed in this Chapter but the occasion for
considering whether it would be right to regrade certain offences. . . .

---

[53] The Committee had noted at para. 90 that 54 per cent. of those convicted of an offence
not involving a dwelling-house were not sentenced to detention; that a further 6 per cent.
were sentenced to 6 months or less, and some of the remainder had received a longer
sentence because of their criminal record. In other cases the proportion of those not
sentenced to detention was only 45 per cent. even though those convicted of breaking
offences had on average worse criminal records.

98. It would be unfortunate if, on the basis of the arguments put to us, the present jurisdiction of courts were to be permanently frozen, despite changes in patterns of crime, in attitudes to the different offences and in the organisation of the various types of court. Indeed, the link between the status of the court of trial and the seriousness of the offence can be broken in two ways. It can be argued that to try a large number of trivial offences at a superior court is just as likely to impair respect for the law as to try grave offences at a magistrates' court.

Eighth Report of the Criminal Law Revision Committee. Theft and Kindred Offences
Cmnd. 2977 (1966)

The Streatfeild Committee on the Business of the Criminal Courts had recommended that burglaries of a dwelling house should not be triable summarily on the grounds that they were more serious than other breakings. At paragraph 89 they had noted: " Where a dwelling house is broken into or entered, the inhabitant is put in fear either directly by the breaking or, if he is not then in the house, by the possibility of repetition. This apprehension extends to the neighbourhood and is aggravated by the fear of future crime being accompanied by violence." The question was considered again by the Criminal Law Revision Committee as part of its consideration of the law of theft.

181. The arguments for making burglary triable summarily with consent even though committed in a dwelling seem to be these.

(i) It is the logical consequence of creating a unified offence of burglary which will include cases which should undoubtedly be triable summarily.

(ii) The principal test of whether an offence should be triable summarily with consent should not be whether the worst cases are very serious. This test would rule out many offences such as stealing (especially by persons in positions of trust) and receiving. The test should be whether the offence is ordinarily very serious. Even the present offence of housebreaking, by day at least, is not regarded as within that class, for many cases are dealt with by fine, probation or conditional discharge. The new offence of burglary will cover a large range of offences from the very serious to the comparatively trivial.

(iii) In other offences which may vary greatly in seriousness magistrates' courts have to decide in accordance with the test laid down in s. 19 of the Magistrates' Courts Act whether they should try the case summarily or commit for trial. There seems no reason why they should not be able to decide the question in the case of burglary of a dwelling. S. 19 (2) (quoted in paragraph 176) requires a magistrates' court, before deciding whether to try a case summarily, to have regard to " any representations made . . . by the prosecutor." Many courts always invite such representations and nearly always accept them if made. Even if the case is tried summarily, the accused can be, and often is, committed to quarter sessions for sentence under s. 29 of the Magistrates' Courts Act (referred to in paragraph 176).

(iv) The fact that the place burgled is a dwelling is only one of the possible aggravating features of burglary. Others are the fact that an offence is premeditated or carefully planned, the method of entry, the behaviour of the burglar in the building and the amount which he steals or intends to steal. It is extremely difficult to define exactly the aggravating features which should exclude jurisdiction. To isolate one feature would be not only illogical but also harmful, as magistrates' courts might regard the absence of this feature as enough to justify dealing summarily with serious cases (for example of shopbreaking) which should be dealt with on indictment.

(v) The other ground for excluding the jurisdiction of magistrates' courts is that the offence is likely to raise difficult questions more fit to be tried on indictment. No difficulty would be likely with burglary.

(vi) The Streatfeild Committee's recommendation to extend the jurisdiction of magistrates' courts to offences of breaking and entering buildings other than dwellings was strongly opposed, but the extension has worked well. Cases have been dealt with quickly and satisfactorily; and there is no reason why burglary of a dwelling should not be dealt with equally satisfactorily. Early trial is particularly desirable where, as often, the offender is young. If, for example, a youth of seventeen breaks into an unoccupied house by merely opening the door and steals a small article, it is undesirable that he should have to be tried at quarter sessions (perhaps after two months). A much more serious breaking and entering by a boy of sixteen would ordinarily be tried soon afterwards in the juvenile court.

(vii) With the great and growing pressure of work, both in magistrates' courts and at quarter sessions, any reform which relieves congestion and reduces delay before trial ought to be introduced, as long as it is consistent with the proper administration of justice.

182. The arguments against making all cases of burglary of a dwelling triable summarily with consent seem to be these.

(i) The offence is, and should be regarded as, specially serious by reason of being committed in a dwelling. . . .

(ii) If Parliament were to reverse their decision in 1962 that housebreaking should not be triable summarily, this might give the impression that the offence was regarded as no longer one of the most serious offences against property but was being put on the level of petty thieving.

(iii) Notwithstanding the theoretically strict requirements in s. 19 of the Magistrates' Courts Act which have to be satisfied before a magistrates' court can deal summarily with an indictable offence with the consent of the accused, many courts will assume jurisdiction in cases where they should not. There is a tendency among magistrates' courts to be too ready to assume jurisdiction to deal with any offence in the Schedule of offences within their jurisdiction without giving sufficient consideration to the matters about which they are required to be satisfied before they decide to do so. Experience shows that sometimes the prosecutor and defence request summary trial for reasons which are later criticized by the High Court. In R. v. Middlesex Quarter Sessions, ex p. D.P.P., [1950] 2 K.B. 589, 593–594; 34 Cr.App.R. 112, 116, Lord Goddard C.J. said:

On the many occasions on which I have given addresses to magistrates, I have brought it to their attention that the fact that they have power to deal with a case summarily is by no means a reason why they necessarily should do so. It is not only a question of sentence: many cases brought before justices can be dealt with by them but are very grave and ought to be sent for trial. It may be that there are matters of mitigation as they may think; and it may turn out that the court to which the case is committed in the end only passes a nominal sentence, or binds the prisoner over. That is not the point: serious cases ought to be dealt with by the superior courts. I hope that because Parliament has introduced this new procedure prosecutors will not think that, for the sake of saving trouble, it will be sufficient for the justices to deal with the case and then send the prisoner forward for sentence.[54]

In spite of Lord Goddard's warning the tendency to assume jurisdiction too readily persists. There are two dangers in particular. One is that the court, conscious of the delay, effort and expense of committal proceedings and trial on indictment, may be reluctant to spend the time involved in the inconclusive and wearisome taking of depositions. This is specially so where the court has reason to believe that the accused would plead guilty at the outset if he were allowed to and where there is a general feeling that the case should be brought to a conclusion as soon as possible. The other danger is that an overworked police officer in charge of a case, anxious to get back to his ordinary work and to enable the other officers concerned to get back to theirs, will be too ready, in discussing the question of jurisdiction with the clerk before the hearing, to suggest that a case in fact serious is trivial enough to justify summary trial.

183. The arguments seem to us evenly balanced. The arguments in favour of making all burglary, even of a dwelling, triable summarily with consent seem to us strong. But for the danger that magistrates' courts would deal summarily with cases which were so serious that they should be tried on indictment most members would have regarded these arguments as decisive. They thought that the test laid down in s. 19 of the Magistrates' Courts Act ought effectually to secure that all serious cases would be tried on indictment and that the legislation ought to be framed on the footing that this would be so. But in the end the majority decided, with regret, that the danger of serious cases being tried summarily and dealt with inadequately was too great. We concluded therefore that the most serious cases of burglary involving dwellings should be excluded from the jurisdiction of magistrates' courts.

184. Some of the most serious burglaries of dwellings will, like burglaries of other kinds of buildings, be excepted under the new paragraph 11 (b) in clause 25 (2) because the offence which the burglar committed or attempted or intended to commit in the dwelling is not triable summarily. In the case of dwellings we decided, after considering several possible courses, that jurisdiction should also be excluded where entry was obtained by certain irregular means, that is to say by force, deception or the use of any tool, key or appliance or where a person in the building was subjected to violence or a threat of violence (sub-paragraph (c)). The cases in sub-paragraphs (b) and (c) will make up the most serious cases of burglary, or at least those in respect of which the objection to summary trial is strongest. The exclusion on the ground of violence . . .

---

[54] Cp. Lord Goddard C.J. in R. v. Bodmin Justices, ex p. McEwen [1947] K.B. 321: "... Here is a case in which a man's life has been seriously imperilled and if he had died, this applicant . . . would have been charged with murder. It was never intended that where a man, whether under the influence of drink, or not, takes a bayonet and stabs a fellow soldier in the back, with the consequences which are disclosed in this case, justices should deal with such a case by reason of that section. For justices to exercise jurisdiction under that section by treating a case of this sort as nothing more than a common assault is a most extraordinary state of affairs. Justices should remember that they have to deal with matters of this sort judicially, although they must take into account what the prosecution and defence say with regard to whether or not it is a proper case for the charge to be reduced, they are not bound to assent to dealing with the case summarily because the prosecution want to get the matter dealt with there and then, without the necessity of going to the Assizes where this case undoubtedly should have been sent."

will serve as a recognition of the fact that one of the most serious features of burglary is the attack on the security of the household.   The effect of these proposals will be that burglary which comprises some of the more technical kinds of breaking and entering under the existing law (such as opening an unlocked door) will become triable summarily for the first time. . . .

185. We considered, but rejected, two other possible cases in which the jurisdiction of magistrates' courts might be excluded. The first was where the burglary is committed at night. To many people entry by night, by whatever means, would seem an ample reason for excluding the jurisdiction of magistrates' courts, however trivial the offence was in other respects.   There is undoubtedly substance in this view. But for reasons similar to those given in paragraph 74 [55] for not making burglary by night a separate offence we are against making this distinction for the purpose of jurisdiction. Moreover to exclude jurisdiction on this ground would make little difference to the number of cases triable by magistrates' courts, because entry by night would seldom be gained without the use of one of the illicit means mentioned in sub-paragraph (c). The second test which we rejected was the value of the property stolen. Although simple, this seems to us an undesirable test. The arguments mentioned in paragraph 62 [56] against making the maximum sentence for theft depend on the value of the property stolen seem to us valid in this connection also.

So far as offences under the Theft Act 1968 are concerned the First Schedule of the Magistrates' Courts Act 1952, which in principle contains those indictable offences which can be tried summarily provides:

11. Any indictable offence under the Theft Act 1968 except—

  (a) robbery, aggravated burglary, blackmail and assault with intent to rob; and
  (b) burglary comprising the commission of, or an intention to commit, an offence which is not included in this Schedule, and
  (c) burglary in a dwelling if entry to the dwelling or the part of it in which the burglary was committed, or to any building or part of a building containing the dwelling, was obtained by force or deception or by the use of any tool, key or appliance, or if any person in the dwelling was subjected to violence or the threat of violence; and
  (d) handling stolen goods from an offence not committed in the United Kingdom.

R. v. Coe

Court of Appeal [1968] 1 W.L.R. 1950

LORD PARKER, C.J.: On 3rd July 1968 at Hemel Hempstead Magistrates' Court the applicant, together with his co-accused, one Molyneux, pleaded guilty to a whole series of offences committed between April and about the middle of June; indeed they went on right up to the moment when they were arrested on

---

[55] There the committee had taken the view that with better street lighting night was neither more favourable to criminals nor so much more frightening to householders. Much serious crime took place by day. It was often as upsetting to find one's home had been ransacked in one's absence in the day as to have it burgled by night when people were less likely to be alone. In a case where the fact that it was night made it more serious this could be taken into account in the sentence.

[56] Here the committee had simply said that the value was merely one aggravating feature among others.

15th June. They asked for a number of other offences, in the case of the applicant Coe 18 other offences, and in the case of Molyneux 17 other offences, to be taken into consideration. Without going into the details of all the offences, the general picture disclosed was as follows: six offences of shopbreaking and larceny committed jointly by the applicant and Molyneux involving property valued at more than £3,500; on each occasion a shop window was smashed, in two cases by reversing a car through the window; in addition one further offence of shopbreaking and larceny committed by Molyneux alone. Then there were some 11 offences of taking and driving away committed jointly and one similar offence by each of them, in other words 13 cars in all were taken and driven away. In each case of shopbreaking one such car was used, and the remainder were used for joy-rides. Then there were two offences committed by the applicant while in Molyneux's company of driving while disqualified, two larcenies by the applicant from gas and electricity meters, offences which were in fact charged and admitted as storebreakings and larceny, and, finally, in addition, each of them admitted a number of larcenies, and in the case of the applicant a number of offences including a breach of probation for an original offence, again by taking and driving away. . . .

(i) This court is quite unable to understand how it came about that the prosecution invited the justices, as they did, to deal summarily with the indictable offences. The picture of events known to them, which I have shortly related, disclosed a really shocking state of affairs. Two young men of 22 making wholesale raids on property throughout Hertfordshire and Bedfordshire, using cars taken and driven away for the purpose, and driving whilst disqualified. No doubt it is convenient in the interests of expedition, and possibly in order to obtain a plea of guilty, for the prosecution to invite the justices to deal with indictable offences summarily. But there is something more involved than convenience and expedition. Above all there is the proper administration of criminal justice to be considered, questions such as the protection of society and the stamping out of this sort of criminal enterprise if it is possible. This court would like to say with all the emphasis at its command that the prosecution in a serious case such as this are not acting in the best interests of society by inviting summary trial. This is by no means the first case in which the court has had to make these comments. They were made by LORD GODDARD, C.J., on a number of occasions in the past; they have been made by this court comparatively recently,[57] where really serious charges, maybe cases of violence, maybe, as here, raids on property, are put before the justices as suitable for them to deal with summarily. It is all the more important, now that the jurisdiction of the justices has been enlarged, for the prosecution to take care that they only invite summary trial in cases where the power in the justices to administer punishment is sufficient. This was on any view a very serious case in which both the applicant and Molyneux fully merited a sentence of four years' imprisonment, possibly more.

(ii) The court would like to observe that while in their view the prosecution were at fault, and while no doubt the invitation to the justices was a temptation to them to deal with it summarily, that is no excuse for the justices. Their duty in the case of indictable offences is to begin to enquire into the matter as examining justices, and only to deal with the case summarily if the matter can be brought fairly and squarely within s. 19 (2) of the Magistrates' Courts Act 1952.

[57] e.g. in the case of R. v. Everest (October 7, 1968), unreported, where an application for leave to appeal against a sentence of eight years' imprisonment on a man of hitherto exemplary character was refused. He had pleaded guilty to throwing corrosive fluid with intent at his mistress. Sixteen days before the offence was committed he had pushed a broken glass into the same woman's face and had been dealt with summarily and fined £10.

In 1959 about 107,000 persons aged 17 and over were tried for indictable offences: about 28,000, at assizes or quarter sessions and about 79,000 at magistrates' courts. 3,433 of those convicted at magistrates' courts were committed for sentence.

COURTS FOR CHILDREN AND YOUNG PERSONS

The rules regulating the treatment of children and young persons have recently been transformed by the Children and Young Persons Act 1969 the latest in a long line of reports and statutes dealing with the problems of young people. In a Guide to the Act published in 1970 the Home Office noted:

1. The 1969 Act is one part of a body of law on children which fits together as a whole. This body of law has been built up and developed over the past 100 years or more. Its development has two aspects. The first is the progressive modification of the criminal law in its application to children. The second is the development of provisions for the care of children, culminating in the establishment in 1948 of the children's departments of local authorities and the conferment on those authorities in 1963 of an express duty to undertake preventive work with children and their families. The 1969 Act carries these developments, and the integration of legal and social provisions for the care and control of children, one stage further. Part I of the Act is therefore to be considered as one part of a single, comprehensive body of legislation.

2. The other major statutes comprised in this body of legislation are the Children and Young Persons Acts of 1933 and 1963 and the Children Act 1948. Section 1 of the 1969 Act (which sets out the basic care jurisdiction of the juvenile courts) can be fully understood only as part of a wider corpus of legislation which includes in particular section 1 of the 1963 Act (which established formally in the law the aim of prevention through work with families in the community); the 1948 Act (which established local authority children's departments and gave them responsibility to care for children deprived of a normal home life or committed to care by order of a court); section 44 of the 1933 Act (which laid down that every court dealing with a child brought before it should have regard to his welfare and, in a proper case, take steps for removing him from undesirable surroundings and securing proper provision for his education and training); and other provisions of children and young persons legislation such as those which established juvenile courts in their present form.

We come to discuss this particular area of the system as a part of a general description of the different courts which exist within it. The topic of children and young persons shows up, however, some of the weaknesses of an approach which takes courts as the starting point, and in particular the separation which has been adopted here between a description of the relevant court and the kind of treatment available for those brought before it. In the case of adults there is still a kind of plausibility about the separation, and even about the order in which the topics are dealt with here. This is because in spite of the fact that increasing attention is being given to the problem of what to do with an offender once he has been convicted—and this after all is what much of the system is about, who gets punished and what punishment does he get, who gets damages and how much—it is still the case that no punishment can be given or treatment imposed at all on an adult until he has been convicted of an offence. Hence the primary concern is with the establishment of the breach of law, the investigation, the court by which he is tried, the procedure, the evidence and the final decision, with the treatment coming as the final, but so far as the technical aspects of the legal system are concerned, relatively secondary consideration. However, for children and young persons there has been a growing implausibility about this kind of approach and this has been increased by the provisions of the Children and Young Persons Act 1969.

There have over the years been two parallel developments, the first more directly related to the legal system than the second. The first has been the gradual modification of the legal system's normal way of handling offenders when juveniles are involved. The second has been an increase in the general welfare services, outside the legal system altogther, to deal with the problem families in the community. So far as the modification of the legal system in its treatment of juveniles is concerned, magistrates' courts were given power in the nineteenth century to try a number of indictable offences summarily if they were committed by young persons, and their parents consented. In 1908 the Children Act went further and provided that for the future when courts of summary jurisdiction heard charges against children and young persons they should sit as juvenile courts in a different place or at a different time from their ordinary sittings. Members of the public were to be excluded and, although representatives of the press could be present, restrictions were imposed on what they could report. It was only in exceptional circumstances for example that the identity of the accused could be revealed. The Home Secretary advised magistrates' courts that only those specially qualified to deal with juvenile delinquents should sit in the juvenile courts, and in 1933 the Children and Young Persons Act required each petty sessional division to set up a special panel of justices from whom those who were to sit in the juvenile court were to be chosen. The Act also provided that no child could be prosecuted if he was under eight (the previous minimum age had been seven) and raised the maximum age of a young person to seventeen (instead of sixteen). The minimum age for prosecution was again raised in 1964 to ten.

Juvenile courts were not, however, merely given the task of dealing with juvenile offenders. They were also given jurisdiction to deal with juveniles who were in need of care and protection. A welfare function, in other words, was built into their jurisdiction. It was made even more explicit when it came to the question of the treatment to be imposed in any case in which they found an offence proved, or the juvenile in need of care and protection, or guilty of persistent truancy. Here they were expressly required to have the welfare of the child in mind. Parallel with the modifications that were made to the actual procedures for dealing with children and young persons changes were also made in the forms of treatment available, beginning with the reformatories and industrial schools set up by voluntary societies in the nineteenth century.[58] The former were officially recognised by statute in 1854 and brought under the supervision of the Home Office and the latter followed the same path in 1857. The Children Act 1908 provided that in future no child under the age of fourteen should be sent to prison, and those between fourteen and sixteen who committed offences which would have been punishable by imprisonment if they had been committed by an adult should normally be sent to a reformatory or, for up to one month, to a place of detention, known, after the Children and Young Persons Act 1933 as remand homes. One further change made by the 1933 Act was of special significance because it emphasised further the blurring of the juvenile court's role as a criminal court and as a welfare agency. This was the assimilation of reformatories and industrial schools under the single classification " approved schools." The report of the Departmental Committee on the Treatment of Young Offenders, on which much of the 1933 Act was based, in recommending this change said that " there is little or no difference in character and needs between the neglected and the delinquent child. It is often a mere accident whether he is brought before the court because he is wandering and beyond control, or because he has committed some offence. Neglect leads to delinquency."

The 1969 Act was preceded by a good deal of discussion and a number of reports, some of which made proposals which went beyond what has actually been done. It was argued by some, for example, that the whole problem should be taken away from the courts and transferred to some new bodies such as family councils. In spite of the attempts which had been made to make them more informal than other courts, juvenile courts, it was argued, still bore the marks of their origins as criminal courts; their whole attitude was affected by the necessity of concentrating on the commission of an offence by an offender, whereas the problem with which they were really being asked to deal was one in which the offence was often marginal and for which measures directed against the offender alone would be insufficient. Against this it was argued that those who advocated a more informal approach ran the danger, in concentrating on the child's welfare, of forgetting his and his parents' rights. On this view the modified form of criminal procedure used in the juvenile courts provided an essential safeguard for the liberty of the individual and in this respect children and young persons needed as much protection as adults. This was a matter which much exercised the Kilbrandon Committee on Children and Young Persons (Scotland)[59] for example. The Ingleby Committee[60] took a much broader view and gave much more emphasis to the central role of the family and the need to give it support, even at times against its will. This was also a theme taken up in the Government White Paper " The Child the Family and the Courts."[61] In that paper the Government did in fact suggest that juvenile courts might be replaced by family courts but this proposal was withdrawn in the light of criticism. A second White Paper " Children in Trouble "[62] announced the changes brought about in the

---

[58] See below, p. 539.
[59] Cmnd. 2306 (1964).
[60] Cmnd. 1191 (1960).
[61] Cmnd. 2742 (1963).
[62] Cmnd. 3601 (1968).

1969 Act and the object behind them.[63] The 1969 Act provides little more than a basic framework and it is left very largely to the courts, the local authorities and the police to work out the details, especially as regards treatment. The actual legislation is further complicated by the fact that it is only intended to bring it into effect in stages. Proposals as regards treatment are discussed below at p. 539. It is useful, here as elsewhere, to compare the provisions in England with those in Scotland under the Social Work (Scotland) Act 1968.

The new legislation attempts to see the court appearance of a child or young person as one part, and not necessarily a central part, of his own problems and of the problems which the community has in dealing with him. It is part of a general perspective which treats appearance before a court as only one of the possible methods of dealing with him and which emphasises the need for the courts to co-operate with other social agencies if a real solution to the problems he creates is to be found. This is a perspective which it is useful to have in mind when looking at other parts of the legal system as well. It is not only in relation to children that the case involving an individual before a court is only a symptom of a much larger problem or that the court's power to work out a solution on its own is limited. When a court awards compensation for an injury in a motor-car accident or in a factory it may be doing little to reduce the dangers of an accident black spot or to raise the standards of care and protection in factories. Suggestions have been made from time to time that there might be specific traffic courts which would have as one of their responsibilities communicating with the relevant authorities if a particular case before them seemed to raise general problems.[64] Proposals for family courts have often had the same idea behind them, that the court should have the power to reconcile as well as divorce spouses. It is useful in reading the passages which follow to have in mind the question as to the extent to which they raise problems about the role of courts in general and suggest changes that might be introduced in other parts of the system as well.

Report of the Committee on Children and Young Persons
Cmnd. 1191 (1960)

7. In the past the main problem has been seen as the proper treatment of juvenile delinquents, . . . The whole question has been looked at largely from the point of view of possible action by the court, and the emphasis has been on cure. Until recently, less thought has been given to . . . prevention. Hitherto, therefore, improvement in the procedure of juvenile courts and in the forms of treatment, including punishments, available to them has been regarded as the most pressing need. While the basic pattern of the Children Act of 1908 remains, much has indeed been done to achieve this improvement through the passing of the Children and Young Persons Act 1933, the Criminal Justice Act 1948, and the Mental Health Act 1959. . . . Until recently the immediate question of how best to deal with the individual offender, or with the child in other kinds of trouble, has tended to obscure the wider aspects of the problem. . . .

---

[63] Below, pp. 104 and 541.
[64] See Elliot and Street, *Road Accidents*, p. 160.

8. . . . The primary responsibility for bringing up children is parental. . . . It is the parents' duty to help their children to become effective and law abiding citizens. . . . Parents vary in their capacity to live up to this ideal and children also vary in the degree to which they are a problem to their parents. . . . It is the duty of the community to provide through its social and welfare services the advice and support which such parents and children need; to build up their capacity for responsibility, and to enable them to fulfil their proper role. . . .

10. [T]he child cannot be regarded as an isolated unit. The problem is always one of the child in his environment, and his immediate environment is the family to which he belongs. . . . It is often the parents as much as the child who need to alter their ways, and it is therefore with family problems that any preventive measures will be largely concerned. . . .

12. If this be accepted, it becomes the duty of the State to . . . help in every possible way . . . by the provision of housing, health services and education. Some families will need greater and more specialised help through the welfare services. . . .

13. We do not suggest that an element of compulsion can or should be eliminated. There are circumstances in which legal proceedings should be taken against parents, and however successful preventive methods may become, there will continue to be children who should come before juvenile courts. Nor do we suggest that court proceedings should never be taken until everything else has failed. . . . We do suggest, however, that advice is more likely to be taken and treatment more likely to be successful when they can be offered and accepted at an early stage and on a voluntary basis, and that even when compulsion has to be used it is most effective when the need for it is understood and accepted by those compelled.

61. We have set out . . . our general views on parental responsibility and the principal function of the State. It is implicit in those views that although the State's main function is to assist there are circumstances in which intervention is required. The child may be subjected to punishment or other form of compulsory treatment, and the intervention may, in extreme cases, amount to the State depriving the parents of their position and the transfer of their responsibilities for the custody and upbringing of the child. Under the present system such action is taken ultimately through the agency of a court, a body which has been given the power and duty of having regard to the child's welfare and of making the order which it regards as being appropriate treatment for the problem that has arisen. The association of a law court and considerations of welfare does, however, raise the question whether intervention should continue to be dependent on proof of specified misbehaviour in the child or neglect of the child.

63. The view upon which the present law is based, is that intervention may not take place until one or more of certain defined factors have been established. Such misfortunes as illegitimacy, physical defect or loss of a parent by death, are not sufficient grounds in themselves; the grounds must be the commission by the child of a criminal offence or actions indicating a serious lack of control or care, irregular school attendance or the commission of offences against the child. All these grounds are defined by legislation and judicial decision, and they provide a clear legal basis for proceedings before a court.

64. The strength of the present system is that it is reasonably acceptable to the community because it satisfies the general demand that there should be some defined basis for State intervention. It is also important that those responsible for initiating proceedings, such as the police and local authorities, should have a reasonably clear-cut set of rules to indicate the case that they must be prepared to substantiate before a court. Further, experience has shown that the range

of circumstances which come within the categories of offences, " care or protection," " beyond control," and " school attendance " is wide enough to cover virtually all cases where there may be a good case for intervention. These grounds are in fact recognised " danger signals " which indicate a need for enquiry. . . .

66. The weakness of the present system is that a juvenile court often appears to be trying a case on one particular ground and then to be dealing with the child on some quite different ground. This is inherent in combining the requirement for proof of a specified event or condition with a general direction to have regard to the child's welfare. It results, for example, in a child being charged with a petty theft or other wrongful act for which most people would say that no great penalty should be imposed, and the case apparently ending in a disproportionate sentence. For when the court causes enquiries to be made, if those enquiries show seriously disturbed home conditions, or one or more of many other circumstances, the court may determine that the welfare of the child requires some very substantial interference which may amount to taking the child away from his home for a prolonged period. It is common to come across bitter complaints that a child has been sent away from home because he has committed some particular offence which in itself was not at all serious. Despite this very real difficulty we are in favour of retaining the present basic principle that specific and definable matters must be alleged and that there should be no power to intervene until those allegations have been adequately proved. We think that the maintenance of this basis is essential if State intervention is to be fitted into our general system of government and be acceptable to the community. We think that the present procedure is unsuitable and in some ways positively misleading, and we recommend in later paragraphs a new procedure that should go a long way to remove the apparent inconsistency between the charge that the court tries and the facts that it takes into account in determining the disposal of the case. Under our new procedure all younger children who appear before the courts would do so because it is alleged that they are in need of protection or discipline, and it should then be easier for people to appreciate that the outcome of the proceedings is to be determined by the wider need and so ought not to be related proportionately to a petty theft or other isolated event. . . .

68. A number of witnesses considered that appearance before a court was not the best method of dealing with a child who was suspected of having broken the law or whose circumstances otherwise called for intervention which might result in compulsory remedial measures. They thought that the procedure of the juvenile court, although it was less formal and public than that of the adult court, was still too formal to be understood by many children, and, despite the limitation on those who may attend sittings of juvenile courts, the proceedings were often conducted in the presence of too many people. It was also unnecessarily clumsy, as in most cases the facts were not in dispute and the parents for the most part were prepared to accept some measure of intervention. The criticism was made that the legal apparatus, and in particular the rules of evidence and the need to prove specific allegations, often prevented a child from obtaining the treatment he needed. Many children, we were told, would be brought for help earlier but for the stigma of a court appearance; and the added stigma of a finding of guilt often had unduly harsh consequences for the child in later life.

69. These witnesses generally proposed that the juvenile court should be replaced by a non-judicial or quasi-judicial tribunal. . . .

70. Most of the evidence we received on this question, however, favoured the retention of juvenile courts. . . . Those who held this view thought it necessary for the proper protection of those who are the subject of proceedings that

the tribunal should be a court of law, and that the power to interfere with personal liberty should be entrusted only to a court. They emphasised also the deterrent value of appearance before a court. They admitted that some of the objections to non-judicial tribunals applied with less force where " care or protection " or " beyond control " proceedings were in question, but considered the careful proof required by a court of law, in these cases as in others, to be a valuable protection for the child and a safeguard against abuse.

71. We doubt whether there is any force in the argument . . . that the change would avoid the stigma of a court appearance and the stigma of a finding of guilt. We think it likely that any stigma there may be would come to attach to appearance, as a result of bad behaviour, before any tribunal.

72. We have some sympathy with the other points made. . . . [T]he juvenile court has acquired important characteristics and functions as a social agency, as well as being a criminal court. Yet juvenile courts inherited most of the principles and concepts of the criminal courts, and, while these contain much that is of value to the working of the courts, they have in some respects turned out to be unsuitable for a jurisdiction in which the concept of welfare plays a large part. . . .

73. Other problems and difficulties in the existing system are the need to associate the child's parents more closely with the proceedings than is commonly done at present, . . . and the undesirability of using the machinery of the court for dealing with offences of a comparatively trivial kind in cases where there is no deep-seated trouble in the child or his family, or where any necessary help to them is already being given, or can be given satisfactorily without the intervention of the court. . . .

75. One of the difficulties that has impressed us most in considering the suggested alternatives to juvenile courts is that the treatment arranged, or other measures taken, by a non-judicial tribunal would depend for their effectiveness and continuation on the co-operation of the parents and the child. If, after agreeing initially to the course proposed, the parents or child ceased to co-operate, the only remedy would be to bring the case before a court. This would mean that numbers of children would come before the courts as a result of things that had happened or situations that had existed possibly a considerable time before. We think that the duplication and protraction of proceedings in this way would be undesirable.

76. Furthermore, the disadvantages of the present system seem to us to derive not from entrusting these functions to the judiciary, but from the historical development of the juvenile court from the ordinary criminal courts. It is not the conception of judicial decision that is at fault: the reasons referred to in paragraph 70 for retaining judicial hearings must, we think, carry great weight. What is desirable is that the juvenile court, in dealing with younger children who commit offences and with all children who need care or protection, should move still further away from its origin as a criminal court, along lines which would enable it to deal not more leniently with the younger " offenders," but more readily and more effectively with them and with children needing care or protection, while ensuring that the child's parents are closely associated with the proceedings.

83. . . . We have no doubt that offences against the law and circumstances which come within the established meaning of a need for care or protection or being beyond control should continue to be the substance of the grounds on which proceedings may be taken. The change that we recommend is essentially one of procedure.

84. . . . [W]e propose that the new procedure should be applied to all children whose primary need is for care or protection and to children under the age of twelve who are alleged to have committed offences (with power for the age

to be raised to thirteen or fourteen at some time in the future). . . . [A]ll children under twelve who come before the court would come for the same basic reason, namely, that they are " in need of care, protection, discipline or control. . . ." This would include the commission of offences and all the other grounds upon which proceedings may at present be taken. . . . [B]efore any proceedings are instituted, there should be consultation between the police and the local authority. The purpose of this is to ensure that proceedings are based upon the most appropriate grounds and to eliminate proceedings where a matter can be adequately resolved without a court order. . . .

87. We recommend that authority to initiate proceedings should be confined to the police or the local authority. . . .

105. . . . Children between twelve and seventeen on the other hand will continue to be before the court under the present procedure, that is, either as offenders responsible in law for their own acts, or as in need of protection or discipline. . . .

The Child, the Family and the Courts
Cmnd. 2742 (1965)

6. When local authorities were given new powers under the Children Act 1948, to care for children who had been deprived of a natural home life, it became necessary for them also to undertake work with families so that the children might return home wherever possible.

Services in support of the family were also provided under the National Health Service Act 1946 and the National Assistance Act 1948 by local authorities through their health or welfare departments. This work was developed over the years, and, following the recommendation of Lord Ingleby's Committee, local authorities were required under section 1 of the Children and Young Persons Act 1963, to " make available such advice, guidance and assistance as may promote the welfare of children by diminishing the need to receive them into or keep them in care, or for them to be brought before a juvenile court." Local authorities are making vigorous use of these new preventive powers as well as developing the services of their health and welfare departments; children's departments are being expanded and more social workers are being trained; a number of authorities have set up a central index of families at risk to assist any department of the authority or other organisation to help a family that appears to be in danger of social breakdown; and family advice centres are being established as focal points where the social services can be readily available to those who need them. . . .

8. However successful local authorities and voluntary bodies may be in their work of sustaining the family, it is clear that there are considerable numbers of young people for whom, because of their conduct or background, special arrangements will have to be made. . . .

9. The Government have come to the conclusion that in future children and young persons under the age of 21 should be regarded as falling into two categories; those under the age of 16, and those between the ages of 16 and 21. Sixteen will soon be the upper age for compulsory school attendance. It marks a significant stage in the lives of many young people. It is the age at which they begin to earn, at which many may leave home, at which they may marry. The same considerations lead to the conclusion that this should also be the upper age for the special preventive measures which are applied by law to those children who are in need of care, protection or control and the age after which young persons should in general become subject to the sanctions of the ordinary criminal law. . . .

10. There has been an increasing weight of informed opinion over the last ten years in favour of changes in our methods of dealing with children and young persons under 16 who now come before the juvenile courts. These courts were created in 1908. They have their own simplified procedures and they are served by selected magistrates. But though care is taken to avoid the characteristics of a criminal court, their procedures naturally derive from the criminal courts. We believe that these arrangements should be radically changed, because:

(1) Children should be spared the stigma of criminality.

(2) In the great majority of cases of offenders brought before the juvenile courts, the facts are not in dispute. The problem is to decide the appropriate treatment, and the court procedures, designed essentially for testing evidence, do not provide the best means for directing social inquiries and discussing possibilities with the child's parents and the social services that might be concerned with treatment.

(3) Although when children appear in the juvenile courts their parents attend whenever possible, the present arrangements do not provide the best means of getting parents to assume more personal responsibility for their children's behaviour.

(4) Decisions as to treatment are made in the form of a court order. This does not allow sufficient flexibility in developing the child's treatment according to his response and changing need.

11. We therefore propose to remove young people so far as possible from the jurisdiction of the court, and to empower each local authority, through its children's committee, to appoint local family councils to deal with each case as far as possible in consultation and agreement with the parents. Where the facts were disputed or agreement could not be reached, the case would have to be referred to the family court, to which reference is made later. This of course must be done in such a way as to ensure that, as at present, the full safeguards of the law are available to ensure that the interests of the child or young person are protected.

Family councils

12. It is proposed that there should be appointed by the local authority of each county and county borough, and of each Greater London borough, acting through its children's committee, a number of family councils consisting of social workers of the childrens' service and other persons selected for their understanding and experience of children and, in particular, for their awareness of the problems facing the children and adults likely to come before them. . . . There would be sufficient councils to enable discussions with parents to be conducted in an unhurried manner; . . . They would in no case meet in a court building. Social inquiries required by the councils would be undertaken by the childrens' service for the area.

13. Where it was thought, by any person who can now bring a child or young person before a juvenile court, that a child or young person under 16 had committed what would in an older person be an offence, or was in need of care, protection or control, or had failed to attend school, he would report the circumstances to the family council. Social inquiries would be carried out where necessary and the council would see the child and his parents in those cases which required it. In most cases, there would be no disagreement as to the facts alleged. Where, however, the facts were disputed by the child or his parents, the case would be referred to the family court in order that the facts

might be judicially determined. If the court found the facts proved the case would be referred back to the family council for the discussion of treatment.

14. Before discussing with the parents what action, if any, ought to be taken, the family council would consider all the information available about the child and his background. In some cases it would be clear that the parents could themselves deal adequately with the situation. In others, it might be agreed that the matter should be disposed of by the parents paying compensation to anyone who had suffered loss from the child's delinquency. In yet other cases, agreement might be reached on the desirability of placing the child under the supervision of an officer of the children's service, or of sending him for some form of residential training. Any agreement thus reached would be formally recorded. It could be varied from time to time in agreement with the parents; and the case would in any event be reviewed from year to year. If the agreement was not complied with, it would be open to the family council to refer the case to the family court, who would deal with it as if it had come before them for decision in the first instance.

15. Cases would be referred to the family court if agreement with the parents proved to be impossible, or if for any other reason, for instance the gravity of the case, the council thought such a reference was desirable. It would be open to the family court to make any order which is now appropriate to a juvenile court, except that, where long-term residential training was considered to be appropriate, the child or young person would be committed to the care of the local authority. . . .

24. At present a young person aged 14 or over may claim trial by jury for an indictable offence which is not a summary offence, or for a summary offence for which an adult would be liable to imprisonment for more than three months. A magistrates' court must, before proceeding to try such a case summarily, inform the accused of this right. The right to trial by jury for children under 14 was abolished (except for homicide) by the Children and Young Persons Act 1932, following a recommendation by the Departmental Committee on the Treatment of Young Offenders, 1927. Under the arrangements outlined in this paper it would seem unnecessary and indeed inappropriate to retain any power for a person between the ages of 14 and 16 to insist upon a jury when his case is referred to a family court for determination of the facts.

25. Homicide by children is extremely rare and almost always involves mental abnormality or extreme provocation. Nevertheless, the offence is of such a special kind that it seems right that homicide cases should continue to be dealt with at assizes, on committal from the family court. . . .

27. The training and recruitment of social workers on the scale required will take some time, and it will therefore be necessary for the proposals in this paper to be brought into full operation by stages. This can probably best be done by enabling the proposed family councils to deal with younger children only at first, gradually raising the age to 16.

Family courts

28. It is proposed that special magistrates' courts should be constituted from panels of justices selected for their capacity to deal with young persons. . . . The special magistrates' court would have two distinct jurisdictions. In dealing with matters involving those under the age of 16, it would sit as a family court. . . . When the family courts have become established, it is envisaged that consideration should be given to enlarging the jurisdiction to include other matters affecting the family.

Young offenders' courts

29. . . . The special courts, sitting as young offenders' courts, would exercise criminal jurisdiction over offences alleged to have been committed by persons between the ages of 16 and 21. A youth charged with an offence which in the case of an adult is not triable summarily and is either triable at assizes only or punishable with 14 years' imprisonment or more (*e.g.* murder, rape or robbery) would be committed by the young offenders' court for trial to the appropriate superior court. In all other cases a young offenders' court would deal with the matter unless it thought the offence so serious that it ought to be tried at assizes, or unless the accused claimed trial by jury. The young offenders' court would be presided over by a legally qualified chairman when dealing with indictable offences not triable summarily in the case of an adult (but within the jurisdiction of the young offenders' court) and with cases of grievous bodily harm or actual bodily harm and breaking offences. The hearing would be in public, and there would be no restrictions on the publication of the name of any person.

30. The young offenders' court would sit at separate times from both the adult courts and the family courts to avoid contact between adults accused of crime and the persons of differing ages with which the special courts would have to deal. . . .

Children in Trouble
Cmnd. 3601 (1968)

1. In August 1965 the Government published a White Paper, " The Child, the Family and the Young Offender ", in order to invite discussion of possible measures to support the family, forestall and reduce delinquency, and revise the law and practice relating to young offenders in England and Wales. The objectives and broad strategy of these proposals were widely welcomed. There was, however, less agreement about machinery, and especially about the proposal to establish family councils. . . .

7. The social consequences of juvenile delinquency range from minor nuisance to considerable damage and suffering for the community. An important object of the criminal law is to protect society against such consequences: but the community also recognises the importance of caring for those who are too young to protect themselves. Over recent years these two quite distinct grounds for action by society in relation to young people have been moving steadily closer together. It has become increasingly clear that social control of harmful behaviour by the young, and social measures to help and protect the young, are not distinct and separate processes. The aims of protecting society from juvenile delinquency, and of helping children in trouble to grow up into mature and law-abiding persons, are complementary and not contradictory.

8. The criminal law, in its application to juvenile offenders, has for many years recognised the welfare of the individual as an important criterion, and has made provision for special forms of treatment. There has been for sixty years a separate system of juvenile courts. . . . Voluntary organisations have played a large part in providing residential and other facilities for children. The probation service has played a pioneering role, with the young as with adults, in developing the concepts of diagnosis and treatment, both in its statutory function and in giving informal help and advice. The approved schools have done much to develop the concept of social education based on an understanding of individual needs and circumstances. The institution of juvenile liaison officer schemes in some areas is an example of the distinctive contribution which the police are making in the juvenile field, as part of their primary duty of crime

prevention. The children's departments of local authorities have made great strides in the twenty years of their existence; together with the educational and health services they are now closely involved in preventive work and in providing facilities for treatment.

9. The legislative proposals described in this Paper preserve for each of the services concerned an important role in co-operation with the others.

10. This legislation will establish a new legal basis for steady development over a period of time. The changes will be introduced gradually over a period of years. Sufficient trained staff and other resources are not available to permit all the changes to be introduced at once, or at any one time. . . . The preparation and subsequent implementation of area development plans and schemes of intermediate treatment (described in Part V) will in any event take time. Provision will accordingly be made for different days to be appointed for the commencement of different parts of the new system; these will not necessarily be the same in all parts of the country. The fixing of appointed days will be decided in consultation with the local authorities and other services, in the light of the resources available. In particular, it is likely that the new legal procedures described in Part III will be brought into operation in several stages, possibly starting with children aged ten and eleven only. Meanwhile, the new system of residential care will enable existing resources to be used more productively.

11. The response to " The Child, the Family and the Young Offender " indicated wide support for the aim that, so far as possible, juvenile offenders should be dealt with outside the courts with the agreement of their parents. There were many comments, however, that this could most effectively be done on an informal basis by social workers, rather than through family councils; and that the basic choice over the procedure to be adopted in each individual case should therefore lie between, on the one hand, court proceedings and, on the other, the provision of help and guidance on an entirely voluntary basis. The weight of opinion was in favour of retaining the seventeenth birthday as the upper age limit for the juvenile system, particularly for care, protection or control proceedings. There were also several suggestions that there should be different arrangements for younger and older juvenile offenders. The proposals in this Part give effect to these views.

12. These proposals also take account of the fact that the transition from the young child's dependence on his parents to the independence and responsibility of the young adult is a gradual process. For most, it reaches a critical phase when the child is 13 or 14. The new legal procedures . . . will provide a graduated and flexible system which reflects this process. The procedure for children under 10 will remain as at present; there will be new provisions for those aged 10 and under 14, which will be added to those relating to children under 10; and new provisions also for those aged 14 and under 17 which will be added to those relating to the younger age groups. The procedure for offenders aged 10 and under 14 will narrow down the circumstances in which court proceedings are now possible. It represents a half-way stage between care, protection or control proceedings and prosecution. It is designed to encourage parents to fulfil the responsibilities which are properly theirs, and to ensure that the child's home background is considered before a decision is taken whether court proceedings should be instituted. Proceedings will remain possible where they are necessary for the protection of society or for the sake of the child. For offenders aged 14 and under 17, prosecution will be available in defined circumstances, as well as the new procedure for offenders under 14. The procedure for those aged 14 and under 17 will provide machinery and criteria for deciding whether the interests of society or of the young person require a prosecution or whether these interests can best be served in other ways.

13. These proposals mean the retention of the juvenile courts. Provision will be made for the Lord Chancellor . . . to appoint juvenile court panels in all parts of the country as he already does in Inner London. . . . At present, juvenile court panels in other areas are appointed by the justices. This may involve invidious choices, and difficulties of selection in those areas where the bench is large and its individual members are not closely acquainted with many of their colleagues. . . .

The new legal procedure relating to offenders aged 10 and under 14

14. The commission of an offence by a child of this age will cease to be, by itself, a sufficient ground for bringing him before a court. Where proceedings are necessary, these will be brought under the care, protection or control procedure, which will be widened . . . by adding . . . that the child has committed an offence. . . .

15. Where a ground for proceedings is the alleged commission of an offence, either the police or the local authority will be able to bring the proceedings. Except in cases of urgency, they will consult together before deciding whether to do so. If the child denies having committed the offence, it will be necessary to prove this in the same way as at present. It will normally be for the police to bring forward the necessary evidence. If the court is not satisfied that the child committed the offence, that will be the end of the proceedings. If the offence is admitted or proved, evidence will then be brought forward by the local authority or the police, in the same way as in existing care, protection or control proceedings, that the child is not receiving such care, protection or guidance as a good parent may reasonably be expected to give, or is beyond control. The courses open to the court if it is also satisfied on the latter point will be the same as in care, protection or control proceedings brought on any other grounds. . . .

Restrictions on the prosecution of offenders aged 14 and under 17

16. Prosecution of an offender of this age (except on a charge of homicide) will be possible only on the authority of a summons or warrant issued by a juvenile court magistrate. The magistrate will be empowered to grant an application for a summons or warrant only if one or more prescribed criteria are satisfied. Any person who proposes to make such an application will be required to inform the local authority in advance. The procedure for dealing with the application will be similar to existing procedure. Before the magistrate takes his decision, however, he will hear the views which the local children's department and the police have formed after consulting each other about the case. The proposed criteria for prosecution are set out, and the procedure is described in more detail, in Appendix A. . . .

17. Under this scheme, the normal course of events, where the police identify an offender aged 14 and under 17, the offence is not denied, and something more than an oral warning on the spot seems to be required, will be as follows. The police will consult the children's department. Available information about the young person's background will be considered, and further enquiries made if necessary. In some cases it will be agreed that no question of court proceedings need arise. If informal action seems likely to be helpful, this will then be taken. In some cases the enquiries may show that care, protection or control proceedings would be more appropriate than a prosecution. Such proceedings will then be initiated. The remaining cases will be put to a magistrate to decide whether one of the statutory criteria for prosecution is satisfied and, if so, whether there should be a prosecution.

Co-operation between services

18. One major effect of the proposals described in this Part will be to encourage and strengthen consultation and co-operation between the juvenile court magistrates, the police, the local authority services concerned—including the schools—and the probation service. The regular discussion of individual cases will be valuable in enabling magistrates, police and social workers to appreciate different aspects of the problems of delinquency. It will be suggested to local authorities, chief officers of police, juvenile court panels and probation committees that they should arrange periodic meetings, at which each are represented, to review the operation of the new procedures in their area and to discuss how each can make the most effective contribution; and that others who are concerned might also be invited to attend such meetings. Teachers who already make an invaluable contribution to the work of the juvenile courts by providing information about pupils appearing in court, will take part in these meetings, and children's departments will maintain close liaison with schools when considering the action to be taken in individual cases. The changes will increase the scope for social casework by the local authority under section 1 of the Act of 1963. Informal warnings, and formal cautions, of offenders by the police will continue. It will also be possible to continue and extend the work of police juvenile liaison schemes in areas where it is agreed that police participation in preventive work is valuable. The courts will continue to provide the safeguard of judicial procedures in cases where allegations are denied or compulsion is exercised.

Minor and consequential changes

19. The more important minor and consequential changes are described in Appendix B. These affect police powers, remands, and the definition of " in need of care, protection or control.". . .

Powers of the higher courts to deal with serious offences

22. The proposal in " The Child, the Family and the Young Offender " that the right to claim trial by jury should be abolished for persons up to 16, except those charged with homicide, met with almost unanimous agreement. In view of the decision to retain an upper age of 17 for the juvenile court, this right will be abolished up to that age, but with an additional exception. Section 53 (2) of the Children and Young Persons Act 1933 gives the superior courts power to order a young person found guilty of a grave offence to be detained in a place directed by the Secretary of State for a period specified by the court. This power will be retained. In practice it is exercised at present mainly in relation to young persons aged 16 who commit very serious offences, often involving violence. The effect will be that, where a young person is charged with an offence punishable in an adult by imprisonment for 14 years or more, and the juvenile court considers that the exercise of this power would be warranted if he were found guilty, the court will commit him for trial by a higher court. If he is found guilty, the higher court will have power to order his detention under section 53 (2) of the 1933 Act, in addition to all the powers available to a juvenile court.

Appendix A

RESTRICTIONS ON THE PROSECUTION OF YOUNG PERSONS AGED 14
AND UNDER 17

1. The following provisions will be enacted by statute:

   (a) Where a young person is alleged to have committed an offence, criminal proceedings may be taken only on account of the seriousness of the offence or of some other prescribed circumstance.

   (b) The sole procedure for instituting a prosecution against a young person (except in the case of homicide) will be by applying for a summons or a warrant to a member of the juvenile court panel, sitting in private, who will be under a duty to consider whether any of the prescribed circumstances is satisfied and, if not, to refuse the application.

   (c) It will be open to the magistrate to decline to issue process if, having regard to all the circumstances, he considers that, although one of the prescribed circumstances is satisfied, the case can appropriately be dealt with without recourse to prosecution.

2. Statutory Regulations will:

   (1) Prescribe the circumstances in which it will be possible for criminal proceedings to be taken for an alleged offence, possibly on the following lines:

   (a) the offence is homicide or some other serious offence;

   (b) the offence is of a type causing much public concern;

   (c) the young person appears not to be in need of sustained support or treatment, but the nature of the offence and his home circumstances suggest that a court appearance and a simple deterrent (e.g. a fine) would be appropriate;

   (d) the known circumstances of the young person or his family indicate that action without the backing of a court order would not be likely to succeed;

   (e) the offence is a traffic offence carrying a likelihood of disqualification from driving or endorsement of the licence that will remain effective after he has reached the minimum age for holding a driving licence;

   (f) help or treatment on a voluntary basis would not be feasible because the young person does not reside in England and Wales or has no fixed abode;

   (g) the offence was committed in company with some other person, whether over or under 17, who is to be prosecuted.

   (2) Require an intending prosecutor of a young person to inform the local authority before applying for a summons or warrant.

   (3) Confer on the local authority a right to be heard by a magistrate considering an application for a summons or warrant.

   (4) Require the magistrate to take into account whether the local authority, or some other social agency, is already engaged or proposes to engage in preventive work with the young person or his family and to consider the advice of the agency concerned.

   (5) Empower the magistrate (a) to require the attendance of local authority or police representatives, if either or both are not present; (b) to adjourn the application, either for this purpose or so that further inquiries can be made by the local authority or a probation officer, or by the police.

(6) Provide that a magistrate issuing a summons or warrant in respect of a young person shall not be a member of the court hearing the case.

3. The detailed administration of this scheme will depend to some extent on local arrangements, but will be broadly as described below. (This scheme relates only to cases where the ground on which action is being considered is the commission of an offence. It will not affect existing arrangements for taking care, protection or control proceedings on other grounds, or for help to be given to children and families by children's departments and other services.)

(1) (a) The possibility of action on a voluntary basis will be considered only where the initial investigations by the police indicate that the offence is not denied. Where it becomes known at any stage that the child or his parents deny the offence he is alleged to have committed, it will be for the police to decide in the ordinary way whether to apply for a summons or warrant if one of the statutory criteria is satisfied, or to take no action.

(b) In cases where the police do not now prosecute, but either take no action or issue an infomal warning, there will be no change.

(c) Where it seems clear that, according to the prescribed criteria, there is bound to be a prosecution (e.g. in a case of grave crime) the police will apply for a summons or warrant, first informing the children's department of the local authority; in cases of homicide it will remain possible for the police to charge the alleged offender in the same way as at present, informing the children's department.

(2) In cases not dealt with as in (1) the first step will be consultation between the police and the children's department. This will include, so far as they think it necessary, assembling and considering the available information about the child and his background (e.g. from his teachers), consulting any others known to be involved already with the child or his family (e.g. the probation service), and a home visit if this seems required before the children's department can decide whether voluntary action with the family would be worth attempting.

(3) (a) If, after this consultation, it is agreed that voluntary action without the support of a court order should be tried or continued, or that a formal caution would be appropriate, or that no action is necessary, the case will be dealt with accordingly and there will be no application for process.

(b) If the police and the children's department agree that it is a case for prosecution or for care, protection or control proceedings, process will be applied for accordingly.

(c) Cases not falling clearly under paragraphs 3 (1) (b) to 3 (3) (b) will be referred to the magistrate for a decision, by the police applying for a summons.

(4) Where an application for process is made, the magistrate will consider it in accordance with the provisions set out in paragraphs 1 and 2 (4) and (5) of this Appendix. He will take into account all the information given by the police, the children's department and the probation officer where he is concerned with the case and will be free to ask them questions and to discuss the circumstances and possible courses of action with them before taking his decision.

(5) If voluntary action is tried but the young person or his parents do not in the event prove to be co-operative, no further action will be taken unless

fresh grounds for court proceedings arise. If the young person offends again, paragraph 2 (1) (*d*) will then apply, and it will be possible to apply for a summons or warrant if prosecution seems the appropriate form of court proceedings.

APPENDIX B

MINOR AND CONSEQUENTIAL CHANGES

Ancillary procedure

1. Power will still be required for the police to take immediate preventive action where a child under 14 is found committing an offence. In relation to an offender aged 10 and under 14, they will be given powers to take him to a place of safety in all circumstances in which they would have power to arrest without warrant an offender of 14 or over.

2. The existing power of the police to take to a place of safety, without reference to a magistrate, a child or young person thought to be in need of care, protection or control will be reformulated. It will be made clear that this power may properly be exercised in situations where the protection of the child or young person clearly requires his immediate removal from the place where he is found, although the police are not in a position to establish straightway whether it will be necessary to bring him before a court.

3. Where a young person aged 14 and under 17 is arrested for an offence but not released on bail, the case will be referred to a magistrate within 72 hours. The magistrate will have power to remand on bail, or to the care of the local authority, pending a decision whether court proceedings should be taken.

4. Adjustments will be made in the powers of the courts to remand children and young persons in custody, and to make interim orders. The existing law specifies in detail the precise circumstances in which children and young persons of particular ages may be committed to particular types of institution. These provisions will be replaced by a provision that all remands (otherwise than on bail) of young persons aged 14 and under 17 shall be to the care of the local authority, and all interim orders for children under 17 shall commit to the temporary care of the local authority. The developments outlined in Part V will, in time, make it possible to accommodate all these children and young persons (apart from those accommodated in hospitals) in establishments provided or managed by local authorities. In the meantime, the Government will continue to provide remand centres or other establishments for those young persons aged 14 and under 17 whose behaviour is such that they cannot be contained satisfactorily in local authority establishments.

Amended definition of " in need of care, protection or control "

5. As explained in paragraph 14 of this Paper, one of the tests in section 2 of the Children and Young Persons Act 1963 is that the child is not receiving such care, protection and guidance as a good parent may reasonably be expected to give. This test will be clarified so as to make it clear that the court may properly consider not only the care, protection and guidance given direct by the child's parents, but also whether the parents are securing for him any care, protection or guidance which they are not themselves able to give but which a good parent might reasonably be expected to secure for his child. This amendment will apply to all children up to the age of 17.

Children and Young Persons Act 1969
1969 c. 54

PART I

Care of children and young persons through juvenile courts

1.—(1) Any local authority, constable or authorised person [67] who reasonably believes that there are grounds for making an order under this section in respect of a child or young person may, subject to section 2 (3) and (8) of this Act, bring him before a juvenile court.

(2) If the court before which a child or young person is brought under this section is of opinion that any of the following conditions is satisfied with respect to him, that is to say—

(*a*) his proper development is being avoidably prevented or neglected or his health is being avoidably impaired or neglected or he is being ill-treated; or

(*b*) it is probable that the condition set out in the preceding paragraph will be satisfied in his case, having regard to the fact that the court or another court has found that that condition is or was satisfied in the case of another child or young person who is or was a member of the household to which he belongs; or

(*c*) he is exposed to moral danger; or

(*d*) he is beyond the control of his parent or guardian; or

(*e*) he is of compulsory school age within the meaning of the Education Act 1944 and is not receiving efficient full-time education suitable to his age, ability and aptitude; or

(*f*) he is guilty of an offence, excluding homicide,

and also that he is in need of care or control which he is unlikely to receive unless the court makes an order under this section in respect of him, then, subject to the following provisions of this section and sections 2 and 3 of this Act, the court may if it thinks fit make such an order.

(3) The order which a court may make under this section in respect of a child or young person is—

(*a*) an order requiring his parent or guardian to enter into a recognisance to take proper care of him and exercise proper control over him; or

(*b*) a supervision order; or

(*c*) a care order (other than an interim order); or

(*d*) a hospital order within the meaning of Part V of the Mental Health Act 1959; or

(*e*) a guardianship order within the meaning of that Act.

(5) An order under this section shall not be made in respect of a child or young person—

(*a*) in pursuance of paragraph (*a*) of subsection (3) of this section unless the parent or guardian in question consents;

(*b*) in pursuance of paragraph (*d*) or (*e*) of that subsection unless the conditions which, under section 60 of the said Act of 1959, are required to be satisfied for the making of a hospital or guardianship order in respect of a person convicted as mentioned in that section are satisfied in his case so far as they are applicable;

(*c*) if he has attained the age of sixteen and is or has been married.

---

[67] *i.e.* the National Society for the Prevention of Cruelty to Children.

(6) In this section " authorised person " means a person authorised by order of the Secretary of State to bring proceedings in pursuance of this section and any officer of a society which is so authorised, and in sections 2 and 3 of this Act "care proceedings " means proceedings in pursuance of this section and " relevant infant " means the child or young person in respect of whom such proceedings are brought or proposed to be brought.

2.— . . . (12) The relevant infant may appeal to [The Crown Court] [68] against any order made in respect of him under the preceding section except such an order as is mentioned in subsection (3) (a) of that section.

(13) Such an order as is mentioned in subsection (3) (a) of the preceding section shall not require the parent or guardian in question to enter into a recognisance for an amount exceeding fifty pounds or for a period exceeding three years or, where the relevant infant will attain the age of eighteen in a period shorter than three years, for a period exceeding that shorter period. . . .

3.— . . . (2) In any care proceedings the court shall not entertain an allegation that the offence condition is satisfied in respect of the relevant infant unless the proceedings are brought by a local authority or a constable.

(3) If in any care proceedings the relevant infant is alleged to have committed an offence in consequence of which the offence condition is satisfied with respect to him . . . the same proof shall be required to substantiate or refute an allegation that the offence condition is satisfied in consequence of an offence as is required to warrant a finding of guilty, or as the case may be, of not guilty of the offence.

(4) A person shall not be charged with an offence if in care proceedings previously brought in respect of him it was alleged that the offence condition was satisfied in consequence of that offence. . . .

(6) Where in any care proceedings the court finds the offence condition satisfied with respect to the relevant infant in consequence of an indictable offence within the meaning of the Magistrates' Courts Act 1952 then, whether or not the court makes an order under section 1 of this Act—

(a) section 34 of that Act (which relates to compensation for loss of property or damage to it) shall apply as if the finding were a finding of guilty of the offence and as if the maximum amount of an award under that section were one hundred pounds; and

(b) the court shall if the relevant infant is a child, and may if he is not, order any sum awarded by virtue of this subsection to be paid by his parent or guardian instead of by him unless it is satisfied that the parent or guardian cannot be found or has not conduced to the commission of the offence by neglecting to exercise due care or control of him. . . .

For the purposes of this subsection an offence under section 14 (1) of the Criminal Justice Administration Act 1914 (which provides for damage committed wilfully or maliciously to be punishable on summary conviction) shall be treated as an indictable offence within the meaning of the said Act of 1952.

(7) Where in any care proceedings the court finds the offence condition satisfied with respect to the relevant infant and he is a young person, the court may if it thinks fit and he consents, instead of making such an order as is mentioned in section 1 (3) of this Act, order him to enter into a recognisance for an amount not exceeding twenty-five pounds and for a period not exceeding one year to keep the peace or to be of good behaviour; and such an order shall be deemed to be an order under section 1 of this Act but no appeal to [the Crown Court] [68] may be brought against an order under this subsection.

[68] The words in brackets were substituted by the Courts Act 1971, s. 56 (2), Sched. 9, Pt. I.

(8) Where in any care proceedings the court finds the offence condition satisfied with respect to the relevant infant in consequence of an offence which was not admitted by him before the court, then—

> . . . (b) if . . . the court decides [not to make any order under section 1 of this Act] . . . ,

the relevant infant may appeal to [the Crown Court] [68] against the finding . . . and a person ordered to pay compensation by virtue of subsection (6) of this section may appeal to [the Crown Court] [68] against the order. . . .

Consequential changes in criminal proceedings etc.

4. A person shall not be charged with an offence, except homicide, by reason of anything done or omitted while he was a child.

5.—(1) A person other than a qualified informant shall not lay an information in respect of an offence if the alleged offender is a young person.

(2) A qualified informant shall not lay an information in respect of an offence if the alleged offender is a young person unless the informant is of opinion that the case is of a description prescribed in pursuance of subsection (4) of this section and that it would not be adequate for the case to be dealt with by a parent, teacher or other person or by means of a caution from a constable or through an exercise of the powers of a local authority or other body not involving court proceedings or by means of proceedings under section 1 of this Act.

(3) A qualified informant shall not come to a decision in pursuance of the preceding subsection to lay an information unless—

> (a) he has told the appropriate local authority that the laying of the information is being considered and has asked for any observations which the authority may wish to make on the case to the informant; and
>
> (b) the authority either have notified the informant that they do not wish to make such observations or have not . . .

but the informant shall be entitled to disregard the foregoing provisions of this subsection in any case in which it appears to him that the requirements of the preceding subsection are satisfied and will continue to be satisfied notwithstanding any observations which might be made in pursuance of this subsection.

(4) The Secretary of State may make regulations specifying, by reference to such considerations as he thinks fit, the descriptions of cases in which a qualified informant may lay an information in respect of an offence if the alleged offender is a young person; but no regulations shall be made under this subsection unless a draft of the regulations has been approved by a resolution of each House of Parliament.

(7) Nothing in the preceding provisions of this section applies to an information laid with the consent of the Attorney General or laid by or on behalf or with the consent of the Director of Public Prosecutions. . . .

(8) It shall be the duty of a person who decides to lay an information in respect of an offence in a case where he has reason to believe that the offender is a young person to give notice to the appropriate local authority unless he is himself that authority.

(9) In this section—

> "qualified informant" means a servant of the Crown, a police officer and a member of a designated police force acting in his capacity as such a servant, officer or member, a local authority, the Greater London Council, the council of a county district and any body designated as a public body for the purposes of this section;

and in this subsection " designated " means designated by an order made by the Secretary of State; . . .

6.—(1) Where a person under the age of seventeen appears or is brought before a magistrates' court on an information charging him with an offence, other than homicide, which is an indictable offence within the meaning of the Magistrates' Courts Act 1952, he shall be tried summarily unless—

(a) he is a young person and the offence is such as is mentioned in subsection (2) of section 53 of the Act of 1933 [69] (under which young persons convicted on indictment of certain grave crimes may be sentenced to be detained for long periods) and the court considers that if he is found guilty of the offence it ought to be possible to sentence him in pursuance of that subsection; or

(b) he is charged jointly with a person who has attained the age of seventeen and the court considers it necessary in the interests of justice to commit them both for trial;

and accordingly in a case falling within paragraph (a) or paragraph (b) of this subsection the court shall, if it is of opinion that there is sufficient evidence to put the accused on trial, commit him for trial.

(3) If on trying a person summarily in pursuance of subsection (1) of this section the court finds him guilty, it may impose a fine of an amount not exceeding fifty pounds or may exercise the same powers as it could have exercised if he had been found guilty of an offence for which, but for section 107 (2) of the said Act of 1952, it could have sentenced him to imprisonment for a term not exceeding three months.[70]

34. (1) The Secretary of State may by order provide—

(a) that any reference to a child in section 4 . . . of this Act shall be construed as excluding a child who has attained such age as may be specified in the order;

(b) that any reference to a young person in section 5 of this Act (except subsection (8)) shall be construed as including a child, or excluding a young person, who has attained such age as may be so specified;

(c) that any reference to a young person in section 5 (8) . . . shall be construed as including a child who has attained such age as may be so specified; . . .

(2) In the case of a person who has not attained the age of seventeen but has attained such lower age as the Secretary of State may by order specify, no proceedings under section 1 of this Act or for an offence shall be begun in any court unless the person proposing to begin the proceedings has, in addition to any notice falling to be given by him to a local authority in pursuance of section 2 (3) or 5 (8) of this Act, given notice of the proceedings to a probation officer for the area for which the court acts; and accordingly in the case of such a person the reference in section 1 (1) of this Act to the said section 2 (3) shall be construed as including a reference to this subsection. . . .

[69] s. 53 (2) of the Act of 1933 provides: " Where a child or young person is convicted on indictment of any offence punishable in the case of an adult with imprisonment for 14 years or more, not being an offence the sentence for which is fixed by law, and the court is of opinion that none of the other methods in which the case may be legally dealt with is suitable, the court may sentence the offender to be detained for such period not exceeding the maximum term of imprisonment with which the offence is punishable in the case of an adult as may be specified in the sentence; and where such a sentence has been passed the child or young person shall, during that period . . . be liable to be detained in such place and on such conditions as the Secretary of State may direct. . . .

[70] Or £10 in the case of a child (s. 34 (5)).

70.—(1) In this Act, unless the contrary intention appears, the following expressions have the following meanings : — . . .

"child ", . . . means a person under the age of fourteen . . . ;

"young person " means a person who has attained the age of fourteen and is under the age of seventeen;

and it is hereby declared that, in the expression "care and control", "care" includes protection and guidance and "control" includes discipline. . . .

73. . . . (2) This Act shall come into force on such day as the Secretary of State may by order appoint, and different days may be appointed under this subsection for different provisions of this Act or for different provisions of this Act so far as they apply to such cases only as may be specified in the order.

(3) . . . [A]n order [made] under the preceding subsection may make such transitional provision as the Secretary of State considers appropriate in connection with the provisions brought into force by the order, including such adaptations of those provisions and of any other provisions of this Act then in force as appear to him appropriate for the purposes or in consequence of the operation of any provision of this Act. . . .

Chapter 2

THE LEGAL PROFESSION

Introduction

Before going on to look at the way the legal system looks at facts and the way it manufactures, discovers and uses the law it might be worth looking at some of the people involved professionally in the process and the legal profession. This chapter looks at the lawyers and the next goes on to say something about the role of the judge and the jury in the legal process. Much of the Englishness of the English legal system is a result of its age, and few parts of it are older or more traditional than the legal profession or professions that keep it going. Not that barristers and solicitors are the only professional people on whom the quality and effectiveness of the legal system depends. The police, probation officers, prison officers, magistrates' clerks, children's officers, law teachers, even Beeching's butler who is becoming so hard to find, have a major part to play. As will be seen below, the police have an essential role in the enforcement process and are entrusted with a wide discretion as regards prevention, detection, apprehension, prosecution and the giving of evidence. The fact that prison officers only receive their charges at the end of the conspicuous part of the legal process does not alter the fact that the effectiveness of the total criminal process depends to an important extent on what they do and the way they do it, their qualities, values and assumptions not to speak of the facilities they are given with which to play their role, This is in some ways even more true of probation officers who not only play an important part in the supervision and rehabilitation of offenders in the community but are one of the primary sources of information which the courts consider when determining sentences. Nevertheless it is the lawyers who lie at the heart of the system and around whose activities the system revolves, and they form the subject-matter of this chapter.

Historical Development

A separate body of men skilled in the preparation and presentation of cases existed as long ago as the thirteenth century. Their status and influence expanded with the extension of the activities of the royal courts of justice and the increasing complexity of the law and legal procedure and even further, in the fourteenth century, when it became the settled practice to appoint the common law judges from among their number rather than make the judiciary a separate parallel profession. Even the organisation of the Bar into Inns dates from the fourteenth century and the four major Inns into which barristers are at the moment organised, Lincoln's, Gray's, Inner Temple and Middle Temple were all in existence by then. The establishment of a recognisably distinct second branch of the profession known at first as attorneys in the common law courts and solicitors in the the civil law courts, and subsequently as solicitors, came later. The Society of Gentleman Practitioners, which was the forerunner of the present Law Society, which is responsible for the admission and discipline of solicitors today, was not founded until 1729, although before that the attorneys had in fact had their own Inns. Until the nineteenth century, however, the profession of solicitor was held in much less esteem than it enjoys today and certainly much less than that enjoyed by the barrister.

The arguments for and against fusion

From time to time proposals have been made for the fusion of the two branches of the profession but these suggestions have always been resisted on the grounds of the importance of retaining a separate Bar. Various reasons have been given for this. It is said that it is essential for the maintenance of standards both of ability and integrity, that advocates, in particular, should work in close contact with one another, in an atmosphere where misconduct on the part of one of them is instantly apparent, where the traditional values can be more easily preserved and communicated, and where the judges can easily see their prospective successors at work. Particular importance is also attached to the independence which is afforded by the fact that it is not the barrister but the solicitor who sees the lay client. This is especially so where there is a continuing relationship between the client and his lawyer. The present structure also allows barristers to specialise and makes them available to a large number of firms of solicitors, even small local ones, rather than having them swallowed up by some larger firm with a monopoly of their work. Stress is also laid on the importance of preserving the economic independence of the barrister. Barristers are not permitted to have partnerships amongst themselves. In 1961 the General Council of the Bar adopted the recommendations of one of its committees to the effect that:

(a) The institution of partnerships at the Bar is wholly incompatible with the traditional conception of members of the Bar as individual practitioners enjoying an independent and individual status.

(b) The institution of partnerships at the Bar could not be effected without working in the long, if not the short run, fundamental changes in this traditional conception.

(c) The present system has been shown by experience to foster the strength and independence of the Bar while affording a satisfactory service to the public.

(d) No case in favour of partnerships has been made out which is sufficient to justify the changes that would be the result of their institution.

(e) There is no real demand for partnerships at the Bar.

(f) Accordingly partnerships at the Bar should not be permitted.

Barristers are, however, grouped together in chambers and share a clerk who is their point of communication with the different firms of solicitors who send briefs to them through him, the theory being that the clerk merely acts as clerk for each individual member of chambers, with work being sent to each barrister by name. It is not a question of the clerk drumming up work for the chambers as a whole and then distributing it amongst the barristers who make up his chambers. The actual way in which the clerk works and the influence he has is not very well known, but what is clear is that the practice is not as clear cut as the theory might suggest.

Those who argue for fusion do so mainly on grounds of economy. In many cases it is said the present system involves the use of two lawyers, first a solicitor and then a barrister briefed by a solicitor, when one would do. The division of function too, it is said, especially that which ordains that barristers may appear as advocates in the superior courts and solicitors may not, is arbitrary, and solicitors may make as good a job of advocacy as any barrister. The arguments based on the need for specialists are countered by the view that lawyers could specialise even if the professions were fused. The argument based on the need to have a small élite group from whom judges can be chosen is met by the assertion that this is to exclude from appointment lawyers who would make perfectly good judges especially having regard to the fact that not every barrister who becomes a judge need have specialised in advocacy.

Up to the present time it is the arguments of those who are in favour of continued separation that have prevailed. Even proposals for a common educational and training programme have been resisted on the thin end of the wedge principle, though in fact so far as legal education in the universities is concerned no distinction is made. If the recommendations of the Ormrod Committee on Legal Education [1] are ever accepted, and the universities are given the task of conducting what is called the "academic" stage of legal education this will formally be the position as well.

BARRISTERS

Admission of a person as a student and, when he is qualified as a barrister, is the responsibility of the Inns of Court. They are also responsible for the maintenance of discipline and the observance by barristers of the rules of professional conduct and etiquette. They exercise their powers under the general supervision of the judges acting as Visitors. The Inns themselves are independent, voluntary organisations though they have common rules and a similar organisation. They have in fact delegated the exercise of a number of their powers. Their responsibilities in regard to the education and the examination of Bar students have been delegated to a Council of Legal Education. In 1967 they delegated their disciplinary power to a Senate of the four Inns which also has wide administrative responsibilities in relation to the Bar. Another important body in relation to barristers is the General Council which is the successor of the Bar Committee set up in 1883 to represent the interests of the Bar on any matter in which its interests might be affected. It is however more than a trade union as it is also responsible for interpreting the rules of etiquette, which play an important part in regulating the conduct of barristers and setting the

[1] Cmnd. 4595, March 1971.

standards of what is and what is not professional and unprofessional conduct. The behaviour of barristers is in fact partly regulated by these, partly of course also by the ordinary law of the land, and partly by the Consolidated Regulations published by the four Inns of Court. Their actual conduct in court is subject to the general power which the judges have of controlling the proceedings before them. It is the judge who is responsible for seeing that the proceedings are conducted with due decorum and the observation of the usual courtesies between counsel and between counsel and the judge. In extreme cases the judge can back up his authority with his power to punish for contempt of court and to report to his Inn any barrister (or to the Law Society any solicitor) whom he thinks has been guilty of professional misconduct.

In some cases the ordinary law of the land gives lawyers special privileges to enable them to perform their functions satisfactorily. They are for example privileged from suit for anything which they say in the course of legal proceedings. They may not be required to reveal communications between themselves and their clients made in the course of asking for or giving legal advice. They have the privilege of conducting " without prejudice " negotiations in an effort to reach a settlement without trial. That is, by heading their negotiations " without prejudice " they can protect them from being used against their clients should negotiations for a settlement break down.

Entry to the Bar is conditional on the passing of qualifying examinations, though holders of university degrees in law are usually exempt from some part of these. A law degree is not at present an essential qualification though the Ormrod Committee on Legal Education whose report was published in 1971 recommended that this should become the rule for both barristers and solicitors. A prospective barrister is also required to eat a number of dinners in the Hall of his Inn and to be a pupil in the chambers of a barrister for six months before he can begin to take work. He must continue a further six months as a pupil before he can practise. There are also fees to be paid at entry and call, though the Inns offer scholarships which will cover the costs of entry and in some cases contribute to maintenance in the early years of work at the Bar. Entry in general, however, remains expensive.

Once qualified, a barrister must find a seat in chambers, often one of the most difficult tasks facing him. Every practising barrister is required to practise in a recognised set of chambers. Those in London are principally in the Temple and within walking distance of the Law Courts but there are also local Bars in such places as Birmingham, Manchester, Norwich, Southampton and Newcastle. A recent ruling by the Lord Chancellor has allowed Queen's Counsel (leading barristers who have " taken silk ") to have chambers in the provinces for the first time and has encouraged them to open new chambers there, in order to provide more places. Once in chambers the barrister is dependent for work on being briefed by a solicitor. He may not advertise or tout for work in any way. Accident and personal contacts apart, he is dependent on his clerk.

Given the separation of the two branches of the profession there are rules which are designed to preserve the barriers between them. A barrister may not have his chambers in an office occupied by a solicitor, or for that matter an accountant. He may not have a solicitor as a pupil and may not himself work in a solicitor's office. Although he may engage in drafting documents including conveyances he is not expected to do any work normally undertaken by a solicitor. He should not for example conduct all the incidental features of conveyancing such as searches, etc. A barrister should normally only accept work from a solicitor. He cannot be briefed by a lay client directly. It is to the solicitor too that he looks for his fee, which is usually fixed by negotiation between his clerk and the solicitor's clerk. What the fee will be is a matter of supply and demand. On his side the solicitor will have to bear in mind what the Taxing Master will allow as a reasonable fee in the case, since it is only this amount that he will be able to recover from the other party if his own client wins. This will also affect the decision as to whether to employ a Queen's Counsel since not only are the fees of the latter likely to be higher, but if briefed he must appear with a junior member as well. In addition to the basic fee, the barrister who is appearing on more than one day as an advocate in a case is entitled to a " refresher," an addition for each day. The unpaid barrister cannot sue for his fee. He may however ask the Bar Council to take up the matter with the Law Society who may themselves in an appropriate case exercise their disciplinary powers over solicitors to secure payment or punish a defaulter. It is said that as a consequence of the fact that the barrister is not able to sue for his fees he cannot himself be sued for negligence in his work. The two rules however are independent and it is likely that public policy would be used to justify the second rule even if the first did not exist.

The barrister owes his special status in part to the traditional position and prestige of his profession but tradition is here backed up by a number of additional supports, the two most important of which are his exclusive right of audience in the superior courts, and his claim on the superior judgeships. The right of audience has long been a bone of contention between barristers and solicitors. The present position is that only a barrister can appear as an advocate in the House of Lords, the Court of Appeal and the High Court, except in the exercise of the latter's bankruptcy jurisdiction. Solicitors however and even managing clerks can appear in chambers in a High Court action in connection with the interlocutory matters that precede a trial. Only barristers can appear in the Crown Court except in those cases which have come to it by way of appeal from a magistrates court or where the accused has been committed to the Crown Court for sentence. Both barristers and solicitors may appear in the county courts but solicitors may only appear in cases which they themselves are conducting. They cannot in other words be " briefed " by another solicitor. Both barristers and solicitors may appear in magistrates' courts. No one else, even though qualified, may appear there, though an accused person is entitled to have someone to assist him in framing questions to witnesses. There is of course nothing to prevent a party presenting his own case, though when it comes to an appeal to the House of Lords, unless leave has been granted by the Court of Appeal, it will be necessary for two Queen's Counsel to certify that it is reasonable to bring the case on appeal.

So far as claims on judgeship are concerned Lords of Appeal in Ordinary are chosen from barristers of at least fifteen years standing or those who have held high judicial office for two years.[2] Lords Justices of Appeal are chosen from barristers of at least fifteen years standing or from High Court judges.[3] High Court judges are chosen from barristers of at least ten years standing.[4] Circuit judges are chosen from barristers of ten years standing or from those who have held the office of Recorder for five years; Recorders from barristers and solicitors of at least ten years standing.[5] This means that a solicitor can now become a Circuit judge if he has previously been a Recorder. Stipendiary magistrates are chosen from barristers and solicitors of at least seven years standing.[6] Masters of the Queen's Bench Division must be barristers of at least ten years standing, though Masters of other Divisions can also be solicitors. The National Insurance Commissioner and the National Insurance (Industrial Injuries) Commissioner are barristers of ten years standing, and the President of the Lands Tribunal a barrister of seven years standing or the holder of a judicial office.

Although a monopoly of advocacy in the superior courts is an important aspect of the special position of the Bar, the line between solicitors and barristers is not simply a question of the latter being advocates and the former not. By no means all barristers are engaged in advocacy. On the other hand many solicitors specialise in advocacy, though of necessity in the lower courts.

The Bar itself is divided up into a number of different specialisms. Much of the work of the Chancery Bar, for example, involves the drawing up of documents and not the conduct of litigation. This is especially true of those engaged in tax work. Even the work of the common lawyer will involve a large amount of paper work, drawing up pleadings, giving advice on evidence, and giving legal advice generally on points of substantive law. Nor is the barrister's attention necessarily centred exclusively on the ordinary courts. Apart from appearing before tribunals, barristers are often engaged in a variety of public inquiries such as planning inquiries or inquiries preceding the compulsory purchase of land. They may also accompany deputations to Ministers or government departments though in such cases they are required to make it clear that they are present as advocates and not as members of the deputation. Not only are there traditional specialisations among members of the Bar, such as tax, company, commercial, criminal, matrimonial, planning, rating, admiralty, patents and copyright, etc. but there is also a division of work according to rank. A Queen's Counsel is not expected to take work which is regarded as part of the staple of the junior such as drawing up pleadings. One of the calculations a junior barrister has to make when he is thinking of applying to the Lord Chancellor for silk—and the decision whether he should be granted silk is a discretionary one—is whether he will make up in other ways the loss he will suffer through having to give much of what has hitherto been his normal work.

[2] Appellate Jurisdiction Act 1876, ss. 6 and 25.
[3] Supreme Court of Judicature Act 1925, s. 9.
[4] Ibid.
[5] Courts Act 1971, ss. 16 and 21.
[6] Justices of the Peace Act 1949, s. 29 (1).

Rules governing practice as a barrister

Rulings of the Bar Council on matters of professional etiquette

(a) Counsel's fees

1. General rules

(1) Counsel is bound to accept any brief in the courts in which he professes to practise at a proper professional fee dependent on the length and difficulty of the case, but special circumstances may justify his refusal, at his discretion, to accept a particular brief.

(2) It is the spirit and tradition of the Bar that counsel is separately instructed and separately remunerated by fees for each piece of work done. It is therefore not permissible for counsel to undertake to represent any person, authority or corporation in all their court work for a fixed annual salary. . . .

(4) . . . [I]t is not permissible for counsel to accept a fixed fee for advising on problems over a fixed period. . . .

(15) It is a breach of professional etiquette to make an agreement with a solicitor to do all his cases of a particular class at a fixed fee in each case, irrespective of the circumstances of each case. . . .

2. Negotiation for fees

(1) Save in a few well-recognised and exceptional cases, such as appearing for a Public Department or for the Police in criminal prosecutions, or for an assisted person under the Legal Aid and Advice Act 1949 a barrister should not appear in court upon a brief which has no fee marked upon it.

(2) Brief fees are fixed by arrangement between the instructing solicitor or his clerk, and counsel's clerk, but it is permissible in cases of special difficulty . . . to discuss the amount of a fee personally with the instructing solicitor.

3. Refresher fees

(1) The circumstances in which a refresher fee may be claimed . . . are defined in the Rules of the Supreme Court. [Annual Statement of the General Council of the Bar (1951) and (1966).]

(b) No counsel can be required to accept a retainer or a brief or to advise or draw pleadings if he has previously advised another person on or in connection with the same matter, and he ought not to do so if he would be embarrassed in the discharge of his duty by reason of the confidence reposed in him by such other person, or if his acceptance would be inconsistent with the obligation of any retainer held by him. . . . [Annual Statement (1938).]

(c) Briefs are as a rule delivered and accepted on the understanding that it is possible that a counsel may be prevented from attending the case. It is a paramount duty of a barrister not to embarrass his client and to allow sufficient time for another counsel to be engaged and to master the brief. A barrister is under a duty to give warning to his instructing solicitor as soon as there is any appreciable danger that he may not be able to attend to a brief and to return the brief if required. Only in most exceptional cases should a brief for the defence of a person charged with a capital offence be returned when once accepted and then only if sufficient time remains for another counsel to master the case. [*Ibid.* (1955).]

(d) [I]f counsel is instructed in a civil case which clashes with the defence of a prisoner in a serious criminal case, then he must return the brief in the civil case. [*Ibid.* (1961).]

(e) (i) It is the duty of every member of the Bar at all times to uphold the dignity and high standing of his profession, and his own high standing as a member of it.

(ii) It is contrary to professional etiquette for a barrister to do, or cause, or allow to be done, anything for the purpose of touting, directly or indirectly, or which is likely to lead to the reasonable inference that it is done for that purpose.

(iii) While a barrister is entitled to such personal advertisement as is a necessary consequence of the proper exercise of his profession or of any act otherwise properly done by him, it is contrary to professional etiquette for a barrister to do, or cause, or allow to be done, anything with the primary motive of personal advertisement, or anything which is likely to lead to the reasonable inference that it is so motivated. . . .   [*Ibid*. (1967).]

(f) 3. (i) A barrister may not advertise that he is in practice, or that he intends to practise, at the Bar. . . .

8. . . . (iii) A barrister may not give an interview or supply information to the press concerning his life, practice or earnings at the Bar.

(iv) A barrister may not give an interview to the press concerning any legal topic, save with the leave of the Council given in the interests of the profession.
                        [*Ibid*. (1956).]

(g) [A]ny barrister who gave any commission or present to anyone introducing business to him would be guilty of most unprofessional conduct, which would if detected imperil his position as a barrister.   [*Ibid*. (1899–1900).]

4. (h) It is not in accordance with professional etiquette for a barrister who has been instructed to draw pleadings, advise or do drafting work or settle indictments to delegate his responsibility to another. This does not preclude the barrister . . . from seeking any assistance which he may require . . . so long as he makes himself personally responsible for their contents. But he may do this only if he is himself competent to do the work, or if the assistance is limited to one specialist aspect of work, the greater part of which is within his own competence. . . .

7. Nothing [in paragraph 4] . . . applies to work done by a pupil, or to any work which any person requests to be and is allowed by a principal in the same chambers to do in order to increase his own skill or experience. . . .
                        [*Ibid*. (1960).]

(i) [T]he general rule is that a barrister should not appear as an advocate on behalf of a client without the intervention of a solicitor. . . .
                        [*Ibid*. (1904–05).]

(j) . . . [I]t is contrary to the practice of the profession that counsel should accept instructions to advise or settle documents from accountants or persons in similar professions acting on behalf of their clients without the intervention of a solicitor.   [*Ibid*. (1923).]

(k) [I]t is not contrary to the etiquette of the profession for a barrister without the intervention of a solicitor (i) to advise on non-contentious matters whether conveyancing or otherwise, or (ii) to draft wills, conveyances or other non-contentious documents, but it is contrary to etiquette so to conduct any other business which is ordinarily conducted by a solicitor.   [*Ibid*. (1919).]

(l) . . . In non-contentious matters it is permissible, though not desirable, for counsel to advise or prepare drafts without the intervention of a solicitor; but it is contrary to . . . etiquette . . . for counsel to carry through conveyancing matters by sending requisitions, executing deeds, and attending completion. This applies whether remuneration is received or not.   [*Ibid*. (1924).]

(m) A firm of publishers desired to have their intended publications specially read by a barrister in an attempt to safeguard themselves against libel actions, infringement of copyright, offences under the Official Secrets Act and the like. . . . The Council is of opinion that counsel is within his rights in such cases in not insisting upon the intervention of a solicitor so long as there is no question of contentious business. . . .   [*Ibid*. (1934).]

(n) (1) A barrister should not become or continue as a barrister unless he is willing for his practice to be his primary occupation.

(2) A practising barrister should refrain from engaging directly or indirectly in any other occupation, his association with which may adversely affect the reputation of the Bar. . . .   [*Ibid*. (1969–70).]

Rondel v. Worsley
House of Lords [1969] 1 A.C. 191

LORD REID: . . . There is no doubt about the position and duties of a barrister or advocate appearing in court on behalf of a client. It has long been recognised that no counsel is entitled to refuse to act in a sphere in which he practises, and on being tendered a proper fee, for any person however unpopular or even offensive he or his opinions may be, and it is essential that that duty must continue: justice cannot be done and certainly cannot be seen to be done otherwise. If counsel is bound to act for such a person, no reasonable man could think the less of any counsel because of his association with such a client, but, if counsel could pick and choose, his reputation might suffer if he chose to act for such a client, and the client might have great difficulty in obtaining proper legal assistance.

Every counsel has a duty to his client fearlessly to raise every issue, advance every argument, and ask every question, however distasteful, which he thinks will help his client's case. But, as an officer of the court concerned in the administration of justice, he has an overriding duty to the court, to the standards of his profession, and to the public, which may and often does lead to a conflict with his client's wishes or with what the client thinks are his personal interests. Counsel must not mislead the court, he must not lend himself to casting aspersions on the other party or witnesses for which there is no sufficient basis in the information in his possession, he must not withhold authorities or documents which may tell against his clients but which the law or the standards of his profession require him to produce. And by so acting he may well incur the displeasure or worse of his client so that if the case is lost, his client would or might seek legal redress if that were open to him.

Is it in the public interest that barristers and advocates should be protected against such actions? Like so many questions which raise the public interest, a decision one way will cause hardships to individuals while a decision the other way will involve disadvantage to the public interest. On the one hand, if the existing rule of immunity continues there will be cases, rare though they may be, where a client who has suffered loss through the negligence of his counsel will be deprived of a remedy. So the issue appears to me to be whether the abolition of the rule would probably be attended by such disadvantage to the public interest as to make its retention clearly justifiable. I would not expect any counsel to be influenced by the possibility of an action being raised against him to such an extent that he would knowingly depart from his duty to the court or to his profession. But although the line between proper and improper conduct may be easy to state in general terms, it is by no means easy to draw in many borderline cases. At present it can be said with confidence in this country that where there is any doubt the vast majority of counsel put their public duty before the apparent interests of their clients. Otherwise there would not be that implicit trust between the Bench and the Bar which does so much to promote the smooth and speedy conduct of the administration of justice. There may be other countries where conditions are different and there public policy may point in a different direction. But here it would be a grave and dangerous step to make any change which would imperil in any way the confidence which every court rightly puts in all counsel who appear before it.

And there is another factor which I fear might operate in a much greater number of cases. Every counsel in practice knows that daily he is faced with the question whether in his client's interest he should raise a new issue, put another witness in the box, or ask further questions of the witness whom he is examining or cross-examining. That is seldom an easy question but I think that most experienced counsel would agree that the golden rule is—when in doubt stop. Far more cases have been lost by going on too long than by stopping too soon. But the client does not know that. To him brevity may indicate incompetence or negligence and sometimes stopping too soon is an error of judgment. So I think it not at all improbable that the possibility of being sued for negligence would at least subconsciously lead some counsel to undue prolixity which would not only be harmful to the client but against the public interest in prolonging trials. . . .

Immunity from action by the client is not the only way in which it has been thought proper to protect counsel. It has long been established that judge, witnesses and barristers alike have absolute privilege with regard to what is said by them in court: and for reasons similar to those which apply to proceedings in Parliament. If there was ever any doubt about that it was removed by the decision in *Munster* v. *Lamb* where a solicitor was sued for defamatory words which he had spoken while defending an accused person. . . .

It would, in my view, be incongruous if counsel were immune from action by any one other than his client in respect of his conduct in court even where that conduct arose from malice, but yet liable to be sued by his client for negligence. . . .

There are other arguments which support the continuance of the present rule: they do not appear to me to be conclusive, but they do have weight. I shall only mention one. Suppose that, as in the present case, a convicted man sues his counsel. To succeed he must show not only that his counsel was guilty of professional negligence, but also that that negligence caused him loss. The loss would be the fact that he was wrongly convicted by reason of his counsel's negligence. So after the plaintiff's appeal against conviction had been dismissed by the Court of Criminal Appeal, the whole case would in effect have to be retried in a civil court where the standard of proof is different. That is something one would not contemplate with equanimity unless there is a real need for it. . . . The main reasons on which I have based my opinion relate to the position of counsel while engaged in litigation, when his public duty and his duty to his client may conflict. But there are many kinds of work undertaken by counsel where no such conflict would emerge, and there I see little reason why the liability of counsel should be different from that of members of any other profession who give their professional advice and services to their clients. The members of every profession are bound to act honourably and in accordance with the recognised standards of their profession. But that does not, in my view, give rise to any such conflict of duties as can confront counsel while engaged in litigation. . . .

Queen's Counsel

A Queen's Counsel is a senior barrister who has been awarded this status by the Lord Chancellor. Barristers who wish to become Queen's Counsel have to make an application and it is then for the Lord Chancellor in his discretion in the light of the barrister's experience and standing at the Bar to decide if he should be appointed a Queen's Counsel. It is common for barristers to apply aften ten years at the Bar. One object in applying is to free oneself from the paper work of preparing pleadings which is a part of the bread and butter of a junior barrister and to be in a position to charge higher fees and so reduce the load of work generally. The decision when to apply thus turns on a calculation as to whether at the higher fees he will retain a sufficient number of clients to make the move sensible.

One rule which applies to them, which makes Queen's Counsel even more expensive is that they cannot appear in court alone but must be accompanied by a junior. The system was defended by the Bar Council in 1965 in a memorandum entitled *The two counsel rule*, June 14, 1965.

> From the point of view of the junior Bar, the merit of the division between leaders and juniors is that the present system skims off each year a score or so busy juniors and thus ensures that the work of the junior is spread downwards through the ranks. Capable juniors are given the opportunity to acquire wider and deeper experience which fits them in turn for advancement. The system thus keeps both parts of the Bar in a healthy state of competitiveness. Court work is not confined to the specialist advocate, the Q.C., but except in the weightiest cases is well spread among juniors. . . .

> The existence of Q.C.s as a class of barrister—about one tenth of those in practice— is advantageous to higher authority as well. . . . The system provides a body of outstanding practitioners, not too numerous to prevent them becoming individually known to the judges, which acts as a reservoir for recruitment to the Bench. It is commonplace for Q.C.s to be invited by government authorities to undertake responsible duties. The status of Q.C. . . . is dependent upon his professional function being different from the majority of the Bar.

An annual general meeting of the Bar in 1971 resolved:

1. That the present two-tier system made up of Queen's Counsel and Junior Counsel should be retained.
2. That the two-counsel rule should be retained, except as regards drafting, without relaxation.
3. That as regards drafting by silks a new rule should be substituted . . . :
   " In general the drafting of documents is appropriate to Junior Counsel only and a Queen's Counsel should in general refuse all such work; but a Queen's Counsel is at liberty to draft letters or parts of documents where the drafting depends wholly or mainly on his own investigation and is ancillary to advice given by him and provided that the length of the draft and the other circumstances of the case are such as not to conflict with the intendment of the general rule; and he is at liberty in consultation with a Junior to settle any draft."
4. That the present formula for the remuneration of Junior Counsel when led should be cancelled and it should merely be stated that the junior should be paid a " proper fee."

Lawyer and Litigant in England, R. E. Megarry

Hamlyn Lectures, No. 14. Stevens, 1962

As an institution, silk has a number of merits for the client. It is a generally recognised guarantee of competence as an advocate and of experience in the law. Silks also can give more time to difficult problems than is usually possible for busy juniors. In most cases "leading counsel's opinion" is (very properly) accorded greater respect than a junior's opinion, even if the junior is very senior. For the Bar, however, silk has its disadvantages; . . . Nobody can know the detailed figures, but probably out of a batch of fifteen silks, the result five years later may be that one has risen to great heights, four have done really well, six are firmly established without being overworked, and the remaining four have never really got going in the front row. For the last four there is no hope of going back to the junior Bar. . . . Sometimes the trouble is self-misjudgment. . . . Sometimes the difficulty is that of supply and demand; . . . But whatever the reason is not the system wasteful and cruel?

It is difficult to answer otherwise than Yes. Almost by definition a man must be a successful junior to be given silk at all. . . . [I]s it not wasteful for some four good juniors to be lost each year to so small a Bar as we have in England? Yet there seems no easy solution. Abolish the rules that distinguish silks from juniors, and you extinguish the reality of silk. What is more you abolish much of the specialisation of function. In any case, the edge is taken off the problems . . . by the opportunities that open with silk. There are many full-time and important part-time legal appointments short of the High Court Bench to which a silk may aspire. . . . Nor are the letters "Q.C." any disqualification for many positions outside the law. . . . There is a price to pay for our system, but it is not exorbitant. . . .

The barrister's clerk

The lawyer's pound of flesh, M. Zander

Sunday Times, October 27, 1968

The man with real control over fees is the barrister's clerk. He controls the flow through chambers, its distribution to the different barristers working there, and all financial negotiations. . . . Unlike the barrister himself, the clerk is not bound by any ethical or disciplinary code. He is free from all restraints, other than his well-tuned sense of what the market will bear. He often has no formal education to speak of, and is unqualified for his job by anything other than experience. Yet the senior clerk in good chambers will often be in the £5,000 to £10,000 a year bracket, depending on how much work he can get for his stable of barristers. Some have identified the commission basis of paying clerks as possibly the most objectionable single aspect of Bar etiquette. It is aggravated by the fact that the client does not do battle himself when counsel's fees are being negotiated. This task is in the hands of a man with no personal interest in keeping the barrister's fee down—namely, his solicitor. The solicitor is an inadequate counterpoise for the clerk's temptation to demand excessive fees. By this same token the Bar has tolerated, and even promoted, a system whereby clerks knowingly take on far more work for their principals than they can possibly complete. This has several consequences, none of them to the public's benefit. It means that all too often there has to be a last minute change of counsel. A solicitor, who has given a brief to barrister A, is told that an earlier case is lasting longer than expected and will prevent barrister A from taking his case to court. In these circumstances, barrister A's clerk is supposed to give the solicitor enough warning for him to get another barrister. But in practice, notice is commonly given so late that a solicitor's only course is to take another barrister from the same chambers. This is obviously the result most beneficial to the clerk himself. But the client may have only the clerk's word that barrister B is as competent in the field as barrister A. The Law Society has elaborated the point: " Shortly before the hearing the lay client may find that his case is in the hands of a young and possibly inexperienced barrister whom he has never met, in whom he may have little or no confidence and who has had but a few hours overnight, or in some cases no time at all, to acquaint himself with the case." . . . The Law Society has said that " it even sometimes happens that chambers provide substitute counsel without the prior consent of the solicitor." Clerks have also been known to accept work suspecting that the barrister specified will not be able to undertake it, but relying on their ability to get the work assigned to another man in chambers. If partnership were permitted at the Bar, the clerk's power could be checked. He would become simply an office manager and the partners themselves would allot the work. Likewise, if there were not a virtual prohibition on advertising, solicitors would be less dependent on clerks than they are now for information about the special skills of particular counsel. A modest amount of publicity among lawyers would be to the benefit of the public. With barristers this might take the form of a circular at least to solicitors listing the qualifications, appointments, important cases and specialities of the men in any given set of chambers. Certainly, in the absence of such positive measures, the grip of the clerk will not be loosened.[8]

The right of audience
Royal Commission on Assizes and Quarter Sessions 1966–69. Written evidence
Cmnd. 4153

At the time when the Beeching Commission reported, the right of audience at Quarter Sessions was governed by each individual court. Solicitors had equal rights of audience in seven courts; in others solicitors were permitted to appear when there were insufficient barristers present. In the great majority barristers had the exclusive right to appear. The Law Society and the Bar Council both included in their memoranda their views on the subject.

Memorandum of the Law Society (Written Evidence No. 47)

29. Out of the 64 (out of 111) Local Law Societies in the provinces who responded to an invitation to submit memoranda, the Council received strong representations from 37 Local Law Societies that a right of audience to solicitors should be permitted at all Courts of Quarter Sessions or at substitute courts of similar jurisdiction; 11 Local Law Societies did not favour a change, and 4 suggested a limited right of audience. . . .

38. Among the reasons given by those favouring an extention of rights of audience to solicitors were:

---

[8] This article led to a reply by Desmond Ackner, Q.C., in the *Sunday Times*, November 3, 1968. He said, *inter alia*: " The statement that the clerk controls the flow of work in chambers and its distribution to the different barristers working there is, for the most part, false. Solicitors normally send briefs to chambers marked with the name of individual counsel. If that counsel is not available, the clerk may, and often does, suggest that the brief be transferred to another member of chambers. The solicitor may agree. But if he does not agree, the brief must be returned to him. In a few cases, mostly involving criminal defences, and often where notice of trial is given for the following day, solicitors may be content, and indeed grateful, for the clerk to select the appropriate member of chambers."

(a) Solicitors have a statutory right to appear as advocates in Magistrates' Courts. If a solicitor is considered competent to conduct a case before a Magistrates' Court, he ought also to be considered competent to conduct the same case where the accused elects trial by jury at Quarter Sessions.

(b) A solicitor who prosecutes in the Magistrates' Court may not deal with the same case, upon the same facts and the same evidence when there is a committal for trial at Quarter Sessions, or committal only for sentence, or when the case is the subject of an appeal, although neither the additional expense nor the change of advocate can be justified.

(c) In cases where the accused is committed for trial at Quarter Sessions, or is committed for sentence only, Counsel must be instructed albeit that a solicitor has conducted the proceedings in the Magistrates' Court, that a plea of guilty is to be tendered, that the role of the advocate is to plead in mitigation of sentence, and that the case does not warrant the additional expense incurred.

(d) Where a solicitor appears as advocate in civil proceedings in a Magistrates' Court (for example, in affiliation proceedings) or conducts a case tried summarily, and it becomes necessary to appeal to Quarter Sessions, there must be a change of advocate at additional expense to conduct the appeal, although the facts and arguments will be the same, and the change of advocacy may be to the disadvantage of the appellant.

(e) In a high proportion of cases it is not possible to obtain from those of the appropriate Circuit Mess the services of suitable Counsel. Often a willing but young and inexperienced barrister takes over the conduct of a case from an experienced and senior solicitor-advocate.

(f) One result of ensuring a right of audience to solicitors in a greater range of cases would be an easing of the problem which flows from the present shortage of barristers and would enable barristers to devote more time to and to accept a greater number of the more substantial types of case.

39. Among the reasons given by those opposed to a change in the present practice were:

(a) The root problem was the present arrangements for the disposal of the increasing volume of business in the Civil and Criminal Courts. If these could be improved so as incidentally to ensure a greater availability of Counsel, the question of rights of representation would be less pressing.

(b) It was vital and in the public interest to preserve a strong body of specialist advocates. Courts of Quarter Sessions provided the range and variety of cases from which specialist experience in advocacy could best be obtained.

(c) There was often an advantage to the client in obtaining a fresh view on the merits of a case or on the way in which it should be presented at the higher Court. If a general right of audience existed, the right to seek Counsel's assistance might be restricted or excluded altogether.

(d) In considering the interests of the public, the saving of expense was not necessarily the primary factor.

(e) With their present commitments, many solicitors would be hard-pressed to undertake more advocacy, and an extension of rights of audience would have no practical effect.

40. The force and validity of the opposing arguments summarised in paragraphs 38 and 39 are self-evident and they are not easy to reconcile. The Council have no doubt that the public interest requires a competent, healthy and independent Bar and that its present strength requires to be substantially increased; they are equally of opinion, as matters now stand, that there is a case in the public interest for some extension of the rights of audience. The Council

believe, however, that the problem can best be considered in the context of such recommendations in respect of any proposed new structure of the Civil and Criminal Courts as the Royal Commission may decide to make when there could then be taken into account, for example, particular local problems, the availability of Local Bars and the sufficiency of suitable advocates generally.

Memorandum of the General Council of the Bar (Written Evidence No. 32)

39. It has been suggested in some of the evidence already submitted to the Commission that it would be in the public interest if all Quarter Sessions were open to solicitor advocates. . . .

41. . . . It is we believe envisaged that if solicitors had this right of audience they would conduct the simpler cases and in particular the pleas of guilty, and it is argued that this would save expense and relieve pressure on the Bar. If pleas of guilty were conducted by solicitors there would be a saving in expense, but we doubt if this would apply to contested cases. We have little doubt that the conduct of pleas of guilty would be only the beginning and that gradually much of the Quarter Sessions advocacy would be taken over by solicitors. If this occurred the effect on the Bar would undoubtedly be very serious and on many local Bars disastrous.

42. . . . [A]dvocates are not made overnight; . . . . At present the newly called young barrister who is going into the general type of practice in Courts of Assizes and Quarter Sessions cuts his teeth at Quarter Sessions. He starts by doing the very simple pleas of guilty, and then gradually as he finds his feet and acquires the skills of his trade solicitors entrust him with the more complex cases. Solicitors already have right of audience in all Magistrates' Courts, County Courts and many administrative tribunals. Undefended divorce going to the County Court will greatly increase their scope for advocacy with a corresponding loss to junior members of the Bar. If now there is to be taken away the simpler if not all the work at Quarter Sessions, how is the young man to start, how is he to learn his trade and how is he to earn a living in the early years?

43. You cannot have a strong healthy Bar and at the same time take away all the nourishment from its young. The results will be that young men will not come to the Bar. . . .

44. We have no doubt there would be a considerable falling off in the standards of advocacy and a consequential adverse effect upon the administration of justice. Advocacy is a very highly specialised art and flourishes with constant practice. Under the present system it is practised by men who are engaged upon it full-time. If solicitors had a general right of audience at Quarter Sessions, many of the advocates then appearing before the Court would be conducting only the occasional case with the result that they could hardly hope to do it as skilfully as those who are now engaged upon the work full-time. The criminal law is technical and the rules of evidence are not easy to master. A mistake by an advocate such as leading inadmissible evidence or putting in character when he should not can be a costly business necessitating the discharge of the jury and a re-trial. Mistakes of this character would be bound to happen with far more frequency if inexperienced advocates conducted cases. We do not suggest that solicitors never make good advocates—of course some solicitors are excellent advocates. But it is not their speciality and so long as our system of trial continues to demand a high degree of expertise on the part of the advocate then so long will it be to the great advantage of the public to have their cases conducted by the Bar.

45. We do realise that in parts of the country there is a need for the Bar to expand to meet the present demand on its services. The position is however considerably aggravated, and the true shortage made to appear more acute than it is, by the present administrative arrangements. . . .

46. The number of those entering practice at the Bar is rising steadily. At the 1st October 1959 the total number in practice was 1,919; it has increased every year since that date and in October 1966 the number in practice was 2,239. A survey of the needs of the profession is being undertaken by the Senate of the Inns of Court and we are confident that recruitment can be encouraged and the Bar expanded to meet the needs of the community. It would be tragic if, because the swing of the pendulum of demand had for the moment slightly overreached the supply, a reform should be introduced which might result in destroying the structure of the Bar.

The Lord Chancellor has issued two Practice Directions on the subject under section 12 of the Courts Act 1971 the first, dated December 7, 1971 [[1972] 1 W.L.R. 5] provides:

1. Solicitors may appear in, conduct, defend and address the court in proceedings mentioned in paragraph 2 of this direction at any sitting of the Crown Court at Caernarvon, Barnstaple, Bodmin, Doncaster or (subject to paragraph 3 hereof) Lincoln.

2. The proceedings in which solicitors may exercise the right of audience conferred by paragraph 1 of this direction are: (a) appeals from magistrates' courts; (b) proceedings on committal of a person for sentence or to be dealt with; (c) proceedings in respect of the offences included in class 4 in the directions given by Lord Widgery C.J. with the concurrence of the Lord Chancellor under sections 4 (5) and 5 (4) of the Courts Act 1971 and reported *Practice Direction (Crime: Crown Court Business)* [1971] W.L.R. 1535; and (d) proceedings under the original or appellate civil jurisdiction of the Crown Court.

3. The right of audience conferred by paragraph 1 of this direction in respect of sittings of the Crown Court at Lincoln shall extend only to proceedings falling within paragraph 2 hereof: (a) on appeal from, or on committal by, a magistrates' court in the County of the Parts of Holland, or (b) which would, but for the passing of the Courts Act 1971, have fallen to be heard by the court of quarter sessions for that county in the exercise of its original or appellate civil jurisdiction.

The second, dated February 9, 1972 [[1972] 1 W.L.R. 307] provides:

1. A solicitor may appear in, conduct, defend and address the court in:

   (a) criminal proceedings in the Crown Court on appeal from a magistrates' court or on committal of a person for sentence or to be dealt with, if he, or any partner of his, or any solicitor in his employment or by whom he is employed, appeared on behalf of the defendant in the magistrates' court;
   (b) civil proceedings in the Crown Court on appeal from a magistrates' court if he, or any partner of his, or any solicitor in his employment or by whom he is employed, appeared in the proceedings in the magistrates' court.

Counsel's fees

Final Report of the Committee on Supreme Court Practice and Procedure

Cmd. 8878 (1953)

45. . . . [T]he evidence has led us to conclude that members of the Bar generally, having regard to their training and to their standards of skill and responsibility, are not over-paid for the work that they do. Instances no doubt occur—more often in cases tried before arbitrators or other special tribunals than

in cases before the Courts—in which very large fees are charged, and these instances gain disproportionate notoriety from their publication (not always accurately) in the Press. But the evidence in our judgment establishes that in the general run of ordinary cases the fees charged on the briefs are reasonable fees. In the few and exceptional cases the high fees are charged by and paid to a few and exceptional or " fashionable " counsel. It is undoubtedly the fact that some litigants insist on being represented by one of these renowned names and that the holders of these names are in a measure compelled for their own protection to make high charges.

46. . . . [I]f the profession is to continue to attract, as it must and should, those of high intellect and character, the reward for long training, skill and extremely hard work must be at the least reasonably attractive.

48. It was also accepted that, as between the litigant (acting through his solicitor) and the barrister, the fee to be charged by the latter must remain a matter of bargain and the majority of the Committee were not satisfied of the desirability or practicability of the establishment, from among members of the Bar itself, of a reviewing authority to decide upon the proper amount of the fee where the circumstances had been such as to impair in some measure bargaining freedom on the solicitor's part. . . .

49. But our study of the schedules [8a] to which we have alluded convinced us that the position in regard to refreshers, i.e., fees paid in addition to the brief fees in cases lasting more than a full day, was not satisfactory. We were satisfied that the system of charging refreshers was, as such, in the interest of the litigants, for thereby the brief fee can be fixed at a lower figure and need not be one sufficient to compensate the barrister however long the case may last (a matter not infrequently very difficult of estimate). But it was noticeable in the schedules that when large amounts were taxed off a winner's bill in respect of counsel's fees, a high proportion was generally attributable to refresher fees. Here we think there is cause on the litigant's part, as things now stand, for reasonable grievance; and we think the grievance is largely attributable to the fact that refresher fees are commonly not fixed at the same time as the brief fee but, perhaps, hurriedly arranged as the case is about to open.

50. . . . We recommend . . . that henceforth the fees payable in respect of refreshers shall, in default of express agreement evidenced by marking on the brief, be related to the brief fees by means of a fixed and descending scale with an over-all maximum for every completed day in addition to the first.

SOLICITORS

The solicitor is traditionally regarded as belonging to the junior branch of the profession, but in terms of numbers, the amount and importance of the work done, and contact with the public, he of course represents the more important branch. However much the quality and character of the legal system, especially in its upper reaches may depend on those of the Bar, no Bar however able or high-minded could maintain its quality or integrity without the support of the vast body of lawyers who are responsible for the day to day working of the law and who are in daily contact with those who need its services.

The responsibility for securing that the requisite number of solicitors is available and for maintaining their quality and integrity has been placed by statute, at present the Solicitors Acts 1957 and 1965, on the Law Society. It is responsible for enrolling solicitors, for prescribing the qualifications and setting examinations, issuing practising certificates and preserving minimum

[8a] Summarising bills presented for taxation in a number of cases.

standards of behaviour. It also runs a compensation fund for those who have suffered from the wrongful acts and defaults of solicitors and supervises the charges made by solicitors for their work. In addition it has statutory responsibility under the Legal Aid and Advice Act 1949 for running the legal aid and advice scheme. This is quite apart from its role as a trade union, which it shares with the British Legal Association established in 1964. Membership of the Law Society in its trade union capacity is voluntary, though about 90 per cent. of practising solicitors belong. Even a great number of the 10 per cent. who belong to the BLA apparently also belong to the Law Society.

Solicitors like barristers must have passed a qualifying examination. A university law degree is not yet necessary, though those who have one will usually be exempt from part of the qualifying examinations. There is at present a further requirement of two or three years in articles with a solicitor though the whole question as to whether this period of practical training should be replaced by some form of institutional training has been in the melting pot for some time. One of the recommendations of the Ormrod Committee was that the universities in future should be associated with some form of institutional professional training in addition to the legal education they already give in their degree courses. The professions have shown themselves unwilling to release this part of a lawyer's training to the universities and are seeking financially viable ways to undertake this very considerable task themselves.

Unlike barristers, solicitors work in firms either for a salary or as partners for a share in the profits. Like barristers however, their special position is protected by a number of monopoly privileges. No one other than a solicitor may issue a writ or process in any court on behalf of another person; no one other than a solicitor can draw documents under seal for gain (though a layman or anyone else can do this if he does not charge a fee). This also applies to the preparation of an instrument for the purpose of land registration or for probate.[9] The monopoly which solicitors have as regards conveyancing is important because profits from conveyancing make up a large part of a solicitor's general profits and often help to subsidise less remunerative work. The fact that conveyancing fees have in the past been charged on a scale which varies with the value of the house conveyed has also meant that solicitors' profits have steadily risen with the rise in house prices.

Unlike barristers the fees charged by solicitors are to a considerable extent regulated by outside bodies or are subject to scrutiny by outside bodies. In the case of contentious business, *i.e.* that which has to do with litigation, they are laid down by three committees: the Supreme Court Rule Committee, the County Court Rule Committee and the Matrimonial Causes Rule Committee. Those for the Supreme Court are set out in Order 62 of the Rules of the Supreme Court. The criteria for non-contentious business are set out in section 56 of the Solicitors Act 1957 and are embodied in Solicitors Remuneration Orders by the Non-Contentious Rules Committee. Section 56 provides:

(4) An Order under this section may, as regards the mode of

---

[9] See Solicitors Act 1957, s. 20.

remuneration, prescribe that it shall be according to a scale of rates of commission or percentage, varying or not in different classes of business, or by a gross sum, or by a fixed sum for each document prepared or perused, without regard to length, or in any other mode, or partly in one mode and partly in another, and may regulate the amount of remuneration with reference to all or any of the following, among other, considerations, that is to say—

(a) the position of the party for whom the solicitor is concerned in the business, that is, whether as vendor or purchaser, lessor or lessee, mortgagor or mortgagee, and the like;

(b) the place where, and the circumstances in which, the business or any part thereof is transacted;

(c) the amount of the capital money or rent to which the business relates;

(d) the skill, labour and responsibility involved therein on the part of the solicitor;

(e) the number and importance of the documents prepared or perused, without regard to length.

The charges made by solicitors, and solicitors' incomes generally, have recently been the subject of three reports of the now defunct Prices and Incomes Board. One of the points it made repeatedly was that in its view there should be a closer relation than existed at the time it reported between the profits of a particular kind of work and the time and capital invested in it. It was particularly critical of the way in which conveyancing charges made up a disproportionate portion of a solicitor's income compared with the costs and expense in skill and time devoted to it. Criticism of the general level of conveyancing charges, which had in the past been dealt with as a special item so far as charging for non-contentious business was concerned, led the Lord Chancellor to announce in March 1972 that instead of the fixed scale fees conveyancing charges should be dealt with on the same basis as other non-contentious business. There is now therefore a single order governing non-contentious business; the Solicitors Remuneration Order 1972, which provides:

2. A solicitor's remuneration for non-contentious business (including business under the Land Registration Act 1925) shall be such sum as may be fair and reasonable having regard to all the circumstances of the case, and in particular to—

(i) the complexity of the matter or the difficulty or novelty of the questions raised;

(ii) the skill, labour, specialised knowledge and responsibility involved;

(iii) the time spent on the business;

(iv) the number and importance of the documents prepared or perused, without regard to length;

(v) the place where and the circumstances in which the business or any part thereof is transacted;

(vi) the amount or value of any money or property involved;

(vii) whether any land involved is registered land within the meaning of the Land Registration Act 1925; and

(viii) the importance of the matter to the client.

3. (1) Without prejudice to the provisions of sections 69, 70 and 71 of the Solicitors Act 1957 (which relate to taxation of costs) the client may require the solicitor to obtain a certificate from The Law Society stating that in their opinion the sum charged is fair and reasonable or, as the case may be, what other sum would be fair and reasonable, and in the absence of taxation the sum stated in the certificate, if less than that charged, shall be the sum payable by the client.

(2) Before the solicitor brings proceedings to recover costs on a bill for non-contentious business he must, unless the costs have been taxed, have informed the client in writing—

(i) of his right under paragraph (1) of this article to require the solicitor to obtain a certificate from The Law Society, and

(ii) of the provisions of the Solicitors Act 1957 relating to taxation of costs.

(3) The client shall not be entitled to require the solicitor to obtain a certificate from The Law Society under paragraph (1) of this article:

(i) after the expiry of one month from the date on which the client was given the information required by paragraph (2) of this article;

(ii) after a bill has been delivered and paid; or

(iii) after the High Court has ordered the bill to be taxed.

4. (1) On the taxation of any bill delivered under this Order it shall be the duty of the solicitor to satisfy the taxing officer as to the fairness and reasonableness of the sum charged.

(2) If the taxing officer allows less than one half of the sum charged, he shall bring the facts of the case to the attention of The Law Society.

5. (1) After the expiry of one month from the delivery of any bill for non-contentious business a solicitor may charge interest on the amount of the bill (including any disbursements) at a rate not exceeding the rate for the time being payable on judgment debts, so, however, that before interest may be charged the client must have been given the information required by article 3 (2) of this Order.

(2) If an application is made for the bill to be taxed or the solicitor is required to obtain a certificate from The Law Society, interest shall be calculated by reference to the amount finally ascertained.

6. A solicitor may take from his client security for the payment of any remuneration, including the amount of any interest to which the solicitor may become entitled under article 5 of this Order. . . .

It has yet to be seen what effect this will have on the general level of conveyancing charges and to what extent it will give rise to a variation of charges between different solicitors of which the lay client can take advantage.

The reports of the National Board for Prices and Incomes

While it was in existence the Prices and Incomes Board made three reports on solicitors in particular in relation to their charges, in February

1968,[10] in November 1969[11] and in March 1971.[12]   Both barristers and solicitors were also subject of a report by the Monopolies Commission on Professional Services in October 1970.[13]   The virtue of the reports of the Prices and Incomes Board lies not so much in their conclusions which on many points were hotly disputed by the professions, but, as to some extent with the Beeching Commission in its consideration of the court system, for its attempt to take a global look at the profession as a whole, in terms of manpower, organisation, overall income and methods of charging. As a result, like Beeching, it provides a useful starting point for looking at the profession as a whole in a broader, if rather flatter perspective. It is also a useful reminder that the profession is more like a bank than a public service. It is a business as well as a profession.

Report No. 54 of the National Board for Prices and Incomes
Cmnd. 3529 (1968)

27. . . . [T]he income received by principals in private practice averages £4,870 per annum. The median income is £4,180. A quarter of the principals receive less than £2,640 and another quarter more than £6,135 per annum. Sole practitioners earn slightly more on average than individual partners in a two-man practice. But apart from that, incomes are higher the greater number of partners in the practice—the highest being found in Central London practices with five or more partners. Taking income by area, Midland practices fare best, and those in Wales and the West least well. . . .

29. . . . [T]he net income of partners increases as the ratio of executive staff to partners increases. Indeed, for the smallest practices, where the number of fee earners cannot economically be increased, there is evidently an economy of scale to be derived from amalgamation of practices.

30. Another way of looking at the size of practices is not in terms of manpower but in terms of capital invested. Again the size and profitability go together—the larger the capital invested, the greater the profitability. The average amount of capital invested in their practices by solicitors in private practice is £7,000. . . .   Nearly a quarter of the profession has less than £2,000 in capital. Another quarter has more than £10,000. The relationship between capital and income varies widely in individual cases, but there is some correlation between low incomes and small amounts of capital and between high incomes and large amounts of capital. Thus, two-thirds of those earning less than £3,000 have less than £3,000 invested, while four-fifths of those earning more than £6,000 have more than £6,000 invested.

31. . . . [M]ovements in revenue, expense and profits for the practices with at least five partners in Central London are quite different from those of other practices. In 1965 their revenue increased faster than their expense, thereby enabling profits to increase by 15 per cent. over 1964. In 1966, however, expense rose faster than revenue, and profits increased by only 2 per cent. Profits of the sole practitioner have fallen by 4 per cent. in the last two years, while those for the largest practices (excluding those in Central London) have risen by 6 per cent. Thus the trend in revenue and profits is moving in favour of large practices.

---

10 Cmnd. 3529.
11 Cmnd. 4217.
12 Cmnd. 4624.
13 Cmnd. 4463.

32. It appears that the larger practices in the large towns attract more remunerative work and, therefore, earn higher profits. But in our opinion this factor is not sufficient to invalidate the conclusion that larger units are in themselves more profitable because they are more economical. The various figures cited above seem to indicate that an increase in the size of practices, which enables the practice to organise its work on a more specialised basis, leads to a more effective use of manpower and, therefore, to a reduction in expense. The question is whether or not it is desirable and practicable to carry this tendency further. If it is, then solicitors' income can be increased without an increase in externally determined charges.

33. Specialisation is recognised in the profession as an important and inevitable development. The Secretary-General of the Law Society, in a Paper written in 1965, said that for both economic reasons and because of the public need for greater expertise from the profession and speed of execution, lawyers in general practice would have to specialise to a much greater extent than at present. The Society's President in his inaugural address at the annual conference in October of last year also referred to this development. But the President went on to explain the limitations to the extent of specialisation and to the formation of larger practices. This point of view was strongly put to us in oral evidence by the Council of the Law Society.

34. The argument over how far specialisation can go stems from a preference for a solicitor/client relationship based on a general professional and personal service, and from the desirability of maintaining a sufficient number of practices spread throughout the country so that everyone, even in relatively thinly populated areas, can have a choice of several fairly easily accessible solicitors.

35. These points are, in fact, at variance with developments within the profession itself. The full personal service of a general practitioner would obviously apply only in the one-man practice, and these solicitors are in a minority. We have already seen that the profession as a whole specialises in conveyancing and probate; many of the operations entailed in conveyancing—and we have been told by the Law Society that there are 73 possible steps in the process—are delegated to legal executives or to articled clerks. Once a practice expands beyond one man, the opportunity to specialise inevitably increases. We should point out that amalgamation to facilitate specialisation does not necessarily mean that work has to be centralised in one place, or the disappearance of the local solicitor's office. What specialisation could mean (apart from helping to spread overheads, through, for example, the centralisation of office machinery) is that the local solicitor would have easier and cheaper access to specialist help. No doubt, larger groupings would to some extent inhibit a client's choice of firm and might mean a longer journey to his solicitor than at present. But we do not consider these factors to be unreasonable if they are the result of measures which keep down costs to the community as a whole. There are, of course, limits to which this process can be carried but there is no doubt that so far little progress has been made.

36. We do not suggest that solicitors can necessarily go to the same lengths as accountants, who have begun to establish themselves as groups both in provincial and in international centres as well as in London, though a few London firms of solicitors do have offices in the provinces and some have started to open branches in Common Market capitals. But we do suggest that their failure to adapt the form of practice to events rather than lack of increases in scale charges has led to the diversion of much tax law work to accountants and held back the expansion of the solicitors' profession.

37. The formation of larger practices will permit the increased use of subprofessional staff—i.e. staff without the full professional training and professional

judgment of a qualified solicitor. There is difficulty in obtaining suitable executive staff with the requisite training and at the rates of pay which solicitors now offer. . . . A substantial increase in the devolution of work to executives would mean that they would have to receive considerably higher rewards. . . .

38. The apparent scope for amalgamation of firms seems to us to throw doubt on the 1965 estimate of a shortage of 5,000 solicitors which was, as we have said, based on an enquiry among solicitors carried out in 1963. We think it likely that this estimate was based on a traditional conception of a solicitor's practice. Therefore, we do not consider it should play any part in our consideration of the level of statutorily determined charges. Nor do we consider that such estimates should in the future be made by the profession without assistance. They should clearly be made in concert with independent advisers and with due regard to the Ministry of Labour's estimates of manpower resources.

39. We would, however, add one qualification though it does not of itself change our conclusion. Solicitors, rather on the same lines as doctors, provide a service which may well be required by all sections of the population. But we have had evidence to show that, in practice, the services are largely provided to the professional and middle income groups with the exception of conveyancing and litigation. Nevertheless, we think it likely that there is, indeed, a large volume of potential and unrecognised demand for legal services, which, if it were brought to the surface, might generate a burden of largely unremunerative work for the profession. We understand a number of possible ideas are under examination. One, for example, is the appointment of salaried solicitors, possibly on the model of the neighbourhood law firms set up in the United States as part of the programme of the war on poverty. We cannot say what extension of legal services might result from experiments of this kind. The numbers of solicitors involved would clearly depend on the kind of organisation adopted. At the moment we content ourselves with noting that the profession's own estimate of the deficiency in its ranks rests on a traditional rather than a forward-looking view of its clientele and organisation. . . .

Conveyancing charges

49. The fact that, even with a charge determined from outside, conveyancing should be so profitable . . . leads us . . . to conclude that certain practices now surrounding the charge should be changed. . . . The fixed charge is, in practice, treated as a minimum. . . . Solicitors should have freedom to ask for less from their clients. . . .

50. The argument advanced against the form of competition we have recommended is that it will lead to a reduction in the quality of work. We see no reason why there should be a guarantee of quality inherent in a fixed charge which is absent in a competitive one. Quality in professional work depends on professional standards.

51. . . . [T]here is also the question of competition from outside. . . . There are those who, though unqualified, have tried to break through the present restrictions and have offered limited conveyancing services at less than the normal charge. These attempts have failed fully to satisfy the courts as to their legality. But apart from this there are at every stage possible legal difficulties which may have a considerable effect on the enjoyment of his title by the buyer. . . . Conveyancing consists not only of a contract to buy, and of the conveyance itself, but of a considerable process of research into issues of various kinds, e.g. in the planning field. Though in practice it may be rare for these issues to raise serious legal problems, they can do so and can cause great difficulty for buyer and seller. It may well be that law reform holds the key to this type of problem. . . . Meanwhile, it is only a minority of clients who can manage

without the help of a qualified solicitor. We cannot, therefore, conclude that the time has yet come to suggest that there should be free competition from the unqualified outsider. . . .

Report No. 164 of the National Board for Prices and Incomes
Cmnd. 4624 (1971)

10. In 1966, at the time of our first survey of the profession, there were 19,223 solicitors in private practice and about 6,720 practices. The profession's gross revenue totalled about £170 million. By 1968 the number of solicitors in private practice had increased to 20,451 but there were fewer practices—about 6,580— indicating some consolidation of the profession into larger units. Even so, 40 per cent of practices were still run by sole practitioners and fewer than 10 per cent had more than four principals. Gross revenue increased in the period to over £200 million. A principal in private practice in 1966 had, on average, a pre-tax profit income of £4,870 (including interest on capital); this had risen by about 5 per cent per annum to £5,373 in 1968.[14]

11. We found in 1966 that conveyancing (including mortgage work) accounted for 56 per cent of the total revenue of solicitors (though only 41 per cent of total expense) while a further 28 per cent of income came from probate, administration of estates, legal advice and other non-contentious work. Litigation was much less remunerative and some of it was done at a loss: overall, it contributed about 18 per cent to income but 27 per cent to the profession's total expense. Since then, charges for County Court and legal advice work have been increased. Conveyancing is more profitable than the other work undertaken by solicitors despite the fact that the charges remain unchanged over long periods. The effect of the *ad valorem* scales is to link conveyancing charges with rises in property values (which as a rule rise faster than prices and costs in the economy generally). On average, conveyancing scale charges rise at about 60 per cent of the rate of increase in property values. This link, coupled with a growing volume of business, has helped the profession to keep up with inflation even when, as in 1966–68, fairly substantial increases in overheads due to S.E.T. and other rising costs have had to be met. . . .

71. In our first survey in 1966, we found that [conveyancing] charges were greater than expense, even after allowing for principals' average profit, by 36 per cent or about £24 million. The present survey confirms that the disparity between charge and expense has not diminished. . . .

72. On the other hand, we had no evidence that levels of remuneration over the professions as a whole are too high. Conveyancing profits are used to subsidise other less remunerative forms of work. The nature of a solicitor's work is such that it is neither desirable nor practicable to attempt to eliminate cross-subsidation completely, though . . . there are serious disadvantages in the extent of the present imbalance. If some classes of work are less profitable than others, this bears harshly on solicitors with a high proportion of such work, and from the point of view of the community the work itself may become neglected in favour of more remunerative work. . . . Equally, if some classes of work are particularly profitable, clients who want such work done are called on to pay more than its costs and so, in effect, to pay for some of the work done for other clients. This is the position in conveyancing today. We therefore continue to regard it as a desirable object of policy . . . to achieve a closer relationship

---

[14] In Report No. 134 it noted: " The average economic rate for principal's time (*i.e.* the amount required to cover overheads and secure the present mean income) is about £6 per hour of productive work."

between charge and expense for each class of legal service—though the profitability of conveyancing overall is so great that progress can be made only gradually. . . . .

The future control of solicitors' charges

100. . . . The criteria which the four statutory committees are required to apply in fixing scales of charges are not clear and their implementation is a matter of judgment. The members of the statutory committees have little means of collecting objective, quantified information. Moreover the committees take decisions in isolation from one another and without adequate information either about the broad trends in the profession's income and in those parts of it which are their own responsibility, or about the profession's manpower needs or the community's needs for particular services.

101. It seems inevitable that the statutory control of litigation and legal advice charges will continue in view of the Government's responsibility for the administration of justice and for financing legal aid work. . . . The question therefore arises whether, with the ending of the standing reference to the Board, the determination of statutory charges should be left once more entirely to the statutory committees on the lines previously followed. Our experience suggests strongly that this would not be satisfactory. Nor, we think, would it be acceptable to the profession, who feel that in an age of inflation some more expert and less cumbersome machinery is required. . . . [W]e conclude that an independent review body to oversee the profession's remuneration would be preferable. . . . Such a body might be in addition to the three review bodies already being established by the Government to deal with the pay of the armed forces; of M.P.'s, Ministers, the Judiciary and other groups; of doctors and dentists; and be constituted in similar form. There would be advantage in the new body making itself familiar with a wider range of professional problems and views by dealing with matters affecting remuneration in other professions, if the Government saw any further requirement of this kind (though the case for an independent review body for solicitors stands independently in view of the extent of statutory regulation of their income). . . .

103. The review body will need to take a broad view of the problems associated with solicitors' remuneration and, in determining charges for services, will have to pay regard to a number of important matters. Of first importance is the desirability of bringing about a closer relationship between charge and expense for various services. The relationship will never be a precise one and there will always be some services which cannot bear the full charge. It may also be judged necessary on occasion to depart from this principle in the public interest. But generally we think it is necessary for practical reasons and for equity to establish a closer relationship between solicitors' costs and charges, based on criteria which so far as possible are objective. The review body will need also to take into account the profession's need to recruit, train and retain manpower, of such calibre and in such numbers as the community's need for legal services requires. It should consider how best to encourage the profession to undertake the various classes of business in which charges are subject to statutory regulation. Finally, the review body will need to consider how to encourage the efficient use of the profession's resources, particularly those of trained manpower, and the part that the regulation of statutory charges can play in this.

104. The relationship between the review body we propose and the existing statutory committees will also have to be determined. The three Rule Committees have extensive responsibilities for the business of the courts and expert knowledge of court procedures and we would accept that there may be a strong

case for them to retain day-to-day oversight of court costs.[15] As regards the Non-Contentious Costs Committee, which deals only with the regulation of charges in non-contentious matters and has no general responsibility for matters of good practice, the situation seems rather different. We do not think it would be difficult for the review body to acquire sufficient familiarity with conveyancing work to enable it to advise on the regulation of the scales of charges equitably while leaving other non-contentious business, as now, broadly in the profession's own control. This would suggest that the fourth statutory committee might no longer be required.

Discipline

The discipline of solicitors is in the hands of the Disciplinary Committee appointed by the Master of the Rolls from among the members of the Council of the Law Society. The Committee has the power to strike a solicitor from the roll, suspend him from practice or impose a penalty of up to £500. There is an appeal to the High Court. The Committee is also responsible for initiating action against unqualified persons acting as solicitors or doing solicitors' work. A brief summary of the activities of the Committee is to be found in the Annual Reports of the Council of the Law Society, which are also a useful source in relation to other activities of the Law Society, and which include memoranda submitted by it to committees and commissions during the year.

The Annual Report for 1971–72 contains the following statement of the Committee's activity over the previous year:

As a result of applications made by The Law Society's solicitors on the Council's instructions, Orders were made by the Disciplinary Committee, constituted under the Solicitors Act, 1957, against 45 solicitors and in respect of 24 clerks. Under the provisions of section 12 of the Solicitors Act, 1957, as substituted by section 6 of the Solicitors Act, 1965, 24 solicitors were informed that they had failed to give satisfactory explanations in respect of matters affecting their conduct and that a discretion has become vested in The Society to refuse, or to grant, subject to conditions, future applications by such solicitors for practising certificates.

The Committee gave instructions for 105 inspections of solicitors' accounts to be carried out under the provisions of the Solicitors' Accounts Rules and the Solicitors' Trust Account Rules. In 4 other cases The Society's Investigating Accountant was instructed to visit solicitors' accountants to clarify their qualifications to their reports.

The Council found it necessary to send 1,291 reminders to solicitors who had failed to deliver their Accountants' Reports by the due date. The reports were subsequently received, or sufficient and satisfactory explanations given for their non-delivery.

---

[15] At the same time, it must be noted that the members of the Rule Committees are drawn from the various parts of the legal profession involved in providing the services, and therefore generating the costs, of the business which is the Rule Committees' concern. There is additional need for some means of examining from time to time the efficiency with which the services are provided, and for assessing possible ways of effecting reductions in costs which would help to lower fees.

Action taken against unqualified persons acting as solicitors

The Solicitors Act 1957

1957 c. 27

19. Any unqualified person who wilfully pretends to be, or takes or uses any name, title, addition or description implying that he is, qualified or recognised by law as qualified to act as a solicitor shall be liable on summary conviction to a penalty not exceeding fifty pounds for each such offence.

20.—(1) Any unqualified person who either directly or indirectly—

(*a*) draws or prepares any instrument of transfer or charge for the purposes of the Land Registration Act, 1925, or makes any application or lodges any document for registration under that Act at the registry; or

(*b*) draws or prepares any other instrument relating to real or personal estate, or any legal proceeding,

shall, unless he proves that the act was not done for or in expectation of any fee, gain or reward, be liable on summary conviction to a fine not exceeding fifty pounds:

Provided that this subsection shall not apply to—

(i) a barrister or duly qualified notary public;

(ii) any public officer drawing or preparing instruments or applications in the course of his duty;

(iii) any person employed merely to engross any instrument, application or proceeding;

and paragraph (*b*) of this subsection shall not apply to a duly certificated solicitor in Scotland.

(2) For the purposes of paragraph (*b*) of the foregoing subsection, the expression " instrument " does not include—

(*a*) a will or other testamentary instrument;

(*b*) an agreement under hand only;

(*c*) a letter or power of attorney; or

(*d*) a transfer of stock containing no trust or limitation thereof.

The responsibility for taking action against unqualified persons is that of the Discipline Committee. The accounts of the activities of the previous year are to be found in the Annual Report of the Council. That for 1971–72 noted:

> The activities of unqualified persons, particularly in the field of conveyancing, have again occupied a considerable amount of the Committee's attention. The Relator Proceedings concerning the National House Owners' Society were disposed of on agreed terms before the Vice-Chancellor in November 1971 and a full statement on this subject was published in the December [Law Society] Gazette (pages 584/5).

The Provision of Legal Services

One particular problem that has caused a great deal of concern in recent years has been the extent to which lawyers generally and in particular solicitors are meeting the needs of the community at large and in particular the poorer sections of the community. A state financed legal aid scheme in relation to civil matters was first introduced by the Legal Aid and Advice Act 1949, following the report of the Rushcliffe Committee on Legal Aid and Legal Advice in 1945.[16] It is organised and run by the Law Society.

The country is divided up into Areas and smaller Districts in each of which there is a Legal Aid Committee consisting of local solicitors and barristers. Application for legal aid is first made to the District Committee. In case of refusal, there is an appeal to the Area Committee. The scheme which was carried into effect piece-meal now applies to all the ordinary civil courts and the Lands Tribunal. Certain actions such as actions for defamation are excluded. So is certain non-contentious work such as conveyancing. An applicant must show that it is reasonable for him to take proceedings and that he falls within the income and capital limits in force at the time. His means are investigated by the Supplementary Benefits Commission. If he is granted a certificate he is entitled to choose a solicitor of his choice from among those who have agreed to take legal aid cases. If the case justifies it, he will also be allowed counsel. He may receive the services free, or he may be required to make a contribution depending on his financial circumstances.

In addition to provision of legal aid to take proceedings there are also provisions for advice and assistance short of bringing an action which have recently been extended by the Legal Advice and Assistance Act 1972. In each of these cases it is the solicitor who decides whether the client qualifies for free advice or assistance or in the case of assistance should pay a contribution. The advice is limited to oral advice. Assistance may involve the writing of letters or the preparation of a claim for full legal aid. It is a condition of this form of assistance that it should not exceed £25 (hence its description " the £25 scheme ").

The impact of Legal Aid even though it was only introduced in stages has been substantial. Each year the Law Society makes an annual report on the previous year and an Advisory Committee makes comments and recommendations. In its fourteenth Report, for 1963–64,[17] it estimated that over 50 per cent of the more serious cases in all the courts were legally aided cases. In its twentieth Report, for 1970–71, it estimated that since 1949 about £90 million had been recovered by legally assisted plaintiffs, mostly in personal injuries litigation, quite apart from those whose defences had been assisted or those cases such as matrimonial cases in which some other remedy had been sought. (Matrimonial cases in fact constitute about 80 per cent of the total number of aid certificates issued.) Legal aid had also made incidental contributions to the law in such cases as *Ridge* v. *Baldwin*,[18] *H. West & Son* v. *Shephard*[19] and *Rookes* v. *Barnard*.[20] It has also made a considerable difference to the prospects of young barristers at the beginning of their careers.

There have however been criticisms. One was the hardship on the unassisted party which the Legal Aid and Advice Act 1964 attempted to mitigate. Another has been the success rate which it is sometimes suggested is

16 Cmd. 6641.
17 H.M.S.O., 1965.
18 [1964] A.C. 40.
19 [1964] A.C. 326.
20 [1964] A.C. 1129.

too high and suggests that the criteria for help are being too strictly applied. It has also been proposed that the scope of the scheme should be extended to cover representation before tribunals and actions for defamation which are at present excluded. More fundamental have been those criticisms which suggest that the provision of financial assistance is not enough and that the existing scheme still leaves unaided a large number of people who need a lawyer's help. Solicitors' offices, it is said, are generally located where their business is and as much of their business is " middle class " there may be no offices in a poorer neighbourhood. They are strange and unfamiliar places and have little experience of dealing with the problems of the poor and in particular with what is often called " welfare " law. People more-over who have problems may not even know that a lawyer could help. A corollary of this has been the view that existing services such as those pro-vided by the Citizens Advice Bureaux are inadequate. It is widely agreed that there is a good basis for much of this criticism. At the risk of over-simplification, three solutions have been proposed.

The Law Society has placed considerable emphasis on the £25 scheme and the prospects that it offers of making legal assistance more readily available and making such work more profitable and so perhaps encourag-ing firms to open branches in hitherto neglected areas. At the same time it has proposed that a number of liaison officers should be appointed in an attempt to bridge the gap which often exists between the voluntary, state and local authority services which already exist, and to which people come with their problems, and the legal profession. A group of Conservative lawyers have advocated subsidies for firms who are willing to open branches in neglected areas (below, p. 154). The Society of Labour Lawyers have put forward the notion of neighbourhood law centres, in which salaried lawyers should be available to give advice and to take action on behalf of clients who come to them from the local community (below, p. 151).

There is no one conception of a neighbourhood law centre. In some cases it is seen as part of a more general community centre which contains a number of specialists of which lawyers would form only one group. In others it is more like a private firm with the difference that it is financed by the state through for example the Law Society or a public corporation and is doing work which a private firm would find unprofitable. In some versions it is more like a centre which acts as a point of referral, passing on cases in which proceedings have to be taken to a private firm. In others it itself undertakes proceedings and is even active in initiating litigation in the interests of the local community, bringing test cases, devising means of challenging evasions and abuses of the law, and compelling private indivi-duals and state and local authorities to perform their legal duties. There has been an increasing number of experiments along these different lines already in existence in the last few years. The Holborn Law Society in London has provided solicitors to give advice in the Citizens Advice Bureau on a voluntary basis. There is a Neighbourhood Law Centre in North Kensington and similar ventures sponsored by local authorities in Camden and Westminster. The Child Poverty Action group have opened a Citizens' Rights Office in London. (Similar ventures are underway elsewhere, *e.g.* in Cardiff and Manchester.) There have been experiments of this kind associated with the Government's Community Development Projects and the Government has also encouraged local authorities to consider extending the services of Citizens' Advice Bureaux by appointing solicitors under its Urban Aid programme. So extensive have these activities become that a Legal Action Group has been formed to provide general information and advice on their activities. Powers have been taken in the Legal Advice and Assistance Act 1972 to enable the Law Society to appoint salaried solicitors to supplement their present Liaison Officer Service. There is also a certain amount of research being conducted into the general problem of "unmet legal need" and how best to deal with it. The Nuffield Foundation has sponsored research of this kind by Dr. Pauline Morris and Miss Marsden-Smedley. The Institute of Judicial Administration in Birmingham is doing research of a similar kind in Birmingham. It is too soon yet to say which of the many projects underway are temporary stop-gaps to fill an immediate pressing need and which will come to form a permanent part of the provision of legal services throughout the country.

It is no accident that much of the inspiration behind the movement in favour of activist neighbourhood law centres comes from the United States where the lawyer in general is used to playing a much more active role in the community than in the United Kingdom. The shift of the American lawyer's interest from the problems of business corporations to the problems of the underprivileged is a change of scene not a change of style or role.

Some of the proposals made in connection with the provision of legal services clearly envisage far more than the bringing of existing services and roles to the service of a neglected section of the community. They involve a radical departure from some of the traditional attitudes of lawyers and in particular solicitors to their function in the community, and will eventually involve an even greater change in the community's attitude to the relevance of a lawyer and his skills in dealing with the problems of daily life. This change of emphasis is behind some of the demands that subjects such as poverty or welfare law should be included in the curricula of the law schools in the universities. If accepted it will be bound to have a radical effect on the orientation of the existing training and educational programmes for future lawyers, a factor as important as regards the future of the profession as the future apportionment of work, roles and skills between lawyers and neighbouring professions such as accountants, economists and estate agents.

This brings us to a further question. It has been suggested from time to time (see *e.g.* below, p. 146) that over the years solicitors have been losing work to other professions such as accountants or even to banks, for example in tax matters, because of their reluctance to develop new skills, backed by contentment with things as they are behind their protective conveyancing monopoly. To this has now been added criticism of their general failure to show any interest in "welfare law." This kind of criticism and Britain's recent entry into the European Economic Community raises some very general and some very particular problems concerning not merely barristers and solicitors but professions and disciplines as a whole. What is it that determines the nature and role of professions in general and the English legal profession in particular? How is it that a particular profession comes to see one job as appropriate for it and another not, and then seeks to reproduce in its schemes of education and training and its rules and values people who will be able to perform the traditional and favoured tasks and not others? Should the roles of barristers and solicitors be the same in 1990 when the present generation of law students will be in positions of responsibility as they are now? Do we have in fact any clear idea what they are now? It is very arguable that the image of a lawyer and his role projected by the courses in many law schools, and the way they are taught, bears little relationship even to the role of law and lawyers at the present time let alone in the future. Only a few years ago the legal profession in conjunction with the BBC produced a film on the legal profession, which the Law Society kindly lends to law schools and which sets out to give an idea of the kind of work lawyers perform and the kind of people lawyers are. But already it is beginning to look dated. It is not simply a question of keeping lawyers up to date with changes in the law, though this problem of continuing education will clearly have to be taken much more seriously in the future than in the past. It is the more fundamental task of keeping under review the whole question of the changing role of law and the changing role of lawyers and of equipping lawyers to cope with these changes. In the last twenty years for example new developments have created new demands for lawyers but not always lawyers trained in the style skills and values of the past. This is so for example in fields such as administrative law and town and country planning with their accompanying appearances before tribunals and inquiries, social security law, and more recently the whole field of industrial relations. A whole new European dimension has now been added.

As the Beeching Commission noted (above, p. 66) the creation of a lawyer, and *a fortiori* a judge, is a very slow process and this can inhibit rapid change. It is for this reason that considerable attention needs to be paid to the problems of legal education and training. Every student of the law should try to identify the assumptions and factors which determine which skills he is being given the opportunity and being required to acquire and which he is not, the job he is being trained to perform and that which he is not, the values which he is being asked to absorb and those which he is not, since it is these skills, these notions of a lawyer's job and lawyers' values that will determine, as much as any rule of substantive law or procedure, the character and quality of the profession in the next three decades. The structure of this book itself rests on assumptions which will themselves probably be out of date in a few years time even though the university in which it is written has gone as far as any at the moment to question many of the existing assumptions, since it is not a matter which is to be decided once and for all. Like the activities of the courts themselves it is something that needs constant rescrutiny if the system as a whole is to play a useful part in the life of the community.

The solicitor's role

In Search of Justice, R. Stevens and B. Abel Smith

Society and the Legal System. Allen Lane, Penguin Press

Over the years, the Law Society has been slow in securing adjustment of the skills of solicitors to the changing needs of clients. In areas where no legislation protects the solicitor there has been considerable 'encroachment' on his work—particularly by accountants but also by banks, company secretaries, estate agents, land developers, debt collectors and the automobile clubs. The Law Society has tried to deal with the problem by concluding demarcation agreements with related professions. The accountants, for example, have agreed (although the agreement does not appear to be adhered to at the local level) not to prepare memoranda and articles of association of companies. The banks have agreed not to draft wills and codicils, while estate agents have promised not to draft contracts of sale. . . .

Because conveyancing and probate work have provided solicitors with a relatively easy and convenient method of earning a comfortable living, the profession as a whole has not always fought hard to extend the work of solicitors in borderline areas. In the last thirty years, however, there has been a change in emphasis. This was marked in the Presidential Address to the Law Society in 1940, when banks, insurance companies, estate agents and accountants were accused of being ' like a flock of sparrows pecking at our preserves '. The banks were put under pressure not to complete conveyances. But in 1966 there were still vigorous complaints about bank managers who took instructions for wills and about the advertising of banks' trustee departments.[21] There were also outbursts from solicitors when insurance companies started to widen the field from which their agents were drawn: it was argued that solicitors should figure prominently among ' bona fide ' agents. Suggestions that surveyors were better qualified than solicitors to handle appeals from a compulsory purchase order were vigorously resisted. Yet, after the passage of the Leasehold Reform Act, 1967, there were advertisements by surveyors and valuers announcing that they would ' be pleased to advise and act for tenants who may be eligible to acquire the freehold or extended lease of their property as a result of the new Act '.

On the other hand, despite the efforts of Mr. Carter, the active and controversial Secretary of the National House Owners' Society, solicitors have so far had little difficulty in maintaining a monopoly of conveyancing work. There are signs, however, that this monopoly may increasingly be invaded. Mr Carter's organization was operating in seven areas by early 1967. Starting in the middle of 1966, a similar organization, the Home Owners' Club, also offered its members a cut-price conveyancing service: it charged £25 for the conveyance of registered property and £35 for the conveyance of unregistered property. . . .

It seems that many new large trusts, whether private or institutional, are now taken directly to investment advisers or merchant banks in the City. But many smaller trusts are still handled by solicitors. Some members of the profession continue to operate uninfluenced by the new competition.[22] Others, particularly the large firms in London, have responded positively. We found firms which used their own accountants to handle the larger trusts, and firms who employed former tax inspectors to advise on the tax planning of trusts.

The relative failure of solicitors to handle the more lucrative trust and investment work can be traced . . . to the failure of the leaders of the profession to appreciate the potential importance of tax law at the turn of the century. As a result, accountancy has become a much more important profession in England than in the United States. It was not until the thirties that solicitors fully appreciated what was at stake: by then accountants were seeking direct access to counsel, as well as moving into other legal areas like the drafting of contracts and the formation of companies. Tax was added to the examination of solicitors in

[21] (1966) 110 S.J. 24. The banks have been accused of having " made off with a huge part of our probate and trust heritage." (1966) 63 L.S.Gaz. 110.
[22] A solicitor in Sussex who handles 100 trusts told us with pride that he never reads the financial page of newspapers, and said that he thought he had " done a jolly good job " for his trusts. He admitted that the capital value of some of the trusts he was handling had not increased since 1939, but took credit for the fact that the beneficiaries had received a steady four per cent. over this long period.

1938. Now younger solicitors have some training in tax law, but it is still generally believed by bank managers and others that tax inspectors prefer negotiating with accountants rather than lawyers. It is, however, possible that in the last four or five years, led by the large and specialized London firms, solicitors have won back some of the lost tax territory. . . .

21st Report of The Law Society on Legal Aid and Advice
H.C. 283. June 1972

Appendix 20

Consolidated Figures For the First Twenty-One Years

Total number of applications received	2,092,831
Total number of applications granted	1,576,677
Total number of certificates issued	1,425,267
Total number of emergency certificates issued	41,097
Total number of results reported	952,203
Total number of successful cases	824,427
Total number of cases closed when all financial matters are concluded	1,104,613
Total amount of contributions received	£23,913,000
Total amount of contributions retained	£11,743,000
Total amount of contributions held in open cases	£6,017,000
Total amount of damages recovered (This figure does not include certain damages recovered but not paid into the Fund prior to 1954; an example of this type of damages is a sum ordered to be invested for the benefit of an infant. It is estimated that if these sums were included the total damages recovered on behalf of assisted persons would exceed £99,000,000) [23]	£94,631,000
Total amount of damages retained in closed cases	£976,000
Total amount of damages held in open cases	£976,000
Total amount of costs recovered	£27,852,000
Total amount of costs and fees paid to solicitors and Counsel ...	£98,685,000
Total amount of grant received	£77,833,000
Total amount deducted as percentage from solicitors' costs and Counsel's fees	£6,470,000

Legal aid in relation to representation before tribunals

17th Report of the Lord Chancellor's Advisory Committee on Legal Aid and Advice
H.M.S.O., 1968

The Advisory Committee in its seventeenth Report recommended that legal aid should be extended to representation before the Lands Tribunal which it said was more akin to an ordinary court of law than to other tribunals. Many and perhaps all of its functions, it said, might equally be

[23] NOTE :—Most legal aid cases are not concerned with the recovery of damages.

performed by the Chancery Division of the High Court. It did not recommend any further extension at the time but expressed the hope that research might be conducted into the extent to which those appearing before tribunals were already represented and how far others would use help, were it available. Their views on legal aid before tribunals other than the Lands Tribunal are printed below. They incidentally throw some light on the role of tribunals in the system, a matter treated somewhat cursorily in Chapter I.

Appendix B

National Insurance Tribunals

2. A Tribunal which satisfies the conditions of the Committee on Administrative Tribunal and Inquiries, that legal aid should be available in proceedings before final appellate Tribunals, are the National Insurance Commissioners. The appellate structure for industrial injury cases has been assimilated in the National Insurance system and the Chief National Insurance Commissioner and his colleagues hear appeals from local Tribunals and Medical Appeal Tribunals which are themselves appellate bodies. There are other reasons to advance for making legal aid available in these proceedings.

3. The financial issues at stake sometimes far exceed the limits of the County Courts jurisdiction or the size of many High Court awards. The right of appeal from a Medical Appeal Tribunal is limited to points of law. Though in some cases the claimant has his union behind him, in many he will not. In many cases it will seem to the claimant that he is fighting the Ministry, and the Insurance Officer, whose original decision he is contesting, or someone on his behalf who makes submissions to the Commissioner and attends the hearing. Sometimes the claimant's success depends on discrediting a witness relied on by the Insurance Officer, producing a vital piece of evidence, or calling expert evidence. All these features point to the need for making legal aid available to him.

4. On the other hand there are arguments against that course. National Insurance law and procedure are in many respects totally different from those in ordinary litigation. There is no *lis inter partes* but an enquiry into the question whether the claimant has a right to a statutory benefit. The ordinary rules of evidence do not apply at any stage. The ministry officials draw the Tribunals' attention to the salient facts, statutory provisions and relevant decisions as well as advising the claimant of the best course to take (sometimes suggesting possible claims that had not occurred to him) and help him in filling up the forms and in making enquiries on his behalf to ascertain the facts. In the majority of cases appeals are determined without a hearing at little or no expense to the claimant; even in oral hearings the losing party does not pay the costs of the other side but, win or lose, he and his witnesses are paid their travelling and subsistence expenses and something for loss of time. He may be represented by anyone and the union frequently appears on his behalf.

5. To provide legal aid in these proceedings would create special difficulties:

(*a*) No leave is required for an appeal from a local Tribunal and fresh evidence can be called before the Commissioners even though the claimant did not attend the local Tribunal hearing. If legal aid were granted before the Commissioner and not before the local Tribunal, the latter could be ignored and every case could end before the Commissioners;

(*b*) The legal aid scheme requires an applicant's means to be investigated by the Supplementary Benefits Commission which claimants might regard as " the other side ";

(c) Owing to the specialised nature of the procedure and law involved there might be initial difficulties in assessing merits and over representation.

6. We have considered whether legal aid could not be introduced on a restricted scale, perhaps limited to appeals on a point of law to Commissioners from the Medical Appeal Tribunals. But the difficulties outlined above would still exist; there would be the danger of elaboration, complication, technicality and delay. Above all little or no cost to the claimant is at present involved and no evidence has been adduced before us that the present system results in miscarriage of justice.

7. In these circumstances we do not think a case has at present been made for extending legal aid to proceedings before the Commissioners. It follows that we do not think it should be introduced before National Insurance Local Tribunals, Industrial Injuries Medical Appeals Tribunals or before the Adjudicator.

Rent Assessment Committees and Rent Tribunals

8. There has been some pressure for extending the Legal Aid Scheme to Rent Assessment Committees on the ground that the landlord can afford representation and the tenant cannot. Figures produced for us by the Ministry of Housing and Local Government, analysing nearly 5,000 cases from all over the country, show that 21 per cent of all landlords were represented by a solicitor and a further 21 per cent by a surveyor. The equivalent figures for tenants are 7 per cent and 2 per cent respectively.

9. On the other hand we have seen an Opinion of the late Sir Sydney Littlewood, who was a member of the Rushcliffe Committee on Legal Aid and then Chairman of the Law Society's Legal Aid Committee and the first President of the London Rent Assessment Panel. He was, therefore, uniquely qualified to give an opinion on whether legal aid was needed in proceedings in Rent Assessment Committees. In his view it was not and all Presidents of Panels share that view. What does appear to be necessary is a Poor Man's Surveyor Service. We are glad to learn that the Chartered Land Societies' Committee have now sponsored a pilot Surveyor's Aid Scheme in Greater London. Under that scheme anyone with £20 0s. 0d. a week or less, after deducting tax, national insurance, family allowances and £1 0s. 0d. for each dependent child (and without realisable capital) will get a surveyor assigned to him on payment from 10s. 0d. to £15 0s. 0d. (which may be paid by instalments) according to income.

10. We think that this is the correct approach to this problem and therefore do not recommend the extension of the Legal Aid Scheme to proceedings before Rent Assessment Committees.

11. Rent Tribunals deal with furnished lettings in much the same way as Rent Assessment Committees deal with unfurnished. They have existed since 1946 and little or no suggestion has been made that legal aid should be extended to proceedings before them. We agree that it is not necessary.

Industrial Tribunals

12. The main functions of these Tribunals arise under the Redundancy Payments Act 1965 and some suggestion has been made that legal aid should be available in these proceedings. The argument is similar to that advanced in connection with Rent Assessment Committees: the employer can afford representation, the employee cannot. In fact employers are rarely legally represented. Where it is a small concern the proprietor attends himself and argues his case. Where it is a big company the Personnel Manager, or some similar member of the management, normally conducts the company's case. Sometimes the employer is represented by his Trade Association. So far as employees are concerned they

are in many cases represented by their Trade Union, officials of which are developing, or have developed, an expertise in the presentation of their cases and a knowledge of the working of the Act. There are, of course, cases where the employee appears in person. We have no evidence that this unduly handicaps him. Proceedings are informal and free of technicality and chairmen recognise that they have a duty to assist both sides in the presentation of their cases.

13. Compensation Appeals, under the 7th schedule to the Act, sometimes involves substantial sums of money and substantial issues of principle. The Compensation Regulations are complex and it is by no means easy to find out the law, but the ordinary general legal practitioner would equally have difficulties. Only 39 cases have so far been heard so there is only the minimum of experience of this branch of the Tribunals' business. There has been no call for legal aid in connection with the other functions of the Tribunals.

14. For all these reasons we do not recommend that legal aid should be made available in any proceedings before these Tribunals.

Mental Health Review Tribunals

15. These Tribunals hear applications for discharge by Patients who are liable to be detained under the Mental Health Act 1959. The Patient cannot know the medical evidence and therefore cannot instruct a Solicitor or Counsel. For him to attempt to do so might be positively detrimental to his health. The Council on Tribunals are studying a scheme for lay assistance through the Mental Health Association and the National Council for Civil Liberties. We welcome this study and, meanwhile, do not make any recommendations.

Supplementary Benefits Appeal Tribunals

16. Although there is provision for legal representation before the Tribunals, which hear appeals brought by persons claiming benefit against determination by the Supplementary Benefits Commission, it is estimated that the right is exercised in only 0·25 per cent of cases. The issues almost invariably contain no matter of law and informality is a feature of tribunal hearings to which great importance is attached because of the personal and sometimes rather intimate nature of the appellant's circumstances. We do not feel that legal aid is either necessary or appropriate for these proceedings.

Justice for All. Report by the Society of Labour Lawyers

Fabian Research Series 273 (1968)

The 1949 Act was a progressive and enlightened measure which has enjoyed a high measure of success. It provided a broad service based on a means test and available to all residents irrespective of nationality or domicile. The means test basis has meant, however, that those outside the limits are often the victims of substantial injustice, in that they are deemed to be capable of meeting their own costs when in fact they cannot do so. This report is not, however, focused on these people but concentrates rather on those at the bottom end of the socio-economic scale. From their point of view, the scheme's limitations may in retrospect be seen to stem from two assumptions—one structural, the other psychological and social. First, the 1949 scheme was wholly and exclusively dependent on the existing private structure of the legal profession and therefore failed to overcome the difficulty that the private practitioner cannot always be found in the poorer areas. He tends to go where there is a prospect of more profitable business.

Secondly, and as a corollary, it was considered sufficient to provide a service only for those with the knowledge, resourcefulness and persistence to seek assistance from a private lawyer. . . . Such a system was bound to work ineffectively where the individual did not succeed in identifying his own need for a lawyer because of ignorance, or did not seek a lawyer's help because of despair or fear, or could not find a lawyer because few worked in the neighbourhood or were not available after his working day had ended; or did not get a lawyer who was truly competent to advise him on his particular problem.

The 1949 Act . . . assumed that the traditional private structure was adequate in composition, training, attitudes and customs to provide legal services to the poorest and worst educated sections of the community, and that the individual would initiate proceedings where he had need of legal aid or advice under the scheme. . . .

The paucity of statistics specifically directed to the problem does not prevent a realistic appraisal of its existence and size. The statistical material which does exist, although to be used with caution, and open as it may in some cases be to differences of interpretation, points, in combination, overwhelmingly in one direction—towards a multiplicity of situations in which laymen need the services of a lawyer, and a vast number of individual cases in which that need remains unfulfilled. But beyond the statistics lies the uncounted experience of the social worker who, each day of his or her life, is brought face to face with that need. . . . On this topic, throughout the investigation and discussion on which this report is based, there was a unanimous certainty: that however many digits a census of unmet need might produce, its volume was enormous and its quality urgent and often desperate. . . . Some would say that if people choose not to use a facility offered them that is their own concern, not society's. . . . In our view this is no longer consistent with the standards of a humane and civilised social system. . . .

We believe that there is a need for a new institution capable of bringing high quality legal services to those parts of our cities where the existing need is greatest, and of attracting men of ability to the service of the community in performing functions which have in the past been regarded as the sole preserve of the private profession. Such an institution would have to be staffed by salaried lawyers. . . . What is needed is a number of local legal centres, sited in those areas where there are at present insufficient numbers of solicitors. . . . Such centres would be able to develop legal services in ways which are necessarily impracticable—even undesirable—within the framework of the private profession. It is not usually practicable, for instance, for solicitors' offices to remain open until say, 7.30 p.m. . . . It is not possible for solicitors, particularly in busy practices, to concern themselves with the education of the public about legal services in general, and the use of the legal system. It is not desirable for solicitors, working within a fee paying system to tout for work by advertising their services. Yet all these activities, including advertising, would be open to local legal centres. . . .

A further consideration . . . is that legal centre lawyers would have the opportunity of acquiring a specialised knowledge of the legal problems and of the law which most directly affect lower income groups. . . . Their experience and expertise would provide a counter weight to the profession's over-emphasis on the problems of the middle classes. . . .

The proposal for a salaried service raises a variety of questions. . . . But . . . there is nothing novel about such a concept in the English system. The 1949 . . . Act which was based largely on the report of the Rushcliffe Committee incorporated that Committee's recommendation that legal advice should be made available by salaried lawyers. The committee recommended that the legal aid area committees should . . . provide at their own offices, or at branch offices, a staff of salaried solicitors, working whole or part time for the purpose of giving legal advice, and simple assistance with advice, such as writing a letter in a situation where one letter would probably dispose of the case, or drafting simple documents. The 1949 Act provides that "legal advice shall consist of oral advice on legal questions given by a solicitor employed whole time or part time for the purpose...." This provision was never brought into effect. When the advice sections of the Act were implemented in 1959 the Government decided that this facility should be offered instead by the private practitioner....

As a working programme, during the experimental stages of the project, it is suggested that the following categories of activity should be excluded from the operations of the local legal centres. First, the centres should undertake no conveyancing work, although this would not exclude advice and simple drafting in connection with tenancy problems. Secondly, the centres should generally limit their activity in criminal matters to the giving of advice except where other means of representation are not at hand. Thirdly, the centres should not undertake any divorce litigation in the High Court or the County Court, or personal injury cases.... The exclusion of the centres from ... any category of work ... would not, of course, prevent them fulfilling a valuable liaison function in passing on such work to private practitioners. Apart from work normally excluded, local legal centres would not, as a general rule, carry on litigation.... [I]n practice they will be concerned with litigation in a limited number of circumstances.... First, the emergency case, as for example where a notice to quit a furnished letting expires in the next 24 hours, or where a county court summons is to be heard next day. Secondly, ... where legal aid is not available, such as representation before a tribunal, or even where representation has been refused. Thus, legal aid may be refused where the amount involved is very small but ... the local legal centre may appreciate that this claim reflects an abuse which is widespread in its area and which could be eliminated by a success in the particular instance. Thirdly, the centres must have discretion to retain litigation which no private solicitor in the area, competent in the subject, is prepared to accept. Next, the centres will ... be sensitive to situations which create the opportunity for a test case....

We recognise ... that lawyers are in short supply and that it is important to reduce to a minimum work done by them that could properly be done by others.... In any event, we believe that any busy local legal centre will probably need to have either on its premises or within easy reach a trained social worker, since there are so many problems (debt, landlord and tenant, petty larceny) whose legal features are only part of a constellation of personal, family and community problems....

Close and formal links should also be established between the centres and the universities.... Law students as such could, through association with the work of the centres, be helped to bridge the gap between the law in books and the law in action, and many of them who might not otherwise do so, might be persuaded by their experience to proceed to a professional qualification, and to take an active part in the work of the centres after they have qualified....

State salaries naturally raise the problem of independence.... [S]ome institutional arrangement is essential to guarantee the insulation of the service from any kind of governmental or other improper pressure. The models of the BBC and the University Grants Committee provide examples of institutions that run their own affairs independently in spite of their reliance on state funds.... In our view the system should be instituted gradually, beginning with a pilot project to test an experimental number of centres, say three or four, for a minimum period of three years.... In the short run, a reasonable aim might be to establish about 10 offices, staffed by 40 to 50 lawyers....

Rough Justice

Conservative Political Centre 1968

Social workers and others concerned with the poorer sections of the community agree that there are ... large numbers of people, many with legal problems, who never get the professional attention that they ought to have. This situation has, we think, three causes. Firstly a straightforward, but very marked, shortage of solicitors in the poorest areas of the country.... Second, for many people the idea of consulting a solicitor is alien, even repugnant. For some people solicitors represent a wholly unknown middle-class realm of life, to be avoided at all costs; and for others the idea of consulting a solicitor simply does not occur to them. Solicitors cannot, of course advertise, and if some social agency suggests a visit to a solicitor, that is a piece of advice that is with surprising frequency ignored.... To solve the problem each of the ... causes must be tackled.... One suggestion is ... the establishment of " neighbourhood lawyers," paid for on a salaried basis, in appropriate areas. As a last resort, we think experiments of this kind could be tried.... But we believe that there is an alternative ... which would take advantage, in terms of independence and integrity, of the present system of private practice, and avoid the risk of state control.... We should attract lawyers to poorer areas and overcome regional shortages of solicitors by making practice in these areas financially more attractive. We propose the payment of capital grants to persons starting practice within appropriately designated areas. Alternatively the grant could be in kind, for example, the provision of premises. In addition we suggest that all solicitors practising in these areas should be paid ... at a higher rate than in the rest of the country....

But the most difficult problem of all remains—how to give legal aid to people who will not go to a solicitor on their own accord. We think the answer is to provide qualified solicitors at all Citizen's Advice Bureaux.... The Bureaux themselves, could advertise the presence of solicitors.... The services of the solicitors at the ... Bureaux would be provided in the legal aid scheme in exactly the same way as those of solicitors elsewhere. Who would these solicitors be? We consider they should be ordinary solicitors in private practice. Thus every firm of solicitors participating in the legal aid scheme ought, we think, to be encouraged to undertake membership of a rota which would provide a solicitor in the local Citizen's Advice Bureaux.... [I]n some areas lawyers in attendance full time, supplied by local practitioners operating the rota system, might be needed....

The future of legal aid in England. Seton Pollock

The Law Society's Gazette, March 1969

Mr. Seton Pollock, the secretary of the Law Society's Legal Aid Committee here explained two of the Law Society's proposals for dealing with unmet legal need. He first described the £25 scheme and then went on to discuss the proposed liaison officers.

The second proposal involves the creation of a full-time salaried advisory liaison service. Its primary function would be to establish an effective link between the many voluntary and official social agencies which are best able to discover cases requiring a lawyer's aid and the profession which can meet that need. It has been suggested that this is an insufficiently radical approach, but it is, in fact, far more radical than has been appreciated. A profession of some 22,000 solicitors distributed all over the country could do no more than scratch the surface of the problem. Only a relatively small proportion of the problems of the citizen are legal and, the legal element is often such as can be dealt with by a sufficiently trained and experienced social worker with knowledge of the facilities available for dealing with them. Again, problems are not by any means divisible into legal and non-legal, and one problem may necessitate help from several quarters. If the profession is to fulfil the function in society for which it is trained, there must be a filter by which those needing legal help can get it promptly and effectively, without overwhelming practitioners with cases in which their special skills are not required. The Seebohm Report, published in August 1968, reached very much the same conclusion as to the need for a sorting-house for welfare problems. Thus, the first task of the proposed advisory liaison team would be to ensure that such bodies as the Citizen's Advice Bureaux were given the help and advice they need in recognising cases in which a solicitor should be consulted and to provide an effective link between the bureaux and the profession to ensure that those needing legal services are put in touch, promptly, with a practitioner willing and able to take up the case.

The team's second task would be to advise the public, disposing of those cases in which reference to a private practitioner would be unnecessary and preparing such statements and notes as might help the solicitor to whom an applicant is referred to gain a grasp of the situation before seeing him.

Though in many parts of the country both practitioners and social workers are satisfied that the existing liaison is already adequate, this is far from being so in London, where there are densely populated districts inadequately manned by the profession and there are sections of the community that regard the solicitor as remote and alien to their interests. It is no cause for surprise that solicitors' offices are at present distributed according to where the private money lies. It could not be otherwise because a practice can only be maintained where there is sufficient paying work. It will take time, even when legal aid work of the type found in disadvantaged districts is realistically remunerated under legal aid, for solicitors to open branches and set up firms in districts where the need for their services is at present unmet.

Accordingly, it may well be necessary, for some considerable time, to maintain effective advisory units in London and, possibly, in other large cities, but until experience has been gained it would be unwise to dogmatise over the extent and character of the services which would need to be provided by such units. It certainly seems likely that there will have to be advisory offices with permanent staff in some parts of London, but it remains to be seen whether such staff may have to fulfil the more extensive functions which are normally performed only by the independent practitioner.

It has been said that there are inherent features of the legal aid scheme which would make any such development impossible and that some entirely new organisation ought to be set up to administer local legal centres. The Law Society already has valuable experience in this field, having set up and successfully administered divorce units, run on the lines of a solicitor's office, to cope with the aftermath of matrimonial problems generated by the War. These continued to function within the legal aid scheme until a point was reached at which their work was found to be less economic than it would be if absorbed by the profession and, accordingly, they were closed down. There is nothing to rule out a comparable service for disadvantaged districts in terms of salaried law offices if experience shows that, without them, sections of the community would be deprived of the help they should receive. As and when normal legal services were to become sufficient, such law offices could be closed.

Nearly a year after the Council's Memorandum was published, reports prepared by lawyers of the two main political parties were published almost simultaneously and have deservedly attracted public interest as well as the keen interest of the profession itself.

The proposals of the Society of Labour Lawyers (December 1968) drew much of their inspiration from developments on the other side of the Atlantic where, since 1964, there have been important advances in legal aid under the aegis of the Office of Economic Opportunity initiated in 1964 by President Kennedy as part of his " War against Poverty " campaign. It is important to remove certain misconceptions which have led some to believe that neighbourhood law firms on the American pattern would provide the right answer for problems in England, though this by no means rules out the question whether local law offices, somewhat along the lines proposed by the Society of Labour Lawyers, should be set up.

In the United States, the rigid rule against unauthorised legal practice has prevented the appearance of such bodies as our Citizen's Advice Bureaux and has created an extensive need for the services of lawyers in respect of matters which, in England, would not be regarded as lying in the lawyer's province. Moreover, American law clung too long to the unrelieved doctrine of the sanctity of contract so that it is harder and harsher than ours. In England, legislation designed to protect the weak and resourceless has been introduced at ever-increasing tempo since Victorian times, with tremendous developments since the First World War continuing right up to the present time. Laws such as those that protect the debtor and the hire purchase customer, coupled with the paternalistic procedures of our county courts, have created a situation that differs radically from the situation in the States.

A typical pattern of the work of a neighbourhood law firm reveals that about half the enquiries are referred elsewhere, mainly to private practitioners who take all damages cases on a contingency fee basis and cases where the applicant is capable of making some kind of payment. The American legal profession is overmanned so that it is almost always possible to find someone prepared to take up a case at a much reduced fee. This leaves the neighbourhood law firm with only those cases which are at indigency level. Of the cases retained, approximately a third relate to debtors who admit owing money but want time to pay or to settle on a reduced payment. Creditors can be induced to take such courses because, otherwise, delaying tactics can be employed that make collection unrewarding. No such service is needed here because our debtors, when in difficulties, are protected by our county courts and can obtain an instalment order. A quarter of the cases relate to grievances against local authorities, mainly in respect of housing or the refusal, reduction or stopping of welfare benefit. Here again, there is far less need for such legal work in England, our own welfare services having developed within the spirit generated in our Welfare State. Of the cases that reach a court, over ninety per cent concern courts of lowest jurisdiction and the few that involve more substantial litigation are mainly test cases designed to achieve social reforms or to establish benefits for sections of the community or some particular neighbourhood. It would be artificial for provision for test cases to be incorporated in our own legal aid scheme because the better remedy would be a separate procedure protecting *all* litigants from the burden of costs incurred in clarifying uncertain law or resolving matters of public policy. The test case in the States has, in any case, little relevance here because, in our legal system, we effect social reforms by legislation rather than, as in the States, by appeals to superior courts of law, with the object of challenging the legislation or common law by reference to the principles of a written constitution.

The director of one important neighbourhood law firm expressed the view, while studying legal aid in England, that the functions being performed by the neighbourhood law firm were in large measure those performed here by Citizen's Advice Bureaux. Neighbourhood law firms are, in fact, a combination of a quasi-political campaign to alleviate the lot of the indigent by developing and enforcing " poverty law " and to resolve the acute problem of the " ghetto " which represents a dangerously explosive feature of American social life. This they set out to achieve by what is, in effect, a " citizen's advice bureau " manned by lawyers engaged in the war against poverty.

A legal aid scheme of that character cannot purport to provide legal aid on the English pattern, namely, as a matter of right for any citizen having a case which he would pursue if he had the means to do so. The neighbourhood law firm must normally confine its activities to a circumscribed district subject, in any case, to a policy laid down by a committee with lay representation from the local community as to the type of case that will be accepted. The primary objective is the general social improvement of the neighbourhood rather than the provision of a legal service for the man who has a right at law. Thus, in California, the legal aid provided is restricted to the defence of Mexican farm workers and actions against welfare authorities. Another neighbourhood law firm has regarded it as part of its function to set up a laundry to compete with one regarded as exploiting the local community. Anxieties are expressed by American lawyers over the influence exerted by pressure groups upon the policy and at the divisive tendency towards two separate legal services, one acting as the champion of the poor and the other serving the rest of the community on ordinary lines. A view that is steadily gaining ground is that the neighbourhood law firm, though it represents (as is probably the case) the right approach in the present socio-legal situation, will in due course break down the barriers existing between the numerous " ghetto " communities of American cities and the lawyers, establishing a situation in which a legal aid scheme broadly comparable to the one that has developed here may prove possible.

A start has been made with the introduction of " judicare " which has features similar to English legal aid but which is hampered because, under American conditions, the cost of handling cases within the existing profession of private practitioners is some three times greater than when they are handled by a neighbourhood law firm. This fact is used as an argument that a local legal centre in England would provide legal aid more economically for the poor than our present system, but this is fallacious. The English lawyer is not called upon to deal with cases which can be adequately dealt with by social workers but only those that need the full facilities of a solicitor's office and these can be more economically handled under our own scheme than in a salaried law firm because the overheads are spread over a practice that includes ordinary paying work. If we are not to develop a " soup kitchen " type of service, the lawyers and their staffs who deal with the poor man's case would need to be remunerated at a level sufficient to maintain the standards of private practice.

LEGAL AID IN CRIMINAL CASES

Legal advice and aid is in many ways more important than in civil cases because the accused's liberty is often at stake. The subject was discussed at length by the Widgery Committee [24] and new provisions are to be found in the Criminal Justice Act 1967. These are omitted here because of shortage of space.

[24] Departmental Committee on Legal Aid in Criminal Proceedings 1964–66, March 1966, Cmnd. 2934.

LEGAL EDUCATION

The education of the common lawyers was for a long time in the hands of the Inns of Court. In the early days these provided lectures, moots and discussions which made them a centre of learning and social life, even for young men who had no intention of practising law. The judges recognised too that they had a part to play in giving young men instruction, and the Year Books make mention of a crib in the Court of King's Bench in which the students sat near to the judge who could then explain what was going on to them. A practice observed, it is said, by Bereford in the thirteenth century and Lord Mansfield in the eighteenth. At these times there were no university courses in the common law. There were law courses at Oxford and Cambridge but in the Roman and Canon Law only, courses which were more suitable for those intending to practise before the prerogative courts, e.g. the Court of Admiralty, than the common law courts. There were textbooks of a kind, but for the most part it seems students of the common law read the Year Books and made notes of cases from them and compiled their own common place books. Later they had Coke on Littleton, and Coke's own Commentaries on the Laws of England to work on, though it was not until Blackstone's *Commentaries* that they really had a book which could be regarded as attractive to read. By the time Blackstone's *Commentaries* were published in 1756 the Inns of Court were no longer thriving centres of legal education. Examinations had been abandoned and right up until the 1840s the only requirement for Call was attendance at dinners and payment of fees, and a formal piece of ritual which was the last remnant of the earlier tests.

In the eighteenth century lawyers learnt their trade by being apprenticed to those already experienced, and by observation in the courts and by private reading. It was Blackstone who made the first attempt to remedy the situation by introducing the common law to Oxford University and becoming its first professor of English law. Although his lectures and his *Commentaries* were a great success and English law obtained a foothold in the universities, no strong tradition of legal education was established there or elsewhere at this time. Professors of law were appointed both at Oxford and Cambridge and in London when University College was established in the 1820s. Some attempts were made at the turn of the century to revive lectures at the Inns, and there were further attempts in the 1820s and 1830s. The famous jurist John Austin was involved both in the university teaching and the lectures at the Inns. But the times were not propitious. The late eighteenth century was not a time for educational innovations in the ancient universities and although there were signs of a revival in the 1830s and 1840s a Select Committee on Legal Education in 1846 [25] concluded that " the present state of legal education in England and Ireland . . . is extremely unsatisfactory and incomplete, and exhibits a striking contrast and inferiority to such education, provided as it is with ample means and a judicious system for their application, at present in operation in all the more civilised states of Europe and America." So far as the Universities of Oxford and Cambridge were concerned this view was confirmed by the

[25] P.P. xi, August 25, 1846.

Royal Commissions into those Universities in 1852 and 1853.[26] Only the University of London seemed to be making any real progress.

By the 1850s however things were beginning to change. The universities were beginning to take seriously the introduction of courses in English Law. The re-establishment of the Vinerian chair of law in Oxford was a mile-stone. Since that time the universities have played the major role in legal education and the Law Society, recognising this, sponsored law courses in a number of universities in the 1920s. Shortage of space prevents further discussion of this vital topic. Good accounts of the past and current situation are to be found in the report of the Ormrod Committee and in the Fabian Pamphlet in 1969 setting out the proposals on legal education of the Society of Labour Lawyers.

[26] 1852 P.P. xxii; 1852–53 P.P. xliv.

CHAPTER 3

JUDGE AND JURY

THE JUDGES

THE CONSTITUTIONAL POSITION OF THE JUDICIARY

Judges began as royal officials attached to the King's Court. Their functions were originally as much administrative as judicial. When they travelled around the country for example in the twelfth, thirteenth and fourteenth centuries they had a general inquisitorial role to fulfil besides the task of deciding cases and trying suspected offenders. They were also closely associated with lawmaking as well as law administration (see *e.g.* the remarks of Hengham C.J. above, p. 3). This close connection had however already declined by the middle of the fourteenth century. By that time too another momentous step had been taken, the appointment of judges from members of the legal profession. English judges have never been a separate profession recruited from those trained to be lawyers as an alternative career to practice at the Bar. Instead they have been chosen from the leading barristers of the day. They have always too played an important part in the life and the government of the profession itself, at first in Serjeants' Inn which they shared with the Serjeants-at-law who were not judges, and at the present time as Benchers of the four Inns of Court. For the most part they are still recruited from barristers and not solicitors, though solicitors are eligible to be Recorders and stipendiary magistrates. Indirectly this means that solicitors may also become Circuit judges, since one of the qualifications for appointment as a Circuit judge is a period of five years as a Recorder. They are not eligible for any of the higher appointments.

Constitutionally great stress is always laid on the independence of the judges, in particular independence from the executive. Although appointed on the recommendation of the executive, judges of the superior courts can only be removed by the Queen on an address of both Houses of Parliament. Their salaries are protected from annual scrutiny by being charged on the Consolidated Fund instead of having to be voted specifically each year. They are protected from incidental criticism in Parliament by the parliamentary rule that the judiciary may only be criticised on a substantive motion and various other rules which prevent the discussion of cases which are *sub judice*. They themselves may not be Members of Parliament. On the other hand they are appointed in effect by the government of the day, and if the government of the day had a majority in the House of Lords as well as the House of Commons an address could be presented to the Queen for removal of any one of them. Their statutory protections are only as secure as statutes themselves and from a legal point of view any statute can be changed by a simple majority in the House of Commons, provided the government either has a majority in the House of Lords or proceeds under the Parliament Acts 1911 and 1949. There are no special constitutional safe-guards protecting the judges because there is no way in which such safe-guards can be established.

Although judges are independent, they have not complete freedom of decision. Any statute passed by Parliament must be applied by them. They have no power to declare it invalid or unconstitutional because it infringes some basic right or is unjust or immoral. This gives them much less leeway than for example a judge of the Supreme Court of the United States. Even their promotion depends on the government of the day. There is no independent commission which determines such matters as to which judge should be promoted to the Court of Appeal or the House of Lords. The fact is that important as the statutory protections were histori-cally, putting an end for example to the claim of the Stuart Kings that judges held office during their pleasure and could be dismissed by them at will, and important as they are in outlining the general framework within which the judges operate, and indeed reflecting the values that underlie the system as a whole, it is these values and their observance in practice which are even more important than the basic statutory rules themselves.

Even more important than the legal rules setting out the independence of the judges is the tradition of independence, a tradition which has been fostered by both the judges and the Bar, and which for the most part has had its influence on those governments and Parliaments which have been inclined to interfere. A judiciary completely subservient to the executive or responsive to every change of popular or party opinion could exist within the English legal system without any change of the formal framework. Too many judiciaries have capitulated in the face of pressure from governments and the community abroad, not to make one curious in the first place about the basis of the English judge's reputation for independence and how it can be preserved, but this is a subject more appropriate for a book on the constitution as a whole than the English legal system part of it.

THE ROLE AND CHARACTER OF THE JUDICIARY

Although the formal dress adds dignity to the proceedings of the courts and gives an air of objectivity and ritual to the whole process the fact is that underneath it judges are lawyers with a professional job to do. The identification of that job is an essential preliminary to asking the question whether they do it well. One important distinction to be drawn is between the trial court judges and those in appeal courts, and between the Crown Court and the Queen's Bench and Family Division of the High Court, on the one hand and the Chancery Division on the other. The former are mostly finders of fact and in the case of the Queen's Bench judges princi-pally finders of fact in criminal cases. From time to time they will be called upon to decide difficult questions of law and then they will have to extract the relevant law from the various statutes and cases, assisted by counsel on both sides. But they are not and are on the whole not expected to be innovators. The doctrine of precedent which is discussed further below at page 236, helps to see to that. It is at the appellate level that one expects to find the judges playing a more active role in lawmaking and law rationalisation. Both of the appeal courts, the Court of Appeal and the

House of Lords, are better equipped for this task not only because the judges in them are more experienced, but also because they have more leisure and a more detached view of the cases, because the trial court will already have pre-digested many of the issues, and because of the simple fact that there are more of them, usually three in the Court of Appeal, and five in the House of Lords.

It is the judges of the appellate courts that have attracted most attention in recent years, though much of the discussion has failed to discriminate sufficiently between them and the trial judges. One of the reasons for this increased attention has been a growing recognition of the role that judges are called upon from time to time to play in making and moulding the law, and not merely a recognition but also an acceptance of the fact. With this acceptance has come realisation of accompanying problems. The judges are appointed not elected. Parliament is elected. Parliament is therefore the primary place in which law should be made. What then is the relationship between the judges as lawmakers and Parliament, and in what sense and to what extent do judges make law? We return to this question in the chapter on law, in particular in relation to the Court of Appeal and the House of Lords. It is generally accepted that judges even in the House of Lords are not as free to make law as the legislature, and that no judge in the United Kingdom has quite the freedom of decision enjoyed by a judge of the Supreme Court of the United States in a marginal constitutional case. But it has nevertheless been strongly argued that this still leaves a good deal of discretion in the hands of at least the higher judiciary as to what exactly they declare to be the law. In relatively technical cases, cases of what is sometimes called lawyers' law, this causes no interest. The cases which, though relatively small in number, do cause concern are those which seem to raise major social or political issues, for although they are small in number they often occur at points of tension where something new is straining with something established, so that for a brief moment even an English court may appear to have become the forum for a major social or political debate. They are also important because the values that they are seen to uphold will flow through the system and affect numerous small and unreported decisions in the lower courts. From the view that the judges have on occasion the power to make law, and in some cases which seem to involve something of moment, it has been a short step to asking, from where do the values which the judges uphold and the assumptions on which they operate come, and more generally from where do the values and assumptions on which the non-statutory part of the law come, and to what extent are they changeable and should they be changed? Some of this curiosity is jurisprudential, based on what is now a long standing interest in the nature of judicial decision making, often influenced to an excessive extent by writings on the Supreme Court of the United States or alarm at the decisions of state and even federal judges across the country in the United States in politically and socially sensitive cases. Some has been itself political and social, following on particular decisions which have been regarded as revealing social and political values of an antagonistic kind, whether to trade unions, freedom of the Press, individual liberty or even to the government. It would not be difficult to cull through the law reports and put together a series of decisions which would reveal the judges in their law decision capacity as authoritarian and slow to respond to changing values, views and circumstances, though it would also be possible to make out an alternative case, showing changes that have been made in the law by the judges themselves without the help of the legislature.

Whatever one's view however on the present state of the English judiciary there are a number of useful points to bear in mind. The first is the distinction between those cases which turn on the judge's individual values, and those which he shares with other members of the judiciary, and even the legal profession as a whole. A second is between those cases which turn on the values which affect a judge's views on the merits of the case and those which turn on values which affect his more general views as to his role as a judge. The latter for example may well affect the extent to which he feels free to depart from precedent or make new law or infuse new ideas into the law. This has accounted for a good many of the disputes between Lord Denning and his colleagues. He has often been prepared to innovate more boldly than they thought consistent with the role of a judge, or a judge in his position in the hierarchy. A third distinction is between the values of the judge and the values embodied in the law at any particular time of which the judge is no more than the means of expression. Fourthly, a distinction lies between the social, political and class origins of a judge and the views and values he expresses on the Bench. Lastly, though without attempting to exhaust the subject, is the distinction with which we started, that between the trial judge and the appellate judge.

So much of the discussion of judges has been in relation to the extent and the way in which they make law that the equally important sphere of the trial court judge, the world of the High Court and Circuit judges, of justices of the peace and stipendiary magistrates, has often been forgotten. As was mentioned above, their functions often have little to do with questions of law as such. The question is not therefore how do they come to decide points of law but rather how they judge character, and find facts. What are their attitudes as reflected in the sentences they impose and the homilies they sometimes deliver to convicted offenders? One should also look at the way in which they conduct their trials, the way in which they treat witnesses, their attitude to the prosecution, the police and the government, the way they sum up, not simply the words (which is all one finds in the reports of those summings up which have been challenged because of the words in which the direction has been given) but the more difficult job of assessing the impression made by the judge when he spoke them. There are the problems of how judges whose practice has been mainly paper work can acquire an expertise in conducting trials with a jury, how judges acquire their knowledge of the world or deal with matters requiring a degree of expert or professional knowledge which they cannot be presumed to have.

The questions are infinite and the answers to them go way beyond the primitive exercises of culling through *Who's Who* and recording the number of judges who went to public schools or the number of lawyers who were Oxbridge trained, which hardly scratch the surface of the problem and which fall well short of the varied and complex range of queries which should be in the front of the minds of those involved in and trying to observe and understand the system. How are judges appointed? Who gets the chance of becoming one? What is the role of the judge in the English system? What supports does he need? How are they provided? What are the checks upon arbitrariness or whimsy? On what does the status, prestige, expertise, ability, independence, function of the judge depend? One perspective one might adopt is that of someone thinking of establishing a legal system for the first time. Another is to look abroad at the position of judges and the way in which they perform their tasks and ask what factors lead to the differences and what the implications of the differences are.

And when one is thinking of research there is one other thing to remember. One is not looking for final conclusions or settled principles or a settled relationship between a given number of variables. It is much more a question of being equipped with a number of questions and a set of criteria for evaluating what is going on at any given moment in the making of decisions, the disposal of cases and the treatment of people and the factors proper and improper which are influencing them.

THE ROLE OF THE JUDGE IN A PARTICULAR CASE

It is usually said that the judge in an English trial is not expected to play an active part in the proceedings before him. In general this is true. In a civil case it is the parties, or rather their legal advisers, who shape their own case, prepare and deliver pleadings, select the evidence which they think is relevant and the witnesses they think are appropriate to give it. In court they conduct the case, calling and examining their own witnesses and cross-examining the witnesses of their opponents, citing the authorities which they think support their case and distinguishing those relied on by the other side. In a criminal case the preparation of the prosecution will be in the hands of the police and their legal advisers. They will determine the charge, in fact they will decide whether there should be a charge in the first place and whether the charge should be followed by a prosecution (see below, p. 313), select the witnesses, attempt to prove their case and put forward any relevant legal arguments.

A civil case arrives before the judge in the form of a bundle of pleadings resulting from the earlier exchange of pleadings between the parties together with relevant documents. He will not usually see the parties or their legal representatives until the opening of the trial. The position in criminal cases is very much the same. At the opening of the criminal trial the judge has the indictment and the depositions or statements of the witness for the prosecution. In addition he will have a list of previous convictions, if any, of the accused and in some cases a pre-trial social inquiry report on him. He will not usually have seen either the accused or the lawyers in the case until the trial opens, unless there has for example been some question of plea bargaining.

The basic function of the judge sitting without a jury in a civil case is to determine in the light of the evidence the facts of the case, and the relevant law, and give his judgment. If the judgment is in favour of the plaintiff, he must then determine the damages or other remedy to which the plaintiff is entitled, and make an order as to costs. In the rare civil case in which he sits with a jury his role will be slightly different. There, it is his task to determine any disputed points of law, review the evidence and sum up the issues and the relevant law for the jury's benefit. It is then for the jury to give their verdict and, if the plaintiff is claiming damages, decide how much he should be awarded. In criminal cases too where a judge is sitting with a jury his role is the same except that it is for the jury to decide whether or not the accused is guilty of the offence charged and for the judge then to determine what sentence should be given, a function which has come to require more sophistication with the increasing range of choice and the emphasis on the individualisation of treatment (see below, p. 500).

Neither in civil nor in criminal cases is the judge expected to play an active let alone a leading part in the actual conduct of the case. To this general picture of non-intervention however there are exceptions. In the first place the judge has a responsibility for seeing that the trial is a fair one,[1] conducted in accordance with the rules and conventions and with reasonable dispatch, and in an atmosphere appropriate to judicial proceedings. There are rules of procedure and pleading to be observed with regard to which he has some discretionary powers, whether or not to allow an amendment of the pleadings for example, or whether to uphold a submission by the defendant that there is no case to answer. There are rules of evidence to be enforced, excluding inadmissible evidence, and in criminal cases excluding evidence which though formally admissible would be unfairly prejudicial to the accused (see below, p. 398). This is a particularly important function since the rationale of many of the exclusionary rules of evidence is that otherwise relevant evidence is treated as inadmissible because of the fear that juries would attach more weight to it than it really deserves. Any argument about admissibility therefore takes place in the absence of the jury. He may put questions to a witness himself or ask counsel to put particular questions, especially when he is sitting with a jury where he has the additional responsibility for seeing that the jury is given as much help as is reasonable in following and understanding what is going on. Hence some of the questions of the " who are the Beatles? " variety. He may even in some cases call a witness himself (see below, p. 386). Although he will leave it in general to the parties to shape their case he may ask them to consider particular points of law which they had overlooked or particular cases or statutory provisions which he may regard as relevant or problematical. This will particularly be the case if he is moved to help an inexperienced counsel. It is also generally accepted that he should to some extent act as an advocate for a party or accused who is unrepresented though the extent to which he can do this is clearly limited; hence the great pressure to make free legal advisers as widely available as possible. If it can be shown that he has gone beyond these limited functions and taken so active a part that he has prevented the parties developing their own case then the decision may be quashed. It may also be quashed if it is shown that he has been partial to one side.

There are two basic rules of natural justice which all those presiding over judicial proceedings are expected to observe, *audi alteram partem*, the obligation to give to each side an opportunity to state his case, and *nemo*

---

[1] Note in relation to this point the intervention by James J. before the beginning of the trial in the " Angry Brigade " case in which he went out of his way to secure as far as possible a jury that would not be prejudiced against the accused. *The Times*, May 31, 1972.

judex in causa sua, or more accurately the obligation not to show improper bias. The first principle is of the essence of the adversary procedure. It has raised very few problems in the higher courts. The leading cases which have arisen on the matter have concerned tribunals and quasi-judicial proceedings in the administrative field, such as public inquiries. The latter has as a legal authority the case of *Dimes* v. *The Grand Junction Canal Company* [2] in which no less a person than the then Lord Chancellor was involved, but it rarely raises problems. It would necessitate in particular a judge declining to hear a case in which he had any financial interest or in which it might appear that he had. It is also automatic for judges to withdraw from cases in which they are acquainted with the parties or a witness.

The qualities of a trial judge are to some degree reflected in the attitude of the appellate courts to their judgments. They are for the most part, as was mentioned earlier, in the Queen's Bench Division, the Crown Court and even more so in the county courts, triers of fact and not deciders of law. Their major task is to listen to and observe the witnesses and to decide so far as they can the truth of the matter. Appellate courts always stress the importance of this role and the advantage it gives the trial judge in deciding the facts, though they are more ready to differ from him where it is a question of the inferences to be drawn from them.

The qualities and functions of a Judge

History of the Criminal Law of England, Sir James Fitzjames Stephen

(1883) Vol. I, p. 544. Macmillan

The duty most appropriate to the office and character of a judge is that of an attentive listener ... not that of an investigator. After performing his duty patiently and fully, he is in a position to give a jury the full benefit of his thoughts on the subject, but if he takes the leading and principal part in the conflict—and every criminal trial is essentially a conflict and struggle for life, liberty from imprisonment, or character ...—he cannot possibly perform his own special duty. He is, and of necessity must be, powerfully biased against the prisoner.

Final Report of the Royal Commission on Delay in the King's Bench Division 1912–14

Cd. 7177 (1913)

57. ... [T]he work of a judge requires unflagging alertness ... [A]nything less than the utmost patience attention and appreciation on the part of a judge is a distinct injustice inflicted upon the suitor; ... [D]uring the hearing of a cause, or criminal trial, the judge needs the full possession and exercise of all his faculties in order to arrive at the truth, which one or other litigant always—and each from time to time—is probably trying to conceal from his opponent, and especially, or at least consequently from the judge, being, moreover aided in this endeavour by advocates often as able and experienced as the judge himself. Lord Sumner in his evidence insisted on the necessity for "mental relief from the perpetual contemplation of human nature not at its best." There can be no doubt that considerable periods of rest from a very fatiguing and perhaps demoralising form of mental activity are in the public interest required. ... The

---

[2] (1852) 3 H.L.Cas. 794.

duties of the judges of the High Court are difficult to discharge—the responsibilities are very onerous and demand the possession not only of learning but of unshaken nerve. It would be disastrous indeed, were the powers of the judiciary in any degree to sink below that high level which has made English justice acceptable at home and respected and imitated abroad. . . .

63. We do not recommend an increase in the judges of the King's Bench Division beyond . . . 18 and it is not possible to tell how many will be required in future. . . . It must be remembered that the field of selection is limited, the more judges appointed the smaller it becomes, and therefore the less certainty of securing in those appointed the high level of ability, legal attainments and mental and physical vigour, which are necessary to maintain the great prestige of the English Bench. The smaller the number of judges the higher will be the standard and the greater the prize for those selected. . . .

64. We have considered . . . whether the administration of justice has been in any way impeded by judges continuing in office who by reason of age, infirmity, or prolonged illness, were incapable of properly fulfilling their duties. We are satisfied that, though such cases have happily been few, they have occurred within the memory of men still in the active practice of the profession of the law. . . . It is especially necessary that the judges of the King's Bench Division should be in full possession of unimpaired physical power; because the nature of their work requires them to be constantly on the alert, sometimes for long hours on circuit, when they are absent from home. . . .

We have therefore considered whether the judges of the King's Bench should be compulsorily retired at a certain age. . . . The principle of compulsory retirement from other kinds of public work has long been accepted in this country. A permanent civil servant . . . may be compelled by the Minister at the head of his department to retire on attaining the age of 60 . . . On attaining the age of 65 he must retire unless his retirement is certified by the head of his department to be detrimental to the public service. . . . A judge is necessarily in a higher and more independent position than any civil servant. He may be called upon at any time to protect the individual against the Executive government; and in order that he should be able, without fear or favour, to hold the scales of justice with an absolutely even hand, it has long been settled that he cannot be removed from his office except on the petition of both Houses of Parliament, and his conduct cannot even be criticised in Parliament except on a special motion to that effect. We believe that the profound respect with which the English Bench is regarded both at home and abroad is in no small measure due to the great and independent position thus secured to its members; and we would certainly not recommend any change which would deprive them of that position, or make their tenure depend on the mere will of the Minister of the day. . . . In fixing the age of retirement it is necessary to bear in mind that knowledge, experience and ripe judgment are more valuable in judicial work than energy or power of initiative. . . . For these reasons we think that the age fixed should be considerably higher in the case of judges than in the case of civil servants; and we agree with the present Lord Chancellor that . . . the judges of the King's Bench Division should be required to retire at the age of 72. . . .

Powell and Wife v. Streatham Manor Nursing Home
House of Lords [1935] A.C. 243

VISCOUNT SANKEY L.C.: . . . Where there has been a conflict of evidence the Court of Appeal will have special regard to the fact that the judge saw the witnesses: see *Clarke* v. *Edinburgh Tramways Co.*, *per* Lord Shaw, where he says: "When a judge hears and sees witnesses and makes a conclusion or inference with regard to what is the weight on balance of their evidence, that judgment is entitled to great respect, ... irrespective of whether the Judge makes any observation with regard to credibility or not. I can of course quite understand a Court of Appeal that says that it will not interfere in a case in which the Judge has announced as part of his judgment that he believes one set of witnesses, having seen them and heard them, and does not believe another. But that is not the ordinary case of a cause in a Court of justice. In Courts of justice in the ordinary case things are much more evenly divided; witnesses without any conscious bias towards a conclusion may have in their demeanour, in their manner, in their hesitation, in the nuance of their expressions, in even the turns of the eyelid, left an impression upon the man who saw and heard them which can never be reproduced in the printed page.... In my opinion, the duty of an appellate Court in those circumstances is for each Judge of it to put to himself ... the question, " Am I—who sit here without those advantages, sometimes broad and sometimes subtle, which are the privilege of the Judge who heard and tried the case ... to come to a clear conclusion that the Judge who had them was plainly wrong? If I cannot ... then it appears to me to be my duty to defer to his judgment."

LORD WRIGHT: ... As the evidence proceeds through examination, cross-examination and re-examination the judge is gradually imbibing almost instinctively, but in fact as a result of close attention and of long experience, an impression of the personality of the witness and of his trustworthiness and of the accuracy of his observation and memory or the reverse. He will not necessarily distrust a witness simply because he finds him inaccurate in some details: he can give such inaccuracy its proper place, particularly if he sees that the witness is tired, or antagonized, or confused, or perhaps impatient, and especially if the matter of the inaccuracy is of minor or collateral importance. But such inaccuracies may appear in a very different light when pointed to as isolated passages in the shorthand notes and abstracted from the human atmosphere of the trial and from the totality of the evidence. The judge will form his impression from the whole personality of the witness: he can allow for the nervous witness, standing up in a crowded Court or worried by the strain of cross-examination. The judge may be deceived by an adroit and plausible knave or by apparent innocence: for no man is infallible; but in the main a careful and conscientious judge with his experience of Courts is as likely to be correct in his impressions as any tribunal, unless perhaps, as some would say, a jury of twelve members is preferable. Yet even where the judge decides on conflicting evidence, it must not be forgotten that there may be cases in which his findings may be falsified, as for instance by some objective fact; thus in a collision case by land or sea the precise nature of the damage sustained by the colliding objects or their relative or final positions may be determinant and indisputable facts, and the same may be true of some conclusive document or documents which constitute positive evidence refuting the oral evidence of the witness. ...

Yuill v. Yuill

Court of Appeal [1945] P. 15

LORD GREENE M.R.: ... I now come to the principal question in the case, which is one of pure fact, namely, did the respondent commit adultery with the co-respondent in the co-respondent's lorry on August 3, 1943? ... From a careful perusal of the whole of the respondent's evidence I have come to the conclusion that she was deliberately seeking out the co-respondent with the intention of renewing her previous relations with him, and that in pursuance of this design she brought about the meeting of August 3, and that with regard to that meeting the evidence of the petitioner and Mr. Young ought to be accepted, and that of the respondent and co-respondent rejected.

But it is said that we are not entitled to take this view because the learned judge believed the evidence of the respondent and the co-respondent, and based his belief, as he said, on a careful observation of their demeanour and the opinion which he formed of their " type and characteristics." He said that much of their evidence—particularly that of the respondent—was given in a very unsatisfactory manner, and that the respondent was on some occasions resentful, and consequently reckless in her answers. Both of them, he said, were affected by nervousness and embarrassment and he was " not satisfied that they were deliberately dishonest in the box." He was, however, satisfied, despite his serious criticism, that they were substantially truthful in their testimony on the vital matters which he mentioned.

We were reminded of certain well-known observations in the House of Lords dealing with the position of an appellate court when the judgment of the trial judge has been based in whole or in part on his opinion of the demeanour of witnesses. It can, of course, only be on the rarest occasions, and in circumstances where the appellate court is convinced by the plainest considerations, that it would be justified in finding that the trial judge had formed a wrong opinion. But when the court is so convinced it is, in my opinion, entitled and indeed bound to give effect to its conviction. It has never been laid down by the House of Lords that an appellate court has no power to take this course. Puisne judges would be the last persons to lay claim to infallibility, even in assessing the demeanour of a witness. The most experienced judge may, albeit rarely, be deceived by a clever liar, or led to form an unfavourable opinion of an honest witness, and may express his view that his demeanour was excellent or bad as the case may be. Most experienced counsel can, I have no doubt, recall at least one case where this happened to their knowledge. I may further point out that an impression as to the demeanour of a witness ought not to be adopted by a trial judge without testing it against the whole of the evidence of the witness in question. If it can be demonstrated to conviction that a witness whose demeanour has been praised by the trial judge has on some collateral matter deliberately given an untrue answer, the favourable view formed by the judge as to his demeanour must necessarily lose its value.

There is one further consideration which is particularly relevant to the present case. A judge who observes the demeanour of the witnesses while they are being examined by counsel has from his detached position a much more favourable opportunity of forming a just appreciation than a judge who himself conducts the examination. If he takes the latter course he, so to speak, descends into the arena and is liable to have his vision clouded by the dust of the conflict. Unconsciously he deprives himself of the advantage of calm and dispassionate observation. It is further to be remarked as everyone who has had experience of these matters knows, that the demeanour of a witness is apt to be very different when he is being questioned by the judge from what it is when he is being questioned by counsel, particularly when the judge's examination is, as it was in the present case, prolonged and covers practically the whole of the crucial matters which are in issue. That it is open to an appellate court to find that the view of the trial judge as to the demeanour of a witness was ill-founded has indeed been recognized by the House of Lords itself. The case to which I refer was one in which I was engaged as counsel in the Court of Appeal and in the House of Lords, and I think it right to place the matter on record as the only report of the case does not bring out the relevant circumstances. The case is that of *Hvalfangerselskapet Polaris A/S* v. *Unilever, Ltd. and Others.*[3] In one respect

[3] (1933) 46 Ll.L.R. 29.

it resembles the present case, since the learned trial judge had himself taken a most active part in the examination of the witnesses. . . .

Watt or Thomas v. Thomas

House of Lords [1947] A.C. 484

Lord Thankerton: . . . [T]he value and importance of having seen and heard the witnesses will vary according to the class of case, and, it may be, the individual case in question. It will hardly be disputed that consistorial cases form a class in which it is generally most important to see and hear the witnesses, and particularly the spouses themselves; and, further, within that class, cases of alleged cruelty will afford an even stronger example of such an advantage. Normally the cruelty is alleged to have occurred within the family establishment, and the physique, temperament, standard of culture, habits of verbal expression and of action, and the interaction between the spouses in their daily life, cannot be adequately judged except by seeing and hearing them in the witness box. The law has no footrule by which to measure the personalities of the spouses. In cases such as the present, it will be almost invariably found that a divided household promotes partisanship, and it is difficult to get unbiased evidence. . . .

Glebe Sugar Refining Co. Ltd. v. Trustees of Port and Harbour of Greenock

House of Lords (1921) 125 L.T. 578

Lord Birkenhead: . . . It is not, of course, in cases of complication possible for their Lordships to be aware of all the authorities, statutory or otherwise, which may be relevant to the issues requiring decision in a particular case. Their Lordships are therefore very much in the hands of counsel, and those who instruct counsel in these matters, and it is the practice of the house to expect, and indeed insist, that authorities that bear one way or the other upon matters under debate should be brought to the attention of their Lordships, . . . irrespective of whether or not the particular authority assists the party who is aware of it. It is an obligation of confidence between their Lordships and all those who assist in the debates in this house in the capacity of counsel. It has been shown that Mr. Sandeman, Sir John Simon, and Mr. Macmillan were unaware of the existence of the section which appears to their Lordships to be highly relevant to, and indeed decisive upon, the matters now under discussion. Indeed, the circumstances in which leading counsel are very often briefed at the last moment render such an absence of knowledge extremely intelligible. But for myself I find it very difficult to believe that some of those who instructed counsel were not well aware of the existence and the possible importance and relevance of the section in question. It was the duty of such persons if they are so aware to have directed the attention of leading counsel to the section and to its possible relevance in order that they in turn might have brought it to the attention of your Lordships.

Annual Statement of General Council of the Bar 1971–72

Counsel's duty to inform the Court of earlier decisions

1. Subject to 3 below, counsel is called upon, as regards a point of law, to put before the court any relevant decision of which he is aware and which he believes to be immediately in point whether it be for or against his contention.

This rule applies to criminal as well as civil cases and to tribunals as well as courts and must be observed with particular care in *ex parte* proceedings or where an opposite party is appearing in person.

2. If after the conclusion of the evidence and argument in a civil case, and where judgment is reserved, counsel discovers a proposition of law which is directly in point and proposes to bring it to the judge's attention, counsel on the other side ought to concur in the proposal even though he knows that the proposition is against him. If he does not concur, it would still be in order for the first counsel to submit the additional authority. . . .

3. If in a criminal case the court, entirely of its own volition and without calling on either the prosecution or the defence, rules that certain facts and documents tendered by the prosecution are inadmissible, counsel for the defence is not bound to draw the court's attention to an authority which it has overlooked even though he knows that the authority renders the court's decision wrong in law and that exclusion of the facts and documents is of great advantage to his case and quite likely to make the difference between conviction and acquittal.

Banbury v. Bank of Montreal
House of Lords [1918] A.C. 626

LORD FINLAY L.C.: . . . It is, of course, within the power of the presiding judge at the trial, if it occurs to him that there is a point of law which is being overlooked by the counsel in the case, to call their attention to it, and if after argument he thinks that it concludes the case, so to decide. This is a power which should be exercised sparingly, as the judge would no doubt think it right to abstain from interfering with the conduct of the case by experienced counsel in the manner which they considered most in the interests of their clients. It would be exercised when it is apparent that, owing to inexperience or some accident, a point material to be considered has escaped the notice of counsel. . . .

Rahimtoola v. Nizam of Hyderabad
House of Lords [1958] A.C. 379

LORD DENNING: . . . My Lords, I acknowledge that, in the course of this opinion, I have considered some questions and authorities which were not mentioned by counsel. I am sure they gave all the help they could and I have only gone into it further because the law on this subject is of great consequence and, as applied at present, it is held by many to be unsatisfactory. I venture to think that if there is one place where it should be reconsidered on principle—without being tied to particular precedents of a period that is past—it is here in this House: and if there is one time for it to be done, it is now, when the opportunity offers, before the law gets any more enmeshed in its own net. This I have tried to do. Whatever the outcome, I hope I may say, as Holt C.J. once did after he had done much research on his own: " I have stirred these points, which wiser heads in time may settle." [4]

Re Lawrence's Will Trusts
Chancery Division [1972] 1 Ch. 418

MEGARRY J.: . . . In the course of this judgment I have referred to certain authorities that were not cited in argument. A judge who, after reserving

---

[4] *Coggs* v. *Bernard* (1703) 2 Ld.Raym. 909, 920.

judgment, comes upon possibly relevant authorities not cited in argument is in a position of some difficulty. Naturally he wishes to avoid the expense and delay of restoring the case for further argument; yet the paramount consideration is that of avoiding any injustice to litigants or their counsel. It seems to me that a distinction can be made. If the authorities are such as to raise a new point, or to change or modify, even provisionally, the conclusion that the judge has already reached, or to resolve his doubts on a point, I can see no alternative to restoring the case for further argument; and, of course, authorities do not always wear the same aspect after they have been dissected in argument as they appeared to wear before. On the other hand, if the authorities do no more than confirm or support the conclusions that the judge has already reached on a point that has been fairly argued, then in most cases I cannot see that it is wrong for the judgment to refer to them without any further argument. A litigant to whom the authorities are adverse would have been defeated in any event, and a litigant whose cause the authorities support is not likely to object to the advent of reinforcements. Further, if an appeal is contemplated, or if the case is reported, the citation of the additional authorities may be of assistance in showing that they were not overlooked and in preventing them from being overlooked in the future. Similarly, I do not think that objection could fairly be taken to the citation of an authority which could not affect the result but merely, for example, provides an apt phrase or extraneous parallel.

It is on this footing that I have cited certain additional authorities in this judgment. Let me make it clear that in doing so I intend no criticism of counsel: certainly I could not complain of any paucity of citation in this case. In the construction of wills, there is, by English standards, a very large number of authorities; and with the almost infinite number of variations of language possible in making most dispositions, it is inevitable that cases which exhibit a helpful similarity of expression may lie hidden until fortune reveals them. Furthermore, the construction of every will turns in the end upon the precise terms of that will, so that, in the old phrase, every will stands on its own bottom. It is accordingly always difficult for counsel to know how much citation of authority will assist the court in any given case. However, although it did not seem to me that in this case there was any need for further argument on this score, if any of the counsel engaged in the case wish to make any application in that respect I shall of course readily listen to it.

Jones v. National Coal Board
Court of Appeal [1957] 2 Q.B. 55

DENNING L.J.: . . . Mr. Gardiner took a further ground of appeal which is stated in the notice of appeal to be " that the nature and extent of the judge's interruptions during the hearing of the evidence called on behalf of the defendants made it virtually impossible for counsel for the plaintiff to put the plaintiff's case properly or adequately or to cross-examine the witnesses called on behalf of the defendants adequately or effectively." Furthermore, Mr. Edmund Davies said that, in case there was any chance of our being persuaded that Mr. Gardiner's three points on liability were correct, he wished himself to give a cross-notice of appeal in similar terms complaining that the judge's interruptions prevented him from properly putting his case. We gave him leave to give a cross-notice to this effect.

We much regret that it has fallen to our lot to consider such a complaint against one of Her Majesty's judges: but consider it we must, because we can only do justice between these parties if we are satisfied that the primary facts have been properly found by the judge on a fair trial between the parties. Once we have the primary facts fairly found we are in as good a position as the judge to draw inferences or conclusions from those facts, but we cannot embark on this task unless the foundation of primary facts is secure. . . . Mr. Mars-Jones appeared for the plaintiff, and opened the case for her. . . . He called . . . an expert, William Charles Davies. This expert had not been down the mine, but he relied on a plan which had been made by the board's surveyor shortly after the accident. This enable him to make criticisms on the same lines as those opened by Mr. Mars-Jones. . . . Mr. Edmund Davies, who appeared for the National Coal Board, then called John Kerr, the manager of the . . . Colliery at the time of the accident. . . . Mr. Edmund Davies began to ask the manager to deal with the criticisms which had been made by Mr. Mars-Jones, and by his expert witness, W. C. Davies. Now, when this happened the judge, we fear, intervened far too much. He had himself made a note of the criticisms and, in his anxiety to understand the manager's replies to these criticisms, he took the examination of the witness out of the hands of leading counsel for the rest of that day and of his junior counsel next morning. Mr. Mars-Jones then cross-examined the witness; but during the cross-examination the judge intervened on several occasions to protect the witness from what he thought was a misleading question, and to bring out points in favour of the witness's point of view.

Next, Mr. Edmund Davies called Thomas George Davies. . . . His examination-in-chief proceeded on normal lines; but during Mr. Mars-Jones's cross-examination the judge seemed to be afraid that he was being misled, intervened at considerable length, and in effect stopped his cross-examination on the important point of chocks. When Mr. Edmund Davies re-examined, the judge cut him short, saying: "This is what has been given again and again." . . . Finally, Mr. Edmund Davies called Cecil Henry Bates, an expert consultant mining engineer. We are afraid that the judge took the examination-in-chief largely out of the hands of Mr. Edmund Davies. He took the points of criticism made against the defendants, went through them with the witness, and appeared to accept his explanations. Mr. Mars-Jones cross-examined the witness, but after a while the judge disclosed much impatience with him and he brought it to a close.

No one can doubt that the judge, in intervening as he did, was actuated by the best motives. He was anxious to understand the details of this complicated case, and asked questions to get them clear in his mind. He was anxious that the witnesses should not be harassed unduly in cross-examination, and intervened to protect them when he thought necessary. He was anxious to investigate all the various criticisms that had been made against the board, and to see whether they were well founded or not. Hence, he took them up himself with the witnesses from time to time. He was anxious that the case should not be dragged on too long, and intimated clearly when he thought that a point had been sufficiently explored. All those are worthy motives on which judges daily intervene in the conduct of cases, and have done for centuries.

Nevertheless, we are quite clear that the interventions, taken together, were far more than they should have been. In the system of trial which we have evolved in this country, the judge sits to hear and determine the issues raised by the parties, not to conduct an investigation or examination on behalf of society at large, as happens, we believe, in some foreign countries. Even in England, however, a judge is not a mere umpire to answer the question " How's that? " His object, above all, is to find out the truth, and to do justice according to law; and in the daily pursuit of it the advocate plays an honourable and necessary role. Was it not Lord Eldon L.C. who said in a notable passage that " truth is best discovered by powerful statements on both sides of the question? " :

see *Ex parte Lloyd*.[5] And Lord Greene M.R. who explained that justice is best done by a judge who holds the balance between the contending parties without himself taking part in their disputations? If a judge, said Lord Greene, should himself conduct the examination of witnesses, " he, so to speak, descends into the arena and is liable to have his vision clouded by the dust of conflict ": see *Yuill* v. *Yuill*.[6]

Yes, he must keep his vision unclouded. It is all very well to paint justice blind, but she does better without a bandage round her eyes. She should be blind indeed to favour or prejudice, but clear to see which way lies the truth: and the less dust there is about the better. Let the advocates one after the other put the weights into the scales—the " nicely calculated less or more "—but the judge at the end decides which way the balance tilts, be it ever so slightly. So firmly is all this established in our law that the judge is not allowed in a civil dispute to call a witness whom he thinks might throw some light on the facts. He must rest content with the witnesses called by the parties: see *In re Enoch & Zaretzky, Bock & Co.*[7] So also it is for the advocates, each in his turn, to examine the witnesses, and not for the judge to take it on himself lest by so doing he appear to favour one side or the other: see *Rex* v. *Cain*,[8] *Rex* v. *Bateman*,[9] and *Harris* v. *Harris*,[10] by Birkett L.J. especially. And it is for the advocate to state his case as fairly and strongly as he can, without undue interruption, lest the sequence of his argument be lost: see *Reg.* v. *Clewer*.[11] The judge's part in all this is to hearken to the evidence, only himself asking questions of witnesses when it is necessary to clear up any point that has been overlooked or left obscure; to see that the advocates behave themselves seemly and keep to the rules laid down by law; to exclude irrelevancies and discourage repetition; to make sure by wise intervention that he follows the points that the advocates are making and can assess their worth; and at the end to make up his mind where the truth lies. If he goes beyond this, he drops the mantle of a judge and assumes the robe of an advocate; and the change does not become him well. Lord Chancellor Bacon spoke right when he said that [12]: " Patience and gravity of hearing is an essential part of justice; and an over-speaking judge is no well-tuned cymbal."

Such are our standards. They are set so high that we cannot hope to attain them all the time. In the very pursuit of justice, our keenness may outrun our sureness, and we may trip and fall. That is what has happened here. A judge of acute perception, acknowledged learning, and actuated by the best of motives, has nevertheless himself intervened so much in the conduct of the case that one of the parties—nay, each of them—has come away complaining that he was not able properly to put his case; and these complaints are, we think, justified.

We have sufficiently indicated the nature of the interventions already, but there is one matter which we would specially mention. Mr. Gardiner made particular complaint of the interference by the judge during the cross-examination of the defendants' witnesses by Mr. Mars-Jones. Now, it cannot, of course, be doubted that a judge is not only entitled but is, indeed, bound to intervene at any stage of a witness's evidence if he feels that, by reason of the technical nature of the evidence or otherwise, it is only by putting questions of his own that he can properly follow and appreciate what the witness is saying. Nevertheless, it

 5 (1822) Mont. 70, 72n.
 6 [1945] P. 15, 20; 61 T.L.R. 176; [1945] 1 All E.R. 183.
 7 [1910] 1 K.B. 327.
 8 (1936) 25 Cr.App.R. 204.
 9 (1946) 31 Cr.App.R. 106.
 10 *The Times*, April 9, 1952; Judgments of the Court of Appeal, 1952, No. 148.
 11 (1953) 37 Cr.App.R. 37.
 12 Essays or Counsels Civil and Moral. Of Judicature.

is obvious for more than one reason that such interventions should be as infrequent as possible when the witness is under cross-examination. It is only by cross-examination that a witness's evidence can be properly tested, and it loses much of its effectiveness in counsel's hands if the witness is given time to think out the answer to awkward questions; the very gist of cross-examination lies in the unbroken sequence of question and answer. Further than this, cross-examining counsel is at a grave disadvantage if he is prevented from following a preconceived line of inquiry which is, in his view, most likely to elicit admissions from the witness or qualifications of the evidence which he has given in chief. Excessive judicial interruption inevitably weakens the effectiveness of cross-examination in relation to both the aspects which we have mentioned, for at one and the same time it gives a witness valuable time for thought before answering a difficult question, and diverts cross-examining counsel from the course which he had intended to pursue, and to which it is by no means easy sometimes to return. Mr. Gardiner submitted that the extent of the judge's interruptions was such that Mr. Mars-Jones was unduly hampered in his task of probing and testing the evidence which the defendants' witnesses gave. We are reluctantly constrained to hold that this submission is well founded. It appears to us that the interventions by the judge while Mr. Mars-Jones was cross-examining went far beyond what was required to enable the judge to follow the witnesses' evidence and on occasion took the form of initiating discussions with counsel on questions of law; further, and all too frequently, the judge interrupted in the middle of a witness's answer to a question, or even before the witness had started to answer at all. In our view it is at least possible that the constant interruptions to which Mr. Mars-Jones was subjected from the bench may well have prevented him from eliciting from the defendants' witnesses answers which would have been helpful to the plaintiff's case, and correspondingly damaging to that of the defendants.

The judge seems to have been under the impression on occasions that Mr. Mars-Jones was asking a misleading question. We do not gain that impression ourselves. It seems to us that the case was conducted by counsel on both sides with complete propriety.

Mr. Edmund Davies asked us to say that the decision reached by the judge was the inevitable decision, but we cannot say that. We have not the material for the purpose. We have some of the primary facts, but not all of those necessary to a decision. . . .

In these circumstances, we think we must grant the widow a new trial. There is one thing to which everyone in this country is entitled, and that is a fair trial at which he can put his case properly before the judge. The widow and the National Coal Board stand in this respect on the level. No cause is lost until the judge has found it so; and he cannot find it without a fair trial, nor can we affirm it.

R. v. Clewer
Court of Criminal Appeal (1953) 37 Cr.App.R. 37

LORD CHIEF JUSTICE GODDARD: . . . In presenting the appeal to this court, Mr. Du Cann . . . frankly admitted that the evidence was such that the jury could properly have convicted. His complaint was that, by reason of the frequency and nature of interruptions by the judge, he never had an opportunity of putting his defence fairly before the jury. No doubt it is sometimes difficult, when the defence is one that appears to the presiding judge . . . to be fantastic or devoid of merit, to treat it with the same consideration as he would pay to a defence not marked by those characteristics. At the same time, the first and most important thing for the administration of the criminal law is that it should appear that the prisoner is having a fair trial, and that he should not be left with any sense of injustice on the ground that his case has not been fairly put before the jury. If counsel is constantly interrupted both in cross-examination and examination-in-chief, and, more especially, as in this case, during his speech to the jury, his task becomes almost impossible. The more improbable the defence, the more difficult it is for counsel to discharge his duty to his client adequately, and, provided that he keeps within the bounds of fair advocacy . . . it is highly desirable that he should be allowed to do his best in presenting his case, leaving it to the judge to deal with, and maybe to demolish, it in his summing-up. . . .

Issues of fact are under our law entirely the province of the jury. Everyday experience shows that juries sometimes accept defences which appear highly improbable to judges, and which would not be accepted if the decision rested with the judge alone. The prisoner is entitled to have his defence, even the most improbable, put to the jury by his counsel, whose task is rendered impossible if he is constantly subjected to the kind of interruptions that occurred in the present case. Moreover, to have his final speech interrupted for so long a period, and on so many occasions, is a most disconcerting experience, as everyone who has been engaged in advocacy can well appreciate. . . .

R. v. Hircock

Court of Appeal [1970] 1 Q.B. 67

WIDGERY L.J.: . . . It was said that the chairman had unfairly interrupted in the course of the evidence . . . and thus prevented the witnesses from giving a connected story or their counsel from examining them properly.

. . . [A]n examination of the transcript does not bear that complaint out. . . .

The real sting of the complaint relates to a matter not in the transcript at all. It can be summarised by saying that the chairman indicated a high degree of impatience during the trial; and, in particular, that . . . he showed impatience in such a degree as to distract the jury from the submissions which were being made, and, in brief, to create an atmosphere in which a fair trial could not be obtained.

Accordingly, Mr. Herbert . . . has sought leave to call evidence from a number of gentlemen who were present at the trial to testify to the matters to which I have referred.

. . . [T]his is an approach which is novel so far as the reports go. There have been cases . . . where a trial has been held to be vitiated and the judge's conduct criticised by reference to the transcript; that is to say by reference to what the judge said in the course of the trial as recorded by the shorthand writer. But there is no case as far as we know where the conduct of the judge was sought to be attacked by evidence given from those present at the trial in respect of matters which the transcript does not disclose. . . .

[S]ection 23 of the Criminal Appeal Act . . . is the present authority regulating the calling of evidence in this court. . . . [U]nder section 23 (1): " . . . the Court of Appeal may, if they think it necessary or expedient in the interests of justice— . . . (c) . . . receive the evidence, if tendered, of any witness." Accordingly, there is nothing in the statute to restrict the evidence which we can receive to witnesses who speak to the offence or the offender; and there is on the face of it no technical bar to our receiving evidence of what happened in the course of the trial.

The section goes on to provide . . . by subsection (2) that . . . one ground upon which the court can refuse to receive tendered evidence is if it is satisfied that the evidence, if received, would not afford any ground for allowing the appeal.

The first question . . . is whether the evidence . . . is evidence which ought to be excluded on that last-mentioned ground. We have looked . . . at the proofs from the witnesses whom the appellants seek to call. . . . It seems that when Mr. Gardner (Counsel for Leggett) was about to address the jury after addresses by all other counsel, he indicated that in order to do justice to his case he was going to run through each defendant's case in turn to establish the position of Leggett during the fight. It is evident that the prospect of this somewhat protracted re-examination of the circumstances was something which did not appeal to the chairman, because all the witnesses say that he observed in a loud voice " Oh, God," and then laid his head across his arm and made groaning noises. There was a silence for a moment, and then the chairman looked up and said to Mr. Gardner " Yes, yes " in what is described as a " testy way," and counsel regarded that as the signal to proceed with his address to the jury, which in fact he then undertook. It is said that throughout the speech the chairman kept sighing and groaning, and one witness at any rate said that he observed " Oh, God " on more than one occasion.

The submission is that that evidence, if received, would form the basis of a further submission that this court should quash the conviction on the footing that the convictions were either unsafe or unsatisfactory. We are referred to *Reg.* v. *Clewer* (1953) 37 Cr.App.R. 37, C.C.A. . . . [I]n that case . . . complaint was being made by defence counsel that he had been frequently interrupted by the judge and never had an opportunity of putting his defence fairly before the jury. Later on it appears that the judge on that occasion had disparaged the defence which was being put forward and referred to counsel as putting up a " dust storm," and had indicated that he regarded the defence as devoid of foundation. . . .

It is to be observed that all those matters . . . arose on the transcript. . . . It is, we think, understandable that in all previous cases of this kind reliance has been placed upon the transcript, because it is on the transcript that one will find interruptions and observations of the judge of the kinds referred to in *Reg.* v. *Clewer.* . . .

There is, in our judgment, a very important distinction between conduct on the part of the presiding judge which may be regarded as discourteous and may show signs of impatience . . . but which does not in itself invite the jury to disbelieve the defence witnesses, and conduct which positively and actively obstructs counsel in the doing of his work. . . . [T]here is nothing here to suggest at all that Mr. Gardner was interrupted in his address in the sense that he was unable to develop to the jury what he wished to say; and certainly there is no suggestion that the chairman was disparaging the defendant, as opposed to the defendant's counsel. If criticism by the chairman is a criticism of counsel in his handling of the case rather than of the case itself, it is obvious that the effect of that criticism upon the trial and its outcome is very different from that which comes from a disparagement of the defendant himself. . . . [W]e are quite satisfied that the kind of conduct spoken to in the evidence of the proposed witnesses . . . is . . . not conduct of the kind which would cause the conviction to be unsafe or unsatisfactory; and, therefore, not conduct which could possibly affect the outcome of the appeal. Accordingly, we refuse leave to call these witnesses, and in the result we must dismiss the appeal against conviction. . . .[13]

[13] *Cf. R.* v. *Jones and Others, The Times,* November 23, 1961.

TRIAL BY JURY

THE ORIGINS OF JURY TRIAL

The idea of referring questions of fact and even of guilt to a body of laymen drawn from the neighbourhood, which is the essence of jury trial, goes back a very long way. It began as primarily an administrative device and was, for example, the method used by the commissioners who compiled the Domesday survey of landholding in England in the eleventh century. It was also the method used by the Commissioners of Eyre who later toured the country making inquiries on behalf of the King into an ever increasing variety of matters ranging from the conduct of royal officials to the non-payment of taxes. Its association with the administration of justice dates from the reign of Henry II (1154–89). In making the royal justices available to try cases of forcible dispossession and ownership of land he stipulated that the issue was to be referred by them to bodies of men chosen from the neighbourhood who were to decide, on the basis of their own knowledge and such information as they could collect, whether in the one case, there had been forcible dispossession and, in the other, whether the plaintiff or the defendant owned the land in question. The juries were known as "assizes" and the remedies the "assize of novel disseisin" and "grand assize." The same method was used to decide whether land was held in spiritual or lay tenure.

Over the years this method became the standard method for deciding disputed facts in civil cases and grew with the growth of the common law courts and the common law, though it never found favour with the other courts such as the Court of Chancery, when it was established. Although a form of presenting or grand jury was established in Henry's reign as well—the Assizes of Clarendon (1166) and Northampton (1176) imposing on each neighbourhood the responsibility of appointing a small body of representatives whose duty it was to present those suspected of serious crimes to the royal justices on their next appearance in the district—trial by jury in criminal cases came later. Up until the thirteenth century trial was by ordeal. At the beginning of the century the clergy were forbidden to take part in the holding of ordeals and this robbed them of their basic justification, the appeal to divine judgment. For a time there was some indecision as to what should take the place of the ordeal. One alternative was to refer the question of guilt to the jury which had presented the accused in the first place, or another presenting jury or an enlarged jury. By the end of the century the practice was firmly settled of referring the question of guilt of those charged with serious offences to a jury of twelve men. The only trace of hesitation in the use of the jury for this purpose was to be found in the requirement that the accused should consent to jury trial. However, the state's conviction of its value as a method of ascertaining or proving guilt was evidenced by the fact that anyone who refused was encouraged to change his mind by the practice known as *peine forte et dure*, which gradually increased in severity up to the point when a man might die as a result of the pressure put on him to agree to jury trial rather than as a result of the jury finding him guilty. It is said that some family men were prepared to suffer in this way since it avoided the forfeiture of property that went with a conviction for felony.

From 1772 the refusal to agree to jury trial or plead was treated as a plea of guilty, and from 1837 as a plea of not guilty. As with the early use of juries in general inquiries like the Domesday survey the idea of having men drawn from the neighbourhood was to have men who were likely to know something about the facts or the reputation of those involved. Sometimes a witness might be added to them to give them more particular information, but in general they were expected to speak from their own knowledge. It followed from this that if it could be shown that they had come to a wrong conclusion there was a presumption that they had behaved improperly and deserved punishment since their false judgment was akin to perjury. In civil cases this punishment came at the end of a hearing by a larger jury of twenty-four on a writ of attaint in which the second jury tried the issue again to see if the first jury had misbehaved. A verdict against the first jury could result in a fine, imprisonment or loss of property. Quite apart from this, the judges and, especially in criminal cases with a political flavour, the Privy Council, and, later in the sixteenth century, the Star Chamber, were always prepared to discipline jurors for misbehaviour, including giving verdicts which in view of the authorities were against the weight of evidence or simply inconvenient. The case of Throckmorton[14] is often cited as an outstanding example.

Juries generally were somewhat roughly treated, being locked up without food, drink or heat until they reached a decision, a practice which continued until the nineteenth century. Examples have been quoted from earlier times when juries were said even to have been carried off from one assize to another in a wagon because they could not reach agreement, which, it had soon been established, had to be unanimous. By the middle of the sixteenth century hesitation was being expressed about the severity of the treatment of juries who gave verdicts which were regarded as false, especially in civil cases. This was partly connected with a change in their role. Over the years they came to speak less from their own knowledge and relied much more on the evidence of witnesses presented to them in court which would often be the first that the jury had heard of the case. Reliance on witnesses meant that if the jury made a mistake it could just as likely be the result of a mistaken inference as a deliberate falsehood, and in Bushell's Case[15] it was finally held that it was wrong to punish a jury for giving a verdict which was regarded as mistaken because, for example, it was against the weight of evidence.

From that time on it was accepted that there was a distinction between giving a dissatisfied party a remedy against an unsatisfactory verdict and punishing the jurors for having given it. At the same time the rule became yet more firmly established that the jury was there to listen to and assess the credibility of witnesses and not to speak from their own knowledge. If they had any personal knowledge of the case they should give evidence as witnesses on oath and subject to cross-examination and not communicate it in the privacy of the jury room. This completed the transition from the

14 (1554) How.St.Tr. 869.
15 (1670) 6 St.Tr. 99.

days when the jury was used to try cases because of the likelihood that the
jurors would know something about the case already, to the present day
when every effort is made to bring the jury to the trial without any prior
knowledge of the case and to confine their attention to the evidence
presented in court. Newspapers for example may be punished for contempt
of court if they publish anything that is likely to prejudice a fair trial, as in
R. v. Bolam [16] and *R. v. Thomson Newspapers Ltd.* [17] even if the publication
was due to mistake, *R. v. Evening Standard Co. Ltd.,* [18] unless it can be
shown that all reasonable care was taken to avoid one. [19] In criminal cases
there are rules which prevent the jury hearing of the accused's previous
record except in special circumstances (though the judge has them before
him and this may affect his summing up). The Criminal Justice Act 1967,
places restrictions on the reporting of committal proceedings unless the
defence wants publicity.

TRIAL BY JURY IN CRIMINAL CASES

Jury trial remains the method of trying cases on indictment but in practice
this means the small minority of cases. The vast majority of criminal cases
are tried summarily without a jury and this includes not only summary
offences but also many which are triable on indictment but which are in
fact tried summarily. In this sense one could say there has been a decline
in the use of the jury even in criminal cases as more indictable offences
have become triable summarily.

Criticisms of the suitability of juries for long and complicated cases of
commercial fraud were rejected by the Departmental Committee on Jury
Service. [20]

TRIAL BY JURY IN CIVIL CASES

Trial by jury was essentially a common law court institution. It was not
used by the other courts which existed before 1875. Until 1854 all civil
cases heard by the common law courts were heard by a judge sitting with a
jury, whereas cases in the other courts were normally heard by a judge
sitting alone. This universal use of the jury was criticised by the Commissioners appointed to look into the process, practice and pleading in the
superior courts, in their second report. [Below, p. 183.]

Following this report the Common Law Procedure Act 1853 provided
that actions at common law could be heard by a judge without a jury if the
parties agreed. In addition, matters involving the taking of accounts were
to go to an arbitrator. The Supreme Court of Judicature Acts 1873–75 in
section 57 provided that a judge could direct that matters requiring prolonged examination of accounts, documents or any scientific or local
examination could be sent to a referee if, in the view of the court or judge,
they could not conveniently be dealt with by a jury. A further important

[16] (1949) 93 S.J. 220.
[17] [1968] 1 W.L.R. 1.
[18] [1954] 1 Q.B. 578.
[19] Administration of Justice Act 1960, s. 13.
[20] Cmnd. 2627 (1965).

step was taken in 1883. The Rules of the Supreme Court, published in that year, provided that in future an order of a judge would be necessary if trial was to be with a jury, except in case of slander, libel, false imprisonment, malicious prosecution, seduction or breach of promise, where only notice had to be given.

Owing to a shortage of jurors at the end of the war, the Juries Act 1918 provided that no case other than those for which an order was not necessary, and cases involving an allegation of fraud, should be heard with a jury unless the judge thought that it was more fit that it should be so tried. There was a return to the pre-war position in the Administration of Justice Act 1920 with the addition of fraud to the cases in which an order was not necessary. In 1925 the additional case of fraud was dropped. Finally in 1933 the present position was reached in the Administration of Justice (Miscellaneous Provisions) Act 1933, as part of a more general drive for cheaper litigation. The result of this statute is that apart from the cases specifically mentioned the question whether or not a civil case is to be tried with a jury is in the discretion of the judge, exercised in the first instance by the Master in charge of the case at the preliminary stage. The presumption is that a jury will only be granted in exceptional cases. In *Ward* v. *James*, for example (below, p. 186), the Court of Appeal advised against granting an application for a jury in personal injury cases, *i.e.* the great majority of cases in the Queen's Bench Division.

JUDGE AND JURY

When a judge is sitting with a jury the broad division of functions between them is that the judge deals with questions of law and the jury questions of fact, but there are a number of overlaps. In actions for defamation, for example, the judge must decide whether the words used are capable of being defamatory before putting them to the jury to decide whether they in fact are. He also decides whether or not damage suffered by a plaintiff is too remote in law to make the defendant responsible for it. He may withdraw a civil case from the jury altogether, or in a criminal case direct the jury to acquit the accused, if in his view the evidence presented by the plaintiff in the civil, or the prosecution in the criminal case would not justify a verdict in their favour. Moreover although the main function of the jury is to decide the facts, their verdict, unless it is a " special " verdict, involves an application of the law as they understand it to the facts as they find them. Their verdict is a final decision of mixed fact and law, not in the sense that they formally determine what the law is, that is for the judge to determine, and to explain in the course of his summing up, but their verdict is a simple verdict of guilty or not guilty in a criminal case or for the plaintiff or the defendant in a civil case, with a sum of damages if that is claimed, without any explanation as to how they arrived at their decision or how they combined fact and law in it. Their decision is, like Marcia, inscrutable.

It is one of the essential features of jury trial that the jury conduct their discussions in secret, with a foreman chosen by themselves as chairman. They are under no obligation to explain or justify their decision to anyone, not even the judge, and their verdict can only be overturned on appeal if it can be shown that it was so unreasonable that no twelve jurors properly directed could reasonably have reached it on the evidence. A similar protection is given to their award of damages. Appellate courts have shown great reluctance to allow evidence to be presented to them of what went on during the discussion, or what the real intentions of the jury were, once a verdict has been given. The courts have also discouraged any discussion by the jurors of the case and their part in it after it is over, and in particular any attempt at re-trial by newspaper. Gossip, anecdote and some research has suggested that this is perhaps a good thing since the general public may not yet be ready to accept the fact that twelve laymen chosen at random with anyone connected with the administration of justice specifically excluded, do not automatically become " the jury " praised by Blackstone.

At the end of the case the judge sums up the evidence for the jury and spells out the main issues and explains the relevant rules of law which they are to apply in reaching their verdict. In the course of his summing up he may comment upon the plausibility of some of the evidence and even the credibility of particular witnesses and the strength and weaknesses of different versions of the facts and the case that has been put forward. He can also give guidance as to the inference which can be drawn from evidence which the jury accepts. In some cases he is bound to tell them to ignore evidence, where for example inadmissible evidence has been given inadvertently or where, on the trial of more than one accused, evidence admissible against one of the accused is not admissible against another. In other cases he is bound to warn the jury of the dangers of acting on the basis of uncorroborated evidence, for example in the case of the unsworn evidence of children or the evidence of accomplices (below, p. 387). He may even withdraw the case altogether from the jury or in a criminal case direct the jury to acquit the accused if, in his view, the evidence presented by the plaintiff or the prosecution would not support a verdict in their favour. Although he is not expected to express his own view on the case he may comment, for example, on the failure of the accused to give evidence on oath and so expose himself to cross-examination in the witness box, just as he may comment on the failure of a party to call a particular witness. He may not, at the moment, comment on the failure of the accused to make any statement to the police (*R.* v. *Davis* [21]; *R.* v. *Leckey* [22]).

There is clearly scope in the summing up for influencing a jury which is looking for guidance, though juries may see guidance where it does not exist and may get the wrong message when there is one. Judges vary in the clarity and force with which they communicate such views as they have formed in a case and the extent to which they attempt to give a positive lead to the jury, just as juries vary in their ability to recognise a lead when it is given and their willingness to take it. It is during the trial and in the summing up that the judge must exercise any influence he wishes to exercise, in public, and subject, therefore, to criticism. He does not retire with the jury or preside over their discussions. Once they have retired to consider their verdict they are kept apart and even during the trial they are

[21] (1959) 43 Cr.App.R. 215.
[22] [1944] K.B. 80.

warned not to discuss the case with other people. Any communication with them requires the leave of the judge and the questions are limited to asking them if they are agreed or if they have any idea whether they are likely to agree in a limited time or whether they need help. They themselves can consult the judge through written communications through their foreman. Any communication of this kind must be read out in open court or at least be shown to counsel. They may also come back into court to ask a question.

Two problems have caused particular difficulty in the past. The first has been explaining to the jury the burden of proof and the extent to which they must be satisfied that it has been fulfilled before they can give a verdict for the person on whom the burden rests (below, p. 192). Secondly has been the question of the degree of influence that the judge can bring upon a jury to agree. As was mentioned above, until the nineteenth century some pressure was brought upon a jury to come to an early verdict by depriving them of fuel and food. The problem has been to balance the desire for a reasonably speedy decision against the feeling that if a small minority cannot conscientiously agree with the majority then it should not be bullied into conformity, even though this brings with it all the disadvantages of a new trial. The problem was accentuated by the commitment to unanimous verdicts. More recently concern has been expressed not about the juror who could not agree in good faith but the juror who would not agree from fear or partiality. In part, the problem of the partial juror has been tackled by punishing those who wrongfully attempt to influence a juror, and in a more general way by disqualifying as jurors those who have recently been in prison (see below, p. 208). The Criminal Justice Act 1967, at some cost as regards principle, has provided a better safeguard in permitting a majority verdict in certain circumstances in criminal cases, and the Courts Act 1971, has provided for a similar majority verdict in civil cases.

Trial by jury in civil cases

Second Report of the Commissioners Appointed to Inquire into the Process, Practice and System of Pleading in the Superior Courts of Law at Westminster

P.P. (1852–53) xl

. . . Trial by jury, long the peculiar feature of the law of England, has in recent times been much canvassed, and its excellence as a judicial institution questioned. It has been urged, that twelve men, taken at hazard from the body of society, unused to judicial duties or forensic discussions, cannot possess the same aptitude for judicial investigation as a judge, in whom a professional education, the habit of considering the effect of evidence, a long course of training and experience, have developed all the faculties which are required for the judicial office. To this it is added, that the sense of responsibility is weakened by being divided among a number of persons, and that such is peculiarly the case with a jury, who, filling the judicial office only for a moment, merge again, as soon as the trial is over, into the body of society, and are lost sight of, and thus escape the condemnation, in case of an unjust judgment, to which the permanent judge is necessarily exposed. Further, it is urged that the want of permanency in the tribunal precludes the adjournments which some-times, in the course of trials, become necessary to enable complete justice to be done. It is added that, in recent times, trial by jury has been much dispensed with. The jurisdiction of courts of equity to try questions of fact without a jury, in certain cases where juries have hitherto been required, has been recently extended. Justices of the peace and commissioners of various kinds exercise jurisdiction in criminal and other matters without the assistance of a jury. And the experience of county courts, in which the suitors may, if they think proper, demand a jury, but in point of practice do not, is referred to, to show that cases may be left, with perfect satisfaction to the suitor, to the decision of a judge, without the intervention of a jury.

On the other side, it is urged that there is a fallacy in the argument which places trial by jury in abrupt antagonism, as it were, to the trial by a judge, inasmuch as it treats the jury as left entirely to their own unaided resources; whereas in fact, according to the practice of our law, the judge sums up the case to the jury, lays the evidence again before them, and makes such observations as his intelligence and experience suggest, to guide them in their decision. The trial is, in fact, a trial by a jury assisted by a judge. And if it be asked why, when the superior aptitude of the judge is acknowledged, the jury should be admitted to discharge functions which might better be left in his hands, it is answered, that if in many respects the superior knowledge and intelligence of the judge is admitted, the jury also bring with them a varied stock of information which the judge cannot be expected to possess, and which is of the most essential advantage in the administration of justice. The merchant, the man of business, the agriculturalist, the man of the world, the man of science, bring each his peculiar knowledge and experience to assist in determining the varied questions which arise in judicial investigations. Moreover, being called upon to act on a temporary occasion only, the juryman enters on his duties with a freshness and an interest which the permanent judge, more accustomed to the daily routine of judicial duty, can hardly be expected to feel. No one familiar with our courts can have failed to be struck with the attention paid by juries to the cases they have to try, and their anxiety to arrive at a right conclusion. Again, the tendency, natural to the professional judge, to look only to the strict letter of the law, is corrected and tempered by the opposite tendency of the jury to take a more enlarged and liberal view, according to the morality and equity of the case. Each acts as a check upon the other, and the result is the administration of the law in a liberal and enlightened spirit. The knowledge of this tends to keep harsh and discreditable cases out of court. The presence of the jury operates also beneficially on the judge in another respect: the duty of summing up the case to them compels him to keep his attention unceasingly alive throughout the trial, and the necessity of making a complete exposition of his views is a security to the suitors and the public for impartiality and honesty on his part. Not the least, however, of the advantages of this institution is, that it familiarises the people with the law, and popularises the administration of it. The beaten suitor, who would be disposed to question the integrity of the single judge who had just decided against him, will not readily bring himself to believe that twelve of his fellow-citizens have unanimously pronounced a dishonest verdict, even though it has been adverse to his expectations. The result is a general reliance and confidence on the part of the public in the administration of justice. Cases, no doubt, occur where juries go wrong; but who will say that, on questions of fact, judges are not also liable to err? There is, besides, a corrective to the occasional mistakes of juries in the authority exercised by the courts, where the verdict is plainly against the weight of evidence, and the judge is dissatisfied with the result, to send the case to another jury for further trial. With respect to courts of equity, their peculiar constitution, for reasons supposed to be generally inapplicable to the matters litigated in courts of common law, referred questions of fact as well as of law to the judge; and recent legislation has done no more than produce uniformity; whilst as to the matters within the jurisdiction of justices of the peace and other functionaries of a similar character, necessity or extreme convenience requires more speedy and summary proceedings than are consistent with the intervention of a jury.

As regards the argument derived from the experience of the county courts, it is to be observed that in these courts, as a general rule, no cause, whether defended or undefended, is determined, except upon a hearing; whilst . . . 97 per cent. of the actions commenced in the superior courts do not proceed to trial; from which, as also from the more extended jurisdiction of the superior courts, it results that the cases which are brought to trial in these courts are of a more important and difficult character than those which occur in the county courts; and further, the practice of the county courts, which makes trial by the judge the rule, and trial by jury the exception, and consequently imposes the necessity of taking an active step to obtain trial by jury, together with the apprehension of giving offence to the judge by so doing, have, no doubt, a considerable effect in preventing litigants from insisting upon trial by jury in those courts.

We are not insensible to the force of this reasoning: at the same time we think it cannot but be admitted that there is a large class of cases in which the intervention of a jury is unnecessary; and others, in which it is mischievous, from the inability of the tribunal to deal with them. Under these heads may be classed first, cases where the question turns on the legal effect of evidence or of undisputed facts, and in which the verdict of the jury must depend on the direction of the judge; second, cases which, when brought before the jury, it is found necessary to withdraw from them and submit to arbitration, including all questions of detailed account, in which figures and vouchers must be referred to.

While, however, we feel that there are cases in which a jury may advantageously be dispensed with, yet, being of opinion that trial by jury on the whole works well and enjoys the confidence of the public we do not think ourselves warranted, except in cases of mere account, to recommend that trial by jury should be superseded, unless the parties themselves prefer that the case should be tried by a judge. We propose, therefore, to continue trial by jury as the rule, but to make it competent to the parties, if both consent, to dispense with the jury, and to leave the decision of the issues of fact to the judge. With regard to cases of mere account, we propose to make it lawful for the court or a judge, on the application of either party, at any time prior to the trial, or if the issue of fact is left to the judge, then to the judge at the time of the trial also, should it appear fitting to him, to direct that matters in issue shall be referred to an officer of the court, or, in country causes, to the judge of any county court, or, if the parties prefer it, to an arbitrator appointed by themselves, upon whose report judgment may be entered up as upon a verdict. The necessity for this latter improvement was pointed out in the Second Report of the former Law Commissioners, pp. 25 to 27, and pp. 77 to 81. . . .

Administration of Justice (Miscellaneous Provisions) Act 1933

1933 c. 36

6. (1) Subject as hereinafter provided, if, on the application of any party to an action to be tried in the King's Bench Division of the High Court . . . the Court or a judge is satisfied that—

(a) a charge of fraud against that party; or

(b) a claim in respect of libel, slander, malicious prosecution, false imprisonment, seduction . . .

is in issue, the action shall be ordered to be tried with a jury unless the Court or judge is of opinion that the trial thereof requires any prolonged examination of documents or accounts or any scientific or local investigation which cannot conveniently be made with a jury; but, save as aforesaid, any action to be tried in that Division may, in the discretion of the Court or a judge, be ordered to be tried either with or without a jury:

Provided that the provisions of this section shall be without prejudice to the power of the Court or a judge to order, in accordance with rules of court, that different questions of fact arising in any action be tried by different modes of trial. . . .

Ward v. James
Court of Appeal [1966] 1 Q.B. 273

LORD DENNING M.R.: . . . Let it not be supposed that this court is in any way opposed to trial by jury. It has been the bulwark of our liberties too long for any of us to seek to alter it. Whenever a man is on trial for serious crime, or when in a civil case a man's honour or integrity is at stake, or when one or other party must be deliberately lying, then trial by jury has no equal. But in personal injury cases trial by jury has given place of late to trial by judge alone, the reason being simply this, that in these cases trial by a judge alone is more acceptable to the great majority of people. Rarely does a party ask in these cases for a jury. When a solicitor gives advice, it runs in this way: " If I were you, I should not ask for a jury. I should have a judge alone. You do know where you stand with a judge, and if he goes wrong, you can always go to the Court of Appeal. But as for a jury, you never know what they will do, and if they do go wrong, there is no putting them right. The Court of Appeal hardly ever interferes with the verdict of a jury." So the client decides on judge alone. That is why jury trials have declined. It is because they are not asked for. Lord Devlin shows this in his book *The Hamlyn Lectures* (eighth series, *Trial by Jury*, Chap. 6), p. 133.

This important consequence follows: the judges alone, and not juries, in the great majority of cases, decide whether there is negligence or not. They set the standard of care to be expected of the reasonable man. They also assess the damages. They see, so far as they can, that like sums are given for like injuries. They set the standard for awards. Hence there is uniformity of decision. This has its impact on decisions as to the mode of trial. If a party asks for a jury in an ordinary personal injury case, the court naturally asks: " Why do you want a jury when nearly everyone else is content with judge alone? " I am afraid it is often because he has a weak case, or desires to appeal to sympathy. If no good reason is given, then the court orders trial by judge alone. Hence we find that nowadays the discretion in the ordinary run of personal injury cases is in favour of judge alone. It is no sufficient reason for departing from it simply to provide a " guinea-pig " case: see *Hennell* v. *Ranaboldo*.[23]

. . . For many years, however, it has been said that serious injuries afford a good reason for ordering trial by jury. At any rate, it is a consideration which should be given great weight. . . . Recent experience has led to some doubts being held on this score. It begins to look as if a jury is an unsuitable tribunal to assess damages for grave injuries, at any rate in those cases where a man is greatly reduced in his activities. He is deprived of much that makes life worthwhile. No money can compensate for the loss. Yet compensation has to be given in money. The problem is insoluble. To meet it, the judges have evolved a

[23] [1963] 1 W.L.R. 1391.

conventional measure. They go by their experience in comparable cases. But the juries have nothing to go by. . . .

. . . [R]ecent cases show the desirability of three things: First, *assessability*: In cases of grave injury, where the body is wrecked or the brain destroyed, it is very difficult to assess a fair compensation in money, so difficult that the award must basically be a conventional figure, derived from experience or from awards in comparable cases. Secondly, *uniformity*: There should be some measure of uniformity in awards so that similar decisions are given in similar cases; otherwise there will be great dissatisfaction in the community, and much criticism of the administration of justice. Thirdly, *predictability*: Parties should be able to predict with some measure of accuracy the sum which is likely to be awarded in a particular case, for by this means cases can be settled peaceably and not brought to court, a thing very much to the public good. None of these three is achieved when the damages are left at large to the jury. Under the present practice the judge does not give them any help at all to assess the figure. The result is that awards may vary greatly, from being much too high to much too low. There is no uniformity and no predictability. . . .

[One] remedy that has been suggested is that the jury should be given more guidance. Two possible ways are put forward: (i) By referring them to awards in comparable cases; (ii) By telling them the conventional figure. . . .

(i) *Comparable cases.* Before 1951 it was not the practice for counsel to refer the court or the jury to awards in comparable cases.

. . . Since *Bird* v. *Cocking & Sons Ltd.* in 1951 a change has set in. When the case is tried by a judge alone, or heard on appeal by the Court of Appeal, counsel is allowed to refer to awards in comparable cases. This is because we now recognise that the award is basically a conventional figure, and in order to arrive at it, it is relevant to refer to comparable cases. If this be so before a judge alone . . . why should it not also be so in trial by jury? . . .

This sounds well in theory, but in practice it is open to strong objection. During the argument before us both counsel agreed that it would not do. See what would happen! Each counsel would refer the jury to cases which he believed were comparable but which were not really so. Speeches would be taken up with the one counsel citing analogies and the other destroying them. Then the judge would have to review them all again in his summing-up. The inevitable result would be that the minds of the jury would be distracted from the instant case and left in confusion.

(ii) *Conventional figures.* Another suggestion is that the jury should be told of the conventional figures in this way, that the judge should be at liberty in his discretion to indicate to the jury the upper and lower limits of the sum which in his view it would be reasonable to award. Thus in the case of the loss of a leg, he might indicate that the conventional figure is between £4,000 and £6,000. This proposal has many attractions. It would give the jury the guidance which they at present lack. But here again we come up against a serious objection. If the judge can mention figures to the jury, then counsel must also be able to mention figures to them. Once that happened, we get into the same trouble again. Each counsel would, in duty bound, pitch the figures as high or as low as he dared. Then the judge would give his views on the rival figures. The proceedings would be in danger of developing into an auction. The objections are so great that both counsel before us agreed that counsel ought not to be at liberty to mention figures to the jury. If this be so, I think that the judge should not do so either.

Apart from this, it seems to me that if the judge were at liberty to mention the upper and lower limits, then in order to be of any real guidance, they would have to be somewhat narrow limits. It would be no use his telling the jury (as judges have done in the past) for the loss of a leg: "Do be reasonable. Don't give as much as £100,000, or as little as £100." The judge would have to come nearer home and say: "The conventional figure in such a case as this is between £4,000 and £6,000." But if he can give them narrow limits of that kind, there is little point in having a jury at all. You might as well let the judge assess the figure himself.

I come to the conclusion, therefore, that we must follow the existing practice, and we cannot sanction any departure from it.

Conclusion. The result of it all is this: that the judge ought not, in a personal injury case, to order trial by jury save in exceptional circumstances. Even when the issue of liability is one fit to be tried by a jury, nevertheless he might think it fit to order that the damages be assessed by a judge alone. . . .

SELLERS, PEARSON, DAVIES and DIPLOCK L.JJ. agreed.

Rothermere and Others v. Times Newspapers Ltd. and Others [23a]

The Times, December 22, 1971

Here the defendants had applied for trial by jury. This had been granted by the Master. The plaintiffs now appealed.

ACKNER J.: . . . If the action were one of the great bulk of cases in the Queen's Bench Division there would nowadays be no likelihood of a judge granting trial by jury. But libel was a type of case in a special category in respect of which an order for jury trial was to be ordered under section 6 (1) of the Administration of Justice (Miscellaneous Provisions) Act 1933, "unless the . . . judge is of opinion that the trial requires any prolonged examination of documents or accounts . . . which cannot conveniently be made with a jury; but, save as aforesaid, any action to be tried in that Division may, in the discretion of the . . . judge, be ordered to be tried with or without a jury".

Whether the law of defamation which had, *per* Lord Justice Diplock in *Boston* v. *W. S. Bagshaw & Sons* ([1966] 1 W.L.R. 1126, 1135), "become bogged down in such a mass of technicalities," should still remain in that special category was doubtless one of the matters currently being considered by Mr. Justice Faulks' committee on defamation. Lord Justice Russell in *Broadway Approvals Ltd.* v. *Odhams Press Ltd.* ([1965] 1 W.L.R. 805, 825), a case which lasted a mere six days at first instance, felt constrained to say that to the comparative newcomer the law of libel seemed to have characteristics of such complication and subtlety that he wondered whether a jury on retiring could readily distinguish their heads from their heels.

Whatever might be the pros and cons for a change, his Lordship must, as he did, take the law as it now stood.

Prima facie the defendants were entitled to a jury. The length of trial and complexities of the issues were in themselves no grounds for basing a claim for trial of a libel action by a judge alone. The plaintiffs had to establish that the trial required prolonged examination of documents or accounts, and that such examination could not conveniently be made with a jury, and that his Lordship should exercise his discretion, which existed solely as a result of the plaintiffs establishing both the foregoing conditions, by refusing a jury.

Mr. Comyn submitted that the degree of depth of the examination was the sole test of whether an examination was prolonged, but that point seemed to be contrary to common sense. In section 6 of the 1933 Act the legislature recognised that, where a trial was such that considerable time had to be spent by a jury in reading and re-reading documents or accounts, an undue strain was likely

[23a] This decision was overruled by the Court of Appeal [1973] 1 W.L.R. 448, while this book was going to press. [Ed.]

to be placed on them, and that was or might be a justification for restricting the trial to the judge alone. It mattered not whether the amount of time that was to be spent on the documents was to be spent on a few rather than many. . . .

The essential defence was justification. . . .

In an affidavit a partner in the plaintiffs' firm of solicitors estimated that he had so far devoted at least 20 working days to preparation of the plaintiffs' list of documents. The contents of upwards of 125 files would be disclosed, and the list of documents would run to over 100 pages.

The particulars of the facts relied on in support of the plea of justification provided a small volume running to nearly 60 pages. Among other documents it would have to go to the jury. . . .

The article made a variety of attacks not only on the honesty and integrity of Lord Rothermere and Mr. Vere Harmsworth—a common enough feature in most libel actions—but on the financial competence with which the *Sketch* and other papers past and present within the group had been and were being run. It alleged that, despite the protestations of losses, the *Daily Sketch* was being closed down to add to their wealth.

His Lordship read an excerpt from the article and said that the defence recognised that such an attack on the policy operated by the plaintiffs and an allegation of misrepresentation as to their true reasons for closing the newspaper would involve considerable investigation into the plaintiff company's accounts. The defendants did not limit themselves to the economics of the *Daily Sketch*. To decide the hotly contested issue—was the decision to close the *Sketch* motivated by the plaintiffs' desire to earn still more money to the detriment of many old employees, or was it genuinely based on financial necessity?—would inevitably involve the consideration of many documents, quite apart from the many chairman's reports referred to in a paragraph of the pleadings. Another paragraph employed every letter of the alphabet in dealing with the position of the *Daily Mail*. That contained reference to the chairman's speech for each of 18 years and brought into issue policy over a period of 40 years.

The plaintiffs maintained that written professional advice was taken before a company—Harmsworth Publications, with the function of owning the three newspapers—was set up and the advice fully justified the action taken. The advice and supporting documents would be material at which the jury would probably have to look.

His Lordship was persuaded that on the imputations involving financial and administrative incompetence alone there were likely to be many documents which a jury would be required to read in whole or in part. To that must be superadded the large number of documents—Mr. Hirst said that there would be many hundreds of sheets of paper—which explained and accounted for the plaintiffs' reasons for closing the *Daily Sketch* and the manner of such closure.

Having spent the entirety of one day considering the submissions on both sides, his Lordship was left in no doubt that the trial would require a prolonged examination of documents and accounts which could not be conveniently made with a jury.

Mr. Comyn urged, as one of his grounds for contending for trial by jury, that a jury did not have to give its reasons. In a complicated case the obligation to give the reasons tended to concentrate the mind admirably. In short, his Lordship was satisfied that, if a jury were to try the case with all its many complicated issues they would be inundated by a sea of documents and that, accordingly, it was in the interest of the administration of justice that trial be by judge alone. The appeal would be allowed.

By consent costs would be costs in the cause.

Leave to appeal to the Court of Appeal was granted.

The summing up

Clouston and Co. Ltd. v. Corry Ltd.

Privy Council [1906] A.C. 122

LORD JAMES OF HEREFORD.: . . . [I]n cases where the trial [is with a jury] the presiding judge has important duties to fulfil. It is for him to say whether there is any evidence to submit to the jury in support of the allegation. . . . If no such evidence has in his opinion been given he should not submit any issue in respect of such allegations. The judge may also direct, guide, and assist the jury. He may direct by informing them of the nature of the acts [in a case of wrongful dismissal] which as a matter of law will justify dismissal. He may guide them by calling their attention to the facts material to the determination of the issues raised, and he may assist them in a manner and to an extent there is no reason to define. There have been judges—more numerous in the past than in the present—who possessed and exercised the power of addressing a jury in terms of apparent impartiality, and yet of placing before them views which seldom failed to secure the verdict desired by the judge. . . .

R. v. O'Donnell

(1917) 12 Cr.App.R. 220

LORD READING C.J.: . . . [A] judge, when directing a jury, is clearly entitled to express his opinion on the facts of the case, provided that he leaves the issues of fact to the jury to determine. A judge obviously is not justified in directing a jury, or using in the course of his summing up such language as leads them to think that he is directing them, that they must find the facts in the way which he indicates. But he may express a view that the facts ought to be dealt with in a particular way, or ought not to be accepted by the jury at all. He is entitled to tell the jury that the prisoner's story is a remarkable one, or that it differs from accounts which he has given of the same matter on other occasions. No doubt the judge here did express himself strongly on the case, but he left the issues of fact to the jury for their decision. . . .

R. v. Hepworth

(1910) 4 Cr.App.R. 128

This case may be compared with the above. In it, counsel for the appellant noted that the Recorder in summing up had told the jury " He practically stands convicted by the evidence of the prosecution " and " You must do your duty; you must leave the other matter to me."

DARLING J.: . . . We have before laid down that a summing up must be fair, and that language proportionate to the occasion must be used. From the beginning of the summing up, one must conclude that appellant's counsel had tried to laugh the case out of Court. He made an eloquent speech. We do not think the summing up a model one. . . . But when we have to consider whether it was so unfair that we ought to quash the conviction, we do not think we ought. We are unable to say that there was anything in the summing up which precluded the jury from doing justice. On the evidence the verdict was justified. . . .

Securing a verdict

Third Report of the Commissioners on Practice and Procedure in the Common Law Courts

P.P. (1831) x

. . . [T]he necessity for the unanimity of the jury carries with it one most valuable advantage. In the event of any difference of opinion it secures a discussion. . . . It is not possible to poll the jury at once, and so, without further trouble or consideration, to come to the conclusion. Any one dissentient person can compel the other eleven, fully and calmly to reconsider their opinions. But there seems to be no good reason why, after a certain period of time sufficiently long for the purpose of reasonable and ample discussion, the jury (if still in disagreement) should not be excused from the necessity of giving a verdict, or why the present principle of keeping them together till unanimity be produced by a sort of duress of imprisonment, should be retained. . . . We propose, therefore, that the jury shall not be kept in deliberation longer than twelve hours, unless at the end of that period they unanimously concur to apply for further time . . . and that at the end of twelve hours, or of such prolonged time for deliberation, if any nine of them concur in giving a verdict, such verdict shall be entered on record, and shall entitle the party in whose favour it is given, to judgment: and in failure of such concurrence, the cause shall be made a *remanet*. . . .

Second Report of the Commissioners Appointed to Inquire into the Process, Practice and System of Pleading in the Superior Courts of Law at Westminster

P.P. (1852–53) xl

We are . . . of opinion that the present rule, requiring the jury to be unanimous, should be maintained. . . . [B]ut that unanimity should not merely be apparent but real. . . . The existing practice, which, upon a division of opinion in the jury, requires them to be shut up, often in an inconvenient room, without accommodation, without fire, without refreshment, for several hours, sometimes for a whole night, is discreditable to the administration of the law. No doubt, unanimity is often thus brought about, but it is the unanimity not of conviction but of exhausted powers—not of intelligence, but of incapacity of physical endurance. The juryman is tempted to escape from prolonged hunger and suffering by compromising his conscience and his oath, and the judge is compelled to receive such a verdict as unanimous. We unhesitatingly recommend that this practice be done away with; that juries during their deliberations shall be furnished with every fitting accommodation, and with necessary refreshment; and we would suggest that cases, in which complicated questions arise, should not be summed up late in the day (as sometimes happens), whereby deliberations of juries are often prolonged late into the night—sometimes through the entire night—at a time when the powers are worn out, and the danger of a submission against conscience and conviction becomes the greater. Further we recommend that the period during which the jury may be kept in deliberation . . . ought not to exceed twelve hours; and that at the expiration of that time, unless the jury themselves desire further time for deliberation, they should be discharged; in which case it should be open to either of the litigant parties to summon a fresh jury, and to try the cause again.[24]

[24] *Cf.* Cockburn C.J. in *Winsor* v. *The Queen* (1866) L.R. 1 Q.B. 289, 305. "Our ancestors insisted on unanimity . . . but they were unscrupulous as to the means by which they obtained it. . . . It was a struggle between the strong and weak, the able-bodied and the infirm, which could best sustain hunger, thirst, and the fatigue incidental to their confinement, and the rest. . . . We, now-a-days, look upon the principles on which juries

R. v. Mills

Court of Criminal Appeal [1939] 2 K.B. 90

LORD HEWART C.J.: . . . Jurymen should not be led, from a desire to acquiesce, or to avoid eccentricity, or to save time and trouble, to represent themselves as holding views which they do not hold. Their verdict must be a true verdict, given according to the evidence, not an untrue verdict given according to some actual or supposed convenience. Nothing is more primary or fundamental in its character than the duty of each juror to form and express his own opinion. Merely to acquiesce would be, not merely indefensible but actually wrong, and a violation of the juror's oath.[25]

R. v. McKenna

Court of Criminal Appeal [1960] 1 All E.R. 326

On Monday, November 23, 1959, at the beginning of the trial Stable J. told the jury that he could not sit after 1 p.m. on Wednesday. He sat until 5 p.m. on Monday and till 6.30 p.m. on Tuesday. He began his summing up on Wednesday morning. At 12 noon he told the jury that once the summing up was over and the jury had retired they could not separate until they had arrived at a verdict.

> Under the rules that govern our procedure once a summing-up is finished and the jury retire they cannot separate until the verdict has been arrived at. If in the middle of a summing-up a break is requested, the jury can go before the conclusion, and come back and hear the conclusion of the summing-up the next day or after the adjournment. The position is this, that I

are to act . . . in a different light. . . . We do not desire that the unanimity of a jury should be anything but the unanimity of conviction. . . . [A] single juryman, or two or three . . . may, if their own convictions are not strong and deeply rooted, think themselves justified in giving way to the majority. . . . [I]f jurymen have only doubts or weak convictions, they may yield to the stronger and more determined view of their fellows; but . . . it [was] the essence of a juryman's duty, if he [had] a firm and deeply rooted conviction, . . . not to give up that conviction, although the majority [is] against him, from any desire to purchase his freedom from confinement or constraint, or the various other inconveniences to which jurors are subject. When, therefore, a reasonable time has elapsed, and the judge is perfectly convinced that the unanimity of the jury can only be obtained through the sacrifice of honest conscientious convictions, why is he to subject them to torture . . . so that the minority, or possibly the majority, may give way, and purchase ease to themselves by a sacrifice of their consciences? . . . ''

[25] In *Walhein* (1952) 36 Cr.App.R. 167 the Court of Criminal Appeal approved the following direction by the judge: '' You are a body of twelve men. Each of you has taken an oath to return a true verdict according to the evidence, but, of course, you have a duty not only as individuals, but collectively. No one must be false to that oath, but in order to return a collective verdict, the verdict of you all, there must necessarily be argument, and a certain amount of give and take and adjustment of views within the scope of the oath you have taken, and it makes for great public inconvenience and expense if jurors cannot agree owing to the unwillingness of one of their number to listen to the arguments of the rest. Having said that, I can say no more. If you disagree in your verdict in relation to one or other of these men, you must say so.''

In *Davey* [1960] 3 All E.R. 533 it rejected the following direction: '' Sometimes in the past judges used to tell the juries that they have to be unanimous, but I always say— and it is true—you all have to agree before you can find anybody guilty, and there is no reason I know of why any judge should worry about that, from my experience, because whereas in lots of your own affairs, on committees, you do not always agree, nevertheless those of you who have experience of board meetings may find that again and again agreement is reached and no vote is taken, and hardly ever is a vote taken at a board meeting, and juries seriously realising what they are doing are united by a passion for the right verdict, a passion for stern or real justice, . . . and the result I should think is that in ninety-nine cases out of one hundred there is not a disagreement at all, but solidarity and sense.''

am very much afraid that I have this engagement and I cannot escape it. I have to get up to London by the 1.35 train, which means I shall have to leave here about ten minutes past one o'clock. If you feel you cannot arrive at a verdict in this case before then I can break off my summing-up at this stage. . . . What I want to guard against is one o'clock coming and you saying, "we still have not arrived at our verdict", in which case I would have to throw this engagement over and it would be very inconvenient and would keep you all locked up overnight.

The foreman consulted the jury and told the judge at 12.15 that they would need more than three-quarters of an hour to arrive at a verdict. The judge however said that he would catch a later train and finished his summing up in five minutes. The jury retired at 12.20. At 2.20 they returned to the court to ask two questions. At 2.38 the judge recalled them and told them that if they did not reach a verdict in ten minutes he would keep them there all night.

I have disorganised my travel arrangements out of consideration for you pretty considerably already. I am not going to disorganise them any further. In ten minutes I shall leave this building and if, by that time, you have not arrived at a conclusion . . . you will have to be kept all night and we will resume . . . at 11.45 a.m. tomorrow. I do not know, and I am not entitled to ask—and I shall not ask—why in a case which does not involve any study of figures or documents you should require all this time . . . May I suggest to you that you go back to your room, that you use your common sense, and do not worry yourself with legal quibbles. That is what you are brought here for: to use your common sense, bring a bit in from outside. . . .

Within six minutes the jury had brought in verdicts of guilty. The accused appealed.

CASSELS J.: . . . It is a cardinal principle of our criminal law that in considering their verdict, concerning, as it does, the liberty of the subject, a jury shall deliberate in complete freedom, uninfluenced by any promise, unintimidated by any threat. They still stand between the Crown and the subject, and they are still one of the main defences of personal liberty. To say to such a tribunal in the course of its deliberations that it must reach a conclusion within ten minutes or else undergo hours of personal inconvenience and discomfort, is a disservice to the cause of justice. In this case the ultimatum no doubt fell with added force on the jury since two of them were women. It may well be that having regard to the steps he had taken from the outset to ensure that the case should finish by mid-day on the third day, steps which included working beyond the normal hours on the Monday and the Tuesday, the learned judge was understandably irritated by the inconvenient slowness of the jury in reaching a verdict in what he thought was a plain straightforward case. But juries do at times take much longer than a judge may think necessary to arrive at a verdict; there are, after all, twelve of them who have to be unanimous and the proper exercise of the judicial office requires that irritation on these occasions must be suppressed or at any rate kept severely in check. To experience it is understandable; to express it in the form of such a threat to the jury as was uttered here is insupportable.

What then, in these circumstances, should this court do? . . .

We subscribe to the view that the evidence against all three appellants was cogent to a degree. We also agree that it is possible that the jury had little doubt about the guilt, at any rate, of Busby and Charles McKenna. The difficulty, however, is that the opposite view cannot, with complete confidence, be excluded.

They had put forward defences which though they may appear to a lawyer to be fanciful, at any rate had the effect that after two hours the jury still had not arrived at a unanimous verdict. At no stage did they say, as they could have done, that they were agreed in the case of some of the prisoners but still not agreed as regards another. And when they were told to reach a conclusion as regards all three prisoners within the next ten minutes or in default to remain together all night it is, at the very least, a reasonable inference that what their minds concentrated on in these last ten minutes was not so much the evidence they had to consider, but the inconvenience and discomfort with which they had been threatened. This being so, the court does not think it right to resort to the proviso to s. 4 (1). The prosecution also submits, as an alternative that a venire de novo should be ordered, but this trial was not in the true sense of the word a nullity.

With regret, therefore, the court feels bound to quash these convictions. Although any jury would have been amply justified in finding all these appellants guilty . . . it is of fundamental importance that in their deliberations a jury should be free to take such time as they feel they need, subject always, of course, to the right of a judge to discharge them if protracted consideration still produces disagreement. Plain though many juries might have thought this case, the principle at stake is more important than the case itself.

The appeals are accordingly allowed and the convictions quashed.

Criminal Justice Act 1967

1967 c. 80

13.—(1) Subject to the following provisions of this section, the verdict of a jury in criminal proceedings need not be unanimous if—

 (*a*) in a case where there are not less than eleven jurors, ten of them agree on the verdict; and

 (*b*) in a case where there are ten jurors, nine of them agree on the verdict;

and a verdict authorised by this subsection is hereafter in this section referred to as " a majority verdict ".

(2) A court shall not accept a majority verdict of guilty unless the foreman of the jury has stated in open court the number of jurors who respectively agreed to and dissented from the verdict.

(3) A court shall not accept a majority verdict unless it appears to the court that the jury have had not less than two hours for deliberation or such longer period as the court thinks reasonable having regard to the nature and complexity of the case.

Courts Act 1971

1971 c. 23

39.—(1) Subject to subsection (3) . . . the verdict of a jury in proceedings in the High Court need not be unanimous if—

 (*a*) in a case where there are not less than eleven jurors, ten of them agree on the verdict, and

 (*b*) in a case where there are ten jurors, nine of them agree on the verdict.

(2) Subject to subsection (3) . . . the verdict of a jury (that is to say a complete jury of 8) in proceedings in a county court need not be unanimous if seven of them agree on the verdict.

(3) The court shall not accept a verdict by virtue of subsection (1) or subsection (2) . . . unless it appears to the court that the jury have had such period

of time for deliberation as the court thinks reasonable having regard to the nature and complexity of the case.

(4) This section is without prejudice to any practice by which a court may accept a majority verdict with the consent of the parties, or by which the parties may agree to proceed in any case with an incomplete jury.

Secrecy of the jury's deliberations

R. v. Thompson

(1962) 46 Cr.App.R. 72

LORD CHIEF JUSTICE: . . . It has for long been a rule of practice, based on public policy, that the court should not inquire by taking evidence from jurymen as to what did occur in either the jury box or the jury room. . . . It is sufficient to refer to a case in the Court of Appeal *Ellis* v. *Deheer* [1922] 2 K.B. 113, before a court consisting of Bankes, Warrington and Atkin L.JJ. It was a civil case, and the question was whether the court could look at affidavits from jurors who would say that the verdict given by the foreman of the jury, albeit in their presence, had not been agreed by them. In the course of giving his judgment Bankes L.J. said . . . " It has for many years been a well accepted rule that when once a verdict has been given it ought not to be open to an individual juryman to challenge it, or to attempt to support it if challenged. I have spoken of this as a rule of law, but it has also been generally accepted by the public as a rule of conduct, that what passes in the jury room during the discussion by the jury of what their verdict should be ought to be treated as private and confidential.

. . . Atkin L.J. . . . put the matter in his own words " . . . The reason why that evidence is not admitted is two-fold, on the one hand it is in order to secure the finality of decisions arrived at by the jury, and on the other to protect the jurymen themselves and prevent their being exposed to pressure to explain the reasons which actuated them in arriving at their verdicts. . . . I do not propose to decide (for it is not before us) whether . . . publication on the part of the Press . . . of the reasons of a particular juryman for arriving at his decision is or is not a contempt of court. . . ."

Th[is] court would also like to refer in passing to what Hewart L.C.J. said on the question of jurymen divulging what occurred, in the case of *Armstrong* (1922) 16 Cr.App.R. 149; [1922] 2 K.B. 555, at pp. 159 and 568 of the respective reports. . . . " If one juryman might communicate with the public upon the evidence and the verdict, so might his colleagues also; and if they all took this dangerous course, differences of individual opinion might be made manifest which, at the least, could not fail to diminish the confidence that the public rightly has in the general propriety of criminal verdicts. . . ."

Boston v. W. S. Bagshaw & Sons

[1966] 1 W.L.R. 1135

LORD DENNING M.R.: . . . [W]e were referred . . . to a case in 1902, *Nesbitt* v. *Parrett*, where a juryman sought to say that he had not agreed to the amount of £1,100. He was staggered by it. He was taken so much aback that he could not speak at the time. The court said they would not possibly receive it. It would be destructive of the whole system of trial by jury if we were to admit evidence of this kind. . . . [I]n *Ellis* v. *Deheer* the jurymen were so placed that they could not hear what the foreman said. In other cases evidence was admitted to show that a juryman was incompetent to act, as, for instance, because he did not understand the language in which the trial was conducted. But, apart from such cases, I know of no case where evidence of jurors has been received to challenge the verdict. . . .

Tenth Report of the Criminal Law Revision Committee

The secrecy of the jury room

Cmnd. 3750

The committee had been asked to consider " whether statutory provision should be made to protect the secrecy of the jury room; and in particular whether, and if so, subject to what exceptions and qualifications, it should be an offence to seek information from a juror about a jury's deliberations or for a juror to disclose such information."

2. In our opinion the conduct referred to in the terms of reference is not a criminal offence . . . except that possibly in some circumstances it might be contempt of court. There is no judicial authority and but little judicial comment. . . . In *Ellis* v. *Deheer* [1922] 2 K.B. 113, Bankes L.J. said at p. 118 that : " it has . . . been generally accepted by the public . . . that what passes in the jury room . . . ought to be treated as private and confidential. . . . I do not think it necessary to express any opinion as to whether such a publication amounts to a contempt of court. . . ." The Departmental Committee on Jury Service . . . in 1965 (Cmnd. 2627) went no further than to say (in para. 355) that : " Gross breaches of the obligation to preserve secrecy might be treated as a contempt of court, especially if the judge in a particular case had expressly told the jury that they must not make any disclosure." [26] The present Lord Chancellor, in a debate in the House of Lords on 6 June 1967 . . . expressed the view that there was no law prohibiting a newspaper from getting a juror to write an account of what happened in the jury room; and this view was not disputed. . . .

3. Since 1951 juries have been reminded of their duty to maintain secrecy by a notice which is displayed on the walls of jury rooms and of which the terms were decided after consultation between the Home Secretary, the Lord Chancellor and the Lord Chief Justice. . .

4. After full deliberation we do not deem it immediately necessary or desirable to make any statutory provision to protect the secrecy of the jury room. . . . We are of opinion that secrecy has been well maintained and that such breaches or attempts to break it as have become known so far have not established a mischief so extensive or serious that it calls for legislation and punishment. . . .

5. . . . It might be said that, now that the subject has been referred to us . . . the publicity for the absence of sanctions for breach of the rule of conduct would

---

[26] The Departmental Committee on jury service noted : " 355. It has sometimes been suggested that there is no need to require jurors not to disclose what happened during their deliberations, and even that the requirement shows a lack of confidence in the jury system and implies that the system would break down if it were generally known what happens when a jury retires to consider its verdict. We recognise that it is impossible to make a proper assessment of the merits of trial by jury in the absence of adequate knowledge of what does happen when the jury retires, but we agree with those of our witnesses who argued that if such disclosures were to be made, particularly to the Press, jurors would no longer feel free to express their opinions frankly when the verdict was under discussion, for fear that what they said later might be made public. In fact they might even fear reprisals from criminals for whose convictions they were responsible, and who had heard about their deliberations. We think there is much force in this argument . . . Gross breaches of the obligation to preserve secrecy might be treated as a contempt of court, especially if the judge in a particular case had expressly told the jury that they must not make any disclosure. The question whether a person who presses a juror to make disclosure is guilty of contempt of court was left open by Bankes L.J. in *Ellis* v. *Deheer*." Ed.

encourage abuses. But ... the absence of sanctions has been well known—at least since an article in *The Observer* of 21 June 1959 ... drew attention to the matter.... Should any newspaper be tempted to ... approach jurors for information in order to prolong the sensationalism of a criminal trial, we should hope that intervention by the Press Council ... would be effectual to check any abuse....

9. ... There are two important reasons that may be advanced why things said during the jury's deliberations should not be disclosed afterwards: (i) the need to protect the jurors themselves, and (ii) the need to preserve the principle that the jury's decision should be treated as final unless upset on appeal. As to (i), obviously jurors might feel inhibited from expressing their opinions freely ... if they knew that their fellow-jurors might disclose what they said, and they might be seriously embarrassed by pressure to give information about what any juror said or how he voted. As to (ii) ... the committee generally takes the view that it is contrary to the public interest that the issue before the jury should be " retried " in public with the use of information supplied by one or more of the jurors. Such a discussion without judicial control of its course and very likely with imperfect knowledge of the evidence given at the trial, might well give a false impression of the reasons for the verdict, especially as other members of the jury might feel inhibited by the obligation of secrecy or by dislike of publicity from coming forward and correcting mistaken statements by the juror who supplied the information. This might lead to unjustifiable dissatisfaction with the result of trials.

10. But the obligation to maintain secrecy cannot be absolute. Jurors are clearly under a duty to inform the court at once of any irregularity which occurs during their deliberations. Even after a trial, disclosure may be necessary in the interests of justice. In *Thompson* (1962) 46 Cr.App.R. 72, where the Court of Criminal Appeal refused, in accordance with practice, to consider an allegation that a member of the jury had said that a number of the jurors were in favour of an acquittal, but that in the course of their deliberations the foreman had produced a list of the prisoner's previous convictions, and thereby influenced the verdict, the court clearly contemplated that this might be inquired into by the Executive.... In the recent case of *Hood* [1968] 1 W.L.R. 773; [1968] 2 All E.R. 56, the Court of Appeal itself considered an affidavit by a juror that he did not disclose to the other jurors his discovery, made during the trial, that the accused was identical with a man whom he knew to have had previous convictions. Moreover service on a jury is to some people an interesting occasion, and clearly there is no objection to jurors discussing their experiences in a general way and without identifying cases.

R. v. Larkin

Court of Criminal Appeal [1943] 1 All E.R. 217

Larkin was charged with the murder or manslaughter of his mistress with a razor. At different times he said he had killed her in a fit of anger because she had taken another lover and that she had fallen on the razor. The judge told the jury that if they accepted either of these defences their verdict should be manslaughter. This was the verdict they returned. The following interchange then took place between the judge and the foreman of the jury. The judge: " May I ask you this question: Did you come to the conclusion that this woman accidentally fell upon the razor?" Foreman: " We did, sir." Judge: " It was an accident? That was the reason? " Foreman: " Yes, it was an accident. We have come to the conclusion that we can find no evidence to prove that it was murder." Judge: " It is not a question of murder. I said if it was done deliberately it was not murder if, in your view there was provocation, and, whether you thought it was provocation or . . . an accident, the verdict would be manslaughter. I do not know whether you did come to any conclusion . . . whether it was an accident or . . . provocation. In either case your verdict is valid. I want to know for my own purposes whether you did come to the conclusion that it was an accident or provocation." Foreman : " Provocation." Larkin appealed.

HUMPHRIES J.: . . . [N]o better illustration could be found of the undesirability of a judge, having accepted in a criminal case a verdict of a jury, then inviting the jury to explain what they mean by their verdict. As we in this country think, trial by jury is the best method yet devised for dealing with serious criminal cases, and the jury is the best possible tribunal to decide whether a man is guilty or not guilty and, if he is guilty, of what he is guilty, subject to the direction in law of the judge; but no one has ever suggested that a jury is composed of persons who are likely to be able to give at a moment's notice a logical explanation of how and why they arrived at their verdict. That was what Oliver J. was inviting the jury to do in this case, and, as has been already observed, inviting the foreman to do so, and accepting from the foreman something with which, perhaps, the other eleven did not agree. The unhappy result was that the foreman, no doubt thoroughly confused, gave two totally inconsistent answers. That incident cannot, in our opinion, be of any importance whatever from the point of view of this appeal against conviction. It was something which happened after the trial was over, so far as the jury were concerned, and if it has any effect at all, it must be an effect upon the sentence. But it must be understood that this court deprecates questions being put to a jury upon the meaning of the verdict which they have returned. If the verdict appears to be inconsistent, proper questions may be put by a judge to invite the jury to explain what they mean, but where a verdict has been returned which is perfectly plain and unambiguous, it is most undesirable that the jury should be asked any further questions about it at all.[27]

Protecting the jury from prejudice

Following the cases of R. v. Griffiths [28] in which W. H. Smith and Son Ltd. was held guilty of contempt for distributing copies of Newsweek which contained material prejudicial to the trial of Dr. John Bodkin Adams, and R. v. Odhams Press [29] in which The People had published material prejudicial to a trial without knowing that a trial was pending, the common law was modified by the Administration of Justice Act 1960 which gave a defence of the exercise of reasonable care in such situations.

Administration of Justice Act 1960

1960 c. 65

11.—(1) A person shall not be guilty of contempt of court on the ground that he has published any matter calculated to interfere with the course of justice in

---

[27] Cf. in civil cases the case of Barnes v. Hill [1967] 1 Q.B. 579 in which Lord Denning M.R. said: " . . . A jury have an absolute right to give a general verdict, that is, to say simply whether they find for the plaintiff or the defendant. They cannot be required to give a special verdict or to answer specific questions. History shows how important is this right, especially in libel actions. And once they have given a general verdict, that is the end of the matter. The judge cannot ask them the grounds of the verdict. . . ."
[28] [1957] 2 Q.B. 192.
[29] [1957] 1 Q.B. 73.

connection with any proceedings pending or imminent . . . if . . . (having taken all reasonable care) he did not know and had no reason to suspect that the proceedings were pending, or . . . imminent. . . .

(2) A person shall not be guilty of contempt of court on the ground that he has distributed a publication containing such matter as is mentioned in sub-section (1) of this section if at the time of distribution (having taken all reasonable care) he did not know that it contained any such matter as aforesaid and had no reason to suspect that it was likely to do so.

(3) The proof of any fact tending to establish a defence afforded by this section . . . in proceedings for contempt of court shall lie upon that person.

In *R. v. Thomson Newspapers Ltd. and Others* [30] the *Sunday Times* published a photograph of Michael Abdul Malik and in the caption with it said he had had an " unedifying career as a brothel-keeper, procurer and property racketeer." Twelve days before, the trial of Malik under the Race Relations Act 1965 had been opened but had been adjourned until a date to be fixed. The Attorney-General applied for an order of committal for contempt. The publishers were fined £5,000.

In *R. v. Bolam* [31] the *Daily Mirror* published an article and photographs of Haigh who was being tried for murder saying that he was a vampire and that not only was he guilty of the murder for which he was being tried but also of other murders as well. The court said that the publication was not simply an error of judgment but was a deliberate act of policy pandering to sensationalism. It imposed a sentence of three months' imprisonment on the editor and fined the newspaper £10,000.

THE VALUE OF TRIAL BY JURY

Much has been claimed for jury trial. It has been argued that it is a bastion of liberty against the state and it has been associated with the provision of Magna Carta that no-one is to be deprived of his liberty or freedom except by the judgment of his peers. And it is true that in the past there have been a number of notable cases in which juries have acquitted men charged with offences against the state, when the odds in many ways seemed against them. Jury trial has also been claimed as an important constitutional right as part and parcel of the more general claim that men accused of offences, and again particularly political offences, should be tried by the common law courts according to common law procedure, including trial by jury, and the common law, and not by some special court like the Court of Star Chamber, and should certainly not be dealt with without any trial. But although it is true that a jury can be a safeguard it is not always so and there is in particular no special reason why they should show favour to a minority group. Many of the most famous acquittals come from a time when there was no universal suffrage and when it was easy for the government to get out of touch with jurors and when they generally were more inclined to use their powers to suppress criticism that would now be more readily tolerated. There is, too, a technical point which weakens the position of juries as protectors of liberty. A surprising number of offences which deal with demonstrations, strikes, and other matters like obstructing

[30] [1968] 1 W.L.R. 1.
[31] (1949) 93 S.J. 220.

the police are dealt with summarily before magistrates, without any jury at all, though it is true that an accused is entitled to a jury in any case where he is liable to three months' imprisonment or more.

The early nineteenth century added a new claim for the jury, that it serves to mitigate the rigour of the law. At a time when society relied on the severity of its penalties rather than an efficient police force some juries paved the way to a more enlightened practice by finding accused persons guilty of lesser offences, lowering the value of things stolen to avoid harsher penalties. It has been argued that this willingness to mitigate the severity of the law both as regards particular laws and also in particular cases is a virtue which the jury has still. It is true that juries do still, it seems, occasionally fail to act as the law intends both in regard to particular laws and in particular cases, though it is questionable whether this is always a virtue. Once jurors became motorists it became much more difficult to persuade them to convict motorists. This was particularly true of the offence of manslaughter by dangerous driving. It was in fact necessary to introduce a new offence of causing death by dangerous driving. There was a similar problem about driving under the influence of alcohol which has been met to some extent by the introduction of the offence of driving with more than a minimum content of alcohol in the blood. It still seems to be true that juries take into account in reaching their verdict factors which, if taken into account at all, should be taken into account in determining the sentence.[32]

A third traditional argument is that it involves every man in the administration of justice and prevents "Judge and Co." dominating the whole affair. This has an advantage for "Judge and Co." as well. The responsibility for deciding guilt rests on the jury and not on the judge, and on a jury which does not have to give reasons. No judgment by a judge would be accepted without reasons. Such is the current general confidence in the jury system that people are still apparently ready to accept all the consequences of a finding of guilt in a criminal court simply because it is made by a jury, subject in certain cases to the control of an appellate court. As juries are constantly changing there is sometimes the additional advantage that criticisms of a particular case does not carry with it the same condemnation of a particular judge or the judges as a whole but can be regarded as the aberration of a particular jury who once their task was done ceased to have any connection with the system at all. But this argument probably underestimates the apparent influence of the judge.

One of the problems involved in assessing the jury system is the difficulty of knowing what exactly its role is. This has come out for example in relation to the question of the facilities provided for jurors. It has been pointed out that in the past jurors have often been asked to follow quite complicated cases for a number of days, cooped up in a small jury box with no facilities or encouragement to take notes. It has been remarked too that the structure of a trial does not always make it easy to follow what is going on, for example the way one witness gives all his evidence at one time, and then the next, so that different issues and events are dealt with in no logical sequence, but the whole comes in bits and pieces. On the other hand it has

[32] See Griew in [1967] Crim.L.R. 555.

been argued that the encouragement of jurors to take notes would be wrong since it would take their minds off what is their true function, which is to sit back and absorb in an impressionistic way what is going on before them, and in particular to reach some notion of who is telling the truth and who is not, leaving it to the judge to sort out the issues and the questions to be answered in his summing up. This is one of the reasons why it has been suggested that some special method should be provided for dealing with difficult cases of commercial fraud where impressions of truth and falsehood are not the main problem.

Explicit criticism has been made in recent years of the jury qualification, though oddly this has come both from people complaining that the quality of juries has declined, and from others who said that the present property basis of jury qualification is now too restrictive. This led to the appointment of a Departmental Committee some of whose comments and recommendations are set out below. Its main recommendations are now embodied in the Criminal Justice Act 1972 (below, p. 205). Some research has been conducted into juries in the United States at Chicago and at the London School of Economics, but mostly in relation to simulated trials. For further reading see W. R. Cornish, *The Jury* and Lord Devlin, *Trial by Jury*.

The Qualifications for Jurors

The qualifications for jurors have recently been changed following the report of the Departmental Committee on Jury Service.[33] For a long time jurors had been, in the words of Lord Devlin in his lectures on the jury "predominantly male, middle aged, middle minded and middle class." This was a result of the fact that the qualifications had been fixed by the Juries Act 1825 and had been linked to the possession of property of a particular value. By the time the committee reported, it was argued that the occupation of property was no guarantee of suitability to be a juror and that the property qualification excluded numbers of people who would make good jurors and who in any event ought to be jurors, particularly large numbers of women. In 1825 it was not unusual to impose a property qualification. It existed also for the parliamentary and local government franchise. It was in the committee's view time that the two qualifications were assimilated again. The committee rejected a suggestion that there should be a minimum age limit of twenty-five instead of twenty-one, pointing out that in 1963 half of those found guilty in the higher courts were under twenty-five and two-thirds under thirty. "If trial by jury," it said, "is to be trial by a representative cross-section of an accused's fellow citizens, good reason must be shown before removing from jury service that section of the adult population nearest in age to the great majority of offenders." They also pointed out that in any jury chosen at random only one or two would be likely to be under twenty-five.

During the passage of the Criminal Justice Bill 1972 through the House of Lords the government introduced an amendment making registration as a parliamentary elector the qualification for jury service, but imposing a

---

[33] Cmnd. 2627 (1965).

minimum age limit of twenty-one although by that time the age for registration as a parliamentary elector had been reduced to eighteen. An amendment reducing the age to eighteen was carried against the government in the House of Commons and this is now embodied in the Criminal Justice Act.

Provisions disqualifying some convicted criminals and also people associated with the administration of justice, previously enacted in the Criminal Justice Act 1967, have also been included in the Criminal Justice Act 1972.

Report of the Departmental Committee on Jury Service

Cmnd. 2627 (1965)

53. . . . It is necessary to have on a jury men and women who will bring common sense to their task of exercising judgment; who have knowledge of the ways of the world and the ways of human beings; who have a sense of belonging to a community; who are actuated by a desire to see fair play; and above all who will strive to come to an honest conclusion in regard to the issues which are for them to decide. We think that in any healthy community there will be a high sense of duty, a fundamental respect for law and order, and a wish that principles of honesty and decency should prevail. A jury should represent a cross-section drawn at random from the community, and should be the means of bringing to bear on the issues the corporate good sense of that community. This cannot be in the keeping of the few, but is something to which all men and women of good will must contribute. . . .

60. . . . [O]ur view is that jury service should be regarded as a duty . . . of a citizen . . . [I]t follows that citizenship should be the basis from which the duty to serve arises. A convenient register of citizens (in the broad sense) is to be found in the register of those qualified to vote. . . . Administrative machinery for the annual compiling of this electoral register is in existence and is accepted as being convenient and efficient. Aliens who are resident here do not qualify to be included in the register, but British subjects and citizens of the Irish Republic do qualify.

61. . . . We therefore *recommend* that the basic qualification . . . should be citizenship as evidenced by inclusion in the register as a parliamentary elector. . . .

63. Our recommendation would make eligible for jury service large numbers of people who do not at present qualify. Inevitably some of these will be unsuitable. But this is true also under the present qualifications, and indeed under any other qualifications that might be devised. . . .

Tests of Education, Intelligence or Literacy

77. . . . We have considered various possible tests which have been suggested to us. One proposal was that each juror should be interviewed on his arrival by some officer of the court, and asked to read aloud from a daily newspaper so that a decision could be made as to whether he seemed to possess a suitable degree of literacy and intelligence. We do not favour the adoption of this proposal. Nor do we consider the fact that an individual did or did not pass some particular examination at school to be a fair or adequate test of his fitness to be a juror in later life. . . .

79. . . . Although it would be possible to devise ingenious tests for prospective jurors, we do not think that they would be appropriate or acceptable here. . . . If the unfortunate summoning officer is not to be left with the invidious task of telling large numbers of people that they have failed to pass whatever test might

be devised, the test itself would have to be of such a simple character as to be practically useless.

80. It is, however, self-evident that a juror will not be able to understand what is going on in court unless he has a good command of the English language. He may have to study documents, and perhaps to take notes. We therefore *recommend* that no one should be qualified to serve on a jury who cannot read, write, speak and understand English without difficulty.

The Case for a Residential Requirement

81. In some of the evidence presented to us concern has been expressed that under the present law immigrants from the Commonwealth and from the Irish Republic are able to qualify for jury service within a few months of first coming to this country.... It has therefore been suggested that ... there should be a requirement that they should have been ordinarily resident in this country ... before being qualified for service.

82. There are two main arguments in favour of such a suggestion. First, it is said that until they have become familiar with and assimilated to the English way of life, immigrants would be bad jurors. An immigrant may experience more than the ordinary amount of difficulty in deciding whether an English witness is lying, or in considering whether certain conduct conforms to a particular standard, e.g. whether driving is dangerous or whether a publication tends to corrupt morals; yet decisions on the credibility of witnesses and the conformity of conduct to a standard are among the primary functions of the jury.

83. The second argument ... is that ... it would be unfair to a very recent immigrant to make him serve on a jury before he has settled down in this country....

84. The arguments against a residential qualification fall under three heads. The first is that it is always possible that the accused in a criminal case, one of the parties in a civil case, or an important witness, would himself be a recent immigrant, in which case there would be much to be said for having one of his own kind on the jury.

85. The remaining arguments simply contradict those mentioned in paragraphs 82 and 83. It is so difficult to tell whether someone is lying that familiarisation with our way of life may in any case be of little assistance. Another point is that although some immigrants make little or no effort to become assimilated, for others no such effort is necessary because the immigrant is already accustomed to a similar way of life, with a legal system which may include trial by jury.

86. As regards the argument based on hardship, it is said that Parliament has in general decided that all British subjects and citizens of the Irish Republic should at once be accorded the full rights and responsibilities of United Kingdom citizens who are ordinarily resident here, and that there is no sufficient case for making a differentiation with regard to jury service.

87. .... [A]fter much deliberation we have concluded that some residential qualification is desirable.... Any decision as [to] the length and commencement of the period of residence required must to a very large extent be arbitrary. Some guidance may possibly be obtained from section 7 of the Commonwealth Immigrants Act 1962, under which a British subject who has been ordinarily resident in this country for five years or more cannot be deported. We *recommend* that no person should be qualified for service who has not, since the age of sixteen, been ordinarily resident in the United Kingdom, Channel Islands or Isle of Man, for a continuous period of five years. This would apply equally to persons who are not immigrants.

99. ... Jury service is a responsibility which should, in general, be shared by all who are qualified. Nevertheless, the nature of some professions and callings is such that their members, even if otherwise qualified, should be excluded from juries. Trial by jury involves a trial by laymen.... [I]t is essential to avoid having as jurors persons whose work is concerned with the administration of justice or the enforcement of the law. Equally, persons with knowledge or experience of a legal or quasi-legal nature might, if on a jury, exercise undue influence on their fellow jurors. There are others who, because of the nature of their religious vocation or function, should also be excluded. In addition, the demands of jury service should not be imposed on those who for reasons of physical or mental disability are unable to sustain them. Last in the group of those who should be excluded are those whose recent criminal record indicates that they may not be fitted to pass judgment on their fellow citizens.

Exclusions from Jury Service

Ineligibility because of connection with the administration of law and justice

103. ... If juries are to continue to command public confidence it is essential that they should manifestly represent an impartial and lay element in the workings of the courts. It follows that all those whose work is connected with the detection of crime and the enforcement of law and order must be excluded, as must those who professionally practise the law, or whose work is concerned with the functioning of the courts. It is impossible, whether desirable or not, to ensure that jurors have no previous knowledge of the law before they begin to hear a case. Many persons without formal legal training, for example, know enough about the way our courts function to be able to make a shrewd guess as to whether the accused has a previous criminal record; and one cannot entirely prevent by legislation the use of such knowledge in the jury room.

104. Nevertheless, it seems to us necessary to secure the exclusion from juries of any person who, in the words of one memorandum submitted to us, " because of occupation or position, has knowledge or experience of a legal or quasi-legal nature which is likely to enable him to exercise undue influence over his fellow jurors." If justice is not only to be done but to be seen to be done, such persons must not be allowed to serve on juries lest the specialist knowledge and prestige attaching to their occupation might cause them to be what has been described to us as " built-in leaders."

115. ... [W]e recommend that the ineligibility ... should continue for ten years after ceasing to follow the occupation in question.

Disqualification of convicted persons

134. There seem to us to be two reasons for excluding from juries persons with criminal records. First, we think it probable that a person who has been convicted, especially if a sentence of imprisonment has been imposed, will find it difficult to regard the police dispassionately.... Second, it seems to us that confidence in the administration of justice is bound to suffer if a person with a recent and serious criminal record is allowed to serve as a juror. An accused person, especially one of previously unblemished character, is entitled to feel that those who are trying him are themselves of good reputation.... In maintaining law and order reliance should not be placed on those who have shown that they pay no heed either to law or to order. It would we wrong to depend upon those whose own understanding of the line that divides right from wrong may be defective; or to entrust the fate of accused persons and the parties in civil suits to those whose own behaviour shows a lack of any proper understanding and recognition of decent behaviour.

141. The best way of excluding persons who are subject to disqualification is to require them to declare the fact to the summoning officer. It follows that the criterion of disqualification must be a simple one which can be quickly understood by prospective jurors. . . . [W]e agree that the seriousness of the offence should be taken into account. . . . [T]his may depend not so much upon what the offence is called, or what the maximum punishment for it may be, but upon the circumstances of its commission. On this basis its gravity could best be judged by the length of the sentence actually imposed. . . .

142. . . . It is true that this will involve accepting as jurors persons who have been convicted and dealt with in other ways, for example by being fined or being placed on probation. But it seems to us consistent with the general approach adopted in the preceding paragraphs to limit disqualification to persons who have been sent to prison or other penal institutions. In the first place, the fact that the court has seen fit to impose a punishment of this nature is some indication that the offence (or the offender's previous record) was of a serious character. Second, we think that a person who has been deprived of his freedom by a court is far more likely to be biased in his judgment as a juror than a person who has been dealt with more leniently.

143. . . . [W]e therefore *recommend* that persons should be disqualified who within the previous five years have been in custodial detention in the United Kingdom, the Channel Islands or the Isle of Man, having been convicted of an offence and sentenced to three months or more, or to an indeterminate sentence, without the option of a fine.

The Committee also recommended the exclusion of ministers of religion and monks and nuns, the blind, the deaf, the physically handicapped and persons suffering from mental disorders. They recommended that excusal as of right should be granted to an occupation because of the special and personal duties to the state, of its members, or their role in the relief of pain and suffering. Members of both Houses of Parliament and the armed forces came under the first head and doctors, dentists, nurses, midwives, vets and pharmaceutical chemists under the second. It also noted at para. 337:

> If our recommendations as to qualifications are accepted we anticipate that many qualified persons will never be called to serve, and that service more than once or twice in a lifetime will be unusual. . . . We do not think it reasonable to require a juror to serve more than once in five years in any court (including a coroner's court), and we recommend that this period should replace the present provisions and be the same for all courts. . . .

Criminal Justice Act 1972

1972 c. 71

25.—(1) Subject to the following provisions, every person shall be qualified to serve as a juror and be liable accordingly to attend for jury service when summoned under Part V of the Act of 1971, if—

(a) he is for the time being registered as a parliamentary or local government elector and is not less than eighteen nor more than sixty-five years of age; and

(b) he has been ordinarily resident in the United Kingdom, the Channel Islands or the Isle of Man for any period of at least five years since attaining the age of thirteen, but not if he is for the time being ineligible or disqualified for jury service; and the persons who are ineligible, and those who are disqualified, are those respectively listed in Parts I and II of Schedule 2 to this Act.

(2) A person summoned for jury service shall be entitled, if he so wishes, to be excused from jury service if he is among the persons listed in Part III of Schedule 2 to this Act, but (except as provided by that Part of the Schedule in the case of members of the Forces and others) a person shall not by this subsection be exempt from his obligation to attend if summoned, where the summons has not been withdrawn under section 31 (6) of the Act of 1971 and he has not under section 34 (2) of that Act been excused from attending.

(3) A written summons sent to any person under Part V of the Act of 1971 shall be accompanied by a notice informing him—

(*a*) of the effect of subsections (1), (2), (4) and (5) of this section; and

(*b*) that he may make representations to the appropriate officer with a view to obtaining the withdrawal of the summons, if for any reason he is not qualified for jury service, or wishes or is entitled to be excused;

and where a person attends in pursuance of such a summons or of a summons under section 33 of the Act of 1971 (summoning without notice in exceptional circumstances), the appropriate officer may put or cause to be put to him such questions as the officer thinks fit in order to establish whether or not the person is qualified for jury service.

(4) Where it appears to the appropriate officer, in the case of a person attending in pursuance of a summons for jury service, that on account of physical disability or insufficient understanding of English there is doubt as to his capacity to act effectively as a juror, the person may be brought before the judge, who shall determine whether or not he should act as a juror and, if not, shall discharge the summons; and for this purpose " the judge " means any judge of the High Court or any Circuit judge or Recorder. . . .

(6) The fact that a person summoned to serve on a jury is not qualified to serve shall be a ground of challenge for cause; but subject to this nothing in this section affects the law relating to challenge of jurors. . . .

27. In section 1 of the Juries Act 1949 (payments in respect of jury service), the following shall be substituted for subsection (1)—

" (1) Subject to the provisions of this Act, a person who serves as a juror shall be entitled, in respect of his attendance at court for the purpose of performing jury service, to receive payments, at the prescribed rates and subject to any prescribed conditions, by way of allowance—

(*a*) for travelling and subsistence; and

(*b*) for financial loss, where in consequence of his attendance for that purpose he has incurred any expenditure (otherwise than on travelling and subsistence) to which he would not otherwise be subject or he has suffered any loss of earnings, or of benefit under the enactments relating to national insurance, which he would otherwise have made or received."

SCHEDULE 2

INELIGIBILITY AND DISQUALIFICATION FOR AND EXCUSAL FROM JURY SERVICE

PART I

PERSONS INELIGIBLE

GROUP A

The Judiciary

Holders of high judicial office within the meaning of the Appellate Jurisdiction Act 1876.

Circuit judges and Recorders.

Masters of the Supreme Court.

Registrars and assistant registrars of any court.

Metropolitan and other stipendiary magistrates.

Justices of the peace.

The Chairman or President, the Vice-Chairman or Vice-President, and the registrar and assistant registrar of any Tribunal.

A person who has at any time been a person falling within any description specified above in this Group.

GROUP B

Others concerned with administration of justice

Barristers and solicitors, whether or not in actual practice as such.

Solicitors' articled clerks.

Barristers' clerks and their assistants.

Legal executives in the employment of solicitors.

The Director of Public Prosecutions and members of his staff.

Officers employed under the Lord Chancellor and concerned wholly or mainly with the day-to-day administration of the legal system or any part of it.

Officers and staff of any court, if their work is wholly or mainly concerned with the day-to-day administration of the court.

Coroners, deputy coroners and assistant coroners.

Justices' clerks and their assistants.

Clerks and other officers appointed under section 15 of the Administration of Justice Act 1964 (Inner London magistrates courts administration).

Active Elder Brethren of the Corporation of Trinity House of Deptford Strond.

A shorthandwriter in any court.

Governors, chaplains, medical officers and other officers of penal establishments; members of boards of visitors for penal establishments.

("Penal establishment" for this purpose means any prison, remand centre, detention centre or borstal institution.)

The warden or a member of the staff of a probation home, probation hostel or bail hostel (as defined in section 53 of this Act).

Probation officers and persons appointed to assist them.

Members of the Parole Board; members of local review committees established under the Criminal Justice Act 1967.

A member of any police force (including a person on central service under section 43 of the Police Act 1964); special constables; a member of any constabulary maintained under statute; a person employed in any capacity by virtue of which he has the powers and privileges of a constable.

A member of a police authority within the meaning of the Police Act 1964; a member of any body (corporate or other) with responsibility for appointing members of a constabulary maintained under statute.

Inspectors of Constabulary appointed by Her Majesty; assistant inspectors of constabulary appointed by the Secretary of State.

Civilians employed for police purposes by a police authority; members of the metropolitan civil staffs within the meaning of section 15 of the Superannuation (Miscellaneous Provisions) Act 1967 (persons employed under the Commissioner of Police of the Metropolis, Inner London justices' clerks, etc.).

A person in charge of, or employed in, any forensic science laboratory.

A person who at any time within the last ten years has been a person falling within any description specified above in this Group.

GROUP C

The clergy, etc.

A man in holy orders; a regular minister of any religious denomination.

A vowed member of any religious order (whether of men or of women) living in a monastery, convent or other religious community.

GROUP D

The mentally ill
(Expressions used in this Group are to be construed
in accordance with the Mental Health Act 1959)

A person who suffers or has suffered from mental illness, subnormality, severe subnormality or psychopathic disorder and on account of that condition either—

(*a*) is resident in a hospital or other similar institution; or
(*b*) regularly attends for treatment by a medical practitioner.

A person who, under Part VIII of the Mental Health Act 1959, has been determined by a judge to be incapable, by reason of mental disorder, of managing and administering his property and affairs.

A person for the time being in guardianship under section 33 of the Mental Health Act 1959.

PART II

PERSONS DISQUALIFIED

A person who has at any time been sentenced in the United Kingdom, the Channel Islands or the Isle of Man—

(*a*) to imprisonment for life or for a term of five years or more; or
(*b*) to be detained during Her Majesty's pleasure or during the pleasure of the Governor of Northern Ireland.

A person who at any time in the last ten years has, in the United Kingdom or the Channel Islands or the Isle of Man—

(*a*) served any part of a sentence of imprisonment or detention, being a sentence for a term of three months or more; or
(*b*) been detained in a borstal institution.

PART III

PERSONS EXCUSABLE AS OF RIGHT

Parliament

Peers and peeresses entitled to receive writs of summons to attend the House of Lords.

Members of the House of Commons.

Officers of the House of Lords.

Officers of the House of Commons.

The Forces

Full-time serving members of—

any of Her Majesty's naval, military or air forces,
the Women's Royal Naval Service,
Queen Alexandra's Royal Naval Nursing Service, or
any Voluntary Aid Detachment serving with the Royal Navy.

(A person excusable under this head shall be under no obligation to attend in pursuance of a summons for jury service if his commanding officer certifies to the officer issuing the summons that it would be prejudicial to the efficiency of the service if the person were required to be absent from duty.)

Medical and other similar professions

The following, if actually practising their profession and registered (including provisionally or temporarily registered), enrolled or certified under the enactments relating to that profession—

medical practitioners,
dentists,
nurses,
midwives,
veterinary surgeons and veterinary practitioners,
pharmaceutical chemists.

SUMMONING A JURY

The sheriff is responsible for summoning the jurors in the first instance. He is required to have the same proportion of men and women in the panel he summons as there are eligible jurors in the lists. Section 35 (1) of the Courts Act 1971 requires the jury for any particular case to be selected by ballot in open court from those summoned. Section 35 (1) of the Criminal Justice Act 1948 gives any person being tried on indictment the right to challenge up to seven jurors without cause. In addition both defence and prosecution may challenge either the whole jury or members of it if they can show cause, though they have no power to examine a juror to see if there is cause. The Departmental Committee at paragraph 247, however, said that it could see no objection to either the parties or the police making inquiries about those summoned to be jurors to see if there was anything in their record which might justify a challenge. If the other side objects to a challenge for cause the judge must decide whether or not to uphold the challenge. The Crown may also ask a juror simply to stand down, provided there are enough jurors left.

Section 35 of the Courts Act 1971 abolishes the old rule which made it possible to obtain an all male or an all female jury though this might result from the way the challenges are used, and a woman could ask for exemption from service on a particular case because of the nature of the evidence or the issues to be tried. It also provides that no one jury should try more than one issue unless the other cases started within twenty-four hours from the time it was constituted. This does not prevent a juror being called upon to sit on another jury.

Selection was supposed to be random before the Act but this did not always happen. Professor Ely Devons described his experience at (1965) 28 M.L.R. 562:

> The text books suggest that this is a random process, with the method of securing this randomness varying from court to court. It certainly was not random in my case. I was called to attend on Monday morning; all day Monday and Tuesday morning I sat at the back of the court hoping that I would be called for a case, but I was not. To put it mildly, by mid-day on Tuesday I was bored, angry and frustrated. I approached the police-sergeant who seemed to be in charge of affairs, and engaged him in general conversation, flattered him not very subtly by saying "How difficult his job must be," explained that I was getting bored just hanging around not being called. He commented in a strong Lancashire accent . . . that sometimes some of those called for the panel did not serve at all. I hoped that that was not going to happen to me. "Leave it to me," he said, "the next case should be quite interesting." Sure enough, the clerk called my name for the next case.

Conditions of Service as a Juror

The Departmental Committee was critical of the existing conditions in which jurors performed their duties. It also made recommendations which throw some light on the role it expected the jury to play.

Departmental Committee on Jury Service
Cmnd. 2627 (1965)

275. When the average juror arrives at the court he finds himself amongst a crowd of total strangers, of both sexes and of all walks of life, who are for the most part as apprehensive and ignorant of the proceedings as he is himself. He may be kept waiting with the other jurors for what seems an unconscionable time, in uncomfortable and dingy surroundings. Eventually he may be informed by an officer of the court that when his name is called out he should answer and go into the jury box. He may then be sworn in as a juror and a case may start immediately. The juror will not have been instructed in any way, and may be quite ignorant of the procedure and nervous of doing the wrong thing. He does not know how or when a foreman is to be chosen; he does not know whether or not a juror may put any questions, and if so at what time and by what method, or whether he may make notes; he may not even know whether or not the verdict must be unanimous. Those who have never been in a court of law may know something in general about the procedure from reading newspapers and from the wireless and television, but their knowledge may be incomplete or

misleading and they may still feel considerable doubt about many aspects of their duties. . . .

278. We *recommend* that prospective jurors should be sent, at the same time as the summons, some general guidance about the nature of their duties. . . .

282. . . . [W]e *recommend* that jurors should be provided, both in jury boxes and in retiring rooms, with adequate facilities to take any notes they wish, but the evidence presented to us has led to the conclusion that it would be unwise to give any positive encouragement to jurors to embark upon note-taking. The process of note-taking is one that requires a good deal of experience and skill. Because of their training, judges are able to make accurate and reasonably complete notes, and at the same time to observe all that is happening and to keep control over the proceedings. Not all jurors can be expected to have the same skill and training. Experience shows that as a general rule it may well be better for jurors to concentrate on listening, observing and reflecting. . . . The provision . . . of writing materials will be an indication that it is permissible to take notes, but beyond that we think it is for individual judges . . . to decide whether to inform jurors of their right to take notes and whether to give any guidance or advice on the matter.

283. Rather similar considerations apply to the problem whether jurors should be told that they may ask questions. We think that there is some peril in encouraging them to do so. If cases are being conducted by advocates on both sides, as they usually are, there is every reason to expect that all relevant questions will be raised at some time before the conclusion of the evidence. If positive encouragement were given to jurors to ask questions there would be a risk in a criminal case of some questions prejudicial to the accused being asked inadvertently, and there would also be some risk of the proceedings getting out of hand. . . . Much must be left to the handling of the proceedings by the judge. . . .

285. Some witnesses have expressed the view that it would often be helpful if, at the commencement of a trial, the judge addressed a few brief words to the jury as to the general nature of their task. . . .

This topic is not strictly within our terms of reference. . . . We therefore do no more than to report the suggestion. . . .

299. The evidence presented to us, and our own investigations, have left us in no doubt that in many court buildings the accommodation provided for jurors is most inadequate. . . .

300. . . . The retiring rooms are often most unsatisfactory. . . . There may be no waiting rooms for jurors. . . . At some courts . . . jurors have to wait around in the corridors, where they may be . . . in close contact with persons intimately connected with a case they are going to try, and with whom in all innocence they may fall into conversation. They could be exposed to approaches from interested parties. . . .

306. . . . We *recommend* that local authorities should as a matter of urgency consider what improvements can . . . be made to the jury accommodation. . . .

CHAPTER 4

FINDING THE LAW

INTRODUCTION

English law is to be found in statutes, delegated legislation such as statutory instruments, statutory Orders in Council and by-laws, and the judgments of past cases. Unlike the continental systems English law has never been codified to any great extent. There have been statutes from time to time which have brought together in one place the rules on the same subject in an effort to simplify an area of law which had become overladen with judicial decisions. The series of criminal statutes passed in the 1860s for example included the 1861 statutes dealing with offences against the person, larceny, malicious damage to property, forgery and coinage offences. Later there were commercial statutes such as the Bills of Exchange Act 1882, the Sale of Goods Act 1893, and the Property Acts of the 1920s. Some modern statutes too, together with the delegated legislation authorised by them, do in fact form a kind of code for a particular area of law, for example the National Insurance Act 1965 and the National Insurance (Industrial Injuries) Act 1946. The Law Commission has as one of its tasks the simplification and codification of different branches of the law; the law of contract being one subject under consideration at the moment. Various parts of the law were codified in former parts of the Empire as well. There was a penal code and codes of contract, evidence and procedure in India. But the English system at home has never been code-oriented. Instead the English lawyer when faced with the task of finding the law on a particular point has in principle to cope with a vast body of miscellaneous statutes and statutory instruments passed at different dates, together with an even greater number of cases distributed throughout law reports, dating from any time between the sixteenth century and the present day, though principally from the last 150 years. One says " in principle " because in his day-to-day practice a lawyer is more likely to rely on secondary sources such as digests, encylopedias like Halsbury's *Laws of England* or the *English and Empire Digest*, or *Current Law* or textbooks. But when it comes to the point, and in particular when it comes to the point of litigation, the statements of law expressed in them rest ultimately on this vast body of materials which of necessity form the bulk of an English law library. One of the major skills which an English lawyer needs is the ability to find his way around this vast body of materials and use them as the basis of any legal advice, argument or decision.

STATUTE LAW AND ITS INTERPRETATION

The constitutional cornerstone of English law is the doctrine of the sovereignty of Parliament. Statutes enacted by Parliament are the supreme law of the land. If there is a statutory provision relevant to a case it is to be applied. No court has the power to ignore a statute or declare it invalid

212

on the grounds, for example, that it infringes some basic constitutional doctrine or basic constitutional right, or that it exceeds the power of Parliament. There are no basic constitutional doctrines or rights which can prevail in law against a statute and there are no legal limits on the power of Parliament to legislate, other than the rule that no Parliament can pass a statute which is incapable of being amended or repealed by it or a subsequent Parliament. Even if a statute can be shown to be contrary to a principle of international law or a treaty the courts will not declare it invalid or ignore or modify the parts which are inconsistent. Whether the courts will modify the principle in relation to European Community law has yet to be seen. The doctrine of the sovereignty of Parliament does not, however, mean that Parliament is the only body with the power to legislate. In practice it delegates powers to legislate to Ministers and government departments, who legislate by means of statutory instruments, and, more rarely, statutory Orders in Council, and local authorities, who legislate by means of by-laws. (In addition the Government has a limited power to legislate by virtue of the Royal Prerogative, but this is not relevant to domestic law.) In form the regulations and decisions of the Council and Commission of the European Community, which, in accordance with the Treaty of Rome, will take direct effect in the United Kingdom, will be delegated legislation since they derive their force, so far as the United Kingdom courts are concerned, from the European Communities Act 1972 which provides that they shall have direct effect in this country. Where they differ from other forms of delegated legislation is of course in the fact that the United Kingdom has less direct control over them than it does over purely domestic delegated legislation, that the grant of powers is intended to be permanent, and that they are more wide-ranging than the powers to legislate which would normally be given to a public authority in this country. One result of Britain's entry into the European Economic Community is that a lawyer may have to refer to the Treaty and regulations made by the Community as well as domestic statutes and domestic delegated legislation when a question of Community law arises.

Delegated legislation differs from statutes, in that, although it prevails over any common law rule, its validity depends upon its being within the power granted by Parliament in the parent statute. It can therefore be challenged on the grounds that it is *ultra vires*, *i.e.* beyond the powers granted, unless statute has succeeded in making it unchallengeable by excluding the jurisdiction of the courts to question it. In other respects it is treated in much the same way as statute.

Discovering or determining the relevant legal rule is often just a question of discovering the relevant statute or statutory instrument and finding the rule there set out, though finding the statute in the first place is not always easy nor is it always easy to keep up with amendments and changes made since the statute was passed. This is one of the reasons why digests like Halsbury's *Laws of England* or Halsbury's *Statutes* are such a necessary part of a lawyer's library. Even when one has discovered the relevant statute and the relevant statutory provision there may still be a problem of interpretation and this often causes difficulty. As the Law Commission noted in its twenty-first report in 1969:

> . . . [T]here are practical limits to the improvements which can be effected in drafting. Account must be taken of the inherent frailty of language, the difficulty of foreseeing and providing for all contingencies, the imperfections which must result in some degree from the pressures under which modern legislation has so often to be produced and the difficulties of expressing finely balanced compromises of competing interests which the draftsman is sometimes called upon to formulate. Difficulties may also arise when words are inserted into a Bill in the course of discussion in Parliament without sufficient regard to its overall structure, as originally planned.

Quite apart from these difficulties the circumstances in which the statute was passed may have changed considerably and the policy of the statute may no longer be in the mainstream of current views and there may be a general desire to interpret its provisions in such a way as to make them conform more to what is regarded as currently desirable.

To aid, and sometimes to limit, the courts, most statutes contain a definition section which contains definitions of some of the leading words and phrases in the statute. In addition there is the more general Interpretation Act 1889 which sets out definitions of common words which apply unless the particular statute makes it clear that some other meaning was intended in the context. The definitions in that Act however have been provided more with the intention of avoiding unnecessary repetition and to cut down the length of statutes than to provide a dictionary of the basic concepts which keep cropping up in statutes of different kinds.

Over the years, too, the judges have developed a number of principles, presumptions and maxims to assist them and others in the interpretation of statutes and to provide some kind of framework within which advocates can urge, and judges justify, one interpretation rather than another. The basic principles known traditionally as the literal, golden and mischief rules are more in the nature of general approaches than real rules, and although they act as guides to interpretation they can in practice be extremely fallible since it is by no means always certain which will be adopted and what the result will be if the court adopts one rather than another. All take the words of the statute as their starting point for, although the courts say that their task is to discover the intention of Parliament, they do not permit any reference to the debates in Parliament, or the recommendations of any commission or committee on which the statute was based, for the purpose of discovering it. The literal rule then provides that if the words are clear, then they best express the intention of Parliament and they should be applied as they stand; the golden rule that if the words are ambiguous they should be applied in their ordinary meaning, unless this would lead to some manifest absurdity; and finally the mischief rule provides that in cases of doubt reference may be made to the state of the law before the statute was passed and the defects in it, which it is presumed the statute was designed to remedy, and then that interpretation is given to the words which will remove the defect and further the remedy. But besides these " basic " rules there are others, equally respectable and fundamental, that have never succeeded in being given a name, like the rule that the words should be considered in the context of the statute as a whole, and that different approaches may be appropriate to different kinds of statute.

Then there are the " presumptions " and the maxims which act as minor aids. Although the courts fully accept that Parliament in a statute can do anything and are willing on occasion to imply things into a statute which have not been expressly stated, there are some things that they regard as so fundamental that they will presume that Parliament did not intend to do them unless it has expressly said so. In *Chester* v. *Bateson* [1] for example they said that they would not presume that Parliament in delegating general powers to a Minister of the Crown intended to include a power to make regulations preventing a landlord taking his tenant to court to recover possession of his house at the end of a lease. In *Att.-Gen.* v. *Wilts United Dairies* [2] they said the same as regards the power to impose a tax or charge. In *Nairn* v. *University of St. Andrews* [3] they took the view that the constitution could not be changed by a sidewind; that it was no use therefore women graduates of the University of St. Andrews putting together a statute giving graduates of the University the parliamentary vote and a statute giving women the right to be admitted to a degree and concluding that Parliament had inadvertently given women graduates the vote when no woman at that time had a vote. In recent years the courts have leaned very strongly against any suggestion that Parliament had intended to oust, or more accurately, succeeded in ousting, their jurisdiction. The courts are unwilling to allow governments to use their majority in Parliament to prevent a citizen aggrieved by the conduct of a Minister, government department or tribunal bringing his grievance to the ordinary courts unless it has managed to make its intention crystal clear and beyond the power of the courts to resist. In a sense, although the presumptions are in form a challenge to Parliament they can be justified as a method of protecting Parliament from being persuaded too easily by the Government of the day to give it powers which in the court's views it should not lightly be given. In this way the courts in some of the presumptions have been developing for Parliament some general principles of administrative law. It is fair to add though that in practice the courts' action has been an almost instinctive reaction to attempted interference with what it regards as basic rights and principles.

The maxims or minor aids are much more technical and of less importance. One, the " *ejusdem generis* " rule, provides that if particular words which refer to members of a class are followed by general words, then it is assumed that the general words are limited to members of the same class. Another, " *expressio unius, exclusio alterius* " provides that the deliberate inclusion of one or more members of a class means the deliberate exclusion of those not mentioned.

It is not at all easy to assess or even describe the weight to be attached to these rules and principles in the application of statutes to particular cases. In part this is because there are so many other factors involved in the interpretation and application of statutes, besides the bare words of the statutes and the basic rules. Statutes vary infinitely in their subject-matter, in their age, even in their style. Some are closely related to and integrated

[1] [1920] 1 K.B. 829.
[2] (1921) 37 T.L.R. 884.
[3] [1909] A.C. 147.

into the common law, like those statutes which have been passed to remedy some defect in the common law or some of those which were passed to consolidate an area of law which had become confused by the proliferation of decided cases. Others are more isolated and form the centre of their own case law, as is the case with the tax statutes. Some, like the tax statutes again, are quite tightly drafted, the response of parliamentary draftsmen over the years to the willingness of the courts to allow taxpayers to find loopholes in them where they can, and to leave it to the Inland Revenue to stop up any gaps that appeared. Others are more loosely worded and leave it to the courts to fill in the gaps, as with the statutes which set out the grounds for divorce or lay down general standards, the detailed application and development of which is left to the courts. The courts, too, have different attitudes to different classes of statute and even to different statutes, and these attitudes may change. In the nineteenth century the courts showed great hostility to statutes which recognised the legality of trade unions and which sought to make some of their traditional weapons, such as the strike and picketing, legal. As a result they interpreted them narrowly and in a manner clearly contrary to the spirit of Parliament's intention. There is still a tradition that taxing and " penal " statutes should be strictly interpreted. Even individual judges themselves sometimes differ not only in their approach to particular statutes or classes of statute but to the problem of statutory interpretation itself. Lord Denning has on a number of occasions recommended a more liberal approach to the interpretation of statutes and has been rapped on the knuckles for his presumption.

The Law Commission has recently recommended on the one hand greater help being given to the courts by Parliament by way of explanation of what the statute is intended to achieve, and on the other hand a broader approach by the courts to the problem of interpretation. A broader approach however, may not be easy and it is not even certain to what extent it is desirable. What is often asserted as desirable is a shift away from a concentration on the mere words of the statute to a more direct assessment of the " intention of Parliament." But quite often the " intention of Parliament " may itself be something of a myth. Parliament operates at the level of general principles. It makes no pretence at being able to foresee all the numerous cases which are likely to arise in the future. Even the notion of Parliament as a single entity has an air of unreality about it. Who can really know what the majority intended on each item, the extent to which Parliament agreed with the interpretation put on the statute by the Government Minister who introduced it and guided it through the various stages, or the exact relationship between amendments and the original provisions?

Even the explanatory statement raises problems: what is to happen as circumstances change and the statute gradually becomes out of date without actually being repealed? Will the judges lose any freedom they may have at the moment to reinterpret its provision to meet changing needs, opinions and circumstances? Attractive and useful as it may be in some cases to resort to debates and the reports of Royal commissions, will this in fact yield benefits commensurate with the time and effort expended? Without necessarily going as far as Lord Halsbury who on one occasion said that the draftsman of a statute was the worst person to interpret it since he only saw what he intended to put into the statute and not what he had in fact put into it, there is a danger that too great an emphasis on matters outside the words will reduce even further the value of a statute as a piece of flexible raw material which can be moulded and adapted and used as a basis for new law creation than is the case at the moment. For in spite of the fact that a great part of English law is now statutory and that series and groups of statutes may over time have a general influence on the assumptions and values of the common law the actual provisions are still limited by the judges to the circumstances they were intended to cover and are not extended by analogy as provisions of the common law are. As Landis put it in *Statutes and the Sources of Law* (Harvard Legal Essays, 1934):

> When the highest tribunal of England in 1868 decided that the land-owner who artificially accumulates water upon his premises is absolutely liable for damages caused by its escape that judgment had an enormous influence throughout Anglo-American law. . . . Had Parliament in 1868 adopted a similar rule, no such permeating results to the general body of Anglo-American law would have ensued. And this would be true, though the Act had been preceded by a thorough and patient inquiry by a Royal Commission into the business of storing large volumes of water and its concomitant risks, and even though the same Lords who approved Mr. Fletcher's claim had in voting " aye " upon the measure given reasons identical with those contained in their judgments. Such a statute would have caused no ripple in the process of adjudication either in England or on the other side of the Atlantic, and the judicial mind would have failed to discern the essential similarity between water stored in reservoirs, crude petroleum stored in tanks, and gas and electricity confined and maintained upon the premises—surely an easier leap than from wild animals to reservoirs. . . .

Statute and international law

Salomon v. Commissioners of Customs and Excise

Court of Appeal [1967] 2 Q.B. 116

DIPLOCK L.J.: . . . [T]he Convention on the Valuation of Goods for Customs Purposes of December 15, 1950 (Treaty Series No. 49 (1954)), which was signed by the United Kingdom on that date and ratified on September 27, 1952, . . . required each contracting party to introduce into its domestic law and apply the definition of value of imported goods set out in Annex I to the convention. The convention is one of those public acts of state of Her Majesty's Government of which Her Majesty's judges must take judicial notice if it be relevant to the determination of a case before them, if necessary informing themselves of such acts by inquiry of the appropriate department of Her Majesty's Government. Where, by a treaty, Her Majesty's Government undertakes either to introduce domestic legislation to achieve a specified result in the United Kingdom or to secure a specified result which can only be achieved by legislation, the treaty, since in English law it is not self-operating, remains irrelevant to any issue in the English courts until Her Majesty's Government has taken steps by way of legislation to fulfil its treaty obligations. Once the Government has legislated, which it may do in anticipation of the coming into effect of the treaty, as it did in this case, the court must in the first instance construe the legislation, for that is what the court has to apply. If the terms of the legislation are clear and unambiguous, they must be given effect to, whether or not they carry out Her Majesty's treaty obligations, for the sovereign power of the Queen in Parliament extends to breaking treaties (see *Ellerman Lines* v. *Murray, White Star Line and U.S. Mail Steamers Oceanic Steam Navigation Co. Ltd*. v. *Comerford*[4]), and any remedy for such a breach of an international obligation lies in a forum other than Her Majesty's own courts. But if the terms of the legislation are not clear but are reasonably capable of more than one meaning, the treaty itself becomes relevant, for there is a prima facie presumption that Parliament does not intend to act in breach of international law, including therein specific treaty obligations; and if one of the meanings which can reasonably be ascribed to the legislation is consonant with the treaty obligations and another or others are not, the meaning which is consonant is to be preferred. Thus, in case of lack of clarity in the words used in the legislation, the terms of the treaty are relevant to enable the court to make its choice between the possible meanings of these words by applying this presumption.

It has been argued that the terms of an international convention cannot be consulted to resolve ambiguities or obscurities in a statute unless the statute itself contains either in the enacting part or in the preamble an express reference to the international convention which it is the purpose of the statute to implement. The judge seems to have been persuaded that *Ellerman Lines etc*. v. *Murray etc*. was authority for this proposition. But, with respect, it is not. The statute with which that case was concerned did refer to the convention. The case is authority only for the proposition for which I have already cited it. . . . If from extrinsic evidence it is plain that the enactment was intended to fulfil Her Majesty's Government's obligations under a particular convention, it matters not that there is no express reference to the convention in the statute. One must not presume that Parliament intends to break an international convention merely because it does not say expressly that it is intending to observe it. Of course the court must not merely guess that the statute was intended to give effect to a particular international convention. The extrinsic evidence of the connection must be cogent. But here we have a convention dealing specifically and exclusively with one narrow topic, the method of valuation of imported goods for the purpose of assessing ad valorem customs duties. Section 258 of and Schedule 6 to the Customs and Excise Act, 1952, deal specifically and exclusively with the same narrow topic. The terms of the statute and convention are nearly identical, save that the statute omits the " Interpretative Notes to the Definition of Value " which appear by the referee and by the judge. . . . The inference that the statute was intended to embody the convention is irresistible, even without reference to its legislative history, to which Russell L.J. will refer. In my view we can refer to the convention to resolve ambiguities or obscurities of language in the section of and the Schedule to the statute.

For my part, had I approached the section and the Schedule without the benefit of knowing what construction had been put upon them by the referee and judge, I might have been misled into thinking that the words were too clear and unambiguous to necessitate any reference to the convention. But as the meaning which my brethren in this court and I ascribe to them differs from that which the referee and judge both thought they bore, it would be hubristic to assert that they are incapable of more than one meaning and to eschew such aid to their construction as the convention can supply. I will, however, observe the rules and first deal with the construction of the words used in the section and the Schedule considered on their own before turning to the convention to seek there confirmation or contradiction of the meaning which I think they bear.

---

[4] [1931] A.C. 126; *sub nom. The Croxteth Hall*; *The Celtic*, 47 T.L.R. 147, H.L.(E.).

Corocraft Ltd. v. Pan-American Airways Inc.
Queen's Bench Division [1969] 1 Q.B. 616

DONALDSON J.: . . . The duty of the courts is to ascertain and give effect to the will of Parliament as expressed in its enactments. In the performance of this duty the judges do not act as computers into which are fed the statute and the rules for the construction of statutes and from whom issue forth the mathematically correct answer. The interpretation of statutes is a craft as much as a science and the judges, as craftsmen, select and apply the appropriate rules as the tools of their trade. They are not legislators, but finishers, refiners and polishers of legislation which comes to them in a state requiring varying degrees of further processing.

All this is familiar to English lawyers. I mention it because the problem with which I am concerned in this case is likely to be of interest to aviation lawyers on the other side of the Atlantic and I should be sorry if they thought, . . . that the English judicial process was such that the judges inhabited Justice Frankfurter's verbal prison, happily unaware of the risks involved in a literal interpretation of Judge Learned Hand's " temperamental beings." Not so. If the English courts might hesitate to adopt so robust an approach as did the Special Referee in the *American Smelting* case,[5] it is not because these courts are less aware of the needs of the commercial community, but rather, perhaps, that there is a difference of opinion between the courts on the two sides of the Atlantic in their evaluation of the commercial advantages of certainty derived from close attention to the words of the statute. A relevant factor may also be differences in the legislative process. In the United Kingdom treaties do not become part of the domestic law by proclamation, but only by enactment after Parliamentary debate, and with the possibility of clarification and amendment. Less therefore may remain to be done by the courts of the United Kingdom by way of interpretation.

There is ample authority for looking at the Convention to which it is the expressed intention of Parliament to give effect (see, for example, *Salomon* v. *Commissioners of Customs and Excise*[6]). There is also authority for the proposition that

> " the judicial interpreter may deal with careless and inaccurate words and phrases in the same spirit as a critic deals with an obscure or corrupt text, when satisfied, on solid grounds, from the context or history of the enactment, or from injustice, inconvenience or absurdity of the consequences to which it would lead, that the language thus treated does not really express the intention and that his amendment probably does "

(see *Swan* v. *Pure Ice Co.*,[7] *per* Romer L.J.[8] and *In re Lockwood*,[9] in which eight words were excised from a statute). . . .

The rules of statutory interpretation

Heydon's Case
(1584) 3 Co.Rep. 1a; 76 E.R. 637

And it was unanimously resolved by Sir Roger Manwood, Chief Baron, and the other Barons of the Exchequer . . . that for the sure and true interpretation

---

[5] U.S. & Ca.Av.Rep. 387 (1956).
[6] [1967] 2 Q.B. 116, C.A.
[7] [1935] 2 K.B. 265, C.A.
[8] *Ibid.* p. 276.
[9] [1958] Ch. 231.

of all statutes in general (be they penal or beneficial, restrictive or enlarging of the common law,) four things are to be discerned and considered:

1st. What was the common law before the making of the Act.

2nd. What was the mischief and defect for which the common law did not provide.

3rd. What remedy the Parliament hath resolved and appointed to cure the disease of the commonwealth.

And, 4th. The true reason of the remedy; and then the office of all the Judges is always to make such construction as shall suppress the mischief, and advance the remedy, and to suppress subtle inventions and evasions for continuance of the mischief and *pro privato commodo*, and to add force and life to the cure and remedy, according to the true intent of the makers of the Act, *pro bono publico*.

Sussex Peerage Case
(1844) 11 Cl. & F. 85; 8 E.R. 1034

TINDAL C.J.: . . . My Lords, the only rule for the construction of Acts of Parliament is, that they should be construed according to the intent of the Parliament which passed the Act. If the words of the statute are themselves precise and unambiguous, then no more can be necessary than to expound those words in their natural and ordinary sense. The words themselves alone do, in such case, best declare the intention of the lawgiver. But if any doubt arises from the terms employed by the Legislature, it has always been held a safe means of collecting the intention, to call in aid the ground and cause of making the statute, and to have recourse to the preamble, which, according to Chief Justice Dyer (*Stowel* v. *Lord Zouch*, Plowden, 353) is " a key to open the minds of the makers of the Act, and the mischiefs which they intended to redress."

Becke v. Smith
(1836) 2 M. & W. 191; 150 E.R. 724

PARKE B.: . . . It is a very useful rule, in the construction of a statute, to adhere to the ordinary meaning of the words used, and to the grammatical construction, unless that is at variance with the intention of the legislature, to be collected from the statute itself, or leads to any manifest absurdity or repugnance, in which case the language may be varied or modified, so as to avoid such inconvenience, but no further.

Inland Revenue Commissioners v. Wolfson
(1949) 65 T.L.R. 260

LORD SIMONDS: . . . It was urged that the construction which I favour leaves an easy loophole through which the evasive taxpayer may find escape. That may be so; but I will repeat what has been said before. It is not the function of a Court of Law to give to words a strained and unnatural meaning because only thus will a taxing section apply to a transaction which, had the Legislature thought of it, would have been covered by appropriate words. It is the duty of the Court to give to the words of this subsection their reasonable meaning and I must decline on any ground of policy to give to them a meaning which . . . I regard as little short of extravagant. It cannot even be urged that, unless this meaning is given to the section, it can have no operation. On the contrary, given its natural meaning, it will bring within the area of taxation a number of cases in which, by a familiar device, tax had formerly been avoided.

LORDS DU PARCQ, NORMAND and REID agreed with this statement of principle.

LORD MORTON OF HENRYTON did not consider it necessary to form a concluded view on the question of principle.[10]

R. v. Bow Road Justices, ex p. Adedigba
Court of Appeal [1968] 2 Q.B. 572

SALMON L.J.: . . . The only matter which has given me any pause is that there has been a great deal of legislation concerning this subject in the last 119 years, and Parliament has never taken the opportunity of correcting *Reg* v. *Blane*.[11] The respondent has contended that since Parliament has not corrected *Reg* v. *Blane*,[11] it must be taken to have approved and endorsed the decision. It is quite true that it is a principle of construction that the courts may presume that when there has been a decision upon the meaning of a statute, and the statute is re-enacted in much the same terms, it was the intention of Parliament to endorse the decision. But this is merely a rule of construction for the guidance of the courts. It is not a presumption which the courts are bound to make: *Royal Crown Derby Porcelain Co.* v. *Russell*.[12] It is always possible that Parliament, however vigilant, may overlook a decision. I think that *Reg* v. *Blane* has been overlooked by the legislature. I am certainly not satisfied that it was the intention of Parliament to endorse it. Indeed, if that decision had been considered by Parliament at any time when the intervening legislation was passed, I have little doubt but that it would have been corrected for it manifestly works gross injustice. It seems to me that the words of Lord Blackburn in *Tiverton & North Devon Railway Co.* v. *Loosemore* [13] can appropriately be applied to the intervening Acts. He said:

> " In construing an Act of Parliament, we ought not to put a construction on it that would work injustice, or even hardship, or inconvenience, unless it is clear that such was the intention of the legislature."

Bank of England v. Vagliano Brothers
House of Lords [1891] A.C. 107

LORD HERSCHELL: . . . The conclusion at which the majority of the Court of Appeal arrived with reference to the construction of the subsection of the Bills of Exchange Act with which your Lordships have to deal . . . was founded upon an examination of the state of the law at the time the Bills of Exchange Act

---

[10] *Cf.* Lord Macnaghten in *Att.-Gen.* v. *Duke of Richmond and Gordon* [1909] A.C. 466: ". . . Your Lordships were warned by the learned counsel for the appellant of the appalling consequences of the decision under appeal. ' Here,' they said, ' is a tremendous hole in the Finance Act discovered by the ingenuity of a Scotch solicitor. The great fishes which the Commissioners look upon as their own will swim through the gap one by one. The duller-witted Southron will follow the lead. And what will become of the revenue of the country? ' My Lords, I do not think the prospect so gloomy, nor can I see that any extraordinary astuteness was required to recommend the course which the late Duke adopted. I should think the eminent solicitor who was the Duke's adviser would be the first to disclaim the left-handed compliments lavished on his skill."

[11] (1849) 13 Q.B. 769.

[12] [1949] 2 K.B. 417, 429. (There Denning L.J. said: " I do not believe that whenever Parliament re-enacts a provision of a statute it thereby gives statutory authority to every erroneous interpretation which has been put upon it. The true view is that the court will be slow to overrule a previous decision on the interpretation of a statute when it has long been acted on, and it will be more than usually slow to do so when Parliament has, since the decision, re-enacted the statute in the same terms. But if a decision is, in fact, shown to be erroneous there is no rule of law which prevents it being overruled.") *Cf.* also Lord Macmillan in *Barras* v. *Aberdeen Steam Trawling Fishing Co.* [1933] A.C. 402.

[13] (1884) 9 App.Cas. 480, 497.

was passed. The prior authorities were subjected by the learned Judges who concurred in this conclusion to an elaborate review. . . .

My Lords, with sincere respect for the learned Judges . . . I cannot bring myself to think that this is the proper way to deal with such a statute as the Bills of Exchange Act, which was intended to be a code of the law relating to negotiable instruments. I think the proper course is in the first instance to examine the language of the statute and to ask what is its natural meaning, uninfluenced by any considerations derived from the previous state of the law, and not to start with inquiring how the law previously stood, and then, assuming that it was probably intended to leave it unaltered, to see if the words of the enactment will bear an interpretation in conformity with this view.

If a statute, intended to embody in a code a particular branch of the law, is to be treated in this fashion, it appears to me that its utility will be almost entirely destroyed, and the very object with which it was enacted will be frustrated. The purpose of such a statute surely was that on any point specifically dealt with by it, the law should be ascertained by interpreting the language used instead of, as before, by roaming over a vast number of authorities in order to discover what the law was, extracting it by a minute critical examination of the prior decisions, dependent upon a knowledge of the exact effect even of an obsolete proceeding such as demurrer to evidence. I am of course far from asserting that resort may never be had to the previous state of the law for the purpose of aiding in the construction of the provisions of the code. If, for example, a provision be of doubtful import, such resort would be perfectly legitimate. Or, again, if in a code of the law of negotiable instruments words be found which have previously acquired a technical meaning, or been used in a sense other than their ordinary one, in relation to such instruments, the same interpretation might well be put upon them in the code. I give these as examples merely; they, of course, do not exhaust the category. What, however, I am venturing to insist upon is, that the first step taken should be to interpret the language of the statute, and that an appeal to earlier decisions can only be justified on some special ground. One further remark I have to make before I proceed to consider the language of the statute. The Bills of Exchange Act was certainly not intended to be merely a code of the existing law. It is not open to question that it was intended to alter, and did alter it in certain respects. And I do not think that it is to be presumed that any particular provision was intended to be a statement of the existing law, rather than a substituted enactment.

21st Report of the Law Commission. The Interpretation of Statutes

H.C. 256, 1969 (Law Com. No. 21)

The rules of statutory interpretation

29. The three so-called rules [of statutory interpretation] do not call for criticism if they are to be regarded simply as convenient headings by reference to which the different approaches of the courts to problems of interpretation may be described. They are less satisfactory, when they, or equivalent propositions in other language, are used to justify the meaning given to a provision. . . .

30. To place undue emphasis on the literal meaning of the words of a provision is to assume an unattainable perfection in draftsmanship; . . . Such an approach ignores the limitations of language, which is not infrequently demonstrated even at the level of the House of Lords when Law Lords differ as to the so-called " plain meaning " of words.[14] Furthermore, the literal approach

---

[14] See *e.g. London and North-Eastern Ry. Co.* v. *Berriman* [1946] A.C. 278.

affords no solution to cases where, for example, a statute prescribes certain consequences which are to attach to a house " unfit for habitation ", and the question before the court is whether a particular house, with the window of one of its two bedrooms with a defective sash cord, is so unfit.[15] This is not a question which could ever be solved by looking at the words alone; in such a case [16] the legislator in effect leaves to the court a limited creative role (even if the court fulfils it in the language of interpretation) within the limits set by the general policy of the statute to be discovered from the context of the statute as a whole and certain other contextual considerations outside the statute.

31. However, although cases may arise from time to time which appear to adopt an excessively literal interpretation of a statutory provision,[17] we would not wish to place undue emphasis upon them.[18] The influence of the literal approach is less directly but perhaps more frequently seen where a court recognises that a provision may have more than one meaning if account is taken of contextual considerations going beyond the ordinarily accepted meaning of the words used; yet the court feels inhibited from examining these considerations where the actual words of the provision are " unambiguous ". We have already referred in this connection to the difficulty created by the decision of the House of Lords in *Ellerman Lines* v. *Murray* [19] and to its apparent inconsistency with the emphasis put by Lord Somervell and Viscount Simonds in *Attorney-General* v. *Prince Ernest of Hanover* [20] on the importance of not assuming that the words of a provision are unambiguous until they have been read in their context. . . .

32. When we turn from the literal rule to the golden rule, we find that this rule sets a purely negative standard by reference to absurdity, inconsistency or inconvenience, but provides no clear means to test the existence of these characteristics or to measure their quality or extent. When a court decides that a particular construction is absurd, it implies, although often tacitly, that the construction is absurd because it is irreconcilable with the general policy of the

---

[15] A problem which faced the House of Lords in *Summers* v. *Salford Corporation* [1943] A.C. 283.

[16] Other examples are provided by the frequent cases in which the courts have had to decide whether an accident arose " out of and in the course of employment."

[17] An extreme example of the application of the literal rule is afforded by the decision in *Whiteley* v. *Chappell* (1868) L.R. 4 Q.B. 147 where personation of " any person entitled to vote " at an election (made an offence by the Poor Law Amendment Act 1851, s. 3) was held not to cover personation of a qualified voter who had died before the election. A modern case with a strong literal flavour is *Bourne* v. *Norwich Crematorium Ltd.* [1967] 1 W.L.R. 691. The literal element in an interpretation does not always involve a preference for the meaning of words in the context of their everyday use. It may arise when a meaning elicited from a particular legal context is adopted and the meaning which the words might bear in a popular context is ignored. Thus in *Fisher* v. *Bell* [1961] 1 Q.B. 394, the Divisional Court, in dealing with a case of flick knives displayed in a shop window, restricted the statutory prohibition (in the Restriction of Offensive Weapons Act 1959, s. 1 (1)) on " offer for sale " of such knives to the technical meaning of " offer for sale " in the law of contract and held that there had been only an " invitation to treat." Lord Parker C.J. cited at p. 400 the statement of Viscount Simonds in *Magor and St. Mellons R.D.C.* v. *Newport Corporation* [1952] A.C. 189, 191 : " It appears to me to be a naked usurpation of the legislative function under the thin disguise of interpretation " [to " fill in the gaps " in legislation]. But this leaves open the question whether the legislature intended the words to be read in the context of contract law. The law was in fact changed by the Restriction of Offensive Weapons Act 1961. *Fisher* v. *Bell* was followed in *Partridge* v. *Crittenden* [1968] 1 W.L.R. 1204, although the relevant statute (Protection of Birds Act 1954, s. 6 (1) and Sched. 4) provided a choice to the prosecutor between selling, offering for sale and having in possession for sale, and he chose to rely on offering for sale.

[18] Cases which appear to adopt a somewhat literal approach to a statutory provision can be balanced by others in which judicial pronouncements emphasise that judges " are not the slaves of words but their masters " (*per* Lord Denning M.R. in *Allen* v. *Thorn Electrical Industries Ltd.* [1968] 1 Q.B. 487).

[19] [1931] A.C. 126.

[20] [1957] A.C. 436.

legislature. Thus in *R.* v. *Oakes* [21] (where the Court read " aids and abets *and* does any act preparatory to the commission of an offence " in s. 7 of the Official Secrets Act 1920 as " aids and abets *or* does any act preparatory to the commission of an offence ") the underlying assumption was that the Act was framed to fit in with the general pattern of the criminal law. Similarly, in *Riddell* v. *Reid* [22] (where the majority of the House of Lords held that the words " outside the area of the building under construction " in the preamble to the Building Regulations 1926 made under s. 79 of the Factory and Workshop Act 1901 could be read in effect as " outside the area used in the building operations ") the finding that a strict construction would be " narrow and unprofitable " (Lord Thankerton),[23] " illogical and inexplicable " (Lord Russell of Killowen) [24] and " paradoxical " and " generally inconvenient and unworkable " (Lord Wright) [25] can only be explained by reference to the purpose of the Building Regulations and their parent Act. In fact the golden rule on closer examination turns out to be a less explicit form of the mischief rule.

33. The mischief rule as expressed in *Heydon's Case* [26] describes in our view a somewhat more satisfactory approach to the interpretation of statutes. But, . . . it reflects a very different constitutional balance between the Executive, Parliament and the public than would now be acceptable. Hence, particularly under its fourth head, in its emphasis on the suppression of the mischief and, in effect, adaptation of the remedy for that purpose, it does not make it clear to what extent the judge should consider the actual language in which the specific remedies contained in the statute are communicated to the public. *Heydon's Case* is also somewhat outdated in its approach, because it assumes that statute is subsidiary or supplemental to the common law, whereas in modern conditions many statutes mark a fresh point of departure rather than a mere addition to, and qualification of, common law principles. Furthermore, the mischief rule was enunciated before the rules excluding certain material, which might bear on the mischief and " true reason of the remedy ", had been developed. If a court has inadequate means of discovering the policy behind a statute, a mere exhortation to consider that policy may not be very effective. . . .

Presumptions

34. . . . Presumptions of intent have been called " policies of clear statement," *i.e.* in effect pronouncements by the courts to the legislature that certain meanings will not be assumed unless stated with special clarity. . . . A court may, for instance, cut down the generality of certain enactments both in order to harmonise them with the existing law and to give effect to prevailing values, *e.g.* in restricting the apparently unfettered generality of provisions which entitle the competent authority to grant planning permission or issue site licences for caravans subject to conditions.[27] Particular presumptions of intention will, however, be modified or even abandoned with the passage of time, and with the modification of the social values which they embody. . . .

35. A judge is not effectively bound by presumptions of intent for the following reasons :

---

[21] [1959] 2 Q.B. 350 (C.C.A.).
[22] 1942 S.C.(H.L.) 51; *sub nom. Potts or Riddell* v. *Reid* [1943] A.C. 1.
[23] 1942 S.C.(H.L.) 51, 58; [1943] A.C. 1, 9.
[24] At pp. 64 and 16 respectively.
[25] At pp. 69 and 22 respectively.
[26] We think it clearer and more accurate to substitute " general legislative purpose " for " mischief " and use the former phrase in our legislative recommendation (para. 81 (*b*) (1)) and in our Draft Clause (Appendix A, Clause 2 (*a*)) dealing with this topic.
[27] See *Hall and Co. Ltd.* v. *Shoreham-by-Sea U.D.C.* [1964] 1 W.L.R. 240; *Mixnam's Properties Ltd.* v. *Chertsey U.D.C.* [1964] 1 Q.B. 214; [1965] A.C. 735.

(a) There is no established order of precedence in the case of conflict between different presumptions.

(b) The individual presumptions are often of doubtful status,[28] or imprecise scope.[29]

(c) A court can give a decision on the meaning of a statute which conflicts with a particular presumption without referring to presumptions of intent at all. The possibility for the court to decide in the first place that the meaning is clear enables it to exclude altogether any operation of a presumption.

(d) There is no accepted test for resolving a conflict between a presumption of intent, such as the presumption that penal statutes should be construed restrictively, and giving effect to the purpose of a statute (the " mischief " of *Heydon's Case*), for example, the purpose of factory legislation to secure safe working conditions.

36. It has been suggested [30] that the difficulties and uncertainties which arise in regard to presumptions of intent might be avoided by the statutory classification of legislation with appropriate presumptions. We do not think that a general classification of this kind would be practicable. Any comprehensive statutory directives would either have to be so generalized as to afford little guidance to the courts, or so detailed that they would lead to intolerable complexity and rigidity of the law. Our consultations confirm this view.

37. In rejecting this approach we nevertheless recognize the force of the arguments, put forward by a number of those whom we have consulted, in favour of laying down statutory presumptions in three difficult areas of interpretation. First, it is notoriously difficult for the courts to decide the precise mental factor required in relation to each prescribed element of a number of statutory offences. The difficulty arises where a statute fails to state whether the criminal liability which it creates is absolute or subject to a requirement of *mens rea* in regard to all or some of its elements. It is true that " in such cases there has for centuries been a presumption that Parliament did not intend to make criminals of persons who were in no way blameworthy in what they did." [31]

---

[28] Thus, the extent to which there is a presumption in favour of the taxpayer in taxation statutes is not entirely clear. Rowlatt J. " whose outstanding knowledge of this subject was coupled with a happy conciseness of phrase " (*per* Viscount Simon L.C. in *Canadian Eagle Oil Co. v. R.* [1946] A.C. 119, 140) in *Cape Brandy Syndicate* v. *Inland Revenue Commissioners* [1921] 1 K.B. 64, 71, said: " In a taxing Act one has to look merely at what is clearly said. There is no room for any intendment. There is no equity about a tax. There is no presumption as to a tax. Nothing is to be read in, nothing is to be implied. One can only look fairly at the language used." Yet in *Inland Revenue Commissioners* v. *Ross and Coulter*, 1948 S.C.(H.L.) 1, 10; [1948] 1 All E.R. 616, 625 Lord Thankerton came near to admitting the continuing existence of a presumption in certain circumstances when he said: " . . . if the provision is capable of two alternative meanings the courts will prefer that meaning more favourable to the subject."

[29] See, for example, *Allen* v. *Thorn Electrical Industries Ltd.* [1968] 1 Q.B. 487, 507, where Winn L.J. said: " I must reject as quite untenable any submission . . . that, if in any case one finds (a) that a statute is worded ambiguously in any particular respect, and (b) finds also clear indications *aliunde* that Parliament intended that they should have the strictest and most stringent meaning possible, the court is therefore compelled to construe the section in the sense in which Parliament would have desired it to take effect, by giving the words their most stringent possible meaning. On the contrary I think the right view is, and as I understand it always has been, that in such a case of ambiguity, it is resolved in such a way as to make the statute less onerous for the general public and so as to cause less interference, than the more stringent sense would, with such rights and liberties as existing contractual obligations." See also Lord Denning M.R. at p. 503 and Danckwerts L.J. at p. 505.

[30] Friedmann, " Statute Law and its Interpretation in the Modern State " (1948) 26 C.B.R. 1277, 1291–1300.

[31] *Per* Lord Reid in *Sweet* v. *Parsley* [1969] 2 W.L.R. 470, 473. It is noteworthy that the Law Lords in that case relied less on this presumption than on the contention that *mens*

This presumption is very strong in regard to offences which, although statutory in form, have their origins in the common law, but it appears to be much weaker in regard to relatively modern statutory offences providing criminal sanctions within the framework of legislation with a broad social purpose, such as the protection of factory workers or the furtherance of road safety. One way of removing the uncertainty might be to provide a statutory presumption, requiring the courts to import *mens rea* in regard to the prescribed elements of any statutory offence in the absence of express words to the contrary. . . .

38. The second area in which a statutory presumption might be helpful concerns the determination of civil liability arising from breach of statutory duty. The courts have endeavoured to isolate the factors by reference to which they decide whether civil liability arises, but it is difficult to ascertain from the cases what measure of authority they enjoy and what is the respective weight to be attached to them.[32] In some recent statutes Parliament has expressly excluded a civil action and occasionally it has expressly provided that an obligation imposed by statute is intended to ground a civil action,[33] but in spite of Lord du Parcq's invitation in *Cutler* v. *Wandsworth Stadium Ltd.*[34] neither of these courses has been generally followed. . . . [W]e recommend that the presumption should take the . . . form . . . that the breach of an obligation is intended to be action-

---

rea was in fact required by the words of the Act—*i.e.* that s. 5 (*b*) of the Dangerous Drugs Act 1965 in referring to a person who " is concerned in the management of any premises used for [the purpose of smoking cannabis or cannabis resin] " meant that the manager must be not only managing the premises as such but conducting them for cannabis smoking.

[32] For example, A. L. Smith L.J. said in *Groves* v. *Lord Wimborne* [1898] 2 Q.B. 402 (C.A.) at p. 407 that a civil remedy is to be implied " unless it appears from the whole purview of the Act . . . that it was the intention of the Legislature that the only remedy for breach of the statutory duty should be by proceeding for the fine." Again, it was suggested by Atkin L.J. in *Phillips* v. *Britannia Hygienic Laundry Co. Ltd.* [1923] 2 K.B. 832 at p. 842 that a civil remedy is not to be implied from the statute if there is an adequate remedy at common law; but this seems difficult to reconcile with the many decisions according civil remedies for breach of statutory duties under factory legislation. Another approach, which might explain the decisions under factory or allied legislation, seeks to determine whether the Act was passed for the benefit of a defined class of persons, in which event the implication would be that a civil remedy was intended, or only for the public at large who would have no civil remedy—see *e.g.* Birkett L.J. in *Solomons* v. *R. Gertzenstein Ltd.* [1954] 2 Q.B. 243 at p. 261, although in *Phillips'* case above Atkin L.J. (at p. 841) had already rejected this test. In *Cutler* v. *Wandsworth Stadium Ltd.* [1949] A.C. 398 an obligation on occupiers of dog tracks to admit bookmakers was held not to give a right of action to a bookmaker who was refused admission on the ground that the Act was passed to give the public a choice between betting with bookmakers and on the totalisator, and not for the benefit of bookmakers. But, as Professor Glanville Williams points out in a survey of this branch of the law (1960) 23 M.L.R. 233, 244 *et seq.*, it is difficult to find the evidence on which the House of Lords concluded that the Act was not intended to benefit bookmakers, and he therefore concludes that the case illustrates a rule that a criminal penalty does not imply a civil right of action unless there is an indication in the statute that it was so intended. If this is true, it is clearly inconsistent with the principle stated by A. L. Smith L.J. in *Groves* v. *Lord Wimborne* (see above) and not obviously true of industrial legislation where a civil remedy is readily implied.

[33] For example, express exclusion in Representation of the People Act 1949, ss. 50 (2) and 51 (2), Radioactive Substances Act 1960, s. 19 (5) (*a*), Water Resources Act 1963, s. 135 (8) (*a*), Medicines Act 1968, s. 133 (2); express provision in Consumer Protection Act 1961, s. 3 (1), Resale Prices Act 1964, s. 4 (2), Restrictive Trade Practices Act 1968, s. 7 (2).

[34] See n. 32 above at p. 410: " To a person unversed in the science or art of legislation it may well seem strange that Parliament has not by now made it a rule to state explicitly what its intention is in a matter which is often of no little importance, instead of leaving it to the courts to discover, by a careful examination and analysis of what is expressly said, what that intention may be supposed probably to be . . . I trust, however, that it will not be thought impertinent, in any sense of that word, to suggest respectfully that those who are responsible for framing legislation might consider whether the traditional practice, which obscures, if it does not conceal, the intention which Parliament has, or must be presumed to have, might not safely be abandoned."

able at the suit of any person who by reason of that breach suffers or apprehends damage, unless a contrary intention is expressly stated.

39. The third area in which we have considered the desirability of a statutory presumption relates to legislation dealing with matters which are subject to international obligations of the United Kingdom (in particular treaties to which the United Kingdom is a party). . . .[35]

The context, outside of the statute

46. It is self-evident that in order to understand a statute a court has to take into account many matters which are not to be found within the statute itself. Legislation is not made in a vacuum, and a judge in interpreting it is able to take judicial notice of much information relating to legal,[36] social, economic and other aspects of the society in which the statute is to operate. . . .

49. The admission of certain material . . . to ascertain the mischief at which the statute aimed—has been allowed by the courts. In *Eastman Photographic Materials Co. Ltd.* v. *Comptroller-General of Patents, Designs and Trade Marks* [37] Lord Halsbury admitted a report of a Commission as a " source of information as to what was the evil or defect which the Act of Parliament now under construction was intended to remedy." [38] And in more general terms in *Govindan Sellappah Nayar Kodakan Pillai* v. *Punchi Banda Mundanayake* [39] the Judicial Committee of the Privy Council held that " judicial notice ought to be taken of such matters as the reports of Parliamentary Commissions and of such other facts as must be assumed to have been within the contemplation of the legislature when the Acts in question were passed." [40] Although it is conceivable that the inference drawn from a committee report as to the mischief which Parliament had in mind in regard to a statute might require modification in the light of statements subsequently made in Parliament, it is doubtful whether the courts can refer to parliamentary statements even to ascertain the mischief at which a Bill under debate is aimed. It is true that in *South Eastern Railway Co.* v. *The Railway Commissioners* [41] Cockburn C.J. spoke of matters which could be " safely asserted " not to " enter into the measure as contemplated nor [to be] present in the mind of the legislature in the Act," [42] having regard to a speech

---

[35] [Author's note] The Commission considered this matter later in their report and concluded that the " *prima facie* presumption that Parliament does not intend to act in breach of international law, including . . . specific treaty obligations," per Diplock L.J. in *Salomon* v. *Commissioners of Customs and Excise* (above, p. 217) should be embodied in a statutory form.

[36] Thus earlier statutes on the same subject-matter as a statute being interpreted and case law in which there is judicial interpretation of the word or words in question may under clearly established present practice form part of the context to be taken into account by the court. Whether such material has the necessary relevance to entitle it to be regarded as part of the context is a question which in our view should be decided by the court according to the circumstances, unfettered by any rigid presumptions as to the intent of Parliament.

[37] [1898] A.C. 571.

[38] At p. 575.

[39] [1953] A.C. 514.

[40] At p. 528. The judgment does not make it entirely clear whether the matters referred to could be taken into account in ascertaining only the mischief or could also be used to elucidate the remedy.

[41] (1880) 5 Q.B.D. 217.

[42] At pp. 236–237. See also the earlier remarks of Lord Westbury L.C. in *Re Mew & Thorne* (1862) 31 L.J.Bcy. 87, 89 which seem to sanction reference to parliamentary debates at least where " it may somewhat assist in interpreting [the words of a section] and in ascertaining the object to which they were directed." The issue was whether the enactment excluded a discretion as to the discharge of bankrupts; the defect revealed by the materials looked at was the evils attendant upon the existence of a discretion under the pre-existing law. In *Municipal Council of Sydney* v. *Commonwealth* (1904) 1 C.L.R.

of the Lord Chancellor in the House of Lords and of the introducer of the Bill in the Commons. But his views were disapproved of by Lord Selborne L.C. on appeal.[43]

50. Material . . . to ascertain the particular remedy which the statute provides to deal with the mischief—would appear to be excluded by the courts. In *Assam Railways and Trading Company Ltd.* v. *Commissioners of Inland Revenue* the question was raised of the admissibility before the House of Lords of certain recommendations of a Royal Commission on Income Tax which had preceded an Act and which counsel for the appellants sought to cite as part of the context of intention of Parliament in relation to a particular section of the Act. Lord Wright said:

> " It is clear that the language of a Minister of the Crown in proposing in Parliament a measure which eventually becomes law is inadmissible and the Report of Commissioners is even more removed from value as evidence of intention, because it does not follow that their recommendations were accepted." [44]

51. It should however be added that some judicial observations since the *Assam* case appear to show a somewhat less strict attitude towards the recommendations of a committee which have been followed by legislation. Thus in *Letang* v. *Cooper* [45] Lord Denning M.R., having said that it was legitimate to look at the report of a committee to see the mischief at which a statute was directed, went on to say:

> " But you cannot look at what the committee recommended, or at least, if you do look at it, you should not be unduly influenced by it. It does not help you much, for the simple reason that Parliament may, and often does, decide to do something different to cure the mischief. You must interpret the words of Parliament as they stand, without too much regard to the recommendations of the committee: " [46]

And in *Cozens* v. *North Devon Hospital Management Committee* and *Hunter* v. *Turners (Soham) Ltd.*[47] Thompson J., while stating that counsel had correctly maintained that a Report of the Committee on Limitation of Actions in Cases of Personal Injury [48] could not be looked at to interpret the Limitation Act 1963, apparently permitted counsel to refer to the report for the negative purpose of showing that there was nothing in the recommendations inconsistent with a particular construction of certain provisions of the Act.[49] But in any event it seems that reference may not be made to parliamentary debates to ascertain the scope or nature of a particular remedy provided by a statute.[50]

208, 213–214 Griffiths C.J. of the High Court of Australia said that parliamentary debates might be referred to " for the purpose of seeing what was the subject of discussion, what was the evil to be remedied and so forth." See P. Brazil, " Legislative History and the Sure and True Interpretation of Statutes in general and the Constitution in particular " (1961) 4 Univ. of Queensland L.J. 1–22.

43   (1881) 50 L.J.Q.B. 201, 203.
44   *Ibid.* p. 458.
45   [1965] 1 Q.B. 232 (C.A.).
46   At p. 240.
47   [1966] 2 Q.B. 318.
48   1962 Cmnd. 1829.
49   See n. 47 at p. 321.
50   It is not uncharacteristic of this rather obscure branch of the law that not even this statement can be left entirely unqualified. Thus in *Beswick* v. *Beswick* [1968] A.C. 58, 105 Lord Upjohn, in construing s. 56 of the Law of Property Act 1925, referred to the report of the Joint Committee on Consolidation Bills which dealt with that Act although, as he pointed out, only for the purpose of ascertaining that the presumption against change in a purporting consolidation measure was not weakened by anything that had taken place in the proceedings.

52. We have considered whether the position summarized in paragraphs 49–51 is satisfactory. In principle it would seem right for the courts to be able to consider any material which " must be assumed to be in the contemplation of the legislature " [51] when the statute in question was passed. The cases in which the point has arisen have for the most part been concerned with the reports of Royal Commissions and official committees, but other documents which have been presented to the legislature by the executive may equally be in its contemplation when considering a statute and form part of the background against which it is passed.[52] This does not of course imply that the meaning which the context provided by this material suggests will be decisive, but only that it is a meaning to be considered by the court. In principle, also, we think that such material should be open to consideration by a court, in ascertaining not only the mischief at which a provision is aimed, but also the nature and scope of the remedy provided. It is, of course, true that the specific recommendations of, for example, an official committee preceding the introduction of legislation may not have been accepted in whole or in part in the first place by the sponsors of the legislation or subsequently by Parliament. If the resulting Act makes clear which recommendations have been accepted and which rejected no problem arises. A practical difficulty may, however, occur where the meaning of a provision in an Act varies according to whether it is, or is not, read in the context of a recommendation of an earlier committee which was before, but not necessarily accepted by, Parliament. But it is also true, although less likely, that Parliament may not have accepted in its entirety a committee's assessment of the mischief to be dealt with by legislation; yet as explained in paragraph 49, the report of a committee could under existing law be considered in ascertaining the mischief. We think that any rigid distinction between the admissibility of material in ascertaining the mischief and in ascertaining the remedy provided is unjustified. It should be borne in mind that a court would not be bound to imply from the presence of a recommended remedy in, for example, a committee report that Parliament accepted the remedy. Furthermore, if a court were entitled to look not only at a committee report but also at a White Paper,[53] published after the appearance of the committee report but before or in connection with the Bill to which it related, the White Paper might inform the court as to the extent to which the recommendations had at that stage been accepted by the Government. The court of course would still have to determine whether any recommendations so accepted were in fact embodied in the resulting Act. This latter consideration, however, raises the question of the admissibility for purposes of statutory interpretation of material relating to the Parliamentary history of an enactment which we consider in paragraphs 53–62 below. Another source of guidance as to the extent to which a committee report had been accepted might in certain cases be provided by an explanatory document, authorised as an aid to interpretation by the Bill and by the subsequent Act to which it relates and subject to such procedure of adjustment (if any) to take

[51] See *Govindan Sellappah Nayar Kodakan Pillai* v. *Punchi Banda Mundanayake* cited in para. 49 above.

[52] In *Katikiro of Buganda* v. *Attorney-General* [1961] 1 W.L.R. 119 the Judicial Committee of the Privy Council held that the contents of a White Paper could not be used to interpret an agreement (having the force of law and to be construed by the rules applicable to the interpretation of statutes). However, it should be noted that the Judicial Committee (at p. 128) said that there was no ambiguity in the relevant part of the agreement " which would justify the admission of extraneous evidence," and added that in any event the contents of the White Paper would have fallen short of establishing the contention which it was said to support (which, it may be noted, suggests that they had in fact looked at it).

[53] Under the present law it is doubtful whether a White Paper would be admissible to elucidate the scope of remedies provided by subsequent legislation—see *Katikiro of Buganda* v. *Attorney-General* (n. 52 above).

account of amendments to the Bill in the course of its passage as Parliament might require. This possibility is dealt with in paragraphs 63–73 below.

The Parliamentary history of an act

53. In considering the admissibility of Parliamentary proceedings, it is necessary to consider how far the material admitted might be *relevant* to the interpretative task of the courts, how far it would afford them *reliable* guidance, and how far it would be sufficiently *available* to those to whom the statute is addressed.

54. If the intention of Parliament is not to be treated as a mere figure of speech, it can hardly be denied in principle that proceedings in Parliament may be *relevant* to ascertain that intention. It is, however, a matter of controversy [54] whether there is a legislative intent capable of discovery apart from the language of the statute. In *Salomon* v. *Salomon & Co. Ltd.*[55] Lord Watson said:

> " ' Intention of the Legislature ' is a common but very slippery phrase, which, popularly understood, may signify anything from intention embodied in positive enactment to speculative opinion as to what the Legislature probably would have meant, although there has been an omission to enact it. In a Court of Law or Equity, what the Legislature intended to be done or not to be done can only be legitimately ascertained from that which it has chosen to enact, either in express words or by reasonable and necessary implication." [56]

And in *Magor and St. Mellons R.D.C.* v. *Newport Corporation* [57] in which Denning L.J. had said in the Court of Appeal:

> " We sit here to find out the intention of Parliament and of Ministers [among other matters the case concerned the interpretation of an Order made by the Minister of Health] and carry it out, and we do this better by filling in the gaps and making sense of the enactment than by opening it up to destructive analysis." [58]

Lord Simonds in the House of Lords made the reply:

> " . . . the general proposition that it is the duty of the court to find out the intention of Parliament—and not only of Parliament but of Ministers also —cannot by any means be supported." [59]

55. The apparent difficulties which arise in the analysis of the concept of the legislative intent may perhaps be clarified if a distinction is drawn between a *particular* legislative intent in the sense of the meaning in which the legislature intended particular words to be understood, and a *general* legislative intent in the sense of the purpose which the legislature intended to achieve.[60] Thus it is possible to agree with Lord Simonds that there are many occasions when it would be unrewarding to seek for the legislative intent in the sense of the intended meaning of particular words, when, for example, Parliament has laid down certain consequences which are to follow an " accident arising out of

---

[54] See in particular Alf Ross, *On Law and Justice*, p. 143; Radin, " Statutory Interpretation " (1930) 43 Harvard L.R. 863; Landis, " A Note on ' Statutory Interpretation ' " (1930) 43 Harvard L.R. 886; Payne, " The Intention of the Legislature in the Interpretation of Statutes," *Current Legal Problems*, 1956, p. 96.

[55] [1897] A.C. 22.

[56] At p. 38.

[57] [1952] A.C. 189.

[58] [1950] 2 All E.R. 1226, 1236.

[59] See n. 57 above, at p. 191.

[60] See Gerald C. MacCallum Jr., " Legislative Intent " (1966) 75 Yale L.J. 754.

and in the course of the employment " [61] while leaving the courts to decide what lies within the course of employment; but it is also possible to accept Denning L.J.'s view that it is the duty of the courts in such a case " to find out the intention of Parliament . . . and carry it out by filling in the gaps and making sense of the enactment ", if the intention of Parliament is here understood to mean the purpose of Parliament in referring to accidents arising out of and in the course of employment in the Workmen's Compensation Act 1897. As regards the reality of legislative intent in the sense of the purpose of the legislature in respect of a statute we see force in the statement that:

> " If [legislative intent] is looked upon as a common agreement on the purposes of an enactment and a general understanding of the kind of situation at which it is aimed, to deny the existence of a legislative intention is to deny the existence of a legislative function." [62]

We do not think therefore that a rule excluding Parliamentary proceedings can be supported solely on the grounds that they can never have any *relevance* to the statute which emerges from them; but the *reliability* and *availability* of Parliamentary material when used for this purpose are more questionable.

56. The *reliability* of Parliamentary history has had many severe critics. It has been said that the purpose of debating a Bill is to secure consent to its terms and to explain the intent and meaning of its precise language only to the extent that the explanation will further the object of getting consent to its passage; that the process of enacting legislation is not " an intellectual exercise in the pursuit of truth but an essay in persuasion or perhaps almost seduction ", and that, in these circumstances, " to appeal from the carefully pondered terms of the statute to the hurly-burly of Parliamentary debate is to appeal from Philip sober to Philip drunk. . . ." [63] Apart from these general dangers, there is the particular danger that if Parliamentary history can be appealed to as evidence of intention, such evidence can be deliberately manufactured during the legislative process by those with an axe to grind. . . .[64]

59. In our system the *reliability* of legislative material for use in the process of interpreting statutes has been called in question by many whom we have consulted. Amongst other considerations there is the fact, . . . that our existing legislative procedures are not especially well adapted for the use of Parliamentary material as an aid to interpretation; in particular, we do not have committee reports of the kind which, as an authoritative summary of the purpose and scope of a legislative proposal, are available to the courts in countries which make use of legislative history. It will be seen that this emphasis on the practical objections [65] to the use of legislative history is no less important in regard to its availability.

---

[61] s. 1 (1) of the Workmen's Compensation Act 1897. Similarly it cannot be said that Parliament had a particular legislative intent in regard to whether a particular number of missing window cords constitute " unfitness for habitation "—see para. 30 above.

[62] " A Re-evaluation of the Use of Legislative History in the Federal Courts " (1952) 51 Col.L.R. 125, 126.

[63] See J. A. Corry, " The Use of Legislative History in the Interpretation of Statutes " (1954) 32 Can. Bar Rev. 624, 621–622.

[64] Charles P. Curtis, " A Better Theory of Legal Interpretation " (1949) 4th *Record of the Association of the Bar of the City of New York*, 328.

[65] In *Beswick* v. *Beswick* (see n. 50 above) Lord Reid (at p. 74) said that " For purely practical reasons we do not permit debates in either House to be cited." However, in *R.* v. *Warner* [1968] 2 W.L.R. 1303 Lord Reid (at p. 1316) suggested that " this case seems to show there is room for an exception where examining the proceedings in Parliament would almost certainly settle the matter immediately one way or the other." In the light of this comment it is interesting to note the legislative history (see the letter by Mr. Graham J. Zellick in (1968) 118 N.L.J. 455) of s. 5 (*b*) of the Dangerous Drugs Act 1965 under

60. In speaking of the criterion of *availability* in regard to the admissibility of legislative material for interpretative purposes. . . . A statute may ultimately have to be interpreted by the courts but it is directed to a wider audience. The citizen, or the practitioner whom he consults, may have a heavy burden placed upon him if the context in which a statute is to be understood requires reference to materials which are not readily available without unreasonable inconvenience or expense. . . . [M]any legal practitioners, notably solicitors in places where library facilities are not conveniently available, may find it difficult to refer to the volumes of Hansard, and in particular to those volumes, not to be found in many libraries, which contain the reports of Parliamentary Standing Committees. We do not wish however to exaggerate this difficulty, as, if the legislative history of statutes was admissible, it is probable that the burden on the lawyer and other users of statutes would be lightened by the inclusion in text-books of significant extracts from the legislative history of the statutes with which they deal.[66]

61. . . . [W]e have reached the conclusion that at present reports of Parliamentary proceedings should not be used by the courts for the interpretation of statutes. . . . In supporting the existing law on this subject we are much influenced by three considerations: (*a*) the difficulty arising from the nature of our Parliamentary process of isolating information which will assist the courts in interpreting statutes; (*b*) the consequent difficulty of providing such information as could be given in a reasonably convenient and readily accessible form; and (*c*) the possibility that in some cases the function of legislative material in the interpretative process could be better performed by specially prepared explanatory material available to Parliament when a Bill is introduced and modified, if necessary, to take account of amendments during its passage through Parliament.

Specially prepared material explaining legislation

63. In this section we deal with the possibility of providing for interpretative purposes specially prepared material which might be used in ascertaining the

which the Court of Appeal in *Sweet* v. *Parsley* [1968] 2 W.L.R. 1360 held the defendant guilty of being " concerned in the management of premises " in which unknown to her the smoking of cannabis took place. S. 5 (*b*) was a reproduction in the consolidation measure of 1965 of an identical provision (s. 9 (1) (*b*) of the Dangerous Drugs Act 1964). The latter was a private member's Bill and in moving the second reading in the House of Lords on April 7, 1964, Lord Amulree said: " Clause 9 strengthens the powers of the police in dealing with cannabis. But it involves the provision that a person cannot be prosecuted unless he knowingly permits his premises to be used for the manufacture or smoking of cannabis " (257 H.L.Deb., col. 12). Another striking example of the disadvantage of our rule excluding judicial reference to parliamentary history is described by Mr. Stephen Cretney in (1968) 112 S.J. 593–594. He points out that in *R.* v. *Wilson, ex p. Pereira* [1953] 1 Q.B. 59 (which involved the interpretation of s. 27 (2) of the Maintenance Orders Act 1950) the Divisional Court followed its decision in *O'Dea* v. *Tetau* [1951] 1 K.B. 184; Lord Goddard C.J. referring (at p. 61) to the earlier decision, said that between July 24, 1950, when *O'Dea* v. *Tetau* was decided, and October 26, 1950, when the Maintenance Orders Act 1950 was passed, there would have been time, had the legislature desired, to reverse that decision and perhaps to deal with it in that Act. But in fact the Government did deal with it. They introduced an amendment of the Maintenance Orders Bill in the House of Lords for the declared purpose of reversing the rule applied in *O'Dea* v. *Tetau*; see the statement of the Lord Chancellor (168 H.L.Deb., cols. 1151–1152) introducing an amendment which was accepted in both Houses and became part of s. 27 (2).

[66] Examples of textbooks, making use of parliamentary material, are those by Magnus & Estrin on the Companies Acts 1947 and 1967. An interesting recent French example is a series of commentaries on the legislation of 1966–67 reforming the law relating to commercial companies. (Hamiaut, *La Réforme des Sociétés Commerciales*, Dalloz, 1966, dealing with the law of July 24, 1966, and Hémard, Terre & Mabilat, *La Réforme des Sociétés Commerciales*, dealing with the decree of March 23, 1967, Dalloz, 1967.)

context in which statutory provisions are to be read.[67] The basic rationale of such a proposal is that an explanatory statement available with a Bill on its introduction (and, if possible, amended to take account of changes in the Bill in the course of its passage) could be a useful aid in determining the meaning of its provisions. It would enable the interpreter of an Act to take into account considerations which were before the legislature when the relevant Bill was under discussion.

It would not give rise to the same problems of availability for interpretative purposes to which we have referred in connection with the use of Parliamentary history, as it could without undue difficulty be made available to the users of statutes. . . .

65. [T]he explanatory statement here under consideration must be distinguished from three types of material which may be produced in connection with a Bill. First, there is the preamble, which, when included in a Bill, is amendable by Parliament in consequence of changes made in the substantive provisions of the Bill and forms an integral part of the resulting Act. . . .[68]

66. Secondly, there is the Explanatory and (where appropriate) Financial Memorandum attached to a Bill on its introduction in each House. These Memoranda are prepared primarily for the information of members of the two Houses and give a highly summarized account of the subject matter of Bills. They are not part of the Bill, and are removed on the first occasion when the Bill is reprinted in either House. . . .

67. Thirdly, there are the Notes on Clauses. The latter are prepared by Government Departments for the use of Ministers or others who have the task of piloting legislation through the various Parliamentary stages; the text is amended as necessary for each House. They provide a general background to the legislation and explain the purpose and effect of each clause, often including practical examples of its application. They contain a proportion of confidential material and are not published outside the Government organization. . . .

68. The explanatory statement which we have in mind would owe something to each of the three devices described in the preceding paragraphs, but it would be more flexible and of wider scope than the preamble or present Explanatory Memorandum, and, unlike Notes on Clauses, would be accessible to users of statutes and admissible before the courts. It would be prepared by the promoters of the Bill (in the case of government legislation by the appropriate department in consultation with the draftsman) and the Bill to which it related would specifically authorise its use as an aid to interpretation. The explanatory statement would thus clearly form part of the contextual background against which the Bill was introduced into Parliament, and, . . . it would seem reasonable that the court should be entitled, in its construction of the Act, at least to consider it. But it would be even more useful if it could be amended, as Notes on Clauses

---

[67] The proposal is not of course new. See pp. 136–137 (Annexe V) of the 1932 Report of the Committee on Ministers' Powers (Cmd. 4060), where Professor Harold J. Laski suggested that a memorandum of explanation might set forth the purposes of a Bill, that authority could be conferred on the courts to utilise the memorandum as an aid in the work of interpretation, a judge not being bound thereby but having it available as " an invaluable guide . . . in his task of discovering what a statute is really intended to mean." See also the amendment to Clause 33 of the Theft Bill 1968 moved (but after debate withdrawn) by Lord Wilberforce (290 H.L.Deb., cols. 897–913). Para. (c) of the amendment was in the following terms : " Reference may be made, for the interpretation of this Act, to the Notes on Draft Theft Bill contained in Annex 2 of Command 2977 [i.e. the 8th Report of the Criminal Law Revision Committee] but this commentary shall be for guidance only and shall have no binding force." An example of the type of material which we have in mind is provided by the Explanatory Notes accompanying the Draft Landlord and Tenant Bill, which forms Appendix I of the Law Commission's Report on the Landlord and Tenant Act 1954, Part II (Law Com. 17).

[68] For a modern example of a preamble to a section, see s. 8 of the Civil Aviation Act 1949.

are in practice amended, at successive stages of the Bill's passage in the light of amendments made at the Committee and Report Stages. It would be more valuable still if the amended statement could be given some form of Parliamentary approval. . . .

70. . . . [T]he views of those whom we consulted through our Joint Working Paper on the proposal for an explanatory statement were divided. . . . [T]hose who expressed . . . a measure of doubt were chiefly concerned with two possible difficulties. First, it was feared that any device for conveying the intention of Parliament by means of two documents instead of one would be as likely to create difficulties as to resolve them and might sometimes present the courts with an irreconcilable conflict of meaning. But . . . the explanatory statement . . . would be no more binding on the courts than much other contextual material (e.g., other provisions of the statute, earlier legislation dealing with the same subject matter and non-statutory material dealing with the mischief) of which under the existing law the courts are entitled to take account. It might however give assistance to the courts in making more explicit the contextual assumptions which at present have to be gleaned sometimes with great difficulty from a number of sources of varying reliability. No interpretative device can relieve the courts of their ultimate responsibility for considering the different contexts in which the words of a provision might be read, and in making a choice between the different meanings which emerge from that consideration. The existence of an explanatory statement would not prevent a court from regarding the meaning of the words in an enacting provision in the light of other relevant contexts as so compelling that it must be preferred to a meaning suggested by the statement.

71. The second difficulty . . . related to the time and labour which would be involved if such a statement had to be prepared for all legislation. We recognised the force of this practical objection, particularly with certain classes of major legislation, although we are inclined to think that it may be somewhat over-emphasised: first, because the practical difficulties might prove, with experience, to be less serious than they appear at first sight; secondly, because a good deal of the material which has in any event to be prepared for Notes on Clauses would be available for inclusion in, or as a basis for, the explanatory statement. However, we reached the conclusion that we should at this stage only recommend the use of an explanatory statement as a selective device, which could be adopted in relation to Bills considered by their sponsors to be appropriate for this purpose. We had particularly in mind Bills giving effect to our own reports or to those of comparable bodies such as the Law Reform Committee and the Criminal Law Revision Committee. In such a case the burden of preparing an explanatory statement would be considerably lightened by the existence of the relevant report; indeed sometimes the form of the report might make it possible to authorise in the Bill direct reference to it for purposes of interpretation, or at least to reproduce in the explanatory statement its relevant passages with any qualifications made necessary by a departure in the Bill in question from the basic rationale or specific recommendations of the committee.

73. An explanatory statement would have a valuable function in connection with the various codification projects which feature prominently in the Programmes of the Law Commission and of the Scottish Law Commission [69] and

---

[69] The Scottish Law Commission has published as Memorandum No. 8 Part I of a Draft Evidence Code for comment and criticism. The draft takes the form of Articles and Commentary. In the introduction to the Code it is explained that, although the Commentary attached to the final version of the Code will differ considerably from that presented with the Draft, it is hoped that Parliament will accept the Commentary as a legitimate extrinsic aid to the construction of the Articles. A similar technique has been adopted by the Law Commissions in their work on the Codification of the Law of Contract

which are likely to form a vital part of the work of both Commissions in the future. The object of a code is, in our understanding, to set out the essential principles which are to govern a given branch of the law. The degree of particularity in which the applications of these principles to specific situations are stated in the code may vary, but, even where detailed application is lacking, a court is expected to discover in the code the principles from which the answer to a particular problem can be worked out. In such a situation we think that an explanatory and illustrative commentary on the code could provide authoritative, but not compelling guidance on the interpretation of the code, which would be particularly valuable in the early years of the operation of the code.

Appendix A

Draft Clauses

1.—(1) In ascertaining the meaning of any provision of an Act, the matters which may be considered shall, in addition to those which may be considered for that purpose apart from this section, include the following, that is to say—

(a) all indications provided by the Act as printed by authority, including punctuation and side-notes, and the short title of the Act;

(b) any relevant report of a Royal Commission, Committee or other body which had been presented or made to or laid before Parliament or either House before the time when the Act was passed;

(c) any relevant treaty or other international agreement which is referred to in the Act or of which copies had been presented to Parliament by command of Her Majesty before that time, whether or not the United Kingdom were bound by it at that time;

(d) any other document bearing upon the subject-matter of the legislation which had been presented to Parliament by command of Her Majesty before that time;

(e) any document (whether falling within the foregoing paragraphs or not) which is declared by the Act to be a relevant document for the purposes of this section.

(2) The weight to be given for the purposes of this section to any such matter as is mentioned in subsection (1) shall be no more than is appropriate in the circumstances.

(3) Nothing in this section shall be construed as authorising the consideration of reports of proceedings in Parliament for any purpose for which they could not be considered apart from this section.

2. The following shall be included among the principles to be applied in the interpretation of Acts, namely—

(a) that a construction which would promote the general legislative purpose underlying the provision in question is to be preferred to a construction which would not; and

under Item I and the heading " Obligations " of their respective First Programmes; see also the propositions and commentary in the Working Party's Provisional Proposals relating to Termination of Tenancies (Published Working Paper No. 16 of the Law Commission) and in its Provisional Proposals relating to the Obligations of Landlords and Tenants (Parts II–IV of Published Working Paper No. 8 of the Law Commission), both sets of proposals falling under Item VIII of the Law Commission's First Programme (Codification of the Law of Landlord and Tenant).

(*b*) that a construction which is consistent with the international obligations of Her Majesty's Government in the United Kingdom is to be preferred to a construction which is not.

3. Sections 1 and 2 above shall apply with the necessary modifications in relation to Orders in Council (whether made by virtue of any Act or by virtue of Her Majesty's prerogative) and to orders, rules, regulations and other legislative instruments made by virtue of any Act (whether passed before or after this Act), as they apply in relation to Acts.

4. Where any Act passed after this Act imposes or authorises the imposition of a duty, whether positive or negative and whether with or without a special remedy for its enforcement, it shall be presumed, unless express provision to the contrary is made, that a breach of the duty is intended to be actionable (subject to the defences and other incidents applying to actions for breach of statutory duty) at the suit of any person who sustains damage in consequence of the breach.

PRECEDENT AND JUDGE MADE LAW

Statutes are the most authoritative source of English law, but, although they form an increasing part of the law, it is the rules developed by the judges, and the techniques for discovering, developing and using them as a basis of argument and justification, that make up the most characteristic feature of the English lawyers' legal technique. Even a statute once interpreted in a case falls under the general technique to this extent, that in future it will be the case that will be looked back to as an authority and not simply the words of the statute themselves.

English judgments are discursive. The judge in deciding a case is not simply expected to give a decision on the merits of the particular case as he sees them. He is expected to give his decision in terms of legal rules, either legal rules already in existence or rules which he formulates for the purpose, and he is expected to derive these rules from a limited number of sources using traditional techniques. This obligation is imposed on him partly as a method of securing consistency between judges, partly to secure objectivity in judgment, partly to keep the law rational, ironing out illogicalities and anomalies, clearing up doubtful points, and partly to keep the law supplied with up-to-date principles which can be used as raw materials for future development. It also has something to do with the way in which the law itself operates. Although one tends to think of legal rules in terms of litigation and the courts, it would be a poor system that depended on a recourse to the courts every time there was a question of what the law was on a particular point. The citizen is entitled to know, or at the least be able to find out by consulting a lawyer, what it is he has to do if he wants to leave his property by will, enter into a binding contract for the supply of goods or services, set up a limited liability company, avoid being ordered to pay compensation to anyone who might suffer damage from what he says or does, or avoid being prosecuted for breach of the criminal law. One of the qualities of a good legal system is that for the most part this is possible. So strong is the requirement in the criminal law that the goal has been stated in the form of a maxim *nulla poena sine lege* which in at least one of its meanings implies that punishment should only be inflicted for a breach of the criminal law which has been clearly formulated beforehand. This is one of the reasons why there has been so much criticism of vague offences such as conspiracy to effect a public mischief (*R. v. Manley*[70]) and conspiracy to corrupt public morals (*Shaw v. D.P.P.*[71] cf. *R. v. Bhagwan*[72]).

One of the major purposes of legal rules is to give notice of what has to be done if certain results are to be achieved and certain unpleasantnesses avoided. Of necessity this cannot be done by prescribing a particular rule for every conceivable factual contingency. Legal rules are general rules. They deal with classes and categories of situation. As Professor Robson notes (p. 242 below) one incidental effect of this way of proceeding is to make everything much more manageable. The use of general rules as part of the actual decision-making process is one of the most distinctive characteristics of a legal system. It is what distinguishes the judgment of a judge from what sometimes goes under the name of " palm-tree justice," or any form of justice where the decision is accepted simply because of the prestige or status, or imputed divine or magical powers of the decision-maker, and it deeply affects the whole process of legal argument and legal reasoning. When counsel is arguing in favour of a particular decision, or a judge is justifying a particular decision, he must do so in terms of rules. He must be able to generalise his argument and show that the rule he is suggesting for the solution of this particular case will also be suitable for other similar cases. This is why one of the standard methods of argument and counter-argument is by means of hypothetical factual examples, in which the advocate or judge shows how the proposed rule would apply in other circumstances. It is also one reason why an argument may be rejected, if the rule suggested is too wide, either because it covers situations where it is felt a different decision would be more appropriate, or where it has always been established that a different decision is the correct one, or simply because it is open-ended and as a result its exact scope is not clear. E. Levi in his book *Introduction to Legal Reasoning* suggests, for example, that one of the reasons why the courts were attached for so long to the notion that in general there was only liability for negligent conduct in relation to " dangerous instruments " and not in relation to articles which were in themselves harmless was that the very phrase " dangerous instruments " not only graphically described the cases where there was liability but also suggested limits to liability that were reasonably clear and justifiable. Compare the reluctance of, for example, Asquith L.J. in the case of *Candler v. Crane, Christmas & Co.* (below, p. 249) to accept a general liability for negligent misstatements.

Besides this reliance on general rules, another peculiar feature of legal reasoning is that the law has developed for its own purposes its own principles of relevance. Here again as we have seen the rules play their part. In their use of classification and categories they are already setting limits to what is relevant. In addition there are quite general principles of relevance which apply almost uniformly throughout the system. Some of these are bound up with notions of fairness and equality. They simply say that some distinctions between people and cases simply do not justify different treatment. It is this principle which really lies at the heart of many of the

---

[70] [1933] 1 K.B. 529.
[71] [1962] A.C. 220.
[72] [1972] A.C. 60.

principles of relevance, and of the very notion of justice according to law. Like cases should be treated alike. To justify a different treatment one must point to an appropriate distinction. Things like appearance, race, religion, political beliefs, even previous criminal record are generally irrelevant. Other things are made irrelevant by the actual rules in particular cases (see below, p. 242). If the rule is that a victim of a motor-car accident can sue the person who negligently caused it, it is irrelevant that the victim subsequently married the defendant or even that the victim was on her way to a robbery.

But quite apart from notions of relevance which rest on general principles of what make good and bad distinctions and on particular legal rules, which it shares with any other legal system, English law has developed its own peculiar system of argument which sharply differentiates what are generally called the common law systems such as the United States, Canada, Australia and New Zealand from the continental code-based systems (though it is not the fact that those systems are code-based that makes the difference but the way in which the codes and the commentaries upon them are used as the basis of legal argument and decision). This is the system or doctrine of precedent.

Where there is no relevant statutory provision and where no question of European Community Law requiring reference to the Court of Justice is involved, English law rests for the most part on decisions in past cases. It is from these that the lawyer and the judge are expected to derive the relevant legal rules either directly or by analogy. The technique of extracting legal rules from past cases is one of the skills of an English lawyer. It is a skill more easily learnt than taught, but there are two distinctions which are important in any understanding of the way in which it works. One is between binding and persuasive precedent, the other between the *ratio decidendi* of a case and obiter dicta. The past cases which are binding on a judge are those he cannot refuse to follow even though he thinks there is good reason for disagreeing with the law laid down in them. The *ratio decidendi* of the case is that part of the judgment in a binding case which lays down the rules by which he is bound. Different courts have different freedoms in this respect. Judges in the High Court and lower courts are bound by all decisions in the Court of Appeal. The Court of Appeal is bound by its own previous decisions except in a limited number of circumstances, and by decisions of the House of Lords. The House of Lords generally regards itself as bound by its own decisions, but announced in 1965 that in future it would not regard itself as absolutely bound but would in exceptional circumstances feel free to reconsider one of its own past decisions. The distinction between the *ratio decidendi* of the case and obiter dicta is a corollary of the fact that there is no limit to the ground that a judge may cover in his judgment. His freedom in this respect is balanced by the rule that not all of what he says in his judgment is binding on future judges, only the *ratio decidendi*.

It would be wrong to pretend that for every case there was a single fixed *ratio*. Quite often much of the legal argument in a later case is on this very question. The general principle is that the *ratio* is that part of the judgment which was necessary to dispose of the material facts of the case. But this will still often leave a good deal of scope for argument, with those who like the case arguing for a broad *ratio* and those who do not for a narrow one. The final decision as to the scope of the *ratio*, too, may itself depend on factors outside the actual case. A case which perhaps started in the mainstream of the law may, over the years, as the area of law around it has been developed, or views and values changed, have been pushed to the side. It may have been constantly distinguished reaching such a point that it would be difficult to ascribe a very broad *ratio* to it. Conversely, a case may have been taken up with enthusiasm and have had a wide *ratio* ascribed to it so often over the years that it would be difficult to maintain that its *ratio* was in fact much narrower. Something like this has happened, for example, to the case of *Donoghue* v. *Stevenson*.[73]

Although it is the *ratio* which is crucial when one is considering whether a case is binding, this is not to say that obiter dicta are of no value. It has been said that obiter dicta for example of the House of Lords cannot be treated lightly [74] and quite apart from this they provide important raw material out of which future law can be made. They also provide an opportunity for tentative formulations of principle which, if they come to be accepted by future judges, can eventually have as much effect upon the law as a true *ratio*. (The same incidentally goes for dissenting judgments.)

Legal argument is persuasive argument and what the doctrine of precedent does is to contribute to the definition of what is regarded as more and less persuasive in English law. It is part of what sometimes is referred to as the hierarchy of sources of English law with statute at the top, then binding precedent, then persuasive precedent and obiter dicta. Textbooks and other books of authority come next. Passages in textbooks sometimes achieve special authority by being quoted by judges as correctly stating the law on a particular point. Persuasive precedents may include cases from other common law jurisdictions. Very low on the list indeed come arguments on the basis of justice, policy, conscience or expediency, though they all may be used to support an argument pressed on other more formal grounds. For although legal argument is persuasive argument, it is an essential feature of it that English courts and judges over the years have developed clear limits to what they will regard as persuasive and to what kinds of argument, therefore, they are prepared to listen. Besides the difference in the extent to which they feel free to change the law, this difference in the scope of the argument by which they are prepared to be persuaded, and the justifications they are prepared to use for any decisions that they make, is one of the major distinctions between the courts and the legislature in this country, and the courts in this country, including the House of Lords, and, say, the Supreme Court of the United States. In general arguments based on the needs of the economy, the virtues or vices of capitalism, the out-of-dateness of monogamy, the economic plight of the north-east, the impossibility of living on less than £20 a week are all regarded as irrelevant. In *Chandler* v. *D.P.P.*,[75] for example, the courts refused to listen to arguments from the " Committee of 100 " that the latter's attempt to invade Wethersfield Air Base and to sit in front of aircraft carrying nuclear weapons was not contrary to the interests of the state (and therefore to the Official Secrets Acts 1911–39) because it

---

[73] [1932] A.C. 562.
[74] *Jacobs* v. *L.C.C.* [1950] A.C. 331.
[75] [1964] A.C. 763.

was not in the interests of the state to have nuclear weapons; just as in *McCormick* v. *Lord Advocate*[76] the Scottish courts told the Scottish Covenant Association that arguments about the Queen not being Queen Elizabeth II in Scotland were better addressed to the electorate. Nor are the courts averse to imposing their standards of relevance on other people, as in *Roberts* v. *Hopwood*[77] when they told the Poplar Borough Council that they could not use their powers to fix wages in such a way as to implement their ideas of a national minimum wage even though the relevant statute authorised such wages as the Council thought fit. The extent to which the courts will themselves take on a legislative function is considered below, pp. 255 and 266.

Judicial Decisions and Legal Reasoning

Justice and Administrative Law, W. Robson
2nd ed., Stevens 1947

. . . [J]udicial institutions do not by themselves suffice to produce justice. . . . [T]he administration of justice requires not merely the establishment of organs of justice, such as courts of law or other tribunals, but also, and perhaps more importantly, that the matters to be adjudicated upon shall be decided by a particular process. That process . . . consists in the application of a body of rules or principles by the technique of a special method of thought, and in the presence of certain psychological elements. . . . The urge towards [the] formulation of principles arises from the desire for consistency. . . . The act which is a crime on Monday must remain punishable on Tuesday; the rule which is binding in Surrey must apply equally in Northumberland. It is this desire for consistency that is at the bottom of that respect for precedent which is so marked a feature of English law. . .

No less important than consistency . . . is the tendency towards equality. . . . This does not mean that everyone has similar rights, or a right to the same things; but all rights of the same kind are equal as between different individuals. . . . [W]hen a given set of facts or a particular group of individuals have been thrown into their appropriate legal categories, the judge must then apply to the individuals concerned the law that governs the entire class of objects or persons situated in those circumstances. Here, indeed, we touch the very essence of what is meant by such phrases as " the impartiality of judges," for the implication of those terms is precisely that the judge shall as far as possible deal with the materials before him by categories, treating equally all the separate items within each category. Every purchaser who has been fraudulently deceived as to the goods which he has bought must be treated alike; there must be no discrimination between them on grounds of religion, or personal attractiveness, or wealth, or nationality, or excellence at golf. All petitioners for divorce must be subjected to the same rules of law: adultery cannot be excused in one respondent because of his laudable war record, or because he and the judge have a mutual friend. This disinterested treatment of each member of a legal category on similar lines, regardless of race, religion, antecedents, physical appearance, intellect, public spirit, or occupation, is the foundation of judicial impartiality. In order that equality before the law shall prevail, . . . the judge is required to distinguish carefully between facts which are relevant to the issue and those which are immaterial. . . . A sense of relevance is, indeed, an essential ingredient in the judicial mind. In the daily procedure of the courts we can observe a continual

---

[76] 1953 S.C. 396.   [77] [1925] A.C. 578.

exclusion from the attention of the judge, of physical, economic, social and moral facts, which are accounted of enormous importance in other departments of life, but which in law have often no significance. A manufacturer of ferro-concrete who treats his wife badly, lies to his children, bullies the servants and cheats at cards, is not on that account placed in a disadvantageous position in regard to a building contract. A woman who is negligently run down by a motor car is not prejudiced in her action for damages because she has squandered her father's fortune or ruined her husband's life. . . .

The law itself, of course, often draws distinctions based on moral grounds between cases which would otherwise call for equal treatment. A man who bets against his horse winning the Derby ought logically to be treated in the same way as a man who bets against the safety of his own cargo on a ship at sea. But the law regards one as a wager which it will not enforce, and the other as a contract of marine insurance. The judge himself is often called upon to mete out unequal treatment to persons whose cases are indistinguishable save on moral grounds. The equitable jurisdiction of the Chancery judges is based on a whole series of moral axioms, such as " He who seeks equity must do equity," and " Who comes for equity must come with clean hands "; and in various other departments of the law moral inequalities are acknowledged to produce legal inequalities. But nothing in all this touches the dominant fact that inequalities of rank, fame and fortune do not call for inequality of treatment from the judge. . . .

It is not sufficient that the administration of justice should be consistent and equal in its treatment. It is necessary that it should be certain. . . . Hence it comes about that the judicial process requires the formulation and promulgation of a definite body of legal doctrine which can be ascertained by all who are subject to its rule. . . . The law must be known, or at least ascertainable, not only so as to enable the citizen to observe whether it is being administered consistently and equally, but also in order to enable him to comply with its provisions. The decisions of the judge must contain some measures of predictability. Even where the decision upon a particular set of facts is in doubt, there must be, in Judge Cardozo's words, " little doubt that the conclusion will be drawn from a stock of known principles and rules which will be treated as invested with legal obligation." It is this stock of rules and principles which is what we mean for most purposes by law. And the law must be ascertainable and certain. . . .

The growth of certainty in the law is closely associated with not only the drawing up of a body of principles but also with the convention which requires judges in the higher courts to give reasons for their decisions. It is difficult to imagine a body of law possessing the certainty which we nowadays expect growing up in a civilised country if the judges were merely to announce their decisions without any statement of the reasons on which they were founded. . . . The achievement of certainty is not the only advantage to be obtained from requiring judicial authorities to justify their conclusions by describing the chain of reasoning whereby they are reached " Good laws," said Jeremy Bentham, " are such laws for which good reasons can be given. . . ." The obligation to give reasons for the conclusion may have an important influence not only in persuading those who are affected by the decision that it is a just and reasonable one but also in developing the mental capacity and sense of fairness of the adjudicator. . . . The practice of giving reasoned decisions should, of course be accompanied by the publication of those decisions in important cases. . . .

[A] judge in court must give reasons for his decision. The jury, on the other hand, are not permitted to state the reasons on which they base their verdict. . . . [B]oth these rules aim at a common purpose: namely, the development of a coherent and impersonal body of law. The judge puts the trained mind of a lawyer on to the case, and is able to reason to the conclusion in terms of legal technique. The juryman . . . is not equipped to express either his thoughts or his feelings in a manner consistent with the body of the law. So like the young colonial judge, he is advised to give his conclusions only.

The artificial reason of the law

John Smith, living in a suburban villa on the outskirts of a city, is never, from the lawyer's point of view, a man of unique personality, who differs in the last resort from all other human beings. The colour of his eyes, his disposition to exaggerate, the peculiar way in which he brushes his teeth, his habit of whistling when asleep, his liking for apricot jam, his interest in pigeon flying, the subtle blend of dislike and admiration with which he regards his domineering wife, his ambition to secure a seat on the local council, the mingled pride and apprehension which he feels towards his strong-minded son : in all this the lawyer takes for the most part no interest. . . . What is legally significant about John Smith is the fact that he is a vendor, a purchaser, a ratepayer, a trustee, a master, a servant, a contractor, a tortfeasor. . . .

This pulverisation of a sentient being into a mere series of categories is an illustration of the classifying process which is going on continually in judicial proceedings, not only in regard to persons, but also in regard to places, things and events. . . . Lawyers look at the complex and moving realities of social life from a special angle, and submit those realities to artificial processes which transform, and sometimes deform, their effective nature. . . . The process of classification, which is one of the principal elements in the " artificial " reason of the law, has two or three great advantages. The attempt to see all things freshly and in detail rather than as types and generalities is exhausting, and among busy affairs practically out of the question. But even apart from the necessities of action, we cannot think in terms of an indefinite multiplicity of detail : our evidence can acquire its proper importance only if it comes before us marshalled by general ideas. Classification simplifies the circumstances relating to the controversy with which the judge has to deal, and reduces the issues to manageable proportions. It relieves the memory from what would otherwise be an intolerable burden by concentrating attention on certain vital aspects of the dispute. It objectifies the administration of justice by eliminating individual differences and insisting on class similarities. It makes for impartiality by securing that individuals and phenomena shall be differentiated according to recognisable objective criteria, and not according to the promptings of the subjective desires of the adjudicator. . . . But there are certain disadvantages which must be taken into account. . . . The " artificial reason " of the law tends to become rigid, and the system of classification may easily acquire an inflexibility which results in the neglect of factors which, though not susceptible to an orderly method of arrangement, are nevertheless of great importance. The disadvantage of the legal method of classification is, briefly, that it excludes imponderables. . . . Yet these imponderables . . . sometimes play an immensely valuable part in human affairs. . . . Mr. Walter Lippmann has indicated in a fine passage the ultimate necessity in intimate human relations for an " individualised understanding." Those whom we love and admire most, he says, are the men and women whose consciousness is peopled thickly with persons rather than with types, who know us rather than the classification into which we might fit. . . .

The Bramble Bush, K. Llewellyn

. . . [A]ll our cases are decided, all our opinions are written, all our predictions, all our arguments are made, on certain four assumptions. They are the first presuppositions of our study. . . .

(1) *The court must decide the dispute that is before it.* It cannot refuse because the job is hard, or dubious, or dangerous.

(2) *The court can decide* only *the particular dispute which is before it.* When it speaks to that question it speaks *ex cathedra*, with authority, with finality, with an almost magic power. When it speaks to the question before it, it announces *law*, and if what it announces is new, it legislates, it *makes* the law. But when it speaks to any other question at all, it says mere words, which no man needs to follow. Are such words worthless? They are not. We know them as judicial *dicta*; when they are wholly off the point at issue we call them *obiter dicta*—words dropped along the road, wayside remarks. Yet even wayside remarks shed light on the remarker. They may be very useful in the future to him, or to us. But he will not feel bound to them, as to his *ex cathedra* utterance. . . . He may be slow to change them; but not so slow as in the other case.

(3) *The court can decide the particular dispute only according to a* general *rule which covers a whole class of like disputes.* Our legal theory does not admit of single decisions standing on their own. If judges are free, are indeed forced, to decide new cases for which there is no rule, they must at least make a new rule as they decide. . . .

(4) *Everything, everything, everything, big or small, a judge may say in an opinion, is to be read with primary reference to the particular question before him.* You are not to think that the words mean what they might if they stood alone. You are to have your eye on the case in hand, and to learn how to interpret all that has been said *merely* as a reason for deciding *that* case *that* way.

Mirehouse v. Rennell

(1833) 1 Cl. & F. 527; 6 E.R. 1015

PARKE J.: . . . The precise facts . . . have never, as far as we can learn, been adjudicated upon in any court; nor is there to be found any opinion upon them of any of our Judges, or of those ancient text-writers to whom we look up as authorities. The case, therefore, is in some sense new, as many others are which continually occur; but we have no right to consider it, because it is new, as one for which the law has not provided at all; and because it has not yet been decided, to decide it for ourselves, according to our own judgment of what is just and expedient. Our common-law system consists in the applying to new combinations of circumstances those rules of law which we derive from legal principles and judicial precedents; and for the sake of attaining uniformity, consistency and certainty, we must apply those rules, where they are not plainly unreasonable and inconvenient, to all cases which arise; and we are not at liberty to reject them, and to abandon all analogy to them, in those to which they have not yet been judicially applied, because we think that the rules are not as convenient and reasonable as we ourselves could have devised. It appears to me to be of great importance to keep this principle of decision steadily in view, not merely for the determination of the particular case, but for the interests of law as a science. I propose, therefore, to inquire, by reference to those sources from which we usually derive them, what the rules and maxims of the common law upon this subject are. . . .

Egerton v. Brownlow

(1853) 4 H.L.Cas. 1; 10 E.R. 359

PARKE B.: . . . The main ground on which it is argued that the provisos are illegal, is that they are against " public policy ". . . . To allow this to be a ground of judicial decision, would lead to the greatest uncertainty and confusion. It is the province of the statesman, and not the lawyer, to discuss, and of the legislature to determine, what is the best for the public good, and to provide for it by proper enactments. It is the province of the judge to expound the law only; the written from the statutes: the unwritten or common law from the decisions of our predecessors and of our existing courts, from text-writers of acknowledged authority, and upon the principles to be clearly deduced from them by sound reason and just inference; not to speculate upon what is the best, in his opinion, for the advantage of the community. Some of these decisions may have no doubt been founded upon the prevailing and just opinions of the public good; for instance, the illegality of covenants in restraint of marriage or trade. They have become a part of the recognised law, and we are therefore bound by them, but we are not thereby authorised to establish as law everything which we may think for the public good and prohibit everything which we think otherwise. The term " public policy " may indeed be used only in the sense of the policy of the law, and in that sense it forms a just ground of judicial decision. It amounts to no more than that a contract or condition is illegal which is against the principle of the established law. If it can be shown that any provision is contrary to well-decided cases, or the principle of decided cases, and void by analogy to them, and within the same principle, the objection ought to prevail. But . . . this cannot be shown here.

Precedents, Lord Wright
(1942–44) 8 C.L.J. 118

. . . In modern days, the judge does not, as it were, start from scratch. He is somewhat like (though the parallel is not exact) a physician diagnosing a case. The physician examines the patient, and does so with his trained sense, with his mental background of physiological, anatomical, pathological knowledge which he has learned, and with his experience of other like cases. Thus he directs his attention to the material symptoms and so diagnoses the complaint and prescribes the remedy. Somewhat in the same way the judge does not approach the case with a blank mind. Subconsciously or consciously, trained mental processes are involved, rules learned in the past function in his mind, his own past experience and his past reading of other cases all combine to lead to a judgment . . . There are in the judge's mind the general principles of law which apart from any specific authority he may not infringe, and there is the background of professional tradition, education, and experience, somewhat like that which the physician possesses. The physician is inspired by his desire to restore health in his patient, the judge by his desire to do justice in the particular matter. Each has to work by rules. The function is rather that of the νοῦς πρακτικός than the νοῦς θεωρήτικός. There is an object to be achieved and an act of will in achieving it.

The Law behind Law : II. John Dickinson
(1929) 29 Col.L.R. 285

Only an adequate understanding of the creative part played by the judges in bringing new law into existence will enable us properly to understand the way in which the growth of law is influenced by legal tradition on the one hand and by contemporary social forces on the other. Too often it is assumed that new law is a direct and immediate product of one or both of these influences—that it grows " organically " out of previously existing law, . . . or that . . . it is passively shaped by the direct pressure of contemporary social forces. The truth of the matter is that these creative agencies are operative only in so far as judges allow them to operate—are effective only in so far as effect is given to them by judges. . . . [I]t is the judges in the exercise of their own capacity and from their own viewpoint who must determine the meaning and significance of legal tradition and who must interpret the influences which we call social forces, measure their intensity and decide the weight which they are entitled to exert. . . . [T]he judges are entitled, and generally in fact tend, to shape new law, and reshape old law, to their reading of the changing convenience of the society which they serve. But such readings are not, and cannot be, absolute, like the readings of a galvanometer. . . . [C]urrent *mores*, factors of social convenience and the like, are things about which there is room for a considerable scope of difference of opinion. . . . The considerations determining a court in the selection of a new rule of law out of a number of possible competing variants can be arbitrarily grouped for convenience in a series of concentric circles . . . with the judges at the centre. In the narrowest circle are the considerations purely personal to the judges, views and value-judgments growing out of the accidents of their individual experience. . . . These personal characteristics of the judges may fairly enough be said to have no appreciable influence on the case-to-case application of well-established rules of law, as, *e.g.* that a contract must rest on consideration, or the rule in *Shelley's Case*. Rules like these possess well understood objective authority in such sense that no competent judge, whatever his temperament or intellectual equipment, feels that he has any choice about giving effect to them. On the other hand the personal bent of the judge is inevitably a strong factor in the formation of the value-judgments underlying the selection of new rules for unprovided cases. Impinging on this original basis of purely personal considerations is a wider circle of other considerations of a more general character—the doctrines and points of view, theories and ideals which are " in the air " at the time. Some of these may be conflicting in character, and the subject of controversy more or less bitter. . . . But apart from these controversial doctrines every age has also its characteristic body of contemporary theory unconsciously saturating the atmosphere of thought and dictating a rough scale of values accepted for the time with tacit unanimity. In one era individual material success may seem the ultimate goal of social life and action; at another the maintenance of an established social order; at still another the widest amount of individual freedom; and again the promotion of an integrated healthy and productive community. These dominant contemporary points of view have a habit of getting themselves theorized and written into books, articles, and newspapers until theory takes on the form of self-evident truth and assumes all the trappings of a body of supposedly inexorable " natural " law. As contemporary theory of this kind influences at given points the formation of new rules of unwritten law, it becomes available to explain these rules, and thus a certain amount of it becomes hardened into and survives as a body of traditional legal theory. Such legal theory forms a highly definite circle of influence surrounding the judges and contributing to the relative sense of values which determines their selection of new rules of law. It is at once more meagre and more stiff than what I have called contemporary theory. Much of it is inherited from the past in more or less stereotyped form. . . .

Legal theory is undoubtedly the most direct and important single intellectual influence operating on the courts in the creation of new rules of law. . . . [L]egal theories like social theories, philosophical theories, and literary theories are subject to continual flux, involving movements of progression and regression, though the rate is slower and the resistance somewhat greater. At times one has a large number of adherents, at other times another, and usually on important points there are twilight zones where competing theories are contending for the mastery, and where neither bears the marks of being properly authoritative. . . . Of course to say that unwritten law is the product of legislative discretion exercised by the courts is by no means to deny the existence of substantial and highly important differences between the legislative process as performed by the courts incidentally to their function of adjudication and that process as performed by a legislature or constituent body charged with the function of making legal or constitutional rules frankly and directly. The process occurs in the two cases under such different conditions as to stamp a different hall-mark on the product.

In the first place, the legislative discretion exercised by the judges necessarily operates for the most part within much narrower limits than that of a legislative body. The courts seldom feel free to effect an important and direct change in an established legal rule in a way that a legislature would have no hesitation in doing. They usually confine themselves therefore to nibbling at the rule by creating distinctions and exceptions, and thus diminishing or deflecting the scope of its direction and operation. . . . When, however, the problem is not that of altering an existing rule but rather of supplying a wholly new rule to meet a new type of case, they cannot well be so circumspect. Here they cannot evade the necessity of creative action on a bolder scale. But here also their method shows a marked difference from that of a legislature. Under the influence of the doctrine that they must apply law which already exists, they are generally concerned, when devising a new rule, to frame one which can be made by some process of reasoning, facile or tortuous, to appear as a necessary logical deduction from some already established rule. This is a necessity from which legislatures are of course free. They can frame their rule to meet a new situation without the need for bringing it into any formal logical alignment with already existing rules. The courts on the contrary, because of the exigencies of theory, are bound to give an important place to considerations of logical symmetry and deductive reasoning. These logical considerations are ingredients which when thrown into the creative process are bound, in most instances, to produce a rule somewhat different from that which would probably have resulted from pure considerations of legislative policy. They deflect the rule more or less in the interest of formal symmetry. This is by no means to be regarded as a wholly unmixed evil. On the contrary, in so far as certainty and uniformity are two of the chief ends to be expected from a regime of law, it serves in part to account for the well-recognized superiority of much judge-made law over that of the statutory variety. The danger is that under the influence of theory the quest for logic may exclude or conceal the necessary operation of considerations of policy. Only by recognizing that policy consciously or unconsciously will and must enter even under cover of logic, can the courts control the work of their own hands. An illusion of logical inevitability is the surest anodyne to prevent a court from facing the practical consequences of a rule which it proposes to lay down and therefore from frankly examining and evaluating the legislative policy underlying the rule. . . .

Administrative Law and the Interpretation of Statutes, J. A. Corry

(1935–36) Univ. of Toronto L.J.

" The intention of the legislature cannot be found, and there is no literal meaning which automatically resolves every case. In many cases, there is no logical compulsion on the judge to accept a single meaning; two or more possible meanings are open to him. In making his choice, he makes law in spite of his protests to the contrary. . . . No science of legislation or interpretation can ever eliminate this creative work of the judge. This does not, however, make him a despot in applying statute law. Many able judges have been forced to conclusions which they genuinely regretted, because the case in question was too clearly within or without the words to allow an assertion of ambiguity in good faith. Every carefully drawn statute has limits beyond which it cannot be extended or restricted. For example, the word 'carriage' in a statute may or may not include a bicycle. So it might or might not include a wheelbarrow or a perambulator. But it would scarcely be possible for judicial ingenuity to make it include a knapsack carried on the back or to exclude a four-wheeled horse-drawn passenger vehicle from its terms. Words can always set limits. But within the limits . . . the judge remains a legislator. . . ."

Transcendental Nonsense and the Functional Approach, F. S. Cohen
(1935) 35 Col.L.R. 809

" We are still in the stage of guesswork and accidentally collected information, when it comes to formulating the social forces which mould the course of judicial decision. We know, in a general way, that dominant economic forces play a part in judicial decision, that judges usually reflect the attitudes of their own income class on social questions, that their views on law are moulded to a certain extent by their past legal experience as counsel for special interests, and that the impact of counsel's skill and eloquence is a cumulative force which slowly hammers the law into forms desired by those who can best afford to hire legal skill and eloquence; but nobody has ever charted, in scientific fashion, the extent of such economic influences."

ENGLISH COMMON LAW REASONING

The five extracts which follow all illustrate the English style of legal reasoning and in particular of judgments. They are taken from cases in which no statute was directly involved and thus show English common law reasoning at its most simple and straightforward, applying and distinguishing past cases and the principles set out in them, testing proposed new rules by applying them to hypothetical instances, examining the consequences of adopting one rule rather than another and at the same time giving a sense of the formal restraints within which the courts operate in dealing with new sets of facts and adapting existing principles to changed circumstances. One thing they cannot do by themselves is to show how the judges can develop the common law over a period particularly within the framework of the doctrine of precedent and the prevailing notions of the limitations on their freedom to innovate and legislate. But *Priestley* v. *Fowler* and the cases which revolve round the principles laid down in *Donoghue* v. *Stevenson* provide useful examples of this long term development, as well as illustrating English legal reasoning techniques in particular cases.

Priestley v. *Fowler* was the case in which the doctrine of common employment was set out. This prevented an employee recovering from his employer in a common law action for damage suffered as the result of the negligence of a fellow employee. Transferred to the context of industry and the factory it caused a good deal of hardship until it was finally laid to rest by the Law Reform (Personal Injuries) Act 1948. The doctrine itself is worth looking at more closely because it provides a convenient case history of what can happen to a principle which falls out of favour but which is difficult to eradicate because it is too well embedded in the law. At first it was in harmony with a more general attitude to the relationship of employer and employee, and went along with such other doctrines as *volenti non fit injuria* which could prevent an employee recovering for damage resulting from a danger of which he was aware, and the doctrine of contributory negligence which, until it was abolished in 1945, would prevent him recovering anything if it could be shown that he had been guilty of the slightest fault himself. The Employers' Liability Act 1880 did something to mitigate the effects of the doctrine of common employment in some cases and the Workmens Compensation Act 1897 was a step towards making employers liable irrespective of fault, but the common law doctrines remained. Over the whole field however the courts in response to changing views and values attempted to mitigate some of the harsher effects of the law. Their success and the limits upon it are a good example of the difference in power to change the law, and of method, between the legislature and the courts, even the House of Lords. So far as the doctrine of common employment was concerned, the furthest the courts managed to go was in *Radcliffe* v. *Ribble Motor Services* [78] in which the House of Lords held that the mere fact that two men were employed by the same employer was not enough to bring the doctrine into play. They had to be engaged in some kind of joint venture. At the same time they attempted an outflanking movement by imposing upon the employer himself a direct obligation to provide a safe system of working which meant that the injured employee could sometimes succeed against the employer without having to rely on the negligence of the fellow employee as such, see *e.g. Wilsons & Clyde Coal* v. *English.* [79] So far as the doctrine of contributory negligence was concerned they took the view that the plaintiff's fault could be ignored if it could be shown that it was not the real cause of the accident. And in *British Columbia Electric Railway* v. *Loach* [80] they even went further and announced that a party who could have avoided the accident but for his own prior fault had the last chance to avoid it and should therefore be regarded as entirely responsible. But even they could not actually get to the point, which had finally to be reached by statute (the Law Reform (Contributory Negligence) Act 1945), that the plaintiff could still recover in spite of the fact that he had been at fault, but that the damages would be reduced by the percentage to which his fault contributed to the accident. The courts were more successful with the doctrine of *volenti non fit injuria*. In *Bowater* v. *Rowley Regis Corporation* [81] it was held that it would be rare for that doctrine to be appropriate in an employer-employee situation, because the requisite degree of voluntariness would normally be difficult to establish because of the nature of the relationship.

Considered by itself, *Priestley* v. *Fowler* offers a good example of reasoning by means of hypothetical concrete cases. It also shows how much the

[78] [1938] 1 All E.R. 71.
[79] [1938] A.C. 57.
[80] [1916] 1 A.C. 719.
[81] [1944] K.B. 476.

plausibility of a particular piece of legal reasoning can depend as much on social values and assumptions taken straight from life as from existing law. *Grant* v. *Australian Knitting Mills*, *Candler* v. *Crane, Christmas & Co.* and *Hedley Byrne* v. *Heller and Partners* are all cases in which principles set out in the most famous case in the law of tort, *Donoghue* v. *Stevenson* [82] were discussed, explained applied and developed. They, together with many other cases dealing with various aspects of the law of negligence also provide as good an example as any of an area of law being developed and adapted over time, as well as individually illustrating again some of the more characteristic features of English legal reasoning and judicial style. In *Donoghue* v. *Stevenson*, Lord Atkin set out two statements of principle, one more general than the other. The first: " You must take reasonable care to avoid acts or omissions which you can reasonably foresee would be likely to injure . . . persons who are so closely and directly affected by my acts that I ought reasonably to have them in contemplation as being so affected when I am directing my mind to the acts or omissions which are called in question." The second: " A manufacturer of products which he sells in such a form as to show that he intends them to reach the ultimate consumer in the form in which they left him, with no reasonable possibility of intermediate examination and with the knowledge that the absence of reasonable care in the preparation or putting up of the products is likely to result in injury to the consumer's life or property, owes a duty to the consumer to take that reasonable care."

The question in *Grant's* case was whether the *ratio* of *Donoghue*, whatever it was, applied to a pair of sulphite impregnated pants which had caused the consumer to contract dermatitis. It provides a clear example of the way in which the courts move by analogy and suggested difference and similarity from one case to another. *Candler*, another case involving the question of the extent of the applicability of *Donoghue* v. *Stevenson*, this time of the broader of the two statements, shows the hypothetical example being used to show that a proposed rule is too open-ended. *Hedley Byrne* is a further example of distinguishing cases and principles, again in the field of negligence.

Entores v. *Miles Far East Corporation* is a contract case. It is a further example of hypothetical arguments, but also raised the question of the adaptation and application of existing rules to new inventions, this time the rules as to the posting of letters to the context of telex machines.

Priestley v. Fowler

(1837) 3 M. & W. 1; 150 E.R. 1030; Court of Exchequer

LORD ABINGER, C.B.: . . . It is admitted that there is no precedent for the present action by a servant against a master. We are therefore to decide the question upon general principles, and in doing so we are at liberty to look at the consequences of a decision the one way or the other.

If the master be liable to the servant in this action, the principle of that liability will be found to carry us to an alarming extent. He who is responsible by his general duty, or by the terms of his contract, for all the consequences of negligence in a matter in which he is the principal, is responsible for the negli-

[82] [1932] A.C. 562.

gence of all his inferior agents. If the owner of the carriage is therefore responsible for the sufficiency of his carriage to his servant, he is responsible for the
negligence of his coach-maker, or his harness-maker, or his coachman. The
footman, therefore, who rides behind the carriage, may have an action against
his master for a defect in the carriage owing to the negligence of the coach-
maker, or for a defect in the harness arising from the negligence of the harness-
maker, or for drunkenness, neglect, or want of skill in the coachman; nor is
there any reason why the principle should not, if applicable in this class of cases,
extend to many others. The master, for example, would be liable to the servant
for the negligence of the chambermaid, for putting him into a damp bed; for
that of the upholsterer, for sending in a crazy bedstead, whereby he was made
to fall down while asleep and injure himself; for the negligence of the cook, in
not properly cleaning the copper vessels used in the kitchen: of the butcher,
in supplying the family with meat of a quality injurious to the health; of the
builder, for a defect in the foundation of the house, whereby it fell, and injured
both the master and the servant by the ruins.

The inconvenience, not to say absurdity of these consequences, afford a
sufficient argument against the application of this principle to the present case.
But, in truth, the mere relation of the master and the servant never can imply
an obligation on the part of the master to take more care of the servant than he
may reasonably be expected to do of himself. He is, no doubt, bound to provide
for the safety of his servant in the course of his employment, to the best of his
judgment, information, and belief. The servant is not bound to risk his safety
in the service of his master, and may, if he thinks fit, decline any service in
which he reasonably apprehends injury to himself: and in most of the cases in
which danger may be incurred, if not in all, he is just as likely to be acquainted
with the probability and extent of it as the master. In that sort of employment,
especially, which is described in the declaration in this case, the plaintiff must
have known as well as his master, and probably better, whether the van was
sufficient, whether it was overloaded, and whether it was likely to carry him
safely. In fact, to allow this sort of action to prevail would be an encouragement
to the servant to omit that diligence and caution which he is in duty bound to
exercise on the behalf of his master, to protect him against the misconduct or
negligence of others who serve him, and which diligence and caution, while they
protect the master, are a much better security against any injury the servant may
sustain by the negligence of others engaged under the same master, than any
recourse against his master for damages could possibly afford.

Grant v. Australian Knitting Mills Ltd.
Privy Council [1936] A.C. 85

LORD WRIGHT: . . . Their Lordships think that the principle of the decision
[in *Donoghue* v. *Stevenson*] is summed up in the words of Lord Atkin: " A
manufacturer of products, which he sells in such a form as to show that he
intends them to reach the ultimate consumer in the form in which they left
him with no reasonable possibility of intermediate examination, and with the
knowledge that the absence of reasonable care in the preparation or putting up
of the products will result in an injury to the consumer's life or property, owes
a duty to the consumer to take that reasonable care." . . . In order to ascertain
whether the principle applies to the present case, it is necessary to define what
the decision involves, and consider the points of distinction relied upon before
their Lordships. . . . In *Donoghue's* case the duty was deduced simply from
the facts relied on—namely, that the injured party was one of a class for whose
use, in the contemplation and intention of the makers, the article was issued to

the world, and the article was used by that party in the state in which it was prepared and issued without it being changed in any way and without there being any warning of, or means of detecting, the hidden danger: . . . In *Donoghue's* case the thing was dangerous in fact, though the danger was hidden, and the thing was dangerous only because of want of care in making it; as Lord Atkin points out in *Donoghue's* case, the distinction between things inherently dangerous and things only dangerous because of negligent manufacture cannot be regarded as significant for the purpose of the questions here involved. . . .

If the foregoing are the essential features of *Donoghue's* case, they are also to be found, in their Lordship's judgment, in the present case. The presence of the deleterious chemical in the pants, due to negligence in manufacture, was a hidden and latent defect, just as much as were the remains of the snail in the opaque bottle: it could not be detected by any examination that could reasonably be made. Nothing happened between the making of the garments and their being worn to change their condition. The garments were made by the manufacturers for the purpose of being worn exactly as they were worn in fact by the appellant: it was not contemplated that they should be first washed. It is immaterial that the appellant has a claim in contract against the retailers, because that is a quite independent cause of action, based on different considerations, even though the damage may be the same. . . . It was argued, but not perhaps very strongly, that *Donoghue's* case was a case of food and drink to be consumed internally, whereas the pants here were to be worn externally. No distinction, however, can be logically drawn for this purpose between a noxious thing taken internally and a noxious thing applied externally: the garments were made to be worn next the skin: indeed Lord Atkin specifically puts as examples of what is covered by the principle he is enunciating things operating externally, such as " an ointment, a soap, a cleaning fluid or cleaning powder."

Mr. Greene, however, sought to distinguish *Donoghue's* case from the present on the ground that in the former the makers of the ginger-beer had retained " control " over it in the sense that they had placed it in stoppered and sealed bottles, so that it would not be tampered with until it was opened to be drunk, whereas the garments in question were merely put into paper packets, each containing six sets, which in ordinary course would be taken down by the shopkeeper and opened, and the contents handled and disposed of separately, so that they would be exposed to the air. He contended that though there was no reason to think that the garments when sold to the appellant were in any other condition, least of all as regards sulphur contents, than when sold to the retailers by the manufacturers, still the mere possibility and not the fact of their condition having been changed was sufficient to distinguish *Donoghue's* case: there was no " control " because nothing was done by the manufacturers to exclude the possibility of any tampering while the goods were on their way to the user. Their Lordships do not accept that contention. The decision in *Donoghue's* case did not depend on the bottle being stoppered and sealed: the essential point in this regard was that the article should reach the consumer or user subject to the same defect as it had when it left the manufacturer. That this was true of the garment is in their Lordships' opinion beyond question. At most there might in other cases be a greater difficulty of proof of the fact. . . . Mr. Greene further contended . . . that if the decision in *Donoghue's* case were extended even a hair's-breadth, no line could be drawn, and a manufacturer's liability would be extended indefinitely. He put as an illustration the case of a foundry which had cast a rudder to be fitted on a liner: he assumed that it was fitted and the steamer sailed the seas for some years: but the rudder had a latent defect due to faulty and negligent casting, and one day it broke, with the result that the vessel was wrecked, with great loss of life and damage to property. He argued that if *Donoghue's* case were extended beyond its precise facts, the maker of the rudder would be held liable for damages of an indefinite amount, after an indefinite time, and to claimants indeterminate until the event. But it is clear that such a state of things would involve many considerations far removed from the simple facts of this case. So many contingencies must have intervened between the lack of care on the part of the makers and the casualty that it may be that the law would apply, as it does in proper cases, not always according to strict logic, the rule that cause and effect must not be too remote: in any case the element of directness would obviously be lacking. . . . In their Lordships' opinion it is enough for them to decide this case on its actual facts.

No doubt many difficult problems will arise before the precise limits of the principle are defined: many qualifying conditions and many complications of fact may in the future come before the Courts for decision. It is enough now to say that their Lordships hold the present case within the principle of *Donoghue's* case. . . .

Candler v. Crane, Christmas & Co.
Court of Appeal [1951] 2 K.B. 164

ASQUITH L.J.: . . . Singular consequences would follow if the principle laid down in the snail case [83] were applied to negligent misrepresentation in every case in which the representee were proximate to the representor. The case has been instanced by Professor Winfield and referred to by my brother Denning of a marine hydrographer who carelessly omits to indicate on his map the existence of a reef. The captain of the " Queen Mary ", in reliance on the map and having no opportunity of checking it by reference to any other map, steers her on the unsuspected rocks, and she becomes a total loss. Is the unfortunate cartographer to be liable to her owners in negligence for some millions of pounds damages? If so, people will, in future, think twice before making maps. Cartography would become an ultra-hazardous occupation. Yet what line can be drawn between the map-maker and the defendants in the present case. If it be said that there is no proximity between the cartographer and those for whose use his map is designed, the reply surely is that there is just as much " proximity " as there was between the manufacturer of the peccant ginger beer bottle and its ultimate consumer.

In the present state of our law different rules still seem to apply to the negligent misstatement on the one hand and to the negligent circulation or repair of chattels on the other; and *Donoghue's* case [83] does not seem to me to have abolished these differences. I am not concerned with defending the existing state of the law or contending that it is strictly logical—it clearly is not. I am merely recording what I think it is.

If this relegates me to the company of " timorous souls ", I must face that consequence with such fortitude as I can command. I am of opinion that the appeal should be dismissed.

Hedley Byrne & Co. Ltd. v. Heller and Partners Ltd.
House of Lords [1964] A.C. 465

LORD REID: . . . The appellants' first argument was based on *Donoghue v. Stevenson*. That is a very important decision, but I do not think that it has any

[83] [1932] A.C. 562.

direct bearing on this case. That decision may encourage us to develop existing lines of authority, but it cannot entitle us to disregard them. Apart altogether from authority, I would think that the law must treat negligent words differently from negligent acts. The law ought so far as possible to reflect the standards of the reasonable man, and that is what *Donoghue* v. *Stevenson* sets out to do. The most obvious difference between negligent words and negligent acts is this. Quite careful people often express definite opinions on social or informal occasions even when they see that others are likely to be influenced by them; and they often do that without taking that care which they would take if asked for their opinion professionally or in a business connection. The appellant agrees that there can be no duty of care on such occasions, and we were referred to American and South African authorities where that is recognised, although their law appears to have gone much further than ours has yet done. But it is at least unusual casually to put into circulation negligently made articles which are dangerous. A man might give a friend a negligently-prepared bottle of home-made wine and his friend's guests might drink it with dire results. But it is by no means clear that those guests would have no action against the negligent manufacturer.

Another obvious difference is that a negligently made article will only cause one accident, and so it is not very difficult to find the necessary degree of proximity or neighbourhood between the negligent manufacturer and the person injured. But words can be broadcast with or without the consent or the foresight of the speaker or writer. It would be one thing to say that the speaker owes a duty to a limited class, but it would be going very far to say that he owes a duty to every ultimate " consumer " who acts on those words to his detriment. . . . So it seems to me that there is good sense behind our present law that in general an innocent but negligent misrepresentation gives no cause of action. There must be something more than the mere misstatement. I therefore turn to the authorities to see what more is required.

Entores Ltd. v. Miles Far East Corporation
Court of Appeal [1955] 2 Q.B. 327

DENNING L.J. When a contract is made by post it is clear law throughout the common law countries that the acceptance is complete as soon as the letter is put into the post box, and that is the place where the contract is made. But there is no clear rule about contracts made by telephone or by Telex. Communications by these means are virtually instantaneous and stand on a different footing.

The problem can only be solved by going in stages. Let me first consider a case where two people make a contract by word of mouth in the presence of one another. Suppose, for instance, that I shout an offer to a man across a river or a courtyard but I do not hear his reply because it is drowned by an aircraft flying overhead. There is no contract at that moment. If he wishes to make a contract, he must wait till the aircraft is gone and then shout back his acceptance so that I can hear what he says. Not until I have his answer am I bound. I do not agree with the observations of Hill J. in *Newcomb* v. *De Roos*.[84]

Now take a case where two people make a contract by telephone. Suppose, for instance, that I make an offer to a man by telephone and, in the middle of his reply, the line goes " dead " so that I do not hear his words of acceptance. There is no contract at that moment. The other man may not know the precise

[84] (1859) 2 E. & E. 271.

moment when the line failed. But he will know that the telephone conversation was abruptly broken off: because people usually say something to signify the end of the conversation. If he wishes to make a contract, he must therefore get through again so as to make sure that I heard. Suppose next, that the line does not go dead, but it is nevertheless so indistinct that I do not catch what he says and I ask him to repeat it. He then repeats it and I hear his acceptance. The contract is made, not on the first time when I do not hear, but only the second time when I do hear. If he does not repeat it, there is no contract. The contract is only complete when I have his answer accepting the offer.

Lastly, take the Telex. Suppose a clerk in a London office taps out on the teleprinter an offer which is immediately recorded on a teleprinter in a Manchester office, and a clerk at that end taps out an acceptance. If the line goes dead in the middle of the sentence of acceptance, the teleprinter motor will stop. There is then obviously no contract. The clerk at Manchester must get through again and send his complete sentence. But it may happen that the line does not go dead, yet the message does not get through to London. Thus the clerk at Manchester may tap out his message of acceptance and it will not be recorded in London because the ink at the London end fails, or something of that kind. In that case, the Manchester clerk will not know of the failure but the London clerk will know of it and will immediately send back a message " not receiving." Then, when the fault is rectified, the Manchester clerk will repeat his message. Only then is there a contract. If he does not repeat it, there is no contract. It is not until his message is received that the contract is complete.

In all the instances I have taken so far, the man who sends the message of acceptance knows that it has not been received or he has reason to know it. So he must repeat it. But, suppose that he does not know that his message did not get home. He thinks it has. This may happen if the listener on the telephone does not catch the words of acceptance, but nevertheless does not trouble to ask for them to be repeated: or the ink on the teleprinter fails at the receiving end, but the clerk does not ask for the message to be repeated: so that the man who sends an acceptance reasonably believes that his message has been received. The offeror in such circumstances is clearly bound, because he will be estopped from saying that he did not receive the message of acceptance. It is his own fault that he did not get it. But if there should be a case where the offeror without any fault on his part does not receive the message of acceptance—yet the sender of it reasonably believes it has got home when it has not—then I think there is no contract.

My conclusion is, that the rule about instantaneous communications between the parties is different from the rule about the post. The contract is only complete when the acceptance is received by the offeror: and the contract is made at the place where the acceptance is received.

In a matter of this kind, however, it is very important that the countries of the world should have the same rule. I find that most of the European countries have substantially the same rule as that I have stated. Indeed, they apply it to contracts by post as well as instantaneous communications. But in the United States of America it appears as if instantaneous communications are treated in the same way as postal communications. In view of this divergence, I think that we must consider the matter on principle: and so considered, I have come to the view I have stated, and I am glad to see that Professor Winfield in this country (55 *Law Quarterly Review*, 514), and Professor Williston in the United States of America (*Contracts*, § 82, p. 239), take the same view.

Applying the principles which I have stated, I think that the contract in this case was made in London where the acceptance was received. It was, therefore, a proper case for service out of the jurisdiction.

The Court of Appeal and Precedent

The primary function of the Court of Appeal is to correct errors in the trial courts, but this is not its only function. It also has a responsibility for ironing out anomalies in the law, keeping it up to date, reconciling conflicting decisions and principles and setting guidelines for the future. Even the notion of correcting errors is not quite as simple as it might seem. When the court says that the trial judge was mistaken in law this does not often mean that he was mistaken in the way that one might say a student had made a mistake in calculation or translation. It more often means that the court takes a different view of what the law should be in the light of the existing cases and current needs, circumstances and values. The court too has greater freedom in this respect because it feels much more free to depart even from a long line of previous decisions at the High Court or Crown Court level, because it is much more used to dealing with the law at leisure than the trial court judge, who is usually heavily involved in the facts of his particular cases, and because there are at least three judges sitting in the court.

But there are limits to what the court can do. It is bound by its own previous decisions, subject to the exceptions laid down in *Young* v. *Bristol Aeroplane Co. Ltd.*[85] and subject to qualifications set out as regards interlocutory matters in *Boys* v. *Chaplin*[86] and in criminal matters in *R.* v. *Taylor.*[87] It is also bound by decisions of the House of Lords, a fact of which it recently had to be reminded in both *Conway* v. *Rimmer* and *Broome* v. *Cassell.*[87a] Both these cases are a reminder that at any given time there may be a difference of view within the court as to how far it may go in departing from the old law, and in particular from its own past decisions. As usual Lord Denning has been the protagonist of a more flexible approach. Like the other courts too it operates within the general principles of precedent and statute, even when there is no question of there being a relevant binding case. It also operates within the general constitutional framework. A further factor which may limit its freedom is the feeling that all courts with power to overrule past cases have, namely that they should not disappoint settled expectations by overruling an old case which has been acted on for a long time even if they think it is wrong. The fact that the court sits as a court of at least three has an incidental advantage besides that of allowing three people to consider the problem instead of one. It makes possible a dissenting judgment in which an alternative view can be put forward and made available for discussion, and even subsequent adoption by the House of Lords. One of the crucial factors in developing the law is the size of the step that a court is being asked to take at any one time. The dissenting judgment can often be used as a stepping-stone which makes a development possible when it could otherwise only have been achieved by what would have seemed too great a leap. It has a role in the development of the law, therefore, similar to that of obiter dicta, or even an unsuccessful argument by counsel, as a means of injecting into the system principles or approaches which, though not accepted at once, may come to

[85] [1944] K.B. 518.   [86] [1968] 2 Q.B. 1.
[87] [1950] 2 K.B. 368.
[87a] Below, pp. 257 and 259.

be accepted if they win support within the system and come to be used as raw material out of which justifications of future decisions are built.

For the role of the Court of Appeal as a reviewing body in particular cases see below Chapter 7.

Young v. Bristol Aeroplane Co. Ltd.

Court of Appeal (Lord Greene M.R., Scott, Mackinnon, Luxmoore, Goddard and du Parcq L.JJ.) [1944] 1 K.B. 718

Lord Greene M.R.: . . . Cases in which this court has expressed its regret at finding itself bound by previous decisions of its own and has stated in the clearest terms that the only remedy of the unsuccessful party is to appeal to the House of Lords are within the recollection of all of us and numerous examples are to be found in the reports. When in such cases the matter has been carried to the House of Lords it has never, so far as we know, been suggested by the House that this view was wrong and that this court could itself have done justice by declining to follow a previous decision of its own which it considered to be erroneous. On the contrary, the House has, so far as we are aware, invariably assumed and in many cases expressly stated that this court was bound by its own previous decision to act as it did.

. . . [W]e can find no warrant for the argument that what is conveniently but inaccurately called the full court has any greater power in this respect than a division of the court consisting of three members only.

The Court of Appeal is a creature of statute and its powers are statutory. It is one court though it usually sits in two or three divisions. Each division has co-ordinate jurisdiction, but the full court has no greater powers or jurisdiction than any division. . . . [W]hat cannot be done by a division of the court cannot be done by the full court.

In considering the question whether or not this court is bound by its previous decisions and those of courts of co-ordinate jurisdiction, it is necessary to distinguish four classes of case. The first is that with which we are now concerned, namely, cases where this court finds itself confronted with one or more decisions of its own or of a court of co-ordinate jurisdiction which cover the question before it and there is no conflicting decision of this court or of a court of co-ordinate jurisdiction. The second is where there is such a conflicting decision. The third is where this court comes to the conclusion that a previous decision, although not expressly overruled, cannot stand with a subsequent decision of the House of Lords. The fourth (a special case) is where this court comes to the conclusion that a previous decision was given per incuriam. In the second and third classes of case it is beyond question that the previous decision is open to examination. In the second class, the court is unquestionably entitled to choose between the two conflicting decisions. In the third class of case the court is merely giving effect to what it considers to have been a decision of the House of Lords by which it is bound. The fourth class requires more detailed examination. . . . Where the court has construed a statute or a rule having the force of a statute its decision stands on the same footing as any other decision on a question of law, but where the court is satisfied that an earlier decision was given in ignorance of the terms of a statute or a rule having the force of a statute the position is very different. It cannot, in our opinion, be right to say that in such a case the court is entitled to disregard the statutory provision and is bound to follow a decision of its own given when that provision was not present to its mind. Cases of this description are examples of decisions given per incuriam. We do not think that it would be right to say that there may not be other cases of decisions given per incuriam in which this court might properly consider itself entitled not to follow an earlier decision of its own. Such cases would obviously be of the rarest occurrence and must be dealt with in accordance with their special facts. Two classes of decisions per incuriam fall outside the scope of our inquiry, namely, those where the court has acted in ignorance of a previous decision of its own or of a court of co-ordinate jurisdiction which covers the case before it—in such a case a subsequent court must decide which of the two decisions it ought to follow; and those where it has acted in ignorance of a decision of the House of Lords which covers the point—in such a case a subsequent court is bound by the decision of the House of Lords.

On a careful examination of the whole matter we have come to the clear conclusion that this court is bound to follow previous decisions of its own as well as those of courts of co-ordinate jurisdiction. The only exceptions to this rule (two of them apparent only) are those already mentioned. . . .

Conway v. Rimmer
Court of Appeal [1967] 1 W.L.R. 1031 [88]

LORD DENNING M.R. [dissenting] : . . . [M]y brethren today feel that we are still bound by the observations of the House of Lords in *Duncan* v. *Cammell, Laird & Co. Ltd.*[89] and by the decision of this court in *Auten* v. *Rayner*.[90] I do not agree. The doctrine of precedent has been transformed by the recent statement of Lord Gardiner L.C.[91] [Practice Statement (Judicial Precedent)]. This is the very case in which to throw off the fetters. Crown privilege is one of the prerogatives of the Crown. As such, it extends only so far as the common law permits. It is for the judges to define its ambit. . . . I take my stand, therefore, on what we said in the trilogy of cases.

DAVIES L.J.: . . . I turn now to the 1964 trilogy of cases, namely, *Merricks*,[92] *Grosvenor Hotel (No. 2)* [93] and *Wednesbury*,[94] mentioned earlier in this judgment and decided in this court by the same trinity of judges, viz., my Lord, Lord Denning M.R., Harman and Salmon L.JJ. The judgments in those cases are, of course, most weighty and most interesting. But, with the greatest respect, I cannot accept them as decisions that English law is other than I have suggested that it is.

Some general observations may be made about those cases. In the first place, in not one of them did the court order production of the documents in question or itself inspect them; so that whether or not the observations made in those cases were obiter, as in that state of affairs I am inclined to think that they were, the Crown had no opportunity of challenging in the House of Lords the validity of the views expressed in this court. . . .

RUSSELL L.J.: . . . It is accepted that *Duncan* v. *Cammell, Laird & Co. Ltd.* is the authority of the House of Lords for the proposition . . . that a claim . . . to Crown privilege from production of documents, on the ground that their contents are such that disclosure would be injurious to the public interest, cannot be questioned or investigated or tested by inspection by the court. . . . The question . . . is whether it is also authority for the proposition . . . that a similar

---

[88] For the circumstances leading up to this case, see below, p. 374.
[89] [1942] A.C. 624.
[90] [1958] 1 W.L.R. 1300.
[91] Below, p. 269.
[92] [1965] 1 Q.B. 57.
[93] [1965] Ch. 1210.
[94] [1965] 1 W.L.R. 261.

claim made on the ground that documents are of a class of which disclosure of any constituent would be injurious to the public interest cannot be questioned or investigated or tested by inspection by the court.... For my part I am unable to elicit from *Duncan's* case any principle other than one which is as applicable to "class" cases as to "contents" cases.... For that reason, in spite of the three valiant attempts made in recent cases in this court (by Athos M.R., Porthos and Aramis L.JJ.) to assert that *Duncan's* case is no authority for a "class" case, I cannot but recognise it as such and must leave it to the House of Lords to reconsider the whole basis of the case, if it wishes to do so. This conclusion entirely accords with the views and decisions of this court in *Auten* v. *Rayner*, which, on the principles stated in *Morelle Ltd.* v. *Wakeling*, I should have thought was of binding authority, although a distinction between "class" and "contents" cases was not suggested in argument. And in *Ellis* v. *Home Office*, also in this court, it was assumed that in a "class" case the absolute proposition was correct, though it cannot be said to be a decision to that effect.

The Master of the Rolls in his judgment has said that the doctrine of precedent has been transformed by the recent statement of Lord Gardiner L.C.... But that statement said nothing to suggest that this court was in any way freed from the hitherto established principles of precedent in relation to previous decisions either of the House of Lords or of this court.

On appeal the House of Lords reconsidered *Duncan's* case and decided they were free to depart from it. The most explicit statement on the position of the Court of Appeal in the case was made by Lord Morris of Borth-y-Gest who said:

> . . . My Lords, it seems to me that that decision [*i.e. Duncan* v. *Cammell Laird*] was binding upon the Court of Appeal in the present case. Your Lordships have, however, a freedom which was not possessed by the Court of Appeal. Though precedent is an indispensable foundation upon which to decide what is the law, there may be times when a departure from precedent is in the interests of justice and the proper development of the law. I have come to the conclusion that it is now right to depart from the decision in *Duncan's* case.

Gallie v. Lee

Court of Appeal [1969] 2 Ch. 17

RUSSELL L.J.: ... I do not support the suggestion that this court is free to override its own decisions, now that the House of Lords has given itself ability to override its own decisions. I am a firm believer in a system by which citizens and their advisers can have as much certainty as possible in the ordering of their affairs. Litigation is an activity that does not markedly contribute to the happiness of mankind, though it is sometimes unavoidable. An abandonment of the principle that this court follows its own decisions on the law would I think lead to greater uncertainty and tend to produce more litigation. In the case of decisions of the House of Lords error, or what is later considered to be error, could only previously be corrected by statute: and the other demands on parliamentary time made this possibility so remote that the decision of the House of Lords not necessarily to be bound by a previous decision was justifiable at the expense of some loss of certainty. But the availability of the House of Lords to correct error in the Court of Appeal makes it in my view unnecessary for this court to depart from its existing discipline.

Salmon L.J.: ... As I have already indicated, the law certainly ought, in my view to be as stated by the Master of the Rolls in his conclusions. I am confident that it would be so stated by the House of Lords were this question to come before it for decision.... I am, however, convinced that so long as this court considers itself absolutely bound by its own decisions I have no power to adopt the Master of the Rolls' conclusions; I must accept the law as stated in the authorities to which I have referred in spite of the fact that it results too often in inconsistency, injustice, and an affront to commonsense. The dicta to the effect that this court is absolutely bound by its own decisions are very strong: see, for example, *Young* v. *Bristol Aeroplane Co. Ltd.* [1944] 1 K.B. 718; [1946] A.C. 163, 169; *Bonsor* v. *Musicians' Union* [1956] A.C. 104, but no stronger than those by virtue of which the House of Lords until recently treated itself as similarly bound by its own decisions. The point about the authority of this court has never been decided by the House of Lords. In the nature of things it is not a point that could ever come before the House for decision. Nor does it depend upon any statutory or common law rule. This practice of ours apparently rests solely upon a concept of judicial comity laid down many years ago and automatically followed ever since: see *The Vera Cruz (No.* 2) (1884) 9 P.D. 96, *per* Lord Brett, at p. 98. Surely today judicial comity would be amply satisfied if we were to adopt the same principle in relation to our decisions as the House of Lords has recently laid down for itself by a pronouncement of the whole House. It may be that one day we shall make a similar pronouncement. I can see no valid reasons why we should not do so and many why we should. But that day is not yet. It is, I think, only by a pronouncement of the whole court that we could effectively alter a practice which is so deeply rooted. In the meantime I find myself reluctantly obliged to accept the old authorities, however much I disagree with them. My only consolation is that in spite of the present unsatisfactory state of this branch of the law, it enables us, on the facts of this case, to reach a decision which accords with reason and justice.

Lord Denning M.R. [dissenting]: ... We are, of course, bound by the decisions of the House [of Lords] but I do not think we are bound by prior decisions of our own, or at any rate, not absolutely bound. We are not fettered as it was once thought. It was a self-imposed limitation: and we who imposed it can also remove it. The House of Lords have done it. So why should not we do likewise? We should be just as free, no more and no less, to depart from a prior precedent of our own, as in like case is the House of Lords or a judge of first instance. It is very, very rarely that we will go against a previous decision of our own, but if it is clearly shown to be erroneous, we should be able to put it right....

Broome v. Cassell & Co.
[1972] A.C. 1027

One of the grounds on which the Court of Appeal had dismissed the appeal from the trial judge in this case was that *Rookes* v. *Barnard* [95] which *inter alia* laid down anew the circumstances in which exemplary damages could be awarded had been wrongly decided and was not binding on the Court of Appeal. They said that it had been arrived at *per incuriam* and without argument from counsel and had ignored two previous decisions of the House of Lords which they said were inconsistent with it. They also said that the decision was " unworkable " and that in the meantime

[95] [1964] A.C. 1129.

"judges should direct juries in accordance with the law as it was understood before *Rookes* v. *Barnard*." [96] On appeal, the House of Lords rejected this approach by the Court of Appeal to one of their decisions.

LORD HAILSHAM L.C.: ... If the Court of Appeal felt, as they were well entitled to do, that in the light of the Australian and other Commonwealth decisions *Rookes* v. *Barnard* ought to be looked at again by the House of Lords, either generally or under the Practice Declaration of 1966, *Practice Statement (Judicial Precedent)* [1966] 1 W.L.R. 1234, they were perfectly at liberty to say so. More, they could have suggested that so soon as a case at first instance arose in which the ratio decidendi of *Rookes* v. *Barnard* was unavoidably involved, the parties concerned might wish to make use of the so-called " leap-frogging " procedure now available to them under the Administration of Justice Act 1969 and thus avoid one stage in our three-tier system of appeals. But to impose on these litigants, to whom the question was, on the court's view, unnecessary, the inevitable burden of further costs after all they had been through up to date was not, in my view, defensible.

Moreover, it is necessary to say something of the direction to judges of first instance to ignore *Rookes* v. *Barnard* as " unworkable." ... [I]t is not open to the Court of Appeal to give gratuitous advice to judges of first instance to ignore decisions of the House of Lords in this way and, if it were open to the Court of Appeal to do so, it would be highly undesirable. The course taken would have put judges of first instance in an embarrassing position, as driving them to take sides in an unedifying dispute between the Court of Appeal or three members of it (for there is no guarantee that other Lords Justices would have followed them and no particular reason why they should) and the House of Lords. But, much worse than this, litigants would not have known where they stood. None could have reached finality short of the House of Lords, and, in the meantime, the task of their professional advisers of advising them either as to their rights, or as to the probable cost of obtaining or defending them, would have been, quite literally, impossible. Whatever the merits, chaos would have reigned until the dispute was settled, and, in legal matters, some degree of certainty is at least as valuable a part of justice as perfection.

The fact is, and I hope it will never be necessary to say so again, that, in the hierarchical system of courts which exists in this country, it is necessary for each lower tier, including the Court of Appeal, to accept loyally the decisions of the higher tiers. Where decisions manifestly conflict, the decision in *Young* v. *Bristol Aeroplane Co. Ltd.* [1944] K.B. 718 offers guidance to each tier in matters affecting its own decisions. It does not entitle it to question considered decisions in the upper tiers with the same freedom. Even this House, since it has taken freedom to review its own decisions, will do so cautiously. That this is so is apparent from the terms of the declaration of 1966. . . .[97]

It is also apparent from the recent case of *Reg.* v. *National Insurance Commissioner, Ex parte Hudson* [1972] 2 W.L.R. 210, where the decision in *Reg.* v. *Deputy Industrial Injuries Commissioners, Ex parte Amalgamated Engineering Union, In re Dowling* [1967] 1 A.C. 725 came up for review under the 1966 declaration, that the House will act sparingly and cautiously in the use made of the freedom assumed by this declaration.

In addition, the last paragraph of the declaration clearly affirms the continued adherence of this House to the doctrine of precedent as it has been hitherto applied to and in the Court of Appeal.

[96] [1971] 2 Q.B. 354, 384.
[97] See below, p. 269.

Boys v. Chaplin [98]

Court of Appeal [1968] 2 Q.B. 1

DIPLOCK L.J.: . . . The first question in this appeal is accordingly whether this court is bound to accept the propositions laid down in *Machado* v. *Fontes* [99] as correct. . . .

The House of Lords in an extra-judicial pronouncement has expressed its intention of loosening its self-imposed fetters of stare decisis; but this was expressly stated not to apply to any other courts. Indeed, it is difficult to see how a pronouncement by the House of Lords which did not form part of the reasons for judgment in any appeal before it could have any binding effect upon any other court. In the Court of Appeal we are bound by judicial decisions of the House of Lords, but so far as concerns the binding effect on the Court of Appeal of its own decisions, our fetters, too, are self-imposed. Their extent was discussed in *Young* v. *Bristol Aeroplane Co. Ltd.*[1] and I concede that the decision in *Machado* v. *Fontes* [2] does not fall within any of the three exceptions to the binding effect of decisions of the Court of Appeal upon a subsequent Court of Appeal of co-ordinate jurisdiction which are set out in *Young's* case.[3] But in *Young's* case it was only final judgments of the Court of Appeal which were under consideration. *Machado* v. *Fontes* [4] was an appeal from an interlocutory order of a judge in chambers, and the order made by the Court of Appeal was an interlocutory, not a final, judgment. In interlocutory appeals the Court of Appeal does not usually have the benefit of a reasoned judgment by the judge against whose order the appeal is brought. The statute constituting the Court of Appeal treats interlocutory appeals as being in a lower category than final appeals; the appeal may be heard by two lords justices, as *Machado* v. *Fontes* was, instead of by three. In practice lengthy and detailed argument in interlocutory appeals is discouraged. *Machado* v. *Fontes*, which raised a question of fundamental importance in the then almost untilled field of conflict of laws, was argued and disposed of by extempore judgments within a single day. In practice, too, appeals to the House of Lords from interlocutory orders of the Court of Appeal are discouraged and leave to pursue them is seldom obtained. These differences in practice in interlocutory and final appeals to the Court of Appeal detract from the weight to be attached to the reasons given for an interlocutory order of the Court of Appeal. *Young's* case, which I loyally, if regretfully, accept as binding upon me, does not, as I think, preclude this court from declining to follow the ratio decidendi of a previous interlocutory order of the Court of Appeal if this court thinks that the ratio decidendi was wrong. In the present state of juristic opinion, I would not extend the doctrine of stare decisis any further.

I think, therefore, that we are entitled to re-examine the two propositions laid down by Lopes and Rigby L.JJ. in *Machado* v. *Fontes* and to form our own view as to whether they are correct. . . .

LORD UPJOHN: . . . If this court thought that *Machado* v. *Fontes* was wrongly decided, it could probably review that case because it was an interlocutory appeal heard by two judges, though this court undoubtedly remains bound by the principles of *Young* v. *Bristol Aeroplane Co. Ltd.* notwithstanding some

---

[98] The decision of the Court of Appeal was later affirmed by the House of Lords, *sub nom. Chaplin* v. *Boys* [1971] A.C. 356.

[99] [1897] 2 Q.B. 231.

[1] [1944] K.B. 718.

[2] [1897] 2 Q.B. 231.

[3] [1944] K.B. 718.

[4] [1897] 2 Q.B. 231.

recent relaxation from the binding effect of precedent in the House of Lords, a relaxation which applies only to that House.

Lord Denning M.R. delivered a concurring judgment.

R. v. Taylor
Court of Criminal Appeal [1950] 2 K.B. 368

Lord Goddard C.J.: . . . I desire to say a word about the reconsideration of a case by this court. The Court of Appeal in civil matters usually considers itself bound by its own decisions or by decisions of a court of co-ordinate jurisdiction. For instance, it considers itself bound by its own decisions and by those of the Exchequer Chamber; and, as is well known, the House of Lords also always considers itself bound by its own decisions. In civil matters this is essential in order to preserve the rule of stare decisis.

This court, however, has to deal with questions involving the liberty of the subject, and if it finds, on reconsideration, that, in the opinion of a full court assembled for that purpose, the law has been either misapplied or misunderstood in a decision which it has previously given, and that, on the strength of that decision, an accused person has been sentenced and imprisoned it is the bounden duty of the court to reconsider the earlier decision with a view to seeing whether that person had been properly convicted. The exceptions which apply in civil cases ought not to be the only ones applied in such a case as the present, and in this particular instance the full court of seven judges is unanimously of opinion that the decision in *Rex* v. *Treanor* [5] was wrong for a reason which I will indicate in a moment.

R. v. Newsome
Court of Appeal (Criminal Division) [1970] 2 Q.B. 711

The appellant had been sentenced to six months' imprisonment. On being told that this would mean that the sentence would have to be suspended the trial judge increased the sentence. The appellant argued that the first sentence should stand and cited previous decisions of the court in which it had allowed appeals in such circumstances and restored the first sentence.

Widgery L.J.[6]: . . . The first thing to observe in this case is that the point is not a novel one. . . . [T]here are two earlier decisions of this court in which the matter was considered. . . .

The first matter which we have had to consider is whether it is open to us, albeit we are sitting as a court of five, to take a different view from that expressed in the two earlier cases. . . . We . . . recognise, as has been recognised for years, that the principle of stare decisis does not apply in its full rigour to decisions of the Court of Criminal Appeal as it used to be and the criminal division of this court as it now is. We have been referred to *Rex* v. *Taylor* [1950] 2 K.B. 368 where a court of seven departed from a previous view assumed by the court and declined to follow an earlier authority. It is perfectly true that Lord Goddard C.J., in giving judgment in that case, justified the action of the court to a very large degree by the fact that in that case a departure from authority was necessary in the interests of the appellant. He took the robust

---

[5] (1939) 27 Cr.App.R. 35.
[6] With Fenton Atkinson L.J. and Melford Stevenson, O'Connor and Eveleigh JJ.

view that, if a man be in prison and in the judgment of the court wrongly in prison, it should not allow such matters as stare decisis to stand in the way. It is, however, also apparent that some importance at any rate was attached by Lord Goddard C.J. to the fact that that was not a normal court of three but in that case a court of seven.

More convincingly on this subject is the more recent case, *Reg.* v. *Gould* [1968] 2 Q.B. 65, a decision of this court in its present form and a decision of a court of three judges. I cite it for a statement of principle by Diplock L.J. giving the judgment of the court. He said, at p. 68:

> "In its criminal jurisdiction, which it has inherited from the Court of Criminal Appeal, the Court of Appeal does not apply the doctrine of stare decisis with the same rigidity as in its civil jurisdiction. If upon due consideration we were to be of opinion that the law had been either misapplied or misunderstood in an earlier decision of this court or its predecessor, the Court of Criminal Appeal, we should be entitled to depart from the view as to the law expressed in the earlier decision notwithstanding that the case could not be brought within any of the exceptions laid down in *Young* v. *Bristol Aeroplane Co. Ltd.* [1944] K.B. 718."

Mr. Hidden says that the court there was not going further than it went in *Rex* v. *Taylor* [1950] 2 K.B. 368, and that that dictum should be regarded as being qualified by *Rex* v. *Taylor*. We do not so read it and I subscribe to that view the more readily because I was a member of the court in *Reg.* v. *Gould* [1968] 2 Q.B. 65.

We do not have in this case to go to extremes in this matter and, in particular, we do not have to consider to what extent a court of five can properly depart from an earlier decision of a court of three when the issue goes to guilt or innocence. One can well see, and these are matters which may have to be dealt with another day, that where the question at issue determined whether an act was criminal or not, then even a court of five should at the very least have far greater reluctance in departing from an earlier decision than it would where such a fundamental issue did not arise.

The matter before us arises in a sphere which is peculiar to the criminal division of the Court of Appeal. It arises out of the well-known duty of this division to lay down principles and guidelines to assist judges of all grades in the application of the discretion which the imposition of sentence requires. And we are all entirely of the opinion that, in the realm which was described by Mr. Cheyne as being a matter of discretion and, as he said, not a matter of practice and procedure but a matter of discretion peculiar to the criminal division; if the court of five is duly constituted to consider an issue of discretion and the principles upon which discretion should be exercised, that court ought to have the right to depart from an earlier view expressed by the court of three, especially where that earlier view is very recent and especially where it was a matter in which the court did not have the opportunity of hearing argument on both sides.

Accordingly, within that restricted sphere, which is the only sphere upon which we have to pronounce today, within that restricted sphere we take the view that a court of five can, and indeed should, depart from an earlier direction on the exercise of a judge's discretion if satisfied that the earlier direction was wrong. . . .

Non-binding precedents of long standing

So far we have considered the position where it is suggested that the Court of Appeal is bound by precedent. It does not follow however that the court will exercise its power to depart from a previous precedent even though it is not bound by it and even though it considers that it was wrongly decided.

Re Hallett's Estate
Court of Appeal (1880) 13 Ch.D. 696

Baggallay L.J.: . . . Repeated decisions have established rules for determining the construction of particular words when used in wills, and other wills have been prepared and executed upon the faith of such words receiving the like construction. Titles have been acquired and lands dealt with upon the footing of the law being as enunciated in the judgments pronounced in other cases. And so, again, in matters of commercial business, contracts have been entered into upon the faith of certain rules, originating in the decisions of the Courts, being recognised as conclusive. Now, in such cases as these, and in others which will readily suggest themselves, the greatest injustice might be occasioned by a Court or judge treating such decisions as having been erroneously arrived at, and thereby creating doubt and uncertainty as to a rule of law which had previously been treated as well and clearly defined. But no such injustice could arise in consequence of our dissenting from the decision in *Pennell* v. *Deffell*. . . .[7]

The Annefield
Court of Appeal [1971] P. 168

Lord Denning M.R.: . . . The only point that we have to consider today is a point of law. . . . The question is whether the arbitration clause which is set out in the charterparty (clause 39) is incorporated into the contract evidenced by the bills of lading by reason of the incorporation clause. . . .

This very point (on this very Centrocon form and bill of lading) came up for decision in 1935, before Sir Boyd Merriman P. It was in *The Njegos* [1936] P. 90. The President there said, at p. 100:

> " Both Sir Robert [Aske] and Mr. Willink agreed, and their experience in these matters is unrivalled, that since the adoption of this form of bill of lading in 1914, attempts made in chambers, under the bill of lading, to enforce the arbitration clause in the charterparty had uniformly failed, and that no one had been hardy enough to test the matter in court."

The President followed that practice. He held that the arbitration clause was not incorporated into the bill of lading.

That case has not been challenged from that time to this. So we have a course of practice from 1914 to 1970, some 56 years. After this time, it would require a very strong case to upset the practice. Once a court has put a construction on commercial documents in standard form, commercial men act upon it. It should be followed in all subsequent cases. If the business community is not satisfied with the decision, they should alter the standard form. In this very case the Centrocon form has, since 1936, been amended in other respects from time to time. But no alteration has been made in this respect. So the construction in *The Njegos* is of special weight.

---

[7] 4 D.M. & G. 372.

R. v. Bow Road Justices, ex p. Adedigba
Court of Appeal [1968] 2 Q.B. 572

The question here was whether a single woman could bring affiliation proceedings under the Affiliation Proceedings Act 1957 when the child was born abroad and she was domiciled abroad. The case of *R. v. Blane* [8] decided under an earlier statute, had said that she could not, and the case had been followed for over a century. As a decision of the Divisional Court it was not however binding on the Court of Appeal.

SALMON L.J.: . . . It is said that however wrong the decision in *R. v. Blane* [8] may have been, it was made 119 years ago. Moreover, it has been followed ever since, as it had to be followed, by the courts upon which it was binding; and accordingly the principle of *stare decisis* should apply. Certainly we do not readily interfere with decisions which have stood for 119 years, or, indeed, for any lengthy period of time. This is particularly true of decisions in fields in which it might be said that the community has arranged its affairs in accordance with what has been regarded as the law for many years past. It is, for example, very true of decisions relating to the law of contract. But even in that field, the courts reverse old decisions when completely satisfied that such decisions were wrong. For example, recently this court (in *C. Czarnikow Ltd. v. Koufos* [9]) overruled *The Parana*,[10] which had stood for nearly 90 years and had been generally accepted as stating the law relating to the measure of damage for breach of contract for the carriage of goods by sea; and the House of Lords upheld the decision of this court.

In the present case none of these considerations underlying the principle of *stare decisis* apply. I do not suppose that the incidence of illegitimate children being conceived and born abroad has been affected in the slightest by the decision in *R. v. Blane.* I think it unlikely that any woman in Nigeria, or indeed anywhere else, would forebear to conceive and give birth to an illegitimate child abroad because she might contemplate that if she and the child came to this country with the putative father, she would not, according to the law as laid down in *R. v. Blane*, ever have a chance of recovering any sum from him by way of maintenance for the child. Nor do I think that putative fathers have arranged their affairs on the basis that *R. v. Blane* was correctly decided; and if they had, I should have no qualms about upsetting it.

LORD DENNING M.R.: . . . If we were to affirm today *R. v. Blane* as being the law of this land, the only consequence would be a reference to the Law Commission; then a report by them; and eventually a Bill before Parliament. It would be quite a long time before the law could be set right. Even then the law would only be set right for future cases. Nothing could be done to set right this present case. The mother here would not get maintenance for the child which she needs now. So I would overrule *R. v. Blane* now. In the days of 1849 the question may not have been of any particular social significance. But now there are many illegitimate children here in England who were born abroad. It is only right and just that the mothers of those children should be able to take out proceedings against the fathers and that the fathers should be ordered to pay reasonable maintenance for their own children. Otherwise what is the position? The children will be left to the care of the state. The National

[8] (1849) 13 Q.B. 769.
[9] [1966] 2 Q.B. 695; [1966] 2 W.L.R. 1397; [1966] 2 All E.R. 593, C.A.; affirmed [1967] 3 W.L.R. 1491; [1967] 3 All E.R. 686, H.L.(E.)
[10] (1877) 2 P.D. 118, C.A.

Assistance Fund will have to pay—the father will get out of his just responsibilities.

EDMUND DAVIES L.J.: . . . However attractive the patina of old age, it ought not to be allowed to conceal clear mistakes, ancient though they were: see the observations of Viscount Simonds in *Public Trustee* v. *Inland Revenue Commissioners*.[11] In *Robinson Bros. (Brewers) Ltd.* v. *County of Durham Assessment Committee*,[12] the House of Lords overruled a decision which had stood for 40 years and which had regulated rating practice throughout that period because it found it erroneous in law and that its operation was unfair in placing an unjustifiable burden on the occupiers of other hereditaments. Lord Macmillan there pointed out [13] that previously cases even more venerable had been overruled. And only yesterday the House of Lords in *Conway* v. *Rimmer* [14] refused to follow one of its own decisions given a quarter of a century ago and which has undoubtedly controlled the course of countless cases decided in the courts during that period.

THE HOUSE OF LORDS

The House of Lords has the power to reverse any previous decision of a lower court and since 1966 has said it is prepared to reconsider any previous decision of its own. It has therefore much greater freedom than either the High Court or the Crown Court or the Court of Appeal. But though it is freer than they from the constraints of binding precedent, it is not as free as the legislature. When it makes or changes the law it must still do so according to the traditional modes, using the traditional arguments and the traditional justification for any departures it may make, and even for refusals to make new law. Though even here it is in a stronger position than the lower courts since at any given moment it is the final judge of where the line is to be drawn between the role of the courts in making and moulding law and the role of the legislature both as a matter of general principle and in particular cases. For it clearly has the final responsibility for deciding how far the courts should go in adapting the law to changing circumstances, needs and views. No legislature could find the time for doing all that is necessary in that respect, even though Parliament is now assisted as we shall see by the Law Commission, in the consideration and preparation of reforms of the law. But quite apart from the limitations imposed by legal technique on what the House of Lords can do, it must also be careful not to cross the line between what society for the time being, or in any particular case, regards as acceptable law-making by a small body of appointed lawyers, and what it insists should be left to Parliament. There are in other words constitutional limitations on what the court can and should do even though there is no written Constitution. This still leaves quite a large amount of discretion to the House of Lords and a good deal of scope for the defence and assertion of controversial values, though the court is never in the position which the Supreme Court of the United States sometimes finds itself in, of being the final arbiter of crucial constitutional issues. For one thing these kinds of issue rarely come before the

---

11 [1960] A.C. 398, 415; [1960] 2 W.L.R. 203; [1960] 1 All E.R. 1, H.L.
12 [1938] A.C. 321; [1938] 2 All E.R. 79.
13 [1938] A.C. 321, 340.
14 [1968] 2 W.L.R. 998.

court, and for another, any decision of the House of Lords can always be corrected by the passing of a statute by Parliament, which has unlimited powers and is not subject to any judicial limitation.

Although from a journeyman's point of view it is the Court of Appeal that plays a more immediate role in shaping the law and preserving uniformity among the lower courts, and keeping the legal rules and principles which come before it up to date, the ultimate character and quality of the law as a whole, and many of the values and assumptions which underlie it, are very much in the hands of the Law Lords. It is in their court that final decisions as to the appropriate blend between the need for stability and the need for change, the preservation and modification, where necessary, of the internal values of the law and the legal and judicial process, the acceptance or rejection of values pressing for recognition, the abandonment or retention of values no longer favoured and the line between proper judicial innovation and improper usurpation of the functions of a legislature have to be made. As its role involves not merely the correct use of logic but judgment and the persuasive use of legal reasoning, its decisions will often be open to serious criticism, especially in controversial areas. There will always be those who in particular cases and at the level of general principle will argue that it is too sluggish, too timid, too conservative; at the same time there will be those who contend that it has gone too far. Its tendency is to be a restraining influence, and to move slowly, because that is the tendency of the law itself. But much depends on the Law Lords themselves and the spirit of the times. The thirties for example seem to stand out as a time when the House of Lords was frequently innovating in an attempt to bring the law up to date without the assistance of the legislature.

After some hesitation in the nineteenth century, the House of Lords finally came down in 1898 with a firm statement that in the interests of certainty it would regard itself as bound by its own decisions. In the 1950s and the 1960s criticism of this restrictive approach to their own past decisions were made by some of the Law Lords. In *Nash (Inspector of Taxes)* v. *Tamplin and Sons Brewery Brighton Ltd.*,[15] for example, Lord Reid said that it was " very unsatisfactory to have to grope for [the *ratio* of] a decision in this way, but the need to do so arises from the fact that this House has debarred itself from ever reconsidering any of its own decisions. It matters not how difficult it is to find the *ratio decidendi* of a previous case, that *ratio* must be found. And it matters not how difficult it is to reconcile that *ratio* when found with statutory provisions or general principles: that *ratio* must be applied to any later case which is not reasonably distinguishable." In *Midland Silicones* v. *Scruttons* [16] he said that although he " would certainly not lightly disregard or depart from any *ratio decidendi* of this House . . . there are at least three classes of case where I think we are entitled to question or limit it: first, where it is obscure, secondly, where the decision itself is out of line with other authorities or established principles, and thirdly, where it is much wider than was necessary for the decision. . . ."

In 1965 Lord Gardiner, the Lord Chancellor, announced that in future the court would take a less restrictive view of their own powers and in parti-

---

15 [1952] A.C. 231.
16 [1962] A.C. 446.

cular cases would be prepared to consider modifying their own past decisions (below, p. 269).

Like the Court of Appeal, the House of Lords can overrule the decision of any lower court and put an end to its authority, but it will not do so if this will disappoint settled expectations. It has no power at the moment to warn that a case will not be followed in the future since the theory which underlies its power to overrule is that the overruled decision is and always was mistaken. It can however say that a particular decision may have to be reconsidered in the future and it can weaken the authority of a decision by casting doubt upon it without actually overruling it.

As with the Court of Appeal the Law Lords usually give separate judgments and there may be dissenting judgments. This may create uncertainty for the future, especially when the Law Lords give different reasons for their decision. At the same time it allows more flexibility than would be the case if only a single judgment were delivered. It is a phenomenon worth noticing in passing that because of the hierarchy of the courts it is possible for the law in a particular case to be finally settled by three Law Lords against the combined opposition of their two colleagues, three judges in the Court of Appeal and the trial judge.

Britain's entry into the European Economic Community has modified the position of the House of Lords in one respect. If a question of Community law arises before it, it is required to refer this to the European Court of Justice for its opinion before giving its own judgment.

London Street Tramways Co. v. London County Council
[1898] A.C. 375

Earl of Halsbury L.C.: . . . My Lords, it is totally impossible, as it appears to me, to disregard the whole current of authority upon this subject, and to suppose that what some people call an " extraordinary case," an " unusual case," a case somewhat different from the common, in the opinion of each litigant in turn, is sufficient to justify the rehearing and rearguing before the final Court of Appeal of a question which has already been decided. Of course I do not deny that cases of individual hardship may arise, and there may be a current of opinion in the profession that such and such a judgment was erroneous; but what is that occasional interference with what is perhaps abstract justice as compared with the inconvenience—the disastrous inconvenience—of having each question subject to being reargued and the dealings of mankind rendered doubtful by reason of different decisions, so that in truth and in fact there would be no real final Court of Appeal? My Lords, " interest rei publicae " that there should be " finis litium " at some time, and there could be no " finis litium " if it were possible to suggest in each case that it might be reargued, because it is " not an ordinary case " whatever that may mean. Under these circumstances I am of opinion that we ought not to allow this question to be reargued.
[Lords Macnaghten, Morris, and James of Hereford concurred.]

Myers v. Director of Public Prosecutions
House of Lords [1965] A.C. 1001

Lord Reid: . . . I have never taken a narrow view of the functions of this House as an appellate tribunal. The common law must be developed to meet changing economic conditions and habits of thought, and I would not be deterred by expressions of opinion in this House in old cases. But there are limits to what we can or should do. If we are to extend the law it must be by the development and application of fundamental principles. We cannot introduce arbitrary conditions or limitations: that must be left to legislation. And if we do in effect change the law, we ought in my opinion only to do that in cases where our decision will produce some finality or certainty. If we disregard technicalities in this case and seek to apply principle and common sense, there are a number of other parts of the existing law of hearsay susceptible of similar treatment, and we shall probably have a series of appeals in cases where the existing technical limitations produce an unjust result. If we are to give a wide interpretation to our judicial functions questions of policy cannot be wholly excluded, and it seems to me to be against public policy to produce uncertainty. The only satisfactory solution is by legislation following on a wide survey of the whole field, and I think that such a survey is overdue. A policy of make do and mend is no longer adequate. The most powerful argument of those who support the strict doctrine of precedent is that if it is relaxed judges will be tempted to encroach on the proper field of the legislature, and this case to my mind offers a strong temptation to do that which ought to be resisted.

Practice Direction (Judicial Precedent)
House of Lords [1966] 1 W.L.R. 1234

LORD GARDINER L.C.: Their Lordships regard the use of precedent as an indispensable foundation upon which to decide what is the law and its application to individual cases. It provides at least some degree of certainty upon which individuals can rely in the conduct of their affairs, as well as a basis for orderly development of legal rules.

Their Lordships nevertheless recognise that too rigid adherence to precedent may lead to injustice in a particular case and also unduly restrict the proper development of the law. They propose, therefore, to modify their present practice and, while treating former decisions of this House as normally binding, to depart from a previous decision when it appears right to do so.

In this connection they will bear in mind the danger of disturbing retrospectively the basis on which contracts, settlements of property and fiscal arrangement have been entered into and also the special need for certainty as to the criminal law.

This announcement is not intended to affect the use of precedent elsewhere than in this House.

R. v. National Insurance Commissioner, ex p. Hudson
House of Lords [1972] 2 W.L.R. 210

LORD REID [having quoted the Practice Direction, continued:] . . . My understanding of the position when this resolution was adopted was and is that there were a comparatively small number of reported decisions of this House which were generally thought to be impeding the proper development of the law or to have led to results which were unjust or contrary to public policy and that such decisions should be reconsidered as opportunities arose. But this practice was not to be used to weaken existing certainty in the law. The old view was that any departure from rigid adherence to precedent would weaken that certainty. I did not and do not accept that view. It is notorious that where an existing decision is disapproved but cannot be overruled courts tend to

distinguish it on inadequate grounds. I do not think that they act wrongly in
so doing: they are adopting the less bad of the only alternatives open to them.
But this is bound to lead to uncertainty for no one can say in advance whether in
a particular case the court will or will not feel bound to follow the old unsatisfactory decision. On balance it seems to me that overruling such a decision will
promote and not impair the certainty of the law.

But that certainty will be impaired unless this practice is used sparingly. I
would not seek to categorise cases in which it should or cases in which it should
not be used. As time passes experience will supply some guide. But I would
venture the opinion that the typical case for reconsidering an old decision is
where some broad issue is involved, and that it should only be in rare cases that
we should reconsider questions of construction of statutes or other documents.
In very many cases it cannot be said positively that one construction is right
and the other wrong. Construction so often depends on weighing one consideration against another. Much may depend on one's approach. If more attention
is paid to meticulous examination of the language used in the statute the result
may be different from that reached by paying more attention to the apparent
object of the statute so as to adopt that meaning of the words under consideration
which best accord with it.

Jacobs v. London County Council
House of Lords [1950] A.C. 361

LORD SIMONDS: . . . It is not . . . always easy to determine how far, when
several issues are raised in a case and a determination of any one of them is
decisive in favour of one or other of the parties, the observations upon other
issues are to be regarded as obiter. That is the inevitable result of our system.
For while it is the primary duty of a court of justice to dispense justice to litigants, it is its traditional role to do so by means of an exposition of the relevant
law. Clearly such a system must be somewhat flexible, with the result that in
some cases judges may be criticised for diverging into expositions which could
by no means be regarded as relevant to the dispute between the parties; in others
other critics may regret that an opportunity has been missed for making an
oracular pronouncement upon some legal problem which has long vexed the profession. But, however this may be, there is in my opinion no justification for
regarding as obiter dictum a reason given by a judge for his decision, because he
has given another reason also. If it were a proper test to ask whether the decision
would have been the same apart from the proposition alleged to be obiter, then a
case which *ex facie* decided two things would decide nothing. . . . The principle . . . is not always easy of application, particularly where the judgments of
an appellate court consisting of more than one judge have to be considered. An
illuminating discussion of the difficulties that may then arise will be found in
an article on *Ratio Decidendi* and *Obiter Dictum* in Appellate Courts by Professor Paton and G. Sawer in 63 *Law Quarterly Review* 461.

Midland Silicones Ltd. v. Scruttons Ltd.
[1962] A.C. 446

LORD REID: . . . It can hardly be denied that the *ratio decidendi* of the *Elder,
Dempster* decision is very obscure. A number of eminent judges have tried to
discover it, hardly any two have reached the same result, and none of the
explanations hitherto given seems to me very convincing. If I had to try, the
result might depend on whether or not I was trying to obtain a narrow *ratio*.

Codification

Codification of the Law of Contract, A. L. Diamond
(1968) 31 M.L.R. 361

Various reasons have been given over the years why codification is desirable. The case for codification in England at this time rests on the following arguments.

1. *Accessibility of the law to the legal profession*

On several occasions [17] Lord Gardiner has stressed the inaccessibility of the law: over 3,000 separate Acts of Parliament, dating from about 1235, contained in 359 different volumes [18]; ninety-nine volumes of subordinate legislation; and well over 350,000 reported cases. . . .

The Lord Chancellor may be right in believing that this is the real case for codification, though it is important not to get carried away by the practical difficulties of the common law. One must not think that the mass of reports and statutes is all that daunting to the practitioner, whatever the effect it may have on the student.

The truth is that there are many practitioners who rarely open a law report more than two years old. Apart from keeping up to date with the latest *Weekly Law Reports* or *All England Law Reports* they will rely for their law on Halsbury's *Laws of England* (forty-two volumes, including index volumes, and a two-volume cumulative supplement), specialist textbooks and books of precedent forms and Halsbury's *Statutes* (forty-seven volumes up to and including the loose-leaf volume for 1967, and two volumes of supplement). Probably they will also take *Current Law* and one or more journals.

Even for those lawyers who do refer to case reports in their daily practice, the figure of 350,000 cases gives a false impression. It must be remembered that a substantial number of those cases have been superseded by later developments in case-law or statutes. For example, a glance at the reports of the nineteenth century will reveal masses of " settlement " cases, where two parishes each claimed that a pauper was settled in the other, and so the responsibility of that other parish for the purposes of the Poor Law. . . .

Nevertheless, the statistics suggest, and common sense tells us, that a code does make the law more accessible than the uncodified common law. . . .

2. *Accessibility of the law to the public*

If a code makes the law more easily accessible to the legal profession, it thereby makes the law accessible to the public. Take the example of delivery by instalments which has just been discussed. The 1890 solicitor would very likely not bother to explain to his client the tortuous processes as a result of which he came to his conclusion. If he had gone to counsel, he might, however, produce a copy of counsel's opinion to his client to confirm the client's impression that the law is a maze into which only the initiated may enter—and that even they would not be very sure whether they would get out again. The 1967 solicitor, by contrast, need have no hesitation. He can produce the Sale of Goods Act to his client and let him read section 31 for himself. The law is accessible to the public in the sense that a lawyer can readily advise his client and, if he wishes, explain the working of the law too.

---

[17] *Law Reform NOW* (1963), Chap. 1; H.L.Deb., Vol. 258, col. 1079 *et seq.* (June 11, 1964); *Proposals for English and Scottish Law Commissions* (1965), Cmnd. 2573; H.L.Deb., Vol. 264, col. 1142 (April 1, 1965).

[18] That was in 1965. Perhaps it should now be 361.

But one suspects that the Lord Chancellor meant something more than that when he wrote in his White Paper that one of the hallmarks of an advanced society is that its laws should be readily accessible to all who are affected by them,[19] for he added that " it is extremely difficult for anyone without special training to discover what the law is on any given topic." [20] Presumably, then, one function of codification is to open the law to the masses: to make it personally available to the person Llewellyn described as the law-consumer. . . .

3. *Improvement of the law*

The real case for codification, I believe, is that it facilitates law reform. We can improve the content of the law when we create the new code; and we can improve it later by revising the code.

There are two kinds of codes. One merely seeks to reproduce the existing law, to translate case-law into statute-law without radical change; the other aims to produce a new set of principles, as the Uniform Commercial Code does. The Law Commission intend the new contract code to be of this second kind: " The intention is to reform as well as to codify." [21]

This differs from our previous experiments in codification. . . .

There are other improvements that may flow from codification. In the field of foreign affairs, it will no doubt be easier to explain our law to our continental partners, whether in EFTA or in the Common Market, and the Law Commission have been " mindful of the importance of achieving harmonisation with continental systems," [22] as well as setting out to draft a code common to England and Scotland.

And one cannot overlook the possible effect on lawyers themselves. As Austin puts it: " If the law were more simple and scientific, minds of a higher order would enter into the profession. . . .[23]

Difficulties of Codification

Commendable as these objectives are, it would be foolish to ignore the difficulties that lie in the way of successful codification. These centre on the problems of statutory interpretation and the limitations of draftsmanship.

(a) *Judicial conservatism*

A code is intended to replace the earlier common law. How can one ensure that the judges, brought up on the common law and familiar with it, will wipe out their knowledge of the cases from their memories and concentrate on the statutory words? This has been a very real problem that has not always been successfully dealt with. . . .

The truth is that it is very difficult to prevent judges from applying the law they know, and have learnt to love, instead of the new and strange statute.

The real difficulty is in envisaging a completely self-contained code. According to the Law Commission: " The object of a code is, in our understanding, to set out the essential principles which are to govern a given branch of the law."

---

[19] Cmnd. 2573 (1965), p. 2.

[20] *Ibid*.

[21] The Law Commission, First Annual Report, 1965–66 (Law Com. No. 4), para. 31. Gardiner and Martin envisaged that reform must precede codification and that accordingly codification could not have a high priority: *Law Reform NOW*, pp. 12, 13.

[22] The Law Commission, Second Annual Report, 1966–67 (Law Com. No. 12), para. 29.

[23] John Austin, *Lectures on Jurisprudence, or the Philosophy of Positive Law* (3rd ed., 1869), Vol. II, Lecture 39, p. 703.

A court, they go on, " is expected to discover in the code the principles from which the answer to a particular problem can be worked out." [24]

This is certainly the theory of continental codes, but it would be a radical departure for a common law code. . . .

The existing English " codes " have not wiped out the old law. In Chalmers' *Sale of Goods Act* nearly half of the cases cited [25] still date from before the Act, and even in the more modern narrative works [26] as many as 20 per cent. of the cases are from before the Act.

(b) *Professional prejudice*

. . . There are still people who distrust a code because it is impossible to foresee everything: but one seldom hears the common law criticised because only things that have already happened come before the courts. The notion of the completeness of the common law is today universally acknowledged to be a legal fiction, but its habits of thought remain.

(c) *The problem of drafting*

David Dudley Field saw clearly the problem: " There should be neither a generalisation too vague nor a particularity too minute, in the Code. . . ." [27]

. . . The Statute Book is littered with phrases that have become battle-grounds—" arising out of and in the course of the employment," [28] " absolutely void," [29] " debt, default or miscarriage of another person." [30] This problem of fixing the right level of abstraction is really: how much discretion should be left to the judge? Some of the difficulties arising from existing codes such as the Sale of Goods Act are due to excessive detail caused by Chalmers' attempt to codify the existing, but still developing, law. What started as the germ of a judicial idea, which might have been distinguished or overruled, became statute-law, binding on all courts including the House of Lords. . . .

With a full-time Law Commission to keep an eye on the code once it has been passed, amending legislation may be quicker and more frequent in the future. But the question arises: must we depend on legislation, or can the common lawyers devise a code which is both precise and flexible?

(d) *Restriction on legal development*

The most telling objection to a code in a common law jurisdiction is that it limits the development of the law. The common law grows and changes. Statute-law is static until it is changed by the legislature. . . . [C]ourts do not see it as their function to mould statute-law or to adapt it to our changing society.

Part of the problem lies in the lawyer's approach to an Act of Parliament. He does not see it as a creative force in the formation of new law, but rather as an interference with the " natural " development of the law by the judges. Hence the notion that Acts of Parliament must be strictly construed and the extraordinary presumption that a statute leaves the common law unchanged. Lawyers do not argue by analogy from statutes as they do from judgments, and many would think it wrong to do so. . . .

---

[24] The Law Commission and the Scottish Law Commission: Published Working Paper on The Interpretation of Statutes, 1967, p. 45.

[25] 15th ed., M. Mark, 1967: 747 cases out of 1610 (46·4 per cent.).

[26] Atiyah, *The Sale of Goods*, 3rd ed., 1966; Fridman, *Sale of Goods*, 1966.

[27] *First Report of the Commissioners of the Code to the New York Legislature*, 1858, cited Honnold, *The Life of the Law*, at p. 109.

[28] Workmen's Compensation Act 1897, s. 1.

[29] Infants' Relief Act 1874, s. 1.

[30] Statute of Frauds 1677, s. 4.

If we could devise a way to stimulate the judicial mind, to distinguish between statutes laying down limited solutions to limited problems and those containing in them more widely applicable truths, progress might be made. The process is not entirely unknown to judges, at least in the Divorce Division if not in the Queen's Bench. Statutes dealing with the divorce jurisdiction of our own courts have led the judges, in *Travers* v. *Holley* [31] and *Indyka* v. *Indyka*,[32] to create new law about our recognition of the jurisdiction of foreign courts. In this way legislation has acted as a source of ideas, rather like a common law analogy.

LAW REFORM

A Law Revision Committee was established on January 10, 1934, " to consider how far, having regard to the statute law and judicial decisions, such legal maxims and doctrines as the Lord Chancellor may from time to time refer to the committee require revision in modern conditions." The first chairman was Lord Hanworth M.R. From 1935 to 1939 its chairman was Lord Wright. It issued eight reports:

1st interim	March	1934, The effect of death on civil liability, Cmd. 4540.
2nd		1934, Recovery of interest in civil proceedings, Cmd. 4546.
3rd	July	1934, Recovery between joint tortfeasors, Cmd. 4637.
4th		1934, Liability of husbands for the torts of their wives, Cmd. 4770.
5th		1936, Statute of limitations, Cmd. 5334.
6th		1937, The statute of frauds and the doctrine of consideration in contract, Cmd. 5449.
7th		1939, The rule in *Chandler* v. *Webster*, Cmd. 6009.
8th		1939, Contributory negligence, Cmd. 6032.

In 1952 it was replaced by the Law Reform Committee which was appointed " to consider, having regard especially to judicial decisions, what changes are desirable in such legal doctrines as the Lord Chancellor may from time to time refer to the committee." By June 1972 it had published eighteen reports:

1st	March	1953, Statute of Frauds and Section 4 of the Sale of Goods Act 1893, Cmd. 8809.
2nd	April	1954, Innkeepers' Liability for Property of Travellers, Guests and Residents, Cmd. 9161.
3rd	October	1954, Occupiers' Liability to Invitees, Licensees and Trespassers, Cmd. 9305.
4th	October	1956, Rule against Perpetuities, Cmnd. 18.
5th	January	1957, Conditions and Exceptions in Insurance Policies, Cmnd. 62.

---

[31] [1953] P. 246, C.A.
[32] [1966] 3 All E.R. 583, C.A. The House of Lords decision ([1967] 2 All E.R. 689) was not based on a statutory analogy.

6th		November 1957, Court's Power to Sanction Variation of Trusts, Cmnd. 310.
7th	July	1958, Effect of Tax Liability on Damages, Cmnd. 501.
8th		December 1958, Sealing of Contracts made by Bodies Corporate, Cmnd. 622.
9th		December 1960, Liability in Tort between Husband and Wife, Cmnd. 1268.
10th	June	1962, Innocent Misrepresentation, Cmnd. 1782.
11th	April	1963, Loss of Services, etc., Cmnd. 2017.
12th	March	1966, Transfer of Title to Chattels, Cmnd. 2958.
13th	April	1966, Hearsay Evidence in Civil Proceedings, Cmnd. 2964.
14th		September 1966, Acquisition of Easement and Profits by Prescription, Cmnd. 3100.
15th		September 1967, The Rule in *Hollington* v. *Hewthorn*, Cmnd. 3321.
16th		December 1967, Privilege in Civil Proceedings, Cmnd. 3472.
17th	October	1970, Evidence of Opinion and Expert Evidence, Cmnd. 4489.
18th		September 1971, Conversion and Detinue, Cmnd. 4774.

A Criminal Law Revision Committee was set up in 1959 " to be a standing committee . . . to examine such aspects of the criminal law of England and Wales as the Home Secretary may from time to time refer to the committee, to consider whether the law requires revision and to make recommendation." By June 1972 it had published eleven reports.

1st	1959, Indecency with children, Cmnd. 835.
2nd	1960, Suicide, Cmnd. 1187.
3rd	1963, Criminal procedure (insanity), Cmnd. 2149.
4th	1963, Order of closing speeches, Cmnd. 2148.
5th	1964, Criminal procedure (jurors), Cmnd. 2349.
6th	1964, Perjury and attendance of witnesses, Cmnd. 2465.
7th	1965, Felonies and misdemeanours, Cmnd. 2659.
8th	1966, Theft and related offences, Cmnd. 2977.
9th	1966, Evidence (Written statements, formal admissions and notices of alibi), Cmnd. 3145.
10th	1968, Secrecy of jury room, Cmnd. 3750.
11th	1972, Evidence (General), Cmnd. 4991.

In 1965 two Law Commissions were set up, one for England and Wales and one for Scotland. Section 3 of the Law Commission Act 1965 provides:

(1) It shall be the duty of each of the Commissions to take and keep under review all the law with which they are respectively concerned with a view to its systematic development and reform, including in

particular the codification of such law, the elimination of anomalies, the repeal of obsolete and unnecessary enactments, the reduction of the number of separate enactments and generally the simplification and modernisation of the law, and for that purpose—

(*a*) to receive and consider any proposals for the reform of the law which may be made or referred to them;

(*b*) to prepare and submit to the Minister from time to time programmes for the examination of different branches of the law with a view to reform, including recommendations as to the agency (whether the Commission or another body) by which any such examination should be carried out;

(*c*) to undertake, pursuant to any such recommendations approved by the Minister, the examination of particular branches of the law and the formulation, by means of draft Bills or otherwise, of proposals for reform therein;

(*d*) to prepare from time to time at the request of the Minister comprehensive programmes of consolidation and statute law revision, and to undertake the preparation of draft Bills pursuant to any such programme approved by the Minister;

(*e*) to provide advice and information to government departments and other authorities or bodies concerned at the instance of the Government with proposals for the reform or amendment of any branch of the law;

(*f*) to obtain such information as to the legal systems of other countries as appears to the Commissioners likely to facilitate the performance of any of their functions.

(2) The Minister shall lay before Parliament any programmes prepared by the Commission and approved by him and any proposals for reform formulated by the Commission pursuant to such programmes.

(3) Each of the Commissions shall make an annual report to the Minister on their proceedings, and the Minister shall lay the report before Parliament with such comments (if any) as he thinks fit.

[A list of its reports will be found in its Annual Reports.]

LAW REPORTS

The earliest law reports are known as the Yearbooks. They run from the reign of Edward I to that of Henry VIII. They were collected together in the sixteenth century but more recently they have been published in a series known as the Rolls Series, and new editions of them are being published by the Selden Society. They are now only of historical interest. At first they were little more than professional magazines containing all kinds of information that might be interesting to practising lawyers, anecdotes and repartee as well as clever arguments, discussions in moots in the Inns mixed up with real cases. Often the decisions are not recorded, because in the early days professional interest centred on pleading and argument. Late in the fourteenth century they assumed a more professional form which has led historians to believe that official editors had been appointed. Long before they ceased to be published lawyers had come to find them too complicated to use and relied instead on abridgments, for example, Fitzherbert's (1516) and Brooke's (1568).

After Coke had published his reports and commentaries at the beginning of the seventeenth century, lawyers were on the whole content to take what he said as summing up what was useful in them for current purposes. By this time new reports were already appearing, compiled by such men as Plowden and Coke himself. They were not necessarily continuous and did not cover all the courts. They were not contemporaneous and the cases had not necessarily been heard by those who were reporting them. They made no pretence to verbal accuracy and some made no claim to substantive accuracy. Coke's aim for example was to state the principles of the law as they arose in litigation and he set out the law as he thought it should be as well as the law as it had been decided. The standard and style of reporting that is current today has grown *pari passu* with the doctrine of precedent which prevails today. In the early days when there was no such doctrine there was no incentive to compile accurate and continuous records of decisions and reasons for them. Lawyers developed the habit of referring to past cases, often from memory but more to illustrate a principle or the fact that a principle had found favour with a particular judge than as a compelling stepping stone in an argument as a relevant case would be today. Many of the early reports were compiled for private use. Many were of poor quality and severely criticised by later judges.

Reports in the modern style, with facts, counsel's argument and the decision carefully set out, are usually said to date from the reports of Burrows in the eighteenth century, and continuous and prompt reporting from the Term Reports at the end of that century. It is from that period too that the notion of an authoritative report appeared, and judges began to revise what they had said before it was published. There had often been in the past complaints about the quality of particular reports and one way of avoiding this, it was hoped, was to nominate particular reports as authoritative in preference to all others. This practice prevailed in the first three decades of the nineteenth century. Unfortunately, monopoly brought with it a decline in quality and in speed of publication and a much wider range of reports was permitted and appeared in the 1830s and the 1840s, for example, the *Law Journal* (1832), the *Jurist* (1837), the *Law Times* (1843), the *Weekly Reporter* (1852) and the *New Reports* (1862). This however gave rise to a new problem. It was expensive for a professional lawyer to buy all the reports and at the same time the reports themselves were not always consistent. Dissatisfaction led to a demand for a return to something more official, a demand that was eventually met by the establishment in 1864 of the (since 1870, Incorporated) Council of Law Reporting, which was given the task of producing a comprehensive set of reports covering the major courts. The Council consists of the law officers of the Crown and representatives of the Inns and the Law Society. The general rule is that any report of a case can be cited in court if a barrister will vouch for its accuracy but the " Official Law Reports " have become the hard core of English Law Reports. Other private enterprise publications continued such as the *Law Times Reports*, the *Law Journal Reports*, the *Times Law Reports* and the *All England Reports* but only these last remain. The

Times Law Reports ceased in 1952. The *Law Times Reports* merged with the *All England Reports* in 1948 and the *Law Journal Reports* in 1950. The Official Law Reports are published in four series:

(1) Appeal Cases, cited [1972] A.C. 1, covering cases heard by the House of Lords and the Privy Council;

(2) Cases in the Queen's Bench Division, the Divisional Court, the Crown Court, the Court of Appeal on appeal from the Queen's Bench Division, and the Court of Appeal (Criminal Division), cited [1972] 1 Q.B. 1;

(3) Cases in the Chancery Division and in the Court of Appeal on appeal from the Chancery Division, cited [1972] Ch. 1;

(4) Cases in the Family Division and cases in the Court of Appeal on appeal from that division, cited [1972] Fam. Until 1971 this series contained the cases heard in the Probate, Divorce and Admiralty Division and those heard on appeal from it and were cited [1971] P. 1.

Since 1953 the Incorporated Society has published another series which aims at getting the reports out more quickly, entitled the *Weekly Law Reports*. Volumes 2 and 3 in the series contain cases which will later appear in the regular series. They are cited [1972] 1 W.L.R. 1. Cases in the Court of Appeal (Criminal Division) are also published in a separate series, cited (1972) 56 Cr.App.R. 1. The leading private series is that published by Messrs. Butterworths, the *All England Reports*, cited [1972] 1 All E.R. 1. Although the series did not begin until 1936 a selection of decisions from earlier cases has been published retrospectively in groups of years. There is also a large number of specialist reports.

CHAPTER 5

PRE-TRIAL PROCEEDINGS

INTRODUCTION

The administration of justice can be broadly divided into two spheres, the criminal and civil, each of which raises slightly different problems for a legal system. The primary purpose of the criminal law is to give notice as to the conduct which is regarded as criminal and will therefore expose those who break its rules to punishment. The criminal process involves the detection of offences against the criminal law, the identification and apprehension of the offender, and at the end of its first stage a decision whether or not to prosecute him. If a prosecution is decided upon there must be a trial. This in turn involves a decision as to the offence with which the accused is to be charged, the collection of evidence and the proof of the facts which constitute the offence, the resolution of any disputed questions of law and finally a decision as to what is to be done with a convicted offender. The civil law plays a much greater variety of roles. One of its primary purposes is often simply to give notice as to what is to be done if a particular legal result is to be achieved, what is to be done if one wants to leave property by will, make a valid contract, set up a company with limited liability, contract a valid marriage. In other cases it plays a role more like that of the criminal law and says what may happen in particular circumstances and sets out the cases in which it is prepared to offer some kind of remedy, in rather the same way in which the criminal law sets out the circumstances in which it will authorise the imposition of punishment. If someone breaks a contract, for example, the other party may sue him for compensation; so, too, if someone negligently causes damage to another person, or defames him, or prosecutes him maliciously. The civil process then involves the collection of facts and a decision as to whether and if so what cause of action has arisen and the preparation of the case for trial. The trial will again involve the proof of relevant facts, the determination of disputed points of law and finally a consideration of the remedy and if the remedy is damages, the amount. These are the bare bones of the system with which the next few chapters are concerned.

At page 242 above, mention was made of the way in which the legal system may sometimes distort issues by the way it classifies facts and people. It is worth saying something more on that theme at this point, since much of what follows in the next chapters may contribute to such distortion as may occur in any particular case, and talking about this problem will throw light on some of the peculiarities which distinguish the way in which the legal system, and especially the English legal system goes about tackling a problem, compared with the way in which other methods of solving disputes and other legal systems go about it.

From one point of view much of the legal system can be seen as a series of filters through which facts, problems and disputes are passed before being finally processed by a judge giving judgment upon them. The judgment is not necessarily the end of the process. There still may be a question of enforcing it, just as in the criminal field there is the necessity of undergoing the treatment imposed. Nonetheless, the judgment is one of the high points in the process. It shapes much of what goes on before it is given, because much of what goes on before it is simply a preparation for it or an attempt to secure it. And though it does not guarantee satisfaction, it forms the essential authority for claiming it in civil cases, just as in criminal cases it forms the formal justification for the treatment subsequently administered.

The filtering element is most easily seen in the civil area where it plays a larger role, though it is present in the criminal as well. It can be seen operating most clearly at the point when a layman decides to ask for legal advice. From the moment a client begins to talk to a solicitor about his problems the sifting process begins to operate. Every trained lawyer approaches any problem with some very general notions of the kinds of thing which the law regards as relevant and what it does not, and the details which are irrelevant according to this criterion are discarded as soon as they are heard. He will also be aware of some of the general categories into which the law is divided and will be making tentative assumptions about what area of law is involved. Within that area legal rules will provide more detailed criteria of what is relevant and what is not, by detailing the kinds of circumstance in which a remedy is available, and setting out any necessary factual conditions which have to be fulfilled before a remedy can be claimed. Finally he will arrive at what for him are the legally relevant details which form the legal problem on which he is being asked to advise. By that time, it is the details of the legal rules which are uppermost in his mind and the main question is how the facts, as described to him, fit into them. All extraneous matters, either in the facts of the story told him or in the nature of the problem or complaint as the layman sees or feels it, will be forgotten. If legal advice is all that the layman wants this may be the end of the matter. If litigation is contemplated then the lawyer must go further, and a further set of filters comes into play.

If the solicitor decides that his client has a good case in law the next problem is how to translate that case into a remedy. Here there will be questions of the proper procedure to be followed, the correct way of framing and pleading the claim. Even more important will be the establishment of his client's version of the relevant facts in the light of the rules of evidence laid down by English law. At each point the relevant rules may well place a quite different emphasis on what is essential and important, and what is not, from that which the layman left to himself would have done, as his complaint is squeezed through the various meshes through which any claim must pass if it is to end up being acknowledged by a judge as justifying a remedy. We take up this question again when we come to examine procedure and pleading in civil cases at p. 338.

In some ways there is less distortion of the original situation or problem as it gets processed on its way to judgment in criminal cases, though here too just as the civil law divides up the world of facts into causes of action, so the criminal law divides it up into offences, and there are still the filters of the procedural forms and the rules of evidence to be gone through before the case is ready for judgment. The definition of criminal offences however, in general, bear a much closer relationship to what a layman would see as the problem to be dealt with than many definitions of causes of action. The gap between the problem as he sees it and the remedy which he may think ought to be applied is opened up more by other factors. One which may arise very early in the process is the failure of the police to detect, identify or apprehend the offender or to prosecute him when he has been found. This is the problem of police discretion (see below, p. 313). Another is the relative freedom the police have in deciding the offence with which they will charge the accused. Criminal factual situations often give rise to more than one criminal offence, some less serious than others. The police may take a different view of the seriousness of the case from the layman, or for reasons of pure convenience, such as the desire to get the case over and done with, may choose to go ahead with a summary offence rather than pursue the longer drawn out process of a trial on indictment. This is the area where what is called " plea-bargaining " may take place, in which the accused may agree to plead guilty to the minor offence in return for the police not proceeding with a more serious charge.

In the criminal field it is more likely that the rules of evidence will play a larger part in distorting the layman's notion of what ought to happen than other aspects of the legal system's way of handling the problem. This is because great emphasis is placed in the criminal process on the method by which an offence is proved, and the method is surrounded by numerous safeguards to secure a fair trial. These operate as a limitation on what the prosecution can do to translate the conviction of the police that the accused is guilty, to an acceptance of this fact by the judge and jury. One example is the rule that in general an accused's previous record is irrelevant. More is said about this when we deal with some of the rules of evidence. First then, the preparation of a criminal case, and in particular the role of the police. Then the preparation of civil cases with particular emphasis on procedure and pleading.

Pre-trial Proceedings in Criminal Cases

In criminal cases it is the police for the most part who are responsible for collecting information, interviewing witnesses, arranging for medical and scientific examinations, identifying and questioning suspects and finally deciding whether to charge and prosecute them. Their powers, and the limits upon them are of crucial importance, since they come at one of the points at which a balance has to be struck between the need to deter and apprehend criminals and to prevent and detect criminal offences, and the desire to allow innocent people the greatest freedom to live their lives without interference from representatives of the state. Different systems draw the line at different points and even the English system has changed the line from time to time.

Powers of arrest and examination of suspects

A policeman may ask questions of anyone whom he thinks may be able to help, but there is in general no obligation to answer. He may ask anyone to attend a police station to assist the police with their inquiries, but there is no legal obligation to attend or stay, unless the police have the power and are prepared to arrest him. Arrest may be with or without a warrant. There is a general power under the Criminal Law Act 1967 to arrest without a warrant anyone whom a police officer suspects, with reasonable cause, to have committed or to be about to commit any arrestable offence, *i.e.* one for which the sentence is fixed by law or which carries a possible sentence of five years or more. In addition a number of particular statutes give a similar power in relation to specific offences. (This is apart from a general power to take such action as is reasonably necessary to prevent a breach of the peace, which can include detaining a person but still would not impose on the person detained an obligation to answer questions.[1]) Otherwise the police must obtain a warrant from a magistrate in accordance with section 1 of the Magistrates' Courts Act 1952. The police have in general no power to detain a person for questioning, short of arresting him. In *Kenlin* v. *Gardiner*[2] for example, the court held that two boys were justified in resisting detention by plain clothes policemen who wanted to ask them what they were doing. The boys said that they thought the policemen were thugs attacking them. On the other hand in *Donnelly* v. *Jackman*[3] it was held that the accused had gone too far when he assaulted a policeman who had tapped him on the shoulder to tell him he wanted a word with him. Talbot J. said " [I]t is not every trivial interference with a citizen's liberty that amounts to a course of conduct sufficient to take the officer out of the course of his duties [and therefore justify retaliation]." There are however some exceptions to the general rule that the police in the course of investigation have no power to detain short of arrest. The Metropolitan Police have long had a " stop and search " power under the Metropolitan Police Act 1839, and the Misuse of Drugs Act 1971 (below, p. 293) gives all police a similar power. The Road Safety Act 1967 (below p. 304), authorises the administration of a breath test in certain circumstances.

Particularly stringent rules have been laid down by the judges in relation to the examination of suspects. There is a general common law rule that no confession may be admitted as evidence against an accused person unless it can be shown to be voluntary in the sense that it was not made in response to a promise or a threat held out by a person in authority. In *R.* v. *Northam*[4] for example, a confession was rejected by the court because it had been made in return for a promise that all the offences of which the accused was suspected including those to which he was confessing would be dealt with at one trial, though it seems that the confession would have been accepted provided a different police officer had made the agreement. It also seems though that, so far as English law is concerned, evidence obtained as a result of an inadmissible confession, *e.g.* stolen property discovered in the place where the accused had confessed he had hidden it is admissible, even though the confession is not, *R.* v. *Warickshall*.[5]

Quite apart from the rule about confessions the judges themselves have added further rules for the guidance of police officers as part of their general

---

[1] *Duncan* v. *Jones* [1936] 1 K.B. 218.
[2] [1967] 2 Q.B. 510.
[3] [1970] 1 All E.R. 987.
[4] (1967) 52 Cr.App.R. 97.
[5] (1783) 1 Leach C.C. 263.

control over the kind of evidence that they will admit against an accused person in a criminal trial. These are set out in the Judges' Rules (below, p. 288). They require the police to warn a suspect, if they have reasonable grounds for believing that he is guilty of an offence, that he need not answer any questions, and to give a further warning when they have decided to charge him. After charging a suspect they may not put further questions except to clear up statements already made. The actual examination may not be continued. All these rules are intended to deter the police from using what is regarded as improper pressure to obtain a confession. The line between what should be permitted and what restrictions should be imposed upon the police in their examination of suspects is always a difficult one to draw and there have been strong criticisms of the present restrictions from the police, which have received some judicial support. In *R.* v. *Northam* (*supra*) for example, Winn L.J. said:

> In these days it really does seem that the undoubtedly well-established doctrines of our law that persons who are minded to make a confession or admission to the police or other authorities must be very strictly safeguarded against any persuasion or inducement to make any such confession or admission is in some respects somewhat out of date. . . . The criminal classes are only too aware of their position of virtual immunity in the hands of the police. It does seem that some of the present doctrines and principles have come down in our law from earlier times when the police of this country were not to be trusted, as they are now to be trusted in almost every single case, to behave with complete fairness towards those who come into their hands or from whom they are seeking information.

The caution however at the moment is simply a strengthening of the general privilege that an accused has to remain silent throughout the whole period from his first contact with the police to the end of his trial, at which he need not go into the witness box at all if he does not wish to, a fact on which the prosecution is forbidden to comment. Even the judge may not comment on the failure of the accused to make a statement to the police.

Besides the rules of law as to confessions and the rules of practice as to cautions, the judges have also said that they will not necessarily admit evidence obtained as a result of a trick, though this in fact depends upon the nature of the deception and the circumstances of the case. To ask a man to write some words on a piece of paper to see if they corresponded in spelling with some writing found at the scene of the crime was held not to be a deception in *R.* v. *Voisin*,[6] even though he was not cautioned, and the same conclusion was reached in relation to the taking of fingerprints in *Callis* v. *Gunn* (below, p. 289). Evidence of a conversation overheard in prison cells was admitted in *R.* v. *Mills.*[7] Evidence obtained by pretending to be a participant in an offence may also be admitted, but here the police have to be careful not to cross the line between legitimate activity and the acts of an agent provocateur (below, p. 290).

[6] [1918] 1 K.B. 531.
[7] [1962] 3 All E.R. 298.

The Criminal Law Revision Committee

Since the above passages setting out the current position were written, the Criminal Law Revision Committee in its Eleventh Report on Evidence (General) [8] has been published. In many ways it follows up the remarks of Winn L.J. quoted above, and in particular it proposes to make some serious inroads into the so-called right to silence, as well as making recommendations on such matters as the necessity of giving a caution, and the admissibility of confessions and other statements made by the accused before the trial. The recommendations dealing with evidence in general are discussed below, at p. 371. The main proposal of the Committee in this connection is that although it should not be made an offence to remain silent during a police interrogation, or on being charged, nonetheless, if the accused has failed when being interrogated or charged to mention a fact which he afterwards relies on either at the committal proceedings or the trial, then the court or jury may draw an adverse inference from his failure to say anything. This means in effect that the court or jury may in appropriate circumstances assume that he had something to hide. They also proposed that in appropriate circumstances silence might even amount to corroboration (for corroboration generally, see below, pp. 376–378). It followed from these recommendations that the cautions in the form required by the Judges' Rules (below, p. 288), which include a statement that the person being cautioned need not make a statement, should also be abandoned. Instead an accused should simply be given a written warning at the time he is charged or officially informed that he may be prosecuted to the effect that if there is any fact on which he intends to rely at this trial, then it would be better to state it there and then. Otherwise the statement would be less likely to be believed if it was first made at the trial. The committee rejected a suggestion that, by way of protection for accused persons, provision should be made in future for interrogation in the presence of a magistrate. They also rejected a suggestion that tape recorders should be used during interrogations by the police. Instead the majority recommended that the use of tape recorders should be tried on an experimental basis in some police stations.

The clear aim of these proposals was to remove some of the existing privileges enjoyed by accused persons and to give the police greater help in obtaining statements which would assist them in their investigations and the actual prosecution, and in addition to allow silence to count against an accused person at his trial. The Committee noted at paragraph 31:

> Some lawyers seem to think that it is somehow wrong in principle that a criminal should be under any kind of pressure to reveal his case before his trial. The reason seems to be that it is thought to be repugnant—or, perhaps rather, " unfair "—that a person should be obliged to choose between telling a lie and incriminating himself. Whatever the reason, this is a matter of opinion and we disagree.

The Committee also made recommendations about the admissibility of confessions with the aim both of simplifying the existing law, by putting it into statutory form, and of putting less emphasis on the existence of a threat

[8] Cmnd. 4991.

or inducement where that was the ground for rejecting the confession and more on the ground that a threat or some inducement was made of a kind likely, in the circumstances existing at the time, to render the confession unreliable. In effect they proposed the separation of the two grounds usually put forward for rejecting involuntary confessions and admissions, namely, the discouragement of the use of oppressive methods of interrogation, and the fact that confessions obtained as a result of threats or inducements may well be false. If a confession is challenged, therefore, the prosecution must in the view of the Committee show both that it was not obtained by oppressive treatment of the accused, or as a result of threats or inducements, but in the latter case only if they were such as were likely to make the confession unreliable. Under the existing law the confession would be rejected if it had been obtained as a result of threats or inducements whether or not these were of a kind likely to make it unreliable.

Discussion and debate of the Committee's proposals, the policy underlying them and their implications will be taking place while this book is going through the press. If by then any of the proposals have been enacted, it will be necessary to monitor the effect of the changes, in particular in relation to changes in police practice, since this is an area where only constant attention to what is actually happening in fact can yield understanding of the issues and values at stake and their preservation.

Interception of communications

The police, customs and excise officers and members of the security services may intercept letters and tap telephones, but only on the authority of a warrant issued by the Secretary of State. A committee of Privy Councillors appointed to consider the subject in 1957 recommended [9] that the police should only be given a warrant where the offence was really serious, where normal methods of investigation had been tried and failed or from the nature of things would be unlikely to succeed, and where there was good reason to think that an interception would result in a conviction. The security services should only be authorised to make interceptions where there was a major subversive or espionage activity that was likely to injure the national interest and the material likely to be obtained would be of direct use in compiling the information that was necessary to enable the security services to carry out their functions.

Search

So far as search of the person is concerned, the Advisory Committee on Drug Dependence in its report on powers of arrest and search in 1970 noted (para. 24):

> There is no general statutory right to search, but the right to do so under certain circumstances is recognised both by common law and by statute. The right of searching persons *in custody* must depend on the circumstances of each particular case. Whatever may be the nature of the charge, a prisoner may be searched who has so conducted himself by reason of violence of language or conduct as to render it prudent and right to do so as well for his own protection as for the constable's. In

[9] Cmnd. 283, 1956–57.

other cases a prisoner may be searched, where it is likely that there are on him (1) stolen articles, or (2) any instruments of violence, or (3) any tools connected with the kind of crime he is alleged to have committed, or (4) other similar articles which may be useful in evidence against him or (5) any documents which may be evidence either for the prosecution or in favour of the prisoner. . . .

The Royal Commission on police powers and procedure [10] had also accepted the practice of search on arrest though they agreed there was little express authority to be found to support it. As was mentioned above the Metropolitan police also have the power to " stop and search " under the Metropolitan Police Act 1839 (as have some other forces under local statutes) (below, p. 294), without arresting the suspect. The police have similar powers under the Misuse of Drugs Act 1971 and the Firearms Act 1965. There are also powers of search under the Customs and Excise Act 1952. The stop and search power was the subject of consideration by the Advisory Committee on Drug Dependence in 1970 (below, p. 293) with particular reference to the factors which led the police to stop and search and the criticism that the police sometimes used this power to harass, and at random. Randomness was one of the objections raised against the original proposals for roadside alcohol tests of motorists in the Road Safety Bill in 1966 (below, p. 301), though it has been accepted in relation to testing the safety of goods vehicles, and seems to be accepted in practice in relation to customs and excise officials.

If a policeman wishes to search property he must either obtain the consent of the occupier or a warrant authorising search from a magistrate. A magistrate can only issue a search warrant in cases where he is specifically authorised to do so by a statute. A large number of statutes authorise search, among them the Public Order Act 1936, the Official Secrets Acts 1911–39, the Theft Act 1968, the Obscene Publications Act 1959, the Misuse of Drugs Act 1971, the Customs and Excise Act 1952, and the Licensing Act 1964. Alternatively if the police can obtain a warrant to arrest a suspect they can enter property on which they reasonably expect him to be to arrest him, and seize any property that may be used as evidence of a crime committed by anyone, *Elias* v. *Pasmore*.[11] This means that they can wait until he is on premises that they would like to search and then enter and search. The police are on occasion prepared to enter premises and conduct a search even though they have no authority (below, p. 306), and there have been complaints from time to time that magistrates are at times too ready to issue warrants on the basis of inadequate information (below, p. 306). The fact that evidence which has been obtained illegally can probably be used in court, *Kuruma* v. *The Queen*,[12] clearly encourages illegal searches to some extent.

Quite apart from their powers to search, the police have also powers of entry under a number of statutes such as the Misuse of Drugs Act 1971 and can also enter public meetings even on private premises if they have reasonable grounds for suspecting an offence might be committed or a breach of

[10] Cmd. 3297, 1929.
[11] [1934] 2 K.B. 164.
[12] [1955] A.C. 197, P.C.

the peace occur, *Thomas* v. *Sawkins*.[13] They can therefore attend and take notes at any public meeting even against the will of the meeting's organisers. They also have the ordinary citizen's implied licence to go on to premises to talk to someone, or to go up to the door of a house to make inquiries (below, p. 305), though they must leave if they are told to (*Davis* v. *Lisle*[14]). They have no right to be on premises simply because they think something may be wrong (*Great Central Ry.* v. *Bates*[15]).

Identification

One of the thorniest problems facing the police is obtaining evidence of identification of the suspect. Both the Home Secretary and the courts have laid down rules as to how identification parades are to be conducted and the circumstances in which photographs of suspected persons can be shown to a witness beforehand. Some of the most notorious cases of proved injustice have involved false identifications, the most famous being that of Adolf Beck, whose case was one of the factors which led to the establishment of a Court of Criminal Appeal in 1907.

Most of the rules so far mentioned impose restrictions upon the police. Others are designed to assist them. Although a mere refusal to co-operate with the police is not an offence, it may amount to obstructing the police in the course of their duty deliberately to mislead them (below, p. 288). The Criminal Law Act 1967 also makes it an offence deliberately to conceal information about the commission of a serious offence (below, p. 312).

The Accused, ed. Coutts

A Comparative Study

British Institute Studies in International and Comparative Law No. 3

The systems of criminal procedure described later in this volume reveal three main methods of regulating events before the trial. At one extreme, the pre-trial stage is left entirely in the hands of the executive officer—the police. Thus, in the case of non-indictable offences in England, the police conduct the investigation, decide whether or not to prosecute and often conduct the prosecution itself in the trial . . . At the other extreme, as in the French system (which is a prototype for the Belgian and German systems, too), the pre-trial stage is subject to the control and guidance of a magistrate . . . A third solution is that adopted in Scotland, where a public prosecutor has charge of the police investigation and of the actual prosecution, the judicial officer merely rubber-stamping the decision to send the accused for trial. These three types of procedure do not, of course, exhaust the possibilities and certain hybrids can be seen. In England, for instance, a Director of Public Prosecutions may have a part to play, though only in a very restricted category of cases. Again, in England, a judicial filter is introduced, in indictable offences, in the shape of the preliminary hearing before a magistrate. . . . In France it is not too much of an exaggeration to say that the pre-trial investigation is in fact a trial of the *inculpé* in private, so thorough and painstaking is the compilation of the dossier. The public trial is, as Professor Anton[16] has remarked, a trial of the dossier rather than of the accused.

---

[13] [1935] 2 K.B. 249.   [14] [1936] 2 K.B. 434.
[15] [1921] 3 K.B. 578.
[16] (1960) Am. Journal of C.L. 1253, " *L'Instruction Criminelle* ": *cf.* " Criminal Proceedings in France," *ibid.* 447.

Examination of suspects

Rice v. Connolly

Divisional Court of the Queen's Bench Division [1966] 2 Q.B. 414

LORD PARKER C.J. . . . It seems to me quite clear that though every citizen has a moral duty or, if you like, a social duty to assist the police, there is no legal duty . . . and indeed the whole basis of the common law is the right of the individual to refuse to answer questions put to him by persons in authority, and to refuse to accompany those in authority to any particular place; short, of course, of arrest.

. . . [I]t is undoubtedly an obstruction [of a police officer in the execution of his duty under s. 51 (3) of the Police Act 1964,] and has been so held, for a person questioned by the police to tell a " cock-and-bull " story; to put the police off by giving them false information . . . In my judgment there is all the difference in the world between deliberately telling a false story—something which on no view a citizen has a right to do—and preserving silence or refusing to answer—something which he has every right to do.

MARSHALL J. . . . In order to uphold this conviction it appears to me that one has to assent to the proposition that where a citizen is acting merely within his legal rights, he is thereby committing a criminal offence. Nor can I see that the manner in which he does it can make any difference whatsoever . . .

JAMES J. . . . For my own part, I would only add this, that I would not go so far as to say that there may not be circumstances in which the manner of a person together with his silence could amount to an obstruction within the section; whether it does remains to be decided in any case that happens hereafter, not in this case, in which it has not been argued.

Practice Note : Judges' Rules

[1964] 1 W.L.R. 152

These rules do not affect the principles:

(a) That citizens have a duty to help a police officer to discover and apprehend offenders;

(b) That police officers, otherwise than by arrest, cannot compel any person against his will to come to or remain in any police station;

(c) That every person at any stage of an investigation should be able to communicate and to consult privately with a solicitor. This is so even if he is in custody provided that in such a case no unreasonable delay or hindrance is caused to the processes of investigation or the administration of justice by his doing so;

(d) That when a police officer who is making inquiries of any person about an offence has enough evidence to prefer a charge against that person for the offence, he should without delay cause that person to be charged or informed that he may be prosecuted for the offence;

(e) That it is a fundamental condition of the admissibility in evidence against any person, equally of any oral answer given by that person to a question put by a police officer and of any statement made by that person, that it shall have been voluntary, in the sense that it has not been obtained from him by fear of prejudice or hope of advantage, exercised or held out by a person in authority, or by oppression.

The principle set out in paragraph (e) above is overriding and applicable in all cases. Within that principle the following rules are put forward as a guide to police officers conducting investigations. Non-conformity with these rules may render answers and statements liable to be excluded from evidence in subsequent criminal proceedings.

Rules

. . . II—As soon as a police office has evidence which would afford reasonable grounds for suspecting that a person has committed an offence, he shall caution that person or cause him to be cautioned before putting to him any questions, or further questions, relating to that offence.

The caution shall be in the following terms:

" You are not obliged to say anything unless you wish to do so but what you say may be put into writing and given in evidence. . . ."

III—(a) Where a person is charged with or informed that he may be prosecuted for an offence he shall be cautioned in the following terms:

" Do you wish to say anything? You are not obliged to say anything unless you wish to do so but whatever you say will be taken down in writing and may be given in evidence."

(b) It is only in exceptional cases that questions relating to the offence should be put to the accused person after he has been charged or informed that he may be prosecuted. Such questions may be put where they are necessary for the purpose of preventing or minimising harm or loss to some other person or to the public or for clearing up an ambiguity in a previous answer or statement.

Before any such questions are put the accused should be cautioned in these terms:

" I wish to put some questions to you about the offence with which you have been charged (or about the offence for which you may be prosecuted). You are not obliged to answer any of these questions, but if you do, the questions and answers will be taken down in writing and may be given in evidence."

Obtaining evidence by subterfuge

Callis v. Gunn

Divisional Court of the Queen's Bench [1964] 1 Q.B. 495

Lord Parker C.J. . . . I take the general law to be as stated by Lord Goddard C.J. in *Kuruma* v. *The Queen*.[17] . . . " [T]he test to be applied in considering whether evidence is admissible is whether it is relevant to the matters in issue. If it is, it is admissible and the court is not concerned with how the evidence was obtained. . . ." That is dealing with admissibility in law, and as Lord Goddard C.J. points out, . . . in every criminal case a judge has a discretion to disallow evidence, even if in law relevant and therefore admissible, if admissibility would operate unfairly against a defendant. . . . [I]n considering whether admissibility would operate unfairly against a defendant one would certainly consider whether it had been obtained in an oppressive manner by force or against the wishes of an accused person. That is the general principle.

When, however, one comes to the admissibility of statements made in answer to the police and to alleged confessions, a much stricter rule applies. There is a fundamental principle of law that no answer to a question and no statement is admissible unless it is shown by the prosecution not to have been obtained in an oppressive manner and to have been voluntary in the sense that it has not been obtained by threats or inducements.

To that principle governing answers to questions and statements made by an accused must be added the Judges' Rules, which are rules of practice indicat-

[17] [1955] A.C. 197.

ing what the judges will exclude within the meaning of oppressive conduct or as not being voluntary statements.

. . . Having said that, it is quite clear that this present case is not concerned in any way with answers to the police or statements made by a defendant. That being so, the Judges' Rules in regard to the giving of a caution do not apply at all. As a matter of law the evidence of fingerprints, if relevant, . . . is admissible subject to the overriding discretion of the court. . . .

That discretion . . . would certainly be exercised . . . if there was any suggestion of it having been obtained oppressively, by false representations, by a trick, by threats, by bribes, anything of that sort. . . . [I]n the present case . . . whatever the defendant knew about the law and his rights, the police never misrepresented it to him. . . . There is no suggestion here that they conveyed to him that he had to accede to the request. . . . [W]hat the justices say is not that the police represented that he had to accede, but that they did not make it sufficiently clear that he had any right to refuse.

In my judgment the justices approached this matter in the wrong way.

[Ashworth and Hinchcliffe JJ. concurred.]

Report of the Departmental Committee on Homosexuality and Prostitution
Cmnd. 247, 1957

121. This particular offence [a male person persistently soliciting or importuning in a public place] necessarily calls for the employment of plain clothes police if it is to be successfully detected and prevented from becoming a public nuisance; and it is evident that the figures of convictions, both for importuning and for indecencies committed in such places as public lavatories, must to some extent reflect police activity. It has been suggested . . . that in carrying out their duty in connection with offences of this nature police officers act as *agents provocateurs*.

. . . It must, in our view, be accepted that in the detection of some offences . . . a police officer legitimately resorts to a degree of subterfuge in the course of his duty. But it would be open to the gravest objection if this were allowed to reach a point at which a police officer deliberately provoked an act; for it is essential that the police should be above suspicion, and we believe that if there is to be an error in the one direction or the other it would be better that a case of this comparatively trivial crime, should occasionally escape the courts than that the police as a whole should come under suspicion.

Sneddon v. Stevenson
Divisional Court of the Queen's Bench Division [1967] 2 All E.R. 1277

Here a policeman had seen two women whom he suspected were prostitutes. He stopped his car near one of them who asked him " Do you want business? " The policeman said, " How much? " She replied, " Two pounds in the car, three pounds inside." He said " Alright " and drove her to a police station where she was charged under the Street Offences Act 1959 with being a common prostitute soliciting for the purposes of prostitution and loitering for the same purpose. She appealed against her conviction on the ground that the policeman was an accomplice and his evidence needed corroboration and that he had incited the commission of the offence.

Lord Parker C.J.: . . . [T]hough a police officer acting as a spy may be said in a general sense to be an accomplice in the offence, yet if he is merely partaking in the offence for the purpose of getting evidence, he is not an accomplice who requires to be corroborated. . . . No doubt this court does frown on the practice of police officers being employed to commit offences themselves, or indeed to encourage others to commit offences. Here . . . the respondent did not commit an offence; in so far as it can be said that he did act so as to enable others to commit offences by making himself available if an offence was to be committed, it does seem to me that, provided a police officer is acting under the orders of his superior and the superior officer genuinely thinks that the circumstances in the locality necessitates action of this sort, then . . . there is nothing wrong in that practice being employed. In a very recent case of *R. v. Murphy*,[18] this matter was considered on a court-martial appeal. The headnote of that case reads:

"The appellant, a soldier serving in the Army, was charged before a district court-martial with the offence of disclosing information useful to an enemy, contrary to s. 60 (1) of the Army Act, 1955. The substance of the case against him was contained in the evidence of police officers who had posed as members of a subversive organisation with which the authorities suspected the appellant to have sympathies, and had elicited the information the subject of the charge by asking the appellant questions concerning the security of his barracks. The appellant was convicted but appealed to the Courts-Martial Appeal Court against his conviction, on the ground that the court-martial which heard the case ought in its discretion to have rejected the evidence of the police officers because of the manner in which it was obtained . . . held: (i) that in criminal proceedings evidence which has been improperly obtained is not thereby rendered inadmissible; . . . (ii) that the court has nevertheless a discretionary jurisdiction to reject evidence which, though admissible, would operate unfairly against the accused; and its discretion is not spent at the time when the relevant evidence has been admitted; (iii) that in the present case the court-martial which tried the appellant was entitled in its discretion to admit evidence of the police officers, and in the circumstances it had been right in doing so." . . .

No doubt action of this sort should not be employed unless it is genuinely thought by those in authority that it is necessary having regard to the nature of the suspected offence or the circumstances in the locality. If, however, it is done for one or other of those reasons, then I myself can see no ground for setting aside a conviction obtained on such evidence, or, as in *R. v. Murphy*, excluding the evidence itself.

[Waller J. delivered a concurring judgment: Swanwick J. concurred.] [19]

---

[18] [1965] N.I. 138.

[19] Note the difficulty which arose in this connection under the Obscene Publications Act 1959. That Act made it an offence to publish an obscene article. In *R. v. Clayton and Halsey* [1963] 1 Q.B. 163 the persons who bought the article were policemen sent there for the purpose. Lord Parker C.J. noted in his judgment: "In the present case the two persons to whom publication was made were experienced police officers employed in the Obscene Publications Department at New Scotland Yard. It was their job to make test purchases such as those in question. Under cross-examination they agreed they had seen thousands of photographs of a similar nature to those in question in the course of their work and that such photographs did not arouse any feelings in them whatsoever. . . . It was argued that the fact that the officers were not in fact depraved or corrupted does not conclude the matter, but here it was urged that these were officers who by the very nature of their employment were not even susceptible of being depraved or corrupted." The court accepted this argument and quashed the conviction for publishing. One result was a change in the law which added to the offence of publication an offence of having

R. v. Birtles

Court of Appeal, Criminal Division [1969] 2 All E.R. 1131

LORD PARKER C.J.: . . . Before leaving this case, the court would like to say a word about the use which, as the cases coming before the court reveal, is being made of informers. The court of course recognises that, disagreeable as it may seem to some people, the police must be able in certain cases to make use of informers, and further—and this is really a corollary—that within certain limits such informers should be protected. At the same time, unless the use made of informers is kept within strict limits, grave injustice may result. In the first place, it is important that the court of trial should not be misled. A good example of that occurred in *R. v. Macro*,[20] again a raid on a sub-post office, which came before this court on 10th February 1969. There the charge was one of robbery with aggravation, with a man unknown. In fact, the man unknown was an informer who together with the police had warned the victim of what was going to take place, and had gone through the pretence of tying-up the victim while the police were concealed on the premises. The effect was that the appellant in that case pleaded guilty to an offence which had never been committed. If the facts had been known, there could not have been a robbery at all, and accordingly it was for that reason that the court substituted the only verdict apt on the facts which was open to it, namely a verdict of larceny. There is of course no harm in not revealing the fact that there is an informer, but it is quite another thing to conceal facts which go to the quality of the offence. Secondly, it is vitally important to ensure so far as possible that the informer does not create an offence, that is to say, incite others to commit an offence which those others would not otherwise have committed. It is one thing for the police to make use of information concerning an offence that is already laid on. In such a case the police are clearly entitled, indeed it is their duty, to mitigate the consequences of the proposed offence, for example, to protect the proposed victim, and to that end it may be perfectly proper for them to encourage the informer to take part in the offence or indeed for a police officer himself to do so. But it is quite another thing, and something of which this court thoroughly disapproves, to use an informer to encourage another to commit an offence or indeed an offence of a more serious character, which he would not otherwise commit, still more so if the police themselves take part in carrying it out. . . .[21]

The power to stop and search

Report of the Commissioner of Metropolitan Police for the Year 1935

Cmd. 5165, 1936

The Stopping and Arresting of Suspects

. . . [I]t has always been an essential part of every policeman's duty to keep his eyes open for those who are searching for the opportunity for committing a crime, and also for those who are coming away from a crime with property in their possession. In such work mistakes must inevitably be made from time to time. The solitary person observed at 3 a.m. carrying a heavy burden may be an honest workman walking home late with the normal tools of his trade, but it is

---

an obscene article for publication: see Obscene Publications Act 1964, c. 74, *cf.* also generally Royal Commission on police powers and procedure, Cmd. 3297, 1929, paras. 104 *et seq.*

[20] *The Times*, February 11, 1969.

[21] As to the non-disclosure of the names of informers, see *Marks* v. *Beyfus* (1890) 25 Q.B.D. 494. Following *R.* v. *Birtles* (1911) 75 J.P. 288, the Home Office sent a confidential circular to chief constables on the use of informants. See *e.g.* (1969) 119 New Law Jo. 513.

the duty of the policeman to assure himself that the bundle does not contain somebody's family plate. In a large proportion of cases a closer glance at the man and the burden, a word of explanation, an apology by the policeman and the incident is closed. These cases occur roughly at the rate of about 1,000 a week in the Metropolitan area. A very considerable number of thieves are caught in this way. . . .[22] The power to arrest persons loitering with intent to commit a felony is quite separate and distinct from the power to stop, search and detain and it is liable to give rise to more serious difficulties. . . . Here again mistakes are always possible. The man who jostles in the crowd at a bus stop, constantly surging forward with each new arrival and as constantly coming back again without any real attempt to board, may be a flustered countryman unacquainted with the London bus routes, but it is quite reasonably likely that he is a pickpocket. The man who hovers round an unattended car park, peering in and trying handles, may be interested in cars and their locking devices, but it is more likely that he is looking for a chance to " lift " a suit case. If he is recognised as a thief, the likelihood is still stronger. . . . Much attention has been drawn in the Press and elsewhere to the number of cases of this kind in which magistrates have dismissed the charges, and the suggestion has been made that police are employing their powers with an excess of zeal or even oppressively. But to deduce improper police action from such decisions indicates possibly some confusion of thought between the function of the court and the function of the police. The court's function is to hear all the evidence that may be brought, and then to decide as to guilt or innocence, with probably—and rightly—a strong inclination to give the benefit of the doubt . . . to the prisoner. The police function is much more limited. The officer has to decide on the basis of what he has observed whether he is justified in leaving a man at liberty who seems to be about to commit a crime. . . . Put shortly, the position is that complete freedom of the individual is not compatible with adequate protection for the community. . . .

Report of the Advisory Committee on Drug Dependence on Powers of Arrest and Search in Relation to Drug Offences 1970

Section 23 (2) of the Misuse of Drugs Act 1971 which replaces in much the same terms the provisions in force at the time the committee reported provides:

> If a constable has reasonable grounds to suspect that any person is in possession of a controlled drug in contravention of this Act or of any regulation made thereunder, the constable may—
>
> (a) search that person and detain him for the purpose of searching him;
>
> (b) search any vehicle or vessel in which the constable suspects that the drug may be found, and for that purpose require the person in control of the vehicle or vessel to stop it;
>
> (c) seize and detain, for the purpose of proceedings under this Act, anything found in the course of the search which appears to the constable to be evidence of an offence under this Act.

---

[22] Cf. P. Laurie, Scotland Yard, p. 65 (Penguin ed., 1972): " section 66 stops produce about 40 per cent. of the Metropolitan Police's 50,000 crime arrests a year, although only 1 stop in 20 is fruitful."

31. The proposal to introduce these powers was foreshadowed by Lord Stonham during the Second Reading debate on the Bill in the House of Lords on 20th June 1967 and the provisions were introduced by a new clause moved by him at the Committee stage of the Bill in the House of Lords on 5th July 1967. . . . The Government arguments in favour of the provisions can be summarised as follows:

    (i) Drug trafficking was widespread and not confined to cities and towns.

    (ii) The existing law gave the police inadequate powers: they could search persons (and their vehicles) by consent, or with a warrant, but otherwise only after arrest, and they could not make an arrest unless they suspected that the person arrested would abscond or had given false particulars of his name and address.

    (iii) Drug pedlars were well familiar with the statutory limitations on search and arrest.

    (iv) Some police forces were able to use local Act powers and these had proved to be of much value. In London the majority of arrests for drug offences had followed exercise of the powers to stop and search available under section 66 of the Metropolitan Police Act 1839.[23]

    (v) There was a strong public demand that young people should be protected from drug pushers and pedlars.

    (vi) It was very difficult to apprehend drug pedlars except in possession of illicit drugs.

No dissent from the proposals was expressed, and the clause was agreed without a division. The new clause was debated in the House of Commons on 23rd October 1967 . . . References were made to the operation " without serious objections " of similar provisions in the Firearms Act 1968, [s. 47,] and the Metropolitan Police Act 1839, [s. 66]. The clause was agreed to without dissent. . . .

104. . . . [T]he procedure followed when a police officer stops and searches a member of the public in the street is broadly as described below.

105. A police officer meets a member of the public in the street and decides that he should stop him and undertake a search. To do this, an officer must have " reasonable suspicion " and this can derive from a number of circumstances. It can be the demeanour of the suspect, his gait or movements, whether he is carrying something suspicious, the state of his dress, the time and place of the encounter or a number of other circumstances. The officer may also have other factors in mind, based on knowledge of the suspect and the place where he is. For any combination of reasons, therefore, an officer may decide to undertake a search and he will normally ask the person concerned if he is prepared to agree to it.

106. If consent is given, the search may take place immediately. If, however, the suspect questions the need or authority for such a search, then the officer discloses not only the reason why he wishes to search—he will usually have done that already—but also the powers under which he is authorised to do so. The search then takes place (although it is open to the officer under existing powers to take the suspect back to the police station). The officer no doubt does what he can to prevent any public embarrassment to the suspect by making the search in a doorway or other convenient place. If nothing is found, the officer asks for the name and address of the person involved, for these or other details of identification are needed in case there is a subsequent complaint (it is always, of

[23] S. 66 of the Metropolitan Police Act 1839, 2 & 3 Vict. c. 47, provides: " [E]very . . . constable may . . . stop, search and detain any . . . person who may be reasonably suspected of having or conveying in any manner any thing stolen or unlawfully obtained. . . ."

course, open to a member of the public to refuse to give his name and address if he so wishes). The officer apologises for the inconvenience caused and, if there is no subsequent complaint, the matter rests there. However, full details of the search, including whether it was resented, are recorded in the officer's pocket book, which is regularly examined by his superior officer. His superior officer should therefore be able to see, among other things, whether the officer has shown a tendency to exercise his powers excessively (and without result) or whether searches have been resented.

107. If, however, something suspicious is found (it is impossible for an officer on the street to identify illicit drugs with certainty) and the suspect does not then give a satisfactory explanation, he is taken in custody to the police station and may be examined and questioned there more fully. . . .

108. Thus described the procedure may give a misleading impression of simplicity. The realities of a given situation are likely to be much less precise. The police officer is trained to be alert and inquisitive. . . . He cannot operate very effectively in that role without talking to people and asking questions. . . . The degree of police inquisitiveness varies according to the prevalence and seriousness of a particular criminal activity; if, for example, many cases of housebreaking are reported in an area, there may be increased police interest in persons carrying suitcases or packages or wearing plimsolls. In the bustle in a public place the police officer has little time for deeply considered judgment. A gesture, a scrap of conversation, the passing of some invisible article, a rapid movement away from observation . . . may raise a " hunch " that leads him to stop and question the person concerned. . . .

109. In the detection of drugs offences (and particularly offences of unlawful possession) police inquisitiveness faces the special difficulty that until any substance found by search has been analysed there is no certainty that it is a drug at all, let alone a controlled drug. Finding a substance, therefore, that *may be* a controlled drug is not the last but much more a first step in a process of enquiry to identify possible criminal actions and transactions. To that extent the stop and search provisions fit logically into a procedure of police action where arrest follows upon suspicions strengthened by what has been found.

110. We heard much criticism from some of our witnesses that the police construe their powers to stop and search on " reasonable grounds " too widely. It can be argued that no reasonable person should resent a request by the police to co-operate in reducing the prevalence of drug abuse; that the police have exceptionally difficult duties in their field and that a vast majority of the public support them in this work. There remains, however, a balance to be struck in all law enforcement between police powers and the individual's rights. . . .

111. On the evidence before us it is difficult for us to judge how far uneasiness about the police interpretation of " reasonable grounds " is justified; whether and how often the line which must be drawn is being transgressed. From the police side it is claimed that complaints on this score are phenomenally rare. On the other side it is argued that the rate of complaints against the police may not reflect the volume of public dissatisfaction with police conduct, and that young people, in particular, are less likely than adults to resort to formal complaints. The main cause for anxiety amongst witnesses who claimed to speak for a substantial minority of young people was that in this field of enforcement against dangerous drugs " reasonable grounds " are too often founded on the appearance and not the action of the individual; that the police are apt to single out young persons with unconventional hair styles, strange dress, beads and the rest of it, and that those who follow these fashions find themselves at special risk. Many illegal drug-takers have an unconventional appearance, as those on the side of the law are swift to stress; most are young. It does not follow that a majority of

young people of unconventional appearance nowadays abuse drugs. Nor does it follow that the factor of " appearance " about which principal disquiet has been expressed will be long-lasting. While it remains in issue, however, we are unanimous in accepting, and we think the police should accept, that hair style and unusual dress should not themselves or together constitute sufficient ground for action. Liberty of the subject must extend to the right to adopt idiosyncratic life styles without exciting police attention and " reasonable grounds " to search. More positive factors must enter a policeman's decision to stop and search, for example, where a person is leaving premises associated with drug abuse, or is seen to make a transaction or is known to the police. In short, appearances cannot always be discounted but they should be a subsidiary and not a principal part of reasonable grounds to stop and search. . . .

Should the statutory powers of search be abolished? The minority view in favour of this

113. The first proposal we considered was one that is favoured by *Mr. Schofield, Professor Williams and Baroness Wootton*, namely that the practice of stop and search should be discontinued and arrest substituted, with search following either in the street or at the police station; where the search revealed nothing, the person could be released forthwith, and where a substance needing analysis was found, the police could release on bail.

The minority argue that this change would have the following advantages

(a) It would simplify the law. Statutory search for drugs is an excrescence on police powers which is not generally thought necessary in other areas of the law. For example, the police have no statutory power to search for concealed weapons other than firearms, even though knife-carrying may be common at some times in some areas. . . . Generally it is thought sufficient that the police should have power to arrest on reasonable suspicion, with consequential powers of search. Why should not the same apply to drug offences?

(b) It would clarify and restrict the power of the police. The law of arrest is well settled, and it clearly requires that suspicion should have focused on the particular person who is arrested. When a statutory power of search is added, . . . [s]eemingly, the police are allowed to search on a suspicion that is too generalised to justify an arrest. Almost inevitably, therefore, the statutory power of search tends to result in some kind of random search, even though it may be confined to particular classes of people or particular localities or times. As the statistics in paragraph 55 show, the proportion of successful to unsuccessful searches varies greatly from area to area, which seems to indicate disparity in police practice. In Birmingham, where a conservative policy is followed, the proportion of successful to unsuccessful searches is better than one in three (43 out of 101). In Northumberland, in the period investigated, it was one in 16, though the absolute figures were low (2 out of 32). In the Cannon Row police station area the proportion was slightly better than one in six (142 out of 812). Regarded as the success rate of a semi-random search this is good, but judged by the standard that would be applied to arrests it is very poor. There is cause for anxiety when five innocent persons are subjected to personal search for every one who is guilty.

114. The minority of the Sub-committee do not think that the object of enforcing the drugs law can justify the infliction of very considerable indignity upon persons against whom there are not sufficient grounds of suspicion to justify an

arrest. When the present power of statutory search for drugs was first placed before Parliament, it was supported by the analogy of the power to search for stolen goods given by the Metropolitan Police Act and other similar local legislation. Later events have shown that the parallel is inexact. Stolen goods in general have an appreciable bulk, and the powers of the Metropolitan Police Act are normally exercised by demanding to see the contents of a suitcase, briefcase or conveyance. But the user of an illicit drug often has only a small quantity, which he can conceal in an intimate part of the body. This necessarily means that a search of drug-users, to be effective, must be vexatious for the person searched. In a paper prepared for us by the Association of Chief Police Officers of England and Wales and the Chief Constables' (Scotland) Association, it was stated that " experience has shown that drugs are concealed in body folds which a routine search of clothing, etc. would not reveal. One cannot carry out a proper search of a person for drugs in a street for instance." . . . This evidence seemed at first to present quite a different picture of police search from the evidence of our assessors summarised at paragraph 107 above. However, when we asked the Association's representative to confirm the record of his evidence for the purpose of this Report, he qualified it by saying that a very detailed personal search is not necessary on every occasion, and that in the majority of cases examination of the contents of pockets or hand-bags has revealed the evidence with very little inconvenience to the persons concerned. Our assessors added the information that searching " the folds of the body " does not imply manual probing, but is effected by requiring the suspect to remove his or her underclothes so that visual examination can be made of the clothes and of the body. Notwithstanding these qualifications, it seems to the minority of the Sub-committee from the evidence given that a superficial search for drugs is likely to be effective only in the case of inexperienced drug-users. The police, therefore, if left in possession of the statutory power of search, are likely to be driven to make a much more embarrassing type of search than the usual search for stolen goods. The minority of the Sub-committee are of the opinion that a search involving the inspection of underclothes and of the naked body should not be allowed in the case of persons who have not been arrested, even if (contrary to their opinion) a search of the pockets and hand-bags of such persons continues to be allowed.

115. In the view of the minority the abolition of the statutory power of search would undoubtedly mean that considerably fewer persons would be stopped and searched, the power to arrest being narrower than the statutory power of search. On their reckoning the proposal would involve a considerable diminution in the vexatiousness of police interference with people who are pursuing their ordinary affairs. . . .

116. . . . . Their broad view is that the control of drug abuse is best achieved by action directed against traffickers and that the power of general search of people on the street is more likely to cause a deterioration in the relations of the police and public than to add substantially to the enforcement of the law. As against traffickers, the minority consider that police powers of arrest, search of vehicles and search on warrant should be sufficient.

Should the statutory powers of search be abolished? The majority view against

117. The rest of us do not accept the arguments advanced by the minority as compelling. Whether search is statutory or following arrest, physical interference and personal inconvenience will be much the same. The risks of either are real and should not be under-estimated nor under-stated. If, however, there are reasonable grounds for search the search should be as thorough as the police

decide to be necessary in the circumstances of the case. The majority of us think this is what the public expects; and, on the police evidence, this is what happens. Evidence we received from non-police sources, however, though critical of some aspects of enforcement, included no complaint about search of " body folds ". There was no reference to what the minority describe as " the infliction of very considerable indignity ". That to the majority suggests strongly that on occasions when the police have exercised their powers of search in this way they have done so in a responsible fashion.

118. The hypothesis of the minority that the police " are likely to be driven to a much more embarrassing type of search than the usual search for stolen goods " may be sound; but we took little evidence about the practice of personal search for stolen goods. We think that a more realistic basis of comparison is with the pattern of personal search made by Customs officers under the Customs and Excise Act 1952. Those who come under suspicion of unlawful possession of drugs or at customs points of possible intent to evade revenue restrictions seem likely to be much the same amalgam of the experienced and the inexperienced in evading the relevant legal restrictions, and correspondingly more or less sophisticated in methods of concealing the article in question. In our view the powers of search must be wide enough to deal with the most skilled suspect in the group. The present law provides for a continuum of powers to act on reasonable grounds: to search before arrest, to arrest and after arrest to search or to search again. We see no grounds for fear that the police would proceed to the most extreme form of personal search, i.e. manual probing of the body cavities, without very strong grounds for suspicion; we should therefore expect that such grounds would lead the police to make an arrest before making such a search; and we recommend that administrative directions should be given to this effect. That, however, does not suggest to us that the police should not have the power to make less thorough forms of search for drugs under statutory powers and before arrest. We question the logic of the minority view . . . that search should be allowed of pockets and hand-bags but not of clothing generally, including underclothes or the external surface of the body.

119. Whether the search is statutory or following arrest the purpose of the search should be explicitly stated. . . . As regards the argument that statutory search is much more " miss " than " hit ", we think that it is impossible to draw reliable inferences from the statistics . . . without relating the comparative success or failure rates of statutory search generally to those for other forms of police enquiry that affect personal liberty in one way or another. Such information as the Sub-committee obtained . . . indicates that stops for searches for drugs are significantly more successful than stops for other purposes. The ratio of arrests to stops for drugs by officers in Kilburn was 2 in 7, and by officers from Cannon Row better than 1 in 6, whereas the ratios of arrests to stops for other purposes by these officers was less than 1 in 12 and 1 in 10 respectively. As regards the argument that the police should concentrate on traffickers, we think that this overlooks the general difficulty in enforcing the drugs law that the dividing line between drug takers and pushers is, as the police witnesses pointed out, obscure, and that the police are not likely to get on to the track of pedlars without evidence of unlawful possession. There are drugs other than heroin, e.g. L.S.D. and injectable amphetamines, unlawful possession of which should be given very active police attention.

120. The crux of the matter lies in the argument that statutory searches tend to be random and that the public would prefer to face the possibility of arrest for purposes of search, particularly if the police were less likely to exercise their power. . . .

121. If there is any tendency for statutory searches to be random—that is, without reasonable grounds—and the majority of us are not convinced that there

is—this ought to be vigorously checked by strict operational supervision. More can indeed be done to improve accounting in this area. Police forces keep records of stops and note those which lead to further action. . . . The majority of us recommend that these figures should be included in their reports in future and published in the Annual Report of Her Majesty's Chief Inspector; that Her Majesty's Inspectors should be able to examine supporting records showing the total of stops for drugs, positive and negative findings, and, if appropriate, sub-totals of searches by individual policemen; and that similar arrangements should be made by the Commissioner of Police for the Metropolis (if statutory powers of search are retained, the minority would also support their recommendation).

122. On the other hand the majority think that, given the special difficulties of detecting illegal trafficking and possession of controlled drugs, it would be against the public interest to tie the hands of the police in such a way that the police become unduly concerned that the possibility of complaint for wrongful arrest would prejudice the proper exercise of their duties and functions as regards drugs offenders. . . . The act of arrest, even if nothing comes of it, carries in most minds serious implications; that was evident from the views of " Release " . . . and substituting arrest-search for statutory-search would exchange one set of apprehensions for another more acutely felt. The rest of us, therefore, recommend that the provisions of section 6 (1) of the Dangerous Drugs Act 1967 should be retained.

Could " reasonable grounds " be positively defined?

123. . . . Criteria which amount to " reasonable grounds " have never been defined. It is not easy to define them. The present unwritten code which is familiar to every police officer, but much less familiar to the public, might be said roughly to include:

(1) the demeanour of the suspect; (2) the gait and manner of the suspect; (3) any knowledge the officer may have of the suspect's character or background; (4) whether the suspect is carrying anything, and the nature of what he is carrying; (5) the mode of his dress, bulges in his clothing, and particularly when these factors are considered in the light of all the surrounding circumstances; (6) the time of observation; (7) any remarks or conversation which he makes to any other person which might be overheard by an officer; (8) the street or the area involved; (9) information from a third party, who may in given circumstances be known or unknown; (10) any connection between that person and any other person whose conduct at that time is reasonably suspect; (11) the suspect's apparent connection with any overt criminal activity.

To any such list must be added the essential fund of common sense, training and experience which every police officer is deemed to possess in some measure and without the exercise of which he may find himself in trouble with his superior officers. It is this crucial element which makes a statutory definition of " reasonable grounds " so difficult. We are unanimously of opinion that it is impossible to draft any such definition in positive terms.

Could " reasonable grounds " be defined by exclusion? The minority view in favour

124. This leaves open the question whether it would be an advantage to effect some definition of reasonable grounds by exclusion. Professor Williams at the request of the Sub-committee drafted the following for consideration as a new provision to follow immediately after section 6 (1) of the Dangerous Drugs Act 1967, which confers the power to stop and search:

" (1A) The following circumstances shall not be sufficient in themselves, whether alone or in conjunction with each other, to establish reasonable grounds of suspicion for the purpose of subsection (1) above.

(*a*) That the person searched appeared to be the kind of person who is frequently found in possession of drugs.

(*b*) That he was carrying any article, other than an article commonly associated with the possession of drugs.

(*c*) That he was found in a locality where drugs were frequently possessed.

(*d*) That he was found in a public place at night or in the early morning." . . .

125. This proposal is supported by Professor Williams and Baroness Wootton as an alternative to their preferred proposal stated in paragraph 113. Mr. Schofield joins them in wishing a similar exclusionary definition to be applied to the " reasonable grounds " justifying an arrest.

126. . . . We do not believe that it is any more practicable to define negative than positive grounds for suspicion, simply because the factors influencing a police officer's judgement cannot be reduced to simple formulae. . . .

127. For the reasons we have stated earlier those of us who object to statutory limitation are prepared to say as strongly as the minority who favour it that dress and hair style should never in themselves or together constitute reasonable grounds to stop and search. We recommend that this principle should become standard police practice and senior officers should accept the need for enforcing it. . . .

135. The National Council for Civil Liberties laid much emphasis on the need for safeguards against " planting " of drugs whether by other persons or the police. . . . " Release " made clear to us that with the Council they were convinced that cases of " planting " occurred from time to time, although they themselves had received many fewer allegations than they had expected. The Law Society told us that in drugs cases the allegations of " planting " were more frequent than in other cases and some years ago were extensive but had decreased. We have found it difficult to assess the significance of the evidence of these bodies. If a person is found in unlawful possession of a drug, there are only two possible lines of defence: " planting ", and wrongful use of police powers. It is to be expected that allegations of " planting " will be made and the three bodies readily conceded this. . . .

137. The National Council and " Release " both proposed . . . that before a suspected person was searched he should be allowed to ask for a third party to be present. The Administrative Directions issued by the Home Office already require this in the case of children. . . . Police representatives assured us that this Direction was faithfully observed, although occasionally circumstances arose where e.g. a child suspected to be in possession of drugs was found a long distance from home late at night and it was not reasonable to delay search until a parent arrived. Children apart, the proposal raises the question whether in the case of drugs there are special factors which justify making search of suspects whatever their age subject to some independent supervision. We do not think that such factors exist. From the practical point of view we see considerable difficulties in the specific proposals made by " Release " and the National Council. . . . Bringing a third party of the suspect's choosing to the scene of the search could be time-consuming, inconvenient and sometimes impracticable. From the wider point of view we think that the introduction of a requirement that a third party should be in attendance during individual police operations to act as an observer would raise issues of confidence and responsibility affecting the

whole conduct of police activity, for which no general justification has been offered to us. . . .

Random checks

Report of the Second Reading of the Road Safety Bill
724 H.C.Deb. c. 655, February 10, 1966

The Government in its White Paper " Road Safety Legislation 1965–66 " [24] proposed that in future it should be made an offence to drive with a blood alcohol concentration of more than 80 mg./100 ml. The problem was how the new law should be enforced. One method proposed was by spot checks at the roadside, *i.e.* stopping vehicles at random and asking drivers to take a screening test. Another was to authorise the police to stop a vehicle and ask the driver to submit to a test only if they had grounds for suspecting that he had taken alcohol. The White Paper concluded:

> The Government consider that random checks would be preferable. These checks would be completely fair and undiscriminating and would cast no slur on the driver who happened to be stopped. They would be the most effective deterrent since any driver would be liable to be stopped at any time to see whether he had exceeded the statutory blood-alcohol level.

A clause to that effect was therefore included in the Road Safety Bill which was introduced into Parliament in 1966. The following extract besides showing some of the issues raised on the Second Reading of the Bill is also a useful reminder that the law is not made by lawyers alone. They operate within the framework and subject to rules laid down by Members of Parliament and it is these rules which not only determine a large part of the substantive law but which also help to shape the values of the system and define its objectives. The style and standard of the debate on the Road Safety Bill is a convenient example of Parliament's role in this regard.

> The Minister of Transport (Mrs. Barbara Castle). . . . We have come to the conclusion that it would be far less invidious and less offensive to the individual to be stopped completely at random, without any stigma being attached to it, rather than be stopped because he has been seen coming out of a public house, or even when he has committed a traffic offence. . . . If we have preliminary tests on suspicion . . . then the presumption is that the driver has drunk more than he should and that is why he is being asked to take a breath test. Anyone seeing him undergoing the test will draw that conclusion. In the case of a random test there can be no such presumption. . . . If we want a deterrent, then there could be no more effective way than for people to realise that there will always be a possibility of their being asked to undertake a random test. . . . [T]o those who maintain that there is a great principle of individual liberty involved, I say that there is no difference in principle between random breath tests and random tests on goods vehicles. . . .

> Sir M. Redmayne . . . [M]any people have written to me expressing their concern at the stopping of drivers—especially of women—on lonely roads by

[24] Cmnd. 2859.

what may appear to be police in uniform, but which may be a trap, and has on occasion been a trap. It seems certain that a test carried out by any method must clearly be seen to be the work of the police; there must be recognisable lighted signs on the police cars fully in evidence. I do not believe that any check of this sort should ever be made—nor can there be any reason for its ever being made—on a deserted road.

I am told that the inventor claims about 5 per cent. false positive reactions, that is, reactions over the level and 5 per cent. false negatives, although other users report a wider variation. It is therefore clear that the error inherent in the instrument used for tests on a random basis, that is, with the great majority of people, who are likely to have less than an 80 blood content—$98\frac{1}{2}$ per cent. of drivers, according to the Indiana test—creates at least the lively possibility of obtaining a false number of positive reactions. Even if only one in a hundred or one in a thousand people are affected, it is important. In such cases following a random test, drivers who have not given any cause for suspicion by their driving or by their behaviour, must be taken to a police station and subjected to further unpleasant ordeals like blood or urine tests. Going to a police station . . . is a serious matter, and they may have to go simply because the machine is not sufficiently accurate. . . . I doubt whether any test . . . will take less than a minute. . . . [S]ome care will have to be taken and drivers will have to be told how to use the instrument. If good relations with the police are to be maintained the operation will have to be conducted with tact and polite-ness, so each test will be fairly slow. . . . In these conditions, the number of drivers tested as a proportion of those on the road will not be very great. . . . The man over the danger mark . . . may be driving home as best he can . . . unchecked because the police are too busy with a largely fruitless search to be on the alert for the careless driving of the man they really want. . . .

There is no real precedent in law for this procedure; namely, that a subject whose actions have in no way given reasonable grounds for suspicion that he may have contravened the law should be compelled, on pain of penalty and arrest, to submit to a physical examination for the purpose of possibly establishing that he has committed an offence. The right hon. Lady quoted vehicle checks. If that is the best precedent the Minister can give for this new proposition, she will have to think again. I have heard other suggestions or parallels. For example, the right hon. and learned Member for Newport (Sir F. Soskice), the former Home Secretary, is on record as having said that there is no difference here from the powers of the Metropolitan Police. Yet the Metropolitan Police Act—and the Liverpool Corporation Act, which is the same in this respect—empowers constables to make an inquiry of a person as to the possession of property only if there is reasonable ground to believe or suspect that the property has been stolen. Similarly, the Customs and Excise Act [25] has been called in aid,

---

[25] s. 298 of the Customs and Excise Act 1952 provides:
    (1) Where there are reasonable grounds to suspect that any person to whom this section applies is carrying any article—
        (a) which is chargeable with any duty which has not been paid or secured; or
        (b) with respect to the importation or exportation of which any prohibition or restriction is for the time being in force . . .
    any officer or any person acting under the directions of an officer may search him and any article he has with him:
    Provided that—
        (i) the person to be searched may require to be taken before a justice of the peace or a superior of the officer or other person concerned, who shall consider the grounds for suspicion and direct accordingly whether or not the search is to take place;
        (ii) no woman or girl shall be searched . . . except by a woman.
    (2) This section applies to the following persons, namely—
        (a) any person who is on board or has landed from any ship or aircraft;

but here again, in one section after another, there must be reasonable grounds
for suspicion. Even in time of war a power as drastic as Regulation 18 B [26] of
the Defence General Regulations imposed on the Secretary of State a duty that
he should have reasonable cause to believe the person concerned to be of hostile
disposition. In spite of these precedents, this Bill proposes that a constable in
uniform can act without reasonable cause for suspicion. . . . [T]he Government
are instituting a method and procedure which will produce new restrictions on
the citizen. I sincerely believe that they are both unnecessary and ineffective.
And the precedent, once established, will be increasingly hard to resist. The
Minister may argue that the public are so anxious to see a reduction in casualties
that they will willingly submit to inconvenience. That may be so, but we at least
have a duty to see that such inconvenience is reduced to a minimum and that it
is justly applied, not to the public at large but to potential offenders. . . .

MR. G. R. STRAUSS . . . The principle of spot checks in other matters has
been well established and in operation for many years. Spot checks are made
on commercial vehicles the whole time. . . . We are all inconvenienced as
individuals by spot checks when we pass through the Customs. . . . Although
the Customs officer has no suspicion that we have offended against the law
by carrying contraband, he stops us and examines our luggage. It is a spot
check. . . .

MR. D. BESSELL . . . Would the right hon. Gentleman agree that the Customs
and Excise Act 1952 requires that a Customs officer shall have reason to suspect?

MR. STRAUSS . . . That may be. I am talking about what happens in practice . . . whatever the legal position might be. I do not think, therefore, that
we can morally object to spot checking, if, in fact, it achieves the purpose of the
Bill better than merely testing people whom a policeman suspects have too great
a concentration of alcohol in their blood. If someone drinks too much he probably thinks that he is likely to be asked to take a breathalyser test, only if he
drives poorly so as to cause a policeman to have suspicion. He will say to himself . . . " Well, I will be all right. My drink will not make me wander across
the road. Therefore, the chance of my being picked up is negligible." . . .
If on the other hand, he knows that he may be stopped by the police anyhow,
he will be more cautious. . . .

MR. RONALD BELL . . . It is perfectly clear to me that there is a most material
distinction between stopping a lorry to spot-check it and stopping an individual
by the road-side and spot-checking him physically to determine his physical condition, in full and open public view of any man, woman or child. . . . I
believe that, on general grounds, this is a most objectionable innovation, and . . .
a great infringement of personal freedom. . . . In my view, the price exacted by
the random checks is higher . . . than I am prepared to pay for any reduction
of deaths or injuries that it might yield. . . . I think that it will be regarded by
most people as a humiliating experience—and it will be a humiliating experience.
We have reticences in this country which are not universally shared. We should
regard it as somewhat undignified to be stopped at the side of the road and made
to blow up one of these beastly little balloons. If I were asked to blow one up

(b) any person entering or about to leave the United Kingdom;
(c) any person within the dock area of a port;
(d) any person at a customs airport;
(e) in Northern Ireland, any person travelling from or to any place which is on
or beyond the boundary.
[26] On this regulation, see the famous case of *Liversidge* v. *Anderson* [1942] A.C. 206.

in one breath in 15 seconds, plus or minus 3 seconds, I would feel it not only undignified but a little difficult. . . .

The function of the police is to detect the guilty, and to detect the guilty inside the rules that the rest of the country choose to make for the operation. It is not their job to . . . cross-check innocence. . . .

Sir Richard Nugent . . . The right hon. Lady claimed that most people would accept the need for roadside spot-checks. But already there has been a very strong reaction from the motoring organisations. . . . [T]he R.A.C. and the A.A. speak for a very large number of people. . . . [W]hat I regard as very important will be the resentment against the police in the carrying out of these tests. . . . [W]e are in a crime wave the like of which this country has never seen, and it must still be in balance whether it will be possible to command the strength and skill to control and defeat this crime wave. One of the vital factors in doing that must be the measure of support which public opinion gives to the police . . . [without which] . . . the . . . job of the police is impossible. . . . [R]ecruitment must be gravely handicapped when public opinion of the Force is adverse. . . . [I]f . . . Clause 2 is put on the Statute Book, the police image will be damaged in the eyes of all the drivers in the country. . . . Our history is littered with examples of unpopular laws which have become dead letters. We need look no further than the traffic laws for the parking of motor cars. Everyone knows . . . that until we introduced the meter system we got no enforcement whatever. The police simply did not wish to implement those laws. They felt that to do so was a difficult and unpleasant job which made bad relations with the public. . . . The reaction of the Police Federation when these plans were announced was seen. The Federation asked from where the men were to come to do this work. . . .

Mr. Peter Thornycroft . . . To stop a vehicle and look at the brakes is quite a different matter from stopping a man and asking him to breathe into a rubber bag. These distinctions must be very clearly drawn. . . . Lord Devlin, to quote from his Frank Newsam Memorial Lecture, . . . used these words . . . :

" The British people . . . are hard taskmasters. They have from the earliest times had a love of freedom which has expressed itself in an intolerance of tyranny and at the same time a desire for order and good government which they know is unobtainable without respect for the law. . . . [I]t is because the British have learnt to measure out stingily their grants of authority, so that it is just enough and no more, that they have, perhaps more successfully than any other nation, held the balance between order and freedom. The police power oscillates uncomfortably at the point of balance and this is what gives every policeman an exacting task. But the British way of life depends to a great extent on the way in which he discharges it." . . .

I am afraid that if one asks the already overburdened police to tour the country and pick up motorists just because they are motorists, one will get beyond the point of balance. Nor am I impressed by the argument that the police should ring public houses, Hunt Balls and the like and start testing people as they approach their motor cars. There are certain things which are clear outside reason from the point of view of asking the police to do them. . . .

The opposition to random checks in the end prevailed. The Road Traffic Act 1972, s. 8 provides:

(1) A constable in uniform may require any person driving or attempting to drive a motor vehicle on a road or other public place to

provide a specimen of breath for a breath test there or nearby, if the constable has reasonable cause—

(*a*) to suspect him of having alcohol in his body, or

(*b*) to suspect him of having committed a traffic offence while the vehicle was in motion. . . .

(2) If an accident occurs owing to the presence of a motor vehicle on a road or other public place, a constable in uniform may require any person who he has reasonable cause to believe was driving or attempting to drive the vehicle at the time of the accident to provide a specimen of breath for a breath test. . . .

Entry and search

Robson v. Hallett

Divisional Court of Queen's Bench Division (Lord Parker C.J., Diplock L.J. and Ashworth J.)
[1967] 2 Q.B. 939

Lord Parker C.J. . . . . [T]hese three police officers, like any other members of the public, had implied leave and licence to walk through that gate up those steps and to knock on the door of the house. . . . [T]he occupier of any dwelling-house gives implied licence to any member of the public coming on his lawful business to come through the gate, up the steps, and knock on the door. . . . [W]e are not here considering the right to enter the front door but merely the right to go . . . up to the front door . . . *Davis* v. *Lisle* [27] . . . is no authority for saying that a police officer on his lawful business making proper inquiries has no right to enter the front gate. . . .

Misuse of Drugs Act 1971

1971, c. 38

23. (1) A constable or other person authorised in that behalf by a general or special order of the Secretary of State . . . shall, for the purposes of the execution of this Act, have power to enter the premises of a person carrying on business as a producer or supplier of any controlled drugs and to demand the production of, and to inspect, any books or documents relating to dealings in any such drugs and to inspect any stocks of any such drugs. . . .

(3) If a justice of the peace . . . is satisfied by information on oath that there is reasonable ground for suspecting—

(a) that any controlled drugs are, in contravention of this Act or of any regulations made thereunder, in the possession of a person on any premises . . . he may grant a warrant authorising any constable acting for the police area in which the premises are situated at any time or times within one month from the date of the warrant, to enter, if need be by force, the premises named in the warrant, and to search the premises and any persons found therein and, if there is reasonable ground for suspecting that an offence under this Act has been committed in relation to any controlled drugs found on the premises or in the possession of any such persons . . . to seize and detain those drugs. . . .

[27] [1936] 2 K.B. 434.

Report of the Inquiry into the Action of the Metropolitan Police in Relation to the Case of Mr. Herman Woolf

Cmnd. 2319, 1964

105. Although Detective Sergeant Bell claimed that he thought that he had implied consent from Mr. Woolf, he added that even if Mr. Woolf had refused, he would still have searched. . . .

106. Detective Superintendent Townsend . . . said . . . that, unless the prisoner or . . . some other person occupying the premises gave permission for them to be searched, a warrant should be obtained. . . . I gathered, however, from the evidence that, generally speaking, the obtaining of the prisoner's consent or alternatively of a warrant, while regarded as desirable if circumstances permitted, was not allowed to be an obstacle to searching the premises if the officer concerned thought that anything material to the charge was likely to be found there and that any delay in carrying out the search might result in the property in question being removed before the search could be made.

107. I appreciate that there may well be circumstances in which delay . . . may result in the property being removed . . . but I do not feel that, unless or until the Legislature sees fit to alter the law . . . unlawful searches of this sort should be countenanced. If the police require greater powers in this respect, the remedy is with the Legislature. The common law requirements with regard to this are an important safeguard of the liberty of the subject which should not be lightly whittled away. . . .[28]

Parliamentary Question

289 H.L.Deb., c. 1224, March 5, 1968

On March 5, 1968, Lord Gladwyn asked the Government " whether they will consider advising magistrates that before issuing, on the sole basis of an anonymous telephone call, a warrant for searching a private house, a magistrate should satisfy himself that inquiries have already been made as to the character and police record of the householder concerned and the inherent probability of his being guilty of the alleged offences."

THE LORD CHANCELLOR (LORD GARDINER): My Lords, when deciding whether to issue warrants, magistrates act judicially and the Government have no power to instruct them as to how they are to exercise their judicial functions. I assume that the noble Lord's question refers to a recent case in which private premises were searched for drugs. In cases of this kind magistrates have statutory power to issue search warrants on being satisfied by an information on oath that there is reasonable ground for suspecting that drugs are on the premises. In this particular instance the information sworn by the police officer applying for the warrant had not disclosed that it was based on an anonymous message.

LORD GLADWYN: My Lords, would it not be a good thing if normally the police could disclose to the magistrate whether the information was based on

---

[28] *Cf.* the statement of H. R. Balmer, the Deputy Chief Constable, Liverpool City Police [1967] Crim.L.R. 19: " . . . Very often, a police officer engaged in the investigation of a serious crime cannot afford to stop his enquiries while he obtains a search warrant from a magistrate because, in this time, vital evidence may have been moved or destroyed. . . . There is much to be said in favour of a general power to search premises on the authority of a superintendent when that officer is satisfied that any delay would result in the removal or destruction of evidence connected with an arrestable offence. . . . I would consider that a superintendent . . . would not issue his authority to support speculative searches or harassment."

an anonymous telephone call? If we are to accept the fact that magistrates have power to issue warrants on the basis of an anonymous telephone call, are we not opening a door for all the enemies of anybody to ring up the police and say that that person is hoarding drugs and his premises ought to be immediately searched? . . .

The Lord Chancellor: My Lords, in this particular case the information on oath was that the officer had received information " from a source which I believe to be reliable ". It would not, I think, have occurred to a magistrate that it was likely to be an anonymous telephone call.

So far as the police are concerned, my right honourable friend the Home Secretary in another place has said that where there is anonymous telephone information the normal procedure is for inquiries to be made, and perhaps observation kept, in order to try to assess the reliability of information of this character. He added that he regretted that this procedure was not carried out. . . .

Lord Gladwyn: My Lords, I was not attempting to accuse the police of any dereliction of duty. My intention was to suggest that sometimes, perhaps, magistrates do not always act in accordance with what is the right procedure. I hope, therefore, that the Government will still manage, somehow or other, to advise the magistrates concerned of the necessities of this case.

The Lord Chancellor: My Lords, I must remind the noble Lord that the case is one in which the police did not follow the usual procedure, and the information which they swore and put before the magistrate, who I think is not to be blamed at all, was not in a form which could have led anyone to think that the information was simply an anonymous telephone call.

Retaining evidence

R. v. Waterfield

Court of Criminal Appeal (Lord Parker C.J., Ashworth and Hinchcliffe JJ.) [1964] 1 Q.B. 164

A policeman wished to prevent a car being taken away before it had been examined to see if there was evidence on it of its having been involved in a collision. The driver drove at the policeman and was subsequently charged with assaulting the police officer while in the execution of his duty. The question was whether he was in the execution of his duty, and in particular whether he had the power to detain the car if he believed it to be evidence of the commission of a serious criminal offence.

Ashworth J. . . . . It is convenient to emphasise . . . that the alleged offences were committed in King's Lynn and that special powers, for example, those conferred upon the Metropolitan Police under section 66 of the Metropolitan Police Act 1839 or powers conferred under a special local Act, cannot be relied on as authorising the action of the two police constables.

. . . [W]hile it is no doubt right to say in general terms that police constables have a duty to prevent crime and a duty, when crime is committed, to bring the offender to justice, it is also clear from the decided cases that when the execution of these general duties involves interference with the person or property of a private person, the powers of constables are not unlimited. To cite only one example, in *Davis* v. *Lisle* [29] it was held that even if a police officer had

---

[29] [1936] 2 K.B. 434, D.C.

a right to enter a garage to make inquiries, he became a trespasser after the appellant had told him to leave the premises, and that he was not therefore acting thenceforward in the execution of his duty, with the result that the appellant could not be convicted of assaulting or obstructing him in the execution of his duty.

In the present case it is plain that the police constables . . . no doubt acting in obedience to the orders of their superior officer, were preventing Lynn and Waterfield taking the car away and were thereby interfering with them and with the car. It is to be noted that neither of the appellants had been charged or was under arrest and accordingly the decision in *Dillon* v. *O'Brien and Davis* [30] does not assist the prosecution.

It was contended that the two police constables were acting in the execution of a duty to preserve for use in court evidence of a crime, and in a sense they were, but the execution of that duty did not in the view of this court authorise them to prevent removal of the car in the circumstance. In the course of argument instances were suggested where difficulty might arise if a police officer were not entitled to prevent removal of an article which had been used in the course of a crime, for example, an axe used by a murderer and thrown away by him. Such a case can be decided if and when it arises; for the purposes of the present appeal it is sufficient to say that in the view of this court the two police constables were not acting in the due execution of their duty at common law when they detained the car. . . . For these reasons appeals against the convictions in respect of the assault on Police Constable Willis must be allowed and the convictions quashed.

Ghani v. Jones

Court of Appeal [1970] 1 Q.B. 693

LORD DENNING M.R. . . . So we have a case where the police officers, in investigating a murder, have seized property without a warrant and without making an arrest and have retained it without the consent of the party from whom they took it. Their justification is that they believe it to be of " evidential value " on a prosecution for murder. Is this a sufficient justification in law?

I would start by considering the law where police officers enter a man's house by virtue of a warrant, or arrest a man lawfully, with or without a warrant, for a serious offence. I take it to be settled law . . . that the officers are entitled to take any goods which they find in his possession or in his house which they reasonably believe to be material evidence in relation to the crime for which he is arrested or for which they enter. If in the course of their search they come upon any other goods which show him to be implicated in some other crime, they may take them provided they act reasonably and detain them no longer than is necessary. Such appears from the speech of Lord Chelmsford L.C., in *Pringle* v. *Bremner and Stirling* [31] and *Chic Fashions (West Wales) Ltd.* v. *Jones.* [32]

Accepting those cases, I turn to two cases where the police acted against a man without the authority of a warrant or of an arrest. The first is *Elias* v. *Pasmore.* [33] . . . Police officers there entered a house in Great Russell Street, of which Elias was the tenant. The police officers had only a warrant for the arrest of a man called Hannington. They had reasonable ground for believing

[30] (1887) 20 L.R.Ir. 300.
[31] (1867) 5 Macph., H.L., 55, 60.
[32] [1968] 2 Q.B. 299.
[33] Reported in [1934] 2 K.B. 164, but the facts are given more fully in (1934) 50 T.L.R. 196.

that he had been guilty of sedition by attempting to cause disaffection among the police. They knew he was in the house. They entered and arrested him. They had no search warrant, authorising them to search the house. No search warrant is permissible to search for seditious papers. That is plain ever since *Entick* v. *Carrington*.[34] Whilst there, however, they searched the place, seized a number of seditious papers and took them to Scotland Yard. These papers implicated, not only Hannington, but also Elias. They showed that Elias had been inciting Hannington to commit sedition. The police prosecuted first Hannington and second Elias. The papers were used at the trial of Elias. Both men were convicted. Elias afterwards said that the police had no right to take his papers and brought an action for their return and for damages for their detention. Horridge J. rejected the claim. He said: " The interests of the state must excuse the seizure of documents, which seizure would otherwise be unlawful, if it appears in fact that such documents were evidence of a crime committed by anyone." [35]

I confess that I think those words " by anyone " go too far. The decision itself can be justified on the ground that the papers showed that Elias was implicated in the crime of sedition committed by Hannington. If they had only implicated Elias in some other crime, such as blackmail or libel, I do not think the police officers would have been entitled to seize them. For that would be a flat contradiction of *Entick* v. *Carrington*. The common law does not permit police officers, or anyone else, to ransack anyone's house, or to search for papers or articles therein, or to search his person, simply to see if he may have committed some crime or other. If police officers should so do, they would be guilty of a trespass. Even if they should find something incriminating against him. I should have thought that the court would not allow it to be used in evidence against him if the conduct of the police officers was so oppressive that it would not be right to allow the Crown to rely upon it: see *King* v. *The Queen*.[36]

The other case is *R.* v. *Waterfield*.[37] . . .

The decision causes me some misgiving. . . . The police had reason to believe that Lynn and Waterfield were implicated in a crime of which the marks on the car might be most material evidence at the trial. If Lynn and Waterfield were allowed to drive the car away, they might very well remove or obliterate all incriminating evidence. My comment on that case is this: The law should not allow wrongdoers to destroy evidence against them when it can be prevented. Test it by an instance put in argument. The robbers of a bank " borrow " a private car and use it in their raid, and escape. They abandon it by the roadside. The police find the car, i.e., the instrument of the crime, and want to examine it for finger prints. The owner of the " borrowed " car comes up and demands the return of it. He says he will drive it away and not allow them to examine it. Cannot the police say to him: " Nay, you cannot have it until we have examined it "? I should have thought they could. His conduct makes him look like an accessory after the fact, if not before it. At any rate it is quite unreasonable. Even though the raiders have not yet been caught, arrested or charged, nevertheless the police should be able to do whatever is necessary and reasonable to preserve the evidence of the crime. The Court of Criminal Appeal did not tell how *R.* v. *Waterfield* is to be distinguished from such a case. The court simply said, at p. 171, that the police constables were under no duty " to prevent removal of the car in

[34] (1765) 19 St.Tr. 1029.
[35] [1934] 2 K.B. 164, 173.
[36] [1969] 1 A.C. 304.
[37] [1964] 1 Q.B. 164.

the circumstance." They did not tell us what was the "circumstance" which took it out of the general rule. It may have been sufficient. I do not know.

Other instances were put in argument to test the position when no one had been arrested or charged. Edmund Davies L.J. drew from his unrivalled experience and told us that the great train robbers, when they were in hiding at Leatherslade Farm, used a saucer belonging to the farmer and gave the cat its milk. When seeking for the gang, before they were caught, the police officers took the saucer so as to examine it for finger prints. Could the farmer have said to them: "No, it is mine. You shall not have it"? Clearly not. His conduct might well lead them to think that he was trying to shield the gang. At any rate it would have been quite unreasonable.

What is the principle underlying these instances? We have to consider, on the one hand, the freedom of the individual. His privacy and his possessions are not to be invaded except for the most compelling reasons. On the other hand, we have to consider the interest of society at large in finding out wrong-doers and repressing crime. Honest citizens should help the police and not hinder them in their efforts to track down criminals. Balancing these interests, I should have thought that, in order to justify the taking of an article, when no man has been arrested or charged, these requisites must be satisfied:

First: The police officers must have reasonable grounds for believing that a serious offence has been committed—so serious that it is of the first importance that the offenders should be caught and brought to justice.

Second: The police officers must have reasonable grounds for believing that the article in question is either the fruit of the crime (as in the case of stolen goods) or is the instrument by which the crime was committed (as in the case of the axe used by the murderer) or is material evidence to prove the commission of the crime (as in the case of the car used by a bank raider or the saucer used by a train robber).

Third: The police officers must have reasonable grounds to believe that the person in possession of it has himself committed the crime, or is implicated in it, or is accessory to it, or at any rate his refusal must be quite unreasonable.

Fourth: The police must not keep the article, nor prevent its removal, for any longer than is reasonably necessary to complete their investigations or preserve it for evidence. If a copy will suffice, it should be made and the original returned. As soon as the case is over, or it is decided not to go on with it, the article should be returned.

Finally: The lawfulness of the conduct of the police must be judged at the time, and not by what happens afterwards.

Tested by these criteria, I do not think the police officers are entitled to hold on to these passports or letters. They may have reasonable grounds for believing that the woman has been murdered. But they have not shown reasonable grounds for believing that these passports and letters are material evidence to prove the commission of the murder. All they say is that they are of "evidential value," whatever that may mean. Nor have they shown reasonable grounds for believing that the plaintiffs are in any way implicated in a crime, or accessory to it. In any case, they have held them quite long enough. They have no doubt made photographs of them, and that should suffice.

...I cannot help feeling that the real reason why the passports have not been returned is because the officers wish to prevent the plaintiffs from leaving this country pending police inquiries. That is not a legitimate ground for holding them. Either they have grounds for arresting them, or they have not.

If they have not, the plaintiffs should be allowed to leave—even if it means they are fleeing from the reach of justice. A man's liberty of movement is regarded so highly by the law of England that it is not to be hindered or prevented except on the surest grounds. It must not be taken away on a suspicion which is not grave enough to warrant his arrest.

I would, therefore, dismiss the appeal.

Edmund Davies L.J. and Sir Gordon Willmer concurred.

Obstructing the police and similar offences

There are a number of offences designed to assist the investigation of offences and the bringing of suspects to trial. One is the general offence of obstructing the police, but it is not obstructing the police simply to refuse to give information which is within one's knowledge. Lord Denning M.R. in *Sykes* v. *D.P.P.*[38] noted at p. 560:

> Take the case in Australia where a man, who was shot and wounded in an affray, refused to disclose to the police the name of the person who had shot him. It would seem that he was engaged in gang warfare, for he said that he would " cop it sweet " if he did disclose the name. He said he would attend to the matter himself, that is, take his own revenge. No civilised community can tolerate such behaviour. But his offence is not obstructing the police.

Another, is interfering with the course of justice, for example, persuading a witness not to give evidence, or fabricating evidence. Following the decision to recommend the abolition of the distinction between felony and misdemeanour, the Criminal Law Act 1967 introduced a number of statutory offences to replace offences which had existed at common law. In proposing the consideration of the form these offences should take the Criminal Law Revision Committee in its seventh report on felonies and misdemeanours [39] noted:

> 40. On the whole . . . the only case needing to be provided for is one in which a person accepts or agrees to accept a bribe not to disclose information . . . about an arrestable offence other than consideration amounting only to the making good of, or reasonable compensation for, any loss or injury caused by the offence. . . . [T]he offence . . . would only apply to information about an arrestable offence which has in fact been committed. . . .
>
> 41. . . . [T]he offence will not apply to a person who refrains from giving information because he does not think it right that the offender should be prosecuted or because of a promise of reparation by the offender. It would be difficult to justify making the offence apply to those cases.
>
> 42. A more questionable limitation is that the offence would not apply to withholding information from the police, even in response to a question, out of mere unwillingness to assist them or to active concealment by positively misleading them. . . . But public opinion would be unlikely to agree to an offence consisting of refusing to answer questions

[38] [1962] A.C. 528.
[39] Cmnd. 2659.

by the police about the commission of offences. This would confer a power on the police, covering a wide range of offences and backed by a substantial penalty, similar to that conferred by section 6 of the Official Secrets Act 1920 (c. 75), under which it is an offence to refuse to answer questions put by an authorised senior officer of police for the purpose of obtaining information about the commission of the most serious offences under the Official Secrets Acts; and even there permission has to be obtained from the Secretary of State before the information can be demanded. In any event the offence would have to be subject to the right of the person being questioned not to give information about an offence to which he was himself a party, which right exists as regards the present offence of misprision.... An offence of actively misleading the police might be easier to justify than an offence of refusing to give them information; but we do not think that there is a sufficient need to create it, and it would be difficult to distinguish between active misleading and mere withholding of information.

44.... [W]e have taken the opportunity to suggest providing for the ... making [of] false reports to the police about the commission of a crime and so causing them to be wastefully employed in investigating the alleged crime.... Cases of this kind occur from time to time and they cause serious loss of time by the police and may well cause suspicion to be cast on innocent people. The offence used to be prosecuted as a public mischief, as in *Manley* [40] ... but in *Newland* [41] ... the Court of Criminal Appeal expressed dissatisfaction with *Manley's* case and doubt whether that offence existed except as part of the law of criminal conspiracy, and they suggested the creation of a specific summary offence aimed at this kind of conduct.

45. We agree that a summary offence should be created to deal with this kind of mischief. ...

Criminal Law Act 1967

1967, c. 58

4.—(1) Where a person has committed an arrestable offence, any other person who, knowing or believing him to be guilty of the offence or of some other arrestable offence, does without lawful authority or reasonable excuse any act with intent to impede his apprehension or prosecution shall be guilty of an offence.

(3) A person committing an offence under subsection (1) above with intent to impede another person's apprehension or prosecution shall on conviction on indictment be liable to imprisonment according to the gravity of the other person's offence, as follows:

(a) if that offence is one for which the sentence is fixed by law, he shall be liable to imprisonment for not more than ten years;

(b) if it is one for which a person (not previously convicted) may be sentenced to imprisonment for a term of fourteen years, he shall be liable to imprisonment for not more than seven years;

(c) if it is not one included above but is one for which a person (not previously convicted) may be sentenced to imprisonment for a term of

[40] [1933] 1 K.B. 529.
[41] [1954] 1 Q.B. 158, 168.

ten years, he shall be liable to imprisonment for not more than five years;

(d) in any other case, he shall be liable to imprisonment for not more than three years.

(4) No proceedings shall be instituted for an offence under subsection (1) above except by or with the consent of the Director of Public Prosecutions:

(5) Offences under subsection (1) above, and incitement to commit them, shall be included in Schedule 1 to the Magistrates' Courts Act 1952 (indictable offences triable summarily with the consent of the accused) where that Schedule includes, or is under any enactment to be treated as including, the arrestable offence to which they relate.

5.—(1) Where a person has committed an arrestable offence, any other person who, knowing or believing that the offence or some other arrestable offence has been committed, and that he has information which might be of material assistance in securing the prosecution or conviction of an offender for it, accepts or agrees to accept for not disclosing that information any consideration other than the making good of loss or injury caused by the offence, or the making of reasonable compensation for that loss or injury, shall be liable on conviction on indictment to imprisonment for not more than two years.

(2) Where a person causes any wasteful employment of the police by knowingly making to any person a false report tending to show that an offence has been committed, or to give rise to apprehension for the safety of any persons or property, or tending to show that he has information material to any police inquiry, he shall be liable on summary conviction to imprisonment for not more than six months or to a fine of not more than two hundred pounds or to both.

(3) No proceedings shall be instituted for an offence under this section except by or with the consent of the Director of Public Prosecutions.

(4) Offences under subsection (1) above, and incitement to commit them, shall be included in Schedule 1 to the Magistrates' Courts Act 1952 (indictable offences triable summarily with the consent of the accused) where that Schedule includes, or is under any enactment to be treated as including, the arrestable offence to which they relate.

(5) The compounding of an offence other than treason shall not be an offence otherwise than under this section.

The decision to prosecute

Once the police think they have collected sufficient information they must decide whether they will charge anyone, and also with what offence they will charge him, just as they decide whether to undertake investigations in the first place and the extent of those investigations. There are no public prosecutors in England with the responsibility for taking these decisions, though from time to time the establishment of such an officer has been proposed. In some cases however the law requires the consent of the Attorney-General or the Director of Public Prosecutions before a prosecution can be brought (below, p. 319) and in others regulations require the Director to be consulted (e.g. the Official Secrets Acts 1911–39, the Public Order Act 1936, the Race Relations Act 1965).

If the police decide not to prosecute there is still the possibility of a private prosecution, though the Director may take over such a prosecution and then not offer any evidence. The Attorney-General also has the power in the case of indictable offences to stop a prosecution by entering a *nolle prosequi.* In the case of a summary offence the magistrates may be asked to dismiss the case. The Attorney-General is a government minister but he is expected to act on his own discretion in these matters and although he may consult his cabinet colleagues in a serious case, the final decision is his own and should be taken in the public and not political party interest (below, p. 319). Many prosecutions are in fact brought not by the police but, for example, by government departments, such as the Inland Revenue and Customs and Excise, Weights and Measures Inspectors, local authorities and public utilities.

The discretion which the police have to prosecute is probably less important than the discretion not to, and indeed the discretion not to investigate in the first place. It is the Chief Constable of each local police force who has the responsibility for deciding how his force should be used (below, p. 316). The local police authority which is made up of representatives of the local authorities and justices of the peace have no power to direct him in this respect. A failure to investigate or prosecute may be due to a variety of reasons. There is the simple question of having limited resources. This was one reason for the controversial statement of the Chief Constable of Southend in 1963 that he would no longer necessarily give assistance in the prosecution of shoplifters.[42] There is the proper exercise of discretion when it is decided to overlook a trivial or technical offence. There is the situation where it is considered that a caution is sufficient. Cautions are part of the standard range of choices open to the police in connection with minor motor offences such as speeding and have been widely used in relation to juveniles. There may be a feeling that some offences are particularly difficult to detect and that their detection requires a degree of searching out, bordering on participation or provocation, which in the absence of special circumstances, is undesirable. On the positive side there may from time to time be a drive against particular kinds of crime in order reduce their incidence (below, p. 315). All these are matters of general policy for the local Chief Constable.

Quite apart from these general considerations there are also those which occur in particular cases. The individual policeman may decide not to notice an offence or report it. Even when reported the police may decide not to follow it up. They may feel that though they are satisfied that the suspect is guilty there is insufficient evidence to convince a court of law or that the circumstances of the accused make it hard to prosecute, or the state of public feeling makes it unwise.

As was mentioned above, the fact that the same set of facts may give rise to more than one offence means that the police may have some discretion not only whether to prosecute but also for which offence. It is here that the practice of plea-bargaining may arise. Rules have been devised by the courts to prevent the fact that the accused may be exposed to the risk of prosecution for more than one offence being used oppressively (below, p. 324).

---

[42] *Cf.* N. Osborough, " Immunity for the English Supermarket Shoplifter " (1964) 13 Am.Jo.Comp.L. 291.

The Policeman and the Community : M. Banton

Tavistock, 1964, pp. 128–131

The decision to invoke the criminal law and put a man on a charge must be in the first place that of the police officer who sees the offence or makes the initial investigation. But there is bound to be variation in the way many thousand different policemen respond in similar circumstances. Quite apart from any variation in their understanding of the law's requirements, some will be temperamentally lenient and others strict. If the initiation of criminal proceedings depended only on the judgment of individual constables there would be serious discrepancies. To guard against this, senior officers lay down rules for the guidance of their subordinates.... However, whereas there are safeguards to prevent the invocation of the law in unsuitable circumstances, it is more difficult to guard against the injustice which may occur when a patrolman improperly neglects to initiate proceedings.... Policemen do not like taking aggressive action unless they believe they have public support, and they often refuse to enforce the law upon their fellow citizens if they believe it would be unfair to do so. Full enforcement would require policemen to be far more detached from society than is possible under the present system.

Report of the Departmental Committee on Homosexuality and Prostitution

Cmnd. 247, 1957

129. To some extent the laws relating to homosexual offences, and for that matter to other sexual offences, are bound to operate unevenly. Obviously many homosexual acts ... never come to light, so that the number of those prosecuted ... constitutes but a fraction of those who from time to time commit such acts. But over and above this obvious fact, we have found that there are variations in the ways in which different police forces administer these laws. In some parts of the country they appear to be administered with " discretion "; that is to say ... no proceedings are initiated unless there has been a complaint or the offence has otherwise obtruded itself upon the notice of the police, for instance by a breach of public order or decency. In other parts of the country, on the other hand, it appears that a firm effort is made to apply the full rigour of the law as it stands....

130. Wide currency has been given ... to a suggestion that a prosecution which took place not long before we were appointed was part of a nation-wide " witch hunt " against homosexuals. We have found no evidence of any " drive " on a national scale. The absence of uniformity in police practice ... is enough to disprove this suggestion.... What we have found is that there may from time to time arise particular local campaigns against this kind of offence, either as the result of a deliberate drive by the police or by reason of local public indignation.

131. We should not wish to imply that it would never be proper for police officers to follow up offences on mere suspicion. But where no clear public interest is involved, we would deprecate any out-of-the-way prying which could soon give rise to suspicions of " witch hunting." [43] ...

[43] In talking of prostitution the Committee noted: " 230. . . . [T]he number of prosecutions must depend to some degree on the number of police available for work of this kind and on the vigour of their activity; and this in turn may well depend on public opinion. At any given moment there may be a state of affairs in the streets which arouses public resentment; this may result in increased police activity and in an increased number of prosecutions." *Cf.* the report of the Inter-Departmental Committee on Abortion, Home

Report of the Departmental Committee on Proceedings before Examining Justices

Cmnd. 479, 1958

5. Before a criminal case appears in court, there must first be a decision to prosecute. In the majority of cases this decision is taken by the Chief officer of police concerned, on the basis of unsworn statements taken from potential witnesses and after consultation in certain cases with the Director of Public Prosecutions. The inquiries that lead up to this decision are confidential like much other police work. The public is not present when the decision is taken, nor is the information on which it is based then normally disclosed. This is true of other prosecutions, such as those by government departments, nationalised undertakings, local authorities, firms and individuals. (In general anyone can initiate a prosecution, and there is an appreciable number of prosecutions every year which are not initiated by the police.)

R. v. Commissioner of the Metropolitan Police, ex p. Blackburn

Court of Appeal [1968] 2 Q.B. 118

In 1966 the Metropolitan Police Commissioner issued a confidential instruction to senior officers in the Metropolitan Police to the effect that they should take no proceedings against clubs for breach of the gaming laws unless there had been complaints of cheating or unless they had become the haunts of criminals. The reason for this instruction was that the law at the time was extremely uncertain and that in view of that the expense and manpower involved in keeping observation upon the clubs, it was not worth while. This is what Mr. Blackburn was told when he asked the Metropolitan Police to help him prosecute clubs in which, he said, illegal gaming was taking place. He thereupon applied to the Divisional Court of the Queen's Bench Division for an order of mandamus calling on the Commissioner to assist him in the prosecution of gaming clubs, to assist him in a particular case, and to reverse the policy decision. His application was rejected and he appealed to the Court of Appeal.

LORD DENNING M.R.: ... I hold it to be the duty of the Commissioner of Police of the Metropolis, as it is of every chief constable, to enforce the law of the land. He must take steps so to post his men that crimes may be detected; and that honest citizens may go about their affairs in peace. He must decide

---

Office, 1939: " 129. The crime of unlawfully procuring abortion is almost invariably committed in circumstances of the greatest secrecy, and it is rare for a case to come to the notice of the police unless the woman who has undergone the abortion becomes seriously ill or dies. If nothing untoward occurs, in the nature of things none of the parties to the offence would ordinarily disclose the occurrence. If for any reason some other person became aware of it, a feeling of sympathy for the woman, which is not uncommon, might still prevent disclosure. . . .

135. . . . [I]n practice proceedings are rarely instituted against a woman who has had an illegal abortion. . . . [T]he view taken by the police is, we gathered, that the prosecution of the abortionist, who may have a widespread practice, should be their primary aim, and since the woman's evidence is required against him, proceedings against her are not taken.

136. A further consideration which weighs with the police . . . is that, in cases in which the evidence is that of accomplices only, the learned judge must advise the jury that it would not be safe to convict on such evidence alone . . . and the necessary corroborative evidence is frequently difficult to obtain."

whether or no suspected persons are to be prosecuted; and, if need be, bring the prosecution or see that it is brought. But in all these things he is not the servant of anyone, save of the law itself. No Minister of the Crown can tell him that he must, or must not, keep observation on this place or that; or that he must, or must not, prosecute this man or that one. Nor can any police authority tell him so. The responsibility for law enforcement lies on him. He is answerable to the law and to the law alone. That appears sufficiently from *Fisher* v. *Oldham Corporation*,[44] and *Attorney-General for New South Wales* v. *Perpetual Trustee Co. Ltd.*[45]

Although the chief officers of police are answerable to the law, there are many fields in which they have a discretion with which the law will not interfere. For instance, it is for the Commissioner of Police of the Metropolis, or the chief constable, as the case may be, to decide in any particular case whether inquiries should be pursued, or whether an arrest should be made, or a prosecution brought. It must be for him to decide on the disposition of his force and the concentration of his resources on any particular crime or area. No court can or should give him direction on such a matter. He can also make policy decisions and give effect to them, as, for instance, was often done when prosecutions were not brought for attempted suicide. But there are some policy decisions with which, I think, the courts in a case can, if necessary, interfere. Suppose a chief constable were to issue a directive to his men that no person should be prosecuted for stealing any goods less than £100 in value. I should have thought that the court could countermand it. He would be failing in his duty to enforce the law.

A question may be raised as to the machinery by which he could be compelled to do his duty. On principle, it seems to me that once a duty exists, there should be a means of enforcing it. This duty can be enforced, I think, either by action at the suit of the Attorney-General: or by the prerogative writ of mandamus. I am mindful of the cases cited by Mr. Worsley which he said limited the scope of mandamus. But I would reply that mandamus is a very wide remedy which has always been available against public officers to see that they do their public duty. It went in the old days against justices of the peace both in their judicial and in their administrative functions. The legal status of the Commissioner of Police of the Metropolis is still that he is a justice of the peace, as well as a constable. No doubt the party who applies for mandamus must show that he has sufficient interest to be protected and that there is no other equally convenient remedy. But once this is shown, the remedy of mandamus is available, in case of need, even against the Commissioner of Police of the Metropolis.

Can Mr. Blackburn invoke the remedy of mandamus here? It is I think an open question whether Mr. Blackburn has a sufficient interest to be protected. No doubt any person who was adversely affected by the action of the commissioner in making a mistaken policy decision would have such an interest. The difficulty is to see how Mr. Blackburn himself has been affected. But without deciding that question, I turn to see whether it is shown that the Commissioner of Police of the Metropolis has failed in his duty. I have no doubt that some of the difficulties have been due to the lawyers and the courts. Refined arguments have been put forward on the wording of the statute which have gained acceptance by some for a time. I can well understand that the commissioner might hesitate for a time until those difficulties were resolved; but, on the other hand, it does seem to me that his policy decision was unfortunate. People might well think that the law was not being enforced,

44 [1930] 2 K.B. 364.
45 [1955] A.C. 457.

especially when the gaming clubs were openly and flagrantly being conducted as they were in this great city. People might even go further and suspect that the police themselves turned a blind eye to it. I do not myself think that was so. I do not think that the suggestion should even be made. But nevertheless the policy decision was, I think, most unfortunate.

The matter has, I trust, been cleared up now. On December 19, 1967, the House of Lords in *Kursaal Casino Ltd.* v. *Crickitt (No. 2)* [46] made it quite clear that roulette with a zero was not rendered lawful simply by the " offer of the bank." Following that decision, on December 30, 1967, the commissioner issued a statement in which he said: " It is the intention of the Metropolitan Police to enforce the law as it has been interpreted." That implicitly revoked the policy decision of April 22, 1966; and the commissioner by his counsel gave an undertaking to the court that that policy decision would be officially revoked. We were also told that immediate steps are being taken to consider the " goings-on " in the big London clubs with a view to prosecution if there is anything unlawful. That is all that Mr. Blackburn or anyone else can reasonably expect.

This case has shown a deplorable state of affairs.... The niceties of drafting and the refinements of interpretation have led to uncertainties in the law itself. The proprietors of gaming houses have taken advantage of the situation. By one device after another they have kept ahead of the law. As soon as one device has been held unlawful, they have started another. But the day of reckoning is at hand. No longer will we tolerate these devices. The law must be sensibly interpreted so as to give effect to the intentions of Parliament; and the police must see that it is enforced. The rule of law must prevail.

SALMON L.J.: ... In my judgment the police owe the public a clear legal duty to enforce the law.... [I]f, as is quite unthinkable, the chief police officer in any district were to issue an instruction that as a matter of policy the police would take no steps to prosecute any housebreaker, I have little doubt but that any householder in that district would be able to obtain an order of mandamus for the instruction to be withdrawn. Of course the police have a wide discretion as to whether or not they will prosecute in any particular case. In my judgment, however, the action I have postulated ... would be so improper that it could not amount to an exercise of discretion.

Mr. Worsley has argued that the discretion is absolute and can in no circumstances be challenged in the courts. He instances the policy decision not to prosecute, save in exceptional circumstances, young teenage boys who have had sexual intercourse with girls just under the age of sixteen. But this, in my view, is an entirely different and perfectly proper exercise of discretion. The object of the Criminal Law Amendment Act 1885 ... was ... to protect young girls against seduction. Unfortunately, in many of the cases today in which teenage boys are concerned, it is they rather than the girls who are in need of protection.... Moreover, experience has shown that if young boys are prosecuted in such circumstances, the courts usually take the humane and sensible course of imposing no penalty. The object of the statute which made housebreaking a crime was quite simply to prevent housebreaking in the interests of society. Similarly, the object of ... the Betting, Gaming and Lotteries Act 1963 and the Betting and Gaming Act 1960 which the statute of 1963 replaced, ... was ... to protect society against the evils which would necessarily follow were it possible to build up large fortunes by the exploitation of gaming. The statutes ... would have been entirely effective to do so had they been enforced. Regrettably they have not been properly enforced ... and ... an immense gaming industry, particularly in London, has been allowed to grow up during the last seven years. This has inevitably brought grave social evils in its train—protection

[46] [1967] 1 W.L.R. 1227.

rackets, crimes of violence and widespread corruption. . . . As long as it remains possible for large fortunes to be made by the private exploitation of gaming, the evils . . . will grow . . . until they threaten the whole fabric of society. Since large fortunes can be made . . . naturally a great deal of ingenuity has been exercised to devise schemes for the purpose of evading the law. With a little more resolution and efficiency, these schemes could and should have been frustrated. . . .

. . . What is now urgently needed is that energetic steps should immediately be taken to prosecute a substantial number of major London gaming houses in which the law is being defied. It may be that even when very heavy fines are imposed, they will be ineffective, in which event the Attorney-General would no doubt consider the advisability of bringing relator actions to restrain the present abuses by injunction.[47] . . . It seems to me fantastically unrealistic for the police . . . to suggest, as they have done, that their policy decision was unimportant because Mr. Blackburn was free to start private prosecutions of his own and fight the gambling empires, possibly up to the House of Lords, single-handed. . . . The only doubt I should have had would have been as to whether Mr. Blackburn had a sufficient personal interest . . . to obtain an order of mandamus. As it is, no order is necessary. . . .

EDMUND DAVIES L.J.: . . . We have ranged far and wide in this case—both chronologically (from Anglo-Saxon times to the present day) and geographically (from Las Vegas to the Edgware Road)—but we have not travelled an inch beyond that made necessary by the urgency and importance of the issues raised. . . . [T]he law enforcement officers of this country certainly owe a legal duty to the public to perform those functions which are the *raison d'être* of their existence. How and by whom that duty can be enforced is another matter, and it may be that a private citizen . . . having no special or peculiar interest in the due discharge of the duty under consideration, has himself no legal right to enforce it. But that is widely different from holding that no duty exists, enforceable either by a relator action or in some other manner which may here-after have to be determined.

[See also *R. v. Metropolitan Police Commissioner, ex parte Blackburn,*[48] in which Mr. Blackburn made an unsuccessful attempt to persuade the court to compel the Metropolitan Police to initiate a more active policy in relation to the sale of pornography.]

The Attorney-General and the Director of Public Prosecutions
483 H.C.Deb. 5s, c. 681, January 29, 1951

THE ATTORNEY-GENERAL (SIR HARTLEY SHAWCROSS) . . . It has never been the rule in this country . . . that suspected criminal offences must automatically be the subject of prosecution. . . . My hon. and learned Friend . . . asked me how I direct myself in deciding whether or not to prosecute in a particular case. . . . [T]he Attorney-General may have to have regard to a variety of considerations, all of them leading to the final question—would a prosecution be in the public interest, including in that phrase of course, in the interests of justice? Usually it is merely a question of examining the evidence. . . . It is not in the public interest to put a man upon trial, whatever the suspicions may be about the matter, when the evidence is insufficient to justify his conviction, or even to call upon him for an explanation. . . . In other cases wider considerations than that are involved. It is not always in the public interest to go through the whole process of the criminal law if, at the end of the day, perhaps because of

---

[47] *Att.-Gen.* v. *Harris* [1961] 1 Q.B. 74.

[48] [1973] 2 W.L.R. 43.

mitigating circumstances, perhaps because of what the defendant has already suffered, only a nominal penalty is likely to be imposed. And almost every day in particular cases, and where guilt has been admitted, I decide that the interests of public justice will be sufficiently served not by prosecuting, but perhaps by causing a warning to be administered, instead. Sometimes, of course, the considerations may be wider still. Prosecution may involve a question of public policy or national, or sometimes international, concern; but in cases like that, the Attorney-General has to make up his mind not as a party politician: he must in a quasi-judicial way consider the effect of prosecution upon the administration of law and of government in the abstract rather than in the party sense. Usually, making up my mind on these matters, I have the advice of the Director of Public Prosecutions, and very often Treasury Counsel as well. I have hardly ever, if ever, refused to prosecute when they have advised prosecution. I have sometimes ordered prosecution when the advice was against it.

I think that the true doctrine is that it is the duty of an Attorney-General, in deciding whether or not to authorise the prosecution, to acquaint himself with all the relevant facts, including, for instance, the effect which the prosecution, successful or unsuccessful as the case may be, would have upon public morale and order, and with any other considerations affecting public policy.... The existence ... and the utility of this discretion ... has been so well recognised that there has been an increasing tendency in recent years to provide that there shall be no proceedings as to particular classes of offences created by statute without the consent of the Attorney-General or the Director of Public Prosecutions. That kind of provision has been made to ensure that there will be no automatic prosecutions and that there will be no frivolous and unnecessary prosecutions in such cases.... But where a provision of that kind does not exist ... the general position in English law ... is that any private citizen can ... set the criminal law in motion. That is really the safeguard if the Attorney-General and the Director of Public Prosecutions and the police all neglect their duties and do not prosecute in cases where, manifestly, prosecutions ought to take place.[49] ... In the case of murder, although a private citizen may initiate proceedings to the extent of ... obtaining a warrant for the arrest of some named individual, it is the statutory duty of the Director of Public Prosecutions to ... take over the conduct of the case, no doubt because Parliament has thought that in cases of such gravity it is important that the prosecution should be conducted with all possible safeguards by an experienced official such as the Director....

Prosecution of Offences Act 1879
42 & 43 Vict. c. 22

2. It shall be the duty of the Director of Public Prosecutions, under the superintendence of the Attorney-General, to institute, undertake, or carry on such criminal proceedings ... and to give such advice and assistance to chief officers of police, clerks to justices, and other persons, whether officers or not, concerned in any criminal proceeding respecting the conduct of that proceeding, as may be for the time being prescribed by regulations under this Act, or may be directed in a special case by the Attorney-General....

2A.[50] (1) Without prejudice to the foregoing section, it shall be the duty of the Director of Public Prosecutions to appear for the Crown or the prosecutor,

---

[49] Note, however, that as regards indictable offences the Attorney-General can issue a *nolle prosequi* to stop the proceedings.
[50] S. 2A was added by Criminal Appeal Act 1968, c. 19, s. 52 (1), Sched. 5.

when directed by the court to do so, on any appeal under section 1 of the Administration of Justice Act 1960 (appeal from High Court in criminal cases) or Part I or Part II of the Criminal Appeal Act 1968 (appeals from the Crown Court to criminal division of the Court of Appeal and thence to the House of Lords).

(2) In subsection (1) of this section " the court " means, in the case of an appeal to or from the criminal division of the Court of Appeal, that division and, in the case of an appeal from a Divisional Court of the Queen's Bench Division, the Divisional Court.

8. The Attorney-General, with the approval of the Lord Chancellor and a Secretary of State, may from time to time, make and when made rescind, vary, and add to, regulations for carrying into effect this Act.

Prosecution of Offences Act 1884

47 & 48 Vict. c. 58

3. The chief officer of every police district in England shall, from time to time, give to the Director of Public Prosecutions information with respect to indictable offences alleged to have been committed within the district of such chief officer, and to the dealing with those offences, and the said information shall contain such particulars and be in such form as may be for the time being required by regulations under the principal Act.

Prosecution of Offences Act 1908

8 Edw. 7, c. 3

1.—(1) . . . [T]he Secretary of State may appoint the Director of Public Prosecutions and may also appoint such number of assistant directors as the Treasury sanction.

(5) An Assistant Director . . . may do any act or thing which the Director . . . is required or authorised to do . . .

2.—(1) The regulations under the Prosecution of Offences Act, 1879 shall provide for the Director of Public Prosecutions taking action in cases which appear to him to be of importance or difficulty, or which from any other reason require his intervention. . . .

(3) Nothing in the Prosecution of Offences Acts, 1879 and 1884, or in this Act, shall preclude any person from instituting or carrying on any criminal proceedings, but the Director of Public Prosecutions may undertake at any stage the conduct of those proceedings if he thinks fit.

Prosecution of Offences Regulations 1946

S.R. & O. 1946 No. 1467

1. It shall be the duty of the Director of Public Prosecutions to institute, undertake or carry on criminal proceedings in the following cases, that is to say—

(a) in the case of any offence punishable with death;

(b) in any case referred to him by a Government Department in which he considers that criminal proceedings should be instituted; and

(c) in any case which appears to him to be of importance or difficulty or which for any other reason requires his intervention.

2. The Director of Public Prosecutions shall give advice, whether on applica-tion or on his own initiative, to Government Departments, clerks to justices, chief officers of police and to such other persons as he may think right in any criminal matter which appears to him to be of importance or difficulty and such advice may be given at his discretion either orally or in writing. . . .

5. The Director of Public Prosecutions shall in all matters, including the nomination of counsel, be subject to the directions of the Attorney-General.

6.—(1) The chief officer of every police district within the meaning of the Prosecution of Offences Act, 1884, shall, as respects offences alleged to have been committed within his police district, report to the Director of Public Prosecutions—

(*a*) every offence punishable with death;

(*b*) every offence in respect of which the prosecution has by statute to be undertaken by or requires by statute the consent of the Director of Public Prosecutions;

(*c*) every indictable case in which the prosecution is wholly withdrawn or is not proceeded with within a reasonable time;

(*d*) every case in which a request for information is made by the Director of Public Prosecutions; and

(*e*) every case in which it appears to the chief officer of police that the advice or assistance of the Director of Public Prosecutions is desirable.

(2) The chief officer of police shall also report, as respects offences alleged to have been committed within his police district, to the Director of Public Prosecutions—

(*a*) offences under the following Acts : —
    (i) Punishment of Incest Act, 1908 [51];
    (ii) Official Secrets Acts, 1911 to 1939;
    (iii) Forgery Act, 1913, sections 2 and 3;
    (iv) Coinage Offences Act, 1936, and Gold and Silver (Export Control etc.) Act, 1920, section 2;

(*b*) offences of sedition (including seditious libel), conspiracies to pervert or defeat the course of justice, public mischief, libel on persons occupying judicial or public offices, bribery and corruption of or by a public official, fraudulent conversion by a public official, solicitor or trustee;

(*c*) offences of manslaughter, attempted murder, rape, abortion, carnal know-ledge of mental defectives, defilement of girls under thirteen years of age, indecent offences upon a number of children or young persons, sexual offences against a child or young person involving the com-munication of a venereal disease, and cases in which there has been a previous conviction for the same or a similar sexual offence and the offence charged is one that can be dealt with summarily;

(*d*) cases of obscene or indecent libels, exhibitions or publications, in which it appears to the chief officer of police that there is a prima facie case for prosecution; and

(*e*) cases under the Extradition Acts, 1870 to 1935, and the Fugitive Offenders Acts, 1881 and 1915.

9. In any case in which the prosecution for an offence instituted before examining justices or a court of summary jurisdiction is wholly withdrawn or is not proceeded with within a reasonable time it shall be the duty of the clerk to the justices or to the court to send to the Director of Public Prosecutions a report of the case and to supply the Director of Public Prosecutions with such further information or documents in relation to the case as he may require.

[51] Now the Sexual Offences Act 1956.

Report of the Royal Commission on the Police
Cmnd. 1728, 1962

Uniformity of law enforcement

379. ... We were asked by the Inns of Court Conservative and Unionist Society, the Magistrates' Association, the Justices " Clerks " Society and other witnesses to recommend the introduction in England and Wales of a system of public prosecutions similar to that in Scotland. The advantages claimed for this were, first, that it would minister to good relations between the police and the public if the decision to prosecute were placed in other hands; secondly, that it would be in the public interest to relieve the police of their present unregulated discretion in this matter; and thirdly, that a system of independent public prosecution would make for a greater uniformity in the enforcement of the criminal law. Such a major change in the machinery for the administration of justice in England and Wales lies doubtfully within our terms of reference, and we have not therefore received or sought the full and detailed evidence on this matter on which any recommendation would have to be based.

380. We do, however, endorse an alternative recommendation made to us by the Magistrates' Association, the Law Society and other witnesses that the police ... should have more legal advice in deciding upon prosecutions or in issuing summonses than is the present practice. We recommend that consideration be given to the appointment of a prosecuting solicitor for every force where this is not already the practice. ...

The police and the motoring public

389. Sensible modern laws, consonant with public opinion and generally understood and accepted, are the indispensable foundation on which the police themselves can enforce the road traffic laws uniformly. But they will still leave a certain amount of discretion to the police. This is partly because of the magnitude of the problem. Enforcement of the law against speeding, for example, cannot but be sporadic. But there are some ways in which the police can exercise their discretion more wisely and more uniformly than they do at present, and thus secure better support and understanding from the motoring public who, because of their mobility between one district and another, are bound to be more sensitive to an uneven pattern of law enforcement than other sections of the public.

390. The motoring associations gave us several examples of ... inconsistent policies adopted by different forces. ... Thus some forces are much more ready than others to issue warnings to motorists for minor offences, in preference to instituting proceedings. ... Lack of uniformity is also seen in the practice adopted in some police forces of preferring alternative charges of dangerous and careless driving where it is reasonably clear that a bench is only likely to convict on the lesser charge. There is no justification for causing anxiety by such a procedure and we recommend that this practice be brought to an end. Yet another example of lack of uniformity of practice concerns the acceptance of pleas of guilty by post. We understand that in some areas the police regard prosecutions of, for example, careless driving as being suitable for the procedure under the Magistrates' Courts Act, 1957, whereby a defendant may plead guilty by post. ... Elsewhere such cases are treated much more seriously.

391. ... We ... recommend that chief officers of police, in consultation with other authorities concerned, formulate uniform policies in regard to the matters to which we have referred. We also recommend that these policies be given adequate publicity, so that the traffic laws can be seen to be consistently enforced throughout the country.

Preventing a multiplicity of prosecutions

Connelly v. Director of Public Prosecutions

House of Lords [1964] A.C. 1254

LORD DEVLIN: ... My Lords, in my opinion, the judges of the High Court have in their inherent jurisdiction, both in civil and criminal matters, power (subject of course to any statutory rules) to make and enforce rules of practice in order to ensure that the court's process is used fairly and conveniently by both sides. I consider it to be within this power for the court to declare that the prosecution must as a general rule join in the same indictment charges that " are founded on the same facts, or form or are part of a series of offences of the same or similar character " (I quote from the Indictments Act, 1915, Schedule 1, rule 3 . . .); and power to enforce such a direction (as indeed is already done in the civil process) by staying a second indictment if it is satisfied that its subject-matter ought to have been included in the first. I think that the appropriate form of the order to make in such a case is that the indictment remains on the file marked " not to be proceeded with ". . . . The doctrine of " autrefois " protects an accused in circumstances in which he has actually been in peril. It cannot, naturally enough, protect him in circumstances in which he could have been put in peril but was not. Yet even the simplest set of facts almost invariably give rise to more than one offence.

In my opinion, if the Crown were to be allowed to prosecute as many times as it wanted to do on the same facts, so long as for each prosecution it could find a different offence in law, there would be a grave danger of abuse and injustice to defendants. The Crown might, for example, begin with a minor accusation so as to have a trial run and test the strength of the defence. Or, as a way of getting round the impotence of the Court of Criminal Appeal to order a new trial [52] when, as in this case, it quashes a conviction, the Crown might keep a count up its sleeve. Or a private prosecutor might seek to harass a defendant by multiplicity of process in the different courts.

There is another factor to be considered, and that is the courts' duty to conduct their proceedings so as to command the respect and confidence of the public. For this purpose it is absolutely necessary that issues of fact that are substantially the same should, whenever practicable, be tried by the same tribunal and at the same time. Human judgment is not infallible. Two judges or two juries may reach different conclusions on the same evidence, and it would not be possible to say that one is nearer than the other to the correct. Apart from human fallibility the differences may be accounted for by differences in the evidence. No system of justice can guarantee that every judgment is right, but it can and should do its best to secure that there are not conflicting judgments in the same matter. Suppose that in the present case the appellant had first been acquitted of robbery and then convicted of murder. Inevitably doubts would be felt about the soundness of the conviction. That is why every system of justice is bound to insist upon the finality of the judgment arrived at by a due process of law. It is quite inconsistent with that principle that the Crown should be entitled to re-open again and again what is in effect the same matter. . . .

The Solicitor-General does not dispute that if the prosecution were in fact to behave in all the ways in which according to his argument they could legally behave, there would be abuses which ought to be corrected. But in his submission the danger of abuse is a matter for the Crown; the Crown itself may

---

[52] The Court of Appeal now has this power in some cases, see below, p. 634.

be trusted not to abuse its powers and if a private prosecutor is abusing his, the Attorney-General can interfere by means of a *nolle prosequi*.

The fact that the Crown has, as is to be expected, and that private prosecutors have (as is also to be expected, for they are usually public authorities) generally behaved with great propriety in the conduct of prosecutions, has up till now avoided the need for any consideration of this point. Now that it emerges, it is seen to be one of great constitutional importance. Are the courts to rely on the Executive to protect their process from abuse? Have they not themselves an inescapable duty to secure fair treatment for those who come or are brought before them? To questions of this sort there is only one possible answer. The courts cannot contemplate for a moment the transference to the Executive of the responsibility for seeing that the process of law is not abused. . . .

I pass now to consider the position in civil suits. . . . The doctrine of *res judicata* occupies the same place in the civil law as the doctrine of *autrefois* does in the criminal. *Autrefois* applies to offences that are charged and not to those that could have been. *Res judicata*, also, if strictly confined, applies only to issues that are raised and not to those that could have been. But from early times it was recognised that some protection must be given to defendants against multiplicity of actions in respect of issues that could have been raised and that were not. At first in the civil law (and I shall note later a similar tendency in the criminal law) it was done by trying to extend the doctrine of *res judicata*. The classic judgment on this point is by Wigram V.-C. in *Henderson v. Henderson.*[53] He said:

> " I believe I state the rule of the court correctly, when I say that where a given matter becomes the subject of litigation in, and of adjudication by, a court of competent jurisdiction, the court requires the parties to that litigation to bring forward their whole case, and will not (except under special circumstances) permit the same parties to open the same subject of litigation in respect of matter which might have been brought forward as part of the subject in contest, but which was not brought forward, only because they have, from negligence, inadvertence, or even accident, omitted part of their case. The plea of *res judicata* applies, except in special cases, not only to points upon which the court was actually required by the parties to form an opinion and pronounce a judgment, but to every point which properly belonged to the subject of litigation, and which the parties, exercising reasonable diligence, might have brought forward at the time."

It will be observed that this rule is not rigid; the plea of *res judicata* applies except in special circumstances.

Macdougall v. Knight [54] was a case in which the plaintiff was suing a second time on a different defamatory statement in the same pamphlet. Lord Esher M.R. said: " even if the plaintiff could in law split up the defamatory matter in the report into different causes of action, I think such a course would be vexatious, so that either way I am of opinion the appeal must be allowed and the action stayed." Actions have been stayed upon the same principle by the Court of Appeal in *Greenhalgh v. Mallard* [55] and *Wright v. Bennett.*[56] In the latter case the court did not reach any conclusion as to whether the plea of *res judicata* would succeed.

I think it is likely that there would have been a similar development in criminal procedure, had it not been that prosecutions fell largely into the hands

[53] (1843) 3 Hare 100, 114–115.
[54] (1890) 25 Q.B.D. 1, C.A.
[55] [1947] 2 All E.R. 255, C.A.
[56] [1948] 1 All E.R. 227, C.A.

of public authorities, who in practice impose restrictions on themselves. Any development would probably have been based on the principle—wider than that of *autrefois* because it comprehended different offences in relation to the same facts—first stated by Cockburn C.J. in *R.* v. *Elrington*[57] ...: " We must bear in mind the well-established principle of our criminal law that a series of charges shall not be preferred, and, whether a party accused of a minor offence is acquitted or convicted, he shall not be charged again on the same facts in a more aggravated form." This was applied in *R.* v. *Miles*[58] and *R.* v. *Grimwood*.[59] In both cases a conviction for common assault was held to be a bar to subsequent charges of wounding, including wounding with intent to cause grievous bodily harm.... To charge the appellant with murder in this case is really only to charge him with robbery in an aggravated form. His guilt consisted in taking part in a robbery in which one of the serious consequences of the threat inherent in the robbery was murder. It is very often only the consequences which differentiate one offence from another. I cannot say that robbery is the same offence as murder any more than I can say that wounding with intent to cause grievous bodily harm is the same offence as common assault.... The facts in the two cases may be substantially the same, but as offences they are quite distinct.... In my opinion, therefore, the principle stated by Cockburn C.J. as applied in *R.* v. *Miles* necessarily goes beyond the principle of *autrefois*. I consider it very desirable that the two principles should be kept distinct, for one gives the defendant an absolute right to relief and the other only a qualified right. I think it is equally desirable that they should be kept distinct in the civil law. *Res judicata* imposes a rigid bar and Wigram V.-C.'s principle a flexible one. I prefer the modern development of this principle which justifies it by the power to stop vexatious process. This, to my mind, is the true principle that is to be extracted from Cockburn C.J.'s statement of the law and the one that I think should be applied in the criminal law as it is in the civil.

... [A] second trial on the same or similar facts is not always and necessarily oppressive, and there may in a particular case be special circumstances which make it just and convenient in that case. The judge must then, in all the circumstances of the particular case, exercise his discretion as to whether or not he applies the general rule. Without attempting a comprehensive definition, it may be useful to indicate the sort of thing that would, I think, clearly amount to a special circumstance.... [W]here the case is one in which, if the offences in the second indictment had been included in the first, the judge would have ordered a separate trial of them, he will in his discretion allow the second indictment to be proceeded with. *A fortiori*, where the accused has himself obtained an order for a separate trial ... [i]f the prosecution considers that there ought to be two or more trials, it can make its choice plain by preferring two or more indictments. In many cases this may be to the advantage of the defence. If the defence accepts the choice without complaint and avails itself of any advantage that may flow from it, I should regard that as a special circumstance; for where the defence considers that a single trial of two indictments is desirable, it can apply to the judge for an order in the form made by Glyn-Jones J. in *R.* v. *Smith*[60] ...

For the rules applying to " plea-bargaining," see for example *R.* v. *Turner*.[61] Consider also this report taken at random from the *Hampstead and Highgate Express and News*, December 24, 1971:

[57] (1861) 1 B. & S. 688, 696.
[58] (1890) 24 Q.B.D. 423.
[59] (1896) 60 J.P. 809.
[60] [1958] 1 W.L.R. 312.
[61] [1970] 2 Q.B. 321.

Police offered no evidence at Hendon court last Thursday against a housewife accused of possessing a .38 revolver, a Smith and Wesson revolver and 365 rounds of ammunition.... Police also offered no evidence on a further charge against her of dishonestly handling a quantity of cigarettes. Appearing with her was ... R ... M ..., of the same address. A charge against him of dishonestly handling £900 cash was also not proceeded with. Mr. M ... pleaded guilty to dishonestly handling £9 worth of Embassy cigarettes at his home.... Detective Chief Superintendant Mooney told the court that no evidence would be offered on the guns and said that both Mrs. C ... and Mr. M ... had been "extremely helpful to the police in their enquiries." This had led to the arrest of another man. Mr. M ... was given a conditional discharge for 12 months and ordered to pay £5 costs on the dishonest handling charge.

The role of the magistrates' court

Once a criminal case is ready it can be brought at once to trial if it is to be tried summarily. If it is to be tried on indictment however it must be brought before the local magistrates for a preliminary investigation.

The character of this preliminary investigation has changed considerably since it was first instituted. The Tucker Committee [62] noted:

11. Before the establishment of a regular police force the role of examining justices was inquisitorial. Their duty was to "pursue and arrest" offenders: they were, in short, detectives and prosecutors. They normally conducted business from and in their private homes. The taking of depositions was first required by Acts of 1554 and 1555.[63] ... [B]efore the accused was committed they served much the same purpose as statements taken by the police today, *i.e.* they formed the basis for the decision whether to prosecute or not. The examination of witnesses was normally held in private and the accused had no right to be present.

In the same vein the Byrne Committee [64] noted:

5. In the seventeenth century it was customary closely to question the accused himself at the preliminary examination. The evidence of the witnesses was not then taken in his presence but was regarded as being solely for the information of the court of trial. Even much nearer to our own times, in 1823, the Grand Jury was told that "when a magistrate was conducting his preliminary examination, he was acting inquisitorially and not judicially; that such proceedings might be communicated to the prosecutor but not to the party accused." Three years

[62] Report of the Departmental Committee on Proceedings before Examining Justices, Cmnd. 479, 1958. The Tucker Committee was appointed in October 1957 "to consider whether proceedings before examining justices should continue to take place in open court, and if so, whether it is necessary or desirable that any restriction should be placed on the publication of reports of such proceedings."

[63] 1 & 2 Ph. & M., c. 13; 2 & 3 Ph. & M., c. 10.

[64] The Byrne Committee was appointed in March 1948 "to inquire into the existing practice with regard to the taking of depositions in criminal cases and to report whether any, and if so, what, alterations in the law were necessary or desirable with a view to securing the more effective despatch of business of the courts while retaining public confidence in the administration of justice." It reported in Cmd. 7639, 1949.

later, however, the procedure on committal for trial was regulated by the Criminal Law Act of 1826 ... and from then onwards the interests of the accused received more consideration. In 1836 the Trials for Felony Act, perhaps better known as the Prisoners' Counsel Act, allowed accused persons at the time of their trial to inspect all depositions taken against them " without fee or reward."

In 1848 the Indictable Offences Act consolidated with amendments the whole law relating to the duties of examining justices and in particular provided that the accused was entitled to be present at the examination of the witnesses. The proceedings are now regulated by the Magistrates' Courts Act 1952 as amended by the Criminal Justice Act 1967.

The Byrne Committee in 1948 rejected the suggestion that it was time the formal taking of depositions before the magistrates should be abandoned. It said:

> 7. ... It has ... been suggested that the taking of depositions is now an anachronism and is merely a waste of time of the justices and of the labour of the clerk.... [W]e are satisfied beyond doubt that the proper taking of depositions before examining justices ... still forms an essential part of our system of justice....
>
> 8. ... [C]ommittal proceedings before examining justices are no mere formality. The justices have to decide not only whether there is a *prima facie* case against the accused but also whether there is, to quote the judgment of the Divisional Court in *R.* v. *Governor of Brixton Prison, ex parte Bidwell*,[65] " such evidence, that if it be uncontradicted at the trial a reasonably minded jury may convict upon it." They have therefore to consider the quality as well as the quantity of the evidence. Since the abolition of the grand jury, committal proceedings have become of even greater importance than before as a safeguard to the accused, and the fact that this preliminary investigation takes place is a valuable safeguard against speculative prosecutions. There are, moreover, a number of cases in which the justices either do not commit for trial or decide, frequently at the instance of the prosecution, to commit for a different offence from the one originally charged.

Since 1967, however, there has been a change and the preliminary investigation has lost much of its importance. The Criminal Justice Act of that year provided that in certain circumstances the proceedings could be merely formal and the statements of witnesses made out of court could be used instead of depositions to establish a *prima facie* case for committal for trial on indictment. Two other important changes that have taken place in recent years have been in relation to the publicity of the preliminary proceedings and the practice which allows the accused not to reveal his defence at this stage. The question of publicity was the particular concern of the Tucker Committee. The reason for their concern was the fact that it was customary at the preliminary proceedings for only the case for the prosecution to be presented. If this was widely reported it was almost inevitable that a member of the jury who eventually came to try the case would have

---

65 [1937] 1 K.B. 305, 314.

seen the report and in a particularly notorious case it might be almost impossible to get a jury which knew nothing of the case beforehand. Its recommendations were followed by the Criminal Justice Act 1967 which made provisions for the proceedings to be conducted without publicity.

The other change has been in relation to the privilege of the accused to reserve his defence until the actual trial. Following a recommendation of the Criminal Law Revision Committee, the Criminal Justice Act 1967 provided that where an accused person intended to rely on an alibi, then he must give formal notice of this before the trial. If he does not do so, then subject to the power of the trial judge to waive the requirement, he will not be allowed to give evidence of it as a part of his defence.

Summary trial

Magistrates' Courts Act 1952

1952, c. 55

13.—(1) On the summary trial of an information, the court shall, if the accused appears, state to him the substance of the information and ask him whether he pleads guilty or not guilty.

(2) The court, after hearing the evidence and the parties, shall convict the accused or dismiss the information.

(3) If the accused pleads guilty, the court may convict him without hearing evidence.[66]

Offences triable on indictment or summarily

18.—(1) Where an information charges any person with an offence that is by virtue of any enactment both an indictable offence and a summary offence, the magistrates' court . . . shall, if the accused has attained the age of seventeen, proceed as if the offence were not a summary offence, unless the court having jurisdiction to try the information summarily, determines on the application of the prosecutor to do so.

(2) An application . . . shall be made before any evidence is called and, if the accused fails to appear to answer to the information, may be made in his absence.

(3) Where a magistrates' court has, in pursuance of subsection (1) of this section, begun to inquire into the information as examining justices, then, if at any time during the inquiry it appears to the court, having regard to any representations made in the presence of the accused by the prosecutor, or made by the accused, and to the nature of the case, that it is proper to do so, the court may proceed to try the case summarily:

Provided that, if the prosecution is being carried on by the Director of Public Prosecutions, the court shall not act under this subsection without the Director's consent. . . .

(5) Where, under subsection (1) of this section, a magistrates' court has begun to try an information summarily, the court may, at any time before the conclusion of the evidence for the prosecution, discontinue the summary trial and proceed to inquire into the information as examining justices. . . .

19.—(1) The following provisions of this section shall have effect where a person who has attained the age of seventeen appears or is brought before a

[66] The Magistrates' Courts Act 1957 makes provision for defendants to plead guilty by post in a number of cases.

magistrates' court on an information charging him with any of the indictable offences specified in the First Schedule to this Act.

(2) If at any time during the inquiry into the offence it appears to the court, having regard to any representations made in the presence of the accused by the prosecutor or made by the accused, and to the nature of the case, that the punishment that the court has power to inflict under this section would be adequate and that the circumstances do not make the offence one of serious character and do not for other reasons require trial on indictment, the court may proceed with a view to summary trial.

(3) For the purpose of proceeding as aforesaid, the court shall cause the charge to be written down . . . and read to the accused and shall tell him that he may, if he consents, be tried summarily instead of being tried by a jury and, if the court thinks it desirable for his information, shall . . . explain what is meant by being tried summarily.

(4) . . . [T]he court shall also explain to him that if he consents to be tried summarily and is convicted . . . he may be committed to the Crown Court under section 29 of this Act if the court, on obtaining information of his character and antecedents, is of opinion that they are such that greater punishment should be inflicted than the court has power to inflict.

(5) After informing the accused as provided by the last two preceding subsections the court shall ask him whether he wishes to be tried by a jury or consents to be tried summarily, and, if he consents, shall proceed to the summary trial of the information.

(6) A person summarily convicted of an indictable offence under this section shall be liable to imprisonment for a term not exceeding six months or a fine not exceeding £400 or both.

(7) Nothing in this section shall empower a magistrates' court to try an indictable offence summarily—

(a) without the consent of the prosecutor in a case affecting property or affairs of Her Majesty or of a public body as defined by section 7 of the Public Bodies Corrupt Practices Act 1889;

(b) without the consent of the Director of Public Prosecutions where the prosecution is being carried on by him.

25.—(1) Where a person who has attained the age of seventeen is charged before a magistrates' court with a summary offence for which he is liable, or would if he were adult be liable, to be sentenced by the court to imprisonment for a term exceeding three months, he may, subject to the provisions of this section, claim to be tried by a jury, unless the offence is an assault or an offence under section 30 or 31 of the Sexual Offences Act 1956 or an offence under section 32 of that Act where the immoral purpose is other than the commission of a homosexual act.

(3) A magistrates' court before which a person is charged with a summary offence for which he may claim to be tried by a jury shall, before asking him whether he pleads guilty, inform him of his right and, if the court thinks it desirable for the information of the accused, . . . explain what is meant by being tried summarily; and shall then ask him whether he wishes, instead of being tried summarily, to be tried by a jury.

(5) Where the accused is charged with an offence that is both—

(a) a summary offence for which the accused may claim to be tried by a jury and

(b) an indictable offence . . .

then, if the court, having begun under subsection (1) of section 18 . . . to proceed as if the offence were not a summary one, proceeds under subsection (3) of that section with a view to summary trial, it shall, before asking the accused whether he wishes to be tried by a jury, explain to him that if he is tried summarily and is convicted he may be committed for sentence to the Crown Court under section 29 of this Act if the court, on obtaining information of his character and antecedents, is of opinion that they are such that greater punishment should be inflicted than the court has power to inflict.

29. Where on the summary trial under subsection (3) of section 18 or section 19 ... of an indictable offence ... a person who is not less than seventeen years old is convicted of the offence, then, if on obtaining information about his character and antecedents the court is of opinion that they are such that greater punishment should be inflicted for the offence than the court has the power to inflict, the court may [in accordance with section 56 of the Criminal Justice Act 1967] commit him in custody or on bail to the Crown Court for sentence in accordance with the provisions of section 29 of the Criminal Justice Act 1948.

Magistrates' Courts Act 1952

Proceedings preliminary to trial on indictment

4.—(1) The functions of examining justices may be discharged by a single justice. . . .

(3) Evidence given before examining justices shall be given in the presence of the accused; and the defence shall be at liberty to put questions to any witness at the inquiry. . . .

7.—(1) Subject to the provisions of this and any other Act relating to the summary trial of indictable offences, if a magistrates' court inquiring into an offence as examining justices is of opinion, on consideration of the evidence and of any statement of the accused, that there is sufficient evidence to put the accused upon trial by jury for any indictable offence, the court shall commit him for trial; and, if it is not of that opinion, it shall, if he is in custody for no other cause than the offence under inquiry, discharge him.

In introducing the second reading of the Criminal Justice Bill in the House of Commons on December 12, 1966 [67] the Home Secretary Mr. Roy Jenkins said, *inter alia*:

[M]y object has been to construct a Bill which would be consistently liberal and rational in its approach to the difficult and emotional questions of crime and punishment, while at the same time being directly relevant in all its approaches to the most menacing crime situation with which this country has recently been confronted.

In seeking to achieve this twin purpose, I have tried to follow three main strands of policy. The first has been that of streamlining our criminal court procedure so as to enable all those concerned with law enforcement, and, certainly not least, the police, to operate within a less time-wasting framework.

... Here the most important provision relates to committal proceedings, dealt with in Clauses 1 to 4. In 1965 there were nearly 30,000 such proceedings before magistrates preliminary to criminal trials on indictment. At these committal proceedings all the prosecution

[67] 738 H.C.Deb. c. 52.

witnesses gave evidence orally to enable justices to decide whether the case should go for trial. In nearly 29,000 of these cases the justices did so decide and the full procedure, time-consuming for all concerned, had to be gone through twice, except where there were initial pleas of guilty.

I considered very carefully whether it would be possible to sweep away committal proceedings completely, but then I became convinced that, although it had its attractions, it would not be right. No one ought to be put on trial at assizes or quarter sessions and perhaps spend about six weeks in custody awaiting trial, without some preliminary judicial investigation.

In certain cases, too, it is a real advantage to the defence, and in some others to the prosecution, to have the evidence sifted at this stage. Furthermore a decision has to be taken as to whether bail should be granted. For all these reasons we cannot, I believe, get rid of committal proceedings entirely, but we can, and I think should, greatly restrict their role.

What I propose in the Bill is that the prosecution will give the accused, in advance, copies of the statements of those of their witnesses whom they do not wish to call to give evidence orally. The defendant will have an absolute right to demand the appearance of all or any of these witnesses. But if he does not require a witness to be called, then that witness will not appear and his statement will be used as evidence at the committal proceedings, which will otherwise take the ordinary form. If all the prosecution evidence is in the form of written statements and the defendant is prepared to accept them as evidence, then, if he does not intend to give or to call evidence himself orally or to argue that the evidence is insufficient for committal to trial, he may be committed for trial in proceedings lasting a few minutes without the justices considering the statements.

This is, in effect, committal by consent and is dealt with in Clause 1. We thought it right in the interests of the defendant to limit this to cases in which the defendant is legally represented so that there is no danger of his so acting without knowledge of the consequences of his action. If these proposals are put into effect, I hope that only a small proportion of witnesses would have to give evidence at the committal stage and that we should produce a substantially time-saving but equally just judicial system. The saving of the time of police witnesses would be considerable.

I have also had to consider what should be the rule about the reporting of committal proceedings in the new circumstances. The Tucker Committee, which reported as long ago as 1958, recommended that there should be a ban somewhat similar to that which has applied for 40 years to the reporting of evidence in divorce cases. It is easy to understand some of the reasons for this. In sensational cases, such as the Moors Murder, the public are served up with the revolting details twice over. In other cases the defence might believe, and believe reasonably, that they were being harmed by the difficulty, after a well-publicised preliminary hearing, of finding an unprejudiced jury. In other cases, substantial damage might be done to a man's reputation by the publication of an uncontested prosecution case and not substantially corrected by the less interesting news six weeks or so later of his acquittal.

To balance these considerations there is the natural repugnance of most of us to court proceedings not being fully publicised. The new rules in relation to committal proceedings will create a new situation. In many such proceedings there will be no evidence to report. For the remainder, I think that the fairest arrangement is that the defence should always be given the right to opt for publicity, but that if they do not do so there should be a restriction on reports of more than the bare details of committal proceedings until the trial has been completed. In this way I think that the main purpose of the Tucker recommendations can be achieved without any unreasonable restrictions on the rights of Press or public.

I should add that in Clause 5 we are restricting the rights of examining magistrates to sit *in camera*. In the past this has been an absolute discretion with the magistrates, although not one very widely used. In the future the magistrates will have to be positively convinced that another enactment, such as the Official Secrets Act, requires them to do so, or that the ends of justice make this necessary, and they should be prepared to give their reasons for this or otherwise always to sit in open court.

Criminal Justice Act 1967
1967, c. 80

Committal for trial without consideration of the evidence

1.—(1) A magistrates' court inquiring into an offence as examining justices may, if satisfied that all the evidence before the court . . . consists of written statements tendered to the court under the next following section, . . . commit the defendant for trial for the offence without consideration of the contents of those statements, unless—

(*a*) the defendant . . . is not represented by counsel or a solicitor;

(*b*) counsel or a solicitor for the defendant . . . has requested the court to consider a submission that the statements disclose insufficient evidence to put that defendant on trial by jury for the offence.

(2) Section 7 (1) of the Magistrates' Courts Act 1952 (committal for trial on consideration of the evidence) shall not apply to a committal for trial under this section.

2.—(1) In committal proceedings a written statement by any person shall, if the conditions mentioned in the next following subsection are satisfied, be admissible as evidence to the like extent as oral evidence to the like effect by that person.

(2) The said conditions are : —

(*a*) the statement purports to be signed by the person who made it;

(*b*) the statement contains a declaration by that person to the effect that it is true to the best of his knowledge and belief and that he made the statement knowing that, if it were tendered in evidence, he would be liable to prosecution if he wilfully stated in it anything which he knew to be false or did not believe to be true;

(c) before the statement is tendered in evidence, a copy of the statement is given . . . to each of the other parties to the proceedings; and

(d) none of the other parties, before the statement is tendered in evidence at the committal proceedings, objects. . . .

(3) The following provisions shall also have effect in relation to any written statement tendered in evidence under this section, that is to say—

(a) if the statement is made by a person under the age of twenty-one, it shall give his age;

(b) if it is made by a person who cannot read it, it shall be read to him before he signs it and shall be accompanied by a declaration by the person who so read the statement to the effect that it was so read; and

(c) if it refers to any other document as an exhibit, the copy given to any other party . . . shall be accompanied by a copy or that document or by such information as may be necessary in order to enable the party to whom it is given to inspect that document or a copy thereof.

(4) Notwithstanding that a written statement made by any person may be admissible in committal proceedings by virtue of this section, the court before which the proceedings are held may, of its own motion or on the application of any party to the proceedings, require that person to attend before the court and give evidence.

(5) So much of any statement as is admitted in evidence by virtue of this section shall, unless the court commits the defendant for trial by virtue of the last foregoing section or the court otherwise directs, be read aloud at the hearing, and where the court so directs an account shall be given orally of so much of any statement as is not read aloud.

(6) Any document or object referred to as an exhibit and identified in a written statement tendered in evidence under this section shall be treated as if it had been produced as an exhibit and identified in court by the maker of the statement.

(7) Section 13 (3) of the Criminal Justice Act 1925 (reading of deposition as evidence at the trial) shall apply to any written statement tendered in evidence in committal proceedings under this section, as it applies to a deposition taken in such proceedings, but in its application to any such statement that subsection shall have effect as if paragraph (b) thereof were omitted.

(8) In section 2 (2) of the Administration of Justice (Miscellaneous Provisions) Act 1933 (procedure for preferring bills of indictment) the reference in proviso (i) to facts disclosed in any deposition taken before a justice in the presence of the defendant shall be construed as including a reference to facts disclosed in any such written statement as aforesaid.

(9) Section 23 of the Magistrates' Courts Act 1952 (use in summary trial of evidence given in committal proceedings) shall not apply to any such statement as aforesaid.

(10) A person whose written statement is tendered in evidence in committal proceedings under this section shall be treated for the purposes of section 1 of the Criminal Procedure (Attendance of Witnesses) Act 1965 (witness orders) as a witness who has been examined by the court.

6.—(1) Examining justices shall sit in open court except where any enactment contains an express provision to the contrary and except where it appears to them as respects the whole or any part of committal proceedings that the ends of justice would not be served by their sitting in open court.[68]

---

[68] Note, however, the restrictions on the publication of the proceedings contained in s. 3.

Notices of alibi

Ninth Report of the Criminal Law Revision Committee
Cmnd. 3145, 1966

31. In contrast to the prosecution the defence in criminal trials are not required to disclose their case before the trial. The accused has the advantage of knowing the case for the prosecution in detail from the evidence given at the committal proceedings and notices of additional evidence. But neither when charged nor at the committal proceedings is he obliged to say what his defence will be or even to say whether he admits or denies the charge. At the committal proceedings, after the evidence for the prosecution has been given and the charge has been read to the accused, the court is required to ask the accused whether he wishes to say anything in answer to the charge but must tell him that he need not say anything unless he wishes to do so (Magistrates' Courts Rules 1952, Rule 5 (4)). Even at the trial the accused need not disclose his defence at the beginning but can wait till it is necessary to do so by cross-examination of the witnesses for the prosecution or by giving or calling evidence himself. He need not inform the prosecution of the names of his witnesses or of the evidence which they are to give. The defence can call a witness at the last moment to give evidence inconsistent with the case for the prosecution when the prosecution may have no time to make inquiries about the witness or to meet the evidence which he is to give.

32. We are considering the whole question of the right of accused persons to remain silent during police investigations and afterwards. Meanwhile . . . we are reporting separately on the question whether provision should be made requiring the accused to disclose in advance a defence of alibi.

35. We believe that it will contribute substantially to the breaking down of false alibis if notice of an alibi has to be given in advance. The present law gives two particular advantages to the defence. First . . . the police may be unable to investigate the alibi before evidence of it is given. It will therefore be of help to them if particulars have to be given before the trial. Secondly, if an alibi witness is kept out of sight till the moment when he is called, the prosecution are deprived of the possibility of finding out something about him which can be put to him in cross-examination and may lessen the value of his evidence. For this reason elaborate precautions are sometimes taken to prevent the police from finding out who the witness is to be until his name is called and he comes into the witness box.

36. We recommend that at a trial on indictment the accused should not without the leave of the court be able to adduce evidence in support of an alibi unless he gives particulars of the alibi during or at the end of the committal proceedings or else by written notice to the solicitor for the prosecutor not later than seven days after the end of the proceedings (not counting Sundays or bank holidays). . . . What will be sufficient particulars of the alibi will depend on the circumstances, but they will in any event include particulars of the place where the accused intends to prove that he was and the time. . . .

37. . . . [T]he court will be expressly empowered to allow the accused to adduce the evidence even if he has not complied with the requirement to give the notice. It seems to us desirable to include this saving in order to provide for a case where the defence are able to produce some reasonable explanation for not having given the particulars in time. For example, the accused may really have been unable to remember where he was or not have found out the name and address until it was too late to give the necessary notice. A witness might in truth not be found until just before the trial . . . , but if the court

thought it desirable, it could in any event adjourn the case to give time for inquiries. . . .

40. Since the object of the requirement to give the names of alibi witnesses is to enable the prosecution to investigate the alibi, we have no doubt that it follows that the police should be able to interview the witnesses. . . . This may give rise to difficulty if allegations are made at the trial that the police acted improperly when interviewing a witness. The trial would then be complicated by the introduction of further issues of fact for the jury. In order to lessen these difficulties it would in our opinion be desirable that chief officers of police should give instructions that before interviewing a proposed alibi witness the police should, wherever possible, give the solicitor for the defence reasonable notice of their intention to do so and a reasonable opportunity to be present at the interview. We do not suggest that it should be the practice to arrange for similar facilities for the accused himself in the uncommon case where he is not legally represented, especially as he may be a long way from where the witness is to be interviewed and may be in custody; but in these cases we suggest that the police should try to arrange for the interview to be in the presence of some independent person. These suggestions relate only to the interviewing of witnesses named in a notice of alibi under the clause. At present if a person on arrest or on being questioned about an offence tells the police that he was somewhere else at the time of the offence, the police are likely to make inquiries at once in order to check his story and may question persons who he says can support him. This practice is obviously valuable and there can be no objection to its continuance, especially as it may show that the person in question is innocent. The matter is different when a formal notice of alibi has been given. . . .

42. We considered whether to include any provision restricting the right of the prosecution to refer at the trial to a notice of alibi . . . or to comment on a discrepancy between the notice and the defence put forward or on the omission of the defence to call an alibi witness indicated in the notice. In our opinion it would be wrong to make a statutory provision on these matters, because the question of what comment is justified will depend on the circumstances. The matter can safely be left to the control of the courts in the exercise of their general power . . . to ensure that the trial is fairly conducted. . . .

43. Our recommendations are limited to trials on indictment. In summary proceedings no real problem is found because of the comparative ease in adjourning the proceedings for the continued hearing of a part-heard case. In practice, surprise evidence of an alibi would be met by a request by the prosecution for an adjournment. This would enable the prosecution . . . to call evidence in rebuttal of the surprise evidence; authority for this course is contained in Rule 17 (3) of the Magistrates' Courts Rules 1952, which provides that: " At the conclusion of the evidence, if any, for the defence, the prosecutor may call evidence to rebut that evidence." . . .

44. Finally, although our present proposals are limited . . . to alibi defences, we wish to emphasise that this should not be taken to mean that this is as far as we think the law should go in restricting the privilege of persons to remain silent when questioned about, or charged with, offences until the time comes to put forward their defence. We are still considering these matters. . . .[69]

Criminal Justice Act 1967

11. (1) On a trial on indictment the defendant shall not without the leave of the court adduce evidence in support of an alibi unless, before the end of the prescribed period, he gives notice of particulars of the alibi.

[69] The Committee's views on these matters are referred to above, p. 284.

(2) Without prejudice to the foregoing subsection, on any such trial the defendant shall not without the leave of the court call any other person to give such evidence unless—

(*a*) the notice under that subsection includes the name and address of the witness or, if the name or address is not known to the defendant at the time he gives the notice, any information in his possession which might be of material assistance in finding the witness;

(*b*) if the name or the address is not included in that notice, the court is satisfied that the defendant, before giving the notice, took and thereafter continued to take all reasonable steps to secure that the name or address would be ascertained;

(*c*) if the name or the address is not included in that notice, but the defendant subsequently discovers the name or address or receives other information which might be of material assistance in finding the witness, he forthwith gives notice of the name, address or other information, as the case may be; and

(*d*) if the defendant is notified by or on behalf of the prosecutor that the witness has not been traced by the name or at the address given, he forthwith gives notice of any such information which is then in his possession or, on subsequently receiving any such information, forthwith gives notice of it.

(3) The court shall not refuse leave under this section if it appears to the court that the defendant was not informed in accordance with the rules under section 15 of the Justices of the Peace Act 1949 (rules of procedure for magistrates' courts) of the requirements of this section.

(4) Any evidence tendered to disprove an alibi may, subject to any directions by the court as to the time it is to be given, be given before or after evidence is given in support of the alibi. . . .

(6) A notice under subsection (1) of this section shall either be given in court during, or at the end of, the proceedings before the examining justices or be given in writing to the solicitor for the prosecutor, and a notice under paragraph (*c*) or (*d*) of subsection (2) of this section shall be given in writing to that solicitor.

(8) In this section " evidence in support of an alibi " means evidence tending to show that by reason of the presence of the defendant at a particular place or in a particular area at a particular time he was not, or was unlikely to have been, at the place where the offence is alleged to have been committed at the time of its alleged commission; " the prescribed period " means the period of seven days from the end of the proceedings before the examining justices. . . .

PRE-TRIAL PROCEEDINGS IN CIVIL CASES

There are two significant differences between pre-trial proceedings in civil and criminal cases. The first is that in civil cases it is left to the parties and their legal advisers to collect the evidence, interview witnesses and prepare the case—at first usually the parties' solicitors, though later a barrister may be called in to give advice on the law or evidence or to draft the pleadings. They identify the cause of action and the remedy they want and set the machinery in motion, though they may take advantage of statements made to the police, for example by witnesses of an accident. The second difference is that the vast majority of civil cases never get beyond the pre-trial stage.

The case is settled after the writ has been issued but before the trial has begun. The Winn Committee on Personal Injuries Litigation [70] noted:

> 59. . . . [O]f all personal injury claims asserted about 20–25% reach the stage of proceedings being started, and only about 10% of these reach the doors of the court, of which between one third and one half are then settled without trial.

The issue of a writ is often simply a method of putting pressure on the defendant and nine times out of ten, especially in cases in the county court, this is enough. In other cases it is merely a step in negotiations while the parties try to test out the strength of their respective cases and of their opponent's will to persevere. A defence for example may be put in simply in the hope that the plaintiff will be prepared to compromise to avoid the expense of a trial.

The English legal system's method of dealing with costs has something to do with the willingness of parties to settle. The general rule is that the winning party in an action will be awarded his costs but this does not mean that he will necessarily recover all he has in fact paid out. The actual amount to which he is entitled will be estimated by a Taxing Master who will only allow, in the case of the normal award of " party and party " costs, expenditure that he regards as reasonably necessary for the conduct of the case. In practice parties are usually willing to spend more than the minimum that is reasonably necessary, in order to be on the safe side, which means that they are bound to be out of pocket even if they win. It is only in exceptional cases where " solicitor and client " costs are awarded that a greater sum will be recovered. If one adds to this the risk that the party who is contending the case may not win, and that even if he wins at first instance he may be taken to the Court of Appeal or even the House of Lords, it is not surprising that there is every incentive to settle before the expense of a full trial is incurred, unless he is supported by some outside body or is legally aided. The frequency and indeed the desirability of settlements before trial is one of the factors that those responsible for shaping pre-trial proceedings have to take into account and was one of the points stressed by the Winn Committee when they were considering the function of pleadings in pre-trial procedure.

Although settlements are common and the pre-trial procedure ought to take this into account, the rules of procedure and pleading are primarily devised with a view to getting the dispute ready for trial. It is in fact a continuation of the process mentioned above, at page 280, which begins when the lay client moves from the stage of merely asking for legal advice to initiating proceedings with a view to litigation, and the rules of procedure and pleading provide another of the filters through which the plaintiff's complaint must be passed before it is ready to be disposed of in a judgment. This means of course that it is another point at which there is a risk of distortion.

As was mentioned earlier it was one of the major objections to the English legal system in the first half of the nineteenth century that the rules of procedure were so technical, and distorted the issues between the parties

---

[70] Cmnd. 3691, 1968.

to such an extent, that not only were the real issues between them not necessarily decided but cases might often be decided on technical points which had nothing to do with the merits of the case at all. It will be remembered that English law was complicated at that time by the sharp distinction which existed between law and equity and between the courts which administered them. One of the tasks facing the nineteenth-century reformers was to bridge this gap, at first by making available the procedural devices used in the one court, such as the procedures for administering interrogatories, and for making orders for discovery, which had been developed by the Court of Chancery, available in the others, and finally by bringing the courts themselves into one single Supreme Court in 1873-75 and devising a single comprehensive set of rules for the whole of the Supreme Court in 1883. But the fact that rules of procedure varied between the different courts—as indeed they still do to some extent between the different divisions of the High Court—and that procedural refinements available in one were not available in the other, were not the only drawbacks of the system of procedure at this time. Even within the common law courts there were considerable variations and a considerable amount of complexity. Two causes of this complexity have already been mentioned: first, the fictions like the Bill of Middlesex in the court of King's Bench, used by the common law courts to steal jurisdiction from one another,[71] and secondly, fictions such as those revolving round Richard Roe and John Doe in the action of ejectment used by the courts to adapt old forms to new circumstances.[72] There were two further aggravating factors. The first had to do with the structure of the law itself. The English common law had grown up around the "forms of action." New remedies had been offered by making available new writs which authorised the initiation of proceedings in the royal courts in the classes of case for which they were introduced. Around each writ there developed a separate "form of action," which specified not only how the action should be begun, but how it should be pleaded and even how the judgment might be enforced. Far from developing as a set of general principles, English law developed in a fragmented way as a number of separate forms of action, and although English lawyers were willing on occasion to develop a particular form of action, such as trespass, from within, so that it could be used to deal with a new class of case, they nonetheless thought it important to keep up what they sometimes referred to as "the boundaries of the forms of action."[73] In framing a claim a lawyer had to be careful to choose the right form of action. Failure to choose the right form of action or failure to observe the rules of procedure appropriate to it would mean loss of the case. And it was the strictness with which the courts insisted on the proper choice of form and a strict adherence to its peculiar procedural rules that constituted the second aggravating factor. Not only was the law and procedure complex, but observance of its form was insisted upon with a rigour that must often have amounted to an injustice.

It was this excessive technicality and complexity that the various Common Law Commissioners set out to remove. The forms of action as such

[71] Below, p. 346.
[72] Below, p. 345.
[73] See e.g. Blackstone J. in *Scott* v. *Shepherd* (1773) 2 W.Bl. 892: the " squib " case.

were abolished—one advantage of which was the fact that the common law could henceforth more easily be developed in terms of general principles, and some of the more bizarre technicalities, in particular the numerous fictions, were removed. Gradually too an attempt was made to bring the different procedures into some kind of uniformity and to relax some of the strictness in observance of the rules which had until then been insisted upon, by allowing a controlled power of amendment, usually on payment of any extra cost that might thereby be incurred by the other party. " To render proceedings shorter, cheaper and more certain," the Common Law Commissioners said in their first report,[74] " is the great object to be proposed in recommending any alteration in the established course of practice. But we are well aware that certainty cannot be attained without precision; that precision is often inconsistent with brevity; and that whatever increases length increases cost. In executing the duty imposed upon us, we shall endeavour in each part of the subject under examination, to point out the shortest and least expensive course, consistent with the safe administration of justice. . . . We shall have no hesitation in proposing the abolition, as far as practicable, of fictions, circuitous courses, and such matters of mere form, as by the progress of time have ceased to be necessary to the purposes for which they were introduced, but which increase the length, and consequently the cost, of proceedings. . . . We shall suggest the abridgement, in many cases, of the forms and language of pleading; some restraint upon the unlimited multiplication of counts and pleas, and an acceleration of every part of the suit. . . ."

In spite of the achievements of the nineteenth century, however, in reducing the technicality and complexity inherited from the past, the legal process remains a formal process. It is this formality, together with its special methods of establishing " the facts " and its disposal of cases by reference to pre-existing or specially formulated rules, that is, " the law," which gives the legal system its distinctive character as a process for resolving disputes. But a legal system must be formal without becoming formalistic. One of the problems that every legal system has is to prevent the form swallowing up the substance of what it is about, and degenerating into ritual. An understanding of some of the reasons for the formality lies close to the heart of understanding some of the purposes of the rules of procedure and pleading.

One particular reason has an air of paradox about it, for one reason why the legal process is formal is because it is an essentially practical affair. The judge is not an armchair moralist. He cannot refuse to give a decision because the case is too complicated, or because he would like to know more facts, have more time to reflect, or because it is impossible to tell who is lying or who has the better powers of observation and memory, or because it is six of one and half a dozen of another. And much of the apparatus of the legal system is shaped by knowledge of this fact and is designed simply to make his task more manageable.

We have already seen that the rules of law themselves go some way towards reducing the issues with which the judge has to deal, by setting limits to the facts which are relevant to his consideration of the dispute

[74] 1829, P.P. ix.

between the parties. Although the forms of action have been abolished, the notion of a " cause of action " has to some extent taken their place. The law is no longer divided up into forms of action but is still divided up into " causes of action " on the civil side and " offences " on the criminal, and the same set of facts can give rise to more than one of them, each with its own legal rules and each looking at the facts in terms of different categories. A motor-car accident may give rise to an action in negligence for damages and a prosecution for dangerous driving. The man who is injured in a railway accident may have an action against the railway in both contract and tort because the law for its own purposes has divided up factual situations into those in which it will award compensation where there has been prior agreement (contract) and those in which it will award compensation whether there was prior agreement or not (tort), and some factual situations will fall into both categories. The railway passenger is an example. He has two causes of action, though he will only recover damages once. So, too, the man who assaults a policeman in Trafalgar Square may find himself charged with assault, assaulting a policeman in the course of his duty, and conduct likely to cause a breach of the peace contrary to the Public Order Act 1936.

As we have seen, the law has to take steps to make sure that the fact that it sees life in terms of separate causes of action and offences does not work oppressively in individual cases.[75] Organising the facts into separate causes of action and separate offences is, however, only the first step in getting the issues which are ultimately to come before the judge into a manageable shape. Within each cause of action and each offence the relevant legal rules break down the situations still further, limiting and defining the issues which are to be treated as relevant and reducing what would otherwise be a multitude of individual facts to manageable proportions. In the words of Professor Robson [76] " John Smith, living in a suburban villa on the outskirts of a city, is never from the law's point of view a man of unique personality.... What is legally significant is the fact that he is a vendor, a purchaser, a ratepayer, a trustee, a master, a servant, a contractor, a tortfeasor." In a very similar passage in *The Bramble Bush* the American Realist Karl Llewellyn says, " It is not a road between Portsville and Arlington; it is a ' highway.' It is not a particular pale magenta Buick, by number 732507, but a ' motorcar.' " [77]

The rules of procedure and pleading carry this process of defining the real issues in dispute between the parties still further by getting them to formulate as precisely as possible the exact nature of their claim and their defence, and getting them to agree so far as possible those facts which are not really in dispute, thus saving the cost of bringing witnesses to prove facts that are not seriously challenged (including where possible such things as medical reports) all in an effort to narrow the range of and clarify the issues that will ultimately have to be tried.

Getting the case into a manageable shape is of course not the only function of pleadings, any more than it is the primary function of rules of law. One of the main reasons underlying the rules of pleading is to prevent

[75] Above, p. 324.
[76] Above, p. 242.
[77] Below, p. 344.

surprise at the trial, and therefore to save parties the expense of having to guard against surprise. This is in contrast to criminal cases where even as a matter of principle, with the exception of the rules as to alibis, only the prosecution is required to reveal its hand before the trial though as a matter of practice even in civil cases, as the Winn Committee pointed out, the spirit of the rules of pleading in this regard is not always fulfilled. The pleadings also incidentally give the judge an opportunity to discover something about the case before he comes to court, and form a part of the record of the case should any question arise either as to its status as a precedent or whether a matter is *res judicata*. They may also have an important influence on the extent to which an appeal court may feel free to upset a judgment of the court below since, as the pleadings are intended to form the basis of the trial, a party is entitled to shape his case and marshal his witnesses and his evidence on the basis of the issues raised by them. This means it may be too late at the appellate stage to allow an amendment so that a new issue on the facts can be raised if the appeal court cannot be sure that the other party might have been able to meet the case had he been prepared to in the lower court.[78]

Procedure and pleading in the Queen's Bench Division

The rules of law prescribe the general circumstances in which a remedy can be claimed. The rules of procedure prescribe the steps which have to be taken to obtain it. In the case of the High Court they are made by the Rules Committee set up under the Supreme Court of Judicature (Consolidation) Act 1925 and are to be found in the *Supreme Court Practice* (or "White Book"), which contains not only the rules themselves but also commentaries on them and reference to relevant judicial decisions. The rules are supplemented by practice directions and practice notes issued by the judges or masters of a particular division of the court for the guidance of those who practise in it.

A typical action in the Queen's Bench Division of the High Court begins with a writ of summons served upon the defendant, who has then to enter an appearance if he wishes to defend. The pleadings which follow are made up of a statement of claim, in which the plantiff sets out his claim, and a defence. There may sometimes be a reply to the defence. Each party may call upon the other for further particulars in order to make the nature of the claim or defence clearer. The formulation and exchange of pleadings are the most important part of the pre-trial civil procedure. They, together with other preparations for the trial, take place under the general supervision of the masters of the Queen's Bench Division[79] sitting in chambers. They deal with all "interlocutory" matters though there is an appeal from their decision to a judge, and there may in some cases be a further appeal to the Court of Appeal and even to the House of Lords. The masters are responsible for seeing that the case is in a fit state for trial. They see that the pleadings are in order, deal with applications like those for further and better particulars or for discovery or the administration of

---

[78] Below, pp. 349 and 603.
[79] In the provinces the work of the masters is performed by district registrars and in the county courts by county court registrars.

interrogatories, and with requests for extension of time, and finally fix the location of the trial and decide such matters as to whether it is to be by judge alone or judge sitting with a jury.

Once the pleadings are closed they may only be amended with leave and leave may be given only on the condition that the party requesting it pays any additional costs incurred. In some cases, and especially on appeal, the court may refuse leave to amend if it takes the view that the amendment raises new issues which have not been properly canvassed in the trial. Unlike the preliminary hearing in criminal cases there is no question of the master having to be satisfied that the plaintiff has made out a prima facie case. Although the pleadings make allegations of fact they do not set out the evidence which will be produced to support the allegations at the trial, so the master has in any event no means of knowing the actual strength of the plaintiff's case. He does have the power to give summary judgment if no defence is made or if he is prepared to strike out a defence as frivolous or vexatious. He may also strike out the claim of the plaintiff as being frivolous, vexatious or oppressive or because it discloses no cause of action. Nor is there anything like a pre-trial conference at which the judge who is to try the case gets together with the parties to prepare the case for trial and even encourage them to reach agreement without the need for litigation. It is much more of an administrative affair. This is no doubt one of the reasons why it is held in private. But, for all that, it can on occasion be decisive. Hence the right of appeal.

The relevance of costs

It is an important principle that no one should be deterred from enforcing his legal rights or raising a legitimate defence because he cannot afford to do so. We have already come across this principle in dealing with the provision of state financial aid, in discussing the demand for an extension of the jurisdiction of county courts and for the establishment of small claims courts, and, by implication, in the discussion of lawyers' fees. In addition, however, the actual costs of proceedings, particularly in the High Court, have also been a matter of anxious concern from the early reports of the Common Law Commissioners onwards. The bulk of the costs of an action which goes to trial are the costs of the trial itself. Here attempts have been made in particular to reduce the necessity for witnesses to attend in person. This has led to an increased willingness to accept written evidence, including hearsay evidence, especially where the evidence is little more than a formality or where the facts to be proved are not seriously in dispute and therefore the elaborate process of examination and cross-examination is not necessary. It has also led to encouragement being given to the parties to agree on such things as experts' reports, and in particular medical reports, before the trial, rather than having a battle of experts at the trial itself. These questions are referred to in the chapter on facts. At the procedural stage attention has been directed to securing that the case is as fully prepared as possible for the trial, with only the real issues in dispute left to be dealt with. This has meant further attention being paid to the clarity of the pleadings, and accounts for the importance attached by, for example, the Evershed Committee to the " summons for directions " which it was hoped would provide an opportunity for a final stock-taking before the trial actually began, though it is not clear in practice how successful a costs-saver the " summons for directions " is.[80]

As was mentioned above, however, the number of actions which actually come to trial is very small. Much of the attention of those who are concerned with saving costs has been concentrated in reducing the cost of the steps leading to trial as well as clarifying the real issues as soon as possible, in order to reduce the expenses incurred before a final settlement is reached. Here much depends on the willingness of the profession to help, and the power of the master to punish unreasonable behaviour with costs. Hence the emphasis put by the Winn Committee on costs as a sanction to support the general suggestion of a " new approach " by the Evershed Committee.[81]

Reducing the facts to order

Bramble Bush : K. Llewellyn

. . . [T]he actual dispute before the court is limited as straitly by the facts as by the form which the procedural issue has assumed. What is not in the facts cannot be present for decision. . . . But how far does that help us out? What are the facts? The plaintiff's name is Atkinson and the defendant's Walpole. The defendant, despite his name, is an Italian by extraction, but the plaintiff's ancestors came over with the Pilgrims. The defendant has a schnautzer-dog named Walter, red hair and $30,000 worth of life insurance. All these are facts. The case, however, does not deal with life insurance. It is about an auto accident. The defendant's auto was a Buick painted pale magenta. He is married. His wife was in the back seat, an irritable, somewhat faded blonde. She was attempting back-seat driving when the accident occurred. He had turned round to make objection. In the process the car swerved and hit the plaintiff. The sun was shining; there was a rather lovely dappled sky low to the West. The time was late October on a Tuesday. The road was smooth, concrete. It had been put in by the McCarthy Road Work Company. How many of these facts are important to the decision? How many of these facts are, as we say, legally relevant? Is it relevant that the road was in the country or the city; that it was concrete or tarmac or of dirt; that it was a private or a public way? Is it relevant that the defendant was driving a Buick, or a motorcar or a vehicle? It is important that he looked around as the car swerved? Is it crucial? Would it have been the same if he had been drunk, or had swerved for fun, to see how close he could run by the plaintiff, but had missed his guess?

Is it not obvious that as soon as you pick up this statement of the facts to find its legal bearings you must discard some as of no interest whatsoever, discard others as dramatic but as legal nothings? And is it not clear, further, that when you pick up the facts which are left and which do seem relevant, you suddenly cease to deal with them in the concrete and deal with them instead in *categories* which you, for one reason or another, deem significant? It is not the road between Portsville and Arlington; it is " a highway." It is not a particular pale magenta Buick eight, by number 732507, but " a motorcar," and perhaps even " a vehicle." It is not a turning round to look at Adorée Walpole, but a lapse from the supposedly proper procedure of careful drivers,

---

[80] See below, p. 366.
[81] *Ibid.*

with which you are concerned. Each concrete fact of the case arranges itself, I say, as the *representative* of a much wider abstract *category* of facts, and it is not in itself but as a member of the category that you attribute significance to it. But what is to tell you whether to make your category " Buicks " or " motorcars " or " vehicles "? What is to tell you to make your category " road " or " public highway "?

Fictions

First Report of the Commissioners on the Practice and Procedure of the Common Law Courts

P.P. 1829 ix

Two sets of commissioners made important contributions to the procedural reforms of the nineteenth century, the first appointed in 1828, the second in 1850. Those appointed in 1828 were asked to: " make a full and diligent inquiry into the course of proceedings in actions and other civil remedies established or used in His Majesty's Superior Courts of Common Law, from the first process to the termination thereof, and into the process, practice, pleading and other matters connected therewith, and to inquire whether any and what parts thereof may be conveniently and beneficially discontinued, altered or improved, and what, if any, alterations, amendments or improvements may be beneficially made therein, and how the same may best be carried into effect, and whether and in what manner the dispatch of the general business in His Majesty's said courts may be expedited."

They made six reports,[82] and those appointed in 1850 published three reports.[83] Extracts from these are to be found at pp. 47, 183, 196. The following passage from the 1829 report deals with two different kinds of fiction in use at the time of the Commissioner's inquiry. The first, the use of fictions in the action of ejectment, had been introduced in order to make that action do the work of the more cumbrous real actions, the second, the Bill of Middlesex, had been introduced to enable the Court of King's Bench to steal jurisdiction from the Court of Common Pleas (see above, p. 3).

In Ejectment, the whole method of proceeding is anomalous and depends on fictions which the courts have devised. . . . This action commences without suing out any original writ or other process, and by delivering to the tenant in possession of the premises, a declaration framed as against a fictitious defendant (for example, Richard Roe) at the suit of a fictitious plaintiff (for example, John Doe). Subscribed to this declaration is a notice, in the form of a letter, from the fictitious defendant to the tenant in possession, apprising the latter of the nature and object of the proceeding, and advising him to appear in court, in the next term, to defend his possession. Accordingly, in the next term, the tenant in possession obtains a Rule of Court, allowing him to be made defendant instead of Richard Roe, upon certain terms prescribed by the court, for the convenient trial of the title; among others, his appearing and receiving, without writ or process, a new declaration like the first but with his own name inserted as defendant. . . .

[82] 1829, P.P. ix 1; 1830, P.P. xi 47; 1831, P.P. x 375; 1831–32, P.P. xxv 1; 1833, P.P. xxii 195 and 1834, P.P. xxvi.
[83] 1851, P.P. xxii 567; 1852–53, P.P. xl 705 and 1860, P.P. xxxi 341.

The peculiarities which attend ejectment . . . are referable to reasons connected with the particular nature of [that action]. . . . The introduction of the Bill of Middlesex and latitat into . . . [the Court of Kings Bench], as ordinary modes of civil process, was owing to a cause of a very different description. . . . [T]he Common Pleas had in former times . . . the exclusive cognisance of all suits merely civil in their nature, where nothing that savoured of violence or crime was imputed to the defendant. The consequence was, that no such action could be entertained in any other court by the ancient and regular method of original writ. But by the use of the Bill of Middlesex and latitat the King's Bench obtained indirectly, and in another shape, a participation in this class of suits; and these modes ultimately became new modes of process to compel appearance in all personal actions of whatever kind, constituting additional exceptions from the ancient method of proceeding by original writ. . . . Similar to this was the motive which led to the adoption of the original *quare clausum fregit* and common *capias* in the Common Pleas, as ordinary forms of process applicable to all modes of personal action. . . .

The Bill of Middlesex and the latitat . . . are chiefly objectionable as founded on certain fictions which are not only useless but inconvenient in their tendency. Whatever be the real form of action intended to be brought, these writs uniformly charge the defendant with a trespass; and whether an arrest is intended or not, they always direct that his body be taken. With respect to the latitat, indeed, it has other false suggestions. It states (almost always contrary to the fact) that a bill of Middlesex has been already issued into Middlesex in the same suit, but without effect; and that the defendant and Richard Roe (or some other ideal personage) run up and down and secrete themselves in another county, and therefore it commands the sheriff of the last mentioned county to take their bodies and have them before the King at Westminster at a certain day. Such is the tenor of this instrument, even when its meaning simply is to summon the defendant to appear on that day in the Court of King's Bench to answer some claim of debt. . . .

We take this early opportunity of expressing our opinion upon the general subject of legal fictions. . . . Considered in its origin, it may be thus accounted for. Our ancient institutions having been adapted to a rude and simple state of society, the courts in later times became sensible of defects of jurisdiction and other inconveniences to which the altered circumstances of the nation had naturally given. In some cases the remedy was supplied by legislative regulation; but where this was wanting, the judges were apt to resort to fiction as an expedient for effecting, indirectly, that which they had no authority to establish as law. But to whatever causes the invention or encouragement of legal fictions may be assignable, we have no doubt that they have an injurious effect in the administration of justice, because they tend to bring the law itself into suspicion with the public, as an unsound and delusive system, while an impression of the ridiculous is also occasionally excited by them, of which the natural effect must be to degrade the science in some measure in popular estimation. . . .

Forms of action and causes of action

First Report of Her Majesty's Commissioners for Inquiring into the Process, Practice and System of Pleading in the Superior Courts of Common Law

P.P. 1851 xxii 567

It may be difficult to define what is meant by a form of action. Practically, however, it may be said to be the peculiar technical mode of framing the writ and pleadings appropriate to the particular injury which the action is intended to redress. By the established practice of pleading, peculiar forms of expression characteristic of each action have been appropriated thereto, many of which are of a purely formal nature, and are wholly independent of the merits of the cause of action. Thus, as an instance, in those cases in which . . . trespass is the appropriate remedy, the plaintiff's declaration must state that the act complained of was done with force and arms, and against the peace, although the trespass may have been unaccompanied by violence; these allegations being unnecessary in case, yet the distinction between the injuries to which these forms of action are respectively appropriate is . . . often of a very shadowy nature and the ground of complaint must in each case be set forth with sufficient distinctness and particularity, independently of these technical forms. . . . The necessity of adhering to these forms sometimes . . . has led to plaintiffs being defeated after establishing a good cause of action, on the ground that the form of action has been mistaken. . . . It appears to us that if the facts which constitute the cause of action be sufficiently set forth in the declaration, all the legitimate purposes of pleading are thereby accomplished, and that to incumber the pleading with formal requirements, which afford no additional information but which open the door to technical and captious objections, is not only useless but mischievous. We feel ourselves, however, bound to state, that much difference of opinion exists in the legal profession on this head. . . .

It is manifest . . . that as the question, whether there is a cause of action or not, must depend upon the facts and not upon the form adopted, the decision of a cause on the merits is not helped by means of these forms of action. . . . [I]f our other recommendations be adopted, forms of action will exist in name only, and as their general effect appears to us to be mischievous, we recommend their abolition. We recommend not only that merely formal expressions shall be unnecessary, but that they shall be disused. This will . . . get rid of formal and capricious objections; it will shorten pleadings, free them from their verbiage, and make them more intelligible by being more like the language of everyday use. . . . It has been frequently stated that causes of action and defence must necessarily be classified, as many, although varying in the particular circumstances, are substantially similar in character. There seems to us no reason why this should not be so under the system we propose; the only difference will be, that the classification will be the natural result of the similarity of the facts, instead of being artificial and technical. . . .

Letang v. Cooper

[1965] 1 Q.B. 232

DIPLOCK L.J. . . . A cause of action is simply a factual situation the existence of which entitles one person to obtain from the court a remedy against another person. Historically, the means by which the remedy was obtained varied with the nature of the factual situation and causes of action were divided into categories according to the " form of action " by which the remedy was obtained in the particular kind of factual situation which constituted the cause of action. But that is legal history, not current law. . . . The Judicature Act, 1873, abolished forms of action. It did not affect causes of action; so it was convenient for lawyers and legislators to continue to use, to describe the various categories of factual situations which entitled one person to obtain from the court a remedy against another, the names of the various " forms of action " by which formerly the remedy appropriate to the particular category of factual situation was obtained. But it is essential to realise that when, since 1873, the name of a form of action is used to identify a cause of action, it is used as a convenient and succinct description of a particular category of factual situation which entitles one person to obtain from the court a remedy against another person. To forget this will indeed encourage the old forms of action to rule us from their graves.

The function of pleadings

First Report of Her Majesty's Commissioners for Inquiring into the Process, Practice, and System of Pleading in the Superior Courts of Common Law
P.P. 1851 xxii 567

Before . . . we address ourselves particularly to the defects complained of and the remedies which we propose, we must dispose of a preliminary question, namely, whether any pleadings or preparatory statements by the parties to a cause should be required. Some persons, irritated by the mischiefs which have followed from the abuse of technical rules, have proposed that parties should come into court without any previous authentic information as to the complaint or answer. From this we wholly dissent. Such a mode of, or rather want of, procedure, may answer the purpose in a rude state of society, or in matters of very trifling moment, in which from the nature of the case the parties know beforehand the precise matter in dispute; but in a highly civilised state, where commercial transactions are numerous and complicated, it would lead to intolerable fraud, oppression, and expense; and we believe that it has never existed in the code of any civilised nation. Dishonest plaintiffs would make unfounded claims, the nature of which could not be ascertained by previous inquiry. The party summoned must either come prepared with all the witnesses who could depose to anything that had ever passed between him and the plaintiff, or must hear the complaint, and then be entitled to an adjournment to bring his witnesses at a future day. In the former case, great and unnecessary expense would be incurred, and frequently incurred with a view to oppression. In the latter case there would, in truth, be a notice given by word of mouth before the judge, which had much better been previously given. In many cases, an adjournment would be necessary for the purposes of justice, but dishonest defendants would equally claim it, and every case would be something like twice tried, each party being at the expense and trouble of twice attending with witnesses. But we do not believe that any one, on reflection, will be found seriously to support this plan; and we, therefore, at once pass on to the next question, viz., What should be the nature of the notice which the parties should give to each other? . . . We . . . think that the plaintiff should state his title to sue, and the nature of his cause of action; that the defendant should likewise be required to state his ground of defence with certainty and precision. This is really the substance of pleading, the object of which . . . is to ascertain the points in controversy, with the view of informing the parties themselves and the tribunal which is to decide between them what are the real questions to be disputed. . . .

Pleadings in personal injuries actions

Final Report of the Committee on Supreme Court Practice and Procedure
Cmd. 8878, 1953

338. Among various suggestions made to us was a proposal that pleadings should be abolished in running-down cases. In our view, if this were done,

some other form of document would have to take the place of the pleadings. The defendant must be informed in some way of the particular accident to which the claim relates and of the personal injuries alleged to have been suffered and special damage sustained. Equally, the plaintiff must be informed of any allegation of contributory negligence or special defence or counterclaim. In our view some form of document setting out the plaintiff's claim and the defendant's defence is necessary in practically every case, and we do not think that the abolition of pleadings is practicable. . . .

340. . . . It is . . . in our opinion, essential that . . . pleadings should contain in broad outline the case alleged respectively by the plaintiff and the defendant, giving particulars of the date, time and place of the accident and, where possible, the direction and course of the persons or vehicles involved therein immediately prior to the accident. . . .

341. In personal injuries actions other than running-down cases we think that pleadings are not only valuable but essential. In such actions the claim is made on the ground of some breach by the defendant of a duty owed to the plaintiff at common law or under some statute. It may be that the duty at common law is owed by the defendant as the owner or occupier of property or as an employer, or because he is under a duty not to create or permit a nuisance. The statutory duty alleged may arise under statute or under one of the many statutory regulations. Unless a statement of claim is delivered the defendant cannot know what case he has to meet. The defendant equally may rely for his defence upon facts which negative the existence of the duty alleged or upon some statutory provision which protects him and which casts the duty upon the plaintiff, and it is essential that the plaintiff should know if such contentions are to be relied upon by the defendants. We are satisfied that pleadings in this type of personal injuries action do raise the issues to be decided. We have heard no complaints about such pleadings and we do not recommend any change in regard to them.

Esso Petroleum Co. Ltd. v. Southport Corporation

House of Lords [1956] A.C. 218

The respondents had brought an action alleging negligence against the master of a ship and against the shipowners as being vicariously liable for the master's misconduct. The trial court held that the master had not been negligent. The respondents then attempted to show that quite apart from the vicarious liability to which they might have been subject, the owners were directly liable as they had failed to show that the damage had not been caused by their negligence in sending to sea an unseaworthy ship. This argument succeeded before the Court of Appeal. The question before the House of Lords was whether the argument was open to them at this stage, given the form of the pleadings.

LORD RADCLIFFE. My Lords, I think that this case ought to be decided in accordance with the pleadings. . . . [T]he appellants . . . were entitled to conduct the case and confine their evidence in reliance upon the further and better particulars of paragraph 2 of the statement of claim which had been delivered by the respondents. It seems to me that it is the purpose of such particulars that they should help to define the issues and to indicate to the party who asks for them how much of the range of his possible evidence will be relevant and how much irrelevant to those issues. Proper use of them shortens the hearing and reduces costs. But if an appellate court is to treat reliance upon them as pedantry or mere formalism, I do not see what part they have to play in our trial system. . . . In my view, where the question is, as here, as to sufficiency of evidence, the state of the pleadings is of more importance than the way in which the case is shaped in argument. It is clear that no application was made to the trial judge to amend the pleadings by altering or extending the particulars, and it is equally clear from what he says at the close of his judgment that he did not regard himself as having expressly or impliedly authorised any such amendment. That being so, I am of opinion that the appellants called as much evidence as was required of them to defend themselves from the charges of negligence that were made in this case. . . . The respondents might have undertaken to make good their claim in more than one way. One way would have been to follow the line taken in *The Merchant Prince*,[84] upon which so much of the argument in this case has turned. That would have meant relying on the view that the mere fact that the ship had grounded on the training wall at all was evidence of negligence, and calling upon the appellants to discharge the onus of disproof thus placed upon them. I do not think that we have sufficient material to enable us to say with certainty whether such an opening attack would have succeeded. . . . But the point is that the respondents did not undertake to make good their case on these lines. It is quite clear from the particulars which they were invited to furnish, and which they furnished, that they decided to rely on certain actions of the master in his navigation of the ship. . . .

Lever Bros. Ltd. v. Bell
Court of Appeal [1931] 1 K.B. 557

Lawrence L.J. . . . . The appellants . . . contended that the learned [trial] judge was not justified in deciding the case on the ground of mutual mistake, as this had not been pleaded. In my opinion this contention ought not to prevail. . . . As . . . all the facts relevant to the question whether there had been a mutual mistake were fully investigated and ascertained at the trial, and the last question to the jury was expressly put by the learned judge in order to elicit whether or not there had been such a mistake, no injustice has been done to the appellants by the decision of the learned judge, and this court ought not to disturb that decision on a mere technical objection which is devoid of merits.

Scrutton L.J. . . . . In my opinion the practice of the courts has been to consider and deal with the legal result of pleaded facts, though the particular legal result alleged is not stated in the pleadings, except in cases where to ascertain the validity of the legal result claimed would require the investigation of new and disputed facts which have not been investigated. . . .

Greer L.J. thought that mutual mistake had been sufficiently pleaded.

Report of the Committee on Personal Injuries Litigation
Cmnd. 3691, 1968

111. Desirable and valuable though it is that the parties to a personal injuries dispute should settle their differences, it is unthinkable that they should be under any compulsion to do so. It is plainly the function and duty of the

[84] [1892] P. 179.

Court to try and afford proper facilities for the trial of all justiciable disputes. It would be quite wrong were the Court or its officers to impose pressure upon the parties to . . . depart from the seat of justice and to have recourse to negotiation when one or both of them seek the decision of a Judge. . . . It is regrettable that litigants, who want a trial, all too often feel compelled to settle because the list of cases awaiting trial is overloaded and the prospects of a timely hearing are dim.

112. Nonetheless we believe that the provision of facilities for the fostering of settlements is an objective which should be pursued by those who mould law and practice. . . .

113. We justify the prominence which our Report gives to settlements not only on the ground that the promotion of just settlements is one way of relieving congestion in the courts but because the number of personal injury claims which are compromised is vastly greater than the number tried or indeed litigated at all; this is true to an extent of all types of actions. . . .

121. The process of settlement has a special significance for the machinery of the Courts when personal injury actions are settled after setting down or at the trial. . . .

125. On the . . . figures and from our own experience we do not hesitate to comment that far too many personal injury cases proceed to the court before they are settled. A case which the parties prefer to settle . . . should be settled so soon as both parties know all that they can expect to learn, without having the relevant witnesses cross-examined. . . .

127. Thus we were led to the conclusion . . . that one of the most important contributions which we could make to the early disposal of personal injury actions, was to devise a framework which would favour the object that as many as possible are speedily and justly settled and as few as possible reach trial. . . .

129. We had in mind the consideration that solicitors of relevant experience and claims managers, like skilled chess players, are for the most part, well able to foresee the outcome of a contest once the pieces are set to a recognisable pattern on the board. Indeed we venture to think that a solution which such persons regard as acceptable in a given case for their respective clients or companies is likely to approximate as closely to the perfectly just answer as the decision or award of a Judge.

130. We have concluded that a major stumbling block to the promotion of settlements is the lack of information on one or both sides concerning material matters which may be within the knowledge of the other party, or may not be available to either party because it is in the hands of an authority which will not disclose it. . . .

132. Thus it was that the first Working Paper which we circulated widely for consultation carried the title " Cards on the Table." In this paper we put the question: " Is it a correct proposition to state ' fair settlements are facilitated when as much information as possible is available to all parties at the earliest possible stage and if each party knows as much as possible about the other side's case and evidence '? " Of those who replied 34 answered " Yes " and 6 " No.". . .

133. Qualifications were naturally placed upon some of the affirmative answers. We ourselves concur with the solicitor . . . who commented that in reality the parties do not seek a " fair " settlement but a favourable one. We also think it is realistic, as another solicitor advised us, that " all that one can hope to do is to create an atmosphere where a settlement is more profitable than litigation." In the same vein . . . was the comment of the National Coal Board that: " The problem is not so much one of deciding a procedure which will

enable the parties to make full disclosure but to create an atmosphere in which the parties will make proper use of that procedure." [85]

353. We have given considerable attention to the idea that a pre-trial conference presided over by a Judge or Master should always or usually be held. . . . With this general notion in mind we posed the following query in our first Working Paper:

" Is there any advantage in bringing the parties together at a certain stage in interlocutory proceedings, for example at the stage of adjourned summons for directions, to enable the possibility of a settlement to be explored? This could take place between the parties alone, or could take place in a situation where a Master of the Supreme Court was available to assist if required: in either case this would be without prejudice. The case would have to be sufficiently prepared for a full assessment of liability and quantum to be made. Counsel would be fully briefed and an appropriate fee would be payable to solicitors and counsel. Advantages would be to compel the full preparation of the evidence at a reasonably early stage in the case before trial brief fees or witness costs had been incurred; it would enable exchanges of view to take place such as now sometimes take place at a late stage or even at the doors of the Court, and it might (though, on this, views may differ) simulate to some extent the atmosphere of the doors of the Court, at which it is well known many settlements now take place."

354. The replies we received were almost unqualifiedly hostile to the idea. . . . The Protection and Indemnity Association told us: " The Associations have had very considerable experience of pre-trial conferences in the U.S.A. and as a result hold the firm conviction that it is a most undesirable practice which frequently results in the judge, without any proper knowledge of all the facts and without having seen the witnesses, suggesting and even pressing the parties to accept a figure for a compromise settlement. In the result, the plaintiff is often not amenable to a negotiated settlement on a reasonable basis " . . . In " Dollars, Delay and the Automobile Victim," p. 167, it is stated that: " Intensive research by means of a controlled official experiment in New Jersey has established that pre-trial conferences in negligence cases did not have any marked tendency to get cases settled. Furthermore they did not observably shorten trial."

355. We ourselves concluded that the adoption of this idea would so complicate, delay and increase the cost of litigation that it should be rejected. We have also concluded that the associated ancillary machinery available in those jurisdictions of " examination for discovery " (Canada) and of pre-trial examination of opposed parties and of potential witnesses (U.S.A.) stand on a like footing and are no less open to the same objections.

Rules of the Supreme Court. Pleadings
R.S.C. 1965

Order 18

Service of statement of claim

1. Unless the court gives leave to the contrary or a statement of claim is indorsed on the writ, the plaintiff must serve a statement of claim on the

---

[85] *Cf.* Report of Committee on Supreme Court Practice and Procedure, para. 21: " It must not be forgotten that of all the actions started only a small fraction ever come to trial. . . . It is therefore to the public advantage that the cost of the early stages of a proceeding should be kept as low as reasonably possible. . . ."

defendant . . . either when the writ, or notice of the writ, is served . . . or at any time after service of the writ or notice but before the expiration of fourteen days after that defendant enters an appearance.

Service of defence

2. (1) Subject to paragraph (2), a defendant who enters an appearance in, and intends to defend, an action, must, unless the court gives leave to the contrary, serve a defence on the plaintiff before the expiration of fourteen days after the time limited for appearing or after the statement of claim is served on him, whichever is the later.

(2) If a summons under Order 14, rule 1,[86] is served on the defendant before he serves his defence, paragraph (1) shall not have effect in relation to him unless by order made on the summons he is given leave to defend the action and, in that case, shall have effect as if it required him to serve his defence within fourteen days after the making of the order or within such other period as may be specified therein.

Service of reply

3. (4) A reply to any defence must be served by the plaintiff before the expiration of fourteen days after the service on him of that defence. . . .

Pleadings subsequent to reply

4. No pleading subsequent to a reply . . . shall be served except with the leave of the court. . . .

Facts, not evidence, to be pleaded

7. (1) Subject to the provisions of this rule and rules 7A, 10, 11 & 12, every pleading must contain and contain only, a statement in a summary form of the material facts on which the party pleading relies for his claim or defence . . . but not the evidence by which those facts are to be proved, and the statement must be as brief as the nature of the case admits. . . .

(2) Without prejudice to paragraph (1), the effect of any document or the purport of any conversation referred to in the pleading must, if material, be briefly stated, and the precise words of the document or conversation shall not be stated, except in so far as those words are themselves material.

(3) A party need not plead any fact if it is presumed by law to be true or the burden of disproving it lies on the other party, unless the other party has specifically denied it in his pleading.

Matters which must be specifically pleaded

8. (1) A party must in any pleading subsequent to a statement of claim plead specifically any matter . . . :
    (a) which he alleges makes any claim or defence of the opposite party not maintainable; or

[86] O. 14, r. 1, provides : " (1) Where in an action to which this rule applies a statement of claim has been served on a defendant and that defendant has entered an appearance in the action, the plaintiff may, on the ground that that defendant has no defence to a claim included in the writ, or to a particular part of such a claim, or has no defence to such a claim or part except as to the amount of any damages claimed, apply to the court for judgment against that defendant.

(2) . . . [T]his rule applies to every action in the Queen's Bench Division or Chancery Division begun by writ other than one which includes—
    (a) a claim by the plaintiff for libel, slander, malicious prosecution, false imprisonment, or
    (b) a claim by the plaintiff based on an allegation of fraud.
(3) This Order shall not apply to an action to which O. 86 applies."

(*b*) which, if not specifically pleaded, might take the opposite party by surprise; or

(*c*) which raises issues of fact not arising out of the preceding pleading. . . .

Matter may be pleaded whenever arising

9. Subject to rules 7 (1), 10 and 15 (2), a party may in any pleading plead any matter which has arisen at any time, whether before or since the issue of the writ.

Departure

10. (1) A party shall not in any pleading make an allegation of fact, or raise any new ground, inconsistent with a previous pleading of his.

(2) Paragraph (1) shall not be taken as prejudicing the right of a party to amend, or apply for leave to amend, his previous pleading so as to plead the allegations or claims in the alternative.

Points of law may be pleaded

11. A party may by his pleading raise any point of law.

Particulars of pleading

12. (1) Subject to paragraph (2), every pleading must contain the necessary particulars of any claim, defence or other matter pleaded . . .

(3) The court may order a party to serve on any other party particulars of any claim, defence or other matter stated in his pleading, or in any affidavit of his ordered to stand as a pleading, or a statement of the nature of the case on which he relies, and the order may be made on such terms as the court thinks just.

(5) An order under this Rule shall not be made before service of the defence unless, in the opinion of the court, the order is necessary or desirable to enable the defendant to plead or for some other special reason.

(6) Where the applicant for an order under this Rule did not apply by letter for the particulars he requires, the court may refuse to make the order unless of opinion that there were sufficient reasons for an application by letter not having been made.

Admissions and denials

13. (1) Subject to paragraph (4), any allegation of fact made by a party in his pleading is deemed to be admitted by the opposite party unless it is traversed by that party in his pleading or a joinder of issue under rule 14 operates as a denial of it.

(2) A traverse may be made either by a denial or by a statement of non-admission and either expressly or by necessary implication.

(3) Subject to paragraph (4), every allegation of fact made in a statement of claim . . . which the party on whom it is served does not intend to admit must be specifically traversed by him in his defence . . . ; and a general denial of such allegations, or a general statement of non-admission of them, is not a sufficient traverse of them.

(4) Any allegation that a party has suffered damage and any allegation as to the amount of damages is deemed to be traversed unless specifically admitted.

Denial by joinder of issue

14. (1) If there is no reply to a defence, there is an implied joinder of issue on that defence.

(2) Subject to paragraph (3)—

- (*a*) there is at the close of pleadings an implied joinder of issue on the pleading last served, and
- (*b*) a party may in his pleading expressly join issue on the next preceding pleading.

(3) There can be no joinder of issue, implied or express, on a statement of claim . . .

(4) A joinder of issue operates as a denial of every material allegation of fact made in the pleading on which there is an implied or express joinder of issue, unless, in the case of an express joinder of issue, any such allegation is excepted from the joinder and is stated to be admitted . . .

Statement of claim

15. (1) A statement of claim must state specifically the relief or remedy which the plaintiff claims; but costs need not be specifically claimed.

(2) A statement of claim must not contain any allegation or claim in respect of a cause of action unless that cause of action is mentioned in the writ or arises from facts which are the same as, or include or form part of, facts giving rise to a cause of action so mentioned; but, subject to that, a plaintiff may in his statement of claim alter, modify or extend any claim made by him in the indorsement of the writ without amending the indorsement. . . .

Striking out pleadings and indorsements

19. (1) The court may at any stage of the proceedings order to be struck out or amended any pleading or the indorsement of any writ in the action, or anything in any pleading or in the indorsement, on the ground that—

- (*a*) it discloses no reasonable cause of action or defence, as the case may be; or
- (*b*) it is scandalous, frivolous or vexatious; or
- (*c*) it may prejudice, embarrass or delay the fair trial of the action; or
- (*d*) it is otherwise an abuse of the process of the court;

and may order the action to be stayed or dismissed or judgment to be entered accordingly, as the case may be.

(2) No evidence shall be admissible on an application under paragraph (1) (*a*). . . .

Close of pleadings

20. (1) The pleadings in an action are deemed to be closed—

- (*a*) at the expiration of fourteen days after service of the reply or, if there is no reply but only a defence to counterclaim, after service of the defence to counterclaim, or
- (*b*) if neither a reply nor a defence to counterclaim is served, at the expiration of fourteen days after service of the defence.

(2) The pleadings in an action are deemed to be closed at the time provided by paragraph (1) notwithstanding that any request or order for particulars has been made but has not been complied with at that time.

Trial without pleadings

21. (1) Where in an action to which this Rule applies any defendant has entered an appearance in the action, the plaintiff or that defendant may apply

to the court by summons for an order that the action shall be tried without pleadings or further pleadings as the case may be.

(2) If, on the hearing of an application under this Rule, the court is satisfied that the issues in dispute between the parties can be defined without pleadings or further pleadings, or that for any other reason the action can properly be tried without pleadings or further pleadings . . . the court shall order the action to be so tried, and may direct the parties to prepare a statement of the issues in dispute or, if the parties are unable to agree such a statement, may settle the statement itself.

(3) Where the court makes an order under paragraph (2), it shall, and where it dismisses an application for such an order, it may, give such directions as to the further conduct of the action as may be appropriate, and O. 25, rules 2 to 7, shall, with any . . . necessary modifications, apply as if the application under this Rule were a summons for directions.

(4) This rule applies to every action begun by writ other than one which includes—

(a) a claim by the plaintiff for libel, slander, malicious prosecution, false imprisonment . . . ; or

(b) a claim by the plaintiff based on an allegation of fraud.

Pleading in personal injuries actions

Report of the Committee on Personal Injuries Litigation
Cmnd. 3691, 1968

237. A perusal of R.S.C. Order 18 . . . with all notes and quotations, constitutes a fascinating experience for a practitioner, in the nature of a trip through territory unknown to him and in a climate which he has not experienced in his daily life. No set of rules could have been more carefully devised; no judicial comment could be more cogently expressed; practice all too regrettably often reveals little relationship to the Rules; the judicial comments pass unregarded.

238. After the reforms in pleading . . . in the latter half of the nineteenth century, Cotton L.J. was able to say in *Spedding* v. *Fitzpatrick* [87] with blissful optimism . . . "The old system of pleading at common law was to conceal as much as possible what was going to be proved at trial." The "old system" has been kept alive too long. . . .

239. Of course pleaders owe a duty to their clients. It is a perfectly proper professional attitude for them to adopt that to tie their clients too tightly to any particular case to be made at trial is not to give the best service; something may crop up between pleading and trial; to have to amend to cover a new situation would reveal that knowledge of it was belated. So it is that many careful and perfectly honourable pleaders . . . in practice, evade the effect of the modern rules.

240. The foregoing is no criticism of the Bar, but may be of the Bench. Order 18 provides a specific and mandatory code which . . . empowers and directs the court to be adamant in excluding new claims or " surprise " defences: should there be any doubt about this, the Rule should be strengthened. As to the former, Order 18, rule 7 governs; as to the latter, Order 18, rule 8 viz.: " A party must in any pleading, subsequent to a statement of claim plead specifically any matter . . . which, if not specifically pleaded, might take the opposite party by surprise."

[87] (1888) 39 Ch.D. 410, 414.

241. There are few bad pleadings produced by the Bar . . . in the sense that they are uncommunicative through ineptitude, not by design. But many others are bad by the standards prescribed by Order 18, whilst being models . . . in the art of permitted . . . concealment.

242. We regard it as . . . essential . . . that the judges should . . . terminate the too long extended life of this " old system " of pleading. Pious exhortations to the Bar would be otiose. It is not the task of the Bar to make things more difficult for their clients. However, we venture to hope that some attention may be given by the Bar to the comments we offer. . . . In the majority of cases where the difficulty is encountered at trial it may well seem right to shut out the undisclosed material, in others an adjournment on strict terms may be more appropriate. . . .

244. Undoubtedly a lot of " dead wood " could and should be cut out of pleadings in personal injury cases. Scottish pleadings . . . merit study. Whilst . . . they tend to loquacity . . . they are framed so as clearly to highlight, in isolation and in logical relevance and significance, the issues to be determined. . . . By contrast in English pleadings there is far too often foliage serving no other purpose than that of a screen.

The statement of claim

248. A statement of claim should found the case to be presented to the Court. Any judge would confirm that he has often been annoyed to find that pleas over which he has expended time and thought before coming into court, are abandoned or ignored when the case is opened.[88]

249. In actions for industrial injuries . . . [t]here is . . . no justification for the malpractice of pleading everything which the pleader, stimulated perhaps by recollection of another accident, thinks might be conceivably relevant.

250. Furthermore, it is at the stage of advice on evidence, not at the trial, that allegations no longer relied upon should be abandoned by notice. . . .

254. In road traffic cases, the statement of claim seldom requires any great intellectual effort and, perhaps for this reason, tends to be a shoddy product. Far too many such pleadings follow a stock form of which the dominant characteristic is that no cause of collision known to practitioners is omitted.

256. There is no reason why a statement of claim . . . should not be accompanied by . . . a form incorporating a notice to admit facts pursuant to Order 27, rule 2,[89] specifying " the several facts set out in paras. . . . [of the statement

[88] Cf. Communication from Best, L.C.J.C.P. Appendix B, 2nd Report of Commissioners on Courts of Common Law, P.P. 1830–31 : " . . . [T]he law says the pleadings ought to be certain and true, so that parties may know from them by what proof they are to be met at the trial, and the judge may know what sort of case he is about to try. . . . No man can say that in complicated cases judges ought not to have some opportunity of thinking of them before they go into court, and sometimes consulting some other judge. A court of justice has to decide questions arising out of all the various transactions that the pleasures, the vices, the follies, and the business of mankind give rise to. These often present so much of novelty and difficulty as to render consideration and assistance necessary to a just and satisfactory decision of them. Criminal cases are much less complicated than civil, yet where is the judge that does not think it necessary to inform himself by reading the depositions taken before magistrates of the cases that he is about to try, and where any difficulty occurs does not avail himself of the assistance of the judge who goes the same circuit with him. A *nisi prius* judge can neither think for himself, or have the benefit of the thoughts of others before he is called on to act. . . . On complicated facts, and on contradictory testimony, he must give to the jury his first impression, an impression made in the noise of a crowded court, and before he has had time to detect any fallacy which the ingenuity of counsel, who has an opportunity of considering the mode of putting his case most favourable to his client before he came into court may have presented. . . ." Ed.

[89] This provides : " (1) A party to a cause or matter may not later than 14 days after the cause or matter is set down for trial serve on any other party a notice requiring him to admit, for the purpose of that cause or matter only, the facts specified in the notice." Ed.

of claim]." This Rule is far too seldom invoked . . . yet Order 62, rule 5 provides expressly a costs sanction for unreasonable failure to comply. Masters might well adopt the practice of applying this sanction on hearing the summons for directions. This initial extra but small cost of serving such a notice should be outweighed by the saving of investigation and formal proof of facts of which admissions are thus obtained.

257. . . . [W]herever it may be practicable the parties should agree a medical report or reports on the basis of which . . . the court can assess damages. . . .

258. It ought never to happen that such a case is called without a serious attempt to reach prior agreement of all special damages related to loss of earnings, save in so far as there may be an issue as to capacity to resume pre-accident type of work or the date of recovery of such capacity. . . .

The defence

259. Traditionally defendants are considered to be immune from demands for particulars or sanctions in costs if they merely traverse, by denial or non-admission, allegations of fact other than " pregnant negative " allegations.

260. Some of the experienced solicitors and litigants accustomed to defending . . . have asserted . . . that this tradition must be maintained intact because the whole system of litigation rests upon the fundamental basis that " the onus of proof is squarely upon the plaintiff." . . . [A]nd it may sometimes be true as they assert . . . that defendants when called upon to plead do not even know whether the alleged accident occurred or at least are unaware how or why it occurred or whether the plaintiff's allegations, or any of them, are true.

261. It is said that in such cases—and because they exist, in all cases—defendants should be entitled to preserve their freedom not only to continue to investigate and search for witnesses but to put forward subsequently any affirmative explanation of the accident or injuries, without delivering any further pleas or any qualification or explanation of their traverse, notwithstanding . . . Order 18, rule 7 (1), rule 8 (1) (b) and (c) and rule 12 (1). . . . There may . . . be cases where a defendant wishes to put the plaintiff to proof of his case and is not prepared to make admissions. Where this happens we think it as well to remind practitioners of the consequence, described by Lord Evershed M.R. in *Regina Fur Co. Ltd.* v. *Bossom*.[90] " . . . Where such is the form of pleading, it is not only obligatory upon the defendants but it is not even permissible for them to proceed to put forward some affirmative case which they had not pleaded or alleged; and it is not, therefore, right that they should, by cross-examination of the plaintiffs or otherwise, suggest such an affirmative case. The defendants are acting correctly if they follow the course adopted in this case—that is, so to challenge, at each point, and by proper evidence, where it is admissible, and by cross-examination the case which the plaintiffs seek to make good. . . . [T]he judges will watch carefully that defendants do not attempt . . . to establish some affirmative case . . . and second, do not attempt to lead evidence solely directed to the credit of witnesses."

262. Mere denials in a defence should be opened up by an order to give particulars of the substance of the defendants factual case. Some guidance . . . is to be derived from the decision of the Court of Appeal in *Fox* v. *H. Wood (Harrow) Ltd.*[91]

263. It seems to us that a defendant would be protected in these respects adequately and so far as proper, having regard to the fact that his interest is not alone involved, if he were required to distinguish at the stage at which he pleads between what he knows to be correct and what he still does not know.

[90] [1958] 2 Lloyd's Rep. at p. 428.   [91] [1962] 3 All E.R. 1100.

Of course he would then expose, in certain cases, the relatively belated nature of the information or theory of causation on which he ultimately contests the claim; this very fact may be a helpful indication to the Court. . . .

264. Therefore, both plaintiffs and defendants must set out in their pleadings what they know or suppose to have happened: changes of knowledge or belief must be revealed by amendment. . . .

266. We have no hesitation in saying that it is in defences that the current practice of pleading calls for the harshest criticism. One of the most experienced Queen's Bench Masters . . . regrets that trial judges seem too unwilling to penalise unsuccessful formal denials by an order of costs (which it is not easy to frame). . . .

271. Before we leave the topic of pleading, we must also make it clear we have not overlooked the position in the Admiralty Division where the established practice is to require the parties to " plead blind " i.e. each must set out openly his case, without first seeing the version of facts asserted by any other party in a " Preliminary Act." [92]

272. We do not advocate the adoption of any like practice in the Queen's Bench Division or in County Courts where personal injury litigation is already too similar to a game of Blind Man's Buff; any changes should minimise rather than increase the part played by guesswork. We think that the reason why the Admiralty practice is appropriate in marine collision cases may be that each ship involved is in substance a plaintiff. . . .

Summary of Recommendations

(6) The following periods are recommended for pleadings in personal injury actions:

    (a) For service of statement of claim—one month from service of writ.
    (b) For service of defence—six weeks from service of statement of claim.
    (c) For service of reply and defence to a counter-claim—three weeks.

The above periods should only be extended in exceptional circumstances. . . .

The problem of delay

Allen v. Sir Alfred McAlpine & Sons Ltd.
Court of Appeal [1968] 2 Q.B. 229

One of the recommendations made by the Winn Committee was that the judges should be more prepared to use their powers, and any additional powers that might be necessary, to secure the speedy resolution of disputes. The Limitation Acts provide a time limit within which actions should be brought. The rules of procedure also lay down times within which things are to be done. But long delays still occur. Hence the interest attached to the robust use of the court's powers in the present case to dismiss an action because it had not been pursued with sufficient despatch.

LORD DENNING M.R. In these three cases the law's delays have been intolerable. . . . In the first case a widow lost her husband nearly *nine* years ago. . . . Her case has not yet been set down for trial. . . . In the second case, a nurse complained that she strained her back *nine* years ago. . . . [T]he hospital authorities . . . have not even yet put in a defence to the claim. In the third case, a man of business bought shares nearly *fourteen* years ago. . . . He brought an action complaining that he was deceived in the deal. . . . Yet the suit has

[92] *Cf.* O. 75, r. 18.

not yet been entered for trial. In none of these three cases has the party himself been at fault. . . . The fault, I regret to say, has been with the legal advisers. It is not that they wilfully neglected the cases. But they have put them on one side, sometimes for months, and even for years, because of the pressure of other work or of other claims on their time. Hence these ills. And these are not the only examples. A few months age we had a couple of cases of like sort. One was on March 9, 1967, *Reggentin* v. *Beecholme Bakeries Ltd.*[93] The other was on March 17, 1967, *Fitzpatrick* v. *Batger & Co. Ltd.*[94] . . . We struck out those cases for want of prosecution. This meant that the injured plaintiffs could not recover their compensation from the defendants. But they could recover it from their own negligent solicitors. These cases have brought home to lawyers that they must get on. A note in the Supreme Court Practice, 1967, 2nd sup. p. 4, para. 25/1/3, says that:

> " These emphatic decisions of the Court of Appeal, which lay down a more stringent practice than was formerly followed, have injected a new element of expedition in the conduct and preparation of cases before trial, especially in relation to ' accident ' cases. Plaintiffs' solicitors who do not ' get on ' with their cases will be at risk of having the plaintiff's action dismissed for want of prosecution and themselves rendered liable for negligence to the plaintiff as their own former client."

Following those decisions, several other cases have been struck out for delay. These three are among them. . . .

All through the years men have protested at the law's delay and counted it as a grievous wrong, hard to bear. Shakespeare ranks it among the whips and scorns of time.[95] Dickens tells how it exhausts finances, patience, courage, hope.[96] To put right this wrong, we will in this court do all in our power to enforce expedition: and, if need be, we will strike out actions when there has been excessive delay. This is a stern measure. But it is within the inherent jurisdiction of the court. And the Rules of Court expressly permit it. It is the only effective sanction they contain. If a plaintiff fails within the specified time to deliver a statement of claim, or to take out a summons for directions, or to set down the action for trial, the defendant can apply for the action to be dismissed, see R.S.C. (Rev. 1965), Ord. 19, r. 1; Ord. 25, r. 1; Ord. 34, r. 2. It was argued before us that the court should never on the first application, dismiss the action. Even if there was long delay, the court should always give the dilatory solicitor one more chance. . . . Such has been the practice, it was said, for a great many years. . . . I cannot accept this suggestion. If there were such a practice, there would be no sanction whatever against delay. The plaintiff's solicitor could put a case on one side as long as he pleased without fear of the consequences.

. . . The principle upon which we go is clear: When the delay is prolonged and inexcusable, and is such as to do grave injustice to one side or the other or to both, the court may in its discretion dismiss the action straightaway, leaving the plaintiff to his remedy against his own solicitor who has brought him to this plight. Whenever a solicitor, by his inexcusable delay, deprives a client of his cause of action, the client can claim damages against him; as, for instance, when a solicitor does not issue a writ in time, or serve it in time, or does not renew it properly. We have seen, I regret to say, several such cases lately. Not a few are legally aided. In all of them the solicitors have, I believe, been quick to compensate the suffering client; or at least their insurers have. So the wrong done by the delay has been remedied as much as can be. I hope this will always be done.

93 (1967) 111 S.J. 216.   94 [1967] 1 W.L.R. 706.
95 *Hamlet*, Act III, sc. 1.   96 *Bleak House*, Chap. 1.

Dealing with interlocutory matters

The Queen's Bench Master. Master A. S. Diamond
(1960) 76 L.Q.R. 504

The Queen's Bench Master in 1960

The master is the tribunal to which interlocutory applications are made; and the litigant, if he wishes, goes to the judge in chambers on appeal. Since 1880 the jurisdiction of the Queen's Bench masters has been increased over the years in various respects, and in 1960 is as follows:

1. They hear and decide all interlocutory applications, with one large qualification, namely, that they have no jurisdiction in regard to matters involving the liberty of the subject—*e.g.,* attachment and committal for contempt of court— and they have generally no jurisdiction to grant injunctions, since injunctions are enforceable by imprisonment. On these matters application must be made, in some cases, to the judge in chambers, in some cases to three judges sitting as a Divisional Court of the Queen's Bench Division, which takes the place of the old common law courts sitting *in banc.*

2. They hear applications to the court for leave to compromise actions involving infants—mainly claims by infants for personal injuries and under the Fatal Accidents Acts—and they invest the money recovered by infants, and money recovered by widows under those Acts, and pay out capital as needed.

3. When judgment is given in default for damages to be assessed, they try the claim as to the amount of the damages.

4. They have jurisdiction to try any action by consent of the parties.

5. They have jurisdiction under the Married Women's Property Act, 1882, to try claims between husband and wife to the ownership or possession of property.

6. They have jurisdiction to try garnishee issues.

7. They have jurisdiction to try interpleader proceedings with the consent of one of the claimants, and in fact try the great bulk of them.

8. They control the clerks of the Central Office.

9. They are available to give advice to the practitioner on matters of practice and procedure.

Outside this the masters issue practice directions which have no statutory force but do control the work of the Central Office. They may also, with the approval of the Lord Chancellor, prescribe forms for general use in the Central Office. The senior master is also Queen's Remembrancer and has some additional functions of a public and legal character.

Aims and ideals

What then should be the aims of a tribunal handling such proceedings and of a system of administration that provides for them? First, to see that the procedure is as simple and economic as it is apt and expeditious—and expeditious not merely because justice may not be justice unless it is speedy, but because the longer a case is pending the higher the costs. This involves judgment without a trial where there is nothing to try, and speedy trial where there is a triable issue. It also involves control of pending actions by the court—a delicate and tactful control, consistent with proper freedom of action by litigant and solicitor (especially since, at the commencement of an action, neither party usually intends a trial) but still, a firm control. Such control will be given, first, by the rules of procedure, which lay down a series of steps to be taken by the litigant at defined intervals and give the opposite party a right to judgment or dismissal if the steps are not taken. The master's function is to supplement the rules by enabling the court to keep control and mould the action into proper form. He will order no more particulars, discovery of documents or interrogatories than is useful; . . . he will endeavour to see that the pleadings do justice to both sides and that they raise clearly the issues for trial; he will see that there is no unnecessary or lavish expenditure on expert witnesses, that evidence is given in the most economic and effective form, and that all is agreed that can be agreed. Further, he will endeavour to educate and train all who have a part to play in interlocutory business (especially, in these days of shortage of labour, the junior solicitors' clerks), so that they may play that part with industry and knowledge and . . . in accordance with the ideal that all alike, including judge and master, are officers of the administration of justice. . . .

[T]he Queen's Bench master . . . hears . . . some 4,000 applications a year; his knowledge of London solicitors and clerks is phenomenal: some he has seen several thousand times. He has a good idea of what happens in the offices of a hundred attorneys; how they prepare their cases, their virtues and their foibles. He knows that it is vital to maintain a certain practice, which he has helped to build up, and fatal to countenance another. Nay, he knows well certain litigants, their problems and their habits, and he even recognises an affidavit that he has seen before. He has a pretty good recollection of what has happened earlier in the same action. He has even a certain compensating advantage that arises from the fact that, as a rule, he will not be the tribunal that tries the action. He can be franker in the views he expresses on the merits of the action, and the desirability of a settlement. He need not be afraid of giving the advocates an impression that he has formed a view about a case before he tries it. Even in America, the judge who has taken the pre-trial conference has often to assign the action to another judge for trial, either because the state rule or statute so provides, or because of something he has learned at the conference. Lastly, the object of interlocutory procedure should be to aid the settlement of an action on just terms, but the master will best serve that end by doing what is indicated above, and especially by helping to keep the case moving. The approach of the day of trial powerfully stimulates a settlement—just as (in the opinion of Dr. Samuel Johnson) "when a man knows he is to be hanged in a fortnight, it concentrates his mind wonderfully."

Costs and the cost of litigation

The Supreme Court of Judicature Act 1925

1925, c. 49

50.—(1) Subject to the provisions of this Act and to rules of court and to the express provisions of any other Act, the costs of and incidental to all proceedings in the Supreme Court, including the administration of estates and trusts, shall be in the discretion of the court or judge, and the court or judge shall have full power to determine by whom and to what extent the costs are to be paid.

Rules of the Supreme Court. Costs

ORDER 62

3.—(1) Subject to the following provisions of this Order, no party shall be entitled to recover any costs of or incidental to any proceedings from any other party to the proceedings except under an order of the Court.

(2) If the Court in the exercise of its discretion sees fit to make any order as to costs of or incidental to any proceedings, the Court shall, subject to this

Order, order the costs to follow the event, except when it appears to the Court that in the circumstances of the case some other order should be made as to the whole or any part of the costs.

4.—(2) In the case of an appeal the costs of the proceedings giving rise to the appeal, as well as the costs of the appeal and of the proceedings connected with it, may be dealt with by the Court hearing the appeal. . . .

5. The Court in exercising its discretion as to costs shall, to such extent, if any, as may be appropriate in the circumstances, take into account . . .

(b) any payment of money into court and the amount of such payment.

7.—(1) Where in any cause or matter anything is done or omission is made improperly or unnecessarily by or on behalf of a party, the Court may direct that any costs to that party in respect of it shall not be allowed to him and that any costs occasioned by it to other parties shall be paid by him to them.

(2) . . . [T]he Court shall . . . have regard in particular to . . .

(a) the omission to do anything the doing of which would have been calculated to save costs;

(b) the doing of anything calculated to occasion, or in a manner or at a time calculated to occasion, unnecessary costs;

(c) any unnecessary delay in the proceedings.

8.—(1) . . . [W]here in any proceedings costs are incurred improperly or without reasonable cause or are wasted by undue delay or by any other misconduct or default, the Court may make against any solicitor whom it considers to be responsible . . . an order—

(a) disallowing the costs as between the solicitor and his clients; and

(b) directing the solicitor to repay to his client costs which the client has been ordered to pay to other parties in the proceedings; or

(c) directing the solicitor personally to indemnify such other parties against costs payable by them.

Report of the Committee on Supreme Court Practice and Procedure
Cmd. 8878, 1953

This committee spent six years considering the problems of practice and procedure and the extracts here cannot do justice to the report as a whole. Along with the report of the Winn Committee however it constitutes the major contribution to the problems since the war.

13. There is . . . no doubt . . . that the litigant who loses may be ruined by the costs of the case, and even the winner, if he is left with a large bill to pay, may think that his victory was too dearly bought. . . .

20. The terms of reference of the Hanworth Committee [97] and the Peel Commission [98] seem to have required them to concentrate upon administrative efficiency and despatch of business. Our own required us to regard the problem of costs as our prime task. To the best of our belief, the common complaint of "the law's delays" is less justified in England than in many, perhaps most,

[97] The Business of Courts Committee (Cmd. 4265, 1933; Cmd. 4471, 1934; Cmd. 5066, 1936) was appointed "to consider the state of business in the Supreme Court, and to report whether greater expedition in the despatch of business or greater economy in the administration of justice in the court, is practicable and would be effected by any, and, if so, what rearrangement, in the constitution of the Supreme Court and of the Divisions comprised in the High Court of Justice. . . ."

[98] The Royal Commission on the Despatch of Business at Common Law (Cmd. 5065, 1934–36) was appointed "to enquire into the state of business in the King's Bench Division of the High Court of Justice and to report whether, with a view to greater despatch, any reforms should be adopted."

other countries. . . . But the burden and the fear of costs are most serious for the many citizens who now find any form of saving from income a matter of extreme difficulty. Since we began our work, the legal aid scheme under the Legal Aid and Advice Act, 1949, has come into operation in the Supreme Court. The scheme may have removed a cause of anxiety and of grievance (and therefore a sense of injustice) from those whose means bring them within the scope of its benevolence; but it has perhaps thrown into sharper relief the case of those who have too much money to qualify for legal aid but not enough for independent litigation. There are numbered, no doubt, among those who have recourse to our Courts many corporations possessed of great resources; but " the average litigant " still means a much larger class who have neither the affluence of great corporations nor the limited means which would enable them to prosecute or defend their rights wholly or partly at public expense. In one way the lot of the litigant of the " average " class has been worsened by the legal aid scheme, for if he finds himself opposed by a legally aided litigant, he may, however just his claim or defence, be unable to recover any costs at all either at the trial or upon appeal. There is also no doubt, in our judgment, that the present high rates of taxation are, in the heavy type of action, responsible (at least in part) for the high level of the cost of the proceedings, particularly if one party is able to charge his costs of the litigation wholly or partly against trading profits for income tax purposes.[99]

21. It must not be forgotten that of all the actions started only a small fraction ever come to trial. This is because to a great many claims there is no defence at all, and many more lend themselves to an early settlement. It is therefore to the public advantage that the cost of the early stages of a proceeding should be kept as low as reasonably possible. . . . No doubt the costs of the trial operate powerfully as an inducement to settle early out of Court, and it is proper that this should be so, for otherwise the Courts would be flooded with frivolous litigation, but it is not desirable that *high* costs should induce a litigant to accept a settlement which appears to him to be a denial of his just rights.[1]

37. . . . The broad principle of English procedure is that he who has successfully prosecuted or defended a claim is *prima facie* entitled to recover his costs

---

[99] *Cf.* Third Report of the Law Commission, para. 12: " . . . Today trade unions, trading associations, many friendly and benefit societies, provide their members with financial assistance in pursuing claims or defences in certain classes of civil action.

13. Similarly, there is widespread throughout our society the beneficent practice of third party liability insurance, under which insured persons are entitled to indemnity against damages and costs awarded against them in actions based upon negligence, nuisance or breach of statutory duty and under which the conduct of the proceedings is normally in the hands of the insurers. . . . Ed.

15. The truth is that today the great bulk of litigation which engages our courts is maintained from the resources of others, including the state. . . ."

[1] *Cf.* the communication of Best L.C.J.C.P., Appendix B, 2nd Report of the Commissioners on the Common Law Courts, 1830, P.P. xi 547: " The great evil of excessive litigation is that it produces angry feelings between neighbours. If legal proceedings were rendered so cheap that the costs of actions would not be much felt, it would become necessary to contrive some means of restraining people from bringing trifling and vexatious actions. But . . . if litigation is to be kept down by expenses that bring ruin on unsuccessful suitors, you will not suppress angry feelings by preventing suits at law. If a man is convinced that he has been injured by an opulent neighbour, and fears that the attempt to obtain redress may reduce himself and his family to poverty, he will feel more bitter and lasting hatred both against his neighbour, and the government that permits such injustice, than any litigation can excite. The ruin of a man from the loss of his cause, particularly if that cause were a just one, is a greater evil than can arise from the prosecution of twenty causes which have been attended with no injurious consequences to the parties. There are many worthy persons now tormented with anguish from being obliged to submit to wrongs and insults; there are some who have been stripped of all their property to pay costs, and others who are languishing in prisons because they have no means of paying

of so doing. In practice the principle is subject to the important (and necessary) qualification that the loser cannot be asked to pay for costs improperly or unreasonably incurred by the winner through undue caution, extravagance or otherwise. There thus arises the distinction between what are known as *party and party costs*, being the costs which the loser will be ordered to pay to the winner, and the *solicitor and own client bill*, that is, the total charge which the solicitor is entitled to make to his client (winner or loser) for his professional services and disbursements (*i.e.* out-of-pocket expenses such as fees for counsel and witnesses, Court fees and the like). In a small case tried in a single day, or two days at the most, the difference between the bill which the winner is liable to pay to his own legal adviser and the sum which he is entitled to recover from the other side is not likely to be large; in a heavy action lasting many days the difference as things at present are is likely to be very considerable. In all cases the gap is there, great or small. It is the inevitable consequence of the limitations necessarily imposed upon indemnity. . . .

39. Two of our Sub-Committees devoted a great deal of time and attention to this important matter and some of the members were inclined to favour the adoption, for party and party bill purposes, of some kind of scale which would fix more rigidly, by reference to the value or estimated value of the subject matter in issue, the costs recoverable by the winner from the loser. . . .

40. . . . [W]e have decided not to recommend the adoption of a scheme for more rigidly limiting the party and party bill by scales or similar devices. We think, for one thing, that there is real difficulty in arriving at a scale which would do justice to the great variety of cases to which it would apply. . . . [T]he proper principle, in our view, is not to attempt a reduction of charges for work in fact done, but, wherever possible, to avoid the necessity for doing the work. We therefore attach the greatest significance . . . to the summons for directions. . . . [T]he summons for directions . . . must be the occasion for cutting away all non-essential matter and confining the questions to be tried to the real issues. To . . . this proceeding we look for the avoidance on either side of unnecessary expense. . . .

41. . . . Though it is . . . dangerous to generalise, it may fairly be taken that in a witness action lasting not more than two days (and the majority of actions tried are of this character) the bill may be divided into three parts, of which the first two would be roughly of equivalent amount, and each would be somewhat larger than the third, *viz.* (*i*) counsel's brief fees, (*ii*) solicitor's profit costs (*i.e.* professional remuneration) including the item " instructions for brief " which is a discretionary figure including the solicitor's general reward for his professional skill, and (*iii*) disbursements (other than brief fees) including Court fees and witnesses' fees. And in such a case the gap between the total bill presented to the winning party by his own solicitor and the amount recovered from the loser should not be large. . . .

43. There were in our schedules examples of much more substantial cases. . . . In these cases the total bill ran into four figures and the sums taxed off (and the resultant gap) were very considerable. In some cases the gap itself amounted to four figures also. In such cases large sums were taxed off counsel's fees, particularly for refreshers. . . .

costs. To these evils all men in the lower and middling classes are at present liable. Whilst these evils are suffered to exist, excellent as our laws are in other respects, no honest man can say that they require no amendment.

My object is to reduce the expense of and to prevent delay in trials at law, and at the same time to restrain parties from proceeding when they have no right to expect success; to prevent justice from being defeated by form, and to secure decisions on the merits, and to make those who have unjustly brought or defended actions pay all the costs that their folly or malignity has occasioned." Ed.

71. The Judges, it is said, must be more " costs-conscious." We hope indeed that they will. The subject of costs, when the trial is ended and judgment delivered, is not generally attractive to a Judge anxious to start upon the next case. But the gravity of the incidence of costs is such that real injustice may be done if questions of costs are insufficiently considered. If our examination, which we claim at least to have been thorough, is shown to have found no effective means of reducing costs, it appears to us at any rate that further search will not be likely to prove fruitful within the framework of our legal institutions as we know them. We hope, therefore, that the Bar Council and the Law Society will feel able to impress upon their members the principles involved and the need for the utmost co-operation if the desired end is to be achieved.[2]

The summons for directions

The Summons for Directions. Master A. S. Diamond
(1959) 75 L.Q.R. 43

At paragraph 40 of its report [3] the Evershed Committee noted: " We . . . attach the greatest significance . . . to the summons for directions. . . . [T]he summons for directions . . . must be the occasion for cutting away all non-essential matter and confining the questions to be tried to the real issues. To . . . this proceeding we look for the avoidance on either side of unnecessary expense."

The Bar is probably now satisfied of the usefulness of the summons for directions as a " general stocktaking " of the action. The usual complaint of the barrister is or was that his case has not been adequately prepared, and that the solicitor has not consulted him early enough on the preparations for trial and on the question whether the case ought to be settled or fought; that he is instructed to advise on evidence on the eve of trial, if at all, and that too little

---

[2] *Cf.* Report of the Winn Committee on Personal Injuries Litigation (Cmnd. 3691): para. 210. To encourage the prompt assertion of claims and to mitigate the manifest disadvantages of stale trials, material inducements are required: mere exhortation is not enough. At the same time there is a need to discourage by any practicable means, including financial deterrents, any unreasonable prolongation of personal injury litigation or any tendency to regard such litigation as a money-making enterprise of which the rewards are greater in proportion to the degree to which it is prolonged. . . .

212. It is our view that an effective improvement in the present situation can be produced by monetary inducements or sanctions. . . .

213. It has been suggested to us that a sanction imposed in costs is unlikely to be sufficiently strong to secure compliance with the aims which we propose. This may well be true in the present climate of judicial practice regarding special orders as to costs. Though a judge in theory has unlimited discretion in awarding costs, in practice his discretion is fettered by well-established rules, and imaginative orders as to costs are understandably rare; . . . special orders are rarely made.

214. It is no doubt because the Bench and the Bar realise the limitations under which a judge labours, that argument as to costs tends to be very brief. At the moment, nothing is to be achieved by counsel pressing for a sophisticated order. Thus at the end of a three-day trial in which the damages are, say, £750, costs are usually disposed of in three minutes, even though there may be some special point on costs which would be well worth arguing if the Court had a freer discretion. Since the person who has to pay the costs of both sides is likely to meet a bill of up to £1,000, which outweighs the damages, it should not be at all incongruous, in a suitable case, that argument as to costs should occupy a more substantial period of time.

215. As a general proposition we recommend that a judge should be disposed more generally than is the present practice, should he disapprove of the conduct of the action by either party . . . to exercise his powers as to costs under R.S.C., Order 62, rules 7 and 8. For example, unnecessary refusal to deal properly with medical reports might well result in a special order relating to costs connected with the medical reports and the attendance of doctors. Ed.

[3] Above, p. 365.

regard is paid to the advice he gives. Now, in a substantial action, he is more commonly asked to advise what directions should be applied for on the summons, and more often than not he will also, in such a case, himself appear on the summons. [Counsel probably appears in 25 per cent. to 30 per cent. of the summonses for directions.] Often relief will be granted on such a summons that would previously have involved several summonses, and a summons for directions on which counsel appears will last anything from ten minutes to two hours. On the summons small savings in costs of proof at the trial will be effected at the suggestion of counsel on one side or of the Master, and the Master will sometimes persuade a party represented by counsel to admit some allegation not admitted in the pleadings (*e.g.* that the premises where the accident occurred are a factory, or that the plaintiff was in the defendant's employ or that the accident happened on a pedestrian crossing). Moreover, as the Master will not try the case, he can be outspoken on occasion in a way that a judge who would try the case could hardly be, and sometimes may be able to discourage a party or encourage a settlement. Then sometimes, where it is necessary, counsel may be asked to advise again on evidence after particulars and discovery. The summons for directions as a " general stocktaking " is an added element of efficiency in the preparation of the trial, though it must not be regarded as new, or more than an improved version of a pre-existing procedure. Has then the summons effected an overall saving of costs? It would be difficult to assert that it has. Whatever savings there may be are usually small and too commonly offset by a small increase in costs. The new summons is necessarily somewhat more expensive than the old, and more than half the actions will be subsequently settled. In a substantial action, if counsel is asked to advise on evidence a second time after advising for the purposes of the summons, the costs of the second opinion must be allowed in an appropriate case. . . . On the other hand, some modest savings at the trial are brought about by this " general stocktaking."

Report of Committee on Personal Injuries Litigation
Cmnd. 3691, 1968

351. We think that the summons for directions is in the vast majority of actions for personal injuries a useless and wasteful step. The employment of counsel on the hearing of such a summons does, no doubt, occasionally—but rarely—result in a preliminary bout of negotiation for a settlement.

352. We recommend the adoption in personal injury actions of a stock form draft order for main directions. Such directions would take effect automatically within fourteen days of service of the defence unless one or other party has applied for further or special directions. By " main directions " we intend to include such matters as: agreement of medical evidence or the number of witnesses in default of agreement, agreement of reports by specified expert or experts, plans and photographs, discovery. . . . In so far as either party modifies the draft order without the concurrence of the other party he should be required to issue a summons for that purpose.

Chapter 6

FINDING THE FACTS

Introduction

It is a mistake to think that lawyers and judges are solely concerned with questions of law. Much of their time, and much of the time and the machinery of the legal system is taken up with facts, ascertaining them, selecting them and proving them. The majority of contested cases raise serious conflicts about the facts and the inferences to be drawn from them, either because someone is lying, or more often because there is an honest difference of opinion about what happened, what was said or what was intended. An essential feature therefore of every legal system is its provision of some method of establishing the relevant facts.

As has been mentioned already, the task of ascertaining the facts is in the first instance a matter for the police in criminal cases, and for the parties and their legal advisers in civil cases, though the latter may have access to statements made to the police, for example in road accident cases, and they may of course employ their own inquiry agents where necessary. It is however one thing to collect the facts together and to decide whether one has a case in law for bringing a prosecution or starting an action, and another to prove it to the satisfaction of a court; for, quite apart from the practical difficulties involved in finding witnesses, and all the problems which arise from their varying abilities to observe and remember accurately what in fact happened, the legal system sets its own standards of proof and lays down rules as to how the facts may, or, more often, may not, be proved. It is these rules, the rules of evidence and proof, which make up another of the filters through which the original case has to pass before a court will give a decision upon it.

The most favoured method of proving a fact in English law is by producing a witness in court and subjecting him to examination and cross-examination about things he can speak of from his own knowledge. In English law this is generally both required and sufficient to prove a fact. This reliance on the virtue of seeing and hearing the witness being examined and cross-examined has already been mentioned in connection with the attitude of appellate courts to findings of fact by trial judges. It appears too in the rule against hearsay which in general prohibits a witness from reporting what he has been told as evidence of the truth of the facts contained in that statement to him. It shows, incidentally, in the view of the Departmental Committee on the Jury [1] when it recommended that although juries should be given facilities for taking notes they should not be positively encouraged to take them since their task was to get a general impression rather than attempt to make a detailed record of what was being said. It comes out too in decisions like that in *Meek* v. *Fleming*,[2] in which

---

[1] Above, p. 211.

[2] [1961] 2 Q.B. 366.

the Court of Appeal ordered a new trial of an action of false imprisonment because in the trial counsel for the defendant, a police officer, had connived with others to keep from the court the fact that the defendant had been reduced in rank from inspector to sergeant as a result of another disciplinary offence relating to a false charge. It was clear from the summing up of the trial judge that he had placed some weight on the fact that the defendant was a superior officer in the Metropolitan Police Force and by implication someone worthy of belief. As a method of discovering the truth it received a recent affirmation by Lord Widgery C.J. in his report on the deaths in Londonderry.[3]

There are two particular difficulties about the general reliance upon evidence which can be given by witnesses produced in court speaking directly of their own experience and observations or producing documents for whose authenticity they can personally vouch, and being subject to cross-examination. One is that this may exclude evidence which may be relevant and useful in determining the facts of the case; the other is that it may add unnecessarily to the costs of the trial, which is of particular importance in civil litigation. For both these reasons there have been moves in recent years to relax some of the restrictions on the use of other kinds of evidence. It has been suggested for example, that many of the exclusionary rules of evidence were developed by the courts at a time when most important cases, civil and criminal, were tried by a jury. One of the reasons for insisting that only evidence that could be vouched for personally by the witness should be allowed was the fear that the jury might find it difficult to assess the true weight to be attached to the evidence, unless they could actually see the witness and hear him cross-examined. There was the further reason, though, that until the early nineteenth century neither the parties in a civil case nor the accused in a criminal case could give evidence themselves and so were not in a position to contradict evidence of this kind which was not subject to cross-examination. Now that most civil cases are tried without a jury, justifications for the old practice which related to the danger that juries might not be able accurately to assess the due weight to be attached to evidence have to a great extent disappeared in civil cases, and even in criminal cases there is a greater willingness to accept evidence that is in some sense second-hand, provided that the way that it has come into existence provides some kind of guarantee of its authenticity and accuracy.

The extent to which changes have been made can be measured to some degree by the modifications which have been introduced by statute into the rule against hearsay evidence; that is the rule which in general prevents a witness stating in court what someone else has told him as evidence of the truth of the facts stated. Quite apart from statute the judges by themselves at common law had introduced a number of exceptions to the rule against hearsay, where for example evidence would otherwise be unavailable and where there was some presumption in favour of it being accurate and authentic, the most conspicuous example being their willingness to admit statements made by deceased persons when they were already under a settled expectation of death and therefore presumed to be more likely than not to be telling the truth. The initial impetus for change has however not come so much from a desire to broaden the range of evidence available to the courts but to save expense, especially in civil cases, and to avoid the necessity for producing witnesses unnecessarily, in particular of facts which are not seriously in dispute. Attacks on the rule against hearsay from this point of view have been part of the more general move towards cheaper litigation, and the reduction of costs by reducing the number of witnesses. They go along with the basic requirement that pleadings should be clear so that parties should know before the trial the case they have to meet and so do not have to have more witnesses available than is actually necessary to meet the case put by the other party and to prove facts which are actually in dispute. They go along too with the encouragement of parties in civil cases to admit facts that they do not seriously intend to deny, with a sanction in costs for unreasonable refusals, and to agree on reports of experts, in particular medical reports, before the trial, to save the expense of having each side produce rival expert witnesses before the court, to dispute, for example, basic facts of the extent of the injuries suffered by a plaintiff in personal injury cases. Quite apart however from questions of costs there is also a growing preference for taking as a starting point the principle that all relevant evidence should be admitted unless there is some good reason why it should not (for example in a criminal trial that the value of the evidence was outweighed by its possible prejudicial effect on the accused, or in civil or criminal trials that admission of the evidence would lead to a proliferation of issues, particularly in relation to the credibility of a witness, or because it fell within one of the specific rules relating to privilege) and that it should be left to the judge, or where there is a jury, the jury under the guidance of the judge, to assess the weight to be attached to it.

Examples of the statutory relaxation of the rule against hearsay are to be found in the Evidence Act 1938 which has now been replaced by the Civil Evidence Acts of 1968 and 1972, and the Criminal Evidence Act 1965. This last statute contains typical provisions designed to deal with typical cases that could arise under the old law because of the strictness of the doctrine against hearsay, admitting the records of statements made to the record-keeper in circumstances which provide some guarantee that they are not likely to be fabricated and where the original maker of the statement would be very difficult to find. The kind of case with which this particular provision was designed to deal had arisen in the case of *Myers* v. *D.P.P.*[4] where the House of Lords had rejected the records of a firm which recorded the numbers it had stamped on the cylinder blocks it manufactured as evidence of identification of a car, on the grounds that the employee who had actually stamped the number on the block was the only person who could give direct evidence of the fact. The Criminal Law Revision Committee in its Eleventh Report proposes that the rules against hearsay evidence in criminal cases should be further modified in much the same way in which they have been modified for civil trials by the Civil Evidence Act 1968. It would however be a mistake to see these developments as an abandonment of the central reliance of the English legal

---

[4] [1965] A.C. 1001.

system on evidence produced by witnesses in court speaking from their own experience and subject to cross-examination. Two other recommendations of the Criminal Law Revision Committee for example, that an accused should no longer have the right to make an unsworn statement not subject to cross-examination, and should actually be called upon in court to give evidence on oath, so that his refusal would be plain for all to see, go in exactly the opposite direction. One unhappy result of the gradual whittling away of the old rule against hearsay while the basic English method of fact-finding is retained, as will be seen below where some of the relevant statutes are set out, is that many of the statutory provisions have an extremely technical and piecemeal air about them.

Rules of Evidence in Criminal Cases

Although in many respects the rules of evidence in criminal and civil cases are similar, there is one important element in trials in criminal cases that looms much larger than in civil cases, and that is the notion of a fair trial. This is seen most clearly in the rule which gives a judge in a criminal case a general discretion to exclude evidence which though technically admissible in law is in his view unfairly prejudicial to the accused, by which it is usually meant that although technically admissible for one purpose it might have the effect of influencing the jury prejudicially against the accused in some other respect, *e.g.* by revealing that he has a criminal record or that he has been involved in similar cases in the past, in circumstances where the evidence would not be admissible for this purpose alone. The problem as to where the line should be drawn between admitting evidence which is relevant and excluding evidence because it is felt that the jury might attach more weight to it than is considered desirable or than it deserves, was one which was considered by the Criminal Law Revision Committee in its Eleventh Report. Two particular areas where the exact location of this line is important is in relation to evidence about the previous convictions of the accused and about his involvement in similar situations in the past which tend to suggest that his part in the present situation was not an innocent one. The general rule at the time of the Committee's Report was that no evidence could be given of the previous convictions of the accused, and that no evidence could be given of the similar past conduct of the accused, at least if this was designed simply to suggest that he was the kind of person likely to have committed the offence with which he was now charged. Each rule was based on the belief that an accused person was entitled to have the evidence of his guilt in the present case proved on the basis of his conduct in relation to the facts charged, without regard to his previous record, that he was in fact to be treated as innocent until proved guilty in the particular case. Although therefore the trial judge had a list of the accused's previous convictions available to him before the trial, these were not available to the jury, though they might of course affect the way in which the judge summed up the case to the jury. This is in marked contrast to continental systems where the past record of the accused is from the very beginning treated as part of the evidence in a criminal case.

To each of the general rules there were already, when the committee reported, a number of exceptions. The principal exception as regards evidence of previous convictions rested on the Criminal Evidence Act 1898, the Act which first laid down that as a general rule an accused person could give evidence on oath on his own behalf, while allowing him also to make an unsworn statement not subject to cross-examination, if he preferred, though there were others as well. Section 1 (2) of the Official Secrets Act 1911, for example, allows the past record of the accused to be proved in order to show that the purpose for which something was done was prejudicial to the safety or interests of the state. The exception based on the Criminal Evidence Act 1898 was part of the compromise made when the accused was first given a general right to give evidence on his own behalf.

An accused was first given an opportunity to make an unsworn statement in cases of felony in 1836. A number of statutes from 1872 made him competent to be examined and cross-examined on oath if he wished. The Criminal Evidence Act 1898 made this a general rule, without compelling him to give evidence if he did not wish to. The prosecution was expressly forbidden to make any comment on his failure to do so. Then section 1 (f) of the Act provided that no question might be put to him which tended to show that he had committed or been convicted of any offence previously, or that he was of bad character, unless he attempted in cross-examination to establish that he was a person of good character, or attacked the character of the witnesses for the prosecution or the prosecutor. If he did either of these things, then he could be questioned about his own character and past conduct. Since the Act was passed the judges have gradually established the principle that the accused does not lose the protection that the Act gave him if he attacks the prosecution witnesses or the prosecutor as an integral part of his denial of the charge, e.g. particularly in cases of rape where the defence was that the prosecutrix consented.

As regards past conduct in general, or evidence of " similar facts " as it is usually known, the exceptions related to such matters as discounting a defence that what had happened had happened innocently or by accident, or showing that the way in which an offence was committed was similar to the way in which the offender had behaved in the past. In R. v. Smith,[5] where Smith was accused of murdering his wife, evidence was admitted to show that his two previous wives had died in similar circumstances with a similar resulting benefit to Smith, in order to rebut any suggestion that his last wife had died by accident. In Makin v. Att.-Gen. for New South Wales [6] a couple were charged with the murder of a child entrusted to their care. Evidence was admitted to show that the bodies of other children entrusted to their care in return for small sums of money had been found buried in gardens of houses previously occupied by the couple, as a means of rebutting any suggestion that the present victim had died of natural causes. Before similar fact evidence, however, can be introduced, there

[5] (1915) 11 Cr.App.R. 229.
[6] [1894] A.C. 57.

must be a sufficiently strong link between the accused and the previous events to outweigh any prejudicial effect the evidence might have. In *Harris* v. *D.P.P.*,[7] for example, evidence that the accused had had the opportunity to commit any one of a series of offences of a similar type which had occurred in a closed market while he was on duty nearby was rejected as evidence that he had committed the latest offence, when the evidence to connect him with the last offence was stronger but still circumstantial. Other examples of evidence more clearly showing disposition being admitted have been cases where the evidence has been admitted as a means of identifying the accused as the person who had committed the offence, *i.e.* where the characteristics of the offender and the accused were so similar and peculiar that they amounted to evidence of identification almost in the same way as if the accused had left his fingerprints at the scene of the crime. In *R.* v. *Straffen*,[8] for example, evidence was admitted to show that Straffen, who was accused of having murdered a small girl while absent from Broadmoor, had previously admitted murdering two small girls. In each case no attempt had been made to hide the body and in each case there had been no sexual assault. In each case the child had been strangled. These features of the murders were all regarded as sufficiently peculiar to be admitted as evidence in the nature of identification, even though it incidentally also amounted to evidence of disposition. More controversial have been the cases where evidence has been admitted that the accused had homosexual tendencies, as a means of identifying him as the man who had committed indecent assaults on boys, as in *R.* v. *Thompson*.[9] The circumstances in which such evidence would be admitted today is a matter of some doubt—see *R.* v. *Morris*[10] and *R.* v. *Twomey*.[11] In all cases, even where the evidence of previous convictions or past conduct is prima facie admissible, it is of course subject to the overriding discretion of the judge to exclude it if he considers it unfairly prejudicial to the accused, and this is particularly the case in respect of evidence which tends to show a disposition to commit a particular kind of offence.

The Criminal Law Revision Committee made no major recommendations so far as evidence of past conduct and previous convictions is concerned. It was divided over the question whether or not to retain the rule under the Criminal Evidence Act 1898 that the accused exposes himself to questions about his previous convictions if he attacks the character of the witnesses of the prosecution. They suggested that in future it should be made clear that he was only to lose the general protection of not having his past convictions revealed if the purpose of his cross-examination of those witnesses was to weaken or destroy their credibility, *i.e.* attempting to show that they were of such a character that what they said should not be believed, and that even then the only questions that could be put to him would be questions strictly relevant to his own credibility as a witness rather than simply showing that he had a criminal record. So far as evidence of " similar facts " was concerned they recommended that the

[7] [1952] A.C. 694.
[8] [1952] 2 Q.B. 911.
[9] [1918] A.C. 221.
[10] (1969) 54 Cr.App.R. 69.
[11] [1971] Crim.L.R. 277.

present law should be both clarified and extended so that where the accused admitted the conduct which was the subject of the charge but asserted that his involvement in it was innocent, then evidence could be brought of other conduct which suggested that he had a disposition to commit that kind of offence (i) in order to show that he possessed the relevant state of mind that would make his involvement a guilty one, *i.e.* that he had the necessary *mens rea* or (ii) to show that the conduct itself was not accidental or involuntary or (iii) to show that there was no lawful justification or excuse for it, and that this evidence should be admissible although the past conduct was not strictly similar, provided that it was sufficiently relevant for these purposes. The evidence of involvement could be simply evidence of a previous conviction. They also recommended that all the law on the subject of when evidence tending to show in the accused a disposition to commit the kind of offence with which he was now charged should be put on a statutory basis and they included a clause giving effect to this in the draft bill attached to their report.

It has already been mentioned that confessions are only admissible as evidence if they are to be shown to be voluntary. In addition any statement may be excluded if it can be shown to have been obtained as the result of some trick which the courts regard as unfair, or oppression, or in breach of the Judges Rules.[12] Apart from this there is no general rule excluding evidence simply because it has been obtained illegally.

CROWN PRIVILEGE

In addition to the rules which exclude some kinds of evidence the Crown, even in cases in which it is not a party, has the power to prevent documents being disclosed if it is contrary to the public interest for them to be revealed. This has in the past been a highly controversial area. In *Duncan* v. *Cammell Laird*[13] the House of Lords recognised that a Minister of the Crown could claim privilege to prevent the production of a document on the grounds that it would be contrary to the public interest to do so, even in cases in which the Crown was not itself a party. The House of Lords also suggested that such a claim was conclusive and could not be challenged by the courts; nor could the document be examined by the court to see if the claim was proper. This ruling met with considerable criticism, particularly as it was said to cover not only documents which themselves contained confidential matter but also documents which belonged to a class which should be protected as such, however innocent the particular document might be. In *Ellis* v. *Home Office*[14] a prisoner in Winchester prison sued the Home Office for negligence after he had been assaulted by another prisoner whom he said the Home Office knew was dangerous and whom they should therefore have kept under control. A vital link in the chain of his argument was to show that the Home Office knew the man was dangerous. The Crown however refused to disclose the prison medical report on the man and the case collapsed.

In response to criticism the government itself modified its practice in 1956 and 1962. At the same time the courts attempted to do something to

---

12 Above, p. 288.
13 [1942] A.C. 624.   14 [1953] 2 Q.B. 135.

mitigate the effect of the rule, in particular as regards class documents. In *Re Grosvenor Hotel Ltd. (No.* 1),[15] for example, Cross J. rejected one affidavit by the Crown on the ground that it did not specify with sufficient particularity the exact ground on which the public interest would be damaged. Much bolder was the attempt of one of the divisions of the Court of Appeal, Lord Denning M.R., Salmon L.J. and Harman L.J. to challenge the authority and scope of the decision of *Duncan* v. *Cammell Laird* itself and in a series of cases they suggested that that case had gone further than necessary in laying down that the claim of privilege was conclusive, in particular in class cases. They claimed that the courts had a discretion to grant and refuse the claim. At the same time they exercised their discretion in favour of the Crown and effectively prevented the line of authority they were developing from being challenged in the House of Lords. Their adventure was finally brought to an end in *Conway* v. *Rimmer*[16] when another division of the Court of Appeal refused to go along with them and asserted the authority of the *Cammell Laird* case. The House of Lords on appeal supported the view that Lord Denning M.R. and his colleagues had gone too far, as a Court of Appeal, but as a House of Lords they themselves departed from the principles laid down in *Duncan* v. *Cammell Laird.*[17]

In theory it is possible for the Crown to object to oral evidence being given as well. There are however technical difficulties in explaining to the court beforehand the exact grounds of objection and there are practical difficulties involved in counsel for the Crown having to intervene at every point at which an answer falling within the objection is likely to be given: *Broome* v. *Broome.*[18]

WITNESSES

It is for the parties to find and present their witnesses and examine them and cross-examine the witnesses of the other side. The judge in a criminal case has the power to call a witness himself; in civil cases he can only do this with the consent of the parties. He may also put questions to a witness either directly or through counsel, and he is more likely to do this when sitting with a jury if he thinks that some point has not been sufficiently or clearly enough brought out for their benefit. In addition he may take " judicial notice " of well-known facts, which means that they need not be formally proved.

In general anyone can be called as a witness. Restrictions which prevented interested persons, parties and their spouses giving evidence were removed as regards civil cases by the Evidence Acts 1843 and 1851, and the Evidence Further Amendment Act 1869. As was mentioned above, an accused person was finally allowed to give evidence in all criminal cases by the Criminal Evidence Act 1898, subject to certain safeguards, though he was under no obligation to do so, and had the right to make an unsworn

[15] [1964] Ch. 464.
[16] [1968] A.C. 910.
[17] See above, p. 257.
[18] [1955] P. 190.

statement instead. The accused's spouse was made a competent witness for the defence at the same time. In general one spouse is not competent to give evidence for the prosecution against the other but to this there are a number of exceptions, statutory and common law, mostly relating to cases where the wife herself has been a victim, *e.g.* section 39 of the Sexual Offences Act 1956 or where the offence was against her property or involves a failure to maintain her and her children. Section 30 (2) of the Theft Act 1968 also provides generally that a spouse is a competent witness for the prosecution in any case brought by her against the accused. In cases of attempted murder and grievous bodily harm against her, a spouse is not only a competent witness for the prosecution but can be compelled to appear (*Leach* v. *R.*,[19] *R.* v. *Lapworth* [20]). In these last cases she can also be compelled to appear for the accused as well. Where a spouse is a competent witness for the defence the prosecution may not comment on her failure to give evidence on her husband's behalf. Even when called as a witness she may still refuse to disclose any communications made to her by her husband during the marriage. As was mentioned above the Criminal Law Revision Committee proposed that in future the accused should lose his right to make an unsworn statement and that he should be called on to give evidence so that his refusal can clearly be seen by the jury. So far as spouses were concerned the Committee recommended that a spouse should be a competent witness for the prosecution in all cases and should be compellable not only in cases involving violence to herself but also in cases involving violence or sexual assault upon a child under sixteen belonging to the same household. In their view too a spouse should be a compellable witness for the accused in all cases. The rule preventing the prosecution commenting on the failure of the spouse to give evidence on behalf of the accused should be abandoned. They also recommended that the special rules about the competence and compellability of spouses should only continue while they are married even in relation to matters which occurred during the marriage. They also recommended the abolition of the privilege of a spouse to refuse to reveal a communication made to her by her husband, which had already been abolished in civil proceedings by the Civil Evidence Act 1968.

Evidence may be given by accomplices but in such cases the jury has to be warned of the danger of relying on their evidence in the absence of some corroboration of it, *i.e.* "independent testimony which affects the accused by connecting or tending to connect him with the crime . . . evidence which implicates him, that is, which confirms in some particular not only the evidence that the crime has been committed, but also that the prisoner committed it. . . ." (*R.* v. *Baskerville*,[21] *per* Lord Reading L.C.J.). An accused person however cannot be called by the prosecution to give evidence against someone charged with him, though he can give evidence of the latter's guilt during his own examination or cross-examination. Alternatively he may plead guilty or even be tried separately and be acquitted, perhaps as a result of the prosecution not offering any evidence against him, and then appear as a witness for the prosecution. If he pleads

[19] [1912] A.C. 305.
[20] [1931] 1 K.B. 117.
[21] [1916] 2 K.B. 658.

guilty he should normally be sentenced before he gives his evidence in order that he does not shape his evidence in the hope of securing more favourable treatment, though this does not always happen. The Criminal Law Revision Committee recommended a number of changes in connection with corroboration. So far as accomplices were concerned they recommended that the absolute rule that the judge should warn the jury in every case should be relaxed and that instead it should be left to the judge's discretion in every case to give a warning whenever he thought it necessary, even where the witness was not strictly an accomplice, wherever there was in fact some danger in relying on his uncorroborated evidence alone.

Children may give evidence on oath if they understand what it involves. Otherwise they may give unsworn evidence provided they at least understand the duty to tell the truth.[22] In *R. v. Wallwork* [23] however, the Court of Criminal Appeal commented on the fact that in that case a child of five had been called as a witness in a case of an alleged assault upon her and the Lord Chief Justice said that " to call a little child of five seems to us most undesirable, and I hope it will not occur again." Here again there is a requirement of corroboration if a jury is to rely on the unsworn evidence of a child and the requirement of a warning of the danger of relying on the uncorroborated evidence of a child even when it is given on oath. The Criminal Law Revision Committee proposed that in future evidence by everyone of fourteen and over should be on oath. In order to determine whether a child under fourteen is competent to give evidence at all the court should be satisfied that the child " is possessed of sufficient intelligence to justify the reception of his evidence and understands the importance of telling the truth in [the] proceedings." They also recommended that in future, so far at least as non-sexual offences were concerned, the need for corroboration or a warning of the dangers of convicting on the evidence of children without corroboration should be abolished.

There are some other cases where corroboration is relevant under the existing law where the Committee also made new proposals. A number of statutes require corroboration, *e.g.* in cases of perjury under the Perjury Act 1911 in some cases under the Sexual Offences Act 1956 and in charges of speeding under the Road Traffic Act 1960, though in this last case it is enough for the witness to say that he checked his speed on his speedometer, whereas in other cases the corroborative evidence, as has been seen in the quotation from *Baskerville*, above, must come from an independent source. In referring to the need for corroboration in the case of sexual offences in his book *The Proof of Guilt* Professor Glanville Williams notes: " There is sound reason for it, because these cases are particularly subject to the danger of deliberately false charges, resulting from sexual neuroses, phantasy, jealousy, spite or simply a girl's refusal to admit that she consented to an act of which she is now ashamed." The rule relating to perjury is to avoid the problem of having to weigh one statement against another, and a proliferation of trials. The Criminal Law Revision Committee has recommended that the requirement of corroboration should be retained in the case of perjury and speeding. So far as sexual offences are

---

[22] s. 38 (1) of the Children and Young Persons Act 1933.
[23] (1958) 42 Cr.App.R. 153.

concerned they recommended that corroboration should still be required where the victim is under fourteen. Where the victim is fourteen or over the judge should simply warn the jury of the special need for caution in convicting on her uncorroborated evidence. The Committee also took the view that there was an area not at present covered by any requirement of corroboration or a warning that should be covered, namely, cases of disputed identification. " We regard mistaken identifications," it said, " as by far the greatest cause of actual or possible wrong convictions." It therefore proposed that the judge should in future warn the jury of the special need for caution before convicting the accused where the case against him depended wholly or substantially on the correctness of one or more disputed identifications of him. They did not propose that corroboration should be required or even that the warning should be of the dangers of convicting without corroboration, but simply that a warning should be given of the need for caution. The Committee also made two other important recommendations in relation to corroboration; that in future evidence that needed corroboration could be corroborated by evidence which itself needed corroboration; secondly that the silence of the accused when questioned by the police, or the refusal of the accused to give evidence could itself in certain circumstances amount to corroboration. This latter recommendation is particularly important as it is a further aspect of the general pressure that the Committee tried to put on an accused person to make some kind of statement or to give evidence, and to remove his immunity of silence.

Examination and Cross-examination

Counsel are responsible for examining their own witnesses. The basic rule is that they are not to ask leading questions, questions framed, that is, in such a way as to suggest the hoped-for answer, except as regards such formal matters as the witness's name, address and occupation. Witnesses are expected to give evidence of facts within their own personal knowledge—things they have seen, heard, touched or smelt, statements made to them, subject to the rules against hearsay, and by them. They are not expected to be asked their opinions on the issues of the case since these are for the judge and jury to decide—though the distinction between fact and opinion is not as clear as it sounds at first, since much so-called observation involves a good deal of opinion and inference—and it can be particularly difficult in relation to expert witnesses who may be asked their professional opinions on matters of fact and whose answers can often come very near to stating an opinion on the main issues of the case.

As a general rule counsel may not challenge the answer given by one of his own witnesses, though he may bring other evidence to show that it is mistaken. In exceptional cases a judge may allow counsel to treat one of his own witnesses as a " hostile " witness if he has in fact shown himself hostile to the party on whose behalf he has been called. If that happens counsel may not only call evidence to contradict the witness but may cross-examine him, usually by putting to him previous inconsistent statements he has made. Greater freedom is allowed in cross-examination. Counsel is not only permitted to cross-examine a witness for the other side about the facts in issue, but may also seek to raise doubts as to his reliability and credibility as a witness both in relation to the particular facts and generally. He may seek to show that he is unreliable because his powers of observation or memory are weak, or that he is biased against the other party, or lacks credibility because of his general reputation or his previous criminal record. As a general rule any answer given to a question relating to the general credibility of a witness has to be accepted, a rule which is related to a theme already touched upon in relation to the rules of procedure and pleading. It was noted above that these rules, and indeed to some extent the rules of substantive law themselves have it as one of their objects to make the case in hand more manageable by limiting and defining the issues and making it possible to dispose of the case in a reasonable way within a reasonable time limit. Some of the rules of evidence have the same purpose. The rule limiting the extent to which counsel can follow up and challenge answers relating to a witness's credibility is one of these. So are some of the rules restricting the questions which counsel may put in the first place. It is one of the functions of the judge to keep the scope of cross-examination within reasonable bounds. Hence the traditional " I do not see where all this is leading us, Mr. —." There are however a number of exceptions to the rule that a witness's answers to questions affecting his credibility cannot be challenged. If he denies a previous conviction this can be proved; so too can previous inconsistent statements.[24]

The Criminal Law Revision Committee recommended a relaxation of the rule that a party could only cross-examine one of his own witnesses if he proved " hostile." Instead, they recommended that if the witness gave evidence which was adverse to the party calling him or was inconsistent with a previous statement he had made it should be possible for counsel to ask the judge for leave to cross-examine him, not to challenge his general credibility but, for example, to put his previous inconsistent statement to him. They also proposed that in future the previous statement should not only be introduced to show that the witness was unreliable but should be permitted to stand as evidence of the facts stated in it.

Although a witness is generally under an obligation to reply to any questions put to him and may be punished for contempt if he refuses to answer a question without lawful justification witnesses have a number of privileges to refuse to answer. A witness can refuse to answer a question on the ground that the answer will tend to expose him to a criminal charge, or on the ground that no one should be required to condemn himself. It is the same principle which underlies the accused's right or immunity of silence, and which protects him from having to make any statement to the police or give evidence subject to cross-examination in court. In some cases this immunity has been taken away by statute, often in return for a prohibition of the use of any answer he may give in any subsequent criminal proceedings, e.g. under the Bankruptcy Act 1914 and the Representation of the People Act 1949. In the latter case an election court can give a certificate of indemnity to a witness whom it considers has answered the questions put to him fully and truthfully.

The position of the accused who gives evidence is not entirely clear. The Criminal Evidence Act 1898 expressly allows the putting of questions

---

[24] See Criminal Procedure Act 1865, below, p. 396.

which tend to incriminate him as to the offence with which he has been charged. The Criminal Law Revision Committee recommended that this should continue to be the case and that he should have no privilege as regards any other offence which tended directly or indirectly to show that he had committed the offence with which he was now charged, but that he should have the privilege in relation to questions tending to show he had committed other offences when these were merely relevant to his credibility.

Other privileges exist to protect the confidentiality of certain relationships or undertakings. Parties are not required to reveal the contents of communications between themselves and their legal advisers when seeking advice. Nor may the contents of negotiations for a settlement before the trial which have been conducted " without prejudice " be revealed (*Jones* v. *Foxall* [25]; *Walker* v. *Wilsher*.[26] The Civil Evidence Act 1968 abolished the privilege of a witness not to reveal a communication made to him by his spouse during marriage, in civil cases. The Criminal Law Revision Committee has recommended the abolition of the privilege in criminal cases as well. Other confidential relationships such as those between a doctor and his patient or a priest and his parishioner are given no formal protection though they may be protected in practice. This is also true in relation to journalists in relation to their sources and the police in relation to their informers. (The rationale of privileges in general are discussed in the Sixteenth Report of the Law Reform Committee " Privilege in Civil Proceedings." [27])

Quite apart from the strict law, counsel is also restricted by rules of professional etiquette.[28] These prohibit him from asking questions which are simply designed to humiliate a witness—and the judge will himself disallow questions which he regards as vexatious. Etiquette requires too that counsel should have some assurance that there is a foundation in fact for any imputation he makes on the character of a witness. This applies particularly to an imputation of fraud—here again witnesses for the prosecution are already protected to some extent by the rule which exposes the accused's past record if he attacks them.

The mere fact that a question or answer is embarrassing is no ground for refusing to answer it though the court may be cleared where particularly embarrassing evidence is being given and there are a number of restrictions on what may be reported in the press, especially as regards matrimonial cases (see *e.g.* the Judicial Proceedings (Regulation of Reports) Act 1926). Other restrictions on reporting exist in relation to juvenile courts and proceedings before examining magistrates.

Interference with witnesses may be punished as contempt of court, and may amount to conspiracy to pervert the course of justice. A witness who makes a false statement under oath may be prosecuted for perjury though it may not always be easy to prove which of two inconsistent statements is false. The Criminal Law Revision Committee considered this matter in its Sixth Report but finally considered that it would be unwise to make it an offence as such to make inconsistent statements. Witnesses are protected from actions for defamation for anything which they say in court.

---

[25] (1852) 15 Beav. 388.   [26] (1889) 23 Q.B.D. 335.
[27] Cmnd. 3472.   [28] Below, p. 395.

THE STANDARD OF PROOF

There is one important difference between criminal and civil cases which remains to be mentioned and that has to do with the standard of proof. It is generally enough in civil cases for the plaintiff to persuade the court that his version of the facts on which his case depends is true on what is usually called the " balance of probabilities." There is a higher standard for the prosecution in criminal cases. It must generally satisfy the judge or jury beyond reasonable doubt. If a reasonable doubt remains in the minds of a jury, or even a minority of the jury (subject to the rules set out above p. 194), or the magistrates in the case of a summary trial, the accused is entitled to be acquitted.

The difference in the degree of persuasiveness that has to be shown in civil and criminal cases has given rise to problems which themselves throw some light on the weight the system is prepared to give to a court's finding of fact, in particular by a criminal court. On the basis of such a finding, the system authorises sentences of imprisonment, fines or other penalties, and in civil cases the award of what may be substantial damages or a decision that what may well be a very severe loss shall be suffered without compensation. Nonetheless until the Civil Evidence Act 1968 the courts attached no weight in civil cases to a previous finding of guilt in a criminal case. As a result it was possible for a man acquitted by a criminal court to fail in an action for defamation against a defendant who published an article saying he was in fact guilty. It was also possible for a man who had been convicted by a criminal court to succeed in an action of defamation against a defendant who had said no more than that the plaintiff had been guilty of the offence. In neither case would the civil court treat the previous acquittal or conviction as evidence of the fact of innocence or guilt. Finally in *Hollington* v. *Hewthorn* [29] a civil court trying an action for negligence arising out of a motor accident refused to admit as evidence the fact that the defendant had been convicted of dangerous driving as a result. This question was eventually considered by the Law Reform Committee [30] and a change of the law made in the Civil Evidence Act 1968. [31]

Judicial notice

Not every fact relevant to a case has to be proved. Both judges and juries may take note without formal proof of facts of common knowledge.

Vosper v. Great Western Railway Co.
[1928] 1 K.B. 340

ATKIN L.J.: . . . Every one knows that in these days hand luggage is constantly carried in such circumstances that there is no room for it in the carriage in which the passenger travels, and that, with the consent and approval of the railway company, it is carried in the corridor of the carriage, either in

[29] [1943] 2 K.B. 587.
[30] Below, p. 419.
[31] Below, p. 424.

close proximity to the compartment in which the passenger is travelling, or in as close proximity as the luggage can be put, very often in a corner at the end of the coach. It is obvious also that there cannot be a duty upon the passenger to remain in the carriage during the whole time of the journey, for there may be occasions on which he may reasonably leave and be absent from it, and indeed, he is invited by the railway company itself on occasion to be absent from it for considerable times while taking meals in the restaurant cars which the company provides for the purpose of supplying meals. To my mind it is further an ordinary incident of railway travel that a passenger who has chosen the carriage in which he is to travel may afterwards for different reasons change his mind and travel a substantial part of the journey, or indeed, the whole of the journey, in some other carriage, as, for instance, where he has procured a seat in a non-smoking carriage and he desires to smoke, or where he has taken a seat in one carriage and joins friends whom he finds in an adjoining or some other carriage. . . . [O]ne knows that third-class passengers do from time to time, for different reasons, travel in first-class carriages. Sometimes they do so in open violation of their rights. Sometimes they do so because there is no room in the third-class carriages and they think that that absolves them from paying the extra fare if they travel first-class. Sometimes they do so because they think it convenient to take a third-class ticket and intend to pay the first-class fare. Sometimes there is a reservation, no doubt, that they will not pay the higher fare if no one comes and asks them for it. Apart from that last case, however, those are lawful forms of user of a railway. A third-class passenger is not an outlaw when he travels in a first-class carriage. When he does so the railway company are still under a duty to him personally, and, as it appears to me, they are also under a duty to him in respect of his luggage. . . .

Balfour v. Balfour

[1919] 2 K.B. 571

Atkin L.J.: . . . It is quite common, and it is the natural and inevitable result of the relationship of husband and wife, that the two spouses should make arrangements between themselves . . . agreements for allowances, by which the husband agrees that he will pay to his wife a certain sum of money, per week, or per month, or per year, to cover either her own expenses or the necessary expenses of the household and of the children of the marriage, and in which the wife promises either expressly or impliedly to apply the allowance for the purposes for which it is given. . . . All I can say is that the small Courts of this country would have to be multiplied one hundredfold if these arrangements were held to result in legal obligations. They are not sued upon, not because the parties are reluctant to enforce their legal rights when the agreement is broken, but because the parties . . . never intended that they should be sued upon. . . . The common law does not regulate the form of agreements between spouses. Their promises are not sealed with seals and sealing wax. The consideration that really obtains for them is that natural love and affection which counts for so little in these cold Courts. The terms may be repudiated, varied or renewed as performance proceeds or as disagreements develop. . . . The parties themselves are advocates, judges, Courts, sheriff's officer and reporter. In respect of these promises each house is a domain into which the King's writ does not seek to run, and to which his officers do not seek to be admitted.

Cf. The following examples of a similar use of " common knowledge " as an element in legal reasoning.

Donoghue v. Stevenson

[1932] A.C. 562

LORD ATKIN: . . . The doctrine supported by the decision below would not only deny a remedy to the consumer who was injured by consuming bottled beer or chocolate poisoned by the negligence of the manufacturer, but also to the user of what should be a harmless proprietary medicine, an ointment, a soap, a cleaning fluid or cleaning powder. I confine myself to articles of common household use, where everyone, including the manufacturer, knows that the articles will be used by other persons than the actual ultimate purchaser—namely, by members of his family and his servants, and in some cases his guests. I do not think so ill of our jurisprudence as to suppose that its principles are so remote from the ordinary needs of civilized society and the ordinary claims it makes upon its members as to deny a legal remedy where there is so obviously a social wrong. . . .

Fender v. St. John-Mildmay

[1938] A.C. 1

LORD ATKIN: *Spiers* v. *Hunt* [32] and *Wilson* v. *Carnley* [33] . . . were both cases in which a husband during the lifetime of his wife had promised to marry another woman on the death of his wife. . . . [T]he judges appear to have thought that a promise made in such circumstances tended to cause immoral relations. They may be right; speaking for myself I really do not know whether that result would follow as a rule. I can only say that if the lady yields to a promise with such an indefinite date she is probably of a yielding disposition. . . .

The English system of fact finding

Final Report of the Committee on Supreme Court Practice and Procedure

Cmd. 8878, 1953

250. . . . (*a*) There is no doubt that the difference between the English and the Continental systems in regard to evidence, *i.e.* in regard to the rules of evidence and the way in which evidence is taken, is very marked; and equally there is no doubt that the difference is one of the main reasons for the fact that litigation in England is substantially more costly. . . .

(*b*) In both France and Germany all (oral) witnesses are the Court's witnesses, though generally speaking they are tendered by the parties. In both countries the system is . . . unlike the English system, " inquisitorial." There is substantially no cross-examination and for practical purposes none at all by the parties or their legal representatives. The witness in effect makes a deposition before the examining Judge who decides what witnesss shall be summoned. The process of taking evidence is almost invariably at an early stage of the proceedings, long before the " trial " proper.

(*c*) The witness makes his statement in his own words—there being no " hearsay " rule. It is for the Court to decide the value of what has been said. . . . [T]he parties themselves are, generally, not competent witnesses in Germany; and in France parents, relatives and servants of the parties and certain other categories of persons are not competent.

---

[32] [1908] 1 K.B. 720.
[33] [1908] 1 K.B. 729.

(*d*) In both France and Germany, oral testimony is regarded as of far less significance than in England. . . . The main emphasis is on written evidence including notarially attested records of every sort of transaction. . . .

(*e*) Types of action which are common in England and which depend, with us, *par excellence*, upon oral testimony either do not occur or are of far less importance in France and Germany. For example, in France the absence of any " exemplary damages " means that libel cases are rare; and in both France and Germany, owing largely to the doctrine of *risque créé*, personal injuries actions are far less common.

251. We considered carefully whether it would be right to recommend the adoption in England wholly or in part of the Continental practice . . . but we have come to a conclusion against so doing. . . . [T]o do so would obviously strike at the root of the English ideas of the administration of justice. There are no doubt two views on the question which system is better adapted to elicit the truth. We are not prepared to say that in his respect the French or German systems are superior; and there is no demand, so far as we have been able to discover, for such a sweeping change. The Bar Council and the Law Society were opposed to it. . . . It is of the essence of the English system . . . that generally speaking (*i.e.* save where expressly provided to the contrary by some statute) no writing or other formality is required to prove a right. Under the system, therefore, the greatest weight and importance is attached to the oral testimony of the parties and their respective witnesses. A change to the Continental system would logically involve a shifting of this very characteristic emphasis. We do not think that such a change could be effectively made unless the Continental system of the administration of justice were adopted in its entirety. The law and rules of evidence are adapted to the English system of justice. Those in France and Germany are adapted to the French and German systems. They are not interchangeable. The adoption here of Continental rules and practice in regard to evidence would mean a new kind of judiciary with many hundreds of local examining magistrates. It would mean also (at any rate if the French model were followed) the creation of a system of notaries all over the country before whom every transaction of any significance would have to be recorded if it were to be legally enforceable in practice. We are not prepared to recommend such changes even if they were within our terms of reference.

252. We are therefore thrown back upon . . . the consideration of possible relaxations or amendments to our own code. And it is of the essence of that code that normally the real or principal issues of fact will be decided by the trial Judge upon the oral evidence of the contestants and their witnesses. It is because of this . . . that there has grown up . . . our peculiar rules in regard to the admissibility of evidence, particularly such rules as those relating to " hearsay " and *res inter alios acta*. It is one of the peculiar functions of the barrister that he assists in the ascertainment of the truth by his cross-examination of the witnesses called by the other side; and it is fundamental to our system that the evidence of every witness should be given on oath and should be subjected to this test. Hearsay evidence cannot be treated by this characteristic method and is not given under the sanction of the oath, and it is largely for these reasons that . . . it is held to be inadmissible. By contrast, under the Continental systems oral evidence . . . is taken more or less in the form of depositions by an examining magistrate before the " trial." The examining magistrate decides what he shall . . . and . . . shall not receive and makes his report thereon. So far as regards oral evidence that is the end of the matter, and it follows that there is no room for the . . . rules about hearsay. . . .

365. Suggestions were made to us that in personal injuries actions the oral evidence at the trial should be restricted. It was suggested that written statements of witnesses should be accepted as evidence and that oral testimony should not be allowed unless the opposite party gives notice requiring the witness to attend for cross-examination. This procedure obviously involves an exchange of witnesses' statements between the parties, a proposal which we have already rejected.[34] . . . In any event, we are satisfied that it is essential in personal injuries actions that the Judge or jury should see the witnesses and hear their evidence, both in chief and in cross-examination. The decision of the Judge or jury depends on the view formed of the witness in the box, *i.e.* not merely his honesty or truthfulness but also his capacity to observe accurately and the reliability of his recollection. In our view, so far as concerns witnesses to the events which give rise to the claim, it is undesirable to alter the present procedure in personal injuries actions.

Report by Widgery L.C.J. into the Events on Sunday, January 30, 1972, in Londonderry
H C. 220, April 18, 1972

54. . . . I am entirely satisfied that the first firing in the courtyard was directed at the soldiers. Such a conclusion is not reached by counting heads or by selecting one particular witness as truthful in preference to another. It is a conclusion gradually built up over many days of listening to evidence and watching the demeanour of witnesses under cross-examination. It does not mean that witnesses who spoke in the opposite sense were not doing their best to be truthful. On the contrary I was much impressed by the care with which many of them, particularly the newspaper reporters, television men and photographers, gave evidence. . . . The photographs . . . confirm that the soldiers' initial action was to make arrests and there was no reason why they should suddenly have desisted and begun to shoot unless they had come under fire themselves. If the soldiers are wrong they were parties in a lying conspiracy which must have come to light in the rigorous cross-examination to which they were subjected. . . .

Wooldridge v. Sumner
Court of Appeal [1963] 2 Q.B. 43

SELLERS L.J.: . . . Another feature of the case is that it provides a striking illustration and reminder of how uncertain can be the raw material of the court's inquiry, the evidence. The event at the time of the accident was being closely watched by the judges of the competition, expert and experienced commentators and many interested spectators, informed in the ways of horses and in horsemanship, and yet from this most unusually qualified body of observers it has been difficult to get a wholly satisfactory account of what occurred, especially in the detail of the last and most vital stages.

DANCKWERTS L.J.: . . . Although there were a number of eye-witnesses of the accident from different positions, most of whom were experts in regard to horse-shows and the nature of horses, a remarkable feature of this case is the variation in their accounts of an occurrence which, of course, took place in a very short space of time. The judge was satisfied that all the witnesses were

---

[34] *Cf.* below, p. 391.

endeavouring to give him a true account of what happened and did not question their veracity. It is possible from these different accounts to ascertain in outline the somewhat unexpected course which this horse took, but doubts remain as to the details and the actual cause of the mishap.

DIPLOCK L.J.: . . . The relevant events took place in the course of a few seconds; all or some of them were seen by 12 different witnesses including the rider and the injured man, and, as is inevitable when honest witnesses give their recollections of what occurred in a very brief space of time there were wide divergences in their respective accounts. In such a case an appellate court will not lightly disturb the findings of the trial judge as to what in fact occurred. The conviction which the evidence of a particular witness carries may depend as much upon the way he says it as upon what he actually says. The way in which each witness gives his evidence, what he says and the intrinsic probability of the events which he asserts took place, are all factors to be weighed in determining what are the true primary facts, and while an appellate court is in as good a position as the trial judge to evaluate the two latter factors the trial judge alone is in a position to assess the first. Although, therefore, a detailed study of the transcript of evidence, taking what I hope is no more than legitimate judicial notice of the vagaries of equine behaviour, would lead me to the conclusion that the strong probability was that the horse shied into the line of tubs after it was already galloping down the straight on the arena side of the shrubs I am, I think, bound by the specific findings of Barry J. that this did not occur.

WITNESSES

(i) *Witnesses called by the judge*

R. v. Dora Harris

Court of Criminal Appeal [1927] 2 K.B. 587

The Court of Appeal in *Re Enoch and Zaretzky Bock & Co.*[35] held that although a judge could call a witness himself if neither party objected, he could not call a witness against the will of one of them. The reason it gave was that there was no right in the parties to cross-examine such a witness which would mean, said Fletcher Moulton L.J. that " the civil rights of a man might be decided by evidence given by persons whose credibility he would have no right to test by cross-examination."

AVORY J.: . . . [I]t has been clearly laid down by the Court of Appeal in *Re Enoch and Zaretzky, Bock & Co.* that in a civil suit the judge has no right to call a witness not called by either party, unless he does so with the consent of both of the parties. It also appears to be clearly established that that rule does not apply to a criminal trial where the liberty of a subject is at stake and where the sole object of the proceedings is to make certain that justice should be done as between the subject and the state. The cases of *R. v. Chapman*[36] and *R. v. Holden*[37] establish the proposition that the presiding judge at a criminal trial has the right to call a witness not called by either the prosecution or the defence, and without the consent of either the prosecution or the defence, if in his opinion this course is necessary in the interests of justice.

[35] [1910] 1 K.B. 327.
[36] 8 C. & P. 558.
[37] 8 C. & P. 606.

(ii) The accused and his spouse

Criminal Evidence Act 1898

1 & 2 Vict. c. 36

1. Every person charged with an offence, and the wife or husband . . . of the person so charged, shall be a competent witness for the defence at every stage of the proceedings, whether the person so charged is charged solely or jointly with any other person. Provided as follows:

(*a*) a person so charged shall not be called as a witness in pursuance of this Act except upon his own application:

(*b*) the failure of any person charged with an offence, or of the wife or husband, as the case may be, of the person so charged, to give evidence shall not be made the subject of any comment by the prosecution:

(*c*) The wife or husband of the person charged shall not, save as in this Act mentioned, be called as a witness in pursuance of this Act except upon the application of the person so charged:

(*d*) Nothing in this Act shall make a husband compellable to disclose any communication made to him by his wife during the marriage, or a wife compellable to disclose any communication made to her by her husband during the marriage:

(*e*) A person charged and being a witness in pursuance of this Act may be asked any question in cross-examination notwithstanding that it would tend to criminate him as to the offence charged:

(*f*) A person charged and called as a witness in pursuance of this Act shall not be asked, and if asked shall not be required to answer, any question tending to show that he has committed or been convicted of or been charged with any offence other than that wherewith he is then charged, or is of bad character, unless—

   (i) the proof that he has committed or been convicted of such other offence is admissible evidence to show that he is guilty of the offence wherewith he is then charged; or

   (ii) he has personally or by his advocate asked questions of the witnesses for the prosecution with a view to establish his own good character, or has given evidence of his good character, or the nature or conduct of the defence is such as to involve imputations on the character of the prosecutor or the witnesses for the prosecution; or

   (iii) he has given evidence against any other person charged with the same offence: . . .

(*h*) Nothing in this Act shall affect . . . any right of the person charged to make a statement without being sworn. . . .

4. (2) Nothing in this Act shall affect a case where the wife or husband of a person charged with an offence may at common law be called as a witness without the consent of that person.

(iii) Accomplices

Davies v. Director of Public Prosecutions

House of Lords [1954] A.C. 378

LORD SIMONDS L.C.: . . . What is the scope and effect of the rule that a judge ought to warn juries in connection with the evidence of an " accomplice "? . . . [F]or over a century and a half it has been customary for judges to warn juries that it is dangerous to convict on such evidence. . . . For most of that period it has been laid down that such a warning was not a precondition of a valid conviction, but was within the judge's discretion to give or to withhold . . . and the whole current of the decisions until the 20th century is in this sense. But after the enactment of the Criminal Appeal Act in 1907, what was no more than a " practice " manifests an increasing tendency to assume the hard lineaments of a rule of law: and as such, many of the decisions of the Court of Criminal Appeal, especially since *R.* v. *Baskerville*,[38] treat it. But in other decisions of the same court the older, the " discretionary " view still finds expression. . . . [T]he " discretionary " school of thought is illustrated by such authorities as *R.* v. *Tate* [39] and *R.* v. *Moore*,[40] and the " peremptory " school of thought (if for brevity I may so call it) by decisions such as *R.* v. *Davies*,[41] *R.* v. *Lewis*,[42] and *R.* v. *Farid* [43]; and subject to certain qualifications . . . the case of *R.* v. *Baskerville* itself. . . .

My Lords . . . I have formed the opinion that whichever might be preferred if the matter were res integra, as things are the latter cases, laying down the stricter rule, have the preponderant weight of authority on their side, and should be adopted by your Lordships on this appeal. The true rule has been, in my view, accurately formulated by the appellant's counsel in his first three propositions, more particularly in the third. These propositions as amended read as follows:

" First proposition :

In a criminal trial where a person who is an accomplice gives evidence on behalf of the prosecution, it is the duty of the judge to warn the jury that, although they may convict upon his evidence, it is dangerous to do so unless it is corroborated.

Second proposition :

This rule, although a rule of practice, now has the force of a rule of law.

Third proposition :

Where the judge fails to warn the jury in accordance with this rule, the conviction will be quashed, even if in fact there be ample corroboration of the evidence of the accomplice, unless the appellate court can apply the proviso to section 4 (1) of the Criminal Appeal Act, 1907."

The rule, it will be observed, applies only to witnesses for the prosecution.

[LORDS PORTER, OAKSEY, TUCKER and ASQUITH OF BISHOPSTONE concurred.]

(iv) Experts

Seventeenth Report of the Law Reform Committee : Evidence of Opinion and Expert Evidence
Cmnd. 4489, 1970

7. It frequently occurs . . . that a judge has to form an opinion upon a matter which calls for some kind of specialised knowledge or experience which he does not possess. . . .

---

[38] [1916] 2 K.B. 658.
[39] [1908] 2 K.B. 680.
[40] (1942) 28 Cr.App.R. 111.
[41] (1930) 22 Cr.App.R. 33.
[42] (1937) 26 Cr.App.R. 110.
[43] (1945) 30 Cr.App.R. 168.

8. There are various ways in which information of this kind can be provided. One way is by expert assessors sitting with the judge. . . . Another would be to appoint an expert to make a report to the court and to the parties. . . . The third, which is the way usually adopted, is for the judge to be supplied with the relevant information by expert witnesses selected and called by the parties and subject to the usual procedure of examination-in-chief, cross-examination and re-examination.

Assessors

9. Under the Rules of the Supreme Court (Ord. 33, r. 6), there is power for a judge to sit with expert assessors—though this power is seldom exercised in practice except in the Admiralty Division. In Admiralty cases the function of an assessor is to advise the judge on matters of nautical skill, knowledge and experience, particularly seamanship. . . .

12. . . . [W]e do not think that any general extension of the use of assessors would be likely to lead to any saving in time or cost of litigation or to raise the standard of judicial decision upon matters involving special knowledge or experience. . . .

Court experts

13. In countries whose procedure is that of the civil law, the common practice is for the court itself to refer matters of expertise to an expert for report. In these countries the courts adopt a more inquisitorial role than is consonant with the adversary system upon which the practice of the English courts is based; but even under the adversary system there would appear at first sight to be merits in obtaining from an acknowledged expert appointed by the court a wholly independent opinion upon a technical matter which is in issue. Provision for the appointment of a court expert is made by Order 40 of the Rules of the Supreme Court; but little use has been made of this power . . . and we do not recommend this course except in a particular class of case. . . .

16. There is . . . one type of case in which it may be desirable that the court should be able to obtain of its own motion a report by an expert appointed by the court itself. That is a case involving the custody or control and care of an infant. In such a case, it is the duty of the court to treat the interests of the infant as paramount. It is the common practice in these cases for the court itself to call for a report from one of the welfare officers appointed for this purpose. . . . [T]heir reports generally contain a great deal of factual information which the welfare officer has obtained as a result of his or her inquiries. This is not the kind of " expert report " which we have been considering. . . . We do not recommend any change in the existing practice in relation to their reports. But there may be circumstances in which it is desirable that the court should be informed upon some matter of expert medical opinion which lies outside the professional qualifications of its welfare officer. One way of dealing with the situation is for the court to appoint the Official Solicitor to represent the infant and to make his own arrangements for a medical examination. This course is frequently adopted but adds to the expense of the litigation. A convenient alternative sometimes employed in the Divorce Division is for the court to order a medical examination of the infant by an independent medical expert to be agreed between the parties or, in default of agreement, to be nominated by the President of the Royal College of Surgeons. The . . . report . . . should be supplied to the parties. They should be entitled to require the maker . . . to be called to be cross-examined orally upon it. They should also have the right to adduce medical evidence themselves.

Oral evidence of experts

21. We do not recommend any fundamental change in the method of providing the court with the information necessary to enable the judge to form a correct opinion on matters requiring special knowledge or experience. . . . We think that it should continue to be left to the parties to choose and call their own expert witnesses, whose evidence should (except in proceedings where it is the practice to adduce affidavit evidence) be subject to the ordinary process of oral examination, cross-examination and re-examination. . . . On the other hand, we think that there are a number of procedural changes which would have the result of reducing controversy on matters of expertise to a minimum and of increasing the usefulness of oral expert evidence on any matters which remain in controversy.

Order for directions

22. Under the current Rules of the Supreme Court (Ord. 38, r. 4) provision may be made in the order for directions limiting the number of expert witnesses. . . . We recommend that the general rule should be that no expert evidence should be admissible . . . unless the order for directions so provides. . . . [H]owever, there should . . . be a discretion in the judge at the trial to admit expert evidence not provided for by the order for directions if for special reasons he considers that the justice of the case so requires.

Admissibility in evidence of experts' reports

23. The recommendation as to the admissibility of hearsay evidence in civil proceedings which were contained in our Thirteenth Report and given statutory effect in Part I of the Civil Evidence Act 1968 were limited to statements of fact. We see no reason in principle why statements of expert opinion should not be similarly admissible. . . .

Compulsory disclosure and exchange of experts' reports

27. Among the recommendations contained in the recent report of the Winn Committee is an important proposal that in actions for damages for personal injuries the parties should, as a general rule, be required to disclose the relevant reports of expert medical witnesses upon whose evidence they propose to rely at the hearing.[44]. . .

28. The object . . . is to reduce to a minimum the matters of expertise which are in issue at the trial. This assists in reaching a fair settlement of the action—and, after all, most actions are settled. In the case of medical evidence where settlement is not reached exchange of reports frequently leads to agreed reports and obviates the need for the attendance of expert witnesses at the trial. Where full agreement on the dual reports cannot be obtained . . . the prior exchange of written reports . . . identifies in advance of the trial the matters of expert opinion which are really in controversy between them, makes it possible for their oral evidence at the trial to be limited to these matters . . . and enables them to prepare more thoroughly and helpfully to the judge their reasons for differing. . . . Whether these objects are likely to be attained by the exchange of experts' reports, however, depends upon the nature of the issues upon which evidence of expert opinion is needed.

---

[44] *Cf.* also the report of the Evershed Committee, paras. 351–357.

The nature of experts' reports

29. All expert opinion is based upon facts which the expert, for the purposes of his opinion, assumes to be true. . . . If they are facts of a kind which . . . can be ascertained before the trial with reasonable certainty by the expert himself by the exercise of his own powers of observation, or are within his general professional knowledge or experience, a report made by him before the trial is likely to be directed to the actual issue upon which his assistance is needed. . . . If, on the other hand, the report is based upon facts which are in dispute between the parties to the action the expert's opinion given before the trial upon a version of the facts supplied by the party on whose behalf he is instructed will only be of assistance if that version is ultimately accepted as the true version by the judge at the trial. Furthermore, experts' reports in the latter category involve disclosing alleged facts which the party instructing the expert will seek to prove at the trial by witnesses other than the expert himself and to this extent involve disclosing material which will be included in the proofs of those witnesses. If the opinion of the expert based upon the alleged facts so disclosed is unfavourable to another party to the action there might be a temptation to that other party to trim the version of the facts presented by him or his witnesses at the trial so as to weaken or deny the factual basis of the unfavourable expert opinion. . . . Most witnesses of fact . . . are honest and intend to be candid. But human memory is fallible and parties in particular are prone to convince themselves without any intentional dishonesty that what would most assist their own case was what actually happened. The fear that this may occur we believe to be the underlying reason why under English procedure, apart from that of the Restrictive Practices Court, there is no disclosure of proofs of witnesses of fact before the hearing. . . . The Winn Committee in their Working Paper No. 1 . . . raised the question of the desirability of exchange of proofs of witnesses of fact. An overwhelming majority of those who replied rejected the proposal. . . .

Suitability of reports for compulsory disclosure

30. These considerations point to the conclusion that compulsory disclosure prior to the hearing of written reports of evidence of expert opinion upon which a party to civil proceedings intends to rely at the trial;

(a) is appropriate in cases where the expert's report may be expected to be based upon facts which are either agreed or can be ascertained with reasonable certainty by the expert . . . but

(b) is *not* appropriate in cases where the expert's report may be expected to be based to any material extent upon a version of facts in dispute . . . which has been supplied to him by the party on whose behalf he has been instructed. . . .

Medical expert evidence; the general rule

31. In considering the application of this test . . . it is convenient to deal first with medical evidence, since this is a class of report which is commonly exchanged voluntarily . . . and has been the subject of proposals by the Winn Committee for compulsory exchange.

The current practice

32. . . . [I]n actions for personal injuries the order for directions has, for the last thirty years at least, almost invariably provided that medical reports be agreed between the parties if possible and that, failing agreement, the medical evidence be limited to a specific number of witnesses on each side. . . . [T]he normal method of attempting to reach agreement . . . is for the parties to disclose to one

another the reports obtained from their respective medical advisers. . . . In the majority of actions for personal injuries . . . such an exchange . . . results in a sufficient degree of agreement to obviate the need for either party adducing oral medical testimony at the trial. . . .

34. If the test of suitability for compulsory disclosure suggested in para. 30 were to be applied, expert medical evidence would in the great majority of cases . . . fall into the category in which disclosure and exchange . . . should be ordered. . . . The opinion expressed by the medical expert, diagnostic or prognostic, is based upon what he himself has observed with his own physical senses, including what was said to him by the patient in the course of his examination, and upon information obtained by him from other doctors or from hospital records. He may have been mistaken in what he thought he himself observed. He may have been misinformed by the patient about his symptoms. These are matters which can be probed in cross-examination at the trial; but the prior disclosure of the information upon which the experts diagnosis and prognosis were based does not in the generality of case create any temptation to the party examined to trim the evidence adduced on his behalf at the trial. We therefore support the recommendation of the Winn Committee that, as a general rule, reports of expert medical witnesses upon whose evidence a party intends to rely should be subject to compulsory disclosure and exchange before the hearing. The onus of showing that this course was inappropriate in the circumstances of a particular case should rest upon a party seeking to avoid disclosure. . . .

37. We think, however, that actions for medical negligence should be treated as an exception to the general rule that the onus should be on the party objecting to disclosure of medical reports to show good cause why they should not be disclosed. These actions will nearly always involve disputed facts as to what actually occurred in the course of the surgical operation or medical treatment . . . and those parts of the reports which dealt with diagnosis and prognosis of the plaintiff's subsequent medical condition might not be easily severable from the remainder. . . .

Non-medical expert evidence

47. Two objections have been advanced to the compulsory disclosure of reports of non-medical experts. Disclosure . . . may, it is suggested assist a dishonest expert to give plausibility to an expression of opinion which is not bona fide, or an incompetent expert to avoid disclosing his incompetence. . . . We should not feel justified in rejecting a practice which would be beneficial if the experts instructed by parties were honest because there may be one or two black sheep among those experts who give evidence in the courts. They soon become known to the bench as well as to the bar and, if cross-examination cannot expose a dishonest witness, even though he is giving expert evidence, our adversary system is less effective than we believe.

48. But the competence of expert witnesses is liable to vary considerably and incompetence is less easy to expose . . . when advocate and judge are unfamiliar with the subject of the witness' expertise. . . .

49. We think that this objection to disclosure could be met . . . if there were provision for simultaneous exchange of experts' reports. . . .

50. The second objection . . . is that it may add to the costs of preparing for trial. Expert reports . . . would have to be considered and might have to be settled by counsel before disclosure. . . .

51. In addition to doctors, the commonest classes of experts who are called to give evidence . . . are probably professional surveyors, valuers, actuaries, architects and engineers. . . . Most witnesses in these classes . . . are accustomed

to giving evidence in courts of law . . . and to preparing reports for submission to the opposing party in the course of negotiations before litigation is started. . . . We do not think that in general they would have any greater difficulty than doctors in preparing reports suitable for compulsory disclosure and exchange without redrafting by counsel. But in any event, if a party proposes to call an expert who lacks experience in giving testimony or himself preparing a written statement of the substance of the evidence which he proposes to give, a task similar to that entailed in editing his report for disclosure would fall upon the solicitor or counsel when the time came to prepare his proof of evidence for the oral hearing.

52. We think, therefore, that, where . . . it is apparent that the reports of non-medical experts will be of a kind which satisfies the requirements of the test proposed in para. 30 above, such reports should be subject to compulsory disclosure and exchange.

Non-medical experts: the onus of showing suitability of reports for disclosure

54. It is really the practical experience of the legal profession over several decades which has enabled the Winn Committee to conclude that the proportion of cases in which the evidence of expert medical opinion required at the trial satisfies the test is so large as to justify putting the onus upon a party objecting to disclosure and exchange of medical reports to show good cause why it should not be ordered. But, while voluntary exchange of other experts reports, particularly those of surveyors and valuers, is quite common . . . there is no comparable volume of experience of the practical results of disclosure. The one apparent exception is the provision in Order 28, rule 6 of the Rules of the Supreme Court, whereby a party to a motor accident case who proposes to call expert engineering evidence at the trial, must disclose the substance of the evidence of the expert before the date of the hearing. . . . The application of this rule has not aroused any significant volume of criticism. . . . We think that in the case of motor accident claims past experience justifies us in recommending that expert engineering evidence should be treated in the same way as expert medical evidence. It should as a general rule be subject to compulsory disclosure and simultaneous exchange, unless the party objecting thereto, satisfies the master that there is good cause for not ordering this.

55. But, with this minor exception, we do not think it right, initially at any rate, to lay down a general rule that reports of the substance of non-medical evidence . . . must be disclosed and exchanged prior to the trial unless the party objecting thereto satisfies the master that there is good cause to the contrary. We think that the onus of satisfying the master that such an order would be appropriate should be upon the party who seeks it. . . .

The judge's discretion at the trial

66. . . . [I]t is, we think, essential that any rules of court which may be made as a result of our recommendation should be subject to the overriding discretion of the judge at the trial to admit expert evidence in cases where the rules have not been complied with. . . .

Three members of the committee dissented from the proposal for compulsory exchange of non-medical experts' reports. They noted that the proposal had been opposed by the General Council of the Bar, the Law Society and the British Insurance Association, and added that in their view " the proposals in the report are impracticable and will if implemented, have the great disadvantage of increasing the costs both of preparation for trial and of the trial." Effect was given to the principal recommendations of the Committee in the Civil Evidence Act 1972.

Civil Evidence Act 1972
1972, c. 30

1.—(1) Subject to the provisions of this section, Part I (hearsay evidence) of the Civil Evidence Act 1968, except section 5 (statements produced by computers), shall apply in relation to statements of opinion as it applies in relation to statements of fact, subject to the necessary modifications and in particular the modification that any reference to a fact stated in a statement shall be construed as a reference to a matter dealt with therein.

(2) Section 4 (admissibility of certain records) of the Civil Evidence Act 1968, as applied by subsection (1) above, shall not render admissible in any civil proceedings a statement of opinion contained in a record unless that statement would be admissible in those proceedings if made in the course of giving oral evidence by the person who originally supplied the information from which the record was compiled; but where a statement of opinion contained in a record deals with a matter on which the person who originally supplied the information from which the record was compiled is (or would if living be) qualified to give oral expert evidence, the said section 4, as applied by subsection (1) above, shall have effect in relation to that statement as if so much of subsection (1) of that section as requires personal knowledge on the part of that person were omitted.

2.—(1) If and so far as rules of court so provide, subsection (2) of section 2 of the Civil Evidence Act 1968 (which imposes restrictions on the giving of a statement in evidence by virtue of that section on behalf of a party who has called or intends to call as a witness the maker of the statement) shall not apply to statements (whether of fact or opinion) contained in expert reports.

(2) In so far as they relate to statements (whether of fact or opinion) contained in expert reports, rules of court made in pursuance of subsection (1) of section 8 of the Civil Evidence Act 1968 as to the procedure to be followed and the other conditions to be fulfilled before a statement can be given in evidence in civil proceedings by virtue of section 2 of that Act (admissibility of out-of-court statements) shall not be subject to the requirements of subsection (2) of the said section 8 (which specifies certain matters of procedure for which provision must ordinarily be made by rules of court made in pursuance of the said subsection (1)).

(3) Notwithstanding any enactment or rule of law by virtue of which documents prepared for the purpose of pending or contemplated civil proceedings or in connection with the obtaining or giving of legal advice are in certain circumstances privileged from disclosure, provision may be made by rules of court—

    (*a*) for enabling the court in any civil proceedings to direct, with respect to medical matters or matters of any other class which may be specified in the direction, that the parties or some of them shall each by such date as may be so specified (or such later date as may be permitted or agreed in accordance with the rules) disclose to the other or others in the form of one or more expert reports the expert evidence on matters of that class which he proposes to adduce as part of his case at the trial; and

    (*b*) for prohibiting a party who fails to comply with a direction given in any such proceedings under rules of court made by virtue of paragraph (*a*) above from adducing in evidence by virtue of section 2 of the Civil Evidence Act 1968 (admissibility of out-of-court statements), except with the leave of the court, any statement (whether of fact or opinion) contained in any expert report whatsoever in so far as that statement deals with matters of any class specified in the direction.

5.—(3) Nothing in this Act shall prejudice—

(*a*) any power of a court, in any civil proceedings, to exclude evidence (whether by preventing questions from being put or otherwise) at its discretion; or

(*b*) the operation of any agreement (whenever made) between the parties to any civil proceedings as to the evidence which is to be admissible (whether generally or for any particular purpose) in those proceedings.

6. . . . [S]ections 1 and 4 (2) to (5) shall come into force on such day as the Lord Chancellor may by order made by statutory instrument appoint. . . .

Examination and cross-examination

Ruling of the Bar Council 1965

Cross-examination

1. In all cases it is the duty of the Barrister to guard against being made the channel for questions which are only intended to insult or annoy either the witness or any other person, and to exercise his own judgment both as to the substance and the form of the questions put. . . .

Cross-examination which goes to a matter in issue

2. In such a cross-examination it is not improper for counsel to put questions suggesting fraud or misconduct or the commission of any criminal offence (even though he is not able or does not intend to exercise the right of calling affirmative evidence to support or justify the imputation they convey), if he is satisfied that the matters suggested are part of his client's case and has no reason to believe that they are only put forward for the purpose of impugning the witness's character.

Cross-examination as to credit only

3. Under the rules of evidence, affirmative evidence cannot in general be called to contradict answers given to questions asked in cross-examination directed only to credit.

4. Questions which affect the credibility of a witness by attacking his character, but not otherwise relevant to the actual enquiry, ought not to be asked unless the cross-examiner has reasonable grounds for thinking that the imputation conveyed by the question is well-founded or true.

5. A barrister who is instructed by a solicitor that in his opinion the imputation is well-founded or true, is entitled *prima facie* to regard such instructions as reasonable grounds for so thinking and to put the questions accordingly.

6. A barrister should not accept the statement of any person other than the solicitor instructing him that the imputation is well-founded or true, without ascertaining so far as is practicable in the circumstances, whether the person has substantial reasons for his statement.

7. Such questions should only be put if, in the opinion of the cross-examiner the answers would or might materially affect the credibility of the witness; and, if the imputation conveyed by the question relates to matters so remote in time or of such a character that it would not materially affect the credibility of the witness, the question should not be put.

Criminal Procedure Act 1865
28 & 29 Vict. c. 18

1. [T]he provisions of sections from three to eight . . . shall apply to all courts . . . as well criminal as all others, and to all persons having, by law or by consent of parties, authority to hear, receive, and examine evidence. . . .

3. A party producing a witness shall not be allowed to impeach his credit by general evidence of bad character; but he may, in case the witness shall in the opinion of the judge prove adverse, contradict him by other evidence, or, by leave of the judge, prove that he has made at other times a statement inconsistent with his present testimony; but before such last-mentioned proof can be given the circumstances of the supposed statement, sufficient to designate the particular occasion, must be mentioned to the witness, and he must be asked whether or not he has made such statement.

4. If a witness, upon cross-examination as to a former statement made by him relative to the subject matter of the indictment or proceeding and inconsistent with his present testimony, does not distinctly admit that he has made such statement, proof may be given that he did in fact make it; but before such proof can be given the circumstances of the supposed statement, sufficient to designate the particular occasion, must be mentioned to the witness, and he must be asked whether or not he has made such statement. . . .

6. A witness may be questioned as to whether he has been convicted of any felony or misdemeanour, and upon being so questioned, if he either denies or does not admit the fact, or refuses to answer, it shall be lawful for the cross-examining party to prove such conviction. . . .

Toohey v. Metropolitan Police Commissioner
House of Lords [1965] A.C. 595

Lord Pearce: . . . From olden times it has been the practice to allow evidence of bad reputation to discredit a witness's testimony. . . . Where a witness's general reputation, so far as concerns veracity, has been . . . demolished, it seems that it may be reinstated by other witnesses who give evidence that he is worthy of credit or who discredit the discrediting witness. . . . Thus far, and no further, it appears, may the process of recrimination go. . . . How far the evidence is confined to veracity alone or may extend to moral turpitude generally seems a matter of some doubt. . . . The . . . general principles which can be derived from the older cases are these. On the one hand, the courts have sought to prevent juries from being beguiled by the evidence of witnesses who could be shown to be, through defect of character, wholly unworthy of belief. On the other hand, however, they have sought to prevent the trial of a case becoming clogged with a number of side issues, such as might arise if there could be an investigation of matters which had no relevance to the issue save in so far as they tended to show the veracity or falsity of the witness who was giving evidence which *was* relevant to the issue. Many controversies which might thus obliquely throw some light on the issues must in practice be discarded because there is not an infinity of time, money and mental comprehension available to make use of them.[45]. . . Human evidence shares the frailties of those who give it. It is subject to many cross-currents such as partiality, prejudice, self-interest and, above all, imagination and inaccuracy. Those are matters with which the jury, helped by cross-examination and common sense, must do their best. But when a witness through physical (in which I include mental) disease or abnormality is not capable of giving a true or reliable account to the jury, it must surely be allowable for medical science to reveal this vital hidden fact to them. If a witness purported to give evidence of something which he believed that he had seen at a distance of 50 yards, it must surely be possible to call the evidence of an oculist to the effect that the witness could not possibly see anything at a greater distance than 20 yards, or the evidence of a surgeon who had removed a cataract from which the witness was suffering at the material time and which would have prevented him from seeing what he thought he saw. So, too, must it be allowable to call medical evidence of mental illness which makes a witness incapable of giving reliable evidence, whether through the existence of delusions or otherwise. It is obviously in the interests of justice that such evidence should be available. The only argument that I can see against its admission is that there might be a conflict between the doctors and that there would then be a trial within a trial. But such cases would be rare and, if they arose, they would not create any insuperable difficulty, since there are many cases in practice where a trial within a trial is achieved without difficulty. And in such a case (unlike the issues relating to confessions) there would not be the inconvenience of having to exclude the jury since the dispute would be for their use and their instruction. Medical evidence is admissible to show that a witness suffers from some disease or defect or abnormality of the mind that affects the reliability of his evidence. Such evidence is not confined to a general opinion of the unreliability of the witness but may give all the matters necessary to show, not only the foundation of and reasons for the diagnosis, but also the extent to which the credibility of the witness is affected.

R. v. Richardson

[1969] 1 Q.B. 299

EDMUND DAVIES L.J.: . . . The principal ground relied upon by both accused involves a point of pure law. . . . It was considered in detail by Lord Goddard C.J. in *R.* v. *Gunewardene*,[46] which in this respect was unaffected by—and indeed approved of in—*Toohey* v. *Metropolitan Police Commissioner*.[47] The legal position may be thus summarised:

---

[45] *Cf.* Rolfe B. in *Att.-Gen.* v. *Hitchcock* (1847) 1 Exch. 91: "The laws of evidence on this subject, as to what ought and what ought not to be received, must be considered as founded on a sort of comparative consideration of the time to be occupied in examinations of this nature, and the time which it is practicable to bestow upon them. If we lived for a thousand years instead of about sixty or seventy, and every case were of sufficient importance, it might be possible, and perhaps proper, to throw a light on matters in which every possible question might be suggested, for the purpose of seeing by such means whether the whole was unfounded, or what portion of it was not, and to raise every possible inquiry as to the truth of the statements made. But I do not see how that could be; in fact, mankind find it to be impossible." And Willes J. in *Hollingham* v. *Head* (1858) 4 C.B.(N.S.) 388: " . . . No doubt, the rule as to confining the evidence to that which is relevant and pertinent to the issue, is one of great importance, not only as regards the particular case, but also with reference to saving the time of the court, and preventing the minds of the jury from being drawn away from the real point they have to decide."

[46] [1951] 2 K.B. 600.

[47] [1965] A.C. 595.

1. A witness may be asked whether he has knowledge of the impugned witness's general reputation for veracity and whether (from such knowledge) he would believe the impugned witness's sworn testimony.

2. The witness called to impeach the credibility of a previous witness may also express his individual opinion (based upon his personal knowledge) as to whether the latter is to be believed upon his oath and is *not* confined to giving evidence merely of general reputation.

3. But whether his opinion as to the impugned witness's credibility be based simply upon the latter's general reputation for veracity or upon his personal knowledge, the witness cannot be permitted to indicate during his examination-in-chief the particular facts, circumstances or incidents which formed the basis of his opinion, although he may be cross-examined as to them.

This method of attacking a witness's veracity, though ancient, is used with exceeding rarity.

EVIDENCE IN CRIMINAL CASES

(i) *The general power to exclude prejudicial evidence*

D.P.P. v. Christie
House of Lords [1914] A.C. 545

LORD MOULTON: . . . The law is so much on its guard against the accused being prejudiced by evidence which, though admissible, would probably have a prejudicial influence on the minds of the jury which would be out of proportion to its true evidential value, that there has grown up a practice of a very salutary nature, under which the judge intimates to the counsel for the prosecution that he should not press for the admission of evidence which would be open to this objection, and such an intimation from the tribunal trying the case is usually sufficient to prevent the evidence being pressed in all cases where the scruples of the tribunal in this respect are reasonable. Under the influence of this practice, which is based on an anxiety to secure for everyone a fair trial, there has grown up a custom of not admitting certain kinds of evidence which is so constantly followed that it almost amounts to a rule of procedure. . . .

Noor Mohammed v. R.
Privy Council [1949] A.C. 182

LORD DU PARCQ: . . . [T]he judge ought to consider whether the evidence . . . is sufficiently substantial, having regard to the purpose to which it is professedly directed, to make it desirable in the interest of justice that it should be admitted. . . . [C]ases must occur in which it would be unjust to admit evidence of a character gravely prejudicial to the accused even though there may be some tenuous ground for holding it technically admissible. The decision must then be left to the discretion and the sense of fairness of the judge. . . . If an examination of it shows that it is impressive just because it appears to demonstrate, in the words of Lord Herschell in *Makin's* [48] case " that the accused is a person likely from his criminal conduct or character to have committed the offence for which he is being tried," and if it is otherwise of no real substance, then it was certainly wrongly admitted.

[48] [1894] A.C. 57, 65; *cf. Selvey* v. *D.P.P.* [1970] A.C. 304.

(ii) Previous convictions and past conduct

The Accused, ed. J. A. Coutts (1966)

A Comparative Study

British Institute Studies in International and Comparative Law, No. 3

Perhaps the most fundamental cleavage of opinion between the common lawyers and continental lawyers is upon the question whether the trial court should learn of the accused's past—and particularly whether he has been previously convicted or is notoriously of bad character. In a continental trial, the presiding judge begins with the cross-examination of the accused expressly in terms of his past—who is he? What has he done earlier in his life? and so on. All the details of the accused's personal standing and habits are in the dossier in the hands of the judge. In France and in Germany, the whole record of the accused will be known to the whole of the court—professional and lay members alike. The accused's criminal record will be considered as part of his whole record and as part of the whole record in the case. In Russia, where this is also the practice, it is, moreover, the function of the prosecutor and the defence counsel (often named from the factory in which the accused worked) to give the court supplemental information as to the social background of the accused's life, of the offence, of the possibility of his being taken back into the factory and so on. In these systems, the history of the accused is taken to throw light on his " personality " and so upon the question (*inter alia*) of the likelihood of his committing the offence. That this is so cannot be denied. But the common law countries proceed upon the assumption that such evidence should be kept from those who have to decide issues of fact until their decision upon such issues has been given, and this exclusionary rule is based quite simply on the belief that such evidence will inevitably be unfairly prejudicial. . . . Scotland, which at one time revealed the accused's past to the court, no longer does so. . . . In England and America, therefore, evidence of the accused's previous convictions or of his bad character is never before the jury unless he himself reveals it or " lets it in " by attacking the prosecution—the latter possibility being one which often places him and his advisers in a dilemma from which there is no hope of escape. The judge who presided over the trial has, however, at least the means of learning all. He has had the depositions and we may surmise that he has read them. He has on the bench before him a folder containing a list of the accused's previous convictions. The practice among judges no doubt differs; some read the folder beforehand, some do not; it has been surmised that most do.

Practice Note (Previous Convictions)

[1955] 1 W.L.R. 139

The judges of the Queen's Bench Division have considered the question as to the information and history of accused and convicted persons that should be given to the court, counsel and solicitors by police officers before and after conviction. They have resolved as follows:

(1) Details of previous convictions must always be supplied by the police to the defending solicitor, or if no solicitor is instructed, to defending counsel, on request. The judges are of opinion that there is no obligation on a police officer to satisfy himself that the prisoner has authorised a statement of previous convictions to be given as it is clearly within the ordinary authority of solicitor and counsel to obtain this information. In order that the defence may be properly

conducted the prisoner's advisers must know whether they can safely put the prisoner's character in issue.

(2) There is no need for police officers to supply a list of previous convictions to the Court before conviction because the previous convictions are always set out in the confidential calendar with which the Judge is supplied by the Governor of the gaol whose duty it is to supply it. The police will of course give any information to the Governor that he may require to enable him to perform his duty.

(3) A proof of evidence should be prepared by a police officer containing a factual statement of the previous convictions, date of birth (if known), education and employment, the date of arrest, whether prisoner has been on bail, and if previously convicted, the date of his last discharge from prison (if known). It may also contain a short and concise statement as to the prisoner's domestic and family circumstances, his general reputation and associates, and if it is to be said that he associates with bad characters, the officer giving evidence must be able to speak of this from his own knowledge. This proof may be given either with his brief or at the outset of the case to Counsel for the prisoner and to no one else, as, unless the accused is convicted, it has no relevance. It need not be prepared in two parts. If the accused is convicted it is to be given to the Court and to Counsel for the Defence but it will be for Counsel for the Prosecution in the first place to decide how much of this he asks the officer to prove, while it will of course be open to the presiding judge to put any questions he may think fit. The statement should not be handed to the Counsel or the Defence Counsel until the officer is sworn. It may by leave of the Court be given to the short-hand writer, who may use it to check his notes, but he must only transcribe so much of it as is given in evidence.

Maxwell v. Director of Public Prosecutions

House of Lords [1935] A.C. 309

The accused was charged with manslaughter of a woman by performing an illegal operation upon her. He was asked whether he had not been tried and acquitted once before, following the death of a previous woman patient. The court held that although the accused had given evidence of his good character and therefore he could be asked about his character the questions had to be relevant.

Viscount Sankey L.C.: ... When Parliament by the Act of 1898...made the prisoner in every case a competent witness, it was in an evident difficulty, and it pursued the familiar English system of a compromise. It was clear that if you allowed a prisoner to go into the witness-box, it was impossible to allow him to be treated as an ordinary witness. Had that been permitted, a prisoner who went into the box to give evidence on oath could have been asked about any previous conviction, with the result that an old offender would seldom, if ever, have been acquitted. This would have offended against one of the most deeply rooted and jealously guarded principles of our criminal law, which, as stated in *Makin* v. *Att.-Gen. for New South Wales*,[49] is that " it is undoubtedly not competent for the prosecution to adduce evidence tending to show that the accused has been guilty of criminal acts other than those covered by the indictment, for the purpose of leading to the conclusion that the accused is a person likely from his criminal conduct or character to have committed the offence for

[49] [1894] A.C. 57, 65.

which he is being tried." Some middle way, therefore, had to be discovered, and the result was that a certain amount of protection was accorded to a prisoner who gave evidence on his own behalf. As it has been expressed, he was presented with a shield and, it was provided that he was not to be asked and that, if he was asked, he should not be required to answer, any question tending to show that he had committed or been convicted of or been charged with any offence other than that wherewith he was then charged, or was a bad character. Apart, however, from this protection, he was placed in the position of an ordinary witness.... [T]he prisoner who was a witness in his own case could not be asked questions which were irrelevant or had nothing to do with the issue which the Court was endeavouring to decide.... [T]he prisoner in the present case threw away his shield and, therefore, the learned counsel for the prosecution was entitled to ask him, and he could be required to answer, any question tending to show that he had committed or been convicted of or been charged with an offence, but subject to the consideration that the question asked him must be one which was relevant and admissible in the case of an ordinary witness.... Proviso (f)... is dealing with matters outside, and not directly relevant to, the particular offence charged; such matters, to be admissible at all, must in general fall under two main classes: one is the class of evidence which goes to show not that the prisoner did the acts charged, but that, if he did these acts, he did them as part of a system or intentionally, so as to refute a defence that if he did them innocently or inadvertently, as for instance in *Makin* v. *Att.-Gen. for New South Wales*.... The other main class is where it is sought to show that the prisoner is not a person to be believed on his oath, which is generally attempted by what is called cross-examination to credit. Closely allied with this latter type of question is the rule that, if the prisoner by himself or his witnesses seeks to give evidence of his own good character, for the purpose of showing that it is unlikely that he committed the offence charged, he raises by way of defence an issue as to his good character, so that he may fairly be cross-examined on that issue.... All these matters are dealt with in proviso (f). The substantive part of that proviso is negative in form and as such is universal and is absolute unless the exceptions come into play.... Exception (i) deals with the former of the two main classes of evidence referred to above, that is, evidence falling within the rule that where issues of intention or design are involved in the charge or defence, the prisoner may be asked questions relevant to these matters, even though he has himself raised no question of his good character. Exceptions (ii) and (iii) come into play where the prisoner by himself or his witnesses has put his character in issue, or has attacked the character of others.... [I]t is clear that the test of relevance is wider in (ii) than in (i); in the latter, proof that the prisoner has committed or been convicted of some other offence, can only be admitted if it goes to show that he was guilty of the offence charged. In the former ... the questions permissible must be relevant to the issue of his own good character and if not so relevant cannot be admissible. But it seems clear that the mere fact of a charge cannot in general be evidence of bad character or be regarded otherwise than as a misfortune. It seemed to be contended on behalf of the respondent that a charge was per se such evidence that the man charged, even though acquitted, must thereafter remain under a cloud, however innocent. I find it impossible to accept any such view. The mere fact that a man has been charged with an offence is no proof that he committed the offence. Such a fact is, therefore, irrelevant; it neither goes to show that the prisoner did the acts for which he is actually being tried nor does it go to his credibility as a witness. Such questions must, therefore, be excluded on the principle which is fundamental in the law of evidence as conceived in this country, especially in criminal cases, because, if allowed, they are likely to lead the minds of the jury astray into false issues; not merely do they tend to introduce suspicion as if it were evidence, but they tend to distract the jury from the true issue—namely, whether the prisoner in fact committed the offence on which he is actually standing his trial. It is of the utmost importance for a fair trial that the evidence should be *prima facie* limited to matters relating to the transaction which forms the subject of the indictment and that any departure from these matters should be strictly confined.... There may ... be cases in which a prisoner may be asked about a charge ... in order to elicit some evidence as to statements made or evidence given by the prisoner in the course of the trial on a charge which failed, which tend to throw doubt on the evidence which he is actually giving, though cases ... must be rare and the cross-examination permissible only with great safeguards. Again, a man charged with an offence against the person may perhaps be asked whether he had uttered threats against the person attacked because he was angry with him for bringing a charge which turned out to be unfounded. Other probabilities may be imagined.... But these instances all involve the crucial test of relevance.... [I]ndeed the question whether a man has been convicted, charged or acquitted ought not to be admitted, even if it goes to credibility, if there is any risk of the jury being misled into thinking that it goes not to credibility but to the probability of his having committed the offence of which he is charged.

In *Stirland* v. *D.P.P.*[50] the House took a similar view of questions put to the accused about the circumstances in which he had left the bank at which he had been working. Here again although the accused said that he had never been charged he had not denied that he had been suspected so that the questions were not relevant to his truthfulness. Nor were they relevant to disprove good character as "the most virtuous may be suspected." At the same time such questions might mislead a jury and so the judge should have excluded them. *Per* Viscount Simon:

> [W]hen *Maxwell's* case[51] decided that where the prosecution had enough evidence to indict a man for a crime, but not enough to convict, no questions can be asked about that incident in a later trial at which he puts his character in issue, how can mere suspicion alleged to have been entertained by his previous employer on an earlier occasion be a legitimate topic for cross-examination to credit?

R. v. Cook

Court of Criminal Appeal [1959] 2 Q.B. 340

DEVLIN J.: ... It is clear from the subsection [s. 1 (*f*) of the Criminal Evidence Act 1898] as a whole that it does not intend that the introduction of a prisoner's previous convictions should be other than exceptional. The difficulty about its phraseology is that unless it is given some restricted meaning, a prisoner's bad character, if he had one, would emerge almost as a matter of course. Counsel for the defence could not submit that a witness for the prosecution was untruthful without making an imputation upon his character; a prisoner charged with assault could not assert that the prosecutor struck first without imputing to him a similar crime. ... Cases of rape have given rise to a peculiar difficulty; the prisoner cannot assert that the connection was with the consent of the prosecutrix without making imputations against her chastity.

---

[50] [1944] A.C. 315.
[51] [1935] A.C. 309.

There was for a long time a difference of opinion about the effect of this; it was not definitely settled in favour of the defence until *R.* v. *Turner*,[52] a case which was shortly after approved by the House of Lords in *Stirland* v. *D.P.P.*[53]... The point that under this subsection the judge had a discretion was first made by Lord Sankey L.C. in *Maxwell* v. *D.P.P.*[54] It was made again by Lord Simon L.C. in *Stirland* v. *D.P.P.* The principle was first elaborated in *R.* v. *Jenkins*.[55] In that case this court reaffirmed *R.* v. *Hudson*[56] and then dealt with the question of discretion. Singleton J. said:

> "The subsection was intended to be a protection to an accused person. A case ought to be tried on its own facts and it has always been recognised that it is better that the jury should know nothing about an accused person's past history if that is to his discredit. Just as it was recognised by the legislature that this was fair and proper, so it was recognised that if the nature or conduct of the defence was such as to involve imputations on the character of the prosecutor or the witnesses for the prosecution, it was equally fair and proper that counsel for the prosecution should have the right to ask questions tending to show that the accused person has committed or been convicted of an offence other than that which is under investigation. If and when such a situation arises, it is open to counsel to apply to the presiding judge that he may be allowed to take the course indicated, as was done in this case. Such an application will not always be granted, for the judge has a discretion in the matter. He may feel that even though the position is established in law, still the putting of such questions as to the character of the accused person may be fraught with results which immeasurably outweigh the result of questions put by the defence and which make a fair trial of the accused person almost impossible. On the other hand, in the ordinary and normal case he may feel that if the credit of the prosecutor or his witnesses has been attacked, it is only fair that the jury should have before them material on which they can form their judgment whether the accused person is any more worthy to be believed than those he has attacked. It is obviously unfair that the jury should be left in the dark about an accused person's character if the conduct of his defence has attacked the character of the prosecutor or the witnesses for the prosecution within the meaning of the section. The essential thing is a fair trial and that the legislature sought to ensure by section 1 (*f*)."

... It may be that, as indicated in *O'Hara* v. *H.M. Advocate*,[57] cases of rape should be regarded as sui generis; certainly the peculiar questions to which they give rise have been settled by *R.* v. *Turner* and that case has determined how the discretion should be exercised. No equally clear guidance can be given in cases where the subject-matter is not so specialised.

Makin v. Att.-Gen. for New South Wales

Privy Council [1894] A.C. 57

LORD HERSCHELL L.C.: ... [T]he principles which must govern the decision of the case are clear, though the application of them is by no means free from difficulty. It is undoubtedly not competent for the prosecution to adduce

---

[52] [1944] K.B. 463.
[53] [1944] A.C. 315.
[54] [1935] A.C. 309.
[55] (1945) 31 Cr.App.R. 1.
[56] [1912] 2 K.B. 464.
[57] 1948 S.L.T. 372.

evidence tending to show that the accused has been guilty of criminal acts other than those covered by the indictment, for the purpose of leading to the conclusion that the accused is a person likely from his criminal conduct or character to have committed the offence for which he is being tried. On the other hand, the mere fact that the evidence adduced tends to shew the commission of other crimes does not render it inadmissible if it be relevant to an issue before the jury, and it may be so relevant if it bears upon the question whether the acts alleged to constitute the crime charged in the indictment were designed or accidental, or to rebut a defence which would otherwise be open to the accused. The statement of these general principles is easy, but it is obvious that it may often be very difficult to draw the line and to decide whether a particular piece of evidence is on the one side or the other.

Harris v. D.P.P.

House of Lords [1952] A.C. 694

VISCOUNT SIMON: . . . There is a second proposition which ought to be added under this head. It is not a rule of law governing the admissibility of evidence, but a rule of judicial practice followed by a judge who is trying a charge of crime when he thinks that the application of the practice is called for. . . . This second proposition flows from the duty of the judge when trying a charge of crime to set the essentials of justice above the technical rule if the strict application of the latter would operate unfairly against the accused. If such a case arose, the judge may intimate to the prosecution that evidence of " similar facts " affecting the accused, though admissible, should not be presented because its probable effect " would be out of proportion to its true evidential value " (*per* Lord Moulton in *D.P.P.* v. *Christie*[58]). Such an intimation rests entirely within the discretion of the judge. It is, of course, clear that evidence of " similar facts " cannot in any case be admissible . . . unless they are connected in some relevant way with the accused and with his participation in the crime. (See Lord Sumner in *Thompson* v. *The King*.[59]) . . . [E]vidence of other occurrences which merely tend to deepen suspicion does not go to prove guilt.

PRIVILEGES OF WITNESSES

Second Report of the Commissioners on Practice and Procedure in the Common Law Courts

1852–53, P.P. xl 701

The law of England protects a witness from answering any question where the answer will tend to subject him to a criminal prosecution, a penalty, or a forfeiture. That such a question may, however, be put to the witness, subject to his privilege of refusing to answer, seems established by the weight of authority and by the every day practice of the courts, though decisions to the contrary are not wanting in the books. The propriety of the rule . . . has been questioned, and it has been proposed to make it obligatory on the witness to answer, with a proviso that no answer . . . shall be admissible in evidence in any proceeding against him, or shall subject him to any punishment. But this proviso does not meet the whole difficulty; for though it might prevent the admission of an offence by the witness from being made the means of convicting him on a future charge it would not prevent a series of questions from being put, the answers to which might afford the means of procuring evidence where-

---

[58] (1914) 24 Cox C.C. 249, 257. [59] [1918] A.C. 221, 234.

upon afterwards to convict him; now to the latter course there are two very grave objections: the one, founded on the fundamental rule of our criminal jurisprudence, that a person accused shall not be subjected to interrogation with a view to his conviction; which rule, so long as it obtains in the penal law, obviously ought not to be violated in a civil proceeding: the other, that the dread of being exposed to such an order might deter the witness from coming forward, and induce him to conceal his knowledge on the subject of the suit, or make him prefer incurring the penalties of a contempt of ocurt to giving evidence. It will readily be seen how effectual a means of intimidation the threat of such an examination would be in the hands of a party against whom such a witness was about to be called. We are therefore averse to the proposed alteration of the law. . . .

Eighth Report of the Criminal Law Revision Committee. Theft and Related Offences

Cmnd. 2977, 1966

203. There is a substantial argument that a person should not get any protection in respect of criminal proceedings merely because he has disclosed his offence in civil proceedings, even on compulsion. But we decided that it would be too severe to take away the privilege of non-incrimination without giving some protection in return. This being so, the choice is between giving the offender immunity from criminal liability . . . and merely making his statement or admission inadmissible in evidence against him in the criminal proceedings. . . . It may be said that to give a person complete immunity if he makes disclosure would produce more information. But it seems to us that this would give more protection than would be justifiable or reasonably necessary. It seems wrong, for example, that an offender should by making an admission escape criminal liability notwithstanding that enough evidence has been obtained from other sources to make a conviction likely even without evidence of his admission. The fact of the disclosure would no doubt be taken into account in the sentence. . . .

204. The right course in our opinion is to make the statement or admission in the civil proceedings inadmissible in evidence against the maker in the criminal proceedings. This would leave the prosecution free to proceed on other evidence in its possession. . . .

205. In the case of bankruptcy proceedings we have come to the conclusion that disclosure concerning an offence should not give any protection in relation to subsequent criminal proceedings for the offence. According to our information the existing provisions making a disclosure inadmissible in criminal proceedings do not in practice operate as an encouragement to debtors to make disclosure. Experience seems to show that the provisions are not in general known or understood. When they are, it is usually by a debtor who is sufficiently informed (or advised) to know that any disclosure by him, though protected, may set off inquiries which will result in other evidence of the offence being obtained on which charges can be founded.

Theft Act 1968

1968, c. 60

31.—(1) A person shall not be excused, by reason that to do so may incriminate that person or the wife or husband of that person of an offence under this Act—

(a) from answering any question put to that person in proceedings for the recovery or administration of any property, for the execution of any trust or for an account of any property or dealings with property; or

(b) from complying with any order made in any such proceedings; but no statement or admission made . . . shall, in proceedings for an offence under this Act, be admissible in evidence against that person or (unless they married after the making of the statement or admission) against the wife or husband of that person.

Civil Evidence Act 1968

1968, c. 64

Privilege

14.—(1) The right of a person in any legal proceedings other than criminal proceedings to refuse to answer any question or produce any document or thing if to do so would tend to expose that person to proceedings for an offence or for the recovery of a penalty—

(a) shall apply only as regards criminal offences under the law of any part of the United Kingdom and penalties provided for by such law; and

(b) shall include a like right to refuse to answer any question or produce any document or thing if to do so would tend to expose the husband or wife of that person to proceedings for any such criminal offence or for the recovery of any such penalty.

(3) In so far as any existing enactment provides (in whatever words) that in any proceedings other than criminal proceedings a person shall not be excused from answering any question or giving any evidence on the ground that to do so may incriminate that person, that enactment shall be construed as providing also that in such proceedings a person shall not be excused from answering any question or giving any evidence on the ground that to do so may incriminate the husband or wife of that person.

16.—(2) The rule of law whereby, in any civil proceedings, a party to the proceedings cannot be compelled to produce any document relating solely to his own case and in no way tending to impeach that case or support the case of any opposing party is hereby abrogated.

(3) Section 3 of the Evidence (Amendment) Act 1853 (which provides that a husband or wife shall not be compellable to disclose any communication made to him or her by his or her spouse during the marriage) shall cease to have effect except in relation to criminal proceedings.

(4) In section 43 (1) of the Matrimonial Causes Act 1965 (under which the evidence of a husband or wife is admissible in any proceedings to prove that marital intercourse did or did not take place between them during any period, but a husband or wife is not compellable in any proceedings to give evidence of the matters aforesaid), the words from " but a husband or wife " to the end of the subsection shall cease to have effect except in relation to criminal proceedings.

(5) A witness in any proceedings instituted in consequence of adultery, whether a party to the proceedings or not, shall not be excused from answering any question by reason that it tends to show that he or she has been guilty of adultery; and accordingly the proviso to section 3 of the Evidence Further Amendment Act 1869 and, in section 43 (2) of the Matrimonial Causes Act 1965, the words from " but " to the end of the subsection shall cease to have effect.

The Rules Against Hearsay Evidence

The Law Revision Committee was asked by the Lord Chancellor in September 1964 " to review the law of evidence in civil cases and to consider whether any changes are desirable in the interests of the fair and efficient administration of justice; and in particular to consider what provisions should be made for modifying rules which have ceased to be appropriate in modern conditions." In their Thirteenth Report on hearsay evidence in civil proceedings [60] they noted:

> This part of the law ought not to be as complicated as it is. We think that the ultimate aim of any review of the law of evidence should be to produce a statutory code. But that will take a very long time and we do not think that all reform should wait upon its completion. There are, we think, branches of the law of evidence which are sufficiently self-contained to warrant separate consideration and to form the subject of interim reports and, we hope, of interim legislation pending the enactment of a comprehensive code.

They chose as their first topic the hearsay rule, because they said:

> The hearsay rule in its present form with its numerous exceptions in our view lacks rational basis, results sometimes in injustice and often in avoidable expense, and introduces much unnecessary complication in the preparation and hearing of civil actions. It is a convenient starting point for reform not only because its abolition would greatly simplify the whole law of evidence but also because the problem has already been broached in the Evidence Act 1938, which has provided useful experience of the effect of admitting particular kinds of hearsay evidence.

Thirteenth Report of the Law Revision Committee on Hearsay Evidence in Civil Proceedings

Cmnd. 2964, 1966

6. The purpose of " evidence " is to enable the court at the trial to ascertain what in fact happened in the past and sometimes what are likely to be its consequences in the future, so that the court can determine whether what did happen entitles the plaintiff to any, and, if so, what, legal reparation from the defendant. *Prima facie* any material which is logically probative of a fact in issue, *i.e.*, which tends to show that a particular thing relevant to the cause of action or to the defence happened or did not happen or is likely or unlikely to happen, is capable of assisting the court in its task and should be capable of being tendered in evidence, unless there are other reasons for refusing to admit it. We are not concerned here with rules which prohibit a party from proving a particular fact at all, but only with rules which exclude the use of a particular kind of material to prove a fact which a party is permitted to prove in some other way. Such rules should have a rational basis. It should be possible to point to some disadvantage flowing from the admission of the particular kind of material as evidence of a fact which would outweigh the value of any assistance which the court would derive from the material in ascertaining what in fact happened.

[60] Cmnd. 2964, 1966.

The arguments for the Hearsay Rule

7. The hearsay rule developed during a period when all, or nearly all, issues of fact in civil as well as criminal cases were determined by juries. Their standard of education was lower than today and it may be that they were ill-qualified to estimate the comparative probative value of alternative methods of proof. Today most civil cases are tried by a judge alone. Trial by jury in civil cases is rare and when it does occur the members of the jury are probably more sophisticated than they were a hundred years ago. Nevertheless, save for the amendments made by the Evidence Act 1938, the hearsay rule remains unchanged.

The reasons most commonly advanced for the hearsay rule are:

    (*a*) the unreliability of statements, whether written or oral, made by persons not under oath nor subject to cross-examination;

    (*b*) the desirability of the " best evidence " being produced of any fact sought to be proved; and

    (*c*) the danger that the relaxation of the rule would lead to a proliferation of evidence directed to establishing a particular fact.

We do not think that on examination either of the first two reasons constitutes a sufficient ground for excluding hearsay evidence. The third reason can, we think, be appropriately dealt with by procedural safeguards. All three reasons can be advanced against the admission of the kind of hearsay evidence which has been admissible for the last twenty-seven years under the Evidence Act 1938 without any apparent disaster to the English system of trial.

8. As respects unreliability it is quite impossible to generalise. A contemporaneous record of some kinds of facts, such as those in issue in *Myers* v. *D.P.P.*,[61] is probably the most reliable evidence of such facts. It would be neither more nor less reliable if the maker of the record had been identifiable and dead at the time of the trial, when it might have been admissible under a common law exception to the hearsay rule, or if the maker of the record were allowed to " refresh his memory " by looking at the record he had made. A statement about events which he had observed shortly after he observed them may well be more reliable than his account of the same events given years later in the witness box. . . . It is always admissible in cross-examination to destroy the probative value of the witness's credibility. . . . Yet such a statement could not logically be used by a witness to refresh his memory unless it were more likely to be true than false, nor could it be treated as destroying the probative value of a witness's oral evidence unless it had at least as much probative value of its own as the oral evidence; that is to say, unless it was as likely to be true as the oral evidence of the same witness.

9. As respects hearsay not being the " best evidence " of a fact, this is merely another way of saying that statements of fact made by persons otherwise than pursuant to the process of oral examination and cross-examination upon oath are not the best, i.e. the most reliable, evidence of a fact. We accept that in most cases of disputed facts of which the court's knowledge must depend upon the honesty and accuracy of recollection of persons who claim to have witnessed them, the method of eliciting the witness's account by question and answer upon oath in examination-in-chief, cross-examination and re-examination is generally the most reliable method of ascertaining the truth under the adversary system of procedure. . . .

We would not recommend a change which would deprive a party of the right to require the recollections of witnesses of *disputed* facts to be tested by the process where it is feasible. . . . A defendant is entitled to require the

---

[61] [1965] A.C. 1001.

plaintiff to prove his case. . . . But the need to call oral evidence of facts which in the result are not disputed adds to the cost of litigation. While recognising the desirability of the " best evidence " being produced of disputed facts . . . we think that this must yield to the need to do justice where the " best evidence " is not available and that there is no need to produce the " best evidence " of facts . . . which are not really in dispute but have not been formally admitted.

10. As respects the danger of proliferation of evidence, we think that this can easily be exaggerated. The Evidence Act 1938 itself presented such a possibility; but it has not happened. Litigation is conducted by lawyers, and with the object of winning. It is to each party's interest to adduce that evidence which has the highest probative value of any disputed fact in issue which he desires to establish and, where direct oral evidence of such a fact is available, he will, we think, continue to call it. Safeguards against his seeking to buttress this unnecessarily by superfluous hearsay can be devised. The proposals which we make below will, we think, shorten and cheapen litigation and not lengthen it.

The Evidence Act 1938

12. We have . . . found it convenient to take as our starting point the Evidence Act 1938 and to treat it as abolishing the hearsay rule as respects statements of fact subject, however, to exceptions. We shall examine each exception to see to what extent it is justified. . . .

Hearsay excluded by the Evidence Act 1938

14. *No statement which is not contained in a written document is admissible.* A written statement speaks for itself. There can be dispute as to whether what it says is accurate; there can be no dispute . . . as to what it says. It is otherwise with an oral statement the maker of which is not called as a witness. The court's knowledge of what was said . . . depends upon the honesty and accuracy of recollection of the witness who gives evidence of it. There is a double source of error; the statement may not only be innacurate, it may also be misreported. But this criticism goes to probative value. . . . Because of its limited probative value it is unlikely that any party to litigation would seek to rely upon an oral statement of a fact which was really in dispute, if the maker of the statement were available to be called as a witness. But if he is not available there is no reason in principle why his oral statement should not be admissible for what it is worth. And, if the fact which the oral statement tends to establish is one which is not really in dispute, the oral statement may be sufficient proof of it.

15. *No statement, not being part of a continuous record, is admissible unless made by a person who had personal knowledge of the matters dealt with in the statement.* Subject to what is said later about documentary statements made in the course of duty, this exception, which excludes second-hand hearsay or rumour, seems to us to be justified and should be retained. The probative value of second-hand hearsay is in any event too small. Its admission might lead to undue proliferation of evidence. In recommending in the preceding paragraph that oral statements should be admissible we had in mind that the reporter of the oral statement would be called to prove it and that the circumstances in which it was made and the accuracy of the recollection of the reporter could be probed in cross-examination. But where John gives evidence of what George said that William (who alone had personal knowledge of the matter) said, the honesty and accuracy of George is a necessary link in the chain. . . . There is no way of estimating the strength of that link unless George is called as a witness. . . . Second-hand hearsay in the form of a written statement by John of what William, who was under no duty to report to John, had said to him

about events that William said had occurred depends for its probative value not only upon the accuracy of John's report . . . but also upon the accuracy and veracity of William, who was under no duty to be either accurate or veracious and may have been reporting what he himself had heard. To admit John's written statement as evidence of the facts stated to have been reported to him would open the door to the admission of all sorts of rumours and involve the risk of proliferation of hearsay evidence of minimal probative value. The line must be drawn somewhere and we think that the Evidence Act 1938 draws it at the right place in excluding second-hand hearsay where there is no duty to report information to the recipient of the report.

16. *No statement, if made by someone without personal knowledge of the matters dealt with, is admissible unless it is (a) part of a continuous record (b) made in the performance of a duty to record information (c) upon information supplied to the maker of the statement by a person who had or might reasonably be supposed to have personal knowledge of the matters dealt with.*

(*a*) The requirement that the statement must be part of a continuous record is presumably based upon the assumption that an entry in a continuous record is more difficult to fabricate. This is merely one aspect of probative value. The limitation excludes many business records. . . . In criminal cases it has been abandoned in the Criminal Evidence Act 1965,[62] and we see no sufficient ground for its retention in civil cases.

(*b*) The requirement that the statement must have been made in the performance of a duty to record information is, we think, a valid one. . . . [T]his requirement also has been abandoned in the Criminal Evidence Act 1965; but that Act is concerned with business records and the requirement that the record should have been compiled " in the course of trade or business " is substantially similar to a requirement that the information should have been supplied pursuant to a duty. This latter requirement is more appropriate to a general statute which would apply to such things as regimental or hospital records as well as those relating to a trade or business. We think, however, that in this context " duty " should be broadly defined so as to cover duties imposed by trade and professional practice as well as contractual duties.

(*c*) The requirement that the maker of the statement must have received the information recorded directly from a person who had or might reasonably be supposed to have personal information of the matters . . . is, we think, unduly narrow. Direct reporting to the record-keeper is not usual in modern business methods. The operative stamps the serial number of the car upon the engine; the inspector inspects it and makes his own note which is handed to the office; from that the appropriate record is entered in the books and the inspector's note destroyed. The recording may, indeed, be done mechanically. The requirement . . . has been abandoned in the Criminal Evidence Act 1965 and should be abandoned in civil cases also. Provided . . . there is a duty all the way down the chain . . . to pass on the information, the statement should be admissible. The length of the chain goes to probative value only insofar as it increases the risk of error in transmission of the information.

17. *No statement is admissible unless it is in the handwriting of or signed or initialled by the maker or otherwise recognised by him in writing as one for the accuracy of which he vouches.* . . . This limitation . . . goes solely to authenticity and restricts the means by which authenticity may be proved. We do not think it is justified. It has been abandoned as respects trade and business records in the Criminal Evidence Act 1965.

18. *No statement is admissible if made by a person interested at a time when proceedings were pending or anticipated involving a dispute as to any*

fact which the statement might tend to establish. This limitation goes to probative value only. . . . We recommend the abolition of this limitation. . . . A
court is, we think, quite capable of assessing the weight to be attached to
statements by whomsoever made. . . .

Summary of recommendations on principle of admissibility of hearsay

19. The effect of the above recommendations would be . . . [that] . . .
[a]ll statements, whether written or oral, which tended to establish a fact, of
which direct oral evidence would be admissible, would themselves be potentially
admissible if proved to have been made by a person who had, or might reasonably be supposed to have, personal knowledge of the matters dealt with in the
statement. So would written or mechanically recorded statements made by
any person in performance of a duty to record information supplied to him by
a person who either himself had personal knowledge of the facts so recorded or
was under a duty to transmit such information, where the information trans-
mitted originated from a person who had such personal knowledge. . . .

Procedural conditions of admissibility

20. We accordingly turn next to a consideration of the circumstances in
which such potentially admissible statements should in practice be allowed to
be given in evidence. . . . [T]he method of oral examination, cross-examination
and re-examination of witnesses to a disputed fact provides a most effective aid
in ascertaining the truth. We do not recommend that this method should be
dispensed with where the fact is really in dispute and the witness is available
to be called at the trial.

21. The Evidence Act 1938 makes it a condition of admissibility that the
maker of the statement should be called as witness, unless he is dead, or unfit
by reason of his mental or bodily condition to attend . . . or is beyond the
seas and it is not reasonably practicable to secure his attendance, or if all
reasonable efforts to find him have been made without success; but the Act also
empowers the court to admit the statement without calling the maker if the
court is satisfied that undue delay or expense would otherwise be caused.

Unavailability of maker of statement

22. It is, we think, obviously right that the statement should be admissible if
the maker of the statement is unavailable for any of the reasons specified. But
if . . . the categories of admissible statements are to be extended . . . we think
it reasonable that the adverse party should be afforded an opportunity to make
his own enquiries as to the unavailability of the maker and also as to the
authenticity of the statement, before he is confronted with it at the trial. . . .

Admissibility of statement where maker available

23. . . . We regard it as essential to devise a simple procedure to safeguard
a party's right to require vital witnesses to be produced for cross-examination,
if available, and to enable all parties to know what preparations they must make
for the trial. . . .

Admissions

29. Inculpatory statements made by parties to proceedings, their agents in
that behalf and persons in privity with them are at present admissible at
common law as informal " admissions." . . . We recommend that a party
should, without serving any notice, be allowed to rely as against an adverse
party upon any statement of fact made by that adverse party or by any person

authorised to make admissions on his behalf, or by anyone falling within those miscellaneous categories of persons whose inculpatory statements are admissible against him under the existing law.

32. . . . The Evidence Act 1938 enables statements of the kinds to which it relates to be tendered in evidence whenever the maker of the statement is called as a witness. The Act appears to entitle a party to call a witness and to tender his signed proof instead of examining him in chief, leaving him to be cross-examined on his proof. This, we think, is unsatisfactory. . . . Examination-in-chief by question and answer without leading questions on matters in dispute plays an important part in our system of eliciting the truth under the adversary system. As every judge and advocate knows, witnesses often fail to " come up to their proofs " in examination-in-chief, and this is one of the commonest ways in which the truth will out. A proof is not really the witness's own narrative, but a summary by the proof taker of the witness's answers to questions put by him which may themselves have suggested the answers. Had different questions been asked, the resulting narrative might have been different. When the witness goes into the box to give his evidence-in-chief, often different questions are asked. When the evidence is about disputed facts, we do not think that this process should be omitted. . . .

Impeaching credibility of maker of statement who is not called

33. Where hearsay evidence is admitted . . . but the maker of the statement is not called because he is not available . . . the credibility of the maker . . . should be impeachable by the adverse party in the same way as if the maker of the statement had been called as a witness. Thus any inconsistent statement by the same maker which was tendered by the adverse party should be admissible . . . to discredit the statement relied on, but not as evidence of the facts contained in the inconsistent statement unless the inconsistent statement had itself been the subject of a notice by the adverse party of intention to rely upon it or unless the judge, in his residual discretion . . . admitted it as evidence of those facts. Any other evidence tending to impair or to support the credibility of the maker of the statement should also be admitted if it would have been admissible had he been called as a witness, but no evidence should be admissible on matters affecting credibility alone as to which the maker's denials in cross-examination would have been final if he had been called as a witness.

34. Where . . . the maker . . . although available, is not called because no counter-notice has been served, we do not think that the adverse party should be entitled to impeach the credibility of the maker. . . . [I]f he wishes to do so, he should serve a counter-notice so that the maker of the statement may have an opportunity to defend himself.

Admissibility of previous statements by a witness who gives evidence at the trial

35. The question of admitting a previous statement made by a person who is called as a witness at the trial . . . has led to a difference of view. At common law, such a statement may be used by the adverse party to attack the credibility of the witness and may also be used by the party calling the witness either to rebut a suggestion made in cross-examination (e.g. that the witness's evidence was fabricated) or to discredit the witness if the court allows him to be treated as " hostile." The use of the statement for these purposes . . . does not make the statement evidence of the facts contained in it. . . . We are all agreed that, if such a statement is to be admitted at all as evidence of the facts contained in it, it should be so admitted only at the discretion of the judge. . . .

36. A substantial minority of us take the view that it should not . . . be permissible to adduce, as evidence of the facts contained in it, a previous statement made by a person who is called as a witness at the trial. . . . [W]hile in favour of admitting hearsay evidence where it is necessary (because direct evidence is not available) or convenient and innocuous (because no adverse party wishes seriously to dispute it), they regard as particularly valuable oral evidence given in answer to questions which are not leading questions. To admit a statement made outside court when the maker is . . . called as a witness is, in their opinion, a departure from the " best evidence " principle for which there is no sufficient justification. . . . The minority see no reason why a party should be permitted where his witness fails to " come up to proof," to remedy the defect in his evidence by showing that on another occasion the witness made a different statement. They are, therefore, opposed to the admission of previous inconsistent statements in any circumstances. They recognise, however, that there are exceptional cases where a previous consistent statement could properly be admitted at the judge's discretion: for instance, a contemporary statement made by an eye-witness to an event who has subsequently lost nearly all recollection of what happened.

37. A narrow majority of us consider that, whether consistent or inconsistent . . . a previous statement . . . should be admissible at the judge's discretion. . . . They attach considerable importance to conferring on the judge a residual discretion to admit statements, as evidence of the facts which they tend to establish, where those statements appear to him likely to assist in ascertaining the truth. A proof of evidence taken from a witness for the purposes of the trial is of small probative value and they would not normally expect a judge to admit it, except in rebuttal of suggestions made in cross-examination; but a statement made by an eye-witness shortly after the event . . . is sometimes more likely to be accurate than his recollection of the event extracted from him in the witness box years later. Whether consistent or inconsistent with his oral evidence, the majority think not only that it may sometimes be a useful aid in assessing the probative value of the latter, but also that it may occasionally possess . . . a higher probative value than the so-called " best evidence " with which it is inconsistent. They would expect statements made while the witness's recollection was still fresh to be freely admitted. . . .

39. We should expect, . . . too, the residual discretion to be used to relax the rule against hearsay where this prevents a witness from telling his story in the natural way and sequence. It only confuses a witness and makes the law look silly when he is asked: " Did your wife say something to you?—Don't tell us what she said, just answer, ' Yes or No.' As a result of what she said, did you do something? " We hope that the judge will let the witness say what his wife did say, although her statement was not the subject of a notice or counter-notice and will also let the witness tell what he said to his wife, if that is the natural way for him to tell his story of what happened.

Objects of the proposed modifications to Evidence Act

40. The rule against hearsay has five disadvantages. First, it results in injustice where a witness who could prove a fact in issue is dead or unavailable to be called; secondly, it adds to the cost of proving facts in issue which are not really in dispute; thirdly, it adds greatly to the technicality of the law of evidence because of its numerous exceptions in addition to those provided by the Evidence Act 1938 . . . ; fourthly, it deprives the court of material which would be of value in ascertaining the truth; and, fifthly, it often confuses witnesses and prevents them from telling their story in the witness box in the natural way.

These disadvantages have long been recognised. It is high time they were tackled boldly. . . .

Criminal Evidence Act 1965
1965, c. 20

This Act and the Civil Evidence Acts 1968 and 1972 are given here in somewhat extensive form not merely for the sake of their contents but to provide an opportunity for a close reading of a statute to elicit its meaning. The Act of 1968, which was passed to give effect to the recommendations of the Law Reform Committee above, is particularly useful since it gives some insight into the gap which has to be bridged between the form in which recommendations, even by lawyers, can be expressed, and the formal enactment of those recommendations in a statute. It is therefore some measure of the degree of formality imposed during the transformation from intention into law.

1.—(1) In any criminal proceedings where direct oral evidence of a fact would be admissible, any statement contained in a document and tending to establish that fact shall, on production of the document be admissible as evidence of that fact if—

(a) the document is, or forms part of, a record relating to any trade or business and compiled, in the course of that trade or business, from information supplied (whether directly or indirectly) by persons who have, or may reasonably be supposed to have, personal knowledge of the matters dealt with in the information they supply; and

(b) the person who supplied the information . . . is dead, or beyond the seas, or unfit by reason of his bodily or mental condition to attend as a witness, or cannot with reasonable diligence be identified or found, or cannot reasonably be expected (having regard to the time which has elapsed since he supplied the information and to all the circumstances) to have any recollection of the matters dealt with in the information. . . .

(3) In estimating the weight, if any, to be attached to a statement admissible . . . by virtue of this section regard shall be had to all the circumstances from which any inference can reasonably be drawn as to the accuracy or otherwise of the statement, and, in particular, to the question whether or not the person who supplied the information recorded in the statement did so contemporaneously with the occurrence or existence of the facts stated, and to the question whether or not that person, or any person concerned with making or keeping the record containing the statement, had any incentive to conceal or misrepresent the facts.

(4) In this section . . . " document " includes any device by means of which information is recorded or stored. . . .

Civil Evidence Act 1968
1968, c. 64

Hearsay evidence

1.—(1) In any civil proceedings a statement other than one made by a person while giving oral evidence in those proceedings shall be admissible as evidence of any fact stated therein to the extent that it is so admissible by virtue of any provision of this Part of this Act or by virtue of any other statutory provision or by agreement of the parties, but not otherwise.

2.—(1) In any civil proceedings a statement made, whether orally or in a document or otherwise, by any person, whether called as a witness in those proceedings or not, shall, subject to this section and to rules of court, be admissible as evidence of any fact stated therein of which direct oral evidence by him would be admissible.

(2) Where in any civil proceedings a party desiring to give a statement in evidence by virtue of this section has called or intends to call as a witness in the proceedings the person by whom the statement was made, the statement—

(*a*) shall not be given in evidence by virtue of this section on behalf of that party without the leave of the court; and

(*b*) without prejudice to paragraph (*a*) above, shall not be given in evidence by virtue of this section on behalf of that party before the conclusion of the examination-in-chief of the person by whom it was made, except—

(i) where before that person is called the court allows evidence of the making of the statement to be given on behalf of that party by some other person; or

(ii) in so far as the court allows the person by whom the statement was made to narrate it in the course of his examination-in-chief on the ground that to prevent him from doing so would adversely affect the intelligibility of his evidence.

(3) Where in any civil proceedings a statement which was made otherwise than in a document is admissible by virtue of this section, no evidence other than direct oral evidence by the person who made the statement or any person who heard or otherwise perceived it being made shall be admissible for the purpose of proving it:

Provided that if the statement in question was made by a person while giving oral evidence in some other legal proceedings (whether civil or criminal), it may be proved in any manner authorised by the court.

3.—(1) Where in any civil proceedings—

(*a*) a previous inconsistent or contradictory statement made by a person called as a witness in those proceedings is proved by virtue of section 3, 4 or 5 of the Criminal Procedure Act 1865 [63]; or

(*b*) a previous statement made by a person called as aforesaid is proved for the purpose of rebutting a suggestion that his evidence has been fabricated,

that statement shall by virtue of this subsection be admissible as evidence of any fact stated therein of which direct oral evidence by him would be admissible.

(2) Nothing in this Act shall affect any of the rules of law relating to the circumstances in which, where a person called as a witness in any civil proceedings is cross-examined on a document used by him to refresh his memory, that document may be made evidence in those proceedings; and where a document or any part of a document is received in evidence in any such proceedings by virtue of any such rule of law, any statement made in that document or part by the person using the document to refresh his memory shall by virtue of this subsection be admissible as evidence of any fact stated therein of which direct oral evidence by him would be admissible.

4.—(1) Without prejudice to section 5 of this Act, in any civil proceedings a statement contained in a document shall, subject to this section and to rules of court, be admissible as evidence of any fact stated therein of which direct oral

---

[63] See above, p. 396.

evidence would be admissible, if the document is, or forms part of, a record compiled by a person acting under a duty from information which was supplied by a person (whether acting under a duty or not) who had, or may reasonably be supposed to have had, personal knowledge of the matters dealt with in that information and which, if not supplied by that person to the compiler of the record directly, was supplied by him to the compiler of the record indirectly through one or more intermediaries each acting under a duty.

(2) Where in any civil proceedings a party desiring to give a statement in evidence by virtue of this section has called or intends to call as a witness in the proceedings the person who originally supplied the information from which the record containing the statement was compiled, the statement—

(*a*) shall not be given in evidence by virtue of this section on behalf of that party without the leave of the court; and

(*b*) without prejudice to paragraph (*a*) above, shall not without the leave of the court be given in evidence by virtue of this section on behalf of that party before the conclusion of the examination-in-chief of the person who originally supplied the said information.

(3) Any reference in this section to a person acting under a duty includes a reference to a person acting in the course of any trade, business, profession or other occupation in which he is engaged or employed or for the purposes of any paid or unpaid office held by him.

[Section 5 deals with information stored in a computer.]

6.—(1) Where in any civil proceedings a statement contained in a document is proposed to be given in evidence by virtue of section 2, 4 or 5 of this Act it may, subject to any rules of court, be proved by the production of that document or (whether or not that document is still in existence) by the production of a copy of that document, or of the material part thereof, authenticated in such manner as the court may approve.

(2) For the purpose of deciding whether or not a statement is admissible in evidence by virtue of section 2, 4 or 5 of this Act, the court may draw any reasonable inference from the circumstances in which the statement was made or otherwise came into being or from any other circumstances, including, in the case of a statement contained in a document, the form and contents of that document.

(3) In estimating the weight, if any, to be attached to a statement admissible in evidence by virtue of section 2, 3, 4 or 5 of this Act regard shall be had to all the circumstances from which any inference can reasonably be drawn as to the accuracy or otherwise of the statement and, in particular—

(*a*) in the case of a statement falling within section 2 (1) or 3 (1) or (2) of this Act, to the question whether or not the statement was made contemporaneously with the occurrence or existence of the facts stated, and to the question whether or not the maker of the statement had any incentive to conceal or misrepresent the facts;

(*b*) in the case of a statement falling within section 4 (1) of this Act, to the question whether or not the person who originally supplied the information from which the record containing the statement was compiled did so contemporaneously with the occurrence or existence of the facts dealt with in that information, and to the question whether or not that person, or any person concerned with compiling or keeping the record containing the statement, had any incentive to conceal or misrepresent the facts; and

(*c*) in the case of a statement falling within section 5 (1) of this Act, to the question whether or not the information which the information contained in the statement reproduces or is derived from was supplied to the relevant computer, or recorded for the purpose of being supplied thereto, contemporaneously with the occurrence or existence of the facts dealt with in that information, and to the question whether or not any person concerned with the supply of information to that computer, or with the operation of that computer or any equipment by means of which the document containing the statement was produced by it, had any incentive to conceal or misrepresent the facts.

(4) For the purpose of any enactment or rule of law or practice requiring evidence to be corroborated or regulating the manner in which uncorroborated evidence is to be treated—

(*a*) a statement which is admissible in evidence by virtue of section 2 or 3 of this Act shall not be capable of corroborating evidence given by the maker of the statement; and

(*b*) a statement which is admissible in evidence by virtue of section 4 of this Act shall not be capable of corroborating evidence given by the person who originally supplied the information from which the record containing the statement was compiled.

7.—(1) Subject to rules of court, where in any civil proceedings a statement made by a person who is not called as a witness in those proceedings is given in evidence by virtue of section 2 of this Act—

(*a*) any evidence which, if that person had been so called, would be admissible for the purpose of destroying or supporting his credibility as a witness shall be admissible for that purpose in those proceedings; and

(*b*) evidence tending to prove that, whether before or after he made that statement, that person made (whether orally or in a document or otherwise) another statement inconsistent therewith shall be admissible for the purpose of showing that that person has contradicted himself:

Provided that nothing in this subsection shall enable evidence to be given of any matter of which, if the person in question had been called as a witness and had denied that matter in cross-examination, evidence could not have been adduced by the cross-examining party.

(2) Subsection (1) above shall apply in relation to a statement given in evidence by virtue of section 4 of this Act as it applies in relation to a statement given in evidence by virtue of section 2 of this Act, except that references to the person who made the statement and to his making the statement shall be construed respectively as references to the person who originally supplied the information from which the record containing the statement was compiled and to his supplying that information.

(3) Section 3 (1) of this Act shall apply to any statement proved by virtue of subsection (1) (*b*) above as it applies to a previous inconsistent or contradictory statement made by a person called as a witness which is proved as mentioned in paragraph (*a*) of the said section 3 (1).

9.—(1) In any civil proceedings a statement which, if this Part of this Act had not been passed, would by virtue of any rule of law mentioned in subsection (2) below have been admissible as evidence of any fact stated therein shall be admissible as evidence of that fact by virtue of this subsection.

(2) The rules of law referred to in subsection (1) above are the following, that is to say any rule of law—

(*a*) whereby in any civil proceedings an admission adverse to a party to the proceedings, whether made by that party or by another person, may be given in evidence against that party for the purpose of proving any fact stated in the admission;

(b) whereby in any civil proceedings published works dealing with matters of a public nature (for example, histories, scientific works, dictionaries and maps) are admissible as evidence of facts of a public nature stated therein;

(c) whereby in any civil proceedings public documents (for example, public registers, and returns made under public authority with respect to matters of public interest) are admissible as evidence of facts stated therein; or

(d) whereby in any civil proceedings records (for example, the records of certain courts, treaties, Crown grants, pardons and commissions) are admissible as evidence of facts stated therein.

In this subsection " admission " includes any representation of fact, whether made in words or otherwise.

(3) In any civil proceedings a statement which tends to establish reputation . . . and which, if this Act had not been passed, would have been admissible in evidence by virtue of any rule of law mentioned in subsection (4) below—

(a) shall be admissible in evidence by virtue of this paragraph in so far as it is not capable of being rendered admissible under section 2 or 4 of this Act; and

(b) if given in evidence under this Part of this Act (whether by virtue of paragraph (a) above or otherwise) shall by virtue of this paragraph be admissible as evidence of the matter reputed or handed down;

and, without prejudice to paragraph (b) above, reputation shall for the purposes of this Part of this Act be treated as a fact and not as a statement or multiplicity of statements dealing with the matter reputed.

(4) The rules of law referred to in subsection (3) above are the following, that is to say any rule of law—

(a) whereby in any civil proceedings evidence of a person's reputation is admissible for the purpose of establishing his good or bad character;

(b) whereby in any civil proceedings involving a question of pedigree or in which the existence of a marriage is in issue evidence of reputation or family tradition is admissible for the purpose of proving or disproving pedigree or the existence of the marriage, as the case may be; or

(c) whereby in any civil proceedings evidence of reputation or family tradition is admissible for the purpose of proving or disproving the existence of any public or general right or of identifying any person or thing.

(5) It is hereby declared that in so far as any statement is admissible in any civil proceedings by virtue of subsection (1) or (3) (a) above, it may be given in evidence in those proceedings notwithstanding anything in sections 2 to 7 of this Act or in any rules of court made in pursuance of section 8 of this Act.

(6) The words in which any rule of law mentioned in subsection (2) or (4) above is there described are intended only to identify the rule in question and shall not be construed as altering that rule in any way.

10.—(1) In this Part of this Act— . . .

" document " includes, in addition to a document in writing—

(a) any map, plan, graph or drawing;

(b) any photograph;

(c) any disc, tape, sound track or other device in which sounds or other data (not being visual images) are embodied so as to be capable (with or without the aid of some other equipment) of being reproduced therefrom; and (*d*) any film, negative, tape or other device in which one or more visual images are embodied so as to be capable (as aforesaid) of being reproduced therefrom;

" film " includes a microfilm;

" statement " includes any representation of fact, whether made in words or otherwise.

The weight to be attached to a conviction

Fifteenth Report of the Law Reform Committee. The Rule in Hollington v. Hewthorn

Cmnd. 3391, 1967

4. It is in a sense true that a finding by any court that a person was culpable or not culpable of a particular criminal offence or civil wrong is an expression of opinion by the court. But it is of a different character from an expression of opinion by a private individual. In the first place, it is made by persons, whether judges, magistrates or juries, acting under a legal duty to form and express an opinion on that issue. In the second place in forming their opinion they are aided by a procedure, of which the law of evidence forms part, which has been evolved with a view to ensuring that the material needed to enable them to form a correct opinion is available to them. In the third place, their opinion, expressed in the form of a finding of guilty or not guilty in criminal proceedings or a judgment in civil proceedings, has consequences which are enforced by the executive power of the state. . . .

6. A finding of culpability or lack of culpability under our system of procedure may be the result of a number of component opinions reached in the course of the decision-making process : opinions as to the credibility of the accounts of individual witnesses of what they claim to have seen or heard, opinions as to the proper inferences to be drawn from primary facts established by credible testimony, opinions of law as to whether the facts proved and inferred constitute the criminal offence or civil wrong with which the person is charged. Basically the decision-making process is the same in both criminal and civil proceedings, but there are two significant differences which are relevant to the probative value of findings of culpability or lack of culpability by criminal courts and civil courts. A finding of culpability by a criminal court must not be made unless the court is satisfied beyond reasonable doubt that the accused is guilty of the offence with which he is charged. If not so satisfied, the criminal court must make a finding of lack of culpability, even though it may be of opinion that it is more likely than not that the accused was guilty. In civil proceedings a finding of culpability must be made on a balance of probabilities, *i.e.* if the court is of opinion that it is more likely than not that a party was culpable of the civil wrong in respect of which he is sued. Secondly, although in both criminal and civil proceedings the court must form its opinion upon the evidence adduced before it, in civil proceedings in general the parties have complete liberty of choice as to how to conduct their respective cases and what material to place before the court, and, except in matrimonial cases, the court has no duty to inquire whether all material relevant to its decision has been brought to its notice. In criminal cases, on the other hand, it is the practice and the duty of the prosecution, as well as adducing evidence which tends to show the culpability of the accused, either itself to adduce or to make available to the defence any material of which it has knowledge which tends to show his non-culpability. There is no corresponding duty on the defence as respects evidence of culpability. It is also the duty of the presiding

judge in trials on indictment to exclude evidence against the accused if he considers that its prejudicial effect would outweigh its true probative value. For these reasons, a finding of culpability against a person upon a contested trial in criminal proceedings is of higher probative value than a finding of culpability against him in civil proceedings, and a finding of lack of culpability against a person in criminal proceedings is of lower probative value than such a finding in civil proceedings.

7. Matrimonial causes in the High Court for dissolution of marriage differ from other civil proceedings in that the judge has a statutory duty to satisfy himself of the existence of valid grounds for dissolution and in so doing he is not confined to the evidence which the parties themselves choose to submit to him.

8. We approach the rule in *Hollington* v. *Hewthorn & Co.*[64] from the premise stated in our Report on Hearsay Evidence . . . that any material which has probative value upon any question in issue in a civil action should be admissible in evidence unless there are good reasons for excluding it. Our further premise is that any decision of any English court upon an issue which it has a duty to determine is more likely than not to have been reached according to law and to be right rather than wrong. It may therefore constitute material of some probative value if the self-same issue arises in subsequent legal proceedings.

Criminal proceedings

9. The issue in criminal proceedings is whether the conduct of the accused has been shown beyond reasonable doubt to constitute the criminal offence with which he has been charged. The same issue, save that culpability would only be shown upon the balance of probabilities, may arise in a civil suit in a number of different ways. It is most likely to arise in a civil suit against the person who was the defendant in the criminal proceedings, for many criminal offences, at any rate if they cause damage to another person, are civil wrongs actionable at his suit. Exceptionally the defendant in the criminal proceedings may be the plaintiff in civil proceedings, as in an action for damages for a defamatory statement that he committed the offence of which he was acquitted or convicted. It may also arise in civil proceedings to which the defendant in the criminal proceedings is not a party, as in an action brought against his employer as vicariously liable for his tortious act or in an action brought against an insurer, as for example under a burglary policy. Provided that the issue decided in the criminal proceedings is the same as an issue in the subsequent civil suit, we do not think that either the admissibility or the effect of the conviction or acquittal should depend upon who are the parties to the civil suit. We are concerned not with estoppel but with the probative value of the opinion of the criminal court expressed in its decision. . .

10. . . . A criminal trial may have three results; a conviction upon a contested trial, a conviction upon plea of guilty, or an acquittal. The probative values of these three results upon the question in issue in the civil action, as to whether upon balance of probabilities the conduct of the accused constituted the criminal offence with which he was charged, are not the same.

Conviction upon a contested trial

11. A conviction upon a contested trial is consistent only with the opinion of the criminal court's being that it has been established . . . beyond reasonable doubt, that the conduct of the accused did constitute the criminal offence with

[64] [1943] K.B. 587.

which he was charged and that it has been so established upon the material known to the prosecution or the defence and considered by either to be relevant to the issue of guilt. Any layman would, we think, regard the fact of such conviction as a firm foundation for the belief that the accused had conducted himself in such a manner as to constitute the criminal offence of which he was convicted and, if such criminal offence would also constitute a civil wrong, that the accused had committed a civil wrong also. We, too, share this common-sense view. We consider that such a conviction has high probative value. . . . We have no doubt in principle that evidence of the conviction should be admissible.

Conviction upon plea of guilty

12. . . . . Where a plea of guilty can be proved under the existing law, considerable weight attaches to it, for people, if they are innocent, do not usually plead guilty to criminal offences which render them subject to punishment. We see no reason in logic or in common sense why the conviction resulting from a plea of guilty should not have probative value in establishing that the accused . . . was guilty of the conduct of which he was convicted. We think it should be admissible in subsequent civil proceedings in the same way as a conviction upon a contested trial.

The weight to be given to convictions

13. We have considered whether in subsequent actions a conviction should be conclusive as to the culpability of the convicted person; but we do not think that, apart from certain actions for defamation, it would be right to go so far. Our premise is that the decision of an English criminal court upon an issue which it has a duty to determine is more likely to be right than wrong—not that it is infallible. Error may arise for a number of reasons. The evidence upon which the criminal court's decision was based may have been incomplete—particularly in summary proceedings for minor offences in which professional lawyers are not engaged. Further evidence may have come to light before the subsequent civil proceedings. The defence may have been inadequately presented at the criminal trial. Unreasonable inferences of fact may have been drawn by the court, or it may have fallen into error in law, but the smallness of the penalty imposed may have made it not worth while to appeal to a higher court. The accused may have pleaded guilty, particularly to a minor offence, not because he had no defence but for reasons of personal convenience—to save time and expense or to avoid disclosing some embarrassing though non-criminous fact which would come to light if the case were defended. We do not suggest that erroneous convictions for these or any other reasons are common, but they may occasionally occur and we do not think that a party to a civil action, who may not be the convicted person himself, should be debarred from proving if he can that a conviction was erroneous. But we have no doubt that the onus should be upon him to prove it. We accordingly recommend that, where any person has been charged with any conduct alleged to constitute a criminal offence and . . . has been convicted . . . the fact of such conviction shall be admissible in any civil proceedings and such person shall be taken to be guilty of such conduct and of such offence unless it is proved that such conviction was erroneous. . . .

Acquittal

15. Because of the higher onus of proof in criminal cases, an acquittal proves no more than that the criminal court was of opinion that it had not

been proved beyond reasonable doubt that the conduct of the accused did constitute the criminal offence with which he was charged. . . . [O]f itself a verdict of not guilty is equally consistent with that court's opinion being that on the balance of probabilities the accused's conduct did constitute the criminal offence—and this would be sufficient to establish his culpability in a civil action. . . . It is at first blush tempting to suggest that . . . evidence of an acquittal should nevertheless be admissible in subsequent civil proceedings " for what it is worth," and that it should be left to the civil court to determine what weight, if any, should be attached to it. . . . But, on reflection, we think this can be shown to be specious. In civil proceedings the onus of proving that the defendant's conduct constituted an actionable wrong lies upon the plaintiff. . . . [A]n acquittal is incapable of shifting the onus and the plaintiff would be obliged to adduce evidence of the conduct of the defendant which he alleges to be actionable. The civil court would have to form its own opinion whether the evidence adduced at the hearing established . . . on the balance of probabilities, that the defendant's conduct was such as to constitute a civil wrong. . . . [T]he civil court's conclusion, whether in favour of the plaintiff or the defendant, would be consistent with the defendant's acquittal in the criminal proceedings. So the acquittal . . . would be without any probative value in the issue in the civil proceedings—which is another way of saying it is irrelevant.

The committee, having regard to the fact that in petitions for dissolution of marriage the judge is under a statutory duty to make inquiry to satisfy himself that the grounds for dissolution are made out and of the high standard of proof required in affiliation proceedings, also recommended that a finding of adultery or of paternity, should be treated in the same way as a criminal conviction.

One other question which the committee considered was the extent to which a person who had been convicted or acquitted in a criminal trial could subsequently challenge in an action for defamation someone who later wrote that he was in fact guilty of the offence. Would it be a defence to such an action simply to show that he had been convicted? On the basis of its previous proposals the conviction would only raise a presumption that he was guilty but would not be conclusive, and the case in which a man who had been acquitted was said to have been guilty would not be affected. In either case it would be open to the civil court in the action for defamation to reconsider the matter. This is exactly what had happened in two recent cases and in each case the civil court had come to a different conclusion from that of the criminal court. Was this desirable?

Defamation

29. . . . The state, nominally the Crown, has a direct interest in all prosecutions for criminal offences. It has established a special system of trial and appellate courts for dealing with them. These courts apply a procedure different from that in civil actions and adopt a different standard of proof, the purpose of which is to safeguard the interests of the accused and to ensure that the innocent are not convicted. The penal sanctions which the criminal courts impose upon those whom they find guilty are enforced by the executive power of the state. No civil court has jurisdiction to alter or affect them. Those whom they acquit cannot be put on trial again. . . . It can only undermine public confidence in the administration of criminal justice if civil courts in actions between private individuals can be forced to re-try the issue of guilt which has already been determined by a criminal court and reach a different conclusion.

To a trained lawyer it is no doubt intelligible that a civil court should reach a different conclusion from that of the criminal court without there having been an error in the finding of the criminal court. The re-trial in the civil action may take place many years later, when the witnesses, upon whose evidence the finding of guilty or not guilty at the criminal trial was based, have died or disappeared or forgotten what happened. Legal aid is not available in actions for defamation and one or other of the parties may lack the resources to trace witnesses and documents and marshal the relevant evidence. In any event, the onus of proof will be different from that which the law regards as essential in a criminal trial. But this is much too technical for the layman. His reaction cannot fail to be: here are two English courts, one says that A was guilty, the other says that he was not; one of them must be wrong. And the law is made for laymen. . . . When such a prosecution . . . results in a conviction which is not set aside upon appeal, any citizen, should, we think, be entitled to say without risk of incurring any civil liability that the convicted person did commit the offence of which he was convicted. And, by parity of reasoning, when a prosecution results in an acquittal, we do not think that he is entitled to say that the acquitted person did commit the offence. . . . [W]e have not overlooked the argument that there may be exceptional cases in which the public interest could be served by the Press, or a private citizen, being free to challenge the correctness of an acquittal, and that our recommendation could be criticised as tending to restrict freedom of discussion. But we think that, on balance, the greater public interest lies in inhibiting attempts to use defamation actions as a means of challenging the findings of criminal courts.

30. . . . [T]he change in the law which we think desirable would be a qualification of our general recommendation about the admissibility and effect of previous convictions in subsequent civil proceedings, by providing that in any civil action for defamation brought in respect of a statement imputing that a person was guilty of any criminal offence, proof that such person stands convicted of such offence . . . should be conclusive evidence that he was guilty of such offence, and proof that such person stands acquitted . . . (or has been pardoned by the Crown) should be conclusive evidence that he was not guilty. . . .

31. . . . It would still be open to the defendant to rely upon privilege, whether absolute or qualified, or leave and licence. . . .

Other civil proceedings

38. With the exceptions with which we have already dealt,[65] an issue of fact in one civil action is seldom the same as an issue of fact in another civil action between different parties. In practice it is only likely to arise where a number of different persons are injured in the same accident by the same acts of negligence. Such cases are most conveniently dealt with by all the injured parties joining in the same action, by consolidation, or by agreeing to treat one action as a test action. It is, however, theoretically possible (and has occasionally happened) that separate actions brought by different passengers in the same vehicle have been tried at different times by different courts with different results. This is undesirable and should be avoided by one or other of the means referred to above. But we do not think that, where there are two civil actions between different plaintiffs against the same defendant or by the same plaintiff against different defendants which do raise the same issue of fact, the finding of the court should be admissible in the second action. As we have already pointed out, in civil proceedings the parties have complete liberty of choice as to how to conduct their respective cases and what material to place

---

[65] *i.e.* findings of adultery and of paternity.

before the court. The thoroughness with which their case is prepared may depend upon the amount at stake in the action. We do not think it just that a party to the second action who was not a party to the first should be prejudiced by the way the party to the first action conducted his own case, or that a party to both actions, whose case was inadequately prepared or presented in the first action, should not be allowed to avail himself of the opportunity to improve upon it in the second. The difference between ordinary civil actions and suits for dissolution of marriage in which there are findings of adultery is that in the latter, unlike the former, the parties are not at liberty to present their respective cases as they please and the judge himself is under a statutory duty of inquiry. . . .

Civil Evidence Act 1968

1968, c. 64

Convictions, etc. as evidence in civil proceedings

11.—(1) In any civil proceedings the fact that a person has been convicted of an offence by or before any court in the United Kingdom or by a court-martial there or elsewhere shall (subject to subsection (3) below) be admissible in evidence for the purpose of proving, where to do so is relevant to any issue in those proceedings, that he committed that offence, whether he was so convicted upon a plea of guilty or otherwise and whether or not he is a party to the civil proceedings; but no conviction other than a subsisting one shall be admissible in evidence by virtue of this section.

(2) In any civil proceedings in which by virtue of this section a person is proved to have been convicted of an offence by or before any court in the United Kingdom or by a court-martial there or elsewhere—

(*a*) he shall be taken to have committed that offence unless the contrary is proved; and

(*b*) without prejudice to the reception of any other admissible evidence for the purpose of identifying the facts on which the conviction was based, the contents of any document which is admissible as evidence of the conviction, and the contents of the information, complaint, indictment or charge-sheet on which the person in question was convicted, shall be admissible in evidence for that purpose.

(3) Nothing in this section shall prejudice the operation of section 13 of this Act or any other enactment whereby a conviction or a finding of fact in any criminal proceedings is for the purposes of any other proceedings made conclusive evidence of any fact. . . .

(5) Nothing in any of the following enactments, that is to say—

(*a*) section 12 of the Criminal Justice Act 1948 (under which a conviction leading to probation or discharge is to be disregarded except as therein mentioned) . . . shall affect the operation of this section. . . .

12.—(1) In any civil proceedings—

(*a*) the fact that a person has been found guilty of adultery in any matrimonial proceedings; and

(*b*) the fact that a person has been adjudged to be the father of a child in affiliation proceedings before any court in the United Kingdom,

shall (subject to subsection (3) below) be admissible in evidence for the purpose of proving, where to do so is relevant to any issue in those civil proceedings, that he committed the adultery to which the finding relates or, as the case may be, is (or was) the father of that child, whether or not he offered any defence to the allegation of adultery or paternity and whether or not he is a party to the civil proceedings; but no finding or adjudication other than a subsisting one shall be admissible in evidence by virtue of this section.

(2) In any civil proceedings in which by virtue of this section a person is proved to have been found guilty of adultery as mentioned in subsection (1) (*a*) above or to have been adjudged to be the father of a child as mentioned in subsection (1) (*b*) above—

(*a*) he shall be taken to have committed the adultery to which the finding relates or, as the case may be, to be (or have been) the father of that child, unless the contrary is proved; and

(*b*) without prejudice to the reception of any other admissible evidence for the purpose of identifying the facts on which the finding or adjudication was based, the contents of any document which was before the court, or which contains any pronouncement of the court, in the matrimonial or affiliation proceedings in question shall be admissible in evidence for that purpose.

(3) Nothing in this section shall prejudice the operation of any enactment whereby a finding of fact in any matrimonial or affiliation proceedings is for the purposes of any other proceedings made conclusive evidence of any fact. . . .

13.—(1) In an action for libel or slander in which the question whether a person did or did not commit a criminal offence is relevant to an issue arising in the action, proof that, at the time when that issue falls to be determined, that person stands convicted of that offence shall be conclusive evidence that he committed that offence; and his conviction thereof shall be admissible in evidence accordingly.

(2) In any such action as aforesaid in which by virtue of this section a person is proved to have been convicted of an offence, the contents of any document which is admissible as evidence of the conviction, and the contents of the information, complaint, indictment or charge-sheet on which that person was convicted, shall, without prejudice to the reception of any other admissible evidence for the purpose of identifying the facts on which the conviction was based, be admissible in evidence for the purpose of identifying those facts. . . .

(4) [Subsection 5] . . . of section 11 of this Act shall apply for the purposes of this section as [it applies] . . . for the purposes of that section. . . .

Chapter 7

REMEDIES

Introduction

In the last resort it is the existence of adequate and effective remedies which give force and effect to the rights that the legal system purports to protect and the duties it seeks to impose. Just what is it that the English legal system offers by way of remedy and redress? The answer is very varied. It can release spouses from the legal bonds of marriage, assist in the distribution of the assets of deceased persons, authorise the winding-up of a company, cancel the debts of a bankrupt, provide for the custody or adoption of children, settle accounts between partners at the end of their partnership, sanction variations of a settlement, order that someone illegally detained should be released, declare an election void, quash decisions of inferior courts and tribunals, and even of Ministers of the Crown if they are acting in a judicial or quasi-judicial capacity. It may order a factory to stop interfering with the enjoyment of neighbouring property or polluting a river, order students to leave a building they are occupying or direct someone to hand over a house he has sold or even to pull down a house he has built in breach of an undertaking.

The most conspicuous remedy however is the traditional common law remedy of an award of damages. This has long been regarded as the English legal and in particular common law remedy *par excellence*, and it is a healthy reminder of the limitations of the law as a means of solving problems. At the end of the day most people prefer to have their contracts performed and their expectations fulfilled; they do not want to limp through life maimed as a result of a car accident or an accident in a factory. Although in some cases the courts will order the specific performance of a contract just as it will order some one by way of injunction to stop doing something, for the most part all it can do is make an award of damages to go some way towards compensating in money for losses that the victim would probably have preferred to avoid in the first place. Moreover even the court can only make an *award* of damages or *order* someone to do something. It cannot guarantee payment or the observance of the order. The recalcitrant defendant can be harassed to some extent by sale of his property to meet the award. But he may in fact have insufficient assets, and at that point there is nothing the courts can do. When the court orders something to be done, in the last resort it can do no more than order the imprisonment of a defendant who refuses to obey the order for contempt. Imprisonment, as has been seen in relation to the Industrial Relations Court, is a double-edged weapon. It can as well make a defendant more unwilling to comply as more willing and is of no direct help to the plaintiff.

The effectiveness of a remedy, the likelihood of its being enforced and the wisdom of either obtaining it in the first place or enforcing it after it has been obtained are very important matters when it comes to the consideration of the use of law as a matter of policy or to secure the solution of a general problem and also to the consideration of whether to go to law in a particular case. At the level of policy it is important to bear these matters in mind when considering demands that " there should be a law against it." Will tenants for example really be better protected if they are given a legal right to take a landlord to court if they are being harassed by him or if he fails to undertake necessary repairs? Does giving a deserted wife a legal right to maintenance in practice solve her problem of making ends meet? What role can law and lawyers (and the answer in the latter case may be different from that in the former) and courts usefully play in such situations? What are the conditions which have to exist in order to make the law and its remedies adequate and effective? What other supporting or additional facilities or agencies or conditions have to be present if the real problem is to be dealt with satisfactorily? We have already touched upon this matter in dealing with the juvenile courts [1] but it is not confined to them. We have seen too how the need to have legal aid and advice readily available is a necessary condition of an effective use of the law in the first place. Now we are at the other end of the process asking whether the remedy offered will really provide a solution.

Similar considerations apply when we move from general policy to particular cases. A lawyer must be skilled not only in knowing what legal rights a client has; he must also know how to translate them into a remedy and whether that remedy will solve the client's problems. Should one sue one's neighbour for nuisance or one's business colleague for breach of contract and then hope to live in peace with the one or do business with the other in the future? If one challenges a decision as *ultra vires* because the proper procedure was not observed, will the only result be that the same decision will be taken again, this time observing the proper procedure? Should one bring the law onto campus or as a weapon in an industrial dispute? If the remedy itself is inadequate, will the trial itself provide a remedy by way of publicising a grievance or a point of view? How can one use the system to get what one wants from it?

Many rights are observed and duties performed and many infringements of rights and breaches of duties compensated without recourse to the courts. But, even though this is so, in practice the availability of the remedies and an assessment of just what they amount to in practice will often play an important part in the calculations which lead to observance and performance and the settlement of claims without court action. If the remedies are inadequate or ineffective, then so far at least as the unscrupulous are concerned, and those too who make nice calculations as to just exactly what it is that they can get away with, which is the professional posture of many lawyers, then the rights and duties set out in the substantive law are not worth the paper on which they are written. It is considerations of this kind that make the provision of adequate and effective remedies an integral part of the institutions and procedures that make up the total legal system.

---

[1] See also below, p. 539.

DAMAGES

As was said above, damages are the most conspicuous of the remedies and raise problems which are both difficult and typical of legal remedies in general. The basic principles relating to them have been developed by the judges, chiefly in cases of contract and torts. The extracts which follow discuss a number of these. First there is the question of the kinds of damage for which a defendant will be held liable. Secondly how the damage for which he is held liable is to be assessed. The first question so far as the law is concerned raises questions of both general legal liability and more limited questions of what is usually called " remoteness of damage." So far as the latter are concerned the courts have said that, even if a plaintiff can show that the defendant has been guilty of some wrongful act, it is not for every loss that the plaintiff suffers in consequence that he can recover compensation. Quite apart from common sense and scientific notions of cause and effect which may make it impossible to say that the wrong caused the damage in any real sense, the courts themselves as a matter of policy and principle have said that they will regard some losses as " too remote." The courts have had some difficulty in formulating satisfactory general principles, let alone applying them to particular cases, and have changed their minds from time to time, but extracts from two of the leading cases are set out below.[2] Closely connected with the question of remoteness, though not so far as the law is concerned technically a part of it, are the rescue cases and the problem of recovery of damages for nervous shock. The rescue cases raise the general question as to the extent to which the fact that the victim voluntarily ran a risk and suffered damage as a result relieves the defendant of liability. The second is interesting for a number of reasons but in particular because of the way in which it shows the courts slowly moving from the position where they would only contemplate awarding damages for nervous shock if it accompanied more obvious physical damage to the present position where they are prepared to award damages to someone who has suffered shock not from any fear for his own safety but as a result of shock suffered from what he saw, heard and feared might happen to another, provided it could reasonably be foreseen that a person in his position might suffer in this way.

This leads on to other cases which raise the more general question as to the extent to which a person can recover for loss he has suffered as a result of damage inflicted by the defendant on a third party. The general rule is that there can be no recovery. But to this there are a number of exceptions. Those discussed below are the rights which arise under the Fatal Accidents Acts 1946–59 for the dependants of someone killed as a result of a tort. The Law Reform (Miscellaneous Provisions) Act 1934 which enables representatives of the dead man to sue on behalf of his estate may have the same effect but this, subject to the provisions of the Inheritance (Family Provisions) Act 1938 depends on whether and how he has distributed his estate by will. Two other minor exceptions are that an employer may recover for damage to his employee, and a husband for damage to his wife. The Law Reform Committee has recommended that this latter right should be abolished.[3]

---

[2] See pp. 437–440.   [3] 11th Rep., April 1963, Cmnd. 2017.

The assessment of damages

So far as the assessment of damages is concerned there may often be no real problem. Quite apart from an agreement to compromise or settle, the parties to a contract may have stipulated a sum to be paid in case of breach in the contract itself and provided the courts do not regard the sum as a " penalty " this will be the sum that is due. In other cases, too, the assessment may be relatively straightforward. Where the wrong is a breach of contract to pay a debt the sum due is easy to calculate. Prima facie the measure of damages for failure to supply or accept goods is the loss suffered from the necessity of having to buy or dispose of goods elsewhere and, provided there is a ready market for the goods, the damages are based on the difference between the contract price and the market price. More difficult problems may arise when the claim is for loss of profit or for losses which are not readily calculable in money terms. Two general principles apply however both in contract and in tort. The first is that the plaintiff should so far as possible be put into the position he would have been in if the contract had been performed or the tort not been committed, though this has been qualified by some judges in the case of tort who have suggested that what is due is fair, and not absolute, compensation.[4] The second is that difficulty of assessment is no bar to recovery. The court must simply do the best it can. This applies in particular of course to losses which are difficult to quantify in money terms such as physical injury, and to losses whose extent in the future it is difficult to assess. These include not only things like physical injury itself but other matters which prima facie ought to be more readily quantifiable, but whose amount depends in fact on a large number of contingencies, e.g. loss of future earnings. One thing that adds to the difficulty here is the rule that in general the courts must award a single fixed sum, once and for all. They have no power to make an award of damages by instalments, which could be altered in the light of changing circumstances, as they can for example when they are making an award of maintenance to a deserted wife, or as a tribunal can under the Industrial Injuries Acts in relation to serious injury. The plaintiff can of course wait to see how serious his injuries turn out to be but there are limits to this imposed by the Limitation Acts. In exceptional circumstances he may be able to bring fresh evidence relating to his injuries to an appeal court, but this will be rare and even here there are time limits which can only be exceeded with the leave of the court. In general it is the assessment of the seriousness of the damage made at the trial, based on the evidence presented to it at the time, which finally determines the damage for which compensation has to be assessed.

The only apparent exception to the rule that the damages must be assessed once and for all arises from the fact mentioned above that the same set of facts can give rise to different causes of action. English law for example distinguishes between actions in negligence for damage to property and actions for damage to the person. As a result it was held in *Brunsden* v. *Humphrey* [5] that the fact that the plaintiff had already been awarded a sum in compensation for loss to his cab did not prevent him bringing a

[4] Below, p. 456.
[5] (1884) 14 Q.B.D. 141.

subsequent action for damage to his person. What he may not do is to bring an action for damage to his person and then make a further application to the court when the damage turns out to be more serious than was expected, any more than the defendant can if the injury turns out to be less serious. Another apparent exception is where a cause of action only arises when damage actually occurs. In such a case an action can be brought as often as damage occurs, and not before. This is the case, for example, with damage caused by subsidence. But this is by no means a benefit to the plaintiff since it means that he can only recover for loss actually suffered. He cannot recover for the loss in value of his property which arises from the prospect of future damage resulting. Moreover even though successive actions may be technically possible the court may strike them out if it regards this as oppressive.[6]

Payment of a lump sum has been recommended in the past because it settles the matter once and for all and may, if the sum is large, enable the plaintiff to start a new life with a capital sum which may allow him to undertake some new enterprise. It has been opposed because of the element of uncertainty in its assessment and because of the danger of its being squandered. In general the courts have taken the view that the use made of any damages they awarded is not their concern, the major exception being in the case of sums awarded under the Fatal Accidents Acts. Until recently all sums awarded to widows under these Acts were controlled but since the Administration of Justice Act 1965, s. 19 (2), a widow without children can now receive the whole sum at once. Sums awarded to widows with children are, however, still subject to supervision.

The introduction of the new schemes of social insurance raised problems concerning the relationship between that scheme and the common law action for damages. The ordinary action for damages had long been regarded as an unsatisfactory solution for the injuries which arose in an industrial context. Hence the Workmen's Compensation Act of 1897 and its successors, which provided that a workman could recover compensation without having to prove negligence. Dissatisfaction with the working of those Acts and the role of the courts in them led to their replacement by the social insurance schemes administered by tribunals and the National Insurance (Industrial Injuries) Commissioner. The Committee on Alternative Remedies[7] recommended that a workman should be allowed to choose whether to bring an action at common law or to rely on social insurance, but that he should not recover twice over. The Law Reform (Personal Injuries) Act 1948 compromised and provided that half the sum due under the state scheme should be taken into account in making an assessment of the common law damages. Sums received under private insurance schemes are not taken into account.

All awards of damages for loss of earnings are made after a deduction has been made to take account of liability for tax, though this has caused some controversy. It was the subject of a report by the Law Reform Committee in August 1958.[8] Recent cases have established that some account may be taken of the possibility of inflation.

[6] Above, p. 325.
[7] Cmd. 6860, July 1946.
[8] 7th Rep., Cmnd. 501.

Exemplary damages

In some cases exemplary damages may be awarded over and above what is regarded as adequate compensation. Lord Devlin's statement of principle in *Rookes* v. *Barnard* [9] as to the circumstances when such an award is appropriate was subsequently criticised by the Court of Appeal in *Broome* v. *Cassell*,[10] which advised trial judges not to follow it. On appeal, however, the House of Lords explained and affirmed Lord Devlin's views, and chastised the Court of Appeal for usurping its functions.[11]

Proposals for change

One question which has been discussed for some time is whether the trial of the action and the assessment should be conducted by the same tribunal or at the same time. This was one of the questions discussed by the Winn Committee on Personal Injury Litigation.[12] Much more fundamental is the question whether the whole system of litigation about personal injuries should be replaced by some scheme of insurance as has been done to some extent in the case of industrial injuries. The whole question of whether actions in court for damages are the best way of handling personal injury cases has been the subject of debate for some time. It raises some of the same kinds of question as were raised at the beginning of this chapter. On December 19, 1972, the Government announced the appointment of a Royal Commission under Lord Pearson—

> to consider to what extent, in what circumstances and by what means compensation should be payable in respect of death or personal injury (including ante-natal injury) suffered by any person (a) in the course of employment; (b) through the use of a motor-vehicle or other means of transport; (c) through the manufacture, supply or use of goods or services; (d) on premises belonging to or occupied by another; or (e) otherwise through the act or omission of another when compensation under the present law is recoverable only on proof of fault or under the rules of strict liability, having regard to the cost and other implications of the arrangements for the recovery of compensation, whether by way of compulsory insurance, or otherwise.

EQUITABLE REMEDIES

The award of damages is the remedy *par excellence* of the common law. The old Court of Chancery offered the more direct remedies of injunction and specific performance. One of the steps taken in the middle of the nineteenth century towards bringing the common law and equity into greater harmony was to make the equitable remedies available in the common law courts and to authorise the Court of Chancery to award damages in lieu of an injunction. All these remedies are now available in each division of the High Court as a result of the Judicature Acts 1873–75. They are also available in the county courts.

---

[9] [1964] A.C. 1129.
[10] [1971] 2 Q.B. 354.
[11] Below, p. 464.
[12] Below, p. 472.

Injunctions

Injunctions are a discretionary remedy but the courts have developed guides as to the circumstances in which they will be granted. One of the classic statements of the principles which guide the courts is that of A. L. Smith in *Shelfer* v. *City of London Lighting Co.*[13] They may be used both to prevent and restrain the commission of a tort or a breach of contract. Some of the common uses are the restraint of a nuisance where money compensation would be inadequate or where repeated actions would have to be brought each time damage is caused; to restrain the publication of a libel; to order people unlawfully occupying property to leave it; to order a trade union official to stop interfering with the free movement of goods; or to prevent the breach of a covenant not to do something, *e.g.* not to work for someone else, not to set up a business in competition with one one has just sold; not to build or use a building in a particular way. The use of restrictive covenants of the latter kind, supported by the availability of an injunction in case of breach, played an important part in preserving the character and standards of a neighbourhood long before there was any question of statutory town and country planning. Many of London's squares were built and preserved using this technique and even with the introduction of town and country planning it still has a role to play.

It will be noted that quite apart from the technical rules as to when the court will and will not grant an injunction the way in which the courts have exercised their discretion and have changed their attitudes over the years is one of the points at which one can see the way in which the courts have come to emphasise different values at different times. The way in which they exercise discretions like that to grant or withhold an injunction reveals some at least of the assumptions on which they operate and where at any given time they strike the balance between conflicting interests. Injunctions may be issued before anything unlawful has actually been done or before any damage has actually been caused. An interim injunction may be granted on the application of the plaintiff only, *ex parte*, pending a trial of the issue, in order to preserve the status quo or prevent further damage. It is usual for an interim injunction to be for a limited period at the end of which the other party may appear and object to its continuance. Although an interim injunction is usually issued with a view to a later trial, if those against whom it is issued cease for example to occupy the plaintiff's property and do not challenge the injunction, there is no obligation on the plaintiff to issue a writ. The injunction will simply lapse or if it has no time-limit an application can be made to have it discharged. One special use of an injunction is on the application of the Attorney-General to restrain the commission of an offence or a public nuisance, *e.g.* where the imposition of fines has proved inadequate to stop the illegal activity; where, for example, an unlawful business was profitable enough to be able to treat the fine as a business expense (*Att.-Gen.* v. *Harris*[14]).

Orders for specific performance

Like injunctions an order for the specific performance of a contract is discretionary. It may be ordered however where damages would not be

---

[13] [1895] 1 Ch. 287; below, p. 475.　　　　[14] [1961] 1 Q.B. 74; below, p. 532.

regarded as a reasonable substitute, as for example in the case of a contract for the sale of a specific and unique thing. Traditionally the courts have been prepared to order the specific performance of a contract for the sale of real property. It is this fact that has made the contract for the sale of property or the grant of a lease something equivalent in equity to a legal right to the property or lease in law. One area where the court will traditionally not order specific performance is of a contract for the performance of services, mostly because of the difficulties of supervision. The object of such an application may sometimes however be achieved indirectly by enforcing by injunction the negative part of an agreement of services in which a promise has been made not to work for someone else, though the courts will not enforce even this negative covenant if the effect would be that the defendant must either perform his contract or starve.[15] Quite apart from any question of remedy the courts as a matter of substantive law may declare a covenant not to work for someone else void, as being in restraint of trade.

The Prerogative Orders

Damages, injunctions and orders for specific performance are the principal remedies offered in non-matrimonial civil cases between private citizens and corporations. In addition there are a number of important remedies available in the public law field. These are the prerogative orders mandamus and certiorari, the prerogative writ of habeas corpus, and declaration. English law has no separate system of administrative law in any strict sense and no special administrative remedies. With the growth in the power of governmental and administrative agencies came the need to control them and to settle disputes which arose in the course of the exercise of or failure to exercise their powers. But more often than not, especially in the early days of this development more attention was paid to giving them powers than to giving an aggrieved citizen any specific remedy. As was noted in Chapter 1 this situation has been remedied in some spheres by the creation of special tribunals to hear disputes. In other cases, e.g. in relation to the compulsory acquisition of land and town and country planning, statute has given anyone aggrieved a specific right to apply to the courts. But there still remains a fairly wide field in which no specific remedy has been given. To meet these situations at a time when hardly any specific statutory provision was made the common law courts extended some of the remedies that they already had at their disposal and adapted them to this new task. Mandamus for example is available against statutory bodies and amounts to an order to them to perform their public duties and to exercise their powers. Certiorari is used to challenge decisions made by bodies which are under a duty to act judicially, if they have failed to do so, or if they have exceeded their powers, or if they have made a mistake of law. Originally intended to apply to inferior courts this remedy has now been extended by the courts to cover decisions by tribunals and indeed any other administrative body, including a Minister of the Crown, even if the final decision is not a judicial one, provided that the process by which it

---

[15] Below, p. 473.

has to be reached has some judicial element in it. The use of certiorari differs from an appeal in that if it is successful the decision is not replaced by one of the court's own but is simply quashed.

Habeas corpus was more important in the past in this context than at the present time. It is the means by which anyone can challenge his unlawful imprisonment. It was a more widely used remedy when the government was more ready to imprison people without lawful justification, but it is by no means obsolete. Touching, as it does, the basic physical liberty, it has long been regarded as one of the most significant of the constitutional remedies in the courts' armoury and very closely connected with the whole notion of government under law.

Declarations, hypothetical cases and preliminary points of law

Declaration is in many ways a more interesting remedy and has also come to play an important part in the sphere of administrative law and in any sphere in which the exercise of power is being challenged. But it is related to a much more general point about the English legal system's attitude to its functions, in particular in relation to the granting of remedies. As a matter of general principle the system does not offer itself as an advisory service on points of law, or as the system itself puts it, will not deal with hypothetical cases. There must be a real issue between the parties. This does not mean that the parties have to be hostile to one another. But it does mean that there must be a real question between them. This sometimes creates difficulties. Some of these can be avoided by bringing a test case which will settle the point for numerous other cases. The Inland Revenue for example may take a case all the way up to the House of Lords in order to get a doubtful point settled, though even here they have to be careful. The House of Lords refused to hear a case in which the Court of Appeal had granted leave to appeal on the condition that the appellants would not only pay the costs of the respondent in any event but would also abide by the Court of Appeal's decision on the merits in any event. This, said the House of Lords, meant that the parties had no further interest in the action and they refused to hear the case. Nor will the courts hear a test case on a concocted set of facts. Alternatively if the question is the courts' reaction to a scheme of tax avoidance it is possible in principle to prepare a much smaller pilot scheme and test this out before embarking on the main scheme. In other cases something may be done deliberately to raise the issue. Someone who wished to test out the question whether he needed planning permission for example could start building and wait for an enforcement notice to be issued.

It is not only the courts themselves who have resisted being called upon to give legal advice. There was also strong resistance in Parliament to a proposal made in the Rating and Valuation Bill in 1924 that the government should have the power to refer difficult questions of law arising under it to the courts for their general opinion, and the clause was dropped. Resistance to giving advice on general points of law seems to rest mainly on the view that the common law method is essentially a case-oriented method and that its whole approach involves the consideration of a legal problem

only in the context of a particular case, and then only to the extent necessary to dispose of that particular case. Even the validity of their decision
as a precedent is tied up with the facts of the case in which the general
principles are laid down (as we have seen in discussing the doctrine
precedent [16]). Nonetheless there are exceptions to this general rule. The
Privy Council for example can be called on to give advice on legal problems as it did in *Re Piracy Jure Gentium*,[17] *Re MacManaway* [18] and *Re
Parliamentary Privilege Act* 1770.[19] The judges used to be called on to
give advice to the House of Lords as they did for example in *M'Naghten's*
case [20] though this practice has lapsed, now that professional lawyers sit
there. Moreover, although the courts will not decide hypothetical cases
they are authorised to state what the law is in a particular case even
though no other remedy is sought or even though no other remedy could
be sought at the time. This is where the declaration comes in as a form
of remedy. Parties may simply ask the courts to declare the law in the
case they have brought before them. Although it is within the discretion
of the courts whether or not they will do so they have shown themselves
willing in cases where, for example, no other remedy is available. In the
case of *Barnard* v. *National Dock Labour Board* [21] for example they
declared that the purported dismissal of dockers was *ultra vires*. In *Pyx
Granite* v. *Minister of Housing & Local Government* [22] they declared that
the plaintiff did not need planning permission for what he wanted to do.
In *Ridge* v. *Baldwin* [23] they declared that the Chief Constable of Brighton
had been wrongfully dismissed. Declaration has proved an effective
remedy because of the readiness of public authorities to conduct their
affairs in accordance with the law so declared.

Order 33 of the Rules of the Supreme Court which provides for the
preliminary trial of an issue of law before the facts are established is set
out below.[24]

THE ADMINISTRATIVE ROLE OF THE COURTS

Quite apart from these specific remedies there are the many situations in
which citizens can apply to the courts for assistance of one kind or another.
This is particularly true of the Chancery Division, *e.g.* in relation to the
administration of trusts, the distribution of assets of deceased persons or in
relation to companies where the consent of a court is sometimes required
before something can be done. The Family Division too has much more
to do than divorce married couples. Apart from its jurisdiction over the
financial problems which arise when marriages break up, it has an extensive jurisdiction in relation to children. For although on the whole the
materials in this book have concentrated on the dispute, settlement and
guilt-proving side of the system, the system itself performs what one might

[16] Above, p. 243.
[17] [1934] A.C. 586.
[18] [1951] A.C. 161.
[19] [1958] A.C. 331.
[20] (1843) 10 Cl. & Fin. 200.
[21] [1953] 2 Q.B. 18.
[22] [1960] A.C. 260.
[23] [1964] A.C. 40.
[24] See p. 486.

call a large judicial-administrative function. Indeed as we have seen in dealing with the county courts, for a good number of firms those courts are little more than a debt-collecting agency. (See the extracts from the Payne Committee on the Enforcement of Judgment Debts.[25])

THE ENFORCEMENT OF JUDGMENTS

Here we come back to the point raised at the beginning of this chapter. Many rules of substantive law are effective because of the willingness of people to observe them without more, subject to their disputing any questions of law or fact which are not reasonably clear. In a clear case the mere threat of an action will usually help to secure observance or the payment of compensation for failure to observe. In other cases the plaintiff may have to go to court but as soon as the decision is given the defendant is willing to comply with it. There remains the hard core of cases in which neither the rules of law by themselves nor even an adverse judicial decision are of any avail. In this last resort the system depends on the power of the courts to enforce their judgments either by ordering the sale of the defendant's goods, removing him forcibly from premises, or imprisoning him for contempt of court for refusing to obey a court order. More recently the courts have been given power to order the attachment of the earnings of a defaulter which means that the sum due will be deducted from his income at source. These are the last formal resources of the law. Even they cannot cater for the " man of straw " who flits in and out of the pages of law books, the wrongdoing man with inadequate assets to compensate for the damage he has caused. To deal with him the legal system has used various devices. It has made employers vicariously liable for the acts of their employees in order to make the employers' assets available to compensate those who have been damaged by the employees' wrongful acts. It has insisted that all motor-car drivers should be insured against damage caused to third parties, and has backed up its requirements with criminal penalties. It has introduced a scheme quite outside the normal process of litigation for compensating victims of crimes of violence. It has made the local community pay for damage caused to property as a result of anything that can be called a riot, even damage resulting from the desire of football spectators to find a back entrance to the match over a nearby house and garden.[26]

Little research is done on the effectiveness of the English legal system in all these respects but there is of course an urgent and constant need to discover just how far the system is achieving its goals and implementing the values which it sets out in the substantive law. Just as the rules of substantive law are exactly that, simply rules which do not purport to describe what actually happens in fact, so too with the law relating to remedies. This chapter is concerned with the remedies offered in principle. There still remains the very large question as to what they mean in fact. One of the purposes of the present materials is to provide a framework in which that kind of question can be asked and answered, to make it clear

[25] Below, p. 492.
[26] Below, p. 488.

what the system purports to do, as a preliminary to discovering what it actually does in fact.

GENERAL PRINCIPLES OF LIABILITY AND REMOTENESS OF DAMAGE

Remoteness of damage in contract

The Heron II
House of Lords [1969] 1 A.C. 350

LORD REID: . . . For over a century everyone has agreed that remoteness of damage in contract must be determined by applying the rule (or rules) laid down by a court including Lord Wensleydale (then Parke B.), Martin B. and Alderson B., in *Hadley* v. *Baxendale*.[27] But many different interpretations of that rule have been adopted by judges at different times. . . . The rule is that the damages " should be such as may fairly and reasonably be considered either arising naturally, i.e., according to the usual course of things, from such breach of contract itself, or such as may reasonably be supposed to have been in the contemplation of both parties, at the time they made the contract, as the probable result of the breach of it." . . . I am satisfied that the court did not intend that every type of damage which was reasonably foreseeable by the parties when the contract was made should either be considered as arising naturally, i.e., in the usual course of things, or be supposed to have been in the contemplation of the parties. Indeed the decision makes it clear that a type of damage which was plainly foreseeable as a real possibility but which would only occur in a small minority of cases cannot be regarded as arising in the usual course of things or be supposed to have been in the contemplation of the parties: the parties are not supposed to contemplate as grounds for the recovery of damage any type of loss or damage which on the knowledge available to the defendant would appear to him as only likely to occur in a small minority of cases. In cases like *Hadley* v. *Baxendale* or the present case it is not enough that in fact the plaintiff's loss was directly caused by the defendant's breach of contract. It clearly was so caused in both. The crucial question is whether, on the information available to the defendant when the contract was made, he should, or the reasonable man in his position would, have realised that such loss was sufficiently likely to result from the breach of contract to make it proper to hold that the loss flowed naturally from the breach or that loss of that kind should have been within his contemplation. The modern rule in tort is quite different and it imposes a much wider liability. The defendant will be liable for any type of damage which is reasonably foreseeable as liable to happen even in the most unusual case, unless the risk is so small that a reasonable man would in the whole circumstances feel justified in neglecting it. And there is good reason for the difference. In contrast, if one party wishes to protect himself against a risk to which the other party would appear unusual, he can direct the other party's attention to it before the contract is made, and I need not stop to consider in what circumstances the other party will then be held to have accepted responsibility in that event. But in tort there is no opportunity for the injured party to protect himself in this way, and the tortfeasor cannot reasonably complain if he has to pay for some very unusual but nevertheless foreseeable damage which results from his wrongdoing. . . . Some importance was attached in argument to *Slater and Another* v. *Hoyle & Smith Ltd.*[28] and the

---

[27] (1854) 9 Exch. 341.
[28] [1920] 2 K.B. 11, C.A.

earlier cases there cited. Those cases deal with sale of goods, and I do not think it necessary or desirable in the present case to consider what the rule there is, whether it conflicts with the general principles now established as to measure of damages, or whether, if it does, it ought or ought not to stand. Those are much too important questions to be decided obiter in the present case, and I refrain from expressing any opinion about them.

[LORDS MORRIS OF BORTH-Y-GEST, HODSON, PEARCE AND UPJOHN delivered concurring judgments.]

Overseas Tankship (U.K.) Ltd. v. Morts Dock and Engineering Co. Ltd. (The Wagon Mound)
Privy Council [1961] A.C. 388

The plaintiffs in this case owned a wharf at Morts Bay, Balamain, Sydney. The defendants were the charterers of the S.S. *Wagonmound*. While the ship was moored about 600 feet away from the wharf the employees of the charterers negligently allowed a large quantity of oil to spill into the water which spread as far as the wharf. At the time a ship was being refitted at the wharf and electric and oxy-acetylene equipment was being used. Molten metal fell from the wharf and set light to some cotton waste or rag on a piece of debris under the wharf, which in turn set light to the oil and damaged both the wharf and the ship which was being refitted. The plaintiffs sued the defendants for their negligence. The defendants argued that the damage was too remote because the defendants could not reasonably have been expected to foresee that the oil would catch fire when spread on the water. The Supreme Court of New South Wales held that the defendants were liable because although they could not foresee the exact damage they could have foreseen some damage—in fact there had been damage to the wharf as a result simply of the oil reaching the wharf—and that the damage was a sufficiently direct result of their original negligence in fact to make them liable. In reaching their decision they relied heavily on the case of *Re Polemis* in the Court of Appeal.[29]

VISCOUNT SIMONDS delivered the judgment of the Privy Council (VISCOUNT SIMONDS, LORDS REID, RADCLIFFE, TUCKER and MORRIS OF BORTH-Y-GEST): . . . It is inevitable that first consideration should be given to the case of *Re Polemis and Furness Withy & Co. Ltd.* . . . [T]he Court of Appeal held that the charterers were responsible for all the consequences of their negligent act even though those consequences could not reasonably have been anticipated. The negligent act was nothing more than the carelessness of stevedores (for whom the charterers were assumed to be responsible) in allowing a sling or rope by which it was being hoisted to come into contact with certain boards, causing one of them to fall into the hold. The falling board hit some substances in the hold and caused a spark; the spark ignited petrol vapour in the hold; there was a rush of flames; and the ship was destroyed. The . . . arbitrators found that the causing of the spark could not reasonably have been anticipated from the falling of the board, though some damage to the ship might reasonably have been so anticipated. . . .

[29] [1921] 3 K.B. 560.

There can be no doubt that the decision of the Court of Appeal in *Polemis* plainly asserts that, if the defendant is guilty of negligence, he is responsible for all the consequences whether reasonably foreseeable or not. . . . [U]p to that date it had been universally accepted that the law in regard to damages for breach of contract and for tort was, generally speaking, the same. . . . Their Lordships refer to this aspect of the matter, not because they wish to assert that in all respects today the measure of damages is in all cases the same in tort and in breach of contract, but because it emphasises how far *Polemis* was out of the current of contemporary thought. . . . If the line of relevant authority had stopped with *Polemis*, their Lordships might, whatever their own views as to its unreason, have felt some hesitation about overruling it. But it is far otherwise. It is true that both in England and in many parts of the Commonwealth that decision has from time to time been followed; but in Scotland it has been rejected with determination. It has never been subject to the express scrutiny of either the House of Lords or the Privy Council, though there have been comments upon it in those Supreme Tribunals. Even in the inferior courts judges have, sometimes perhaps unwittingly, declared themselves in a sense adverse to its principle. . . .

Enough has been said to show that the authority of *Polemis* has been severely shaken though lip-service has from time to time been paid to it. In their Lordships' opinion it should no longer be regarded as good law. It is not probable that many cases will for that reason have a different result, though it is hoped that the law will be thereby simplified, and that in some cases, at least, palpable injustice will be avoided. For it does not seem consonant with current ideas of justice or morality that for an act of negligence, however slight or venial, which results in some trivial foreseeable damage the actor should be liable for all consequences however unforeseeable and however grave, so long as they can be said to be " direct." It is a principle of civil liability, subject only to qualifications which have no present relevance, that a man must be considered to be responsible for the probable consequences of his act. To demand more of him is too harsh a rule, to demand less is to ignore that civilised order requires the observance of a minimum standard of behaviour. . . . [I]f it is asked why a man should be responsible for the natural or necessary or probable consequences of his act (or any other similar description of them) the answer is that it is not because they are natural or necessary or probable, but because, since they have this quality, it is judged by the standard of the reasonable man that he ought to have foreseen them. . . . For, if some limitation must be imposed upon the consequences for which the negligent actor is to be held responsible— and all are agreed that some limitation there must be—why should that test (reasonable foreseeability) be rejected which, since he is judged by what the reasonable man ought to foresee, corresponds with the common conscience of mankind, and a test (the " direct " consequence) be substituted which leads to nowhere but the never-ending and insoluble problems of causation. " The lawyer," said Sir Frederick Pollock, " cannot afford to adventure himself with philosophers in the logical and metaphysical controversies that beset the idea of cause." Yet this is just what he has most unfortunately done and must continue to do if the rule in *Polemis* is to prevail. . . .

Their Lordships conclude this part of the case with some general observations. They have been concerned primarily to displace the proposition that unforeseeability is irrelevant if damage is " direct." In doing so they have inevitably insisted that the essential factor in determining liability is whether the damage is of such a kind as the reasonable man should have foreseen. This accords with the general view . . . stated by Lord Atkin in *Donoghue* v.

Stevenson.[30]. . . . It is proper to add that their Lordships have not found it necessary to consider the so-called rule of " strict liability " exemplified in *Rylands* v. *Fletcher* [31] and the cases that have followed or distinguished it. Nothing that they have said is intended to reflect on that rule.

Nervous shock

Hambrook v. Stokes

Court of Appeal [1925] 1 K.B. 141

SARGANT L.J. (dissenting): . . . There seems to me to be no magic in actual personal contact. A threatened contact producing physical results should be an equivalent. The principle on which a threatened battery may justify damages for assault is in my view strictly analogous. In the case of a threat of imminent danger to a plaintiff resulting in illness through nervous shock, there is, in my view, as real and direct an interference with the personality of the plaintiff as if the illness had been caused by actual physical contact with him. And the duty of a defendant to avoid acts or omissions which will result in the illness of the plaintiff seems to me as clear and definite in the one case as in the other, though no doubt the occasions on which illness will result are much less frequent in the first case than in the second.

Bourhill v. Young

House of Lords [1943] A.C. 92

LORD MACMILLAN : . . . The crude view that the law should take cognizance only of physical injury resulting from actual impact has been discarded, and it is now well recognized that an action will lie for injury by shock sustained through the medium of the eye or the ear without direct contact. The distinction between mental shock and bodily injury was never a scientific one, for mental shock is presumably in all cases the result of, or at least accompanied by, some physical disturbance in the sufferer's system. And a mental shock may have consequences more serious than those resulting from physical impact. But in the case of mental shock there are elements of greater subtlety than in the case of an ordinary physical injury and these elements may give rise to debate as to the precise scope of legal liability.

King v. Phillips

Court of Appeal [1953] 1 Q.B. 429

DENNING L.J.: . . . [T]here can be no doubt since *Bourhill* v. *Young* [32] that the test of liability for shock is foreseeability of injury by shock. But this test is by no means easy to apply. . . . Some cases seem plain enough. A wife or mother who suffers shock on being told of an accident to a loved one cannot recover damages from the negligent party on that account. Nor can a bystander who suffers shock by witnessing an accident from a safe distance: *Smith* v. *Johnson* (unreported), cited in *Wilkinson* v. *Downton*,[33] *Bourhill* v. *Young*, *per* Lord Porter. But if the bystander is a mother who suffers from shock

[30] [1932] A.C. 562, 580.
[31] (1868) L.R. 3 H.L. 330, H.L.
[32] [1943] A.C. 92.
[33] [1897] 2 Q.B. 57.

by hearing or seeing, with her own unaided senses, that her child is in peril, then she may be able to recover from the negligent party, even though she was in no personal danger herself: *Hambrook* v. *Stokes Brothers*.[34] Lord Wright said that he agreed with that decision. So do I. This brings me to the real question: Is the present case covered by *Hambrook* v. *Stokes Brothers* or not? I think that we should follow *Hambrook* v. *Stokes Brothers* so far as to hold that there was a duty of care owed by the taxi driver not only to the boy, but also to his mother. In that case the negligence took place 300 yards from the place where the mother was standing. In this case it was only 70 or 80 yards. In that case the mother was not herself in any personal danger. Nor was she here. In that case she suffered shock by fear for the safety of her children from what she saw and heard. So did she here. In that case the mother was in the street, and in this case at the window of the house. I do not think that makes any difference. Nevertheless, I think that the shock in this case is too remote to be a head of damage. It seems to me that the slow backing of the taxicab was very different from the terrifying descent of the runaway lorry. The taxicab driver cannot reasonably be expected to have foreseen that his backing would terrify a mother 70 yards away, whereas the lorry driver ought to have foreseen that a runaway lorry might seriously shock the mother of children in the danger area.

The above case may be compared with *Boardman and Another* v. *Sanderson and Another*[35] where a father recovered for nervous shock which followed his hearing his son's screams and seeing his foot trapped under the car of his friend with whom he had gone to a garage. There Ormerod L.J. noted:

> . . . Mr. Richardson has endeavoured to submit that the line of distinction must be drawn somewhere and that must depend on whether the accident was witnessed by the plaintiff. . . . There has been no authority produced to the court to bear out that submission and, for my part, I must say I find it difficult to understand why the line should be drawn in that arbitrary fashion. It may be that, in some cases, that is a proper line to draw. . . . On the other hand, clearly the facts in these cases are infinitely variable and it would be difficult, if not impossible, to draw any line of distinction and say in one case the plaintiff should succeed and in another case he should not.

Dooley v. *Cammell Laird and Co. Ltd.*[36] was a case where a crane driver recovered damages for nervous shock which he suffered when he thought that a load, which had fallen because of a weak rope provided by the company, might have injured his fellow workers below. There Donovan J. said:

> Here the following questions arise: (1) Were Mersey Insulation under a duty towards Dooley to take reasonable care to avoid acts and omissions which they could reasonably foresee would be likely to injure him? . . . (3) If so, did such breach result in injury to Dooley? . . . If you load a sling and hoist it, using a weak rope, the rope may break and the contents of the sling be precipitated on to the deck or down the hold of the vessel being loaded. And if men are working on the

---

[34] [1925] 1 K.B. 141.
[35] [1964] 1 W.L.R. 1317, C.A.
[36] [1951] 1 Lloyd's Rep. 271.

deck or down in the hold, it is obvious that they may get severely injured and possibly killed in consequence. Furthermore, if the driver of the crane concerned fears that the load may have fallen upon some of his fellow workmen, and that fear is not baseless or extravagant, then it is, I think, a consequence reasonably to have been foreseen that he may himself suffer a nervous shock. . . . Accordingly I answer the first question in the affirmative. . . . It is clear to me on the medical evidence that Dooley suffered a nervous shock on this occasion, which nervous shock I find was due to fear that some of his fellow workmen may have been injured through the fall of the load, which fear was not unreasonable in the circumstances. The damage he suffered was not too remote, and I answer the third question also in the affirmative.

Chadwick v. British Railways Board

Queen's Bench Division [1967] 1 W.L.R. 912

The plaintiff sued for injuries suffered by her husband, who had since died, at the scene of a railway accident at Lewisham on December 4, 1957, in which ninety persons were killed. The accident occurred 200 yards from his home. He went to help and stayed there through the night administering injections and helping people out of the wreckage. Before the accident he was a cheerful busy man carrying on a successful window cleaning business, with many spare time activities. Afterwards he became psychoneurotic and spent six months in a mental hospital. His health deteriorated, he no longer took an interest in life and he could not work.

WALLER J.: I do not see any objection in principle to damages being recoverable for shock caused other than by fear for one's own safety or for the safety of one's children. . . . The scene described by Mrs. Taylor was the kind of thing to be expected if trains collided as these did and it was one which could, in my view, properly be called gruesome. In my opinion, if the defendants had asked themselves the hypothetical question: "If we run one train into another at Lewisham in such circumstances that a large number of people are killed, may some persons who are physically unhurt suffer injury from shock?" I think that the answer must have been "Yes."

Injuries to others and rescue cases

Cattle v. Stockton Waterworks Co.

Court of Queen's Bench (1875) L.R. 10 Q.B. 453

BLACKBURN J.: . . . In the present case the objection is technical and against the merits, and we should be glad to avoid giving it effect. But if we did so, we should establish an authority for saying that, in such a case as that of *Fletcher* v. *Rylands* [37] the defendant would be liable, not only to an action by the owner of the drowned mine, and by such of his workmen as had their tools or clothes destroyed, but also to an action by every workman and person employed in the mine, who in consequence of its stoppage made less wages that he would otherwise have done. And many similar cases to which this

[37] (1866) L.R. 1 Ex. 265.

would apply might be suggested. It may be said that it is just that all such persons should have compensation for such a loss, and that, if the law does not give them redress, it is imperfect. Perhaps it may be so. But, as was pointed out by Coleridge J., in *Lumley* v. *Gye*,[38] courts of justice should not " allow themselves, in the pursuit of perfectly complete remedies for all wrongful acts, to transgress the bounds, which our law, in a wise consciousness as I conceive of its limited powers, has imposed on itself, of redressing only the proximate and direct consequences of wrongful acts." In this we quite agree. No authority in favour of the plaintiff's right to sue was cited, and, as far as our knowledge goes, there was none that could have been cited . . . In *Lumley* v. *Gye* the majority of the Court held that an action would lie for maliciously procuring a third person to break her contract with the plaintiff. But all three of the judges who gave judgment for the plaintiff relied upon malicious intention. It would be a waste of time to do more than refer to the elaborate judgments in that case for the law and authorities on this branch of law.

Best v. Samuel Fox & Co. Ltd.

House of Lords [1952] A.C. 716

LORD GODDARD: . . . It may often happen that an injury to one person may affect another; a servant whose master is killed or permanently injured may lose his employment, it may be of long standing, and the misfortune may come when he is of an age when it would be very difficult for him to obtain other work, but no one would suggest that he thereby acquires a right of action against the wrongdoer. Damages for personal injury can seldom be a perfect compensation, but where injury has been caused to a husband or father it has never been the case that his wife or children whose style of living or education may have radically to be curtailed have on that account a right of action other than that which, in the case of death, the Fatal Accidents Act, 1846, has given. . . .

Baker v. T. E. Hopkins & Son Ltd.

Court of Appeal [1959] 1 W.L.R. 966

The plaintiff's husband, a doctor, had been overcome by fumes when he had been lowered down a well in an attempt to rescue two workmen, who had themselves been overcome by fumes, as the result of their employer's negligence.

WILLMER L.J.: . . . It seems to me that in this case, as in any case where a plaintiff is injured in going to the rescue of a third party put in peril by the defendants' wrongdoing, the questions which have to be answered are four-fold: (1) Did the wrongdoer owe any duty to the rescuer in the circumstances of the particular case? (2) If so, did the rescuer's injury result from a breach of that duty, or did his act in going to the rescue amount to a novus actus? (3) Did the rescuer, knowing the danger, voluntarily accept the risk of injury, so as to be defeated by the maxim volenti non fit injuria? (4) Was the rescuer's injury caused or contributed to by his own failure to take reasonable care for his own safety? All these questions are raised by the circumstances of this case, and have been much canvassed in argument before us. I will endeavour to deal with each in turn.

---

[38] (1853) 22 L.J.Q.B. 463, 479.

(1) The question whether the wrongdoer owed any duty to the rescuer must be determined, in my judgment, by reference to Lord Atkin's familiar statement of the law in *Donoghue* v. *Stevenson*,[39] when he said: "You must take reasonable care to avoid acts or omissions which you can reasonably foresee would be likely to injure your neighbour." In the circumstances of the particular case is the rescuer in law the "neighbour" of the wrongdoer, in the sense that he is so closely and directly affected by the wrongdoer's act that the latter ought reasonably to have him in contemplation as being so affected? Where the act of the wrongdoer has been such as to be likely to put someone in peril, reasonable foresight will normally contemplate the probability of an attempted rescue, in the course of which the rescuer may receive injury. In the American case of *Wagner* v. *International Railway Co.*[40] Cardozo J., as it seems to me, foreshadowed in a remarkable way Lord Atkin's statement of principle, and applied it to a typical rescue case. He said: "Danger invites rescue. The cry of distress is the summons to relief. The law does not ignore these reactions of the mind in tracing conduct to its consequences. It recognises them as normal. It places their effects within the range of the natural and probable. The wrong that imperils life is a wrong to the imperilled victim; it is a wrong also to his rescuer." Then a little later he went on: "The risk of rescue, if only it be not wanton, is born of the occasion. The emergency begets the man. The wrongdoer may not have foreseen the coming of a deliverer. He is accountable as if he had." The judgment of Cardozo J. was referred to with approval by Lord Wright in *Bourhill* v. *Young* [41] and Lord Wright went on to say: "This again shows how the ambit of the persons affected by negligence or misconduct may extend beyond persons who are actually subject to physical impact. There may, indeed, be no one injured in a particular case by actual impact, but still a wrong may be committed to anyone who suffers nervous shock or is injured in an act of rescue." I should also refer to *The Oropesa*,[42] where Lord Wright, quoting from the speech of Lord Haldane in *Canadian Pacific Railway Co.* v. *Kelvin Shipping Co.*[43] said: "Reasonable human conduct is part of the ordinary course of things." Assuming the rescuer not to have acted unreasonably, therefore, it seems to me that he must normally belong to the class of persons who ought to be within the contemplation of the wrongdoer as being closely and directly affected by the latter's act.

Fatal Accidents Act 1846 [44]

9 & 10 Vict. c. 93

Whereas no action at law is now maintainable against a person who by his wrongful act, neglect or default may have caused the death of another person, and it is oftentimes right and expedient that the wrongdoer in such case should be answerable in damages for the injury so caused by him. . . .

1. Whensoever the death of a person shall be caused by wrongful act, neglect or default, and the act, neglect, or default is such as would (if death had not ensued) have entitled the party injured to maintain an action and recover damages in respect thereof . . . the person who would have been liable if death had not ensued shall be liable to an action for damages, notwithstanding the death of the person injured. . . .

[39] [1932] A.C. 562, 580.
[40] (1921) 232 N.Y.Rep. 176, 180.
[41] [1943] A.C. 92, 108, 109.
[42] [1943] P. 32, 39.
[43] (1927) 138 L.T. 369, 370.
[44] As amended by the Law Reform (Limitation of Actions) Act 1954, c. 36.

2. Every such action shall be for the benefit of the wife, husband, parent, and child of the person whose death shall have been so caused . . . and in every such action the jury may give such damages as they may think proportioned to the injury resulting from such death to the parties respectively for whom and for whose benefit such action shall be brought; and the amount so recovered, after deducting the costs not recovered from the defendant, shall be divided amongst the before-mentioned parties in such shares as the jury by their verdict shall find and direct.

3. Provided . . . that . . . such action shall be commenced within three years after the death of such deceased person. . . .

5. The word " parent " shall include father and mother and grandfather and grandmother and the word " child " shall include son and daughter, and grandson and granddaughter. . . .

Fatal Accidents Act 1959
7 & 8 Eliz. 2, c. 65

1.—(1) The persons for whose benefit or by whom an action may be brought under the Fatal Accidents Act, 1846, shall include any person who is, or is the issue of, a brother, sister, uncle or aunt of the deceased person.

(2) In deducing any relationship for the purposes of the said Act and this Act—

(a) an adopted person shall be treated as the child of the person or persons by whom he was adopted . . . and, subject thereto,

(b) any relationship by affinity shall be treated as a relationship by consanguinity, any relationship of the half blood as a relationship of the whole blood, and the stepchild of any person as his child; and

(c) an illegitimate person shall be treated as the legitimate child of his mother and reputed father. . . .

2.—(1) In assessing damages in respect of a person's death in any action under the Fatal Accidents Act, 1846, . . . there shall not be taken into account any insurance money, benefit, pension or gratuity which has been or will or may be paid as a result of the death.

(2) In this section—

" benefit " means benefit under the National Insurance Acts, 1946 (as amended . . .) . . . and any payment by a friendly society or trade union for the relief or maintenance of a member's dependants;

" insurance money " includes a return of premiums; and

" pension " includes a return of contributions and any payment of a lump sum in respect of a person's employment.

[For calculation of damages in such a case see *e.g. Mallett* v. *McMonagle*[45] and *Taylor* v. *O'Connor*.[46]]

Law Reform (Miscellaneous Provisions) Act 1971
1971, c. 43

4.—(1) In assessing damages payable to a widow in respect of the death of her husband in any action under the Fatal Accidents Acts, 1846 to 1959, there shall not be taken into account the remarriage of the widow or her prospects of remarriage.

[45] [1970] A.C. 166.   [46] [1971] A.C. 115.

Law Reform (Miscellaneous Provisions) Act 1934
24 & 25 Geo. 5, c. 41

1.—(1) Subject to the provisions of this section, on the death of any person . . . all causes of action subsisting against or vested in him shall survive against, or, as the case may be, for the benefit of, his estate. Provided that this subsection shall not apply to causes of action for defamation. . . .

(2) Where a cause of action survives . . . for the benefit of the estate of a deceased person, the damages recoverable . . .

(*a*) shall not include any exemplary damages . . .

(*c*) where the death of that person has been caused by the act or omission which gives rise to the cause of action, shall be calculated without reference to any loss or gain to his estate consequent on his death, except that a sum in respect of funeral expenses may be included. . . .

(5) The rights conferred by this Act . . . shall be in addition to and not in derogation of any rights conferred . . . by the Fatal Accidents Acts. . . .

Successive actions on the same facts

Brunsden v. Humphrey
Court of Appeal (1884) 14 Q.B.D. 141

The plaintiff was here bringing an action for damage suffered by him in an accident when he was driving his cab. He had previously brought an action in the county court for damage to his cab. The defendant argued that he could not sue twice for the same wrongdoing.

BOWEN L.J.: . . . According to the popular use of language, the defendant's servant has done one act and one only, the driving of the one vehicle negligently against the other. But the rule of law . . . is not framed with reference to some popular expressions of the sort, but for the sake of preventing an abuse of substantial justice. Two separate kinds of injury were in fact inflicted, and two wrongs done. The mere negligent driving in itself, if accompanied by no injury to the plaintiff, was not actionable at all, for it was not a wrongful act at all till a wrong arose out of the damage which it caused. One wrong was done as soon as the plaintiff's enjoyment of his property was substantially interfered with. A further wrong arose as soon as the driving also caused injury to the plaintiff's person. . . . It certainly would appear unsatisfactory to hold that the damage done in a carriage accident to a man's portmanteau was the same injury as the damage done to his spine, or that an action under Lord Campbell's Act by the widow and children of a person who has been killed in a railway collision, is barred by proof that the deceased recovered in his lifetime for the damage done to his luggage. It may be said that it would be convenient to force persons to sue for all their grievances at once and not to split their demands; but there is no positive law (except so far as the County Court Acts have from a very early date dealt with the matter) against splitting demands which are essentially separable (see *Seddon* v. *Tutop* [47]), although the High Court has inherent power to prevent vexation or oppression, and by staying proceedings or by apportioning the costs, would have always ample means of preventing any injustice arising out of the reckless use of legal procedure. . . .

[47] (1796) 6 Term.Rep. 607; 101 E.R. 729.

LORD COLERIDGE C.J. (dissenting): . . . [I]t seems to me a subtlety not warranted by law to hold that a man cannot bring two actions, if he is injured in his arm and in his leg, but can bring two, if besides his arm and leg being injured his trousers which contain his leg, and his coat-sleeve which contains his arm, have been torn. The consequences of holding this are so serious, and may be very probably so oppressive, that I at least must respectfully dissent from a judgment which establishes it.

Darley Main Colliery Co. v. Mitchell
House of Lords (1886) 11 App.Cas. 127

LORD HALSBURY: . . . No one will think of disputing the proposition that for one cause of action you must recover all damages incident to it by law once and for ever. A house that has received a shock may not at once shew all the damage done to it, but it is damaged none the less then to the extent that it is damaged, and the fact that the damage only manifests itself later on by stages does not alter the fact that the damage is there; and so of the more complex mechanism of the human frame, the damage is done in a railway accident, the whole machinery is injured, though it may escape the eye or even the consciousness of the sufferer at the time; the later stages of suffering are but the manifestations of the original damage done, and consequent upon the injury originally sustained. But the words "cause of action" are somewhat ambiguously used in reasoning upon this subject; what the plaintiff has a right to complain of in a Court of Law in this case is the damage to his land, and by *the* damage I mean the damage which had in fact occurred, and if this is all that a plaintiff can complain of, I do not see why he may not recover toties quoties fresh damage is inflicted. Since the decision of this House in *Backhouse* v. *Bonomi* [48] it is clear that no action would lie for the excavation. It is not, therefore, a cause of action; that case established that it is the damage and not the excavation which is the cause of action. I cannot understand why every new subsidence, although proceeding from the same original act or omission of the defendants, is not a new cause of action for which damages may be recovered. . . . A man keeps a ferocious dog which bites his neighbour; can it be contended that when the bitten man brings his action he must assess damages for all possibility of future bites? A man stores water artificially, as in *Fletcher* v. *Rylands* [49]; the water escapes and sweeps away the plaintiff's house; he rebuilds it, and the artificial reservoir continues to leak and sweeps it away again. Cannot the plaintiff recover for the second house, or must he have assessed in his first damages the possibility of any future invasion of water flowing from the same reservoir? ..

In *West Leigh Colliery Co. Ltd.* v. *Tunnicliffe & Hampson Ltd.* [50] Lord Macnaghten, having cited Lord Halsbury in the case above noted:

If this be so, it seems to follow that depreciation in the value of the surface owner's property brought about by apprehension of future damage gives no cause of action by itself. . . . But if depreciation caused by apprehension of future mischief does not furnish a cause of action by itself, because there is no legal wrong, though the damage may be very great, it is difficult to see how the missing element can be supplied

---

[48] (1861) 9 H.L.Cas. 503.
[49] (1866) L.R. 1 Ex. 265.
[50] [1908] A.C. 27.

by presenting the claim in respect of depreciation tacked on to a claim in respect of a wrong admittedly actionable.

ASSESSMENT OF DAMAGES

Difficulty of assessment no bar to recovery

Chaplin v. Hicks

Court of Appeal [1911] 2 K.B. 786

In a competition among newspaper readers the plaintiff had reached the last fifty from which twelve winners were to be chosen. She claimed that the defendant had robbed her of her chance to be one of those by failing to give her sufficient notice, in breach of contract.

VAUGHAN WILLIAMS L.J.: . . . It was said that the plaintiff's chance of winning a prize turned on such a number of contingencies that it was impossible for anyone . . . to say that there was any assessable value of that loss. . . . I am unable to agree with that contention. I agree that the presence of all the contingencies upon which the gaining of the prize might depend makes the calculation not only difficult but incapable of being carried out with certainty or precision. . . . I do not agree with the contention that, if certainty is impossible of attainment, the damages for a breach of contract are unassessable. . . . In the case of a breach of contract for the delivery of goods the damages are usually supplied by the fact of there being a market in which similar goods can be immediately bought, and the difference between the contract price and the price given for the substituted goods in the open market is the measure of damages. . . . Sometimes, however, there is no market for the particular class of goods; but no one has ever suggested that, because there is no market, there are no damages. . . . [T]he fact that damages cannot be assessed with certainty does not relieve the wrong-doer of the necessity of paying damages. . . . There are cases, no doubt, where the loss is so dependent on the mere unrestricted volition of another that it is impossible to say that there is any assessable loss resulting from the breach. In the present case there is no such difficulty. It is true that no market can be said to exist. None of the fifty competitors could have gone into the market and sold her right; her right was a personal right and incapable of transfer. But a jury might well take the view that such a right, if it could have been transferred, would have been of such a value that everyone would have recognised that a good price could be obtained for it. . . .

FLETCHER MOULTON L.J.: . . . It is impossible in many cases to regard the damage that has followed the breach as that for which the plaintiff is to be compensated, for the injury to the plaintiff may depend on matters which have nothing to do with the defendant. For example, an innkeeper furnishes a chaise to a son to drive to see his dying father; the chaise breaks down; the son arrives too late to see his father, who has cut him out of his will in his disappointment at his not coming to see him; in such a case it is obvious that the actual damage to the plaintiff has nothing to do with the contract to supply the chaise. Therefore at an early stage the limitation was imposed that damages for breach of a contract must be such as might naturally be supposed to be in the contemplation of the parties at the time the contract was entered into; damages, in order to be recoverable, must be such as arise out of the contract and are not extraneous to it. This limitation has been appealed to here. It has been contended in the present case that the damages are too remote; that they are not the natural consequences of a breach with regard to which the parties intended to contract. To my mind the contention that they are too remote is unsustainable. The very object and scope of the contract were to give the plaintiff the chance of being selected as a prize-winner, and the refusal of that chance is the breach of contract complained of and in respect of which damages are claimed as compensation for the exclusion of the plaintiff from the limited class of competitors.

In *Cook* v. *S.*[51] the court awarded £160 for loss of maintenance money for which the defendant solicitor had failed to apply and £200 because the defendant had failed to put in a defence to a petition for divorce and failed to enter a cross petition for divorce on the ground of adultery when the petitioner put in a discretion statement. Lord Denning M.R. said:

> What damages should be obtainable? That depends on what were the prospects of a successful outcome. The judge said that, even if the case had been fought, the probabilities were that the husband would still have got a divorce on the ground of desertion. That may be true; but there was quite a chance that both might have got decrees, the husband on the ground of the plaintiff's desertion, and the plaintiff on the ground of the husband's adultery. There was an outside possibility of the plaintiff herself getting a decree. She is entitled to general damages for the loss of the chance of a more favourable outcome, for the simple reason that it does affect a person's standing to be found the guilty party instead of the innocent party. The judge assessed the damages on this loss at £200. That was essentially a matter for him. I do not think we should interfere with the figure. . . .

Scott v. Musial

Court of Appeal [1959] 2 Q.B. 429

MORRIS L.J.: . . . When someone has suffered the torment of having his body so crushed or battered that the whole course of his life will be changed, it is a task of supreme difficulty to endeavour to assess the monetary sum which will fairly compensate him. A judge or jury can but essay to preserve a sense of proportion, of moderation, and of fairness. It will be reasonable to bear in mind what relation the injuries under consideration bear to other injuries to which the misfortunes of life may make man subject. It will be essential to make calm reason gain the mastery over the urges which pity may inspire. It will be necessary to harness those qualities of balanced common sense which form a sure guide to decision.

West v. Shepherd

House of Lords [1964] A.C. 326

LORD MORRIS OF BORTH-Y-GEST: . . . My Lords, the damages which are to be awarded for a tort are those which, " so far as money can compensate will give the injured party reparation for the wrongful act and for all the natural and

---

[51] [1967] 1 All E.R. 299; *cf. Hall* v. *Meyrick* [1957] 2 Q.B. 455.

direct consequences of the wrongful act." (*Admiralty Commissioners* v. *S.S. Susquehanna* [52]). The words " so far as money can compensate " point to the impossibility of equating money with human suffering or personal deprivations. A money award can be calculated so as to make good a financial loss. Money may be awarded so that something tangible may be procured to replace something else of like nature which has been destroyed or lost. But money cannot renew a physical frame that has been battered and shattered. All that judges and courts can do is to award sums which must be regarded as giving reasonable compensation. In the process there must be the endeavour to secure some uniformity in the general method of approach. By common assent awards must be reasonable and must be assessed with moderation. Furthermore, it is eminently desirable that so far as possible comparable injuries should be compensated by comparable awards. When all this is said it still must be that amounts which are awarded are to a considerable extent conventional. . . .

The Quantum of Damages

Quantum in Contract

Dunlop Pneumatic Tyre Co. Ltd. v. New Garage and Motor Co. Ltd.

House of Lords [1915] A.C. 79

The courts will enforce a provision in the original contract which fixes the sum payable in the event of breach provided it does not amount to a " penalty."

Lord Dunedin : . . . My Lords, we had the benefit of a full and satisfactory argument, and a citation of the very numerous cases which have been decided on this branch of the law. The matter has been handled, and at no distant date, in the Courts of highest resort. I particularly refer to the *Clydebank* case [53] in your Lordships' House and the cases of *Public Works Commissioner* v. *Hills* [54] and *Webster* v. *Bosanquet* [55] in the Privy Council. In both of these cases many of the previous cases were considered . . . I shall content myself with stating succinctly the various propositions which I think are deducible from the decisions which rank as authoritative :

1. Though the parties to a contract who use the words " penalty " or " liquidated damages " may prima facie be supposed to mean what they say, yet the expression used is not conclusive. The Court must find out whether the payment stipulated is in truth a penalty or liquidated damages. This doctrine may be said to be found passim in nearly every case.

2. The essence of a penalty is a payment of money stipulated as in terrorem of the offending party; the essence of liquidated damages is a genuine covenanted pre-estimate of damage (*Clydebank Engineering and Shipbuilding Co.* v. *Don Jose Ramos Yzquierdo Y Castaneda*).

3. The question whether a sum stipulated is penalty or liquidated damages is a question of construction to be decided upon the terms and inherent circumstances of each particular contract, judged of as at the time of the making of

---

[52] [1926] A.C. 655, 661.
[54] [1906] A.C. 368.
[53] [1905] A.C. 6.
[55] [1912] A.C. 394.

the contract, not as at the time of the breach (*Public Works Commissioner* v. *Hills* and *Webster* v. *Bosanquet*).

4. To assist this task of construction various tests have been suggested, which if applicable to the case under consideration may prove helpful, or even conclusive. Such are:

(*a*) It will be held to be penalty if the sum stipulated for is extravagant and unconscionable in amount in comparison with the greatest loss that could conceivably be proved to have followed from the breach. (Illustration given by Lord Halsbury in *Clydebank* case.)

(*b*) It will be held to be a penalty if the breach consists only in not paying a sum of money, and the sum stipulated is a sum greater than the sum which ought to have been paid (*Kemble* v. *Farren* [56]). This though one of the most ancient instances is truly a corollary to the last test. Whether it had its historical origin in the doctrine of the common law that when A promised to pay B a sum of money on a certain day and did not do so B could only recover the sum with, in certain cases, interest, but could never recover further damages for non-timeous payment, or whether it was a survival of the time when equity reformed unconscionable bargains merely because they were unconscionable—a subject which much exercised Jessel M.R. in *Wallis* v. *Smith* [57]—is probably more interesting than material.

(*c*) There is a presumption (but no more) that it is a penalty when " a simple lump sum is made payable by way of compensation on the occurrence of one or more or all of several events, some of which may occasion serious and others but trifling damage " (Lord Watson in *Lord Elphinstone* v. *Monkland Iron and Coal Co.* [58]).

On the other hand,

(*d*) It is no obstacle to the sum stipulated being a genuine pre-estimate of damage that the consequences of the breach are such as to make precise pre-estimation almost an impossibility. On the contrary, that is just the situation when it is probable that pre-estimated damage was the true bargain between the parties. [59]

[*Cf. Campbell Discount Co. Ltd.* v. *Bridge.* [60]]

British Westinghouse Electric and Manufacturing Co. Ltd. v. Underground Electric Railways Company of London Ltd.

House of Lords [1912] A.C. 673

VISCOUNT HALDANE L.C.: . . . The quantum of damage is a question of fact, and the only guidance the law can give is to lay down general principles which afford at times but scanty assistance in dealing with particular cases. . . . Subject to these observations I think that there are certain broad principles which are quite well settled. The first is that, as far as possible, he who has proved a breach of a bargain to supply what he contracted to get is to be placed, as far as money can do it, in as good a situation as if the contract had been performed. The fundamental basis is thus compensation for pecuniary loss naturally flowing from the breach; but this first principle is qualified by a second, which imposes on a plaintiff the duty of taking all reasonable steps to mitigate the loss consequent on the breach, and debars him from claiming any part of the damage

---

[56] (1829) 6 Bing. 141.
[57] (1882) 21 Ch.D. 243.
[58] (1886) 11 App.Cas. 332.
[59] *Clydebank* case, Lord Halsbury [1905] A.C. 11; *Webster* v. *Bosanquet*, Lord Hersey [1912] A.C. 398.
[60] [1962] A.C. 600.

which is due to his neglect to take such steps. In the words of James L.J. in *Dunkirk Colliery Co.* v. *Lever*,[61] " The person who has broken the contract is not to be exposed to additional cost by reason of the plaintiffs not doing what they ought to have done as reasonable men. . . ."

[T]his second principle does not impose on the plaintiff an obligation to take any step which a reasonable and prudent man would not ordinarily take in the course of his business. But when in the course of his business he has taken action arising out of the transaction, which action has diminished his loss, the effect in actual diminution of the loss he has suffered may be taken into account even though there was no duty on him to act. . . . The subsequent transaction, if to be taken into account, must be one arising out of the consequences of the breach and in the ordinary course of business. This distinguishes such cases from a quite different class illustrated by *Bradburn* v. *Great Western Railway Co.*,[62] where it was held that, in an action for injuries caused by the defendants' negligence, a sum received by the plaintiff on a policy for insurance against accident could not be taken into account in reduction of damages. The reason of the decision was that it was not the accident, but a contract wholly independent of the relation between the plaintiff and the defendant, which gave the plaintiff his advantage.

Again, it has been held that, in an action for delay in discharging a ship of the plaintiffs' whereby they lost their passengers whom they had contracted to carry, the damages ought not to be reduced by reason of the same persons taking passage in another vessel belonging to the plaintiffs: *Jebsen* v. *East and West India Dock Co.*,[63] a case in which what was relied on as mitigation did not arise out of the transactions the subject-matter of the contract.

[LORDS ASHBOURNE, MACNAGHTEN AND ATKINSON concurred.]

Addis v. Gramophone Company Ltd.

[1909] A.C. 488

LORD ATKINSON : . . . I have always understood that damages for breach of contract were in the nature of compensation, not punishment. . . . There are three well-known exceptions to the general rule . . . namely, actions against a banker for refusing to pay a customer's cheque when he has in his hands funds of the customer's to meet it,[64] actions for breach of promise of marriage, and actions like that in *Flureau* v. *Thornhill*,[65] where the vendor of real estate, without any fault on his part, fails to make title. I know of none other. The peculiar nature of the first two of these exceptions justified their existence. Ancient practice upholds the last, though it has often been adversely criticised, as in *Bain* v. *Fothergill*.[66] If there be a tendency to create a fourth exception it ought, in my view, to be checked rather than stimulated. . . .

[I]n actions of tort motive . . . may be taken into account to aggregate damages . . . [and] to mitigate them, as may also the conduct of the plaintiff himself who seeks redress. Is this rule to be applied to actions of breach of contract? There are few breaches of contract more common than those which arise

---

[61] (1878) 9 Ch.D. 20, 25.
[62] (1874) L.R. 10 Ex. 1.
[63] (1875) L.R. 10 C.P. 300.
[64] This is now limited to cases where the customer is a trader: *Gibbons* v. *Westminster Bank* [1939] 2 K.B. 882. Actions for breach of promise have been abolished.
[65] (1776) 2 W.Bl. 1078.
[66] (1874) L.R. 7 H.L. 158.

where men omit or refuse to repay what they have borrowed, or to pay for what they have bought. Is the creditor or vendor who sues for one of such breaches to have the sum he recovers lessened if he should be shewn to be harsh, grasping, or pitiless, or even insulting, in enforcing his demand, or lessened because the debtor has struggled to pay, has failed because of misfortune, and has been suave, gracious, and apologetic in his refusal? On the other hand, is that sum to be increased if it should be shewn that the debtor could have paid readily without any embarrassment, but refused with expression of contempt and contumely, from a malicious desire to injure his creditor? Few parties to contracts have more often to complain of ingratitude and baseness than sureties. Are they, because of this, to be entitled to recover from the principal, often a trusted friend, who has deceived and betrayed them, more than they paid on that principal's behalf?

[LORDS LOREBURN L.C., JAMES OF HEREFORD, GORELL AND SHAW OF DUNFERMLINE delivered concurring judgments. LORD COLLINS dissented.]

Quantum in Tort

Personal injuries

British Transport Commission v. Gourley

[1956] A.C. 185

LORD GODDARD: ... In an action for personal injuries the damages are always divided into two main parts. First, there is what is referred to as special damage, which has to be specially pleaded and proved. This consists of out-of-pocket expenses and loss of earnings incurred down to the date of trial, and is generally capable of substantially exact calculation. Secondly, there is general damage which the law implies and is not especially pleaded. This includes compensation for pain and suffering and the like, and, if the injuries suffered are such as to lead to continuing or permanent disability, compensation for loss of earning power in the future. ...

LORD REID (dissenting): ... [D]amages must be assessed as a lump sum once and for all, not only in respect of loss accrued before the trial, but also in respect of prospective loss. Such damages can only be an estimate, often a very rough estimate, of the present value of his prospective loss.

Law Commission Working Paper 41 : Personal Injury Litigation : Assessment of Damages

9. The framework within which negotiated settlements are achieved is provided by the judges, who have devised a more or less precise conventional scale for the compensation of the non-pecuniary loss involved in specific injuries, and methods for the computation of pecuniary loss. This scale and these methods are comparatively easily applied in most cases. If it were not possible to settle cases in the numbers that are at present settled, the courts would be overwhelmed with personal injury litigation. Without prejudging the questions which arise as to the way in which the scale is made, the evaluations found therein or the correctness of the methods devised, we think it extremely important, therefore,

to continue to provide in the system for the assessment of damages sufficient certainty to enable settlements to be negotiated. . . .

96. . . . [T]he judges have achieved a high degree of uniformity. . . . Uniformity as Diplock L.J. pointed out in *Hennell* v. *Ranaboldo* [67] is maintained by the existence of a consensus between judges and by the Court of Appeal's power to alter a judge's award if it is out of line with current patterns. Judges and members of the Bar are also in the habit of discussing awards among themselves, and of regularly consulting certain publications which classify awards and make a wider selection of them accessible than do the Law Reports. . . .

Hennell v. Ranaboldo
Court of Appeal [1963] 1 W.L.R. 1391

DIPLOCK L.J.: . . . When one is translating physical injuries into pounds, shillings and pence one is seeking to equate the incommensurable. There is no absolutely right answer. The answer can only be an empirical one and depends on a general consensus of damage-awarding tribunals as to what is the proper measure of recompense in pounds, shillings and pence for pain and suffering, physical injuries, lack of amenities and the like. Justice is not done between the plaintiff and the defendant in a particular action unless the award of compensation, if any, is in reasonably close approximation to that empirical scale. . . . That scale is maintained at present in two ways: one, by the general consensus of opinion of judges trying these cases and the other by the ability to appeal to the Court of Appeal which, in a case tried by judge alone, can alter an award which is unreasonably out of scale and thus ensure that justice is done between the particular plaintiff and the particular defendant in the particular action which has been tried without putting the parties to the expense and delay of a new trial.

See also *Bastow* v. *Bagley & Co. Ltd.*[68] where the Court of Appeal had refused to alter the sum of £1,150 awarded by the trial judge even though they felt it lower than they would have awarded. Before final judgment was entered another division of the court increased an award in a comparable case from £850 to £2,200. The present division therefore met again and raised its figure to £1,800.

Wise v. Kaye
Court of Appeal [1962] 1 Q.B. 638

DIPLOCK L.J. (dissenting): . . . There are, I believe, two main empirical considerations which determine the maximum sum to be awarded for the worst injury that can be foreseen to occur; worst, in this context, meaning: causing the greatest amount of unhappiness to the victim.

The first consideration depends upon the social environment in which we live. In the days before insurance against liability for damages for personal injuries was almost universal it was useless to award damages greater than the defendant could pay; and if the datum were set so high that a substantial proportion of defendants could not pay the damages awarded in respect of very

[67] [1963] 1 W.L.R. 1391, 1393.
[68] [1961] 3 All E.R. 1101.

serious personal injuries, but only some lesser sum dependent on their individual means, the just proportion as between the damages recovered by one plaintiff and those recovered by another would seldom be achieved . . . ; and it was lest juries should in individual cases be tempted to depart from this scale and so work injustice as between the plaintiff and another that they were not allowed to be told whether a defendant was insured or not. Today, when the vast majority of defendants are insured, this consideration does not operate so directly. Insurance removes the immediate burden of paying damages from the individual defendants and spreads it ultimately over the general body of premium-paying policy-holders. Here it increases in most cases the general cost of goods and services, in some cases merely the cost of private motoring, with consequent hardship to the public as a whole. To avoid fixing the scale at a level which would materially affect the cost of living or disturb the current social pattern is a factor, Benthamite no doubt in origin, in the empirical process by which the maximum/datum is determined.

The second consideration stems from the conception that damages are awarded as compensation for the victim. So long as pecuniary damages are the only remedy the courts can give for loss of happiness we must assume that they are in some respects commensurate or that the possession of more money makes a man happier—an assumption on which the acquisitive habits of the human race under a money-economy are based. But even today we are sufficiently Aristotelian to believe that wealth beyond a moderate share is not usually conducive to happiness, and that to increase an award of damages beyond that moderate share could not, whatever use be made of it, ensure an additional happiness to a normal human being to compensate him for that of which he has been deprived by his personal injuries. What sum constitutes the golden mean of wealth will vary with current social conditions, and, in particular, the general standard of living. To avoid misunderstanding I would stress that these two empirical considerations which take into account the social environment and characteristics of what I may call the average plaintiff and the average defendant are directed solely to arriving at the yardstick to be used where loss of happiness is to be measured, as it must be by the court, in money. The cardinal principle is that there should be a just proportion between the damages awarded to one plaintiff and those awarded to another. Money is all that the court can award and equivalent losses of happiness, whoever the plaintiffs or defendants may be, should result in the award of equal sums. It would thus be wrong to award an individual plaintiff a greater or lesser sum according to whether or not the defendant was rich or poor, insured or uninsured. So, too, the fact that an individual plaintiff, as in this case, cannot use or in the case of a very rich or ascetic patient does not need the money damages is not a relevant factor. I agree with, and need not repeat what Upjohn L.J. has already said upon this topic.

The two considerations which I have discussed are, I think, the main factors which lead empirically, without precision but within broad limits, to the maximum figure which provides the datum for the proportion sum which is involved consciously or unconsciously in any estimate of damage for personal injuries. The common consensus of damage-awarding tribunals, today mainly judges but still occasionally juries, would appear to assess it at a figure of the order of £20,000 to £25,000, and an award of this order would include a substantial sum for loss of earnings and for additional expenses on care and nursing necessitated by the physical disability. Whether in accepting as appropriate this maximum the courts have taken sufficiently into account not only the fall in value of money but also the increase in the standard of living and the real value of the average wage may be debatable; but a figure of this order is, I think, the current maximum and thus the yardstick by which the propriety of the damages awarded to the respondent in the present case should be assessed.

Any attempt, such as I have sought to make, to analyse the principles on which damages for personal injuries are assessed tends to suggest that there is some precise formula by which the correctness of the damages awarded in a particular case can be judged. This, of course, is not so. There is inevitably a very wide margin for differences of opinion at each stage of the process of arriving at the appropriate figure in each particular case. It is impossible to say that any particular figure within that wide margin is more " right " than another. All that one can say is that it is " wrong " if it is out of all proportion to the damages currently awarded in other cases of personal injuries when judged by the criterion of the loss of happiness to the victim which is involved.

Fletcher v. Autocar and Transporters Ltd.
Court of Appeal [1968] 2 Q.B. 322

LORD DENNING M.R.: . . . Whilst I acknowledge the care which the judge devoted to this case, I think that his conclusion was erroneous. In the first place, I think he has attempted to give a perfect compensation in money, whereas the law says that he should not make that attempt. It is an impossible task. He should give a fair compensation. That was settled 90 years ago by *Phillips* v. *London & South Western Railway Co.*[69] . . . Field J. . . . said: " In actions for personal injuries of this kind . . . [p]erfect compensation is hardly possible, and would be unjust. You cannot put the plaintiff back again into his original position." This direction was approved by Cockburn C.J. . . . Those passages were quoted with approval by Lord Devlin in *H. West & Son Ltd.* v. *Shephard*,[70] and undoubtedly represent the law. It is true that in these days most defendants are insured and heavy awards do not ruin them. But small insurance companies can be ruined. Some have been. And large companies have to cover the claims by their premiums. If awards reach figures which are " daunting " in their immensity, premiums must be increased all the way round. The impact spreads through the body politic. Consider also the position of the plaintiff. He is the person entitled to be compensated. What good does all this money do for the poor plaintiff? He cannot use it all by any means. Halve it. Still he cannot use it in his lifetime. In order to give him fair compensation, I should have thought that he should be given a sum which would ensure that he would not . . . want for anything that money could buy; and that his wife should be able to live for the rest of her life in the comfort that he would have provided for her; and that any savings that he would have made if uninjured would be available for his family. . . .

DIPLOCK L.J.: . . . In *Wise* v. *Kaye* [71] I suggested that the common standard of comparison for assessing the degree of worsening was based upon the effect of the injuries on the happiness of the victim. But I was wrong: see the majority judgments in that case and the majority speeches in *H. West & Son Ltd.* v. *Shephard*. I think that the result of the decisions in these cases is that the standard of comparison which the law applies, if it is not wholly instinctive and incommunicable, is based, apart from pain and suffering, upon the degree of deprivation—that is, the extent to which the victim is unable to do those things which, but for the injury, he would have been able to do.

69 (1879) 4 Q.B.D. 406; (1879) 5 Q.B.D. 78, C.A.
70 [1964] A.C. 326.
71 [1962] 1 Q.B. 638, 665.

The use of actuarial evidence

Watson v. Powles

Court of Appeal [1968] 1 Q.B. 596

LORD DENNING M.R.:... The next point which Mr. Howe took was also important. He submitted it should be the general practice to work out the loss of future earnings on an actuarial basis with the assistance, if need be, of an actuary. This may sometimes be helpful, but I do not think it should be the general practice. Take this case. Mr. Howe put before us some figures giving the average working life of a working man. It would be more useful if he gave us the average life of a benchman with the South Durham Steel Company, and that was not available. If actuaries were called in on these cases, it would add much to the time and expense of the trial: and there are so many intangibles that it might not be found particularly helpful. I would add that none of Mr. Howe's figures were before the court below: and on this account alone I do not think we need go further into them now.

WINN L.J.:... I have listened with very great interest to the lucid and very pleasantly presented arguments of Mr. Geoffrey Howe and had, of course, read the article upon which he has relied in his submissions [Continuing Loss Element in Damages by J. C. Walker].[72] I read it when it was published with great interest and, if I may be allowed to say so, admiration for the original thinking that had been put by the author into that article and into his tables. I am sorry to say that I remain quite unconvinced that, at present at least, the actuarial approach or technique affords the court such a precise tool as it would desire to have in its hand, if it were by direction of this court or of their Lordships' House compelled to set aside instinct in favour of what has been called, attractively enough, by Mr. Geoffrey Howe, the rational approach so that justice may be done to plaintiffs, and no less to insurers and those who provide insurers with their working capital and it may be the taxpayers as a general body. Of course, one wants people who have been injured to receive proper compensation in accordance with the law, but I think what Mr. Geoffrey Howe is contending for would be a substantial alteration in the present law as to the proper procedure and the proper result of the process of assessment of damages. I cannot regard this set of figures or table as a precise instrument [The Length of Working Life of Males in Great Britain].[73] It was published in 1959. It gives a table as at 1955 showing, as at different ages, survivors in working life out of 10,000 males born. It, therefore, includes all Her Majesty's judges, or almost all of them, up to the age of 70 or some aged between 70 and 80, and it includes directors of companies proceeding to their offices in comfort, with no hazards of transport, save in so far as a substantial car might crumple in a collision, and not bound to retire or tender resignation until 70. My own opinion is that this table presents a very imprecise and therefore non-scientific mode of assessing damages for loss of earnings which would have been derived from employment but for the accident....

See also Lord Guest in *Taylor* v. *O'Connor* [74]:

> ... It has been suggested that a more precise method of arriving at the extent of the loss would be to obtain actuarial figures as to what sum would be required, based on the widow's expectancy of life, to

[72] 111 S.J. 223.
[73] Ministry of Labour and National Service, Official Statistics Study No. 4, H.M.S.O. 1959.
[74] [1971] A.C. 115.

purchase an annuity of the extent of the loss. This method has been disapproved in the past and never adopted except as a very rough guide. . . . I would not be in favour of its adoption for this or any similar type of case. This method would require actuarial evidence which would increase the length and expense of trials and would unduly complicate matters which might have to be considered by juries.

Other miscellaneous factors in assessing damages

In estimating future loss of earnings the incidence of tax is taken into account (*B.T.C.* v. *Gourley*[75]). This question was the subject of the Seventh Report of the Law Reform Committee 1958.[76] Unemployment benefit is also deducted but not supplementary social security benefit (*Parsons* v. *B.N.M. Laboratories Ltd.*[77]). The Law Reform (Personal Injuries) Act 1948 provides that one-half the value of any industrial injury benefit, industrial disablement benefit or sickness benefit received during the five years beginning when the cause of action accrued shall, in assessing damages for personal injuries, be taken into account against any loss of earnings or profit which has accrued or possibly will accrue. No reduction is made for any sum received as the result of a private insurance policy. It seems from *Taylor* v. *O'Connor*[78] that some account may be taken of inflation and other general financial trends. The judgment of Lord Morris illustrates some of the factors to be taken into account in deciding the appropriate sum to be awarded to a dependant under the Fatal Accidents Acts. The same reasoning would apply to an assessment of future loss of earnings.

Taylor v. O'Connor
[1971] A.C. 115

LORD REID: . . . It will be observed that I have more than once taken note of present-day conditions—in particular rising prices, rising remuneration and high rates of interest. I am well aware that there is a school of thought which holds that the law should refuse to have any regard to inflation but that calculations should be based on stable prices, steady or slowly increasing rates of remuneration and low rates of interest. That must, I think, be based either on an expectation of an early return to a period of stability or on a nostalgic reluctance to recognise change. It appears to me that some people fear that inflation will get worse, some think that it will go on much as at present, some hope that it will be slowed down, but comparatively few believe that a return to the old financial stability is likely in the foreseeable future. To take any account of future inflation will no doubt cause complications and make estimates even more uncertain. No doubt we should not assume the worst but it would, I think, be quite unrealistic to refuse to take it into account at all.

LORD MORRIS: . . . On these facts what sum was it reasonable for the learned judge to award? It would, in my view, be a sum having reference both to the

75 [1956] A.C. 185.
76 Cmnd. 501.
77 [1964] 1 Q.B. 95.
78 [1971] A.C. 115; below.

annual loss of benefit and also to the future loss of capital sums. The learned judge took both of these into computation. It is to be remembered that the sum which is awarded will be a once-for-all or final amount which the widow must deploy so that to the extent reasonably possible she gets the equivalent of what she has lost. A learned judge cannot be expected to prophesy as to future monetary trends or rates of interest but he need not be unmindful of matters which are common knowledge, such as the uncertainties as to future rates of interest and future levels of taxation. Taking a reasonable and realistic and commonsense view of all aspects of the matter he must try to fix a figure which is neither unfair to the recipient nor to the one who has to pay. A learned judge might well take the view that a recipient would be ill-advised if he entirely ignored all inflationary trends and if he applied the entire sum awarded to him in the purchase of an annuity which over a period of years would give him a fixed and predetermined sum without any provision which protected him against inflationary trends if they developed. A learned judge would be entitled to award a sum which would be gradually drawn upon over a number of years but which until exhausted would yield interest (though in annually decreasing amounts) and so would produce during each of the years the annual sum which he had decided to be the appropriate sum. Where, as in the present case, the figures being considered are large it would be necessary to have the incidence of tax in mind. The sum awarded is not to be regarded as a sum the capital of which can be kept intact and which for all future years will yield an annual income. The sum is one the capital of which will gradually be used up: but until it is so used up the current and remaining amount of it will produce interest. That interest will, however, bear tax. In the present case the annual amount which must be produced is the amount of £3,750 (taking the figure of the learned judge) as a net spendable figure.

The learned judge was disposed in the present case to take ten as the multiplier. He varied it to 12 because he considered that the present era is not one of stable money values. I would not regard that as a valid reason. Nor would I think that ten need be considered as unreasonably low in the present case. Learned judges have a range of experience in these matters and in a realm where there are many imponderables and where mathematical accuracy is not possible the recognised methods of approach have proved rational and workable. In fixing a multiplier judges do the best they can to make fair allowance for all the uncertainties and possibilities to which I have earlier referred. It may well be that in cases where high figures are involved courts could derive assistance from skilled evidence concerning ways in which a sum of money could be used and managed to the best advantage. Such evidence should, however, only afford a check or a guide. It could not resolve those matters which in the nature of things must be uncertain or decide those issues to which the art of judgment must be directed.

Periodic payments

Report of the Committee on Personal Injuries Litigation
Cmnd. 3691, 1968

374. . . . . [W]e would next like to consider whether it would be appropriate to introduce any scheme whereby awards of damages could be reviewed and increased or reduced from time to time. . . .

375. The experience of those who practised in Workmen's Compensation Acts cases does not, so far as we are aware, incline any of them to favour variable periodic payments as a method of compensating tortiously injured

persons. We are convinced that, in general, plaintiffs in personal injury actions, whether or not they are workers or are complaining of an industrial accident would prefer an out-and-out award to periodical variable payments; a lump sum can be used to acquire a business, such as a shop, or to discharge or reduce a mortgage.

376. The medical advice which we received and our own experience, fortified by that of a number of judges and leading counsel, strongly suggests that complete and rapid recovery may be seriously impeded in the case of many plaintiffs by continuing uncertainty as to periodic reassessment of their compensation.

377. We cannot rationally assess but feel bound to envisage that were the Court to have to entertain in every action or in many actions after judgment one or more applications supported and opposed on medical and other evidence for the variation upwards or downwards or the termination of periodical payments or, it may be, for their commutation for a capital sum the system would become unworkable. The increase in costs payable by the parties or the Legal Aid Fund and the additional judicial and ancillary manpower which would be necessitated would be so enormous as to be utterly unacceptable if not literally insupportable. For our part we reject any idea that awards should be made in the form of periodical payments.

See also W. R. Frank, "Employers' Liability in Great Britain " [79]:

Lump sum settlements were strenuously opposed by trade unions. They were objected to because they tended to unsettle the recipient by giving him what may have appeared to be a substantial sum of money. This capital sum was often improvidently invested or used up for daily expenditure, leaving the workman then dependent on the poor law. Many workmen resisted the offer of a lump sum settlement until the accumulation of debts forced them to give way. . . .

National Insurance (Industrial Injuries) Act 1965

1965, c. 52

5.—(1) Subject to the provisions of this Act, where an insured person suffers personal injury caused after 4th July 1948 by accident arising out of and in the course of his employment, being insurable employment, then—

(a) industrial injury benefit . . . shall be payable to the insured person if during such period as is hereinafter provided he is, as the result of the injury, incapable of work;

(b) industrial disablement benefit . . . by way of disablement gratuity or disablement pension shall be payable to the insured person if he suffers, as the result of the injury, from such loss of physical or mental faculty as is hereinafter provided;

(c) industrial death benefit . . . shall be payable to such persons as are hereinafter provided if the insured person dies as a result of injury. . . .

12.—(3) Where the extent of the disablement is assessed . . . as amounting to less than twenty per cent., disablement benefit shall be a disablement gratuity. . . .

(b) payable, if and in such cases as regulations so provide, by instalments.

[79] *Law and Contemporary Problems* 1954, p. 336.

Libel actions

McCarey v. Associated Newspapers

Court of Appeal [1965] 2 Q.B. 86

DIPLOCK L.J.:... In an action for defamation, the wrongful act is damage to the plaintiff's reputation. The injuries that he sustains may be classified under two heads: (1) the consequences of the attitude adopted towards him by other persons as a result of the diminution of the esteem in which they hold him because of the defamatory statement; and (2) the grief or annoyance caused by the defamatory statement to the plaintiff himself.... Under head (1)... it may be possible to prove pecuniary loss, such as loss of practice or employment, or inability to obtain fresh appointments.... But the major consequences under head (1) may be purely social and lie in the attitude adopted towards the plaintiff by persons with whom he comes into social or professional contact. Neither this kind of injury under head (1) nor the grief or annoyance caused to the plaintiff himself under head (2) involves pecuniary loss. In putting a money value on these kinds of injury... damage-awarding tribunals... are being required to attempt to equate the incommensurable. As in the case of damages for physical injuries, it is impossible to say that any answer looked at in isolation is right, or that any answer is wrong. But justice is not justice if it is arbitrary or whimsical, if what is awarded to one plaintiff for an injury bears no relation at all to what is awarded to another plaintiff for an injury of the same kind, or, I would add, if what is awarded for one kind of injury shows a wrong scale of values when compared with what is awarded for injuries of a different kind which are also incommensurable with pounds, shillings and pence. ... I am convinced that it is not just (and I do not think that it is the law ...) that in equating incommensurables when a man's reputation has been injured the scale of values to be applied bears no relation whatever to the scale of values to be applied when equating those other incommensurables, money and physical injuries. I do not believe that the law today is more jealous of a man's reputation than of his life or limb. That is the scale of values of the duel. Of course, the injuries in the two kinds of cases are very different, but each has as its main consequences pain or grief, annoyance or unhappiness, to the plaintiff. In this court recently we refused by a majority to disturb a verdict of a jury awarding £2,000 to a woman 30 years of age who had, after considerable suffering for many months and two operations in hospital, had a leg amputated below the knee, and her knee permanently immobilised. In that case it was the view of the Court of Appeal that a proper measure of damages, had the award been made by a judge, would have been in the neighbourhood of £4,000 to £6,000, a figure which is in scale with the amount of damages which are commonly awarded (and have been approved by this court) in serious physical injury cases. If £2,000 is not inappropriate, or if £4,000 to £6,000 is appropriate, compensation for a life-long injury of that character, which has its physical effect every day of the plaintiff's future life, and £9,000 is the appropriate award for the injury done to the plaintiff in this case, then I can only say that the scale of values is wrong, and if that is the law, so much the worse for the law. But I do not accept that that higher scale of values in defamation cases is sanctioned by the law. It is, I think, legitimate as an aid to considering whether the award of damages by a jury is so large that no reasonable jury could have arrived at that figure if they had applied proper principles to bear in mind the kind of figures which are proper, and have been held to be proper, in cases of disabling physical injuries. If, as I have said, figures much lower than that awarded in this case are the proper compensation for loss of an eye or limb, or for other life-long disabling injuries, a sum of £9,000 as compensation for this injury, serious, distressing and annoying though it was, but in any event evanescent and in this case followed by a vindication of the plaintiff's reputation at a time of his own choice, is a figure that no reasonable jury, applying correct principles which included a proper scale of values, could have reached.

Exemplary damages

Rookes v. Barnard

House of Lords [1964] A.C. 1129

LORD DEVLIN: . . . Exemplary damages are essentially different from ordinary damages. The object of damages in the usual sense of the term is to compensate. The object of exemplary damages is to punish and deter. It may well be thought that this confuses the civil and criminal functions of the law; and indeed, so far as I know, the idea of exemplary damages is peculiar to English law. There is not any decision of this House approving an award of exemplary damages and your Lordships therefore have to consider whether it is open to the House to remove an anomaly from the law of England.

It must be remembered that in many cases of tort damages are at large, that is to say, the award is not limited to the pecuniary loss than can be specifically proved. In the present case, for example, and leaving aside any question of exemplary or aggravated damages, the appellant's damages would not necessarily be confined to those which he would obtain in an action for wrongful dismissal. He can invite the jury to look at all the circumstances, the inconveniences caused to him by the change of job and the unhappiness maybe by a change of livelihood. In such a case as this, it is quite proper without any departure from the compensatory principle to award a round sum based on the pecuniary loss proved.

Moreover, it is very well established that in cases where the damages are at large the jury (or the judge if the award is left to him) can take into account the motives and conduct of the defendant where they aggravate the injury done to the plaintiff. There may be malevolence or spite or the manner of committing the wrong may be such as to injure the plaintiff's proper feelings of dignity and pride. These are matters which the jury can take into account in assessing the appropriate compensation. Indeed, when one examines the cases in which large damages have been awarded for conduct of this sort, it is not at all easy to say whether the idea of compensation or the idea of punishment has prevailed.

But there are also cases in the books where the awards given cannot be explained as compensatory, and I propose therefore to begin by examining the authorities in order to see how far and in what sort of cases the exemplary principle has been recognised. The history of exemplary damages is briefly and clearly stated by Professor Street in Principles of the Law of Damages (1962) at p. 28. They originated just 200 years ago in the cause célèbre of John Wilkes and the North Briton in which the legality of a general warrant was successfully challenged. Mr. Wilkes' house had been searched under a general warrant and the action of trespass which he brought as a result of it is reported in *Wilkes* v. *Wood*.[80] Serjeant Glynn on his behalf asked for "large and exemplary damages," since trifling damages, he submitted, would put no stop at all to such proceedings. Pratt C.J., in his direction to the jury, said: "Damages are designed not only as a satisfaction to the injured person, but likewise as a punishment to the guilty, to deter from any such proceeding for

[80] (1763) Lofft. 1.

the future, and as a proof of the detestation of the jury to the action itself." The jury awarded £1,000. . . .

[T]he authorities convince me of two things. First, that your Lordships could not, without a complete disregard of precedent, and indeed of statute, now arrive at a determination that refused altogether to recognise the exemplary principle. Secondly, that there are certain categories of cases in which an award of exemplary damages can serve a useful purpose in vindicating the strength of the law and thus affording a practical justification for admitting into the civil law a principle which ought logically to belong to the criminal. . . . I am well aware that what I am about to say will, if accepted, impose limits not hitherto expressed on such awards and that there is powerful, though not compelling, authority for allowing them a wider range. . . .

The first category is oppressive, arbitrary or unconstitutional action by the servants of the government. I should not extend this category—I say this with particular reference to the facts of this case—to oppressive action by private corporations or individuals. Where one man is more powerful than another, it is inevitable that he will try to use his power to gain his ends; and if his power is much greater than the other's, he might, perhaps, be said to be using it oppressively. If he uses his power illegally, he must of course pay for his illegality in the ordinary way; but he is not to be punished simply because he is the more powerful. In the case of the government it is different, for the servants of the government are also the servants of the people and the use of their power must always be subordinate to their duty of service. It is true that there is something repugnant about a big man bullying a small man and, very likely, the bullying will be a source of humiliation that makes the case one for aggravated damages, but it is not, in my opinion, punishable by damages.

Cases in the second category are those in which the defendant's conduct has been calculated by him to make a profit for himself which may well exceed the compensation payable to the plaintiff. . . . It is a factor also that is taken into account in damages for libel; one man should not be allowed to sell another man's reputation for profit. Where a defendant with a cynical disregard for a plaintiff's rights has calculated that the money to be made out of his wrong-doing will probably exceed the damages at risk, it is necessary for the law to show that it cannot be broken with impunity. This category is not confined to moneymaking in the strict sense. It extends to cases in which the defendant is seeking to gain at the expense of the plaintiff some object—perhaps some property which he covets—which either he could not obtain at all or not obtain except at a price greater than he wants to put down. Exemplary damages can properly be awarded whenever it is necessary to teach a wrongdoer that tort does not pay.

To these two categories which are established as part of the common law there must of course be added any category in which exemplary damages are expressly authorised by statute.

I wish now to express three considerations which I think should always be borne in mind when awards of exemplary damages are being considered. First, the plaintiff cannot recover exemplary damages unless he is the victim of the punishable behaviour. The anomaly inherent in exemplary damages would become an absurdity if a plaintiff totally unaffected by some oppressive conduct which the jury wished to punish obtained a windfall in consequence.

Secondly, the power to award exemplary damages constitutes a weapon that, while it can be used in defence of liberty, as in the *Wilkes* case, can also be used against liberty. Some of the awards that juries have made in the past seem to me to amount to a greater punishment than would be likely to be incurred if the conduct were criminal; and, moreover, a punishment imposed without the safeguard which the criminal law gives to an offender. I should not allow the respect which is traditionally paid to an assessment of damages by a jury to prevent me from seeing that the weapon is used with restraint. It may even be that the House may find it necessary to follow the precedent it set for itself in *Benham* v. *Gambling*,[81] and place some arbitrary limit on awards of damages that are made by way of punishment. Exhortations to be moderate may not be enough.

Thirdly, the means of the parties, irrelevant in the assessment of compensation, are material in the assessment of exemplary damages. Everything which aggravates or mitigates the defendant's conduct is relevant.

Thus a case for exemplary damages must be presented quite differently from one for compensatory damages; and the judge should not allow it to be left to the jury unless he is satisfied that it can be brought within the categories I have specified. But the fact that the two sorts of damage differ essentially does not necessarily mean that there should be two awards. In a case in which exemplary damages are appropriate, a jury should be directed that if, but only if, the sum which they have in mind to award as compensation (which may, of course, be a sum aggravated by the way in which the defendant has behaved to the plaintiff) is inadequate to punish him for his outrageous conduct, to mark their disapproval of such conduct and to deter him from repeating it, then it can award some larger sum. If a verdict given on such direction has to be reviewed upon appeal, the appellate court will first consider whether the award can be justified as compensation and if it can, there is nothing further to be said. If it cannot, the court must consider whether or not the punishment is, in all the circumstances, excessive. There may be cases in which it is difficult for a judge to say whether or not he ought to leave to the jury a claim for exemplary damages. In such circumstances, and in order to save the possible expense of a new trial, I see no objection to his inviting the jury to say what sum they would fix as compensation and what additional sum, if any, they would award if they were entitled to give exemplary damages. That is the course which he would have to take in a claim to which the Law Reform (Miscellaneous Provisions) Act, 1934, applied. . . .

Broome v. Cassell

House of Lords [1972] A.C. 1027

LORD HAILSHAM L.C.: . . . Of all the various remedies available at common law, damages are the remedy of most general application at the present day, and they remain the prime remedy in actions for breach of contract and tort. They have been defined as " the pecuniary compensation obtainable by success in an action for a wrong which is either a tort or a breach of contract." They must normally be expressed in a single sum to take account of all the factors applicable to each cause of action and must of course be expressed in English currency : *Mayne and MacGregor on Damages*, 12th ed. (1961), para. 1.

In almost all actions for breach of contract, and in many actions for tort, the principle of restitutio in integrum is an adequate and fairly easy guide to the estimation of damage, because the damage suffered can be estimated by relation to some material loss. It is true that where loss includes a pre-estimate of future losses, or an estimate of past losses which cannot in the nature of things be exactly computed, some subjective element must enter in. But the estimate is in things commensurable with one another, and convertible at least in principle

[81] [1941] A.C. 157.

to the English currency in which all sums of damages must ultimately be expressed.

In many torts, however, the subjective element is more difficult. The pain and suffering endured, and the future loss of amenity, in a personal injuries case are not in the nature of things convertible into legal tender. The difficulties arising in the paraplegic cases, or, before *Benham* v. *Gambling*,[82] in estimating the damages for loss of expectation of life in a person who died instantaneously, are only examples of the intrinsically impossible task set judges or juries in such matters. Clearly the £50,000 award upheld in *Morey* v. *Woodfield (No. 2) (Note)*[83] could never compensate the victim of such an accident. Nor, so far as I can judge, is there any purely rational test by which a judge can calculate what sum, greater or smaller, is appropriate. What is surprising is not that there is difference of opinion about such matters, but that in most cases professional opinion gravitates so closely to a conventional scale. Nevertheless in all actions in which damages, purely compensatory in character, are awarded for suffering, from the purely pecuniary point of view the plaintiff may be better off. The principle of restitutio in integrum, which compels the use of money as its sole instrument for restoring the status quo, necessarily involves a factor larger than any pecuniary loss.

In actions of defamation and in any other actions where damages for loss of reputation are involved, the principle of restitutio in integrum has necessarily an even more highly subjective element. Such actions involve a money award which may put the plaintiff in a purely financial sense in a much stronger position than he was before the wrong. Not merely can he recover the estimated sum of his past and future losses, but, in case the libel, driven underground, emerges from its lurking place at some future date, he must be able to point to a sum awarded by a jury sufficient to convince a bystander of the baselessness of the charge. . . . This is why it is not necessarily fair to compare awards of damages in this field with damages for personal injuries. Quite obviously, the award must include factors for injury to the feelings, the anxiety and uncertainty undergone in the litigation, the absence of apology, or the reaffirmation of the truth of the matters complained of, or the malice of the defendant. The bad conduct of the plaintiff himself may also enter into the matter, where he has provoked the libel, or where perhaps he has libelled the defendant in reply. What is awarded is thus a figure which cannot be arrived at by any purely objective computation. This is what is meant when the damages in defamation are described as being " at large." In a sense, too, these damages are of their nature punitive or exemplary in the loose sense in which the terms were used before 1964, because they inflict an added burden on the defendant proportionate to his conduct, just as they can be reduced if the defendant has behaved well—as for instance by a handsome apology—or the plaintiff badly, as for instance by provoking the defendant, or defaming him in return. In all such cases it must be appropriate to say with Lord Esher M.R. in *Praed* v. *Graham*[84]:

> " . . . in actions of libel . . . the jury in assessing damages are entitled to look at the whole conduct of the defendant " (I would personally add " and of the plaintiff ") " from the time the libel was published down to the time they give their verdict. They may consider what his conduct has been before action, after action, and in court during the trial."

It is this too which explains the almost indiscriminate use of " at large," " aggravated," " exemplary " and " punitive " before *Rookes* v. *Barnard*.[85] . . .

---

[82] [1941] A.C. 157.
[83] [1964] 1 W.L.R. 16.
[84] (1889) 24 Q.B.D. 53, 55.
[85] [1964] A.C. 1129.

It was not until Lord Devlin's speech in *Rookes* v. *Barnard* that the expressions "aggravated," on the one hand, and "punitive" or "exemplary," on the other, acquired separate and mutually exclusive meanings as terms of art in English law.

The next point to notice is that it has always been a principle of English law that the award of damages when awarded must be a single lump sum in respect of each separate cause of action. Of course, where part of the damage can be precisely calculated, it is possible to isolate part of it in the same cause of action. It is also possible and desirable to isolate different sums of damages receivable in respect of different torts, as was done here in respect of the proof copies. But I must say I view with some distrust the arbitrary subdivision of different elements of general damages for the same tort as was done in *Loudon* v. *Ryder* [86] . . . In cases where the award of general damages contains a subjective element, I do not believe it is desirable or even possible simply to add separate sums together for different parts of the subjective element . . . [I]n the words of Windeyer J. in *Uren* v. *Fairfax & Sons Pty. Ltd.*[87]:

> "The variety of the matters which, it has been held, may be considered in assessing damages for defamation must in many cases mean that the amount of a verdict is the product of a mixture of *inextricable* considerations." (Italics again mine.)

In other words the whole process of assessing damages where they are "at large" is essentially a matter of impression and not addition.

The true explanation of *Rookes* v. *Barnard* is to be found in the fact that, where damages for loss of reputation are concerned, or where a simple outrage to the individual or to property is concerned, aggravated damages . . . can, and should in every case lying outside the categories, take care of the exemplary element. . . .

As regards the meaning of the particular categories, I have come to the conclusion that what Lord Devlin said was never intended to be treated as if his words were verbally inspired. . . . It may very well be that, in deciding in favour of the two exceptional categories, he was making an unnecessary concession to tradition. But he made the concession after a careful analysis of the authorities and, speaking for myself, and given the cautious approach indicated in Lord Gardiner L.C.'s practice declaration,[88] and by a majority of this House in *R.* v. *National Insurance Commissioner, ex parte Hudson*,[89] I do not think there is any reason for disturbing them. . . .

I regard it as extremely important that, for the future, judges should make sure in their direction to juries that the jury is fully aware of the danger of an excessive award. . . . Damages remain a civil, and not a criminal remedy, even where an exemplary award is appropriate, and juries should not be encouraged to lose sight of the fact that, in making such an award they are putting money into a plaintiff's pocket, and not contributing to the rates, or to the revenue of central government. . . .

Rookes v. *Barnard* has not perhaps proved quite the definitive statement of the law which was hoped when it was decided. This is often the case. I remember . . . that in his judgment in *Robert Addie & Sons (Collieries) Ltd.* v. *Dumbreck* [90] my father believed he was putting a final end to the debate about the limits of occupiers' liability to trespassers, licensees and invitees. But the way forward lies through a considered precedent and not backwards from it. . . .

[86] [1953] 2 Q.B. 202.
[87] (1965) 117 C.L.R. 118, 150.
[88] [1966] 1 W.L.R. 1234.
[89] [1972] A.C. 944.
[90] [1929] A.C. 358.

LORD REID: . . . The whole matter of exemplary damages was dealt with in this House in *Rookes* v. *Barnard* in a speech by Lord Devlin with which all who sat with him, including myself, concurred. . . .

The very full argument which we have had in this case has not caused me to change the views which I held when *Rookes* v. *Barnard* was decided or to disagree with any of Lord Devlin's main conclusions. But it has convinced me that I and my colleagues made a mistake in simply concurring with Lord Devlin's speech. With the passage of time I have come more and more firmly to the conclusion that it is never wise to have only one speech in this House dealing with an important question of law. My main reason is that experience has shown that those who have to apply the decision to other cases and still more those who wish to criticise it seem to find it difficult to avoid treating sentences and phrases in a single speech as if they were provisions in an Act of Parliament. They do not seem to realise that it is not the function of noble and learned Lords or indeed of any judges to frame definitions or to lay down hard and fast rules. It is their function to enunciate principles and much that they say is intended to be illustrative or explanatory and not to be definitive. When there are two or more speeches they must be read together and then it is generally much easier to see what are the principles involved and what are merely illustrations of it.

I am bound to say that, in reading the various criticisms of Lord Devlin's speech to which we have been referred, I have been very surprised at the failure of its critics to realise that it was intended to state principles and not to lay down rules. But I suppose that those of us who merely concurred with him ought to have foreseen that this might happen and to have taken steps to prevent it. So I shall try to repair my omission by stating now in a different way the principles which I, and I believe also Lord Devlin, had in mind. I do not think that he would have disagreed with any important part of what I am now about to say. . . .

It has long been recognised that in determining what sum within that bracket should be awarded, a jury, or other tribunal, is entitled to have regard to the conduct of the defendant. He may have behaved in a high-handed, malicious, insulting or oppressive manner in committing the tort or he or his counsel may at the trial have aggravated the injury by what they there said. That would justify going to the top of the bracket and awarding as damages the largest sum that could fairly be regarded as compensation.

Frequently in cases before *Rookes* v. *Barnard*, when damages were increased in that way but were still within the limit of what could properly be regarded as compensation to the plaintiff, it was said that punitive, vindictive or exemplary damages were being awarded. As a mere matter of language that was true enough. The defendant was being punished or an example was being made of him by making him pay more than he would have had to pay if his conduct had not been outrageous. But the damages though called punitive were still truly compensatory: the plaintiff was not being given more than his due.

On the other hand when we came to examine the old cases we found a number which could not be explained in that way. The sums awarded as damages were more—sometimes much more—than could on any view be justified as compensatory, and courts, perhaps without fully realising what they were doing, appeared to have permitted damages to be measured not by what the plaintiff was fairly entitled to receive but by what the defendant ought to be made to pay as punishment for his outrageous conduct.

That meant that the plaintiff, by being given more than on any view could be justified as compensation, was being given a pure and undeserved windfall at the expense of the defendant, and that in so far as the defendant was being required to pay more than could possibly be regarded as compensation he was being subjected to pure punishment.

I thought and still think that that is highly anomalous. It is confusing the function of the civil law which is to compensate with the function of the criminal law which is to inflict deterrent and punitive penalties. . . .

Those of us who sat in *Rookes* v. *Barnard* thought that the loose and confused use of words like punitive and exemplary and the failure to recognise the difference between damages which are compensatory and damages which go beyond that and are purely punitive had led to serious abuses, so we took what we thought was the best course open to us to limit those abuses.

Theoretically we might have held that as purely punitive damages had never been sanctioned by any decision of this House (as to which I shall say more later) there was no right under English law to award them. But that would have been going beyond the proper function of this House. There are many well-established doctrines of the law which have not been the subject of any decision by this House. We thought we had to recognise that it had become an established custom in certain classes of case to permit awards of damages which could not be justified as compensatory, and that that must remain the law. But we thought and I still think it well within the province of this House to say that that undesirable anomaly should not be permitted in any class of case where its use was not covered by authority. . . .

I must now deal with those parts of Lord Devlin's speech which have given rise to difficulties. He set out two categories of cases which in our opinion comprised all or virtually all the reported cases in which it was clear that the court had approved of an award of a larger sum of damages than could be justified as compensatory. Critics appear to have thought that he was inventing something new. That was not my understanding. We were confronted with an undesirable anomaly. We could not abolish it. We had to choose between confining it strictly to classes of cases where it was firmly established, although that produced an illogical result, or permitting it to be extended so as to produce a logical result. In my view it is better in such cases to be content with an illogical result than to allow any extension.

. . . I do not agree with Lord Devlin's view that in certain classes of case exemplary damages serve a useful purpose in vindicating the strength of the law. That view did not form an essential step in his argument. Concurrence with the speech of a colleague does not mean acceptance of every word which he has said. If it did there would be far fewer concurrences than there are. So I did not regard disagreement on this side issue as preventing me from giving my concurrence.

I think that the objections to allowing juries to go beyond compensatory damages are overwhelming. To allow pure punishment in this way contravenes almost every principle which has been evolved for the protection of offenders. There is no definition of the offence except that the conduct punished must be oppressive, high-handed, malicious, wanton or its like—terms far too vague to be admitted to any criminal code worthy of the name. There is no limit to the punishment except that it must not be unreasonable. The punishment is not inflicted by a judge who has experience and at least tries not to be influenced by emotion: it is inflicted by a jury without experience of law or punishment and often swayed by considerations which every judge would put out of his mind. And there is no effective appeal against sentence. All that a reviewing court can do is to quash the jury's decision if it thinks the punishment awarded is more than any twelve reasonable men could award. The court cannot substitute its own award. The punishment must then be decided by another jury and if they too award heavy punishment the court is virtually powerless. It is no excuse to say that we need not waste sympathy on people who behave outrageously. Are we wasting sympathy on vicious criminals when we insist on proper legal safeguards for them? The right to give punitive damages in certain cases is so firmly embedded in our law that only Parliament can remove it. But I must say that I am surprised by the enthusiasm of Lord Devlin's critics in supporting this form of palm tree justice. . . .

Lord Devlin's first category is set out on p. 1226. He said:

"The first category is oppressive, arbitrary or unconstitutional action by the servants of the government. I should not extend this category—I say this with particular reference to the facts of this case—to oppressive action by private corporations or individuals."

This distinction has been attacked on two grounds: first, that it only includes Crown servants and excludes others like the police who exercise governmental functions but are not Crown servants and, secondly, that it is illogical since both the harm to the plaintiff and the blameworthiness of the defendant may be at least equally great where the offender is a powerful private individual. . . . I think that the context shows that the category was never intended to be limited to Crown servants. The contrast is between "the government" and private individuals. Local government is as much government as national government, and the police and many other persons are exercising governmental functions. It was unnecessary in *Rookes* v. *Barnard* to define the exact limits of the category. I should certainly read it as extending to all those who by common law or statute are exercising functions of a governmental character.

The second criticism is I think misconceived. I freely admit that the distinction is illogical. The real reason for the distinction was, in my view, that the cases shewed that it was firmly established with regard to servants of "the government" that damages could be awarded against them beyond any sum justified as compensation, whereas there was no case except one that was overruled where damages had been awarded against a private bully or oppressor to an amount that could not fairly be regarded as compensatory, giving to that word the meaning which I have already discussed. I thought that this House was therefore free to say that no more than that was to be awarded in future.

We are particularly concerned in the present case with the second category. With the benefit of hindsight I think I can say without disrespect to Lord Devlin that it is not happily phrased. But I think the meaning is clear enough. An ill disposed person could not infrequently deliberately commit a tort in contumelious disregard of another's rights in order to obtain an advantage which would outweigh any compensatory damages likely to be obtained by his victim. Such a case is within this category. But then it is said, suppose he commits the tort not for gain but simply out of malice, why should he not also be punished? Again I freely admit there is no logical reason. The reason for excluding such a case from the category is simply that firmly established authority required us to accept this category however little we might like it, but did not require us to go farther. If logic is to be preferred to the desirability of cutting down the scope for punitive damages to the greatest extent that will not conflict with established authority then this category must be widened. But as I have already said I would, logic or no logic, refuse to extend the right to inflict exemplary damages to any class of case which is not already clearly covered by authority. On that basis I support this category.

Control of the use of damages

Oliver v. Ashman

Court of Appeal [1962] 2 Q.B. 210

HOLROYD PEARCE L.J.: . . . It was argued that if a jury think that the right figure would be £10,000, but are satisfied that the plaintiff cannot spend more than £5,000, they should award only £5,000. . . . For the plaintiff is only entitled to damages, it is argued, as compensation and he can only have them if they can be used to compensate. But what warranty is there for such a proposition? The plaintiff having made out his cause of action in negligence and proved his damages is entitled to his judgment. There is no condition that he should spend or use the damages. They are his to save or to spend or to dissipate in any useful or useless manner that he may choose. His needs or his ability to use his damages are, as it seems to me, irrelevant to their assessment. It would be undesirable to introduce the suggested principle into the law of tort. If that were done, an attempt would no doubt be made to extend it to cases where the plaintiff was rich so that he could never need the damages to which he was entitled.

Control of widows' damages

Report of the Committee on Funds in Court

Cmnd. 818, 1959

16. The Fatal Accidents Acts did not contain any provision for the control by the Court of widows' damages. Under the Workmen's Compensation Acts, however, if a workman died as the result of an accident arising out of and in the course of his employment, compensation was payable for the benefit of his dependants, including his widow, and there was provision for control by the Court of such compensation. . . .

17. . . . [P]ower for the Court to control widows' damages was conferred by . . . section 21 of the Administration of Justice Act, 1925. . . .

27. In an action under the Fatal Accidents Acts, a widow with dependent children will normally have awarded to her the major part of the total sum of damages. It is assumed that she will use her damages for the maintenance and benefit of the children as well as herself. . . . There is however the need to ensure the conservation of the fund by safeguarding it against early disappearance in some imprudent investment or undertaking and against too rapid depletion by excessive drawings. Most of the widows have no training or experience in the technique of handling large sums of money and in particular of distinguishing between income and capital. The Court has a duty, in performance of one of its traditional functions, to protect the interests of the children. . . . In our opinion, subject to paragraphs 32 and 33 of this Report, the Court's power to control widow's damages in cases where there are dependent children should undoubtedly be continued.

28. As there are special reasons for continuing the power to control widows' damages in the case of widows with dependent children, there is a possible intermediate view that the power should be continued only in relation to widows with dependent children and should be abolished in relation to those without dependent children. . . . The intermediate view is tenable, but is not held by us. . . .

31. . . . [W]e are of opinion that the Court's power to control the investment and application of widows' damages even in the case of widows without dependent children should be continued. . . . The majority of widows, used to

receiving their housekeeping money weekly, have no training or experience in the handling of sums running into four figures. There is a minority of widows who are perfectly capable of handling large sums of money and of distinguishing clearly between capital and income. The Court should have a discretionary power and should exercise it in such a way that the majority will have their money controlled for them and the minority will have their money released to them immediately or at an early stage. There ought not to be in relation to the majority, who need the control for their protection, a *laissez-faire* attitude based on the general principle of sex equality. Moreover the question is not whether a new control should be introduced, but whether an existing control, affirmed by Parliament . . . should be abolished. After careful consideration of the argument based on discrimination . . . we are in the end not impressed by it. . . .

32. On the assumption that the Court's power to control widows' damages is to remain . . . it is . . . in our view undoubtedly right, that the power should remain as a discretionary power. . . . What then is the right test or formula for deciding whether the money should be paid into or retained in Court or paid to the widow? We suggest that the money should be directed to be paid to the widow whenever the Court is satisfied that control of the money is not necessary for the purpose of securing the sufficient preservation and prudent application of the money. . . . It should be incumbent on the widow, personally or by her solicitor or counsel, to satisfy the Court on this point, because the Court will often need information as to the widow's situation and resources and expectations as a guide to the decision, and the widow has the knowledge and can supply the information. . . . [S]ometimes the trial Judge might be able to decide at the end of the trial without further information, if he had from seeing and hearing the widow giving evidence in the witness-box in the course of the trial formed a clear view as to her capacity or incapacity for sufficiently preserving and prudently applying the money if she immediately had full possession and unrestricted disposal of it. . . . The wishes of the widow and the opinion of her solicitor would of course be relevant and important factors to be taken into account, but not conclusive. If there are dependent children, their interests have to be considered and an order for payment of the whole fund to the widow is less likely to be appropriate. . . . The question will arise for decision in the first instance when the widow's damages have been recovered, whether by trial and judgment or by approval of an agreed settlement. . . . The question however may arise at any later time be it assumed that the money has been paid into Court under the initial directions, and that the fund in Court so created is being administered by the Master in the High Court or by the Judge or Registrar in the County Court: then the widow may at any time apply to him for a direction that the remainder of the money be paid out to her. We suggest that a comparatively cautious attitude would be appropriate at the stage of the initial directions as to disposal, and that there might be a somewhat greater readiness to accede to a subsequent application made some years later. At the first stage the widow may be still emotionally affected by the death of her husband, and she may be unduly impressed by the apparent magnitude of the financial resources now available to her, and it is at this time that the vendors of bankrupt businesses and indigent relatives may be expected to gather round. After a period of initial control she will have some experience of owning capital and spending income (perhaps supplemented by contributions from capital), and she will be better able to understand the system of control and investment and to judge between the advantages and disadvantages of control and those of decontrol for her purposes. The Master or Judge or Registrar administering the fund, if the widow after some years applies to him for a direction that the remainder of the money be paid to her, should decide the application on its

merits in the light of the situation then existing, and should not regard the initial decision in favour of control as necessarily being a decision in favour of permanent or prolonged control.

Split trials

Report of the Committee on Personal Injuries Litigation
Cmnd. 3691, 1968

486. . . . [I]n its broadest and most robust setting the split trial means:

    (*a*) that after liability (or in some cases quantum) has been established . . . there will be a separate trial of the damages (or liability) issue, not necessarily before the same judge; and that

    (*b*) the medical and financial loss issues are not considered at the first trial. . . .

489. The principal advantages claimed for the split trial system can be summarised as follows:

    (*a*) Delay in resolving claims and evidentiary inadequacies attributable to frailty of memory will be reduced if a party may at a comparatively early stage ascertain whether he is entitled . . . to receive or . . . pay compensation . . . without embarking upon an inquiry about the extent and nature of the injuries suffered. . . .

    (*b*) Since a significant proportion of cases reaching trial result in a finding against the plaintiff on the issue of liability, the time and labour (and the cost of both) involved in dealing with the injuries and loss issues would all be saved. . . .

    (*c*) Plaintiffs' solicitors would be enabled to negotiate (without instituting proceedings) a sensible compromise of the issue of liability, without being met by a refusal by the defendants' representatives to negotiate at all while the extent of the injuries is unknown or uncertain.

    (*d*) It is argued that once liability is established there is what some writers on the subject have called " a compulsive urge " to settle by making a sensible and realistic offer to the plaintiff. . . .

    (*e*) If liability is established at an early stage, impecunious or needy plaintiffs may be able to obtain a payment on account of their ultimate entitlement. . . .

    (*f*) It is said that there is . . . a hard-core of cases where defendants (arguing between themselves which of them is liable to the plaintiff) could make use of this procedure to sort out their internal liability problems, at a minimum of inconvenience or cost to the plaintiff.

490. The principal arguments advanced by those who oppose any radical change in the existing system are:

    (*a*) That it is unsatisfactory to separate the trial of the two issues because both contain factors a consideration of which contributes to a just and careful resolution of the other. . . . A plaintiff who exaggerates his injuries or one who dishonestly or recklessly inflates his special damage may . . . emerge as someone upon whose version of the accident itself no reliance should be placed. . . . A plaintiff's attitude towards his claim frequently enhances his general credibility. . . . The overwhelming body of both judicial and practitioners' opinion sets great store by these considerations. . . .

(*b*) It is said that the split trial will . . . cause parties to be subjected to waiting in two queues instead of one. . . . The T.U.C. told us that where there follows after liability has been established any prolonged period of anxiety about the amount of damages . . . there is no room for doubt that injured plaintiffs and their families suffer harmful consequences. . . .

(*c*) It is urged too, that . . . if the liability issue was capable of speedy decision, defendants and their insurers would be reluctant to compromise claims, since an element of uncertainty could be removed. In this sense it is feared that more rather than fewer trials would result. . . .

(*d*) [A]fter liability is established, a defendant . . . will not know with any degree of accuracy what his ultimate financial involvement is likely to be. . . .

(*e*) . . . Defendants argue with cogency that in assessing payments into Court they take into consideration their prospects on the liability as well as the damages issues. They say that split trials would deprive them of this important safeguard in the liability trial.

A separate tribunal for assessing damages

Final Report of the Committee on Supreme Court Practice and Procedure

Cmd. 8878, 1953

368. The second suggestion was that in all personal injuries actions the assessment of damages should be referred to a tribunal which would confine itself solely to the question of quantum. . . . [I]t was said that the amounts assessed as damages for apparently similar injuries vary considerably with the Judges who try the cases and that greater uniformity would be achieved if there were tribunals which would consult together and would in all cases assess the damages to be awarded. The suggested tribunal was to consist of a lawyer and a medical man, drawn from a small panel, who would sit together. It was also proposed that solicitors should have a right of audience before the tribunal. We appreciate the object underlying this suggestion but we are unable to recommend its adoption. It would involve the setting up of special tribunals in London and also at various towns throughout the country. The view of the majority of the witnesses before us was that it would not produce much more uniformity in the assessment of damages than there is at present; they felt also, and we agree, that it would probably result in an increase of costs in many cases. We think that consultation between the Judges would probably be the best method of achieving greater uniformity in awards of damages, and for the same reason it does not appear to us to be necessary (even if it were at present practicable) to adopt the further proposal . . . that questions of damages should be decided by a bench of three Judges.

INJUNCTIONS

Whitwood Chemical Co. v. Hardman

Court of Appeal [1891] 2 Ch. 416

LINDLEY L.J.: . . . We are dealing here with a contract of a particular class. It is a contract involving the performance of a personal service, and, as a rule, the Court does not decree specific performance of such contracts. That is a general rule. There has been engrafted upon that rule an exception, which is explained more or less definitely in *Lumley* v. *Wagner* [91]—that is to say, where a person has engaged not to serve any other master, or not to perform at any other place, the Court can lay hold of that, and restrain him from so doing; and there are observations, in which I concur, made by Lord Selborne in the *Wolverhampton and Walsall Railway Company* v. *London and North Western Railway Company*,[92] to the effect that the principle does not depend upon whether you have an actual negative clause, if you can say that the parties were contracting in the sense that one should not do this, or the other—some specific thing upon which you can put your finger. . . . What are we to say in this particular case? What injunction can be granted in this particular case which will not be, in substance and effect, a decree for specific performance of this agreement? It appears to me the difficulty of the Plaintiffs is this, that they cannot suggest anything which, when examined, does not amount to this, that the man must either be idle, or specifically perform the agreement into which he has entered. . . . I think the court, looking at the matter broadly, will generally do much more harm by attempting to decree specific performance in cases of personal service than by leaving them alone; and whether it is attempted to enforce these contracts directly by a decree of specific performance, or indirectly by an injunction, appears to me to be immaterial. It is on the ground that mischief will be done to one at all events of the parties that the Court declines in cases of this kind to grant an injunction. . .

Warner Bros. Pictures Inc. v. Nelson

King's Bench Division [1937] 1 K.B. 209

BRANSON J.: . . . The case before me is . . . one in which it would be proper to grant an injunction unless to do so would in the circumstances be tantamount to ordering the defendant to perform her contract or remain idle or unless damages would be the more appropriate remedy. . . . It was . . . urged that the difference between what the defendant can earn as a film artiste and what she might expect to earn by any other form of activity is so great that she will in effect be driven to perform her contract. That is not the criterion adopted in any of the decided cases. The defendant is stated to be a person of intelligence, capacity and means, and no evidence was adduced to show that, if enjoined from doing the specified acts otherwise than for the plaintiffs, she will not be able to employ herself both usefully and remuneratively in other spheres of activity, though not as remuneratively as in her special line. She will not be driven, although she may be tempted, to perform the contract, and the fact that she may be so tempted is no objection to the grant of an injunction.

Dowty Bolton v. Wolverhampton Corporation

Chancery Division [1971] 1 W.L.R. 204

Wolverhampton Corporation had undertaken in a conveyance to allow the company to use its airfield and subsequently in breach of its undertaking proposed to develop the site as a housing estate. The company applied for an injunction. The court held that it would have to be content with damages.

---

[91] (1852) 1 D.M. & G. 604.
[92] (1873) L.R. 16 Eq. 443.

PENNYCUICK V.-C.: . . . I turn now to consider the remedy available to the company should the corporation persevere in its intention to appropriate this land for housing. It seems to me that the remedy of the company must lie in damages only and that the company is not now entitled, and will not be entitled at the hearing of the action, if it is then otherwise successful, to any relief by way of injunction or mandatory order. The right vested in the company necessarily involves the maintenance of the airfield as a going concern. That involves continuing acts of management, including the upkeep of runways and buildings, the employment of staff, compliance with the Civil Aviation Act 1949, and so forth, i.e. in effect the carrying on of a business. That is nonetheless so by reason that so far the corporation has elected to engage Don Everall Aviation Ltd. to manage the airfield on its behalf. It is very well established that the court will not order specific performance of an obligation to carry on a business or, indeed, any comparable series of activities. See in this connection 36 Halsbury's Laws (3rd Edn) pp. 267–269, paras 365, 366:

> " The court does not enforce the performance of contracts which involve continuous acts and require the watching and supervision of the court . . .
>
> A judgment for specific performance is not pronounced, either at the suit of the employer or the employee, in the case of a contract for personal work or service . . . This principle applies not merely to contracts of employment, but to all contracts which involve the rendering of continuous services by one person to another, as, for instance, a contract to work a railway line."

The cases cited in the note under that last sentence are a number of cases in the middle of the last century. It would not be useful to refer to them. The principle is established, I should have thought, beyond argument. For this purpose there is no difference between an order for specific performance of the contract and a mandatory injunction to perform the party's obligation under the contract. In the present case, the notice of motion is expressed as one for a negative injunction, but one has only to look at it to see that it does involve a mandatory order on the corporation to maintain the airfield. In order that the corporation could continue to allow the company to use the airfield, it is essential that the corporation should maintain the airfield. It would be quite impossible for the company to use the airfield if the corporation did not maintain it. So an injunction in the terms asked would put on the corporation a duty, to be observed for something over 60 years, to maintain the airfield.

Shelfer v. City of London Electric Lighting Co.
Court of Appeal [1895] 1 Ch. 287

The Chancery Amendment Act 1858 authorised the Court of Chancery to award damages in lieu of an injunction. The present case has for long been a *locus classicus* for the statement of the circumstances in which it would do this. There has since been some modification in practice but it remains the starting point.

A. L. SMITH L.J.: . . . In my opinion, it may be stated as a good working rule that—

(1) If the injury to the plaintiff's legal rights is small,

(2) And is one which is capable of being estimated in money,

(3) And is one which can be adequately compensated by a small money payment,

(4) And the case is one in which it would be oppressive to the defendant to grant an injunction:—then damages in substitution for an injunction may be given.

There may also be cases in which, though the four above-mentioned requirements exist, the defendant by his conduct, as, for instance, hurrying up his buildings so as if possible to avoid an injunction, or otherwise acting with a reckless disregard to the plaintiff's rights, has disentitled himself from asking that damages may be assessed in substitution for an injunction. It is impossible to lay down any rule as to what, under the differing circumstances of each case, constitutes either a small injury, or one that can be estimated in money, or what is a small money payment, or an adequate compensation, or what would be oppressive to the defendant. This must be left to the good sense of the tribunal which deals with each case as it comes up for adjudication.

Fishenden v. Higgs and Hill Ltd.

Court of Appeal (1935) 153 L.T. 128

LORD HANWORTH M.R.: . . . In *Kine* v. *Jolley* [93] (at p. 504), Cozens-Hardy L.J. says this: " I think it is impossible to doubt that the tendency of the speeches in the House of Lords in *Colls* v. *Home and Colonial Stores* [94] is to go a little further than was done in *Shelfer* v. *City of London Electric Lighting Company*,[95] and to indicate that as a general rule the court ought to be less free in granting mandatory injunctions than it was in years gone by." It seems to me, therefore, that we ought to incline against an injunction if possible. It is not possible to say what the injury to the plaintiff will be when estimated in money. I think the damages that he may be given will be a substantial sum— not a trivial sum like £50 or £100, but a substantial sum. On the other hand, the defendants have certainly acted with circumspection, and I think with a desire to avoid any unreasonable invasion of the plaintiff's rights, and certainly not to take him or catch him at a disadvantage. Their conduct inures to their benefit, and therefore we have to consider what would be the result to them if they had to modify their plans and to cut off a portion of their building. They may be unable to use the site in a manner in which they have a right to use it when they are making use of this now vacant piece of land and building upon it in a manner which is not uncommon at the present time, a liberty which cannot be restrained because of what Lord Halsbury said in the *Colls* case, namely, that there is a right to build upon a piece of land like this within the City of Westminster.

I have come to the conclusion on the whole that this is a case in which damages will be a sufficient remedy. Even though those damages may sound a not inconsiderable sum, we are dealing with sites of large value. The plaintiff himself has to pay a high rental, and he is subject to a covenant under which he had to make a large outlay when he took possession of these premises. . . . But I also think that one ought to consider whether the defendants will be oppressed in the sense that they will lose so very large a *quantum* of the enjoyment of their site as to amount to oppression.

[93] [1905] 1 Ch. 480.
[94] [1904] A.C. 179.
[95] [1895] 1 Ch. 287.

Redland Bricks Ltd. v. Norris
[1970] A.C. 652

LORD UPJOHN: . . . The grant of a mandatory injunction is, of course, entirely discretionary and unlike a negative injunction can never be " as of course." Every case must depend essentially on its own particular circumstances. Any general principles for its application can only be laid down in the most general terms:

1. A mandatory injunction can only be granted where the plaintiff shows a very strong probability on the facts that grave damage will accrue to him in the future. As Lord Dunedin said [96] it is not sufficient to say "timeo." It is a jurisdiction to be exercised sparingly and with caution but, in the proper case, unhesitatingly.

2. Damages will not be a sufficient or adequate remedy if such damage does happen. This is only the application of a general principle of equity; it has nothing to do with Lord Cairns' Act [97] or *Meux's* case.[98]

3. Unlike the case where a negative injunction is granted to prevent the continuance or recurrence of a wrongful act the question of the cost to the defendant to do works to prevent or lessen the likelihood of a future apprehended wrong must be an element to be taken into account: (*a*) where the defendant has acted without regard to his neighbour's rights, or has tried to steal a march on him or has tried to evade the jurisdiction of the court or, to sum it up, has acted wantonly and quite unreasonably in relation to his neighbour he may be ordered to repair his wanton and unreasonable acts by doing positive work to restore the status quo even if the expense to him is out of all proportion to the advantage thereby accruing to the plaintiff. As illustrative of this see *Woodhouse* v. *Newry Navigation Co.*[99]; (*b*) but where the defendant has acted reasonably, although in the event wrongly, the cost of remedying by positive action his earlier activities is most important for two reasons. First, because no legal wrong has yet occurred (for which he has not been recompensed at law and in equity) and, in spite of gloomy expert opinion, may never occur or possibly only on a much smaller scale than anticipated. Secondly, because if ultimately heavy damage does occur the plaintiff is in no way prejudiced for he has his action at law and all his consequential remedies in equity.

So the amount to be expended under a mandatory order by the defendant must be balanced with these considerations in mind against the anticipated possible damage to the plaintiff and if, on such balance, it seems unreasonable to inflict such expenditure on one who for this purpose is no more than a potential wrongdoer then the court must exercise its jurisdiction accordingly. Of course, the court does not have to order such works as on the evidence before it will remedy the wrong but may think it proper to impose on the defendant the obligation of doing certain works which may on expert opinion merely lessen the likelihood of any further injury to the plaintiff's land. Sargant J., pointed this out in effect in the celebrated " Moving Mountain " case, *Kennard* v. *Cory Brothers & Co., Ltd.*[1] (his judgment was affirmed in the Court of Appeal).

4. If in the exercise of its discretion the court decides that it is a proper case to grant a mandatory injunction, then the court must be careful to see that the defendant knows exactly in fact what he has to do and this means not as a matter of law but as a matter of fact, so that in carrying out an order he can give his contractors the proper instructions.

---

[96] In *Att.-Gen. for the Dominion of Canada* v. *Ritchie Contracting and Supply Co. Ltd.* [1919] A.C. 999, 1005.
[97] *i.e.* the Chancery Amendment Act 1858.
[98] [1895] 1 Ch. 287.
[99] [1898] 1 I.R. 161.   [1] [1921] 1 A.C. 521.

Eleventh Report of the Law Commission : Transfer of Land and Restrictive Covenants, 1967

Propositions and Commentary

Proposition 10—Enforcement Jurisdiction of the Courts

(*a*) *In the exercise of its enforcement jurisdiction in the case of restrictive land obligations, the Court should award damages in lieu of granting an injunction notwithstanding that there would be no oppression upon the defendant by such grant, where it is satisfied that the plaintiff entitled to the benefit of the obligation can be adequately compensated in money in respect of the harm done to his interests by the actual or contemplated breach complained of.*

(*b*) *The Court should have jurisdiction to grant declaratory relief in proceedings instituted by a person intending to carry out specific development which may contravene a restrictive land obligation. In the exercise of such jurisdiction the Court should be empowered, in appropriate cases, where a legally enforceable land obligation would be contravened, to award damages to any objecting party if the Court considers that he can thereby adequately be compensated in money in respect of the harm which will be done to his interests if such development proceeds.*

NOTES

1. Paragraph (a) of this Proposition reflects recent tendencies in the Courts in restrictive covenant cases to depart from the somewhat inflexible principles formerly applied to the exercise of the jurisdiction conferred upon the Chancery Courts by the Chancery Amendment Act 1858 (Lord Cairns' Act) to grant damages in lieu of an injunction in appropriate cases. These principles are best stated in the " working rule " propounded by A. L. Smith L.J. in *Shelfer v. City of London Electric Lighting Company* [2] that—

" (1) If the injury to the plaintiff's legal rights is small,
(2) And is one which is capable of being estimated in money,
(3) And is one which can be adequately compensated by a small money payment,
(4) And the case is one in which it would be oppressive to the defendant to grant an injunction : —
then damages in substitution for an injunction may be given."

The reason for the application of this working rule to restrictive covenant cases is thought to have been that, before the advent of planning controls, the judicial enforcement of covenants was the only means by which undesirable development of land could be prevented. Study of the reported cases shows how the development of the law upon restrictive covenants and of the powers of the Courts regarding their enforceability is the ancestor of modern planning law, particularly in " scheme " cases. Recent decisions (for example, *Baxter v. Four Oaks Properties Limited*,[3] where damages of £500, £100 and £150 respectively were awarded to three plaintiffs and an injunction to enforce a covenant, of the terms of which the defendant was aware at the time of his purchase of the burdened land, was refused) illustrate a more flexible attitude on the part of the Courts. We consider this to be a welcome tendency. We do not think, at the present time, that in these cases the Court would adhere to the

[2] [1895] 1 Ch. 287, 322–323.
[3] [1965] Ch. 816.

" working rule's " requirements that only a *small* sum should be entertained when damages are to be contemplated or that the element of " oppression to the defendant " should necessarily have to be shown. Whilst the introduction of planning control by local authorities has not replaced the need for and the usefulness of privately imposed restrictions upon land development, these processes of controlling land use should be regarded as complementary. Paragraph (a) is directed at facilitating this approach to the problems of the control of land use.

2. Paragraph (b) contemplates a variety of cases. For example, a developer may have brought, or may propose to buy, land which appears to be affected by a restrictive land obligation. He may be in doubt whether the obligation is enforceable or, if so, whether his proposed development would contravene it, and he may want the Court's ruling on either of those points. Alternatively, he may admit both those matters but consider that the contravention would be slight. In any of those cases he may think that the persons who will be truly affected by the development can be adequately compensated and may wish to ascertain the Court's view on this aspect of the matter. This is a new jurisdiction but it is one which we think that the Court should have. The result would not be dissimilar to that which was reached in the case of *Baxter* v. *Four Oaks Properties Limited* (*supra*) and we would regard it as both a clarification and a logical extension of the jurisdiction, exercised in *Re Gadd's Land Transfer* [4] by Buckley J. under R.S.C. Ord. 5 Rule 4, to decide whether restrictive covenants would be enforceable against an intended purchaser of the burdened land.

Warwick University v. Presland and Others
(Unreported)

The following injunction was issued to recover possession from students occupying the Registry Building at the University of Warwick in February 1970.

In the High Court of Justice
Queen's Bench Division   1970 T No. 840
Between the University of Warwick *Plaintiffs*
and
[21 names] *Defendants*

Upon hearing Counsel for the Plaintiffs *ex parte* it is ordered that the Defendants [21 names] and each of them:

1. By 9.00 am on Friday 13 February 1970, or within thirty minutes after service of this order whichever is the later, do give up occupation of and leave the building known as the Administration Building and Registry in the University of Warwick.

2. Be restrained until further order by themselves, their servants or agents or otherwise from re-entering the said Administration Building and Registry save for such purposes as the Plaintiffs permit them in accordance with the statutes and usages of the University so to do.

3. Be restrained until further order by themselves, their servants or agents or otherwise from entering upon or occupying or otherwise using any part of the buildings or premises of the Plaintiffs save for such purposes as they are permitted by the statutes and usages of the University so to do.

4. Be restrained until further order by themselves, their servants or agents or

[4] [1966] 1 Ch. 56.

otherwise from further damaging any part of the Plaintiffs' buildings or premises or any property of the Plaintiffs thereon, or otherwise harming the same.

5. By 9.00 am Friday 13 February 1970, or within thirty minutes of the service of this order whichever is the later, deliver to the plaintiffs all such books, papers or documents of whatsoever kind as the defendants have removed from the Administration Building and Registry in the University of Warwick, including all copies of any such documents, and be restrained by themselves, their servants or agents or otherwise from removing or copying any further such documents.

6. Forthwith be restrained by themselves, their servants or agents or otherwise from publishing or otherwise in any way disclosing the contents of or making any use of any documents removed by the defendants from the Administration Building or Registry in the University of Warwick, or any copies of any such documents, or of any other confidential documents the property of the Plaintiffs.

Notice

If you, the within-named Defendants, neglect to obey all or any of the orders recited in paragraphs 1 or 5 of this order, or if you disobey all or any of the orders recited in paragraphs 2, 3, 4 and 6 of this order, you will be liable to process of execution for the purpose of compelling you to obey the same.

[In handwriting] Leave to Plaintiffs to serve this order, if necessary, by substituted service either by communicating the words therein to the Defendants by loud-hailer or by leaving a copy of it in the Administration and Registry.

Hypothetical Cases, Declaration and Preliminary Points of Law

M'Naghten's Case

(1843) 10 Cl. & F. 200; 8 E.R. 718

The House of Lords put a number of questions to the judges concerning the defence of insanity on charges of murder:

1st. What is the law respecting alleged crimes committed by persons afflicted with insane delusion, in respect of one or more particular subjects or persons . . . ?

2nd. What are the proper questions to be submitted to the jury, when a person alleged to be afflicted with insane delusion respecting one or more particular subjects or persons, is charged with the commission of a crime (murder, for example), and insanity is set up as a defence?

3rd. In what terms ought the question to be left to the jury, as to the prisoner's state of mind at the time when the act was committed?

4th. If a person under an insane delusion as to existing facts, commits an offence in consequence thereof, is he thereby excused?

5th. Can a medical man conversant with the disease of insanity, who never saw the prisoner previously to the trial, but who was present during the whole trial and the examination of all the witnesses, be asked his opinion as to the state of the prisoner's mind at the time of the commission of the alleged crime, or his opinion whether the prisoner was conscious at the time of doing the act, that he was acting contrary to law, or whether he was labouring under any and what delusion at the time?

LORD BROUGHAM: . . . [T]here can be no doubt of your Lordships' right to put, in this way, abstract questions of law to the Judges, the answer to which might be necessary to your Lordships in your legislative capacity. There is a precedent for this course, in the memorable instance of Mr. Fox's Bill on the law of libel; where, before passing the Bill, this House called on the Judges to give their opinions on what was the law as it then existed.

LORD CAMPBELL: . . . It was most fit that the opinions of the Judges should be asked on these matters, the settling of which is not a mere matter of speculation; for your Lordships may be called on, in your legislative capacity, to change the law; and before doing so, it is proper that you should be satisfied beyond doubt what the law really is. . . . Your Lordships have been reminded of one precedent for this proceeding, but there is a still more recent instance; the Judges having been summoned in the case of the Canada Reserves, to express their opinions on what was then the law on that subject. The answers given by the Judges . . . will be of the greatest use in the administration of justice.

LORD COTTENHAM: . . . It is true that they [the Judges] cannot be required to say what would be the construction of a Bill, not in existence as a law . . . but they may be called on to assist your Lordships, in declaring their opinions upon abstract questions of existing law.

MAULE J.: I feel great difficulty in answering the questions put by your Lordships on this occasion: — First, because they do not appear to arise out of and are not put with reference to a particular case, or for a particular purpose, which might explain or limit the generality of their terms, so that full answers to them ought to be applicable to every possible state of facts, not inconsistent with those assumed in the questions: this difficulty is the greater, from the practical experience both of the bar and the Court being confined to questions arising out of the facts of particular cases: — Secondly, because I have heard no argument at your Lordships' bar or elsewhere, on the subject of these questions; the want of which I feel the more, the greater are the number and extent of questions which might be raised in argument: — and Thirdly, from a fear . . . that as these questions relate to matters of criminal law of great importance and frequent occurrence, the answers to them by the Judges may embarrass the administration of justice, when they are cited in criminal trials.

Rating and Valuation Bill

70 H.L.Deb. cc. 631 and 914, 1928

The government in this Bill had proposed that the Minister of Health should be able to refer points of law under it to the courts for advice. Lord Hailsham, the Lord Chancellor, explained the justification for this proposal at c. 915:

> [U]nder the Act of 1925 a committee was set up called the Central Valuation Committee, whose duty it is to advise upon certain points of rating law, since one of the purposes of the Act of 1925 was to ensure uniformity in that law. . . . [T]hey have discovered that there are in the law of rating certain matters which are certainly obscure and with regard to which practice in different parts of the country has not been uniform. . . . In those circumstances . . . the . . . Committee . . .

were anxious that a speedy and inexpensive means should be provided of obtaining the judicial decision which would guide rating authorities all over the country upon matters of general importance which, without that decision, would remain in doubt and with regard to which no one ratepayer had sufficient interest probably to incur the expense or the risk of fighting the case up to the High Court with the possibility of being taken even to your Lordships' House. . . . It was with that purpose that the clause was inserted.

LORD CARSON: . . . [I]f there is one matter above all others that this House ought to take care that a Government should not be allowed to do, it is that they should not be allowed to take from litigants the right of decision by the courts and the right to argue their cases before them. That is what this clause does. . . .

LORD HANWORTH: . . . [T]he courts have always set themselves, and rightly set themselves, against giving any opinion upon theoretical facts, and apart from concrete facts, and for this very legitimate and cogent reason. If you give an opinion without having the particular facts before you, you may find that you have overlooked some consideration that ought to be borne in mind, and a later appreciation of facts may show that the interpretation given was either too wide or perhaps did not go far enough. . . .

LORD HAILSHAM: . . . I confess it does not seem to me that the provision can fairly be described as one which made the judiciary subject to or the advisers of the Executive. . . . But it has seemed to us that there is another matter which is to be considered. Not only is it important that the Judiciary should be independent of the Executive, but it is also of vital importance that the public should be satisfied that the Judiciary and Executive are independent. We have thought that the undoubted fact that members of your Lordships' House occupying high judicial positions have seriously and sincerely believed that this principle of independence was being infringed, necessarily must arouse doubt and distrust in the public mind and that it was far better that we should abandon the effort to obtain a power of this kind than that we should run any risk of an impression being created, rightly or wrongly, in the minds of the public that there was any connection being established between the Executive and the Judiciary and any infringement of that independence of the Judiciary which is the palladium of the liberty of the subject. . . .

Glasgow Navigation Co. v. Iron Ore Co.
[1910] A.C. 293

The House (Lord Loreburn L.C. and Lords Atkin and Shaw of Dunfermline), being of opinion that the action was brought to try a hypothetical case . . . declined to make any order, except that the action be dismissed and that no costs be allowed to either party here or below.

Lord Loreburn L.C. stated that it was not the function of a Court of law to advise parties as to what would be their rights under a hypothetical state of facts.

The following order was made:— . . . " [I]t appearing to their Lordships that the pursuers and defenders, though without any wrong purpose, concurred in asking for an order upon the footing that they were bound by a contract different from the contract by which they were actually bound, the

House declined to make any other order than the following, viz.: —" *Ordered and adjudged that this action be dismissed; and it is further ordered that no costs be allowed to either side here or below.*

Sun Life Assurance Co. of Canada v. Jervis
[1944] A.C. 111

Here the appellant insurance company had only been given leave to appeal by the Court of Appeal on the condition that the costs of the appeal would be met by the appellants in any event and that the respondent's award would not be affected.

VISCOUNT SIMON L.C.: . . . I do not think that it would be a proper exercise of the authority which this House possesses to hear appeals if it occupies time in this case in deciding an academic question, the answer to which cannot affect the respondent in any way. If the House undertook to do so, it would not be deciding an existing lis between the parties . . . but would merely be expressing its view on a legal conundrum. . . . What is sometimes called a " friendly action " is not necessarily open to this objection . . . for the respective parties in such an action are arguing for different results and the winner gains something which he would not gain if he lost, but the objection here is that, if the appeal fails, the respondent gains nothing at all from his success. No doubt, the appellants are concerned to obtain, if they can, a favourable decision from this House because they fear that other cases may arise . . . in which others who have taken out policies . . . with them will rely on the decision of the Court of Appeal, but if the appellants desire to have the view of the House of Lords on the issue . . . their proper and more convenient course is to await a further claim and to bring that claim, if necessary, up to the House of Lords with a party . . . whose interest it is to resist the appeal. . . . I think it is an essential quality of an appeal fit to be disposed of by this House that there should exist between the parties a matter in actual controversy which the House undertakes to decide as a living issue.

This decision is by no means designed to discourage, in suitable cases, the putting of an unsuccessful litigant " on terms " as a condition of his being given leave to appeal from the Court of Appeal to this House. Terms requiring that . . . the appellant should undertake to ask for no costs in this House, or even should undertake to meet the costs of both sides in any event, may be perfectly proper. Again, cases may sometimes arise where the term is imposed that the respondent shall keep, at any rate, a portion of his damages whatever the result of the appeal, but what is objectionable is that the terms for leave to appeal should be so framed as to take away from the respondent any interest in the result of the appeal whatever.

LORD ATKIN, THANKERTON, RUSSELL OF KILLOWEN and PORTER agreed.

See also the statement of Warrington L.J. in *Stephenson, Blake & Co. v. Grant, Legros & Co.*[5]: " The function of the Court is not to decide abstract questions of law, but to decide questions of law when arising between the parties as the result of a certain state of facts."

See also *Adams* v. *Naylor.*[6] Before the Crown Proceedings Act 1947 made the Crown liable in tort for the actions of its employees it was the

[5] (1917) 86 L.J.Ch. 439.
[6] [1946] A.C. 543.

practice of the Crown on occasion to put forward a nominal defendant and then *ex gratia* pay the damages awarded against him. The House of Lords helped to precipitate the passing of the 1947 Act which had been recommended by a committee in 1929 by rejecting this practice. Lord Uthwatt for example said: " It was not open to the parties to this suit by agreement to have the matter dealt with on the footing, proved to be false, that the defendant was in occupation of the land in question. The matter could not be dealt with on the basis wished by the Crown."

Declarations

Vine v. National Dock Labour Board

House of Lords [1957] A.C. 488

The plaintiff, a dock labourer, complained that the defendants, in purporting to dismiss him, had not exercised their powers in the manner required by the Dock Workers (Regulation of Employment) Order 1947 which governed his terms of service. He therefore asked the court for a declaration that the dismissal was invalid.

VISCOUNT KILMUIR : . . . The granting of a declaration is a matter of discretion, and, in view of the opinion expressed by the majority of the Court of Appeal, I have considered what was said on this subject in your Lordships' House in *Russian Commercial and Industrial Bank* v. *British Bank for Foreign Trade Ltd.*[7] In that case Lord Finlay said, in the course of his dissenting opinion: " The question in what cases the jurisdiction to give a declaratory judgment should be exercised has been considered in a number of cases. . . ." Lord Finlay then cited expressions used in those earlier cases: " sparingly," " with great care and jealousy," " with extreme caution." I agree that the discretion should not be exercised save for some good reason. On the other hand, I find helpful the Scottish tests set out in that case by Lord Dunedin, who said: " The question must be a real and not a theoretical question; the person raising it must have a real interest to raise it; he must be able to secure a proper contradictor, that is to say, someone presently existing who has a true interest to oppose the declaration sought."

It seems to me that, however " cautiously " or " sparingly " the discretion is to be exercised, this is a case in which the judge was right to grant a declaration.

Pyx Granite Co. Ltd. v. Minister of Housing and Local Government

House of Lords [1960] A.C. 260

The plaintiff company proposed to quarry in the Malvern Hills. They claimed that they were authorised to do so by the Malvern Hills Act 1924. The Minister took the view that planning permission was needed for development of the kind proposed. The company asked the court for a declaration that their view of the position was correct.

VISCOUNT SIMONDS : . . . The appropriateness of the remedy was the final point in this part of the case. It was urged that, even if the court had jurisdiction to make the declaration claimed, it was a discretionary jurisdiction which

[7] [1921] A.C. 438.

should not be exercised in this case. My Lords, this plea should not, in my opinion prevail. It is surely proper that in a case like this involving, as many days of argument showed, difficult questions of construction of Acts of Parliament, a court of law should declare what are the rights of the subject who claims to have them determined. I do not dissent from the contention of the respondents that, where the administrative or quasi-judicial powers of the Minister are concerned, declaratory judgments should not readily be given by the court. But here, if ever, was a case where the jurisdiction could properly be invoked. It might even be thought surprising that the Minister should not be glad to have such questions authoritatively determined. . . .

Re Barnato, decd.

Court of Appeal [1949] 1 Ch. 258

COHEN L.J.: The Master of the Rolls asked Mr. Christie to cite any case in which a purely future and hypothetical question had come before the courts and the courts had held that they had jurisdiction to consider it. Mr. Christie could not put forward any such case, but founded his argument on the cases of *Dyson* v. *Att.-Gen.*,[8] *Esquimault and Nanaimo Railway Co.* v. *Wilson*[9] and in *Re Chamberlain's Settlement*.[10] . . .

In *Dyson* v. *Attorney-General* the matter arose in this way: Under the Finance (1909–10) Act, 1910, a number of notices had been issued by the Commissioners of Inland Revenue requiring the person to whom they were respectively addressed to fill in a form commonly known as " Form No. 4," and notifying the addressee that unless he did so within thirty days of the date of the notice, he would be subject to a penalty not exceeding £50. It, therefore, was a case in which the plaintiff found himself in the position that he would have to fill up a form which he contended he was under no liability to complete, or subject himself to the risk of incurring a penalty of £50. Accordingly, he asked for a declaration under Ord. 25 that he was under no obligation to comply with the notice or to furnish any of the said particulars. The court came to the conclusion that a declaratory judgment could be made against the Attorney-General representing the Crown. . . . It is to be observed . . . that in that case there was an immediate question to be decided between the subject and the Crown, for the Crown was seeking to compel the plaintiff to fill in the form and had threatened him with a penalty if he failed to do so. . . . In the present case, as I see it, there is no immediate question between the plaintiffs and the Crown . . . Mr. Christie, and Mr. Jopling for Mrs. Sanges and her children . . . said it was contrary to justice and equity that they should be kept in the state of uncertainty in which they are at present as to their possible liability under s. 8, subs. 4, of the Finance Act 1894. That is a state, I am afraid, which often exists in the minds of the subject under the various taxing statutes. It does not seem to me that the existence of that state of uncertainty can justify us in creating the precedent of compelling the Crown to subject itself to the decision of a purely hypothetical case which can never arise unless Mrs. Asher dies before the expiration of five years, and which may never arise, for other reasons—for instance, as the Master of the Rolls suggested in the course of the argument, if Parliament in its wisdom were in the meantime to think fit to alter the law. . . .

[R]e *Clay* seems to show that there would be no jurisdiction to make a declaratory order in a case of this kind as between subject and subject. . . . The

[8] [1911] 1 K.B. 410.
[9] [1920] A.C. 358.
[10] [1921] 2 Ch. 533.

effect of the decision is, I think, sufficiently summed up in two short passages. The first from the judgment of the Master of the Rolls, is as follows: " And it is not open to a person, certainly not to one against whom no claim in fact has been made, to cut the matter short by bringing an action at his own option, and saying: ' I wish to have it determined that you have no claim whatever against me.' " The second is from the judgment of Eve J., and is as follows: " So soon as it was demonstrated that no specific right had been asserted and no claim formulated, the court had . . . no jurisdiction to deal with the petition. . . ."

LORD GREENE M.R.: . . . Mr. Jopling emphasized the fact that for the trustees this was a practical instant question, because, he said, without guidance from the court . . . the trustees will be unable to act in the way they would like to act. Unfortunately, it is not only trustees who may find themselves in that kind of difficulty owing to the uncertain construction of some taxing Act. Any ordinary subject may find himself in precisely the same difficulty, and if these trustees could ask the court to bring the Crown here and insist upon deciding a doubtful question which may or may not arise between them according to events, merely because they want guidance as to the ordering of their affairs, I can see no end to the litigation that would inevitably follow. But the argument, in my opinion, is fallacious, and for this reason, that although the trustees at the moment require guidance, the question which it is suggested we ought to decide is a question as between the trustees and the Crown, and that is a purely hypothetical and future question. The fact that it is a doubtful question and may or may not arise no doubt is embarrassing for the trustees in deciding on their present course; but the actual question which we are asked to decide is a purely hypothetical and future question. The Crown will be able to put forward a claim, rightly or wrongly, in the event of the tenant for life dying before the expiration of five years, and if we were to decide this here and now, and the tenant for life were to live for more than five years, we should have given a decision binding on the Crown and effective either in favour of or against all other taxpayers, on a question which had never arisen, on a liability which had never matured; and, in my opinion, if it is desired that these courts should have power to decide hypothetical questions, on the construction of taxing Acts for the guidance of the subjects of the King that ought to be done by legislation and not by this court arrogating to itself jurisdiction to do it. I agree that the appeal must be dismissed.

SOMERVELL L.J. delivered a concurring judgment.

The Judicial Committee Act 1833, c. 41, provides in section 4 that " It shall be lawful for His Majesty to refer to the said Judicial Committee [of the Privy Council] for hearing or consideration any such other matters whatsoever as His Majesty shall think fit; and such committee shall thereupon hear or consider the same, and shall advise His Majesty thereon . . ."

Preliminary points of law

Rules of the Supreme Court

ORDER 33

3. The court may order any question . . . arising in a cause or matter, whether of fact or law or partly of fact and partly of law, and whether raised by the pleadings or otherwise, to be tried before, at or after the trial of the

cause or matter, and may give directions as to the manner in which the question or issue shall be stated.

Carl Zeiss Stiftung v. Herbert Smith and Co.
Court of Appeal [1969] 1 Ch. 93

LORD DENNING M.R.: . . . I know that it has been said on one or two occasions that a preliminary issue should be ordered only when, *whichever way it is decided*, it is conclusive of the whole matter. That was said by Lord Evershed M.R. in *Windsor Refrigerator Co. Ltd.* v. *Branch Nominees Ltd.*[11]; and Harman L.J. in *Yeoman Credit Ltd.* v. *Latter.*[12] I do not think that is correct.

The true rule was stated by Romer L.J. in *Everett* v. *Ribbands* [13]:

> " Where you have a point of law which, *if decided in one way*, is going to be decisive of litigation, then advantage ought to be taken of the facilities afforded by the Rules of Court to have it disposed of at the close of pleadings, or very shortly after the close of pleadings."

I have always understood such to be the practice. I quite agree that in many cases the facts and law are so mixed up that it is very undesirable to have a preliminary issue. I always like to know the facts before deciding the law. But this is an exceptional case.[14] . . .

COMPENSATION FOR VICTIMS OF CRIMINAL OFFENCES

A number of statutes authorise the criminal courts to order a convicted person to pay compensation to his victim. The Theft Act 1968, s. 28, for example, authorises orders to be made to compensate the owner of stolen goods from money taken from the offender on his apprehension. The Criminal Justice Act 1972, following recommendations made by the Advisory Council on the Penal System in its report, " Reparation by the Offender," goes further, and in section 7 authorises a criminal bankruptcy order to be made where loss or damage, other than by way of personal injury, has been suffered in excess of £15,000. Statute had already authorised a court to order an offender convicted of an indictable offence before it to pay up to £400 for any loss or damage to property caused by him, other than a loss caused as a result of an offence involving a motor car, and section 1 of the Criminal Justice Act 1972 has now extended this to personal injury suffered as a result of a criminal offence, other than a motoring offence.

In addition to the statutes authorising reparation by the offender there are also a number of statutes which provide for a system of public compensation for victims of criminal offences. One of long standing is the Riot (Damages) Act 1886 which enables anyone who has suffered damage to his property as the result of a " riot " to recover compensation from the local authority—and " riot " in this context may cover anything from a

[11] [1961] Ch. 88.
[12] [1961] 1 W.L.R. 828, 835.
[13] [1952] 1 K.B. 112.
[14] *Cf.* the remarks of Lord Radcliffe in *David* v. *Abdul Cader* [1963] 1 W.L.R. 834 and Lord Wilberforce in *Nissan* v. *Att.-Gen.* [1970] A.C. 179.

violent demonstration to the efforts of football spectators to see a football match.[15]   More important is the state scheme of compensation for victims of crimes of violence.   In a White Paper " Penal Practice in a Changing Society " in February 1959, the government announced that it had decided to set up a Working Party to consider the question of state compensation for victims of crimes of violence.   Its report " Compensation for Victims of Crimes of Violence "[16] was not encouraging.   Some kind of state compensation was however advocated by " Justice " and a group of Conservative lawyers, and in 1964 the government published proposals for a scheme in a further White Paper.[17]   These were put into effect in the same year. The details of the scheme and the criteria used in determining who should receive compensation, which is given not as of right but *ex gratia*, can be found in the Annual Reports of the Criminal Injuries Compensation Board, which administers the scheme.

Compensation orders and criminal bankruptcy

Criminal Justice Act 1972
1972, c. 71

COMPENSATION ORDERS

1.—(1) Subject to the provisions of this Part of this Act, a court by or before which a person is convicted of an offence, in addition to dealing with him in any other way, may, on application or otherwise, make an order (in this Act referred to as " a compensation order ") requiring him to pay compensation for any personal injury, loss or damage resulting from that offence or any other offence which is taken into consideration by the court in determining sentence.

(2) In the case of an offence under the Theft Act 1968, where the property in question is recovered, any damage to the property occurring while it was out of the owner's possession shall be treated for the purposes of subsection (1) above as having resulted from the offence, however and by whomsoever the damage was caused.

(3) No compensation order shall be made in respect of loss suffered by the dependants of a person in consequence of his death, and no such order shall be made in respect of injury, loss or damage due to an accident arising out of the presence of a motor vehicle on a road, except such damage as is treated by subsection (2) above as resulting from an offence under the Theft Act 1968.

(4) In determining whether to make a compensation order against any person, and in determining the amount to be paid by any person under such an order, the court shall have regard to his means so far as they appear or are known to the court.

(5) The compensation to be paid under a compensation order made by a magistrates' court in respect of any offence of which the court has convicted the offender shall not exceed £400; and the compensation or total compensation to be paid under a compensation order or compensation orders made by a magistrates' court in respect of any offence or offences taken into consideration in determining sentence shall not exceed the difference (if any) between the amount or total amount which under the foregoing provisions of this subsection is the maximum for the offence or offences of which the offender has been

15 *Munday* v. *Metropolitan Police District Receiver* [1949] 1 All E.R. 337.
16 Cmnd. 1406, June 1961.
17 Cmnd. 2323, March 1964.

convicted and the amount or total amounts (if any) which are in fact ordered to be paid in respect of that offence or those offences.

(6) Section 4 of the Forfeiture Act 1870, section 4 of the Protection of Animals Act 1911, section 11 (2) of the Criminal Justice Act 1948, section 34 of the Magistrates' Courts Act 1952 and section 8 of the Criminal Damage Act 1971 shall cease to have effect. . . .

3. At any time before a compensation order has been complied with or fully complied with, the magistrates' court for the time being having functions in relation to the enforcement of the order may, on the application of the person against whom it was made, discharge the order, or reduce the amount which remains to be paid, if it appears to the court—

(a) that the injury, loss or damage in respect of which the order was made has been held in civil proceedings to be less than it was taken to be for the purposes of the order; or

(b) in the case of an order in respect of the loss of any property, that the property has been recovered by the person in whose favour the order was made.

4.—(1) This section shall have effect where a compensation order has been made in favour of any person in respect of any injury, loss or damage and a claim by him in civil proceedings for damages in respect thereof subsequently falls to be determined.

(2) The damages in the civil proceedings shall be assessed without regard to the order; but where the whole or part of the amount awarded by the order has been paid, the damages awarded in the civil proceedings shall not exceed the amount (if any) by which, as so assessed, they exceed the amount paid under the order.

(3) Where there is an amount unpaid under the compensation order (whether the whole or part of the amount awarded) and the court awards damages in the civil proceedings, then, unless the person against whom the order was made has ceased to be liable to pay the amount unpaid (whether in consequence of an appeal, of his imprisonment for default or otherwise), the court shall direct that the judgment—

(a) if it is for an amount not exceeding the amount unpaid under the order, shall not be enforced; or

(b) if it is for an amount exceeding the amount unpaid under the order, shall not be enforced as to a corresponding amount,

without the leave of the court. . . .

CRIMINAL BANKRUPTCY

7.—(1) Where a person is convicted of an offence before the Crown Court and it appears to the court that—

(a) as a result of the offence, or of that offence taken together with any other relevant offence or offences, loss or damage (not attributable to personal injury) has been suffered by one or more persons whose identity is known to the court; and

(b) the amount, or aggregate amount, of the loss or damage exceeds £15,000,

the court may, in addition to dealing with the offender in any other way (but not if it makes a compensation order against him), make a criminal bankruptcy order against him in respect of the offence or, as the case may be, that offence and the other relevant offence or offences.

(2) In subsection (1) of this section "other relevant offence or offences" means an offence or offences of which the person in question is convicted in the same proceedings or which the court takes into consideration in determining his sentence.

(3) A criminal bankruptcy order shall specify—

    (*a*) the amount of the loss or damage appearing to the court to have resulted from the offence or, if more than one, each of the offences;

    (*b*) the person or persons appearing to the court to have suffered that loss or damage;

    (*c*) the amount of that loss or damage which it appears to the court that that person, or each of those persons, has suffered; . . .

(6) The Secretary of State may by order made by statutory instrument direct that subsection (1) . . . shall be amended by substituting . . . such amount as may be specified in the order; and any order . . . shall be subject to annulment in pursuance of a resolution of either House of Parliament. . . .

The Criminal Injuries Compensation Scheme

Report of the Criminal Injuries Compensation Board
Cmnd. 4812, 1971

APPENDIX E

1. The Compensation Scheme will be administered by the Criminal Injuries Compensation Board, appointments to which will be made by the Home Secretary and the Secretary of State for Scotland, after consultation with the Lord Chancellor. The Chairman will be a person of wide legal experience, and the other members of whom there are at present eight, will also be legally qualified. . . .

4. The Board will be entirely responsible for deciding what compensation should be paid in individual cases and their decisions will not be subject to appeal or to Ministerial review. . . .

5. The Board will entertain applications for *ex gratia* payment of compensation in any case where the applicant or, in the case of an application by a spouse or dependant (see paragraph 12 below), the deceased, sustained in Great Britain, or on a British vessel, aircraft or hovercraft, on or after 1st August 1964 personal injury directly attributable to a crime of violence (including arson and poisoning) or to an arrest or attempted arrest of an offender or suspected offender or to the prevention or attempted prevention of an offence or to the giving of help to any constable who is engaged in arresting or attempting to arrest an offender or suspected offender or preventing or attempting to prevent an offence. In considering for the purpose of this paragraph whether any act is a criminal act, any immunity at law of an offender, attributable to his youth or insanity or other condition, will be left out of account.

6. Compensation will not be payable unless the Bord is satisfied—

    (*a*) that the injury was one for which compensation of not less than £50 would be awarded; and

    (*b*) that the circumstances of the injury have been the subject of criminal proceedings or were reported to the police without delay; and

    (*c*) that the applicant has given the Board all reasonable assistance particularly in relation to any medical reports that they may require.

Provided that the Board at their discretion may waive the requirement in (*b*) above.

7. Where the victim who suffered injuries and the offender who inflicted them were living together at the time as members of the same family no compensation will be payable. . . . [W]here a man and woman were living together as man and wife they will be treated as if they were married to one another.

8. Traffic offences will be excluded from the scheme, except where there has been a deliberate attempt to run the victim down.

9. The Board will scrutinise with particular care all applications in respect of sexual offences or other offences arising out of a sexual relationship, in order to determine whether there was any responsibility, either because of provocation or otherwise, on the part of the victim (see paragraph 17 below), and they will especially have regard to any delay that has occurred in submitting the application. The Board will consider applications for compensation arising out of rape and sexual assaults, both in respect of pain, suffering and shock and in respect of loss of earnings due to pregnancy resulting from rape and, where the victim is ineligible for a maternity grant under the National Health Scheme, in respect of the expenses of childbirth. Compensation will not be payable for the maintenance of any child born as a result of a sexual offence.

10. Subject to what is said in the following paragraphs, compensation will be assessed on the basis of common law damages and will take the form of a lump sum payment, rather than a periodical pension. More than one payment may, however, sometimes be made—for example, where only a provisional medical assessment can be given in the first instance.

11. Where the victim is alive the amount of compensation will be limited as follows—

(a) the rate of loss of earnings (and, where appropriate, of earning capacity) to be taken into account will not exceed twice the average of industrial earnings at the time that the injury was sustained;

(b) there will be no element comparable to exemplary or punitive damages.

12. Where the victim has died in consequence of the injury no compensation will be payable for the benefit of his estate but . . . compensation will be payable to any person entitled to claim under the Fatal Accidents Acts 1846 to 1959. . . .

13. Where the victim has died otherwise than in consequence of the injury, the Board may make an award in respect of loss of wages, expenses and liabilities incurred before death as a result of the injury where, in their opinion, hardship to dependants would otherwise result. . . .

17. The Board will reduce the amount of compensation or reject the application altogether if, having regard to the conduct of the victim, including his conduct before and after the events giving rise to the claim, and to his character and way of life it is inappropriate that he should be granted a full award or any award at all.

18. The Board will have discretion to make special arrangements for the administration of any money awarded. . . .

23. Procedure at a hearing will be as informal as is consistent with a proper determination of the application, and the hearing will be in private.

ENFORCEMENT OF JUDGMENTS

Enforcing the Law : R. M. Jackson
Macmillan, 1972

A judgment may be sufficient in itself, as where a marriage is dissolved, but apart from decisions as to status the ordinary result is that the judgment provides for one or more of several forms of remedy. If the defendant does not comply, further steps must be taken where a judgment is for the recovery of land or buildings, sheriff's officers (with police help if need be) will eject the wrongful occupant and put the successful plaintiff into possession. An injunction, that is an order that a person do some specified thing or refrain from doing something, and a somewhat similar order for specific performance of a contract, is enforced by regarding wilful failure as contempt of court, so that the defaulter may be sent to prison; the committal is usually for an indeterminate time and it will end when he " purges " his contempt by apology and promises to comply with the order. A judgment for damages may lead to the defendant's property being seized and sold so that the plaintiff may be paid out of the proceeds. More elaborate remedies exist to make intangible property such as a bank balance, and other assets available for the judgment creditor....

All forms of enforcement ultimately depend on the power of the State. If sheriff's officers are prevented by force or threatened violence from seizing goods or entering upon property they must call on the police; and if the police cannot tackle the job the armed forces must be brought in....

When a judgment has been given there is no automatic enforcement: no enforcement procedures will take place unless the plaintiff sets them in motion, and he decides whether to pursue his remedies to the full or to be content with less than his pound of flesh.

County Courts Act 1959
7 & 8 Eliz. 2, c. 22

124.—(1) Every bailiff or officer executing any warrant of execution issued from a county court against the goods or chattels of any person may by virtue thereof seize—

(*a*) any of the goods and chattels of that person, except the wearing apparel and bedding of that person or his family, and the tools and implements of his trade, to the prescribed value, which shall to that extent be protected from seizure; and

(*b*) any money, banknotes, bills of exchange, promisory notes, bonds, specialties or securities for money belonging to that person.

(2) The prescribed value for the purposes of the foregoing subsection shall be the same as that for the purposes of section eight of the Small Debts Act, 1845, namely, twenty pounds or such larger amount as is for the time being prescribed under subsection (2) of section thirty-seven of the Administration of Justice Act, 1956, by order of the Lord Chancellor....

128. No goods seized in execution under process of a county court shall be sold for the purpose of satisfying the warrant of execution until the expiration of a period of at least five days next following the day on which the goods have been so seized unless—

(*a*) the goods are of a perishable nature; or

(*b*) the person whose goods have been seized so requests in writing.

Report of the Committee on the Enforcement of Judgment Debts
Cmnd. 3909, 1969

46.... Nowadays credit has become as indispensable to the economy of ordinary families as it was to the development of industrialism.... [I]t is no part of our enquiry to examine the ethical and economic aspects of the credit system. We start from the assumption that citizens ought to repay legally binding debts and that the community recognises a social and moral obligation to honour obligations freely contracted.... The function of law is to compel observance of the rule in those marginal cases where moral and social sanctions fail. Accordingly, the legal machinery must be efficient, capable of reaching out to all the assets of a debtor and yet sensitive both to the needs and social circumstances of debtors and to the rights of creditors.

Contractual debts

58. Apart from civil actions in which damages are claimed and matrimonial proceedings, the main civil business of the High Court, particularly in cases which do not proceed to trial, is the recovery of contractual debts.... [W]e estimate that writs of summons for the recovery of debts represent about 85 per cent. of the total of the writs issued. In the county court, the proportion of claims for the recovery of debts is about the same....

59.... [A] tiny proportion only of the total value of contractual debts are sued for and most actions are uncontested and are brought in the county court for sums under £100. Indeed, were it otherwise, the credit and legal system would collapse. Nevertheless the aggregate amounts involved are large.

60. ... In 1967 the amounts [recovered in the High Court and sued for in the county courts] . . . were of the order of £30 million and £37 million respectively.... [Between 1956–67 the number of default and Order 14 judgments was over 90 per cent. in the High Court and those disposed of by consent or on admission or in default of appearance or defence in county courts was 62–70 per cent.]

68. Very little is known about the debtors. We estimate that some one million persons are sued for debt every year and that on the average judgment debts are discharged in three years. We think that the largest group of debtors consists of married, male wage-earners who have contracted multiple obligations and lack resources other than their weekly earnings.

69. We regard the multiple debtor as an important figure in our enquiry. The evidence we have received shows that one debtor is very likely to be owing many other debts at the same time. If he is in arrear with his hire purchase instalments, he is very likely to be in arrear also with his rent or with his rates or with his gas and electricity bills. Indeed, this situation extends over a wider field. If a man is in arrears with his maintenance orders, he is very likely to have hire purchase and other debts at the same time; in some cases the civil debtor may also be discharging a fine imposed on him by a magistrates' court.

70. This has a very important bearing upon what should be the proper machinery for the recovery, and more especially the enforcement, of debts. It is undesirable from the social and economic point of view that the civil debts of one debtor should be dealt with individually and a very great burden must fall upon the legal machinery if each debt can be pursued separately, and if each creditor is allowed to pursue the enforcement of his debt without regard to other creditors. Such a system harms both debtor and creditor. So far as a debtor is concerned, the satisfaction of one of several debts relieves him hardly at all from the burden of his debts and a continual pursuit by the other creditors through the courts. From the point of view of the creditors, each is induced to seek priority for his own debt, if necessary at the expense of other creditors. The machinery of the courts becomes a game in which the prize goes to the swiftest and sometimes to the least deserving. The game becomes a " free for all " and the reasonable or indulgent creditor may be overtaken by the demanding or exacting creditor....

76. . . . Enforcement is predominantly a matter of legal rights but it would be foolish to ignore its crucial effects not only upon the individual debtor but also upon his family. We have received a considerable body of opinion, some of it expressed in strong, even virulent, language to the effect that the courts lean heavily in favour of debtors, and that the present enforcement system is designed to help the debtor and not the creditor. We think that these complaints are misguided and misconceived. The truth is that all courts, judges and registrars alike, are aware that it is necessary to have regard to the social needs of the debtor while at the same time enforcing the legal rights of the creditor, and it is in the endeavour to find a fair and proper balance between these conflicting interests that they incur the wrath of the creditors.

77. . . . . It is perhaps a remarkable feature of our present legal system that, although it is possible for the enforcement of a civil debt to sell up a man's home or to commit him to prison, there is no such individual study or consideration of his circumstances and welfare as is devoted to a man who has been found guilty of a criminal offence, and for whom the Probation Service exists. We have accordingly thought it right to consider, without, we stress, diminishing the effectiveness of the enforcement system, how far and in what ways it would be useful and proper to improve the administration of justice by introducing the provisions of the social services into the enforcement procedures of the courts.

311. . . . Dissatisfaction and disillusion with the present system are widespread and there is evidence . . . of creditors who will not pursue their remedies in the courts because of the feeling that it is a waste of time and of others who have recourse to private and sometimes ugly methods of enforcement. . . .

313. . . . We have had to consider whether the existing system could be amended and modified or whether more fundamental changes are necessary. . . . [W]e are agreed that mere reforms in the present framework will be no solution of the problems disclosed by our examination. . . . [A] fresh approach to the whole question is essential so that new modern machinery can be devised.

314. . . .

> (a) There should be an integrated system for the enforcement of the judgment debts of all civil courts subject to specified exceptions.
>
> (b) The process for the enforcement of judgment debts should be capable of reaching out to all the income, assets and property of the judgment debtor subject to specified exceptions.
>
> (c) The modes of enforcement should be capable of being employed concurrently or consecutively in one continuous process.
>
> (d) Full information about the means, property, assets and circumstances of the debtor should be ascertained before enforcement is pursued and the onus of disclosing the information should be placed upon the debtor.
>
> (e) The proceeds recovered in the course of the enforcement of judgment debts should be fairly distributed amongst the judgment creditors subject to specified priorities between them.
>
> (f) The procedure should provide for the fair treatment of the judgment debtor.
>
> (g) The system should contain methods for the control of credit of judgment debtors.
>
> (h) The system should be operated by machinery which should be efficient, effective, expeditious and fair. . . .

316. The first and vital step is to replace the present miscellany of enforcement courts and processes by a new office in which an integrated system of enforcement of judgment debts can be operated. . . .

338. Accordingly we recommend the establishment of an " Enforcement Office " to which the enforcement of all civil judgment debts (subject to exceptions hereinafter mentioned) should be channelled. . . .

346. . . . [W]e think that the matrimonial and affiliation orders made by the magistrates' courts should normally remain for enforcement in the magistrates' court but that the magistrates should be able, on the application of the wife or other complainant or the Ministry of Social Security and at their discretion, to transfer them to the Enforcement Office, if it is desired to use the modes of enforcement there available. . . .

348. Precisely the same situation will apply to the enforcement of fines and other judgment debts arising in criminal proceedings. We envisage that the enforcement of fines and other criminal judgment debts including costs, which may now under the Criminal Justice Act 1967 be enforced in the county court, should be undertaken in the new Enforcement Office if they are transferred by the appropriate criminal court. In this event imprisonment . . . will not be available. . . .

351. Only the maintenance orders of the High Court and the county court will not be enforceable through the Enforcement Office. These will remain for enforcement in the courts which made them unless transferred by them to the Enforcement Office or to magistrates' courts. . . .

Execution upon goods

631. . . . [I]n all the evidence which we have received there has been no suggestion that execution upon goods should be abolished. . . . The ultimate justification for the levy of an execution as a method of enforcement . . . is that it is wrong for the debtor to continue to have and enjoy the use of any goods and property which are not exempt from seizure whilst he remains under the obligation to discharge his judgment debt.

632. The sale of goods seized under an execution in the county court is in practice very rare indeed. . . .

This appears from the following table:

Year	Number of Executions	Number of Sales
1963	1,651,577	5,505
1964	1,758,451	4,113
1965	1,789,519	3,269
1966	1,655,439	3,206
1967	1,608,905	3,445

633. So far as the High Court is concerned . . . for the first six months of 1964–1965 . . . out of 18,262 writs of *fi. fa.* there were 568 sales. . . .

634. Every effort is made to avoid a sale, partly because of the obvious hardship to debtors and their families but no less because the price of second hand furniture and other goods is so low that the sums realised are often hardly worth the trouble involved. . . .

635. There can be no doubt that the effectiveness of execution . . . rests in the threat to sell. . . . This threat is, of course, effective against the honest and the dishonest debtor alike. . . . [F]or the six months period of the shrievalty year 1965–66, execution by writ of *fi. fa.* resulted in satisfaction to the extent of 68 per cent. in the case of judgments under £75 and to the extent of 47 per cent. in the case of judgments over £75. On the other hand, in no fewer than 30 per cent. of the writs of *fi. fa.* issued for execution there were no goods. . . .

637. . . . [I]t seems likely that, of the goods sold, a higher proportion are the goods of traders rather than of private householders. . . .

642. Our conclusion that the judgment debts of all the civil courts should be enforced through an Enforcement Office applies as much to execution upon goods as to all the other modes of enforcement. . . .

675. There is . . . one point of exceptional importance and urgency. . . . In relation to the exemption of goods from seizure attention has been brought to the fact that the disruption which sometimes takes place in the family of the debtor when the furniture and furnishings are removed and sold under an execution far outweighs any possible advantage that may accrue to the judgment creditor. . . . This point was emphasised to us by the Under Sheriffs' Association. . . .

> " This Association is concerned at the hardship that can be caused to detbors' families by the removal of household goods that are virtually essential to the maintenance of the family as a whole. Sheriffs' Officers would welcome authority to leave on debtors' premises sufficient chattels to prevent disruption of the debtor's household. . . ."

We agree . . . and recommend that a list of exempted articles should be prescribed, after consultation with social welfare and other interested organisations, and founded upon the general principle that a tradesman should retain such tools of trade and goods as are necessary to enable him to maintain his earnings, and that such household goods and personal clothing should be exempted as are necessary to provide a clean and decent home for the whole family.

Attachment of Earnings Act 1971
1971, c. 32

1.—(1) The High Court may make an attachment of earnings order to secure payments under a High Court maintenance order.

(2) A county court may make an attachment of earnings order to secure—

(*a*) payments under a High Court or a county court maintenance order;

(*b*) the payment of a judgment debt, other than a debt of less than £5 or such other sum as may be prescribed by county court rules; or

(*c*) payments under an administration order.

(3) A magistrates' court may make an attachment of earnings order to secure—

(*a*) payments under a magistrates' court maintenance order;

(*b*) the payment of any sum adjudged to be paid by a conviction or treated (by any enactment relating to the collection and enforcement of fines, costs, compensation or forfeited recognisances) as so adjudged to be paid; or

(*c*) the payment of any sum required to be paid by a legal aid contribution order. . . .

6.—(1) An attachment of earnings order shall be an order directed to a person who appears to the court to have the debtor in his employment and shall operate as an instruction to that person—

(*a*) to make periodical deductions from the debtor's earnings in accordance with Part I of Schedule 3 to this Act; and

(*b*) at such times as the order may require, or as the court may allow, to pay the amounts deducted to the collecting officer of the court, as specified in the order.

Law Commission : Landlord and Tenant : Interim Report on Distress for Rent

Law Com., No. 5, 1966

15. There is little indication either that the threat of distraint is abused or that abuses occur in the course of distress, or that unjustifiable hardship is caused by distress. Nevertheless, some warning notes were sounded; and in particular, cases cited by the National Citizens' Advice Bureaux Council are significant. Another reply pointed to the emotional upset caused to tenants' families by the law of distress, and another to the fact that on account of the disproportionately low second-hand value of goods today, a family could lose all its possessions in satisfying a minimal debt. Clearly the second-hand value of such things as washing machines, cookers, radio and T.V. sets (favoured objects of distress) bears no relation to their cost when new. Although tenants do not lose their homes by distress yet the loss of their furniture and domestic equipment makes it likely that these will be replaced and that this will lead to heavy new hire-purchase liabilities, thus conducing to further arrears of rent. The answer might be that the tenant would do better to give up his tenancy and find one at a rent within his means. But it must be appreciated that rent arrears are just as likely to arise from unemployment, sickness or matrimonial disturbances, as from careless mismanagement. In cases of misfortune it is undoubtedly the practice of most landlords, if they know tenants to be in such difficulties, to stay their hand, but too often tenants make no attempt to explain their problems and it is only on the bailiff's arrival that they come to light. From the information provided it appears that bailiffs generally do what they can to avoid loss under distress, where there is a genuine case of misfortune or hardship. On the other hand it can be said that distress is less disastrous to the tenant than eviction, and certainly less expensive than a judgment for arrears. The timeous use of distress in appropriate cases may save the tenant from accumulating further arrears of rent thus adding to his difficulties.

16. The replies to the questionnaires demonstrate quite clearly that the threat of a levy of distress is, in the overwhelming majority of cases, sufficient to produce payment of arrears and rent. . . . Where, in the very small minority of cases, levy of distress is pursued to its conclusion, the indications are that the result is frequently unsatisfactory, either because there are insufficient saleable goods or because the sale proceeds do not satisfy the debt and the costs of distress and auction. It does not appear that the common law and statutory exceptions protecting certain categories of goods from distress have any material effect upon the effectiveness of the threat of a distress warrant as a means of producing payment.

17. Distress for rent has to a large extent fallen into disuse. . . .

18. It is clear that landlords are in a less favourable position than most other creditors. Once a landlord has taken a tenant he is compelled to give credit until he can recover possession, whilst a tradesman gives and can withhold credit upon his assessment of the customer's position. What the landlord wants, therefore, when he has to deal with a tenant in arrears, is a speedy effective remedy and certainly one that is going to satisfy him more quickly and at less cost than the action for recovery of arrears at present provides. . . .

19. Where application to the court is a pre-condition to the levy of distress, the delay involved at the present time is of the order of two to three weeks. This delay is likely to produce further arrears of rent which may have, in due course, to be the subject of a fresh application. . . .

21. So far as local authorities are concerned those that employ the remedy . . . do so to a limited extent and only when they are reasonably satisfied that the appearance of the bailiff will produce payment. Many such authorities accept

an obligation and exercise a tolerance not only in hardship cases but also to bad tenants who otherwise might not find accommodation. Such authorities go to extreme lengths (by repeated warning notices, use of welfare offices etc.) not only to avoid eviction proceedings but even to avoid levying distress. . . .

23. The Law Commission approaches its recommendations upon distress for rent with the following conclusions in mind:

A. Distress for rent is a remedy of which little use is made in practice; but where it is invoked the first step, the issue of a warrant—or its equivalent—is more productive of results in obtaining payment of arrears than the pursuit of distress to the point of sale.

B. The archaic and extrajudicial character of the remedy makes it unattractive to contemporary society, although there is little evidence of abuse of the remedy or of substantial hardship occasioned by its exercise.

C. Arrears of rent, whether the results of bad management or of misfortune on the part of the tenant, are merely one aspect of the problem of overall individual indebtedness and their recovery is one aspect of the wider problem of satisfactory enforcement processses.

D. In the rare cases where the remedy is used, even when leave is required, the process is speedy and inexpensive compared with the present available remedies of an action for arrears or for possession.

E. The extended requirement of leave of the court for distress imposed by the Rent Act 1965 is likely further to restrict its use by private landlords.

F. There is no major criticism of the existing features of the remedy other than of the requirement of the court's leave, where this exists, by landlords and of the absence of such a requirement, where it does not exist, by tenants.

G. In the case of landlords of dwelling houses to whom Part I of the Rent Act 1965 does not apply (mainly local authorities), no reason has been given why they should receive more favourable treatment in respect of this use of the remedy than private landlords. Local authorities rentals are, to an increasing extent, determined by realistic standards. Further, in respect of recovery of possession, the policy appears to be to assimilate the local authorities' position to that of private landlords (see e.g. section 35 of the Rent Act 1965). Finally, it is desirable that self-help remedies should be brought under judicial control, as has, for example, occurred with the retaking of goods within the Hire Purchase Act 1965 let on hire-purchase terms. Contemplation of the possibility of a modernised and comprehensive debt enforcement machinery also supports the removal of the present differentiation of private and other landlords.

24. Although the extremely limited use of distress for rent . . . does support a case for the immediate abolition of the remedy. . . . The real demand is for a review of remedies for non-payment of rent and for the provision of an effective machinery for debt recovery from those members of the community whose practices or misfortunes lead them into a condition of chronic indebtedness towards their landlords and other creditors. The former, a review of remedies, is currently being examined under Item VIII of the Law Commission's First Programme (Codification of the law of landlord and tenant). The latter, enforcement procedures and machinery, is under consideration by the Payne Committee. Pending the completion of these examinations, it is . . . considered that distress for rent should not be abolished. . . .

Chapter 8

PENALTIES

Introduction

Looking at penalties requires a quite different attitude and approach from much that has been considered so far. It seems almost inevitable, as was said earlier, that in studying the legal system one's attention is drawn especially to the decision-making part of it, and in particular the decision which takes place when a judge finally decides the case at the end of the legal process, in the narrow sense of the process of litigation and trial, even though it is clear that legal rules and the legal profession itself play a role which goes far beyond this narrow area. One tends therefore to arrive at the problem of disposal and treatment as something which comes at the end of the process. In fact the problems of penal policy and the treatment of offenders are problems in their own right and are not simply an end product of the trial process. This is even more the case now that attention has shifted increasingly from treatment as punishment to treatment as a process of rehabilitation and reform. There is a greater plausibility in seeing the sentence as merely the end product of the detection, apprehension, prosecution and conviction sequence when treatment takes the form of the appropriate penalty. Once the reform element enters into the matter and the court is faced with an ever increasing variety of possibilities and is being asked to consider what is best for the offender and the community, it is more plausible and certainly more helpful to see the whole trial process as simply the condition that has to be fulfilled before measures can be taken without the offender's consent which will offer the best hope that he and others will not commit further offences. Alternatively one can readjust one's perspective by recalling that litigation and the trial process itself which makes up much of the contents of this book, is only one of the ways in which the legal system as a whole is attempting to deal with the social problems with which at any given time it is called upon to cope. From this perspective the real problems which face the legal system are not the technical problems of how to get a dispute into manageable shape, how to find the facts, how to make the law; these are simply problems of method and technique; the real problems relate to the provision of facilities to enable people to carry on their daily affairs in a peaceful and orderly way, the satisfaction of their legitimate expectations, the prevention and settlement of disputes, the maintenance of order and the protection of persons and property, the definition and discouragement of intolerable behaviour, the reduction of death and injury on the roads and in the factory, oiling the wheels of the economy, smoothing out the business and work relations of companies and individuals, and the personal relations of families, parents and children, subject always to the qualification that the contribution that the legal system can make is always limited by its powers and its own particular style. The real problem with which this chapter is concerned is what to do with those whom society has labelled offenders to prevent them and to discourage them and others from committing more of what society has labelled offences, and it is a problem which requires a quite different technique from those relevant to many of the technical matters that have been discussed before. This chapter deals first with the problems of sentencing and then discusses some of the sentences available.

The problems of sentencing

Committee on Homosexuality and Prostitution
Cmnd. 247, 1957

169. In general, to decide the most appropriate method of treatment of a particular offender is a much more difficult problem for the courts than the decision as to his guilt, and this is particularly true of the offences with which we are here concerned. It is, however, of the utmost importance, not only to the offender but to the whole community, that the sentence should be right and effective. Harsh treatment can undoubtedly create in the offender a sense of injustice and induce in him a frame of mind likely to make him more inclined to commit further offences. On the other hand, leniency may not only have the same effect, by encouraging the offender to believe that he has nothing to fear if he commits further offences, but may also encourage potential offenders to believe that they have nothing to fear if they commit similar offences.

170. It is, we understand, now generally accepted that apart altogether from any considerations of retribution the objectives of penal sanctions are deterrence, prevention and reformation. Thus the law provides for the punishment of certain acts in the hope that persons will be deterred from committing such acts. Where the law itself has not proved a sufficient deterrent, it may be necessary, for the protection of others, to prevent the offender from doing further wrong, even by putting him in prison. And for the common good it is desirable that an offender should be subjected to such form of treatment as is most likely to improve his character and make him a better citizen.

171. The courts are faced with the problem of reconciling, in an individual case, these three main objectives, which are not always compatible. It is not enough to look only to the details of the offence or the circumstances of the offender. In doing justice to the individual offender the courts cannot overlook their duty to protect other citizens and to ensure respect for the criminal law, and they must necessarily ask themselves in every case which of these three objectives should be paramount before considering the method most likely to be successful in a particular case. Thus, for example, when a particular offence is rife at a particular time or in a particular place, it may be right for the courts to attach more weight to the deterrent and preventive aspects than would otherwise be the case. At the same time, the ultimate purpose is more likely to be achieved if the treatment of the offender is constructive and not merely punitive, and it follows that the personality of the individual offender must be a decisive factor in determining the appropriate treatment.

Report of the Inter Departmental Committee on the Business of the Criminal Courts
Cmnd. 1289, 1961

257. Sentencing used to be a comparatively simple matter. The primary objective was to fix a sentence proportionate to the offender's culpability, and

the system has been loosely described as the " tariff system." The facts of the offence and the offender's record were the main pieces of information needed by the court, and the defence could bring to notice any mitigating circumstances. The information was about past events which could normally be reliably described; and it was readily available.

258. In addition, the courts have always had in mind the need to protect society from the persistent offender, to deter potential offenders and to deter or reform the individual offender. But in general it was thought that the " tariff system " took these other objectives in its stride. Giving an offender the punishment he deserved was thought to be the best way of deterring him and others and of protecting society.

259. Over the last few decades, these other objectives have received increased attention. The development has been most obvious in the increased weight which the courts give to the needs of the offender as a person. It is realised that whatever punishment is imposed, he will eventually return to society, and sentences are increasingly passed with the deterrence or reform of the offender as the principal objective; and in assessing the offender's culpability his social and domestic background is more closely examined. In addition, sentencers give special attention to the need to protect society from persistent offenders and a special form of sentence, preventive detention, is available in appropriate cases; and increases in crime have emphasised the need to deter potential offenders.

263. This wider range of objectives naturally calls for different information. The information which enabled the court to assess culpability is not necessarily the information which indicates how the offender should be reformed, much less how potential offenders should be deterred.

267. Where the court is considering culpability there is little room for doubt about the sort of information which is relevant. The facts of the offence indicate its seriousness, and it is reasonably clear what additional information will count in mitigation. But where the court is seeking, for instance, to deter or reform the individual offender it is less clear what constitutes relevant information. . . .

268. . . . . There are many gaps in our knowledge, and it must be frankly recognised that some of the objectives which sentencers have in view require information which is not at present available. . . .

269. In our view the key to advance in this field is to recognise the fundamental difference between assessing culpability and pursuing the other objectives of sentencing: namely, that where the court is seeking to reform, to deter or to protect, it is seeking to control future events rather than simply to pass judgment on past events. The court can never know for certain that the sentence will in fact control events in the way desired, but if such an objective is to be based on more than a hunch, the court must, in logic and justice, have reasonable grounds for believing that the sentence is likely to have the desired effect. . . .

270. The most satisfactory ground for such beliefs is that similar sentences previously imposed in similar circumstances have had the desired result; for although these objectives are concerned with future events, the events are—in theory at any rate—capable of being subsequently observed. Unless the results of this observation are properly marshalled and systematically made available to the courts, sentences aimed at controlling future events are largely speculative, and the courts cannot even know whether such objectives are practicable. . . .

274. The sentencer . . . can profitably reflect on the lessons to be drawn from his own experience, but his experience is necessarily restricted. At quarter sessions and petty sessions he can see reports from probation officers on offenders whom he has placed on probation, and in the course of time he sees a good many offenders who have previous convictions and have therefore not been

deterred or reformed by previous sentences. But this is only a narrow picture. Every day he passes sentences without knowing whether they achieve what they aim at. For all he knows, every offender whom he seeks to reform or deter may commit another offence within a few days of finishing the sentence imposed to prevent this happening. But unless he has information of this kind, he can never make an informed re-appraisal of his practice. . . .

280. . . . [O]ccasionally the need to deter others is regarded as so pressing that it becomes the dominant consideration and the court passes a sentence which is specially designed to be exemplary. It may be, for instance, that a sentence of three years' imprisonment would normally be the appropriate sentence for a particular assault, but assaults of that type have recently been prevalent in the area and the court imposes a sentence of five years with the specific aim of reducing the number of such assaults or of arresting the increase.

281. The justification for exemplary sentences lies in the supposition that they deter, and it is important that the courts should have reliable information bearing on this supposition. . . . It is also desirable, in fairness to the offenders who are made an example of. . . .[1]

297. In addition, the greater complexity of sentencing has increased the information needed about what the different forms of sentence themselves involve. In the latter half of the 19th century practically the only sentence imposed at assizes and quarter sessions was one of detention, which was called imprisonment if the term was shorter than three years [or at one stage, 5 years] and penal servitude otherwise, and there were few refinements within the system. But only about half the sentences now imposed at the superior courts are strictly sentences of imprisonment. The additional objectives which sentences aim at have widened the range of sentences available. . . . Each is designed to deal with different types of offenders and has its own characteristic regime, with which the court should be familiar if a sentence is to bear some relation to the offender's culpability. . . .

298. In recent years the authorities have put out a certain amount of general information to courts about what the different forms of sentence involve, what they are designed to achieve and what they do achieve. A Stationery Office publication " Prisons and Borstals," which is revised every few years, has been circulated to courts.[2] The Home Office have also issued occasional circulars to courts about what new sentences involve and, more recently, about the results of research into the efficacy of these sentences (e.g. detention in a detention centre).

299. . . . We recommend that there should be a standing booklet covering all forms of sentence and written specially for sentencers. . . .

300. The booklet should be revised, as necessary, every few years, and supplemented every six months, say, by information about national trends in crime, together with additional research material as it becomes available. . . .

301. We recommend that the dissemination of this information should be the responsibility of the Home Office. . . . This does not infringe the principle

---

[1] Cf. Hall Williams, The English Penal System in Transition, p. 9: " Illustrations which are frequently used by English judges as evidence to justify deterrent penalties are: 1. The decline in post office fraud following the harsh penalties adopted by the judges in the immediate post-war years; 2. The decline in racial violence following the severe sentences passed in the cases of the Notting Hill disturbances; 3. The decline in telephone kiosk thefts following the tough line taken with offenders by the Birmingham courts. It may be true that the harsh penalties inflicted contributed to controlling each of these situations, but close analysis reveals that there were in each situation other factors which affected the situation equally strongly, such as, in cases 1 and 3, changes in post office techniques and equipment and in case 2 a falling off in racial tension which preceded the actual sentence."

[2] The last edition was in fact published in 1960.

that the Executive should not interfere with the judiciary or seek to control its work. The information we have in mind does not point to decisions going a particular way in individual cases or in groups of cases. It is the basic factual material on which such decisions have to be based and it is proper that the Executive should supply it. . . .

The committee also placed great emphasis on the importance of sentencers visiting penal institutions and also recommended a procedure by which sentencers could follow up particular cases and receive information about how an offender had progressed, his response to after-care, probation and any subsequent conviction within three years of his finishing his sentence. The recommendation that a book on sentences be published has been put into effect by the publication of *The sentence of the court*. In addition the Home Office publishes a series of specific studies undertaken by or on behalf of its own Research Unit. From time to time " sentencing conferences " have been organised for judges and magistrates. It is also one of the functions of the Divisional Court of the Queen's Bench Division, the Court of Appeal and the Lord Chief Justice to give general guidance on matters of sentencing in the course of their judgments. The Lord Chancellor and the Lord Chief Justice also from time to time make extrajudicial statements of general policy.

Information related to individual offenders

THE PROSECUTION

325. In order to assess culpability, the court needs to have, first, full details of the offence which it is dealing with. The prosecution assumes responsibility for placing these facts before the court; and there is manifestly no difficulty in this type of information being available.[3]

THE POLICE

326. . . . [T]he police . . . provide a statement of the antecedents of every person appearing for trial or sentence. The scope of this statement has varied a little over the years, but since 1955 the police have had a clear direction, in the form of a resolution of the judges of the Queen's Bench Division, that it should contain " a factual statement of the previous convictions, date of birth (if known), education and employment, the date of arrest, whether the prisoner has been on bail, and if previously convicted, the date of his last discharge from prison, if known. It may also contain a short and concise statement as to the prisoner's domestic and family circumstances, his general reputation and associates, and if it is to be said that he associates with bad characters, the officer giving evidence must be able to speak of this from his own knowledge." . . .

327. . . . Before the development of the probation service, the court rarely looked for more than a brief picture of the offender from the police officer in

---

[3] At para. 289 the committee had noted: " Under the system we have in this country the parties in the case give the court less direct help in arriving at the right sentence than they do in other judicial matters." *Cf.* the ruling of the Bar Council in 1952: " Counsel for the prosecution should state all the relevant facts of the case dispassionately whether they tell in favour of a severe sentence or otherwise; but he should not attempt by advocacy to influence the court towards a more severe sentence. It is, however, a common and proper practice, especially in the case of an unrepresented offender, for prosecuting counsel to draw the attention of the court to any mitigating circumstances as to which he is instructed."

charge of the case. But courts now place increased emphasis on the offender's social and domestic background, particularly where he is young or has no previous convictions. . . . This deeper study of the offender is better entrusted to a probation officer, as a trained social worker serving the court; and in any event it would be inappropriate for the police to enquire into some of the background matters which a probation officer finds it useful to examine. . . .

328. On the other hand, we do not think that the police statement should be restricted to those matters (e.g. criminal record and tendencies) with which the police are automatically concerned. In a case where a probation report is not thought to be necessary or cannot be available upon conviction, it would be foolish to deprive the court of information about the offender's education record, employment and home conditions which it would not otherwise have and might find helpful in almost every case. For instance, information of this kind helps the court to avoid imposing a fine which is either nugatory or oppressive. Moreover, if the police are encouraged to see the defendant in the wider context of his background, their report on the purely criminal aspects of his antecedents will be more balanced and therefore more valuable; and this broader conception of their functions also has important advantages for the police themselves from the point of view of their position in the community.

330. We . . . recommend that at least 24 hours before a defendant is due to appear in a superior court, the prosecution should, where possible, furnish the clerk of the court with a copy of the proof of the antecedents statement. . . . We later recommend that the court should have at this stage a copy of any probation report to be made. . . . The statement would not be seen by the jury, who alone are concerned with the issue of guilt, but by the judge, who is already supplied with a confidential list of the previous convictions of the prisoners for trial and with the Prison Commissioners' reports on suitability for preventive detention, corrective training and borstal training. . . .

331. We consider that, as at present, the police officer who prepares the statement should always be present in court to give evidence on the lines of his statement. . . . [T]here is always the possibility that the defence will wish to cross-examine him on the antecedents. . . .

The probation service

333. The first function of a probation report is to provide information about the offender and his background which will help the court in determining the most suitable method of dealing with him. Originally, the information was used primarily where the court was considering putting the offender on probation, but it has also been found helpful where the court is considering whether any other form of sentence might divert the offender from crime. In addition, the information has been found relevant to the court's assessment of culpability. . . .

334. Secondly, probation officers have been encouraged at some courts to express an opinion about the likely response of the offender to probation and other forms of sentence.

335. We endorse these aspects of the probation report. . . .

336. We cannot formulate a comprehensive list of the items with which a probation report should deal. . . . But we agree with the National Association of Probation Officers that in most cases it should include, among other things, essential details of the offender's home surroundings, and family background; his attitude to his family and their response to him; his school and work record and spare-time activities; his attitude to his employment; his attitude to the present offence; his attitude and response to previous forms of treatment following any previous convictions; detailed histories about relevant physical and mental conditions; an assessment of personality and character. . . .

337. There may also be cases where the probation officer feels able, as the court's informant on social matters, to provide information relating to other aspects of sentencing. He may know, for instance, that a particular young offender has recently collected in his criminal activities a number of hangers-on, who could shortly become a determined criminal gang; and he may consider, in his experience, that this development would be stopped if the offender were removed from contact with the others for a substantial period. The probation officer would obviously have to exercise great care in forming, and expressing, such an opinion, but, subject to that, we think that he could properly deal with such matters in a probation report. . . .

339. Although it is not universally recognised that a probation officer may express an opinion in his report on an offender, we have no doubt that in many cases he can give a useful opinion. In our view the provision of such opinions should be regarded as an integral part of the probation officer's function.

346. Opinions of this sort, however frank and comprehensive they may be, relate to only one of the possible considerations in the court's mind: how to stop the offender from offending again. The court has still to consider the nature of the offence and the public interest, and it has the sole responsibility for the sentence which is ultimately passed. The probation officer should never give his opinion in a form which suggests that it relates to all the considerations in the court's mind. It is not a recommendation, but an informed opinion proffered for the assistance of the court on one aspect of the question before it. Provided that this is understood by all concerned, there can be no grounds for thinking that in expressing a frank opinion on the likely effect on the offender of probation or other forms of sentence the probation officer is in any way usurping the functions of the court.[4]

349.[5] A considerable number of our witnesses thought that enquiries of the kind made by probation officers should not be undertaken before the trial

---

[4] The Departmental Committee on the Probation Service (Cmnd. 1650, 1962) was more sceptical. At para. 40 it noted: " We fully agree with the Streatfeild Committee so far as the committee endorses the volunteering of informed opinions by probation officers about offenders' likely responses to probation. . . . 41. . . . . The proposal . . . that they should also offer opinions on offenders' suitability for other methods of treatment is more innovatory. Even the most experienced probation officer, with his wide knowledge of offenders and their records, would, we believe, find difficulty at present in making such forecasts. His first-hand information about the treatment offered in prisons, borstals, approved schools, and detention centres will derive from two sources. He will probably have visited some of these institutions; and he will have known offenders who have been to them. His knowledge of the alternative treatments to probation can never approach that of the officers of the institutions by which the treatments are provided, and the extent to which he can aspire to comprehensive knowledge will be diminishing as the treatments which the penal system provides become more complex. A relationship with an offender from a " closed " borstal may not, for example, entitle him to draw conclusions about how a like offender would respond in an " open " borstal. . . . So, too, for prisons and approved schools. Moreover . . . knowledge of the comparative effects of treatments on like offenders is rudimentary. We do not make these remarks as a criticism of the Streatfeild Committee's recommendation since that Committee has said clearly that a probation officer should offer an opinion only when he feels that it is reliable and relevant and that his opinion should be based on actual and substantial experience and on the results of research. Our point is that probation officers are not now equipped by their experience, and research cannot yet equip them, to assume a general function of expressing opinions to the courts about the likely effect of sentences. . . . [W]e do not see scope at present for more than a very gradual development towards the function that the Streatfeild Committee envisaged. . . ."

[5] The committee had already noted at para. 310: " We share the view of the majority of our witnesses that it is desirable on general grounds that sentence at the superior courts should follow immediately upon conviction. Where an offence is serious, there is usually considerable local interest in the outcome, and those concerned in the case itself have a legitimate interest in knowing as soon as possible what the sentence is. Many sentences are designed not so much to secure the reformation of the offender but, for example, to

unless it was known that the accused intended to plead guilty. They thought it wrong in principle that employers and others should be asked questions which became relevant only if the accused was found, or pleaded, guilty. They suggested that there was a distinction between the informal subjective answers which the probation officer was seeking and the formal, objective statement of employment history and the like which the police obtained, apparently without difficulty, in practically every case. Moreover, the defendant cannot discuss the offence in a way which is helpful to the probation officer and it may often be impossible to offer an opinion on the likely effect of probation or other forms of sentence. . . .

352. We recognise the force of the objections put to us, but in our view pre-trial enquiries cannot satisfactorily depend on whether the accused intends to plead guilty or not. Some defendants who fully intend to contest the case may be perfectly willing for enquiries to be made, and the representatives of the Law Society who gave evidence before us said that most solicitors advised their clients, whatever the character of the defence, that it was not contrary to their interests to co-operate with those whose duty it was to make enquiries. Other defendants, even though they have virtually no defence to the charge, may think that they would be embarrassed or prejudiced by enquiries, and however unjustified this view may be, they are entitled to be treated as innocent persons until they plead, or are proved, guilty. Moreover, because no formal plea is taken until a case appears at the court of trial, an intention to plead guilty or not guilty is known with certainty only occasionally. When the accused is asked by the committing justices whether he has anything to say in answer to the charge, he often makes a non-committal reply, even if he has already made a statement to the police which is tantamount to a full confession. At the trial, however, 76 per cent. of defendants plead guilty.

353. The procedure which we prefer is that an accused person should be given the opportunity of objecting before enquiries are made. He should be . . . asked, in a specific question, whether he has any objection.

354. . . . In our view the probation officer who would make the report is the right person to explain the position. . . . Where it is known that the accused is legally represented, the question should be put through the defending solicitor or with his concurrence.

355. Provided that this safeguard is introduced, we are satisfied that . . . pre-trial enquiries may be properly undertaken. . . .

356. Ordinarily the probation officer should not make any move until after the accused has been committed for trial, but where it seems likely, before the committal proceedings are concluded, that if the accused is committed for trial, the interval before his appearance at the higher court will be too short for adequate enquiries, we see no objection to the probation officer starting his enquiries at any time after the accused has been charged. The overriding consideration is the need to avoid the necessity of a post-conviction adjournment,

demonstrate that persons who commit serious offences are punished; and the public impact of the sentence is much reduced if it is made known at a later date than the finding of guilt. . . .

311. Further, even where the court can readily be reassembled . . . the court has usually to spend a fair amount of time in recapturing the atmosphere of the case. It still has to bear in mind the facts of the offence, which in the type of case dealt with at the superior courts are an important factor in determining sentence and are often complicated in themselves. Otherwise, the results of the enquiries for which the adjournment was ordered might assume a disproportionate importance to the exclusion of some important feature (whether aggravating or mitigating) of the offence itself. . . .

312. . . . [I]f post-conviction adjournments are to be kept to a minimum, pre-trial enquiries on a fairly extensive scale are unavoidable and may be properly undertaken, subject to suitable safeguards. . . .'' On the power to defer sentence, see below, p. 515.

and although some accused persons are discharged by the magistrates and not committed for trial, the proportion is small. We recognise that if the sort of case we have in mind is to be picked out in time, there will have to be a high degree of intelligent anticipation and co-operation by those concerned, including the clerk to justices. . . .

358. Having regard to the sentencing aims to which probation reports are relevant, we recommend that, where practicable, a probation officer should prepare a pre-trial report on every defendant who has not been previously convicted of an offence punishable with imprisonment or is not over 30 years old. These two categories contain a substantial proportion of cases where there may be some hope of stopping the criminal career by positive action or where there may be a need for detailed information about background before culpability can be assessed. . .

359. We also recommend that a report should be available on any other defendant who has recently been in touch with the probation service, e.g. on probation or for after-care. In such a case the probation service will have direct experience of the success or failure with the offender of one form of sentence at any rate. . . .

361. The[se] categories are minimum categories, to which individual courts may wish to add others. The probation liaison officer . . . should also have a general discretion to authorise enquiries in cases in which he thinks that the court may be helped by a report, but we cannot agree with the suggestion . . . that the defence should be entitled to have enquiries made by a probation officer on request.

Post-conviction reports

364. There will remain some cases where the court would be helped by a probation report but one is not available upon conviction. . . .

365. . . . In some cases it may be possible for a report to be obtained during the sitting of the court, but the court should be careful to ensure that this is genuinely practicable. Probation officers can be embarrassed by being asked to make a report within a matter of hours, perhaps only on the basis of an interview with the offender in the cells. On the one hand, the probation officer wants to give the court all the help he can. On the other hand, he is not in a position to verify any information provided by the offender, and he fears that he is putting forward a shallow assessment which may be unreliable.

The committee went on to discuss reports from prison authorities, for example, on the offender's previous custodial sentences or of psychiatric or medical examinations conducted by the prison medical officer. It is also noted that it was always open to the defence to draw the court's attention to mitigating circumstances and to emphasise favourable aspects in the reports.

Criminal Justice Act 1967
1967, c. 80

57.—(1) The Secretary of State may by rules make provision requiring that in any case to which the rules apply a court of any prescribed class shall before passing on any person a sentence to which the rules apply consider a social inquiry report, that is to say a report about him and his circumstances, made by a probation officer or any other person authorised to do so by the rules.[6]

[6] The Departmental Committee on the Probation Service (Cmnd. 1650, 1962) had noted: " We think that it would be consistent with the developing range of cases in which probation officers make enquiries if the terms ' probation report ' and ' probation officer's

(2) Rules under this section may apply to a sentence of imprisonment or detention of any class prescribed by the rules and may make different provision for different cases.

(3) No sentence shall be invalidated by the failure of a court to consider a social inquiry report in accordance with rules under subsection (1) of this section, but any other court on appeal from that court shall consider such a report in determining whether a different sentence should be passed on the appellant from the sentence passed on him by the court below.

(4) In this section "sentence of imprisonment or detention" means a sentence of imprisonment, borstal training or detention in a detention centre or a sentence of detention passed under section 53 of the Children and Young Persons Act 1933 (young offenders convicted of grave crimes).

The Report of the Probation and After-Care Department for 1966–68 [7] noted in relation to section 57 of the Criminal Justice Act 1967:

105. . . . For the present the Home Secretary has decided to proceed under the provision informally by making recommendations to the courts rather than by exercising the rulemaking power.

106. Accordingly, he has recommended (Home Office Circular No. 189/1968) [8] to superior courts that they should, as normal practice, consider a social enquiry report before imposing on an offender aged seventeen or over a sentence of detention in a detention centre; of borstal training; of imprisonment (including a suspended sentence) for two years or less where the offender has not received a previous sentence of imprisonment (including a suspended sentence) or borstal training; or, in the case of a woman, any sentence of imprisonment. The superior courts have in most cases been obtaining pre-trial reports since 1963 over almost the whole range of offenders in these categories, the only exceptions being (a) men over thirty who have one or more previous convictions but have not received a previous custodial sentence, and for whom the court has in mind a sentence of two years' imprisonment or less, and (b) women over thirty who have one or more previous convictions of an offence punishable with imprisonment. The Home Secretary has suggested that the courts consider modifying their arrangements for the provision of pre-trial reports so as to include these categories.

107. The Streatfeild committee were concerned with the needs of the higher courts but they made it clear that the principles underlying their recommendations were equally applicable to magistrates' courts, and it has been the practice of many of these courts, particularly since 1963, to ask for social enquiry reports in a wide range of cases. (The practice is of much longer standing in the juvenile courts.) The Home Secretary has accordingly felt justified in recommending (Home Office Circular No. 188/1968) [8] to magistrates' courts that they too should

report ' were avoided in describing reports they prepare. These terms suggest, the former particularly, that the scope for such enquiries is limited to cases where probation is in prospect and they may encourage false optimism in an offender about the course which the court intends to take. We have considered alternatives, including ' pre-sentence report,' but this has the disadvantage that a sentence may not follow. Indeed, probation itself is not a sentence. We recommend that ' social enquiry report ' be used. . . ."

[7] Cmnd. 4233, 1969.
[8] The Report of the Probation and After-Care Department 1969–71 (Cmnd. 5158), noted that the Home Office had issued fresh circulars in February 1971 but that they were for the most part of a consolidating nature.

obtain and consider such reports in the categories of cases mentioned in the previous paragraphs; and additionally, before committing an offender to Quarter Sessions for sentence under section 28 or 29 of the Magistrates' Courts Act 1952. Both the higher courts and the magistrates' courts were reminded of the view expressed by the Morison Committee that a social enquiry report should normally be obtained before a probation order is made. For practical reasons, the probation officer's enquiries for the magistrates' courts are usually made on remand, but pre-trial enquiries are undertaken wherever possible.

108. While the primary purpose of social enquiry reports is to assist the courts in determining the most suitable method of dealing with the offenders before them, these reports may also prove to be of value, in a number of ways, after sentence has been passed. Then, they often enable much needed help to be given urgently to a prisoner's wife and family; they alert the prison welfare officer to any special needs and provide a point of contact; and they are a valuable source of information when the grant of parole to a prisoner is under consideration.

THE SENTENCES AVAILABLE AND THEIR USE

How the courts dealt with persons found guilty in 1971

Criminal Statistics for England and Wales in 1971
Cmnd. 5020, July 1972

Table 9: Persons found guilty shown by age group, sex, sentence or order, and type of court

9a : Magistrates' courts—indictable offences

Sentence or order	Under 14		14 & under 17		17 & under 21		21 & over		All ages	
	M	F	M	F	M	F	M	F	M	F
Absolute discharge .	383	47	694	137	472	102	955	395	2,504	681
Conditional discharge	4,512	538	7,315	1,288	5,007	1,505	10,473	5,416	27,307	8,747
Probation . .	—	—	—	—	6,742	1,887	7,301	3,853	14,043	5,740
Supervision order .	5,099	541	8,338	1,343	82	9	—	—	13,519	1,893
Fine . . .	3,473	415	17,100	1,746	35,588	3,662	67,759	16,486	123,920	22,309
Detention centre .	—	—	1,415	—	3,987	—	—	—	5,402	—
Care order .	2,261	168	3,394	457	24	5	—	—	5,679	630
Suspended sentence .	—	—	—	—	1,753	137	14,585	1,203	16,338	1,340
Imprisonment (immediate) .	—	—	—	—	702	22	10,888	378	11,590	400
Attendance centre .	2,183	—	3,202	—	160	—	—	—	5,545	—
Committal to quarter sessions for sentence under s. 28 Magistrates' Courts Act 1952 . .	—	—	1,344	41	1,389	99	—	—	2,733	140
Committal to quarter sessions for sentence under s. 29 Magistrates' Courts Act 1952 . .	—	—	—	—	3,628	142	5,183	177	8,811	319
Otherwise dealt with	53	3	175	23	986	42	1,043	145	2,257	213
Total . . .	17,964	1,712	42,977	5,035	60,520	7,612	118,187	28,053	239,648	42,412

9b: Magistrates' courts—non-indictable offences

Sentence or order	Under 14		14 & under 17		17 & under 21		21 & over		All ages	
	M	F	M	F	M	F	M	F	M	F
Absolute discharge .	183	13	840	69	1,010	28	9,054	1,283	11,087	1,493
Conditional discharge .	1,160	65	3,463	336	2,976	527	8,757	2,019	16,356	2,947
Probation . .	—	—	—	—	2,186	432	2,262	715	4,448	1,147
Supervision order .	620	46	1,755	168	22	2	—	—	2,397	216
Fine . . .	1,902	97	33,727	1,598	155,190	7,490	1,010,816	88,432	1,201,635	97,617
Care order .	215	14	716	65	7	—	—	—	938	79
Suspended sentence . .	—	—	—	—	917	112	5,545	507	6,462	619
Imprisonment (immediate) .	—	—	—	—	429	49	5,173	357	5,602	406
Otherwise dealt with .	294	3	1,817	42	5,496	103	4,135	805	11,742	953
Total . .	4,374	238	42,318	2,278	168,233	8,843	1,045,742	94,118	1,260,667	105,477

9c: Higher courts—persons found guilty at higher courts

Sentence or order	Under 14		14 & under 17		17 & under 21		21 & over		All ages	
	M	F	M	F	M	F	M	F	M	F
Conditional discharge	6	—	96	16	513	50	868	177	1,483	243
Probation . .	—	—	—	—	1,803	266	1,947	466	3,750	732
Supervision order .	4	—	205	36	4	1	—	—	213	37
Fine . . .	1	—	93	1	1,449	46	4,572	236	6,115	283
Detention centre .	—	—	293	—	1,523	—	—	—	1,816	—
Care order . .	5	—	99	9	4	—	—	—	108	9
Borstal training .	—	—	257	3	3,072	78	—	—	3,329	81
Suspended sentence .	—	—	—	—	533	24	4,956	299	5,489	323
Imprisonment (immediate) .	—	—	—	—	1,302	18	12,930	308	14,232	326
Extended sentence .	—	—	—	—	—	—	78	2	78	2
Otherwise dealt with	2	—	39	2	472	14	534	64	1,047	80
Total . .	18	—	1,082	67	10,675	497	25,885	1,552	37,660	2,116

9d: Higher courts—persons sentenced after committal for sentence

Sentence or order	Under 14		14 & under 17		17 & under 21		21 & over		All ages	
	M	F	M	F	M	F	M	F	M	F
Conditional discharge	—	—	38	5	103	5	97	4	238	14
Probation . .	—	—	—	—	797	97	785	52	1,582	149
Supervision order .	—	—	75	1	2	1	—	—	77	2
Fine . . .	—	—	29	—	318	8	206	3	553	11
Detention centre .	—	—	307	—	647	—	—	—	954	—
Care order .	—	—	91	5	4	—	—	—	95	5
Borstal training .	—	—	859	27	2,996	150	—	—	3,855	177
Suspended sentence .	—	—	—	—	240	11	870	28	1,110	39
Imprisonment (immediate) .	—	—	—	—	509	5	3,691	68	4,200	73
Extended sentence .	—	—	—	—	—	—	17	—	17	—
Otherwise dealt with	—	—	47	6	358	9	184	3	589	18
Total . .	—	—	1,446	44	5,974	286	5,850	158	13,270	488

Table 10: Persons found guilty of non-indictable offences shown by sentence or order separately for motoring offences and other offences

Sentence or order		Motoring offences		Other offences		Total	
		Number of persons	Per-centage	Number of persons	Per-centage	Number of persons	Per-centage
Absolute discharge	.	7,177	0·7	5,403	1·4	12,580	0·9
Conditional discharge	.	3,222	0·3	16,081	4·2	19,303	1·4
Probation	. . .	1,035	0·1	4,560	1·2	5,595	0·4
Supervision order	.	700	0·1	1,913	0·5	2,613	0·2
Fine	. . . .	965,369	97·8	333,883	88·2	1,299,252	95·1
Care order	. . .	439	—	578	0·2	1,017	0·1
Suspended sentence	.	2,595	0·3	4,486	1·2	7,081	0·5
Imprisonment (immediate)	. .	2,022	0·2	3,986	1·1	6,008	0·5
Otherwise dealt with	.	4,979	0·5	7,716	2·0	12,695	0·9
Total	. . .	987,538	100·0	378,606	100·0	1,366,144	100·0

Persons cautioned by the police

18   Table 11 shows the number of persons to whom written or oral cautions for (i) indictable offences and (ii) non-indictable offences other than motoring offences were given by, or on the instructions of, senior police officers, as an alternative to taking proceedings in court. The figures for females include 4,187 women cautioned ' for loitering or soliciting for the purpose of prostitution '.

Table 11 : Persons cautioned for indictable offences and persons cautioned for non-indictable offences (other than motoring offences) shown by age group and sex

Age group and sex		Indictable offences	Non-indictable offences other than motoring offences
Under 14	M	27,389	3,740
	F	6,683	208
14 and under 17 . . .	M	20,160	6,415
	F	5,668	694
17 and under 21 . . .	M	3,684	2,378
	F	532	1,729
21 and over	M	4,761	14,457
	F	3,537	4,988
All ages	M	55,994	26,990
	F	16,420	7,619
All persons		72,414	34,609

CONDITIONAL RELEASE

The first group of methods includes absolute discharge and those which involve releasing the offender under a condition that he does not commit a further offence within a given period of time (*i.e.* an order of conditional discharge or a suspended sentence, the main difference between the two being that in the latter case the court must have come to the conclusion that a sentence of imprisonment was in fact warranted in the particular case

w.—18

though there were reasons why it should be suspended), or under a condition that he keeps the peace and is of good behaviour (binding over) or under condition that he commits no further offence and puts himself under the supervision of a probation officer (probation).

Absolute and conditional discharge

Sections 7 and 8 of the Criminal Justice Act 1948 as amended by the Criminal Justice Act 1967 provide that where a court " is of opinion, having regard to the circumstances including the nature of the offence and the character of the offender, that it is inexpedient to inflict punishment and that a probation order is not appropriate," it may make an order discharging him absolutely or subject to a condition that he commits no further offence during the specified period, which may not exceed three years. If he does commit an offence he is liable to be sentenced for the original offence. If the offender is subsequently convicted the court " may deal with him, for the offence for which the order was made, in any manner in which the court could deal with him if he had just been convicted . . . of that offence."

Binding over

An offender may be bound over to come up for judgment at some time in the future if he fails to observe some condition imposed at the same time, or fails to keep the peace or be of good behaviour. The courts also have the power to bind over a person to keep the peace or be of good behaviour even though he has not been convicted of an offence. A refusal to be bound over in such a case may result in his being sent to prison.

Suspended sentences

The Advisory Council on the Treatment of Offenders had considered the question of a suspended sentence in 1952. It took the view that such a sentence was " wrong in principle and to a large extent impracticable. It should not be adopted, either in conjunction with probation or otherwise." It argued that if it was used in conjunction with probation it could prejudice the chances of success of the probation by putting an emphasis on the need to avoid conduct that would bring the suspended sentence into effect rather than more positive attempts to make a success of the probation period. Although it might be appropriate in cases where effective supervision was not possible there was a danger that in practice it might be used in other cases. There was also the problem as to whether on a breach of condition the sentence would be imposed automatically in which case someone who had made a genuine attempt to conform would be treated in the same way as someone who had made no effort. If the court had a discretion then there was no point in fixing a sentence in the first place. The Council considered the matter again in 1957 and came to the same conclusion. Nonetheless provision was made for suspended sentences in the Criminal Justice Act 1967. The only condition that is attached to them is the commission of another offence. They cannot be imposed in conjunction with probation. They can be imposed in addition to a fine, otherwise a person who was fined might be worse off than someone who because his offence or record was more serious was sentenced to imprisonment but this was suspended. In some cases suspension was made mandatory. The Criminal Justice Act 1972 removed the mandatory provisions and changed the period of suspension from a maximum of three years to a maximum of two years. The 1972 Act also makes provision for a supervision order to be made in conjunction with a suspended sentence.

Criminal Justice Act 1967
1967, c. 80

39.—(1) A court which passes a sentence of imprisonment for a term of not more than two years for an offence may order that the sentence shall not take effect unless, during a period specified in the order, being not less than one year or more than [two] years from the date of the order, the offender commits in Great Britain another offence punishable with imprisonment. . . .

(2) A court which passes a suspended sentence on any person for an offence shall not make a probation order in his case in respect of another offence of which he is convicted by or before the court or for which he is dealt with by the court.

(8) Where a court has passed a suspended sentence on any person, and that person is subsequently sentenced to borstal training, he shall cease to be liable to be dealt with in respect of the suspended sentence. . . .

40.—(1) Where an offender is convicted of an offence punishable with imprisonment committed during the operational period of a suspended sentence and either he is so convicted by or before a court having power . . . to deal with him in respect of the suspended sentence or he subsequently appears or is brought before such a court, then . . .—

(a) the court may order that the suspended sentence shall take effect with the original term unaltered;
(b) it may order that the sentence shall take effect with the substitution of a lesser term for the original term;
(c) it may by order vary the original order under subsection (1) of the last foregoing section by substituting for the period specified therein a period expiring not later than [two] years from the date of the variation; or
(d) it may make no order with respect to the suspended sentence;

and a court shall make an order under paragraph (a) of this subsection unless the court is of opinion that it would be unjust to do so in view of all the circumstances which have arisen since the suspended sentence was passed, including the facts of the subsequent offence, and where it is of that opinion the court shall state its reasons.

(3) Where under subsection (1) (a) of this section a court orders that a suspended sentence shall take effect with a term of not more than six months and the court would have had power to sentence the offender to be detained in a detention centre for that term if it had convicted him of the original offence on the occasion of the order, the order may include a direction that he shall serve the sentence in a detention centre.

41.—(1) An offender may be dealt with in respect of a suspended sentence by [the Crown Court] [9] or, where the sentence was passed by a magistrates' court, by any magistrates' court. . . .

[9] As amended by the Courts Act 1971, s. 56 (1), Sched. 8, para. 48.

(2) Where an offender is convicted by a magistrates' court of an offence punishable with imprisonment and the court is satisfied that the offence was committed during the operational period of a suspended sentence passed by [the Crown Court] [9]—

> (a) the court may, if it thinks fit, commit him in custody or on bail to [the Crown Court] [9]; and
>
> (b) if it does not, shall give written notice of the conviction to the clerk of the court by which the suspended sentence was passed.

Criminal Justice Act 1972
1972, c. 71

11.—(3) An offender shall not be dealt with by means of a sentence of imprisonment suspended under section 39 of the . . . Act of 1967 unless the case appears to the court to be one in which a sentence of imprisonment would have been appropriate in the absence of any power to suspend a sentence.[10]

12.—(1) Where a court sentences an offender for a single offence to imprisonment for a term of more than six months and makes an order suspending the sentence under section 39 (1) of the Criminal Justice Act 1967, the court may make a suspended sentence supervision order . . . placing the offender under the supervision of a supervising officer for a period specified in the order not exceeding the period which under . . . section 39 (1) is the operational period in relation to the suspended sentence.

(2) The Secretary of State may by order—

> (a) direct that subsection (1) above be amended by substituting, for the number of months specified in the subsection . . . such other number (not more than six) as the order may specify; or
>
> (b) make in that subsection the repeals necessary to enable a court to exercise the powers of the subsection in the case of any suspended sentence, whatever the length of the term.

Orders under this subsection shall be made by statutory instrument subject to annulment by resolution of either House of Parliament. . . .[11]

The power to defer sentence

Report of the Advisory Council on the Penal System. Non-custodial and Semi-custodial Penalties 1970

The case for a specific power to defer the imposition of sentence on conditions

71. We are convinced . . . that a power to defer sentence would be a useful addition to the penal armoury. . . .

---

[10] In *R.* v. *O'Keefe* [1969] 2 Q.B. 29 the Court of Appeal had noted: "This court has found many instances where suspended sentences are being given as what one might call a "soft option," when the court is not quite certain what to do; and in particular this court comes across many cases when suspended sentences have been given when the proper order was a probation order. This court would like to say as emphatically as can be said that suspended sentences should not be given when, but for the power to give a suspended sentence, a probation order was the proper order to make. After all, a suspended sentence is a sentence of imprisonment. . . . [I]t ranks as a conviction, unlike the case where a probation order is made, or a conditional discharge is given. . . . [B]efore one gets to a suspended sentence at all, the court must go through the process of eliminating other possible courses such as absolute discharge, conditional discharge, probation order, fines, and then say to itself: this is a case for imprisonment, and the final question, it being a case for imprisonment, should be: is immediate imprisonment required, or can I give a suspended sentence?"

[11] *Cf.* the provisions for supervision at pp. 527 and 592, below.

72. . . . [E]very court at present necessarily has to rely on guess work. The advantage of deferring sentence is that the court can . . . see how in fact the offender does behave. . . . On the other hand, it is argued that an offender has the right to have his case disposed of at the earliest opportunity following conviction. We see some substance in this argument . . . and . . . we think that there should be a maximum period of deferment of 6 months. . . .

80. There are, we think, two quite distinct categories of case where courts are currently desirous of using power to defer sentence: (a) to ensure future good conduct or to enable the court to await the happening of an event, e.g., the obtaining of specific employment, or the return of the offender to his family home; and (b) to await the outcome of the offender's undertaking to make reparation to his victim. . . .

81. We are firmly of the opinion that there is a definite place in the penal code for the deferment of sentence to provide an opportunity for the offender to show good behaviour, to repay money which he has acquired dishonestly, to pay compensation for damage which he has caused maliciously, or to perform some other act which would indicate ability to stay out of trouble. We would think that this sentence could be used effectively in some cases of vandalism and hooliganism. . . .

83. . . . [T]he Scottish courts are free on deferring sentence to impose any conditions that they like. We considered carefully whether we should recommend the same freedom of action for English sentencers, bearing in mind that among lay magistrates there may be a few who would indulge in fanciful and inapt conditions. . . . We considered whether the conditions might not be restricted to three categories: (a) restitution/compensation; (b) residential requirements; (c) employment. While we would think it important that the conditions should never be offensive, impracticable or degrading, on the whole we have come down against tying the hands of the sentencers. Most of the situations in which it would be appropriate to defer sentence would, we think, fall within categories (a) (b) and (c), but there might conceivably be other circumstances in which the power might be useful. We would favour a right of appeal to quarter sessions or to the Court of Appeal (Criminal Division), both against the court's order to defer sentence and against any conditions attached. . . .

Criminal Justice Act 1972
1972, c. 71

22.—(1) Subject to the provisions of this section, the Crown Court or a magistrates' court may defer passing sentence on an offender for the purpose of enabling the court to have regard, in determining his sentence, to his conduct after conviction (including, where appropriate, the making by him of reparation for his offence) or to any change in his circumstances.

(2) Any deferment under this section shall be until such date as may be specified by the court, not being more than six months after the date of the conviction; and where the passing of sentence has been deferred under this section it shall not be further deferred thereunder.

(3) The power conferred by this section shall be exercisable only if the offender consents and the court is satisfied, having regard to the nature of the offence and the character and circumstances of the offender, that it would be in the interests of justice to exercise the power.

(4) A court which under this section has deferred passing sentence on an offender may pass sentence on him before the expiration of the period of deferment if during that period he is convicted in Great Britain of any offence. . . .

(7) Nothing in this section shall affect the power of the Crown Court to bind over an offender to come up for judgment when called upon or the power of any court to defer passing sentence for any purpose for which it may lawfully do so apart from this section.

Probation

Criminal Justice Act 1948
11 & 12 Geo. 6, c. 58

3.—(1) Where a court by or before which a person [who has attained the age of 17] is convicted of an offence (not being an offence the sentence for which is fixed by law) is of opinion that having regard to the circumstances, including the nature of the offence and the character of the offender, it is expedient to do so, the court may, instead of sentencing him, make a probation order, that is to say, an order requiring him to be under the supervision of a probation officer for a period to be specified in the order of not less than one year nor more than three years.

(2) A probation order shall name the petty sessional division in which the offender resides or will reside; and the offender shall . . . be required to be under the supervision of a probation officer appointed for or assigned to that division.

(3) Subject to the provisions of the next following section, a probation order may . . . require the offender to comply during the whole or any part of the probation period with such requirements as the court, having regard to the circumstances of the case, considers necessary for securing the good conduct of the offender or for preventing a repetition by him of the same offence or the commission of other offences: Provided that (without prejudice to the power of the court to make an order under subsection (2) of section 11 of this Act) the payment of sums by way of damages for injury or compensation for loss shall not be included among the requirements of a probation order.

(4) . . . [A] probation order may include requirements relating to the residence of the offender : Provided that—

(a) before making an order containing any such requirements, the court shall consider the home surroundings of the offender; and

(b) where the order requires the offender to reside in an approved probation hostel, an approved probation home or any other institution, the name of the institution and the period for which he is so required to reside shall be specified in the order, and that period shall not extend beyond twelve months from the date of the order.

(5) Before making a probation order, the court shall explain to the offender in ordinary language the effect of the order . . . and that if he fails to comply therewith or commits another offence he will be liable to be sentenced for the original offence; and the court shall not make the order unless he expresses his willingness to comply with the requirements thereof.

Section 4 provides that the court may make it a condition of a probation order that he submits to treatment by or under the direction of a duly qualified medical practitioner.

6.—(3) If it is proved to the satisfaction of the court before which a probationer appears or is brought . . . that the probationer has failed to comply with any of the requirements . . . that court may without prejudice to the continuance of the probation order, impose on him a fine not exceeding ten pounds or, in a case to which section 19 . . . applies,[12] make an order under that section requiring him to attend at an attendance centre, or may—

    (*a*) if the probation order was made by a court of summary jurisdiction, deal with the probationer, for the offence in respect of which the probation order was made, in any manner in which the court could deal with him if it had just convicted him of that offence;

    (*b*) if the probation order was made by the [Crown Court] [13] commit him to custody or release him on bail (with or without sureties) until he can be brought or appear before the [Crown Court].

(4) (*b*) . . . [T]he [Crown Court] . . . may deal with him, for the offence in respect of which the probation order was made, in any manner in which the court could deal with him if he had just been convicted before that court of that offence. . . .

(6) A probationer who is required by the probation order to submit to treatment for his mental condition shall not be treated for the purposes of this section as having failed to comply with that requirement on the ground only that he has refused to undergo any surgical, electrical or other treatment if, in the opinion of the court, his refusal was reasonable having regard to all the circumstances; and without prejudice to the provisions of section 8 . . . a probationer who is convicted of an offence committed during the probation period shall not on that account be liable to be dealt with under this section for failing to comply with any requirement of the probation order.

8.—(5) Where it is proved to the satisfaction of the court by which a probation order or an order for conditional discharge was made, or, if the order (being a probation order) was made by a court of summary jurisdiction, to the satisfaction of that court or the supervising court, that the person in whose case that order was made has been convicted . . . of an offence committed during the probation period, or during the period of conditional discharge . . . the court may deal with him, for the offence for which the order was made, in any manner in which the court could deal with him if he had just been convicted by or before that court of that offence.

(6) [14] If a person in whose case a probation order or an order for conditional discharge has been made by a court of summary jurisdiction is convicted before the [Crown Court] of an offence committed during the probation period or during the period of conditional discharge, or is dealt with by the Crown Court for an offence so committed in respect of which he was committed for sentence to that court, the [Crown Court] may deal with him, for the offence for which the court of summary jurisdiction could deal with him if it had just convicted him of that offence.

(7) If a person in whose case a probation order or an order for conditional discharge has been made by a court of summary jurisdiction is convicted by another court of summary jurisdiction of any offence committed during the probation period, or . . . conditional discharge, that court may, with the consent of the court which made the order or, in the case of a probation order, with the consent of that court or the supervising court, deal with him, for the offence for which the order was made, in any manner in which the court could deal with him if it had just convicted him of that offence.

---

[12] s. 20 of the Criminal Justice Bill 1972 now provides that this should be £50. Alternatively the court may make a community service order. See below, p. 539.
[13] All references to Crown Court enclosed in square brackets are amendments by s. 56 (1), Sched. 8, para. 24 of the Courts Act 1971.
[14] This section has been extended by s. 9 of the Criminal Justice Act 1961.

FIFTH SCHEDULE

3.—(5) It shall be the duty of probation officers to supervise the probationers and other persons placed under their supervision and to advise, assist and befriend them, to inquire, in accordance with any directions of the court, into the circumstances or home surroundings of any person with a view to assisting the court in determining the most suitable method of dealing with his case, to advise, assist and befriend, in such cases and in such manner as may be prescribed, persons who have been released from custody and to perform such other duties as may be prescribed or may be imposed by any enactment.

The First Schedule of the Criminal Justice Act 1948 provided *inter alia* that the court by which a probation order was made could discharge it on the application of the probationer or the probation officer. The Criminal Justice Act 1967, s. 54 (1) provided that this power in future was to be exercised by the supervising court unless the order had been made by the Crown Court and that court had made a direction to the contrary in the order. Section 53 of the Criminal Justice Act 1967 provides that instead of discharging the probation order absolutely the court may substitute an order for conditional discharge, on the condition that the probationer commits no offence between the making of the order and the expiration of the probation period.

Report of the Departmental Committee on Social Service on Courts of Summary Jurisdiction

Cmd. 5122, 1936

49. . . . Long before probation was thought of courts made use of their power to bind offenders to come up for judgment if called upon; the idea of placing these offenders under supervision flowed naturally from this practice. It is not surprising that the credit for being the first to combine the two principles is disputed. . . . In England, according to the Young Offenders Committee, " the honour, it would appear, belongs to some Warwickshire Magistrates of whom it is recorded as early as 1820 that in suitable cases they passed sentence of imprisonment for one day upon a youthful offender, on condition that he returned to the care of his parent or master to be by him more carefully watched and supervised in the future." [15] The same report describes how the practice was developed by the well-known Recorder of Birmingham, Matthew Davenport Hill, who in 1841 instituted a register of these forerunners of the modern probation officer. . . . The experiments of the Warwickshire Magistrates and Matthew Davenport Hill are . . . examples of the humaner spirit which under the influence of reformers like John Howard and Elizabeth Fry entered and ultimately changed the harsh penal system of the eighteenth and early nineteenth century. Like the reformatory and industrial schools probation was a product of this movement; but it was easier to convert public opinion to generous experiments for young offenders than for adults. Twenty years after the passing of the Reformatory Schools Act of 1854 and the Industrial Schools Act of 1857, the first police court missionary of the Church of England Temperance Society appeared in the London Police Courts. This appointment

---

[15] Report of the Departmental Committee on the Treatment of Young Offenders, Cmd. 2831, 1927, p. 10.

was the result of a suggestion made in 1876 by a working printer, who urged that the Society should make an attempt to arrest the downward careers of men who made their first appearance in the Police Court.

50. Supervision now became for the first time a practicable method for courts which were fortunate enough to possess the services of a police court missionary, and while the primary object of the first appointment was the reclamation of offenders whose downfall was the result of drink, it was soon found that other offenders could be helped in the same way. More missionaries were soon appointed in London and elsewhere, and their employment was facilitated by the Summary Jurisdiction Act of 1879, which provided (section 16) that where a court of summary jurisdiction thought that, though the charge was proved, the offence was of so trifling a nature that it was inexpedient to inflict any punishment, the court, upon convicting the prisoner charged, could discharge him, conditionally on his giving security, with or without sureties, to appear for sentence when called upon, or to be of good behaviour. This provision was, however, limited to summary cases, and adults convicted summarily of an indictable offence on a plea of guilty, were, for technical reasons, expressly excluded from its benefits. In the previous year in the State of Massachusetts, where supervision of offenders had been tried informally, and where the term " probation " first came into use, the legislature passed an important measure, which provided for the appointment of a paid probation officer for the City of Boston. This was a significant step which was soon followed in other American states and later in England, where great interest was taken in the American experiment. A Bill for the establishment of a system of supervision on bail failed to reach the statute book in 1881, and the provisions for supervision on American lines were embodied in the First Offenders Bill, which was introduced into Parliament in 1887, but were deleted before the Bill became law as the Probation of First Offenders Act of the same year. The Act of 1887, in which the term " probation " made its first appearance in English law, extended the provisions of the Act of 1879 to first offenders convicted of larceny, false pretences or other offences punishable with not more than two years' imprisonment, and was not limited to courts of summary jurisdiction. Whereas the Act of 1879 merely referred to the trifling nature of the offence, under this Act regard was to be had to the youth, character and antecedents of the offender, to the trivial nature of the offence, and to any extenuating circumstances under which the offence was committed. The Act of 1887 was afterwards repealed but its title seems to have left an indelible impression on the minds of some who still think that probation is solely or primarily intended for first offenders, and indeed that all first offenders should be given the benefit of it.

51. Though the work of the police court missionaries of the Church of England Temperance Society and the agents of other voluntary societies was considerably handicapped by the lack of any legal sanction to enforce their efforts, they rendered invaluable services to the courts. Using the powers given by the Acts in force " many magistrates were accustomed to bind over the offenders charged before them for a specified term and to inform them that, meanwhile, they would be under the supervision of the police court missionary of the district. Some magistrates adjourned the case to a fixed date, the offender being similarly placed under that supervision." [16] It appears that the second method had the advantage that the observance of conditions other than those permitted by the Act of 1887 could be imposed. The courts were quick to recognise the value of the services of the missionaries, and their numbers increased rapidly. . . .

[16] Report of the Departmental Committee on the Probation of Offenders Act 1907, Cd. 5001, 1909, p. 3.

It was a remarkable illustration of the strength of voluntary effort in English social life. The work of the missionaries also grew in other directions, until they became in many ways the handymen of the courts. The Summary Jurisdiction (Married Women) Act of 1895 brought with it new functions, for it was to the missionaries that the courts naturally turned for help in applying conciliation to matrimonial disputes.

52. Although probation was in common use in many courts by 1907, it was still informal and its employment was only possible where there were police court missionaries. The Probation of Offenders Act 1907 remedied both deficiencies. Supervision was given statutory effect. Probation was distinguished from binding-over, and the courts were enabled to appoint paid probation officers, who might be the agents of voluntary societies. It is interesting to observe that before legislating the Government collected information as to the working of probation in the United States, which was published as a Parliamentary paper. . . .[17]

The courts were not slow to take advantage of the new Act. . . . The Departmental committee appointed in 1909 to enquire into its working reported " that the Act was already proved to be of great value in a large number of cases and, that, actively used, when the conditions allow, it may become in future a most useful factor in our penal law."

Departmental Committee on the Probation of Offenders Act 1907
Cd. 5001, 1909

3. The Probation [of Offenders] Act [1907] provides a method by which a person who has offended against the law, instead of being punished by imprisonment or fine, or, in the case of a child, being sent for a prolonged period to a reformatory or an industrial school, may be brought under the direct personal influence of a man or woman chosen for excellence of character and for strength of personal influence; and, lending authority to that supervision, securing that it shall not be treated as a thing of little account, the Act keeps suspended over the offender the penalties of the law, to be inflicted or to be withdrawn according as his conduct during the specified period is bad or good.

4. There are many persons on whom the effect of such influence, applied at the moment when the commission of an offence reveals the special need for it, may be as valuable as the skilled help of a doctor to a person suffering from disease. Often without friends of their own, more often with friends only of a degraded type, out of touch with any civilising influence, the probation officer comes to them from a different level of society, giving a helping hand to lift them out of the groove that leads to serious crime. He assists the man out of work to find employment. He puts the lad into touch with managers of a boys' club, where he can be brought under healthy influences. He helps to improve the bad homes which are the breeding grounds of child offenders. He persuades the careless to open accounts in the savings bank. Securing for him a respectful hearing, and furnishing a motive for the acceptance of his counsels, there is always in the background the sanction of the penal law—the knowledge that the probation officer is the eye of the magistrate; that misbehaviour will be reported to the court, and will bring its penalty. So great, however, is the influence which a good probation officer is able to exercise over an offender

---

[17] Memorandum on the probation system as at present in force in the United States of America, Cd. 3401, 1907.

during the specified period of probation, that his friendly interest is often sought after that period has expired, and his advice continues to carry weight, although the powers that supported it are ended.

5. To the magistrate also the probation officer may be of much assistance. The reports furnished by the probation officer inform him of the results, in practice, of his action; he can tell whether his clemency has been justified or not. He gathers material to guide him in future cases. . . .

7. The Act has not yet been long enough in operation to allow an opinion to be formed on the results attained. . . .

8. The evidence we have received has led us to the clear conclusion . . . that the Act has already proved to be of great value in a large number of cases, and that, actively used, when the conditions allow, it may become in future a most useful factor in our penal law. . . .

11. . . . [B]efore 1908 the enactments dealing with the probation of offenders were section 16 of the Summary Jurisdiction Act 1879 and the Probation of First Offenders Act 1887. . . . These Acts set up no machinery for the supervision of the probationer, and it was left to the court missionaries and other voluntary workers to do their best, without any legal sanction to enforce their efforts. . . .

23. . . . There are indeed many classes of cases for which probation is quite unsuited. The graver offences must receive their punishment for the sake of deterring others, though, indeed, it is necessary to regard the character of the offender as well as the character of the offence, and instances may possibly occur in which a person, having committed even a serious offence, may be best dealt with by being placed under a probation order. Except on very rare instances, probation appears to be useless for habitual offenders, for tramps and for prostitutes. Some cases, such as those of casual breaches of byelaws or threats uttered in a moment of temper, do not warrant a prolonged supervision.

24. There remain a great number of cases where the person charged is neither a first offender nor a child, in which a probation order should properly be made. . . .

28. The value of probation must necessarily depend on the efficiency of the probation officer. It is a system in which rules are comparatively unimportant, and personality is everything. The probation officer must be a picked man or woman, endowed not only with intelligence and zeal, but, in a high degree, with sympathy and tact and firmness. On his or her individuality the success or failure of the system depends. Probation is what the officer makes it. . . .

41. There are certain dangers attached to the system of probation against which the officers should be continually on their guard. The chief is the danger of too great laxity when the offender's behaviour is unsatisfactory. There is always a temptation to the officer to show in his annual report as large a proportion as possible of satisfactory cases. If a considerable percentage of the cases committed to his charge have been brought back before the court, he fears that the fact may be regarded as a reflection upon his own competence. We do not wish to suggest that the probation officer should regard it as his duty to bring the probationer again before the court for any slight breach of decorum or even for infraction, if it is trivial, of one of the conditions of the order. But he should be careful to make him feel—and the magistrates may be expected to support their officer in so doing—that probation is a reality, that it is not equivalent to acquittal and discharge. Firmness is as necessary in a probation officer as sympathy. Too much laxity can only result in an unwillingness on the part of the magistrates to use the probation officer's services at all. . . .

51. . . . [T]here could be no greater encouragement to a probation officer and no more potent means of contributing to the success of the probation system than for the magistrates themselves to . . . watch the result in each case, and to discuss with the probation officer the action he has taken. . . .

Report of the Departmental Committee on the Probation Service

Cmnd. 1650, 1962

13. . . . Society must protect itself against the wrongdoer. It must show its disapproval of crime. But we take it as axiomatic that . . . society . . . must seek, in fulfilling these objects, the minimum interference with life and liberty that is consistent with them. . . . We see probation as epitomizing the principle because, while it seeks to protect society through the supervision to which the offender is required to submit, it both minimizes the restriction placed upon him and offers him the help of society in adjusting his conduct to its demands. It seeks to strengthen the offender's resources so that he may become a more responsible member of the community which must also play a part in rehabilitating him. The offender is conditionally entrusted with freedom so that he may learn the social duties it involves; but his failure does not automatically lead to his punishment as when a sentence has been suspended.

14. The value of probation is not, however, to be judged only, or even primarily, by the rights that it seeks to preserve to the offender. Custodial treatment removes the offender from his family and community and suspends his social and economic obligations to them. He becomes, indeed, a burden upon society. Probation exacts from the offender a contribution, within the limits of his capacity, to the well-being of others, whether it be through his useful employment in the community or through his participation in the life of the family or other social group. In so doing, it minimises the economic and social disruption caused by the probationer's offence, preserves him from the penal or reformative institution, whose constructive work must inevitably be limited by the delinquent community in which the offender is placed, and seeks to avoid the harm to others that follows, for example, the imprisonment of a breadwinner.

15. We conclude that there is an *a priori* case for the use of probation when four conditions exist. Firstly, the circumstances of the offence and the offender's record must not be such as to demand, in the interests of society, that some more severe method be adopted in dealing with the offender; secondly, the risk, if any, to society through setting the offender at liberty must be outweighed by the moral, social and economic arguments for not depriving him of it; thirdly, the offender must need continuing attention, since otherwise, if the second condition is satisfied, a fine or discharge will suffice; and, fourthly, the offender must be capable of responding to this attention while he is at liberty.

16. It is customary to refer to probation as a method of " treatment " but the attention which society pays to offenders through the probation service takes many forms in which the element of treatment varies. At one extreme the probationer may be an unruly schoolboy whose primary need is for guidance and discipline and whose delinquency is superficial; at the other he may be an inadequate or aggressive personality who poses major therapeutic problems. It is a merit of probation that it caters for a wide range of cases, some requiring intensive therapy, others help and advice, others primarily needing regular control. In each case the object of the probation order is " the ultimate re-establishment of the probationer in the community." [18] Probation is, in our view, properly used if it serves this purpose and we should deprecate any tendency to regard such purpose as other than therapeutic even although its fulfilment requires guidance and control of the probationer. On the other hand, it would be inconsistent with the objects of probation to employ it solely as a discipline to show an offender that he had not " got away with it."

[18] Report of the 1936 Committee, para. 83.

54. The responsibility of probation officers towards their probationers is expressed by statute in words which have been in use since the Probation of Offenders Act, 1907. It is their duty " to supervise the probationers and . . . to advise, assist and befriend them." . . . But, although the terminology remains broadly valid, it obscures major changes in the ways in which probation officers establish and use the personal relationships on which their success depends. . . . Today, the probation officer must be seen, essentially, as a professional case-worker, employing, in a specialised field, skill which he holds in common with other social workers. . . . It must be added that while, as a caseworker, the probation officer's prime concern is with the well-being of an individual, he is also the agent of a system concerned with the protection of society and as such must, to a degree which varies from case to case . . . seek to regulate the probationer's behaviour. He must also be prepared, when necessary, to assert the interests of society by initiating proceedings for breach of the requirements of the probation order. This dichotomy of duties should not be over-stressed: the offender cannot realise his own potential for contented living while he is at odds with society, and one of the probation officer's tasks is to help him to perceive that, in this sense, his interests and those of society are identical. Nevertheless, the dichotomy is one which the probation officer cannot cease to be conscious, and the probationer's recognition of him as a representative of " authority " will affect the casework technique that the officer employs. We found wide-spread agreement among those who gave us evidence that the probation officer's need to overcome the fear, suspicion and resentment of authority felt by many probationers called for special skill. Yet the probation officer's possession of authority is not necessarily an obstacle to casework: it may assist him to exert the firm, consistent and benevolent control which some probationers require and many have never experienced.

55. . . . [T]here has been no abrupt or planned change of function. . . . The new methods have . . . evolved from the gradually accumulated experience of social work teachers and practitioners in this and other fields as they have learnt to apply and test a growing body of psychological and sociological theory. . . . [Moreover] the purposes for which the courts use probation are too varied, and accurate selection for probation still too difficult, for intensive casework to be necessary or appropriate in more than a proportion of cases. Every probation officer will have some cases in which he needs to or can do little. This leavening of " easy " cases and cases where only a " holding " operation is possible can, on the other hand, be identified only by the exercise of the probation officer's diagnostic skill. The superficially straight-forward case may prove complex and the probationer's true problem may emerge only as the probation period progresses.

56. Casework, as we understand it, is the creation and utilisation, for the benefit of an individual who needs help with personal problems, of a relationship between himself and a trained social worker. . . . Initially, the caseworker may know no more than that the probationer has engaged in anti-social behaviour or that there has been some other disturbance in his emotional or social life. . . . [E]ven if the probationer offers a rational and specific exposition of his problems, their true nature may be different and their causes deeper-seated than he realises. Accordingly, careful appraisal of his personality, family and social setting, and his problems must precede any attempt at helping him to resolve or modify his difficulties [In his emotional or social life]. . . .

This can, itself, be a lengthy and exacting process. . . . Rare sensitivity may be needed in establishing and developing the casework relationship at this stage, and sympathetic interest must be matched by objective and critical analysis of the data obtained.

57. ... Failings, anxieties and problems are the outcome of diverse causes which may be understood and altered. There may, in the first place, be scope for altering external influences by helping the individual to change his home or economic circumstances, his habits or companions. ... Fundamentally, however, his [*i.e.* the caseworker's] purpose is more profound than any environmental alteration he can achieve. He seeks to establish a relationship which will, itself, be a positive influence, counteracting and modifying the ill-effects of past experiences and of irremovable factors in the present. ... The caseworker must secure acceptance as a friend and confidant and he cannot do this unless he shows that ... he accepts the individual, whatever his inadequacies and limitations, as a person who deserves consideration and respect. The caseworker must be a realist, and must recognise that external influences, beyond his altering, may outweigh any influence that he, himself, can exert. He must realise that the most deeply-rooted difficulties may be a psychiatrist's province rather than his own and must understand his own personality, prejudices and attitudes and the ways in which these influence his professional relationships. He must also appreciate that in many instances there will be limited capacity for change and little or no desire to change. Indeed, this lack of desire to change personal behaviour, together with a tendency to attribute personal failures to outside causes, is characteristic of many probationers.

58. If, however, the probationer feels free and has sufficient desire to explain and examine, with the caseworker's help, the feelings and attitudes which underlie or accompany his problems, or have made him a problem to society, he may be able, with continuing help, gradually to see himself and his place in society in a new and more mature way. In so far as this happens, he will become better able to cope with the stresses of living. At the same time, we recognise that a relationship with an individual caseworker cannot necessarily be expected to bring about substantial changes in the anti-social behaviour of individuals who live in districts with a high delinquency rate, and whose behaviour conforms to that of many of their fellows in the neighbourhood.

59. It is the appreciation of, and concentration upon, the probationer's ability to benefit from a developing personal relationship with the probation officer that principally distinguishes probation supervision today from that of a quarter of a century ago. ... This development has been both facilitated and encouraged by full employment and growing material prosperity, for if the welfare state has freed the probation officer from preoccupation with the material needs of offenders, it has also shown ... that crime is not primarily the product of economic hardships. ...

Fines

Many statutes in creating an offence make a fine one of the penalties. In addition the Criminal Law Act 1967 makes a fine an alternative for most indictable offences and the Magistrates' Courts Act 1952 makes a fine an alternative to imprisonment or detention and as a possible penalty for indictable offences tried summarily. It is in fact the penalty most commonly used in magistrates' courts. Several problems have been frequently discussed; the question of fixing the amount which includes both the problem of making the fine in some way proportionate to the offender's means and of achieving some kind of uniformity; securing payment, and thirdly its effectiveness as a penalty. So far as the problem of enforcement is concerned the aim has been to devise ways in which defaulters can be dealt with without putting them into prison, on the assumption that one of the reasons for imposing a fine in the first place was the court's view that prison was not an appropriate method of treatment in the particular case. In this respect there has been a gradual development, giving offenders longer time to pay, conducting inquiries into the reasons for default, and devising alternative means of securing payment. The Criminal Justice Administration Act 1914 for example provided that the courts should allow more time for payment unless there was some good reason for not doing so, such as the fact that the offender had no permanent address. This itself led to a reduction in the numbers imprisoned. The Money Payments (Justices Procedure) Act 1935, following on the report of a Departmental Committee on Imprisonment by Courts of Summary Jurisdiction in default of payment of fines and other sums of money,[19] provided that no one was to be imprisoned for failure to pay a fine or maintenance under a maintenance order until an inquiry had been made into his means. The Criminal Justice Act 1967 introduced further safeguards [20] and also the power to make an attachment of earnings order.

Criminal Law Act 1967
1967, c. 58

7.—(3) Where a person is convicted on indictment of any offence other than an offence for which the sentence is fixed by law, the court, if not precluded from sentencing the offender by its exercise of some other power (such as the power to make a probation order), may impose a fine in lieu or in addition to dealing with him in any other way in which the court has power to deal with him, subject however to any enactment limiting the amount of the fine that may be imposed or requiring the offender to be dealt with in a particular way.

Magistrates' Courts Act 1952
15 & 16 Geo. 6 & 1 Eliz. 2, c. 55

19.—(6) A person summarily convicted of an indictable offence under this section shall be liable to imprisonment for a term not exceeding six months or a fine not exceeding [four hundred pounds] [21] or both.

27.—(3) Where under any . . . enactment a magistrates' court has power to sentence an offender to imprisonment or other detention but not to a fine, then, except where an Act passed after the thirty-first day of December, eighteen hundred and seventy-nine, expressly provides to the contrary, the court may, instead . . . impose a fine not exceeding [one hundred pounds] [22] and not of such an amount as would subject him, in default of payment of the fine, to a longer term of imprisonment or detention than the term to which he is liable on conviction of the offence.

31.—(1) In fixing the amount of a fine, a magistrates' court shall take into consideration among other things the means of the person on whom the fine is imposed so far as they appear or are known to the court.

[19] Cmd. 4649, 1934.
[20] Below, p. 528.
[21] This was raised to £400 by s. 43 (1) of the Criminal Justice Act 1967.
[22] Originally £25. Raised to £100 by s. 43 (2) of the Criminal Justice Act 1967.

Children and Young Persons Act 1933

22 & 23 Geo. 5, c. 12

55.—(1) [23] Where a [. . .] young person is [charged with] any offence for the commission of which a fine, damages, or costs may be imposed, if the court is of opinion that the case would be best met by the imposition of a fine, damages, or costs, whether with or without any other punishment, the court may [. . .] order that the fine, damages, or costs awarded be paid by the parent or guardian of the [. . .] young person instead of by the [. . .] young person, unless the court is satisfied that the parent or guardian cannot be found or that he has not conduced to the commission of the offence by neglecting to exercise due care [or control] of the [. . .] young person.

The enforcement of payments of fines

Departmental Committee on Imprisonment by Courts of Summary Jurisdiction in Default of payment of Fines and Other Sums of Money

Cmd. 4649, 1934

The committee was appointed in June 1933 to review the existing law relating to the enforcement of fines imposed by Courts of Summary Jurisdiction and to the enforcement of wife maintenance and affiliation orders and of payment of rates, and to consider whether by changes in the law or in the methods of administration it is possible to reduce the number of imprisonments in default of payment, due regard being given to the importance of securing compliance with orders made by the courts.

2. If there is general agreement that the courts must have a power of imprisonment in the cases falling within our terms of reference, there is equally general agreement that the power should be used as seldom as possible. As the Lord Chancellor said in the speech which foreshadowed the appointment of this Committee—"The bad effect which imprisonment may have on a man's character and self-respect, the suffering caused to his family and dependants, and the fact that he is cut off from any possibility of earning while in prison and will probably find it more difficult than ever to secure employment on release—all these evil results cannot be disputed." . . . We are glad to report that in our opinion it is practicable to reduce considerably the number of imprisonments. . . .

27. In the majority of cases where fines are imposed, the nature of the offence and the character of the offender are such that a sentence of imprisonment is inappropriate, because it is too severe and liable to have too damaging an effect on the future career of the offender. The court expects that the fine will be paid and that there will be no question of imprisonment. If imprisonment follows because of failure to pay the fine, the intention is frustrated. . . .

28. Defaults in the payment of fines may often be due, not to wilful refusal or to deliberate neglect, but to the difficulty experienced by poor people in paying what is to them a large sum unless the payments are made by weekly instalments. . . .

[23] Material in square brackets in this section has been amended by Children and Young Persons Act 1969, s. 72 (3), Sched. 5, para. 5.

29. Most defaulters are poor people with little knowledge of court procedure and they frequently do not realise the serious consequences of failure to make provision for the fine. . . .

30. In cases of this class and in many others imprisonment might be avoided if some pressure were put on the offender to pay small weekly sums, or even if the payment of instalments were facilitated. . . .

36. Amongst the defaulters sent to prison, as a result of non-payment of fines or of sums due under maintenance or affiliation orders or of rates, there are many whose indifference to their obligations is gross and inexcusable; and of most of the defaulters it may be assumed that their will to meet their obligations and to economise for the purpose is weaker than average, since they are a minority compared with the many people who, though no better off, manage to meet similar obligations. But many of those with a poor capacity of saving would pay if the fine or the rate were levied by weekly instalments . . . and if earlier pressure were exerted to prevent the accumulation of arrears. While therefore the defaults are partly due to the defaulter's own character, they are also partly due to a system which does not take sufficient account of human weakness and human habits. . . .

37. . . . Perhaps the greatest defect of the existing system is that in many cases commitment automatically follows on default and the court has no opportunity of giving specific attention to the question whether the case is one for imprisonment or whether further consideration ought to be granted to the defaulter. The defect is most evident in the enforcement of fines and in rate cases though it is also a contributory cause of unsatisfactory results in maintenance and affiliation cases. When a fine is imposed, the practice of most courts, is to provide simultaneously for . . . a term of imprisonment in default. In the great majority of these cases that part of the adjudication which relates to imprisonment is regarded by the court at the time as a consequential formality; it is not expected that imprisonment will follow and in 97 cases out of 100 this expectation is justified. Consequently at that point the question of imprisonment is not prominent in the mind of the court. Later, if the fine is not paid, the question of issuing a commitment warrant arises. The issue of such warrants, which is the critical step determining imprisonment, is an administrative act which can be performed by any justice, not a judicial act of the court. It is anticipated that in most cases the issue of the commitment warrant will result in payment of the fine, and accordingly, unless the attention of the justice is called to some special case, he has not when signing such warrants expressly in mind the question whether the particular defendant ought to be sent to prison. . . .

39. In the result, a survey of the practice of courts of summary jurisdiction and of the circumstances in which orders are made for commitment to prison of persons who have defaulted in the payment of money, leads us to the conclusion that it is desirable to lay down as a general principle that no one should go to prison for non-payment of money under an adjudication of a court of summary jurisdiction unless and until the mind of the court has been specifically directed to the question of imprisonment. . . .

Magistrates' Courts Act 1952

15 & 16 Geo. 6 & 1 Eliz. 2, c. 55

71.—(1) Where any person is adjudged to pay a sum by a summary conviction and the convicting court does not commit him to prison forthwith in default of payment, the court may, either on the occasion of the conviction or on a subsequent occasion, order him to be placed under the supervision of such person as the court may from time to time appoint.

(2) An order placing a person under supervision in respect of any sum shall remain in force so long as he remains liable to pay the sum or any part of it. . . .

(4) Where a person under twenty-one years old has been adjudged to pay a sum by a summary conviction and the convicting court does not commit him to prison forthwith in default of payment, the court shall not commit him to prison in default of payment of the sum, or for want of sufficient distress to satisfy the sum, unless he has been placed under supervision in respect of the sum or the court is satisfied that it is undesirable or impracticable to place him under supervision.

(5) Where a court, being satisfied as aforesaid, commits a person under twenty-one years old to prison without an order under this section having been made, the court shall state the grounds on which it is so satisfied in the warrant of commitment.

(6) Where an order placing a person under supervision . . . is in force, a magistrates' court shall not commit him to prison in default of payment . . . or for want of sufficient distress . . . unless the court has . . . taken such steps as may be reasonably practicable to obtain from the person appointed for his supervision an oral or written report on the offender's conduct and means. . . .

The Third Schedule to the Act sets out maximum periods of imprisonment in default of payment (as amended by the Criminal Justice Act 1967) as follows:

An amount not exceeding £2 .... seven days
An amount exceeding £2 but not exceeding £5 .... fourteen days
An amount exceeding £5 but not exceeding £20 .... thirty days
An amount exceeding £20 but not exceeding £50 .... sixty days
An amount exceeding £50 .... ninety days

Criminal Justice Act 1967
1967, c. 80

44.—(2) A magistrates' court shall not on the occasion of convicting an offender of an offence issue a warrant of commitment for a default in paying any such sum unless—

(a) in the case of an offence punishable with imprisonment, he appears to the court to have sufficient means to pay the sum forthwith;

(b) it appears to the court that he is unlikely to remain long enough at a place of abode in the United Kingdom to enable payment of the sum to be enforced by other methods; or

(c) on the occasion of that conviction the court sentences him to immediate imprisonment or detention in a detention centre for that or another offence or he is already serving a term of imprisonment or detention in a detention centre.

(3) A magistrates' court shall not in advance of the issue of a warrant of commitment fix a term of imprisonment which is to be served by an offender in the event of a default in paying a sum adjudged to be paid by a conviction, except where it has power to issue a warrant of commitment forthwith, but postpones issuing the warrant under section 65 (2) of the Magistrates' Courts Act 1952 (power to fix a term and postpone the issue of a warrant).

(4) Where on the occasion of the offender's conviction a magistrates' court does not issue a warrant of commitment for a default in paying any such sum as aforesaid or fix a term of imprisonment under the said section 65 (2) which is to be served by him in the event of any such default, it shall not thereafter issue a warrant of commitment for any such default or for want of sufficient distress to satisfy such a sum unless—

(*a*) he is already serving a term of imprisonment or detention in a detention centre; or

(*b*) the court has since the conviction inquired into his means in his presence on at least one occasion.

(5) Where a magistrates' court is required by the last foregoing subsection to inquire into a person's means, the court may not on the occasion of the inquiry or at any time thereafter issue a warrant of commitment for a default in paying any such sum unless—

(*a*) in the case of an offence punishable with imprisonment, the offender appears to the court to have sufficient means to pay the sum forthwith; or

(*b*) the court has considered or tried all other methods of enforcing payment of the sum and it appears to the court that they are inappropriate or unsuccessful.

(6) After the occasion of an offender's conviction by a magistrates' court, the court shall not, unless—

(*a*) the court has previously fixed a term of imprisonment under section 65 (2) of the Magistrates' Courts Act 1952 which is to be served by the offender in the event of a default in paying a sum adjudged to be paid by the conviction; or

(*b*) the offender is serving a term of imprisonment or detention in a detention centre;

issue a warrant of commitment for a default in paying the sum or fix such a term except at a hearing at which the offender is present . . .

(7) Where a magistrates' court issues a warrant of commitment on the ground that one of the conditions mentioned in subsection (2) or (5) of this section is satisfied, it shall state that fact, specifying the ground, in the warrant.

(8) A magistrates' court may, either before or on inquiring into a person's means under this section, and a justice of the peace acting for the same petty sessions area as that court may before any such inquiry, order him to furnish to the court within a period specified in the order such a statement of his means as the court may require.

(9) A person who fails to comply with an order under the last foregoing subsection shall be liable on summary conviction to a fine not exceeding £50.

(10) Where a fine has been imposed on conviction of an offender by a magistrates' court, the court may, on inquiring into his means or at a hearing under subsection (6) of this section, remit the whole or any part of the fine if the court thinks it just to do so having regard to any change in his circumstances since the conviction, and where the court remits the whole or part of the fine after a term of imprisonment has been fixed, it shall also reduce the term by an amount which bears the same proportion to the whole term as the amount remitted bears to the whole fine or, as the case may be, shall remit the whole term.

In calculating the reduction in a term of imprisonment required by this subsection any fraction of a day shall be left out of account.

46.—(1) If it appears to a magistrates' court by which a sum has been adjudged to be paid by a conviction that the offender has defaulted in the payment of that sum and that he is a person to whom earnings fall to be paid, the court may, after inquiring into his means under section 44 of this Act, make one or more attachment of earnings orders within the meaning of the Maintenance Orders Act 1958. . . .

47.—(1) [If the Crown Court imposes a fine on any person . . . the court] [24] shall, subject to the next following subsection, make an order under section 14 (1) of the Criminal Justice Act 1948 . . . fixing a term of imprisonment which that person is to undergo if the sum . . . is not duly paid or recovered.

(2) No person shall on the occasion when a fine is imposed on him . . . be committed to prison in pursuance of such an order unless—

(a) in the case of an offence punishable with imprisonment he appears to the court to have sufficient means to pay the sum forthwith;

(b) it appears to the court that he is unlikely to remain long enough at a place of abode in the United Kingdom to enable payment of the sum to be enforced by other methods; or

(c) on the occasion when the order is made the court sentences him to immediate imprisonment or detention in a detention centre for that or another offence . . . or he is already serving a term of imprisonment or detention.

Report of the Advisory Council on the Penal System. Non-custodial and Semi-custodial Penalties 1970

14. The fine is the most commonly used of all the penalties available to the criminal courts as a whole and appears to be one of the most effective in relation to offenders of almost all age groups and criminal histories.[25] Provisional criminal statistics for 1969 show that fines were imposed on 95 per cent. of offenders who were found guilty of non-indictable offences; 98 per cent. of offenders found guilty of non-indictable motoring offences and 89 per cent. of those found guilty of other non-indictable offences were so dealt with. Of the offenders found guilty of indictable offences at magistrates' courts 49 per cent. were fined. The last two decades have seen an increase in the use of fines by higher courts: in 1950 of those found guilty on indictment 6 per cent. were fined: by 1967 the proportion had risen to 21 per cent. although it fell to 13 per cent. in 1968 and 1969 after the introduction of suspended sentences.[26]

15. Several radical changes in the law concerning fines and their enforcement were made by the Criminal Justice Act 1967. The Act increased the maximum fines which magistrates' courts may impose for a wide range of offences; placed responsibility on magistrates' courts for the collection and enforcement of all fines and recognizances, irrespective of whether these were imposed on indictment or on summary conviction; made further provision to ensure that in general offenders were given time to pay and were not committed in default unless a means enquiry had been held and all other means of enforcement found inappropriate or unsuccessful; gave magistrates' courts power to remit fines in whole or in part; and introduced enforcement by attachment of earnings and by proceedings in the civil courts. . . .

---

[24] As amended by Courts Act 1971, s. 56 (1), Sched. 8, para. 53 (1)–(3).
[25] *The Sentence of the Court*, 1969, H.M.S.O., Annex, para. 13.
[26] The statistics given in this paragraph and in para. 106 are on the basis used in the Criminal Statistics. That is, the figures relate to penalties imposed on offenders for their principal offence; penalties imposed for subsidiary offences have been disregarded.

16. We have considered whether there are any steps which could be taken to improve the use of the fine as a penal measure. One suggestion commonly made is that the fine should be related more accurately to the offender's means....

17. In considering the offender's means, a distinction must be made between cases where the offender is present in court and where he is not.... It is clearly not easy for account to be taken of the means of a defendant who pleads guilty by post or is otherwise dealt with in his absence, although it is open to the court to adjourn and to summon the defendant if they have in mind to impose a relatively high fine or where they think it desirable to have information about his means. Specific provision is now made in the form for pleading guilty by post to enable the defendant to draw attention to his financial circumstances ... if he thinks that they constitute grounds for leniency. We understand, however, that few give helpful information on this form. In practice, it may safely be assumed that it is rare for a court imposing a fine in the absence of the offender to be aware of his means, and that the tendency is towards standardising fines for these less serious offences. There have in fact been moves in recent years designed to assist magistrates' courts to achieve a greater consistency in fining, and ... information has been circulated to justices' clerks by the Lord Chancellor's Office and the Home Office about the average fines imposed for exceeding the speed limit on public roads.

18.... We suspect that, even where the offender is present in court, means are often ignored and that, where they are taken into account, ... the courts fix the fine by reference to the seriousness of the offence and scale it down if it seems excessive in relation to the offender's means, so that there is no corresponding upward adjustment in the case of the better-off offender.... [T]he preliminary findings ... of a study carried out by Dr. Roger Hood of the sentencing in magistrates' courts of offenders convicted of serious motoring offences ... indicate that a substantial minority of magistrates think that income should be taken into account, if at all, only when adjusting time allowed for payment.... We recognise that in this area we are at the mercy of what it is possible to achieve, and that it would be unrealistic to think that hard-pressed magistrates' courts, in dealing with the very large numbers of offenders who are sentenced in their absence, could accurately differentiate between all of them according to their means, even if the relevant information were made available. In general, however, we think that fines should be assessed according to the offender's ability to pay, and that it is not enough to give effect to this principle solely by the exercise of mitigation. In our view, it is right that penalties for similar offences should as far as possible be designed to make an equal impact on offenders, and that the well-to-do should pay more than the less affluent. The fine will be equitable only if it is assessed in this way and constitutes something more than payment for a licence to commit the particular offence.

26.... [V]ery little information is available about the ... effectiveness of enforcement procedures.... We are not satisfied that magistrates courts are adequately equipped to carry out the thorough investigation of means which the law requires before a fine defaulter is committed to prison. Too often the evidence available does not amount to much more than repeated failure to comply with demands for payment.... [I]n some areas an officer has been appointed to the staff of justices' clerks to supervise the payment of fines—a development commended by the Payne Committee.[27]

27. The Payne Committee has recently recommended the abolition of imprisonment for civil debt.[28]... [A] civil debt is an obligation voluntarily

[27] Report of the Committee on the Enforcement of Judgment Debts 1969, Cmnd. 3909, para. 1269.
[28] Ibid., paras. 955–966.

incurred, whereas a fine is imposed by authority; nevertheless we do not think that this distinction justifies the use of the sanction of loss of liberty merely for failure to pay, as distinct from recalcitrance, in the case of the fine-defaulter any more than in that of the civil debtor. The Payne Committee further recommended the establishment of an Enforcement Office to enforce the collection of civil debts.... We...think that the Enforcement Office should be concerned with the collection of overdue fines as well as civil debts. It should have the power to make instalment orders, to defer payment on such terms and conditions as it thinks fit, to levy execution against defaulter's property, to issue attachment of earnings orders against the defaulter's employer, to appoint a Receiver of all the defaulter's property and to make the defaulter bankrupt. It should also retain a register of defaulters to which reference could easily be made by the courts imposing fines. ...

28. At this point our views are divided. A minority, comprising Mr. Blom-Cooper, Professor Trasler and Baroness Wootton . . . propose that it should be a criminal offence for any person persistently to refuse or to neglect to pay a fine when he has the means to do so. Such a proposal would be analogous to section 30 of the Ministry of Social Security Act 1966, which makes it a criminal offence for a person persistently or negligently to refuse to maintain himself or his family, and in consequence to draw benefit from the Supplementary Benefits Commission. The proposed new offence would...be the subject of a formal charge, and would have to be proved in the same way as any other criminal charge; and a social enquiry report should be available to the court before sentence of imprisonment is imposed. If proved, it could lead to a sentence of imprisonment: this, however, would not necessarily have to be suspended under section 39 (3) of the Criminal Justice Act 1967 if the analogy of section 104 (1) of that Act were followed. In the opinion of the minority, without the introduction of such an offence, the recalcitrant and the impoverished defaulter will continue to be inextricably mixed up together, both alike at risk of committal to prison . . . Only when persistent and unjustified default becomes an offence in its own right, will the...fine become...a genuinely non-custodial penalty.

29. The majority of us...doubt the practicability of the step which our colleagues advocate. We are not reassured by the analogy of...the Ministry of Social Security Act 1966, for we note that the Payne Committee were told that the difficulties of prosecuting under that section seemed to be considerable, and that it was little used.[29] Fine-default is a larger problem, and we have been told that a substantial number of fines are paid at the stage when a warrant of commitment to prison is made out. To interpose the necessity to prosecute would not merely create a great deal of work for law-enforcement agencies; it would seriously weaken the only sanction which seems likely to affect the wilful defaulter who does not mind giving up or changing his job. . . .

Attorney-General v. Harris
Court of Appeal [1961] 1 Q.B. 74

If fines prove to be ineffective the courts will in certain circumstances, on the application of the Attorney-General issue an injunction.

PEARCE L.J.:...It is not, of course, desirable that Parliament should habitually rely on the High Court to deter the lawbreaker by other means than the statutory penalties instead of taking the legislative step of making the

---

[29] *Ibid.*, para. 1038.

penalties adequate to prevent the offence which it has created. Especially is this so where the offences are of a trivial nature. Yet it is, on the other hand, highly undesirable that some member of the public should with impunity flout the law and deliberately continue acts forbidden by Parliament. And in cases where, under the existing law, this court alone can provide a remedy, it should in general lend its aid to enforce obedience to the law when that aid is invoked by the Attorney-General on behalf of the public. . . . The Attorney-General exercises an administrative discretion in deciding whether the action should be brought. The court does not inquire into the rightness of that decision. The bringing of the proceedings has shown that in the opinion of the Attorney-General the acts warrant an injunction. This opinion, though *ex parte*, will obviously carry weight with the court. Where, as in the present case, deliberate and still continuing breaches of the law have been proved, the court will in the exercise of its discretion normally grant an injunction, unless after hearing both sides it comes to the conclusion that the matter is too trivial to warrant it, or that an injustice will be caused by it, or that there is some other good reason for refusing to enforce the general right of the public to have its laws obeyed. I do not . . . agree . . . that the Attorney-General is in no better position than any other litigant. For the Attorney-General represents the community, which has a larger and wider interest in seeing that the laws are obeyed and order maintained. It is this wider element that is apt to be overlooked or undervalued when one considers injury to the public merely in terms of immediate injury. In *Attorney-General* v. *Sharp* [30] there was no injury to the public in this sense. In that case, probably some extra omnibuses were, on the short view, a convenience rather than otherwise, yet an injunction was granted. There are many statutes and by-laws whose breach by one man only, even though repeated, would do no injury (in the narrower sense) to the public. Indeed, it is one of the difficult problems of administration to decide what acts, harmless in themselves in isolated instances, must be forbidden in the interest of public order and well-being. And a breach with impunity by one citizen leads to a breach by other citizens, or to a general feeling that the law is unjustly partial to those who have the persistence to flout it. Moreover, a breach of one law leads to a breach of another. It is in this respect that I find myself unable to agree with the judge in his finding that the acts done by the defendants do not tend to injure the public.

Other Alternatives to Imprisonment and Custodial Sentences

One of the most notable features of penal policy in the last seventy years has been the move away from imprisonment as the typical form of punishment. This can be seen at the beginning of the century in relation to young offenders with the limitations imposed upon the imprisonment of the very young offender and the introduction of borstal training as an alternative to imprisonment for the young offender. But although the movement began in relation to young offenders it has extended beyond them and become a part of general policy that imprisonment is to be avoided as a method of treatment whenever possible. The motivation behind this development has been partly practical and partly as a result of changing views as to the value of custodial sentences generally, and especially custodial sentences that have to be served in a prison. The practical reason has been that prisons are overcrowded and expensive. The changing view has been

[30] [1931] 1 Ch. 121.

a growing acceptance of the fact that far from having a remedial effect on an offender a prison sentence may have exactly the opposite effect, both because of the danger of further contamination by association with more professional or more habituated criminals and because of the danger that, in particular in the case of the younger offender, early experience of prison will rob it of some of its unfamiliarity and therefore of some of its deterrent effect. Hence there has been particular emphasis on keeping first offenders and young offenders out of prison so far as possible. One result of this change in policy has been the need to develop alternatives. So far as young offenders are concerned this has led to the introduction of detention centres and attendance centres, as forms of custodial and semi-custodial treatment, and to suggestions that attendance centres might be extended to cater for older offenders either generally or in particular classes of case. It has also led to the introduction of community service orders in the Criminal Justice Act 1972 and suggestions that such methods as reporting to police stations might be used, again as a way of dealing with particular classes of case, such as football hooligans. Within the prison system itself it has led to the introduction by the Criminal Justice Act 1961 of the indeterminate sentence for young offenders, to make it possible to order an early release of an offender who has responded well to treatment, a separation of young offenders prisons from those of other offenders and an assimilation between borstal training and the sentences of imprisonment for these offenders. It has also led to the development of a greater variety of institutions with differing régimes to cater more particularly for the specific needs of different classes of prisoner.

Limitations on imprisonment

Criminal Justice Act 1948
11 & 12 Geo. 6, c. 58

17.—(1) . . . [A] [Crown Court] [31] shall not impose imprisonment on a person under [seventeen] [32] years of age.

(2) No court shall impose imprisonment on a person under twenty-one years of age unless the court is of opinion that no other method of dealing with him is appropriate; and for the purpose of determining whether any other method of dealing with any such person is appropriate the court shall obtain and consider information about the circumstances, and shall take into account any information before the court which is relevant to his character and his physical and mental condition.

Magistrates' Courts Act 1952
15 & 16 Geo. 6 & 1 Eliz. 2, c. 55

107.—(2) A magistrates' court shall not impose imprisonment on any person under seventeen years old.

(3) Where a magistrates' court imposes imprisonment on a person under twenty-one years old under powers contained in subsection (2) of section seventeen

[31] Amended by s. 56 (1), Sched. 8, para. 24, of the Courts Act 1971.
[32] Amended by s. 2 (2) of the Criminal Justice Act 1961.

of the Criminal Justice Act, 1948 ... the court shall state the reason for its opinion that no other method of dealing with him is appropriate, and cause that reason to be specified in the warrant of commitment and to be entered in the register.

Criminal Justice Act 1972
1972, c. 71

14.—(1) A court shall not pass sentence of imprisonment on a person who has attained the age of twenty-one and has not previously been sentenced to imprisonment unless the court is of opinion that no other method of dealing with him is appropriate; and for the purpose of determining whether any other method of dealing with any such person is appropriate the court shall obtain and consider information about the circumstances, and shall take into account any information before the court which is relevant to his character and his physical and mental condition.

(2) Where a magistrates' court sentences to imprisonment any such person as is mentioned in subsection (1) of this section, the court shall state the reason for its opinion that no other method of dealing with him is appropriate, and cause that reason to be specified in the warrant of commitment and to be entered in the register.

(4) Subsection (1) of this section does not affect the power of a court to pass sentence on any person for an offence the sentence for which is fixed by law.

Report of the Advisory Council on the Treatment of Offenders on Alternatives to Short Terms of Imprisonment 1957

7. . . . [H]owever useful a reduction in short-term prisoners would be for prison administration, that is not the main ground on which the need has been put to us for suitable alternatives to short terms of imprisonment. The argument is rather that in a substantial number of cases a short term of imprisonment does no good and may do some harm. These are the cases with which our inquiry is concerned. None of our witnesses has denied that there are such cases and that there is a need for suitable alternatives for them. This is not, however, the same as saying that alternatives should be found for all short-term sentences. In our view there is nothing to justify such sweeping condemnation. The short sentence has a definite and necessary place in our criminal law. There are many cases in which a sentence of imprisonment is inevitable, but the nature and circumstances of the offence do not require a long sentence. There is nothing inherently wrong in a short sentence being the only sentence of imprisonment open to magistrates' courts, the courts which deal with over 95% of criminal charges. Nor is there any reason why a short sentence should not be socially and penally useful in certain circumstances.[33]

8. We agree that there nevertheless remain the short-term sentences for which some alternative is desirable. Exactly what this group comprises and how large it is, is difficult to judge. There are, perhaps, two distinct categories within it. First there is the prisoner whose offence suggests that *prima facie* prison is unsuitable and useless; the fine defaulter, the chronic alcoholic, the woman convicted of child neglect, the husband who has defaulted on a maintenance order. These are all recognisable groups and the problem is how to deal with

---

[33] *Cf.* the Report of the Advisory Council on Detention Centres, 1970, below, p. 552.

the group rather than with individual prisoners. The second is the prisoner convicted of a criminal offence such as larceny, breaking or assault and given without the option of a fine a sentence of imprisonment which, it is said, will neither train nor deter but possibly contaminate him and for which there does not at present exist a suitable or adequate alternative. This is a much more elusive category. It would need the most extensive research to form even a tentative estimate of the number it contains. We have, however, formed the opinion that it exists in sufficient numbers to constitute a problem. It can be expected to consist principally of first offenders and offenders who have not been in prison before, and in support of our opinion we point to the 1,297 first offenders sentenced to imprisonment [in 1954] without the option of a fine for six months or less for non-indictable offences and the further 1,309 who had one or more previous offences but had not been sentenced to imprisonment before. . . .

The committee considered a number of possibilities. Their proposals for experimental adult attendance centres are set out below at p. 555. Among other things they recommended as well the possibility of a heavy fine being drawn to the attention of the court as an alternative to imprisonment, provided the means of the convicted person were taken into account, together with a reminder of their power to make a supervision order pending payment. They also recommended that a system of attachment of wages should be introduced if there had been a default in the payment of a maintenance order. One of the other possibilities was reporting to a police station.

23. It has been suggested to us that some of the administrative problems involved in setting up attendance centres would be removed by adopting as an alternative the practice of some other countries of ordering offenders to report at fixed times to a police station. This reporting would undoubtedly be a nuisance and the suggestion has a certain superficial attraction. It is, however, open to the fundamental objection of principle . . . that the police should not be associated with punishment. The reporting that was required of penal servitude licence holders is no precedent, since it was intended not as a punishment but as a means of helping the police in their true task of preventing and detecting crime by enabling them to keep track of the whereabouts of released criminals. Nor do we consider that the courts would be likely to regard such reporting as an adequate alternative in those cases where they now impose imprisonment.

Report of the Advisory Council on the Penal System. Non-custodial and Semi-custodial Penalties 1970

6. In general our concern has been with the average run of minor offenders. Although we have been directed to pay particular regard to the professional criminal, we have not seen much scope for the development of non-custodial penalties for offenders in this category, unless the definition of professional criminal can be said to embrace the ineffective and feckless minor recidivist who makes a precarious living from crime. There was general agreement among those whom we consulted about the need for supportive treatment which would enable this type of offender to be dealt with in the community. . . .

8. In the light of the inquiries we have made of the courts we are in no doubt that they themselves feel that their powers are too limited. . . . [I]t was for example a common experience to have to deal with cases where the offence

required the imposition of an effective deterrent both to the offender and others; where a fine was in effect no penalty, because the offender was either well-to-do or dependent on his parents; and where a custodial sentence was ... too harsh, or inappropriate in the sense that it would be likely to embitter or contaminate an offender who was not already steeped in criminal behaviour.

9. ... Imprisonment is not only harmful and inappropriate for many offenders ... ; often it is also wasteful of limited resources. Cost is not the only factor, but it is worth observing, that, quite apart from the increased risk that the state would have to support the family of an offender ... the cost of maintaining an inmate in a prison ... is on the average about £22 a week. No official estimate has been made of the average cost of supervising a probationer but we would judge it to be of the order of £1 a week.

10. As to the form that new non-custodial penalties should take, sentencers ... were generally baffled. ... Those suggestions that did emerge amounted in the main to some form of community service ... ; a wider use of some form of attendance centre; semi-custodial penalties under which the offender either worked in the community during the day and returned to a residential establishment at night, or was detained during weekends; and hostels for inadequates. ...

Service to the community

30. ... [O]ur inquiries revealed a widespread recognition on the part of sentencers that some entirely new type of custodial penalty was required. ...

31. It was thus that we were led to what is the most ambitious proposal of this report—namely, that, in appropriate cases, offenders should be required to engage in some form of part-time service to the community. ...

37. We have not attempted to categorise precisely the types of offenders for whom community service might be appropriate, nor do we think it possible to predict what use might be made by the courts of this new form of sentence. While inappropriate for trivial offences, it might well be suitable for some cases of theft, for unauthorised taking of vehicles, for some of the more serious traffic offences, some cases of malicious damage and minor assaults. ... [W]hile in general we could hope that an obligation to perform community service would be felt by the courts to constitute an adequate alternative to a short custodial sentence, we would not wish to preclude its use in, for example, certain types of traffic offence which do not involve liability to imprisonment. Community service should, moreover, be a welcome alternative in cases in which at present a court imposes a fine for want of any better sanction, or again in situations where it is desired to stiffen probation by the imposition on the offender of an additional obligation other than a fine. It might also be appropriate as an alternative to imprisonment in certain cases of fine default. We do not think, however, that it should be possible to combine a requirement to perform community service with a fine in respect of the same offence. ...

38. We recognise that community service might be particularly valuable in the treatment of the young offender, especially in view of the association which we envisage with volunteers, many of whom are teenagers: indeed, such service is one of the forms of treatment which are envisaged for offenders under seventeen by the Children and Young Persons Act 1969. But we do not think it should be confined to any particular age group.

39. ... [W]e do not include in this context any proposal for full time compulsory service, which we regard as fundamentally different in principle. ...

41. ... The scheme that we have in mind ... is intended, not to compel the offender to undergo some form of penance directly related to his offence ... but to require him to perform service of value to the community or to those in need.

43. . . . [W]e have been assured that there is an abundance of opportunity for community service. . . . But the administrative problems involved in promoting a sufficient range of suitable tasks and in matching these tasks to the offenders—who would not come in a steady flow and who would represent a wide range of ability, and possibly of willingness to co-operate—would be considerable. It would be necessary to ensure that offenders . . . did not slack . . . and for the court to be satisfied that its sentence was being effectively carried out. . . .

44. Difficult problems are raised by the question how much information about offenders working alongside volunteers should be disclosed. . . . [W]e think that it would be premature to lay down hard and fast rules in advance of practical experience. . . .

49. . . . We have discussed the matter in general terms with the representatives of the Conference of Principal Probation Officers, the National Association of Probation Officers and the Central Council of Probation and After Care committees and . . . with the Advisory Council for Probation and After Care. . . . They have all readily accepted the proposition that the probation and after care service would be the appropriate organisation to administer a scheme of community service for offenders. . . .

56. . . . There would need to be provision for dealing with breaches of a direction to undertake community service, such as failure to report or to work satisfactorily. The court should have power to deal with minor offences by imposing a fine, and with more serious transgressions by revoking the original direction and dealing with the offender in any way in which he could have been dealt with for his original offence. . . .

Reporting to a police station

113. It is commonly suggested that it would be useful to be able to prevent football hooligans from gaining attendance to a football match by making them report to a police station or elsewhere shortly after kick-off. . . .

115. . . . The representatives of the police service felt that it was undesirable in principle for the police to be associated with punishment, and that it would cause administrative difficulty if police stations . . . were used for reporting purposes. We recognise that this argument has some force; but it seems to us that the proposed penalty would require minimum involvement of the police with punishment and that there should be no appreciable additional administrative burden. It is, after all, a common practice for motorists stopped by the police to be required to produce their driving licences and insurance and test certificate at a police station, and a person admitted to bail may be required to report to the police pending his reappearance in court.

116. We therefore recommend that police stations should be used as reporting centres, and we see no reason why the Greenwich and Manchester senior attendance centres should not also have this function. . . .

The committee again considered the question of adult attendance centres.[34]

Section 15 of the Criminal Justice Act 1972 now authorises a court which has convicted an offender of seventeen or over of an offence punishable with imprisonment to make a community service order requiring him to perform unpaid work for not less than forty nor more than 240 hours. No such order can be made without the offender's consent. Section 20 provides that such an order can also be made where there has been a breach

[34] See below, p. 556.

of a probation order instead of imposing a fine. Section 40 authorises a magistrates' court to make such an order instead of imposing imprisonment in the case of default in payment of a fine.

Criminal Justice Act 1972

1972, c. 71

Community service orders

15.—(1) Where a person who has attained the age of seventeen is convicted of an offence punishable with imprisonment, the court by or before which he is convicted may, instead of dealing with him in any other way (but subject to subsection (2) of this section), make an order (in this Act referred to as " a community service order ") requiring him to perform unpaid work in accordance with the subsequent provisions of this Act for such number of hours (being in the aggregate not less than forty nor more than two hundred and forty) as may be specified in the order.

(2) A court shall not make a community service order in respect of any offender unless the offender consents and the court—

(*a*) has been notified by the Secretary of State that arrangements exist for persons who reside in the petty sessions area in which the offender resides or will reside to perform work under such orders; and

(*b*) is satisfied—

(i) after considering a report by a probation officer about the offender and his circumstances and, if the court thinks it necessary, hearing a probation officer, that the offender is a suitable person to perform work under such an order; and

(ii) that provision can be made under the arrangements for him to do so. . . .

SPECIALISED MEASURES FOR DIFFERENT CATEGORIES OF OFFENDER

Children and young persons

As we have already seen in connection with juvenile courts it has long been an aim of the English legal system to keep children and young persons separate from adults so far as court hearings are concerned. And the same is true of treatment. Already in the nineteenth century the Reformatory Act of 1854 had provided that children could be committed to a reformatory instead of being sent to prison. By virtue of the 1857 Industrial Schools Act a child in need of care and protection could be sent to an industrial school. Both of these types of institutions had been established as voluntary institutions. Once they had been given statutory recognition in this way they came under the inspection of the Home Office. By 1933 there was little to choose between the two different types of school and they became known as approved schools. Until approved school orders were abolished by the Children and Young Persons Act 1969 they remained one of the common ways of dealing with children and young persons brought before the courts.

In 1908 two further custodial institutions were introduced. First, the Children Act 1908 which provided that in future no one under fourteen should be sent to prison also provided for the establishment of " places of detention " to which those between the ages of fourteen and sixteen could be sent if they were remanded in custody awaiting trial or by way of punishment or in default of payment of a fine, for detention of up to one month. A young person who was too unruly or depraved to make it safe or suitable for him to be sent to such a place would still have to be remanded in prison. These " places of detention " became known as " remand homes " after the Children and Young Persons Act 1933. Secondly, the Prevention of Crime Act 1908 introduced another new form of custodial treatment, Borstal detention (later Borstal training) for those between the ages of sixteen and twenty-one, again, as an alternative to imprisonment (see below, p. 545). The minimum age for Borstal training has now been raised to seventeen. Further possibilities were introduced by the Criminal Justice Act 1948 which provided for detention centres for those between the ages of fourteen and twenty and attendance centres for those between the ages of twelve and twenty. It also provided for " remand centres " to which those between the ages of seventeen and twenty could be remanded in custody and also for those who were too unruly or depraved to be sent to a remand home.

The Children and Young Persons Act 1969 introduced substantial changes in the existing structure with the general aim of increasing the involvement of the local authority services in the treatment of those under seventeen and also with the aim of providing a much greater flexibility and variety in their treatment. The Act was preceded by the White Paper " Children in Trouble " which set out what it was hoped to achieve. In future approved schools, junior attendance centres and detention centres so far as they catered for the under seventeen are all to be absorbed or replaced by the new forms of " intermediate treatment " or the new system of " community homes."

Second Reading of the Children and Young Persons Bill 1969
779 H.C.Deb., c. 1176, March 11, 1969

THE SECRETARY OF STATE FOR THE HOME DEPARTMENT (MR. JAMES CALLAGHAN): . . . Clause 1 (3) and clause 7 give the courts three basic options which are available in all care and criminal proceedings. They apply to all children up to the age of seventeen. The first option is to bind over the parents. We regard this as appropriate in cases where the court judges that the parents are capable of taking the necessary action themselves, but have grown slack and need pulling up. It is part of the principle and the philosophy that where possible the responsibility should be put on the parents and upon the family.... The second option is the supervision order, which will take the place of probation orders, and supervision orders under the present law. The third option is the care order, which is very similar to the existing so-called fit-person order.... The supervision order and the care order ... will be extremely flexible, and will embrace a wide range of possibilities.... They rest upon the principle that it is for the court to decide the nature and extent of the compulsory powers to be exercised and that, within well specified limits, the responsibility for decisions on treatment in individual cases should be placed on those who undertake the treatment. But in all cases there is the safeguard of appeal to Quarter Sessions and, throughout the life of a care or supervision order the Bill provides a right to apply to a juvenile court for a revocation or the variation of the order with, again, appeal to Quarter Sessions against refusal of an application. The courts will also retain their powers in criminal cases to fine, to order the payment of compensation, to discharge conditionally or absolutely, and, in the case of older young persons, to order disqualification or endorsement in motoring cases. . . . Clause 13 (2) defines the relationship between the functions of the children's service and those of the probation service in this field. . . . The children's service will assume general responsibility for supervision under court orders for children under fourteen and the courts will have the choice of supervisor for children between fourteen and seventeen. I referred to the flexibility in the new forms of treatment for children placed under supervision by the courts. Of course, they might not go to court, since there could be an informal agreement. This is in clauses 12 and 19, where it is called " intermediate treatment." The object is to give the supervisors access to resources which are denied to many children from poorer backgrounds, providing them with opportunities for new experiences and relationships to help them mature and to learn to stand on their own feet. The function is to bring youngsters in trouble in contact with others taking part in normal constructive activities of young people of their own age—social, educational, recreational, helping others. These activities may take place in the evenings or at weekends, and the children may go away under supervision, perhaps, for longer periods. They may involve going away, for instance, for adventure training or to a harvest camp. In some cases, a supervision order might involve spending as much as three months away from home. For example, a period might be spent in a community home . . . or a term at a boarding school. . . .

Children in Trouble
Cmnd. 3601, 1968

20. The aim of the changes is to increase the effectiveness of the measures available to deal with juvenile delinquents. Effectiveness means helping children whose behaviour is unacceptable to grow up, to develop personal relationships and to accept their personal responsibilities towards their fellows, so that they become mature members of society; in some cases it also means firm control of anti-social behaviour. In order to achieve these aims it is necessary to develop further our facilities for observation and assessment, and to increase the variety of facilities for continuing treatment, both residential and non-residential. Increased flexibility is needed so as to make it easier to vary the treatment when changed circumstances or fuller diagnosis suggest the need for a different approach. Organisational changes are also desirable so as to provide a setting for closer co-operation between the services concerned.

21. Three main changes in the powers of the juvenile court will be made for this purpose. First, the approved school order will be abolished; an order for the compulsory removal of a child from home will in all cases take the form of committal to the care of the local authority. Second, provision will be made for the development of new forms of treatment, intermediate between supervision in the home and committal to care. Third, all supervision of children under fourteen will be by the local authority. The first change was proposed in " The Child, the Family and the Young Offender ", and was widely supported. The third is a modification of a proposal in that White Paper. The second is new. . . .

23. At present young persons of fifteen and sixteen may be committed to quarter sessions, and sent to borstal by quarter sessions, if no other method of dealing with them is appropriate. Power will be retained for the present to commit to borstal young people of this age for whom committal to, or a continuation in, care would be unsuitable. This power will be discontinued when new arrangements have been made for treating, where necessary under conditions of security, children and young persons whose behaviour presents serious problems.

Supervision

24. At present children and young persons who have committed an offence may be placed on probation and are supervised by probation officers. Those found in need of care, protection or control may be placed under the supervision of a probation officer, the local authority or any other person. Under the new arrangements, the supervision of a child under fourteen found to be in need of care, protection or control will be by the local authority. . . . For young persons aged fourteen and under seventeen, supervision following both criminal proceedings and care, protection or control proceedings will be by the local authority or by a probation officer (but not, as at present, by any other person) as decided by the court. This means that the association of the probation service with young persons aged fourteen and under seventeen will be preserved. Supervision will be for a specified period of not more than three years.

Intermediate forms of treatment

25. Existing forms of treatment available to the juvenile courts distinguish sharply between those which involve complete removal from home and those which do not. The juvenile courts have very difficult decisions to make in judging whether circumstances require the drastic step of taking a child away from his parents and his home. The view has often been expressed that some form or forms of intermediate treatment should be available to the courts, allowing the child to remain in his own home but bringing him also into contact with a different environment. The junior attendance centres go some way towards meeting this need, but the time spent by an individual offender in an attendance centre is short (up to 24 hours at most, spread over a number of Saturdays), and it has not been possible to provide centres outside the more populous areas. The junior detention centre involves removal from home which, although relatively brief, is sudden and complete. A new legal and administrative framework will therefore be established for the development of a variety of forms of intermediate treatment for children and young persons placed under supervision by the juvenile courts. One object is to make possible the use for this purpose of facilities not provided expressly for those who have been before the courts. These new methods of treatment will be linked to supervision, but a straightforward supervision order will remain possible. . . .

26. Intermediate treatment will fall into two categories. The first will involve temporary residence, attendance or participation, for a period or periods totalling not more than one month during each year of supervision. The court will fix the actual period, within this maximum. The supervisor (*i.e.*, the local authority or probation officer) will decide on the particular place to be attended or activity to be undertaken, selecting the most appropriate of the facilities available under the local scheme mentioned in paragraph 28. These powers will be capable of use in a wide variety of ways. Possible instances are attendance for a number of evenings, or week-end afternoons, or entire week-ends, at a place for training, treatment or recreation; or taking part for a specified total of hours or days in some organised work project, or social service, or adventure training. There are

many other possibilities. The aim will be to bring the young person into contact with a new environment, and to secure his participation in some constructive activity.

27. The second category will involve residence at a specified place for a fixed period of not more than three months, beginning within the first year of supervision. Again the actual length of the period of residence will be set by the court, within the statutory maximum. Its timing and nature will be decided by the supervisor, who will be responsible for selecting the most appropriate of the facilities available under the local scheme. This type of treatment will be available for use where the basic need is for help and supervision in the home, but a short period away from home also seems desirable. It will, for example, enable a child or young person to be placed for a short time in a home or hostel, or with relatives who are willing to receive him, while help is offered in remedying a difficult family situation. It will also be suitable for use in cases where the child himself needs some form of short-term treatment in a residential establishment or the kind of residential experience now being provided by a number of local education authorities.

28. It will be the responsibility of the local authorities, . . . to prepare schemes setting out the range of intermediate treatments which they propose to make available, whether directly or by arrangement with voluntary bodies. Representatives of the juvenile court justices and of the police and probation services in each area will be associated with the planning committee in preparing these schemes. The facilities included in each scheme will have to come within general categories authorised by the Secretary of State, or to be approved expressly by him; the local authorities and other services will be consulted about the types of facilities to be authorised.

29. . . . When adequate facilities for attendance or participation are provided under a scheme the existing powers of those courts to make junior attendance centre orders will lapse. Similarly, when adequate facilities for short term residence are provided under a scheme, existing powers to commit to a junior detention centre will lapse. In the meantime, the Government will continue to maintain junior attendance centres and junior detention centres, and will be ready to discuss with local authorities ways in which these facilities might be incorporated within new schemes of supervision or residence. In particular, it is important that the valuable work of police officers in the junior attendance centres should not be lost.

Residential treatment

30. The abolition of the approved school order means that children and young persons who would now be committed to approved schools will come into the care of the local authority in whose area they live. The basic duty of local authorities towards children in their care will remain that of providing the care, protection, guidance or treatment which they consider appropriate in the interests of each child. This duty will include restoring the child to his home as soon as practicable and desirable, having regard to the need to protect society while children and young persons whose behaviour is difficult to control are undergoing treatment. The Secretary of State will have a reserve power to give directions to a local authority in any case where he is satisfied that a particular form of control is necessary for the protection of the public.

31. Local authorities will be responsible for developing a comprehensive system of residential care and treatment for the children received or committed into their care who are not boarded out with foster parents. . . . A considerable variety of provision will be needed within this system, which will be described for legal purposes as the public system of community homes for children and

w.—19

young persons. The needs of the great majority of children will be met by homes which, as now, will care for them as nearly as possible in the same way as a good family, making use of the education, health, and other services which are generally available. . . . Even in the long term, however, there will remain a substantial minority of children whose needs cannot be met in this way. There will thus be a continuing need for some establishments providing education and treatment on the premises. In some cases this will be with the limited aim of preparing for an early return to the use of the normal services. In others the first priority will be a therapeutic approach to social education. Some of these children, particularly those whose behaviour is most difficult, will also need control in secure conditions, or very specialised forms of treatment.

32. These proposals will not diminish the need for residential facilities. [A]ll the existing approved schools, including the senior schools, will probably be required for the accommodation of children and young persons in care. The schools will retain an important role within the new system of community homes, in continuing to provide for the needs of both offenders and non-offenders.

33. Centres for observation and assessment will form an essential part of the system. They will provide facilities on both a residential and a day-attendance basis for children remanded or subject to interim orders by the courts, and will advise on the treatment of children in care, so that decisions can be soundly based on the best possible diagnosis of the child's needs and circumstances. Observation centres will not be distinguished in law, however, from other community homes. The present legal distinctions between remand homes, reception centres, children's homes and approved schools impose unnecessary restrictions on making the best use of these resources.

34. A young person who is now committed to an approved school at the age of sixteen is liable to be detained up to his nineteenth birthday. Committal to the care of a local authority ends at the eighteenth birthday. A period of little over one year may not be sufficient for the treatment of a young person who is nearly seventeen when committed to care. Accordingly, where a young person has already reached the age of sixteen, committal to care will be until the nineteenth birthday. Provision will also be made for a young person to be retained in care up to this age, even if he came into care before reaching the age of sixteen, if he has been admitted to a special establishment for the treatment in secure conditions of very disturbed and difficult young people. The right to apply at any time for the revocation of an order committing to care will remain.

V. COMMUNITY HOMES FOR CHILDREN AND YOUNG PERSONS

35. The public system of community homes for children in the care of local authorities will be an integrated system; " community home " will be the common legal description for a wide range of establishments meeting the needs which are now served by local authority children's homes and hostels, remand homes, reception and remand centres, local authority and voluntary approved schools, and some voluntary children's homes which regularly accommodate children in care. The Government attaches great importance to the further development of partnership between public and voluntary bodies in meeting these needs, and the public system will therefore include both local authority and voluntary homes. . . .

37. The powers and duties of children authorities will . . . be extended. To enable each authority to fulfil its duties towards the children in its care, . . . its duties will also include :

(a) the preparation, in co-operation with the other authorities in a joint
    planning area designated by the Secretary of State, of
    (i) a comprehensive plan for the development of a full range of
        residential facilities for children and young persons in care, and
        of facilities for observation and assessment; and
    (ii) a scheme specifying the facilities to be made available for the
        intermediate forms of treatment described in Part IV;
(b) the provision, or assistance with the provision, of the facilities specified in
    the development plan and scheme of intermediate treatment.

These recommendations were given effect in the Children and Young
Persons Act 1969. The actual dates of the particular changes depend however on the availability of the new facilities required, and the relevant provisions are to be brought in, for the most part, when the Home Secretary
makes an order. It is too soon to say what effect they will have.

The young offender

Apart from the special provisions for children and young persons,
special provision has also been made for the treatment of the young offender,
especially the offender between the ages of seventeen and twenty-one.
Many of the non-custodial methods of treatment such as probation were
originally introduced with the young offender in mind and the introduction
of new methods of treatment such as community service orders have a
similar motivation. Even where it has been decided that some form of
custodial treatment is necessary, attempts have been made to provide treatment geared to the special needs of the young offender, as an alternative to
imprisonment, with the additional intention of preventing his being con-
taminated by older and more experienced prisoners and becoming
accustomed at an early age to prison conditions. One of the earliest forms
of special treatment that was introduced was Borstal training which has
now become the standard alternative to imprisonment for the young
offender. More recently detention centres and attendance centres have been
introduced as kind of half way houses to a long period of custodial
treatment.

Borstal Training

Borstal institutions were introduced by the Prevention of Crime Act 1908
for those between the ages of sixteen and twenty-one as an alternative to
imprisonment. They were then described as " places in which young
offenders . . . may be given such industrial training and other instruction,
and be subjected to such disciplinary and moral influences as will conduce
to their reformation and the prevention of crime." A court was authorised
to impose a sentence of Borstal training if it seemed that it was expedient
that the offender " by reason of his criminal habits or tendencies, or association with persons of bad character . . . should be subject to detention for
such term and under such instruction as appears most conducive to his
reformation and the repression of crime." The sentence was an indefinite
one and the offender could be released at any time after six months. Over
the years there was also developed within the prison system a number of

young prisoners' centres which had a regime different from that of the run-of-the-mill adult prison. Following proposals by the Prison Commissioners, who at the time were responsible for running the prison system, which were accepted by the Advisory Council on the Treatment of Offenders in their report " The Treatment of Young Offenders " in 1959 these two systems were brought together by the Criminal Justice Act 1961. That Act provided that in future a young offender between the ages of seventeen and twenty-one should not be sentenced to imprisonment except for a period of less than six months or more than three years. Any custodial sentence for an intermediate period had to be one of Borstal training. It was envisaged that the short term of imprisonment would gradually be replaced by a sentence of detention in a detention centre provided for by the Criminal Justice Act 1948 as these became available.

Report of the Advisory Council on the Treatment of Offenders. The Treatment of Young Offenders 1959

In May, 1958, you asked the Council to consider proposals put forward by the Prison Commissioners for dealing with offenders between the ages of sixteen and twenty-one. The three principal proposals were: —

(a) that a system of detention centres should be developed to the point at which it could replace short-term imprisonment (*i.e.*, for six months or less) for young offenders;

(b) that the principle of the indeterminate sentence, which already exists in the borstal sentence, should be extended to all young offenders for whom a court consider that a period of detention of between six months and two years is required;

(c) that the courts should be prohibited from sentencing young offenders to imprisonment unless they consider a sentence of at least three years to be appropriate.

7. . . . The main objects of the Prison Commissioners' proposals are:

(*a*) to keep young offenders under the age of twenty-one out of prison; and

(*b*) to ensure the protection of society by providing that such offenders can be given the amount and type of training best suited to their needs, and from which they are likely to derive the most benefit. The objects conform with the fundamental principle which has long been accepted . . . that the penal treatment of young offenders should be primarily remedial and be carried out in separate institutions or separate sections of institutions. . . .

9. These proposals . . . will provide a means of dealing with the problem . . . created by the alarming increase in the amount of crime now committed by young people. This has led to great pressure on the accommodation available in borstals and young prisoners' prisons and has caused many youths sentenced to borstal training to wait for long periods in local prisons before they can be sent to a borstal institution.

10. The . . . proposals will make it possible . . . to build up a system of custodial treatment for young offenders (other than the small number sentenced to long terms of imprisonment) which will be entirely separate from the prison system for adult offenders. This will extend to all young offenders sentenced

to custodial treatment the benefits of individual study and treatment which are the objects of the borstal system and which have been achieved to a limited extent at detention centres.

Criticism of the proposals

12. We think that these proposals may be criticised on two main grounds:—

   (a) that they will deprive the courts of the power to pass sentences which they consider to be appropriate to the offences committed; and
   (b) that the proposed methods of treatment will be too " soft " either to punish offenders adequately for the offences they have committed or to act as a deterrent.

In our view neither of these criticisms would be well founded.

13. It is true that there will be some restriction of the power of the courts to select the sentence they consider most appropriate . . . and that, in the case of the indeterminate sentence of custodial training, the Prison Commissioners and not the court will decide how long a particular offender shall remain in custody. We do not think, however, that objections on those grounds are as valid in relation to young offenders as they might be in relation to adults. . . . The commission of an offence serious enough to warrant a custodial sentence shows in most cases that a youth requires training if he is to be diverted from crime; his sentence should therefore be related primarily to that need and he should be detained long enough for adequate training to be given. This period cannot usually be judged before the sentence begins. . . . The principle of the indeterminate sentence is already fully established in the borstal sentence and we see no objection to its proposed extension.

14. We do not think that the methods of treatment now proposed can be regarded as " soft " or as being less severe than the existing methods. . . . [W]hile the living conditions in detention centres may be better than those in prison, the regime will certainly be more exacting. The mere fact that the proposed sentence of custodial training will be indeterminate will in itself act as a deterrent, for what impresses offenders most in a sentence is time. . . . If these proposals are accepted the Prison Commissioners will have at their disposal a wide variety of establishments, and a wide variety of regimes. If a youth shows that he needs to serve his sentence in rigorous conditions, we are sure that the Prison Commissioners will see that he does.

16. . . . In a serious case . . . it will remain open to the court to pass a sentence of three years imprisonment or more. Such sentences are likely to be rare. In addition we recommend . . . that where a youth who has served one indeterminate sentence is convicted again the court should have power at their discretion to impose a determinate sentence of not less than 18 months instead of another indeterminate sentence. It will thus be possible for the courts to deal adequately with persistent or serious offenders. . . .

47. If it is accepted that the regime provided for young offenders should be in all cases remedial and educational . . . it is in principle no longer necessary to provide a separate form of sentence, such as the borstal sentence, to secure those ends. The present system of two forms of sentence makes for difficulties. . . . Some young persons are sentenced to borstal training whose needs could better be met by the type of regime provided at a young prisoners' centre, and some . . . to imprisonment who would benefit from the type of training provided at a borstal institution. It is also impossible to make the most advantageous and economical use of establishments available.

49.... [T]he courts already show a marked preference for the indeterminate sentence, with its emphasis on training, provided by the borstal sentence. In 1957, only 387 youths under the age of twenty-one were sentenced to imprisonment for more than six months; in the same year 2,367 youths were sentenced to borstal training. The proposals would have little effect on the conditions in which young offenders serve their sentences, for there is already little difference between the principles of training in a young prisoners' prison and those in borstal institutions....

51.... [W]e think that there would be considerable advantages in retaining the familiar name " borstal training " which is already generally recognised as meaning an indeterminate sentence with the emphasis on constructive training.

Criminal Justice Act 1948

11 & 12 Geo. 6, c. 58

20.—(1) Where a person is convicted on indictment of an offence punishable with imprisonment, then if on the day of his conviction he is not less than [seventeen] [35] but under twenty-one years of age . . . the court may, in lieu of any other sentence, pass a sentence of Borstal training.

Magistrates' Courts Act 1952

15 & 16 Geo. 6 & 1 Eliz. 2, c. 55

28—(1) Where a person is convicted by a magistrates' court of an offence punishable on summary conviction with imprisonment, then, if on the day of the conviction he is not less than [seventeen] [35] but under twenty-one years old . . . the court may commit him in custody [or on bail] [36] to [the Crown Court] [37] for sentence in accordance with the provisions of section twenty of the Criminal Justice Act 1948.

Criminal Justice Act 1961

9 & 10 Eliz. 2, c. 39

1.—(2) The power of a court to pass a sentence of borstal training under . . . section twenty [of the Criminal Justice Act 1948] . . . shall be exercisable in any case where the court is of opinion, having regard to the circumstances of the offence and after taking into account the offender's character and previous conduct, that it is expedient that he should be detained for training for not less than six months . . .

(3) Before passing a sentence for borstal training in the case of an offender of any age, the court shall consider any report made in respect of him by or on behalf of the Secretary of State....

(4) The foregoing provisions of this section shall apply in relation to committal for a sentence of borstal training under section twenty-eight of the Magistrates' Courts Act, 1952....

[35] Originally 16. Lowered to 15 by the Criminal Justice Act 1961, s. 1, and raised to 17 by the Children and Young Persons Act 1969.
[36] As added by Criminal Justice Act 1967, s. 103 (1), Sched. 6, para. 11.
[37] As amended by Courts Act 1971, s. 56 (1), Sched. 8, para. 34 (1).

3.—(1) Without prejudice to any other enactment prohibiting or restricting the imposition of imprisonment on persons of any age, a sentence of imprisonment shall not be passed by any court on a person within the limits of age which qualify for a sentence of borstal training except—

(*a*) for a term not exceeding six months; or

(*b*) (where the court has power to pass such a sentence) for a term of not less than three years.

(2) Subsection (1) of this section shall not apply in the case of a person who is serving a sentence of imprisonment at the time when the court passes sentence. . . .

(3) In relation to a person who has served a previous sentence of imprisonment for a term of not less than six months, or a previous sentence of borstal training, subsection (1) of this section shall have effect as if for the reference to three years there were substituted a reference to eighteen months; . . .

(5) Her Majesty may by Order in Council direct that paragraph (*a*) of subsection (1) of this section shall be repealed, either generally or so far as it relates to persons, or male or female persons, of any age described in the Order:
Provided that—

(*a*) an Order in Council shall not be made under this subsection unless the Secretary of State is satisfied that sufficient accommodation is available in detention centres for the numbers of offenders for whom such accommodation is likely to be required in consequence of the Order;

(*b*) no recommendation shall be made to Her Majesty in Council to make an Order under this subsection unless a draft of the Order has been laid before Parliament and has been approved by resolution of each House of Parliament.

Prison Act 1952
15 & 16 Geo. 6 & 1 Eliz. 2, c. 52

45.—(2) [38] A person sentenced to Borstal training shall be detained in a Borstal institution for such period, not extending beyond [two years] [39] after the date of his sentence and not being less than six months from that date, as the Secretary of State may determine, and shall then be released: Provided that the Secretary of State may, if he thinks fit, direct that any such person shall be released from a borstal institution before the expiration of the said six months.[40]

Detention Centres

Detention centres were established by the Criminal Justice Act 1948. The idea behind them was to provide a short sharp shock in an attempt to bring a young offender to his senses and also to act as a deterrent. It was intended to provide a good deal of work, with little leisure, done at the double. There were senior detention centres for those between the ages of seventeen and twenty-one and junior detention centres for those between

[38] As amended by the Prison Commissioners Dissolution Order 1963, S.I. 1963 No. 597.
[39] As amended by Criminal Justice Act 1961, s. 41 (1) (3), Sched. 4.
[40] For s. 45 (3), see below, p. 592.

fourteen and sixteen. There was originally a centre for girls but this was subsequently abandoned.

Penal Practice in a Changing Society
Cmnd. 645, 1959

32. Detention centres were intended by Parliament to provide a sanction for those who could not be taught to respect the law by such milder measures as fines, probation and attendance centres, but for whom long-term residential training was not yet necessary or desirable. In the first (junior) detention centre (Campsfield House, Kidlington, 1952—for boys aged 14 to 17) emphasis was placed on the elements of hard work, brisk tempo, and strict discipline. From the outset, however, it was understood that these stricter elements should be used as part of a constructive reformative system in which the staff would make a real effort to find out what was wrong with a boy and put it right.

33. It was realised that within the short period of the sentence, which is normally three months and only in exceptional cases up to six months, no such constructive all-round training as is possible in an approved school or borstal could be attempted; indeed, boys in need of such training should not be sent to detention centres. Nevertheless, with the growth of experience, and the addition first of a senior centre (Blantyre House, Goudhurst—for boys aged 16 to 21) and later of another junior and another senior centre, it has been found possible to adapt the original conception of the " short sharp shock " to include that of a limited but positive form of training. From the outset, at the request of the Prison Commissioners, the experiment at the first two centres was followed by Dr. Max Grünhut, the Reader in Criminology at Oxford University. He has now completed a report based on a study of 434 boys before, during and after treatment. Dr. Grünhut concludes that the results are encouraging, in terms both of reappearances in court and of character improvement, and that the detention centre " has a legitimate place in a variegated system of treatment for young offenders. . . ."

Criminal Justice Act 1961
9 & 10 Eliz. 2, c. 39

Detention Centre and Remand Home

4.—(1) In any case where a court has power, or would have power but for the statutory restrictions upon the imprisonment of young offenders, to pass sentence of imprisonment on an offender under twenty-one . . . years of age, the court may, subject to the provisions of this section, order him to be detained in a detention centre.

(2) An order for the detention of an offender under this section may be made for the following term, that is to say—

(a) where . . . the maximum term of imprisonment for which the court could (or could but for any such restriction) pass sentence in his case exceeds three months, any term of not less than three nor more than six months;

(b) in any other case, a term of three months.

(3) An order under this section shall not be made in respect of any person unless the court has been notified by the Secretary of State that a detention

centre is available for the reception from that court of persons of his class or description, or an Order in Council under subsection (5) of section three of this Act is in force in respect of persons of his age. . . .

(4) An order under this section shall not be made in respect of a person who is serving or has served a sentence of imprisonment for a term of not less than six months or a sentence of borstal training unless it appears to the court that there are special circumstances (whether relating to the offence or to the offender) which warrant the making of such an order in his case; and before making such an order in respect of such an offender the court shall—

(a) in any case, consider any report made in respect of him by or on behalf of the Secretary of State,

(b) if the court is a magistrates' court and has not received any such report, adjourn the hearing under subsection (3) of section fourteen of the Magistrates' Courts Act, 1952, and remand the offender in custody to enable such a report to be made; . . .

5.—(1) Where a court has power to commit a person to prison for any term for a default and that person has attained the age of seventeen and is detained in a detention centre under a previous sentence or warrant, the court may, subject to the provisions of this section, commit him to a detention centre for a term not exceeding the term aforesaid or six months, whichever is the shorter.[41]

(2) Except as provided by the following provisions of this Part of this Act, a person shall not be committed under this section to a detention centre . . . (b) for any term exceeding six months. . . .

(4) This section applies in relation to the fixing of a term of imprisonment to be served in the event of default of payment of a fine or other sum of money as it applies in relation to committal to prison in default of such payment; and in any such case subsection (2) of this section shall apply in relation to the term fixed by the court, and not to that term as reduced by virtue of any subsequent payment.

6.—(3) Where, after a warrant or order has been issued or made by a magistrates' court—

(a) committing a person to prison, . . . for any default; or

(b) fixing a term of imprisonment, . . . to be served by him in the event of any default,

it is made to appear to a justice of the peace that that person is for the time being detained in a detention centre, the justice may amend the warrant or order by substituting that centre for the prison . . . named therein and, where . . . the term of imprisonment specified in the warrant or order exceeds six months, by reducing that term to six months.

7.—(1) Subject to the provisions of this section, any court which makes an order or issues a warrant for the detention of any person in a detention centre may direct that the term of detention under the order or warrant shall commence on the expiration of any other term for which that person is liable to be detained in a detention centre by virtue of an order or warrant made or issued by that or any other court. . . .

(3) Where a direction under subsection (1) of this section is given in connection with the making of an order under section four of this Act, the term of detention specified in that order may, if the court thinks fit, be a term of less than three months; . . .

[41] As amended by Children and Young Persons Act 1969, s. 72 (3), Sched. 5, para. 44.

(4) The aggregate of the terms for which a person may be ordered to be detained in a detention centre by virtue of any two or more orders made by the same court on the same occasion shall not in any case exceed six months.

(5) Without prejudice to subsection (4) of this section, the total term for which a person may be detained in a detention centre shall not exceed nine months at a time; and accordingly so much of any term for which a person is ordered to be so detained as, together with any other term on which it is wholly or partly consecutive, exceeds nine months shall be treated as remitted.[42]

Report of the Advisory Council on the Penal System. Detention Centres 1970

56. Most of our witnesses have been in no doubt that there is a need for a short custodial sentence such as detention in a detention centre for young males. . . . Some witnesses take the view that detention . . . is an effective form of punishment, while others see it as a means of providing a change of environment, in preparation for a period of after-care, and the opportunity for reformative treatment without taking the offender away from his home for the much longer period required for Borstal training (6 months to 2 years, on an indeterminate basis).

57. We consider that these two views are not incompatible. When a court makes a detention centre order, it has probably opted for a short-term custodial sentence either because of the seriousness of the current offence or because less drastic sanctions, such as fines and probation, have not prevented a repetition of earlier offences. The court probably sees the order as a means of bringing home to the offender the seriousness of his course of conduct (and as a deterrent to the offender's contemporaries) rather than as a means of providing reformative treatment in the sense in which borstal training is so regarded. There is, however, in our view an element of reformative treatment in any sentence . . . since an offender's attitude may be influenced by his appearances in court, by the process of investigation associated with them and by the pattern of sentences imposed.

58. Our own view is that while . . . short term custodial treatment has little relevance to young women and girls, as regards young men loss of liberty must in present circumstances be available as a sanction, and whenever possible it should be short rather than long. . . . [A] power should be maintained to impose short custodial sentences at least until such time as the treatment of young offenders has been reviewed in all its aspects. We hope, however, that in due course it may prove possible to introduce new forms of non-custodial or semi-custodial penalty that may reduce the need for custodial treatment, and that research may shed further light on the type and length of sentence most suited to different offenders.

59. As we are in no doubt that imprisonment of young offenders should be avoided whenever possible, the standard short term custodial treatment would need to be detention in a detention centre or an entirely new form of custodial treatment. We doubt, however, whether it would be wise to abolish short term imprisonment of young offenders . . . until the whole range of penalties has been reviewed, since research has established that the majority of young offenders sent to short term imprisonment (of whom there were on average some 300 in custody during 1968) are criminally sophisticated and unlikely to be readily assimilated with those sent to detention centres. . . .[43]

---

[42] See also s. 13 below, p. 592.
[43] Cf. the Report of the Advisory Council on Alternatives to short terms of imprisonment, 1957, above, p. 535.

61. We have examined the available research into detention centres and have been made aware of certain studies . . . in progress. The deduction that we draw from these studies is that for young men with not very serious criminal careers detention in a detention centre is as effective as short term imprisonment and possibly as effective as the longer term borstal training. The principal advantages . . . are . . . that it is shorter and to that extent cheaper than borstal training and that it provides a valuable alternative to prison. . . .

62. The statutes do not prescribe the type of treatment to be given during the period of detention. . . . [I]t is no longer possible to determine to what extent the regime . . . has ever concentrated on the " short, sharp shock ". . . . The requirement to adhere to a prescribed timetable and to attain and maintain unaccustomed standards of performance and behaviour are bound to be, initially at least, unpleasant and even punitive, although for some offenders they can . . . also be therapeutic and reformative. If the centres have ever been solely punitive, it is evident that over the years wardens and staff have moved towards a more positive approach. We are sure that in this their judgment has been sound, but we consider it important that in the future the aims and the philosophy of detention in a detention centre should be defined as clearly as possible. . . .

63. In our view the punitive function of detention . . . should be regarded as fulfilled by the deprivation of an offender's liberty. Although he will inevitably regard other constraints and requirements as punitive they should not be designedly so. The shortness of the period in custody . . . places limitations on what can be done by way of reformation, but . . . with young offenders an attempt must be made to help them towards a change of behaviour . . . to prepare for life in the community and to instil . . . an appreciation of some of the disciplines that a populous society is bound to impose on its members. . . .

105. . . . The Estimates Committee in their report on prisons, borstals and detention centres,[44] expressed the view that the three month sentence was by far the most effective within the present detention centre system. We consider that it will remain so under the concept that we envisage. . . .

142. We have reached the conclusion (which is contrary to our initial expectations) that there are no grounds for proposing that the power to make a detention centre order should be further circumscribed by statute so as to exclude specific categories of offender. . . .

143. . . . [W]e consider that:

(a) when dealing with an offender who has been to an approved school as a result of delinquency, the court would be well advised to consider whether borstal training might not be more appropriate than detention in a detention centre;

(b) if detention in a detention centre is to be effective, it needs to be applied before a young offender has a long string of previous convictions;

(c) it is undesirable to make a detention centre order in respect of an offender who is seriously handicapped physically or mentally or needs immediate medical treatment;

(d) where it appears possible that an offender is seriously handicapped . . . or needs immediate . . . treatment, a medical report should be obtained if the information in the social inquiry report is insufficiently detailed to enable a firm conclusion to be reached;

(e) where an offender appears to be dependent on drugs, courts should make a practice of obtaining a medical report as well as a social inquiry report before passing sentence. . . .

44 Eleventh Report from the Estimates Committee, Session 1966–67, para. 124.

145. . . . [O]ffenders with few or no previous convictions, from reasonably good homes and without institutional experience are the least likely to lapse after a period of detention in a detention centre. But this is so in relation to any form of penal treatment and . . . we do not consider that detention in a detention centre should be confined to those with a good prognosis. Since it provides the standard, and potentially the only form of short term custodial treatment . . . we consider that . . . the detention centre system . . . should aim to deal with the widest possible range of offenders. . . .

148. This report, inasmuch as it does not look . . . to other methods of custodial treatment of young offenders is limited in scope. . . . [T]here is a need for a wide ranging review of the treatment of young offenders. . . . We should therefore emphasise that . . . our proposals . . . should be regarded as provisional to the extent that they should not be regarded as binding upon whoever undertakes such a review.

Report of the Detention Centre Subcommittee of the Advisory Council on the Penal System. Detention of Girls in a Detention Centre

4. . . . Girls get into trouble much less frequently than boys, but when they do they are generally much more difficult. They are usually unhappy and disturbed, often sexually promiscuous, and often rejected by their families. They are usually in great need of help and understanding, however reluctant to accept sympathy and affection they may appear to be. Frequently they need protection while they are given a chance to sort out their problems. Generally this can be done under the guidance of a probation officer either at home or in a probation hostel, but if they do need custodial training, it should be in a place where all the ancillary services are readily available, that is to say specialist medical care, psychiatric help and assistance from social workers such as children's officers and probation officers. We are sure that the detention centre concept is not appropriate to girls. Most of the written evidence we have received suggests that detention centre training in particular and short-term custodial treatment in general are of little value in respect of girls. Our own review of the problem leads to the same conclusion. In our view most if not all the girls at present sent to Moor Court [at that time the only detention centre for girls] would derive more benefit either from non-custodial treatment or from the longer period of treatment provided by borstal training.

Attendance Centres

Criminal Justice Act 1948

11 & 12 Geo. 6, c. 58

19.—(1) Where a court of summary jurisdiction has power, or would but for [the statutory restrictions upon the imprisonment of young offenders] [45] have power to impose imprisonment on a person who is . . . under twenty-one years of age, or to deal with any such person under section 6 of this Act for failure to comply with any of the requirements of a probation order, the court may, if it has been notified by the Secretary of State that an attendance centre is available for the reception from that court of persons of his class or description, order him to attend at such a centre . . . for such number of hours . . . as may be so specified :

[45] Amended by Criminal Justice Act 1961, s. 41 (1) (3), Sched. 4.

Provided that no such order shall be made in the case of a person who has been previously sentenced to imprisonment, Borstal training or detention in a detention centre, or has been ordered to be sent to an approved school.

48.—(2) The Secretary of State may provide attendance centres, that is to say places at which offenders . . . under twenty-one years of age may be required to attend, in pursuance of orders made under section 19 of this Act, on such occasions and at such times as will avoid interference so far as is practicable with their school hours or working hours, and be given under supervision appropriate occupation or instruction; and for the purpose aforesaid the Secretary of State may make arrangements with any local authority or police authority for the use of premises of that authority.

The minimum age for attendance centres was originally twelve. It was reduced to ten on the recommendation of the Ingleby Committee [46] by the Criminal Justice Act 1961. The Children and Young Persons Act 1969 has raised the minimum age to seventeen with the object of absorbing junior attendance centres into its general provisions for " intermediate treatment." [47] The idea is to bring the offender to a centre for a maximum of three hours on a maximum of eight occasions. During that time he is to take part in some form of disciplined activity and training as well as being given the opportunity of receiving advice. The Advisory Council on the Penal System noted:

> 101. The activities pursued have included first-aid, life-saving drill, artificial respiration, road safety, cycle repairs, carpentry, leather work, painting and decorating, electrical repairs, map-reading, toy-making and model making.

The question of senior attendance centres for those between the ages of seventeen and twenty-one was considered by the Advisory Council on Treatment of Offenders in 1957 (below), and the Advisory Council on the Penal System in 1970.[48]

Report of the Advisory Council on the Treatment of Offenders. Alternatives to Short Terms of Imprisonment 1957

As was mentioned above, one of the possibilities that the committee considered was the setting up of adult attendance centres.

Adult Attendance Centres

18. . . . [I]n our view there could be no question of the police being associated with adult centres in the same way as they are associated with juvenile attendance centres. It would be contrary to our traditional system of justice for punishment to be administered by the police. We accordingly agree that the Prison Commissioners would have to be responsible for running and staffing the centres; this would have the added advantage of emphasising the connection between the centres and imprisonment. . . .

19. Administration by the Prison Commissioners would mean . . . that in the foreseeable future the regime of adult centres would be merely deterrent. Sewing mailbags or other work on that level would be the staple task and

---

[46] Cmnd. 1191, 1960.
[47] Above, p. 543.   [48] Below, p. 556.

imprisonment the ultimate sanction for misconduct at the centre and failure to attend. . . .

20. It is clear that in this respect at any rate the suggested adult attendance centres cannot be regarded as a logical extension of the present juvenile attendance centres. We think that instead there would be a danger that attendance at an adult centre might too closely resemble being kept in after school and come to be regarded with contempt. There is also the danger that the deterrent atmosphere would make the offender unresponsive. In short the centres might annoy but, lacking the stigma attaching to prison, would not deter. If this happened, the whole scheme would hardly appear to be in keeping with either the dignity or the interests of justice and so become unacceptable to the courts as an alternative to imprisonment. We do not think that this would inevitably happen, but we consider that in view of the possibility the suggestion should be developed with particular caution.

21. In our view the way to proceed is first to set up on an experimental basis a centre providing for male 17–21 year olds. Statutory power already exists for providing centres for offenders up to the age of 21. . . . [T]he Prison Commissioners should be responsible for running it, particularly if it is to be a genuine alternative to imprisonment for such youths. We regard it as essential, however, that with this age group the regime should have some training element, and the Prison Commissioners have told us that although such a regime could be beyond their resources if adult centres for all ages had to be established throughout the country, they would make the regime for a centre for 17–21 year olds as constructive as the available time and resources permitted. After this centre has become established we think that further consideration should be given to establishing other centres for the same age group. . . .

Report of the Advisory Council on the Penal System. Non-custodial and Semi-custodial Penalties 1970

Senior attendance centres and analogous forms of treatment

90. . . . [I]n accordance with a recommendation of the Advisory Council . . . in their 1957 Report on Alternatives to Short Terms of Imprisonment, an experimental attendance centre for youths aged 17 and under 21 was opened in Manchester in December 1958 and a similar centre was opened in Greenwich in April 1964. . . .

102. . . . Were we not putting forward proposals relating to community service . . . we might well have thought it right to recommend some expansion of the present experiment by an increase in the number of senior centres and by inclusion in their regimes of extra-mural activities of the community service type. But . . . [i]t seems open to doubt whether there is room for both. . . . It seems to us that, where a penalty involves deprivation of liberty or leisure, the deprivation itself should supply the punitive element, and that the offender's time thus put at the disposal of the penal system should be used constructively. . . . [E]xternal activities of service to the community are the more promising alternative, in that they provide not only an identifiable return to the community in recompense for the offence, but also a better prospect of modifying the offender's attitudes, and a sanction which would be more comprehensible both to him and to the staff administering the service. . . .

103. In the light of these considerations we are disposed to think that the right course is to defer any question of setting up further senior attendance centres designed for offenders in general . . . until the practicability of com-

munity service has been demonstrated and some assessment made of its effectiveness.

Attendance centres for traffic offenders

105. . . . [W]e consider that there might be scope for an extension of the attendance centre idea alongside community service if centres were designed for special categories of offender. The obvious example is the traffic offender. . . .

106. . . . [I]n practice fines are used for the majority of motoring offences. . . . The only other measures which are widely used—usually in conjunction with fines—are disqualification and endorsement, the latter being in effect a step towards disqualification; and courts are reluctant in certain cases to impose disqualification because of the loss of employment or severe inconvenience which it may entail. There seems to be room for some measure which is not simply an individual deterrent or attempt at temporary incapacitation but which makes an effort to educate bad drivers, and especially those who have failed to respond to fines. . . .

109. The programme of activity of these special centres should be wholly directed towards improving, not only the offender's competence, but also his attitudes as a driver. . . .[49]

The persistent or habitual offender

The habitual offender has been a major concern of those responsible for penal policy since he is a constant witness to the failure of the system. Although some persistent offenders are skilled professional criminals many are not. They frequently commit relatively minor offences and they frequently get caught. The penal system is faced with two major tasks in trying to deal with the problem. The first is to prevent as many people as possible from becoming persistent offenders in the first place. Hence the concentration on the young offender, the special provisions for juveniles, the use of attendance centres and detention centres, and the principles underlying Borstal training, and the postponement of imprisonment as a penalty for as long as possible, both because of the fear of contamination and of habituation to prison life. The second is to provide some method of dealing with those who are already persistent offenders which will make the greatest use of any chance there may be of integrating them into the community as law-abiding citizens, and at the same time to reduce the nuisance value of their offences. The present system of " extended sentences " for persistent offenders was introduced by the Criminal Justice Act 1967. Earlier attempts to deal with the problem are illustrated in the extracts which follow.

Report of the Commissioners Appointed to Inquire into the Operation of the Transportation and Penal Servitude Acts

1863, P.P. xxl

36. It is also desirable that longer sentences should be passed on habitual thieves, and professional criminals, than on persons of a different character, convicted of similar offences. There is in the metropolis and other large towns,

---

[49] Other proposals considered by the committee are set out above, p. 536.

a class of persons who are so inveterately addicted to dishonesty, and so averse
to labour, that there is no chance of their ceasing to seek their existence by
depredations on the public, unless they are compulsorily withdrawn for a very
considerable time from their accustomed haunts.   Such persons may sometimes
be guilty of minor offences; yet by the continual repetition of such offences they
may inflict more loss upon the public, while they are also much less likely to
become reformed, than men who under great temptation commit a grave but
single crime.   The law already recognises the propriety of awarding heavier
punishment to criminals on a second conviction, but this principle requires to
be more fully acted upon. . . .

Report of the Departmental Committee on Prisons
c. 7702, 1895

Habitual criminals

85. We recommend that this class of prisoners should be kept as a class
apart from others.   We think that they are a most undesirable element in a
mixed prison population, and that they require and deserve special treatment.
It is clear from the evidence that while the habitual prisoner is orderly and
easily managed, the prison regime has little or no deterrent effect upon him
unless he is subjected to long periods of imprisonment and penal servitude,
which, however, frequently make him desperate and determined, when again
at large, not to be taken alive.   But there is evidently a large class of habitual
criminals not of the desperate order, who live by robbery and thieving and
petty larceny, who run the risk of comparatively short sentences with comparative indifference.   They make money rapidly by crime, they enjoy life after
their fashion, and then on detection and conviction they serve their time quietly
with the full determination to revert to crime when they come out.   We are
inclined to believe that the bulk of the habitual criminals at large are composed of men of this class. . . . Upon the evidence given to us we are strongly
of the opinion that further corrective measures are desirable for these persons.
When under sentence they complicate prison arrangements, when at large they
are responsible for the commission of the greater part of undetected crime; they
are a nuisance to the community.   To punish them for the particular offence
in which they are detected is almost useless; witnesses were almost unanimous
in approving of some kind of cumulative sentence; the real offence is the wilful
persistence in the deliberately acquired habit of crime.   We venture to offer the
opinion found during this inquiry that a new form of sentence should be placed
at the disposal of the judges by which these offenders might be segregated for
long periods of detention during which they would not be treated with the
severity of first-class hard labour or penal servitude, but would be forced to work
under less onerous conditions.   As loss of liberty would to them prove eventually
the chief deterrent, so by their being removed from the opportunity of doing
wrong the community would gain. . . .

In 1908 the Prevention of Crime Act provided that " habitual criminals "
i.e. those who had since the age of sixteen been convicted of crime on three
occasions and whom the jury found to be leading " persistently a dishonest
or criminal life " or who had already been found to be habitual criminals
could be sentenced to an additional period of preventive detention over
and above any sentence of penal servitude that had been imposed on them
for their current offence, if the court was of the opinion that " by reason of
his criminal habits and mode of life it is expedient that the offender should

be kept in detention for a lengthened period of years." The extra period was to be between five and ten years. The Home Secretary was given the power to discharge someone undergoing " preventive detention " on licence if he was satisfied that there was " reasonable probability that he will abstain from crime and lead a useful and industrious life or that he is no longer capable of engaging in crime or that for any other reason it is desirable to release him from confinement in prison." Anyone who was released on licence could be put on probation. It was made clear by the Home Secretary at the time that preventive detention was intended for the professional criminal, the " advanced dangerous criminal " or the " persistent dangerous criminal " or " the most hardened criminals," and not just the persistent inadequate. It was not for those who were " a nuisance rather than a danger to society " or to those who were " partly vagrants, partly criminals, and who were to a large extent mentally deficient." " [M]ere pilfering, unaccompanied by any serious aggravation, can never justify proceedings under the Act. . . . On the other hand, violence conjoined with other crime, skill in crime, the use of high class implements of crime, and the possession of firearms or other lethal weapons, will always count as important adverse factors."

The system, however, was not a success and sentences of preventive detention declined from 178 in 1910 to 37 in 1930. In April 1931 therefore another committee was appointed " to inquire into the existing methods of dealing with persistent offenders, including habitual offenders who are liable to sentences of preventive detention and other classes of offenders who return to prison repeatedly, and to report what changes, if any, are desirable in the present law and administration."

Report of the Departmental Committee on Persistent Offenders
Cmd. 4090, 1932

4. No statistics are available showing what proportion of those who come to prison for the first time do not return, but all persons who are experienced in prison administration agree that a very large proportion of these " first-timers " are not reconvicted. Of the comparatively small number of persons who return to prison on a second sentence a large proportion, however, come back repeatedly; the probability of relapse increases with the number of previous sentences, and a substantial part of the prison population consists of a " stage army " of individuals who pass through the prisons again and again.

5. The inference is that the present methods not only fail to check the criminal propensities of such people, but may actually cause progressive deterioration by habituating the offenders to prison conditions, which weaken rather than strengthen their characters. That the present methods of dealing with persistent offenders are unsatisfactory is the general burden of all the evidence we have received. . . .

8. Moreover, the present system not only fails to provide the treatment of which many persistent offenders stand in need. Amongst the offenders who are at present sentenced again and again to short terms of imprisonment, there are some who, if subjected to a substantial term of training, might respond to such treatment; there are others who require control for their own protection; and there are others who might be deterred from continuing their criminal careers, if the consequences to be apprehended were not a short term of imprisonment

for the offence which happens to be detected but a long term of detention for persistence in crime.

9. The evidence of prison authorities is to the effect that these persistent offenders may be divided into three classes. First there are the offenders of relatively strong character and mentality who deliberately choose a life of crime. Many of them are young and they might be amenable to reformative treatment. Secondly there are the offenders of weaker moral character who drift into crime because they are unable to face the difficulties of ordinary social life. Thirdly there are the pathological cases . . . who may be amenable to medical and psychiatric treatment. There is of course no sharp distinction between those categories especially as between the first and the second, and many cases belong to a border region in which various causes of widely differing character appear to be at work.

19. The primary consideration in determining the nature of the sentence to be imposed is the intrinsic character of the particular offence committed. In order that there may be a proper grading of sentences to fit the many degrees of gravity presented by the various cases which fall within the same legal category, it is necessary that the maximum sentence authorised by law should be reserved for the rare offences which are exceptionally heinous, that sentences approaching the legal maximum should be reserved for offences falling within the next degree of gravity, and so on—with the result that for ordinary offences (such as form the great majority of cases coming before the courts) the heaviest sentence which the court feels justified in imposing is usually far below the maximum. . . . In assessing the gravity of the offence numerous factors have to be taken into account. In no two cases are the facts precisely similar, and it is the duty of the court to take into consideration all the circumstances and consequences of the offence. For example if a persistent office-breaker breaks into a railway booking office with intent to steal large sums of money and for some reason or other only manages to obtain a few trifling articles, the court will probably consider appropriate a very much lighter sentence than if he had succeeded in his object.

20. In addition to considering the facts and circumstances of the offence it may be necessary for the court to have regard to such points as the offender's age, his health, his circumstances, the prevalence of the offence and other matters. Moreover, views may change from generation to generation as to the sentences appropriate to particular types and classes of offences. The very long sentences which were often passed twenty years ago are now usually regarded as harsh and excessive and are seldom imposed. All these factors prevent any precise standardisation of sentences, but nevertheless there is among judicial authorities a large measure of agreement on general principles and the practice of the courts creates certain general standards. Sentences heavier than are warranted by these standards are liable to be reduced on appeal.

21. As we understand the position, it is only within the limit of the heaviest sentence warranted by these standards for the particular offence that the offender's record falls to be considered. For example, the legal maximum sentence for larceny is five years' penal servitude, but the Recorder of London told us that for larceny of a bicycle he would never feel justified in giving a longer sentence than twelve or fifteen months' imprisonment, no matter how often the offender had been previously convicted. If the record of the offender is good, this may influence the court towards a lenient sentence; conversely, a bad record will influence the court towards a heavier sentence; and the difference resulting from an offender's record may be great. For example a man with a good record may be merely bound over for an offence which if committed by a man with a bad record would entail a substantial term of imprisonment; but however bad

the record may be, it is not open to the court to pass upon him a sentence heavier than is warranted by the standards indicated above for the specific offence on which the court is adjudicating. Accordingly when a persistent offender with numerous previous convictions, which perhaps include convictions of grave offences, is convicted of some less serious crime his sentence on this occasion must not exceed the term which is appropriate to the less serious crime. . . .

24. It is of course necessary to preserve the general legal principle that there should be some grading of sentences according to the gravity of offences. If a man with a bad record were liable to receive the same sentence whether he were convicted of a minor larceny or of robbery with violence, there is a danger that he might more often commit the grave offence on the principle that it is better to be hanged for a sheep than a lamb. We think, however, that while giving due weight to the importance of the principle behind the present gradation of sentences. . . .

25. . . . the judicial authorities would welcome an extension of their powers to enable them in suitable cases, and subject to proper safeguards, not merely to order terms of imprisonment of such length as is warranted by the facts of the particular offence, but instead to order detention of such character and length as seems to be requisite either for the training of the offender or for the protection of society. . . .

38. . . . It is particularly important to make proper provision for persistent offenders between the ages of twenty-one and thirty. Statistics show that a large amount of crime is committed by persons between those ages. . . .

39. Measures for preventing persistence in crime are obviously more likely to be effective in the early than in the later stages of an offender's career. . . .

40. . . . [W]e recommend . . . that courts should be given power . . . to order . . . detention for any period being not less than two nor more than four years with the object, not of imposing a specific penalty for a specific offence but to subjecting the offender to such training, discipline, treatment or control as will be calculated to check his criminal propensities. . . .

42. The proposed new sentence . . . will not remove the need for a sentence involving longer terms of detention. There is a class of habitual criminal for whom detention for such periods is inadequate either because of the serious nature of their crimes or because sentences for such periods have already proved ineffective. We have in mind particularly the " professional " criminals who deliberately make a living by preying on the public. Danger from this class of criminal lies not merely in the offences which they commit, but also in their contamination of others—particularly younger men. . . . Among the criminals against whom the community ought to be adequately protected are those who practise thefts or frauds on a comparatively small scale—the victims usually being poor people to whom the loss of a small sum may inflict a more serious injury than the loss of valuable property in persons of means. There are also certain sexual offenders for whom a long term of detention is necessary, particularly those who commit repeated offences against children or young people and those who corrupt boys.

43. These classes of offenders include, no doubt, some who are suitable subjects—in the first instance at any rate—for detention for two to four years; no fixed and fast line can be drawn between the types of offender for whom the shorter sentences are appropriate and the types for whom longer sentences are necessary. . . .

45. It is, however, clearly desirable that courts should have the power of imposing prolonged sentences of detention for the protection of the public on

certain types of persistent offenders for whom a shorter sentence is inadequate. . . . [W]e recommend that . . . there should be provisions empowering . . . Assizes or Quarter Sessions. . . . when dealing with a persistent offender . . . to impose . . . a sentence of detention for such period as the court may determine, being not less than five nor more than ten years, if the court is of opinion that the offender is of such criminal habits and mode of life that his detention for a lengthened period of years is expedient for the protection of the public. This power should only be exercisable when the offender is convicted of a serious crime and has been at least thrice previously convicted of crime. . . .

Reasons for the repeal of Part II of the Prevention of Crime Act 1908

153. The evidence we have received shows that the existing scheme of adding a sentence of preventive detention to a sentence of penal servitude is regarded with general disfavour. . . .

154. One object of requiring a preliminary sentence of penal servitude was to restrict the sentence of preventive detention to offenders convicted of serious crimes, and to prevent its application to " such petty offenders as are a nuisance rather than a danger to society.". . . The requirement . . . has had the effect of preventing a court from sentencing to preventive detention a habitual criminal whose crimes have been grave, if the particular offence of which he is convicted is not such as would . . . justify a sentence of penal servitude. . . .

155. . . . [M]any offences which would in 1908 have been punished by sentences of penal servitude, are today punished by sentences of imprisonment; and this change in the practice of the courts excludes from the operation of the Act many offenders who would in 1908 have been liable to preventive detention. . . .

158. It may be added that the dual sentence is apt to create the impression that the offender is being punished twice over. Theoretically the preliminary sentence of penal servitude is imposed in respect of the specific offence and the sentence of preventive detention . . . in respect of the persistence in crime, but the prisoner can hardly be expected to appreciate the force of the distinction. . . . If a persistent, housebreaker has been bound over for his first offence, given six months for his second, a year for his third, eighteen months for his fourth and on the fifth occasion when he commits a crime which is similar in character and gravity to the preceding ones, gets a sentence of three years' penal servitude plus five years' preventive detention, he not unnaturally feels that the sentence of three years' penal servitude takes account of his criminal record and that the sentence of preventive detention is a second punishment.

159. We, therefore, in drawing up proposals for revised methods of dealing with persistent offenders have excluded any idea of combining sentences of detention with sentences of penal servitude or imprisonment, and for this reason we recommend that Part II of the Act of 1908, should be repealed.

Effect was finally given to the recommendations of the Persistent Offenders Committee by the Criminal Justice Act 1948. The special sentence for young offenders known as " corrective training " was made available for offenders over twenty who were found guilty of an offence punishable by imprisonment for two years or more and who had been convicted at least twice before of similar offences since they had reached the age of seventeen, where the court took the view that a period of corrective training for a substantial time was desirable. The sentence was to be for between two and four years followed by a period of supervision if the offender was released before the completion of the sentence. The longer " preventive detention " was reserved for those who were not less than thirty who had been found guilty of a similar offence with three previous convictions of similar offences on at least two of which they had been sentenced to Borstal training, corrective training or imprisonment. In his case the court had simply to be satisfied that " it is expedient for the protection of the public that he should be detained in custody for a substantial time." The sentence could be for between five and fourteen years. A Practice Direction in 1962 [50] advised that a sentence of preventive detention should only be given as a last resort to those nearing forty years of age or over. This system was considered by a subcommittee of the Advisory Council on the Treatment of Offenders which was appointed in May 1961 " to review the working of the preventive detention system established by the Criminal Justice Act 1948 and to report."

Report of the Advisory Council on the Treatment of Offenders. Preventive Detention 1963

48. . . . [O]ur inquiry has brought to our attention several major defects in the system of preventive detention established by the Criminal Justice Act, 1948. The system deals with only a very small proportion of persistent offenders, and many of these offenders have committed crimes which are not in themselves serious, although they mostly have a long record of similar offences. The public is undoubtedly protected by the system to the extent that persons dealt with by it are segregated from the community during the period of their sentence. But this period of segregation is demoralising and embittering and does little, or nothing, to prepare most of them for life in the outside world on their release; thus at the end of their sentence they are usually no more able to keep out of crime than they were before they began it, and the majority are reconvicted within a few years of release. . . .

Sentencing practice

59. Ever since the passing of the Prevention of Crime Act in 1908 . . . it has been recognised that the sentence passed on a persistent offender may have regard as much to his previous record as to his current offence. In this sense a sentence of preventive detention differs from a sentence of ordinary imprisonment which, although it takes account of the previous record, relates primarily to the gravity of the current offence. . . .

60. The validity of this distinction between the principles on which sentences of preventive detention and sentences of imprisonment are imposed does, however, seem to us to be open to question. . . . [W]e do not regard it as inequitable for a persistent petty offender to be deprived of his liberty for a longer period than his current offence would warrant, and we see no advantage in describing such a sentence as preventive detention rather than imprisonment. Prevention of the offender from the commission of further crime is one of the objects of all sentences. . . .

61. The disadvantages of the present preventive detention sentence may . . . be summed up by saying that it creates an unduly rigid and largely artificial distinction between preventive detainees and other persistent offenders. . . . The few who receive preventive detention feel that they have been unjustly treated and they have reason to do so. There is too great a difference between

[50] [1962] 1 W.L.R. 402.

the punishment of those who just manage to avoid preventive detention and those who fall just on the other side of the line. . . .

62. These difficulties would be removed if instead of having to choose between what may, in the case of a minor offender, be a comparatively short sentence of imprisonment, and a substantial term of preventive detention, the courts were able to make a wider use of the whole range of sentences of imprisonment for those offenders whose persistence in crime makes it necessary to give added weight to the need for the protection of the public.

63. We recognise that there is a natural disinclination on the part of the courts to pass sentences of imprisonment not commensurate with the gravity of the current offence, and we therefore suggest that . . . Parliament should make it clear . . . that the protection which is at present afforded to the public by preventive detention should in future be provided where necessary, by longer sentences of imprisonment. For most offences for which preventive detention has in the past been imposed the existing maximum terms of imprisonment are already sufficiently high for the purpose. There are, however, some offences . . . for which the maximum sentence . . . is considerably lower than the average term of preventive detention. . . . We, therefore, recommend that it should be provided . . . that where a person aged 21 years or over is convicted on indictment of an offence punishable with imprisonment for a term of 5 years or more, and the court is satisfied, having regard to his antecedents and the need to protect the public, that it is necessary to impose a longer term of imprisonment than is at present permitted for the offence in question, the court should be empowered to pass a sentence of up to 10 years' imprisonment. Such a provision would, of course, in no way affect the court's power to impose a larger sentence than 10 years imprisonment where this was already permitted by law.

64. Although the time must come when an offender who persists in petty crime can properly be sentenced to imprisonment for a longer term than is appropriate to the particular offence, we think that it is right to maintain some proportion between the gravity of the offences in the prisoner's record and the severity of the sentence and that the longest terms of imprisonment should be reserved, save in exceptional circumstances, for those whose crimes are of a serious character. It is also our view that a sentence of imprisonment longer than the existing maximum should not be imposed on an offender under 40 years of age except as a last resort. . . .

The need for a new type of prison régime

65. . . . . The question which now arises for consideration is whether the persistent offender requires different treatment from other prisoners. . . .

66. An essential preliminary to any consideration of the treatment which persistent offenders require is an analysis of the characteristics of these offenders and the different types that are to be found among them. . . . Except that it excludes the very small group who commit offences of violence against the person or sexual offences, the following quotation from Dr. Hammond's [51] conclusions sums up the position:—" The analysis shows broadly three types of offender are sentenced to preventive detention. These are the housebreakers who are generally professional criminals in their 30's or 40's; their offences can be regarded as serious in themselves, both for the loss and hardship they occasion and because the offences may lead to more serious acts if the offender is disturbed in the course of committing his offence. Then there is the group of fairly serious larceny or fraud offenders who manage to make away with large sums of money. This group is numerically small. A third group consists of

[51] *Persistent Criminals*, vol. 5, *Studies in the Causes of Delinquency and the Treatment of Offenders*, by W. H. Hammond and Edna Chayen, H.M.S.O. 1963.

the persistent petty thief or false pretence offender who is often quite old and who has failed to make a satisfactory adjustment to life generally. He has few ties, he holds a job for a short period only, he tends to have no roots and lives from day to day in hostels, lodging houses or on the streets, and he tends to be a drain on the social services whether in prison or not. Moreover he has been in and out of prison most of his life and appears to be better adjusted to prison life than to any other. It would seem fairly obvious that these three types of offender cannot be dealt with satisfactorily by one form of sentence. . . ."

67. All the information we have received suggests that it is this last group which present a special problem in terms of treatment. Broadly speaking the other groups can be provided for within the existing prison system, and such problems as they present are not peculiar to persistent offenders. . . . It is the petty offender against property whose criminal behaviour is the result of inadequacy rather than deliberate choice who . . . could with advantage be detained in rather more open conditions. . . .

68. We have in mind that those who were fit to do so might be allowed, at a comparatively early stage in the sentence, to work in ordinary jobs in the neighbourhood of the prison as the " hostellers " do at present in the third stage of preventive detention. For those who could not be trusted to work outside the prison, or as a preliminary to outside work we hope that it would be possible to provide a full day's work within the prison. We suggest in particular, that consideration should be given to the setting up of one or two special establishments . . . where the prison staff work with the men and are tradesmen rather than discipline officers. . . .

After care

75. In view of the difficulties experienced by persons released from preventive detention, particularly those who have no relatives or friends to give them a home, in trying to settle down in the community, we think it would be well worthwhile for consideration to be given to the establishment of a number of homes or hostels to which they could go on release. . . .

The recommendations of the Advisory Council were approved by the government in a White Paper " The Adult Offender " and effect given to them by the Criminal Justice Act 1967.

The Adult Offender
Cmnd. 2852, 1965

9. There are at present two forms of special sentence which may be imposed on persistent offenders—corrective training and preventive detention. The former is for the younger man, usually in his twenties, and the latter for the older criminal.

10. Corrective training . . . is generally agreed to be now inappropriate. Today all suitable prisoners, whatever their sentence, are given training. The number of sentences of corrective training has fallen steadily to about 200 a year. There are at present only some 260 men and women serving such sentences.

11. It is proposed that the special sentence of corrective training should be abolished.

12. . . . Preventive detention sentences, too, have decreased in number. In 1964 there were 40 such sentences, and there are only about 500 preventive detainees in prison at the present time.

13. The public have a right to be protected from offenders who persistently commit serious offences, and the courts must have adequate powers to deal

with them. The Government agree, however, with the endorsement by their predecessors of the recommendation of the Advisory Council on the Treatment of Offenders in their 1963 Report on Preventive Detention that this special sentence should be abolished as no longer necessary or appropriate for the purpose it was designed to serve and arbitrary and unfair in its incidence. It is proposed, therefore, to abolish it.

14. Instead Courts will be given jurisdiction when they have before them a person who has committed an offence and who is in addition shown by evidence to be a persistent offender to impose a longer sentence than they would have imposed had they been sentencing him only for the crime itself of which he is convicted. . . .

15. . . . [I]t is essential for this purpose that the persistent offender must be clearly defined in a definition in the statute in such a way as to apply only to delinquents whose character and record of offences are such as to put it beyond all doubt that they are a real menace to society, and to exclude the petty criminal who commits a series of lesser offences. He is certainly a nuisance but not the menace against whom special protection is necessary. . . .

16. . . . As with the ordinary prisoner, the man sentenced as a persistent offender would be eligible for release after one-third of his sentence but, whatever the date of release, he would be on licence until the whole of his sentence expired. . . .

Criminal Justice Act 1967
1967, c. 80

37.—(1) No person shall be sentenced by a court to preventive detention or corrective training.

(2) Where an offender is convicted on indictment of an offence punishable with imprisonment for a term of two years or more and the conditions specified in subsection (4) of this section are satisfied, then, if the court is satisfied, by reason of his previous conduct and of the likelihood of his committing further offences, that it is expedient to protect the public from him for a substantial time, the court may impose an extended term of imprisonment under this section.

(3) The extended term which may be imposed under this section for any offence may exceed the maximum term authorised for the offence apart from this section if the maximum so authorised is less than ten years, but shall not exceed ten years if the maximum so authorised is less than ten years or exceed five years if the maximum so authorised is less than five years.

(4) The conditions referred to in subsection (2) of this section are:—

(a) the offence was committed before the expiration of three years from a previous conviction of an offence punishable on indictment with imprisonment for a term of two years or more or from his final release from prison after serving a sentence of imprisonment, corrective training or preventive detention passed on such a conviction; and

(b) the offender has been convicted on indictment on at least three previous occasions since he attained the age of twenty-one of offences punishable on indictment with imprisonment for a term of two years or more; and

(c) the total length of the sentences of imprisonment, corrective training or preventive detention to which he was sentenced on those occasions was not less than five years and—

(i) on at least one of those occasions a sentence of preventive detention was passed on him; or

(ii) on at least two of those occasions a sentence of imprisonment (other than a suspended sentence which has not taken effect) or of corrective training was so passed and of those sentences one was a sentence of imprisonment for a term of three years or more in respect of one offence or two were sentences of imprisonment each for a term of two years or more in respect of one offence.

(5) Where an extended term of imprisonment is imposed on an offender under this section, the court shall issue a certificate (hereafter in this Act referred to as " an extended sentence certificate ") stating that the term was so imposed.

38.—(2) For the purposes of subsection (4) (*b*) of the last foregoing section a person who has been convicted by a magistrates' court of an indictable offence and sentenced for that offence by a court of quarter sessions, or on an appeal from such a court, to imprisonment, corrective training or preventive detention shall be treated as if he had been convicted of that offence on indictment.

IMPRISONMENT

As has already been mentioned imprisonment has become the sentence of last resort. It came into its own as a form of treatment with the reduction in the number of capital offences in the early nineteenth century and the abolition of transportation. This resulted in the building of such prisons as Parkhurst, Wormwood Scrubs and Pentonville. There have been considerable changes since then. One, already mentioned has been the development of alternative modes of treatment, both for particular classes of offender and generally. The other has been in the philosophy underlying the prison régime and the purposes of imprisonment.

The big change in prison régime and the aims of penal policy was marked by the publication of the report of the Gladstone Committee in 1895.[52] The emphasis has shifted from a régime that was intended to deter to a régime which is intended to assist reformation. More emphasis too is placed on the classification of prisoners and the provision of a variety of institutions and régimes to cater for different types of prisoner and for the same prisoner at different stages of his term of imprisonment. Closer attention has been paid to the problems of the transition of the prisoner from the prison back into the community and this has affected both the atmosphere and régime in the prisons themselves, and the provision of transitional facilities towards the end of an offender's term and the provision of services of after-care once the offender has returned to the community. Provision is made for compulsory supervision of those released on parole or on licence after a sentence of life imprisonment[53] those under twenty-one at the time of their sentence and sentenced to less than eighteen months, those released from Borstal,[54] or from detention centres[55] or from an approved school[56] and those under eighteen convicted of murder and

---

[52] Below, p. 580.
[53] Criminal Justice Act 1967, ss. 60, 61.
[54] *Ibid.*, s. 45; Criminal Justice Act 1961, s. 11.
[55] 1961 Act, s. 13.
[56] 1961 Act, s. 14.

detained during Her Majesty's pleasure or children and young persons convicted of an offence punishable in the case of an adult with a sentence of fourteen years imprisonment or more and released on licence.[57] In any other case in which a prisoner is released on licence it may be made a condition of the licence that he is under supervision. Supervision is usually by a probation officer.

Particular problems remain. The persistent offender and the young offender still raise special problems in relation to sentencing. The long term prisoner raises special problems in relation to the form his treatment should take. Some of the considerations that have played a part in shaping present policy are touched on below.

Factors determining the length of sentence

Normally the courts are given some kind of discretion within a maximum when they are deciding the length of sentence, or even whether to impose a sentence of imprisonment at all, though in some cases the sentence is mandatory as in the case of life imprisonment on a conviction of murder.

Where statute specifies imprisonment as a punishment, a maximum term is usually attached and section 7 of the Criminal Justice Act 1967 prescribes a maximum of two years for any statutory offence to which no maximum is attached. Common law offences do not have maxima attached to them though section 7 also provides that a person who is convicted on indictment of an attempt to commit an offence which is punishable by imprisonment should not be sentenced to a longer term (or if the punishment was a fine a greater fine) than the maximum set for the completed offence. It is usually assumed that the maximum is intended for the most serious example of the offence and that other examples are to be dealt with accordingly. But this does not invariably follow in practice since if the maximum was fixed some time ago the courts may have come to regard it as too severe or too lenient, and in any event the court takes other factors into account in determining the sentence. There is for example the offender's past record, including not only his previous convictions but also his conduct generally, the length of time since a previous offence and his conduct in the meantime. (This and his response to previous measures may of course lead to his not being given a sentence of imprisonment at all.) The court may also take into account other offences admitted by the offender though not tried by the court. An especially long sentence may be imposed to deter others, or to prevent the offender enjoying the fruits of his crime or because he may still be a security risk for some time. In the case of an habitual offender the court may impose a special "extended sentence."[58] Co-operation with the police, the recovery of stolen property, penitence, the seriousness of injury to the victim may all be taken into account. The courts have held, though, that judges should not take into account the fact that in normal circumstances a prisoner will be entitled to remission or to release on parole, and then add a term of years to defeat the effect of the remission or release on parole, except where the object of

[57] Children and Young Persons Act 1933.
[58] See above, p. 566.

fixing the length in the first place was to secure that enough time was available for a particular course of treatment.[59]

Besides the maxima linked to specific offences, section 19 (6) of the Magistrates' Courts Act 1952 imposes a general limitation on magistrates' courts which cannot impose a sentence longer than six months, though, as was mentioned earlier[60] they can, after having tried an indictable offence summarily, commit an offender to the Crown Court for sentence if they think a longer sentence is more appropriate. Sometimes minima have been laid down by statute but these have been mostly in connection with special forms of treatment other than imprisonment where it is felt that to be successful the treatment should last for a minimum period. The minimum for Borstal training for example is six months, and for detention in a detention centre three months and for probation one year. Magistrates' courts may not in any event sentence to a term of imprisonment of less than five days though they can order an offender to be detained for the rest of the day and in the case of a fine defaulter, overnight.[61]

The Criminal Justice Act 1961 also imposes a minimum on the sentence which can be imposed on a young offender.[62]

The use of maxima

Eighth Report of the Criminal Law Revision Committee. Theft and Related Offences

Cmnd. 2917, 1966

10. Except in three cases (burglary, criminal deception and taking a motor vehicle or other conveyance without authority) we have provided single maximum penalties for the offences in place of the widely different penalties depending on various factors—the kind of property involved, the relation between the offender and the owner, the method by which or the place where the offence is committed, whether it is a first or subsquent offence and so on. The present different maximum penalties date from times when maximum sentences were passed much more commonly than they are now and when Parliament was less willing to trust to the discretion of the courts in sentencing. The policy of drawing distinctions of detail for the purpose of punishment is to a large extent the cause of the multiplicity of offences and the great complications under the present law. In the past century the attitude of the courts to sentencing has greatly changed. Nowadays their practice is to reserve maximum sentences for the worst conceivable cases of the offence, and for some offences the maximum is never given. In *Harrison*[63] Channell J. said in giving the judgment of the Court of Criminal Appeal:— " The maximum sentence must, as presumably the law intended, be reserved for the worst cases."[64] . . . In *Ball*[65] Hilbery J. said in giving the judgment of the Court of Criminal Appeal:— " Our law does not . . . fix the sentence for a particular crime, but fixes a maximum sentence and leaves it to the court to decide what is, within that maximum, the appropriate sentence for each criminal in the particular

[59] See below, p. 574.
[60] Above, p. 331.
[61] ss. 107, 109, 110 of the Magistrates' Courts Act 1952.
[62] See above, p. 549.
[63] (1909) 2 Cr.App.R. 94, 96.
[64] The Committee here quoted para. 19 of the Report of the Departmental Committee on Persistent Offenders, above, p. 560.
[65] (1951) 35 Cr.App.R. 164, 166.

circumstances of each case." As a result maximum sentences for serious offences are rarely passed; and it is common for offences punishable with long terms of imprisonment, even life imprisonment, to be dealt with by short terms or even in ways not involving imprisonment. For example, manslaughter is punishable with life imprisonment but is not infrequently dealt with by a conditional discharge or probation order.

11. It seems to us better, and more in accordance with modern theories of sentencing, to fix a maximum for each offence which will be high enough for the worst cases, even though it will rarely be imposed, and to leave a wide discretion to the courts, than to lay down scales related to particular aggravating features. Since the seriousness of an offence always depends on a combination of factors, it is in general misleading to single out certain factors for the purpose of providing maximum penalties. Moreover the simplification of the law which is obviously desirable could not be achieved unless the present policy of graded maximum penalties were for the most part abandoned. . . .

People in prison

People in Prison
Cmnd. 4214, 1969

29. The people in custody are predominantly young. About 28% . . . are under 21, while of the men over that age, almost half are under 30. . . . [T]he majority of convicted offenders have been found guilty of offences against property (theft or burglary) and . . . only a small proportion are first offenders—less than 1 in 10 of adult men sent to prison, and less than 1 in 30 of young men at borstal. Moreover . . . the majority of convicted offenders in prisons and borstals are not serving their first sentence but have been in custody before.

30. The majority of convicted offenders are in custody for less than 12 months. . . . Young offenders sent to detention centres normally serve a fixed sentence of 3 to 6 months, on which one-third remission is now granted, and the normal period of detention at borstal is a little over a year. Only about 1 in 5 of adult offenders in prison have to spend more than 2 years in custody.

Note to Part II : Changes in prison population and length of sentence

i. The number of offenders in custody at any one time depends on several factors : the number convicted by the courts, the number committed to custody

TABLE 1

People Committed to Custody (Males and Females)

	1913	1938	1948	1958	1961	1964	1967	1968
Remands, etc.[66]	15,402	9,506	11,667	18,059	18,682	22,591	29,394	30,864
Detention Centre	—	—	—	1,302	2,311	5,890	7,220	7,675
Borstal	487	1,347	2,115	3,162	3,715	3,863	5,160	5,153
Sentenced to imprisonment [67]	138,570	30,772	35,277	34,239	40,581	44,013	48,333	36,069
Civil prisoners and others	14,987	8,246	5,372	9,377	9,676	9,633	8,011	7,505
Total	169,446	49,871	54,431	66,139	74,965	85,990	98,118	87,266

[66] Persons remanded or committed in custody who did not return to custody on sentence.

[67] Imprisonment includes court martial sentences, life sentences and death sentences commuted to life imprisonment. This section also includes those committed to prison in default of payment of fines. (The big drop between 1913 and 1938 reflects, in particular, the fall in the number of short sentences. See para. iii.)

TABLE 2

Average Daily Number of People in Custody in Different Types of Institution
(Males and Females)

					Prisons	Borstals	Detention Centres	Total
1913	...	...	...	...	17,227	928	—	18,155
1938	...	...	...	...	8,926	2,160	—	11,086
1948	...	...	...	...	16,659	3,106	—	19,765
1958	...	...	...	...	21,209	3,899	271	25,379
1961	...	...	...	...	23,948	4,615	462	29,025
1964	...	...	...	...	23,701	4,604	1,295	28,800
1967	...	...	...	...	27,652	5,749	1,608	35,009
1968	...	...	...	...	25,320	5,563	1,578	32,461

and the length of sentence imposed. The work of the prison service is therefore crucially affected not only by the total rise in the number of offenders but by changes in the sentencing practices of the courts. . . .
ii. Table 1 shows how many people were committed to custody in selected years from 1913 onwards. Table 2 shows how many people, on an average day, were in custody in the same years.

Short sentences

iii. Fewer people now go to prison for a short period. . . . [T]he courts are now dealing in other ways—for example by probation and by allowing offenders reasonable time to pay fines—with those who formerly spent a few days or weeks in prison. . . .

Criminal Justice Act 1967

vi. It has been the policy of successive Governments throughout this century to attempt to limit the number of people sent to custody and to encourage other effective ways of dealing with offenders. In particular there has been a series of statutes aimed at reducing to the minimum the number of young people and first offenders sent to prison. One of the main purposes of the Criminal Justice Act 1967 was to accelerate the shift of emphasis away from imprisonment. One major innovation introduced by that Act was the suspended sentence. . . . The offender serves his sentence only if, within the period of suspension, he commits a further offence punishable with imprisonment; in that event, the suspended sentence is put into effect unless the court considers that it would be unjust to do so in view of any circumstances that have arisen since it was passed.
viii. The 1967 Act contained other measures designed to reduce the number of people sent to prison for short periods. These included legislative restrictions on remands in custody, the freer use of bail, the more widespread use of social inquiry reports as a guide to sentencing, increased powers to fine offenders, and modified fine-enforcement procedures. Here also the preliminary results are encouraging. The number of people received into custody before sentence—and this, for almost all adults, means detention in grossly overcrowded local prisons —fell by 1,564 (or 3 per cent.) in 1968 compared with 1967 and the number of those sent to prison in default of fines fell by 4,395 or 34 per cent. . . .

Very long sentences

x. There is a widespread impression that more very long sentences are now being imposed. Table 7 gives some information about the number of offenders sentenced to imprisonment for 10 years or over (including life) in each year since

1958. It shows that while there has been an increase in the number of offenders received with life sentences, the number of *fixed* sentences of 10 years and over has not changed greatly in the last decade. On the other hand, there has been a change in the number of offenders received with fixed sentences of 14 years and over. Table 8 shows the number of such sentences imposed in each year since 1949. As the Advisory Council on the Penal System pointed out in their Report on the Regime for Long-Term Maximum Security Prisoners,[68] the secure yet humane containment of this very small group of prisoners creates special problems for the prison service.

TABLE 7

Proportion of Sentences of Ten Years or Over (Males)

	Total Number of Receptions	Number of receptions under sentence of ten years or over excluding life	Life Sentences	Percentage [69]
	(1)	(2)	(3)	(4)
1958	31,749	50	34	0·26
1959	34,605	33	46	0·23
1960	35,561	41	48	0·25
1961	38,007	54	49	0·27
1962	43,152	59	37	0·22
1963	43,420	47	54	0·23
1964	41,724	47	54	0·24
1965	43,382	43	73	0·27
1966	47,770	90	84	0·36
1967	46,183	54	91	0·31
1968	34,671	57	92	0·43

TABLE 8

Number of Fixed Sentences of Fourteen Years and Over (Males)

Years	1949	50	51	52	53	54	55	56	57	58	59	60	61	62	63	64	65	66	67	68
14		5	4	1	2	5	3		6	2	2	1	4	6	1		1	5	2	2
15	1	2		3			2				1	3	4	1	3	5	1	7	3	2
16–20					3	1		1					3	1	1	1		3	2	4
21–25													3			3	2		1	1
30																7				
42												1								

Life sentences

xi. New problems have also been created for the prison service by the increase in the number of prisoners serving life sentences. Ten years ago, at the end of 1958, there were 139 prisoners serving life sentences or detention " during Her Majesty's Pleasure ". Five years later the figure was 329. By 31st December 1968 it had risen to 598. It seems likely that the number will continue to rise. The term of imprisonment actually served by prisoners sentenced for life is determined according to the circumstances of every particular case—and every case is different. Since the war most life sentence prisoners have served a term

---

[68] *The Regime for Long-Term Prisoners in conditions of Maximum Security*, H.M.S.O. 1968.
[69] This percentage is the total of Cols. 2 and 3 expressed as a percentage of Col. 1 to show the proportion of sentences of ten years and over imposed by the courts in each year.

equal to that served by a prisoner with a long fixed sentence of between 10 and 18 years. Out of 180 such prisoners released in the 10 years 1959–1969 all but 19 had served for periods equivalent to a fixed sentence of 10½ years or longer on which the normal one third remission had been granted. A few life sentence prisoners were detained for much longer periods. One had spent 15 years in prison, one 20, and two were released after 21 years. Such very long periods have been unusual since the war. But the position is changing partly as a result of the abolition of capital punishment. There are some men who have already spent a considerable period in custody (in one case more than twenty years) and whom it would not in the present state of knowledge be safe to release into the community. A few may have to be detained for something approaching the term of their natural life.

Remission and Release on Licence

A prisoner may not serve the full term of his sentence because of the practice of remission and the system of release under licence (parole).

Remission

Prison Act 1952
15 & 16 Geo. 6 & 1 Eliz. 2, c. 52

25.—(1) Rules made under section 47 of this Act may make provision whereby, in such circumstances as may be prescribed by the rules, a person serving a sentence of imprisonment for such a term as may be so prescribed may be granted remission of such part of that sentence as may be so prescribed on the ground of his industry and good conduct, and on the discharge of a person from prison in pursuance of any such remission as aforesaid his sentence shall expire.

The Prison Rules
S.I. 1964 No. 388 [70]

5.—(1) A prisoner serving a sentence of imprisonment for an actual term of more than one month may, on the ground of his industry and good conduct, be granted remission in accordance with the provisions of this Rule: Provided that this Rule shall not permit the reduction of the actual term to less than 31 days, or in the case of a prisoner (other than a prisoner within paragraph (2) (*b*) of this Rule) who has been released on licence and recalled to prison, permit his release before the 30th day following his return to prison on recall.

(2) The remission granted under this Rule shall not exceed—

> (*a*) one-third of the total of the actual term and any period spent in custody by the prisoner after his conviction awaiting sentence which is taken into account under section 67 of the Criminal Justice Act 1967 . . . or
>
> (*b*) in the case of a prisoner in respect of whom an extended sentence certificate was issued when sentence was passed on him, and who has been released on licence and recalled to prison, one-third of that part of his sentence unexpired at the time of his recall. . . .

[70] As amended by the Prison (Amendment) Rules 1968, S.I. 1968 No. 440.

(4) This Rule shall have effect subject to any disciplinary award of forfeiture of remission, and shall not apply to a prisoner serving a sentence of imprisonment for life....

The Court of Appeal held in *Maguire* v. *Enos*[71] that it is generally wrong for the trial court in determining the sentence to take the prospect of remission into account.

> The business of a court is to consider what is the proper length of imprisonment to impose for a particular offence.... [I]t is not right for a court to say to a prisoner: "We are going to sentence you to seven years' imprisonment, because we want you to be kept in prison for four years and so many months" because it is equivalent to saying: "We think the proper sentence ... is four years and so many months and not seven years.".... A prisoner has a prospect and a hope of remission, but the question of remission is not to be taken into account when sentence is being imposed.

According to the Court, however, in *Turner*[72] it may be different where the court is considering not punishment but reform or mental treatment where a minimum period of detention may be necessary for the treatment to be given a chance. In such a case, it seems, remission can be taken into account. The Murder (Abolition of Death Penalty) Act 1965 expressly gives a judge the power to make a recommendation that someone sentenced to life imprisonment should not be released until he has served fifteen years, but this is not binding on the prison authorities.

Release under licence (parole)

The introduction of a system of parole was announced in the White Paper " The Adult Offender "[73] in December 1965. It stated:

> 4. The central feature of the Government's proposals is that prisoners whose character and record render them suitable for this purpose should be released from prison earlier than they are at present. Prisoners who do not of necessity have to be detained for the protection of the public are in some cases more likely to be made into decent citizens if, before completing the whole of their sentence, they are released under supervision with a liability to recall if they do not behave. Other countries have used systems of this kind with success....
>
> 5. At present a prisoner is released after completing two-thirds of his sentence unless he misconducts himself in prison. What is proposed is that a prisoner's date of release should be largely dependent upon his response to training and his likely behaviour on release. A considerable number of long-term prisoners reach a recognisable peak in their training at which they may respond to generous treatment, but after which, if kept in prison, they may go downhill. To give such prisoners the opportunity of supervised freedom at the right moment may be decisive in securing their return to decent citizenship.

[71] (1957) 40 Cr.App.R. 92, 94.
[72] [1957] Crim.L.R. 118.
[73] Cmnd. 2852, 1965.

The Criminal Justice Bill which was introduced into Parliament in 1966 authorised the release of prisoners at the discretion of the Home Secretary on licence. There were however objections to giving a Minister this power and the Government therefore introduced an amendment which set up a Parole Board which must include:

(a) a person who holds or has held judicial office;
(b) a registered medical practitioner who is a psychiatrist;
(c) a person appearing to the Secretary of State to have knowledge and experience of the supervision or after care of discharged prisoners; and
(d) a person appearing to the Secretary of State to have made a study of the causes of delinquency or the treatment of offenders.

Particular cases are considered in the first instance by a local review committee in the particular prison. The Local Review Committee Rules, S.I. 1462, 1967 provide that it shall include:

(a) a probation officer who is not a prison welfare officer;
(b) a member of the board of visitors or visiting committee of the prison;
(c) a person who is not a probation officer or a member of that board or committee.

No officer of the prison other than the governor may be a member. The committee must review the case of any prisoner referred to them by the Home Secretary, and subject to the consent of the prisoner, the case of any prisoner serving a sentence of two years or more, other than for life, at some time before he becomes eligible for release under section 60 of the Criminal Justice Act 1967 and subsequently at intervals of not less than ten months or more than fourteen months. The committee then reports to the Home Secretary on the suitability of the prisoner for release on licence. He may either release a person on licence on the recommendation of the local review committee or refer a favourable recommendation to the Parole Board for its decision. He has reserved the right to refuse to release a prisoner even if release has the support of the Board.[74]

In the case of a person sentenced to imprisonment for life there is normally a review after four years at the Home Office to see if, exceptionally, the local review committee should be asked to review the case in the next two years. It is more usual to refer the case to the local review committee after seven years have been served. Whether or not the local committee supports release, the case then goes to the Parole Board.

The report of the Probation and After Care Department for 1966–68 [75] noted, at para. 197, that the standard conditions of the licence under which a prisoner is released are that:

(a) the prisoner shall report to the officer in charge of the probation and after care office . . . forthwith

(b) he shall place himself under the supervision of whichever probation officer is nominated for this purpose from time to time

[74] 767 H.C.Deb. Written Answer c. 63, June 25, 1968.
[75] Cmnd. 4233.

(c) he shall inform his probation officer at once if he changes his address or changes or loses his job

(e) he shall be of good behaviour and lead an industrious life.

The Parole Board may recommend the addition of a condition relating to where he may live or work. The current statute regulating parole is the Criminal Justice Act 1967.

Criminal Justice Act 1967
1967, c. 80

59.—(1) For the purpose of exercising the functions conferred on it by this Part of this Act as respects England and Wales there shall be a body to be known as the Parole Board ... consisting of a chairman and not less than four other members appointed by the Secretary of State.

(3) It shall be the duty of the Board to advise the Secretary of State with respect to—

(a) the release on licence under section 60 (1) or 61 and the recall under section 62, of this Act of persons whose cases have been referred to the Board by the Secretary of State;

(b) the conditions of such licences and the variation or cancellation of such conditions; and

(c) any other matter so referred which is connected with the release on licence or recall of persons to whom the said section 60 or 61 applies.

(6) The Secretary of State may by rules make provision—

(a) for the establishment and constitution of local review committees having the duty of reviewing at such times or in such circumstances as may be prescribed by or determined under the rules the cases of persons who are or will become eligible for release under section 60 or 61 of this Act and reporting to the Secretary of State on their suitability for release on licence ... and rules under this subsection may make different provision for different cases.

60.—(1) The Secretary of State may, if recommended to do so by the Parole Board, release on licence a person serving a sentence of imprisonment, other than imprisonment for life, after he has served not less than one-third of his sentence or twelve months thereof, which expires the later. . . .

(3) Without prejudice to his earlier release under subsection (1) of this section the Secretary of State may direct that—

(a) a person serving a sentence of imprisonment in respect of whom an extended sentence certificate was issued ... ; or

(b) a person serving a sentence of imprisonment for a term of eighteen months or more who was under the age of twenty-one when the sentence was passed;

shall, instead of being granted remission . . . be released on licence at any time on or after the day on which he could have been discharged from prison if the remission had been granted.

(6) A licence granted to any person under this section shall, unless previously revoked under section 62 of this Act, remain in force until a date specified in the licence, being—

(a) in the case of a licence granted to a person in respect of whom an extended sentence certificate was issued ... or to a person under the age of twenty-one when sentence was passed on him, the date of the expiration of the sentence;

(b) in any other case, the date on which he could have been discharged from prison on remission. . . .

61.—(1) The Secretary of State may, if recommended to do so by the Parole Board, release on licence a person serving a sentence of imprisonment for life or a person detained under section 53 of the Children and Young Persons Act 1933 (young offenders convicted of grave crimes), but shall not do so in the case of a person sentenced to imprisonment for life or to detention during Her Majesty's pleasure or for life except after consultation with the Lord Chief Justice of England together with the trial judge if available.

62.—(1) Where the Parole Board recommends the recall of any person who is subject to a licence . . . the Secretary of State may revoke that person's licence and recall him to prison.

(2) The Secretary of State may revoke the licence of any such person and recall him . . . without consulting the Board, where it appears to him that it is expedient in the public interest to recall that person before such consultation is practicable.

(7) If a person subject to any such licence is convicted on indictment [of an offence punishable with imprisonment] or is committed to [the Crown Court] [76] for sentence . . . the court by which he is convicted or to which he is committed . . . may, whether or not it passes any other sentence on him, revoke the licence.

Criminal Justice Act 1972
1972, c. 71

35.—(1) If, in any case falling within such class of cases as the Secretary of State may determine after consultation with the Parole Board, a local review committee recommends the release on licence of a person to whom subsection (1) of section 60 of the Criminal Justice Act 1967 applies, the Secretary of State shall not be obliged to refer the case to the Parole Board before releasing him under that subsection. . . .

Report of the Parole Board for 1968
H.C. 290, June 1969

7. An effective parole system must be complementary to and not in conflict with the sentencing policy of the courts. . . . For example, the prevalence at any given time of a particular class of offence or the expressed view of the courts that a particular class of offence merits exemplary punishment are factors which the Parole Board should not ignore when assessing the suitability for release on licence of an offender convicted of such an offence. Correspondingly the courts in the exercise of their functions of determining the right sentence for an offender recognise that within the period of that sentence the parole system will operate. . . .

50. . . . The Board's concern is to make in each case the decision whether it will be of greater benefit to the prisoner, his family and the public to release him on licence early than to keep him in prison for the normal portion of his sentence. The selection of a prisoner as one suitable for parole depends upon

---

[76] As amended by s. 56 (1), Sched. 8, para. 48, of the Courts Act 1971.

his history prior to the start of his current sentence, his behaviour during his current sentence, his plans for the future and the circumstances into which he will go if and when he is released.

51. A prisoner's ... past record—domestic, occupational and social—is a relevant factor. Has he had a settled and stable home life? Has he had a good record of regular employment? Has he been previously convicted, and, if so, of what type of offence? At what age was he first convicted and with what frequency has he appeared before the courts? Has he previously been under the supervision of a probation officer and, if so, what was his response? What was the nature and gravity of the offence resulting in the current sentence of imprisonment? Did the presiding judge make any observations relevant to parole in sentencing him? ... The weight to be attached to these matters varies from case to case and may be influenced by any change of circumstances affecting prospects for the future. ... [77]

THE PRISON RÉGIME

The Prison Act 1952 places the responsibility for the administration of the prison system on the Home Secretary. The old system by which the Prison Commissioners were responsible was abandoned in 1963. Section 47 of the Act authorises him to " make rules for the regulation and management of prisons, remand centres, detention centres and Borstal institutions respectively, and for the classification, treatment, employment, discipline and control of persons required to be detained therein." It is for the prison authorities to classify prisons and prisoners.

Report of the Committee to Review Punishments in Prisons, Borstal Institutions, Approved Schools and Remand Homes
Cmd. 8256, 1951

6. Modern prison legislation may be said to date from Peel's Gaol Act of 1823. This statute represented the efforts of the legislature to get rid of the evils and abuses in the prisons of the country which John Howard and his friends and followers had brought to public notice. The preamble to the Act is interesting because it expresses the intentions of those who framed its provisions and because it proves that the good intentions of the legislature are valueless if there are not the means or the will to carry them into effect. The preamble runs as follows: " Whereas ... it is expedient that arrangements should be made in prisons as shall not only provide for safe custody but shall also tend effectually to preserve the health and improve the morals of the prisoners confined therein and shall insure the proper measure of punishment to convicted offenders: and whereas the due classification, inspection, regular labour and employment and religious and moral instruction are essential to the discipline of a prison and to the reformation of offenders, be it enacted. ..." Such a declaration might with slight alteration serve as a statement of the intentions of the Prison Commissioners today. ...

8. ...In 1832 and again in 1835 Parliamentary Committees found ample cause to condemn the lack of discipline and uniformity in the prisons and recommended a more efficient form of administration. In 1850 a Select Committee of the House of Commons reported that the state of the prisons was so unsatisfactory that " proper punishment, separation or reformation was impossible in

[77] Cf. the statement of Lord Stonham, 288 H.L.Deb. c. 746, June 12, 1967.

them " and suggested that the remedy was to be found in delegating responsibility for their administration to a central authority.

9. Despite the exhortations of successive committees, the introduction of a system of inspection by Home Office officials and general agreement with the principle that complete segregation of the individual prisoner was necessary if the prison system was to prove adequately punitive and deterrent, the evidence given to the famous Select Committee of the House of Lords in 1863 revealed bewildering differences of ideas and practice between one prison and another. The prison in Wales which evaded the problem of treatment and forestalled possible criticism by contriving to remain without any prisoners at all was, it is true, unique; but there were others where a handful of prisoners were left to their own devices while the Governor attended to more pressing business elsewhere. In contrast, the evidence of the Governor of the large and overcrowded establishment at Coldbath Fields revealed that conditions there were little better than those which had moved Howard a hundred years earlier to indignant protest; while even at prisons where the separate system was in operation and the rules had been approved by the Home Secretary, governors and justices still had widely divergent ideas of discipline and prison punishments. . . .

11. The impression to be gained from reading the evidence given to the Committee and the reports of the Inspectors of Prisons of those days is that the efforts of the prison authorities were directed to making prison conditions harsh and uncomfortable so that prisoners might thereby be persuaded to reform. But hard labour on the crank and treadwheel and a diet which by any standard was inadequate for health did not serve to render prisoners submissive to authority even while they were in prison. There were very few prisons in 1864 in which the incidence of punishments for prison offences was lower than it is today. . . .

13. The uniformity of administration which the Act of 1823 had aimed at but failed to achieve was secured by the passing of the Prison Acts of 1865 and 1877. By the latter all prisons were brought under the control of the Prison Commissioners, who were under an obligation to make annual reports to the Secretary of State on their administration.

14. In the twenty years following the 1877 Act the prisons of the country were run efficiently and economically. In so far as the Prison Commissioners had aimed at placing the administration of prisons on a proper basis, they succeeded most admirably. It was unfortunately true that they failed to appreciate the necessity of dealing with prisoners as individual human beings. The first Chairman of the Commission was a warm advocate of the advantages of the separate system, and he reflected informed public opinion of his time in giving precedence to the punitive and deterrent elements in prison administration. The prisons were designed as containers for the anti-social members of the community. Not only had these persons to be punished for their misdeeds but the punishment had to take such form as would deter others from rendering themselves liable to the penalties of the criminal law.

15. The rigid administration of the Prison Commissioners at length evoked considerable public criticism, and in 1894 the Home Secretary was moved to appoint a departmental committee to inquire into the prison system. The report of the Gladstone Committee marks the beginning of the present day prison administration. . . .

16. Apart from the great value of the report itself the proceedings of the Committee provide evidence of a new spirit and outlook among those concerned with the treatment of offenders. As in 1863 there was an appreciation of the social evil of a large criminal population. But there was a world of difference between the approach of the Gladstone Committee to the whole problem of prison maintenance and that of the House of Lords Committee of 1863. In 1894 the members of the Committee and many of the witnesses who gave

evidence expressed disagreement with those who held that the reformation of
the prisoner could not be one of the purposes of imprisonment, and the Report
stated that " the prisoners have been treated too much as a hopeless or worthless
element of the community. . . ."

Report of the Departmental Committee on Prisons
C. 7702, 1895

17. If the condition and treatment of prisoners at the present time are
compared with what they were 60, 40, or even 20 years ago, the responsible
authorities can justly claim credit for great and progressive improvement. . . .
Nevertheless, we feel that the time has come when the main principles and
methods adopted by the prison Acts should be seriously tested by the light of
acquired experience and recent scientific research. . . .

19. . . . It is easy to find fault, to form ideal views, and to enunciate lofty
speculations as if they were principles arrived at by experience. It is extremely
difficult to organise and carry out a perfect system with reasonable regard to
economy, which should provide equal advantages and similar methods of treatment, not in one great centre, which would be comparatively easy, but in
greater or less degree in all the considerable centres of a great population distributed throughout the country, and which should apply uniformly to all the
varying classes of offenders undergoing sentences from a day's imprisonment to
penal servitude for life.

20. The difficulty of laying down principles of treatment is greatly enhanced
by the fact that while sentences may roughly speaking be the measure of
particular offences, they are not the measure of the characters of the offenders;
and it is this fact which makes a system of prison classification which shall be at
once just, convenient, and workable, so difficult to arrive at. . . .

Prison Act 1877

23. . . . [T]he centralisation of authority [as a result of the Prison Act 1877]
has been a complete success in the direction of uniformity, discipline and
economy. On the other hand it carried with it some inevitable disadvantages.
The great and, as we consider, the proved danger of this highly centralised
system has been, and is, that while much attention has been given to organisation, finance, order, health of the prisoners and prison statistics, the prisoners
have been treated too much as a hopeless or worthless element of the community,
and the moral as well as the legal responsibility of the prison authorities has been
held to cease when they pass outside the prison gates. The satisfactory sanitary
conditions, the unbroken orderliness of prison life, economy and high organisation, are held, and justly held, to prove good administration. But the moral
condition in which a large number of prisoners leave the prison, and the serious
number of recommittals have led us to think that there is ample cause for a
searching inquiry into the main features of prison life. From the evidence submitted to us it appears that as a criminal passes into the habitual class, prison
life, subject to the sentences now given, loses its terrors as familiarity with it
increases.

Character of necessary changes

25. . . . We think that the system should be made more elastic, more capable of
being adapted to the special cases of individual prisoners; that prison discipline
and treatment should be more effectually designed to maintain, stimulate, or

awaken the higher susceptibilities of prisoners, to develop their moral instincts, to train them in orderly and industrial habits, and whenever possible to turn them out of prison better men and women, both physically and morally, than when they came in. Crime, its causes and treatment, has been the subject of much profound and scientific inquiry. Many of the problems it presents are practically at the present time insoluble. It may be true that some criminals are irreclaimable, just as some diseases are incurable, and in such cases it is not unreasonable to acquiesce in the theory that criminality is a disease, and the result of physical imperfection. But criminal anthropology as a science is in an embryo stage, and while scientific and more particularly medical observation and experience are of the most essential value in guiding opinion on the whole subject, it would be a loss of time to search for a perfect system in learned but conflicting theories, when so much can be done by the recognition of the plain fact that the great majority of prisoners are ordinary men and women, amenable, more or less, to all those influences which affect persons outside....

27. Upon what does the reformatory influence which we desire to bring to bear more fully on the prison population depend? We answer (i) the administrative authority, (ii) individual effort, (iii) a proper classification of prisoners.

(i) The population of every prison is a community in itself, changing with greater or less rapidity, but composed of individuals of varying character, aptitude, and history. For purposes of prison discipline it is comparatively easy to mass them together, to call each of them by a number, and by a cast-iron system to make them all go through the same tasks, observe the same hours, and lead the same lives. But under this orderly equality there exist the most striking inequalities. The hardened criminal bears the discipline without much trouble. Others are brutalised by it. Others suffer acutely and perhaps are permanently weakened by it in mind and body. What is a temporary inconvenience to the grown criminal, may be to lads and younger men a bitter disgrace from which they never recover to their dying day. It is impossible to administer to each man a relatively exact amount of punishment. But yet it is these very inequalities which often must produce that bitterness and recklessness which lead on to habitual crime. These inequalities must exist under the best available system. But the responsible authorities of the prison should have sufficient time at their command to observe prisoners individually, and sufficient discretionary power to give or obtain for an individual prisoner that guidance, advice, or help, which at such a crisis in his life may make a priceless change in his intentions or disposition. And it should be the duty of the central executive to cooperate with the local officials in carrying out satisfactorily this most important part of their functions.

(ii) Without an excessive and impossible increase in the number of higher prison officials adequate individual attention to prisoners could not be given. But the warders could be trained to do some of this work, and under proper rules and regulations outside helpers could be brought in to supplement the work of the prison staff. Ordinary amateurs, as a rule, would be worse than useless. There are, however, many men and women in every centre of population who by training and temperament are amply competent to render valuable assistance.

(iii) The probabilities of success would be largely increased by a careful classification of prisoners. At present a large prison contains almost every type of offender. They are mixed up in hopeless confusion.... Old and young, good and bad, men convicted of atrocious crimes, and those convicted of non-criminal civil offences, are all to be found in the same prison.... A sound and wise system of classification would make it more possible to deal with prisoners collectively by reason of their circumstances being at any rate to some extent of a like nature. Efforts could then be concentrated on the individuals who were contumacious, and with better chances of ultimate success....

Memorandum by the Home Office to the Royal Commission on the Penal System on the Concepts and Purposes of the Penal System [78]

Written Evidence, Vol. I

17. One of the first improvements after 1895 was in the classification of prisoners. The "Wakefield" system was introduced in 1923, earnings schemes were started experimentally in 1929, and the first open prison for selected prisoners was started in a camp outside Wakefield in 1936. This experiment was extended in wartime, but the vigorous programme of open prisons did not really get under way until after the war. This relaxation of physical security was one of the main results of the emphasis on reform, since open institutions offer the best conditions for a training regime.

18. Some deterrent features lasted for a long time. Hard labour and flogging (as sentences available to the courts) were not abolished until 1948, and until 1945 hard labour prisoners were without a mattress for the first fourteen days of their sentence. But it may now be said that the prison regime no longer contains any deliberately imposed deterrents. Such deterrent features as remain are the necessary consequences of the duties of the prison authorities to retain in custody those whom the courts have sentenced to imprisonment and to ensure reasonable standards of behaviour in a disciplined and closed community. The time has passed when every development of the regime was the outcome of an anxious balancing of the conflicting considerations of deterrence and reform. The underlying concept is now that there should be progressive development of the prison regime and prison methods in order to produce a coherent system of training. . . .

26. The reformative aspects of a custodial sentence are not confined to the period in custody. It is now recognised that *after-care*, in the form of supervision, personal guidance and support after discharge, should be available to discharged offenders generally. Sentences such as borstal training have long included such a period of supervision, and steps to provide a more general service are now being taken. . . .

Departmental Committee on Persistent Offenders

Cmd. 4090, 1932

15. . . . The question was raised by one or two witnesses whether more offenders would not be deterred from incurring the risk of a second experience

---

[78] The Royal Commission on the Penal System was appointed in April 1964 " in the light of modern knowledge of crime and its causes and of modern penal practice here and abroad, to re-examine the concepts and purposes which should underlie the punishment and treatment of offenders in England and Wales; to report how far they are realised by the penalties and methods of treatment available to the courts, and whether any changes in these, or in the arrangements and responsibility for selecting the sentences to be imposed on particular offenders, are desirable; to review the work of the services and institutions dealing with offenders and the responsibility for their administration; and to make recommendations " (693 H.C.Deb., c. 601, April 16, 1964). On April 27, 1966, the Prime Minister announced the dissolution of the Commission. " While no fundamental differences within the Commission on philosophy and principles have manifested themselves, six of the members have felt increasingly that the time is not opportune for a single review of the penal system, leading to a comprehensive report, which could set the direction for a generation. They are in favour of early experimental changes in the system, but they believe that such changes, combined with the relative lack of conclusive research results, will make it difficult in the near future to offer recommendations designed to last for a lengthy period. These members recently tendered their resignations; and two others felt that, in these circumstances, the Royal Commission could not usefully continue, and they also tendered their resignations " (727 H.C.Deb., c. 703, April 27, 1966). In place of the Commission an Advisory Council on the Penal System was established.

if prison conditions were made somewhat harder. Imprisonment would be more effective if prison industries were improved and harder work were done in prisons; but a return to the policy of severity for severity's sake would provide no remedy.[79] As the long history of the penal system shows, severity is a double-edged weapon and if the offender leaves prison a worse man and a more embittered enemy of society than he was when he came in, society is injured equally with the offender. The object of modern changes in prison treatment has been to remove or modify the features which conduced to deterioration of mind or character and to make imprisonment, so far as possible, a period of training. This aim is not inconsistent with the deterrent function of imprisonment. In addition to the deterrence resulting from loss of liberty, training—if the system is efficient—is a deterrent experience. It should demand from the prisoner a higher standard of effort in work and behaviour and self-discipline than is demanded by a purely punitive system.

16. For many an offender it is said that his punishment begins not when he goes into prison, but when he comes out. Imprisonment often causes an almost irreparable break with home, friends, work and character; and unless an ex-prisoner can find employment and be restored to some social status, the chances of his relapsing into crime are increased. The arrangements made for helping a prisoner on discharge—especially prisoners serving a first sentence—have an important bearing on our problem.

People in Prison
Cmnd. 4214, 1969

The complexity of the task

24. The work of the prison service is inherently complex because a prison must be, in most respects, a micro-copy of the world outside. People live, eat, work and sleep in prison. There must be hospitals, chapels, classrooms and workshops within the perimeter of the prison, as within the confines of other " total " institutions. There is the further responsibility for security. " Rehabilitation " itself is complex. There is no such person as the average offender.... All generalisations about the characteristics of people in custody are therefore suspect. (There are exceptions even to the generalisation that people in custody are there unwillingly). The prison service has to deal with offenders, some of whom are dangerous and many of whom are afflicted by emotional and personality disturbance and social inadequacies. It is also true that the prison service has to cope with many with whom other social agencies have in some way failed.

25.... There is now a wide variety of penal institutions.... Increasingly, moreover, the service aims to provide a range of regimes even within one type of institution and has to assess that suitability of offenders for transfer from one to another. Obviously it is simpler to organise a prison in which the inmates

[79] *Cf.* Report of the committee to review punishments, etc. (Cmd. 8256, June 1951): " 4. . . . [W]e accept without question the principle held today by the authorities . . . that the punishment of imprisonment, to which a man or woman is sentenced for an offence against the community, consists in loss of liberty—the fact of being in prison *is* the punishment—and that there is no advantage whatever to the community, to the prison or to the prisoner in making his lot more unpleasant than it needs must be. A discipline and a regime unreasonably harsh or severe would not assist the administration or improve the tone of the prison; it could only result in the prisoner returning to freedom at the end of his sentence embittered and more hostile to law and order and to his fellow-creatures than he was when he went in; whereas the object and the ideal of prison discipline and training are to send the prisoner back to the community a better citizen, if possible, than he was before. . . ." Ed.

are held in solitary confinement than one in which they can associate with each other. It is also easier in such a prison to provide security against escapes. It is simpler to organise and control the hand-sewing of mail bags than the modern types of industrial work now being introduced. . . .

Discipline

35. The entire regime must rest on a foundation of discipline and good order. . . . But discipline depends far more on the attitudes of staff and of the offenders in their charge than it does upon sanctions. . . . There will always be a small minority of offenders needing strict control and supervision and there are some offenders who, if given any opportunity to do so, will dominate the larger group of which they form a small part. For the majority of offenders no more restrictions need be imposed than are necessitated by the efficient performance of the task of the establishment with the limited space available, and by the maintenance of good order. . . .[80]

Association

36. . . . Restrictions on prisoners talking to each other have long since been abolished, and it is the Government's policy to allow them to associate with each other at work, at mealtimes and in the evenings. . . . [P]rogress is still hampered by Victorian buildings, designed for solitary confinement and by shortages of staff. In many local prisons most prisoners have to eat in their cells, because there is no room for them to do so anywhere else, and spend the evening hours in their cells because of the lack of space for classes or other activities. . . .

Report of the Advisory Council on the Penal System on the Regime for Long-term Prisoners in Conditions of Maximum Security 1968

Giving or earning

74. . . . [B]ecause certain facilities ought to be available in a prison it does not follow that they should be *given* to prisoners; there are considerable advantages for the regime of the prison, and for the self-respect of the prisoner, if they are earned and not given.

75. We do not mean by this that the regime should be based on an automatic system of reward for outward conformity, and punishments for all minor breaches of the rules laid down for the outwardly smooth running of the institution. Such a regime does not increase self respect. We mean rather that the aim should be to create an atmosphere within the prison which will make the prisoner wish to earn for himself improvements in the conditions of his existence. The prisoner can earn these by work. We shall suggest, for example,

---

[80] *Cf.* the Report of the Committee to review punishments, etc. (Cmd. 8256, June 1951):
"94. . . . The average prisoner is well-behaved in prison; his main desire is that his time there should be passed with as little unpleasantness and as little delay as possible. He is not, however, as a rule prepared to suffer any deprivation of his rights without strong protest; and apart from legitimate protest he can find endless opportunities for making awkward and anxious the life of a person against whom he has a grievance. The prison officer has to live with the prisoners. They may not come to love one another, but they must if they are to have a quiet life contrive to tolerate one another. We have talked with many prison officers; we have seen them at their duties and have heard them giving evidence at adjudications by governors and visiting committees. Our judgment—supported very generally by the testimony of ex-prisoners—is that they treat the prisoners under their charge with forbearance and understanding, and as human beings. . . ." Ed.

that prisoners should have better clothes, but they should make a contribution towards the cost out of the earnings of their work. If a record library is available we see no reason why prisoners should not ... make a small financial contribution towards the cost of the records.... Small practical measures of this kind go a little way towards reducing the gap between the situation in prison and the situation as it will be after release when the former prisoner will not have everything provided for him. The prisoner should also be able to earn the opportunities for greater variety in his daily and yearly routine by his response to his fellow prisoners and to the efforts of the staff....

Personal possessions

91. Subject only to the limitations of security and space a prisoner should be allowed to keep certain personal possessions, books, a wireless, photographs, calendars, and if he so chooses, pin-ups in his cell. In a long-term prison we see no reason why he should not be allowed to paint his cell with a colour-scheme of his own choice ... or to make himself a bookshelf at a woodwork class. If a prisoner has personal possessions and letters and other things that he values in his cell he should be able to know that they are not likely to be stolen or damaged when he is not in it....

93. The present rules allow what is known as " private cash " to be used only for certain limited items, of which radios for long-term prisoners are the most important. With the present level of prison earnings there is no reasonable prospect of a prisoner purchasing from his earnings even the small number of personal possessions that we think it reasonable for him to be allowed. Nor do we think the taxpayer should meet the whole cost. We do not propose any changes at present. Subject to the existing limitations and careful scrutiny to limit abuse, the use of private cash should continue. But the whole subject should be re-examined if, as we hope, there is, in future, a substantial increase in the rate of earnings in prison.

Sanitation

94. There is no disagreement about the need to provide better sanitation in British prisons....

Appearance

96.... We believe that a dramatic improvement in prison clothing would be relatively cheap and should be made as soon as possible, and that no other single change would do more to raise the self-respect of prisoners....

97. There should not be a regulation hair cut, and subject to such administrative safeguards as are necessary to prevent unrecorded changes of appearance a prisoner should be able to grow a beard or a moustache.

Penal Practice in a Changing Society
Cmnd. 645, 1959

Work in prison

65. Offenders do not come to prison because they have failed as workmen, and the task of the prison is to train the whole man: a prison is not therefore, and should not be, first and foremost a factory. Nevertheless a prisoner's work must always be in some ways the basis of his training. It fills the greater part of his day, and his response to it and to the conditions in which he has to do it may well affect his response to other forms of training. It should therefore be

obviously purposeful, efficiently organised, and carried out so far as possible in conditions similar to those in outside workshops. It should at least enable him to acquire habits of regular and orderly industry, and at best give him a trade skill which he can use when he goes out. Above all, there should be enough of it to keep him busy for a full working day, week in and week out.

72. . . . In this country, before the war, the system had been adopted of making payments, known as " earnings," which though trifling in themselves were found to serve as a substantial incentive to prisoners to work faster and better. This system, with minor adjustments, has continued to the present time with occasional increases in the average level, which is now about 2s. 8d. a week. It not only provides an incentive to effort, but also allows the prisoner to have something to spend which he has earned, and to think about how he shall spend it. This has a training value in more than one way. It does, for example, allow the prisoner the opportunity, rare in a prison, to do something unselfish for somebody else. It is remarkable how much of these small sums is spent in the canteens on Christmas and birthday cards, or on chocolates for the children when they visit.

73. Nevertheless, a system under which a week's hard work by a good workman may not earn him the price of a packet of cigarettes is hardly consistent with the view of the prisoner as an ordinary member of the working community; for this reason, it has often been suggested that a prisoner should be paid " the economic rate for the job." This means that he should receive wages on the same basis as workers outside, and out of them should pay for his keep in prison, maintain his dependents, keep up his social insurance contributions, save a fixed proportion for use on release, and retain the balance for personal spending in prison. In favour of this scheme it has been argued that it would make for greater self-respect and self-responsibility, for greater interest and industry at work, and for a stronger position on release. It ought also to make it easier for prison industry to be accepted as a normal part of the national economy, since prisoners would then be employed in conditions similar to those of free industry.

74. . . .[I]t is clear that, apart from the many practical and economic difficulties, there are important questions of principle involved. For example, would such a system really contribute to a prisoner's training by encouraging responsibility and the faculty of choice, since he would have little real control over the disposal of his earnings? And what would be the moral basis of such a system if it were not linked with changes in the law which would enable prisoners also to be required to make restitution from their earnings to the victims of their offences? . . . [W]hatever conclusions may be reached on the conflicting arguments of principle, it seems clear that this conception of the " economic rate " cannot provide a general solution of the prison earnings problems until the general level of productivity and efficiency of prison industry approximates much more closely to that of outside industry.

Report of the Advisory Council on the Employment of Prisoners. Organisation of Work for Prisoners 1964

Prisoners' pay

31. We are convinced that adequate pay incentives are of great importance in prison industries. As the industries become more highly organised, pay will become even more important. . . .

32. Prisoners pay can be considered (a) purely as pocket money for spending in prison (b) as pocket money plus an additional amount for compulsory savings and (c) on the level of full wages.

33. . . . There is clearly a limit to the amounts which prisoners ought to be allowed to spend in prison. A reasonable relationship ought to be maintained between prisoners' pocket money and the pocket money allowed to people who, through no fault of their own, are dependent on national assistance. . . .

34. We have not been able to give detailed consideration to the question of increasing prisoners' pay to a level which permits compulsory savings, but it seems to us that this would provide a much higher incentive than mere pocket money and would help to give prisoners a start in life on discharge instead of being subsidised by the social services out of the taxpayers' pockets. . . .

35. The question of paying prisoners full wages is still more complicated and we have not so far tried to reach any conclusions on the advantages and disadvantages of this. . . .

Prisons and Borstals. Report of the Work of the Prison Department for 1963

Cmnd. 2381, 1964

On March 31, 1963, the Prison Commission was dissolved and its staff and functions transferred to the Home Office. It then became the duty of the Home Secretary to prepare and present the annual reports on the prison service. In a foreword to this report the Home Secretary, Henry Brooke, referred to some of the handicaps under which the Prison Commissioners had been labouring in recent years.

Prison buildings

2. First of all, I want to pay my tribute to the many wise and enlightened men among the Prison Commissioners and their staffs who assisted successive Home Secretaries to bring about the transformation of practice and outlook in and about the prisons of England and Wales between 1878 and 1963. . . .

3. Their heavy handicap in recent years has been the age and character of many of the buildings, particularly the local prisons. Anyone who wishes material evidence of this should first visit Pentonville, acclaimed as the new model prison in 1842 (when indeed transportation was about to give place to imprisonment as the ordinary punishment for criminals), and then one of our newest prisons, Blundeston in Suffolk, occupied for the first time in July 1963. . . .

4. Pentonville, like many of its Victorian successors, was designed simply as an efficient place of containment. The main star-shaped building consisted almost entirely of cells, easy to supervise from the centre of the star. Surrounding it was and is a high wall. In the prisons of the mid-Victorian age, men worked alone in their cells, or on a treadmill; the wall surrounded the exercise ground. It was a life completely cut off from the outside world, into which the prisoner was discharged, totally unprepared for freedom, at the end of his sentence.

5. Blundeston has no prison wall. Its extensive site is surrounded by a high chain-link fence, through part of which one can look out on to the countryside. Security is in the buildings themselves, with windows guarded by manganese steel bars which will resist any file. The main building has classrooms, dining and recreation rooms, chapels, a library and gymnasium as well as cells; about a quarter of the prisoners sleep in dormitories. Nearly all the furniture, here as in other establishments, is prison made. Alongside are a number of workshops, much like small factory buildings on an industrial estate—for a modern

prison should make its inmates work, and work hard, with plant and under conditions as similar as possible to those they will find in an ordinary factory when they come out of prison and have to earn their own living and support their families again.

6. Pentonville was built as a vast undifferentiated place, with some 850 cells, all alike; other prisons of the same era are similar in design, though few are as large. Blundeston is designed for 300 prisoners, divided physically into four sections of 75, each of which can be run as a distinct community for many purposes.... All this reflects the change in attitude over a hundred years. We have come to recognise that people received into prison are not simply creatures to be kept locked up, but persons to be studied and handled in manageable groups according to their characters and weaknesses, with a view to building up their capacity and will to live good and useful lives when they have served their sentences and are free again.

7.... One must not judge a prison, any more than a school, by its age; it is the people in charge that matter. Nevertheless the design of the old prisons negates the purpose of modern prison treatment. One cannot do all that one would because solid out-of-date structures frown on it and delay it....

9. Why is this country so loaded with old prisons?... Part of the answer lies in past history. For many years before the last war the prison population had remained fairly static. There had therefore been no felt need to build new prisons for accommodating more prisoners; and the mere replacement of old prison buildings seemed to deserve less priority than, for example, the clearance of slums and the proper housing of law abiding people.... [W]hen I opened Blundeston last summer ... it was the first purpose-built secure prison used for men since Camp Hill in the Isle of Wight, which was officially opened in 1912 by the then Home Secretary, Mr. Winston Churchill.

10. The second reason why old prisons remain in use is that resources have deliberately been concentrated on the young. Only seven borstals and two detention centres are in buildings used by the prison service before the war.... Resources are now being directed to a much greater extent to the construction of new accommodation for men prisoners whose numbers are three times as large as in 1939; but until we have conquered overcrowding we cannot afford to pull down the old. That is why Pentonville and other old prisons remain....

The Adult Offender
Cmnd. 2852, 1965

Contacts with the outside world

21. It is of the utmost importance to maintain contact between the prisoner and his family.... A man who has won the trust and affection of a wife and children must have good in him. His bond with his family is as it were the bridge over which he can pass back from prison to the companionship of his fellow citizens.... Moreover such a man also suffers a far more agonising punishment confined in prison away from his family than the rootless introvert who has never thought of anybody but himself.

22. Under the existing system a prisoner may be far removed from his wife and family and from other home ties and may only see his family on rare occasions. He may ... save up accumulated visits and then be sent back to his local prison in order to receive frequent visits from his family during a short period of time. At present such accumulated visiting periods are only allowed when a prisoner has served at least two years. It is proposed ... to reduce this ... to one year. In addition visits ... should be facilitated. Advance ... must ... be cautious and gradual in order not only to overcome the ...

administrative difficulties . . . but also to avoid abuse. . . . [E]xtended opportunities might be given to prisoners who show themselves worthy of trust to have from time to time . . .day or week-end home leave. . . .[81]

Report of the Advisory Council on the Penal System on the Regime for Long-term Prisoners in Conditions of Maximum Security 1968

Conjugal visits

138. . . . . [I]f it could be established that the introduction of conjugal visits in the regime of a prison increased the chances of the rehabilitation of the prisoners concerned, and kept in being marriages that would otherwise collapse, we would think these were important advantages to be weighed against possible disadvantages. We mean also that, although there are special considerations applying to some abnormal offenders, we do not regard the deprivation of marital relationships, and enforced celibacy, as being among the purposes of imprisonment. . . .

139. What empirical evidence is there? We . . . did not find any conclusions based on controlled and carefully observed studies. . . .

140. A good many of our witnesses stressed the very great practical difficulties of arranging conjugal visits in conditions that combined security with decency and human dignity, and the administrative problems of deciding which prisoners should receive visits, and from whom. . . . But most of the witnesses who were opposed to conjugal visits raised other objections. They argued that in the outside world the sexual relationship between a man and his wife was but one part of the sharing of everyday living together. It would be not only artificial, but wrong, and degrading to both parties, to envisage brief sexual encounters in a prison setting. Witnesses suggested to us partly for these reasons that several countries in Western Europe . . . are considering . . . experiments in the grant of home leave. One very relevant point is that home leave enables a man to resume contact not only with his wife but with his children. If we are thinking of ways of keeping family relationships viable against release the link between parent and child is as important as that between man and wife. Moreover, home leave can be granted to enable an unmarried prisoner to visit his parents, or other relatives, and need not be confined to married men. . . .

141. There is a further complex of arguments. . . . Very little is reliably established about sexuality in prison, and the reactions of prisoners to sexual frustration. . . . Long-sentence prisoners make some form of adaptation to the institution . . . and . . . one method of doing this involved a form of regression to a state of emotional, intellectual and sexual inactivity. . . . [F]ollowing this line of argument it was suggested that the provision . . . of infrequent opportunities for marital relations might increase sexual tension and frustration. . . .

142. . . . Some witnesses argued that the provision of infrequent opportunities for marital relations could cause great misery to both parties. . . .

144. . . . [W]e cannot feel that such a radical change in one prison system as the introduction of conjugal visits can be introduced in [a maximum security prison] . . . until a great deal of experience has been gained elsewhere.

145. . . . We support the extension of home leave, though we are very conscious of the practical difficulties of selection. But we think something

[81] *Cf.* People in Prison (Cmnd. 4214, November 1969): " 91. The limits which are still placed on the number of letters, and the number and the length of visits, reflect the demands on staff resources for censorship and supervision and the lack of space in visiting rooms. . . . There are security and general reasons why the censorship of letters is necessary."

more is needed if the prison service is to meet the challenge of containing men for long periods and treating them with a view to return to a community of men and women. . . . We suggest that selected prisoners should be allowed, two or three times a year, to spend a day or a week-end with their families in . . . accommodation which was near a long-term prison but not inside the perimeter wall . . . although the arrangement could clearly not be envisaged for prisoners of the higher security category. . . .[81a]

The long-term prisoner

200. . . . Since 1961 an average of about 10 prisoners a year have received determinate sentences that involve their being continuously in custody for at least 9 years, and in a few cases for as much as 20 years. . . . There are now prisoners serving life sentences who would previously have been executed. Some life sentence prisoners . . . may have to be securely contained for something approaching the term of their natural life. . . .

201. A considerable proportion of those now serving long determinate sentences, and a smaller proportion of those serving life sentences, are violent anti-social recidivist criminals. . . . Some of these people can be as difficult to control inside prison as they are dangerous outside it. . . . In addition the increase in organised violent crime means that some criminal gangs may be able to command considerable resources that could be used to assist a member of the gang to escape from custody. . . .

202. . . . Our conclusion . . . is that (i) there needs to be an increase in the coefficient of security in our closed prisons, especially those in which long-term prisoners are contained. This need not, and must not, be obtained by a reversal of the trend towards a more liberal and constructive regime inside our long-term prisons, still less by a partial or complete return to the restricted and solitary life for the prisoners for which our 19th century prisons were designed. Our conclusions are that (ii) given an adequate, well-led, alert and well-trained staff, the necessary general increase in security can be obtained by a very considerable strengthening of perimeter security, and also that (iii) within such perimeter security, and with adequate staff and buildings, it becomes possible to continue and develop a liberal regime for the human and constructive treatment of long-term prisoners. . . .

Principles of a prison regime

203. . . . [O]ur society cannot treat as less than human those men it finds it necessary to send to prison. This means that the community must provide for the prison service the necessary resources to enable men to be contained for long periods in conditions that combine security with humanity. It means also that (iv) the regime of a prison must aim to meet the needs of human beings in custody. . . .

The prison and the community

205. . . . We have said something in section xi of our report about the importance of trying to maintain links between a prisoner and the outside world.

[81a] During a debate in the House of Commons on November 15, 1968 the Home Secretary said that the necessary conditions did not exist in closed prisons for conjugal visits and that it was doubtful whether they would in the foreseeable future. In his view it would not be possible to arrange for such visits in a way which would combine security with human dignity. Instead he hoped to make a modest extension in the system of grants of home leave.

Equally the prison staff must be in touch with the community. The community must be concerned about what goes on in the prison, and about the work of the staff, and the prison authorities both locally and centrally must be willing to provide the necessary information. Even a maximum security prison should not be a secret place known to the outside world only if something goes wrong in it. Another very important link with the outside world is that the community, and thus the taxpayer, should share with the prisoners the benefit of the goods that can and should be produced in the prison workshops. This . . . is a field in which our prison system has fallen behind those of other countries. . . .

208. . . . [W]e are in no doubt that (v) there are prisoners who for the protection of the public need, and can be recognised as needing, the very highest degree of security that a prison system can provide. Some of these prisoners though by no means all, will be men who are so violent, or whose influence is so disruptive in the prison community, that their presence in a larger recidivist prison is likely to jeopardise the development of a liberal and constructive regime in the prison. Others may make persistent attempts to escape.

209. It would be possible to concentrate the most difficult and dangerous prisoners in one small maximum security prison. The alternative is to disperse such prisoners among three or four secure long-term recidivist prisons where the majority would be absorbed into the general population of those prisons, although a minority would from time to time have to be transferred to small segregation units. . . . Our conclusions are: (vi) there are grave disadvantages for both prisoners and staff in the proposal to concentrate the most difficult and dangerous prisoners in one small expensive maximum security prison . . . ; (viii) the problem of satisfactory containment of a small number of violent and disruptive prisoners can best be met by the establishment of small segregation units within larger prisons. . . .

210. . . . We have considered the security measures needed in a long-term prison which might contain a proportion of the most difficult and dangerous prisoners. . . . Our conclusions include . . . ; (ix) adequate perimeter security, and confidence of the prison staff in it, are a necessary concomitant of the development of a liberal regime; (x) present security plans should be supplemented by the use of observation towers . . . ; (xi) the Home Office Scientific Advisory Group should consider how research into the development of non-lethal weapons can be advanced . . . ; (xii) bearing in mind both the nature of the regime desirable within the prison, and the risk of outside help for escape, it is an essential though regrettable part of the security measures that officers on observation duty in the towers should be armed. . . .[82]

---

[82] *Cf.* Report of the Committee on Punishments in Prisons, etc. (Cmd. 8256, June 1951): " 87. A proposal was made to us by witnesses who appeared on behalf of the Prison Officers' Association that a special prison should be set aside for the prisoners who were proved or known to be tobacco barons, racketeers and gang leaders. We were assured by officers of long experience that there are in every prison a few prisoners—perhaps 12 in a prison holding 1,000 men—whose activities give rise to much serious disciplinary trouble, and that if they could be removed it would be possible to introduce a more benevolent regime. We were told for instance of an occurrence at one prison where a prisoner made a violent attack on a prison officer. . . . In the course of this attack two elderly prisoners went to the officer's assistance. The following morning these two were set upon and beaten up by a gang of 12 prisoners. The trouble was said to have been instigated by two gang leaders who had cause to dislike the officer; but neither of them took any active part. . . .

90. We accordingly recommend that very fully consideration be given to the suggestion that a prison be set aside for those prisoners who by continued misconduct and defiance of authority prove themselves unfitted to ordinary prison conditions. . . . "

SUPERVISION AND AFTER-CARE

There is not space here to deal with the provisions for after-care of released prisoners. The main principles are set out in the Report of the Advisory Council on the Treatment of Offenders, " The Organisation of After-Care," 1963. The periodic reports of the Probation and After-Care Department of the Home Office [83] provide useful information. There are a number of statutory provisions for compulsory supervision after release. Supervision by *e.g.* a probation officer may also be imposed as a condition in the licence when a prisoner is released on licence under the provisions of the Criminal Justice Act 1967.

Criminal Justice Act 1961
9 & 10 Eliz. 2, c. 39

13. Every person who is detained in a detention centre in pursuance of an order made under section four of this Act ... shall, after his release from the detention centre, be subject to supervision ...

Criminal Justice Act 1967
1967, c. 80

63.—(1) A person serving a sentence of imprisonment for a term of less than eighteen months who was under the age of twenty-one when the sentence was passed shall be subject after his release from prison to supervision . . . as if he had been released from a detention centre ...

Prison Act 1952
15 & 16 Geo. 6 & 1 Eliz. 2, c. 52

45.—(3) A person shall, after his release from a Borstal institution and until the expiration of [two years from the date of his release],[84] be under the supervision of such society or person as may be specified in a notice to be given to him by the [Secretary of State] ... on his release ...

---

[83] Cmnd. 3107 for 1962–65; Cmnd. 4233 for 1965–68 and Cmnd. 5158 for 1969–71.
[84] As amended by Criminal Justice Act 1961, s. 41 (1) (3), Sched. 4, and the Prison Commissioners Dissolution Order 1963, S.I. 1963 No. 597.

CHAPTER 9

APPEALS

APPEALS IN CIVIL CASES

THE COURT OF APPEAL (CIVIL DIVISION)

The role of an appeal court

One party to a lawsuit is always disappointed and sometimes his disappointment is justified. Judges do make mistakes, mistakes about what the law is, about the weight to be given to particular evidence or particular facts or about the kind or amount of compensation which should be given. Sometimes the trial itself may be unsatisfactory because for example the judge intervened so much that a party was prevented from making his case, or because a member of the jury communicated with one of the parties during the trial. In all these cases some review body is needed to correct these mistakes or provide for a new trial. But the role of an appeal court goes well beyond that. Although one may find a Court of Appeal reversing a decision of a lower court on the ground that it has made a mistake of fact or law, there are mistakes and mistakes. Simple straightforward errors like a complete misreading of a statute or the complete failure to notice a relevant authority are comparatively rare. More often what a disappointed party is doing is asking the Court of Appeal to take a different view of the facts or the law from that taken by the trial judge, in a situation where different views are possible. In this, the Court of Appeal is presumed to have some advantages, some practical and some technical. The practical advantages include the fact that the appeal court is being asked to give a second opinion, after the facts and the issues have been clarified and the authorities have been fully discussed in the lower court, in a detached atmosphere, away from the hurly-burly of the trial itself, where in the Queen's Bench Division at any rate, much of the judge's time must be spent in sorting out the facts and the issues and assessing the reliability and truthfulness of the various witnesses. By the time the Court of Appeal gets to the case the original facts and disputes have been processed by solicitors and counsel on both sides, the pleadings, the trial itself and the judgment of the trial judge. The professional advisers have twice, once at the trial and once in the Court of Appeal, searched out and discussed the relevant authorities. It may be that by the time the case has got to the Court of Appeal more experienced counsel have taken over the case so that the court may even receive help of a higher quality than the trial judge had in coming to his decision. One drawback which the Court of Appeal recognises is that in avoiding the immediate pressures of the trial, they also miss the opportunity of seeing the witnesses, and are deprived of the contribution that seeing and hearing them gives for assessing their credibility. But this does not matter when the disagreement is simply about questions of law or compensation; and even when the dispute is about the facts they are in as good a position to draw inferences from agreed facts, for example as to whether particular conduct amounted to negligence, as the trial judge. The fact that the Court of Appeal is not itself a trial court is also an advantage. Reviewing cases is what the court is doing all the time. It has the further advantage that it consists of a minimum of three judges, against the trial judge's one. It was one of the major criticisms of the changes that took place in 1873–75 that in future the common law courts of four judges would be replaced by the single judge procedure, and the possibility of a review by three senior judges to some extent makes up for that change.

The technical advantage enjoyed by the Court of Appeal has to do with the doctrine of precedent. Judges sitting in the High Court do not have the same freedom of departing from previous decisions, and especially a line of previous decisions, as the Court of Appeal. It is true that the Court of Appeal has decided that in general it, too, is bound by its own previous decisions, but it can overrule previous decisions of the High Court and has as a matter of practice a greater power to innovate and to depart from even an established line of authority than the High Court judge. Moreover the role of the Court of Appeal goes beyond that of reviewing particular cases in order to see if a different decision should be given on the merits of the case or a new trial ordered. It is not only a reviewing body. It is also a supervising body, and one of its tasks is to preserve some kind of uniformity in the decisions of the lower courts and to lay down principles which will guide them in the future, so that decisions do not vary according to the particular trial court in which the case happens to be brought. Here the doctrine of precedent gives it support. Besides having the power to reverse a decision because it is out of line with other decisions or because as between two approaches to a problem it prefers that of another lower court, it can also lay down rules and principles of law which are binding on all lower courts in future cases. It not only aims therefore to give just decisions in particular cases, but also to harmonise the rules and principles of law, fact-finding and compensation that are applied in the lower courts.

Finally, the court has a responsibility not only for ironing out inconsistencies and anomalies in the law but also a more positive role in keeping the law up to date with changing circumstances. Some of these matters we have already discussed in looking at the role of the appeal courts in lawmaking, and there has also been some discussion of the advantages enjoyed by the trial judge as a finder of facts. This chapter deals a little more with the way in which the appeal courts go about their task of reviewing particular cases.

The origins of the appeal system

Although it is now readily accepted that there is a need for a review body with wide powers to oversee and if necessary overrule the decisions of the lower courts, the idea of an appeal in this broad sense was slow to grow. From the earliest days, the Court of King's Bench heard appeals from the Court of Common Pleas. In 1357–58 a Court of Exchequer Chamber was set up to hear appeals from the Court of Exchequer. In 1585 a second court of Exchequer Chamber was set up to hear appeals from the

Court of King's Bench when it was hearing cases at first instance. This had become necessary because of the expansion of this jurisdiction at the expense of the Court of Common Pleas. Any decision of the King's Bench whether sitting as an appeal court or court of first instance could be reviewed in Parliament, whose functions came to be exercised in this respect by the House of Lords. In 1830 the two Courts of Exchequer Chamber were replaced by a third. It was created to hear appeals from all three common law courts and consisted of the judges of the courts other than that from which the appeal was brought. The King's Bench lost its jurisdiction to hear appeals from the Court of Common Pleas.

However, although there was this appellate structure on the common law side, the actual scope of the appeal was limited. Procedure was by writ of error and the basis of the complaint was an error appearing on the record of the case. At first any error sufficed, however technical, and only an error on the record sufficed. As time passed authority was given to correct technical errors without affecting the validity of the original judgment. The other limitation was however never completely overcome, the main defect of the procedure being that only a limited number of things appeared on the record and could be used as the basis of complaint. The position was mitigated to some extent by the introduction of the Bill of Exceptions in which a party could ask the trial judge to note that a particular defence had been rejected and the Bill and its contents were then treated as part of the record for the purpose of the procedure on error. A further disadvantage remained. The result of a successful appeal was that the judgment below was quashed but no new judgment could be substituted. Instead a new trial was necessary.

Appeals on questions of fact were even more difficult. In the days when juries were expected to speak from their own knowledge, mistaken verdicts were treated as something akin to perjury and the writ of attaint was available to try the truth of the jury's verdict, and punishment followed if the jurors of the attaint jury, which was twice as large as the original jury, came to a different conclusion. The notion of a mistake of fact based on mistaken but honest assessment of, or inference from, the evidence was slow to develop, along with the development of jurors from being a body of men who knew the facts of a case to being a body which was expected to know nothing other than what had been presented as evidence in court. It was then, from the seventeenth century on, that juries ceased to be punished for their verdicts and that the common law courts would order new trials, at first where it was shown that the jury had behaved improperly in some way and later where the verdict was regarded as being against the weight of evidence.

It was in the Court of Chancery that the notion of a full appeal by way of rehearing was developed. At first both the Master of the Rolls and the Lord Chancellor were themselves prepared to rehear cases which they had already heard. In 1851 a Court of Appeal in Chancery was established, composed of two Lords Justices in Chancery.

When the Judicature Commissioners came to consider the matter, therefore, in 1869 they found a number of appeal courts, and competing approaches to the problem of how to handle appeals. So far as the courts were concerned, besides the Court of Exchequer Chamber and the Court of Appeal in Chancery, appeals from the Court of Admiralty which had earlier gone to delegates appointed for the purpose by the Crown, had since 1832 been referred to the Privy Council and since 1833 to the Judicial Committee of the Privy Council. Appeals from the Divorce Court established in 1857 were from the single judge to the full court and from 1868 to the House of Lords, and appeals from the Probate Court also established in 1857 to the House of Lords. The Commissioners recommended that in future there should be a single Court of Appeal from the High Court into which all the lower courts were to be combined, and that the style of appeal should be the Chancery appeal by way of rehearing.

The composition of the Court of Appeal

The composition of the Court of Appeal is set out in the Supreme Court of Judicature (Consolidation) Act 1925. In practice the Court of Appeal consists of Lords Justices of Appeal appointed especially for the purpose by the Crown on the advice of the Prime Minister, and the Master of the Rolls. The Lord Chancellor also has the power to ask a judge of the High Court to sit. The Lord Chancellor himself, the Lord Chief Justice, the President of the Family Division, Law Lords, former Lord Chancellors, Lords Justices and judges of the High Court are also eligible to sit but rarely do so. The court usually sits in divisions of three but it sometimes sits in a full court of five or even seven. The Administration of Justice Act 1968 fixed the maximum number of Lords Justices at thirteen but provided that the Queen could increase the number at any time by Order in Council, the draft of which had been approved by a resolution of both Houses of Parliament. The Supreme Court of Judicature Act 1925 provides for the appointment of a Vice-President to preside over the sittings of the court, but in practice this role has been assumed by the Master of the Rolls. It has happened on occasion that different divisions of the Court of Appeal have taken different views about the law or about the appropriate sum of damages to be awarded in a particular type of case. In normal circumstances the only way in which such a conflict can be resolved is by an appeal to the House of Lords.

Jurisdiction, procedure and powers

The jurisdiction of the Court of Appeal is set out in the Supreme Court of Judicature (Consolidation) Act 1925, the County Courts Act 1959 and a number of other statutes giving specific rights of appeal. The Court of Appeal has all the powers of the appeal courts which it replaced and of the High Court, including the power to authorise the amendment of the pleadings. It can hear appeals on interlocutory matters before the trial has begun, though where a discretion has been left to the judge in these matters it will not interfere with his exercise of the discretion simply because it would have exercised it in a different way. The appeal is said to be by way of rehearing but this is not a genuine rehearing of the witnesses. The proceedings are conducted on the basis of the pleadings and any documents that went with them, and a transcript of the evidence or the judge's note.

There have been suggestions for a more extensive use of written briefs, but at present reliance is still placed on oral argument. It is possible for one party to take a new point not made below and even to raise a new issue not raised on the pleadings, but the court will be reluctant to allow this where it would put the other party at a disadvantage, in particular in relation to the case he might have made at the trial and the evidence he might have brought had the point been pleaded or the case made out in that particular way earlier. It has also been said that another reason for reluctance is because it deprives the Appeal Court of the considered opinion of the lower court on the point. There are cases, however, where this reluctance gives way to other principles, for example the principle that it is the responsibility of the court not to give effect to illegal agreements, even though the illegality was not expressly pleaded or taken in the court below. The practice here seems to be somewhat stricter in the case of appeals from county courts than from the High Court. The Court of Appeal can also receive fresh evidence but will only do so in exceptional circumstances and where the evidence was not reasonably available at the trial. Its willingness to review findings of fact is limited by its recognition of the advantage enjoyed by the trial judge in having seen the witnesses.

Appeal may lie not only against the decision but also against the compensation awarded. In cases where damages are at large, and in particular personal injury cases, the Court of Appeal has moved towards the position in which it tries so far as possible to achieve some kind of consistency between awards, whether by judges alone or by juries, though it will not interfere simply because, if left to itself, it would have fixed a different figure.

Where the trial below was conducted with a jury, the proceeding before the Court of Appeal is not by way of appeal but by motion to set aside the verdict, or motion for a new trial, though in many ways the procedure is the same. The court's power to upset a verdict is more restricted than its power to upset a finding of fact or an award of damages from a judge sitting alone. The appeal is not a rehearing. To upset the verdict the appellant will have to show that there was not sufficient evidence to go to the jury, or that the judge failed to put the issues to the jury satisfactorily, or that the verdict cannot be supported having regard to the evidence, or that no reasonable jury properly directed could have reached it. If the court decides that there was insufficient evidence or that the verdict cannot be supported having regard to the evidence, it can enter judgment for the appellant. In other cases it can order a new trial. Appeals against an award of damages by a jury are made more difficult because the jury does not explain how it has arrived at the sum or what it has allocated to different heads of damage.

There are other circumstances in which the court may order a new trial, for example where the judge has improperly admitted or rejected evidence, or where there has been some irregularity in the trial (*e.g.* where the status of a party was misrepresented to the court), where the judge wrongly refused leave to amend, or where the jury has awarded excessive or inadequate damages. In this last case the court can substitute a new figure with the consent of the parties.

Supreme Court of Judicature (Consolidation) Act 1925

15 & 16 Geo. 5, c. 49

27.—(1) Subject as otherwise provided in this Act and to rules of court, the Court of Appeal shall have jurisdiction to hear and determine appeals from any judgment or order of the High Court, and for all the purposes of and incidental to the hearing and determination of any appeal, and the amendment, execution and enforcement of any judgment or order made thereon, the Court of Appeal shall have all the power, authority and jurisdiction of the High Court:

Provided that an appeal from a judgment or order of the High Court when acting as a prize court shall not lie to the Court of Appeal, but shall lie to His Majesty in Council in accordance with the provisions of the Naval Prize Acts, 1864 to 1916. . . .

30.—(1) Every motion for a new trial, or to set aside a verdict, finding or judgment, in any cause or matter in the High Court in which there has been a trial thereof or of any issue therein with a jury, shall be heard and determined by the Court of Appeal.

(2) Nothing in this section shall alter the practice in any criminal cause or matter or in bankruptcy. . . .

31.—(1) No appeal shall lie . . .

> (*b*) from an order allowing an extension of time for appealing from a judgment or order;
>
> (*c*) from an order of a judge giving unconditional leave to defend an action;
>
> (*d*) from the decision of the High Court or of any judge thereof where it is provided by any Act that the decision of any court or judge, the jurisdiction of which or of whom is now vested in the High Court, is to be final;
>
> (*e*) from an order absolute for the dissolution or nullity of marriage in favour of any party who having had time and opportunity to appeal from the decree nisi on which the order was founded, has not appealed from that decree;
>
> (*f*) without the leave of the divisional court or of the Court of Appeal, from the determination by a divisional court of any appeal to the High Court . . .
>
> (*h*) without the leave of the court or judge making the order, from an order of the High Court or any judge thereof made with the consent of the parties or as to costs only which by law are left to the discretion of the court;
>
> (*i*) without the leave of the judge or of the Court of Appeal from any interlocutory order or interlocutory judgment made or given by a judge, except in the following cases, namely—
>
>> (i) where the liberty of the subject or the custody of infants is concerned;
>>
>> (ii) where an injunction or the appointment of a receiver is granted or refused; . . .
>>
>> (iv) in the case of a decree nisi in a matrimonial cause or a judgment or order in an admiralty action determining liability;
>>
>> (v) in the case of an order on a special case stated under the Arbitration Act, 1889;
>>
>> (vi) in such other cases, to be prescribed, as are in the opinion of the authority having power to make rules of court of the nature of final decisions; . . .

(*l*) from an order refusing leave for the institution or continuance of legal proceedings by a person who is the subject of an order for the time being in force under section fifty-one of this Act.

(2) An order refusing unconditional leave to defend an action shall not be deemed to be an interlocutory order within the meaning of this section.

(3) In matters of practice and procedure every appeal from a judge shall be to the Court of Appeal.

32. The jurisdiction vested in . . . the Court of Appeal . . . shall, so far as regards procedure and practice, be exercised in the manner provided by this Act or by rules of court, and where no special provision is contained in this Act or in rules of court with reference thereto, any such jurisdiction shall be exercised as nearly as may be in the same manner as that in which it might have been exercised by the court to which it formerly appertained.

68.—(1) Subject to the provisions of this Act every appeal to the Court of Appeal which is an appeal against a final order or judgment, or is by way of motion for a new trial or to set aside a verdict, finding or judgment in any cause or matter in the High Court in which there has been a trial thereof or of any issue therein with a jury, shall be heard before not less than three judges of the Court of Appeal, and every such appeal shall, when it is an appeal against an interlocutory order or judgment, be heard before not less than two judges of that court.

(4) No judge of the Court of Appeal shall sit as a judge on the hearing of an appeal from a judgment or order made in any case by himself or by any divisional court of the High Court of which he was a member.

(5) Notwithstanding anything in the foregoing provisions of this section, if all parties to an appeal or motion before the hearing file a consent to the appeal or motion being heard and determined before two judges of the Court of Appeal, the appeal or motion may be heard and determined accordingly. . . .

69.—(1) In any cause or matter pending before the Court of Appeal, any direction incidental thereto not involving the decision of the appeal may be given by a single judge of that court. . . .

Rules of the Supreme Court 1965

ORDER 59

1. This Order applies, subject to the provisions of these rules with respect to particular appeals, to every appeal to the Court of Appeal . . . not being an appeal for which other provision is made by these rules).

2. This Order (except so much of rule 3 (1) as provides that an appeal shall be by way of rehearing and except rule 11 (1)) applies to an application to the Court of Appeal for a new trial or to set aside a verdict, finding or judgment after trial with or without a jury, as it applies to an appeal. . . .

3.—(1) An appeal to the Court of Appeal shall be by way of rehearing. . . .

(2) Notice of appeal may be given either in respect of the whole or in respect of any specified part of the judgment or order of the court below; and every such notice must specify the grounds of the appeal and the precise form of the order which the appellant proposes to ask the Court of Appeal to make.

(3) Except with the leave of the Court of Appeal, the appellant shall not be entitled on the hearing to rely on grounds of appeal, or to apply for any relief, not specified in the notice of appeal. . . .

10.—(1) In relation to an appeal the Court of Appeal shall have all the powers and duties as to amendment and otherwise of the High Court including . . . the powers of the Court under Order 36 to refer any question or issue of fact for trial before, or inquiry and report by, an official referee. . . .

(2) The Court of Appeal shall have power to receive further evidence on questions of fact, either by oral examination in court, by affidavit, or by deposition taken before an examiner, but, in the case of an appeal from a judgment after trial or hearing of any cause or matter on the merits, no such further evidence (other than evidence as to matters which have occurred after the date of the trial or hearing) shall be admitted except on special grounds.

(3) The Court of Appeal shall have power to draw inferences of fact and to give any judgment and make any order which ought to have been given or made, and to make such further or other order as the case may require.

(4) The powers of the Court of Appeal under the foregoing provisions of this rule may be exercised notwithstanding that no notice of appeal or respondent's notice has been given in respect of any particular part of the decision of the court below . . . or that any ground for allowing the appeal or for affirming or varying the decision of that court is not specified in such a notice; and the Court of Appeal may make any order, on such terms as the Court thinks just, to ensure the determination on the merits of the real question in controversy between the parties.

(5) The Court of Appeal may, in special circumstances, order that such security shall be given for the costs of an appeal as may be just.

11.—(1) On the hearing of any appeal the Court of Appeal may, if it thinks fit, make any such order as could be made in pursuance of an application for a new trial or to set aside a verdict, finding or judgment of the court below.

(2) The Court of Appeal shall not be bound to order a new trial on the ground of misdirection, or of the improper admission or rejection of evidence, or because the verdict of the jury was not taken upon a question which the judge at the trial was not asked to leave to them, unless in the opinion of the Court of Appeal some substantial wrong or miscarriage has been thereby occasioned.

(4) In any case where the Court of Appeal has power to order a new trial on the ground that damages awarded by a jury are excessive or inadequate, the Court may, in lieu of ordering a new trial—

(a) with the consent of all parties concerned, substitute for the sum awarded by the jury such sum as appears to the Court to be proper;

(b) with the consent of the party entitled to receive or liable to pay the damages, as the case may be, reduce or increase the sum awarded by the jury by such amount as appears to the Court to be proper in respect of any distinct head of damages erroneously included in or excluded from the sum so awarded;

but except as aforesaid the Court of Appeal shall not have power to reduce or increase the damages awarded by a jury.

12. Where any question of fact is involved in an appeal, the evidence taken in the court below bearing on the question shall, subject to any direction of the Court of Appeal, be brought before that Court as follows:— . . .

(b) in the case of evidence given orally, by a copy of so much of the transcript of the official shorthand note as is relevant or by a copy of the judge's note, where he has intimated that in the event of an appeal his note will be sufficient, or by such other means as the Court of Appeal may direct.

Report of the Committee on Supreme Court Practice and Procedure
Cmd. 8878, 1953

67. We have carefully considered but have decided to reject the procedure generally favoured in other countries, including the United States of America, of " written briefs " for the Court of Appeal in addition to, but in large measure in substitution for, the oral arguments. The grounds for our rejection appear in paragraph 574. We mention here only one of them. Approximately one-third of the cases coming before the Court of Appeal are County Court appeals normally conducted by junior counsel and normally occupying less than a day for hearing. In addition, an appreciable number of the appeals from the three Divisions of the High Court are cases of no greater duration or (sometimes) substance. The separation of the two branches of the legal profession is here an important consideration. For the preparation of the written brief counsel, we assume, would be instructed. He would charge, and be entitled to charge, a proper fee. And, although it is possible that the separate fee for the oral argument might be reduced, we feel little doubt that in a substantial number of the total appeals the result would be to increase rather than to reduce costs. Nor can we see that the hearing of appeals would be likely to be accelerated. On the other hand we recommend that an appellant, in his notice of appeal, should be bound to state the grounds upon which he proposes to rely, and also that a respondent should be bound to give notice to an appellant of any new point he proposes to take on the hearing of the appeal in support of the judgment. . . .

574. . . . Our reasons for arriving at these conclusions are briefly as follows:

(a) We are satisfied that there are real and substantial advantages in our system of unrestricted oral argument, whereby every point in a party's case is thoroughly sifted in the process of discussion between counsel and the members of the Court. Furthermore, our system enables the members of the Court to work together as a team, each member having the advantage of hearing the questions put by the other members and of weighing the answers of counsel thereto. Under this system, it is thought, there is a far greater chance of the Court arriving at a common conclusion, so that in the majority of cases the parties have the advantage of a unanimous decision, and the Court's decision on the question in issue carries all the greater authority.

(b) By contrast, the system prevailing in the United States leads to a higher proportion of dissenting judgments. It has seemed to us that the members of the appellate Court, reading the " briefs " and documents for themselves, and without the advantages of hearing unrestricted oral argument together, must tend to bring their individual minds to the case rather than work as a team.

(c) Under the American system there is likely to be much greater delay in reaching a decision. Having regard to the time which must be allowed for filing the " briefs "—first that of the appellant, then that of the respondent, and possibly a " brief " in reply by the appellant—a considerable time must elapse before the case can be brought on for hearing. What is perhaps more serious is the fact that the Court can rarely deliver judgment at once. . . . [A]lmost every judgment must be reserved, and we were informed that it is not uncommon for a substantial time to elapse, often extending to many months, before the judgments are delivered.

(d) Perhaps the strongest objection to the introduction in this country of anything resembling the American system for conducting appeals arises from the fact that here the legal profession is divided into two branches. The system works in America largely because the profession is differently organised. The American lawyer is a member of a firm and has at his disposal an office staff of trained lawyers. The lawyer who is conducting the case can thus be relieved of the spade-work of preparing the written "brief", which a more junior member of the firm's staff can do. It is not difficult to fix a fair inclusive fee to cover the whole conduct of an appeal, including both the preparation of the "brief" in the office and the oral argument in Court. If a similar system were adopted in this country, it is not to be thought that solicitors would find it possible, even if it were otherwise desirable, to prepare the "briefs" in their offices. Few solicitors' offices in this country would have the staff to do so; and in any case it would be unfair to counsel who would be instructed to conduct the oral argument that he should have no hand in preparing the written "brief". In practice it would be inevitable that counsel would be employed to settle the "brief". The time which counsel would spend on doing so would not usually be less than and might often far exceed, the time which under the present system would be occupied in conducting the oral argument.... It is true that a somewhat smaller fee than that now paid would possibly be sufficient to cover the abbreviated oral argument and there would be no refreshers. At the same time it is to be remembered that counsel would have to get up the case twice—once for the purpose of preparing the "brief" and again for the oral argument, for which purpose he would have to be prepared for any point that might be raised against him in Court. Bearing in mind this additional burden on counsel, we do not think that any marked reduction in counsel's fees could be expected. On the contrary, the over-all total of counsel's fees for the preparation and hearing of an appeal might well be greater than it is at present. . . .

Practice Note

[1962] 1 All E.R. 897

The following statement was read by Lord Evershed, M.R., at the sitting of the court on March 22, 1962.

It will be generally known that there came to London last July, as guests of H.M. Government, a distinguished party of lawyers from the U.S.A. representing the Institute of Judicial Administration. . . . The object of the visit was to examine and compare the work in our two countries of appellate courts, civil and criminal. . . . [A]ll the American visitors, without exception, have drawn attention to the length of time so frequently taken in this court by the reading of documents, including the judgment under appeal and the cases therein cited; and it has been pointed out (with truth) that the result must often be substantially to increase the costs which, under our system, one or other of the parties or (in appropriate cases) in whole or part the legal aid fund will have to pay. . . .

It has not been suggested by any member of the English "team" [which paid a return visit to the United States] that we should in this country adopt the American system of written briefs and the limitation of time spent on oral arguments. On the other hand the unanimity of the American comments, when added to the recommendations of the Committee on Supreme Court Practice and Procedure, have persuaded my colleagues and myself in this court that it would be worth while making an experiment aimed at a real reduction in the time taken, through mere recitation, in this court and therefore at a real reduction in costs; but without at all fettering the right of counsel to full oral argument of their cases. For the purposes of such experiment each member of the court will have read (a) the pleadings or the originating summons (or their equivalent) (b) the order under appeal (c) the notice of appeal and respondent's notice (if any) and (d) the judgment of the learned judge, together with any cases cited by him in his judgment. It is proposed to introduce the experiment in this court with the appeals tribunal list next week and so in each such appeal we shall all have read beforehand the Case Stated, the order made by the tribunal, the notice of appeal and the decision, together with any cases cited in the decision.

I wish to emphasise again that what is suggested is by way of experiment; the results will depend on the event. . . .

One final point: the recommendation of the Committee on Supreme Court Practice and Procedure about stating the grounds of appeal in notices of appeal has, of course, been implemented by amendment of the rules of court. There is, however, in our experience, considerable variation in the quality of the stated grounds. When the grounds have been carefully and thoughtfully prepared their usefulness has been very great—both in assisting the court to appreciate the points involved and also in limiting the scope of the arguments and therefore assisting the respondent and limiting the costs, e.g., of copying of documents. At the other end of the scale the grounds of appeal may be comparable to a pleading in a personal injury case in cumulative numbers and uninformative brevity of individual items. May I then take this opportunity of asking counsel, in the best interests of our system of administration of justice and of the litigants who come to this court, to pay real regard to the purpose and therefore the formulation of grounds of appeal.

Compare Danckwerts L.J. in *Rondel* v. *Worsley* [1]:

The solicitor acting for Rondel was allowed to present to us a typewritten document of 116 pages, in which he set out the legal arguments on behalf of the plaintiff's case, something in the style of the briefs which are allowed under the quite different procedure of the courts of the United States of America. Secondly, at the conclusion of the arguments by counsel on behalf of the defendant, Rondel was allowed to read nine typewritten pages, in the form of a reply which had obviously been prepared for him, notwithstanding that the arguments on his behalf had been presented by counsel instructed by the Official Solicitor, who were ready to make such arguments in reply as were proper. Both these matters were wholly irregular and contrary to the practice of the court, and in my opinion should not be allowed as a precedent for future proceedings. It appears that counsel was in fact available to appear for Rondel without a fee, and the course mentioned above was deliberately adopted.

THE SCOPE OF THE APPEAL

Raising new points

See *Esso Petroleum Co. Ltd.* v. *Southport Corporation* and *Lever Bros.* v. *Bell.* [2]

North Staffordshire Ry. Co. v. Edge
[1920] A.C. 254

LORD BIRKENHEAD L.C.: . . . The efficiency and the authority of a Court of Appeal, and especially of a final Court of Appeal, are increased and

[1] [1967] 1 Q.B. 443.
[2] [1956] A.C. 218; [1931] 1 K.B. 557, above, pp. 349–350.

strengthened by the opinions of learned judges who have considered these matters below. To acquiesce in such an attempt as the appellants have made in this case is in effect to undertake decisions which may be of the highest importance without having received any assistance at all from the judges in the Courts below. Decisions of this House have laid it down that in very exceptional cases, and in spite of the considerations above referred to, new matters may be considered by your Lordships: see the judgment of Lord Halsbury in *Sutherland* v. *Thomson* [3] and the judgment of Lord Watson in *Connecticut Fire Insurance Co.* v. *Kavanagh.* [4] I have carefully examined the cases upon the subject which have been decided in this House, and my examination of them has led me more and more to the conclusion that such attempts must be vigilantly examined and seldom indulged. . . .

See also *Snell* v. *Unity Finance Co. Ltd.,* [5] where the Court of Appeal said that where it was satisfied that it had all the facts before it and it was clear from them that the contract it was being asked to enforce had an illegal object, then it would not enforce the contract whether the illegality had been pleaded or not.

Fresh evidence

Order 59, rule 10 (2) provides that the Court of Appeal will only receive fresh evidence which existed at the time of the trial " on special grounds." The cases of *Braddock* v. *Tillotson's Newspapers Ltd.* [6] and *Ladd* v. *Marshall* [7] set out the general principles. *Meek* v. *Fleming* [8] is an unusual case as it has not to do with the substance of the case but the way in which it was conducted. It is less a case in which " fresh evidence " is being brought than a case in which evidence about the trial itself is being used to challenge the judgment. It should be compared with those cases in which attempts have been made to challenge a decision because of alleged misconduct by the jury. There the court has always been reluctant to admit the evidence if it concerned what went on in the jury room. There have been problems in connection with awards of damages, because of the principle that damages should be assessed once and for all. Unlike the other cases, here the cases have been concerned chiefly with events occurring since the judgment in the court below.

Braddock v. Tillotson's Newspapers Ltd.
Court of Appeal [1950] 1 K.B. 47

TUCKER L.J.: . . . It has been the invariable practice of the Court of Appeal in this country to confine the admission of fresh evidence, in circumstances such as this, to evidence which could not reasonably have been discovered before the trial, and to evidence which, if believed, either would be conclusive or, as has been said by some judges, to evidence which would lead to the reasonable probability that the verdict would have been different. But the practice has

---

[3] [1906] A.C. 51.
[4] [1892] A.C. 473.
[5] [1964] 2 Q.B. 203.
[6] [1950] 1 K.B. 47.
[7] [1954] 3 All E.R. 745.
[8] [1961] 2 Q.B. 366.

hitherto been confined to evidence relating to an issue in the case, or at any rate to an issue which could and might yet be raised if there were a new trial in the action. No case has been cited in which this court has ever admitted or has ever been asked to admit evidence going to credit only. That, of course, is not conclusive . . . but the invariable practice is clear, and furthermore, when one comes to apply the first test, namely, whether the evidence could have been discovered by reasonable diligence before the trial, that language is really hardly applicable to evidence of this kind, because in the ordinary normal events a solicitor or a client would not be expected, in the absence of unusual circumstances, to go rummaging about, if I may so call it, into the past records of any witness he may think was to be called. In fact, generally speaking, he would not know who the witnesses were who were going to be called. . . . There has been some variation in the language used by judges as to the quality of new evidence required by the court, before it shall be admitted, namely, whether it must be such as is presumably to be believed, and if believed would be conclusive; or that it is sufficient if there is a reasonable possibility that, if brought before the jury, a different verdict would have been given. In the case of *Brown* v. *Dean*,[9] Lord Loreburn L.C., said this: " My Lords, the chief effect of the argument which your Lordships have heard is to confirm in my mind the extreme value of the old doctrine ' Interest reipublicae ut sit finis litium,' remembering as we should that people who have means at their command are easily able to exhaust the resources of a poor antagonist. . . . When a litigant has obtained a judgment in a court of justice . . . he is by law entitled not to be deprived of that judgment without very solid grounds; and where (as in this case) the ground is the alleged discovery of new evidence, it must at least be such as is presumably to be believed, and if believed would be conclusive." With regard to that, Lord Atkinson concurred; Lord Shaw, however, said: " My Lords, I concur, but I hope your Lordships will forgive me for expressing doubt upon a single point . . . Speaking for myself, I do not at present see my way to go the whole length of the proposition my noble and learned friend the Lord Chancellor has proposed, to the effect that the res noviter veniens must, if believed, be conclusive. It is possible to figure cases in which it might be so gravely material and so clearly relevant as to entitle the court to say that that material and relevant fact should have been before the jury in giving its decision.". . .

These varying expressions have, so far as the decisions of the courts in this country are concerned, always been directed to evidence directly relevant to the main issue in the action, or to some issue which could, or would, have been raised at the trial if the evidence had been discovered. It is not necessary in this case to express any opinion as to which is the better view with regard to the quality of the evidence in such a case. If, however, this court is to depart from its invariable practice of confining such evidence to the relevant issues and is to admit fresh evidence directed solely to credit, I am of opinion that such a course would, if ever, only be justified where the evidence is of such a nature and the circumstances of the case are such that no reasonable jury could be expected to act upon the evidence of the witness whose character had been called in question. It would, in my view, be wrong for this court to admit fresh evidence directed solely to credit, merely because there is a possibility, or merely a reasonable probability, that such evidence would result in a different verdict. There are two conflicting principles always operating in these matters; one is that everything should be done in order to ascertain the truth; the other is that there should be some finality in litigation, and, so far as possible, a reasonable limitation of costs. It is in order to achieve the latter result that it is necessary

[9] [1910] A.C. 373, 374.

for the court to impose some limit to the reopening of decided issues, even at the risk that injustice may result, or it may appear that there is a possibility of injustice resulting. . . .

COHEN L.J.: . . . This application is, . . . so far as this court is concerned, without precedent. . . . When I say " without precedent," I am not overlooking the case in the Court of Criminal Appeal . . . *Rex* v. *Hamilton*,[10] . . . but . . . that . . . case is different in two material respects. First, the evidence which it was sought to adduce in that case as to credit was evidence disproving facts alleged at the trial; and secondly, there is a radical distinction between criminal and civil cases. In civil cases the interest of the republic is " ut sit finis litium "; whereas in criminal cases the dominant and paramount interest is that an innocent man should not be pronounced guilty. It was no doubt for this reason that the Crown, in *Hamilton's* case (1), did not seek to oppose the application to have the witness recalled for cross-examination. . . .

[SINGLETON L.J. delivered a concurring judgment.]

Ladd v. Marshall

Court of Appeal [1954] 3 All E.R. 745

LORD DENNING M.R.: . . . In order to justify the reception of fresh evidence or a new trial, three conditions must be fulfilled: first, it must be shown that the evidence could not have been obtained with reasonable diligence for use at the trial; second, the evidence must be such that, if given, it would probably have an important influence on the result of the case, although it need not be decisive; third, the evidence must be such as is presumably to be believed, or in other words, it must be apparently credible, although it need not be incontrovertible. We have to apply those principles to the case where a witness comes and says: " I told a lie but nevertheless I now want to tell the truth." It seems to me that the fresh evident of such a witness will not as a rule satisfy the third condition. A confessed liar cannot usually be accepted as credible. To justify the reception of the fresh evidence, some good reason must be shown why a lie was told in the first instance, and good ground given for thinking the witness will tell the truth on the second occasion. If it were proved that the witness had been bribed or coerced into telling a lie at the trial, and was now anxious to tell the truth, that would, I think, be a ground for a new trial, and it would not be necessary to resort to an action to set aside the judgment on the ground of fraud. Again, if it were proved that the witness made a mistake on a most important matter and wished to correct it, and the circumstances were so well explained that his fresh evidence was presumably to be believed, then again there would be ground for a new trial: see *Richardson* v. *Fisher*.[11] This, however, is not a case of bribery or coercion, nor of mistake. . . . I am afraid it is simply a case of a witness who has told a lie at the first hearing now wishing to say something different. It would be contrary to all principles for that to be the ground for a new trial.

HODSON L.J.: . . . I wish to make only a brief reference to the well-known case of *Brown* v. *Dean* [12] where . . . Lord Loreburn . . . says: " . . . [T]he . . . new evidence . . . must at least be such as . . . if believed would be conclusive." . . .

[10] 13 Cr.App.R. 32.
[11] (1823) 1 Bing. 145; 130 E.R. 59.
[12] [1910] A.C. 373.

[T]he more modern cases have proceeded on the view that perhaps " conclusive " is too strong a word. . . .

[PARKER L.J. agreed.]

Meek v. Fleming

Court of Appeal [1961] 2 Q.B. 366

The plaintiff was claiming damages for assault and wrongful arrest. The defendant was a chief inspector at the time of the incident who had arrested the plaintiff. Unknown to the plaintiff and his advisers, between the issue of the writ and the trial the defendant had been reduced to the rank of station sergeant after he had been found guilty of a disciplinary offence involving the deception of a court. The defendant's advisers decided that it would prejudice their client's case if this were known and they and the witnesses who appeared on his behalf were careful not to reveal the fact and not to correct the judge or plaintiff's counsel when they referred to the defendant as an inspector. It was clear to the Court of Appeal that the trial court and the jury were influenced by the fact that the defendant was in their view a senior officer of the Metropolitan Police Force and as such entitled to be believed. In the circumstances the plaintiff was allowed to bring before the court the evidence of what had happened to support his application for a new trial.

HOLROYD PEARCE L.J.: . . . This court is rightly loth to order a new trial on the ground of fresh evidence. Interest reipublicae ut sit finis litium. . . . In the case of fresh evidence relating to an issue in the case, the court will not order a new trial unless such evidence would probably have an important influence on the result of the case . . . *Ladd* v. *Marshall*. . . . Where . . . the fresh evidence does not relate directly to an issue, but is merely evidence as to the credibility of an important witness, this court applies a stricter test. . . . *Braddock* v. *Tillotson's Newspapers Ltd.* . . . Where [however] a party deliberately misleads the court in a material matter, and that deception has probably tipped the scale in his favour (or even, as I think, where it may reasonably have done so), it would be wrong to allow him to retain the judgment thus unfairly procured. Finis litium is a desirable object, but it must not be sought by so great a sacrifice of justice which is and must remain the supreme object. Moreover, to allow the victor to keep the spoils so unworthily obtained would be an encouragement to such behaviour, and do even greater harm than the multiplication of trials.

In every case it must be a question of degree, weighing one principle against the other. In this case it is clear that the judge and jury were misled on an important matter. . . . [S]ince the defendant and his advisers thought fit to take so serious a step, they must, in the light of their own intimate knowledge of their case, have regarded the concealment as being of overwhelming importance to their success. . . . It may well be that it was not so clear in prospect as it is in retrospect how wide the web of deceit would be woven before the verdict came to be given. But in the event it spread over all the evidence of the defendant. It affected the summing-up of the judge, and it must have affected the deliberations of the jury. The defendant and his legal advisers, and probably some at least of his witnesses . . . were aware of the facts, and intent not to reveal them, in order . . . that the defendant might be thereby enabled to masquerade as a chief inspector of unblemished reputation enjoying such advantage as that status and character would give him at the trial. It would be an intolerable infraction of the principles of justice to allow the defendant to retain a verdict thus obtained. I would, accordingly, allow the appeal with costs, and order a new trial.

WILLMER and PEARSON L.JJ. delivered concurring judgments.[13]

APPEALS ON QUESTIONS OF FACT

Watt or Thomas v. Thomas

House of Lords [1947] A.C. 484

VISCOUNT SIMON:... If there is no evidence to support a particular conclusion (and this is really a question of law), the appellate court will not hesitate so to decide. But if the evidence as a whole can reasonably be regarded as justifying the conclusion arrived at at the trial, and especially if that conclusion has been arrived at on conflicting testimony by a tribunal which saw and heard the witnesses, the appellate court will bear in mind that it has not enjoyed this opportunity and that the view of the trial judge as to where credibility lies is entitled to great weight. This is not to say that the judge of first instance can be treated as infallible in determining which side is telling the truth or is refraining from exaggeration. Like other tribunals, he may go wrong on a question of fact, but it is a cogent circumstance that a judge of first instance, when estimating the value of verbal testimony, has the advantage (which is denied to courts of appeal) of having the witnesses before him and observing the manner in which their evidence is given. What I have just said reproduces in effect the view previously expressed in this House—for example by Viscount Sankey L.C. in *Powell* v. *Streatham Manor Nursing Home*,[14] and in earlier cases there quoted. Lord Greene M.R. admirably stated the limitations to be observed in the course of his judgment in *Yuill* v. *Yuill*.[15]... It not infrequently happens that a preference for A.'s evidence over the contrasted evidence of B. is due to inferences from other conclusions reached in the judge's mind, rather than from an unfavourable view of B.'s veracity as such: in such cases it is legitimate for an appellate tribunal to examine the grounds of these other conclusions and the inferences drawn from them, if the materials admit of this; and if the appellate tribunal is convinced that these inferences are erroneous, and that the rejection of B.'s evidence was due to the error, it will be justified in taking a different view of the value of B.'s evidence. I would only add that the decision of an appellate court whether or not to reverse conclusions of fact reached by the judge at the trial must naturally be affected by the nature and circumstances of the case under consideration. What I have said applies to appeals from a judge sitting alone. Conclusions of fact embodied in the verdict of a jury cannot be subjected to the same degree of re-examination—for the course of reasoning by which the verdict has been reached is not disclosed—and consequently the verdict of a jury on fact must stand if there was any evidence to support it and if the conclusion is one at which a reasonable jury when properly directed might reasonably arrive....

[13] *Cf. Skone* v. *Skone* [1971] 1 W.L.R. 812, where the House of Lords admitted fresh evidence which suggested that the respondent in a divorce petition had not been telling the truth and granted a new trial.
[14] [1935] A.C. 243, 250. Above, p. 167.
[15] [1945] P. 15, 19. Above, p. 168.

Compare Scrutton L.J. in *Place* v. *Searle*,[15a] where he said:

> ... An enormously strong case is needed before the Court of Appeal
> can say that though there is evidence given by a witness it cannot
> reasonably be believed by the jury. Unless we get such a case as that,
> we must assume in considering the question whether there is any
> evidence on which the jury could reasonably find a verdict for the
> plaintiff, that they accepted the evidence in favour of the plaintiff and
> disbelieved the evidence given in favour of the defendant....

See also Lord Sumner in *S.S. Hontestroom* v. *S.S. Sagaporack*.[16]

APPEALS ON QUESTIONS OF DAMAGES

Scott v. Musial

Court of Appeal [1959] 2 Q.B. 429

MORRIS L.J.: ... In the present case there was a jury. It is now said that
their award was excessive. In considering this matter, the approach of the court
is different from its approach in cases tried by a judge alone. Where there is an
appeal from the decision of a judge sitting alone, the appeal is by way of
rehearing. The rehearing applies to the issue of damages as well as to other
issues. But it is recognised that the fixation of damages is so largely a matter
of opinion or of impression that differences of calculation or assessment are
be be expected. There is, to some extent, an exercise of judicial discretion.
It is for this reason that, if three judges of the Court of Appeal consider
that the amount of general damages that they would have awarded would
have been a figure different from that decided by the trial judge, they will not,
for that reason alone, give preference to their own figure; they will only do so
if satisfied that the judge has acted on a wrong principle of law or has misappre-
hended the facts, or has, for those or other reasons, made a wholly erroneous
estimate of the damage suffered: see the speech of Lord Wright in *Davies* v.
Powell Duffryn Associated Collieries Ltd. (*No.* 2).[17] But, if there has been an
assessment of damages by a jury, the function of the Court of Appeal on a complaint that the damages are too high or too low is different. Where the order
of the court has been that trial is to be with a jury, then twelve jurors have
collectively (and, be it remembered, unanimously) to decide on an assessment.
On appeal, always assuming that the trial has been properly conducted and that
the jury have been properly directed, it is not for the members of the Court of
Appeal to seek to substitute their assessment and their judgment for that of the
jury; the function of the Court of Appeal is then directed to considering whether
or not the figure stated by the jury is out of all proportion to the circumstances
of the case. Unless it is, this court must not interfere. The jury do not have
to give reasons, and it may be impossible to deduce how the jury have regarded
the particular individual features of a claim, such as, for example, in a personal
injuries case, pain and suffering, deprivation of the amenities of life, and future
possible loss of earnings. To warrant any interference with the award of a jury
it is not enough to say that the award is more, or even much more, or less, or
even much less, than what the judges of the Court of Appeal would consider
to be the appropriate amount. The Court of Appeal will not interfere if the
figure is one which a jury, acting properly, might award. Interference will be

---

15a [1932] 2 K.B. 497.
16 [1927] A.C. 37.   17 [1942] A.C. 601, 616.

justified if it is made to appear that the jury must have acted improperly and so have brought about a palpably wrong result. If the figure of an award seems to be outrageous, or so extravagant that no other jury would repeat it, then there might, in some cases, be ground for suspecting that a jury has been partial or perverse. But, as the Court of Appeal will only have the figure, as announced by the jury, to consider, the court will have to decide, on a consideration of the figure itself, whether it appears so excessive or so inadequate that no twelve reasonable jurors could reasonably have awarded it; or, stated otherwise, whether the figure appears to be out of all proportion to the circumstances of the case: see the speech of Lord Wright in *Mechanical & General Inventions Co. Ltd.* and *Lehwess* v. *Austin and Austin Motor Co. Ltd.*[18]

In the present case we were referred by Mr. Skelhorn ... to some figures of awards in cases resembling the present one which had been tried by judges alone. He submitted that the award of the jury in the present case should be regarded as being higher than those awarded by judges in comparable cases. Whether this be so or not cannot be in any way decisive in this case.

In cases which are comparable but which are decided by different judges, a certain pattern or level of awards of damages may emerge. If, however, an award of a jury does not seem to conform to such pattern, that is not to prove that the jury is necessarily wrong. The views of juries may form a valuable corrective to the views of judges. The jury will not necessarily have knowledge of any pattern or level which judges have thought to be appropriate, and the jury are not bound by any such pattern or level.

Of course it is inevitable that members of the Court of Appeal, when considering a complaint against the award of a jury, will formulate individual views as to the figure of damages which they themselves would have deemed appropriate. That will be comprehended within, and will be one part of the process of deciding, whether the jury's award is out of all proportion to the circumstances of the case. It must, however, be no more than a part of that process. The figure of an award by a jury is not to be deemed to be wrong merely because judges might have arrived at a different figure....

The judge dealt most carefully with the injuries which the plaintiff has suffered.... The judge was careful to invite the jury to be moderate.... The summing-up of the judge ... was a fair and balanced summing-up which left the matter to the jury for their good judgment. The injuries are undoubtedly grave; the figure of the award is certainly high. On the principles which must guide us, I do not feel that it would be right for us to upset that decision of the jury or to say that their award cannot stand....

McCarey v. Associated Newspapers Ltd.
Court of Appeal [1965] 2 Q.B. 86

WILLMER L.J.:... [I]t is only in exceptional cases that this court can be justified in interfering with an award of damages by a jury, and I think that that applies with particular force to an award of damages in a libel action. I think that the reason for that is to be found in the statement of principle by Lord Herschell in *Bray* v. *Ford*.[19] ... Lord Herschell said:

"In the case of an action for libel not only have the parties a right to trial by jury, but the assessment of damages is peculiarly within the province of that tribunal. The damages cannot be measured by any standard

[18] [1935] A.C. 346, 378.
[19] [1896] A.C. 44.

known to the law; they must be determined by a consideration of all the circumstances of the case, viewed in the light of the law applicable to them. The latitude is very wide."

That being so, I have, as I have said, entertained grave doubts as to whether we should be justified in interfering with the award of damages made by the jury in this case, large though the sum of damages is. There being no standard known to the law whereby to measure the damages which ought to be awarded, one may well ask with what superior wisdom we in this court are endowed which entitles us to set aside an award of a jury on the basis that it is such that no twelve reasonable persons could have arrived at it. . . .

Broome v. Cassell

House of Lords [1972] A.C. 1027

LORD REID: . . . There remains what is perhaps the most difficult question in this case—whether the additional award of £25,000 as punitive damages is so excessive that we can interfere. I think it was much too large, but that is not the test. I would like to be able to hold that the court has more control over an award of punitive damages than it has over an award of compensatory damages. As regards the latter it is quite clear that a court can only interfere if satisfied that no twelve reasonable men could have awarded so large a sum and the reason for that is plain. The court has no power to substitute its own assessment for the verdict of a jury. If it interferes it can only send the matter back to another jury. So before it can interfere it must be well satisfied that no other jury would award so large a sum. I do not see how this House could arrogate to itself any wider power with regard to punitive damages. We could not deprive the plaintiff of his right to a new trial so we must adhere to the established test. Any diminution or abolition of the functions of a jury in libel cases can only come from Parliament. If this case brings nearer the day when Parliament does take action I for one shall not be sorry.

Whether or not we can interfere with this award is a matter which is not capable of much elaboration. In considering how far twelve reasonable men might go, acting as jurors commonly do act, one has to bear in mind how little guidance the court is entitled to give them. All they can be told is that they must not award a sum which is unreasonable. In answer to questions whether anything more definite could properly be said neither counsel in this case was able to make any suggestion and I have none to offer. The evidence in this case is such that the jury could take an extremely unfavourable view of the conduct of both defendants. I do not say that they ought to have done so, but they were entitled to do so. And they must have done so. I find it impossible to say that no jury of reasonable men inexperienced but doing their best with virtually no guidance, could reach the sum of £25,000. Or, to put it in another way. I would feel no confidence that if the matter were submitted to another jury they must reach a substantially different result. So with considerable regret I must hold that it would be contrary to our existing law and practice if this House refused to uphold this verdict.

It is true that in this case the parties agreed that if the verdict for £25,000 were quashed they would leave it to this House to substitute another figure. But that agreement cannot justify us in doing otherwise than we would have done if the parties had stood on their legal rights. The obvious reason for that agreement was a common desire to avoid the enormous expense of a new trial. This is not the first occasion on which I have felt bound to express my concern about the undue prolixity and expense of libel actions. I would not blame any individuals. It may arise from the conduct of a trial before a jury being more expensive than a trial before a judge. If so that is an additional argument for taking these cases away from juries. Or it may be that it suits wealthy publishers of newspapers, books and periodicals that the cost of fighting a libel action is so great that none but a person with large financial backing can sue them effectively. Whatever be the reason the costs of this case have already reached a figure which many laymen would call scandalous. I think that those in a position to take effective action might take note.

Murphy v. Stone-Wallwork Ltd.

House of Lords [1969] 1 W.L.R. 1023

In fixing the amount of damages to be awarded to the appellant for breach of statutory duty by his employers the trial judge had assumed that the appellant would continue to be employed by them on lighter work as he had been for the 2½ years between the accident and the trial. The same assumption was made by the Court of Appeal six months later. A fortnight after the Court of Appeal had given its judgment the appellant was dismissed. The only reason given was his accident.

LORD PEARSON: . . . (1) If it had been established that the defendants were in material respects guilty of bad faith or negligence or oppression in their treatment of the plaintiff, that would undoubtedly have been a good ground for allowing the fresh evidence and reopening the assessment of damages. But to my mind, . . . no such misconduct on the part of the defendants has been established. . . .

(2) The plaintiff is seeking to adduce fresh evidence, not as to any event occurring or condition existing before the date of the judgment appealed from, but only as to an event which has happened after that date. This makes a difference according to the practice of the Court of Appeal, which I think can usefully be taken into account in considering what should be done here. R.S.C., Ord. 59, r. 10 (2) (formerly R.S.C., Ord. 58, r. 9 (2)), provides:

> "The Court of Appeal shall have power to receive further evidence on questions of fact, either by oral examination in court, by affidavit, or by deposition taken before an examiner, but, in the case of an appeal from a judgment after trial or hearing of any cause or matter on the merits, no such further evidence (other than evidence as to matters which have occurred after the date of the trial or hearing) shall be admitted except on special grounds."

Thus, in the Court of Appeal no special grounds are needed for the admission of evidence as to matters which have occurred after the decision of the Court below. The conditions laid down in *Ladd* v. *Marshall* [20] would not be applicable, or not fully applicable, in relation to the admission of evidence of such matters. There must, however, be a discretion to decide whether such evidence is to be admitted or not.

(3) There is not in this case any difficulty arising from any lapse of time. No extension of time is required.

(4) I think it is useful to take into account another aspect of the practice in the Court of Appeal. Under R.S.C., Ord. 59, r. 3 (1) " an appeal to the Court

[20] [1954] 1 W.L.R. 1489.

of Appeal shall be by way of rehearing. . . ." In *A.-G. (at the relation of Tamworth Corpn.)* v. *Birmingham, Tame and Rea District Drainage Board*,[21] where the continuance of an injunction was in question, Lord Gorrell said [22]:

> " Under the Judicature Acts and Rules the hearing of an appeal from the judgment of a judge is by way of rehearing, and the Court has power to give any judgment and to make any order which ought to have been made, and to make such further or other order as the Court may think fit. . . . The Court also has power to take evidence of matters which have occurred after the date of the decision from which the appeal is brought. . . . It seems clear, therefore, that the Court of Appeal is entitled and ought to rehear the case as at the time of rehearing. . . ."

This passage was cited and relied on in *Curwen* v. *James*.[23] That was a case under the Fatal Accidents Act 1846, and the widow had remarried after the judgment of the trial judge but before the hearing in the Court of Appeal. The damages were reassessed in the light of the known fact of the remarriage. Harman L.J., cited *Bwlfa and Merthyr Dare Steam Collieries (1891), Ltd.* v. *Pontypridd Waterworks Co.*[24] and *Re Bradberry, National Provincial Bank, Ltd.* v. *Bradberry, Re Fry, Tasker* v. *Gulliford*,[25] and said [26]:

> " Why should we, when we know that the lady has married, pretend that we do not know it and assess the damages, as we are assessing them anew here, on the footing that she may or may not marry? As we know the truth, we are not bound to believe in a fiction."

I think it is quite clear that if on appeal fresh evidence is admitted as to subsequent events (events occurring after the date of the judgment appealed from) and the fresh evidence justifies a reassessment of the damages, the damages should be reassessed in the light of the relevant facts as known at the date of the reassessment.

(5) But there is still the question whether the fresh evidence should be admitted. It is in general undesirable to admit fresh evidence on appeal, because there ought to be finality in litigation. Interest reipublicae ut sit finis litium. . . . As I said in *Curwen* v. *James* [27]:

> " . . . the normal rule in accident cases is that the sum of damages falls to be assessed once for all at the time of the hearing. When the assessment is made, the court has to make the best estimate it can as to events that, may happen in the future. If further evidence as to new events were too easily admitted, there would be no finality in such litigation. There are quite often uncertain matters which have to be estimated and taken into account to the best of the ability of the judge trying the action."

In *Jenkins* v. *Richard Thomas & Baldwins, Ltd.*,[28] Salmon L.J. said:

> " The general rule is that damages in actions of this type have to be assessed once and for all at the trial. It not infrequently happens that, when damages are assessed at the trial on the basis that the plaintiff will in the future probably be able to earn such and such a sum, it turns out that he is actually able to earn, and does earn, either substantially more or substantially

---

[21] [1912] A.C. 788.
[22] *Ibid.* at p. 801.
[23] [1963] 1 W.L.R. 748, 751, 752, 754.
[24] [1903] A.C. 426, 431.
[25] [1943] Ch. 35, 42.
[26] [1963] 1 W.L.R. 748, 754.
[27] [1963] 1 W.L.R. 748, 755.
[28] [1966] 1 W.L.R. 476, 479.

less. It must not be thought that, whenever this occurs, one side or the other can come to this court and appeal and ask for leave to call further evidence with a view to having the damages reduced or increased as the case may be. If the basis on which the damages have been assessed proves to be wrong very shortly after the trial and the point is promptly taken up, with the other side, then, in the exceptional circumstances, there may be good grounds for this court giving leave, as we have done here, to call further evidence."

I think the question whether or not the fresh evidence is to be admitted has to be decided by an exercise of discretion.... It can be said in the present case that the basis on which the case had been conducted on both sides and decided both at the trial and in the Court of Appeal was suddenly and materially falsi-fied by the change of wind, involving a reversal of policy, on the part of the defendants, and in the circumstances it would not be fair ... to allow the defendants to retain the advantage of the decision given by the Court of Appeal on the basis which has been so falsified. . . .

LORD PEARCE: . . . Our courts have adopted the principle that damages are assessed at the trial once and for all. If later the plaintiff suffers greater loss . . . than was anticipated at the trial, he cannot come back for more. Nor can the defendant come back if the loss is less than was anticipated. Thus, the assess-ment of damages for the future is necessarily compounded of prophecy and calculation. The court must do the best it can to reach what seems to be the right figure on a reasonable balance of the probabilities, avoiding undue optimism and undue pessimism. Although periodic payments and a right of recourse whenever circumstances change might seem an attractive solution of the difficulty, yet they, too, have serious drawbacks such as an unending possibility of litigation which, in the view of the law, have hitherto been held to outweigh the disadvantages of an assessment of damages once and for all. The present case is a classic example of the latter disadvantages if no remedy is available to the appellant. . . .

Appeals Against the Exercise of a Discretion

Evans v. Bartlam

House of Lords [1937] A.C. 473

LORD WRIGHT: . . . The Masters admirably exercise their discretion in routine matters of pleading, discovery, interrogatories, venue, mode of trial, and other interlocutory directions, without any appeal being necessary. But such matters may on occasion raise questions most vital to the final issue of the case. The decision of such questions is properly for the judge who will no doubt consider carefully the order of the Master. If a further appeal is taken to the Court of Appeal it is the judge's discretion which that Court has either to support or vary or reverse. . . . It is clear that the Court of Appeal should not interfere with the discretion of a judge acting within his jurisdiction unless the Court is clearly satisfied that he was wrong. But the Court is not entitled simply to say that if the judge had jurisdiction and had all the facts before him, the Court of Appeal cannot review his order unless he is shown to have applied a wrong principle. The Court must if necessary examine anew the relevant facts and circumstances in order to exercise a discretion by way of review which may reverse or vary the order. Otherwise in interlocutory matters the judge might be regarded as independent of supervision. . . . [T]here are many cases in the books where it has been held that the appellant has satisfied the onus of showing that the exercise of the discretion by the judge was not justified on the facts. A judge's order fixing the date of trial or refusing to grant an adjournment is a typical exercise of purely discretionary powers, and would be interfered with by the Court of Appeal only in exceptional cases, yet it may be reviewed by the Court of Appeal. Thus in *Maxwell* v. *Keun* [29] the Court of Appeal reversed the trial judge's order refusing to the plaintiff an adjournment. . . . A recent case in which the Court of Appeal set aside a judge's order remitting an action in tort to the County Court was *Stevens* v. *Walker*,[30] where it was held that the circumstances did not justify the order. . . . [I]n *Watt* v. *Barnett* [31] . . . the Court of Appeal . . . reversed the order of the judge who had refused to set aside a default judgment. . . .[32]

Ward v. James

Court of Appeal [1966] 1 Q.B. 273

LORD DENNING M.R.: . . . REVIEWING DISCRETION. This brings me to the question: in what circumstances will the Court of Appeal interfere with the discretion of the judge? At one time it was said that it would interfere only if he had gone wrong in principle; but since *Evans* v. *Bartlam*,[33] that idea has been exploded. The true proposition was stated by Lord Wright in *Charles Osenton & Co.* v. *Johnston*.[34] This court can, and will, interfere if it is satisfied that the judge was wrong. Thus it will interfere if it can see that the judge has given no weight (or no sufficient weight) to those considerations which ought to have weighed with him. A good example is *Charles Osenton & Co.* v. *Johnston* [35] itself, where Tucker J. in his discretion ordered trial by an official referee, and the House of Lords reversed the order because he had not given due weight to the fact that the professional reputation of surveyors was at stake. Conversely it will interfere if it can see that he has been influenced by other considerations which ought not to have weighed with him, or not weighed so much with him, as in *Hennell* v. *Ranaboldo*.[36] It sometimes happens that the judge has given reasons which enable this court to know the considerations which have weighed with him; but even if he has given no reasons, the court may infer from the way he has decided, that the judge must have gone wrong in one respect or the other, and will thereupon reverse his decision; see *Grimshaw* v. *Dunbar*.[37]

[29] [1928] 1 K.B. 645.
[30] [1936] 2 K.B. 215.
[31] (1878) 3 Q.B.D. 363.
[32] The approach adopted by Lord Wright in this case has also been followed in cases involving the exercise of discretion not concerning interlocutory matters, *e.g. Thornely* v. *Palmer* [1969] 1 W.L.R. 1037, where the question was whether the Court of Appeal would interfere with the trial judge's decision in a case under the Family Inheritance Act 1938. In *Smith* v. *Smith* [1970] 1 W.L.R. 155, which involved the exercise of discretion in a divorce case, Edmund Davies L.J. said: " [N]owadays this court regards itself as being freer to differ from a trial judge regarding the manner [in which] he has exercised his discretion than it formerly did. It may not be able to pinpoint any error in law; it may find it impossible to say that any m[a]terial matter of fact has been overlooked or that there has been any misapprehension regarding points of evidence. Yet, even in the absence of any patent errors of that sort, if this court nevertheless is clearly convinced that by some means or other the discretion has been exercised in an erroneous manner, then it can rectify such error: see the cases referred to in *Re Thornley Decd.* [1969] 1 W.L.R. 1037, 1042."
[33] [1937] A.C. 473.
[34] [1942] A.C. 130, 148.
[35] [1942] A.C. 130.
[36] [1963] 3 All E.R. 684.
[37] [1953] 1 Q.B. 408.

RULES TO GUIDE DISCRETION. In *Sims* v. *William Howard & Son, Ltd.*,[38] this court laid down a rule for the guidance of the judges. It said that in personal injury cases a jury should not be ordered except in special circumstances. This rule has been challenged. It is said to be an unwarranted fetter on the discretion of the judges. Yet it is of the first importance that some guidance shall be given—else you would find one judge ordering a jury, the next refusing it, and no one would know where he stood. It might make all the difference to the ultimate result of the case. This would give rise to much dissatisfaction. It is an essential attribute of justice in a community that similar decisions should be given in similar cases, and this applies as much to mode of trial as anything else. The only way of achieving this is for the courts to set out the considerations which should guide the judges in the normal exercise of their discretion. And that is what has been done in scores of cases where a discretion has been entrusted to the judges. . . .

The cases all show that, when a statute gives a discretion, the courts must not fetter it by rigid rules from which a judge is never at liberty to depart. Nevertheless the courts can lay down the considerations which should be borne in mind in exercising the discretion and point out those considerations which should be ignored. This will normally determine the way in which the discretion is exercised and thus ensure some measure of uniformity of decision. From time to time the considerations may change as public policy changes, and so the pattern of decision may change. This is all part of the evolutionary process. We have seen it in the way that discretion is exercised in divorce cases. So also in the mode of trial. Whereas it was common to order trial by jury, now it is rare.

APPEALS IN OTHER CIVIL CASES

There are appeals from magistrates' courts in civil cases to the High Court. More important on the civil side however are the provisions for appeal from tribunals on points of law to the High Court, since this links them with the traditional court system and gives the High Court a power of supervision. The courts had already established a wide supervisory jurisdiction over tribunals through the prerogative writs, in particular certiorari. This enabled someone aggrieved by the decision of a tribunal to bring the decision before the High Court and seek to have it quashed if it could be shown that it was given in excess of jurisdiction, or if the rules of natural justice had not been observed, or if there was an error of law appearing on its face.[39] Following on the report of the Franks Committee on Tribunals and Inquiries[40] this jurisdiction was strengthened to some extent by the Tribunals and Inquiries Act 1958, which imposed an obligation on a number of tribunals to give reasons for their decisions, thus exposing any error in their legal reasoning and attracting certiorari if it included an error of law. But the Act went further than this and expressly provided for an appeal on point of law from a number of tribunals, the difference in the case of an appeal being that the High Court can substitute its own judgment and not simply quash the decision that has been brought before it as in the case of certiorari.

---

[38] [1964] 2 Q.B. 409.
[39] *R.* v. *Northumberland Compensation Appeal Tribunal, ex p. Shaw* [1952] 1 K.B. 338.
[40] Cmnd. 218, 1957.

It is important to emphasise that there is no general right of appeal from tribunals to the courts. In some cases it is expressly excluded. The Social Insurance tribunals for example are regarded as a self-contained unit with the Insurance Commissioner as the final court of appeal. In each case it is necessary to see whether a right of appeal has been given by statute. So far as review by certiorari is concerned the reverse is true. All tribunals are subject to supervision by way of certiorari unless this jurisdiction has been excluded by statute.

APPEALS IN CRIMINAL CASES

The Court of Appeal (Criminal Division)

Until 1848 there was no appeal from convictions on indictment. A judge could refer a question of law to his fellow judges informally before he delivered judgment or before sentence was executed. If they took the view that a conviction was mistaken then a recommendation was made that the convicted man should be pardoned. In 1848 this informal procedure was made formal and a Court for Crown Cases Reserved was established. Its scope was broadened by making it available to chairmen of quarter sessions and recorders as well as judges. There was still no appeal on a question of fact, but if it could be shown that the verdict was against the weight of evidence, or that the trial was irregular in some way then a new trial might be ordered. Pressure to establish a proper Court of Appeal for criminal cases was reinforced as a result of the mistaken convictions and imprisonment of Adolf Beck in 1896 and 1904, and in 1908 the Court of Criminal Appeal was set up by the Criminal Appeal Act 1907. The court was not however made a part of the Supreme Court which had been set up by the 1873–75 legislation, though it was staffed by the Lord Chief Justice and judges from the Queen's Bench Division.

In August 1965 an interdepartmental committee [41] recommended that the court should at the least become part of the Supreme Court, but it also recommended that it should cease to exist as a separate court altogether and that criminal appeals should in future be heard by a new Criminal Division of the Court of Appeal. The main reason for this recommendation was the hope that it would lead to the development of more uniform and consistent policies in criminal cases at the appellate level. Although the Court of Criminal Appeal was staffed by the Lord Chief Justice and the judges of the Queen's Bench Division, the actual composition of the court for particular cases was constantly changing. Some amelioration of the position had resulted from the Lord Chief Justices' practice of appointing a senior

---

[41] The committee under Lord Donovan was appointed in February 1964 to consider and report: " (1) Whether it would be in the public interest to transfer the hearing of all or some of the cases now heard by the Court of Criminal Appeal . . . to the Court of Appeal or some other court; and if so, as to the manner in which that Court should be constituted, the powers it should have and the procedure to be followed; (2) If in the view of the committee the Court of Criminal Appeal should retain the whole or part of its current jurisdiction whether any and if so what changes are desirable (a) in the constitution, powers, practice and procedure of the court; (b) in the system and procedure for giving notice of appeal and applications and in the functions and practice of the Criminal Appeal Office." It reported in August 1965 (Cmnd. 2755).

judge for a year at a time to sit with him and preside over a second division when that was needed but this had not solved the problem. The committee cited examples of inconsistencies which still occurred, *e.g.* in relation to the relevance to sentence of the fact that the appellant had not been convicted of an offence for some time before and the effect of a judge's failure to ask the accused if he had anything to say before sentence was passed on him. The Hanworth Committee on the Business of the Courts which had considered the question in its Second Interim Report had come to a similar conclusion and had in fact recommended that the appellate jurisdiction of the Divisional Court should be transferred to the Court of Appeal as well. The later Evershed Committee had taken a contrary view. It had, however, considered the question mainly from the point of view of possible conflict between decisions of the Court of Appeal on the civil side and the Court of Criminal Appeal on the criminal, as had occurred in the cases of *Hardie and Lane Ltd.* v. *Chilton* [42] and *R.* v. *Denyer,* [43] a conflict which was not resolved until the House of Lords decision in *Thorne* v. *Motor Trade Association.* [44] In the view of the Evershed Committee such conflicts were too rare to justify a transfer of jurisdiction.

The recommendation of the Donovan Committee was carried into effect in the Criminal Appeal Act 1968. Other recommendations of the Committee were carried into effect at the same time.

One aspect of the court's jurisdiction, its power to order new trials, had already been considered by an earlier committee appointed in 1952. [45] Its recommendation that the court should be given this power when it allowed fresh evidence to be considered was given effect by the Criminal Appeal Act 1964, now sections 7 and 23 of the Criminal Appeal Act 1968. There is no appeal against acquittal in cases tried on indictment. There may be an appeal against conviction even after a plea of guilty.

Report of the Departmental Committee on New Trials in Criminal Cases

Cmd. 9150, 1954

5. When the Criminal Appeal Bill was introduced into Parliament in 1907, it was decided not to proceed by way of new trial and not to give a right of appeal by way of rehearing, as in civil cases. . . . In respect of convictions the Court of Criminal Appeal were, however, given the power to grant a writ of *venire de novo* in cases where they held that the trial had been a nullity. The Bill was framed to afford a right of appeal on certain specific grounds and to impose on the Court of Criminal Appeal the duty to quash the conviction and substitute a verdict of acquittal if the appeal succeeded, subject, however, to the proviso that the Court may dismiss the appeal " if they consider that no substantial miscarriage of justice has actually occurred " (section 4 (1) of the

---

[42] [1928] 2 K.B. 306.
[43] [1926] 2 K.B. 258.
[44] [1937] A.C. 797.
[45] The committee under Lord Tucker was appointed to consider: " Whether the Court of Criminal Appeal and the House of Lords should be empowered to order a new trial of a convicted person who has appealed to the Court . . . or whose case has been referred to the Court by the Secretary of State, and, if so, in what circumstances and subject to what safeguards." It reported in May 1954 (Cmd. 9150).

Criminal Appeal Act, 1907).... But the Court were given very wide supplemental powers ... and not limited to applications to call fresh evidence, to require the attendance of any witness, whether he gave evidence at the trial or not, to be examined before the Court and to take other action " if they think it necessary or expedient in the interests of justice " (section 9 of the Criminal Appeal Act, 1907).

6. .... [I]t may well have been thought by some, at the time the Act was passed, that the powers given to the Court of Criminal Appeal by section 9 coupled with the proviso to section 4 (1) ... would enable the Court, in suitable cases, virtually to re-try the case. It is clear, however, that from the time they were established the Court of Criminal Appeal have never considered it to be any part of their duty to substitute their verdict for that of the jury....

7. Once the proviso to section 4 (1) ... was approached by the Court of Criminal Appeal from the standpoint that they could not substitute themselves for the jury, it became obvious that the cases in which the proviso can be used are comparatively few, though it has been useful where there has been some trivial irregularity or misdirection at the trial. It has also been laid down by the House of Lords that the proviso cannot be applied in the case of misdirection unless the Court are satisfied that a reasonable jury properly directed would have reached the same conclusion (*D.P.P.* v. *Stirland* [46]).

8. This being the way the Criminal Appeal Act, 1907 has worked in practice, it was soon found that there were a number of cases in which there had been some irregularity or misdirection at the trial which could not be dismissed as trivial, and it being impossible to apply the proviso, the Court of Criminal Appeal had no alternative but to quash the conviction and enter a verdict of acquittal, although they might feel little doubt of the appellant's guilt and although in some cases it could be truly said that the appellant's guilt had never really been properly tried....

12. We sought the views of the judiciary and the legal profession on the questions before us. . . . Of the Judges of the Queen's Bench a small majority were in favour of the Court ... having power to order a new trial.... The Bar Council said that widely different views ... were held by members of the Bar.... The Law Society were opposed to the proposal in principle as a violation of the rule that once there has been an acquittal or conviction for an offence, there should be no second trial for the same offence. They also considered ... the proposal open to objections on the grounds of delay and expense....

New trial on a count on which appellant has been acquitted

29. .... [W]e are all agreed that a new trial should not be ordered on a count on which [the accused] ... has already been acquitted....

New trials in cases of fresh evidence

30. We are agreed that ... the Court should be empowered to order a new trial in cases where under the existing law and practice fresh evidence would be admissible on appeal.... [I]n many cases it is impossible to assess the value of new evidence without weighing it against evidence given at the trial. This can properly be done only by a jury who hear and see all the witnesses, including both those who gave evidence at the trial and those whose evidence has subsequently become available....

31. Although we recommended that the Court of Criminal Appeal should be given power to order a new trial in such cases, we are of opinion that this would

[46] [1944] A.C. 315.

not obviate the necessity for the Home Secretary to set up extra-judicial inquiries in certain cases. Cases from time to time occur where the appellant relies on testimony which would not be admissible in evidence at a second trial or where another person is alleged to have confessed to the commission of the crime of which the appellant has been convicted.... [A]n extra-judicial inquiry will be necessary to enable the Home Secretary to decide whether to recommend the exercise of the Prerogative of Mercy. In our view, for example, the existence of power to order a new trial would not have made it possible to dispense with the inquiries which were held in the cases of Rowland in 1947 [47] and of Devlin and Burns in 1952.[48] The first case involved a " confession " to the murder by another man, of which the authenticity could not have been determined by a second trial of Rowland. The second case also involved an alleged confession by another man and evidence by a girl in a form which would not have been admissible at a second trial of the appellant.

New trials in other cases

33. .... [T]here is a difference of opinion among members of the Committee on the question whether the Court ... should have power to order a new trial in all cases.... The following paragraphs (34 to 37) represent the views ... of five members (Mr. R. F. Levy, Sir Theobald Mathew, Mr. Noel Leigh Taylor, Mr. G. P. Coldstream and Mr. F. Graham-Harrison) who are opposed to the proposal that the Court should have power at large to order new trials. The views of the three members (Lord Tucker, Sir Travers Humphreys and Judge Bass) in favour of the proposal are given in paragraphs 38 and 39.

Views of members opposed to the Court of Criminal Appeal having unlimited power to order new trials

34. The cases, other than those involving fresh evidence, in which the question of the desirability of a new trial is generally raised are those where there has been a misdirection or non-direction at the trial by a presiding judicial officer; where evidence has been wrongly admitted or excluded; where a " repugnant " verdict has been returned; or where some other irregularity on the part of the judicial officer or the prosecution has occurred. In such cases the disadvantages of the present system lie in the fact that the Court of Criminal Appeal are occasionally obliged to allow an appeal in circumstances which result in a guilty man going free.... But this difficulty arises only rarely, and we have no evidence that cases have occurred where responsible public opinion has been seriously disturbed, ... because of the possible or actual consequences of quashing a conviction. If they were of frequent occurrence we should expect the Judges to be united in support of the grant of new powers to the Court.... But the fact is that the Judges are not of one mind on this matter....

35. .... [T]here are objections, both of principle and practice, to giving the Court ... a power at large to grant new trials in these cases.... We deal first with the objections of principle.
It is of the essence of the administration of the criminal law in this country that justice should be swift and should be final.... Any provision for appeals necessarily involves derogation from the principle of finality, but we should regard any further derogation as a misfortune which could be justified only if the need for it were established by clear and conclusive evidence. Furthermore, it is undoubtedly repugnant to public opinion that a man should be put in peril twice for the same offence. This may appear to happen under the present law

[47] Cmd. 7049.
[48] Cmd. 8522.

in certain circumstances, for example where the jury disagree.... [W]e should be most loth to make a proposal which would extend the ambit of these circumstances any further.

36. We turn now to the practical objections....

[T]he prolongation of criminal proceedings might often be unfair and oppressive to the appellant. The uncertainty and lack of finality over a long period, with all its attendant anxiety, must inevitably lead to great hardship, and indeed injustice. In most cases the accused would be kept in custody whilst awaiting the second trial... on account of some irregularity in the first for which he was almost certainly not responsible.

Secondly,... [t]he jury at the second trial would almost certainly learn in the course of the trial that the accused had previously been convicted of the charge, and if the proceedings at the first trial attracted much publicity they might well be aware of any previous convictions of the accused, of his private circumstances, and of any damaging comments made by the Judge at the first trial in sentencing him. They might also infer that the Court of Criminal Appeal had ordered a new trial only because they considered the appellant to be probably guilty.... [E]ven if we accept the view that the jury would be able to dismiss from their minds, anything that they had previously read or heard about the case and that the trial would in fact be fair, it is at least doubtful whether justice would appear to be done, because of the natural impression in the public mind that the jury cannot fail to be prejudiced....

Thirdly, there is, in our opinion, a substantial danger that if the power to order new trials at large were now to be given, a practice would gradually grow up of ordering them more and more frequently....

Views of members in favour of the Court of Criminal Appeal having unlimited power to order new trials

38....(a) There is no real substance in the objection that a general power to order new trials is contrary to fundamental principle, provided the power is confined to counts upon which there has been a conviction and against which conviction there has been an appeal....

(b)... Juries can be trusted to confine their attention to the evidence adduced before them and not to be influenced by... extraneous matters....

(c) Although all trials are necessarily ordeals to the persons accused... it would occasionally be in the public interest that an accused person should have to undergo two trials before a verdict is properly reached, rather than that a guilty man, whose guilt or innocence has never been properly ascertained, should go free....

(d) Apprehension that a power at large to order new trials would tend to make courts of trial become lax with regard to technicalities cannot be supported in view of the well known dislike of trial Judges of their cases being sent back for a new trial.

(e) The power to order new trials would not tend to make the Court of Criminal Appeal unduly insistent on technicalities, particularly as all courts seek to avoid new trials whenever possible....

(g) The most serious objection... is the difficulty that may arise in deciding in what type of case the power should be exercised. It has been stated by the Lord Chief Justice and others that the power, if given, would be sparingly exercised. It appears unwise to attempt to define by statute the cases in which the power might be exercised as any such definition would be a matter of great difficulty and would inevitably lead to a mass of case law on its interpretation. If the power is to be given, it should then be left to the unfettered discretion of the Court.... The way in which the Court of Criminal Appeal have exercised their jurisdiction over the last forty or fifty years certainly gives no grounds for thinking that the Court could not be trusted to exercise with care and discretion any further power given to them. . . .

Cases referred to the Court of Criminal Appeal by the Secretary of State

41. We all consider that the power of the Court of Criminal Appeal to order a new trial in a case which has been referred to them by the Secretary of State under section 19 of the Criminal Appeal Act, 1907, should be the same as in a case of a person who has appealed to the Court.

More than one new trial

42. . . . We are all agreed, . . . that if . . . the Court . . . were given power at large to order a new trial, this power should not be exercised more than once in a particular case, as when it comes to a third and a fourth trial of a convicted person being held, the excessive delay in bringing the proceedings to finality outweighs any possible advantages of a further trial; . . . [B]ut if the power of the Court of Criminal Appeal were restricted to ordering new trials only in cases involving fresh evidence, cases where there were grounds to justify ordering more than one new trial would in practice so rarely arise that we think it would be unnecessary to deal with the matter by an express statutory provision.

Procedure and costs

43. If the Court of Criminal Appeal are given power to order a new trial, we think that . . . the Court . . . would no doubt also be given power to order, if necessary, the costs incurred by the accused at the first or second trial to be paid from public funds.

House of Lords

44. We are all agreed that the House of Lords must necessarily be given the same powers to order a new trial in criminal cases as the Court of Criminal Appeal.

Report of the Committee on the Court of Criminal Appeal
Cmnd. 2755, 1965

Court of Appeal (Criminal Division)

59. In 1909 the first full year in which the Court was in operation, it disposed of . . . 618 cases . . . In 1938 the total . . . was almost identical.

60. But by 1961 . . . this total had risen to 2,930. Of these no less than 1,867 were applications for leave to appeal against sentence only. . . .

61. . . . The number of judges available to deal with the work in 1909 was 17. In 1964 it was 34. These figures include the Lord Chief Justice.

62. In order to dispose of the volume of work (which is still increasing) the Court has to sit in more than one division. . . .

63. In consequence of the Criminal Justice (Administration) Act 1962, implementing the Report of the Interdepartmental Committee on the Business of the Criminal Courts (under the Chairmanship of Mr. Justice Streatfeild, Cmnd. 1289), and designed to reduce delays in criminal trials, the judges of the Queen's Bench Division now spend more time on circuit. . . .

64. The result is that the composition of the Court (i.e. as regards the individual judges who sit) is never constant for any appreciable length of

time.... The opportunities for all those who may from time to time sit in the Court to get together and formulate consistent policies, for the lack of which separate divisions of the Court may go different ways, are few.... On the same topic therefore different divisions of the Court may speak with different voices; and in the important matter of sentences, proceed on different lines.

71. It should not be supposed that conflicts... are frequent; but it is important to reduce the risk of their occurrence....

72.... It can never be entirely removed, for it would be both impracticable and unwise to have the same judges hearing nothing but appeals and applications in criminal cases for the whole of their judicial lives....

83. At the moment, the Court of Criminal Appeal would appear to stand on its own. The Supreme Court of Judicature consists of the Court of Appeal and the High Court.... The Court of Criminal Appeal is a separate court. There would seem to be no reason why it should not formally be made part of the Supreme Court of Judicature and we think this should be done in any event.

84. Next, after careful consideration, we think that the Court of Appeal should be reconstituted so as to consist of a Civil Division and a Criminal Division. The work of the Civil Division would be the same as that of the existing Court of Appeal. To the Criminal Division would be transferred the whole of the present jurisdiction of the Court of Criminal Appeal.... The Criminal Division of the Court of Appeal would, in order to cope with the volume of work ..., need to sit in two courts and, for part of the year, in three.

85. The Lord Chief Justice should preside in the first of these courts, assisted by a Lord Justice of Appeal and one puisne judge from the Queen's Bench Division. This court would be concerned principally with appeals, whether against conviction or sentence. The second and third courts should be presided over by a Lord Justice of Appeal assisted by two puisne judges from the Queen's Bench Division. These two courts would be concerned principally with applications for leave to appeal, whether against conviction or sentence. All three courts should, however, have jurisdiction to deal with appeals and applications for leave to appeal as the flow of work from time to time might require.

88.... If in an appeal there were a division of opinion in any one of the divisions ... the case should be re-heard before a court of five judges, and that court should be composed of the Lord Chief Justice, two Lords Justices of Appeal and two puisne judges, or three Lords Justices and two puisne judges. Here the majority opinion should prevail.

89. The reasons for retaining puisne judges as members of the courts are two. First, to retain the experience that they are continually acquiring in the trial of crime and sentencing of offenders, which must necessarily be greater than can be acquired by any Lord Justice of Appeal, even if the latter from time to time goes on circuit. Second, because the experience a puisne judge obtains by doing appellate work is of great advantage to him in his work at first instance. It is objected by some that it is not right that a new and inexperienced judge should sit on appeal in criminal cases simply to learn how to try crime. In fact he does not do so. If he has not tried any criminal cases before being appointed to the Bench (which is most unlikely) he would have to learn by doing the work. But he will learn it more quickly and more thoroughly by seeing the mistakes that others sometimes make and the dangerous pitfalls he must avoid. In this respect appellate work is most valuable.[49]

---

[49] The committee noted at para. 277: " Whatever the technical position the rule to-day is almost invariably that a judge who has presided over a trial does not sit on the appeal or on the application for leave to appeal of a prisoner convicted at that trial.

278. The Law Society asked that, however rarely this rule may be departed from, it should be made absolute. This would need legislation but we think effect should be given

94. The new Criminal Division will not be manned always by the same three Lords Justices. They will have to be relieved after a spell—say of two to three months—and and we think it is essential that they should also spend a few weeks each year on circuit or at the Central Criminal Court trying criminal cases themselves. To allow for these requirements there should be a panel of some six or seven Lords Justices having experience of criminal work from whom the complement of the Criminal Division should from time to time be chosen. The panel should be chosen by the Lord Chancellor with the consent of the Lord Chief Justice.

95. We see no convincing reason why all the judges of the Queen's Bench Division should not continue to be eligible to sit on criminal appeals. . . .

97. The present right of appeal to the House of Lords on a point of law should be continued, subject to the same conditions as are specified in the Administration of Justice Act 1960.

The requirement of leave to appeal

107. The Act of 1907 gave to every person convicted on indictment an unconditional right to appeal . . . against his conviction on any ground which involved a question of law alone.

108. It also gave a conditional right of appeal against conviction to any such person on any ground involving a question of fact alone, or a question of mixed law and fact, or on any other ground which appeared to the Court to be sufficient. In all of these cases the condition is that the would-be appellant obtains leave to appeal either from the Court of Criminal Appeal or (by way of certificate) from the judge who tried him.

109. The reason for distinguishing in this way between appeals on questions of law alone and all other appeals was, no doubt, the expectation that the former would be comparatively few in number, whereas the latter might be very numerous; and that some sort of sieve would be required to prevent the Court from being overwhelmed. The sieve would hold back the hopeless cases.

110. In the various representations made to us there has been general approval of this arrangement. . . .

111. Two witnesses, however, . . . suggested that . . . the necessity for obtaining leave to appeal . . . should be abolished. Abstract justice, it was urged, required this change.

112. There would be little point in making it, however, unless an appreciable number of potential appellants took advantage of it; and if they did the consequences for the Court of Criminal Appeal would be serious. These consequences would have to be faced if there were grounds for supposing that significant numbers of potential appellants with good reasons for appealing are today deterred by the need of obtaining leave to appeal. We do not believe this to be the case. There may be some such who today are deterred from making an application for leave because of the prospect that, if leave is refused, they will spend longer in prison than otherwise; but we propose some amelioration of this position later on in this Report. Apart from these persons, however, there are a vast number of others who, under present conditions, make no application for leave to appeal against conviction, but who might be expected to do so if the prior necessity to obtain leave were abolished. To take the year 1963 for example, there were 22,267 convictions on indictment. During the

to the Law Society's request. Though we are quite sure the trial judge in such a case would not (to use Mr. Justice Darling's expression in *R. v. Bennett and Newton* (1913) 9 Cr.App.R. 146, 157) ' fight for his own hand ' we think the appearance of justice being done is enhanced if the trial judge does not sit.''

same year the Court disposed of 2,531 applications and appeals, including 19 appeals as of right.... [N]early 20,000 persons convicted ... did not appeal. If only one third of these took advantage of a new absolute right of appeal the Court would have to deal with more than 6,500 additional cases, and many more judges would be needed. Bearing in mind that this increase in the work would be provided by those who today do not contest their convictions, the strong likelihood is that these additional appeals would be as much devoid of merit as are most of the applications for leave to appeal which are heard under the present law. In the end, therefore, no real good is likely to be done. We conclude that the grant of an unconditional right of appeal ... however attractive in theory, is not a practical proposition.

115. For reasons similar to those given in paragraph 112 we think there should be no unconditional right to appeal against sentence but that the leave of the Court should continue to be required.

230. ... [T]he power of the Court to grant leave to appeal may be exercised by any judge of the Court. This is called in practice " the single judge proce-dure," and the judge himself ... " the single judge." By way of contrast the Court consisting of three judges is called " the full Court."

231. In practice it is more usual for an application for leave to appeal against *conviction* to go direct for decision by the full Court, sitting in public. Applica-tions for leave to appeal against *sentence*, on the other hand, are usually con-sidered first by the single judge sitting in his private room. But this division of work is not invariable. Applications for leave to appeal against sentence are sometimes heard by the full Court without going to the single judge. Applica-tions for leave to appeal against conviction are now with increasing frequency referred for initial consideration by a single judge. . . .

233. ... In practice ... an application which would otherwise be dealt with by the single judge would be placed before the full Court for determination when it became known that it was to be argued by counsel.

234. Ordinarily an application for leave to appeal will be heard by the full Court without either the prosecution or the applicant being legally repre-sented. Before the single judge this is always the case. The full Court and the single judge come to a conclusion on the papers before them, which will include a precis of the facts of the case prepared in the Registrar's office and the transcript of the arraignment of the applicant, the plea, the judge's summing-up to the jury, the verdict, any evidence as to character and antece-dents, and the sentence.[50]

235. If the full Court decides to grant leave to appeal, it announces its decision to that effect. . . . If it decides to refuse leave to appeal, it likewise announces its decision to that effect, and one of the three judges comprising the Court will deliver a short judgment giving the essential facts of the case and stating the Court's reasons.

236. If the single judge decides to grant leave to appeal he simply makes a note to that effect on a form which is sent to him with the papers. . . . If he decides to refuse the application, he simply makes a note to that effect on the same form. As a rule he gives no reason for his refusal. The applicant may,

---

[50] The Committee noted, para. 271 : " . . . [T]he course of practice until some years ago was for the Registrar, on receiving notice of appeal or of application for leave to appeal, to invite the trial judge to submit a report if he wished to do so. If a judge sent in such a report it was treated as private to the Court and not disclosed to the appellant.

272. This practice has now been discontinued except in any case where the notice of appeal or application for leave to appeal contains an allegation that the judge misconducted himself in some way at the trial. He may then be asked to submit a report. The Bar Council and the Law Society ask that a copy of any such report should be supplied to the appellant. In fact this is now done."

however, within five days of this refusal being communicated to him require that his application shall be heard by the full Court.

237. Accordingly it could happen that an application for leave to appeal will be considered by four judges, i.e. the single judge plus the three judges of the full Court. If the application succeeds, the appeal will be heard by the full Court, again consisting of at least three judges. So that in all seven judges will deal with the case. Some of the judges who have dealt with the application for leave to appeal may sit on the hearing of the appeal itself. More often, however, the composition of the Court will, owing to the demands of circuit, civil work, etc., have entirely changed by the time the appeal comes to be heard. . . .

238. One witness from the Bench criticised this procedure as wasteful of " judge power " and time. . . .

240. The remedy suggested was that an application for leave to appeal, whether against conviction or sentence or both, should be heard by two judges. If one of them considered that there was an arguable case, leave would be granted. Otherwise it should be refused and the refusal should be final unless some fresh circumstances arose. . . . We are by no means insensible to the desirability of eliminating waste both of " judge power " and of time, but we are unable to recommend any change which will deprive prisoners of a chance of putting their applications before the full Court. Furthermore it must be remembered that the necessity for obtaining leave to appeal is itself an arrangement for reducing the burden of work which would otherwise fall on the full Court, and though it absorbs the time and attention of some of the judges it saves the time and attention of others.

241. Another witness from the Bench suggested that the Registrar of the Court should be empowered to grant or refuse leave to appeal, with the proviso that any applicant to whom he refused leave could have his application next heard by the single judge. We are unable to recommend this suggestion. In the first place it is doubtful whether any time of the judge would be thereby saved since most unsuccessful applicants would (we think) not rest content with the decision of the Registrar. In the second place, and as a matter of principle, we do not think the task of adjudicating upon a matter which affects the liberty of the subject should be discharged otherwise than by a judge.

Appeals on questions of fact

137. [Section 4 (1) of the Court of Criminal Appeal Act 1907 provides:]

" The Court of Criminal Appeal on any such appeal against conviction shall allow the appeal if they think that the verdict of the jury should be set aside on the ground that it is unreasonable or cannot be supported having regard to the evidence. . . ."

138. From the outset the Court has acted upon the view that its functions are circumscribed in appeals which raise issues of fact. . . .

139. . . . [The] general principle . . . was expressed by Lord Chief Justice Goddard in 1949 . . . : " Where there is evidence on which a jury can act, and there has been a proper direction to the jury, this Court cannot substitute itself for the jury and re-try the case. . . . If we took any other attitude it would strike at the very root of trial by jury " (R. v. McGrath [51]).

140. The view that the Court cannot re-try cases is clearly correct. What has been questioned . . . is whether the Court is, or should be, debarred from interfering with a jury's verdict because there was *some* evidence to support it, and because it cannot therefore be described as unreasonable.

[51] [1949] 2 All E.R. 495, 497.

143. Where a crime has been committed, and the proof that a particular person committed it rests solely upon his identification by a witness or witnesses for the prosecution, then if the jury accepts that evidence, and rejects the evidence of an alibi tendered by the defendant, the latter would have little hope of successfully appealing against his conviction in face of the construction of section 4 (1) of the Act adopted by the Court. Yet the verdict could be wrong, and the defendant innocent.

144. Upon the first trial of Adolf Beck in 1896, ten women swore that he was the man who defrauded them, and Beck served a sentence of seven years' penal servitude. Upon his second trial in 1904 five women swore that he was the man who had defrauded them, and Beck was again convicted. Yet all these fifteen witnesses were mistaken. . . . [A] man named McGrath was convicted in October 1948 on a charge of receiving stolen property and was sentenced to three years' penal servitude. His defence was that his identification by two police officers was mistaken, and that at the material time he was far from the scene. The jury, however, rejected his alibi and found him guilty. His appeal against conviction was dismissed by the Court of Criminal Appeal in 1949, there being evidence upon which the jury could act. It was discovered later, however, that McGrath did not return to London (where the crime was committed) until a time which made it most unlikely that he was involved; and on a reference by the Home Secretary to the Court under section 19 of the Act the further evidence was considered and the conviction quashed in July 1949. The evidence of identification by the two police officers though honest was mistaken. In the meantime McGrath had spent nine months in prison (*R. v. McGrath, supra*).

147. It is noteworthy that . . . the Court has sometimes acted as though [it] . . . was entitled to quash a verdict which it considered to be unsafe or unsatisfactory, in spite of there being some evidence to support it. . . .

148. In these cases . . . the Court has acted as a jury and come to the conclusion that on the totality of the evidence, some of which was one way and some the other, it would be unsafe to allow a verdict of guilty to stand.

149. There are some who would argue that this is within the words of section 4. . . . We think the better view is that in order to do justice (which includes the avoidance of possible injustice) the Court has assumed a power the existence of which is doubtful. We think . . . that the Court . . . should be given an express power to allow an appeal where, upon consideration of the whole of the evidence, it comes to the conclusion that the verdict is unsafe or unsatisfactory.

150. If this recommendation be accepted two adverse results may follow: (1) there may be an increase in the number of appeals or applications for leave to appeal because undeserving appellants may see new hope in the new provision; and (2) some appellants who are guilty may escape on appeal. The first possible consequence is probably of little moment. It is common for appellants today to urge that the verdict against them was unreasonable and contrary to the weight of the evidence, which is not very different from urging that it was " unsafe or unsatisfactory ". We doubt therefore if the number of additional appellants would be large. As to the second consequence, we think reliance can safely be placed upon the experience and acumen of Her Majesty's judges to reduce this risk to minimum. The advantage to be gained from the provision we suggest, however, is that the safeguards for an innocent person, wrongly identified and wrongly convicted, are sensibly increased. . . . It might operate in other cases besides those of disputed identity, *e.g.* some cases of alleged rape where there is substantial evidence of consent which the jury reject in favour of the woman's denial.

Fresh evidence

132. The Court of Criminal Appeal is not a court of re-trial, and an appeal to it is not an appeal by way of a re-hearing of the case. It is not surprising that the Court has had this situation well in mind when considering when it would, and when it would not, exercise its power to hear fresh evidence. If fresh evidence were admitted as a matter of course there would clearly be a risk that the Court would on occasions find itself re-trying the case—a function which Parliament did not intend it to discharge, and for which it is in any event inadequately equipped. The Court in the past formulated rules for the exercise of its discretion. They were that fresh evidence would not be admitted unless—

    (1) it was not available at the trial;
    (2) it was relevant to the issues; and
    (3) it was credible evidence, i.e. well capable of belief.

See in this connexion *R. v. Parks*.[52] Where fresh evidence is admitted the Court considers whether, if admitted at the trial, the addition of such evidence might have led to a reasonable doubt of guilt in the mind of the jury.

133. The above conditions prescribed by the Court for the exercise of its discretion have been criticised as too narrow. . . . The condition which has given rise to most disquiet is the first. . . .

134. The Court has usually regarded any evidence which was known, and which could have been produced with reasonable diligence, as being evidence available at the trial. There may have been various reasons, however, why it was not produced, *e.g.* a decision not to do so on the part of the appellant's legal adviser which in retrospect can be seen to have been mistaken; . . . the incompetence of a prisoner defending himself; and the failure to trace and serve a witness although more determined and sustained efforts might have yielded results.

135. During the debates on the Criminal Appeal Bill in 1964 efforts were made to introduce a provision widening the grounds for the admission of fresh evidence by the Court. On the Third Reading of the Bill in the House of Commons the Home Secretary said: " I knew of the interest which honourable Members had taken in the point, and I therefore thought it right to consult the Lord Chief Justice about it. He has authorised me to say that, while it is essential for the court to decide what evidence it will treat as admissible, it is not bound by its previous practice as to the admission of evidence, and that it can and will review the practice in the light of the Bill, the governing principle being to ensure so far as possible that there has been no miscarriage of justice." [53]

136. We construe this as meaning that the Court will exercise its power to hear fresh evidence in such a way as to ensure that any miscarriage of justice will so far as possible be avoided or corrected. It will, we think, conduce to this and if the condition as to the evidence not having been available at the trial were discarded; and we recommend that additional evidence should be received, if it is relevant and credible, and if a reasonable explanation is given for the failure to place it before the jury. The recent decision of the Court in the case of *R. v. Kelly*,[54] indicates that the Court may already be acting on these lines.

Appeals against sentence

187. . . . If . . . the Court were to think that nine months was a proper sentence it will seldom, if ever, reduce an existing sentence of twelve months. *Per contra* it will seldom, if ever, increase a sentence of nine months to twelve

[52] (1961) 46 Cr.App.R. 29.
[53] Parliamentary Debates, House of Commons, April 30, 1964, col. 722.
[54] [1965] 2 All E.R. 250.

months merely because it thinks that twelve months is the sentence which
" should have been passed ". The Court will not, to use the language it has
itself employed at times, "tinker" with sentences. This reluctance can be
justified on reasonable grounds. If the members of the Court would themselves have passed a different sentence, but the difference is small, is it possible
to say with any confidence that the different sentence *should* have been passed
by a trial judge who has had the advantage of considering the matter at first
hand, of seeing and perhaps hearing the accused, and, it may be, of being
familiar with local circumstances either mitigating or aggravating the offence?
Again, to modify sentences by taking a little off here and putting a little on
there would be bound to have an unsettling effect on those presiding at criminal
trials, who would be at a loss to know where they stood. They might soon
cease to give the important matter of sentencing the careful consideration it
deserves, because in their view the Court of Criminal Appeal would in all probability alter the sentence anyway. It is not surprising therefore that the Court
has formulated its policy on this matter in the following words, taken from *R.*
v. *Ball* [55] :—

> " In the first place, this Court does not alter a sentence which is the
> subject of an appeal merely because the members of the Court might have
> passed a different sentence. . . . It is only when a sentence appears to err
> in principle that the Court will alter it. . . ."

188. The Court has no general power to alter the sentence if the appellant has
appealed against conviction only. This may be contrasted with the . . . powers
. . . of quarter sessions, which can on appeal against *conviction or* sentence
" award any punishment, whether more or less than that awarded by the
court of summary jurisdiction, which that court might have awarded " (section
31 of the Summary Jurisdiction Act 1879, as amended). At quarter sessions,
however, there is the material difference that the appeal is a complete rehearing
of the case, in which fresh evidence may be offered, and in which the court
may make a complete re-assessment of the case.

194. Among the witnesses whom we heard opinion was fairly evenly divided
on the question whether the Court should retain its power to increase sentences. . . . Generally speaking, those witnesses in legal practice favoured
abolition; those who were members of the judicial Bench favoured retention. . . .

195. The principal reasons for retaining the power seem to be these:

> (1) If a sentence . . . is manifestly inadequate, justice requires that it
>   should be increased, as much as justice requires that a sentence
>   which is manifestly excessive should be reduced.
> (2) The existence of the power serves to deter unmeritorious appeals.
> (3) The use of the power has some effect in removing disparity between
>   sentences in comparable cases.

196. The first of these reasons is beyond controversy. But if the doing of
justice is the principal reason for the power, then it would seem that the prosecution ought to be able to bring before the Court cases where, in its view, the
sentence was so inadequate that justice had not been done. The idea that the
prosecution should be able to appeal against the sentence . . . would be a complete departure from our tradition that the prosecutor takes no part, or the
minimum part, in the sentencing process. The question then is whether the
existence of the power is warranted on the ground that the doing of justice in
only a few cases is to be preferred to leaving those cases, however few,
uncorrected. . . . [I]n 1963 there were six cases in which the power was
exercised.

[55] (1951) 35 Cr.App.R. 164.

197. The Court would have had no power to increase the sentence even in these few cases had not the appellant himself invoked the Court's consideration of it. In response the Court granted his application for leave to appeal, and assigned to him the benefit of counsel, thus indicating to him in all probability that his plea for a reduction was regarded as having substance. The Court was privately of opinion, however, that the sentence ought to be increased, but was careful to let no hint of this view reach the appellant. In the end the increase of his punishment must have come to the prisoner as a very rude shock, and the granting of leave to appeal as nothing but the setting of a trap.

198. No criticism of the Court is intended, or would be justified, by this description of what in fact happens. . . . For if the Court frankly stated its opinion that the sentence was inadequate, and said that leave to appeal against it was given so that it could be increased if the Court remained of that opinion, the appeal would promptly be abandoned. But the procedure to which the Court is unavoidably driven is not an edifying spectacle.

199. As to the deterrent effect of the power, the Court has no authority to increase a sentence merely because it thinks the application for a reduction is frivolous. . . . But the increase of a sentence periodically does, we think, have the effect of reducing for a time the numbers of those who apply for leave to appeal against sentence. . . . Some of those thus deterred may be prisoners with a reasonable case for reduction of their sentences. Just how many unmeritorious applications are prevented is quite impossible to say. If there were reliable evidence that it was substantial, the argument in favour of the retention of the power to increase sentences would certainly be stronger; and it would hardly matter that this effect of the power was not its real purpose.

200. The usefulness of the power in avoiding disparity of sentence is minimal. It is exercised in so few cases that its retention cannot be justified on this ground. . . .

201. One way of avoiding to some extent the deceptive procedure which at present must be adopted, . . . is to give the Court power to review the sentence in all cases of appeals (as distinct from applications for leave to appeal) against conviction; even though the appellant does not seek to question his sentence. . . . Apart from its being a complete break with the system which has now been in force for over half a century, the number of cases in which the sentence would be increased would, judging from experience, not be worth the additional work involved. The Court would be looking at a considerable number of sentences only to refrain from interfering. In those cases where the sentence ought to be reduced it is a reasonable expectation that the prisoner himself would be found appealing not only against conviction but against sentence also. One undesirable feature of the innovation would also be that some meritorious appeals against conviction would not be prosecuted because of fear that, in the event of failure, the sentence might be increased.

202. Another proposal put to us was that all sentences of more than a specified length should be automatically reviewed by the Court. This seems to us to have nothing to do with the machinery of appeal. Automatic review of sentences raises wide questions of penal policy and the treatment of sentenced offenders which are outside our terms of reference. It is, in any case, a function which we should regard as inappropriate for a Court of Criminal Appeal. . . .

204. We have come to the conclusion that the undesirable features inseparable from the existence of the present power to increase sentence outweigh the benefit resulting from the circumstance that in a very few cases each year an adequate sentence is substituted for an inadequate one. . . . In these circumstances we think the power should be abolished, if only experimentally. If this were to lead to a flood of unmeritorious appeals against sentence the matter could be reviewed.

206. The power of the Court to vary the kind of sentence originally imposed, *e.g.* by substituting a sentence of borstal training, or a hospital order with a restriction order, should be preserved, even though the latter might carry a liability to a longer period of detention than under the original sentence.

273. One chairman of quarter sessions asked that, whenever leave to appeal against sentence is given, a report should be called for by the Court from the judge by whom the sentence was passed. He could then explain the reasons for it. We think a formal rule to this effect is unnecessary. If some special reason prompted a particular sentence the judge would normally explain it to the prisoner at the time and his remarks would appear in the shorthand note. If some case should arise in which the Court of Criminal Appeal needs clarification of the reasons for a particular sentence it could always enquire of the trial judge. Any report made by him in such a case should likewise be made available to the appellant.

Forfeiture of time by unsuccessful appellants

167. Under the present law and practice an unsuccessful appellant may serve up to 63 days more in prison than he would have done had he not appealed at all.....

169. . . . subject to the overriding discretion of the Court to order that no time, or more or less time, shall be discounted in any particular case. . . .

172. The primary justification for the present law remains the need to impose some restraint upon hopeless applications to the Court. . . .

173. The device has frequently been criticised on the general grounds that a prisoner ought not to be penalised for presuming to exercise his rights of appeal, and that it discourages prisoners who have genuine grounds of appeal without effectively deterring applications without merit. But the most common source of complaint is that the provision is applied without discrimination to virtually all cases where the Court does not feel justified in granting leave to appeal. Since the Court so rarely exercises its discretionary powers to mitigate the loss of time there is no distinction between the flagrantly frivolous applicant and the applicant who only just failed to persuade the Court to grant leave.

174. The proportion of cases in which the application is wantonly frivolous, in the sense that the appellant himself knows it to be without merit, is probably relatively small, but there are some. The facilities for unlimited letters and visits allowed to prisoners for the purpose of the appeal are capable of abuse. . . . Dr. Terence and Pauline Morris referred to this in their book *Pentonville, a Sociological Study of an English Prison.* . . . " . . . A most reliable prisoner informant stated: ' It's true that some people appeal just to get extra letters and visits, especially where a man has had a lot of domestic or business troubles at the time of his conviction.' " The authors returned to the subject in a later chapter on " influences from over the wall," where they said: " Those who have friends outside, particularly those who belong to well-integrated criminal groups, are on the other hand often able to keep ' businesses ' running and maintain their position, as it were, by proxy. Visits are generally crucial for this purpose, and men not infrequently lodge appeal notices, not because they entertain serious hope of obtaining a lighter sentence, but simply because the additional visits available to appellants are most useful for tidying up ' loose ends.' "

175. The majority of appellants, however, sincerely believe that they have grounds for appeal. In some cases this belief may be quite misconceived . . . but to the prisoner himself his application is far from frivolous. At the opposite

end of the scale there are other cases (and this occurs especially in appeal against sentence) where the prisoner may have reasonable grounds for believing (perhaps on legal advice) that he can persuade the appeal court to intervene. Generally all these cases are treated alike for the purpose of loss of time.

178. The position is [quite] different in Scotland. . . .

180. It is also relevant to mention that by section 17 of the Criminal Justice Administration Act 1962 the whole time spent by an accused person in prison awaiting trial (during which time he has wider privileges than those of an appellant) now counts as part of the sentence subsequently imposed. . . .

184. We were impressed by the volume of criticisms of the unfairness of the present English practice and we have no doubt that the Scottish system is in principle more equitable. We recognise the dangers of weakening the barriers against unmerited appeals, but it seems to us that the effect of the alteration of the Scottish law has not been as serious in this respect as might have been feared. In our opinion the time has come when the like alteration should be made here, even if only as an experiment. We recommend therefore that the time during which an appellant is in custody pending the determination of his appeal should, subject to any direction which the Court may give to the contrary, be reckoned as part of any term of imprisonment under his sentence. The Court will thus retain power to penalise an appellant whose appeal is totally devoid of merit, but it will be required to bring its mind to the problem instead of operating an almost automatic rule. In any case where the Court orders the forfeiture of time we think it should give its reason, and that this should be communicated to the appellant if he has not been present.

Criminal Appeal Act 1968

1968, c. 19

PART I

Appeal to Court of Appeal in Criminal Cases

Appeal against conviction on indictment

1.—(1) A person convicted of an offence on indictment may appeal to the Court of Appeal against his conviction.[56]

(2) The appeal may be—

    (a) on any ground which involves a question of law alone; and

    (b) with the leave of the Court of Appeal, on any ground which involves a question of fact alone, or a question of mixed law and fact, or on any other ground which appears to the Court of Appeal to be a sufficient ground of appeal;

but if the judge of the court of trial grants a certificate that the case is fit for appeal on a ground which involves a question of fact, or a question of mixed law and fact, an appeal lies under this section without the leave of the Court of Appeal.

---

[56] In R. v. Forde [1923] 2 Q.B. 400, the Court of Criminal Appeal noted that there could be an appeal even after a plea of guilty " if it appears (1) that the appellant did not appreciate the nature of the charge or did not intend to admit he was guilty of it, or (2) that upon the admitted facts he could not in law have been convicted of the offence charged."

2.—(1) Except as provided by this Act, the Court of Appeal shall allow an appeal against conviction if they think—

    (a) that the verdict of the jury should be set aside on the ground that under all the circumstances of the case it is unsafe or unsatisfactory; or [57]

    (b) that the judgment of the court of trial should be set aside on the ground of a wrong decision of any question of law; or

    (c) that there was a material irregularity in the course of the trial,

and in any other case shall dismiss the appeal:

Provided that the Court may, notwithstanding that they are of opinion that the point raised in the appeal might be decided in favour of the appellant, dismiss the appeal if they consider that no miscarriage of justice has actually occurred.[58]

(2) In the case of an appeal against conviction the Court shall, if they allow the appeal, quash the conviction.

(3) An order of the Court of Appeal quashing a conviction shall, except when under section 7 below the appellant is ordered to be retried, operate as a direction to the court of trial to enter, instead of the record of conviction, a judgment and verdict of acquittal.

3.—(1) This section applies on an appeal against conviction, where the appellant has been convicted of an offence and the jury could on the indictment have found him guilty of some other offence, and on the finding of the jury it appears to the Court of Appeal that the jury must have been satisfied of facts which proved him guilty of the other offence.

(2) The Court may, instead of allowing or dismissing the appeal, substitute for the verdict found by the jury a verdict of guilty of the other offence, and pass such sentence in substitution for the sentence passed at the trial as may be authorised by law for the other offence, not being a sentence of greater severity.

---

[57] Cf. R. v. Cooper (Sean) [1969] 1 Q.B. 267. Cooper had been convicted of assault occasioning actual bodily harm after a majority verdict of 10 to 2. Although the victim had had no hesitation in identifying him, another witness had suggested that someone else had told him that he had been responsible. Widgery L.J. said: " [T]his . . . is . . . a case in which every issue was before the jury and in which the jury was properly instructed, and, accordingly, a case in which this court will be very reluctant indeed to intervene. It has been said over and over again . . . that this court must recognise the advantage which a jury has in seeing and hearing the witnesses, and if all the material was before the jury and the summing-up was impeccable, this court should not lightly interfere. Indeed, until the passing of the Criminal Appeal Act 1966—provisions which are now . . . in section 2 of the Criminal Appeal Act 1968—it was almost unheard of for this court to interfere in such a case.

However, now our powers are somewhat different, and we are indeed charged to allow an appeal against conviction if we think that the verdict of the jury should be set aside on the ground that under all the circumstances of the case it is unsafe or unsatisfactory. That means that in cases of this kind the court must . . . ask itself a subjective question, whether we are content to let the matter stand as it is, or whether there is not some lurking doubt in our minds which makes us wonder whether an injustice has been done. This is a reaction which may not be based strictly on the evidence as such; it is a reaction which can be produced by the general feel of the case as the court experiences it. . . . After due consideration, we have decided we do not regard this verdict as safe, and accordingly we shall allow the appeal and quash the conviction. . . ."

[58] In R. v. Brown (1971) 55 Cr.App.R. 478, Cairns L.J. said: " [I]t has been rightly said . . . that for the proviso to be applied, there must be an overwhelming case against the accused. It is put in this way in Archbold (37th ed.), para. 925, in two sentences, which, in the view of the Court, correctly state the law: ' A miscarriage of justice within the meaning of the proviso has occurred where by reason of a mistake, omission or irregularity in the trial the appellant has lost any chance of acquittal which was fairly open to him. The court may apply the proviso and dismiss the appeal if they are satisfied that on the whole of the facts and with a correct direction the only proper verdict would have been one of guilty.' "

6.—(1) Where, on an appeal against conviction, the Court of Appeal are of opinion—

(a) that the proper verdict would have been one of not guilty by reason of insanity; or

(b) that the case is not one where there should have been a verdict of acquittal, but that there should have been a finding that the accused was under disability,

the Court shall make an order that the appellant be admitted to such hospital as may be specified by the Secretary of State. . . .

Retrial

7.—(1) Where the Court of Appeal allow an appeal against conviction and do so only by reason of evidence received or available to be received by them under section 23 of this Act and it appears to the Court that the interests of justice so require, they may order the appellant to be retried.

(2) A person shall not under this section be ordered to be retried for any offence other than—

(a) the offence of which he was convicted at the original trial and in respect of which his appeal is allowed as mentioned in subsection (1) above;

(b) an offence of which he could have been convicted at the original trial on an indictment for the first-mentioned offence; or

(c) an offence charged in an alternative count of the indictment in respect of which the jury were discharged from giving a verdict in consequence of convicting him of the first-mentioned offence.

Appeal against sentence

9. A person who has been convicted of an offence on indictment may appeal to the Court of Appeal against any sentence (not being a sentence fixed by law) passed on him for the offence. . . .

10.—(1) This section has effect for providing rights of appeal against sentence when a person is dealt with by [the Crown Court] (otherwise than on appeal from a magistrates' court) for an offence of which he was not convicted on indictment.

(2) The proceedings from which an appeal against sentence lies under this section are those where an offender convicted of an offence by a magistrates' court—

(a) is committed by the court to be dealt with for his offence [before the Crown Court;] or

(b) having been made the subject of a probation order or an order for conditional discharge or given a suspended sentence, appears or is brought before [the Crown Court] to be further dealt with for his offence.

(3) An offender dealt with for an offence [before the Crown Court] in a proceeding to which subsection (2) of this section applies may appeal to the Court of Appeal against sentence in any of the following cases:—

(a) where either for that offence alone or for that offence and other offences for which sentence is passed in the same proceeding, he is sentenced to imprisonment for a term of six months or more; or

(b) where the sentence is one which the court convicting him had not power to pass; or

(c) where the court in dealing with him for the offence makes in respect of him—

    (i) a recommendation for deportation; or

    (ii) an order disqualifying him for holding or obtaining a licence to drive a motor vehicle under Part II of the Road Traffic Act 1960; or

    (iii) an order under section 40 of the Criminal Justice Act 1967 (orders as to existing suspended sentence when person subject to the sentence is again convicted).

11.—(1) An appeal against sentence, whether under section 9 or under section 10 of this Act, lies only with the leave of the Court of Appeal.

(3) On an appeal against sentence the Court of Appeal, if they consider that the appellant should be sentenced differently for an offence for which he was dealt with by the court below may—

(a) quash any sentence or order which is the subject of the appeal; and

(b) in place of it pass such sentence or make such order as they think appropriate for the case and as the court below had power to pass or make when dealing with him for the offence;

but the Court shall so exercise their powers under this subsection that, taking the case as a whole, the appellant is not more severely dealt with on appeal than he was dealt with by the court below.

(4) The power of the Court of Appeal under subsection (3) of this section to pass a sentence which the court below had power to pass for an offence shall, notwithstanding that the court below made no order under section 40 (1) of the Criminal Justice Act 1967 (power of court on conviction of further offence to deal with suspended sentence) in respect of a suspended sentence previously passed on the appellant for another offence, include power to deal with him in respect of that suspended sentence where the court below—

(a) could have so dealt with him if it had not passed on him a sentence of borstal training quashed by the Court of Appeal under subsection (3) (a) of this section; or

(b) did so deal with him in accordance with paragraph (d) of the said section 40 (1) (power of Court of Appeal to make no order with respect to suspended sentence).

Sections 12–15 deal with appeals against a verdict of not guilty by reason of insanity and findings that the accused is unfit to stand trial.[59]

Review by Court of Appeal of cases tried on indictment

17.—(1) Where a person has been convicted on indictment, or been tried on indictment and found not guilty by reason of insanity, or been found by a jury to be under disability, the Secretary of State may, if he thinks fit, at any time either—

(a) refer the whole case to the Court of Appeal and the case shall then be treated for all purposes as an appeal to the Court by that person; or

(b) if he desires the assistance of the Court on any point arising in the case, refer that point to the Court for their opinion thereon, and the Court shall consider the point so referred and furnish the Secretary of State with their opinion thereon accordingly.

---

[59] S. 15 (2) reproduces s. 1 (2); s. 16 (1) reproduces s. 2 (1).

(2) A reference by the Secretary of State under this section may be made by him either on an application by the person referred to in subsection (1), or without any such application.[60]

19. The Court of Appeal may, if they think fit, on the application of an appellant, admit him to bail pending the determination of his appeal.

20. If it appears to the registrar of criminal appeals of the Court of Appeal (hereafter referred to as "the registrar") that a notice of an appeal purporting to be on a ground of appeal which involves a question of law alone does not show any substantial ground of appeal, he may refer the appeal to the Court for summary determination; and where the case is so referred the Court may, if they consider that the appeal is frivolous or vexatious, and can be determined without adjourning it for a full hearing, dismiss the appeal summarily, without calling on any one to attend the hearing or to appear for the Crown thereon.

23.—(1) For purposes of this Part of this Act the Court of Appeal may, if they think it necessary or expedient in the interests of justice—

    (a) order the production of any document, exhibit or other thing connected with the proceedings, the production of which appears to them necessary for the determination of the case;

    (b) order any witness who would have been a compellable witness in the proceedings from which the appeal lies to attend for examination and be examined before the Court, whether or not he was called in those proceedings; and

    (c) subject to subsection (3) below, receive the evidence, if tendered, of any witness.[61]

(2) Without prejudice to subsection (1) above, where evidence is tendered to the Court of Appeal thereunder the Court shall, unless they are satisfied that the evidence, if received, would not afford any ground for allowing the appeal, exercise their power of receiving it if—

    (a) it appears to them that the evidence is likely to be credible and would have been admissible in the proceedings from which the appeal lies on an issue which is the subject of the appeal; and

    (b) they are satisfied that it was not adduced in those proceedings but there is a reasonable explanation for the failure to adduce it.

(3) Subsection (1) (c) above applies to any witness (including the appellant) who is competent but not compellable, and applies also to the appellant's husband or wife where the appellant makes an application for that purpose and the evidence of the husband or wife could not have been given in the proceedings from which the appeal lies except on such an application.

(4) For purposes of this Part of this Act, the Court of Appeal may, if they think it necessary or expedient in the interests of justice, order the examination of any witness whose attendance might be required under subsection (1) (b) above to be conducted, in manner provided by rules of court, before any judge or officer of the Court or other person appointed by the Court for the purpose, and allow the admission of any depositions so taken as evidence before the Court.

---

[60] S. 29 of the Criminal Justice Act 1972 gives the Attorney-General power to refer points of law to the court in the case of acquittal after trial on indictment, without affecting the original decision.

[61] In R. v. Lomas [1969] 1 W.L.R. 306 it was said: " . . . The normal case where fresh evidence is tendered and received under this section is on a question of fact, where, for example, some eye-witness or alibi witness not previously available has later been discovered. Although the section in its terms appears wide enough to embrace fresh evidence of scientific or medical opinion, it seems to this court that only in most exceptional cases would it be possible to say that there was any reasonable explanation for not adducing such evidence at the trial. . . . However, in this case we decided to admit the evidence. . . ."

Other matters depending on the result of appeal

29.—(1) The time during which an appellant is in custody pending the determination of his appeal shall, subject to any direction which the Court of Appeal may give to the contrary, be reckoned as part of the term of any sentence to which he is for the time being subject.[62]

(2) Where the Court of Appeal give a contrary direction under subsection (1) above, they shall state their reasons for doing so; and they shall not give any such direction where—

(a) leave to appeal has been granted; or

(b) a certificate has been given by the judge of the court of trial under section 1 of this Act; or

(c) the case has been referred to them by the Secretary of State under section 17 ...

(3) When an appellant is admitted to bail under section 19 of this Act, the time during which he is at large after being so admitted shall be disregarded in computing the term of any sentence to which he is for the time being subject.

(4) The term of any sentence passed by the Court of Appeal under section 3, 4, 5, 11 or 13 (4) of this Act shall, unless the Court otherwise direct, begin to run from the time when it would have begun to run if passed in the proceedings from which the appeal lies.

31.—(1) The powers of the Court of Appeal ... of this Act which are specified in subsection (2) below may be exercised by a single judge in the same manner as they may be exercised by the Court and subject to the same provisions.

(2) The said powers are the following:—

(a) to give leave to appeal;

---

[62] In April 1970 [1970] 1 W.L.R. 663 the Lord Chief Justice made the following announcement: " . . . In 1969 there were approximately 9,700 applications for leave to appeal to the Court of Appeal. This year the number may well exceed 12,000. . . . In each of the . . . applications, the Criminal Appeal Office must obtain papers from the court of trial, and, in most cases, a transcript. . . . All the papers have to be read by one or more of a small group of judges. . . . In the first instance, with some exceptions, the papers . . . are read by one judge (known as the ' single judge '). In 75 per cent. of the cases, at a conservative estimate, it then becomes apparent . . . that the application is unarguable. Such applications delay those in which there are arguable points of substance and merit and absorb the time of the judges who are much needed for other work. . . . Both the court and the single judge have power in their discretion to direct that part of the time during which the prisoner is in custody after putting in his notice of application shall not count towards his sentence. Nevertheless, the power of the single judge to direct that time shall be lost has, hitherto, been exercised only in rare cases. The power has been used sparingly, because, until recently, a prisoner might be without legal advice, and, until the refusal by the single judge, might have thought that there were grounds to support his application. However, provisions for advice on appeals under legal aid were made in the Criminal Justice Act 1967 and those provisions have been in force since October 1968. There has been, therefore, sufficient time, since then, for the provisions to become generally known, and understood. Now, no prisoner need be without advice. A form of letter is provided in prison to enable him to ask for it. Further, if he has made his application without advice, because in some special circumstances he has been unable to obtain it, it is open to him to ask this court for assistance. Where, therefore, an application which is unarguable is made . . . the single judge has no reason to refrain from directing that time shall be lost if he thinks it right so to exercise his discretion. . . . As from April 7, 1970, those who contemplate putting in a notice of application for leave to appeal, and their legal representatives, must bear this matter in mind. . . . It follows that it is important that those contemplating an appeal should seek advice. They should remember that it is useless to appeal without grounds and that the grounds should be substantial and particularised. . . . Where grounds . . . are settled, and . . . signed by counsel, it will be plain to the single judge that there were reasons for making the application. . . . As the court has pointed out already (. . . 50 Cr.App.R. 290), counsel should not draft grounds of appeal unless they are prepared to support them by argument before the court. . . ."

    (*b*) to extend the time within which notice of appeal or of application
for leave to appeal may be given;

    (*c*) to allow an appellant to be present at any proceedings;

    (*d*) to order a witness to attend for examination;

    (*e*) to admit an appellant to bail;

    (*f*) to make orders under section 8 (2) of this Act and discharge or vary
such orders [63];

    (*g*) to make orders for the payment of costs under section 25 of this Act;

    (*h*) to give directions under section 29 (1) of this Act.

(3) If the single judge refuses an application on the part of an appellant to
exercise in his favour any of the powers above specified, the appellant shall be
entitled to have the application determined by the Court of Appeal.

PART III

Miscellaneous and General

45.—(1) Subject to rules of court made under section 1 (5) of the Criminal
Appeal Act 1966 (power by rules to distribute business of Court of Appeal
between its civil and criminal divisions), all jurisdiction of the Court of Appeal
under Part I or Part II of this Act shall be exercised by the criminal division
of the Court; and references in those Parts to the Court of Appeal shall be
construed accordingly as references to that division of the Court.

50.—(1) In this Act, " sentence ", in relation to an offence, includes any
order made by a court when dealing with an offender (including a hospital
order under Part V of the Mental Health Act 1959, with or without an order
restricting discharge) and also includes a recommendation for deportation.

(2) Any power of the criminal division of the Court of Appeal to pass a
sentence includes a power to make a recommendation for deportation in cases
where the court from which the appeal lies had power to make such a
recommendation.

OTHER APPEALS IN CRIMINAL CASES

A person convicted by a magistrates' court may appeal to the Crown Court
against conviction or sentence, unless he pleaded guilty, in which case he
can only appeal against sentence.[64] Sentence here, though, does not include
a probation order or an order for conditional discharge. Either party may
then make a further appeal to the Divisional Court of the Queen's Bench
Division on a point of law although the Crown Court may refuse to state
a case for the purpose if it thinks the application for it to do so is frivolous,
unless it is the Attorney-General who wants to appeal. The would-be
appellant who has had his application for a case to be stated refused can
apply to the High Court for a mandamus directing the Crown Court to
state a case.

    Alternatively either party to the proceedings before the magistrates'
court may question a conviction or order on the ground that it is wrong in

---

[63] S. 8 (2), *inter alia*, authorises the Court of Appeal on ordering a retrial to make orders
for the custody or admission on bail of the person to be retried.

[64] Courts Act 1971, Sched. 1: " There shall be vested in the Crown Court all appellate and
other jurisdiction conferred on any court of quarter sessions, or on any committee of a
court of quarter sessions, by or under any Act, whether public general or local. . . ."

law or in excess of jurisdiction by applying to the justices to state a case for the High Court. The justices can refuse to state a case if they consider the application frivolous, unless the application is by the Attorney-General. The applicant, if refused, can apply to the High Court for a mandamus to the justices.

On an appeal to the Crown Court the appeal is by way of rehearing with the court rehearing the whole case including the witnesses. It may award any punishment that the magistrates' court could have awarded including one that is more severe than was awarded in the case.

THE HOUSE OF LORDS

Appeals in Civil Cases

The Judicature Commissioners in their First Report in 1869 made no recommendation about the House of Lords, which they regarded as outside their terms of reference. It was the original intention of the 1873 legislation to remove its jurisdiction as a final court of appeal and to rely instead on an appeal to a full Court of Appeal, but after a change of government and some parliamentary agitation its jurisdiction was restored. There is now therefore the possibility of a double appeal, to the Court of Appeal and from the Court of Appeal to the House of Lords (and this also applies to criminal cases), provided the necessary leave can be obtained.[65] It is a moot point whether this has been a better solution than that originally envisaged.

The House of Lords is to all intents and purposes a part of the judicial structure rather than a part of the parliamentary structure. The Appellate Jurisdiction Act 1876 provided for the appointment of special Law Lords to sit in it in order to prevent a recurrence of the situation where its composition and quality depended on the accident of which members of the House of Lords as a legislative body happened to have had judicial experience and were therefore entitled to sit and vote on appeals. It was already the convention that lay peers should not take part. The strongest link between the House of Lords in its legislative and the House of Lords in its judicial capacity is in the person of the Lord Chancellor who sits in both and can be active in both. The Law Lords who are life peers sit in the legislative body but their participation is normally confined to questions affecting the law and the administration of justice.

The system of double appeal has some advantages, but such as they are, they are probably advantages for the legal system as a whole than for the litigant who goes through the double process. For the litigant there is a positive advantage in having an early end to litigation. Litigation is already expensive and time-consuming enough without adding to it the risk of having to pay for two appeals and to wait for two more hearings before getting a final decision. It is in fact one of the major criticisms of the common law system that it is too dependent on litigation and litigants for the clarification and development of the law, and the existence of a higher appellate court is a constant temptation to the rich and the legally aided.

---

[65] See below, p. 642.

There is a sense in which appeals may be welcomed by the court and the profession because of the opportunity they give to have an authoritative decision on a doubtful point, to have an area of law reviewed and perhaps revised, or to remove some anomaly or obstacle to growth. The higher up the appellate structure one goes the more it gives the appearance of being involved in its own purposes, either in correcting its own mistakes or renovating its own raw materials at the expense of the parties before it. The Law Society in its report on the provision of legal aid is always concerned to draw attention to important cases which have been decided in which the parties had legal aid, to show the important role that legal aid plays in this aspect of the appellate process.

Some of the arguments used in favour of an appeal court in connection with the Court of Appeal,[66] however, lose their force when one comes to a second appeal, in particular that based on numbers; for it is possible for a party to win his case in the House of Lords by a vote of three to two having lost in both the lower courts and it is difficult to see in what sense the judgment of three Law Lords which in an extreme case may rest on different grounds, should be preferred to that of two Law Lords, three Lords Justices and a trial judge, at least in a case in which the lower courts were free to reach the same decision but rejected the opportunity. The requirement of leave helps to mitigate the burden of a double appeal to some extent, and legal aid also. In some cases too it is the practice of a party who wishes to appeal because of the importance to him of getting the law settled (the Inland Revenue Commissioners for example) to pay the costs of the appeal of the respondent, and the Court of Appeal in giving leave may make this a condition. The House of Lords has however said that a prospective appellant cannot be asked to guarantee both the costs of the respondent and also to promise not to take from him the benefit of the decision of the Court of Appeal in any event, since in that case the appellant ceases to have an interest in the case, which becomes hypothetical. One particular difficulty, the situation where it is clear that the Court of Appeal cannot give a different decision from that of the lower court because of the state of the legislation or the precedents, has been met in part by providing the possibility of a leap-frog appeal by which the appellant can go straight from the lower court to the House of Lords without engaging in a fruitless appeal to the Court of Appeal.

Appellate Jurisdiction Act 1876

39 & 40 Vict. c. 59

3. Subject as in this Act mentioned an appeal shall lie to the House of Lords from any order or judgment of any of the courts following; that is to say,

(1) Of Her Majesty's Court of Appeal in England; and
(2) Of any Court in Scotland from which error or an appeal at or immediately before the commencement of this Act lay to the House of Lords
by common law or by statute. . . .

[66] Above, p. 593.

4. Every appeal shall be brought by way of petition to the House of Lords, praying that the matter of the order or judgment appealed against may be reviewed before Her Majesty the Queen in her Court of Parliament, in order that the said Court may determine what of right, and according to the law and custom of this realm, ought to be done in the subject-matter of such appeal.

5. An appeal shall not be heard and determined by the House of Lords unless there are present at such hearing and determination not less than three of the following persons, in this Act designated Lords of Appeal; that is to say,

(1) The Lord Chancellor of Great Britain for the time being; and

(2) The Lords of Appeal in Ordinary to be appointed as in this Act mentioned; and

(3) Such Peers of Parliament as are for the time being holding or have held any of the offices in this Act described as high judicial offices.[67]

6. For the purpose of aiding the House of Lords in the hearing and determination of appeals, Her Majesty may by letters patent appoint qualified persons to be Lords of Appeal in Ordinary.[68]

A person shall not be qualified to be appointed by Her Majesty a Lord of Appeal in Ordinary unless he has been at or before the time of his appointment the holder for a period of not less than two years of some one or more of the offices in this Act described as high judicial offices, or has been at or before such time as aforesaid, for not less than fifteen years, a practising barrister in England or Ireland, or a practising advocate in Scotland.

Every Lord of Appeal in Ordinary shall hold his office during good behaviour, and shall continue to hold the same notwithstanding the demise of the Crown, but he may be removed from such office on the address of both Houses of Parliament.

Every Lord of Appeal in Ordinary, unless he is otherwise entitled to sit as a member of the House of Lords, shall by virtue ... of his appointment be entitled ... to a writ of summons to attend, and to sit and vote in the House of Lords; his dignity as a Lord of Parliament shall not descend to his heirs. ...

A Lord of Appeal in Ordinary shall, if a Privy Councillor, be a member of the Judicial Committee of the Privy Council, and, subject to the due performance by a Lord of Appeal in Ordinary of his duties as to the hearing and determining of appeals in the House of Lords, it shall be his duty, being a Privy Councillor, to sit and act as a member of the Judicial Committee of the Privy Council.

Administration of Justice (Appeals) Act 1934

24 & 25 Geo. 5, c. 40

1.—(1) No appeal shall lie to the House of Lords from any order or judgment made or given by the Court of Appeal ... except with the leave of that Court or of the House of Lords.

(2) The House of Lords may by order provide for the hearing and determination by a Committee of that House of petitions for leave to appeal from the

---

[67] s. 25 provides that " high judicial office " means: " the office of Lord Chancellor . . . or of Judge of one of Her Majesty's superior courts of Great Britain and Ireland." This includes judges of the High Court and the Court of Appeal and the Court of Session and according to the Appellate Jurisdiction Act 1887 Lords of Appeal in Ordinary and members of the Judicial Committee of the Privy Council.

[68] The Administration of Justice Act 1968 provides that the maximum number of Lords in Ordinary is to be eleven but that this number can be increased by Order in Council, the draft of which has been approved by both Houses.

Court of Appeal: Provided that section five of the Appellate Jurisdiction Act 1876, shall apply to the hearing and determination of any such petition. . . .

(3) Nothing in this section shall affect any restriction existing, apart from this section, on the bringing of appeals from the Court of Appeal to the House of Lords.[69]

Administration of Justice Act 1969

1969, c. 58

PART II

Appeal from High Court to House of Lords

12.—(1) Where on the application of any of the parties to any proceedings to which this section applies the judge is satisfied—

(a) that the relevant conditions are fulfilled in relation to his decision in those proceedings, and

(b) that a sufficient case for an appeal to the House of Lords under this Part of this Act has been made out to justify an application for leave to bring such an appeal, and

(c) that all the parties to the proceedings consent to the grant of a certificate under this section,

the judge, subject to the following provisions of this Part of this Act, may grant a certificate to that effect.

(2) This section applies to any civil proceedings in the High Court which are either—

(a) proceedings before a single judge of the High Court (including a person acting as such a judge under section 3 of the Judicature Act 1925), or

(b) proceedings before a commissioner acting under a commission issued under section 70 of the Judicature Act 1925, or

(c) proceedings before a Divisional Court.

(3) Subject to any Order in Council made under the following provisions of this section, for the purposes of this section the relevant conditions, in relation to a decision of the judge in any proceedings, are that a point of law of general public importance is involved in that decision and that that point of law either—

(a) relates wholly or mainly to the construction of an enactment or of a statutory instrument, and has been fully argued in the proceedings and fully considered in the judgment of the judge in the proceedings, or

(b) is one in respect of which the judge is bound by a decision of the Court of Appeal or of the House of Lords in previous proceedings, and was fully considered in the judgments given by the Court of Appeal or the House of Lords (as the case may be) in those previous proceedings.

---

[69] e.g. s. 27 (2) of the Supreme Court of Judicature (Consolidation) Act 1925, which provides: " The decision of the Court of Appeal on any question arising under the provisions of this Act relating to matrimonial causes and matters and to declarations of legitimacy and of validity of marriage shall be final, except where the decision is either on the grant or refusal of a decree on a petition for dissolution or nullity of marriage or for such a declaration as aforesaid, or on a question of law on which the Court of Appeal gives leave to appeal "; or s. 114 of the County Courts Act 1959, which provides: " No appeal shall lie from the decision of the Court of Appeal on any appeal from a county court in any probate proceedings."

(5) No appeal shall lie against the grant or refusal of a certificate under this section.

(6) Her Majesty may by Order in Council amend subsection (3) of this section by altering, deleting, or substituting one or more new paragraphs for, either or both of paragraphs (*a*) and (*b*) of that subsection, or by adding one or more further paragraphs.

(7) Any Order in Council made under this section shall be subject to annulment in pursuance of a resolution of either House of Parliament.

13.—(1) Where in any proceedings the judge grants a certificate under section 12 of this Act, then, . . . any of the parties to the proceedings may make an application to the House of Lords under this section.

(2) Subject to the following provisions of this section, if on such an application it appears to the House of Lords to be expedient to do so, the House may grant leave for an appeal to be brought directly to the House; and where leave is granted under this section—

(*a*) no appeal from the decision of the judge to which the certificate relates shall lie to the Court of Appeal, but

(*b*) an appeal shall lie from that decision to the House of Lords.

(3) Applications under this section shall be determined without a hearing.

(4) Any order of the House of Lords which provides for applications under this section to be determined by a committee of the House—

(*a*) shall direct that the committee shall consist of or include not less than three of the persons designated as Lords of Appeal in accordance with section 5 of the Appellate Jurisdiction Act 1876, and

(*b*) may direct that the decision of the committee on any such application shall be taken on behalf of the House.

15.—(3) Where by virtue of any enactment, apart from the provisions of this Part of this Act, no appeal would lie to the Court of Appeal from the decision of the judge except with the leave of the judge or of the Court of Appeal, no certificate shall be granted under section 12 of this Act in respect of that decision unless it appears to the judge that apart from the provisions of this Part of this Act it would be a proper case for granting such leave.

(4) No certificate shall be granted under section 12 of this Act where the decision of the judge, or any order made by him in pursuance of that decision, is made in the exercise of jurisdiction to punish for contempt of court.

APPEALS IN CRIMINAL CASES

Criminal Appeal Act 1968

1968, c. 19

Appeal to the House of Lords from Court of Appeal (Criminal Division)

33.—(1) An appeal lies to the House of Lords, at the instance of the defendant or the prosecutor, from any decision of the Court of Appeal on an appeal to that court under Part I of this Act.

(2) The appeal lies only with the leave of the Court of Appeal or the House of Lords; and leave shall not be granted unless it is certified by the Court of Appeal that a point of law of general public importance is involved in the

decision and it appears to the Court of Appeal or the House of Lords (as the case may be) that the point is one which ought to be considered by that House.[70]

35.—(1) An appeal under this Part of this Act shall not be heard and determined by the House of Lords unless there are present at least three of the persons designated Lords of Appeal by section 5 of the Appellate Jurisdiction Act 1876.

(2) Any order of the House of Lords which provides for the hearing of applications for leave to appeal by a committee constituted in accordance with section 5 of the said Act of 1876 may direct that the decision of that committee shall be taken on behalf of the House.

(3) For the purpose of disposing of an appeal, the House of Lords may exercise any powers of the Court of Appeal or may remit the case to the Court.

Administration of Justice Act 1960

8 & 9 Eliz. 2, c. 65

1.—(1) Subject to the provisions of this section, an appeal shall lie to the House of Lords, at the instance of the defendant or the prosecutor,—

(a) from any decision of a Divisional Court of the Queen's Bench Division in a criminal cause or matter.

(2) No appeal shall lie under this section except with the leave of the court below or of the House of Lords; and such leave shall not be granted unless it is certified by the court below that a point of law of general public importance is involved in the decision and it appears to that court or to the House of Lords, as the case may be, that the point is one which ought to be considered by that House.

(3) Section five of the Appellate Jurisdiction Act, 1876 (which regulates the composition of the House of Lords for the hearing and determination of appeals) shall apply to the hearing and determination of an appeal or application for leave to appeal under this section as it applies to the hearing and determination of an appeal under that Act; and any order of that House which provides for the hearing of such applications by a committee constituted in accordance with the said section five may direct that the decision of that committee shall be taken on behalf of the House.

(4) For the purposes of disposing of an appeal under this section the House of Lords may exercise any powers of the court below or may remit the case to that court.

---

[70] In *Att.-Gen. for Northern Ireland* v. *Gallagher* [1963] A.C. 349 Lord Tucker noted: ". . . [O]nce the court from which the appeal is brought has certified that a point of law of general public importance is involved in the decision, and leave to appeal has been given, either by that court, or this House, the jurisdiction of this House to hear the appeal is established, and there is nothing in the Administration of Justice Act 1960 in any way limiting its jurisdiction. It will always be a matter for the exercise of its discretion whether to allow a point in no way connected with the certified point of law to be argued on the appeal, and it is not to be assumed from the decision in this case that an appellant can as a matter of right raise any such point. . . ."

INDEX